Buddhist Landscapes in Central India

Buddhist Landscapes in Central India:

Sanchi Hill and Archaeologies of Religious and Social Change, c. Third Century BC to Fifth Century AD

Julia Shaw

The British Association for South Asian Studies
The British Academy
London

Published by the British Association for South Asian Studies,
14 Stephenson Way, London NW1 2HD

British Library Cataloguing in Publication Data
A catalogue record of this book is available from the British Library.

ISBN 978-0-9553924-4-3

Designed by Andrew Shoolbred
Produced by Felicity Awdry and Colin Grant
Printed in England by CPI Antony Rowe, Chippenham

Contents

Preface

This book builds on my PhD dissertation (Shaw 2002) and related research carried out between 1998 and 2001 at the University of Cambridge, and incorporates various phases of the Sanchi Survey Project (hereafter SSP) undertaken in subsequent years. The main aim of this study was to situate the well-known Buddhist complex of Sanchi, a UNESCO World Heritage site in central India, within its wider archaeological setting in order to address a number of problems regarding the social, religious and economic background of Buddhism in the late centuries BC. Sanchi is one of India's best preserved and most studied Buddhist sites with a continuous constructional sequence from c. third century BC to twelfth century AD. The establishment of Buddhism here was closely tied to the spread of the Mauryan empire and related processes of urbanisation, the latter well represented by the early-historic city-site of Vidisha, several km to the north. However, despite a large body of scholarship on these two sites, a number of major questions remained unaddressed. For example, how did the incoming Buddhist *saṅgha* establish itself in the area? How did it relate to the pre-existing social, religious, and economic landscape? What were the factors that led to certain places being chosen for the construction of monasteries and stupas? And how did the local history of Buddhism relate to contemporary developments in the Brahmanical traditions, as well as to wider social and economic processes such as urbanisation, and changes in local agrarian practices and food customs?

Two underlying themes can be delineated here: i) the continuities, discontinuities, and transformations that fuel the formation of a multi-layered ritual landscape; and ii) the political, economic and 'practical' underpinnings of religious change and propagation. My interest in both of these themes is a long-standing one, stemming as much from my upbringing in the Highlands of Scotland, as from my more formal studies in the history and archaeology of Indian religions. I was initially drawn to the south Indian 'megaliths' and the enigmatic question of their relationship (both morphologically and topographically) to Buddhist stupas, which, as with a long stream of Scottish and Irish observers in the eighteenth and nineteenth centuries before me (in particular, the polymath, Meadows Taylor), evoked a similar set of relationships in landscapes closer to home. More recently, Gregory Schopen (1996b) has re-visited these questions focusing on the relationship between Buddhist and protohistorical burial traditions in the Deccan and south India, as well as textual and secondary archaeological evidence for the development of a 'cult of the monastic dead' at numerous Buddhist sites (including some of those in the Sanchi area) from at least the second century BC. Schopen's argument is that many of the smaller stupas found at Sanchi and other well-known Buddhist sites were not simply 'votive' as previously assumed, but rather contained the mortuary remains of 'ordinary' monks or laity, and were placed in relation to more important relic stupas following a similar rationale as burial *ad sanctos* traditions in Christian contexts. Lars Fogelin (2004 2006) during his survey around Thotlakonda in Andhra Pradesh has discovered whole burial grounds consisting solely of stupas of this category, while similar findings were documented during the SSP.

Another focus of research has been the *saṅgha*'s relationship to pre-existing cults, drawing on textual accounts of the Buddha's 'taming' of dangerous local deities such as *yakṣa*s and *nāga*s, or on the presence of shrines to these deities within later monastic compounds (Cohen 1998). There were problems in applying any of these approaches to the Sanchi area, largely because there are no protohistorical burial mounds to speak of, and the earliest free-standing *yakṣa* or *nāga* images postdate the arrival of Buddhism by several centuries. What was possible, however, was to draw on consistencies in the location of Buddhist remains across an extensive (c. 750 km^2), relatively well-preserved archaeological landscape and to examine how these sites related to other aspects of the ritual landscape (Brahmanical and otherwise) as well as habitational settlements and agrarian systems. By doing so, it became possible to assess theories of religious change, with regard both to Buddhism's relationship to other religions and to its wider economic and social infrastructure.

This brings me to the second major theme of this book: the social and economic dimension of Buddhist monasticism. A particularly enduring memory from my first visit to Thailand is the 'clanging' sound of a stream of coins being dropped into a metal bucket in a Buddhist temple in Bangkok. The temple was crowded with poor devotees, mainly women, and I was struck by the complete absence of monks, whom I later spotted poking their heads out of an air-conditioned hall in a separate part of the compound. Quite obviously these monks, despite their renunciate status were not cut off from society, or from the fruits of its labour which were trickling steadily into the temple bucket! Again, closer to home, I was reminded of the economic influence of the medieval Christian monasteries in Scotland and Ireland, which today mostly lie in ruins. That Buddhist monasteries from their very inception have not only been dependent on the generosity of the laity, but have also grown into powerful and wealthy institutions in their own right, is a well known fact, as attested by modern examples in Southeast and East Asia; in Sri Lanka, the earliest evidence for 'monastic landlordism' is datable to c. second century BC.

A key question that this study sought to address was how and when did this level of social embeddedness begin in central India? And how did the monks on arriving in the area set up exchange networks with local populations? These and related questions regarding the social and economic background of Buddhist monasticism have long since been pondered by Indologists, with two main areas of interest: i) how the actual emergence of Buddhism in the sixth or fifth centuries BC related to wider changes such as the rise of urban culture and monarchical states in the Gangetic valley (Bailey and Mabbett 2005); and ii) the economic and political factors that propelled and supported the later spread of Buddhism into other parts of India during the late centuries BC. While some scholars have looked at the medical underpinnings of Buddhist monasticism (Zysk 1991), of particular interest has been the *saṅgha*'s link with trade, as studied through generalised observations regarding the positioning of Buddhist monasteries (e.g., Ray 1986; Heitzman 1984), the content of donative inscriptions, and textual accounts of the development of the ritual exchange of gifts and merit between monastic and lay populations (Schopen 1996a; 1996c). However, when I began my research at Sanchi in 1998, no systematic archaeological investigations of the landscape setting of Buddhist monasteries had hitherto been carried out. The main aim of the study was to approach the social and economic background of Buddhism in the Sanchi area by going beyond the site's formal monastic boundaries and examining its relationship with other forms of religious, social, and agricultural sites in the wider archaeological landscape. Since the project began, a number of studies with similar objectives have also been initiated in other areas, including Lars Fogelin's (2004, 2006) survey at the Buddhist site of Thotlakonda in Andhra Pradesh, and more recently Jason Hawkes's (in press) survey at Bharhut in Madhya Pradesh. Although Fogelin's study extends 'beyond the monastery walls', its geographical scope is much less extensive than the SSP, covering an area of less than 8 km^2. His monograph was only published at a late stage in the completion of this book, so unfortunately it has not been possible to make more than passing reference to this important work.

Various research papers synthesizing results of the SSP, or else concentrating on single aspects of the dataset have already been published elsewhere. It was felt necessary to incorporate some of this work into the present book in order to provide the necessary context for newly published material. This applies in particular to chapters 6, 12 and 14, which draw heavily on previously published papers (Shaw 2004a; Shaw and Sutcliffe 2001, 2003a–b, 2005; Shaw *et al.*, 2007). The aim of this book was not to provide another, albeit longer, synthesis of results, but rather to publish the complete dataset in a coherent and comprehensive manner, amounting to a report of the first ten years of the SSP. The sheer volume of data thus makes for a rather unwieldy book whose main text is frequently interrupted by numbered data references which correspond to entries in the long appendix at the end of the book. However, whilst illustrations have been provided for many of the key archaeological finds, restrictions over space meant that over half of the data presented in the appendix is lacking accompanying illustrations. Further, the tabulated format of the appendices does little justice to the complexity of the multi-layered, 'relational' database upon which they are based. In order to remedy this situation, a web-based version of the original database complete with site-by-site illustrations and maps, will be launched in due course (see www.britac.ac.uk/institutes/SSAS/projects/sanchi.htm for details of availability). The book includes five sections of Plates in black and white, while Figures in black and white (maps and line drawings) are integrated with the text. One Plate (no. 15) and a number of other Figures are reproduced in colour in a separate section between pp.232 and 233. Diacritics have only been applied to transliterated words given in italics, usually titles of texts and technical terms, not proper names.

Largely on account of the book's 'data-heaviness', it is likely to have more appeal to scholars with a particular interest in the archaeology of Indian religions than to the general reader. However, dealing as it does with wider theoretical and methodological issues relating to landscape archaeology, and the study of religious, social and environmental change, it will hopefully be of some use to scholars working in other regions, too.

List of Figures

Page references are given for Figures in black and white, while Figures in colour are to be found between pp.232 and 233.

List of Tables

List of Plates

Abbreviations

Publications

ASIAR	*Archaeological Survey of India Annual Reports (*1902 onwards*)*
ASIR	*Archaeological Survey of India Reports*, vols. I–XXIII (1861/2–1883/4).
Bhandarkar CII, III	*Corpus Inscriptionum Indicarum, vol. III: Inscriptions of the Early Guptas*. New Delhi: Archaeological Survey of India. Revised edition, by D.R. Bhandarkar, edited by B. Chhabra and G.W. Gai (1981).
CII	*Corpus Inscriptionum Indicarum.* Vols. I–IV. Calcutta: Superintendent of Government Printing, India.
EI	*Epigraphica Indica*, from 1892. Calcutta: Government of India Press.
Fleet CII, III	*Corpus Inscriptionum Indicarum, vol. III: Inscriptions of the Early Gupta Kings and their Successors*. Calcutta: Superintendent of Government Printing, India. By J.F. Fleet (1888).
IAR	*Indian Archaeology: A Review*
Imp Gaz.	The Imperial Gazetteer of India. Vol. 8: Berhampore to Bombay; vol. 12: Einme to Gwalior; vol. 9: Bomjur to Central India. Oxford: Clarendon Press (1908)

Ceramics

BRW	Black and Red Ware
NBPW	Northern Black Polished Ware
PGW	Painted Grey Ware

Museums, institutions and others

AMG	Archaeological Museum Gwalior
ASI	Archaeological Survey of India
NMD	National Museum, Delhi
GGMM	Gwalior Gujari Mahal Museum
SAM	Sanchi Archaeological Museum
SAMRC	Sanchi Archaeological Museum Research Collection
SSP	Sanchi Survey Project
VM	Vidisha Museum
VMRC	Vidisha Museum Reserve Collection

Select Glossary

cabutra	Platform, often found in villages as base for sculptural fragments under worship
caitya	Buddhist shrine, often rock-cut
Camundai	Durga in her emaciated form
dāna	Religious gift
dharma	Religious teachings
ekamukhaliṅga	*Liṅga* with single face of Siva on its shaft
liṅga	Phallic symbol for the Brahmancial deity Siva
Mahiṣāsuramardinī	Form of Durga showing the goddess killing the demon Mahisa
mātṛkā	'Mother' goddess, often shown in a group of seven (*sāpta*)
nāgakal	Theriomorphic snake stone
nāga/nāgarāja	Anthropomorphic snake deity
pūṇya	Religious merit
saṅgha	Collective 'order' of Buddhist monks
sindhūr	Red paint often daubed onto sculptures to indicate their sacred status
sucika	Cross-bar of stupa railing
śāsana	Collective Buddhist teachings
śikhara	Tower of Hindu temple
stupa	Domed building for storing Buddhist relics
tope	Term used by nineteenth-century writers for stupa
varṇa	One of the four Brahmanical 'classes'
vedikā	Upright stupa railing
vessana	Buddhist monsoon retreat
vihāra	Buddhist monastery
yakṣa	Male deity of fertility and nature

Acknowledgements

This book began life in 1997 as a PhD research project at the University of Cambridge, under the supervision of Dilip K. Chakrabarti whose guidance I gratefully acknowledge. Subsequent phases of research were carried out during a Visiting Fellowship at the University of Stanford, USA; a British Academy Post-doctoral Fellowship at the University of Oxford (Merton College, and Institute of Archaeology); and since 2005 a Lectureship at the Institute of Archaeology, University College London. Key fieldwork seasons have been funded by the British Academy, the Society for South Asian Studies, Merton College, INTACH UK, and the Nehru Trust.

This research could not have been undertaken without the permission of the Archaeological Survey of India (ASI). I am indebted to the officers of the ASI, Bhopal Circle, and Madhya Pradesh Directorate of Archaeology, Archives and Museums for all kinds of support and assistance. Particular thanks to S.B. Ota, K.K. Mohammed, Narayan Vyas, S.K. Verma, P.K. Mukherjee, and O.P. Misra.

Others who have contributed to the project's success include: Rakesh Tewari (Director of Uttar Pradesh State Archaeology Department, Lucknow); K.K. Chakravarty (formerly Director of Museum of Man, Bhopal); the officers and staff of the Vidisha Museum and the Sanchi Archaeological Museum; R.G. Naidu, the former Collector of Vidisha; Anuradha Shankar, Superintendent of Police; Thera Somaratna, former Chief Incumbent of the Mahabodhi Society, Sanchi; and the Manager and staff at Madhya Pradesh State Tourism Travellers' Lodge, Sanchi.

So many people have been involved, directly or indirectly, in the project over the years that it is impossible to acknowledge everyone by name. I first visited Sanchi with Michael Willis to whom I am particularly grateful for introducing me to many crucial aspects of working in central India and for being a constant source of academic encouragement, support and inspiration in subsequent years. I would like to thank Michael for editing this book with so much care, and also Colin Grant and Andrew Shoolbred, who saw the book through to publication with endless patience and attention to detail. Others who have read earlier versions of parts of the book or offered helpful suggestions, include (in alphabetical order), Hans Bakker, Ian Hodder, Derek Kennet, Alexis Sanderson, Andrew Sherratt (sadly no longer with us), Janice Stargardt, John Sutcliffe, and Jonathan Walters. I am particularly indebted to John Sutcliffe with whom I have worked closely on the irrigation side of the project since our serendipitous meeting in the Museum of Man, Bhopal, back in 1998. The hydrological calculations in chapter 14, which draw on several previously published papers (Shaw and Sutcliffe 2001, 2003a, 2003b, 2005; Shaw *et al.*, 2007), are the result of significant collaboration. I also owe an enormous debt to John for proof-reading earlier versions of the book and offering suggestions for improvement. Any extant errors, however, are entirely my own responsibility.

The project has also involved collaborations, at various stages, with Anthony Beck (Universities of Durham, and Leeds), Lindsay Lloyd-Smith (University of Cambridge), M.S. Chauhan (Birbal Sahni Institute of Palaeobotany, Lucknow), and S.R. Patidar (Nikhil Land Survey and Civil Consultancy, Bhopal). Anthony Beck helped greatly in improving the project's database and GIS structure, often through long and gruelling brain-storming sessions on the complexities of 'ordering' landscapes of the past.

Since beginning this project, the Vidisha, Sanchi, Bhopal area has become a second home to me. In Bhopal, the warmth and generosity of spirit received in the home of Meera and Ishwar Dass formed a central core to my life while carrying out fieldwork. In Vidisha, Dharmacaitanya (Swami ji) and Ma Pushpa (Babhi ji) Jain opened their house and embraced me within their remarkable family. Their boundless support and nourishment (on mental, emotional and nutritional levels) are treasures that remain with me always. The friendship of Ashutosh Vyas and Chitra Singh made my social life in Vidisha as eventful and enjoyable as any newcomer could have wished for.

An enormous debt goes to Santosh Kumar Dvivedi, my principle research assistant during the initial phases of the project. His keen archaeological eye, his endless stamina and patience, and above all, boundless good humour, all contributed greatly to the success and enjoyability of fieldwork. Other team-members at various points included Arvind and Raju Dvivedi, Adityashekar Gupta, Dhiraj and Chhaya Shah, Brajesh Sharma, Gurudas Shete, Mahindra Singh, Dharmendra Vishwakarma, Pratap Yadav (who sadly died in 2002), Manoj Kumar Manhi, and Sravan Singh Rajput.

I am indebted to the numerous villagers, farmers and landowners whose cooperation and warmth were central to the smooth running of the project. Many welcomed me into their houses, responded to my endless, and in many cases, puzzling questions about potsherds and 'old stones', shared their knowledge of local archaeological sites, landmarks, and sacred places, and tramped with me for miles through fields and jungles in search of *Purāne jagah*. Particular thanks to the following: Rahesh Bhai (Devrajpur village); Mubeen Akhtar (Chopra); Munshilal Chow-ksee (Ratanpur); Phulgir Goswami (Salera); Shahid Mohammad (Umariya); Ashok Kumar Tiwari (Bhoriya); Patel Rakesh Tiwari

(Nonakhera); Natu Ram Chaudhary (Besar talai); and Mohar Singh (Karaiya Khera).

The memories of walking through lush wheat fields into the evening sun at the end of the day and driving back to Vidisha on the trusted M80 motorbike, are some of the happiest I have. A heartfelt thanks to everyone, many of whom are not listed here, for helping me realise what was only a dream when I first arrived in Sanchi over ten years ago, and particularly to my family, and Alexandre G. Mitchell, without whose love and understanding I might never have finished this book.

All photographs are by the author, apart from Plates 202 and 204 (Williams 1982, pls. 45–6). Grateful thanks to Joanna Williams for granting permission to reproduce copies of these images. I am grateful to the ASI for granting me permission to photograph sculptures in both the main and reserve collections of the Sanchi Archaeological Museum. Permission to take photographs in the State Museum, Lucknow, the Vidisha Museum, and the Gujari Mahal Museum, Gwalior, is also gratefully acknowledged.

Institute of Archaeology, University College London
October 2007

CHAPTER 1

Introduction

The archaeology of Buddhist landscapes

The archaeology of Buddhism has generally been the study of stupas, monasteries, sculpture and epigraphy. The primary geographical focus of interest has been the Gangetic valley, where places such as Sarnath, Bodhgaya, Sravasti, Rajgir or Vaisali were closely connected to events relating to the life and teachings of the historical Buddha (Figure 1.1). Some of the best-preserved monastic sites, however, are situated beyond the cradle of Buddhism in central India and the Deccan. The establishment of Buddhism at sites such as Sanchi and Bharhut coincided in part with the westward expansion of the Mauryan empire in c. third century BC, with major building programmes taking place slightly later between the second century BC and early centuries AD. Some of the early rock-cut *caitya*s and monasteries in the Deccan, such as Karle, Bhaja, Bedsa, and Pitalkhora, seem also to have been part of this 'second propagation' of Buddhism. All of these sites have generated a significant body of scholarship, largely because of their art-historical appeal. Sanchi has been of particular interest because of its continuous history of Buddhist occupation from c. third century BC to twelfth century AD. Its remarkably well-preserved monuments and sculptures have provided a kind of blueprint for the history of art and architecture over this period.

However, one of the major problems that this study seeks to address is that until recently scholars have rarely looked beyond the art-historical value of important ritual sites to their wider archaeological or cultural setting.[1] Little consideration has been given to how Buddhist sites related to less tangible or 'monumental' aspects of the landscape, such as topography, local settlement patterns, water-resource structures or, indeed, sites belonging to other religious traditions.[2] This lacuna reflects the fact that the archaeology of Indian religions has tended to focus on well-known monuments, with little reference to recent theoretical shifts, which amongst other things have led to the recognition of entire landscapes as foci of archaeological enquiry. This has obviously hampered our understanding of the early history of Buddhism and its relationship to other key processes taking place during the early-historic period such as state formation, urbanisation, population shifts, and changes in food production and consumption practices. Secondly, there is still little understanding of how the *saṅgha* aligned itself with the pre-existing social, economic and religious infrastructure of the new areas into which it arrived. Further, although some scholars of Buddhist history have, through their use of secondary archaeological evidence, spearheaded a departure from the subject's traditional reliance on texts (Schopen 1997; Trainor 1997), the lack of coordination between active archaeological research and text-based analysis means that many received models of Buddhist history have gone unchallenged. A similar lack of integration between the methods and results of archaeology and history has also had a detrimental effect on the study of state formation and urbanisation in ancient India, something which is taken up for discussion at various points in this book.

The Sanchi Survey Project: a case study

In an attempt to redress some of these problems, it was decided to choose a relatively tightly focused area in which the archaeological setting of monastic sites could be studied in detail. The primary archaeological focus of the Sanchi Survey Project (SSP), which has undergone various stages of research since its inception in 1998, is the well-known monastic complex at Sanchi, a recently designated UNESCO World Heritage Site in Madhya Pradesh (Figures 1.1, 1.2). Its earliest documented history dates to c. third century BC and it is associated with the patronage of the Mauryan empire whose expanding boundaries mirrored in part the early movement of Buddhist monks from their base in the middle Gangetic plains. Both its distance from the 'cradle' of Buddhism and its proximity to the early-historic city of Vidisha make it an ideal case-study for examining the socio-economic and religious background of Buddhist propagation. Another reason for choosing Sanchi is that a number of well-preserved Buddhist sites were already known in the surrounding area: Satdhara, Morel khurd, Andher and Sonari. These are all situated within a radius of about 15 km from Sanchi and were originally documented in the mid-nineteenth century in Alexander Cunningham's (1854) famous monograph entitled *The Bhilsa Topes;* throughout this study these sites are referred to as the 'Bhilsa Tope' sites.

However, the way in which Sanchi has been studied acts as an exemplar for the theoretical and methodological problems already mentioned, relating to South Asian archaeology in general and the study of Buddhism in particular. Despite the large body of art-historical and epigraphical scholarship at Sanchi (notably Marshall 1940) prior to the present study, its relationship to neighbouring Buddhist sites, or to other aspects of the archaeological landscape, remained unexamined. Thus, the history of Sanchi has hitherto remained disconnected from other social and religious histories based on the distribution of local

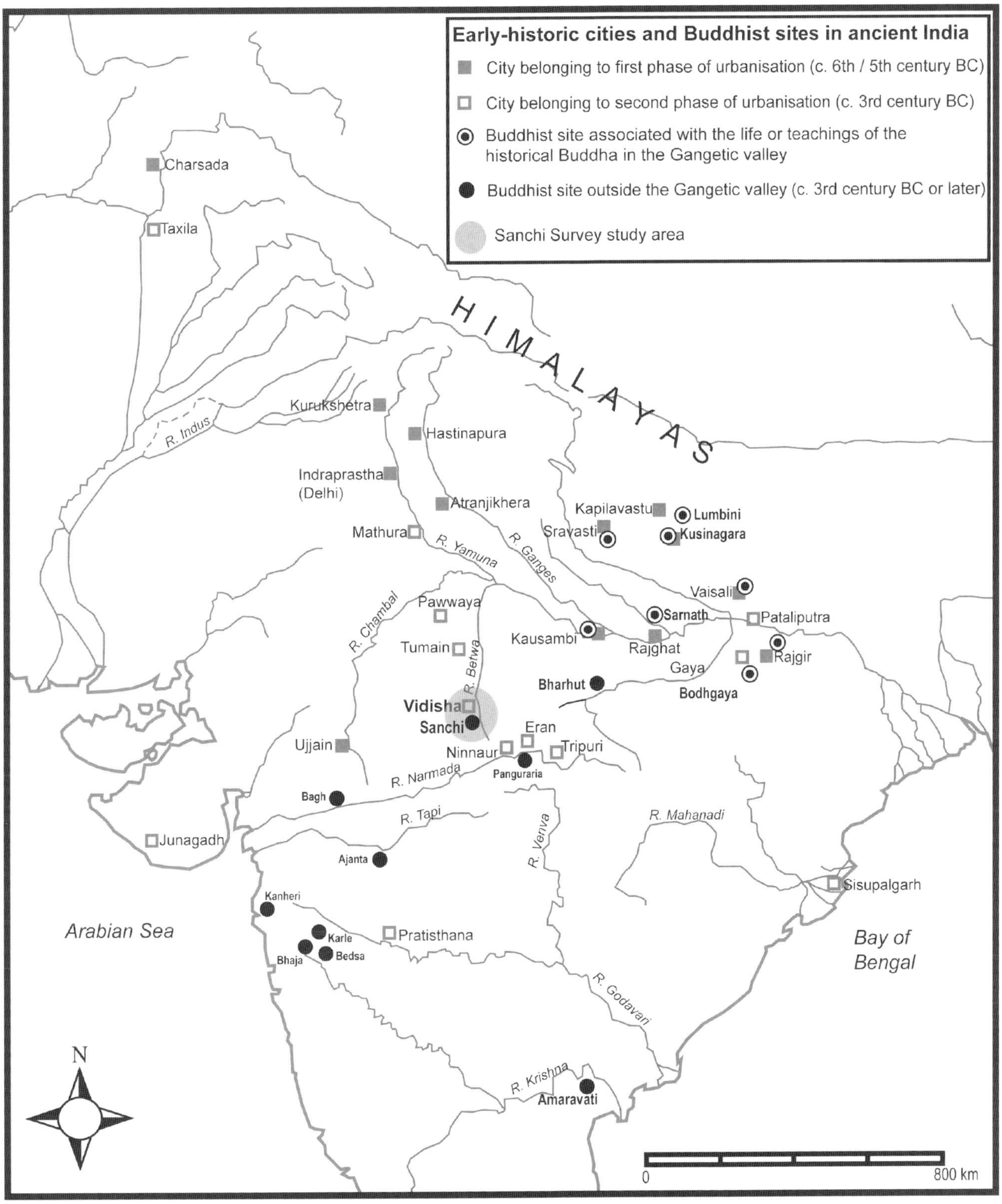

Figure 1.1 Map of India showing key Buddhist sites and early-historic urban centres

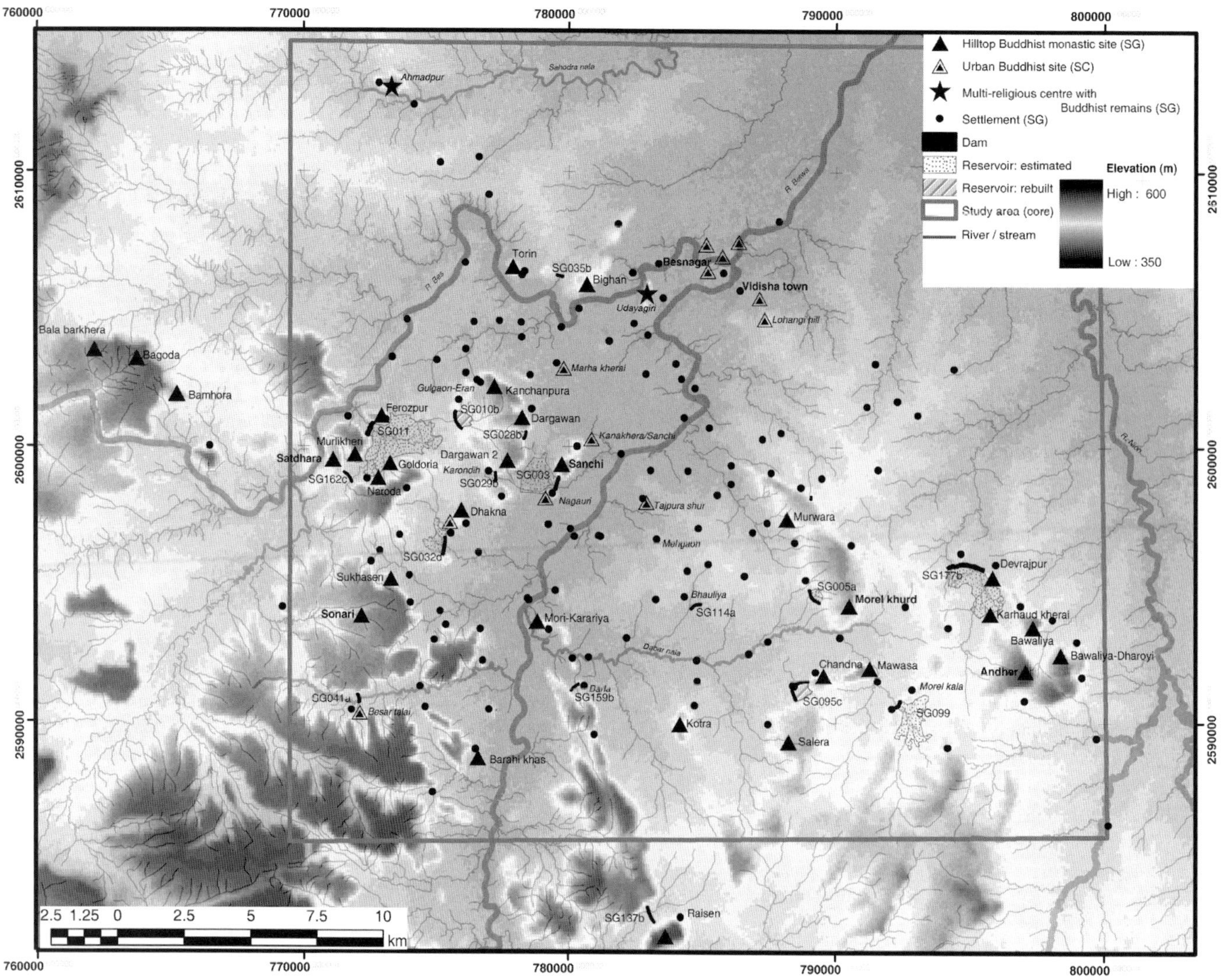

Figure 1.2 Map of key archaeological sites in the Sanchi-Vidisha area

habitational settlements, agricultural systems and both Buddhist and non-Buddhist ritual sites.

The primary aim of the fieldwork that formed the basis of this book was to achieve a less fragmented picture of Buddhist history by combining the methods of landscape archaeology, and art and architectural history, while drawing on debates generated within religious studies and ancient Indian history. The field-based project consisted of a multi-stage archaeological survey carried out over 750 km^2 with Sanchi roughly at its centre. The principal fieldwork was conducted over two six-month seasons between 1998 and 2000 (Shaw 2000a; 2000b; 2001; Shaw and Sutcliffe 2001), with several follow-up seasons in subsequent years (Shaw 2004a; 2004b; 2005; Shaw and Sutcliffe 2003a; 2003b; 2005; Shaw *et al.*, 2007). The survey resulted in the documentation of over 35 Buddhist sites, 145 settlements, 17 irrigation works and over 1000 sculpture and temple fragments. Each of these site categories provides valuable information relating to the history of Buddhist monasticism, settlement history, the changing configuration of the multi-layered ritual landscape, the development of new forms of land use and changing attitudes towards food during the early-historic period. However, one of the primary contentions of this study is that these sites do not exist in isolation from each other, but form integrated components of a series of what may be termed 'archaeological complexes' (Shaw and Sutcliffe 2001), or 'site groups', as they are referred to in this book. An analysis of the internal spatial dynamics of these groups provides an empirical basis for assessing theories of social and religious change, and the emergence of exchange networks between monastic and non-monastic sections of society, between c. third century BC and fifth century AD.

History of archaeological research in the Sanchi area

Sanchi hill

Since its discovery almost 200 years ago, the Buddhist monuments on Sanchi hill have attracted considerable scholarly interest.[3] The site was first noticed in 1818 by General Taylor of the Bengal Cavalry (Burgess 1902) and was revisited in the following year by Captain Edward Fell (1819). In subsequent years, the site was subjected to various bouts of haphazard digging, constituting little more than ill-conceived treasure hunts. The most ambitious project carried out in 1822 resulted in considerable damage to the site

(Marshall 1940, 47), so much so that by the time J.D. Cunningham visited in 1847, many of the monuments were already in complete ruins (Cunningham 1847).

The first serious excavations were initiated in 1851 by Alexander Cunningham and F.C. Maisey and formed the primary focus of Cunningham's *Bhilsa Topes* (1854). These resulted in the retrieval of relics and inscribed reliquaries from Stupas 2 and 3; the former bear the names of the Hemavata school of monks (Willis 2000), thus providing a crucial framework for understanding the identity of early Buddhist schools in the area. Restoration work began in 1881 (Cole 1884), continuing in later years under John Marshall (1940), whose excavations between 1912 and 1919 represent the most comprehensive and authoritative study to date. Marshall's six-phase sequence between c. third century BC and twelfth century AD still provides the primary framework for ongoing studies, as does Foucher's art-historical analyses of the stupa railing carvings published in the same volume. Finally, N.G. Majumdar's chapter on the site's epigraphical record, including the Asokan edict, a large body of second-century-BC donative inscriptions and a later group of Gupta-period land-grants, provides the primary basis for ongoing scholarship on the history of patronage at Sanchi (Dehejia 1992; Singh 1996).

Several excavations have been carried out since Marshall's time. In 1936, Hamid (1940) excavated a large courtyard-type monastery immediately to the west of Stupa 1, while in 1995–6, clearance by the Archaeological Survey of India (ASI) of an area SW of Stupa 1 revealed a group of small stupas (Plate 20; Willis 2000). As discussed in chapter 9, similar stupas, found at a wide range of north Indian sites, were traditionally viewed as performing a 'votive' function. However, recent scholarship on the stupa and relic cult (Schopen 1987) suggests that they belonged to a burial *ad sanctos* tradition, possibly containing the mortuary remains of 'ordinary' monks or lay followers.[4] Recent clearance work undertaken around the large stone platform known as Building 8, resulted in the discovery of a stairway built into the body of the structure (Plate 76). Both Marshall and Cunningham were unclear as to the function of this building, but comparisons with similar buildings at neighbouring sites (Willis 2000; Shaw 2000) provide strong evidence that it formed the base of an early monastery. The significance of this and other 'monastery platforms' in the area for challenging received assumptions regarding the history and chronology of monasticism is discussed in chapters 9 and 11. A large trench opened in the upper terrace above Stupa 1 by the ASI under S.B. Ota, who also cleared areas around the smaller stupas on the lower ground immediately to the east of the main Stupa, revealed paving stones and other features. Further, several 'new' monasteries were uncovered by P.K. Mukherjee around the seventh-century monastery cluster in the southern part of the site. These and other repairs and soundings have not yet been published.

Neighbouring monastic sites

As already mentioned, Sanchi is not the only published Buddhist site in the area. Four other well-preserved stupa sites, Sonari, Satdhara, Morel khurd and Andher (Figure 1.2), all situated within about 15 km of Sanchi, were first documented by Cunningham (1854). Excavations carried out together with Maisey resulted in the retrieval of reliquaries from a number of the stupas at these sites. Some of these were found to bear names which correspond to those of the Hemavata monks listed in the reliquary inscriptions from Stupa 2, Sanchi. This demonstrates that all five sites were linked under the Hemavata school, which under the leadership of a teacher called Gotiputa, appears to have played a major role in the 'second propagation' of Buddhism in the last quarter of the second century BC (Willis 2000). All four of these sites are under the protection of the ASI. However, apart from basic conservation measures, they have received meagre archaeological attention since Cunningham's time. The exception is Satdhara, which has undergone renewed excavation and conservation in recent years. The most important discoveries have been described in a summary report (Agrawal 1997), but have yet to be digested in a scholarly way.

A summary report of a sixth monastic site, Bighan, about 3 km NW of Vidisha, was published by H.H. Lake (1910b) around 60 years after Cunningham's explorations. Until it was taken up for renewed investigation during the present study, this important site had not received any scholarly interest in subsequent years. Consequently it has escaped state protection, and is increasingly in danger of destruction from ongoing stone-quarrying and tree-planting programmes at the site.

Ancient Vidisha

The other key archaeological site is the ancient city of Vidisha whose mounds are situated in the fork of the Rivers Betwa and Bes, around 8 km north of Sanchi. Also referred to as Besnagar after the village Bes which occupies a key position on the city mounds, the city is thought to have moved to its new location as represented by the modern town of Vidisha, approximately 1 km to the south, some time during the post-Gupta period in the sixth or seventh century AD. However, as discussed in chapter 6, there is evidence for occupation of the 'modern' site during earlier periods also (Figure 1.2).

The earliest archaeological examination of the site was conducted by Cunningham (1880), whose site-plan illustrates the main city mound protected by a massive earthen rampart in the west. Cunningham's excavations were mainly concerned with some of the smaller mounds overlying various Brahmanical, Buddhist and Jain structures, and thus contributed little to the understanding of the site's urban history. Several of these mounds were re-excavated in later years by H.H. Lake (1910a), but it is difficult to relate Lake's numbered mounds to those studied by Cunningham due to the absence of a site-plan which is nevertheless referred to in the former's report. Both scholars were principally interested in the sculptural remains at these sites, many of which are now stored in the Gujari Mahal Museum, Gwalior. Of particular interest was a group of pillars and capitals to the north of the River Bes, in the vicinity of a site known at the time as Kham Baba. It was only following Lake's (1910a, 137–9) discovery of the associated inscription buried beneath layers of *sindhūr* on the principal pillar there that the site's link with Heliodorus of Taxila became known (Plates 27, 34). The inscription records that the pillar was set up by the Greek ambassador of king Antialcidas in honour of a temple of Vasudeva during the time of king Bhagabhadra (Marshall 1909; Sircar 1965, 88). Although the genealogy of Bhagabhadra is problematic, coins from the North-West which bear the name Antialcidas suggest a date of c. 115–80 BC (Willis 2000, 57). The importance of this inscription for understanding the religious and political history of the area, as well as for providing the first reliable chronological marker after the Asokan pillar at Sanchi, is discussed at various points in this book.

Further excavations were carried out by J. Bhandarkar between 1913 and 1915 (Bhandarkar 1914; 1915) and later in the 1960s by M.D. Khare (1969; *IAR* 1963–4, 17; 1964–5, 19–20). Both projects centred upon the area around the Heliodorus pillar, and in particular on the foundations of the Vasudeva shrine mentioned in the inscription. During Khare's excavations, trenches were sunk at seven additional locations across the city mounds, resulting in the identification of six occupational levels ranging from c. 2000 BC to the sixth century AD (Figure 9.2). By the end of the fifth season, this sequence had been modified to incorporate pre-pottery microlithic levels underlying a small three-phase Chalcolithic mound at Rangai, about 4 km to the south of the city mounds (*IAR* 1976–7, 33–4). The foundations of the city rampart, dated to c. third century BC on the basis of associated Northern Black Polished Ware (NBPW), marked the earliest urban phase at the site. This sequence accords with the chronology and history of urban development in central India: with the exception of the fortified city site of Ujjain to the west, which as the capital of one of the *mahājanapadas* listed in early Buddhist texts, had already reached a level of urbanism by the sixth century BC, it was not until the 'second' phase, from about third century BC onwards, that Vidisha and many other sites in central India became fully fledged cities (Chakrabarti 1995a; Allchin, ed., 1995).

Unfortunately, apart from several summary reports (*IAR* 1963–4, 16–17; 1964–5, 18; 1965–6, 23; 1975–6, 30–1; 1976–7, 33–4), the full excavation report from Vidisha has never been formally published. As Upinder Singh (1996, 7) aptly puts it, 'in the absence of horizontal excavation at this site, in view of the disparities in the sequences revealed at BSN 1–4, and the meagreness of the published details, it is difficult to reconstruct a coherent, detailed archaeological profile of the history of ancient Vidisha'. This is an extremely important point and one which needs to be borne in mind when it comes to evaluating a particularly problematic, but enduring, theory in ancient Indian history, itself strongly informed by the later stratigraphic levels at Besnagar. As discussed in chapters 9 and 13, the suggested abandonment, and relocation of the city during the post-Gupta period, has featured prominently in theories regarding 'urban decline', originally put forward by the historian R.S. Sharma (1987). As discussed recently by Derek Kennet (2004), the endurance of this problematic and hitherto untested theory is partly the result of outdated archaeological techniques, which, together with inadequate publication, leave the archaeological record open to misunderstanding by non-specialists.

Other archaeological sites

The other major published archaeological site in the study area is Udayagiri hill, situated just 1.5 km to the west of Vidisha's city rampart. The hill contains a number of rock-cut shrines containing a mixture of Vaisnava, Saiva and Jain carvings. The main dating evidence is provided by an inscription of Candragupta II dated to AD 401, although there is evidence for earlier periods of religious activity dating back to the second century BC. As discussed in chapters 11 and 12, the site's religious history and its relationship to the wider archaeological landscape has undergone major revision following recent field investigations of Michael Willis (2004) and Meera Dass (2001; Dass and Willis 2002).

The Sanchi area is also renowned for its numerous prehistoric rock-shelters and associated paintings and stone tools (Plates 45–8). The primary focus of rock-art research in Madhya Pradesh has been in the Betwa source area, and amongst the dense hills around Raisen. However, Sanchi hill itself contains painted rock-shelters, some of which figure on John Marshall's site-plan, and numerous rock-shelters have been reported, albeit in summary form, in the surrounding area (*IAR* 1976–7, 77; *ibid.*, 1982–3; 39–40; *ibid.*, 1992–3, 127). Prominent examples include those at Nagauri hill (Neumeyer 1978), less than 0.5 km south of Sanchi, and Ahmadpur (Khare 1976; *IAR* 1976–7, 32–3) around 10 km north of Vidisha.

The wider archaeological landscape

Other than Sanchi and the limited number of published archaeological sites described above, the surrounding countryside has seen little in the way of systematic archaeological exploration. In recent years, a number of unsystematic surveys have been carried out by the ASI (e.g. *IAR* 1976–7; 1982–3). However, the resulting reports comprise little more than single-line entries, usually without map coordinates, meaning that they provide, at the very most, a preliminary means of orientation in the landscape. Secondly, they usually consist of lists of ancient sites ranging from sculptural fragments to settlement mounds and associated surface ceramics. Generally absent is any reference to their wider geographical or archaeological context or to their spatial and historical relationship to better-known sites in the area. Finally, since the survey methods used to collect these data are rarely made explicit, and there are often gaps in the areas chosen for exploration, this material is of little use for building up quantitative spatial patterns in the landscape. More recently, a number of village-to-village surveys have been carried out in the area by the Madhya Pradesh State Archaeology Department (Maheswari 1997). Although they are as yet unpublished, these surveys are much broader in scope, and have resulted in fairly detailed reports, complete with a large quantity of colour photographs.[5]

Theoretical issues

Despite the rich history of archaeological, art-historical and epigraphical research in the area, there is a pronounced fragmentation between these various fields of enquiry. Scholars have tended to study either the prehistoric or early-historic period with little consideration of how the two relate to each other. This is illustrated, for example, by the general lack of reference to the close spatial relationship between prehistoric rock-shelters and Buddhist sites. The fragmentation between the aims, objectives and methods of the two strands of enquiry is further reflected in the structure of many conferences, which are frequently divided into separate 'early-historic' and 'prehistory' panels. While the first tends to focus on art history and architecture, wider considerations of landscapes and micro-environmental data are usually confined to the prehistory panel. Secondly, despite various textual references to the link between Vidisha and Sanchi during the Mauryan empire, the archaeological linkages between these two sites have not been adequately addressed. Both these factors have helped to perpetuate a fissured archaeological landscape in which the Buddhist monuments at Sanchi are separated from their wider setting. There are also other factors to be considered, which may be divided into a number of major groups, namely i) archaeological method and theory; ii) the social and economic background of Buddhism; iii) the spread of a Buddhist geography and world-view; iv) theories of state and urbanisation; v) irrigation technology and agrarian change; and vi) models of religious change. These points are taken up in detail in the following chapters but are of sufficient importance to be briefly introduced here.

Archaeological method and theory: monuments v. landscapes

The major theoretical shifts that have occurred in European archaeological circles over the last few decades and have led to an interest in archaeological landscapes have seen little application within the Indian context. The perpetuation of nineteenth-century archaeological paradigms, dominated by a 'monumental' and site-based vision, has meant that art-historically 'impressive' sites like Sanchi are usually studied in isolation from lesser known archaeological remains in the surrounding countryside. This study calls for a sensitivity to the type of archaeological vision which recognises the importance of the contextual setting of the material record (Hodder 1992) and looks beyond the myopic trench-based focus of the 'site', artefact or monument to the landscape as a whole. The present study thus seeks to combine the methods of art-historical analysis with those developed in landscape archaeology, examining sculptural and architectural remains not as isolated objects of enquiry, but as components of multifaceted cultural landscapes. The Sanchi area is well suited to this kind of approach, largely because of the rich archaeological, epigraphical and textual dataset relating to early Buddhism in general and to Sanchi in particular. However, as I shall argue in chapters 7–8, the 'blind' application to India of ready-made theoretical and methodological models developed by Western landscape archaeologists is to be avoided; a sensitivity to local requirements and conditions is needed to produce results which are viable.

The social and economic background of Buddhism

As discussed in chapter 2, the 'sociology' of Buddhism has generated a significant body of scholarship, with a number of apparently conflicting models describing the relationship between the rise of Buddhism and wider socio-economic developments such as urbanisation and state development in the Gangetic valley. Further, there is considerable uncertainty regarding the social and economic underpinnings of the spread of Buddhism out of its 'homeland' into areas further afield during the Mauryan and post-Mauryan periods. An understanding of these issues has in part been hampered by the perpetuation of a 'theological' or 'passive' model of Buddhism, which has traditionally viewed the *saṅgha*'s participation in social relations as a distortion of its original position as a body of renouncers concerned solely with individual enlightenment (e.g. Conze 1975). Further obstacles have been created by the lack of proper interaction between archaeology and text-based scholarship, a relationship in which archaeology continues to be cast in its traditional role as 'handmaiden' to history. For example, although the differences between orthodoxy and orthopraxy in Buddhist texts are well known (Schopen 1994b), the absence, prior to the first century AD, of inscriptions recording 'permanent endowments' in the form of buildings or agricultural land has been taken as proof that the 'domestication' of the *saṅgha* did not occur until the Kusana period (*ibid.*, 547). Further support for this argument has been presented by the apparent absence of 'planned and ordered' monastery architecture at Sanchi prior to the Gupta period (*ibid.*; Marshall 1940, 63–4). The main problem with this kind of reasoning is that the archaeological evidence upon which it is based is the product of the 'monumental' site-based paradigm discussed earlier, with little reference to more recent discoveries or developments in archaeological method and theory. Secondly, being based solely on the history and chronology of the courtyard monastery, this understanding overlooks other early forms of monastery architecture which do not conform to this plan. Finally, by relying solely on monumental and epigraphical evidence, little attention is given to other forms of evidence for long-term relationships between the *saṅgha* and local populations. The material documented for this study therefore presents an empirical basis for challenging many of these received assumptions. This includes evidence for early monasteries and other indicators of a 'domesticated' *saṅgha* based on the relative configuration of monasteries and habitational settlements and irrigation systems, which point to monastic participation in social relations outside the prescriptive parameters of the Buddhist texts, or at least the parameters set by occidental scholarship.

The spread of a Buddhist geography and world-view

Buddhism was the first religious tradition in India to conceive of itself within a broad ritual geography that transcended its regional origins in the Gangetic valley. This was effected through i) the spread of the relic cult, which meant that each stupa was envisaged as a part of a larger 'Buddha-body' (Walters 2002); ii) the spread of pan-Indian modes for visually representing the Buddhist narrative; and iii) the spread of the Mauryan empire and its support of the *saṅgha*, at least in the initial stages of Buddhist propagation. It would not be an understatement to say that the effective spread of Buddhism across South Asia (and later Asia as a whole) was a remarkable religious and cultural feat. How this was achieved is one of the major questions that this book seeks to address.

Theories of state and urbanisation

The relationship between Buddhism, urban populations and the state is another significant concern in this book. The main emphasis is on developments in central India during the Mauryan and post-Mauryan periods and, in particular, the role of smaller regional polities within the pan-Indian political scene. However, it is important to examine the earlier antecedents of these relationships in the Buddhist heartland during the mid-first millennium BC. To this end, the earlier history of Buddhism and its relationship to the re-appearance of urbanism and monarchical statehood, following the demise of urban culture within the Harappan context over 1000 years earlier, are discussed in chapter 2, along with a critical review of the state in ancient India.

Irrigation technology and agrarian change in ancient India

The subject of irrigation and land ownership has occupied a central position in the study of ancient Indian states, which traditionally has been informed by uncritical readings of problematically dated texts such as Kautilya's *Arthaśāstra*, as well as Orientalist and Marxist-inspired notions regarding despotic and centralised Asian polities. The received view, until recently, is that the appearance of urban-based states was dependent on agricultural surpluses brought about by centrally administered irrigation systems. This, and alternative approaches to water-management in ancient India, will be discussed in chapter 2 as a theoretical basis for the assessment, in chapter 14, of a group of irrigation systems documented during the SSP. Their spatial and temporal relationship to Buddhist sites in the area has provided an empirical basis for suggesting parallels with Sri Lanka where a rich body of archaeological, textual and epigraphical evidence attests to a system of 'monastic landlordism' from c. second century BC. The Sri Lankan material has been important for building an 'active' model of religious change in relation to Buddhism, and also for presenting, along with similar evidence in Southeast Asia, a more devolved picture of water-management than that portrayed by traditional Asian models of state and irrigation.

Models of religious change
There are also gaps in our understanding of the relationships between the incoming *saṅgha* and pre-existing religious frameworks. Despite a body of literature on 'tribal absorption' or 'cultic integration' in the Brahmanical tradition (e.g. Kulke 1993), the issue of which model of 'religious change' best fits the Buddhist context is a subject of ongoing debate. Approaches to this subject have tended to be dominated by 'theological' models, based largely on textual accounts of the Buddha's 'conversion' or subordination of 'local' deities such as *nāga*s and *yakṣa*s. In recent years, the issue of whether the *saṅgha* was overtly interested in converting local populations has come under doubt, with scholars such as Cohen (1998) or Bloss (1973) arguing instead that the *saṅgha*'s assimilation of local folk deities was a mechanism for 'localising' itself in new areas. However, a principal contention of the present study is that the assumed 'pan-Indian' v. 'local' polarisation, upon which both of the above narratives rest, may be inappropriate when it comes to assessing spatial and temporal patterns in Sanchi's archaeological landscape. The fact that the appearance of *nāga* and *yakṣa* sculptures there postdates the arrival of Buddhism by several hundred years should warn us against viewing them as clear-cut indicators of 'pre-Buddhist' cultic practice, as is usually assumed to be the case. Rather, their representation in pan-Indian sculptural conventions may have been just as much the result of Buddhism's own view of local deities as that of their actual devotees. As discussed in chapter 12, a particularly instructive historical parallel here is the introduction of Buddhism to eighth-century-AD Tibet, which involved, amongst other things, the renaming and re-ordering of local spirits and deities into a 'Buddhist' or 'Indian' typological framework.

Another key thread of this book is the argument that in order to construct a more socially integrated model of religious change it is necessary to move beyond the 'ritual' landscape *per se* to an examination of the archaeological landscape as a whole. This point is discussed further in chapter 6, drawing on 'practical' models of religious change, hitherto restricted to the context of Islamic and Christian traditions, which have stressed the non-religious motives of 'conversion' (Eaton 1993; Peel 1968; Goody 1975), such as, for example, access to medicine, water supplies and improved agricultural resources. In the Sanchi area, the empirical basis for assessing these models is provided by the spatial and temporal distribution of habitational settlements and irrigation systems discussed in chapters 13 and 14 respectively. In particular, I will argue that the *saṅgha* aligned itself with local agricultural deities such as *nāga*s, because the latters' perceived ability to control the monsoon rains was directly in keeping with the *saṅgha*'s own vested interests in water and land management. Not only did its involvement with water provide an instrument for generating lay patronage, but it acted as a very practical means for alleviating suffering (*dukkha*), which lay at the heart of the Buddhist message. Finally, there are strong suggestions that the Sanchi dams were built for irrigating rice-agriculture which, as discussed in chapters 4 and 14, raises a number of questions regarding the wider cultural, religious and ideological underpinnings of food change during the late centuries BC.

Research questions

The aim of this study was to tackle these theoretical issues through the documentation of Buddhist sites and their topographical and archaeological setting. This included the documentation of habitational settlements, irrigation works, rock-shelters and sculpture in the Vidisha hinterland. The primary research questions may be summarised as follows:

i) What was the full extent of Buddhist propagation in the area beyond the context of Sanchi and Cunningham's four other 'Bhilsa Tope' sites?
ii) What inferences can be drawn regarding the pre-existing religious, cultural and economic significance of the places at which monastic sites were established following the *saṅgha*'s arrival in the area?
iii) What evidence is there for early monastery dwellings prior to the early centuries AD? How does this evidence impact on the received models of understanding regarding the 'domestication' of the *saṅgha*?
iv) How does the configuration of monastic sites relate to local settlement patterns, water-resource structures and non-Buddhist cult spots? What do these relationships tell us about a) the wider socio-economic and religious background of Buddhist propagation; b) the terms of exchange between the incoming *saṅgha* and local agricultural populations; c) the *saṅgha*'s relationship to local belief systems; and d) the administrative underpinnings of water-management and its relationship to political and religious institutions?
v) How did the spread of Buddhism and related developments influence local agricultural practices and patterns of food consumption?
vi) What were the forces that allowed Buddhism to propel, and conceive of, itself within a pan-Indian 'Buddhist geography', before similar concepts had arisen within Brahmanical traditions?

Structure of the book

Following the present introductory chapter, this book is organised into two major sections, with chapters 2–10 providing a theoretical, historical and methodological background to the new data presented in chapters 11–14.

The theoretical framework
Chapter 2 aims to situate the newly documented material in this book within a broader historical and theoretical framework through an examination of theories regarding the social and economic background of Buddhism in the Gangetic valley during the mid-first millennium BC. Chapter 3 deals with the physical and archaeological geography of central India, and provides the basis for the account, in chapters 4–6, of the physical geography and political and religious history of the SSP study area. Chapter 7 discusses the main theoretical and methodological influences behind the emergence of landscape archaeology in Europe and considers how these approaches might be adapted to India.

Field methodology and ordering the archaeological landscape

Chapter 8 provides an account of the field methods used during the present study, drawing in particular on the challenges of tempering European survey techniques with a more localised research design. It also provides a framework for defining the various levels of archaeological remains in the landscape. A major contention is that sites do not exist in isolation but form components of larger site groupings, and also that not all sites exist at the same scale. Thus, in the project database, a 'Site Group' (SG) refers to a site at its broadest spatial level, e.g. a habitational settlement, hilltop ritual site or reservoir. Each Site Group has its own number (e.g. SG24) and may contain within its boundaries several smaller 'Site Clusters' (e.g. SC124) with more tightly defined categories, e.g. 'settlement mound', tank, stupa cluster, temple, etc. Again, each Site Cluster contains one or more 'Sites' (e.g. S55), operating at an even higher level of definition; e.g. sculpture pile or building cluster. Finally, a site may comprise one or more 'installations' (e.g. I-335), which refer to its individual architectural or sculptural constituents, such as 'pilaster', 'stupa railing' or *nāga* sculpture.

Whilst this was an effective way of structuring the database, there are also broader inter-Site Group relationships which are not so easy to fit into neat tables and categories, but rather are recognised when repeated with sufficient regularity across the study area as a whole. Thus, clusters of inter-related Site Groups constitute what can be called an 'archaeological complex' or, in more historically specific terms, an 'early-historic complex' (Shaw and Sutcliffe 2001). The early-historic complex at Sanchi, for example, consists of the hilltop Buddhist monuments (SG001), together with the settlements at Kanakhera (SG002) and Nagauri (SG003a) and the reservoir to the south (SG003), and acts as a kind of 'microcosmic' model for identifying similar patterns throughout the study area. It is only by treating these individual elements as interrelated parts of dynamic but spatially bounded complexes that we can begin to address the historical aims of the study and assess hypotheses regarding the role of Buddhism in its socio-economic landscape.

The data chapters

Chapter 9 deals with the archaeologies of Vidisha and Sanchi, with a critical appraisal of existing chronological sequences. A basic account of Sanchi's immediate archaeological context is also given, including habitational settlements, dams and non-Buddhist cult spots. Taken together, these patterns provide a model for evaluating the archaeological setting of Buddhist monasteries throughout the area as a whole. The chronological framework used for dating newly documented sites is described in chapter 10, including the revised sequences at Vidisha and Sanchi, and the surface pottery assemblages from the SSP.

Chapters 11–14, which deal with the newly documented data across the study area, are aimed at assessing the regional manifestation of the archaeological patterns at Sanchi. Given the historical and theoretical aims of this study, it was important to organise and represent the data so as to bring out as clearly as possible the relationship between sites through time and space. I was presented with the choice of whether to organise the data according to site-category, and perhaps lose out on the element of inter-site relationships, or to break up the study area into different geographical sectors, describing the major archaeological complexes as I went along. This would have helped to bring out the internal cohesion of each 'archaeological complex', but would also have led to a rather 'cluttered' dataset and, consequently, confused arguments. In the end, therefore, I chose a compromise between the two options. Each of the four data chapters, on Buddhist sites, non-Buddhist sites, habitational settlements and irrigation systems respectively, include two or more sections, consisting of a site-gazetteer followed by thematic discussions.

There is some variation between the internal structuring of the site-gazetteer in each of the four data chapters (11–14); this reflects fundamental differences in the nature of the material being discussed. In chapters 11 and 14, the Buddhist sites and ancient dams are ordered according to their geographical rather than chronological distribution. This is because, with a few exceptions, most of these sites belong to a single phase (II). By contrast, there is much more variety, both in sectarian affiliation and chronology, with respect to the non-Buddhist sculpture described in chapter 12. In this case, the data were arranged according to phase rather than geographical sector, in order to highlight the changing configuration of the ritual landscape through time. In both cases, the decision to describe the data in prose rather than tabular form stemmed from the conviction that the ensuing discussion would otherwise lack adequate context. By contrast, many of the habitational settlements described in chapter 13 have already been mentioned in previous chapters, and are thus listed in a more summarised, note-format. The chapter follows a sector-by-sector structure, with the provision of Site Group (SG) names and numbers to enable easy cross-referencing with the ensuing discussion in Part II of the chapter.

Although this way of ordering the data effectively separates out individual components of the broader site-group categories, references to the wider archaeological setting of archaeological remains are made throughout the study. Further details on particular inter-site relationships are provided in Appendix I, which is organised according to 'Site Group' number and name, together with associated Site Cluster and Site descriptions. This system was chosen in order to highlight the internal spatial relationships within a single Site Group. All sculptural and architectural fragments are listed in Appendix IIa, with associated details such as site name, stone type, dimensions, iconography, context and present-day condition. To enable easy-cross referencing, every sculpture mentioned in the main text is accompanied by its respective Site Group and 'Instalment' no. (e.g. SG099/I-156). Appendix IIa also includes several previously published sculptures or those stored in museum collections. Appendix IIb lists the major types and phases of monastic buildings and their associated sites. Appendix IIc consists of a phase-by-phase list of non-Buddhist cult spots and temple sites whose primary context is known. As mentioned in the Preface, the structure of the appendices is a simplified version of the project's primary relational database. However, the transformation into a 'flattened' tabular version involves a reduction in the level of complexity that a relational database can bring to the analysis of archaeological data at a landscape level, especially when linked to GIS spatial attributes. The complete dataset in its original form will shortly be made available in web format, with linked figures, plates and maps.[6] This resource will include a comprehensive, illustrated gazetteer of the entire sculpture dataset to supplement the unavoidably incomplete version here: while this book provides plates of most of the 'early' (c. third century BC to sixth century AD) sculptures, only limited selections of the later examples could be included.

Appendix III (a–d) deals with the ceramic material collected during the survey. The methodology for studying this material is described in chapter 10, while references to ceramic phasing are given throughout the book, with corresponding sample numbers listed in footnotes. Full details of the latter, and their associated sites are provided in Appendix IIIa. The main fabric and vessel types, discussed in detail in chapters 10 and 13, are listed in Appendices IIIb and IIIc respectively, with illustrations of the most diagnostic vessel types in Appendix IIId.

Conclusion: transcending disciplinary boundaries

By challenging received models of ancient Indian religion and calling for a greater level of integration between textual, art-historical and archaeological approaches to the subject, this book is not intended to undermine the quality of existing scholarship in any of these individual fields. Further, although several approaches from different disciplines have been combined in this study, it is possibly some way off before an acceptable level of integration might be achieved. Bridging the boundaries between the various disciplines that deal with ancient India is a tricky problem that requires a concerted degree of long-term effort on the part of all concerned. Much of the problem is locked into the underlying academic infrastructure, changes to which would be necessary to achieve an acceptable level of integration. For example, at least in the UK, most subjects relating to ancient India are still taught within regionally, rather than disciplinarily defined departments with labels such as 'Oriental Studies' or 'South Asian Studies'. In such contexts, archaeology plays a marginal, secondary or non-existent role, and usually with little emphasis on theory or method. Conversely, students studying India within archaeology departments have the advantages of a strong methodological or theoretical background, but are likely to lack the necessary training in language, religious or political history.[7]

Two extremes can be envisaged here: on the one hand are the philologists, theologians and textual historians, absorbed in a particular religious tradition, language or set of textual sources. For such scholars it is difficult enough to find time to assimilate the key archaeological evidence relevant to their subject, let alone keep up with more specialised theoretical and methodological debates within archaeological circles. The problem is, however, that without the latter it is difficult to judge the soundness of archaeological interpretations. The obverse situation applies to archaeologists, who are increasingly being directed into methodological specialisms which can involve extended periods of time in the field or laboratory. Students with a background in 'general archaeology', or those without a particular geographical focus, often lack the language or history background to situate their findings within a meaningful cultural framework. Quite clearly, if we stray too far from our respective disciplines we are in danger of compromising the quality of what we are trained to do or of being labelled a 'jack of all trades but master of none'! We are far removed from ninteenth-century polymaths such as Alexander Cunningham or James Prinsep who managed to transcend these limitations and at the same time hold down 'day jobs' as senior engineers and government employees.

The current academic restraints today mean that what is now required is meaningful and focused dialogue across and between the various disciplines. However, while archaeology sits easily with the physical and social sciences such as geography, geophysics, geology, biology and anthropology, its relationship with text-based scholarship is still an uneasy one. This may have something to do with the fact that most of the above cited disciplines are by their very nature dependent on team work, and, indeed, most modern archaeological projects are exercises in interdisciplinarity, involving collaboration between a wide range of specialists from different fields. By contrast, most text-based research is a fairly solitary activity. In order to work together in a meaningful way, we each need to be aware of the potentials and limitations of our respective datasets. For example, it is as difficult for an uninformed archaeologist to ask the right questions of a scholar of Buddhist texts as it is for the latter to recognise the potential contribution of a pile of potsherds or hydrological data to their own research. In recent years, several groups, including the Vijayanagara Research Project and the Vidisha Research Group (with which the SSP is connected), have been established to try to redress these problems by bringing together scholars from different fields, yet all united in their interest in a particular geographical region. It is the hope of the current author that more such groups will develop in years to come in order to tackle specific problems through a range of disciplinary approaches and methods.

CHAPTER 2

Buddhism, Urbanisation and the State

Introduction

The aim of this chapter is to position the research agenda outlined in the previous chapter within a broader temporal, geographical and theoretical framework. Although the book's primary focus is on the social and economic underpinnings of Buddhist propagation in central India from c. third century BC, it is important to consider the earlier history of Buddhism in the Gangetic valley, and its relationship to urbanisation, state-formation and other major economic and political processes taking place during the mid-first millennium BC. This will involve a summary of the prevalent models of state in ancient India, highlighting a number of methodological shortcomings in the archaeological contributions to these debates, as well as the problematic relationship between archaeology and history in the study of early Indian polities. The archaeology of irrigation and land-ownership will also be explored in light of the prominent position that irrigation-based agricultural surplus has occupied in traditional explanations for the rise of cities and monarchical states during this period. A major aim will be to assess the degree to which the archaeological record supports the received view that ancient Indian irrigation was dependent on centralised administration. To this end, I will draw on evidence for 'monastic landlordism' in Sri Lanka, which presents a more devolved model of irrigation control than suggested by the traditional view. The Sri Lankan material provides a helpful parallel for assessing the ancient dams in the Sanchi area, discussed in chapter 14, and their relationship to wider aspects of the religious and economic landscape.

Buddhist history

Notwithstanding ongoing disagreement over the dating of the historical Buddha (Bechert, ed., 1991), the Buddha's life and teachings are usually placed sometime between the sixth and fifth centuries BC. Although some of the main pilgrimage sites and other important places associated with key events in the story of Buddha have been identified, there is a paucity of archaeological material relating to the earliest history of Buddhism at these sites (Coningham 2001). The first time that Buddhism enters the archaeological record at these sites and others, both in and beyond the Buddhist heartland, is during the third century BC, following the Mauryan emperor Asoka's conversion to Buddhism. The overlapping processes of Buddhist propagation and imperial expansion can be tracked through the distribution of Asokan edicts which extend from Afghanistan to south India (Falk 2006); many of these, like the Asokan pillar at Sanchi, stand within Buddhist compounds.

For the earlier period, we are heavily dependent on the Pali Canon, the earliest texts being sections of the *Dīgha Nikāya*, *Majjhima Nikāya, Saṃyutta Nikāya* and *Anguttara Nikāya*, which purport to have been composed during the lifetime of the Buddha. In addition to providing the main framework of Buddhist theology, these texts also contain incidental references to the social, economic and political conditions that formed the backdrop to the rise of Buddhism in the Gangetic valley.[1] A number of major cities (e.g. Rajgir, Sravasti, Vaisali, Kausambi) are described as places frequented by the Buddha, or as locations for the first monasteries donated by the Magadhan kings and other personages, including merchants and other patrons. Although these monasteries have been identified archaeologically, they have yielded no material evidence datable prior to the early centuries AD (Coningham 2001). This absence probably reflects the makeshift nature of the monasteries during the time of the Buddha, when the *saṅgha* consisted of a body of monks compelled to wander for most of the year apart from the monsoon months when they were required to take up communal residence in temporary rain retreats (*vessana*). In time, these retreats grew into permanent monasteries, although the question of when the transition from peripatetic to sedentary monasticism took place has not been settled. This transition is central to discussions regarding the 'domestication' of the *saṅgha*, as it is seen as providing the basis for the formalisation of exchange networks between monastic and lay populations. The latter, which revolves around the ritual giving of gifts (*dāna*), ranging from food to buildings, land and water-resource structures, in exchange for merit (*pūnya*), are discussed below. However, as stressed by Strenski (1983) it is important to acknowledge the potential that such relationships existed outside the context of sedentary monasticism, the foundations for which were already laid down during the earliest history of Buddhism: as we shall see, these developments cannot be understood without consideration of wider social, political and economic processes taking place in the Gangetic valley during the mid-first millennium BC.

Urbanisation in the Gangetic valley

As mentioned earlier, Buddhist texts have shed some light on the political and economic milieu of the time. The *Anguttara Nikāya* provides the names of sixteen major states (*mahājanapadas*) and their capital cities, extending from Afghanistan in the north to the Deccan in the south. Over half of these state capitals have been identified in the archaeological record as fortified settlements associated with Northern Black Polished Ware (NBPW), a diagnostic pottery which marks the earliest phase of urbanisation in the Indo-Gangetic divide and the upper Gangetic valley, datable to the mid-sixth century BC. For example, Rajgir, described as the capital of Magadha, Rajghat, capital of Kasi, and Champa, capital of Anga, all appear to have reached a level of 'incipient urbanism' by this time (Figure 1.1). Other urban centres beyond the Gangetic region are also mentioned, including Ujjain in central India, the capital of ancient Avanti, and Taxila and Charsadda in the North-West, both of which were associated with the annexation of Gandhara and the Indus valley by the Achaemenid empire, whose capital was at Persepolis.

Increasing inter-state warfare and expansionism eventually led to the consolidation of the sixteen *mahājanapadas* into four larger states: Avanti, Vatsa, Kosala and Magadha. By 400 BC, the focus of power had become concentrated upon Magadha, whose territory under the Nanda dynasty extended as far as Orissa in the east and Karnataka in the south. It is during this period that punch-marked and uninscribed coins first appear in the archaeological record and texts attest to a professional bureaucracy and a rising class of merchants and traders. Meanwhile, much of the Achaemenid territory to the north came under Hellenistic rule following the invasion of Alexander the Great in c. 326 BC (Allchin, ed., 1995).

By c. 321 BC, the whole of Magadha and the Hellenistic colonies in the North-West had become incorporated into the Mauryan empire under its first ruler, Candragupta Maurya. The Magadhan capital subsequently shifted to Pataliputra (modern Patna) described in Classical sources of the early fourth century BC as a well-planned city with enormous fortifications.[2] These descriptions are matched by excavated remains of a pillared hall and a wooden palisaded rampart datable to the same period. This represents the beginning of the second major stage of urbanisation culminating in the third century BC under Candragupta's grandson emperor Asoka (r. 273–236 BC). The older fortified capitals become fully fledged cities, while urban culture spread into previously undeveloped areas: Vaisali in the middle Gangetic valley, Vidisha, Eran, Tumain and Tripuri in central India, and the earliest cities in south India all belong to the later phase of urbanisation (Allchin, ed., 1995).

As discussed below, there are still major uncertainties over the precise nature of political administration across and between the different states. Although this is partly a problem of historiography, it can also be attributed to methodological shortcomings within Indian archaeology. First, many of the above city sites were excavated long before the development of scientific sampling and dating techniques, and secondly, apart from several diagnostic wares, many of the more ubiquitous ceramic types remain undated.[3] Further, the archaeological basis of the above chronology for the most part consists of sequences from limited vertical trenches at key points (usually through the city rampart), with little in the way of horizontal excavation or systematic survey to relate the city sequences to settlement patterns in their rural hinterlands. Exceptions including two oft-cited settlement distribution surveys in the Gangetic valley (Lal 1984; Erdosy 1988) are discussed in chapter 7. Erdosy's (1988) survey carried out over 1200 km^2 in Allahabad district, around Kausambi in the ancient Janapada of Vatsa, suggests that by 400 BC there was a three-tier settlement hierarchy which had increased to five-tier by the late NBPW period (c. 400–100 BC). Further, as sites towards the upper end of the settlement hierarchy grew in scale, there was a corresponding increase in the number of villages in 'interior' areas, away from major rivers. As discussed later, and in chapter 7, these findings have figured prominently in theories regarding the link between iron technology and urbanisation. However, they need to be viewed with some caution as they are based on inferences regarding phase-by-phase changes in surface pottery scatters, which are highly susceptible to distortions caused by site-formation and post-depositional processes (Hodder and Malone 1984).

Theories of urbanisation and state

State formation

Various theories have been put forward to explain the reappearance of urban culture in the Gangetic valley area between c. 1000 and 300 BC following the disintegration of the Harappan urban civilization in the North-West some 1000 years earlier. Key amongst these is a set of major economic and political transformations assumed to have occurred over this time-frame (Thapar 1984; Sharma 1983a). In particular, comparative analyses of the Vedic and early Buddhist texts have suggested a shift from a pre-monetary, tribal economy based on agriculture and exchange to a more complex economy based on a diverse range of craft specialisation, guilds and cities organised according to occupational groups. Incidental descriptions in Buddhist texts attest to a primarily 'urban based economy supported by a large agricultural sector, operating at different levels of development, and with inter-regional trade providing luxury goods' (Bailey and Mabbett 2003, 63).

The other major development thought to have occurred during this period is the transition from non-monarchical tribal republics ruled by elected chiefs to monarchical states governed by hereditary rulers. The former (*gaṇa dhīna*/*gaṇa saṅgha*) first finds reference in Vedic texts (c. 1500–800 BC) within the context of a four-tier *varṇa* (class) structure: *kṣatriya*, *brāhmana*, *vaiśya*, *śudra*.[4] This system was characterised by democratic rule whereby leaders were elected from the *kṣatriya varṇa* with rule legitimised by the support of fellow elites. By contrast, the monarchical states (*rājā dhīna*) of the Buddhist texts, were centred on royal capitals and based on a hereditary system of descent whereby the ruler's power was legitimised by the priestly class which had now taken the place of the *kṣatriyas* at the top of the *varṇa* hierarchy. There was also a third category of political organisation, represented by small non-monarchical states based on towns ruled by oligarchies or tribes with hereditary leaders.

Archaeologies of state

There are considerable difficulties when it comes to distinguishing between these political categories in the archaeological record. Notwithstanding the methodological problems outlined above, the archaeological manifestations of monarchical and non-monarchical states can be remarkably similar, with common features such as standardised monetary and weight systems, fortified capitals, taxation, local and inter-regional trade, state and privately owned land, multi-tiered settlement hierarchies based around an administrative capital, and hereditary classes of elites and occupational groups (Kenoyer 1997). Additional problems stem from Orientalist-inspired notions regarding the centralised nature of ancient Indian states, assumed to have been ruled over by tyrannical despots. The roots of these ideas are traceable to the historical and political writings of Classical Greece and also underscore European political thinking from the Renaissance to the eighteenth and nineteenth centuries (Sinopoli 2003, 1–12). Marx and Engels's theory of the 'Asiatic Mode of Production' has been influential, particularly in its later form as developed by Karl Wittfogel (1957). Wittfogel's hydraulic theory, to be discussed later, was based on the belief that Asia's predominantly semi-arid environment watered by several large river systems created a unique situation whereby agricultural surplus, upon which urbanisation is assumed to depend, was itself dependent on large-scale centrally administered irrigation systems (Sinopoli 2003, 1–12).

According to this model, India is seen as the polar opposite of European dynamism, its past presented as despotic and timeless, defined by stable and unchanging technologies and political systems, upset only by external factors such as foreign invasions. The archaeological identification of such processes has traditionally taken place within a 'culture-history' framework, which rests on the assumption that specific polities and 'peoples' are identifiable on the basis of spatially and temporally bound material culture traits, with any change being explained in diffusionist terms. As summarised by Johansen (2003, 197), 'the construction of closed spatio-temporal "cultural" units considered coterminous with ethnolinguistic human groups from typologically derived packages of material traits became by far the dominant episteme in South Asian archaeology following Wheeler's work'. The problem with these 'cultures' is that, as descriptive rather than explanatory categories, they say little about social meaning, political systems or individual agency. Such clear-cut correlations between material 'cultures' and peoples have left the culture-history model open to abuse, as illustrated most forcefully by the legitimising role that Gustav Kossina's archaeology, with its emphasis on the material-culture traits of the 'Germanic' peoples, played in the ideology of Nazi Germany (Johansen 2003). Similarly, theories that link the appearance of iron and Painted Grey Ware (PGW) in c. 1100 BC with the movement of Indo-Aryan speaking groups into the Gangetic valley are now largely dismissed as products of an outdated interpretative model (Shaffer 1984; Chakrabarti 1997; Thapar 1999). The scientific focus of 'processual' archaeology, itself partly a reaction to the abuses of the culture-history framework, and the more recent 'post-processual' trends have made an impression on South Asian archaeology (Fuller and Boivin 2002a; 2002b; Paddaya 1995), but neither have helped develop a more nuanced model of state in ancient India.

Whilst the lack of secure regional ceramic sequences is a major culprit here, further misassumptions about the Indian state, and in particular the Mauryan empire, have stemmed from a text-dominated framework of analysis, which has helped to shape the traditional vision of Indian history as one based on long dynastic sequences pivoted around the two highly centralised imperial states of the Mauryan and Gupta dynasties.[5] The periods following the demise of each of these empires are characterised by political fragmentation and, in the case of the post-Gupta period, urban decline, a situation which is seen as leading to feudalism, closely paralleling the situation in medieval Europe (Sharma 1987). As discussed in chapter 5, there are serious methodological shortcomings associated with the archaeological evidence upon which the historian, R.S. Sharma, based his 'urban decay' model (Kennet 2004). Further criticisms of the 'feudal' model draw on the lack of attention given to the economic or political processes that led to such levels of supposed political centralisation, and the failure to take account of smaller local polities and the nature of their interaction with pan-Indian power structures. Other misassumptions regarding the centralised nature of the Mauryan empire have stemmed from uncritical readings of the *Arthaśāstra*, a manual on statecraft traditionally attributed to Kautilya, the chief minister of Candragupta I (r. 326–313 BC). Despite an enduring reluctance to acknowledge its anachronistic qualities, it is now thought to be a much later text probably not reaching its final form until the third century AD or later (Trautmann 1971). Finally, the traditional view that the distribution of the Asokan edicts represent the boundaries of a unified political entity is no longer taken for granted, the current understanding being that the edicts mark the furthest extent of Mauryan interaction with neighbouring polities (Fussman 1987–8; Sugandhi 2003). A growing body of numismatic and epigraphical evidence relating to small yet powerful local oligarchies during the post-Mauryan period has also helped to build a more complex picture of political administration within and between states, as discussed in relation to the Sanchi area in chapter 5.

In recent years, scholars have argued against the viability of a single universal model of state for South Asia, proposing a number of regionally and temporally specific models. Developed largely by historians drawing on textual, epigraphical and architectural sources, notable studies include Heitzman's (1995) analysis of the Cola state between the ninth and thirteenth century AD; Kulke's (1995b) account of 'early medieval' Orissa, and Chattopadhyaya's (1994) of state-formation in Rajasthan. Examples of more interdisciplinary studies include the Chanderi project in central India (Fussman 2003) and the Vijayanagara project in south India (Sinopoli 2003).[6] The latter, dealing with the fourteenth to seventeenth centuries AD, combines historical analysis with both excavation and survey-based archaeological techniques and provides a working model for the kind of focused inter-disciplinary collaboration needed to address some of the major questions regarding the nature of early Indian polities.

The Iron Age

Limited quantities of iron objects, largely in the form of hunting weapons and craft tools, first appear in the archaeological record at sites such as Atranjikhera and Hastinapur in the Gangetic valley from c. 1000 BC, in association with PGW. Rare occurrences of iron in earlier Chalcolithic contexts have also been reported. However, it is only with the rise of urbanism in the mid-sixth century BC that iron appears in significant quantities, with the addition of tools of production such as axes and ploughshares. Consequently, developments in iron metallurgy lie at the heart of technological determinist explanations for the transition from Chalcolithic village-based economies to the urban culture of the early-historic period (Kosambi 1963; Sharma 1983b). There are two slightly different hypotheses here. The first, centred upon excavation sequences and settlement patterns in the Deccan Chalcolithic (Shinde 1988), is that the iron ploughshare enabled cultivation of heavy black-cotton soils in interior areas away from naturally cleared floodplains. The second, drawing largely on the two settlement studies in the Gangetic valley mentioned earlier (Lal 1984; Erdosy 1988), is that iron axes enabled clearance of dense forests that opened up new areas for cultivation and settlement.

The central hypothesis of the Deccan-based research is that, due to the absence of iron tools during the Chalcolithic, farmers were unable to cultivate the heavy clayey soils beyond the narrow patches of alluvium on the floodplains (Kosambi 1963, 309–18; Agrawal 1982). Hence the positioning of so many Chalcolithic settlements on the banks of major rivers despite the fact that such locations were prone to flooding, as attested by evidence for repeated inundation from excavated sequences at Kayatha (Ansari and Dhavalikar 1975, 7–8), Dangawada (Chakravarty *et al.*, 1989), with close parallels at Rangai, near Vidisha (Khare 1981; *IAR* 1976–7: 33–4). It is only after c. 1100 BC that significant numbers of settlements appeared in interior areas. The argument that this was due principally to developments in iron technology has been challenged on a number of accounts, the main contention being that adequate ploughing can be achieved with wood and chalcedony blades, not to mention the fact that black-cotton soil is renowned for its 'self-ploughing' properties (Dhavalikar 1973, 142).

Hypotheses regarding the role of iron in the clearance of forests in the Gangetic valley area are based largely on settlement distribution studies in the Kanpur (Lal 1984) and Allahabad (Erdosy 1988) regions which have provided additional empirical evidence for a shift from river bank to interior settlement locations between the Chalcolithic and early-historic periods. Lal's (1984) survey, for example, revealed that all the Chalcolithic Black and Red Ware (BRW) sites were situated on river banks as compared to 40 out of 46 sites during the subsequent PGW phase. By the NBPW phase, however, the majority of a total of 99 sites were located away from river-bank locations.

More recent scholarship, however, has shed doubt on the posited link between deforestation and urbanisation on the basis of independent textual evidence which suggests that the bulk of deforestation in the Ganga-Yamuna Doab area occurred in the post-Industrial era (Erdosy 1998; Lal 1986). Another counter-argument draws on the absence of evidence for any significant change in iron technology during the time under question (Chakrabarti 1985), while a growing body of evidence for a much longer chronology of iron technology in the Gangetic valley area (Tewari 2003) sheds additional doubt on these theories. Indeed, moving to our study area in central India, considerable quantities of iron have been found in pre early-historic levels at Vidisha (*IAR* 1963–4).

Archaeological assemblages and literary evidence suggest that the use of iron weapons in inter-regional warfare might have had a greater impact on the formation of states and cities than agricultural surplus which had already reached significant levels during the pre-iron period. Another important point to bear in mind is that the Bronze Age urban civilisation of the Indus valley grew up before the development of iron technology, most probably without centrally administered irrigation and land-ownership systems (Miller 2006), and that other factors such as the consolidation of trading networks, stable political structures and a strong agricultural base are now considered more relevant in the re-emergence of urban culture during the early-historic period (Chakrabarti 1985).

Irrigation in ancient India

Another central tenet in the traditional accounts of state formation and urbanisation outlined above is that the agricultural surplus upon which these processes are assumed to depend is itself the result of irrigation systems administered at a centralised state-level. This view has stemmed largely from references to state-controlled irrigation systems in texts such as the *Arthaśāstra*, but also from verses in Asoka's edicts which include the provision of water as one of the responsibilities of a king. Wittfogel's hydraulic theory has also helped to shape the idea that irrigation was the sole prerogative of the state. It is important to assess the archaeological basis for these arguments, especially given the prominence that this book gives to dams and irrigation systems and their temporal and spatial relationship to Buddhist sites in Sanchi's archaeological landscape.

Until recently the study of ancient Indian irrigation has been dominated by a textual framework, which is largely responsible for the traditional view that the building and management of irrigation works were dependent on centralised forms of state administration (Chakravarty 1998). Most studies to date (e.g. Puri 1968; Venkayya 1906) have consisted of compilations of textual references ranging from the *Ṛg Veda* to the *Arthaśāstra*. Generally absent is any critical attention to problems of historicity, authorship, chronology or regional context. Particularly problematic in this respect is the *Arthaśāstra*, which, despite evidence that it was not codified until the third century AD or later (Trautmann 1971), is often treated as a kind of guidebook to the Mauryan empire.

Theories regarding the centralised nature of irrigation management are not unique to India but are common to Asia as a whole, largely as a result of 'Orientalist' models of state discussed earlier, but also because centralised irrigation is often regarded as essential to agricultural surplus, one of the key factors, along with accelerated trade and craft production, used to explain the rise of urbanisation and state-formation.[7] Wittfogel's (1957) hydraulic theory, for example, which was a direct product of these influences, has continued to shape interpretations of Asian economic systems until relatively recent times (Geertz 1980).[8] In Sri Lanka, evidence relating to the monastic ownership of irrigation systems as an instrument of lay patronage from c. second century BC onwards (Gunawardana 1971), together with ethnographic accounts of small-scale irrigation works built and managed by village councils (Leach 1959), have helped to challenge the 'Oriental despot' theory, attesting instead to a 'multicentred society with power devolving on the gentry and the monastic institutions' (Gunawardana 1971, 26). In Bali, observations regarding the priestly control of irrigation systems (Lansing 1991) have also led to more devolved models of irrigation control,[9] with additional insights provided by archaeological investigations of irrigation systems in Thailand (Stargardt 1983; 1990; 1998). Stargardt's work is particularly useful because of its comprehensive geographical focus, and its strong emphasis on the cultural links between Southeast Asia and southern India. Not only does it bring together hydrological and archaeological analyses, but also focuses on the link between water-management and religious institutions.

For ancient India, however, the traditional 'centralised' model has until recently remained unchallenged due in part to the paucity of archaeological research on specific irrigation traditions. Further, material evidence has usually consisted solely of inscriptions, with three key examples frequently cited in support of textually generated theories for the centralised nature of irrigation management (Chakravarty 1998): i) a body of dams and associated inscriptions in south India, traditionally associated with the Colas on the basis of descriptions in Tamil *Sangam* literature but rarely datable before c. seventh century AD (Venkayya 1906); ii) a first-century-BC inscription referring to the royal construction of a canal at Hathigumpha, Orissa, in c. fourth century BC (Sircar 1965, 213–21); iii) an inscription issued during the reign of the Saka ruler, Rudradaman (second century AD), in association with the Sudarsana lake (*taṭāka*) at Junagadh, Gujarat (Kielhorn 1905–6). The inscription records Rudradaman's repair of the dam following a major storm and describes its original construction during the reign of Candragupta Maurya and subsequent improvements under the orders of Asoka (*Ep. In.* VIII, 36–49; X, 99). Later repairs are also mentioned in the inscription of Skandagupta (Bhandarkar *CII*, III, 296–304; Fleet *CII*, III, 56–65).[10]

Although the content of these inscriptions generally supports the view that the construction and maintenance of big dams were the prerogative of an overarching centralised authority, little consideration had been given to the wider context of these inscriptions and their associated dams. Further, inadequate attention has been given to the capacity of material evidence to stand as independent data with the ability to contradict textual readings. This is particularly important given the rhetorical if not polemical style of elite texts and the multiple interpretations that may be drawn from them, but also because aspects of the archaeological landscape can shed independent light on their administration and function. At Junagadh, for example, consideration of the wider ritual landscape, including a group of rock-cut structures immediately downstream of the reservoir, supports suggestions of a link between water-management and Buddhism from at least third century BC (Shaw and Sutcliffe 2003a), while during the Gupta period, this relationship appears to have been reframed within a Brahmanical context, as suggested by a Visnu temple mentioned in the inscription of Skandagupta (*ibid.*).[11] This fits with patterns across north India as a whole from the Gupta period, when evidence for devolved systems of irrigation management is provided in the form of land-grants attesting to the management of agrarian resources by Brahmanical institutions (Kulke 1993, 11). In subsequent years, this system becomes fully entrenched, as illustrated by the tradition of temple-owned tanks described in the Pallava and Cola inscriptions of south India (Morrison 1993, 145).

Despite these data, focused archaeological studies of ancient irrigation systems are few and far between, as already mentioned. A number of irrigation systems in Neolithic south India are known (Allchin 1954, 130, 510–11; Ludden 1979), but these are largely restricted to primitive, unlined tanks, while other more focused studies (Davison-Jenkins 1997; Morrison 1993) relate to much later water-resource structures in and around the pre-modern city of Vijayanagara. In Baluchistan, a group of siltation tanks known as 'Gabarbands' have also generated interest, but there are still major uncertainties over their dating (Possehl 1975). Theories which link the rise of Harappan urbanisation with irrigation-based agricultural surpluses usually draw on assumptions regarding the use of river inundation, small-scale canal networks, and well and lift irrigation. However, clear archaeological evidence for the nature of Harappan irrigation is still lacking (Miller 2006). The other major body of evidence, more in line with the chronological focus of the present study, comes from Gujarat. Although the aforementioned Sudarsana reservoir at Junagadh has been known for over a century from the inscriptions of Rudradaman and Skandagupta, the dam's physical remains were only relatively recently located (Mehta 1968), together with a number of similar dams in Sabarkantha district around the Buddhist site at Devnimori (Mehta 1963).[12] In 2002, the opportunity was taken to visit Junagadh (Shaw and Sutcliffe 2003a) in order to verify Mehta's archaeological claims, which appear not to have been fully incorporated into subsequent historical scholarship. For example, Thapar (1998, 285) states that 'the [Sudarsana dam] has yet to be conclusively identified', adding (*ibid.*, n. 56) that Mehta's discovery 'is an attempt at locating the site and seems probable but not certain'. As discussed in chapter 14, the Sudarsana dam provides the closest comparative framework for studying the design and function of newly documented dams in the Sanchi area, as well as their relationship to political authority and religious institutions.

Several other accounts of early-historic irrigation technology in ancient India do exist but these relate to canals discovered by chance during unrelated excavation projects. In Vidisha, for example, the remains of a third-century-BC canal, which would have drawn water from the River Betwa, were discovered during excavations at the Heliodorus pillar site (Bhandarkar 1915, 69–70). Other early canals have been identified at Benares (*ASIAR* 1914–15, 69) and Kaveripattam in Tamil Nadu (*IAR* 1963–4, 20), while another, as just noted, is mentioned in the first-century-BC inscription from Hathigumpha, Orissa (Sircar 1965, 213–21). This limited body of evidence has helped to shape the view that, in contrast to the use of reservoirs in Sri Lanka, canal-based irrigation was the dominant form of irrigation in ancient India (Puri 1968, 54). The lack of reference to dam-based irrigation is probably a reflection of a vertical, trench-based focus of Indian archaeology which, as discussed in chapter 7, has until recently lacked the 'horizontal' perspective achievable through modern survey methods. A more comprehensive image might have been formed had attention been paid to surface remains throughout these cities' rural hinterlands.

Comparisons are also possible with the more or less contemporary developments in the dry zone of Sri Lanka, where information is available on advances in dam construction and control structures from c. third century BC onwards (Parker 1909; Brohier 1934 [reprint 1979]; Bohingamuwa 2005). The physical survival of these structures, which were examined and described before their reconstruction in the nineteenth century, means that the study of irrigation in Sri Lanka is better developed than anywhere else in South Asia. Although the scale of the larger reservoirs is considerably greater than the central Indian dams and the hydrological background different, there are historical and technical similarities between the two developments. As discussed elsewhere (Shaw and Sutcliffe 2003a), there is sufficient evidence of similarity in the dating and design of the Sri Lankan dams and those around Sanchi to suggest that there could have been exchange of technical expertise between the two areas, which were of course in touch during the period of Buddhist evangelism. These inter-regional comparisons shed considerable light on the possible history and function of the Sanchi dams, as well as the administrative systems that lay behind their construction and upkeep. As discussed later, they also provide the basis for building an integrated model of religious and social change. The principal working hypothesis is that the control of water harvesting and irrigation facilities was not only a means of political legitimisation for local rulers, but also formed a central component of the Buddhist *saṅgha*'s propagation strategies. The second hypothesis is that they were built to provide irrigation for rice, which, based on limited evidence from the Deccan and south India, is unlikely to have been introduced into central India before the late centuries BC.

Its spread from the Gangetic valley where it had formed the staple crop for at least the previous three millennia, would have been an effective response to increased population levels suggested by the distribution of Buddhist sites and settlements in the Sanchi area. Moreover, a major contention in this book is that rice was also part of the wider cultural package that accompanied the spread of urban culture and new religious values from eastern India. The Sanchi dams thus provide an empirical basis for assessing the broader religious and ideological underpinnings of food change in the late centuries BC.

Buddhism and urbanisation

The rise of Buddhism and Jainism, both closely connected with mercantile and trading communities, is also posited as an influencing factor in the appearance of states and urban culture during the mid-first millennium BC (Ghosh 1973). The relationship between Buddhism and urbanism has been explored in depth by textual scholars, but has not been assessed archaeologically; this is largely because of the narrow focus of the regional site-distribution surveys carried out to date, which, as discussed in chapter 7, have tended to prioritise habitational settlements at the expense of other aspects of the landscape such as ritual centres or agricultural systems.

Although this book is concerned with the later history and spread of Buddhist monasticism, the way in which the earliest Buddhist *saṅgha* related to its wider social and economic environment has a direct bearing on subsequent developments and therefore warrants further discussion here. A recent study by Bailey and Mabbett (2003) provides a useful synthesis of the various approaches to date. As they point out, there are two apparently contradictory models concerning the relationship between Buddhism and the rise of urban culture: i) the 'positive' model, wherein Buddhism is viewed as growing out of, and encouraging, urbanisation, because it provided a means of legitimisation for non-Brahmin elites such as merchants and traders (e.g. Thapar 1984) – Buddhist monasticism was an instrument of monarchical statehood, its success being largely attributable to the close relationship between monks and kings; and ii) the 'negative' model, which regards the Buddhist preoccupation with suffering (*dukkha*) as a reaction to the social upheaval, poverty and illness caused by urbanisation (e.g. Gombrich 1988, 58–9). Buddhism offered a means of tackling this suffering, while monasticism, that is, the monastic collective in the form of the *saṅgha*, represented an idealised form of pre-state tribal organisation (*gaṇa saṅgha*) described in Vedic texts.[13] The principal argument here is that Buddhism was able to flourish because monks acted as mediators between the political and economic forces of the time, benefiting from the social changes that other groups were finding difficult to digest, i.e. they capitalised on what for others was a source of adversity.

Bailey and Mabbett (2003, 13) remark on the irony that 'scholars argue on both sides often without seeming to notice the contradiction' between the two positions. Thus one side regards Buddhist theology as appealing to non-monastic populations because it in some way fitted the needs of these rising urban states, and the other sees it as a spiritual salve, an opiate, for those who suffered from the effects of urbanisation. There are also inherent contradictions in each of these positions, that of the 'positive' model being that Buddhism was designed as an ascetic path for those renouncing society, not for those in its upper echelons: 'the gap between the austere ascetic impulse and the needs of expanding urban kingdoms is great indeed' (*ibid.*, 6). For the negative model, the fundamental question is why did the Buddhist version of *dukkha* grow specifically out of an urban milieu when suffering can be assumed to have been common to all places and times? The irony of focusing on suffering at a time when significant sections of society must have been enjoying the economic rewards of urbanisation and development has also been remarked upon: 'early Buddhism ... is a social and religious movement *adapting itself to an expanding society where the economy is experiencing steady growth and a degree of prosperity*' (*ibid.*, 28, their emphasis). However, the downsides of development and urbanisation are all too apparent from modern parallels in Asia where common 'side-effects' include overpopulation, unemployment, environmental stress, the break up of close-knit communities and the erosion of traditional values.

The fundamental question, however, posed by scholars of Buddhist theology and history is why would the *saṅgha*, as a community of ascetics who had renounced material wealth, be so entwined economically and religiously with the merchant class? Further, why did the latter support the *saṅgha*, and what kind of economy allowed such a group to emerge and prosper?

As a first step to addressing these questions, it is important to stress that the Buddhist message was intended not only for monks but for the collective well-being of society (*ibid.*, 54–5). Not only did its emphasis on self-improvement and individual advancement accord with urban values, but, unlike the message of the Brahmanical ascetic, it applied to society at large, rather than to specific caste groups. This point is well illustrated in the oft-cited passage from the *Mahāvagga* (Vin I 226) in which the Buddha extols to the laity the five-fold virtues of following a high moral path, the main point being that by alleviating *dukkha* one is more likely to achieve one's material goals (Bailey and Mabbett 2003, 52–3). Monks may have opted out of society, but they are still concerned with society's material and spiritual welfare. As discussed below, they also have a vested interest in helping to maximise profitability outside the monastery because ultimately the *saṅgha*'s livelihood is dependent on society's material support. As noted by Benavides (2005, 82), 'a degree of abundance is the prerequisite for asceticism'. In other words, large communities of both sedentary and peripatetic renouncers could not have survived without a developed level of agricultural production to support them.

Benavides (2005, 82) thus argues that, rather than viewing Buddhism as either a rejection, or affirmation, of the economic changes that were taking place during the mid-first millennium BC, it should be seen rather as a 'commentary', a 'meditation' or a 'distillation' of the new, urban way of life which was intricately bound up with a new attitude to labour and consumption. An oft-cited passage in relation to these developments (Benavides 2005, 80; Green 1992, 227–34) comes from the *Aggañña Sutta* of the *Dīgha Nikāya* (v. 27) (Walshe 1995, 407–14). This story, which has close parallels with Buddhist myths in Laos, Thailand and Cambodia, describes the various social and economic stages that lead to the need for royalty, on the one hand, and renunciate communities, on the other: 'in the beginning', everyone's nutritional needs were provided for by wild rice crops which were so abundant that they could be harvested as and when required. However, men eventually became lazy and instead preferred to cultivate and store the rice rather than having to work in the fields every day. They also became driven by sexual desire and thus needed houses in order to have sex in private. These changes had a number of knock-on effects including a reduction in the rice grains' size, the need for kings to regulate an increasingly unruly society, and communities of renunciate monks in order to counterbalance its excesses. Because both kings and monks were exempt from having to cultivate the rice they ate, it became necessary for the rest of society to produce extra rice to feed them.

Dāna: ritual giving and receiving

The mythical link between Buddhism and rice offers a useful gloss for the discussion in chapter 14 (alluded to earlier) regarding the religious underpinnings of food change in ancient India. Benavides (2005, 87) has also argued that the concept of *dāna*, the system of ritual giving and receiving whereby the laity donates goods (primarily food, but also shelter and, later on, land and permanent structures) to the *saṅgha* in exchange for merit, was a particularly Buddhist way of responding to these new attitudes to production and consumption (Benavides 2005, 87). In other words, by creating an arena for *dāna* which lies at the very heart of the monk-laity dynamic, the monastery acted as a 'mirror' to the new emphasis on wealth. Daud Ali (1998) comes to a similar conclusion regarding the *saṅgha*'s relationship with urban or courtly society. Although the aims of both sections of society were very different, both used a similar set of 'technologies' or 'signs', as illustrated by the prominence of courtly imagery and aesthetics in Buddhist literature and thought. Taken together, these developments help to reconcile the two apparently contradictory models that have been used to explain the relationship between Buddhism and urbanisation. Indeed, Benavides (*ibid.*) goes as far as to say that 'to solve the mystery of giving and receiving, of sacrifice and asceticism, of work, leisure, and agency, would be to solve the mystery of religion'!

The irony of this dynamic is obvious: although monks are exempt from labour, the *dāna* on which they depend is the direct result of others' work; in other words, the monks' survival depends on the laity breaking the monastic precepts that they live by, including agricultural labour and the killing of animals. The layperson has to endure the burden of not only the work itself, but also the resultant pollution believed to be inherent in all work. However, all is not lost! By agreeing to give some of the fruits of their labour to the *saṅgha*, donors are cleansed of resultant sins by the merit that they receive from the monk in exchange for gifts: 'the villagers thus free the monks for higher pursuits, [while] ... their labors – even though polluting – are positively virtuous, too, and merit is their reward' (Tambiah 1970, 148).

'Passive' v. 'active' models of Buddhism

While the advantages of this arrangement for the monk are clear, the benefits for the laity, beyond a purely spiritual sphere, are less obvious. What other incentives might there have been for supporting the *saṅgha*? Insights into this question have been hampered by the 'theological' or 'passive' model of Buddhism, which regards the *saṅgha*'s participation in social relations as a distortion of its original position as a body of renouncers concerned solely with individual enlightenment (Conze 1975; Ortner 1978).

The passive model is typified by the views of Weber (1963), for whom Buddhism was essentially concerned with an 'otherworldly' ideal which undermined the commercial world and represented the antithesis to modern capitalism. With regard to the Mauryan period, Weber acknowledged Asoka's concern with social welfare, but saw it as a coincidence that was essentially at odds with the original spirit of Buddhism. For the laity, the sole incentive for economic activity was to produce surplus in order to generate good *karma*, rather than a means for 'capitalist reinvestment'.

The earliest Buddhist monks are thus regarded as passive recipients of such gifts with any reciprocation of merit being interpreted as superficial and essentially 'passive' (Schopen 1996a), while evidence for more commercial forms of exchange, such as 'monastic landlordism' in Sri Lanka, is regarded as a deterioration of 'true' Buddhist values. For example, the second-century-BC donative inscriptions at Sanchi which record donations of individual building components are generally viewed as indicators of a one-way system of gift-giving, in which the *saṅgha*'s role is regarded as one of passive non-reciprocity. These are contrasted with the inscriptions of the Gupta period, which for the first time refer to the donation of entire buildings and to permanent endowments of land and interest.

The 'passive' model of Buddhism has been challenged from a number of angles, one view being that Buddhism's active role in the present-day economy, especially of Southeast and East Asia, had been overlooked by Weber (Harvey 2000; Tambiah 1976).[14] With regards to ancient India, additional problems with this framework should be noted at the outset. Not only is any reciprocity on the part of the monks denied, but the deeper social implications of the early donative inscriptions, for example, their possible function as 'advertisements' of the donors' piety for reasons of social prestige, have been overlooked by a body of scholarship which has focused entirely on the 'ritual' motives of gift-giving (Schopen 1996a). Further, little consideration has been given to the degree of social integration required for this kind of fund-raising exercise: Buddhism appears to have provided the earliest arena in ancient India for 'competitive giving' and the very public recording of this act in perpetuity. Finally, it is important to broaden the scope of evidence to include other indicators of exchange between the *saṅgha* and local populations. For example, certain practical skills such as water-harvesting, represented by the abundance of cisterns at second-century-BC rock-cut monasteries in the Deccan (Shaw and Sutcliffe 2003a), evidently played a significant role in the propagation of Buddhism. As discussed in relation to models of religious change in chapter 6, these skills appear to have formed part of a very practical form of evangelism which tackled suffering (*dukkha*) on an every-day subsistence level, but also provided incentives for locals to give their economic support to the monastery.

Medicine

Another 'practical' skill of importance, aimed at the alleviation of suffering but also central to the propagation of Buddhism, was medicine. Zysk (1991, 6–7) argues that the roots of Ayurveda were closely connected with heterodox ascetic traditions, which needed to do more than provide spiritual guidance if they were to survive. The classical medical treatises of Caraka and Susruta represent a later Sanskritised version of this pre-existing knowledge. Wandering physicians collecting *materia medica* and practising a mixture of empirical rational medicine and magical healing had much in common with ascetics, who had also abandoned the norms of society. These ascetics were referred to in the Pali and Greek sources as *Śramaṇa*s (McCrindle 1979, 67–8; *Geography* 15.1.70), of whom the wandering physicians seem to have been a subgroup (Zysk 1991, 32). It is likely that 'the first documented codification of this medical lore took place as wandering ascetics assumed a more stationary existence, cloistered in the early Buddhist monasteries', where treatment of the laity became a regular part of the monastic duties (*ibid.*, 37). Indeed, access to superior medical treatment appears to have been one of the many 'non-religious' motives for joining the *saṅgha*, including escaping poverty or military service (Brekke 1997); allusions to this are provided in the *Mahāvagga* of the *Vinaya Piṭaka* (I.39). As Zysk (1991, 4) points out, the positioning of medical centres within religious compounds was later appropriated by Hindu institutions following the demise of Buddhism (see also Willis, forthcoming a, ch. 2)

Buddhist economics

The recognition that the *saṅgha* has from its very inception maintained a vested interest in social welfare, eventually becoming an active agent in social and economic development, has also had some impact on modern economic thinking. In Southeast Asia where recent economic and political regimes have oscillated between capitalist and communist ideologies, there has been a growing movement towards a specifically 'Buddhist economics', with close parallels to other religiously determined economies such as those of the Islamic Middle East. The call for an economic system based on 'Buddhist' principles has now become a religio-political movement which draws upon ancient exchange networks in Sri Lanka, although often tinged with idealised and moralistic interpretations reflecting a Victorian version of the Buddhist past (Harvey 2000, 215–19; Green 1992). An early proponent of these views was E.F. Schumacher (1973), an economic adviser in 1950s Burma who advocated 'intermediate technology' as a reaction to Western development models. Schumacher sought to highlight the downsides of 'modernisation', which he regarded as being responsible for the 'collapse of the rural economy, a rising tide of unemployment in town and country, and a growth of a city proletariat without nourishment of either body or soul' (*ibid.*, 56). Instead, he called for an economic system based on Buddhist ethics, i.e. a 'Middle Way between materialist heedlessness and traditionalist immobility', which considers the social and environmental impact of business transactions rather than profit at the expense of both of these factors (*ibid.*, 48).

Integrated exchange networks

One of the aims of this book is to consider to what degree we can talk of a specifically Buddhist economic system in the late centuries BC. To this end, it is important to look beyond epigraphical and archaeological evidence from individual sites to the landscape as a whole, and to build up a more localised picture of interaction between the *saṅgha* and lay sections of society. It was with this aim in mind that the documentation of the settlements and water-resource structures in the vicinity of monasteries in the Sanchi area was carried out. A major driving question was: 'How did the monks survive on a day-to-day basis?' Did they beg for alms in neighbouring villages or were they supported by the kind of permanent endowments like those described in the *Mūlasarvāstivāda-Vinaya*? Schopen (1994b, 546) has noted how, according to these texts, this type of endowment only came about when permanent monasteries began to be donated to the *saṅgha*. This is because, according to the 'web of mutual obligation' upon which such acts of giving were based, the donor was rewarded with religious merit for only as long as the building continued to be occupied by the *saṅgha*. In order for this 'open system of indebtedness' to continue in perpetuity, permanent supplies in the form of money, agricultural land and labour, and sometimes entire 'maintenance villages', had to be provided for the upkeep of the *vihāra* and its residents.

Domestication of the saṅgha

These developments are thought to have led eventually to the eradication of the traditional, mendicant path of monasticism as expounded in the Canon, and are thus central to discussions of the 'domestication' of the *saṅgha*. As discussed by Strenski (1983), academic perceptions of this subject have been distorted by the narrow criteria by which domestication has been defined. Scholars have tended to focus disproportionately on the *saṅgha*'s transition from a peripatetic to a sedentary lifestyle, rather than on other indicators of domestication, such as the development of exchange networks with non-monastic communities, which do not necessarily presuppose the adoption of permanent monastic establishments. For example, the fact that Sri Lankan forest-dwelling monks of the third to second centuries BC were able to involve themselves in local patronage networks has been demonstrated by the large body of donative inscriptions in the associated rock-shelters (Coningham 1995).

Sri Lanka: monastic landlordism

By the second century BC, the main focus of patronage in Sri Lanka had shifted to irrigation works with the resulting system of 'monastic landlordism' providing the earliest empirical 'proof' for the kinds of textually attested exchange networks discussed above. Many of the ancient dams there bear inscriptions linking them to nearby monasteries, whose involvement in agrarian modes of production as instruments of lay patronage played a major role in the emergence of socially integrated monasticism (Gunawardana 1971). These inscriptions show that Buddhist monasteries were in possession of large tracts of property, including irrigation works and fields, donated by local chieftains (*parumakas*) as well as private individuals (*ibid.*, 24; Paranavitana 1970, vol. I, lxii, lxxxiv). Buddhaghosa, writing some centuries later, describes how the *saṅgha*, having received an irrigation work as a gift, would take over the responsibility of its management and profit-control, while local farmers would be granted access to the irrigation works as long as they paid a certain 'percentage' of their yields in the form of a 'donation' to the *saṅgha* (*Samantapāsādikā*, vol. III, 697; Gunawardana 1978a; 1979, 57–9). Monasteries were thus ensured the proceeds from land irrigated by their own tanks, or else given privileged access to the tanks of others. By making the monastery the focus for the 'accumulation of property and the concentration of administrative authority' (*ibid.*, 72–3), the *saṅgha* assured itself a secure livelihood without compromising canonical rules that prohibit monks from participating in agriculture. The dynamics of monastic landlordism thus unfolded through a 'three-way mutually beneficial relationship' between patrons, monks and farmers (Gunawardana 1971, 24). The success of this arrangement was further ensured by the donation of 'service villages' (*aramīkagāma*) or 'maintenance villages' (*bhogagāma*), which provided constant supplies of labour to the *saṅgha* (Gunawardana 1979; *Cūḷavaṃsa* 46.15).

Non-monastic labour

The practice of employing non-monastic staff for work that was prohibited to monks was an effective means for allowing monasteries to engage with the wider economic world without breaking the monastic code. The term *ārāmika* is known from the time of the Pali Canon (*Vinaya* I, 207) and applies to a wide range of employees from slaves to agricultural labourers, cooks and cleaners, while the *kappiyakāraka* belonged to a higher order of staff responsible for administrative duties and the *saṅgha*'s financial and business dealings (Gunawardana 1979, 97–9; Gombrich 1998, 101–2). The *kappiyakāraka* was known as 'the legitimiser' because it was he who 'accepted donations of property, administered them on behalf of the *saṅgha*, and diverted the proceeds to the provision of "allowable articles"' (Gombrich 1988, 102). While selected monks would have been responsible for overseeing such activities, this system ensured that the *saṅgha* remained connected with the commercial world without subjecting its members to worldly duties.

India: the development of exchange networks

While the relationship between monasteries and irrigation reservoirs in Sri Lanka represent the archaeological embodiment of this paradox, identifying these developments in the archaeological record remains problematic. This is partly because of the lack of question-orientated collaboration between textual and archaeological scholars, one of the consequences being that both parties are susceptible to misinterpretation of each other's respective primary sources; as discussed in chapter 1, there is no easy solution to this problem. One case in point is the uncritical manner in which archaeological reports from major monastic sites have been interpreted by text-based scholars of Buddhist history. The resulting framework of understanding regarding the development of institutionalised monasticism rests on a number of mutually intertwined assumptions: first, that the donation of permanent endowments presupposes the existence of permanent monasteries and, second, that the 'planned, ordered and settled community' described in these texts assumes a level of architectural sophistication which has, for some unknown reason, been linked exclusively to the courtyard type of monastery (Schopen 1994b, 547). Since this style of monastery is not believed to have developed in the North-West until c. first century AD, the texts in which these descriptions occur are thus thought to be datable to no earlier than the Kusana period (*ibid.*). As discussed in chapter 9, the fact that neither the courtyard type of monastery nor inscriptions relating to permanent endowments of land and property appear at Sanchi until at least the Gupta period has been taken as evidence for the late development of institutionalised monasticism in central India.

The central problem with this line of reasoning, discussed further in chapters 9 and 11, is that other types of monasteries which pre-date the courtyard style have not figured in these debates. Additional problems stem from the predominantly 'site-based' focus of Buddhist archaeology which has hitherto given little consideration to patterns in the archaeological landscape. Although the symbiotic relationship between monasteries and local elites as donors of land and property has been recognised, as well as the role of monasteries in facilitating inter-regional trade (Heitzman 1984; Ray 1986; Morrison 1995a),[15] any possibility of the *saṅgha*'s 'active' role in the local forces of production has been underplayed, largely due to the 'canonical' model of Buddhism outlined earlier, but also because of the lack of systematic survey that could relate Buddhist monasteries to their social and agricultural setting. A notable, and recently published, exception to this trend is Lars Fogelin's (2006) 'total survey' carried out over an area of less than 8 km^2 in and around the monastery of Thotlakonda in Andhra Pradesh. Although the limited area under survey means that wider regional patterns are lacking, the results of this study offer interesting parallels to my own. As discussed in chapter 13, comparative analysis of pottery found both within the monastic compound and a nearby settlement suggests a high level of economic interaction between monastic and lay populations, while large numbers of storage jars at Thotlakonda suggest that food was being stored and produced on-site, most probably by non-monastic staff.

The earlier preconceptions help to explain Heitzman's (1984, 131) theory that the apparent spatial dislocation between monasteries and centres of economic production rules out any direct political or economic role on the part of the *saṅgha* (cited in Bailey and Mabbett 2003, 69). While the begging of one or two wandering monks might be supported with little difficulty by a village or set of households, Bailey and Mabbett (*ibid.*) argue that a settled monastery with large numbers of monks could not have been sustained without considerable pressure on the forces of production. In order to test this hypothesis archaeologically, Bailey and Mabbett (*ibid.*, 68) argue that what is needed is:

> a systematic effort in locating and statistically analysing the number of villages grouped in close proximity to a given monastery. Nor, and maybe this is of greater significance if only because of the potential size, do we know how the presence of a monastery might have increased demand in the local economy of the area in which it was located. Two factors should be relevant: i) the simple function of the *saṅgha* as a purchaser of goods and services from the local area, hence a stimulator of demand for certain goods, and ii) the role of the *saṅgha* in creating an ideational motivation for increasing production or in modifying the methods of distribution.

Conclusion

Although the above passage was published some time after the primary documentation and analysis of the SSP had already been completed, it acts as a useful, albeit coincidental, framework in which to situate the data presented in this book. In other words, Bailey and Mabbett's challenge is to a certain degree met by the results of the SSP, which include data relating to the relative configuration of monasteries and settlements, as well as a group of ancient irrigation systems which shed additional light on the relationship between Buddhist history and changes in agricultural production.

CHAPTER 3

Physical Geography and Archaeology of Central India

Introduction

Sanchi and Vidisha are situated at the convergence of several major early-historic trade routes at the very heart of the Indian subcontinent in what is generally known as central India. The aim of this chapter is to discuss the geography and archaeology of this area in order to provide a physical and cultural background for the more tightly focused (both regionally and chronologically) survey that ensues in the following chapters.

Geography

The Sanchi area belongs to a geographical entity known as Malwa, which forms a triangular plateau based on the Vindhyan hills, in the North-West corner of Madhya Pradesh (Figure 3.1 colour). The Vindhyan range (21–26° lat., 78–83° long.) traverses almost the entire breadth of peninsular India. Extending for about 1050 km from west to east, it covers most of modern-day Madhya Pradesh and the districts of Allahabad and Mirzapur in eastern Uttar Pradesh. The average elevation is 300 m (984 ft). In the west it forms the southern boundary of the triangular-shaped Malwa plateau and includes the Satpura range, which runs parallel to it in the south. The latter extends for 900 km from Ratanpur in the west to Amarkantak in the east and ranges in height from 500 to 1000 m (1640–3280 ft). The main river is the Narmada, which runs between the two ranges, while the Malwa plateau is drained by the Chambal, Sipra, Betwa and Bes rivers, the last two being the principal rivers in the Sanchi area. The Vindhyan and Satpura ranges act as a physical and cultural dividing line between north India and the Deccan plateau to the south. In the eastern zone the Vindhyas include the Kaimur range, which is drained by the Ganga-Yamuna system and major tributaries such as the Son and Belan.

The name Malwa is generally applied to the regions of the old Central India Agency, including the former states of Gwalior, Indore, Dhar and Bhopal. Following Independence in 1947, most of the area was incorporated into the new state of Madhya Bharat, which subsequently became Madhya Pradesh.

There are two principal topographical and cultural zones: i) the hilly regions, rich in prehistoric painted rock-shelters and stone-tool scatters, as well as Buddhist monastery and stupa remains datable to the late centuries BC; and ii) fertile black-cotton-soil plains with evidence for agricultural settlements from the Chalcolithic period onwards.

Broadly speaking, the hilly regions can be divided into two major geological sectors: the northern sector consists of Vindhyan sandstone scarpland, which extends from Rohtasgarhon on the River Son to Ginnurgarh, just to the west of Bhopal. Situated in the north-east plateau of Malwa, Sanchi forms an outcrop of this formation. The southern sector comprises the Deccan basalt trap of the Vindhyan range (not to be confused with Vindhyan sandstone). Due to the rapid weathering of the horizontal lava flows, these basaltic hills are usually much lower and less steep and dissected than the sandstone hills to the north. A smaller third zone, largely restricted to the northern area around Gwalior, consists of a much older igneous formation called Bundelkhand gneiss. This is a granitic stone which can sometimes be found underlying sandstone cliffs.

Prehistoric archaeology

Three main areas of prehistoric research, to be outlined below, have been conducted in the Vindhyan region: i) rock-shelter research, ii) open-air stone-tool production studies, and iii) river-bed stone-tool sequence studies.

i) Rock-shelter research

Over three-fourths of India's rock-shelters occur in the Vindhyas, particularly the western zone. Most rock-shelter surveys to date have been extensive and unsystematic, ranging from D.H. Gordon's 1930s study in the Mahadeo hills of the Narmada valley to later studies in the Betwa basin carried out variously by V.S. Wakankar and R.R.R. Brooks (1976) and Erwin Neumeyer (1993). The two best-known sites where surface remains have been supplemented by excavated sequences are Adamgarh in the Narmada valley and Bhimbetka near the source of the Betwa, to the south of Bhopal (Figure 3.1 colour). The latter has been excavated over various seasons from 1971 onwards and in 2003 was declared a UNESCO World Heritage site. Other significant rock-shelter complexes include Pangurariya in Hoshangabad district (*IAR* 1975–6, 28–30) (Plate 47), and Kharwai, Putli Karar, Satkunda and Ghatla (*IAR* 1982–3, 39) in Raisen district.[1] Numerous rock-shelter sites were documented during the SSP. Many of these, such as Sanchi hill itself, Nagauri and Ahmadpur (*IAR* 1976–7, 77) to the north of Vidisha (Figure 11.1; Plates 45–6), occur with later Buddhist remains and are described in chapters 9 and 12.

Many of the shelters contain stone tools from the lower Palaeolithic to the Chalcolithic period. However, test-pits at

Bhimbetka (Jacobson 1980) have demonstrated that most of the c. 0.6–0.9 m-deep cultural material there belongs to the microlith-using phase. Paintings are also found in over half of the 240 shelters at Bhimbetka and many of the other rock-shelter sites. Dating is problematic, drawing largely on stylistic typologies and observations of superimposition. Two main phases have been classified: 'prehistoric', with five sub-phases, consisting of wild animals and hunting scenes; and 'historic', consisting of religious processions, battle-scenes, horses, metal-tipped weapons, etc. (Mathpal 1984). Most of the prehistoric paintings are thought to date to the Chalcolithic period. However, earlier dates have also been proposed: the 'green earth' found in Upper Palaeolithic levels at Bhimbetka IIIA-28 has been related to the earliest green painting layers there. Ochre fragments found within Mesolithic levels have also led to inferred Mesolithic dates for some of the red ochre paintings at Bhimbetka (Wakankar and Brooks 1976).

The 'historic' phase also includes Brahmi inscriptions, datable to between the third and first centuries BC, and shell inscriptions (*śankhalipi*), datable to as late as the Gupta period. The Brahmi inscriptions, as found for example at Bhimbetka and Pangurariya, form part of a wider body of evidence, including solid stone platforms constructed at their entrances, and nearby stupas, for the Buddhist adaptation of prehistoric rock-shelters for use as monastic dwellings. These are referred to in this study as 'monastic rock-shelters'. Of the above-mentioned sites, similar evidence occurs at Bhimbetka (Gupta, 1967, 83), Pangurariya (*IAR* 1975–6, 28–30) (Plate 52), Kharwai and Ghatla, as well as numerous hilltop Buddhist sites in the SSP study area including Sanchi itself (Figure 11.23; Plates 48–51).

ii) Open-air stone-tool production studies

Various surveys aimed at locating surface sites have also been carried out in the Vindhyan region. These include J. Jacobson's (1980; 1985) documentation of Acheulian tool production sites over an area of about 175 km^2 in Raisen district; a number of surveys in the Narmada valley by Deccan College from the 1960s onwards, resulting in, amongst others, excavations at Mahadeo Piparia and Samnapur; another survey of vertebrate fossils in the Narmada valley (Narsinghpur district) carried out in the early 1990s by Deccan College and the Museum of Man, Bhopal; and, finally, the Son valley survey carried out by the Universities of Allahabad and Berkeley (Clark and Sharma 1983).

iii) River-bed stone-tool sequence studies

The river-bed sites, often situated at some distance from raw sources, consist of tools found in cross-bedded, sandy, pebbly gravels overlying Acheulian-yielding horizons. Sequences from the Narmada river basin around Hoshangabad were first provided by De Terra and Paterson (1939). Others from Maheshwar (Sankalia 1974), Damoh (Joshi 1961), Mahanadi valley (Pandey 1987) and the Upper Son valley (Clark and Williams 1990) have been studied in subsequent years. The last consists of five phases with lower palaeolithic flakes, cores and bifaces of quartose sandstone and quartzites appearing in alluvial gravels of the Middle Pleistocene (Phase I). Upper Acheulian to Middle Palaeolithic tools occur in gravelly clays and fluviatile sands of the Middle to Upper Pleistocene (Phase III). Middle to Upper Palaeolithic tools appear in sands and clays of the Upper Pleistocene (Phase IV), while the last phase spans the Upper Pleistocene and Holocene, yielding tools of the Upper Palaeolithic, Mesolithic and Neolithic.

The Palaeolithic

Thermoluminescence dating of the Loess deposit overlying the Acheulian tool level in the Son valley has produced a date of 103,800 +- 19,800 BP for the Lower Palaeolithic. C14 dates from geological deposits of the Baghor formation and from the Upper Palaeolithic site of 'Baghor I' have produced an Upper Palaeolithic date of 10,000–12,000 BP. Further dates have been obtained from ostrich egg shells at the following sites: Chandrasal, Chambal valley (36,550 +- 600 BP, and 38,900 +- 750 BP); Nagda (31,000 BP); and Mehtakheri (41,900 BP). Freshwater shells from Mehtakheri have also produced a date range of 30,680 +- 1040–920 BP (Chakrabarti 1999).

Stone tools occur frequently in rock-shelters from the Lower Palaeolithic onwards, as revealed by excavation sequences at Bhimbetka and Adamgarh. Other Lower Palaeolithic finds include a line of cup marks at Bhimbetka, shelter III.F-24 (Bednarik 1993) and a hominid fossil skull from Hathnora, near Narsinghpur, in the Narmada valley, and interpreted variously as modern *Homo erectus* (Sonakia 1986) or archaic *Homo sapiens* (Badam and Sathe 1995).

Of the 94 Lower Palaeolithic seasonal camp sites found in Raisen district by Jacobson (1985), the majority are located at the raw material sources, such as chert, chalcedony, jasper and agate occurring in sedimentary formations and as intertrappean beds. There is an increase in site density during the Middle and Upper Palaeolithic, with sites often exceeding several hectares in area and consisting of thousands of tools and waste products. The Upper Palaeolithic marks the first appearance of portable art: a bone object from Upper Palaeolithic gravels (C14 dated to 19715 +- 340 BP) at Lohanda Nala in the Belan valley has been interpreted variously as a 'mother goddess' image or a harpoon (Bednarik 1993). Excavations at Baghor I, Sidhi district, have revealed the remains of what appear to be an Upper Palaeolithic shrine datable to c. 9000–8000 BC (Kenoyer *et al.*, 1993).

The Mesolithic (c. 10,000–4000 BC)

There are two types of Mesolithic sites in the Vindhyan region: i) the aforementioned rock-shelter dwellings, many of which show continued occupation from the preceding Palaeolithic phase; and ii) open-air seasonal camps, such as Baghor II, Sidhi district, with others (e.g. Chopani Mando, Sarai Nahar Rai, Mahadaha, Langhnaj and Morhana Pahara) in the Ganga valley on the banks of ox-bow lakes in Allahabad and Pratabgarh districts.

The tool assemblage consists of microblades mass-produced by the pressure technique, as opposed to the earlier percussion-flaking method. Chert and chalcedony are the main source materials. Similar microliths are found throughout the Sanchi area although some may date to much later periods.

Few plant remains datable to this period have been reliably identified, but shallow querns and rubbers at Bhimbetka attest to the use of plant foods. At Adamgarh, faunal assemblages of wild and domesticated animal species attest to a combination of hunter-gathering and stock-breeding subsistence strategies. Evidence for simple structures with post-holes and hearths occur at some sites, such as Sarai Nahar Rai, while a shelter at Bhimbetka contains a stone partition-wall datable to this period. Others contain human burials with grave offerings such as bone ornaments and pieces of antlers and ochre pieces. The latter have been used to infer a Mesolithic date for some of the rock-paintings.

Protohistoric archaeology

Neolithic-Chalcolithic sites

The Vindhyan Neolithic may have begun as early as 6000 BC but is more commonly placed between c. 4000 and 1500 BC. In the eastern zone, the best-studied sites are Koldihawa, Mahagara and Chopani Mando, all on the Belan river. The ceramic assemblage at Koldihawa (Ghosh 1990) is fairly representative of this period: handmade plain red wares (occasionally corded and incised) and crude Black and Red Ware (BRW). Levels datable to the early second millennium BC have yielded grains of wheat, barley and several Southwest Asian pulses (peas, lentils, grass pea and chick pea). These crops appear to have resulted from a process of diffusion from the North-West, where sites such as Mehgarh in the western borderlands of the Indus river have yielded the earliest evidence for agricultural domestication in the Indian subcontinent. Plant and bone assemblages from Mehgarh and related sites in Baluchistan suggest that wheat, barley and various pulses, as well as goats, sheep and cows, were domesticated from at least c. 7000 BC. This was evidently the result of a much broader sphere of domestication with its centre in the Jordan valley area further to the west, although individual components of this assemblage, for example, barley and cattle, appear to have been domesticated locally (Fuller 2002; 2003).

The introduction of this North-West crop package into the Gangetic valley appears to have supplemented a pre-existing agrarian economy based largely on rice cultivation: at Chopani Mando and Koldihawa, pottery containing rice (*Orzya sativa*) husks and charred grains has been dated to the fourth and fifth millennia BC respectively (Sharma *et al.*, 1980). However, there are considerable uncertainties over the stratified context of these finds and the mid-third millennium BC is the generally accepted date for the beginnings of rice cultivation in the Gangetic valley, based on excavations at Damadama (Fuller 2002; 2003). Recent phytolith analysis at Lahuradewa may push this date back further (Fuller, in press; Saxena *et al.*, 2006).

The element of continuity between the Neolithic and Chalcolithic (early to mid-second millennium BC) at these sites is fairly pronounced, as confirmed by assemblages at numerous riverside Chalcolithic settlement mounds in the Gangetic valley. Neolithic pottery types, as well as microliths, generally continue into these later periods, in association with newly introduced, fine, wheel-made, BRW, black-slipped and red wares, often with geometric decorations. Kakoria, excavated by the University of Allahabad, also has megalithic cairn circles and cists datable to the pre-Iron Age (Ghosh 1990).

In the western zone, most of the documented Neolithic-Chalcolithic sites are situated on river banks in the fertile Malwa plateau and characterised by well-made, round and rectangular houses, with mud-plastered reed screens.[2] Neolithic celts and microliths continue in association with Kayatha Ware (c. 2000–1800 BC), a wheel-made pottery with a dark brown slip and linear paintings in deep red. It is best represented by the assemblage at Kayatha in the Chambal valley (Wakankar 1967) and related sites in central India, including Dangawada (Chakaravarti *et al.*, 1989); Maheswar-Navdatoli (Sankalia *et al.*, 1971); Nagda (*IAR* 1955–6); Pipalda, Badada, Chikalda and Khedi in the Narmada valley (Ghosh 1989); Eran (*IAR* 1960–1); Vidisha and Rangai (*IAR* 1963–4, 1964–5, 1965–6, 1975–6, 1976–7); Amakheda, Pipalia Lorka, Nayakheda and Nandur (Sharma and Misra 2003) in the Betwa valley; and several of the Bhimbetka rock-shelters.

Banas ware (1700–1500 BC) marks the second main Chalcolithic phase in the Malwa plateau area. First identified at Ahar in the Banas valley of Rajasthan, it is also found at Kayatha, Navdatoli and other sites in the Chambal valley. It is a black and red ware, wheel-turned, with white painted geometric designs. Unlike Rajasthan where there is an abundance of copper tools, the ware continues to be produced alongside a rich stone blade industry.

The third main phase is represented by Malwa ware (1500–1200 BC), a buff/orange slipped ware with black or dark brown designs, found at Maheshwar-Navdatoli, Eran and many other sites in central India. As in earlier periods, it occurs in association with stone tools and mud huts with mud-plastered bamboo screens, but a significant development is the appearance in large numbers of copper tools such as axes, chisels, arrowheads and daggers. The earliest evidence for carbonised wheat in Madhya Pradesh occurs at Navdatoli-Maheshwar in c. 1660–1440 BC and Kayatha in c. 1380 BC, that is, around the same time as sites further to the east. Other elements of the modern crop assemblage, such as black gram, green gram, lentil and grass pea, are all in evidence by this period. Bones of both wild and domesticated animals, such as cattle, pig, sheep and goat, attest to a combined animal husbandry and hunter-gathering based economy. There are also limited rice finds, but in such meagre quantities that it cannot be regarded as having played any significant role in subsistence patterns during this period; as discussed in the following chapter, limited archaeobotanical samples from the Deccan and south India suggest that the westward spread of rice agriculture from its base in the Gangetic valley did not occur until the late centuries BC, when it coincided with the consolidation of the Mauryan empire as well as the spread of new religious and economic movements. However, the lack of systematic archaeobotanical sampling in central India means that there are still significant gaps in our understanding of early agricultural history. Nevertheless, the existing evidence suggests that, as in the Gangetic valley, the basic framework of agriculture had already been laid down by this time and that the area played a pivotal role in inter-regional trade (Ansari and Dhavalikar 1975; Chakravarty *et al.*,1989).

Historical archaeology

Urban sites

Many of the major early-historic cities in Madhya Pradesh, such as Vidisha, Eran and Ujjain, were first documented by Alexander Cunningham in the nineteenth century, and in subsequent years have continued to undergo study and excavation by various archaeological departments (Sharma and Misra 2003). The major excavations include Vidisha, Ujjain, Tumain (Bajpai and Pandey 1984), Tripuri (Dikshit 1955), Nandur and Ninnaur, all in the Narmada valley; and Amilkoni in Rewa district (Sharma and Misra 2003). Since the late 1980s, the Madhya Pradesh State Government has been engaged in a large rescue archaeology exercise as areas become submerged as a result of the Narmada Sagar dam project; this has revealed a great deal of new information about Chalcolithic and early-historic settlements in the western zone (*ibid.*). In the eastern zone, a number of major settlements in Rewa district (Misra *et al.*, 2000–1) and Allahabad/Varanasi districts have been located during various surveys carried out by the Uttar Pradesh State Archaeology Department. Many of these sites are located in close proximity to major trade routes which pass through the Vindhyan region (Chakrabarti 2001; Chakrabarti and Tewari 2003)

There are considerable uncertainties regarding the history of urbanism in the Vindhyan region, due to a paucity of published reports, limited systematic surveys and vague ceramic sequences.[3] Compared to the Gangetic valley, less is known about the transition between the Chalcolithic and early-historic period. Whilst the onset of urbanisation in the Gangetic valley is generally positioned between c. 1000–600 BC, along with the appearance of PGW and iron, in central India these developments take place slightly later during what is referred to as the 'second' phase of early-historic urbanism. There are relatively few occurrences of PGW in Madhya Pradesh, with the highest concentration on the northernmost fringes adjoining Rajasthan and Uttar Pradesh. The exception is Ujjain, the state capital of Avanti, one of the sixteen *mahājanapadas* listed in the *Anguttara Nikāya*. Here, PGW datable to c. 750–500 BC has been found in the city ramparts in association with BRW and punch-marked coins. However, the main thrust of urbanism at sites such as Vidisha, Tumain, Tripuri, Maheshwar, Eraich and Eran occurs in c. 500–300 BC, as marked by the appearance of NBPW, in association with BRW of the immediately preceding period. Punch-marked coins and iron appear in large quantities during this period.

Ancient Vidisha

The mounds of ancient Vidisha cover an area of over 290 ha and offer several challenges to scholars interested in early historic urbanisation and its relationship to earlier and later developments. Excavations were carried out on the main city mounds over five seasons between 1963 and 1977. Unfortunately, these were never fully published, apart from several summarised accounts (*IAR* 1963–4, 16–17; 1964–5, 18; 1965–6, 23; 1975–6, 30–1; 1976–7, 33–4). Nevertheless, the available sequence, which reveals six occupational levels dating from the Chalcolithic to post-Gupta periods, is useful for the purposes of the present study. The full details are given in chapter 9, but the main point here is that the urban phase (Periods IIIb–c), datable to between the third and second centuries BC on the basis of NBPW and punchmarked coins in the city rampart, puts Vidisha in line with the chronology and history of urban development in central India.

Although, as discussed above, Ujjain further to the west follows a similar chronology to the fortified capitals of the Gangetic valley, which had already reached a level of urbanism by c. sixth century BC, Vidisha appears to have been only a small town at this time (Bhattacharyya 1977, 194–5). However, the lack of horizontal excavation makes it difficult to assess the character of the settlement in pre-Mauryan times. The received understanding is that it is only during the third century BC, following the western expansion of the Mauryan empire (under Asoka) from its base in the Gangetic valley, that Vidisha became the capital city of the former state of Avanti (Chakrabarti 1995a; Allchin, ed., 1995), later to be known as Dasarna or Akara (Sircar 1969; Kalidasa's *Meghadūta* I, 24–5). However, there are still uncertainties about the earliest history of urbanism at Vidisha during both the Mauryan and pre-Mauryan periods. Some information can be gleaned from passages in the Sri Lankan chronicles, the *Dīpavaṃsa* and *Mahāvaṃsa* (fourth to fifth century AD), which have a special link with Vidisha as it is from here that Asoka's son, Mahinda, is supposed to have arrived in Sri Lanka with the Buddhist message. The texts inform us that Vidisha was the native town of Devi, the wife of Asoka, who was based as viceroy in Ujjain (*Mahāvaṃsa*, 13:7; *Dīpavaṃsa* 12:14). Sanchi is described in these texts as Cetiyagiri or Vedisagiri, the setting of the 'beautiful monastery' which queen Devi and her son, Mahinda, visited while at Vidisha. Asoka's marriage to a local woman demonstrates Vidisha's prominence within the pan-Indian political scene, but also alludes to its importance in the pre-Mauryan period, although the precise character of the place during this period remains largely unknown.

This unsatisfactory situation is exacerbated further by uncertainties over the chronology of NBPW, but also because the nature of the transition between the Chalcolithic and early-historic period has not yet been understood; there are major problems when it comes to relating Vidisha's urban occupation levels to the preceding Chalcolithic levels. One of the wider aims of the excavations at Vidisha was to address this very question. In addition to Vidisha itself, an independent Chalcolithic village site was also excavated at Rangai Amkhera, a low mound on the eastern bank of the River Betwa, just below the railway bridge between Vidisha and Sanchi (Khare 1981; *IAR* 1976–7, 33–4).[4] Excavations revealed a three-phase Chalcolithic sequence, overlying two pre-pottery microlithic levels. The earliest ceramic level was dominated by red wares with geometric designs, animal figures painted in black and BRW-bearing white-painted designs. Their similarity to wares from Kayatha II (Ansari and Dhavalikar 1975) suggested a date of c. 2000–1800 BC. The uppermost levels contained some PGW and related wares, attesting to continued occupation until c. 1000 BC.

Of particular interest to the excavators was the fact that prior to its final abandonment, the site showed evidence of having undergone repeated inundation by monsoon flooding. This pattern is paralleled by evidence at Chalcolithic sites in the Ujjain area, such as Kayatha (Ansari and Dhavalikar 1975, 7–8) and Dangawada (Chakravarty *et al.*, 1989). Observations of similar processes in the Gangetic valley area lie at the heart of theories regarding major shifts in settlement patterns between the Chalcolithic and early-historic period (Lal 1984; Erdosy 1988). Some scholars have argued that increased movement away from flood-prone riverside locations into 'interior' areas during the early-historic period was made possible through the introduction of iron tools which enabled the clearance of large areas of forest (Banerjea 1965). As discussed in chapter 2, this theory is no longer taken for granted following a growing body of scholarship on the chronology of deforestation and iron technology in the Gangetic valley area. Other scholars have focused on the possible ideological, political and religious underpinnings of these changes in settlement patterns (such as, for example, the rise of Buddhism), but these have not hitherto been addressed archaeologically.

Ritual sites

As in other parts of India, aspects of central India's religious geography were first examined archaeologically by Alexander Cunningham, who was responsible for the first systematic documentation of the Buddhist remains at Sanchi and the four other 'Bhilsa Tope' sites (Cunningham 1854; 1880) that delineate the outer boundaries of the SSP study area. The first horizontal excavations at Sanchi, described in detail in chapter 9, were not carried out until Marshall's time (1940). Other major Buddhist sites in central India include Ujjain, in western Madhya Pradesh, and Bharhut, about 300 km NE of Sanchi in Rewa district. The latter was documented for the first time by Cunningham (1879) and only in recent years taken up for renewed investigation in the form of a PhD-based survey project aimed at relating the site to its wider archaeological landscape (Hawkes, in press). More recent discoveries include a second-century-BC stupa complex at Deokothar in Rewa district (Misra 2001) and a large complex of stupas and 'monastic rock-shelters' (*IAR* 1975–6, 28–30), as well as an Asokan edict, at Pangurariya, near Hoshangabad, Sehore district (Sircar 1979; Sarcar 1983; Allchin and Norman 1985; Falk 2006). As mentioned earlier, the latter site is also known for its large number of prehistoric painted rock-shelters, as is Kharwai, near Raisen, which also contains several second-century-BC stupas. The other major religious practice during the late centuries BC is the proto-Pancaratra system of the Bhagavata tradition, as represented by the Heliodorus pillar site at Vidisha. Datable to the late second century BC following the chronology of Antialcidas, the Indo-Greek king mentioned in the pillar inscription, the material here belongs to a larger body of archaeological, epigraphical and textual evidence from a variety of north Indian sites believed to represent the earliest phase of the Bhagavata religion. Foundations of an earlier apsidal building underlying the associated temple remains may be as early as the third century BC (Khare 1967; *IAR* 1963–4; 1964–5).

CHAPTER 4

Sanchi Study Area: The Physical Environment

Introduction

Having discussed the geography and archaeology of the central Indian region to which the SSP study area belongs, this chapter will take a micro-regional approach to the latter's physical environment, touching upon elements of local geology and pedology, as well as the history of land use, agriculture and climate. These details provide the necessary background for later accounts of the project's field methodology (chapter 8), itself partly shaped by local terrain; they also inform the methods used to interpret the ancient irrigation systems described in chapter 14.

Location

Sanchi hill is situated approximately 50 km NE of Bhopal in the modern state of Madhya Pradesh (Figures 3.1; 4.1; 4.2). The boundary between the modern districts of Vidisha and Raisen lies just to the north of Sanchi hill. The district administrative towns, Vidisha and Raisen, are situated 7 km to the north-east and 11 km to the south respectively. Prior to Independence in 1947, these district divisions also marked the boundary between the two princely states, Bhopal to the south and Gwalior to the north.

Geological zones

Sanchi hill is an outcrop of Vindhyan sandstone at the boundary between the sandstone hills to the south and west and the basalt-floored valley of yellow and black-cotton soils to the north and east. The local distribution of sandstone is therefore the precise opposite of the broader regional patterns described in the previous chapter.

The area comprises two major geological zones: i): flat black-cotton-soil plains formed from denuded basalt, interspersed by ii): sandstone inliers covered in thin (0.3 m) sandy soils. These zones are distributed in various combinations over the study area (Figure 4.1). Thus, the area to the west and south of Sanchi is dominated by long hill-ranges separated by narrow, cultivated valleys, whereas the opposite – large expanses of flat plains dotted with isolated, prominent hillocks – prevails to the north and east. Enclosed by these hilly zones and forming the central core of the study area is a large expanse of predominantly flat agricultural land. The elevation in the plains ranges between 410 to 440 m above mean sea level with an average slope of between 3 and 1% (Hodnett and Bell 1981, 3). The hilly areas range in elevation from 440 to 580 m. In several places, such as Ahmadpur and Saleiya hills NW of Vidisha, outcrops of basalt overlie the much older Vindhyan sandstone formations. This is due to volcanic inundations, resulting in basalt flows over the sedimentary deposits.

Although this geological classification is arbitrary in that each zone is part of an interrelated physical and cultural landscape, it does correspond quite closely to spatial trends in the archaeological landscape: the plains, mostly under cultivation, also contain habitational (both ancient and modern) settlement mounds, distributed at an average density of 1 per 2 km^2; the majority of Brahmanical and Jain temples also occur within such settlement contexts. By contrast, the hills provide refuge from monsoon flooding in the lower terrain. Most of the Buddhist sites occur on these hilltops, while rock-shelters formed by the jagged sandstone cliffs around their upper edges show occupation from at least the Chalcolithic period, with habitational settlements common on their lower slopes (Plate 1). The hills are exploited for their sandstone and other raw mineral resources and are covered with a semi-permanent scrub which is heavy on the slopes and lighter on the top. Coverage is dense in the west and south, whereas some forest clearance has taken place in the north and east (Figures 4.1, 4.2 colour). Further discussion of the relationship between ecology, land use and human occupation is given in the following sections.

Pedology and modern land use

The hilly zones

The soils on the hills are thin and sandy, with depths rarely exceeding 0.3 m (Hodnett and Bell 1981, 2). The native vegetation consists of broad-leaved, deciduous forest species such as teak, *tendū* (*Diospyros tementosa*), *sāl* (*Shorea robusta*) and *salai* (*Boswellia serrata*) (*Imp. Gaz.* viii, 127).[1] However, these native trees are rapidly being replaced by open-canopy species such as acacia and prickly scrub, more common to the shallower soils of the Deccan trap. Nowadays most of the hills are covered with a fast-spreading, prickly shrub called lantenna, originally introduced as an ornamental garden plant from Australia during the nineteenth century (Plate 8). Unlike broad-leaved species which shed their leaves during the summer, lantenna remains in leaf throughout the year. As discussed in chapter 8, this presents a major hindrance to transectual exploration; it also undermines the effectiveness of satellite remote-sensing as a reconnaissance

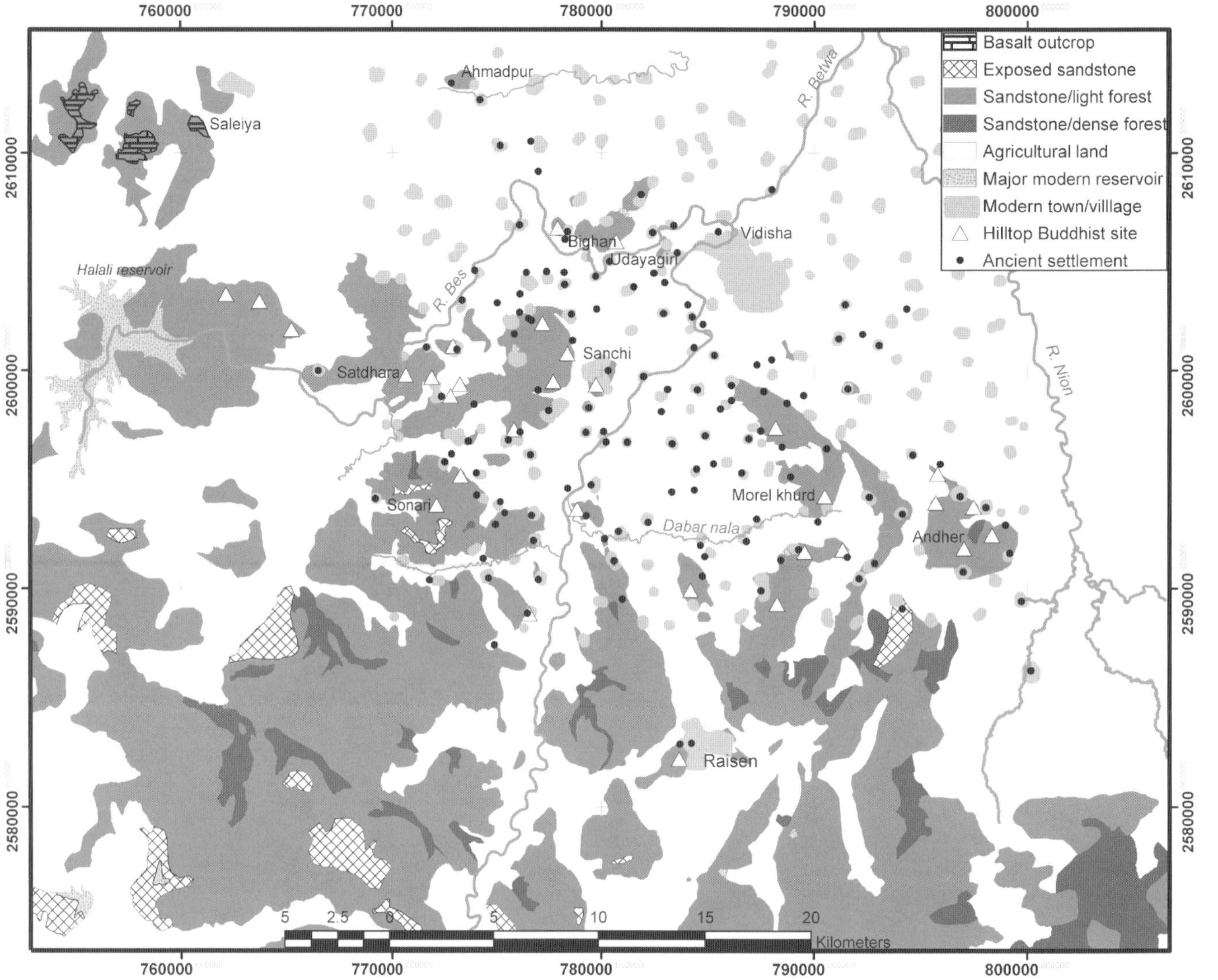

Figure 4.1 Map showing study area with main geological and land-use zones, and modern settlements, together with ancient settlements and Buddhist sites (SG level)

method. One of the few surviving native broad-leaved forests in the area occurs on a basaltic outcropping at Saleiya hill, to the NW of Vidisha (Figure 4.1). Because the leaves are shed by the middle of the dry season, it is one of the rare hilltop areas in the study area suitable for satellite remote-sensing (Plate 4).

In addition to these changes in flora, recent deforestation has also had a negative impact on soil erosion and drainage; in the 1970s, forests accounted for just 11% of the total land area in the Vidisha region (Singh, ed., 1971, 592). This figure is likely to have reduced even further in subsequent years as a result of the acceleration of non-sustainable industries such as wood planking and stone-quarrying.

Although surviving forests are nowadays mostly restricted to the hilly zones, small patches of scrub or rough grass occasionally extend to areas of shallow soil in the low-lying river basins: these strips of uncultivated land, important for grazing and hay production, comprise approximately 15% of the plains area (Hodnett and Bell 1981, 4) and can be found at the edges of settlements and along field boundaries, tracks and stream beds.

In addition to the collection of wood and forest plants, the quarrying of sandstone is also one of the major economic activities associated with the hilly regions. There are four major varieties (Kaimur, Rewah, Baindar and Bijawar), which, because of their distinctive colours and textures, have been favoured variously at different stages in the history of local sculptural and architectural production. For example, while most of Sanchi's Phase II monuments are built from the buff-coloured variety quarried from Nagauri, the Phase III gateways use the white sandstone from Udayagiri hill. By contrast, from the late ninth century onwards, the purple Baindar variety was preferred. Precious and semi-precious stones and minerals also occur throughout both the Vindhyan and Deccan trap zones. The quartzite tools of the Palaeolithic and Mesolithic-Neolithic are generally sourced from the Vindhyan sandstone (Pandey 1990, 5), while the Deccan trap, outcrops of which are frequently found overlying the sandstone base, contains intertrappean beds of silica-related minerals such as chert, chalcedony, agate and quartz (*ibid.*, 3). All of these minerals occur as microlithic tools throughout the Vidisha district, as does jasper, an opaque mineral found in the banded layers in the Bijawar series of sandstone. Since historical times, the red variety of jasper has provided a primary ingredient for use in local inlay decoration industries (*Imp. Gaz.* ix, 329).

The sandstone hills are also valued for their banded lateritic deposits. Laterite is used in the brick-making industry and is also a major source for locally produced iron-ore. Central India is acclaimed as an 'iron country *par excellence*' (Chakrabarti 1992, 27) and, until the industry came to an end following the famine of 1899–1900 (*Imp. Gaz.* viii, 136–7), the Sanchi area was particularly well known as an important source of high-quality iron (Malcolm 1832; Chakrabarti 1992, 27). This reputation evidently goes back to the early-historic period, as attested by finds of high-grade iron at Sanchi, as well as in the foundations of the Heliorodus pillar at Vidisha (Dass 2002–3). Further, numerous samples of iron slag were collected from ploughed settlement mounds during the SSP (chapter 13).

The agricultural plains

The black-cotton soils of the low-lying plain, by virtue of their high clay content and, consequently, high moisture storage capacity, are greatly valued for agricultural purposes, with wheat being the dominant crop. Approximately 85% of these soils are under cultivation (Hodnett and Bell 1981, 4). In the deeper soil areas the depth of the black-cotton soil and the underlying yellow clay is generally between 2 and 10 m, but may be deeper in the central part of the basin. Due to their high clay content, the soils have marked swelling and shrinking qualities. During the dry season they crack deeply; these cracks are up to 75 mm wide at the surface and reach a depth of 1.5 to 2 m under cultivated sites and up to 6 m under perennial grass and scrub. Thus the soils are able to receive soil moisture recharge rapidly at the outset of the monsoon; the local practice of harrowing the soil surface at the end of the monsoon closes the cracks and prevents excessive soil moisture loss due to evaporation (Hodnett and Bell 1986).

Local black-cotton soils are associated with land-use practices easily distinguishable from regions further to the north or east, an important point when it comes to assessing the function of the ancient dams described in chapter 14. The almost complete absence of irrigation and manure for either *kharif* (autumn) or *rabi* (spring) crops has long since been noted (Watt 1889–93, vi, 150). In 1908, only 5% of the total cultivated land in Malwa was under irrigation, whilst Vidisha district, with only 1% of irrigated land, had the lowest levels for the whole of central India (*Imp. Gaz.* xii, 429). Irrigation was usually confined to areas on the outskirts of larger towns, for crops such as poppy, sugar-cane and vegetables (*Imp. Gaz.* viii, 135). For wheat and barley, irrigation was only required in areas to the north, around Gwalior and Baghelkhand, where 'the yield is always inferior to that obtained without irrigation from the rich soils of Malwa' (*Imp. Gaz.* ix, 360). Irrigation generally took the form of wells, operated by means of a leather bucket lift (*charas*) or a beam with weight (*dhenkli*), or, in Gwalior, by a 'Persian Wheel' (*rahat*) (*Imp. Gaz.* ix, 363; Singh, ed., 1971, 587). In Baghelkhand, temporary earthen dams were used for constructing small irrigation tanks (*Imp. Gaz.* ix, 363). There is little evidence for the practice of extracting water from perennial rivers until the recent adoption of motorised pumps. This is largely because most river beds in Malwa are too far below the surrounding landscape for effective water extraction (*Imp. Gaz.* xii, 430).

This pattern is largely consistent with the figures for Vidisha during the early 1980s when only 1% of the total cultivated land was under irrigation. However, limited exploitation of groundwater resources by pump irrigation was already in evidence at this time (Sutcliffe *et al.*, 1981, 150). The most significant variable appears to be soil type: the shallower sandy soils to the north have higher irrigation requirements. However, other factors may also have contributed to the low levels of irrigation in the Vidisha area. It has been suggested that major depopulation following the famines of 1899–1900 may partly account for these trends. According to Watt (1889–93, vi, 151–2), this situation led to 'low farming on a large scale' rather than 'high farming on a small scale', and although the 'outturn of the land is ... far smaller than in more crowded tracts ... the surplus produce per head is considerably larger'. In addition to an adequate monsoon, only 50–75 mm of winter rain is required to ensure sufficient yields. It is therefore hardly surprising that most farmers are unwilling to pay the overheads for irrigation facilities. However, Watt (*ibid.*, 152) did refer to contemporary experiments which suggested that irrigation would bring about the necessary increase in yields to cope with potential population growth.

There are also records of earlier famines, and consequent cycles of depopulation, in 1344, 1595 and 1630 (*Imp. Gaz.* ix, 374). This is an extremely important point when it comes to assessing the function of the irrigation reservoirs described in chapter 14, and the possible reasons for the radical changes in land use between the early-historic period and the present day.

Ancient agriculture and archaeobotanical research

As discussed in chapter 3, wheat, known in central India from the mid-second millennium BC, is the principal crop in the Sanchi-Vidisha area today. By contrast, there is strong evidence, discussed in chapter 14, that the dams in the Sanchi area, datable to the late centuries BC, were built principally for the irrigation of rice (Shaw and Sutcliffe 2001; 2003a; 2003b; 2005; Shaw *et al.*, 2007). However, the precise history of rice agriculture in this part of central India has not been assessed archaeobotanically. To date, the main focus of archaeobotanical investigation has been on the Gangetic valley area where agricultural production appears to have been based on wet-rice cultivation from at least the mid-third millennium BC (Fuller 2002; 2003, 352).[2] Rice finds have been reported from Chalcolithic sites in northern Maharashtra and the Narmada valley (Dhavalikar 1985). However, neither sample quantity nor collection strategy justifies viewing rice as having played a significant role in subsistence patterns until much later periods (Fuller 2002). Limited samples from the Deccan and south India (Fuller 2002) suggest that the introduction of rice in these areas did not occur until the late centuries BC, with the westward spread of Buddhism and monarchical state systems from the Gangetic valley (Chakravarty 1988, 96–7). This evidence is generally in keeping with our working hypothesis, based on archaeological, hydrological and limited palynological (Shaw *et al.*, 2007) analyses of the Sanchi dams, that the history of rice in central India followed a similar pattern. Further, the introduction of wet-rice agriculture in the Sanchi area would have been an effective response to increased population and economic complexity indicated by settlement and monastery patterns documented during the SSP, and also this particular aspect of food change was an inevitable co-factor of the westward spread of Buddhist and urban culture, both of which grew out of a predominantly rice-growing environment: not only does rice have a number of dietary and environmental advantages over other grains, in India it also has a range of medicinal and ritual associations which even today marks it out as the favoured crop.

As mentioned earlier, the kind of archaeobotanical research required to test these hypotheses is still in its infancy in central India. Ancient pollen sequences from central Indian lake cores have hitherto focused on the history of woodland and grassland species, rather than agricultural crops (Chauhan 1995; 2000; 2002). This is due to the difficulty of identifying cereal types from pollen alone, a problem exacerbated by wind-borne spores which can travel considerable distances. Samples may not, therefore, reflect the immediate environment.. However, even a general profile can contain suggestive indicators of a rice-growing environment. For example, preliminary pollen analysis of reservoir deposits from the Sanchi area (Shaw and Sutcliffe 2005; Shaw *et al.*, 2007) revealed a predominance of spores from wet, marshland plant species. This fits closely with the kind of water-logged environment expected of an upstream cropping system.

By contrast, phytoliths, the non-organic opaline silica bodies formed within and between living plant cells, can lead to the identification of individual species such as rice and wheat (Rosen 1992; Ball *et al.*, 1993). The potential of this technique has already been demonstrated in South Asia (Fujiwara *et al.*, 1992; Madella 2003; Eksambekar *et al.*, 1999; Kajale and Eksambekar 2001; Harvey *et al.*, in press). However, identification is only reliable at the genus level, and it is difficult to distinguish between wild and domesticated rice (Houyuan 1997; Madella 2003; Harvey *et al.*, in press). Unfortunately, as confirmed during a recent pilot-project (Shaw *et al.*, 2007), reservoir deposits are not generally useful for phytolith analysis due to the poor preservation of phytoliths in ancient water bodies as compared to crop post-processing sites and ceramic tempers.[3]

Drainage

The Sanchi area is drained by two major rivers: the Betwa and the Bes or Halali. Both rivers have had an important influence on the positioning of settlements, ritual sites and communication routes. The River Betwa, a tributary of the Yamuna, drains from the hilly region to the SW, and passes about 1 km east of Sanchi hill to meet its tributary, the Bes; the mounds of ancient Vidisha are enclosed within their fork (Figures 1.2 and 9.2). The Bes flows through the Sanchi area from SW to NE. Its high rocky banks are more suitable for settlement than the low, flood-prone banks of the Betwa; in addition to settlements such as Fatehpur Marmata in the west, several major ritual sites (e.g. Udayagiri and Satdhara) overlook the Bes. As discussed in chapter 8, the fordability of these rivers and, in particular, the limited places on the Betwa suitable for crossing (Figure 8.3) are also determining factors in the positioning of settlements, hence the decision in this study to divide the landscape into a number of 'geographical sectors'.

The area is also drained by numerous, either perennial or seasonal, streams (*nālas*), whose banks are in many cases more suitable for villages as they are less prone to monsoon flooding. The damming of these *nālas* formed the basis of the early-historic reservoirs discussed in chapter 14. Further, because of the close association between water, fertility and local perceptions of the divine, these streams are frequently worshipped as the embodiment of the goddess (*devī*) and continue to have a profound impact on the construction of both social and ritual geographies. The frequency with which such *nālas* are omitted from settlement studies and site distribution maps reflects a disjuncture between academic and local perceptions of the historical landscape (cf. Lahiri and Singh 1999, 176).

Climate

Modern climate

The annual average rainfall of the whole Betwa basin is about 1140 mm (Table 4.1), with the average decreasing (Figure 4.3) from over 1300 mm on the hills to the east of Vidisha to about 900 mm to the north of the basin near Jhansi. This places it within India's 'moist climate zone' (Singh *et al.*, 1972, 496). The rainfall is highly seasonal, with on average over 90% occurring between the middle of June and the end of September. The seasonal rainfall distribution is illustrated in Figure 4.4. The balance between average monthly rainfall and potential transpiration, important for understanding the function of the Sanchi dams, is described in chapter 14.

Climatic and environmental change

Since the present climate and hydrology form the basis for calculations about irrigation and land use during the early-historic period, it is important to consider the evidence for climatic and environmental change over the past 2000 years. Unfortunately, there is very little palaeo-ecological information for the early-historic period; most of the emphasis hitherto has been on a major phase of aridification at the beginning of the third millennium BC which has been linked to theories regarding the decline of the Harappan civilisation (Singh 1971). Pollen and sedimentary analysis of lakes in the Thar desert in Rajasthan, together with pollen and oxygen isotope ratios in the Arabian Sea, have indicated the beginning of an arid phase in the second millennium BC, reaching present levels around AD 100 (Fuller 2002). Roughly similar patterns have been inferred from sequences in African regions affected by the Indian Ocean monsoon (Grove 1993; Fuller 2002). Although it is difficult to relate these sequences to the humid and arid phases supposed to have influenced major archaeological events during the proto and early-historic periods (Dhavalikar 1995), it is generally assumed that by the late centuries BC, a general movement towards present-day levels of aridity had begun to set in. However, the global sequence needs to be tempered with consideration of micro-climate change; remains of

Table 4.1 Average rainfall and evaporation (mm): Betwa basin, 1926–75 (after Sutcliffe *et al.*, 1981)

	Jan	Feb	Mar	Apr	May	Jun	Jul	Aug	Sep	Oct	Nov	Dec	Year
Rainfall over Betwa basin (mm)	15	7	6	2	5	111	390	351	196	31	15	8	1138
Potential transpiration, Bhopal	83	102	152	193	241	197	134	115	133	127	90	75	1643
Open water evaporation, Bhopal	113	135	193	241	293	237	164	143	167	165	123	103	2077

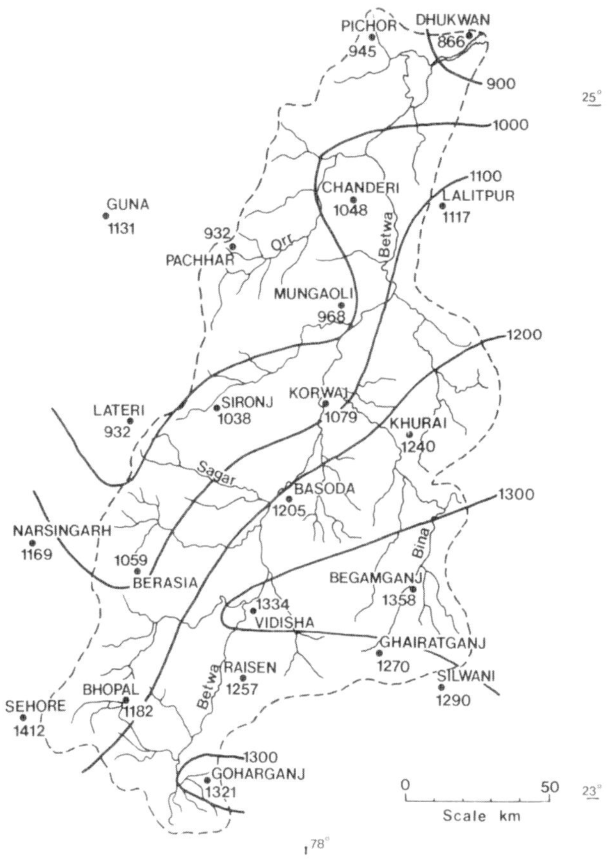

Figure 4.3 Annual average rainfall (mm): Betwa basin, 1926–75 (after Sutcliffe *et al.*, 1981, fig. 4)

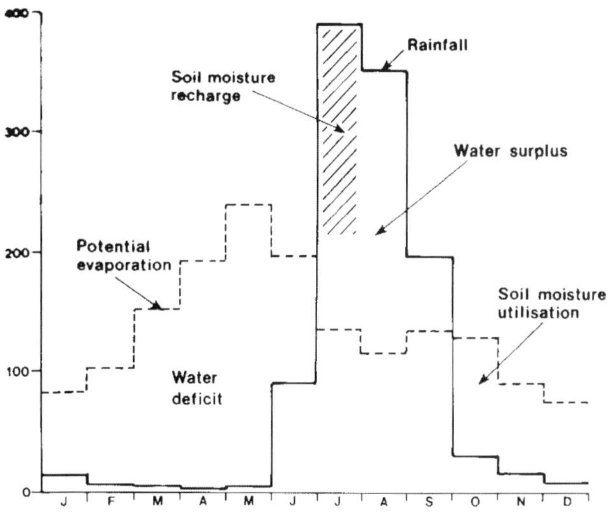

Figure 4.4 Seasonal rainfall and potential transpiration (mm) (after Sutcliffe *et al.*, 1981, fig. 2)

dried-up water-channels at Udayagiri, near Vidisha,[4] and Pangurariya in the Narmada river may suggest higher water-flow levels than today.

Some scholars have sought to explain changes in the positioning of Gangetic-valley settlements between the Chalcolithic and early-historic periods by the theory that widespread forest clearance was made possible by innovations in iron technology (Erdosy 1998). However, others argue that most deforestation in north India has resulted from relatively recent changes in land use (Lal 1986). Although the practice of 'slash and burn' shifting cultivation (*dahiyā*) may have had some negative impact (*Imp. Gaz.* IX, 363), the onset of the industrial revolution is probably the most influential factor. This supposition is supported by pollen and faunal analysis (Chowdhury 1977) and a body of textual evidence which suggests that at least until the Moghul period many parts of north India were still under forest (Erdosy 1998; Lal 1986). For example there are vivid descriptions of dense jungles throughout the Gangetic plain in the *Śatapatha Brāhmaṅa* (14.1; 4.14; Lal 1986), whilst the *Mahābhārata* depicts the city of Hastinapura as being surrounded by forest. Similar descriptions occur in the seventh-century accounts of the Chinese pilgrim, Xuanzang; and a record dating to the time of Mahmud Ghazni's campaigns in the eleventh century AD (Erdosy 1998, 51). Later still, the sixteenth-century *'Ain-i-Akbari* (283–93) describes royal forests around Agra, Meerut and Allahabad, areas which are now almost completely devoid of woodland (Erdosy 1998, 65). Central India appears to have been equally well forested: the same text mentions large herds of wild elephants in the forests around Raisen. The Moghul emperors were known to have hunted wild elephants until the seventeenth century (*Imp.. Gaz.* ix, 366), while in the Guna district, wild lions were still being hunted in the late nineteenth century (*ibid.*).

Conclusion

An obvious point, but one which needs to be stressed before considering the study area's political and religious history, is its location at the very centre of India. It is situated at the convergence of several ancient trade routes, at least one of which is represented by the modern Delhi–Bombay railway line which passes through Vidisha and Sanchi, less than 1 km to the west of the hill itself. The constant movement of trains through the area is a powerful reminder of its strategic position within the larger, pan-Indian sphere. As discussed in the following chapters, Vidisha has been the centre of major religious, political and artistic movements from at least the third century BC onwards. These were not localised, regionally specific phenomena, but rather resulted from far-reaching political and economic alliances that stretched as far as Taxila in the North-West.

CHAPTER 5

Political History of the Sanchi area

Introduction

This chapter will summarise what is known about the Sanchi area's position in Indian political history, based on published epigraphical, textual and archaeological material. The chronological focus is between c. third century BC and sixth century AD, which according to most historical accounts, is usually divided into four main phases: Mauryan (c. third century BC), post-Mauryan or 'Sunga' (c. second to first century BC), Satavahana/Ksatrapa (c. first to fourth century AD), Gupta (c. fourth to sixth century AD). Although these broad dynastic categories are useful for contextualising the newly documented archaeological material discussed in this book, it is important to temper the pan-Indian political framework with a consideration of more localised power structures.[1] To this end, the discussion in chapter 2, based on models of state in ancient India, is balanced here by a micro-regional approach to political organisation in the Sanchi area. Consideration is also given to the political situation from the sixth century AD, following the downfall of the Guptas, to the twelfth century; this will include a crucial appraisal of theories of urban decline during this period.

The pan-Indian dynastic framework: the Mauryas up to the Guptas

Phase Ic: third to second century BC (Mauryan)

The earliest inscriptions in central India are the Asokan edicts found at Sanchi, as well as at Rupnath, Jabalpur district, and Gurjara, Datia district, and two more recently discovered edicts at Pangurariya, Sehore district (Sircar 1979; Allchin and Norman 1985). The edict at Sanchi is carved on the Mauryan pillar which stands outside the southern gate of Stupa 1, its four-lioned capital now stored in the Sanchi Archaeological Museum. Although, as discussed in chapters 9 and 11, a pre-Mauryan, 'pre-monumental' phase of Buddhism in the area cannot be ruled out, the Asokan edict provides a time frame of c. 269–232 BC for the first Buddhist monuments there (Marshall *et al.*, 1940, 287; Hultzch 1925, I, 160). The earliest identifiable urban phase at nearby Vidisha is also datable to the Mauryan period, marked by the presence of NBPW in the city ramparts. Although the intertwined histories of Buddhism and urbanisation in this area appear to have coincided in part with the expansion of the Mauryan empire from its epicentre in the Gangetic valley, the precise nature of this relationship is still open to question. As discussed in chapter 2, for example, the Mauryan empire may have been considerably less centralised than implied by the distribution of Asokan edicts (Fussman 1987–8), and the expansion of heterodox religious institutions such as Buddhism and Jainism may have been just as significant as the state in the forging of pan-Indian political and economic unity. Such a view is supported by a growing body of textual and archaeological scholarship on the *saṅgha*'s active involvement in trade (Smith 2001, 32), as well as agrarian production (Gunawardana 1979; Shaw and Sutcliffe 2001; 2003a; 2003b). As discussed in chapters 1 and 6, Buddhism also appears to have been the first religious institution to conceive of itself within a pan-Indian ritual geography (Walters 2002).

Phase II: second century BC to first century AD

In most historical accounts, the period following the dissolution of the Mauryan empire in c. 232 BC is referred to as the Sunga period, a dynastic designation based largely on textual accounts which describe Pusyamitra Sunga as the successor to the Mauryan empire. Although Pataliputra remained the state capital, Vidisha is reputed to have played a significant role, first as the residence of Agnimitra, the viceroy and Pusyamitra's son, and later as the Sunga capital, following the Indo-Greek invasion of Pataliputra (Sircar 1969, 59–60). Vidisha's link with the Sungas is further attested by two inscriptions, both from Vidisha itself. The first is the Heliodorus pillar inscription, which after the Asokan inscription at Sanchi provides the second major chronological marker in the area (Sircar 1965, 88; Salomon 1998, 265–6). Closely linked with the proto-Pancaratra system of the Bhagavata tradition, it records the erection of a Garuda pillar by Heliodorus of Taxila, an ambassador of the Indo-Greek king Antialcidas; coins bearing the latter's name in the North-West provide a time frame of c. 115–80 BC (Bopearachchi, 1989, no. 401, 63–4). The inscription also mentions the local ruler, king Bhagabadra, who is usually identified as the fifth ruler of the Puranic list of ten Sunga kings (Sircar 1965, 88, no. 2). The second inscription, also from Vidisha, refers to the construction of a Bhagavata temple by king Bhagavata, generally identified as the ninth Sunga king of that name (Bhandarkar 1914, 190; Chanda 1920, 152). However, much of the uncertainty surrounding the Sungas stems from the fact that, apart from the epigraphical evidence from Vidisha, there are only two other inscriptions connected with a dynasty of that name: i) an inscription from Bharhut which mentions Dhanabhuti of the Sunga kingdom (Sircar 1965, i, 87; Majumdar and Pusalker 1954, 95–8); and ii) the inscription of king Dhanadeva (second century BC) from the Hamunangarhi temple in Ayodhya which mentions two Asvamedha sacrifices performed by his predecessor, Pusyamitra (*EI* 1929, 20, 54).

Further, the nature of the 'state' at this time remains obscure. That it may have been less centralised than traditionally assumed is suggested by the frequency of 'tribal coins' bearing the names of what appear to have been autonomous city-states (Bopearachchi and Pieper 1998, 35, 126, figs. 2–11). The two most important series are those bearing the names Bhagila and Kurara, both of which appear to have been urban sites in the Vidisha area (*ibid.*; Willis 2000, 59). The latter may correspond to the Kurara of the Sanchi donative inscriptions, where it occurs more frequently than any other place-name. The place itself may well correspond to the modern village of Kurawar, situated on a prominent mound to the north of Vidisha (Singh 1996). The fact that these 'cities' were issuing their own coins suggest that, even if the Sungas were ruling from Vidisha, their local authority may only have been of a titular nature. Further, as discussed in the next chapter, in contrast to the preceding Mauryan period when the establishment of Buddhism was closely connected with the patronage of the emperor himself, it is inaccurate to refer to the post-Mauryan monuments at Sanchi as Sunga. Not only was Pusyamitra reputedly animical to Buddhism, but most of the donative inscriptions during this period attest to predominantly collective and non-royal modes of sponsorship.

Phase III: c. first to third century AD (Satavahana/Ksatrapa)

During the third major phase, the control of central and western India oscillated between the Satavahanas and their long-standing rivals, the western Ksatrapas. Copper coins from Vidisha, Ujjain and Eran bearing the name Sri Satakarni (or simply Sata) show that by the first century AD this part of central India had already been incorporated into the Satavahana empire, with its base in the Deccan.[2] The same name is also mentioned in the inscription on the top architrave of the southern gateway at Sanchi (Marshall *et al.*, 1940, 342, inscrip. 398).[3] The inscription of Rudradaman at Junagadh shows that the Satavahanas had been temporarily ousted by the Ksatrapas during the second century AD (Sircar, 1969, 67). By the mid-third century AD, the Sanchi-Vidisha area had also come under Ksatrapa rule, as demonstrated by coins found here bearing the name Rudrasena II (c. 255–78) (Jha and Rajgor 1992, 38; 71). That the Ksatrapas were still in control of the area as late as the late fourth century AD is attested by the well inscription from Kanakherha village on the lower saddle of Sanchi hill (Sircar 1965, 186–7; Mirashi 1955a; Marshall *et al.*, 1940, 392–3, inscrip. 839), which describes the construction of a well by the Saka chief and 'righteous conqueror' (*dharmavijayī*) *mahādaṇḍanāyaka* Sridharavarman. As discussed later, the same ruler is mentioned alongside his Naga military commander in an inscription from Eran (Mirashi 1955b). This evidence helps to strengthen the view that Kusana rule, which covered most of the Gangetic valley and the North-West during this time, did not extend into this part of central India. As discussed in chapter 9, several Kusana-style images from Mathura have been found at Sanchi, but none of these appear to be local products. By contrast, many of the sculptures documented during the SSP in the surrounding countryside are closely related to the typical Kusana style at Mathura. However, this probably attests to the spread of pan-Indian artistic idioms rather than to the actual political control of the Kusana dynasty.

Phase IV: fifth to sixth century AD (Gupta)

The major event towards the beginning of this period is the defeat of the Ksatrapas by the Guptas. Samudragupta's (c. AD 335–75) Allahabad pillar inscription alludes to the subjugation of Saka Mahaksatrapa Rudrasena III during the mid-fourth century AD, while his Eran inscription attests to the conquest of east Malwa (Sircar 1965, 268–70; Bhandarkar *CII*, III, 220–3). Gupta control over the western part of the Ksatrapa dominions, including the Sanchi-Vidisha area, was consolidated in the reign of Candragupta II (c. AD 376–412). The main evidence to this effect comes from Udayagiri where the Cave 7 inscription records the commission of a *Śaṃbhu* (Siva) shrine by Śabaravirasena, minister of Candragupta II (Fleet, *CII*, III, 34–6). A second inscription from Cave 6 provides the date of GE 82 (AD 400/401), and refers to a gift made by a king of the Sanakanika who meditated at the feet of the '*paramabhaṭṭarāka mahārājadhirāja*, the glorious Candragupta' (Fleet *CII*, III, 21–5; Sircar 1969, 271–2). The Guptas' support of Brahmanism, particularly Vaisnavism, was a major factor influencing the changing configuration of the ritual landscape during this period. The sculpted panel in Cave 5 shows Varaha rescuing the goddess Earth from the primordial ocean. This is usually taken as an allegory of Candragupta's restoration of political and moral 'order' after years of foreign domination, although as discussed in chapter 12, there is some disagreement between scholars over the interpretation of individual iconographic details (Willis 2004). The rescue of the Earth may also be connected to the story, retold in a Sanskrit drama, of Candragupta's rescue of Dhrudevi, the wife of his elder brother Ramagupta. Ramagupta's shameful surrender of his wife to the Sakas is presented as one of the primary factors behind Candragupta's final campaign against the Sakas. Although the historicity of Ramagupta was once doubted (Majumdar and Altekar 1967, 389–93), the local presence of a king of that name in the latter half of the fourth century AD is attested by the discovery of coins and three inscribed Jain images at Vidisha bearing the name Ramagupta (Gai 1969; Sircar 1970; Williams 1982, 25).

The close link between Udayagiri and Candragupta is testimony to the supreme importance of the Vidisha area in the dissemination of political power. Indeed, the defeat of the Sakas led to the Guptas' dominance over most of north and west India. Candragupta's ongoing presence in the area is attested by an inscription at Sanchi dated GE 93 (AD 412/13). This records a grant of land by Amarakarddava, a military officer in Candragupta II's army (Marshall 1940, 388; inscrip. 833; Fleet *CII*, III, 29–34; Bhandarkar *CII*, III, 247–51; Sircar 1965, 280–2). However, while some have stressed that any ruler who wished to rule north India had first to gain control of Vidisha (Misra 1994), history has shown that attempts to build a power base from there repeatedly failed (Bakker 2006).

The post-Gupta period

Phases V–VII: c. sixth to twelfth century AD

Following the dissolution of the late Guptas at the end of the sixth century AD, the dominion became divided into a number of small, separate principalities. The Malwa area came under the control of the Kalacuri dynasty (Sircar 1966, 16–17). However, as discussed in chapter 2, there is little supporting evidence for the theory of widespread urban decay (Sharma 1987) during this period. This view, based largely on problematically dated texts such as the *Arthaśāstra*, has emphasised a clear-cut polarity between the assumed overarching nature of the state during the early-historic period and the disintegrated, 'degenerate' nature of statehood during the 'medieval' period; these theories are critically reviewed in Chattopadhyaya 1994. Much has been made of the occupational sequence at ancient Vidisha and the assumed shift in location from the mounds at Besnagar to the modern town of Vidisha sometime in the seventh century AD. It is only once a substantial number of early-historic city sites have been subjected to horizontal excavation, and related to their hinterlands through systematic settlement survey, that such theories can be properly assessed. The establishment of secure regional ceramic sequences is also an urgent requirement.[4] However, as discussed in chapters 11–12, documentation during the SSP of second-century-BC sculptural and architectural remains within Vidisha town suggests that the boundary between the pre- and post-Gupta settlements may have been overstated. Additional indications to this effect are provided by the second-century-BC pillar remains on the summit of Lohangi hill, a prominent rocky outcrop which rises dramatically out of the 'modern' town of Vidisha (Plates 3, 32). Vidisha's political importance during the post-Gupta period is further attested by the Vadner plate inscription of the Kalacuri king Buddharaja which was issued from Vidisha in Kalacuri year 360 (AD 608) (*EI* XXX, 210). The acceleration of building activity at Sanchi during this period also sheds doubt on the feasibility of the 'urban-decay' theory.

The Kalacuri kings were evidently still ruling in the Vidisha region during the mid-ninth century AD, as attested by an inscription from the Maladevi temple in Gyaraspur. They were by now tributaries of the Gurjara Pratiharas, who had become prominent towards the end of the eighth century AD (Salomon 1996; 1998, 77–8). Willis (1996a, 14–16; 2000, 78) has suggested that since the Kalacuri king Vopparaja of the Gyaraspur inscription may be the same as the Vappakadeva mentioned in the Temple 43 inscription at Sanchi (Marshall 1940, 394, inscrip. 842), we may viably regard Temple 43 and another of Sanchi's later monuments, Temple 45, as being under the direct patronage of the early Kalacuris. The last Pratihara ruler was Mahendrapala I (c. AD 885–910), while in the Malwa area the start of the tenth century witnessed the beginning of Paramara rule under Vakpatiraja I (c. AD 895–920) (Willis 2000, 77; Trivedi 1991, 7–9). The most powerful of the Paramara rulers was king Bhoja (c. AD 1000–55), during whose reign a large number of temples were built in the Vidisha area, the most well known being the Bijal Mandal in Vidisha and the Bhojpur temple to the south of Bhopal (Nagarch 1990).

Localised polities in central India: city states and Naga oligarchies

While the foregoing summary helps to place Vidisha's political history within a broad dynastic framework, relatively little is known about how these pan-Indian forces played out at a local level. The post-Mauryan Bhagila and Kurara series coins indicate that from around the second century BC local elites were issuing their own city coins, but the position of these rulers within the larger political arena is unclear. Similar uncertainties surround the Naga dynasty, which from at least the second century AD appears to have been one of the most prolific coin-issuers at Vidisha; large quantities of tiny copper Naga coins were retrieved during the Besnagar excavations (*Bhandakar* 1914, 210–11; 1915, 88); they continue to be collected by local farmers from the ploughed city mounds and sold on the local market. Analyses of these coins, and other numismatic, epigraphical and textual evidence, have led to the suggestion that the dynasty originated in Vidisha during the second half of the second century AD, from where it moved north to Mathura, Pawaya and Kantipurya, the three major Naga centres mentioned in the *Viṣṇu Purāṇa*.[5] That the Nagas were connected with Vidisha during earlier periods, however, is suggested by the high number of Naga-related names in the first-century-BC donative inscriptions at Sanchi.[6] It is also likely that the *nāga* sculptures in the area doubled as symbols of the Naga clan and, in particular, their patronage of major irrigation projects in the area (Shaw and Sutcliffe 2003a).

Although the Nagas' later history is relatively well attested from indirect references in Gupta and Vakataka inscriptions, how they related chronologically or politically to earlier pan-Indian dynasties such as the Ksatrapas is less clear. Preliminary insights are provided, however, by an inscription from Eran, which mentions the Saka chief *Mahādaṇḍanāyaka* Sridharavarman, also the subject of the Kanakherha well inscription at Sanchi. The object of the Eran inscription is to record the erection of a memorial pillar (*yaṣṭi*) by Sridharavarman's military commander (*senāpati*), a Naga chief from Maharashtra called Satyanaga (Mirashi 1955b).[7] This reference supports the image of the Nagas as a powerful oligarchy with family ties extending far beyond the Vidisha-Eran orbit, and with close allegiances to Ksatrapa authority.

Later inscriptions provide clear evidence that the Nagas' political clout came to be seen as a threat to Gupta authority. It is ironic, for example, that although the inscriptions of Samudragupta (AD 350–76) and Skandagupta at Allahabad and Junagadh respectively are primarily concerned with recording their victory over the Ksatrapas, the most dramatic language of subjugation is reserved for the Nagas. Samudragupta's inscription refers to the 'uprooting singly and in a moment' and the 'forcible extermination' of sections of the Naga dynasty (Bhandarkar, *CII*, III, 10–17; Bakker 1997, 10–11). It has been suggested that the three Naga kings mentioned by name, Achyuta, Nagasena and Ganapati, had been part of a coalition aimed at removing Samudragupta from power. In Bhandarkar's (*CII*, III, 11) words, 'that the formation of this confederacy was a great menace to the Gupta power and that its destruction was consequently regarded as the greatest of Samudragupta's military feats is inferred from the fact that this achievement alone has been described in the verse portion with which the Allahabad pillar inscription begins'. There are also epigraphical allusions to the defeat of the Nagas' allies, the Vakatakas, leading to their forcible relocation from their original territory in Bundelkhand to Nandivardhana in the Deccan (Bakker 2002). That the continued enmity of these two subjugated dynasties was considered a dangerous threat to political stability is suggested by the Guptas' concerted efforts to maintain peaceful links between the three houses. This three-way confederacy was consolidated by the marriage between Samudragupta's son, Candragupta II and the Naga princess Kuberanaga, who in earlier years had been raised in Samudragupta's court (Bakker 1997, appendix I, v. 5). Their daughter, Prabhavati, married a Vakataka prince, Rudrasena II, whose premature death resulted in Prabhavati herself becoming a powerful ruler (Bakker 1997, 11). Although the Guptas clearly kept the upper hand in this alliance, Prabhavati's mixed political and familial allegiances were instrumental in ensuring the political standing of her Naga relatives back in the Vidisha area (Bakker 2002, 1–3).

For instance, the marriage between her daughter and Prabhavati's half-brother, Ghatotkaca, the viceroy in Vidisha, during the reign of her other brother Kumaragupta (AD 415–54) ensured that by the time the latter's illegitimate son Skandagupta (AD 455–67) came to the throne, the three-way ties of the Gupta-Naga-Vakataka alliance were still intricately intermeshed (Bhandarkar *CII*, III, 276–9; Bakker 1997, 17). This marriage may have been an important factor during the battle for the throne between Skandagupta and his uncle Ghatotkaca, and the resulting split between the western and eastern halves of the Gupta dominion. Bakker (2002, 17) writes that during this conflict, 'the Guptas [at Vidisha] may have been supported by Naga feudatories who hadn't yet forgotten their defeat by Samudragupta and were biding their time'. This relationship would have led to the reinforcement of the 'old Vākāṭaka-Vidiśā-Nāga axis' (*ibid*., n. 62), the Nagas here being Ghatotkaca's allies rather than his adversaries, as assumed by earlier writers (Bhandarkar *CII*, III, 81). Bakker (2002, 17) has also noted strong allusions to these developments in the Junagadh inscription, which describes Skandagupta as he 'who forged an order with an effigy, namely Garuda, which rendered devoid of poison, the serpent rulers [i.e. the Nagas] who uplifted their hoods in pride and arrogance' (Bhandarkar *CII*, III, 299, 302; Fleet *CII*, III, 56–65). On a religious level, the reference to Garuda, the traditional slayer of serpents, is a clear pun on the Guptas' strong Vaisnava allegiances and the long-standing relationship of ambivalence between Visnu and *nāgas*.[8] On a political level, though, it seems that the Nagas, once again, had become a force to be reckoned with. These epigraphical sources provide a useful political context for explaining the 'royal' attributes of the Gupta-period *nāga* sculptures in the Sanchi area, which, as discussed in chapter 12, may have embodied references to the local Naga elites.

Conclusion

This and previous chapters have established a basic framework for understanding the physical geography and political history of the Sanchi area. However, while insights into Sanchi's position within the pan-Indian historical situation are provided largely by texts, epigraphy and numismatics, a more localised perspective has been hampered by a paucity of micro-regional archaeological research. The current framework of archaeological understanding is based on a limited number of prominent monumental sites, with much of the intervening countryside remaining unexplored archaeologically. The field methods in this study, to be described in chapter 8, were primarily aimed at filling some of these gaps and at redressing some of the problems, only alluded to in this chapter, regarding the relationship between political and religious history. While the earliest monuments at Sanchi were closely connected with the patronage of the Mauryan emperor Asoka, the proliferation of Buddhist monuments throughout the Sanchi area during the post-Mauryan period occurred with little input from the state. In striking contrast to the royal setting of the Bhagavata cult, as represented by the post-Mauryan pillars and capitals at Vidisha, the second major phase of Buddhist propagation was inspired by more localised political alliances and exchange networks. Quite how such networks came about, however, is not well understood. The documentation of Buddhist monasteries and their archaeological setting provides a starting point for addressing this question.

CHAPTER 6

Religious History and Religious Change in the Sanchi Area

Introduction

In this chapter I will outline the key phases of local religious history and the changing patterns of religious patronage over the timeframe covered by the SSP. This provides the necessary historical and theoretical context for the newly documented archaeological data described in chapters 9–14. I will also discuss the main models of religious change that have hitherto been used to explain the ways that pan-Indian religions integrated themselves within the social and religious environments into which they arrived, and assess their applicability to the SSP study area.

The Sanchi region occupies a key position in the archaeology of early-historic religions, with four main foci having dominated the scene to date: first, the rich body of art-historical, architectural and epigraphical material at Sanchi and neighbouring monastic sites attests to a sequence of Buddhist occupation from around the third century BC to the twelfth century AD (Cunningham 1854; Marshall *et al.*, 1940; Willis 2000). Secondly, the famous Heliodorus pillar site at the nearby city of Vidisha illustrates the local prominence of a proto-Pancaratra system of the Bhagavata cult from at least the second century BC.[1] Thirdly, a strong local Vaisnava presence continues in later years, reaching a climax during the Gupta period, as illustrated by the sculptural programme at Udayagiri.[2] The area is also home to an important group of early *nāga* and *yakṣa* sculptures, which, together with various stupa railing carvings and donative inscriptions at Sanchi, have been used to infer the prominence of these cults in the region (Chandra 1976; Misra 1982; Schopen 1996). Despite a long history of archaeological, art-historical and epigraphical research in the area, the traditional site-based focus of Indian archaeology, discussed more in chapter 7, has meant that little was hitherto known about how each of these religious traditions related to each other.[3]

Buddhism in the Sanchi area: building phases and patronage networks

Phase I (third to second century BC)

The establishment of Buddhism, or at least its monumentalisation, is datable to around the third century BC on the basis of the Asokan inscription and related monuments at Sanchi. There are also suggestions of a Mauryan phase at nearby Satdhara, one of the four outlying sites first documented in the nineteenth century by Alexander Cunningham and recently taken up for renewed investigations (Cunningham 1854; Agrawal 1997). The Asokan edict at Sanchi forms part of a wider body of evidence attesting to the interdependence of the *saṅgha* and the state during the Mauryan period (Gombrich 1988). More specifically, the transition from what had earlier been a regional sect confined to the Gangetic valley into an inter-regional religion was largely facilitated by state patronage. However, it is important to stress that the understanding of Buddhist propagation during the Mauryan period is based principally on sites highest up the 'monumental' scale which were clearly part of a centralised, 'city: monastery' model. Sanchi, for example, forms part of a larger group of stupa sites, including Sarnath, Amaravati (Ramaswami 1975, 7) and Taxila (Marshall 1951), whose proximity to major urban centres conforms to the *Patimokka* rules (*Vinaya* III, 155) which stipulate that monasteries should be situated close to, but nevertheless at a removed distance from, towns.[4] While the earliest monuments at Sanchi were closely linked to Asoka, on the one hand, and Vidisha, on the other, it is important to consider the possible existence, during the Mauryan or even pre-Mauryan period, of 'monumental' monastic establishments, funded by more devolved forms of patronage. As discussed in chapters 9 and 11, for example, some of the 'adapted' prehistoric rock-shelters at Sanchi and neighbouring Buddhist sites may represent a pre-monumental phase of Buddhism. Secondly, an examination of the rural settlements around Sanchi and other Buddhist sites helps to detract from the traditional focus on state forms of patronage during this period.

Phase II (second century BC to first century AD)

It was only during the post-Mauryan period that Buddhist stupas and monasteries began to spread into the surrounding countryside beyond the context of Sanchi and Satdhara. Existing monuments at these two principal sites were further expanded and elaborated, while the three other 'Bhilsa Tope' sites, Sonari, Morel-khurd and Andher (Cunningham 1854), all situated within a 15 km radius of Sanchi, were established for the first time (Cunningham 1854; Willis 2000; Agrawal 1997). Donative inscriptions from Phase II stupa railings at these sites represent a collective form of patronage whereby the funds for individual architectural components such as railings and paving slabs were pooled together from powerful families and guilds throughout central India (Dehejia 1992). The near absence of royalty in these donations at Sanchi provides a striking contrast to the preceding Mauryan period.[5] As discussed in chapter 2, these inscriptions have figured prominently in discussions regarding the 'domestication' of the *saṅgha*. The received view, heavily influenced by the 'passive' model of Buddhism, is that, in contrast to the Gupta period when inscriptions attest to donations of land, villages and non-monastic staff, the monks' response to such gift-giving during Phase II was one of passive non-reciprocity. However, important aspects of the inscriptions, not to mention their wider archaeological setting, have been overlooked by this scholarship. Although the near absence of royal donors in the post-Mauryan inscriptions is notable, the 'local' quality of these patronage networks may have been over-emphasised. First, the fact that the single largest group of donors (200) consists of monks (*bhikkhu*) and nuns (*bhikkuni*) says more about the *saṅgha*'s ongoing access to family wealth than it does about local social relations. Secondly, although many of the places mentioned in the inscriptions are in central India, only 16 refer to Vidisha. Much more numerous are references to Ujjeni (59) and Kurara (68).[6] Others come from as far away as Abu (Aboda) and Pushkara (Pokhra) in Rajasthan, and Paithan (Patithana) in Maharashtra. Even by modern-day standards, these places are hardly 'local'. Furthermore, most of the donors belong to the non-productive, urban and predominantly trading sections of society as opposed to the presumably agricultural populations residing in villages in the immediate vicinity of Sanchi hill.

Finally, inscriptions represent a particular form of patronage, i.e. a one-off, inter-regional fund-raising exercise aimed at the construction of elaborately decorated stupas. In other words, they pertained to capital funding rather than to maintenance. As suggested by Dehejia (1992), it is likely that monks travelled to these places with the sole purpose of pooling subscriptions. Other more sustainable and localised forms of patronage, such as those required for ensuring the daily subsistence of the *saṅgha*, do not find expression in these inscriptions. Furthermore, there is little reference to *local* agricultural populations, upon whom the *saṅgha* must have depended for food and grain. As discussed in the following chapters, in order to construct a more localised picture of interaction between the *saṅgha* and lay-sections of society, it is necessary to look beyond buildings and inscriptions at individual sites to the relative configuration of Buddhist and non-Buddhist ritual complexes, habitational settlements and land-use systems in the landscape.

The Hemavatas

This second major phase in the local history of Buddhism appears to have been closely connected with a school of Buddhist monks known as the Hemavatas, led by a teacher called Gotiputa (Cunningham 1854; Willis 2000, 69–75). Inscriptions bearing the names of these monks figure on the reliquaries from Sanchi Stupa 2, and contemporary stupas at the other four 'Bhilsa Tope' sites (Table 6.1). This evidence shows that all five sites were linked under a single school. All of the names mentioned in the inscriptions are analogous to those given in textual descriptions of the mission dispatched to the Himalayas after the Third Council.[7] Taken together with the archaeological evidence at these sites, and the fact that the stupa railings, discussed in chapters 9 and 11, were presumably built some time after deposition of the relics, Willis (2000, 23) suggests that the Hemavatas arrived at Sanchi 'just after the mid-second century BC', took over the older sites of Sanchi and Satdhara and established new monastic centres at Sonari, Morel-khurd and Andher. The fact that the Hemavatas' relics (along with those of Buddha's chief disciples, Mahamogalana and Sariputa) were taken to central India, rather than the older cradle of Buddhism in the Gangetic valley, is testimony to Sanchi's key position within the broader Buddhist world at this time (Walters 2002, 10).

While their arrival in the area, and the deposition of their relics in 'new' stupas, was evidently central to a 'second propagation' of Buddhism, quite how the Hemavatas related to the newly documented Buddhist sites documented in the study area is unclear. At most of these sites, described in detail in chapter 11, the earliest architectural material dates to Phase II. Contemporary Buddhist remains such as stupas and pillar capitals were also found within habitational settings. Two principal suggestions can be made on the basis of these patterns: i) the growth of the patronage-base of Buddhism between the third and second cen-

Table 6.1 Relics, reliquaries and burial deposits from the Sanchi area

Name/ SG	Stupa no.	SC/S no.	Stupa phase	Stupa deposit description	Relic phase	Current location	Ref.
Sanchi/ SG001	2	SC623	II	Inscribed sandstone box (in BM) containing five inscribed reliquaries. Describe relics of members of the Hemavata school. Contained burnt human bones. Whereabouts currently unknown.	II	Sandstone box: BM. Reliquaries: one in V&A; others in BM.	MW; AC
	3	SC613	II	Two large sandstone boxes inscribed with the names, Sariputa and Mahamogalana, whose initials are carved on steatite caskets found inside each box. Both caskets contained fragments of burnt bones, and one contained seven kinds of precious beads.	II	Boxes: SAM Relics: unknown.	AC, MW
	14	SC623/S890	V	Mathura sandstone Buddha image seated cross legged in *dhyana mudra*.	IIIb	SAM	JM, I, 47; III, pl. 105b. MMH, cat. 19.
	12	SC623/S887	V	Broken pedestal of Mathura sandstone with part of the left foot of a standing image, wearing sandals. Bears Brahmi inscription describing it as a gift of daughter of Vishakula.	IIIb	SAM	JM, I, 47; III, pl 124d, inscrip. 830, MMH, cat. A84.
	29	SC711/S1133	IV	Reliquary made of two earthenware cups, one inverted above the other, and containing bone fragment and broken vase.	II	?	JM, I, 48; III, pl 105d.

Sonari/ SG004	2	SC632	II	Steatite reliquary, carved with a panel of animals on the upper half, and a lotus petal on the lower. Contained five reliquaries, one of crystal, and four of steatite, all carved with single names of Hemavata monks, and containing bone fragments, burnt wood, resin fragments, beads, and metal ornaments.	II	Steatite reliquary: V&A. Four small reliquaries: BM. Other unknown. Relics: unknown.	AC, MW
	1	SC26/S26	II	Fragments of sandstone, two-part reliquary box. Contained three inter-stacked reliquaries culminating in a tiny crystal casket. No relic found.	II	Unknown	AC, MW
Satdhara/ SG007	2 II	SC635	II	Two steatite caskets inscribed with the names Sariputa and Mahamogalana, respectively.	II	Originally in V&A. Currently unknown having been sent to India.	AC, MW
	8 (formerly 7)	SC637	II	Uninscribed, steatite reliquary dish in two parts, surmounted by another two-part reliquary, of a wheel-made ceramic material, with a burnished red slip.	II	BM	AC, MW
Morel khurd/ SG005	2	SC28/S1054	II	Crystal stupa-shaped reliquary with double parasol pinnacle, found in a red earthenware box, whose lid was covered with white-wash, and inscribed in ink with illegible letters. Fragments of bone, gold and precious stones were found in both containers.	II	Reliquary: V&A. relics: unknown.	AC, MMW
	4	SC28/S1056	II	NBPW lidded container containing smaller ceramic bowl inscribed with the word *mun* ('the holy), and itself containing a crystal reliquary. Contained tiny fragments of precious stones and gold.	?	BM	AC, MW
	9c (sometimes called 8c)	SC675/S1062	II	Large red ceramic box containing purple mottled steatite pinnacled reliquary in three tiers. Both uninscribed. Contained large, and many complete, human bones.	II	?	AC
	7	SC675/S1069	II	Two red ceramic pots: i) inscribed with the word 'Patībho'; ii) inscribed with the name 'Upahita kasa'.	II	i) BM; ii) unknown.	AC, MW
	10	SC675/S1063	II	Disturbed deposit of earthenware box, containing bone fragments.	?	Unknown	AC
	11	SC675/S1064	II	Disturbed deposit of earthen jar containing bone fragments.	?	Unknown	AC
	17	SC675/S1070	II	Two relic-chambers containing earthenware pots and bone fragments.	?	Unknown	AC
	23q	?	II	Three earthenware jars.	?	Unknown	AC
Andher/ SG013	1	SC73	II	Rounded stone box containing ashes and 'calcined nut-shells'; lower down was a hemispherical red earthenware jar on top of a second red earthenware container. The latter contained a black ceramic bowl, which itself contained a lidded vase. Both were of a 'bright metallic lustre' a clear allusion to NBPW.	?	Unknown	AC
	2	SC520/S565	II	Large red ceramic box containing three reliquaries inscribed with names of the Hemavata monks, one of Gotiputa himself, the others of his disciples. Two are made of steatite, the other ceramic, all bearing engraved designs (one of the steatite ones bearing animal and lotus designs, similar to that from stūpa 2, Sonari).	II	BM	AC
	3	SC520/S566	II	Swastika shaped relic chamber, containing a large ceramic box, inside of which was a tall steatite reliquary in two parts. The name of a Hemavata monk is engraved on the outside of the latter, and another inscribed in ink on the lid. It contained burnt bone fragments.	II	BM	AC

Abbreviations: MW: Willis 2000; AC: Cunningham 1854;JM: Marshall 1920; MMH: Hamid 1920

turies BC was closely related to the increasingly urban character of settlements in the area; and ii) the spread of Buddhism and that of pan-Indian artistic idioms into the 'interior' were mutually interrelated processes: the only evidence for stone sculpture in these areas prior to the first century BC is found within hilltop monastic settings or at urban stupas or shrines with a strong link to Buddhism.

Sanchi and the creation of a Buddhist landscape

A related set of ideas discussed in detail by Jonathan Walters (2002) is that Buddhism was the first religious tradition to propel itself within a pan-Indian world-view.[8] This vision manifested itself on a number of levels: i) within the ritual sphere, the forging of what Walters (*ibid.*) refers to as a 'Buddhist World Map' was closely tied to the mechanisms of the relic cult; ii) in the political arena, the establishment of early Buddhist centres beyond the Gangetic valley was closely tied to the spread of the Mauryan empire and the ideology of the emperor Asoka; and iii) in the visual realm, Buddhism embraced a set of artistic, stylistic and iconographic conventions that transcended regional traditions. Walters's (2002, 2) theory that the Buddhist World Map was conceived of as an ever-expanding Buddha corpse made up of numerous individual Buddha relics finds sanction in early texts such as the *Mahāparinibbānasutta* (D.II. 164ff) and *Buddhavaṃsa* (ch. 28). These texts support the view that 'individual Buddhist kingdoms were part of a larger Buddhist whole just as their stupas contained parts of a larger whole Buddha' (Walters *ibid.*). As discussed in chapters 9 and 11, although Sanchi Stupa 1 has yielded no relics, there are strong suggestions that it contained, and may still do, a relic of the Buddha himself. However, that there were other Buddhist maps made up of the relics of important monks and saints is suggested by the distribution of the Hemavata relics in the Sanchi area.

Sanchi was also part of a 'Buddhist-Imperial Map': just as Stupa 1 was part of a network of stupas making up the larger Buddha corpse, so the Asokan edict here was part of a network of edicts forming the larger Mauryan world map (Walters 2002, 4). However, Walters's application of a similar model to the post-Mauryan period, whereby the Buddhist map and its individual monuments are now seen as being 'controlled' by the 'Sungas' or the 'Kusanas' (*ibid.*, 5–6), is less credible given the uncertainties, discussed in chapter 5, over the history of these dynasties in central India. Rather, as discussed later, the content of the Phase-II inscriptions at Sanchi suggests that the principal funders and 'controllers' of this post-Mauryan Buddhist landscape were not emperors but rather local oligarchs, land-owners, merchants, and even monks and nuns themselves.

Finally, the creation of a unified Buddhist World Map was closely bound up with the development of a codified artistic vocabulary for representing the Buddhist narrative and world-view. During Phases I and II, there is little in the way of specifically 'Buddhist' narratives, although the sculptural style clearly follows a pan-Indian idiom with influences as far afield as Mathura in the east and Karle in the Deccan (Willis 2000). By Phase III, the *Jātaka* tales are now represented on the Stupa 1 gateway panels, but unlike their earlier counterparts at Bharhut, the labels have been dropped. Presumably, this decision was made with the assumption that the local population had already been sufficiently exposed to the Buddhist story by this time. There is also the aspect of bringing the influence of the Buddhist heartland into new areas, through the representation of scenes and places from Buddhist narratives set in the Gangetic valley, e.g. Sravasti and Rajgir. The questions here, however, are multifold. How were the schools that produced this pan-Indian art organised? How were these 'foreign' scenes and themes received by local populations? What was the *saṅgha*'s 'sales pitch' for attracting sponsorship for the execution of this art?

Phases III–VI (first to twelfth century AD)

The material at Sanchi indicates an unbroken tradition of Buddhist activity up to the eleventh or twelfth centuries AD, with major construction periods taking place around the fifth, seventh and tenth centuries AD. However, there is little evidence at interior sites for ongoing occupation during the post-Gupta period. By the ninth or tenth centuries AD, the proliferation of Brahmanical temples, often within or close to monastic complexes, attests to the diminishing influence of the *saṅgha* and a corresponding shift in the focus of religious patronage.

Significant changes in the objects of donative inscriptions at Sanchi take place from the fifth century AD, with the donation of individual architectural components being replaced by that of land, villages and money, as well as accrued interest, for feeding monks and purchasing lamp fuel (Majumdar 1940, 388–96).[9] As discussed in chapter 2, these fit with textual evidence for the *saṅgha*'s increasing involvement in reciprocal and institutional exchange networks with local lay populations. However, patterns in the wider archaeological landscape provide strong support for the prior existence of such links during earlier periods. The main evidence to this effect is provided by the close spatial and temporal relationship between Buddhist sites and major irrigation systems, both at Sanchi itself and throughout the study area. As discussed in chapter 14, the working hypothesis is that, as in Sri Lanka where 'monastic landlordism' was in evidence from c. second century BC, irrigation systems were central to the development of exchange networks between monks and local agricultural communities (Shaw 2000b; Shaw and Sutcliffe 2001; 2003a; 2005; Shaw *et al.*, 2007).

Brahmanical traditions

The Sanchi-Vidisha area also plays a key role in the development of Hinduism, although its history is more multilinear than its Buddhist counterpart. For sake of simplicity, the associated archaeology can be divided into two groups: a) material relating to the proto-Pancaratra traditions from c. third century BC onwards; and b) material connected with the emergence of orthodox Brahmanical theism from the mid-first millennium AD onwards, a process which reaches a climax during the ninth or tenth century AD.

The Bhagavata cult

At the same time as Buddhism was flourishing at Sanchi, Vidisha was becoming a major centre for a proto-Pancaratra system of the Bhagavata tradition, as represented by the material at the Heliodorus pillar. Situated immediately north of the confluence of the Rivers Bes and Betwa, this material is datable to the late second century BC, based on the chronology of Antialcidas, the Indo-Greek king mentioned in the main pillar inscription.[10] The Heliodorus complex belongs to a larger body of archaeological, epigraphical and textual evidence from throughout northern India, believed to represent the earliest phase of the Bhagavata religion (Härtel 1987, 575, n. 7). Defined by some Indologists as *vīravāda*, it was based on the cult of the heroes of the Vrsni clan, later developing into *vyūhavāda* (system of emanations), and later still into the *avatāravāda* (incarnation system).[11] At the outset, *vīravāda* was dominated by the clan's two principal members, Samkarsana and his elder brother, Vasudeva, but in later years, it grew into a cult of five heroes (*Pañcavīra*).[12] Amongst the earliest material evidence for Samkarsana and Vasudeva is a group of six coins from Ai Khanoum bearing the name of Agathocles in both Greek and Brahmi scripts. Datable to the second century BC, the Greek on the obverse side is shown next to Samkarsana carrying a plough and *musala*, while the Brahmi inscription on the reverse side accompanies a depiction of Vasudeva carrying a wheel and conch (Bernard 1974; Narain 1973; Härtel 1987, 2, pl. II, a–b). Similar depictions are known from rock-painted contexts datable to the second century BC from both North-West and central India.[13] The same deities are mentioned in a number of early texts and inscriptions.[14] In later years, these deities become part of a larger group of five heroes: Samkarsana, Vasudeva, Pradyumna, Samba and Aniruddha.[15] In Härtel's understanding this *vīravada* develops into *vyūhavāda*.[16] The most significant departure from the earlier tradition is that the members of the Vrsni clan are no longer seen as earthly beings; the former family structure is displaced, with Vasudeva taking the supreme position and Samba being discarded or superseded by Aditya. The order of succession thus became Vasudeva, Samkarsana, Pradyumna and Aniruddha.[17]

Despite this body of textual and archaeological material relating to the proto-Pancaratra tradition, several important questions remain unanswered: i) when did the cult of the two heroes develop into five; ii) when did the transition from *vīravāda* to *vyūhavāda* take place; and iii) in what form were the *vīra* deities depicted? A major problem is that prior to the early centuries AD, there is no clear evidence for sculptural images of the *vīra* deities as they appear in the earliest coins and inscriptions.[18] By the Kusana and Gupta period we begin to find images identifiable as Samkarsana as well as Vasudeva in their *vīra* form,[19] but as stated by Härtel (1987, 583), 'we can only hope that the soil of India [will] once yield an *old* vīra also'.

Prior to the Kusana period, the only sculptures with any link to the proto-Pancaratra tradition are of Balarama in his serpent manifestation. Discussed further below, these sculptures are *nāgas*, the only iconographic link with the human figures on the Ai Khanoum coins being the plough and *musala* that they hold. Given the close ritual roles of Samkarsana as an agricultural deity, and the *nāgas* as spirits of water and fertility, the transplantation of these objects from one religious tradition to another would presumably have been a fairly seamless process of 'cultic assimilation'. Härtel (1987, 582) has suggested, however, that it was not until the development of the *vyūha* system that Balarama in his serpent manifestation became fully incorporated into the Bhagavata cult. He argues that during the late centuries BC, it is unlikely that Samkarsana in his *vīra* form was represented as a snake god, but rather as a human deity in the manner of the depictions on the Ai Khanoum coins. The early plough-wielding *nāgas* may thus only have been loosely connected to the Bhagavata tradition and were probably worshipped as independent deities (*ibid.*, 585–6).

As well as providing some historical framework for assessing a group of newly documented Balarama-*nāga* images in the SSP study area described in chapter 12, these issues are also of importance when it comes to considering the proto-Pancaratra material at the Heliodorus pillar site itself. The pillar (Plate 27) is described in the inscription as a 'Garuda *stambha*'.[20] Since Garuda is traditionally the vehicle of Vasudeva (*Mahābhārata* I, 33, 16–17), it is assumed that the pillar was dedicated to this deity. The remains of a Garuda image (Plate 28), now in the Gujari Mahal Museum, Gwalior (henceforth GGMM), evidently stood on the top of the pillar as a standard of Vasudeva. The sculpture consists of a railed abacus, on top of which are the remains of Garuda's claws pinning down part of a snake (Dass 2002–3).[21] This 'Garuda *stambha*' appears to have been part of a row of pillars, as suggested by post-holes found during excavations and associated capitals scattered around the site (Härtel 1987, 577–9; Khare 1967, 23–4; Irwin 1976). Of the latter, the most significant is a group of fan-palm capitals (*tāladhvaja*) (Plate 30),[22] which, together with similar capitals from several other north Indian sites,[23] have been viewed as standards of Samkarsana, a link which is supported by early textual descriptions.[24] However, whilst it is probable that these aniconic standards were associated with Vasudeva and Samkarsana-Balarama respectively, we should not assume that they were set up in lieu of anthropomorphic images: the practice of establishing standards in honour of deities whose images were installed in adjoining shrines was an ancient custom well attested in the textual record.[25] It is very likely that the temple described in the second inscription from Vidisha (mentioned in chapter 5) as having been constructed by king Bhagavata (Bhandarkar 1914, 190) contained images which have not survived and, furthermore, that these images were not dissimilar to those found on the second-century-BC Ai Khanoum coins and contemporary depictions discussed earlier.

Also included within the sculptural material at the Heliodorus pillar site was a large crocodile capital which has been interpreted as the standard of Pradyumna.[26] Härtel suggests that 'the evidence of the pillars for three of the *Pañcavīras* makes it obvious that in this temple at [Vidisha] also all the five heroes were worshipped' (Härtel, 1987, 579–80).[27] However, this final conjecture needs to be considered with some caution; the existence of the crocodile capital cannot be taken as conclusive evidence for the full development of the *Pañcavīra* system during this time. Further, although the standards of Vasudeva and Samkarsana are described in the *Mahābhārata*, those of the other *Pañcavīras* do not find textual sanction until well after the post-Gupta period, and when they do so, it is within the context of the *vyūha* rather than the *vīra* system (Shaw 2004a; Willis, forthcoming a, ch. 3).

A number of points regarding the relationship between the Bhagavata system and the state should be made here. The wide geographical distribution of the material relating to the proto-Pancaratra system is in keeping with the inter-regional political alliances attested by the Heliodorus inscription. Its pan-Indian status is also confirmed by the inter-regional style of the Heliodorus pillar and its associated capitals. As discussed in chapter 9, its inverted lotus capital belongs to a recognisable post-Mauryan pillar type found within both Buddhist and Brahmanical contexts throughout the Sanchi area (Figure 9.4) (Willis 2000, 56–8), while similar fan-palm capitals have been found as far away as Pawaya and Mathura in the north, and Kausambi in the east.[28] The obvious availability of state patronage may be taken as one of the main factors behind the relatively early monumentalisation of the Bhagavata tradition. While thus sharing certain attributes with the early history of Buddhism, it is significant that in contrast to Buddhism, which takes on a very visible presence even in the most interior areas from at least the second century BC, the Heliodorus pillar material finds no direct equivalent in the surrounding countryside. As discussed in chapter 12, the appearance of anthropomorphic depictions of Balarama in his serpent form in these rural areas from the first century BC raises important questions regarding the relationship between the various strands of what have come to be grouped together as a single religious tradition.

The yakṣa and nāga cults

The first deities to be represented in the form of free-standing, anthropomorphic stone sculptures belong to the *yakṣa* and *nāga* traditions. Both *nāgas* and *yakṣas* and their female counterparts, *yakṣinis* and *nāginīs*, were traditionally associated with fertility, agriculture and the natural elements, and worshipped as place-bound tutelary deities. Possibly because they were considered too 'powerful' to be subverted, they were often assimilated into pan-Indian religious traditions as subsidiary deities (Cunningham 1879, 22; Coomaraswamy 1980, I. 9–27). *Yakṣas*, for example, were incorporated into Buddhist contexts as guardians of gates and, in the *Purāṇa* texts, as directional guardians (Misra 1981, 96). Although they figure prominently on the carved stupa railings at Bharhut and Sanchi during the post-Mauryan period, free-standing *yakṣa* and *yakṣini* images appear as early as the third century BC. Whilst these early examples come from east India (Chanda 1921),[29] the Vidisha area is home to a well-known group of slightly later images, datable to the mid-first century BC (chapter 12). However, considering the stylistic maturity of these images, they clearly stemmed from much older cultic traditions and were represented in other media throughout the preceding centuries (Allchin, 1995; Gupta 1980; Ray 1945). For example, the largely unknown pantheons of male and female deities portrayed in terracotta art may well represent prototypes of the later stone *yakṣa* and *yakṣini* sculptures (Pal, ed., 2002).

Although there are no archaeological remains of ancient *yakṣa* shrines, we can infer their appearance from both textual and artistic representations. Early Buddhist and Jain texts, for example, describe the worship of *yakṣas* at places variously called *caitya*, *thūpa* or *devakula*. Whilst later becoming synonymous with Buddhist shrines or stupas, these were probably simple tree shrines that are unlikely to have left archaeological remains (Misra 1981, 91–3; Law 1931; Irwin 1987; Van Kooij 1995). As far back as the Harappan seals, we find depictions of railed trees or spirits residing in trees (Marshall 1931, 63–5); semi-structural tree-shrines with small altars described in the *Saṃyutta Nikāya* (Coomaraswamy 1980, I. 17) are plentiful in Buddhist bas-relief sculpture of the post-Mauryan period at Bharhut, Sanchi or Amaravati (Barua 1926, pl. 20, 35; Misra 1981, 91–3), as well as on early tribal and dynastic coins (Bopearachchi and Pieper 1998; Allan 1936, 122–8).

The chronology of *nāga*, or serpent, sculptures is similar to that of *yakṣas*, and much of our information comes from Buddhist texts, which describe *nāgas* as dangerous deities residing in the nether regions of the earth or in ponds and rivers (Vogel 1926; Misra 1981, 90). This association with water is borne out by the frequency with which *nāga* sculptures, both at Sanchi and elsewhere, are situated in close proximity to water bodies (Shaw and Sutcliffe 2003a; 2001; Puri 1968, 50). They are traditionally believed to have the powers of the forces of nature and are propitiated in order to regulate the monsoon rains. Their ritual status is thus an ambivalent one, because, while they can bring about the rains needed for a healthy crop, they can also bring about floods and storms. Their obvious importance in an agrarian economy made them particularly susceptible to assimilation into both Buddhist and Brahmanical contexts. Their relationship with each of these traditions is discussed below.

Pan-Indian religions and 'local' cults: models of religious change

Hinduisation and royal legitimisation

There is a considerable body of scholarship on the subject of religious change in ancient India, with a particular emphasis on the question of how 'pan-Indian' religions related to the pre-existing cultic framework of the areas in which they established themselves. For the most part, the emphasis has been textual, with the aforementioned descriptions of *yakṣas* and *nāgas* in Buddhist and Brahmanical texts providing the main frame of reference. The prevailing interpretive framework has generally drawn on Brahmanical models of 'tribal absorption' or 'cultic integration' (Kulke 1993), the underlying premise of which is that 'local' deities are incorporated into the mainstream religious framework through a process of 'Hinduisation' or 'Sanskritisation' (Weber 1920; Srinivas 1967). Such discussions, however, rarely relate to contexts prior to the Gupta period when Hinduisation became central to strategies of royal legimitimisation. This is well illustrated by Kulke's (1993) study of the role of 'Hinduisation' in the establishment of early-medieval royal centres in predominantly tribal parts of Orissa. He argues that since the Hindu court was dependent on the support and loyalty of these tribes, they were willing to accept the tribal autochthonous deities as royal tutelary deities. It is for this reason that most important Hindu pilgrimage centres accommodated the older cult deity, usually represented by an unhewn stone, as in the case of the goddess temple Maninagesvari in Ranpur, which is mentioned in two royal land donative inscriptions of the fifth to sixth century AD.

Pan-Hindu pilgrimage centres and ritual geographies

The assimilation of 'local' cults also appears to have played an important role in the rise of major Brahmanical pilgrimage centres such as Mathura and Ayodhya (Bakker and Entwistle 1981, 86; Entwistle 1987; Bakker 1996). Bakker's (1996) survey of the material remains at the main Ramaite pilgrimage sites in and around Ayodhya, alongside a comparative analysis of the various versions of the city's traditional pilgrimage manual, the *Ayodhyāmāhātmya*, attests to a gradual phasing out of *yakṣa*, *nāga* and other non-Vaisnava cult spots. Bakker's study has also shown that the city's reputation as a pan-Hindu pilgrimage centre did not emerge until the twelfth century AD, while evidence for Ayodhya's exclusively Ramaite associations is rare before the sixteenth century. Ironically, its rise to prominence on an 'all-India' level occurred against the backdrop of considerable Muslim oppression, including a ban on Hindu temple construction between the twelfth and eighteenth centuries, as well as increasing rivalry between different sects of orthodox Hinduism (Bakker 1986, 61–3). It has been suggested, therefore, that the creation of pan-Hindu pilgrimage sites such as Ayodhya provided a useful ritual and political counterbalance to the perception of Islam as a homogeneous, 'monolithic' and 'unambiguous' entity (Rao 1994, n. 18).

For the earlier periods, however, we are hindered by the sheer heterogeneity of the Brahmanical tradition, which prior to the emergence of orthodox theism during the Gupta period cannot be reduced to an overarching philosophical or iconographic category but, rather, as illustrated by the discussion of the Bhagavata cult above, tends to consist of multiple and disparate cultic strands. This makes any clear-cut division between 'local' and 'pan-Indian' religions rather futile. The other major limitation is the lack of archaeological correlates for cultic activity prior to the third century BC when stone becomes a medium of religious expression for the first time. Prior to this, we have various instances of portable art (terracottas, for example) but little in the way of place-bound cultic locales. And, as far as the Vidisha region is concerned, there is no indication of any significant degree of terracotta image production.

Brahmanism and 'local' cults in the SSP study area: Balarama in his serpent form

As mentioned earlier, much of the literature on religious change within the Brahmanical framework relates to the Gupta period onwards when Hinduism becomes a pan-Indian phenomenon for the first time. The temporal and spatial patterns in the distribution of temples and sculptures discussed in chapter 12 reflect these wider patterns. For example, the increasing 'royalisation' from c. fifth century AD onwards of not only orthodox Hindu deities such as Visnu but also *nāga* images forms close parallels to patterns in Orissa (Kulke 1993) and appears to be part of the legitimising strategies of the Gupta kings. The archaeological patterns also shed interesting light on inter-religious dynamics during earlier periods. Of particular interest is a group of early *nāga* sculptures in the form of Balarama, who, as discussed earlier, is synonymous with Vasudeva's elder brother, Samkarsana. These begin to appear throughout the rural landscape to the east of Sanchi between the first century BC and first century AD, thus forming a contrast to the exclusively urban context of the proto-Pancaratra-related material at Vidisha and other north Indian city sites. There are also major iconographic differences. Samkarsana's no longer appears as a fan-palm standard or as a deified human hero (*vīra*), but as a serpent deity, with a human body and a serpent canopy outspread over his head. The earliest-known Balarama images in north India, a two-armed Balarama from Jansuti, near Mathura (Plate 149),[30] and two separate images from Tumain,[31] are datable between the second and first centuries BC. These early examples have the god holding a pestle (*musala*) in the right hand and a plough (*hala*) in the other (Plate 149).

By the early centuries AD, a second iconographic model appears as typified by the misnamed *nāga* from Chargaon, dated year 40 of the Kaniska era (Bachhofer 1939, pl. 97a). Now the right hand is raised over the head, the left hand holding a wine goblet against the chest.[32] Balarama's appearance as a *nāga* is thought to coincide with the shift from the *vīravāda* to the *vyūhavāda* system of Vaisnavism (Härtel 1987, 582). Despite references in the *Mahābharāta* (12, 326) to the link between Samkarsana and the snake incarnation of Sesa Narayana, it has been argued that this connection between Visnu as Sesa Narayana and Balarama as *nāga* is a 'confused' one, both stemming from quite separate traditions (Banerjea 1942). Following this line of reasoning, Härtel views Balarama's *nāga* manifestation as a mechanism for keeping the *nāga* cult 'under Orthodox control' (Härtel 1987, 582; Vogel 1926, 89). It is important to stress that *pañcavyūha* and *pañcavīra* iconography does not unfold in a unilinear manner, a point illustrated by the co-existence of various iconographic elements right through to the Gupta period. Thus the lion-headed mace/plough idiom appears in early serpent forms of Balarama as well as later non-serpent forms such as the Gupta-period image from Vidisha mentioned earlier.[33] While Balarama's manifestation as a *nāga* is thought to be a later development involving a process of 'cultic assimilation' into the Bhagavata tradition, there is a danger here of extrapolating back into the past from a set of connections that may only have been formalised in later years.[34] We cannot assume, for example, that the sectarian link between these Balarama-*nāga* images and the representation of the proto-Pancaratra deities in Vidisha was an established fact. This is just one of a set of problems regarding the relationships between the sectarian strands of early Vaisnavism that chapter 12 seeks to redress.

There are also problems when it comes to relating these early strands of Vaisnavism with later developments, as typified, for example, at Udayagiri, whose sculptural programme during the Gupta period reflects wider theological shifts such as the full development of the concept of *avatāra*.[35] Aspects of the wider archaeological context of these plough-wielding *nāga* sculptures, together with an increasing incorporation of more explicitly Vaisnava iconography, also shed light on the changing patterns of religious patronage in the Sanchi area. In particular, their location on the edge of ancient irrigation systems provides an empirical basis for assessing wider theories regarding the involvement of Brahmanical institutions in land-tenure and agrarian production, and for suggesting a level of competition with Buddhism in this respect. The increasing link between orthodox Hinduism, kingship, land-tenure and water-management during the Gupta period is discussed in chapters 12 and 14, with special reference to recent scholarship at Udayagiri (Willis 2004).

Buddhism and local cults

Suggestions have also been posited regarding the pre-existing cultic associations of major Buddhist sites, which in some cases seem to have re-emerged following the demise of Buddhism (Byrne 1995; Kosambi 1962; Bakker 1996). However, these suggestions are based largely on the aforementioned textual references to *nāgas* and *yakṣas* and depictions of semi-structural shrines for their worship in Buddhist bas-relief sculpture of the second century BC. D. D. Kosambi (1962) posited a link between ancient hunter-gatherer tracks and major Buddhist pilgrimage sites in the Deccan, arguing that the Pandhapur pilgrimage was a vestigial form of pre-agrarian seasonal movement.[36] However, his theory of 'Microlithic Tracks' has not yet been archaeologically verified, and specific archaeological evidence for earlier cultic activity at these sites is entirely lacking beyond the existence of natural shrines and painted rock-shelters whose precise ritual associations cannot be ascertained in the absence of excavation.

For this reason, the focus of debate regarding religious change in the Buddhist context has largely been restricted to the *saṅgha*'s relationship with *nāgas* and *yakṣas*, the first Indian deities to be represented in the form of anthropomorphic, free-standing stone sculptures. In the main, two models have been used to interpret this relationship: i) 'conversion' models which draw on textual accounts of the Buddha's subordination and ultimate 'conversion' of powerful local deities as a means of explaining the presence of *nāga* and *yakṣa* imagery at Buddhist sites (Misra 1981);[37] and ii) 'localisation' models premised on the belief that local cults were incorporated into Buddhist ritual practice as a means of legitimising the *saṅgha*'s presence (Cohen 1998; Bloss 1973).

The most common textual sanction for the first model is the story of Buddha's protection by Mucalinda during his quest for enlightenment. There are also numerous textual references to the Buddha challenging and defeating the power of dangerous *nāga*s, notably the story of the subordination of a fierce serpent inhabiting the fire-temple of the Kasyapas;[38] this episode is shown in one of the gate-reliefs at Sanchi (Marshall 1940, pl. 52). *Nāga*s are presented as dangerous and in need of external control because of their venomous bite, but also because of their ability to bring about environmental havoc through either withholding the monsoon rains or causing excessive deluges. Demoted from their position as deities in their own right, they often became guardians of Buddhist relics, a direct adaptation of their role as protectors of subterranean and sub-aquatic treasure: Buddhist texts frequently recount how relics were guarded by *nāga*s until they were made available for human worship.[39] Accordingly, *nāga*s often feature as guardians of entrances to stupas or monasteries: at Sanchi, several of the Stupa 2 railings bear serpent motifs, while at Pitalkhora in the Deccan, two rearing cobras are placed at the entrance of the main monastery, their mouths acting as pipes for draining out the water from the complex above (Plate 77). This link with water, also borne out by the frequency with which *nāga* sculptures, both at Sanchi and elsewhere, are situated in close proximity to water bodies (Shaw and Sutcliffe 2003a; 2001; Puri 1968, 50), is in keeping with the *nāga*s' perceived control over the natural elements.

According to the second model (Cohen 1998, 377–8; Bloss 1973), the reason for their assimilation into Buddhism is that because of their perceived status as guardians of particular places, their appropriation is essential to the *saṅgha*'s establishment or 'localisation' in new areas. By demonstrating his superiority over the local *nāgarāja*, the Buddha adopts the attributes of the divine ruler of the place and thus gains ritual legitimisation for the *saṅgha*'s presence. Drawing on spatial patterns at Ajanta, Cohen (1998, 377) argues that in contrast to the relationship presented in the traditional 'conversion' model, the Cave 16 *nāga* does not represent the newly converted devotee or protector of the Buddha, but rather the recipient of the Buddha's protection under whose auspicious gaze he sits. This explains the rather removed distance of the Cave 16 *nāga* in relation to the Buddha image inside.[40]

Further, because of the close link between *nāga*s and kingship, the Buddha becomes associated in the minds of the populace with the other major symbol of local authority, the king: there are numerous tales which relate how the king's rule is dependent upon the 'authorisation of the *nāga* who is the primary guardian and master of the territory' and who will withdraw his support if the king fails to behave properly (Bloss 1973, 42). Not only does the *saṅgha* adopt a similar legitimising role in its relationship to the Cakravartin kings, it also appropriates the *nāga*'s principal power, by claiming to possess the ultimate control over the natural elements. This is attested by the elaborate rain-making rituals described in Mahayana texts such as the *Mahāmeghasūtra*; although *nāga*s continue to feature as the facilitators (and also withholders) of rain, it is the Buddha who ultimately grants them this power (Bendall 1880; Schmithausen 1997, 58–65).[41] The image that this text presents, of the *saṅgha* having established a monopoly over the 'religious business' of weather control through an alliance with powerful, albeit subordinated, *nāga* deities, is supported by the writings of the fifth-century-AD Chinese pilgrim Faxien, who describes monks worshipping at *nāga* shrines inside monastic compounds in order to ensure adequate rainfall and to protect against 'plagues and calamities' (Cohen 1998, 377–8). According to Cohen (*ibid*., 400), the Cave 16 *nāga* at Ajanta would have been worshipped in a similar way and provides further justification for viewing the Buddhist worship of *nāga*s as 'properly, fully and fundamentally Buddhist practices'.[42]

My own position is that the 'conversion' and 'localisation' models should not be viewed as mutually exclusive, and that both are useful when it comes to assessing the archaeological patterns in the Sanchi area described in chapters 11–12. However, neither is free from problems. My principal contention is that disproportionate emphasis has been placed on the ritual motives behind 'Buddhist' *nāga* worship, as opposed to the possible 'practical', economic or political incentives. This may reflect Indology's overreliance on religious texts which are not directly concerned with economic aspects of society. Although Cohen's and Bloss's studies break ground by introducing a material dimension to the debate, they are both overtly concerned with the ritual sphere. This bias is further exacerbated by their exclusively 'site-based' focus, which, by not taking into account patterns in the archaeological landscape, means that broader questions regarding the *saṅgha*'s ritual, social and economic relationship with surrounding populations cannot be addressed. Secondly, there are striking disparities between the chronologies of the Buddhist and *nāga* traditions as far as their translation into stone mediums is concerned. This sheds serious doubt on the traditional narrative of a pan-Indian Buddhist appropriation of a universal, pre-existing, 'local' tradition. Suggestions for addressing both of these problems, through recourse to landscape-based analysis and the establishment of tight chronological controls, are presented in the following sections.

Ritual v. 'practical' models of religious change

The SSP aimed to develop a more nuanced model of religious change by relating ritual sites to their wider archaeological landscape, and also by drawing on 'functional' models of religious change as developed, for example, in relation to the spread of Islam and Christianity, both in India and further afield. Eaton (1993) has shown how the acceptance of Islam in east Bengal was intricately tied to the introduction of new agrarian schemes. This process was not just a reflection of political or economic change, nor did it represent a transplantation of a fixed religious system on a 'passive' community. Rather, it involved a complex relationship between 'economic base and ideological superstructure' (*ibid*., 297), whereby the 'ideology of forest-clearing and agrarian expansion, [served] not only to legitimise but to structure the very socioeconomic changes taking place on the frontier' (*ibid*., 267). In contrast to traditional 'conversion by the sword' models, Eaton (*ibid*., 218, 264) argues that this system was not overtly concerned with 'conversion' but rather accommodated largely 'non-Brahmanized' communities, which in turn aligned themselves with the Muslim tradition of merging agrarian expansion with religious building activity; wherever a new village was founded, a temple would be established according to the religious affiliation of the local landlord, while the construction of a mosque would ensure that the economic and ideological links with the hinterland were combined with the political ties to the state. Parallels may be drawn here with 'religion as technique' models such as Peel's (1968) study of Christianisation in west Nigeria. Peel uses a medical analogy to understand Yoruba attitudes towards religion, whereby each religious 'technique' is viewed as an independent means of reaching certain spiritual or social goals, just as a new cough medicine may be used alongside a traditional flu remedy (*ibid.*, 124–5). Similarly, Goody (1975) found that for the Lo Dagaa people of West Africa, the acceptance of Christianity was not viewed as 'conversion' because belief in the older gods was still maintained.

Returning to South Asia, and to historical contexts more closely related to the present study, the Sri Lankan systems of 'monastic landlordism' discussed in chapter 2 accord closely with the aforementioned 'practical' models of religious change.[43] Epigraphical and textual evidence suggests that the *saṅgha* was not overly concerned with conversion. Rather, the monastic community's alignment with water and land management from c. second century BC onwards served two interests: for local society it acted as an agent for economic development; and for the *saṅgha* it enabled the propagation of Buddhist ideology in the most interior areas.[44] The promise of religious merit (*pūnya*) is usually cited as the main incentive for buying into this new scheme; there were also worldly advantages such as the promise of increased yields and improved nutrition. Given that the central tenet of Buddhism's Four Noble Truths is the omnipresence of human suffering (*dukkha*) as well as its causes and means of alleviation, the fact that the *saṅgha*'s scheme could also help to tackle some of the more 'mundane' and common causes of suffering, poverty and famine appears to be more than coincidental. Following this line of logic, one may view the *saṅgha*'s involvement with domestic and agricultural water supply as part of a very practical form of evangelism that tackled suffering on an every-day, subsistence level.

As argued in chapter 14, the relative configuration of dams, monasteries and settlements in the Sanchi area is sufficiently similar to the Sri Lankan patterns to infer the existence of similar models in the Sanchi area. Further, the apparent link between the Sanchi dams and wet-rice cultivation suggests that their construction was tied up with major changes in food consumption trends. While these changes cannot be attributed to a single factor, confident assertions regarding the *saṅgha*'s involvement in water management in ancient India are possible, based on observations regarding the ostentatious display of water-harvesting facilities at second-century-BC rock-cut monasteries in western India (Shaw and Sutcliffe 2003a, 92–5). Cisterns and water-collection channels are dominant features at the earliest sites such as Bhaja, Karle and Bedsa. At Kanheri, they are in such abundance that hardly a drop of rainwater would have gone to waste. The entire hillside is carved with monastic cells and halls, each of which is incised by an intricate chain of channels that would ensure a year-round water supply. During the monsoon, this labyrinth of water would have been an awesome spectacle for both monks and local visitors. In a country where 90% of the annual rainfall occurs in two to three months, such water-harvesting strategies were essential to the *saṅgha*'s survival. They would also have set an example to local communities for whom water-storage would have been a key concern.

Again we come back to the issue of *dukkha*, the central tenet of Buddhism's Four Noble Truths. As discussed in chapter 2, before the first permanent monastic establishments, monks were compelled to wander from one place to another teaching the *dharma*. The one time of year when such wandering was forbidden was during the monsoon when monks would take up residence in temporary rain-retreats. An obvious point, but one which needs to be stressed, is that the subject of rain would have dominated monks' thoughts and discussions during this time. The problems of flooding encountered by neighbouring villagers and farmers would also have been impossible for the monks to ignore. They would also have been aware from their travels during the dry months that the problem of drought was another major source of suffering. The development of water-harvesting systems not only provided a practical key to the *saṅgha*'s transition from a peripatetic to a sedentary lifestyle, it could also play a role in its missionary activities. The propagation of these practical skills was, like monastic landlordism in Sri Lanka, a means to alleviate suffering. And, as shown by the donative inscriptions associated with wells and cisterns at the Deccan sites, it was also an instrument for generating patronage networks.

Pan-Indian, local and translocal deities: chronologies and geographies

As mentioned earlier, current frameworks of religious change with regards to Buddhism are also undermined by a number of chronological and geographical contradictions. A notable problem, for example, is the fact that references to *nāga*s in the early Buddhist texts are set almost exclusively in the Gangetic valley, where most of the Buddha's historical life was spent. We have no such evidence for central and western India, areas outside the Buddha's geographical orbit. Current discussions on religious change as illustrated by Cohen's interpretation of the positioning of the *nāga* shrine at Ajanta are thus built on the hitherto untested assumption that similar 'local' cults were a universal phenomenon throughout India prior to the arrival of Buddhism in the third to second centuries BC. As discussed in chapter 11, the chronological and temporal distribution of *nāga*s across the SSP study area provides a starting point for assessing the validity of this underlying assumption. The main problem is that there is no material evidence for *nāga*s or *yākṣa*s in the Sanchi area prior to the mid-first century BC, with the earliest free-standing examples post-dating the establishment of Buddhism by around two hundred years. While there is every possibility that these seemingly local deities were worshipped in non-durable forms during earlier periods, it is perhaps necessary to question the validity of the traditional polarisations between 'Buddhist' and 'non-Buddhist, 'pan-Indian' and 'local', and 'high' and 'low' or 'state-level' and 'folk' upon which most models of religious change are predicated. In north India, for example, a number of apsidal temples, such as Temple no. 2 at Sonkh (Härtel 1993, 425) and the Maniyar Math at Rajgir (Chandra 1938, 53), attest to organised, state-patronised forms of *nāga* worship, which help to challenge the idea of *nāga*s as the 'folk other' of Buddhism into which it is passively assimilated. For a more nuanced understanding, we should distinguish between the practice and the representation of the *nāga* cult. Serpent worship no doubt existed throughout ancient India, as it does today, but in many divergent, regional forms. The appearance of iconographic and stylistic conventions for representing *nāga*s, as well as the label itself, are quite different phenomena which may reflect the *saṅgha*'s attempt to frame a uniformed cultic category, possibly deriving from a specific regional context, on a host of disparate cultic identities.

We know from the aforementioned Mucalinda narrative that individual *nāga* deities with roots in eastern India became part of the standardised Buddhist repertoire in new areas; another example of this kind of 'portable local' deity is Hariti, well known from Buddhist stories as the terrifying local *yakṣī* from Rajgir who is addicted to eating children (Cohen 1998). The Buddha manages to convert her, after which the *saṅgha* agrees to support and feed her, as long as she keeps her promise not to harm children. Hariti images are thus a common feature in Buddhist dining-rooms as an epitome of the Buddhist conversion narrative whereby local deities are propitiated (like the *nāga* examples cited above) to prevent them from returning to their former, innate malevolence (Cohen 1998; Bloss 1973, 45). Drawing again on patterns at Ajanta, Cohen (1998, 12) argues that, in contrast to the 'local' *nāga* who is kept at a slight distance, Hariti is placed at the heart of the monastic compound because she is an 'insider'. Whilst the *nāga* will be worshipped irrespective of his spatial distance from the Buddha, Hariti is placed there by the Buddha himself. Because the spheres of the local laity and the *saṅgha* are thus symbolically intertwined, the distinction between the 'foreign' monks and the locals, of whom Hariti is the symbolic representative, is also broken down. The *nāga* is unavoidable, but Hariti is one of the props of Buddhist propagation. Although aspects of this interpretation are compelling, one should not make too much of this 'foreign-local' distinction, because, over time, Ajanta's monastic population, as in other areas, would have included significant numbers of monks drawn from the local community. There is also a danger of over-emphasising the polarity between the conversion and 'localisation' models as represented by Hariti and the *nāga* at Ajanta. In my view the *nāga*, like Hariti, can be regarded as a kind of transplanted deity. It is quite possible that other specific examples of interaction between Buddhism and local deities in eastern India, other than the Hariti story, may also have influenced the way in which newly encountered deities were interpreted and labelled by the incoming *saṅgha*.

A much later but instructive example of this process is the introduction of Tantric Buddhism to Tibet during the eighth century AD, which involved the 'taming' and ordering of indigenous demons and spirits: 'one of the constant motifs of Tibetan religion over the centuries has been the animated, and often malevolent, landscape, and the need to mollify it, pacify it, or subjugate it' (Dalton 2004, 760). Central to this process of 'demon subjugation' was the application of new systems of naming and codification, whereby a multitude of 'unruly' spirits with similar properties were subsumed within a new, overarching class of deity:

> Tibetans are clearly concerned to make sense out of the chaos of names and places, the shifting iconographies, and the various groupings. The spirit world of Tibet is an unruly one. The Tibetan universe is filled with powerful beings who demand recognition yet are forever evading classification. Tantric Buddhism offered early Tibetans a way to order these chaotic beings. (Dalton 2004, 766–7)

This process of codification may also have involved foreign and indigenous iconographies becoming entwined. A case in point is the set of Seven Goddesses usually associated with the seven major sacred mountains and lakes of Tibet. According to the Tibetan conversion narrative, these are presented as pre-Buddhist deities who are subjugated and converted by Padmasambhava, the monk largely responsible for the introduction of Buddhism to Tibet (Dalton 2004, 766). Some of these deities, as in the Sanchi area, may also have been associated with water, the control of which appears to have played a role in Padmasambhava's manipulation of the Tibetan landscape (Dalton 2004, 769). Curiously, however, there is no evidence for their existence prior to the introduction of Buddhism. It has therefore been suggested that they represent a process whereby a chaotic host of indigenous spirits and demons was simplified to fit the framework of the Indian Saptamatrkas, which, according to some interpretations, appear to be Sanskritised 'local' deities.

Conclusion

The Sanchi-Vidisha area is in many respects ideally suited to addressing some of these problems in the field, principally because of its rich and varied archaeological and epigraphical record. The three principal religious centres, Sanchi, Vidisha and Udayagiri, have already generated a rich body of scholarship against which new material documented during the survey can be evaluated. Further, the relatively slow pace of industrialisation compared to many other parts of India has meant that much of this newly documented material is still in its original context, or else can be provenanced without too much difficulty. This has allowed for sculptures and buildings to be studied not as isolated objects of enquiry but rather as elements of a multi-layered ritual landscape whose various temporal and spatial patterns form the principal foci of interest in the following chapters.

CHAPTER 7

Theory and Method of Landscape Archaeology

Introduction

The aim of this chapter is twofold: i) to examine recent developments in landscape archaeology that have in part informed the theoretical and methodological underpinnings of this study; and ii) to discuss the application of these developments to the South Asian context. Since the late 1970s the recognition of entire landscapes as foci of archaeological interest has led to a proliferation of literature on 'landscape studies', which, broadly speaking, can be divided into two main categories: (a) those dealing with theoretical aspects of landscape research (Tilley 1994; Bender 1993) which draw heavily on parallel movements in cultural geography and anthropology (Gregory 1995) and consider varying modes of interaction with the landscape such as visibility, memory and re-use (Ucko and Layton 1999; Ashmore and Knapp 1999); and (b) those dealing with aspects of survey methodology such as approaches to surface exploration, sampled collection strategies and statistical analysis (Keller and Rupp 1983; Ammerman 1981; Plog *et al.*, 1978).

This chapter will discuss both of these research fields and assess their applicability to the SSP. In South Asia these influences began to take effect in archaeological circles from the 1980s onwards when settlement distribution-based survey studies became an integral part of archaeological research. However, a general interest in landscape can be identified in various strands of scholarship outside the context of modern archaeology such as anthropology, geography and religious studies. While some of these strands reflect the influence of theoretical movements in the West, others seem to be responses to specifically South Asian concerns which need to be made explicit. Another contention, taken up in the second half of this chapter, is that the development of a non-'site-based' landscape archaeology has been hampered by a lack of integration between the theories and methods of landscape research as represented by the two strands of 'landscape studies' scholarship outlined above. Further, inadequate attention has been given to the question of the applicability of methods developed largely for European settings. I will discuss the variables of South Asian survey research design as a background to describing the SSP field methods in the following chapter.

Theoretical roots of 'Landscape Studies'

Geographical and archaeological approaches to landscape

The development of landscape research in archaeology has roots in a variety of disciplines. In history, both W.G. Hoskins (1955) and J.B. Jackson, who founded the U.S. journal *Landscape* were major pioneers in the study of continuities and discontinuities in the landscape through a combination of micro-history, survey work and place-name studies (Meinig 1979). Similar concerns had already been expressed by earlier writers such as Johnson (1908) whose work on the relationship between ancient monuments, place-names and routes resonated closely with later 'Post Processual' interests. However, archaeology's changing attitude towards the landscape over the past four decades is best viewed alongside parallel movements in anthropology and geography. For example, for the 'New Archaeology' of the 1960s, the landscape was regarded as a universal and neutral entity whose artefacts, sites and demography could be measured by objective 'scientific' means, with little regard to issues of power and ideology. The empirical school of landscape archaeology was thus based primarily on survey methods which prioritised material evidence over and above the society which produced it. This approach was paralleled by currents in the 'New Geography', which treated the landscape as an abstract *container* of human action, rather than an integrated element of human agency (Hodder 1987). Geography also led the way methodologically, with Chorley and Haggett's *Models in Geography* (1967), for example, setting the precedent for Clarke's *Models in Archaeology* (1972) and other mathematical spatial analyses (Hodder and Ortner 1976).

Geographers were also the first to spearhead a reaction to these 'utilitarian functional' strands as expressed in a new stream of writing on subjective, historically contextualised perceptions of landscape (Lowenthal 1961; Lowenthal and Bowden 1976; Relph 1976; 1985; Tuan 1974; 1977). Heavily influenced by the work of existential philosophers such as Sartre, Heidegger and Merleau-Ponty, these 'phenomenological' geographers sought to capture the 'every day insider's' view of landscape as opposed to the 'external', objective stance taken by the 'New Geographers'. Tuan's *Topophilia* (1974), for example, addressed the 'affective bond between people and place or setting'. Tuan's interest in the archetypal 'power' of places drew on the earlier work of Bachelard (1964, xxxi), who had also used the term 'topophilia', and, earlier still, on Rudolph Otto's (1925) idea of *numen loci* and *mysterium tremendum*, the sense of awe-inspiring mystery experienced at sacred places. For Tuan (1977), it was this very 'power of place', which existed independently from changes in space and time, that provided the fundamental explanation for the enduring significance of major cultural or ritual centres.

Within archaeological circles, these influences were taken in a number of different directions. First, the idea of *numen loci* impacted on the shifting focus of enquiry within Classical archaeology. In particular, Scully's (1961) view that Greek sanctuaries were not merely buildings, but rather full embodiments of the 'spirit' of places, led to the recognition of the cultic significance of topographic features such as rocks and caves within temple compounds. This approach challenged earlier theories (e.g. Stillwell 1954) which, whilst recognising the elements of Greek geometry in temple planning, viewed the co-existence of 'natural' features as evidence for the haphazard nature of the placing of Greek temples.

Another response was the rise of social and symbolic archaeology (e.g. Hodder, ed., 1982). This included structuralist analyses such as John Fritz's (1978) study of the symbolic function of symmetry in settlement patterns and social structure. Although structuralism had little influence within geography, it is usually placed alongside Tuan's 'mythic' or 'archetypal' approach, both being informed by a belief in universal structures of meaning (Hodder 1987; Gregory 1978). Both approaches have therefore been subjected to similar types of criticism, namely that, by stressing the element of universality, they tend to discount the negotiable nature of meaning, as well as overlooking the issue of historically bound socio-economic or political context (Hodder 1991, 35–55).

In India, too, a body of geographical and anthropological writings, heavily influenced by the ideas of Tuan, Relph and other phenomenological geographers, can be criticised on similar grounds. Their main focus has been on the 'sacred geography' and, in particular, the underlying 'geometric' structure of major pilgrimage centres in north India (Singh, ed., 1994; Jha, ed., 1985, 1995). Whilst breaking ground by introducing a landscape dimension to the study of sacred places and spaces, they generally lack the firm chronological controls provided by archaeological or textual scholarship.

Alternative geographies

Another movement in geography, this time aimed at problematising the overarching narrative of traditional cartography, was a major impetus behind the development of less normative forms of landscape analysis in archaeology. The focus of this new critique was on cartography's tendency to present maps as the 'whole' view of 'reality', rather than a single perspective. Instead, geographers recognised the need to distinguish between the impact of different kinds of culture on the landscape. Out of this recognition grew the concept of 'cartographies of identities' comprising, for example, a combination of 'dominant', 'alternative', 'emergent' or 'excluded' landscapes (Gregory 1995, 475). A distinction was also drawn between 'actual', 'symbolic' and 'ideological' landscapes (Lowenthal and Bowden 1976), or what Gregory (1995) termed 'imaginative geographies'. Studies of landscape as 'text' in Sri Lanka (Duncan 1990), influenced largely by deconstruction theorists such as Derrida or Ricoeur, also highlighted the possibility of multiple 'readings' of the landscape.

The recognition that a single spatial entity may embody a myriad of different historical trajectories was another major influencing factor in landscape archaeology. Tilley's (1991) approach to the 'textual' quality of rock-art landscapes in Scandinavia, for example, paid a major debt to post-structuralist theories, while the elements of contestation, appropriation and transformation have figured prominently in recent interpretations of Neolithic monuments in southern Britain (Bender, ed., 1993).

Pilgrimage studies

Recent developments in the anthropology of pilgrimage, generally framed as a reaction to traditional Durkheimian and structuralist/archetypal models of ritual, have also offered useful lessons to landscape archaeologists by highlighting the 'negotiated' and multi-tiered nature of sacred spaces and landscapes. For example, both Durkheim's theory of pilgrimage as a social mechanism for integration and cohesion (Cohn and Marriott 1958) and Turner's (1973) view of pilgrimage as 'anti-structure', that is, as a subversion rather than reflection of social order, have been criticised for overlooking the interplay between varying or contradictory discourses within a single pilgrimage 'field' (Coleman and Elsner 1994; Eade and Sallow 1991). Eade and Sallow (*ibid.*, 15), for example, argue that the pilgrimage field should be regarded as a 'religious void', which provides an arena for divergent interpretations of the sacred beneath the umbrella of the official discourse. More recently, these concerns have crossed over into the archaeology of pilgrimage, as illustrated, for example, by studies of the pre-Christian origins of major churches and pilgrimage centres (Stopford 1994; Harbison 1994).

In India, the rich body of ethnographic, textual and archaeological material relating to Brahmanical pilgrimage has provided an empirical basis for unravelling the elements of contestation, multivocality and the 'invention of tradition' at major centres such as Ayodhya (Bakker 1986) and Mathura (Entwistle 1987). To date, the most useful approaches have come from Sanskrit studies, as illustrated by Bakker's (1996) comparative analysis of the *Ayodhyāmāhātmya*, together with material remains on the ground, which has helped to highlight the element of conflict between textual and material versions of Ayodhya's past. Diane Coccari's (1989) anthropological study of the configuration of neighbourhood guardian deity shrines in Varanasi has also been useful for demonstrating how the city's *śāstric* spatial geography can be 'upset' by historical and religious traditions transplanted from a rural, folk context. Finally, Nayanjot Lahiri's (1996, 251) study of the sacred geography of Ballabgarh is a good example of archaeology's capacity to highlight the disparity between 'official' and 'local' ritual geographies: 'there was no overarching consensual structure in the sacred geography of the type that is suggested in textual sources, a structure which was uniformly comprehensible and significant to all rural groups'.

The ritual v. profane polarity

Another reaction to essentialised, overarching models of spatial meaning came from the recognition, in both anthropological and archaeological circles, of the arbitrariness by which spaces and landscapes are divided into 'ritual' and 'profane' or 'domestic' spheres. In archaeology, this polarity was particularly firmly entrenched, because of the subject's traditional site-based focus of enquiry and the general lack of investigation into the trajectory of ritual into other, less tangible areas of experience. In anthropology, the prevalence of Turnerian models meant that ritual was often presented as operating in a depersonalised, detemporalised present, disconnected from wider social or political currents. In recent anthropological literature there is a general consensus that ritual should be viewed as just one of a number of competing discourses operating through a network of social practices (Asad 1983, 244–5). Archaeologists have also recognised the need to treat ritual not as a unique kind of action, but rather as an integral 'aspect of action' (Lane 1986). Barrett's (1990) study of the shift from Neolithic long mounds to Bronze Age round barrows, or Hodder's (1984) theory that long mounds represent houses, are examples of attempts to redress this problem. In many respects, the bringing together of both spheres of life has been most successful within regional landscape projects, which, as pointed out by Andrew Sherratt (1996), are 'simultaneously exercises in settlement archaeology and investigations of ritual landscapes'. This is not only because a comprehensive understanding of regional history requires an investigation of both types of sites, but also because the distinction between ritual and secular monuments may depend on differential rates of archaeological preservation or whether the decision to 'monumentalise' was directed towards the ritual or secular domain (*ibid.*).

Some of the earliest applications of these theoretical shifts took place within the context of Classical archaeology with, for example, Snodgrass's (1986) study of the relationship between the configuration of Greek sanctuaries, social identity and peer polity interaction. Another major pioneer in this area was de Polignac (1984, 49–60), whose work on the wider territorial and political function of extra-urban temples laid down the primary foundations for the modern school of Classical landscape archaeology (e.g. Marinatos and Hagg, ed., 1993; Alcock and Osborne 1996).

In India, attempts to redress the ritual-profane polarity have taken place in a number of research areas. Most relevant to the present book are studies of the political underpinnings of pilgrimage (Van de Veer 1988; Bakker 1992), the relationship between temple building, kingship and land-ownership (Kulke 1993), and the economic background of Buddhism (Ray 1986, 1994; Morrison 1995a; Chakrabarti 1995b). However, although there is a material dimension to all of these studies, the geographical focus remains fairly broad; when it comes to micro-regional analyses, the tendency for 'ritual' and 'non-ritual' dimensions to be polarised into separate spheres is still firmly entrenched. As discussed below, most of the South Asian surveys carried out since the 1980s have concentrated on habitational settlements alone, while major temples, Buddhist sites or pilgrimage centres continue to be studied in isolation from settlement patterns, land-use or inter-regional routes. Several exceptions to this trend are discussed later, including Dilip Chakrabarti's (2001; Chakrabarti *et al.*, 2003) extensive study on the configuration of trade routes across north India. However, the latter's inter-regional scale obviously places it in a different category to the rest.

The 'nature'-'culture' polarity

While the dissolution of the ritual-profane polarity was closely connected to a growing interest in the relationships between different types of sites, the opening up of the landscape as a whole, beyond the focus on sites *per se*, was also influenced by reactions to another polarity, that between the 'natural' and 'cultural'. This perpetuation of a Cartesian rhetoric, based on the arbitrary division between natural and cultural features of the environment, meant that large areas of the landscape were being overlooked. A direct repercussion of this reaction, and one which provides a major key for understanding the mutually entwined relationship between the theories and methods of landscape archaeology, was the recognition of the 'non-site', rather than 'site' or artefact, as the minimum unit of archaeological analysis (Plog *et al.*, 1978, 389; Foley 1981; Dunnell and Dancey 1983, 268). It was acknowledged, for example, that certain types of behaviour, especially those associated with non-sedentary groups, leave behind archaeological traces, such as low density artefact scatters, which had generally been excluded from conventional archaeological classifications (Schiffer *et al.*, 1978, 2; Plog *et al.*, 1978: 384). At the same time, the concept of 'non-site' was broadened to include other 'non-archaeological' dimensions of the landscape, such as prominent topographical features or caves, which had previously been overlooked because of their so-called natural status. The importance of 'natural places' for understanding long-term continuities in the landscape is now increasingly accepted in archaeological circles (Bradley 1999), with some (Tilley 1994; 1996) arguing, for example, that many of the Neolithic megaliths in southern England represented a 'monumentalisation' of natural *locales* already established during earlier periods. Since the 1990s, a growing level of conflict between the interests of governmental organisations and indigenous groups in Australia and the USA has led to the rise of new legislative measures to protect places of cultural significance which lack a 'monumental' dimension (Carmichael *et al.*, 1994; Smith 1999; Layton 1999). The recognition of such 'associated landscapes' by the World Heritage Committee in 1993 (Carmichael *et al.*, 1994) was a much belated step towards addressing the deep-seated division between archaeological and 'local' perceptions of the landscape.

In India, the study of prehistoric rock-shelters and associated rock-art is a growing area of archaeological research (Chakravarty *et al.*, 1997; Fu 2001). However, possibly due to its non-monumental status, this material tends to be studied as a universal category, with more points of convergence with rock-art studies in Australia and South Africa than with wider aspects of South Asian archaeology. This is illustrated in the SSP study area, where prehistoric rock-shelters are usually studied in isolation from later aspects of their surrounding landscape such as Buddhist sites or historical settlements, and with little consideration of their continued currency during these later periods. As for other 'non-site' data such as 'natural' shrines and springs, these have received little attention in South Asian archaeology. The importance of these categories for the development of a specifically South Asian survey methodology is discussed later.

Phenomenology of landscapes

Another important development has been a reaction to static forms of visual presentation, such as those provided by plans and maps, which can suppress the experiential ways in which people interacted with buildings and landscapes. A major influence has been Bourdieu's (1977) theory of *habitus*, whereby people interact non-discursively with their environment through long processes of enculturation. Another was Gidden's (1979, 66–73) structuration theory, which presented structures as both the 'medium and outcome of action'. Giddens drew heavily on Hagerstrand's 'Time Geography', the concept of the fusion of time and space in the form of *locales*, which, being the focus of repeated congregation, give meaning and structure to everyday life; and Husserl's idea of the retention of past events in the present. The influence of these wider strands of social theory is evident in recent studies of the 'temporality' or constant 'becoming' of archaeological landscapes (Ingold 1993; Thomas 1991) as well as the more phenomenological approaches of Barrett (1990), Bradley (1991) and Richards (1993). The latter studies, termed 'archaeologies of action', stressed the interactive relationship between people and buildings, as opposed to earlier structuralist theories which tended to focus on the inherent and 'essential' meanings of the built environment. Of particular concern has been the ways in which the physical layout of ritual sites helped to maintain behavioural and ideological regularity, especially through the control and restriction of vision and bodily movement. More recently, archaeologists have focused on the visual dimension, seeking in particular to identify linkages between ancient sites through the element of intervisibility (Tilley 1994; Peatfield 1983; Bender *et al.*, 1997).

Despite introducing an element of human agency into ancient landscapes, the phenomenological approach has been criticised from a number of angles. The first major drawback is the tendency towards ahistoricity, which can undermine the meaning of specific structures and places. Secondly, the people who move around these landscapes and who do the 'seeing' are presented as generic disembodied actors rather than convincing historical agents. There is also a general failure to distinguish between the type of deity propitiated at a particular spot. In response to such criticisms, there has been a call for a 'historical phenomenology' (Thomas 1991). However, in most archaeological settings, this remains little more than optimistic speculation, largely because of the limited dataset available to scholars of European prehistory.[1] This is not to discredit the phenomenological approach altogether: as demonstrated in chapter 11, in early-historic settings such as Sanchi where inferences based on well-preserved archaeological and epigraphical datasets can be substantiated by textual information, it is easier to introduce a plausible spatial dynamic to the landscape.

Annales school

No discussion of landscape archaeology is complete without reference to the Annales school of history, founded with the writings of Lucien Febvre and Marc Bloch, but more commonly associated with Fernand Braudel's (1972) well-known study of sixteenth-century life in the Mediterranean. Described as an exercise in 'total history', the latter conceived of history as unfolding through the interweaving of several different types of time and social structures. Two major levels of temporal rhythms were envisaged: *longue-durée*, an 'almost imperceptible' series of historical currents underlying the long-term relationship between man and his environment; and *événements*, single historical events (*ibid.*, 20). These are bound together by *mentalités*: religious, ideological and behavioural systems which define a particular society. The Annalist school provided an apt model for landscape archaeology, whose ability to identify broad regional patterns was well suited to investigations of *longue-durée* (Bintliff 1991; Knapp 1992). On the other hand, archaeological settings, where information regarding short-term historical events is provided by textual and epigraphical evidence, have benefited most from Braudelian-type investigations. A good illustration of the interdisciplinary nature of Annalist landscape projects of this kind is Graeme Barker's (1995) survey in the Biferno valley of Italy, whose primary aim was to develop a 'unified theory of material culture for the study of the past' (*ibid.*, 2). Barker stressed that it is only once historical texts and archaeological evidence are both viewed as material culture, rather than being relegated to their respective disciplines, that regional history can be approached in the kind of all-encompassing way envisaged by Braudel. This kind of method offers a number of obvious suggestions for regional research in India, where the differences rather than the similarities between the aims and methods of text-based studies and archaeology continue to be stressed.

Survey archaeology

The elevation of survey from its traditional role as a supplementary means of identifying potential sites for excavation to an independent method of archaeological reconnaissance was partly a response to the broader theoretical shifts described in the foregoing account. The most obvious advantage of survey archaeology is that it allows for a 'total', horizontal assessment of large areas of land. Further, due to its non-invasive quality, it requires low levels of manpower and fewer resources, and sidesteps many of the legislative hurdles posed by excavation. Barker (1995, 51), for example, states that although archaeological survey 'cannot make "real maps" of the ancient world ... it can provide reasonably reliable models of settlement forms, densities and patterns that are the critical data we need to understand the long-term settlement history of a region'.

Since the 1980s there has been a growing body of literature on the methodological complexities of survey archaeology. Most of this draws on European and U.S. case-studies (Keller and Rupp 1983; Ammerman 1981; Plog *et al.*, 1978) with several high-profile projects in the Mediterranean (Alcock and Cherry 1996; Jameson *et al.*, 1994; Cherry 1994; Cherry *et al.*, 1991; Renfrew and Wagstaff 1982), America (Flannery 1976) and Western Asia (Adams 1981) providing the primary framework for ongoing landscape research in these regions.

As discussed later, equivalent literature for areas such as Africa or Asia is notably scant. Although some archaeological methods are fairly universal in terms of their geographical applicability, certain physical, historical and cultural particularities call for tailor-made approaches. The aim of the following sections, therefore, is to provide a historical outline of the development of conventional survey methods and assess their applicability to South Asian contexts. A further aim is to highlight the fact that, despite a number of South Asian settlement surveys from the 1980s onwards, the full development of a methodology for the study of the landscape on a scale beyond that of individual sites has been hampered by three major factors: i) an uncritical application of European surveying methods; ii) a failure to develop tailor-made surveying strategies which draw specifically on the cultural, historical and ecological elements of the local landscape; and iii) a lack of integration between the theories and methods of landscape research. Although the broader theoretical literature on 'landscape studies' has included case-studies from non-European regions (Ashmore and Knapp 1999; Ucko and Layton 1999), including South Asia (Lahiri and Singh 1999), there is rarely much integration or overlap with the scholarship on survey archaeology. Thus, the relationship between theory, method and research results often remains unstated. As illustrated by the two-tiered structure of landscape-based scholarship outlined at the beginning of this chapter, a similar disjuncture is evident in European contexts, a problem which a number of recent studies have sought to redress (Sherratt 1996; Bender *et al.*, 1997). These points, and other suggestions for developing an integrated and 'reflexive' methodology for regional landscape research in South Asia, are discussed in the next chapter with reference to the SSP field methods.

The development of European survey methodologies: a one-way track?

Studies on survey methodology customarily begin with a historical outline of the development of archaeological survey, divided into a three-phase process mirroring the paradigm-shifts through which the discipline has moved over the past fifty years. According to one well-known study (Cherry 1982, 14–15), the story begins with the 'topographical studies' or 'exploratory travels' of nineteenth-century Greece and Italy. Unsystematic and text-driven, the primary focus of these early surveys was on large public monuments as opposed to less tangible remains in the surrounding landscape. These gave way to the 'improved' extensive surveys of the 1960s, this second phase being described as 'extensive reconnaissance' (Cherry 1982, 14–15). It coincided with the wider set of theoretical shifts, discussed earlier, which led to the recognition of entire landscapes, as opposed to single monuments, as the minimum foci of archaeological enquiry. However, the large size of the survey areas often led to biases in coverage and representativeness, as well as the perpetuation of the traditional focus on well-known, impressive sites. The elimination of these biases became a central concern of the 'intensive' and systematic surveys, the third phase that arose during the 1980s. Research designs became problem-orientated, geared towards achieving maximum survey coverage over small areas and building models for testing patterns outside the study area (Renfrew and Wagstaff 1982; Jameson *et al.*, 1994). The use of systematic survey transects, together with geophysical and satellite remote-sensing techniques, allowed for the identification of archaeologically less visible sites, often missed by extensive field-walking, and for forms of 'non-site' data whose archaeological importance was increasingly being recognised (Foley 1981).

This three-stage model offers a useful gloss for understanding the mutually entwined relationship between the theories and methods of landscape archaeology and the changing resolution of archaeological knowledge. However, on two main accounts it should not be taken as a universally applicable model. Firstly, the development from extensive to intensive, or unsystematic to systematic, methods is typically presented as a unilinear evolutionary progression in which the element of 'improvement' is taken for granted; in other words, the adoption of systematic methods based on statistical sampling and geophysical techniques is viewed as an inevitable step towards which all landscape projects should ultimately strive. Some commentaries (Plog *et al.*, 1983; Ammerman 1981) take a distinctly condescending stance towards low-budget, small-scale projects, with others (Cherry 1982, 387) questioning whether the resolution they provide justifies the effort. Many of these problems have been overcome since the introduction of cheap handheld GPS technology. However, it is important to note that although the detection of 'non-site' data is generally attributed to the development of systematic survey techniques (Plog *et al.*, 1978, 389; Foley 1981; Dunnell and Dancey 1983, 268), little attention is given to the wider theoretical movements discussed earlier which recognise that the ability to detect rock-shelters or 'natural' cult spots is less dependent on sophisticated reconnaissance techniques than on a particular 'way of looking' at the landscape. In the SSP study area, for example, the outright abandonment of extensive methodologies would have removed important sections of the archaeological dataset from the object of enquiry.

Secondly, much of the literature on survey methodology is based on Western European and U.S. case-studies, with little emphasis on parts of the world with less 'developed' economic or academic infrastructures. In order to avoid unfair criticism, therefore, projects in the latter category need to be evaluated within a broader framework that takes account of specific cultural, ecological and historical criteria.

Survey archaeology in South Asia

These points may be illustrated through an examination of survey archaeology in South Asia. Although archaeological notices began much earlier, the first formal surveys were those of Alexander Cunningham (*ASIR* 1861 onwards; Cunningham 1924; Imam 1966) whose exploratory reports still provide the starting point for most new historical studies in north India. His explorations were aimed at identifying major urban and ritual centres described in the Classical sources and Chinese pilgrims' records, with less interest in smaller sites or those not mentioned in the texts. Unsystematic, text-driven and carried out over vast areas of north India, they may reasonably be placed alongside the so-called 'exploratory travels' of Greece and Italy (Cherry 1982, 14–15).

Cherry's second, 'extensive reconnaissance' phase in the history of European archaeological survey can also be related to developments in South Asia, specifically the proliferation of settlement distribution studies from the 1980s onwards. These are too many to list here, but notable examples include those carried out in Harappan and post-Harappan contexts in Saurashtra (Possehl 1980), Cholistan (Mughal 1980; 1992;) and adjoining areas (Mughal *et al.*, 1996); Chalcolithic contexts in Maharashtra (Shinde 1989), Rajasthan (Hooja 1988) and south India (Murty 1989); and two oft-cited studies in the Gangetic valley which deal with changes in settlement patterns between the Chalcolithic and early-historic periods: the first in Kanpur (Lal 1984) and the second in Allahabad district (Erdosy 1988). All of these studies took as their primary research focus the distribution of habitational settlements as opposed to ritual sites. More diverse in scope was the multi-phase survey of Lahiri *et al.* (1996) carried out over a relatively small study area near Delhi in Faridabad/Ballahbarh districts, as were the inter-regional surveys of Chakrabarti (2001; Chakrabarti *et al.*, 2003) which sought to relate long-distance trade routes between the Gangetic plain and the Deccan to their wider archaeological landscape. Although the broad geographical focus of Chakrabarti's investigations means that their resolution is obviously much lower than the regionally specific studies mentioned above, the datasets are nevertheless immensely rich and varied.

All of these projects were extensive in focus, using a variety of methods to reduce survey coverage biases over relatively large study areas. For example, during Possehl's (1980) survey in Saurashtra the study area of 12 x 15 km was stratified into sampled topographical zones; Mughal's surveys were also defined by sampled topographical zones. However, the unavailability of detailed maps, together with restrictions at the time over the use of aerial photography and satellite imagery, precluded the application of intensive gridding methods. Erdosy and Lal followed a 'village-to-village' surveying strategy, whereby modern habitations provided identifiable points from which transect-based exploration was carried out within a radius of 10 to 12 km. The large areas under survey, 1200 km^2 in the case of the Allahabad study (Erdosy 1988), led to the prioritisation of visually prominent mounds, to the exclusion of more heavily ploughed mounds or hillside settlements. Additional biases can be attributed to the widely spaced transects (up to 5 km in some cases), which may explain why Lal's (1984) survey yielded just 150 sites over 5100 km^2. Further, both studies built their central hypotheses regarding phase-by-phase changes in site location and size on surface ceramic evidence. The susceptibility of these to distortions caused by site-formation and post-depositional processes (Hodder and Malone 1984) was not made sufficiently explicit.

In recent years, a number of intensive and systematic surveys have been carried out, often over more spatially discrete areas. The Vijayanagara Metropolitan Survey (Sinopoli and Morrison 1992, Morrison 1995b; Sinopoli 1997), for example, used an intensive methodology with 20 m intervals between exploration transects, while Monica Smith's (2001; 2002) intensive survey in and around the early-historic city of Sisulapalgarh, Orissa, formed part of a wider excavation-based project there. In contrast to the broad regional focus of earlier studies, both projects were concerned with relating these specific city sites to their immediate hinterland. More intensive still is Lars Fogelin's (2004) recent survey at the Buddhist site of Thotlakonda, Andhra Pradesh, which, unlike other South Asian surveys, was aimed at achieving 'full coverage' over an area of 7.3 km^2, with an additional 0.6 km^2 explored unsystematically (Fogelin 2006, 122–4). Resulting in the documentation of 134 'sites', this approach reflected the project's principal goal of assessing the spatial and temporal links between a single Buddhist site and its immediate archaeological setting. Although the wider manifestation of these patterns beyond the spatially restricted study area thus remains unknown, the resulting dataset offers an extremely useful parallel to the more broadly dispersed patterns documented during the SSP and facilitates the assessment of text-driven theories regarding modes of interaction between monastic and lay populations within a highly localised area.

Another recent survey which has combined systematic and non-systematic reconnaissance methods across the research area is the study of Neolithic and Megalithic landscapes in the Bellary district, south India, by Nicole Boivin *et al.* (2002). Finally, another study with a strong landscape dimension is the multi-disciplinary Indo-French project at Chanderi, which has attempted a 'total history' of the city since its foundation in the thirteenth century AD (Fussman 2003).

Extensive v. intensive survey

Although the development of survey archaeology in South Asia has followed a not-dissimilar trajectory to that in other areas, it is important to stress that just because reconnaissance techniques have improved, the adoption of intensive or systematic survey methods should not be taken as a given when undertaking new landscape projects in the region. In many cases South Asian and European surveys call for quite different levels of resolution. In South Asia, where vast areas remain unexplored, the most viable and justifiable aim is often the establishment of broad archaeological patterns, which can be supplemented later on by more systematic investigations. Thus, Cunningham's surveys, with their enormous geographical focus, made no pretences to representativeness, but rather created a skeletal framework which still forms the primary backbone of India's archaeological map today. Similarly, the surveys of Erdosy and Lal were aimed at identifying settlement types representative of each chronological phase, rather than making claims to quantitative accuracy. While a more representative picture could have been achieved by choosing a smaller area as a model for testing patterns outside the study area, this might have been counterproductive to the projects' broad-scale objectives. Erdosy (1988, 27) himself stresses that it is more important to make one's strategies and aims explicit than 'blindly' apply probabilistic sampling strategies as a means of bestowing 'an unwarranted gloss of accuracy to data which will already be heavily biased due to the vagaries of preservation'. Finally, Chakrabarti's surveys have been aimed at identifying archaeological indicators of inter-regional trading and cultural routes across long distances and periods, rather than the exhaustive documentation of micro-regional data in a spatially or temporally discrete area.

It is also important to acknowledge the environmental, academic, political and cultural variables that can reduce the effectiveness, or indeed rationale, of systematic survey methods. Firstly, in contrast to the Mediterranean where survey information can be readily contextualised by published excavation reports, the paucity of published stratigraphic sequences in South Asia can negate the advantages of sampled ceramic collection strategies; this was a particular problem during the SSP.[2] This problem is compounded further by restrictions over the use of test-trenching and augering in South Asia. Secondly, limited access to aerial photography and the non-availability of maps more detailed than 1:50,000 has been a deterrent against the use of intensive gridding methods (Possehl 1980, 37). Although this has to some extent been remedied by the recent release of affordable satellite imagery for South Asia, remote-sensing is not always a suitable method for primary reconnaissance in the region. As discussed later, the problem of dense forest coverage in much of the SSP study area meant that satellite imagery only became useful after the primary archaeological patterns had been delineated through field-walking (Shaw and Sutcliffe 2005; Beck and Shaw, forthcoming). There is also the question of finance: the high costs and heavy manpower associated with intensive, transect-based investigations are the main obstacles for small-scale, low-budget surveys, especially the kind commonly carried out as part of PhD projects (Gallant 1983; Moody 1989; Fotiades 1983).

Towards an integrated survey methodology for South Asia

In addition to acknowledging the environmental and bureaucratic factors that can undermine the effectiveness of intensive survey methods in South Asia, it is important to consider other cultural factors that have contributed to a range of specifically South Asian survey methods. This may be illustrated by Nayanjot Lahiri's study of the diverse narratives underlying the archaeological landscapes of Ballabgarh district, near Delhi (Lahiri 1996; Lahiri and Singh 1999; Lahiri *et al.*, 1996). Despite using a 'village-to-village' surveying strategy, which seems not to have been supplemented at a later stage by systematic methods, Lahiri was able to transcend the 'site-based' focus of earlier surveys, largely by highlighting the culture-specific underpinnings of her methodology. The point here is that, while sharing traits with other extensive methods, the 'village-to-village' survey has grown out of a set of cultural conditions peculiar to the Indian countryside. As discussed later, the tendency towards settlement continuity, the reinstallation of archaeological material as objects of worship within villages and the commemoration of ancestral links between modern and ancient settlements, all make the configuration of modern villages a suitable basis for exploration. All of these factors mean that a high level of local interaction can be as effective as the use of aerial photography or remote-sensing. Further, a sensitivity to the close relationship between local perceptions of the divine and the configuration of archaeological sites can play a positive role in the reconnaissance process. Lahiri is at pains to emphasise the need for a regionally specific survey methodology which incorporates local practices as integral components of its research design. As I shall discuss later, not only does this kind of approach allow for a degree of compromise between extensive and systematic methodologies, but it also sets the 'village-to-village' survey apart from the generic 'extensive' survey.

Further, I would suggest that Erdosy (1988) and Lal's (1984) surveys could have been improved by a greater level of integration between the theories and methods of landscape archaeology. Despite lengthy accounts of European sampling strategies and statistical spatial analyses (Lal 1984, 158–67), there is little reference to the wider theoretical debates discussed earlier in this book, such as the attempt to break down the traditional polarity between 'ritual' and 'profane' spaces and places in the landscape (Asad 1983; Hodder 1984; Sherratt 1996). Consequently, despite the shift of emphasis from monuments to settlements, Erdosy and Lal's surveys merely result in the replacement of one narrow category by another: both studies concentrate almost solely on settlements and associated pottery to the exclusion of ritual complexes, water bodies, rock-shelters or springs and 'natural' cult spots. The resulting distribution-maps organised according to the periodisation of single-site categories obviously represent a distorted view of the historical landscape. Ironically therefore, despite using methods designed specifically for landscape research, the Gangetic valley surveys remain firmly rooted in a 'site-based' framework of analysis; a similar disjuncture between the theories and methods of landscape archaeology has been noted in some of the early extensive surveys in Europe which, despite adding a new spatial dynamic to archaeological understanding, resulted merely in changes in 'techniques and methods rather than in theory and metaphysics' (Dunnell and Dancey 1983, 283). Finally, it is partly because of the polarised character of Lal and Erdosy's datasets, divided as they are into 'ritual' and 'secular' dimensions of the landscape, that ongoing attempts to draw on ideological and political explanations for new population trends during the early-historic period lack archaeological corroboration (Ghosh 1973; Chakrabarti 1985).

Conclusion

There have been two main points to this chapter. First, while regional research in central India can benefit from some of the recent theoretical and methodological developments in European landscape archaeology, it is important to highlight the possibilities for building independent models which reflect the area's unique cultural and historical environment. This is particularly relevant with regard to the more 'somatic' approaches to landscape archaeology, which have faltered because of the limited dataset available to scholars of European prehistory. This type of approach can be fruitfully adapted to the SSP study area because of the availability of a rich combination of archaeological, epigraphical and textual material. The second major point has been to stress the need for tailor-made research methodologies, which, as with all new projects, need to temper European survey techniques with a sensitivity to local conditions.

CHAPTER 8

The Sanchi Survey Project: Research Design and Field Methodology

Introduction

The aim of this chapter is to describe the field methods as they were applied at various stages of the SSP. The research design was informed in part by some of the theories and methods of landscape archaeology discussed in the previous chapter. However, the ambition here was not simply to find a ready-made methodology and apply it to a new area but, rather, to temper conventional survey methods with a sensitivity to local historical, geographical and cultural conditions.

The Sanchi Survey Project 1998–2005: a multi-stage archaeological survey

The survey design was multi-staged, developing and expanding as the archaeological and environmental patterns became better understood, and as the research questions and hypotheses became more clearly formulated. The primary reconnaissance and documentation work (Stage I) was carried out over two six-month seasons in 1998/9 and 2000/1, with subsequent seasons aimed at improving the quality of the data and testing hypotheses through the application of refined methodologies. From 2002 to 2005, four additional field seasons (Stage II), drawing on new collaborations, were added to refine and develop existing results and to test earlier hypotheses with new methodologies. Particular attention was paid to the history of local irrigation based on the study of surface remains, together with present-day hydrological and climate data. In 2003-4, a pilot study was initiated with the aim of testing hypotheses about the chronology of the dams in the Sanchi area and the land uses associated with them. Existing road-cuttings were scraped back to reveal dam sections which cast new light on aspects of dam construction. This allowed the collection of sediments and ceramics for Optically Stimulated Luminescence (OSL) dating (Shaw *et al.*, 2007).[1] Sediment samples were also collected from cores hand-drilled in dried-up reservoir beds for supplementary OSL dating and pollen analysis. The results of the OSL analysis study confirmed the suitability of local sediments to geological dating methods as well as supporting our working hypothesis that the dams were constructed, along with the earliest Buddhist monuments in central India, in the late centuries BC. The establishment of local pollen sequences also strengthened our hypothesis regarding the dams' link with wet-rice agriculture.

Stage II also included systematic mapping of selected sites and satellite remote-sensing. The latter was aimed principally at testing the degree of concordance between archaeological remains documented during Stage I and levels of visibility within a subset of different satellite imagery; it has also aided the mapping process and led to improvements in the quality of the project's GIS structure (Shaw and Sutcliffe 2005; Beck and Shaw, forthcoming).[2] Considerable time and effort was also invested in redesigning the project's database structure. The result is a more effective tool for organising and analysing the spatial and temporal patterns in the archaeological landscape.

Reconnaissance methods

Stage I (1998–2001): the village-to-village survey

The Stage I reconnaissance procedure consisted of two main aspects: i) the re-exploration of Sanchi and the four outlying 'Bhilsa Tope' sites; and ii) exploration throughout the rest of the study area (approximately 750 km^2). As in the case of the village-to-village survey technique discussed in chapter 7, modern settlements (approximately one village per 2 km^2) formed the foci for following up local leads and exploring the surrounding fields and hills. The reconnaissance process was divided into three main stages: a) the initial journey from Vidisha to the village in question; b) investigations, drawing heavily on local information, in and around the village itself; and c) a combination of systematic (i.e. transect-based) and non-systematic exploration in the surrounding area. Although most exploration was carried out on foot, the initial journey was usually made on motorbike which provided several advantages over the jeep, mainly in the form of maximised mobility and accessibility on narrow, muddy tracks. It is also culturally less imposing than the jeep, the vehicle of choice of most government officials. This is an important point because villagers are often reluctant to impart knowledge about archaeological sites on their land for fear of governmental infringements. Further, the choice to keep team-numbers to a minimum and to use locally familiar modes of transport was found to have a positive impact on the quality of local interaction.

The composition of the survey team also had an effect on survey results. Criteria such as personality, age and social status were found to be just as relevant as prior field experience, especially since my presence as a foreign woman was often cause for curiosity and suspicion. The team usually consisted of myself and one or two other members who formed a pool of local field-assistants. On most days, we were accompanied by a temporary third party: usually a local informant who remained with the team for up to a week at a time, or until we moved into unfamiliar territory; in most cases local knowledge extended to about 3 km from the village of residence. This third member was often a valuable asset, not to mention an indispensable 'go between' when entering new villages.

Stage II (2002 – 2005): satellite remote-sensing
Aerial photography and satellite imagery were not utilised during Stage I due to restricted access to the former and the prohibitive expense of the latter. However, a range of satellite imagery with different spatial and spectral resolutions was purchased between 2003 and 2005 (Stage II) with two major objectives: i) evaluating the applicability of satellite imagery as a prospection and landscape analysis tool against the survey results collected during Stage I; and ii) as a supplementary tool to ground-based site mapping and for improving the analysis and presentation of the existing survey data. The following datasets were purchased over two phases, with an intervening field season in 2003/4 aimed at determining which image-sets best met the projects' needs: Corona, KFA, Landsat ETM, Iconos, co-registered pan and multispectral (MS) Quickbird, and Shuttle Radar Topography Mission (SRTM) elevation data (Table 8.1; Figure 8.1 colour).

Overview of satellite imagery
The Corona imagery was of particular interest as it was collected in 1969–70 prior to the many major landscape modifications (e.g. canal construction, mechanical ploughing and irrigation) that have now affected the area. Most of this imagery has a ground resolution of c. 3 m.

Overall the KFA imagery was disappointing due to camera aberrations or atmospheric distortions. It was not useful for either reconnaissance or mapping purposes, contrary to expectations that the 5 m resolution would highlight a range of natural and cultural features, particularly given that the imagery was taken in May when there is low vegetation.

The Landsat ETM imagery displayed a range of different landscape features despite its relatively low spatial resolution. Two sets of imagery, collected in October and June respectively, were purchased. The former was of little use for detecting mounds and palaeochannels due to high vegetation and soil moisture levels in the post-monsoon season. As discussed later, the imagery collected in the dry summer months yielded positive results in this respect. Overall the Landsat imagery was helpful for creating geological and soil maps.

A sample of Ikonos multispectral imagery was purchased for areas containing a selection of archaeological sites documented during Stage I. The aim was to test the imagery's utility for the detection of mounds, as well as determining the appropriate resolution characteristics for future reconnaissance exercises. The imagery was collected in early May, so as to capitalise on reduced crop height and increased soil colour differential at archaeological sites. The Ikonos image did independently reveal settlement mounds whose existence was verified against the original Stage I survey data. The large size of these sites meant that they were potentially detectable in the Landsat ETM image (Beck and Shaw, forthcoming).

A selection of co-registered pan and multispectral (MS) Quickbird imagery was purchased primarily for site reconnaissance and mapping in the hilly regions, with variable, but generally positive results, as discussed later. The sensor characteristics of the SPOT imagery were simulated from the

Table 8.1 Satellite imagery purchased in 2003–5

Purchase stage	Sensor	Spatial (m)	Bands	Date of collection	Area km²	Comments
1	Corona KH4B	3	1	23/11/70		Unrectified
1	Corona KH4B	3	1	23/11/70		Unrectified
1	Corona KH4B	3	1	23/11/70		Unrectified
1	Corona KH4B	3	1	23/11/70		Unrectified
1	Corona KH4B	3	1	23/11/70		Unrectified
1	KFA	5	3	27/5/89	2120	Orthorectified
1	Landsat 5	30	7	3/10/92	21000	Orthorectified
1	Landsat ETM+	30	8	1/10/00	6108	Orthorectified
1	Landsat ETM+	15	1	1/10/00	6108	Orthorectified
1	Quickbird MS	2.4	4	12/10/02	25	Georeferenced
1	Quickbird pan	0.6	1	12/10/02	25	Georeferenced
1	Quickbird MS	2.4	4	13/12/02	95	Georeferenced
1	Quickbird pan	0.6	1	13/12/02	95	Georeferenced
1	Radar	90	1	21/2/00		DEM
2	Quickbird MS	2.4	4	13/12/02	25	Georeferenced
2	Quickbird pan	0.6	1	13/12/02	25	Georeferenced
2	Ikonos MS	4	4	8/8/01	49	Georeferenced
2	Quickbird MS	2.4	4	5/6/05	106	Georeferenced
2	Quickbird pan	0.6	1	5/6/05	106	Georeferenced
2	Landsat ETM+	30	8	1/6/04	21000	Orthorectified
2	Landsat ETM+	15	1	1/6/04	21000	Orthorectified

Quickbird imagery using two techniques: degradation of 0.6 m pan imagery to 2.4 m and extraction of the first principal component of the MS bands (Beck and Shaw, forthcoming). The high spatial resolution of the pan imagery allowed the identification, in shadow, of wires between pylons. Modern hard and soft detail field systems were easily identified and even narrow scrub field boundaries were visible. However, in some areas, particularly the sandstone hillocks, the imagery was over-saturated.

The 90 m resolution Shuttle Radar Topography Mission (SRTM) elevation data (freely available from NASA) was useful for creating digital terrain models and for extracting contours. The latter were particularly useful for revising Stage I estimates regarding reservoir areas and volumes.

Satellite imagery as a reconnaissance and mapping tool

As mentioned above, a short pilot project was carried out in the field in 2003/4 in order to test a sample of satellite imagery prior to committing to a larger purchase order. A 'blind' examination of the high resolution imagery led to many false leads, with most 'potential' archaeological features, on inspection, turning out to be trees, electrical pylons or quarry pits. When assessed against archaeological sites already documented during Stage I, the imagery, generally speaking, proved to hold more potential as a supplementary mapping aid than a primary site detection tool. However, its relative effectiveness in either capacity varied enormously according to topography and vegetation cover (Beck and Shaw, forthcoming). This is because in the hilly zones many of the settlements or Buddhist sites are obscured by dense vegetation, while in the agricultural zone, most of the sites that are suitable for satellite prospection, i.e. settlement mounds or dams in open plains, are already highly visible: during the primary reconnaissance in Stage I, most of these sites, surviving as prominent earthworks, were visible from surrounding hilltops (Plates 219–20). Secondly, many sites which rarely show up in satellite imagery, such as hillside settlements, rock-shelters, springs or 'natural' shrines consisting of small piles of rocks (Plate 12, 14), are more readily detected through a sensitivity to the role which archaeological sites play in the construction of present-day social and ritual geographies. In many cases, this phenomenon ensures the continuing 'visibility' of less tangible archaeological sites.

Furthermore, many of the caveats used to illustrate the ineffectiveness of traditional surveying methods relate to parts of the world where surface sites are commonly destroyed by heavy industry and intensive agriculture. In the SSP study area, however, the prevalence of traditional shallow ploughing methods,[3] and the relatively slow pace of industrialisation, has contributed towards high levels of archaeological visibility.[4] Finally, in contrast to areas such as Midwest America or Western Asia where sites are often obscured by heavy alluvium (Plog *et al.*, 1978, 384; Adams 1981), the relatively narrow extent of river sedimentation in the Sanchi area has ensured fairly high levels of archaeological 'obtrusiveness' (Shaw and Sutcliffe 2003a, 81).

Site-documentation, recording and mapping

Stage I

Internal site details were recorded on a specially designed record-form, whose format evolved gradually as familiarity with the range of survey data developed. Like most surveys (Plog *et al.*, 1978, 412–13), the record-form consisted of a combination of standardised questions regarding, for example, topographical zone, sector, size and collection strategy, with additional sections for less predictable information based on day-to-day encounters at the village level. However, it differed from settlement-distribution surveys whose principal interest in ceramic scatters makes for a highly reproducible set of surveying tasks. For the SSP, whereas field-walking and pottery collection posed little problem for inexperienced team-members, the sheer variety of data, and the broad range of architectural and sculptural remains encountered during the survey, ruled out the possibility of splitting up the team into different groups.

The method of site-planning varied enormously depending on site-type: settlement mounds were usually measured by pacing out the diameter of the mound, while more complex sites were planned using a simple compass-bearing-and-pacing method. Key architectural complexes were drawn to scale using measured offsets. Irrigation dams and tanks were paced out or measured; individual structures, sculptures, rock-paintings and inscriptions were drawn to scale and photographed, sometimes using a high ladder to gain a vertical perspective (Plate 84). Given the number of sites being documented during Stage I, more precise mapping techniques applied during later stages of the project were considered unnecessary and impracticable.

During Stage I, archaeological sites and features were plotted as single coordinates using a handheld Geographical Positioning System (GPS). Each site record, along with the associated site coordinates, was then entered manually into a relational database (Microsoft Access) which, as discussed later, underwent significant structural changes over the duration of the project. The database was linked to a Geographical Informations System (GIS) mapping package (ArcMap), which enabled the creation of basic site-distribution maps, with sites in the landscape represented as single points overlaying a digitised version of Survey of India 1: 50,000 toposheets.[5] During Stage I, the lack of wider polygon-based information meant that it was difficult to represent each site's relationship to its respective archaeological complex in a visual medium.

Stage II

The problem just mentioned was redressed during Stage II (2002 onwards) as part of a wider attempt to improve and consolidate the existing survey data. This included: i) the purchase of satellite imagery which led to improved reconnaissance and mapping techniques; ii) the purchase of a new GPS machine linked to a handheld computer which enabled sites to be digitised directly in the field and to be represented in more realistic forms in mapping programmes; and iii) a major overhaul of the project's database and GIS infrastructure which allowed for more sophisticated ways of ordering and analysing the survey data (Beck and Shaw, forthcoming).

Many sites originally documented during Stage I were revisited and mapped using a combination of Total Station equipment, Kite Aerial Photography (KAP) and the newly purchased GPS equipment. The last allowed for sites to be digitised as single points, as well as linear features and polygon outlines, in contrast to the single latitude-longitude readings provided by older equipment. By thus recording sites as spatial entities, it was easier to illustrate 'real' spatial patterns in the landscape. For example, the polygon outlines of ancient settlements in Figure

13.2, by representing the total area of habitational occupation, provide a particularly striking indication of the 'surburban' quality of the landscape in contrast to its present-day rural appearance.

For small-scale site mapping, the high-resolution satellite imagery, particularly Quickbird, provided a useful supplementary tool: many previously documented mounds and hilltop Buddhist sites were clearly visible in this imagery and could thus be digitised directly as polygon outlines without the need for additional on-site mapping. As well as architectural planning, some topographical survey was also carried out around selected reservoir sites, with contour mapping at intervals of 1 m providing a check on earlier calculations regarding reservoir area and volume as well as inferences about land use (Shaw and Sutcliffe 2005).[6] The SRTM satellite imagery also generated high resolution contour data which provided the background mapping for most of the individual site-plans produced for this book.

As shown by the imagery and on-site mapping at Ferozpur (Plate 42 colour), there is a close degree of concordance between the satellite imagery and GPS data. However, an offset of approximately 20 m between the site-plan and the Quickbird satellite imagery in Plate 42 is a result of the inherent error margin of hand-held GPS technology, with further errors related to the projection system of the satellite imagery. Such a small error margin is considered acceptable over a 750 km^2 study area.

Database structure

During Stage I, the survey data were stored in a relational database arranged into three main tables: i) the first contained site information at its broadest level, defined as a 'site complex' and comprising a number of site groupings that were regarded as connected in some way. For example, the Sanchi complex included the Buddhist hilltop complex as well as the dam at the base of Sanchi hill, and the settlement remains on Kanakhera and Nagauri hills. Details about these individual components were stored in the second 'site' table, arranged according to functional types such as 'settlement', 'stupa complex', 'temple remains', 'dam', etc. The third, and most detailed, table contained information about sculptural evidence with which some of these sites were associated. Additional tables included information on ceramic collections and other surface finds.

The trouble with this structure was that the boundaries of the broadest grouping were based on subjective interpretations rather than more neutral forms of categorisation. Further, although information about phasing and ritual affiliation was stored in the sculpture and ceramics tables, there were serious limitations when it came to establishing complex chronological and denominational sequences based on different types of evidence, much of it no longer in its primary context or resulting from studies (excavation-based or otherwise) carried out prior to the SSP.

Considerable time and effort were spent during Stage II to remedy these problems and, in particular, to reduce the element of human bias in the ordering of the data. A major concern, for example, was the issue of how boundaries around and between sites were defined, or where one site ended and another began. Sometimes such decisions draw on architectural and topographical divisions such as walls or cliffs, but in most cases they are based on historical inferences or assumptions. For example, during Stage I the decision to include the dam and the Buddhist monuments at Sanchi within a single archaeological complex drew on wider evidence for the role of water management in the history of Buddhist monasticism. Boundaries and groupings are also easier to draw when particular inter-site patterns repeat themselves with sufficient regularity across a region. Chronological divisions, together with the changing use and custodianship of sites, however, are less easy to deal with. For example, do the clusters of prehistoric rock-shelters on the edges of Sanchi hill belong to the same site grouping as the hilltop Buddhist complex? There is no absolute answer to such questions. Data-organisation and cartography are both interpretative processes with the fixing of boundaries around and between sites being less to do with geographical and topographical 'reality' than with history and theory. The redesigning of the database during Stage II thus aimed at avoiding the imposition of preconceptions about inter-site relationships, without losing sight of more 'obvious' patterns in the landscape.

To this end, the number of major interlinked tables in the project database increased from three to four, with a downward migration from the most general to the most specific spatial level; this structure is reflected in the organisation of the Appendices in this book. The first table deals with sites at their broadest level, which are now referred to as 'Site Groups' (SG). 'Site Groups' are defined principally on the basis of function and consist of four main types, a) settlements, b) hilltop ritual sites, c) reservoirs and d) background landscape, the last referring to isolated sites, particularly temples and cult spots, that bear no obvious spatial relationship to larger settlement or ritual centre. The second table contains information regarding the internal organisation of the 'Site Group', which is organised into one or more 'Site Clusters' (SC). For example, every settlement at the SG level will contain one or more smaller 'Site Clusters' (SC) distinguished by types such as 'settlement', 'tank' or 'temple'. The third table introduces a higher level of descriptive detail regarding individual 'Sites' (S) which make up every Site Cluster. For example, a temple at the SC level may contain a number of separate 'Site' categories such as 'settlement pile', 'temple base' or 'natural shrine'. Further a settlement at the SC level may be made up of several 'Sites' ranging from different types of habitational zones such as 'settlement mounds' or 'hillside *bastis*' as well as 'sculpture piles', wells or 'temple remains'. Finally, the fourth table contains information relating to 'Installations' (I-), that is, portable remains found at individual 'Sites', particularly 'stupas', 'temple remains' or 'sculpture piles'. For the last two instances, the Installation table provides details of the associated sculptural and architectural remains. In the case of 'stupas', it provides details of the evidence upon which such an interpretation is based, such as, for example, 'stupa outline', 'stupa base' or 'railing'. It is important to note, however, that religious structures listed at the SC or S level may derive some or all of their dating and cultic information from Installations currently stored at a separate location.[7] Whilst each Installation is listed according to the site in the landscape at which it is currently stored, an additional field in the Installation table (and Appendix IIa) indicates the Site no. of its original context, when known. Thus, while Figure 8.4 (colour) and many of the more detailed sector-by-sector maps reflect the current location of Installations, the lists of cult spots in Appendix IIb, as well as the phase-by-phase maps relating to trends in the ritual landscape of the past (e.g. Figure 12.1), reflect the inferred original context of Installations.

In addition to the four principal tables numerous sub-tables were introduced to deal with information such as multiple dating criteria, changing ritual affiliations through time and records of site visits. The relationships between the key data tables in the database are illustrated in Figure 8.2. This level of complexity reflects the challenges of a project whose subject matter consists of multiple types and periods of archaeological remains, and which operates at a number of different spatial resolutions. For example, some site-categories relate to whole architectural compounds, others to individual sculptural fragments. The database thus needed to be designed so as to withstand queries geared at an intra-site level as well as those of a more regional landscape-based resolution. It also needed to cope with queries based on the changing ritual affiliations of sites at any of the four main site levels, at any point in time and space. This was enabled by the creation of several linked 'update query' tables stored in separate databases, which meant that whenever changes were made at the Installation level, for example, to dating or ritual affiliation, related information at the other three levels would automatically be updated. Unfortunately, there is no such thing as a ready-made database template for dealing with the regional particularities of landscape-based projects such as the SSP. This is something rarely taken into account when embarking on a new survey. As discussed in chapter 7, there is ample literature dedicated to the survey methodology and research design, but little attention has been given to how the resulting dataset should be organised to effectively deal with the underlying research questions, as well as responding to the theoretical underpinnings of various strands of 'landscape studies', such as the interest in multiple readings and reinterpretations of spaces and places through time. Quite clearly, given the recent proliferation in survey-based projects, there is an urgent need for more critical discussion of these issues.

Dating methods

Stage I

During Stage I, the dating of sites was based on a combination of sculptural, architectural, epigraphical and ceramic evidence, which, as discussed in chapter 10, offered chronologies of varying resolution as well as application. The primary chronological framework built on existing art-historical and excavation-based sequences from Sanchi, Vidisha and other published sites in north and central India, with additions and modifications based on new evidence from the SSP.

Stage II

Several steps towards improving the project's chronological framework were taken during Stage II. These included a pilot study initiated in 2003 and aimed at obtaining OSL dates from selected dams and reservoirs in the study area (Shaw *et al.*, 2007). A number of successful dates were obtained, confirming earlier hypotheses that the dams were built between the third and second centuries BC, in line with the first two phases of Buddhist construction in the area. Existing architectural chronologies were also refined through detailed site-mapping, which amongst other things resulted in improved stupa and monastery typologies (Shaw and Sutcliffe 2005).

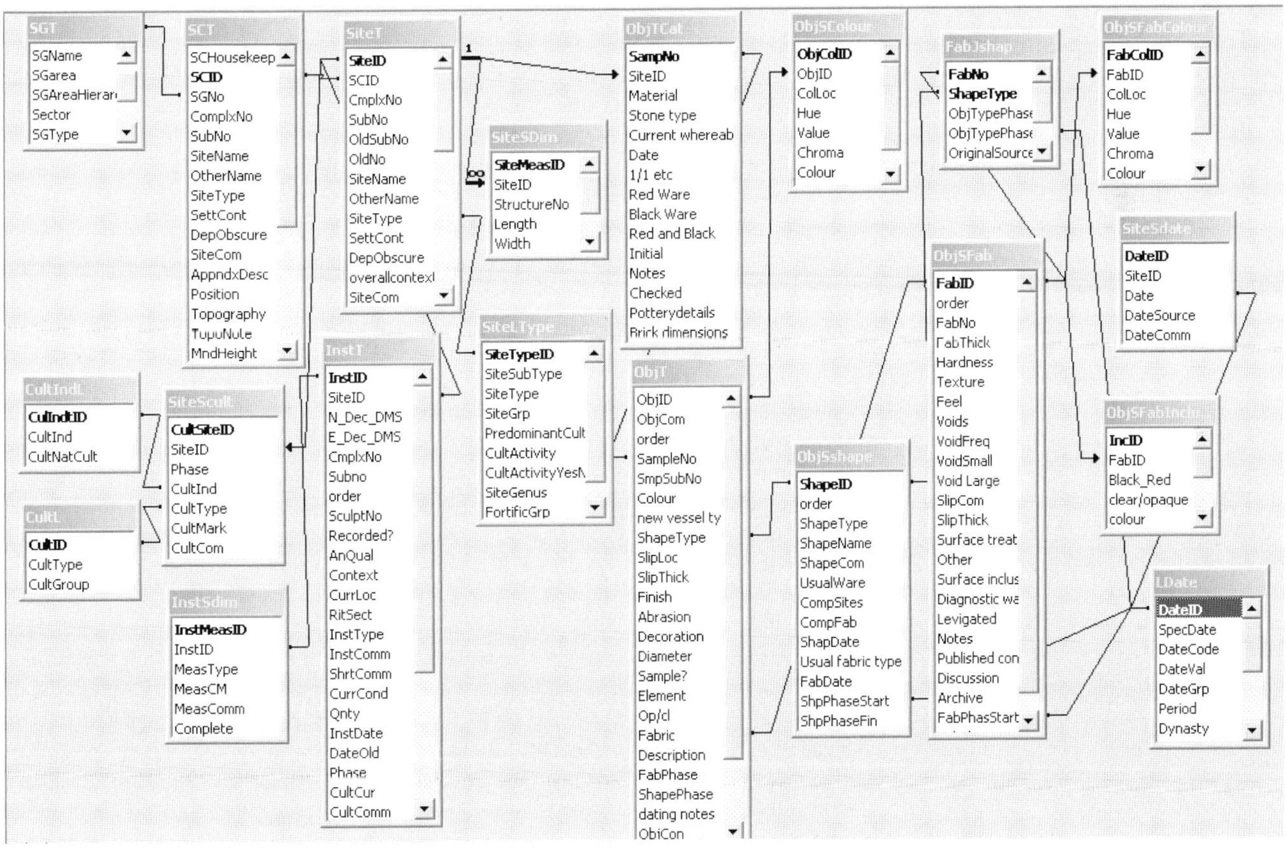

Figure 8.2 Internal structure of the SSP database showing relationships between main data tables

Survey design

In addition to acknowledging the mutual interdependence between local environmental and cultural variables, as well as archaeological methods and results, four broad steps, described further in the following sections, were taken towards achieving an 'improved' village-to-village survey which transcended the site-based focus traditionally associated with extensive surveys:

i) keeping the survey area small enough to allow for maximisation of coverage, without detracting from the broader regional perspective;
ii) following a stratified survey strategy;
iii) bringing the 'village-to-village' survey in line with theoretical movements which have led to a broadened definition and interpretation of 'sites' and their interrelationship in the landscape;
iv) incorporating present-day perceptions of the cultural landscape into the survey design.

Study area: boundaries and geological zones
The survey covered an area of approximately 750 km^2, extending for a radius of 10–15 km in all directions from Sanchi hill (Figure 1.2). The outer boundaries were defined by local topography, together with the configuration of the four 'Bhilsa Tope' sites, Sonari, Andher, Satdhara and Morel khurd, which form a rough circle around Sanchi. For the purposes of this study, the 'cultural' or arbitrary quality of the survey boundaries does not present any particular problem: in order to examine the relationships between the early Buddhist *saṅgha* and its cultural and archaeological landscape, the initial step was to identify a 'sample' area which could act as a model for processes taking place further afield. The existence of several well-preserved, previously published, Buddhist sites made it well suited to the aims of the project.

Geographical sectors
As discussed in chapter 4, the distribution of several well-defined geological zones (Figure 4.1), together with local drainage patterns, provided the basis for the identification of four major geographical sectors (Figures 8.3, 13.1). The latter allowed for a 'stratified' surveying strategy, and a level of transparency regarding the relationship between certain types of sites and their environmental setting. Sector 1 refers to the region around, and to the west of, Sanchi and is divided into two sub-sectors: 1a covers the central agricultural plain enclosed by the Rivers Bes and Betwa between Sanchi and Vidisha, while 1b comprises the small hill-ranges interspersed by narrow agricultural valleys to the west of Sanchi. One of the 'Bhilsa Tope' sites, Satdhara, is situated on the east bank of the River Bes towards its westernmost boundary, the latter being marked by several prominent hills 3–4 km further to the west. Sector 2 refers to the whole area to the east of the River Betwa, and is also divided into two sub-sectors: 2a covers the flat agricultural plains on the Betwa's eastern bank, while 2b takes in the hilly region further to the east which includes the 'Bhilsa Tope' sites of Morel khurd and Andher. Although Sectors 2a and 1a effectively belong to the same geological zone, their separation into two sectors is justified by the natural division created by the River Betwa, and further strengthened by the limited number of natural fording points south of Vidisha (Figures 8.3, 13.1).[8] Sector 3 refers to the area to the south of the Sanchi–Raisen road, and consists of large hilly ranges which become increasingly dense towards the outermost edges of the survey area. The 'Bhilsa Tope' site, Sonari, is situated towards its southernmost boundary, amidst a dense hill range which extends as far as Bhopal. The outer boundary is represented by a large valley 2–3 km further south, whose rich settlement remains, including an urban stupa site, have provided important insights into modes of interaction between monastic and non-monastic populations in the area. Finally, Sector 4 covers the flat agricultural terrain, interspersed by several prominent low-lying hills, to the north of the River Bes. The northernmost hill in this sector is Ahmadpur, beyond which the land levels out again until it meets the hilly Shamshabad district about 50 km further to the north.

'Stratified' exploration methodology
This system allowed for a 'stratified' exploration methodology which, in keeping with other surveys (Maclean 1996; Possehl 1980), allowed for any methodological variability caused by environmental conditions alone to be made explicit. In the flat plains where settlement mounds and dams stand out as fairly visible earthworks, especially from surrounding hilltops (Plates 5, 220), transects were usually separated by 50–100 m, depending on fluctuating levels of visibility and obtrusiveness at different times of the year: during winter (October–February), when most of the Stage I reconnaissance was carried out, low crop height means that field-walking can proceed relatively unhindered. The soil is also better suited to the detection of surface material at this time due to its high moisture content, dark hue and pliable, recently ploughed texture. In February–March, visibility levels are reduced due to dense crop coverage, further exacerbated by dry, cracked soil conditions in the post-harvest months (March–June).

Different reconnaissance methods were needed in the hilly zones because of reduced visibility caused by all-year vegetation cover. This is more of a problem in Sectors 2b and 3, than in areas to the east where more deforestation has taken place. Even without these problems, visibility is already low in the hilly zones since the high reuse value of sandstone blocks from ancient structures means that hillside settlements rarely consist of more than collections of wall outlines. However, most of these hills are small enough for systematic exploration between identifiable points, and, depending on forest cover, transects were usually separated by 5–30 m.

'Stratified' collection methods
Over 1100 potsherds were collected, mainly from the surfaces of ploughed settlement mounds, as a means of supplementing dates provided by sculptural and architectural evidence. Other surface finds included terracotta fragments, iron slag, microlithic tools and coins. The collection strategy varied according to geographical sector and geological zone, with sites in the agricultural zones presenting the least difficulty. At unoccupied settlement mounds, sampled collections were made by walking along two cross-transects intersecting at the centre of the site; at intervals of every 10 metres, a rough circle of about 0.5 m radius was delineated, inside which every sherd with an intact rim or diagnostic surface treatment, was collected. This is similar to methods used in other surveys (Cherry *et al.*, 1991; Jameson *et al.*, 1994), although the use of string or wooden frames was considered unnecessary. Mounds with ongoing occupation (Plate 6) called for alternative collection methods: erosion gullies and

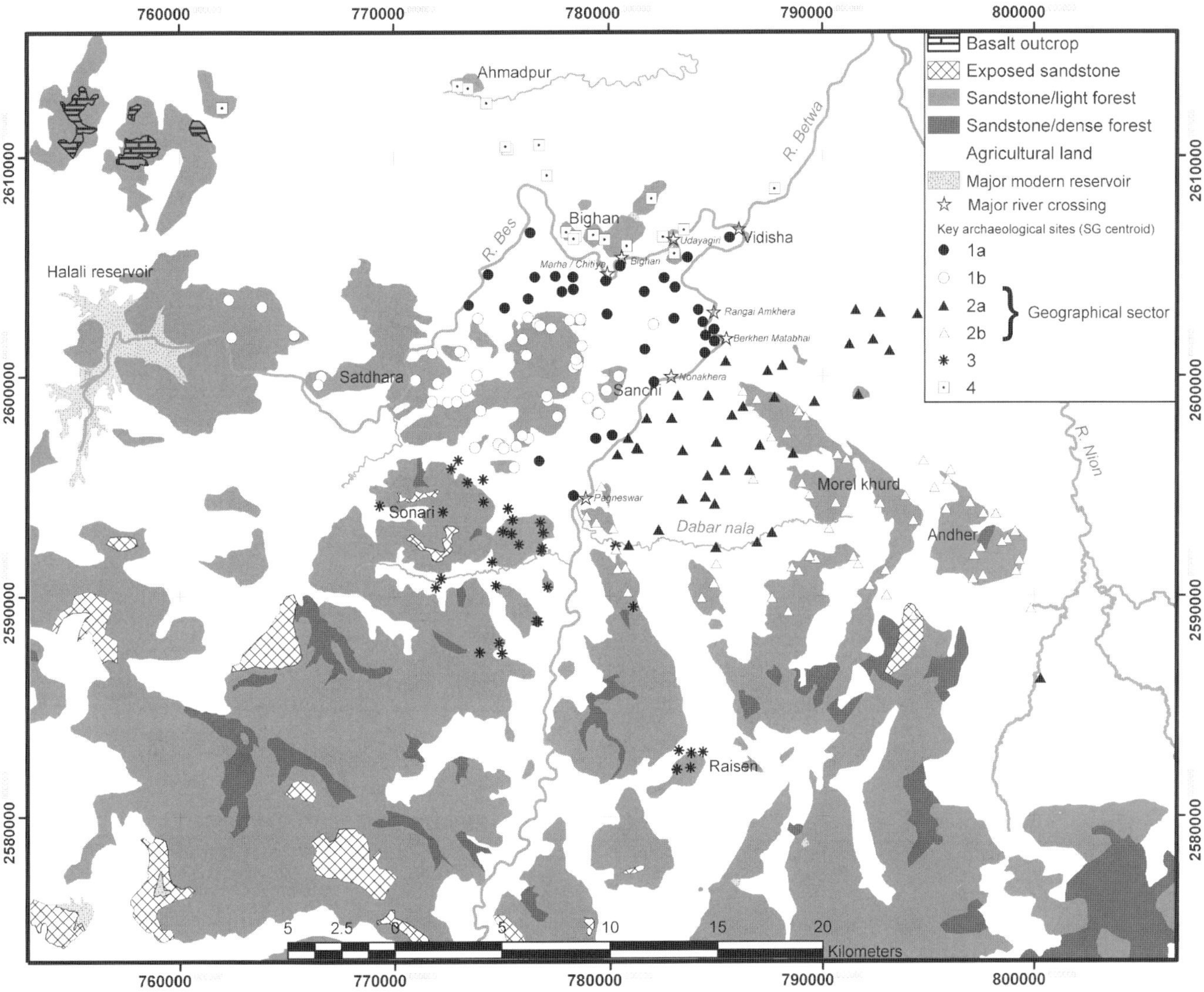

Figure 8.3 Map showing study area with main geographical sectors, key archaeological sites and river crossings

artificial cuts were examined for archaeological finds such as ceramics and walls, with additional chronological information provided by sculptural and architectural fragments stored within the village itself. The lack of exposed sections and ploughed surfaces at most of the hillside settlements prevented systematic collections, with any surface pottery being of little use due to the high probability of it belonging to the site's latest phase of occupation. With the exception of Bilori 2 (SG071) or Karhaud kherai (SG012b), where deep sections had been formed as a result of quarrying activity (Plate 7), comparative chronologies at hillside sites usually drew on sculptural and architectural typologies and consideration of wider contextual information from sites in the immediate vicinity.

'Sites' in the landscape

Another step towards maximising levels of representativeness involved the incorporation of theoretical developments that have led to changes in the definition of archaeological enquiry; it is widely accepted that the quality of survey results is affected by the working definition of 'site' used. Conventional definitions usually revolve around an agreed ratio between artefact density and area, e.g. 'five artefacts per square metre' (Doelle 1977, 202). The SSP followed a less rigid definition as proposed by Dunnell and Dancey (1983, 272): 'a virtually continuous spatial distribution of material over the landscape with highly variable density characteristics'. This approach avoids focusing on a single type or period of site, but rather views the landscape as a fluid entity in which categories such as 'ritual' and 'secular' or 'past' and 'present' play an implicitly interlinked role. Thus, while the SSP yielded a wide range of different site-types described below, it was only when viewed as interrelated parts of a unified landscape that they provided the empirical basis for addressing the project's principal research questions regarding the economic and religious modes of interaction between monastic and non-monastic sections of society.

Buddhist sites

The survey centred on Sanchi, and included the four 'Bhilsa Tope' sites in the outlying hills. These sites consist largely of stupas (stone-faced, spherical earthen mounds designed as repositories for the Buddhist relic), monasteries and temples, most of which have been extensively restored by the ASI. The only available early sketch-plans for these sites are those produced by Cunningham (1854). A major problem that this study sought to remedy was that many of the less well-preserved structures at these sites remained unmapped and often extended far beyond the boundaries of the ASI-protected areas, which, generally speaking, follow those defined during Cunningham's time.[9]

The thirty additional Buddhist sites documented during the SSP contained similar remains in varying states of preservation, as well as miscellaneous buildings such as storerooms or refectories possibly connected with lay personnel. The term stupa encompasses a range of architectural categories ranging from small cairn-like structures with diameters of 1–2 m to large monuments with diameters of up to 30 m, as at Sanchi. As discussed in chapters 9–11, such wide disparities in size may also reflect functional differences, with some of the smaller stupas possibly acting as monastic burials rather than repositories for relics of the Buddha or saintly monks. Remains vary from heavily disturbed stupa outlines (Plate 61) and bases (Plate 62), to more complete stupas reaching heights of up to 5 m (Plates 16, 63). There are also morphological differences relating to date, with three identifiable stupa phases described in chapter 10. In addition to these *in situ* remains, individual elements of stupas, such as railings and pillar fragments, were also documented, often in urban, rather than hilltop ritual locations. In many cases, these could be traced back to nearby Buddhist centres; in others they were used to infer the existence of an urban stupa whose foundations were no longer visible.

Four main types of monasteries, the dating of which is discussed in chapters 10–11, were also identified (Appendix IIb): i) simple single-roomed structures surviving only as boulder outlines with no infill (Plate 94); ii) single- or double-roomed rectangular structures with surviving walls of the rubble-infill, outer facing variety (Plate 93); iii) quadrangular structures consisting of multiple cells, either square or rectangular, arranged around a central courtyard (Plates 88, 91; Shaw and Sutcliffe 2005); iv) large imposing stone platforms originally surmounted by brick and wood superstructures (Plate 80; Shaw 2000b, fig. 13). Differences in function and date between these monastery forms are discussed in chapters 9 and 11. There is also a fifth category of monastic dwelling: 'monastic rock-shelters', as found at Sanchi hill and several other hilltop Buddhist sites in the study area (Plates 49–50). These consist of prehistoric rock-shelters showing signs of adaptation for monastic use in the form of platforms built up in front of their entrances or Buddhist wall-paintings and inscriptions (Plate 51).[10] The question of whether these adapted shelters, also known at better-documented sites such as Bhimbetka and Pangurariya (Plate 52), represent a 'pre-monumental' phase of monasticism, is taken up in chapter 11.

All of the newly documented hilltop Buddhist sites were discovered during Stage I by either transect-based exploration or following up local leads. During Stage II, high-resolution satellite imagery provided a supplementary mapping tool, although its effectiveness depended on the varying environmental conditions of each sector in the study area (Shaw and Sutcliffe 2005, figs. 11–12; Beck and Shaw, forthcoming). For example, the comparatively high forest cover in Sectors 1b and 3, together with the lack of differentiation between stupas and their background sandstone surface, meant that small cairn-like stupas in these areas rarely showed up in the Quickbird imagery. By contrast, many of the stupas in Sector 2b showed up, due to a combination of improved levels of preservation and higher levels of forest clearance (Plate 43). Many of the simplest types of monastery, surviving only in the form of sandstone boulder outlines, were difficult to distinguish from their sandstone backgrounds. However, the platformed and courtyard monasteries were easier to identify, even in densely vegetated areas, due to higher levels of monumentality and the angular edges of masonry walls (Plate 42).

Dams and other water features

A group of 17 ancient dams, discussed in chapter 14, were first documented during Stage I. Visible from nearby hilltops, they survive as pronounced earthworks laid across narrow valleys (Figure 1.2; Plates 219–20). Reaching lengths of up to 1 km, they consist of earthen cores faced with stone slabs (Plate 222). During Stage II, morphological and hydrological studies were supplemented by geological dating analysis (Shaw *et al.*, 2007) and a programme of detailed site mapping (Shaw and Sutcliffe 2005), while a range of satellite imagery was assessed for its ability to identify such sites: many of the dams showed up in the Landsat, KFA and Quickbird imagery, while some palaeochannel activity, possibly relevant for supplementing the hydrological framework of analysis, was identified in the Quickbird imagery (Beck and Shaw, forthcoming). SRTM data were also useful for generating contours, which, together with Total Station-generated contours, have been used for refining calculations made during Stage I regarding reservoir areas and volumes (Shaw and Sutcliffe 2005). Other water features such as 'excavated' domestic tanks and wells were also documented, usually in settlement contexts, but occasionally also within hilltop Buddhist sites (Plate 97). These were all located during the primary reconnaissance in Stage I, but the tanks represented one of the few site-categories that showed up with some regularity in the Quickbird satellite imagery.

Settlements

A total of 145 habitational settlements were documented during Stage 1, with two major types of sites: i) low settlement mounds (average height: 1–6 m) formed from denuded mud-brick structures and found throughout the fluvial plains (Plate 5). The mounds are similar in nature and formation to *tell* sites in the Near East (Rosen 1986), although they are considerably smaller in height and extent and are sometimes overlain by modern villages (Plate 6; Shaw 2000a, fig. 2); ii) hillside settlements known locally as *basti*s (Plate 8) and surviving as clusters of ruined stone structures, often immediately behind or adjacent to modern hillside villages.

As mentioned earlier, each settlement type called for different sets of surface collections. They also called for different reconnaissance procedures. While the mounds stand out as prominent features in the landscape, documentation of the hillside settlements depends on more systematic exploration, following up local leads or, as discussed later, paying close attention to the configuration of modern cult spots, which often commemorate ancient settlement sites. Some of the high resolution satellite imagery, such as Quickbird and Corona, introduced during Stage II, revealed some of the previously documented mounds by virtue of their relatively light soil colour caused by their high ceramic content and other surface finds (Plates 9–10).[11] In contrast to other foci of the project, it appeared thus that mound identification was the one area in which satellite remote sensing might have proven useful as a primary reconnaissance tool during the early phases of the project. By contrast, most of the hillside settlements were ill suited to satellite remote-sensing due to a combination of dense vegetation cover and the lack of colour differentiation between the already highly denuded sandstone structural remains at such sites and their natural sandstone background.

Temple sites and sculpture fragments

Over 1000 individual sculpture and architectural fragments were documented during the survey. Many were still under worship and installed on village platforms (*cabutra*). A total of 313 find-spots were identified (Figure 8.4 colour), approximately one-third of which related to *in situ* architectural and sculptural components of extant temples or, as sculpture piles, in or in close proximity to associated temple mounds or foundations. The remaining two-thirds consisted of isolated sculpture piles with no obvious temple site in the immediate vicinity. In such cases, their original context had to be inferred on the basis of stylistic, denominational or chronological similarities with sculptural assemblages with known provenances. Some assemblages consisted of fragments from more than one phase which may have been taken from a variety of temple sites. Only in a few cases did individual sculptures remain without a clearly identifiable context.

The distinction between those sculptures that are still in their original context and those that are not is crucial to much of the discussion in chapter 12 on temporal and spatial patterns in the ritual landscape, based as it is on the distribution of actual temples and cult spots rather than isolated sculpture piles. However, neither of these site categories is well suited to satellite remote sensing, due to the often highly eroded condition of surviving temple foundations and the dispersed nature of sculpture collections. As discussed later, these sites were more easily detected through a sensitivity to the currency of ancient temple remains in the configuration of the present-day ritual landscape.

'Non-monumental' sites

The project was also informed by the wider recognition by landscape archaeologists of the 'non-site' rather than site or artefact as the minimum unit of archaeological enquiry (Plog *et al.*, 1978, 389; Foley 1981; Dunnell and Dancey 1983, 268). My own stance was that, as well as less tangible remains such as faint structural outlines or stone tool scatters, the 'non-site' category should be broadened to include rock-shelters (with or without paintings), prominently shaped rocks and sacred trees, many of which continue to play an important role in local ritual practices. The ability to detect these sites is often less dependent on sophisticated reconnaissance techniques than on a particular 'way of looking' at the landscape: it was not because of inferior technology that less tangible or well-preserved sites failed to find mention in Cunningham's reports. Indeed, with elephants for transport and large teams of assistant engineers, his technical resources were considerably superior to those of today's student. The main difference is one of archaeological interest: Cunningham (1854) was concerned primarily with retrieving relics and reliquaries from Buddhist stupas and in establishing a broad historical map for any given region based on its most prominent archaeological features. It is hardly surprising, therefore, that lesser sites did not figure prominently in his accounts. On the other hand, the 'small site' category, which holds greater interest to today's archaeologists, would not make much sense without the broader contextual framework provided by two centuries of archaeological, art-historical and epigraphical scholarship.

The *visual* dimension of the archaeological landscape, in particular the issue of intervisibility between key ritual sites, also formed an important part of the survey methodology (Shaw 2000b). Despite parallels with 'phenomenological' approaches to European prehistoric landscapes (Tilley 1994; Bender *et al.*, 1997), it was not simply a case of blindly applying ready-made models to a new area. As discussed in chapter 7, the phenomenological approach suffers from a number of drawbacks due, in part, to the limited range of sources available to scholars of European prehistory. By contrast, inferences regarding the importance of visual linkages between ritual monuments in the Sanchi area can been made with more certainty (Shaw 2000b), thanks to the relatively well-preserved state of the structures and the rich body of textual and epigraphical material with which they are connected. As discussed in chapter 11, the importance of 'divine seeing' at Buddhist sites and, in particular, the visual prominence of stupas are given canonical sanction by textual and epigraphical descriptions of stupas not just as repositories of the Buddhist relic, but as containers of a 'living presence' which projects the power of the Buddha, the dharma and respected monks into and across the surrounding space (Schopen 1997, 116–17; Shaw 2000b, 29, n. 25).

Archaeological sites in today's socio-ritual landscape

The village shrine

Before following up local leads and carrying out exploration in the fields and hills, the initial point of call on a typical survey-day was the village itself. The first task was to enquire about archaeological material such as sculptures, coins and other artefacts stored in the village. While some of this material is often kept in individual houses, in most cases the sculptural and architectural remains collected from the surrounding areas can be found on the ubiquitous *cabutra*, a platform made of mud or stone (Plate 11).

These motley collections can range from several heavily eroded fragments to large piles of sculptures and temple parts, with dates ranging from the second century BC to the thirteenth century AD. Taken from ruined temples of the Brahmanical, Buddhist or Jain traditions, they are a powerful reminder of the radical changes in the structuring of the ritual landscape following the Muslim conquests of the thirteenth century AD. Despite canonical prohibitions against the reinstallation of damaged sculptures (Lahiri 1996, 225), many of these platforms double as village shrines, multiple layers of red paint (*sindhur*) on selected sculptures indicating their ongoing status as objects of worship. The *cabutra* therefore represents the transformation of orthodox 'high culture' into the arena of medieval folk religion (Lahiri 1996, 225). This physical and cultural relocation is often accompanied by a transformation of religious meaning: it is not uncommon to find images of Buddha being worshipped as Visnu or male deities being revered as goddesses.[12] Such examples highlight a wider problem in formal art-historical analysis: by defining objects according to their 'original' religious and temporal designation, their ongoing trajectory of religious meaning according to time and place can be undermined (Shaw 2000b; Davis 1999). The archaeological landscape is not a neutral or 'flat' backdrop, but rather is constantly open to transformation 'through a filter of socio-religious beliefs and memories' (Lahiri and Singh 1999, 176).

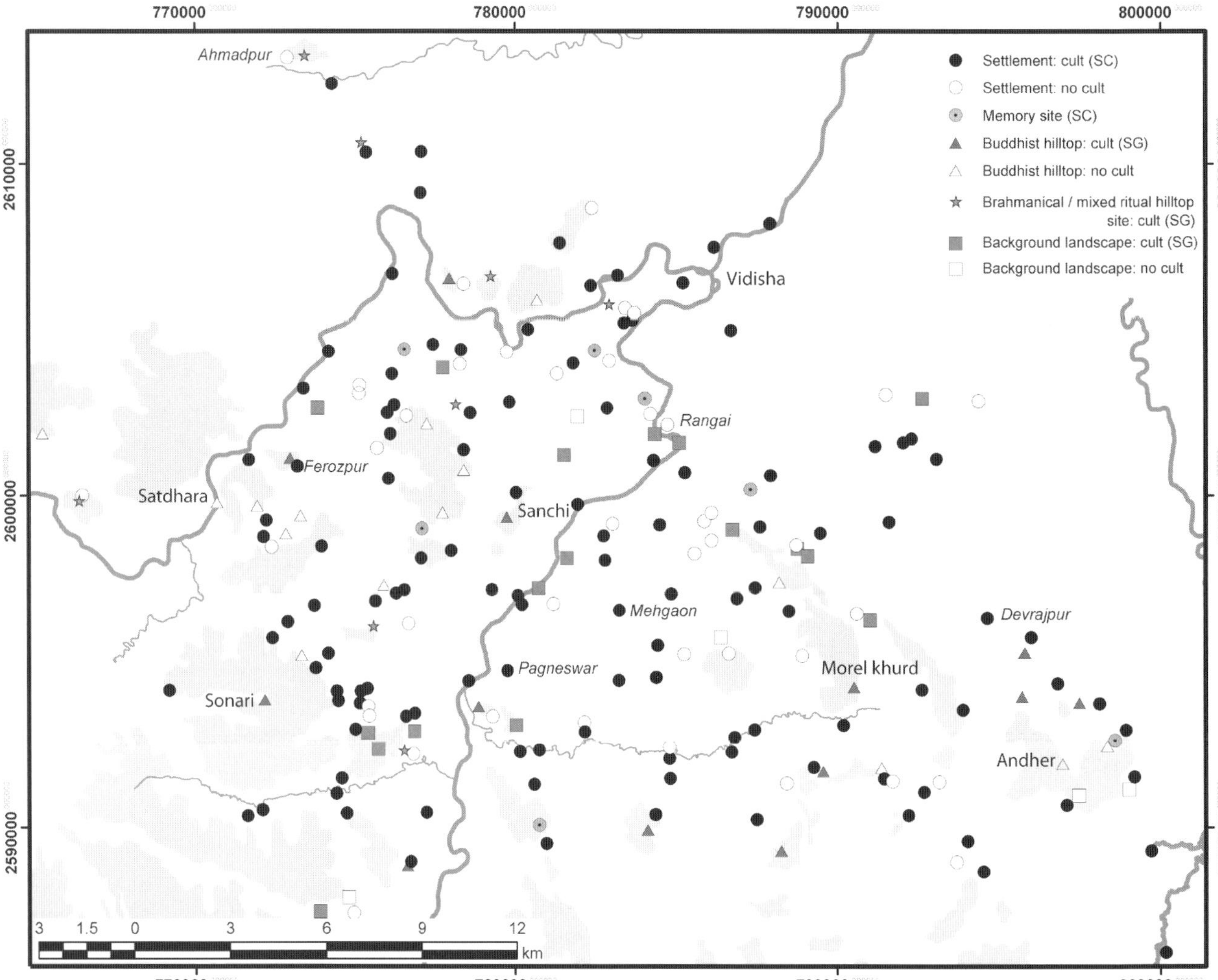

Figure 8.5 Map of the SSP area, showing archaeological sites marked out as modern cult spots and 'memory sites'.

The practice of worshipping ancient remains is not restricted to modern villages alone, but occurs throughout the countryside wherever archaeological sites are located by villagers. A wide range of sites, from settlements to temples and isolated piles of sculptural fragments, are commonly staked out from the surrounding landscape by brightly coloured paint daubed onto the sculptures themselves, and/or by prominent trees and coloured flags hoisted prominently onto high poles. In some cases, the shrines are devoid of sculptural remains but consist solely of 'natural' cairn-like shrines (Plate 12), platforms set into the roots of trees or simple collections of unhewn, triangular-shaped stones believed to be manifestations of the goddess (Plate 14).

Those sites which show evidence of being commemorated in this way are illustrated in Figure 8.5. The continued currency of ancient remains obviously has a powerful impact on archaeological conservation in the face of the increasing threat from destructive industries.[13] However, rather than reflecting a community of avid conservationists, these sites are marked out because of their ongoing association with place-bound deities and tutelary spirits, referred to by a host of names such as *devī* ('goddess'), *māta* ('mother'), *bhūmia*, *bir baba* (a hero deity) or *djinn maharāj*. As illustrated by the last example which has Muslim origins, worship at these shrines usually overrides sectarian affiliation. These tutelary spirits are believed to occupy ancient settlements long after their abandonment. Because many modern villages maintain ancestral associations with nearby archaeological sites, a sense of reverence for the old deity is often maintained (cf. Lahiri 1996, 255). The fact that these commemorated places can be seen from considerable distances has an obvious impact on reconnaissance methods in that they often provide the starting point for exploration in a new area. Further, since many of these shrines also commemorate what in archaeological terms would be described as 'non-site' material, such as strangely shaped stones or rock-shelters, or are situated in otherwise inaccessible places, it is quite likely that they would be missed by systematic sampling methods, as well as widely spaced transect-based exploration. Thus, the configuration of these commemorated sites provides a crucial key for enabling survey over areas unfeasibly large for systematic methods, whilst achieving far greater coverage than would be possible through conventional extensive methods.

These observations are useful for illustrating the close link between the biography of archaeological material in Sanchi's contemporary socio-ritual setting and levels of archaeological visibility and, by extension, the reconnaissance process as a whole. A sensitivity to the interwoven trajectories of the geographies of the past and the present was thus crucial to the success of the SSP, as it allowed a middle course to be steered between systematic and extensive methods of exploration. As discussed in the previous chapter, by failing to draw attention to this dimension of the archaeological landscape, the Gangetic valley surveys of Erdosy and Lal have overlooked the central backbone of the 'village-to-village' survey. This lacuna was in part remedied by Lahiri's study of the diverse cultural and historical processes underlying the rural landscape of Ballabgarh (Lahiri 1996; Lahiri *et al.*, 1996; Lahiri and Singh 1999). Although Lahiri's lack of reference to wider movements in landscape theory and method detracts from the force of her argument, the regional underpinnings of the 'village-to-village' survey are made quite explicit by her point that 'the ways in which peasant and other social groups view their physical environment and the traces of earlier habitations it contains are just as integral to the reconstruction of the settlement history and landscape archaeology of a region as are the usual archaeological approaches' (Lahiri and Singh 1999, 175).

Local perceptions of the archaeological landscape

The practices described in the foregoing account called for a surveying strategy in which local informants played a significant role. This kind of approach has been criticised as unreliable and for perpetuating an overly 'site-based' level of enquiry (Cherry 1983). Also, in parts of Western Europe where local knowledge of the historical landscape is fading, an over-reliance on local information may well turn out to be fruitless. However, such criticisms are less valid for central India, where the configuration of 'non-monumental' sites, such as caves, prominent rocks or 'natural' shrines, often has a greater impact on local perceptions of the historical landscape than do more 'conventional' archaeological sites.

This is not to say that local information should play more than a supplementary role to systematic, transect-based exploration. In keeping with the ideological basis of all archaeological categorisation, the local historical and archaeological knowledge is shaped by a wide range of cultural variables such as age, experience, social position and occupation. It is thus important to ensure that one's pool of informants is as varied as possible. For example, a goat-herder, forager and farmer will tend to interact with quite distinct togographical zones of the landscape, and this will influence the types and locations of archaeological sites about which they are likely to have knowledge. There is also a tendency for the category of archaeological site situated closest to the village to dominate local perceptions of ancient sites in general. Although locals may insist that there is 'nothing' (*kuch nahīn*) on a particular hilltop, actual inspection may reveal a major archaeological site. This type of 'misinformation' can arise from a range of factors, including genuine ignorance, as well as laziness and unwillingness to accompany one to the place in question. Others may suspect one's motives as being those of a 'treasure-hunter' or sculpture thief, and thus refrain from revealing information. More commonly, however, such discrepancies between local and academic perceptions of the landscape stem from different value systems regarding the kinds of places that are worth visiting: some find it incomprehensible why anyone would want to scramble through dense jungle to reach a ruined monastery or stupa that has no currency in present-day religious practice,[14] while an equally arduous journey to a local goddess shrine consisting of no more than a pile of unhewn stones might be positively encouraged. It seems that a site is only regarded as a 'place' (*sthān*) if it maintains linkages with a local divinity, personage or important event. Otherwise it remains *purāne pathar hī hai* ('just a pile of old stones')!

Such discrepancies also work in the obverse direction: some sites, referred to here as 'Memory sites', were encountered during the survey which, despite being commemorated as ancient settlements, yielded no supporting archaeological evidence to this effect.[15] In most cases the site was marked out by a flag and a shrine of unhewn stones dedicated to the presiding deity of the 'abandoned settlement', with which the nearest village was perceived as maintaining ancestral links. However, although villagers sometimes pointed to pebbles or unusually shaped stones as representing 'ancient remains', such claims had no archaeological basis. A possible explanation for these sites is that they represent a kind of 'invented' antiquity. The legitimisation of sacred space by reference to a place's proclaimed antiquity is a common occurrence in South Asia (Bakker 1992; Shaw 2000c). In many cases it is the village *devī* or *bīr baba* which provides the key to this process, because as a potent symbol of 'locality', it asserts a sense of divine right over places whose custodianship may have become the object of dispute. This is well illustrated, for example, by Diane Coccari's (1989) study of modern *bīr baba* shrines in Benares, which have played a powerful role in upsetting orthodox ritual geography and assisting low-caste land claims.

Conclusion

In this chapter I have described the archaeological, cultural and ecological variables that shaped the research design of the SSP. Whilst sharing certain attributes with other types of extensive surveys, it does not fit easily within unilinear evolutionary schemes which, developed largely in European and North American settings, place the intensive/systematic survey as the inevitable culmination of a series of flawed methodologies. Rather I have tried to show that by making explicit the regional underpinnings of the 'village-to-village' survey, it is possible to strike a balance between extensive/unsystematic and intensive/systematic methods. The result is a regional methodology which has enabled the effective analysis of spatial and temporal relationships over regions defined by cultural boundaries, whilst avoiding many of the biases associated with 'traditional' extensive methods. With broad archaeological patterns from the first two seasons (Stage I) thus established, as well as a number of working hypotheses about the social and economic background of Buddhist propagation in central India, subsequent seasons (Stage II) were aimed at testing these hypotheses and strengthening the theoretical and methodological underpinnings of the project. As confirmed during Stage II from preliminary comparisons between a range of satellite imagery and previously documented archaeological sites, much of the archaeological landscape would have remained 'invisible' if remote-sensing had been relied on as a primary reconnaissance tool during Stage I. The extensive and time-consuming explorations carried out during the primary reconnaissance seasons turned out to be far more effective, together with a sensitivity to the the continued currency of archaeological sites in today's ritual and cultural landscape.

1 Sanchi hill

2 Andher hill: 'natural' fortification

3 Lohangi hill (from the north)

4 RIGHT Basalt hill in northern sector (Saleiya) with native broad-leaved forest

5 Barren settlement mound (Pipalia kherai)

6 Settlement mound occupied by modern village (Ahmadpur)

7 Exposed section at hillside site of Bilori 2

8 Hillside *basti*

9 Quickbird imagery: Baheriya settlement with two extant mounds, and pottery scatters shown through soil colour differentiation

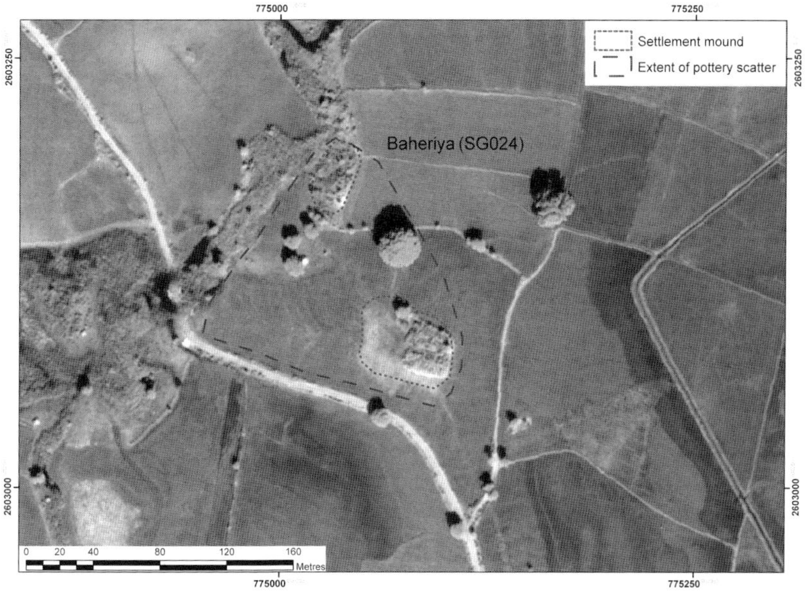

10 Pottery and iron slag on mound surface

11 Mehgaon: sculpture stored on the village *cabutra*

12 Cairn/shrine ('natural')

13 Tree shrine ('natural')

14 Devi shrine ('natural')

CHAPTER 9

Archaeology of Vidisha and Sanchi Hill

Introduction

The primary framework used to date newly documented material in the SSP was provided by excavation sequences and art-historical typologies at Vidisha and Sanchi (Figure 9.1 colour; Tables 9.1, 9.2), which provide the central focus of this chapter. However, because of the divergent time-scales and phasing systems used at these two sites, a level of synchronisation was required in order to produce a coherent regional chronological framework for the region. Further adjustments were needed in order to take account of recent revisions in art-historical and archaeological scholarship. It was also necessary to return to earlier nineteenth-century site reports, including maps and photographs, in order to shed further light on objects whose provenance was not made explicit in earlier studies. The resulting chronological framework is explained further in chapter 10. In the second half of this chapter, I will examine aspects of Sanchi's immediate archaeological context beyond the largely Buddhist and monumental focus of earlier studies. This will involve discussion of non-Buddhist cult spots, habitational settlements and water-management schemes both on and below Sanchi hill. Although most of these features belong to separate 'Site Groups', taken together they comprise what may be envisaged as a coherent 'early historic complex' which provides a working model for examining temporal and spatial relationships between similar categories of Site Groups throughout the SSP study area.

The archaeological sequence at Vidisha

As discussed in chapter 3, excavations carried out at Vidisha in the 1960s and 1970s resulted in the identification of six main occupational levels dating from the Chalcolithic to the post-Gupta period (*IAR* 1963–4, 16–17; 1964–5, 18; 1965–6, 23; 1975–6, 30–1; 1976–7, 33–4); the four ASI trenches, labelled BSN1–4, are indicated in Figure 9.2. The phasing system is somewhat confusing, with little consistency from trench to trench and with new phases being introduced from season to season. The complete sequence as known at the end of the five excavation seasons is summarised in Table 9.2. Period Ia refers to the pre-pottery Chalcolithic period based on excavations at Rangai, a separate settlement mound to the south of Vidisha, discussed later. As far as the main Besnagar mounds are concerned, the earliest occupational level was assigned to the Chalcolithic period (IIa: c. 1800–1100 BC) characterised by painted black-and-red wares, black-slipped wares and microlithic blades, overlapping with iron, PGW and related wares in the uppermost layers (Period IIb: c. 1100–900 BC) (*IAR* 1964–5, 19). Period III (a–c) covers the period between c. 900 BC and the early first century AD, with the first occurrence of NBPW in Period IIIb (c. 500–200 BC), along with iron objects and punchmarked coins. The latter half of this period marks the beginning of the site's earliest urban phase. Period IIIc is assigned to the 'Sunga Satavahana' period, to which the foundations of the 1.5 km-long city rampart at the western edge of the main city mounds are also assigned.[1] This period is characterised by the 'absence of NBPW and BRW' (*IAR* 1975–6, 30). However, the possibility of an earlier, i.e. Mauryan, date cannot be ruled out, especially given the identification of material from this phase in the rampart itself, not to mention the postulated third-century-BC date of the Vasudeva shrine at the Heliodorus pillar site. Period IVa, characterised by plain red wares, red-slipped wares (especially in the form of 'sprinklers'), painted black-on-red wares, votive tanks, terracotta beads and Naga coins, was assigned to the 'Naga-Kusana' period (c. first to third century AD), and Period IVb to the Ksatrapa-Gupta period (c. third to fifth century AD) on the basis of red wares, black-and-red wares, jewellery, Ksatrapa coins and a 'fragmentary terracotta image housed in a shrine' (*IAR* 1964–5, 19), while Periods V and VI were given the labels 'early medieval' (ninth to eleventh century AD) and 'late medieval-modern' (eighteenth to early twentieth century AD) respectively, prior to which the site is argued to have been deserted for several centuries (*ibid.*). For the 'urban decay' interpretation of the latter phases in Vidisha's occupational sequence, see chapter 5.

Excavations were also carried out at a separate settlement site called Rangai Amkhera, a low mound on the eastern bank of the River Betwa, just below the railway bridge between Vidisha and Sanchi (Khare 1981; *IAR* 1976–7, 33–4). These revealed a three-phase Chalcolithic sequence, overlying two pre-pottery microlithic levels, assigned to Period Ia, following the final sequence given in Table 9.2. The earliest ceramic level (Period 1b in Table 9.2) was dominated by red wares with geometric designs and animal figures painted in black, and BRW with white paintings. Their similarity to wares from Kayatha II (Ansari and Dhavalikar 1975) suggested a date of c. 2000–1800 BC, i.e. slightly earlier than the dates for Phase IIa at Besnagar given in Table 9.2. The uppermost levels contained some PGW and related wares, attesting to continued occupation until c. 1000 BC, following which the site appears to have been abandoned. This sequence fits with the Erdosy and Lal models in the Gangetic valley, where the shift

Table 9.1 Marshall's phasing at Sanchi.

Phase	Date range	Monuments	Inscriptions	Sculptures
I	3rd century BC	Stupa 1: brick core. Pillar 10. Temple 40 (apsidal). Temple 18 (apsidal).	Asokan inscription (c. 269–232 BC).	Elephant capital from Temple 40 (?).
II	2nd–1st century BC	Stupas 2, 3, 4. Stupa 1: casing and railings. Temples 18 and 40 (enlargements); Building 8 (platformed monastery).	Donative inscriptions on Stupas 1, 2 and 3 railings; reliquary inscriptions from Stupas 2 and 3.	Pillar by Stupa 2; Pillar 25.
III	1st–3rd century AD	Stupa 1: gateway carvings.	Southern gateway inscription of Satakarni (c. AD 25).	
IV	4th–6th century AD	Temples 17 and 19. Stupas 28 and 29.	Inscription of Candragupta II (Gupta year 131, or AD 450–1).	Stupa 1 *pradaksinapatha* Buddha images; Pillar 25 and crowning Vajrapani image; two Padmapani to the north Stupa 1; *nāga*, *nāginī*, and *yakṣa* sculptures. Various others now in the SAM.
V	7th–8th century AD	Stupas 4, 5, 11, 12, 13, 14 and 16. Temples 18 and 40 (additions); Temples 20, 22 and 31. Monastery complex beneath Building 43; Monasteries 36, 37 and 38, and other newly excavated structures in the southern area; Monastery 51 (?).		
VI	9th–12th century AD	Eastern platform, surmounting monasteries (46 and 47), and temple (45), and boundary wall; Building 43.	Building 43 inscription (mid- to late 9th century AD)	Buddha and Bodhisattva images from Temple 45. Numerous other images in SAM.

Table 9.2 Summary of phasing at Vidisha based on five excavation seasons.

Phase	Dates	Period	Dating criteria
Ia	Pre-c. 2000 BC	Pre-pottery Chalcolithic (Rangai only)	Microlithic blades.
Ib	c. 2000–1800 BC	Chalcolithic (Rangai only)	Painted Black on Red wares, Black and Red ware with white paintings (similar to Kayatha II).
IIa	c. 1800–1100 BC	Pottery Chalcolithic	Painted black-and-red wares; black-slipped wares; microlithic blades.
IIb	c. 1100–900 BC	Iron Age	PGW and related wares; iron.
IIIa	c. 900–500 BC	Late Iron Age	PGW and related wares, iron.
IIIb	c. 500–200 BC	Early-historic/urban phase	NBPW, punchmarked coins, iron.
IIIc	c. 200 BC–early first century AD	Sunga Satavahana (city rampart)	'Absence of NBPW' and Black and Red ware.
IVa	1st–3rd century AD	Naga-Kusana	Plain red, red-slipped wares (especially 'sprinklers'), painted black-on-red wares, votive tanks, teracotta beads, and Naga coins.
IVb	3rd–5th century AD	Ksatrapa-Gupta	Red wares, black-and-red wares, jewellery, Ksatrapa coins.
V	9th–11th century AD	'Early medieval'	
VI	18th–early 20th century AD	'Late medieval-modern'	

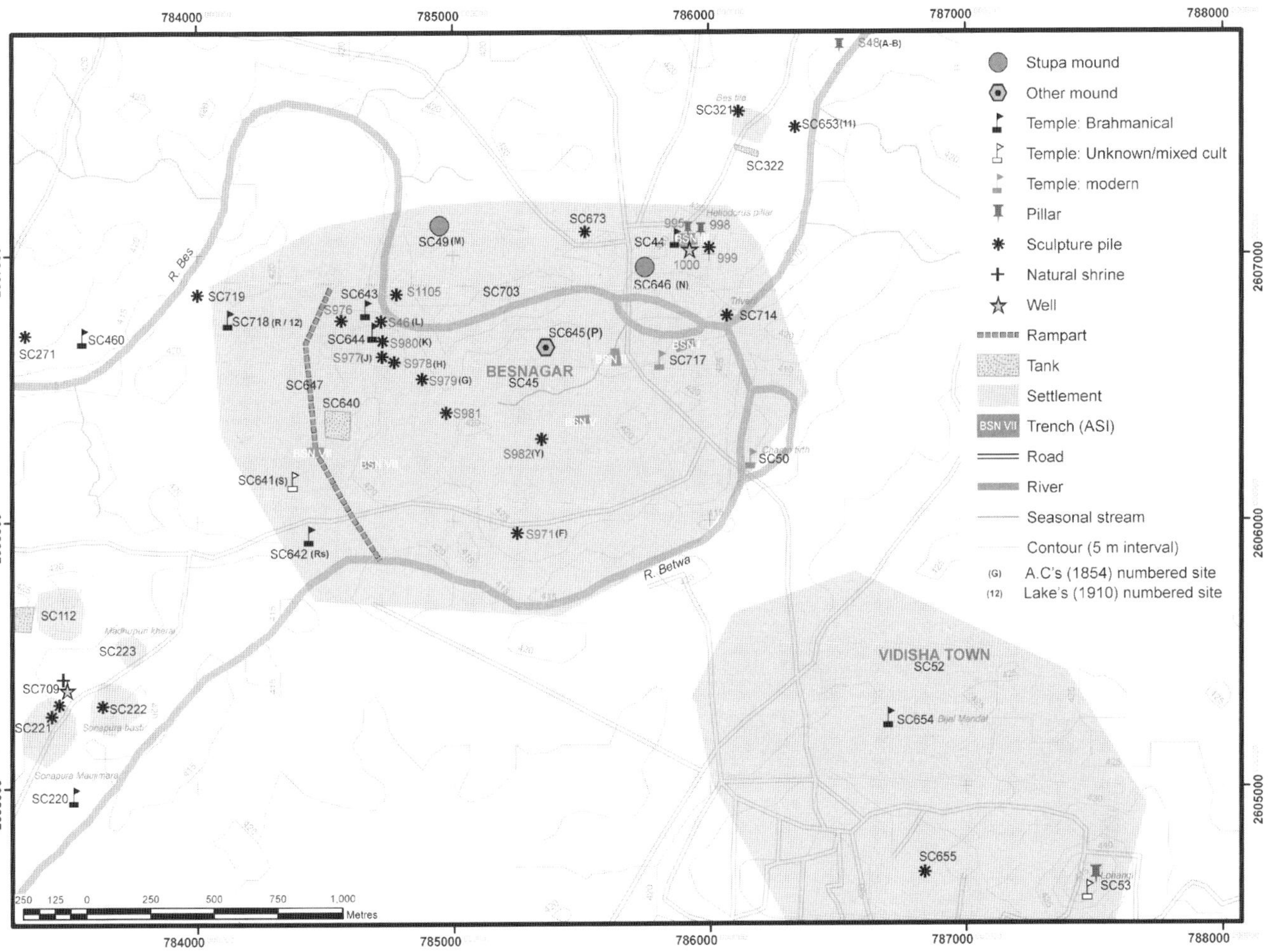

Figure 9.2 Map of ancient Vidisha (including location of trenches)

between Chalcolithic and Iron Age settlement patterns was characterised by a move away from flood-prone, riverside locations. The degree to which the wider settlement patterns in the SSP study area fit with this model is addressed in chapter 13.

Sanchi and its archaeological landscape

As discussed in chapter 11, the quickest way to reach Sanchi from ancient Vidisha is to travel SW from Udayagiri, through an area (Sector 1a) characterised by fertile plains and several ancient settlement mounds, as well as an important 'road-side' stupa site at Marha kherai.[2] This journey is just 8 km, whereas the modern route via Vidisha town is about 4 km longer.

Sanchi hill, which runs from south to north, consists of two small plateaus, separated by a low saddle (Plates 1, 15 colour; Figure 9.3). The Buddhist monuments occupy the higher plateau (height: 520 m) in the south, while the lower plateau (height: 440 m) to the north is occupied by the modern villages of Sanchi and Kanakhera.[3] To avoid confusion, the southern part will henceforth be referred to as 'Sanchi hill'; the northern part, as 'Kanakhera hill'. The site's importance in prehistoric times is attested by a series of rock-shelters, some of which are listed under their modern names on Marshall's (1918, pl. XV) site-plan, immediately above Manchi village and the eastern edge of the lower saddle (Plate 45).[4] Many contain paintings and microlithic tools, datable to the Chalcolithic period or earlier (*IAR* 1978–9, 14). Additional rock-shelters were documented during the SSP on the northern and western edges of the hill. As discussed later, some show signs of adaptation for Buddhist monastic purposes (Plate 49).

The Buddhist remains at Sanchi thus represent a single temporal layer in the site's archaeological trajectory. In spatial terms, too, they do not exist in isolation but form part of a larger, interlinked archaeological landscape, made up of various types of contemporary sites. The remains of a 'large town' were noted by Cunningham (1854, 117) on the lower saddle of the hill between the two villages of Sanchi and Kanakhera (Figure 9.3). No surface pottery was collected during the SSP, due to the unploughed ground conditions, but the fourth-century-AD Kanakhera well-inscription (Sircar 1965, 186–7; Mirashi 1955a; Marshall *et al.*, 1940, 392–3, inscrip. 839), discussed in chapter 5, attests to the settlement's antiquity. Earlier remains were also documented during the SSP, including a second-century-BC bull capital, now lying at the edge of a dried-up pond at the NE foot of the hill (Plate 131; Figure 9.1 colour). As discussed in chapter 11, this may well have come from Sanchi itself, but it is very likely that there was a settlement here during Sanchi's earliest Buddhist history. The remains of an ancient route linking the Sanchi and Kanakherha hills are still visible on the eastern side of the lower saddle.[5] Surviving as several large, worn paving slabs, the route is marked as 'Chikni ghat' on Marshall's (1918, pl. XV) site-plan. Elsewhere, Marshall (1940, 13–14) describes various other

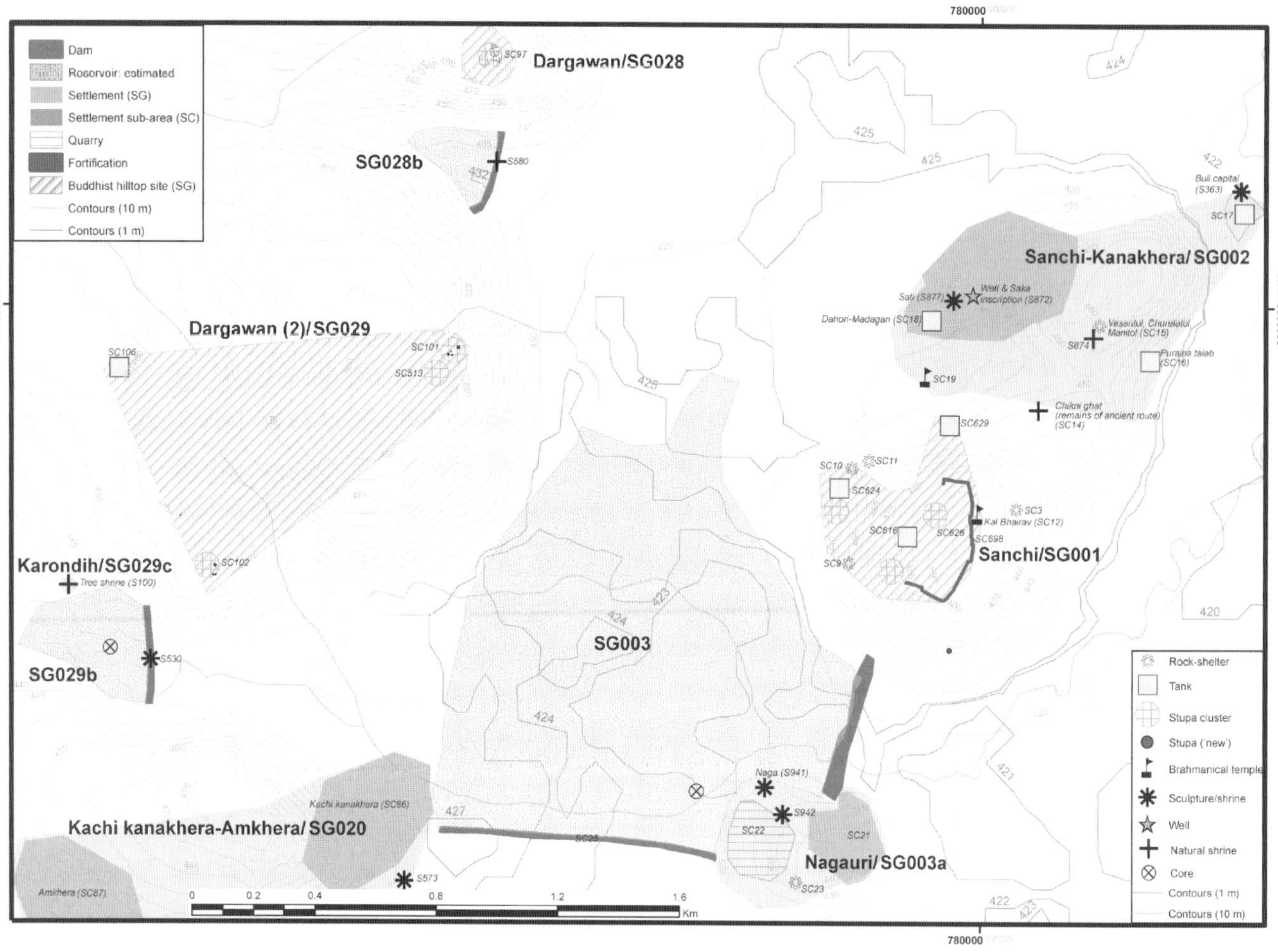

Figure 9.3 Map of Sanchi and wider archaeological landscape (including dam complex below)

approaches, as well as several rainwater storage-tanks at the summit and base of the Sanchi hill (Figure 9.3) (cf. Agarwal and Narain 1997, 170–1).

Nagauri hill (SG003a), approximately 350 m to the south of Sanchi, also has strong prehistoric associations as attested by dense microlithic scatters and a cluster of prehistoric painted rock-shelters on the eastern edge of the hill. However, as discussed further in chapter 11, the hill can also be viewed as forming part of the overall Sanchi complex (Plate 15 colour; Figure 9.3). First, the buff and purple coloured stone used in most of the Buddhist monuments at Sanchi was sourced from the ancient quarry here, signs of which can still be seen all over the hilltop.[6] Secondly, one of the aforementioned rock-shelters[7] contains a historical painted frieze (Figure 9.3) closely related in style to the first-century-AD gateway carvings at Sanchi. Thirdly, as discussed in chapter 12, the first-century-BC *nāga* sculpture on the northern slopes of the hill is also closely related to Buddhist ritual practice. Fourthly, the modern village of Nagauri overlies an ancient settlement,[8] datable by surface pottery to the late centuries BC, in keeping with the chronology of the earliest monuments at Sanchi.

Finally, the archaeological and economic link between Nagauri and Sanchi is further attested by the remains of an ancient embankment which adjoins the two hills (Plate 219; Figure 9.3).[9] A second dam links Nagauri with the hillside settlement at Kacchi Kanakhera in the west. As discussed further in chapter 14, these dams would have formed a reservoir with an area of about 3 km^2, and a storage capacity of about 3.6 m^3 x 10^6, drained by streams running down from the hills to the west. Two smaller reservoirs at Karondih and Dargawan in the shorter valleys to the west were evidently designed to maintain water levels in the main reservoir as part of an upstream irrigation system. Marshall (1940, 13; 1918, pl. XV) gave a basic description of the structure and dimensions of these remains. In the absence of substantiating evidence he offered a rough estimate of about second century BC, in keeping with the second and most prolific phase of building activity at Sanchi and neighbouring Buddhist sites. Detailed archaeological and hydrological analyses of these, and similar dams across the SSP study area, suggest that Marshall's posited dates were roughly correct. The spatial and temporal relationship between the Buddhist monuments on Sanchi hill and the settlements, dams and non-Buddhist cult spots in the immediate vicinity provide a kind of 'microcosmic' model for assessing the dynamics of the 'early-historic complex' throughout the SSP study area.

Phase I (third century BC): establishment of Buddhism at Sanchi

The Phase I monuments

The earliest Buddhist complex at Sanchi was confined to a small area roughly at the centre of the hill and, as far as we know, consisted of three major monuments: i) Stupa 1 (Plate 16), built entirely of brick and at the time devoid of stone facing; ii) the Asokan pillar (Plate 18), immediately to the south of Stupa 1; and iii) a wooden, apsidal shrine (Temple 40), further to the south still.[10] Marshall dated the stupa's brick core (now obscured by subsequent building phases) to c. 269–232 BC, the generally accepted reign of Asoka, on the basis that its surrounding floor shared the same stratigraphic level as the foundations of the Asokan pillar. Further evidence was provided by the 'typical' Mauryan-sized bricks (16 x 10 x 3 in or 41 x 25 x 8 cm) and the polished Chunar sandstone parasol found in the stupa debris. That the original complex extended for some distance towards the east was confirmed by the discovery of a section of the original floor beneath the NW bastion of Building 43, one of the later buildings at Sanchi (Marshall 1940, 60). The pillar bears the Asokan 'schism' edict (Hultzsch 1991; Bechert 1982) and consists of a monolithic spherical shaft of polished Chunar sandstone, part of which is still *in situ*.[11] The crowning element, now stored in the Sanchi Museum, consists of an abacus decorated with the traditional Mauryan pecking-geese and the honey-suckle motif, itself topped by a bell-shaped lotus with cable-necking and four lions seated back-to-back.[12]

The earliest phase of Temple 40 was dated to the same period on the basis of its stratigraphic relationship to the overlying Phase II pillared hall.[13] A small elephant capital retrieved from the debris between the two structural phases was assigned to the Mauryan period, although Marshall (1940, 68, pl. 104i) added that it was 'unlike other sculptures of that period' (Plate 116).[14] What sets it apart is that it is carved from local grey sandstone and, contrary to some accounts, is unpolished. The delicate carving around the face and ears, and the 'ripple' treatment on the neck and chest are also notable features. It is also much smaller than most of the better known Mauryan capitals, for instance the elephant capital from Sankisa (*ASIAR* I, 274–5, pl. xlvi; Irwin 1987) which is about double its size. Further, no other elephant capitals are known at Sanchi, although the elephant is the most frequently depicted animal on the Phase II railing carvings.[15] However, it is important to stress that Marshall's opinion was formed on the basis of a single piece of evidence. A number of recently documented animal capitals from neighbouring sites provide strong evidence that the Temple 40 elephant may in fact belong to the post-Mauryan period. This important, but previously unpublished, body of sculpture, discussed further in chapter 11, includes an elephant capital recently excavated by the ASI during excavations at Satdhara Stupa 1 (Plate 114) and a group of elephant and bull capitals documented at various locations during the SSP (Table 11.1; Figure 9.4; Plate 119). These capitals are associated with a pillar type closely related to the Heliodorus pillar, whose inscription, as discussed at various points in this book, provides a date of c. 115–80 BC and is a major marker for dating Phase II material at Sanchi.

Where are the Phase I monasteries?

The apparent absence of Phase I monastery buildings is usually taken as an indication that despite the site's 'monumental' nature, monks were still living in make-shift structures which no longer survive. It is also possible that the 'adapted' rock-shelters documented during the SSP on the western and southern edges of the hill were used as monastic dwellings. Some of these have platforms built up in front of their entrances; others have clusters of stupas either on the platforms or directly on the overhangs (Plate 49). As discussed in chapter 11, similar 'monastic rock-shelters' occur throughout the study area and are also prominent at the well-known Asokan edict site of Pangurariya in the Narmada valley (Plate 52). Whether they represent a pre-monumental phase of Buddhism or simply a form of 'forest monasticism' which may have continued to co-exist with more communal forms of monasticism during later periods, as was the case in other parts of the Buddhist world such as Sri Lanka and Southeast Asia, can only be assessed through excavation at selected sites. The future excavation of such shelters may also provide the key to determining whether monastic communities were living in the area prior to the Mauryan period. Tentative suggestions to this effect are already hinted at by the very presence of the 'schism' edict at Sanchi. The only two other occurrences of this edict are at Kausambi and Sravasti in the Gangetic valley, which were already important during the lifetime of the Buddha. The fact that it was issued at Sanchi has a number of implications for our understanding of local monastic history. First, Bechert (1982, 67) argues that the received understanding of the schism edict has been distorted by the sectarian rhetoric of later Theravada commentaries which view it as evidence of Asoka's preferential treatment of the Theravada sect and his corresponding condemnation of all others. Bechert argues that the term *nikāya* referred not to 'sect', but rather to a group of monks who shared a common acceptance of the *Vinaya* rules and resided within the same monastic boundary (*sīma*). According to the *Vinaya*, every monk living within the same *sīma* is obliged to attend the *Uposatha* ceremony and, if failing to do so, is guilty of a schism offence (*Mahāvagga* II, 5.1). This particular understanding of the schism edict implies that by the third century BC, the dispersed nature of the monastic landscape had already become a problem at Sanchi. We should thus remain open to the possibility that the earliest permanent monuments at Sanchi represented a formalisation of a pre-existing tradition based on simple adapted rock-shelter dwellings.

Phase II (second to first century BC): the second propagation of Buddhism at Sanchi

Phase II stupas and temples

The most prolific building activity at Sanchi took place during Marshall's Phase II. Existing buildings were renovated and a large number of structures built anew. Stupa 1 was enlarged to almost double its original size, bringing its diameter to 30 m.[1] Stone encasing was added, and a *harmikā* (a square platform enclosed by a *vedikā*) and triple parasol were positioned at its summit. The stupa was surrounded by a ground balustrade (*vedikā*) consisting of upright railing pillars (*stambha*) which rest on a plinth (*ālambana*) and are joined by interlocking horizontal bars (*sūcīka*). The whole railing was surmounted by a curved coping (*uṣṇīṣa*). The railings are undecorated but most bear single-line donative inscriptions, discussed later. Marshall (1940, 27; 1912–13 (I): 22) dated the railings to c. 150 BC on the basis of the relative stratigraphy between the earliest and latest floors around the stupa. A lofty platform (*medhi*) was also built to form an upper *pradakṣiṇāpatha*, reached by a double-stairway (*sopana*). Both this and the stairway were also enclosed by a balustrade, whose upright pillars are carved with simple floral designs, and figural and animal motifs, set within circular and semi-circular medallions. On the basis of these carvings, Marshall assigned the upper railings to a slightly later period than the undecorated balustrade below. The absolute chronology for these railings rests largely on art-historical arguments, which will be presented in the following section. A pavement was built around the stupa which extended for some distance towards the east.[17]

Renovations were also carried out to Temple 40.[18] The original wooden structure was replaced by a stone pillared hall, set on a high platform, and reached by two sets of stairways, set into the main body of the structure (Marshall 1940; 65; *ASIAR* 1913–14 (I): 22; pl. XXIa). Amongst the new additions to the site was Temple 18 to the south of Stupa 1. The stone pillared hall which stands today was built in c. seventh century AD, but the original structure followed an apsidal plan, with a stone wall around the apse (Marshall 1940, pl. 111).[19]

Relic stupas

A number of stupas containing interesting relic deposits were built anew during this period. Stupa 3, immediately NE of Stupa 1, contained the relics of Buddha's chief disciples, Mahamoggalana and Sariputta (Cunningham 1854, 297). Stupa 2, situated half-way down the western side of the hill (Plate 17), contained four steatite reliquaries inscribed with the names of ten Buddhist saints, described as belonging to the Hemavata school (*ibid.*, 291; Willis 2000, 69–5). The significance of this school for understanding the spatial and temporal dynamics of Buddhism in the local landscape is discussed below. Stupa 4, immediately west of Stupa 3, and Stupa 6,[20] to the east of Temple 18, also belong to Phase II. No relics have yet been found in Stupa 1 but, as discussed in chapter 11, textual prescriptions regarding the positioning of relic stupas in relation to the internal hierarchies of the original *saṅgha* suggest that Stupa 1 was intended to house the relics of the Buddha himself (Shaw 2000a).

The Phase II stupas are all considerably smaller than Stupa 1, with average diameters and heights of 15 m and 8 m respectively. Morphologically they are also quite distinct from the mud-brick construction method of Phase I: their cores usually consist of heavy stone blocks interspersed with chippings; their upper terraces built with small rubble, faced with a single course of dressed stone blocks (Marshall 1940, 41).

Carved railings

Stupas 2 and 3 have lower and upper balustrades, although the lower balustrade of Stupa 3 has mostly disappeared. Most of the individual upright railings and crossbars bear donative inscriptions, as well as carved medallions, similar in style and content to the upper railings on Stupa 1. However, there is some stylistic variety between the three sites, with those on Stupa 2 being by far the most adventurous and innovative, and showing evidence for having been carved over a significant period of time. Whilst this complicates the dating of Phase II carvings, in broad terms they share a similar thematic repertoire: wild elephants and lions marauding through the jungle; villagers and forest-dwellers engaged in hunting or battle scenes; and lotus flowers and jungle foliage. The general atmosphere is one of natural abundance and over-flowing fertility. References to specifically 'Buddhist' themes are kept to a minimum.[21] Some of the scenes bring to mind the prehistoric rock-paintings found throughout the neighbouring hills, suggesting that both art-forms were shaped by a similar world view. Generally speaking, there are many common allusions to hunting, men decorated with tattoos, and animal and floral motifs (Plate 21). More specifically, direct comparisons can be made between, for example, the pot-and-flower motif on many of the railings and that in the prehistoric painted rock-shelters at Ahmadpur[22] to the north of Vidisha and, beyond the SSP study area, at Bhimbetka, south of Bhopal.

Dating the Phase II stupas

Since Sanchi provides the primary marker for dating Buddhist remains in the SSP study area, the dating of its Phase II monuments requires further discussion. The relative chronology between Phases I and II has been approached from three main angles, as discussed below.

i) Palaeography

The reliquary inscriptions from Stupa 2 have been dated to the last quarter of the second century BC (Majumdar 1940, 270), largely on the basis of palaeographic links with the Heliodorus pillar inscription at Vidisha, discussed in chapter 5.

ii) Railing carvings

Art-historical analyses of the carved stupa railings have also helped to establish a chronological framework. Marshall (1940, 27; 1912–13 (I): 22) suggested that the undecorated ground railings of Stupa 1 were the earliest, datable to c. 150 BC on the basis of the relative stratigraphy between the earliest and latest floors around Stupa 1.[23] The carved upper balustrade of Stupas 1 and 3, and the ground balustrade of Stupa 2, were positioned somewhat later. Attempts to date these carvings have generally revolved around theories that draw on the element of discontinuity between Mauryan and post-Mauryan art-forms, traditionally characterised as a movement from an 'imperial' courtly idiom to more regionalised styles derived from folk art and carried out by artists more familiar with non-durable media, such as wood or terracotta. This approach is typified by Ray's (1945, 65–81) view that the 'naturalism' of post-Mauryan art was a nationalistic reaction to the foreign-inspired, imperial art of the Mauryan period. After the Mauryan period, everything is referred back to the carvings of Bharhut, whose low-relief and 'flat' features become the defining style of the post-Mauryan age.[24] The dating of Bharhut is far from settled, but nevertheless it generally acts as the base-line against which everything else is measured. For example, the railing carvings of Sanchi Stupa 2 are usually, by virtue of a perceived progression towards three-dimensionality, placed slightly later than Bharhut. Not surprisingly, therefore, much of the disagreement over the dating of Stupa 2 reflects wider differences in opinion regarding the date of Bharhut, itself resting largely on the unresolved dating of the 'Sunga' king Dhanabhuti mentioned in the inscription on the east gateway (Sircar 1965, i, 87). However, if we follow Willis's (2000) postulated date of 150 BC as a general marker for the earliest sculpture at Bharhut, the Sanchi Stupa 2 carvings can be placed in the last quarter of the second century BC.[25]

iii) Post-Mauryan pillars

It is important to temper this framework of analysis with more localised comparisons: the closest reference point is the Heliodorus pillar in Vidisha (Willis 2000, 57; Plate 27), which after the Asokan pillar is the next monument in the SSP study area to be associated with a clearly datable inscription. As discussed in chapters 5 and 6, the pillar inscription, issued by Antialcidas in honour of a temple to Vasudeva, provides a date range of c. 115–80 BC. It is important for dating the Phase II material at Sanchi for two reasons: first, it represents a typical 'post-Mauryan' pillar style which has close equivalents at Sanchi; and secondly, it embodies stylistic features which find direct parallels with carvings on the Phase II stupa railings.

Being one of the key markers of the post-Mauryan style, the Heliodorus pillar should be described in some detail. A number of features such as the bell-shaped lotus capital, the cable necking and the abacus, decorated with pecking-geese and honey-suckle motifs, are direct continuations of the Mauryan pillar idiom (Plate 18). However, there are also a number of new details. First, unlike the circular shafts of the Asokan pillar, the column is divided into three sections: octagonal, sixteen-sided and at the top gently tapering. Secondly, its diameter is less than half that of the Asokan pillar at Sanchi. Another distinguishing feature is the line of sixteen small petals which overlap the upper bulbous end of the 'bell'. This is not found on Asokan lotus capitals. Thirdly, the honey-suckle is carved in lower relief and with less formality than the Asokan examples. Finally, the 'bead-and-lozenge' moulding at the base of the abacus marks a departure from Mauryan conventions. As discussed in chapter 6, it was probably crowned by an image of Garuda (Plate 28), the vehicle of Vasudeva in whose honour the pillar was erected; a fragment of this capital is stored in the Gujari Mahal Museum in Gwalior (Dass 2002–3). Despite these differences, however, it was informed by the preceding Mauryan model. It is thus important to refrain from reproducing the polarised rhetoric of nationalistic art-historical analyses mentioned earlier which tend to emphasise the issue of discontinuity between Mauryan and post-Mauryan art-styles.[26]

The remains of two similar pillars are found at Sanchi itself. The first, a fragment of a 16-sided pillar shaft, lies to the south-west of Stupa 2 (Plate 22; Marshall 1940, 82);[27] its original lotus capital with the distinctive 'petalled' feature, is kept in the Sanchi Museum (Plate 23),[28] together with the crowning lion capital (Plate 24).[29] Although the lion is similar to earlier Asokan examples, such as the Rampurva lion capital, the faceted shaft is identical to the Heliodorus pillar and represents a departure from the smooth surface treatment of the Mauryan pillars. The tradition of placing pillars at the entrances of stupas or temples means that we can be fairly confident that its original location was not far from Stupa 2. It thus provides a *terminus post quem* date for the latter. A second pillar (no. 25) stands *in situ* immediately to the east of Stupa 1 (Plate 25; Marshall 1940, 49).[30] The column is divided into two main sections: a lower octagonal section which rises straight from the ground and an upper, sixteen-sided section. Its lotus capital, now on the ground beside the pillar, follows the general Heliodorus pattern. A novel detail, however, is the cuboid railing

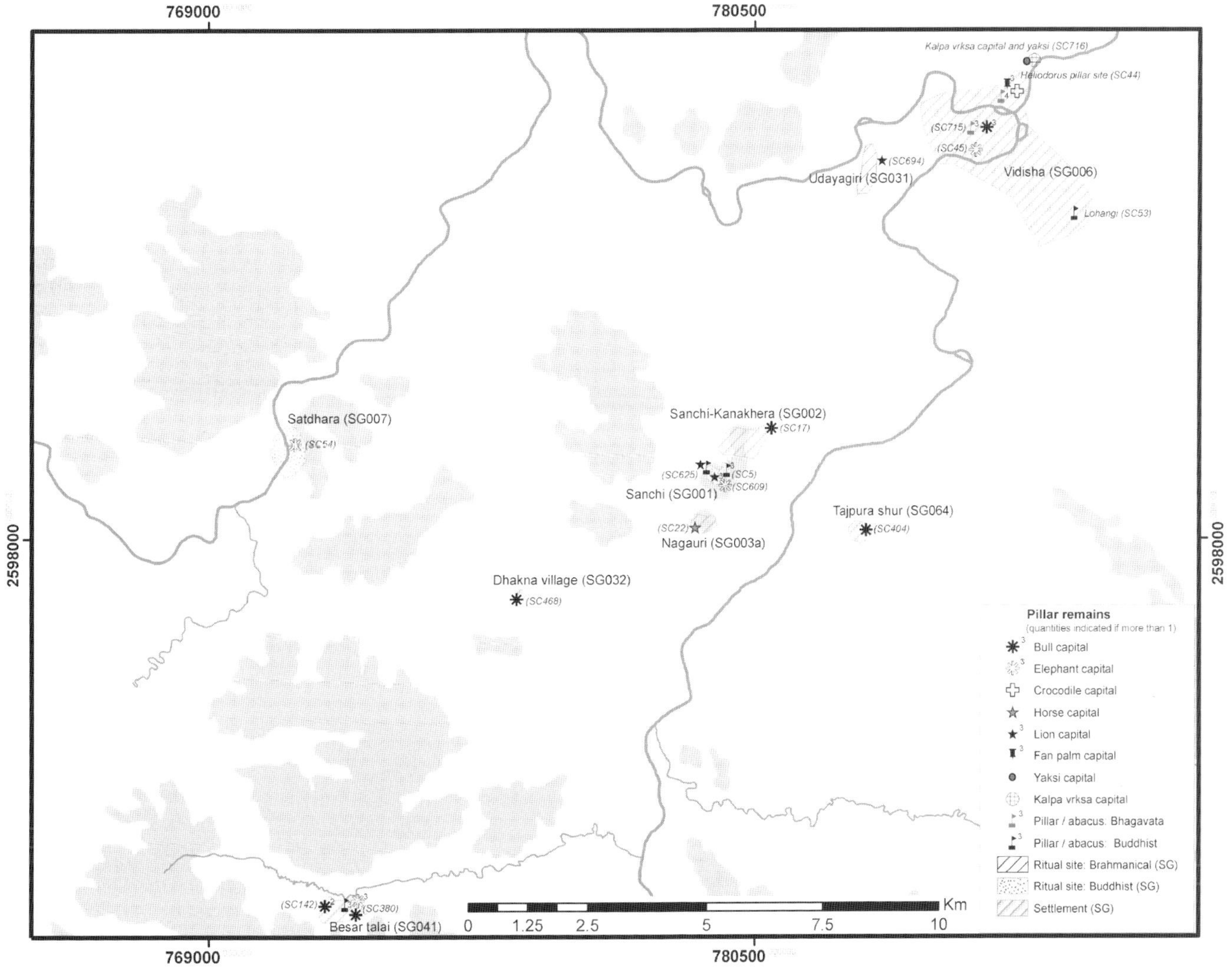

Figure 9.4 Map showing distribution of Phase I–II (c. third to first century BC) pillar remains and capitals in the Sanchi area

decoration on top of the abacus, a feature which, as discussed below, occurs on several other post-Mauryan pillars at Vidisha. Marshall was unclear as to the nature of the crowning capital. However, a second lion capital, now in the Sanchi Museum (Plate 26), is a strong contender as the original crowning piece.[31]

As discussed in chapters 11–12, similar post-Mauryan pillars and capitals occur throughout the SSP study area (Figure 9.4). These include an abacus with a cuboid railing decoration (as on Pillar 25) 1 km to the east of the Heliodorus pillar (Plate 29; Cunningham 1880, 42–3, pl. xiv; Willis 2000, 32).[32] A crocodile capital found nearby probably formed the original crowning element.[33] A closely related pillar and capital (Plate 31) stands in the garden of the Vidisha Museum.[34] Other animal capitals were documented during the SSP, including the bull capital, which, as discussed earlier, was possibly taken from Sanchi but now lies next to a dried-up pond at the eastern foot of Kanakhera hill (Plate 131).

Another link between the Heliodorus pillar and Sanchi Stupa 2 is the band of half-lotus medallions carved immediately above the Heliodorus inscription (Plate 34). As observed by Willis (2000, 57), this is almost identical to some of the more rudimentary carvings on the Stupa 2 railings (Plate 35). Secondly, the honeysuckle and bead-and-lozenge motifs found on the capital and abacus of the Heliodorus pillar and related examples also occur on the stupa railings. A third linking factor, which has not hitherto received scholarly attention, is represented by four separate carvings on the southern and northern gateway railings of Stupa 2 (Plate 33). In each case, the subject matter is a faceted pillar shaft surmounted by a lotus capital with 'overlapping petals' and crowned by a capital of two addorsed lions and elephants.[35] Each of these features occurs on the free-standing post-Mauryan pillars at Sanchi and Vidisha, although the lion/elephant combination is particular to Buddhist settings.[36] These gateway carvings should thus be regarded as fairly accurate representations of the kinds of pillars that artists would have been familiar with at the time.

These comparisons with the Heliodorus pillar and related material provide a strong basis for dating Sanchi's Phase II monuments to between the late second and early first centuries BC. As argued by Willis (2000, 70), the stupa carvings were probably executed over some time, beginning in c. 115 BC with the more rudimentary railing medallions and culminating in c. 80 BC with the more 'mature' and specifically 'Buddhist'-themed gateway carvings; others show evidence for having been re-carved as late as the first century AD (*ibid.*, fig. 25). At the other end of the spectrum are the corner posts of the Stupa 1 staircase, datable to between c. 80 BC and the end of the first century BC (*ibid.*, 57). They show an increased movement away from the Bharhut style and, according to Willis (*ibid.*), represent 'quiet harbingers of the monumental gates to which they are adjacent'.

iv) Carved railings at the other 'Bhilsa Tope' sites

The carved railings at Satdhara, Sonari, Morel khurd and Andher also fit within this broad chronological framework, although those at Andher are the most straightforward to date: only Stupa 1 has a balustrade which, despite the lack of conservation work there, is still largely *in situ* (Plates 65, 102). The style and content of the railing medallions are closely related, and sometimes identical, to the simple floral rosaces and animal motifs at Sanchi Stupa 2 (Willis, 2000, figs. 27–9). At Sonari, both Stupas 1 and 2 were equipped with balustrades, but only very few fragmentary pieces have survived. Willis (2000, 58–9, figs. 84 and 90) notes that the lotus rosaces from Stupa 2 are closer to the simple variety at Sanchi, whilst those on Stupa 1 are more akin to the deeply cut carvings on the staircase of Sanchi, Stupa 1. Similarly, the lotus meander design on the coping stone from Sonari, Stupa 1 (Plate 101) is described as more 'complex' than its counterpart at Sanchi, Stupa 1. Willis (2000, 57) therefore positions the former in the beginning to mid-first century BC. However, given the fragmentary and incomplete nature of the remains, it is difficult to interpret these differences in purely temporal terms. Although Morel khurd is one of the largest Buddhist sites in the area, only one or two of the stupas there appear to have had balustrades. Those railings which survive at the site itself all bear lotus medallion carvings (Willis 2000, figs. 101–2, 108).[37] These follow the 'complex' pattern and are carved in relatively deep relief. Willis (*ibid.*) thus positions them towards the end of the first century BC, in keeping with some of the stairway carvings on Sanchi, Stupa 1.

Summary

In the light of the above, the approach taken in the SSP was to break down Marshall's Phase II into an 'early' (IIa: late second to mid-first century BC) and 'late' (IIb: late first century BC to early first century AD) phase. However, it is important to acknowledge that a number of different carving styles could have co-existed at the same time: whilst recognising regional and temporal trends, one should not lose sight of individual tastes and skills. As suggested by Willis (*ibid.*, 56), the variety in carving style and subject matter may have more to do with the varying abilities and stylistic preferences of the artists who carved them than with the unilinear unfolding of a regional style. The differences between carving styles at different sites may also reflect varying levels of patronage: Satdhara is the only site, apart from Sanchi, whose surviving railings bear donative inscriptions. More remote sites, or those with less generous endowments, would have had to make do with less elaborate carvings. Finally, just because artists were carving in low relief does not mean that they were incapable of three-dimensionality. We already know, from the pillars and capitals discussed above, that three-dimensional sculpture was being produced at the same time as the lower relief carvings on the stupa railings. Whilst the pillars at Sanchi and Vidisha represent a distinctive 'post-Mauryan' style, they nevertheless embody elements of the older Mauryan repertoire. The railing carvings and the pillars were most probably produced by two different sets of craftsmen. But this is not to suggest that both styles did not come together. This is best exemplified by the lotus medallions on the Heliodorus pillar. Whilst these provide a useful marker for dating the more rudimentary railing carvings at Sanchi, it would seem to be a circular argument to use these carvings as a baseline for dating others according to their relative 'complexity' or depth of relief.

Phase II monasteries and dwellings

Platformed monasteries

Also datable to Phase II is Building 8, a lofty platform situated at the SW corner of the circuit wall (Figure 9.1 colour; Plate 76). It consists of a solid square plinth, with a stairway cut into its eastern face. Due to its similarity to the plinth and stairway of Temple 40, Marshall dated it to c. second century BC (Marshall 1940, 68; 1912–13 (I), 19). Similar platforms, described in chapter 11, occur at Satdhara, Sonari, Morel khurd and Andher as well as several of the newly discovered Buddhist sites documented during the SSP (Plates 78–87; Figure 11.24). Apart from the Andher example, which is more ruined than the others, all of the 'Bhilsa Tope' platforms have stairways cut into their main plinth. Their function caused both Marshall (*ibid.*) and Cunningham (1854, 328) some confusion. Both suggested that they were the bases for temples, a supposition informed largely by the remains of a temple on the summit of the Morel khurd platform (Plate 82). These ruins, however, date to at least the seventh century AD, i.e. eight hundred years after the earliest remains at these sites.[38] The later addition of a temple, absent at the other sites, cannot be taken as a useful guide to the original function of these structures. As argued in chapter 11, these platforms were more likely to have formed the bases for monastery buildings. All the platforms are covered with accumulations of crumbling red brick, indicating that the upper walls were once brick-built with, most probably, timber superstructures. Narrative reliefs at Sanchi and other early sites leave no doubt that many prominent buildings in ancient India were raised on poles or large platforms with the upper structure made of wood and other perishable materials.[39] In later years, temples continued to be built on large platforms and this probably inspired the medieval additions to Morel khurd. After about the eighth century AD, the construction of high, vertically orientated monasteries, however, was restricted to Nepal and other parts of the Himalayas. The perpetuation of old ideas in remote areas suggests that the towering, largely wooden monasteries of the Himalayas may also find their ultimate origin in these early platformed buildings, a subject which merits further exploration.

Many of the rock-cut monasteries in the Deccan are also placed on high rock-cut plinths. Cave 4 at Pitalkhora, for example, is reached by a covered flight of steps cut into the high plinth and guarded by two *dvārapāla*s and a *nāga* (Plate 77). The surmounting monastery, datable on the basis of associated inscriptions to the mid-second century BC (Mitra 1971, 173; *IAR* 1957–8, 65–6), consists of a series of cells set around a courtyard. Although courtyard monasteries are not considered to have made an appearance at Sanchi until the late or post-Gupta period, it is not unlikely that the platforms at Sanchi and neighbouring sites were surmounted by structures following a similar plan.

Monasteries and monasticism in Phase II

As discussed in chapter 11, this hitherto unrecognised form of monastery is part of a larger body of evidence documented during the SSP for the existence of permanent monasteries during this phase. Including simple single- and double-roomed structures, this evidence presents a direct challenge to received theories regarding the late development of institutionalised monasticism in central India, itself based on the generally accepted chronology of the courtyard type of monastery. The latter is not thought to have reached Sanchi until the Gupta period at the earliest, the implication being that monks in preceding periods were all living in makeshift, semi-permanent structures.

This line of reasoning is predicated on a set of normative correlations between architectural and social order, that is, that the courtyard type of monastery, and no other, is seen as embodying the required level of architectural refinement expected of a 'domesticated' *saṅgha*. There are two main problems with this line of reasoning. The first is that, until recently, the study of 'domestication' has rested largely on the issue of the *saṅgha*'s adoption of permanent dwellings, rather than on forms of exchange with local populations. Consequently, the possibility that the *saṅgha* may have reached a fully religious social status without actually having settled down is often overlooked. The second major problem is that by assuming a universal (albeit unspecified) measure of spatial order, no other architectural form apart from the quadrangular monastery type has figured in these debates. For example, rock-shelters or even rock-cut monasteries are usually seen as evidence of an 'undomesticated' *saṅgha*. The tendency to look for causal linkages between social and organisational order is typified by Schopen's (1994b, 547) statement that 'planned and ordered space implies a planned, ordered and settled community'. This kind of approach is reminiscent of the normative structuralist spatial models of the 1980s, discussed in chapter 7; it also reflects wider problems regarding the lack of coordination between textual and archaeological approaches to religious history, and the kinds of inaccuracies that can creep in through cross-disciplinary interpretation.

While challenging the received chronology of monastic architectural development, it seems natural to assume some variety in the types of accommodation available to monks in all periods. For example, some monks would have resided in simple 'adapted' rock-shelters, as represented by the group of 'monastic rock-shelters' on the western and southern edge of Sanchi hill. One has small stupa platforms (Plate 49) built directly on top of the overhang; another has a group of stupas immediately in front of the shelter.[40] Together with similar examples from other Buddhist sites described in chapter 11, this evidence is important for showing that even within a single Buddhist complex, the adoption of permanent monasteries was not an overarching or unilinear process.

Phase III (first to third century AD)

The four elaborately carved gateways (*toraṇa*) at each of the cardinal directions of Stupa 1 date to this period (Plate 16). The southern gateway is assignable to c. AD 25 on the basis of the Satakarni inscription of the Satavahana dynasty on its upper architrave.[41] Both the style and content of the carved panels represent a major departure from the Phase II railing carvings. Much of the compartmentalised rigidity has been replaced by an expansive fluidity, and static medallions have given way to narrative panels. Finally, the largely decorative tone of the Phase II carvings has been replaced by specifically 'Buddhist' themes, largely drawn from the *Jātaka* tales. Interestingly, these are no longer labelled as in the case of the earlier carvings at Bharhut, indicating a higher level of local familiarity with the Buddhist tradition. The whole universe has now become ordered and 'landscaped' according to the Buddhist scheme of things. Animals are no longer shown rampaging wildly through the jungle, but rather stand in a docile manner before aniconic symbols of the *dharma*, such as trees set within square railings. Tamed and ordered, the latter form a striking contrast to the overflowing aquatic foliage of Stupa 2. Men and women have been transformed from jungle-dwellers, hunters and tree-spirits into well turned-out urbanites; women are no longer entwined around wild creepers, but rather peek out of city palaces or bow in obeisance before objects of Buddhist ritual. This may reflect the wider process, discussed by Ali (1998), of the increasing preoccupation with 'courtly' culture during this period. As discussed in chapter 6, the proliferation of specifically 'Buddhist' themes, and narratives set in the Gangetic valley, may also reflect the consolidation of the process of Buddhist propagation and the creation of a unified pan-Indian Buddhist geography.

The later part of Marshall's Phase III is almost completely absent at Sanchi, with no structures or locally produced sculptures clearly datable to the Kusana period. A number of Bodhisattva and Buddha images were retrieved from the relic chambers of the post-Gupta stupas to the south of Stupa 1, but the majority appear to be imports from the Mathura region. These include a seated Bodhisattva figure whose inscription, written in Kusana Brahmi and dated to the year 28, records a gift during the reign of king Vasiska (Marshall *et al.*, 1940, I, 387–8; III, pl. 124b; inscrip. 828; Hamid *et al.*, 1922, no. A82); following recent revisions of the Kusana era (Willis 1999/2000, 269–70), this can now be viewed as year 128 (c. AD 253–4). Three other images carved from Mathura sandstone have been found at Sanchi. One of these, a pedestal surmounted by the feet of a standing Buddha and with the lower part of an attendant figure to his right, bears an inscription dated to the year 22 (c. AD 148) and mentions a king called Vaskusana, thought to be a member of the Kusana dynasty (Marshall *et al.*, 1940, I, 386; III, pl. 105c; inscrip. 829; Hamid *et. al.*, 1922, no. A83). The other two Mathura sandstone images were found in Gupta or post-Gupta stupas: i) a broken pedestal with part of the left, sandal-clad foot of a standing image retrieved from the relic chamber of Stupa 12 (Marshall 1940, I, 47; III, pl. 124d; Hamid *et al.*, 1911, no. A84). It bears an inscription in Kusana Brahmi (no. 830) mentioning a dedication from the daughter of an individual named Visakula; ii) a seated Bodhisattva image found in the relic chamber of Stupa 14 (Marshall 1940, I, 47; III, pl. 105b; Hamid *et al.*, 1922, no. 19). The fact that these images were placed in stupas several hundred years after their original manufacture reflects the changing focus of the relic cult during later periods (Willis, forthcoming b).

The torso of another Mathura sandstone Buddha image has also been reported at nearby Gulgaon (*ASIAR* 1972-3, pl. XLIV).[42] This may have been taken from Sanchi but could equally have originated from one of the hilltop Buddhist sites in the western sector. As discussed in chapter 11, despite the absence of locally produced sculpture of this period at Sanchi itself, significant quantities of such material were documented during the SSP in the surrounding countryside. This led to the introduction of an extra sub-phase (IIIb) in order to distinguish between the Satavahana and Kusana sculptural styles, whilst at the same time keeping in mind earlier discussions in chapter 5 regarding the lack of evidence for the actual presence of the Kusana dynasty in the Sanchi area.

Phase IV (fourth to sixth century AD)

Phase IV stupas

Marshall's Phase IV, which corresponds to the Gupta period, saw the construction of several new temples to the south of Stupa 1. These included Temple 17, renowned as the earliest surviving free-standing temple in India, and Temple 9, slightly further to the east; both are datable to c. AD 400 (Williams 1982, 38–9). The discovery of a number of Gupta pilasters reincorporated into, or buried beneath, later structures to the east of Stupa 1 attest to additional temples in this area.[43]

A number of stupas were also built anew during this period. Stupas 28 and 29, just to the west of Temple 31, belong to c. sixth century AD. Others such as Stupas 4 and 5 just behind Stupa 3, Stupa 7 on the SW corner of the plateau and a cluster of stupas (nos. 11, 12, 13, 14 and 16) immediately to the south of Stupa 1 may be as late as c. seventh century AD (Plate 19). However, all belong to a single stupa category, easily distinguishable from the earlier Phase II examples; this is an important point when it comes to dating newly discovered stupas in the field. All are set on circular or square platforms, sometimes with stone footings at their base (average dimensions: 9 x 9 m) (Plate 19). They are considerably smaller than their Phase II counterparts and are all devoid of balustrades. The method of construction is also quite distinct, with rubble-and-earth cores faced with neat, narrow courses of well-dressed masonry blocks (Marshall 1940, 46). Further, as just noted, the retrieval of older images and reliquaries from some of these stupas attests to a shift in the nature of relic deposits during this period.[44]

Phase IV sculpture

A notable development during the Gupta period is the appearance of locally produced, free-standing Buddha and Bodhisattva images, such as the four seated Buddhas placed within the *pradakṣiṇāpatha* of Stupa 1 at each of its entrances. A terminal date for these images is provided by a railing inscription dated to the Gupta year 131 (AD 450–1) which records the donation of a lamp 'in the place of the four Buddhas' (Fleet *CII*, III, 29–34; Marshall 1940, 389–90; inscrip. 834), although on stylistic grounds they are usually assigned to a slightly earlier period of c. AD 435 (Williams 1982, 86).[45] A large number of contemporary Buddha images are stored in the Sanchi Museum (Hamid *et al.*, 1922), while the first locally produced Mahayana images also appear during this period. The Vajrapani image, now stored in the Sanchi Museum, originally stood atop the Gupta pillar (no. 35) to the north of Stupa 1(*ibid.*, 391, pl. 108b).[46] The two Padmapani (Avalokitesvara) images, also in the Sanchi Museum, would have originally stood a little to the north of the northern gateway of Stupa 1 (Plate 36; Figure 9.1 colour).[47] This may be deduced from Cunningham's (1854, 200) description of 'two colossal figures, probably of porters or gateway attendants, at the head of steps … which lead past no. 3 stupa to the road leading to Sanchi village'.[48] Their find-spot, just to the south of the main entrance to the modern ASI complex, is marked on Cunningham's map (*ibid.*, pl. IV). Such a prominent location is evidence of the growing influence of Mahayana during this period.

Phase V (seventh to eighth century AD)

Phase V stupas and temples

The 'post-Gupta' period is also one of major building activity, which in itself provides additional grounds for challenging the problematic theories of post-Gupta 'urban decay' discussed in chapter 2. A new portico was added to Temple 40, while Temple 18 was converted from an apsidal shrine to an elegant pillared hall.[49] The carved doorway decorated with images of Ganga and Yamuna, is assignable to the same period.[50]

As already mentioned, some of the smaller stupas to the south of Stupa 1 also date to this period. However, most of the Phase V monuments are concentrated in the eastern and southern zones. Most of the former are obscured by the 5.3 m-high retaining platform, built in the tenth century AD, evidently to hold up what by this time had become a pile of architectural debris (Marshall 1940, 60).[51] However, some of these monuments still protrude from the base of the platform (Plate 19), such as Building nos. 19, 20 and 22, possibly temples,[52] and no. 21, an ancient cobblestone road. That the larger complex to which these structures belonged extended as far as the eastern edge of the hill is confirmed by the discovery of seventh-century-AD temple remains below Monasteries 46 and 78 (*ibid.*, 76–7). The remains of a seventh-century-AD monastery were also revealed beneath Building 43. The plinth of Temple 31, to the NE of Stupa 1, is the only surviving element of the original Phase V complex (*ibid.*, 58). The superstructure was built during the tenth century AD, but parts of the original temple, such as a number of seventh-century pilasters, can still be seen inside; two of the pilasters were taken from an earlier Gupta-period temple (Plate 207; Williams 1986, 49, pl. 40;). The enshrined Buddha image also belongs to the earlier structure (*ibid.*, pl. 114e; 115a).

Phase V monasteries

The area to the south of Temple 40 consists almost entirely of seventh-century-AD monastery buildings. Three of these (nos. 36, 37 and 38) were excavated during Marshall's time (1940, 68). A number of additional monasteries were revealed during ASI excavations carried out between 1993 and 2003 (*IAR* 1996–7, 65; *IAR* 1997–8, 103–5). All are of the courtyard type, with small cells lining the inner walls. Only the lower courses of rough and uneven dry stone masonry survive. However, the remains of a stairway in Monastery 36 attest to an upper storey, possibly of wood or mud (*ibid.*, 68–9). Excavated finds of defence-related objects (e.g. iron arrow-heads, daggers, spear-heads, javelin, helmet, etc.) and agricultural implements (e.g. axe and ploughshare) have led to the suggestion that these structures were not monasteries, but rather secular buildings for use by non-monastic sections of society (Ota and Khamari 2006, 330–1). Although this view may in part by influenced by a literal reading of canonical rules which prohibit the monks' involvement in worldly activities, it is possible that some of these buildings were used for storing tools and weapons, and that they were overseen by lay employees such as the *ārāmika*, a term that embodies a wide range of staff from slaves to manual labourers including those working in the monastery fields (Gunawardana 1979, 97–8; Gombrich 1998, 101–2). The role of the *ārāmika* and other non-monastic employees such as *kappiyakāraka* and Parivahana are discussed further in chapters 2 and 15.

Similar confusion surrounds the function and date of the courtyard monastery (no. 51) on the lower ledge to the west of Stupa 1 (Plate 88). Largely on account of the large quantities of precious stones and other valuables retrieved from beneath the structure, it was pronounced by the excavator (Hamid 1940) as the 'monastery of Queen Devī', mentioned in the Sri Lankan chronicles. Further suggestions of a Mauryan date were provided by the presence of several 'Mauryan'-sized bricks (16 x 10 x 3 in or 40 x 25 x 8 cm). In subsequent years, however, such remains have come to be viewed as evidence that despite canonical prohibitions, the *saṅgha* did in fact involve itself in commercial activities. In Hamid's time, when the economic underpinnings of Buddhist monasticism were less recognised by scholars of Buddhist history, the traditional association between precious stones and royalty would have been a more plausible explanation. Further, other scholars (Mitra 1996, 17) argue that the structure cannot be earlier than c. seventh century AD, in keeping with the dating of the aforementioned 'monasteries' in the southern part of the site, and the received chronology of courtyard monasteries in central India, discussed in chapter 10.[53] Mitra (*ibid.*) argues that the 'Mauryan' bricks described by Hamid were probably taken from an older structure, while most of the bricks are of the small variety commonly used in later structures.

Phase VI (ninth to twelfth century AD)

The site continued to undergo restoration and renewed construction until the tenth or eleventh century AD. The Phase VI buildings are largely confined to the summit of the retaining platform to the east of Stupa 1, which, as mentioned earlier, appears to have been built over ruined buildings of the preceding phase. The high boundary wall which runs around the eastern and southern edge of the hill belongs to the same period.[54] The eastern platform is dominated by a large, interconnected courtyard monastery complex (nos. 46 and 47), surrounded by a number of small temples (nos. 44 and 32).

Perched at the easternmost edge of the site, in the forecourt of the monastery complex, is Temple 45, possibly built at a slightly earlier date. Its main components are a central *garbagṛha*, the central doorway carved with figures of Ganga and Yamuna; a verandah; and two side shrines. Only part of the surmounting *śikhara* is still standing, but the original *āmlaka*, *bhūmiāmlaka*s and a *kalaśa* lie nearby. The central Buddha image was originally part of a triad, along with Avalokitesvara and Maitreya (Irwin 1972).[55] Additional Mahayana deities include carvings of Pancika and Manibhadra on the doorway, and an image of Manjusri on the rear southern face of the temple.[56]

Marshall divided the temple into two major phases. However, subsequent studies show it to be the result of a single architectural programme executed in the Pratihara style of the late ninth century AD (Willis 2000, 76–7). Insights into its original appearance prior to the destruction of the *śikhara* are provided by the more-or-less intact Bajramath temple at Gyaraspur. Both temples are datable to the late ninth century AD on the basis of the inscription (now in Gujari Mahal, Gwalior) from the Car Khamba, Gyaraspur, dated to VS 936 (AD 879–80) (*ibid.*; 1997, pls. 122–4). The latter structure is in a highly ruinous state, but can be linked with the other two temples by lotus moulding and floral scrolls on the lower plinth.[57]

The other major monument on the eastern platform is Building 43, a cruciform structure with circular bastions at each of its four corners. Marshall (1940, 394) considered it to be one of the latest structures at Sanchi, assigning it to c. tenth to eleventh century AD. A fragmentary inscription found during excavations refers to the construction of a monastery at Botasriparvatta (the medieval name for Sanchi) in honour of Lokanath and Vajrapani (*ibid.*, inscrip. 842). Marshall dated it on palaeographical grounds to the end of the seventh century AD, but the possible linkages, already referred to, between Vappakadeva, mentioned in the inscription, and Vopparaja of the Maladevi inscription in Gyaraspur provide a more likely date of c. 836–85 AD (Willis, 2000, 78).[58] Marshall suggested that Building 43 formed the base of a stupa or shrine (Marshall, *ASIAR*, 1912–13 (I): 21). However, given its apparent military overtones, many questions remain regarding its true rationale and function.

As discussed in chapter 11, structures with a similarly military appearance were documented at other Buddhist sites during the SSP. At Bighan, to the north of Udayagiri, for example, one of the Phase II stupas is set within a quadrangular enclosure with circular towers at each of its four corners.[59] If it is contemporary to the stupa, then it is significantly earlier than Building 43 at Sanchi. Some of the boundary walls that occur at Buddhist sites throughout the study area are fitted with similar towers; these walls are similar to the tenth-century example at Sanchi, but may date to earlier periods. Further, the Phase II monastery platform at Morel khurd has towers at each of its four corners. Finally, many of the hills on which Buddhist sites in the area are situated are themselves naturally fortified (Plate 2). The possible rationale behind this element of fortification will be discussed, along with parallels from other parts of north India, in chapter 11. In particular, it will be suggested that the increasingly fortified aspect of Buddhist sites may be connected with the underlying factors that led to the ultimate downfall of Buddhism in central India.

Buddhist remains from Sanchi in nearby villages

A number of Buddhist remains now stored in neighbouring villages, but possibly originating from Sanchi, were also documented during the SSP. These include a fifth-century-AD votive stupa, carved with an image of Manjusri, now being worshipped as a Siva *liṅga*, in a small rock-shelter shrine above Manchi village on the eastern slopes of Sanchi hill.[60] A fragment of a Phase II stupa railing, carved on the obverse with a goddess, is currently stored on a platform in Nonakhera village, 2 km to the NE of Sanchi, on the western bank of the River Betwa.[61] Thirdly, a fragment of a *śalabanjika* image, very similar to those on the Phase III Stupa 1 gateways, is currently stored outside the modern temple at Bilori, a large village 1 km to the south of Nagauri (Plate 41).[62] It is probably from Sanchi, due to its similarity to the *śalabanjika* figures on the first-century-AD gateways there (Plate 16). Finally, as mentioned earlier, the torso of a Mathura sandstone Buddha image, whose whereabouts are no longer known, has been reported at Gulgaon, 4 km NW of Sanchi (*ASIAR* 1972–3, pl. XLIV).

The 'non-Buddhist' elements of the site

In addition to the Buddhist remains discussed above, reference should also be made to a number of non-Buddhist elements both within and immediately outside Sanchi's formal ASI boundaries. The earliest examples date to c. first century BC and the latest to the twelfth century AD, during which time their ritual context undergoes significant transformations. This material is thus central for assessing the theories discussed in chapter 6, regarding the *saṅgha*'s changing relationship to its wider multi-layered ritual landscape.

Nāgas and yakṣas

As discussed in chapters 6 and 12, prior to the Gupta period there is no archaeological evidence for any independent, non-Buddhist cultic activity within the actual monastic complex at Sanchi. Both *nāga*s and *yakṣa*s, ancient place-bound deities associated with fertility and the natural elements, *do* occur on the Phase II railing carvings, but not in any independent capacity. Their depiction usually takes place within the context of narratives, i.e. following the story of Mucalinda, the serpent king who protected Buddha from the storm during his quest for Enlightenment.

By contrast, there are no free-standing *nāga* sculptures at Sanchi until the Gupta period; all the earlier examples are situated outside the main compound. The earliest such sculptures in the area date to c. 50 BC, and include a *nāga-nāginī* couple on Nagauri hill immediately to the south of Sanchi, whose monuments it overlooks. Since it was first described by Marshall (1940, 244), the *nāginī* has been stolen, but the *nāga* (Plate 139) remains *in situ*. Its stylistic treatment and position within the wider archaeological and ritual landscape are discussed in chapter 12. In particular, I will argue that despite the geographical dislocation between the two sites, the *nāga* was not necessarily external to Buddhist practice. The main justification for this view is that it is situated within a bounded 'early historic complex' which comprises several economically and socially interlinked 'Site Groups': the Buddhist remains on Sanchi hill, the settlement and quarry remains at Nagauri, and the ancient reservoir remains between the two hills. The *nāga*'s proximity to the last conforms to Gupta-period textual accounts from the Gangetic valley that *nāga*s were propitiated by Buddhist monks because of their connection with the powers of fertility and agriculture.

The appearance of *nāga* sculptures at Sanchi itself during the Gupta period marks an obvious change in relationships and reflects the *saṅgha*'s public acceptance of *nāga* worship as an integral component of Buddhist practice. Two *nāga*s, now stored in the Sanchi Museum (Plate 161),[63] are assignable on stylistic grounds to the beginning of the fifth century AD (Williams 1976, 174, n. 5). These sculptures form part of a larger body of Gupta-period *nāga*s which display a marked Visnuisation in terms of apparel and ornamentation. The full significance of this iconographic shift for discussions of religious change is discussed in chapter 12. From Maisey's descriptions (1892, 76), it seems likely that one of the Sanchi *nāga*s originally formed a pair with the *nāginī* that stands outside Temple 31 (Plate 162).[64] This assumption may be confirmed by early photographs showing a *nāga* lying amongst a pile of sculptures outside Temple 31.[65] As Marshall (1940, 59) points out, the tenon at the base of the *nāginī* shows that it was originally set in a plinth and was most probably moved to its present location in the tenth century AD. Maisey (1892, 76) writes that the second *nāga* was discovered on the summit of the tenth-century-AD platform to the east of Stupa 1 and must therefore have been taken from elsewhere on the site. Insights into the original provenance of these images are provided by James Cunningham's (1847, 746) description that 'in some [temples] the halo which usually invests the head is carved to resemble the expanded hood of snakes'. Earlier in 1802, Fell (reprint 1834, 492) described an image of 'Parsvanath' with 'five expanded serpent hoods' in one of the shrines to the east of Stupa 1.[66] Given Fell's lack of familiarity with Indian iconography, one may assume that he was referring to one of the *nāga*s in question. The temple(s) described by Fell and Cunningham must have been destroyed during the early 'excavations' at the site, following which at least one of the *nāga*s was moved to the eastern platform, where it was found by Maisey.[67] As discussed in chapter 11, the suggestion that *nāga*s were worshipped in independent temples at Sanchi accords with textual and archaeological evidence from other parts of India that during the Gupta period *nāga* worship had become an integral part of Buddhist practice, because the perceived ability of serpents to ensure adequate rainfall was in keeping with the *saṅgha*'s interest in agricultural production.

In addition to *nāga*s, several *yakṣa*s were also incorporated into the main monastic complex during the Gupta period. Two are presently stored on the retaining wall to the east of Sanchi

(Plate 38);[68] another three are now in the Sanchi Museum (Plate 39).[69] Their original provenance is unknown, but taken together with the *nāga* images discussed above, they provide evidence of the *saṅgha*'s adoption of more active policies of 'cultic integration' than were evident in earlier periods. The possible rationale behind this apparent shift in policy so long after the establishment of Buddhism, and its impact on wider theories of religious change, will be discussed in chapter 11.

Brahmanical and Jain remains

While the incorporation of non-Buddhist deities during the Gupta period was the result of an active decision on the part of the *saṅgha*, the appearance of Brahmanical sculptural and architectural between the eighth and twelfth centuries AD is suggestive of quite a different process. Many of these are presently stored in the Sanchi Museum (Rao 1994; Hamid *et al.*, 1922). No details regarding original provenance are provided in existing publications (*ibid.*), but most of these sculptures are likely to have originated from one of two ruined temples situated on the lower slopes of Sanchi hill. The first is perched at the eastern edge of the hill, immediately below the boundary wall and Temple 45.[70] Today the site is occupied by a modern temple and a Kal Bhairav shrine set into the side of a small rock-shelter, but the existence of a tenth-century Saiva temple is attested by a large Nandi sculpture in the adjoining shelter (Plate 217). A number of pilasters are incorporated into the modern temple, and others are strewn at various points over the hillside. At the northern foot of Sanchi hill, just to the east of the Government Rest House, is the base of a tenth-century-AD temple, together with various architectural fragments.[71] As shown in chapter 12, a radical increase in Brahmanical temple construction during the Gupta period reaches an overall climax between the ninth and tenth centuries AD. Although both of the temples at Sanchi are situated outside the formal boundaries of the monastic complex, they nevertheless form part of a wider body of evidence attesting to the increasing 'Brahmanisation' of the landscape and the accompanying decline of Buddhism.

There is also evidence for a growing Jain influence in the area from Phase VI onwards. At Sanchi, the construction of a large Jain temple complex sometime between the eleventh and twelfth centuries AD is attested by a number of white sandstone sculptures, stored on the verandah of the Sanchi Archaeological Museum. Their exact provenance is not certain, but Prinsep's (1837, 453) description of 'beautiful Jain temples' on a neighbouring hill to Sanchi, makes Nagauri hill the most likely contender.[72]

Conclusion

In this chapter, the chronological sequences at Sanchi and Vidisha have been described, together with suggested revisions discussed further in chapter 10, based on recent developments in art-historical scholarship. The material at Sanchi also provides a starting point for revisiting debates regarding the history and chronology of monasticism based on evidence for monastic dwellings in the SSP area. Finally, the relationship between Sanchi's Buddhist monuments and aspects of the immediate archaeological landscape, including habitational, ritual and agrarian sites, provides a microcosmic model for assessing spatial and temporal patterns throughout the SSP study area as a whole. The primary hypothesis is that these inter-Site Group relationships, when taken together, provide an exemplar for the internal dynamics of the typical 'early-historic complex'. The rest of this study is aimed at assessing this hypothesis by documenting Buddhist sites throughout the wider study area and relating these sites to other aspects of the archaeological landscape, such as prehistoric rock-shelters, habitational settlements, irrigation works and non-Buddhist sculpture.

16 Sanchi: Stupa 1 – northern gateways

17 Sanchi: Stupa 2

18 Sanchi: Asokan pillar

19 Sanchi: Phase IV stupas and buildings protruding from eastern retaining wall (left)

20 Sanchi: burial *ad sanctos* stupas

21 Sanchi: Stupa 2 – railing carvings

22 Sanchi: Stupa 2 – post-Mauryan pillar shaft (SG001/I-14)

23 Sanchi: Stupa 2 – post-Mauryan pillar lotus capital (SMRC; SG001/I-36)

24 Sanchi: Stupa 2 – post-Mauryan pillar lion capital (SMRC; SG001/I-32)

25 Sanchi: Pillar 25 (SG001/I-15)

26 Sanchi: lion capital, possibly from Pillar 25 (SMRC; SG001/I-72)

27 Vidisha: Heliodorus pillar (second to first century BC) (SG006/I-170)

28 Vidisha, Heliodorus pillar site: Garuda capital (GGMM; SG006/I-561)

29 Vidisha: post-Mauryan pillar capital with crocodile motif (GGMM; SG006/I-560)

30 Palm capital stored at the Heliodorus pillar site (c. second to first century BC) (SG006/I-173)

31 Post-Mauryan pillar in Vidisha Museum garden (SG006/I-171)

32 Vidisha, Lohangi hill: pillar capital (c. second to first century BC) (SG006/I-99)

33 Sanchi: Stupa 2 – pillar carved on entrance railings

34 Vidisha: Heliodorus pillar – lotus carvings

35 Sanchi: Stupa 2 – lotus railing carvings

36 Sanchi: Padmapani image (c. fifth century AD) (SAM, SG006/I-303)

37 Sanchi: Vajrapani image (c. fifth century AD) (SAM; SG006/I-227)

38 Sanchi: one of two seated *yakṣas* on eastern terrace (c. fifth century AD) (SG006/I-12)

39 Sanchi: seated *yakṣa* (c. fifth century AD) (SAMRC; SG006/I-39)

40 Sanchi: standing *yakṣa* (c. first century AD) (SAMRC; SG006/I-34)

41 Bilori: *śalabanjika* fragment outside modern temple (probably from Sanchi) (SG009/I-51)

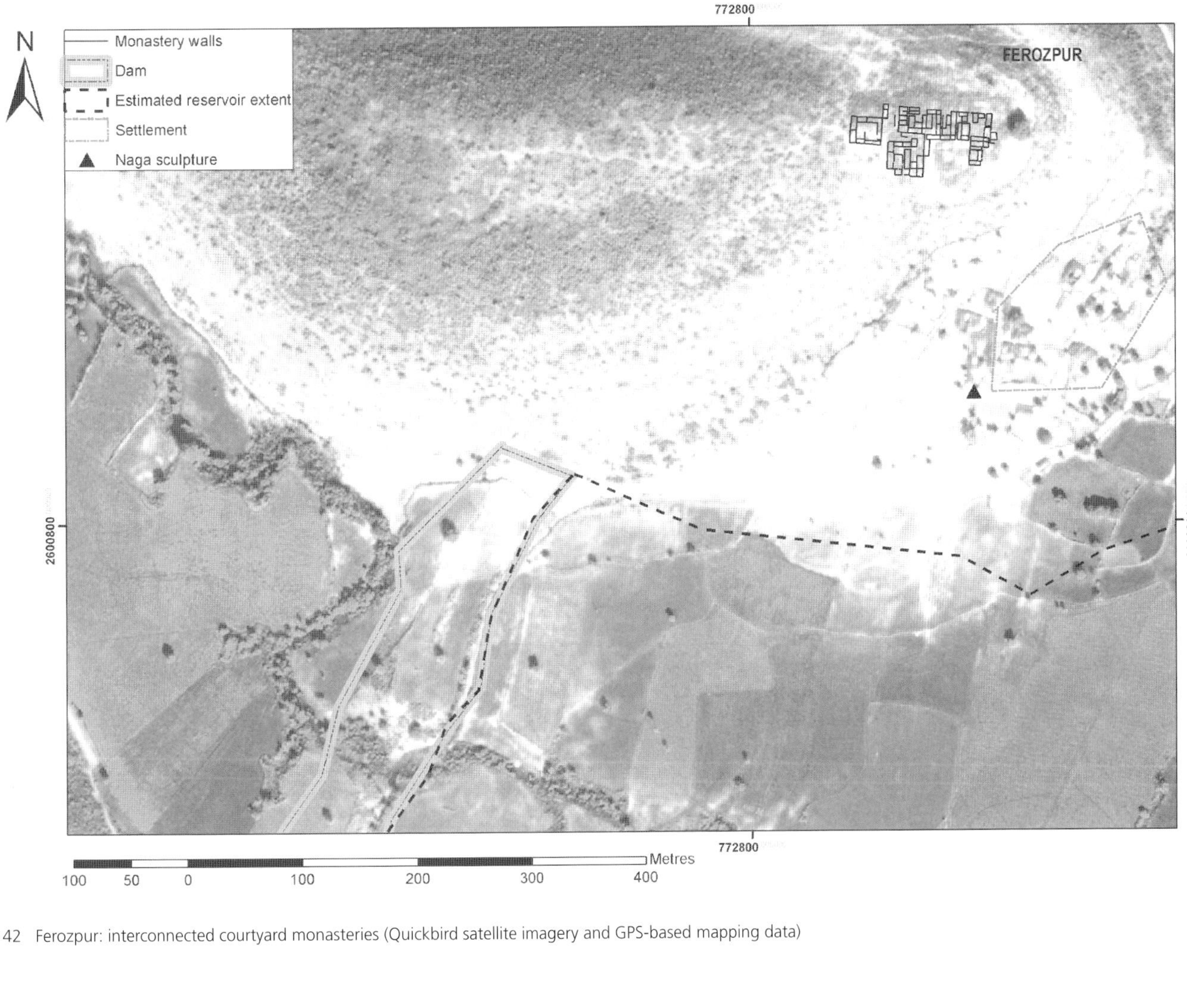

42 Ferozpur: interconnected courtyard monasteries (Quickbird satellite imagery and GPS-based mapping data)

CHAPTER 10

The Sanchi Survey Project: Chronology

Introduction

During Stage I of the SSP, newly documented sites were dated drawing variously on sculptural, architectural, epigraphical and ceramic evidence, with a programme of Optically Stimulated Luminescence (OSL) dating introduced during Stage II. The aim of this chapter is to provide an overview of the chronologies derived from these different datasets.

The final chronological framework used here (Table 10.1) was informed by the excavated and art-historical sequences at Sanchi (Table 9.1) and Vidisha (Table 9.2) discussed earlier, with some modification, including synchronising the different phasing systems used at these two sites and taking into account recent strands in art-historical and archaeological scholarship. Marshall's Phase I at Sanchi (c. third century BC) thus became Phase Id following the incorporation of three earlier periods identified during excavations at Vidisha (Table 9.2); its time-frame was also extended slightly (c. fifth to third century BC) to fit with the 'NBPW'/'urban phase' at Vidisha.[1] Phase Ia refers to the pre-pottery microlithic levels as identified at Rangai; Ib covers the period between c. 2000 and 1000 BC, and corresponds roughly to the Chalcolithic Period (IIa) at Vidisha and Rangai. Phase Ic covers the period between c. tenth to sixth century BC, and incorporates both the 'Chalcolithic/PGW' and 'Pre-NBPW' periods as defined at Vidisha.[2] In the light of recent views regarding the relative chronology between Stupas 1 and 2, Marshall's Phase II was broken down into 'early' (IIa: late second to mid-first century BC) and 'late' (IIb: late first century BC to early first century AD) sub-phases. Phase III was also divided into 'early' (IIIa: first century AD) and 'late' (IIIb: second to third century AD) sub-phases, the former referring to the Satavahana sculpture, and the latter to a number of locally produced sculptures in the surrounding countryside with close links to Kusana sculpture at Mathura. As discussed in chapter 5, there is no evidence that Kusana control extended to the Sanchi area, and apart from a few imported sculptures, this period is largely absent from Marshall's phasing at Sanchi. Phase IV (fourth to sixth century AD) corresponds to the Gupta period. Marshall's Phase V, referring to the 'post-Gupta' to early Pratihara periods (c. seventh to late eighth century AD) was left largely unchanged. Finally, the time-frame of Marshall's phase VI was shortened so as to refer to the late Pratihara-Paramara period alone (c. ninth to tenth century AD), with the addition of Phase VII for the later material of the eleventh and twelfth centuries AD.

As shown in Table 10.1, each type of datable material encountered during the SSP offered a chronology of varying resolution as well as application. For example, the fairly finely tuned chronological framework with respect to the sculptural and architectural evidence reflects the relatively advanced level of art-historical scholarship in central India. This material was helpful in providing *terminus ante quem* dates for settlements and dams and also provided the primary basis for dating various phases in the development of Sanchi's multi-layered ritual landscape, at least as far as the adoption of a stone-working tradition is concerned. By contrast, the ceramic-based chronology is much less detailed or precise, largely due to the lack of reliable regional pottery sequences based on excavated evidence. Thus, the function of the ceramic evidence in the SSP does not extend beyond providing dates based on the 'presence' or absence of surface pottery, itself largely determined by ground conditions. Since surface ceramic collections are more reliable from ploughed contexts, pottery was largely restricted to habitational settlements. Further it is important to stress that, due to the unavailability of sculpture prior to the third century BC and the limitations of ceramic analysis, there may be a degree of under-representation of pre-Phase Id sites.

Sculpture and architecture

Stupa typologies

The basic framework for assessing newly documented stupas was provided by typologies at Sanchi (Marshall 1940) and the four other 'Bhilsa Topes' sites (Cunningham 1854). Sanchi's stupas can be divided into four main morphological and chronological groups: i) the Mauryan type (Phase Id), as represented by the brick core of Stupa 1, closely paralleled by Stupa 1 at Satdhara (Agrawal 1997); ii) the post-Mauryan type (Phase II), as represented by Stupas 2 and 3, and similar examples at Sonari, Satdhara, Morel khurd and Andher – these stupas are often enclosed by a carved balustrade and consist of a core of heavy stone blocks interspersed with chippings and faced with a single course of dressed stone blocks (Marshall 1940, 41); iii) somewhat smaller stupas of the Gupta and post-Gupta periods, such as those clustered around Sanchi Stupa 1, all set on a square or circular platform without the addition of railings (Marshall 1940, 46); iv) even smaller stupas, with diameters of 1 m or less, such as the recently revealed cluster on the lower southern slopes of Sanchi hill (Willis 2000). Traditionally classifed as 'votive' in function, they are now regarded by some scholars as burial *ad sanctos* stupas, built to

Table 10.1 The Sanchi Survey: phasing and dating criteria

		Pottery and stone tools			Sculpture, Architecture and Epigraphy
Phase	Approximate dates	Dating criteria	Sub phase	Dates	Dating criteria
Ia	Pre-2000 BC	Microliths, Neolithic stone tools, painted rock-shelters.			
Ib	c. 2000–1000 BC	Early chalcolithic pottery (e.g. Kayatha ware); Black slipped ware.			
Ic	c. 1000–500 BC	Later chalcolithic and Iron Age pottery: Black and Red ware; Black slipped ware; Coarse grey wares; some red slipped wares.			
Id	c. 500–200 BC	Northern Black Polished ware; Black slipped ware; Coarse grey wares; Buff coloured slipped ware; Red slipped ware.		c. 269–232 BC	Asokan pillar, capital and edict; Stupa 1.
II	c. 2nd–1st century BC	Red slipped ware; Coarse grey wares; Buff coloured slipped ware.	IIa	c. 115–80 BC	Heliodorus pillar and inscription; Early railing carvings on Stupa 2.
			IIb	c. 50 BC–0 BC	Later railing carvings on Stupas 1 and 2, Sanchi.
III	c. 1st–3rd century AD	Micaceous wares; Burnished red ware; Black painted red ware; Thick buff coloured ware.	IIIa	Early 1st century AD	Satakarni inscription, Sanchi Stupa 1, southern gateway.
			IIIb	c. 2nd–3rd century AD	Sculpture found during survey, with comparisons formed with Kusana sculpture from the Gangetic valley area.
IV	c. 4th–6th century AD	Painted red ware.			Inscriptions of Candragupta II at Udayagiri and Sanchi; Gupta period art and architecture.
V–VII	c. 7th–12th century AD	Unslipped red wares and heavy grey wares (type nos. 000).	V	c. 7th–8th century AD	Post-Gupta to early Pratihara art and architecture.
			VI	c. 9th–10th century AD	Late Pratihara-Paramara art and architecture at Sanchi, with dated comparisons from Gyaraspur, and Bhojpur.
			VII	c. 11th–12th century AD	Comparisons from Udayapur and Chandella art.

contain the mortuary remains of ordinary monks and the laity, and positioned at a removed distance from more important stupas in deference to the hierarchical structure of the relic cult. Similar stupas occur throughout the study area, either within wider monastic compounds as at Sanchi, or comprising large burial grounds, as on the small hillock to the north of the Dargawan dam immediately to the west of Sanchi (Shaw and Sutcliffe 2005, 8–12).[3]

Whilst providing the framework for assessing newly documnted stupas in the field, precise dating was often complicated by high erosion and disturbance levels. In many cases, stupas have been reduced to no more than faint circular outlines on the ground or square stupa bases (Plates 61–2), the main building material having been removed for reuse in new structures. Even in better-preserved cases, the outer facing has usually been removed, and the inner core dug down as far as the central relic chamber.

Monastery typologies

Four main types of monastery were recorded during the SSP, only the first two of which are represented at Sanchi itself (Figure 11.23; Appendix IIb): i) the courtyard monastery which is traditionally thought not to have appeared before the Gupta period; ii) the less well-understood platformed variety, which at Sanchi survives in the form of Building 8, with better-preserved examples at Morel khurd, Satdhara, Sonari and Andher. Similar structures occur at five other sites documented during the SSP.[4] As discussed in chapter 11, they probably date to Phase II and were surmounted by towering superstructures of brick and stone. These imposing structures provide a challenge to received views regarding the history and chronology of institutionalised monasticism in central India. These are based entirely on the courtyard monastery which is usually seen as having originated in the North-West during the Kusana period, and not appearing at Sanchi until much later, as represented by the late, or post-Gupta, examples in the southern part of the site (Marshall 1940, 63–4). This framework has been used to support theories regarding the late domestication of the *saṅgha* in central India (Schopen 1994b, 547), drawing largely on the assumption that the courtyard monastery, with its emphasis on planning and 'order', was the key archaeological manifestation of textual allusions to the transition between peripatetic and sedentary monasticism. As argued earlier, the most obvious problem with this line of reasoning is its underlying normative model of spatial order. However, the fact that the courtyard model was already fully developed as early as the second century BC, in the form of rock-cut monasteries of the Deccan (*ibid.*), means that the possibility of earlier prototypical examples of this kind of monastery in central India cannot be ruled out. Additional evidence to this effect is provided by a third category of monastery found at four newly documented sites, but not represented at Sanchi itself. At Mawasa, Barahi khas, Ferozpur, Karhaud kherai and Devrajpur, these consist of rectangular structures arranged around a series of interconnected courtyards (Figures 11.12, 11.17; Plate 91), while one of the Mawasa examples is built on the summit of a monastery platform. As discussed in chapter 11, the latter suggests a Phase II date, while the rectangular shape is suggestive of a dormitory prototype of the single-occupancy cells found in the Phase IV counterparts at Sanchi. A fourth monastery type, represented at seven newly documented sites, consists of simple single- or double-roomed rectangular structures, which appear to be simplified versions of the rectangular type of courtyard monasteries. In some cases the walls consist of a rubble core, faced on both sides with dressed masonry slabs (Plate 99); others are formed from large free-standing boulders, the intervening spaces between which were presumably originally filled with mud or mortar (Plate 94). Examples of the former type were recently revealed during ASI excavations at Satdhara (Agrawal 1997, fig. 7). Their simple form and distance from the principal stupas and platformed monasteries there led to the suggestion that they were occupied by junior monks or pilgrims. Their proximity to Phase II stupas implies a second-century-BC date.

There is also a fifth category of monastic dwelling: prehistoric rock-shelters showing evidence of adaptation for monastic use in the form of platforms built up in front of their entrances, Buddhist paintings/inscriptions on their walls, or nearby stupas (Figure 11.23). Whilst these additional features are datable by reference to art-historical, architectural and palaeographic typologies, the Buddhist occupation of the actual shelters prior to their adaptation is difficult to date in the absence of excavation.

Wall typologies

Further variations in the dates of monastery structures, boundary walls and residential buildings were suggested by different types of wall construction. The most common wall type in all three contexts consists of a rubble core, faced with dressed stone masonry (Plate 99). Consideration of the wider context of these remains meant that this type of wall was usually dated somewhere between Phases II and IV. Indeed, this type of wall is usually regarded as an indication of an 'early' date. For example, similar types of walls with ashlar masonry facing and loose rubble core are regarded as one of the major 'constructional defects' (Chandra 1970b) of Gupta-period temples as found for example at Sanchi (Marshall 1950, 57) and Maṛhia (Chandra 1970b). Later walls usually have a more homogeneous structure. As mentioned above, a third type of wall identified during the SSP survives in the form of simple boulder outlines, which would originally have been held together by some form of mortar (Plate 94). However, it is important to note that this typology need not necessarily relate to a chronological schema; all three wall types could easily have co-existed, and the choice as to which one to was used may have simply reflected varying construction budgets.

Ceramics

Given that stone sculpture and architecture are unknown in the Sanchi area prior to c. third century BC, the dating of sites prior to this depended on other types of evidence. The other major dating criteria consisted of potsherds, over 1100 of which were collected during the survey (Appendix III). The majority were collected from ploughed surfaces, with others coming from exposed sections and ditches. The reliability of surface pottery collections as dating tools is highly dependent on a critical understanding of the complexities of the site-formation processes (Hodder and Malone 1984). A major problem, for example, is that even when collected from ploughed surfaces, surface ceramic assemblages tend to be dominated by pottery belonging to the latest phase of the site. This is especially problematic in central India where traditional ploughing methods still prevail; the ox-drawn plough can only reach depths of about 15 cm, approximately one sixth of the capacity of modern ploughs. As a consequence, lower levels of high settlement mounds are less likely to be represented in surface assemblages. It is therefore important to compare surface collections with archaeological material in eroded sections, or to draw on additional corroborative markers such as the relative heights of mounds. The latter method has its own problems because it is often difficult to determine how much mound-erosion has already taken place at the time of survey (Possehl 1973, 463).

However, the most important factor in the dating of surface assemblages is the availability of localised excavated sequences against which individual sherds can be compared. For example, in many parts of western Europe where there is an abundance of published stratified sequences, creating ceramic typologies on the basis of surface material is a fairly straightforward procedure. In central India, however, the paucity of detailed excavation reports means that the main comparative framework for dating ceramics comes from excavated sequences at Gangetic valley sites such as Hastinapura (Lal 1954) and Ahichchhatra (Ghosh and Panigrahi 1946). This means that more localised variations particular to central India are generally overlooked; furthermore most of these sites were excavated prior to the development of scientific sampling, or characterisation analysis techniques, and are generally framed within a 'culture historical' context, where the tendency is to draw one-to-one correlations between certain wares and period-specific 'peoples'. Thirdly, published sequences are usually divided into a limited number of well-known diagnostic wares such as PGW, BRW, Black Slipped Wares (BSW), NBPW or Red Polished Ware. Other, less distinguishable wares are rarely described in anything but highly generalised terms. For example, sherds without diagnostic surface treatments are usually described simply as 'red ware' or 'black ware'. Such ubiquitous categories obviously subsume a vast amount of diversity both in terms of fabric-type and colour: this problem is compounded by the lack of standardised terminology for describing different colour hues; the same colour may be described by a variety of terms in different publications, rather than referring to standardised Munsell soil colour charts. For example, descriptions such as 'dark red' are reflections of subjective responses which vary from one individual to another. Comparative analysis is hampered further by the fact that photographs of diagnostic wares and surface treatments are rarely provided. Although outline drawings of common vessel shapes provide useful comparisons for assessing surface collections, the main problem with this type of approach is that while some vessel types are confined to fairly precise fabric and period-specific contexts, others occur in a wide variety of fabrics and over long periods of time.

In the SSP study area these problems were exacerbated by the fact that the Vidisha excavations were never published beyond summary form. Although the main ceramic types associated with each chronological layer were listed, there were no detailed descriptions or illustrations. Despite these drawbacks, I am compelled to work within the current framework of understanding. It is not the intention here to challenge the existing framework of knowledge regarding local ceramics, but rather to use the available published resources to build a loose internal typology for supplementing the sculptural and architectural material described in chapters 9, 11 and 12. In Madhya Pradesh, the closest stratified ceramic sequences come from Tumain (Bajpai and Pandey 1984) to the north, and Tripuri (Dikshit 1952) and Kayatha (Ansari and Dhavalikar 1975) in the south. An inter-regional comparative framework is provided by excavation reports from Ahichchhatra (Ghosh and Panigrahi 1946), Hastinapura (Lal 1954) and Kausambi (Sharma 1969) in the Gangetic valley, while recent reports from Sonkh (Härtel 1993) and Sravasti (Aboshi and Sonoda 1997) represent more refined methodologies. The ceramic sequence at Devnimori (Mehta and Chowdhary 1966), although largely a single-phase site datable to the early centuries AD, offers useful parallels for studying the micaceous wares collected during the survey. Although there are problems with inter-regional comparisons, the attested links between the pottery from excavated contexts in central India and the Gangetic valley (Sharma 1969, 126–7) provide justification for drawing on this wider material.

Each sherd collected during the survey was subjected to basic characterisation analysis, described below.[5] Many included rim portions, from which the vessel types in Appendices IIIc–d could be inferred. Incomplete body fragments were only collected when they belonged to diagnostic fabric or surface-treatment groups. A basic pottery typology was then constructed on the basis of vessel and fabric types. The relationship between these two variables is illustrated in Appendix IIIc. Particular emphasis was placed on achieving a high level of standardisation so that, despite the problems outlined above, the internal typology can be easily adjusted at a future stage once a localised stratified sequence eventually becomes available.

There were two major stages in the analysis procedure: i) all sherds with intact rims were drawn to scale and arranged into a shape-based typology – approximately 200 major vessel types are listed in Appendix IIIc with illustrations in Appendix IIId and, where relevant, details regarding comparative material from excavated sites are also given; ii) the sherds were then organised into 28 major fabric types listed in Appendix IIIb. It is important to stress that comparisons based on shape alone can only provide very loose chronological markers, which need to be supplemented by consideration of other factors such as fabric type and surface treatment.

The characterisation analysis was carried out using a magnification of x10, following a simplified version of systems used during selected surface surveys in Nubian and Classical contexts (Smith 1996; Adams 1986; Peacock 1977). The main distinguishing criteria include fabric colour, surface treatment, firing technique, texture and hardness. The use of Munsell soil charts for describing fabric and surface colour introduced an element of standardisation, which will prove essential for reanalysis at any point in the future. The level of levigation was also another major consideration: details regarding voids and inclusion types are given. This framework will be refined at a later point using a range of petrographic and chemical analyses.

Attempts to fit these typologies into a chronological framework were kept to a minimum, with suggestions of phasing only offered when information about both vessel and fabric type was available. For example, a major factor when it comes to assessing the reliability of shape-based comparisons is the degree of correspondence between fabric and vessel type. Dating is thus only ventured when wares occur in association with a limited variety of vessel types. By contrast, there is much less justification for accepting the chronology of a shape-based comparison when there is a significant disparity between the fabrics of the excavated and surface examples. In these cases, no attempt at dating was made, and the sherd was omitted from the final analysis.

Many of the fabric types listed in Appendix IIIb belong to ubiquitous categories of 'red' and 'black' wares, for which direct comparisons are difficult to find. In such cases, therefore, reliance must be placed on shape-based comparisons alone. However, at least ten examples correspond to diagnostic wares which, along with their associated vessel types, are well represented at excavated sites and thus act as relatively secure chronological markers. The earliest ware type (1) found during the survey was Black and Red Ware (BRW). As shown in Appendix IIIc, it is generally restricted to shallow carinated dishes and bowls (Shapes 1, 2, 10, 12). BRW is most common in excavated contexts between c. 1000 and 600 BC (Ansari and Dhavalikar 1975, 96). However, more crude versions (e.g. type 9) continue between c. second century BC and second century AD (*ibid.*; Mehta and Chowdhary 1966, 84). The next diagnostic ware (type 3) is NBPW, characterised by its well-levigated clay, thin body and highly polished surface, which, in the case of the highest quality examples, has a metallic appearance. The generally accepted date range for NBPW is c. 600–100 BC (Ghosh 1990, 255–6). Only two sherds were found during the survey, both belonging to the non-metallic variety. Neither had surviving rims, but the most common NBPW vessel types found during excavations are shallow dishes and cooking vessels (*handi*). The third major ware is Black Slipped Ware (BSW), which is characterised by a thick (type 4) or thin (type 2) slip, usually polished or burnished. As shown in Appendix IIIc, it occurs most frequently in carinated dishes and cooking vessels (e.g. Shapes 75, 76a, 76b). Similar wares and associated vessel types are found throughout north and central India from c. 1000 to c. 200 BC, in association with both BRW and NBPW (Sinha 1971, 10–11; Narain and Roy 1976, 68–9). A variation of this ware has a buff-coloured slip (types 5a and 5b), often with a high polish or burnish. Its associated vessel-type assemblage is much wider than that of other Black Slipped Wares, including cooking vessels (e.g. Shapes 90, 95) and a range of basins and jars. Its chronology in central India appears to overlap with NBPW and continues into the following period (c. second–first century BC). One of the most common wares in the SSP is the Coarse Grey Ware (types 6 and 6b), which is generally unslipped. This, too, occurs in a wide range of shapes, although each vessel type occurs in large quantities (Appendix IIIc). For example, it occurs six times in Shape 101 and seven times in Shape 210, both jars. Another commonly associated vessel type is a shallow cooking dish (Shapes 189a, 96b, c). Similar wares from excavated contexts generally occur between pre-NBPW levels and the first century BC (Ansari and Dhavalikar 1975, 98).

The most common red-coloured ware collected during the SSP was a Red Slipped Ware (types 10a and 10b). It is characterised by a hard-baked fabric, with a slightly metallic ring and medium to thick slip, often polished or burnished. Red Slipped Wares are found in association with both BRW and NBPW levels at Vidisha (*IAR* 1963–4, 16–17) and Tumain (Bajpai and Pandey 1985), and continue into later periods. In the SSP it occurred in a wide range of vessel types, with a few examples such as the bowl (Shape 15) illustrated in Appendix IIId, possibly datable to as early as BRW chalcolithic contexts. The majority, however, may be dated to the early-historic period, on the basis of the chronology of associated vessel types. This applies in particular to Shapes 140, 148a and 148b, all pyriform jars which appear for the first time, and in large numbers, at sites such as Kausambi and Sonkh (Hartel 1993, 364; pl. II. 54) during the late centuries BC (Sharma 1969, 150; pl. 21. 44; 154; pl. 22. 86). Another pyriform jar (Shape 175a–d) occurred as often as 22 times in the SSP. This is also one of the most frequently found vessel types at Kausambi and Sonkh. The fairly tight chronological focus of the vessel type in question therefore suggests a similar date for other examples for which there is a close correspondence between fabric and vessel type. This applies in particular to Shapes 141a and 141b, a jar/pouring vessel which occurred 16 times in the SSP. Another jar type occurring in the same fabric includes Shape 163.

Another similar Red Slipped Ware is type 14a, although this has a much finer fabric, and higher burnish than type 10a. At first appearance, it shows similarities to the well-known Red Polished Ware which is most closely associated with c. first- to second-century-AD levels at sites such as Amreli (Rao 1966) and Baroda (Subbarao 1953, 57–62) in Gujarat. It has also been reported in Madhya Pradesh at sites such as Maheshwar (*ibid.*, 62) and Vidisha itself (*IAR* 1964–5, 19). Although the examples collected during the SSP lack the high levigation typical of Red Polished Ware, the shapes in which it occurs suggest a similar chronology (Phase III). For example, a fragment from a globular pot (Shape 99b) has direct parallels with a Red Polished Ware vessel from Devnimori (Mehta and Chowdhary 1966, 82, pl. 32. 68). Datable to roughly the same period is the Black Painted red ware (type 14b). Examples of this ware are reported in 'Kusana' levels at Vidisha (*IAR* 1963–4, 17) and Kayatha (Ansari and Dhavalikar 1975, 99), continuing into the Gupta period at Sonkh (Hartel 1993, 361, fig. 92).

Another frequently encountered ware during the SSP was the Micaceous Ware (type 13). It is characterised by a light orange/ochre colour and smooth texture. Its high mica content creates a striking 'sparkly' appearance, hence its reputation as a 'de-luxe' ware (Mehta and Chowdhary 1966, 77). Mica is also a powerful flux agent which helps to reduce the rate of firing (Allchin 1960, 27). The relationship between fabric and vessel type is most striking in the micaceous wares (Appendix IIIc). The commonest vessel types include shallow dishes (e.g. Shapes 3a, 3c) and carinated cooking vessels (e.g. Shape 95), the latter occurring 28 times. A Phase III date range is suggested by micaceous wares at Pauni (Deo and Joshi 1972, 65), Tumain (1985, 31; pl. 15.198) and Devnimori (Mehta and Chowdhary) where the repertoire of associated vessel types is almost identical to that represented in the SSP assemblage.

Dams and reservoirs

Further chronological markers were provided by a group of dams located and studied throughout the SSP study area during Stage I. Dams are difficult to date due to the nature of their construction, with building material often sourced from multiple locations and frequent repairs. Assigning an original context to associated archaeological material is rarely straightforward. The dating of Sri Lankan and South Indian dams has usually relied on inscriptions and constructional (particularly sluice) typologies (Venkayya 1906; Parker 1909; Brohier 1934 [reprint 1979]; Davison-Jenkins 1997). During the initial stages of the project, *terminus ante quem* dates varying between c. first century BC and fifth century AD were provided by *nāga* sculptures located on or near some of the embankments (Shaw 2004a; Shaw and Sutcliffe 2001, 68–71; 2003a, 84–5). That they were placed in such locations after the construction of the dams is confirmed by the cultic association between *nāga*s and agriculture, and a similarly close relationship between *nāga*s and tanks or reservoirs in other parts of India and Sri Lanka (Shaw and Sutcliffe 2001). Marshall (1940, 13), who examined the dam below Sanchi hill, suggested a construction date of c. third or second century BC in keeping with the earliest Buddhist monuments at Sanchi and neighbouring sites. During Stage II of the SSP, this hypothesis was tested through a programme of Optically Stimulated Luminescence (OSL) dating of dam and reservoir sediments at Sanchi and Devrajpur, a major site in the eastern sector (2b).

OSL refers to the levels of luminescence (light) emitted on exposure to light as the result of released energy accumulated in crystalline materials through the action of ionising radiation from natural radioactivity. When a sediment is exposed to sunlight prior to deposition, the OSL acquired over geological time is removed; the luminescence 'clock' is thus set to zero. The OSL then accumulates in response to the ionising radiation received during the burial period of the sediment. The level of OSL observed in ancient samples is thus dependent on the absorbed radiation dose, and hence can be related to the time elapsed since last illumination/heating, once the dose received per year (during burial) has been calculated.[6]

In recent years, C14 and OSL techniques have been used to date canal systems in Sri Lanka (Myrdal-Runebjer 1994; Risberg *et al.*, 2002) and southern Cambodia (Bishop *et al.*, 2004, 321) respectively.[7] For the latter, the underlying premise was that the OSL clock was reset to zero when the sediments were last exposed to light during the original excavation or re-excavation of the canals. A similar assumption informed our dating of the Sanchi dams: because sediments need to be disturbed prior to being deposited in a dam, we should be able to date the last disturbance by measuring the amount of OSL accumulation, or time elapsed, since the sediment's last exposure to light. However, in order for the OSL clock to be reset to zero, the sample must: i) contain sufficiently high levels of crystalline material (e.g. quartz/sand); and ii) have undergone sufficient exposure to light prior to deposition in the dam. While the geology of the Sanchi area meant that the former was not a significant problem, the latter was less easy to guarantee, due to the possibility of portions of sediment remaining unexposed during the digging and redeposition process.

Successful dating is also dependent on the avoidance of light-contamination during sampling. Thus, sediments were collected from dam sections using light-resistant plastic tubes. Cores were also drilled in selected reservoir beds, using a hollow-headed (0.25 x 0.10 m) hand auger (Shaw *et al.*, 2007, pl. 2). Samples were collected from within and below the reservoir deposit, using a light-resistant bag to extract sediment from the core-head.

The results of this study showed that local sediments, as well as methods of dam construction, were suitable for OSL dating methods. The most successful samples came from the Sanchi dam, providing a date-range between the third and second centuries BC. This tallies closely with our principal working hypothesis that the Sanchi dams were built around the same time as the earliest Buddhist monuments at Sanchi and neighbouring monastic sites, and that, as in Sri Lanka, they were central to the development of exchange networks between monastic and non-monastic sections of society.

Conclusion

The overall chronology used throughout the following chapters is summarised, along with the associated dating criteria, in Table 10.1. Quite clearly, the ceramic-based typology remains speculative until it can be fitted into a regionalised stratified sequence. Further, it was only used as an independent dating tool when there was a consistent match between shape and fabric types. However, when combined with the higher resolution of the sculpture and architecture-based typologies, it provided an adequate starting point for building a loose framework for dating newly documented sites.

CHAPTER 11

Buddhist Sites and 'Buddhist Landscapes'

Introduction

Sanchi's size, archaeological grandeur and rich patronage base mark it out as the most important Buddhist site in the study area. Despite its spatially distinct hilltop location, its proximity to Vidisha conforms to the traditional city-monastery model propounded in early canonical texts (e.g. *Vinaya* III, 155). Quite clearly it belongs to the 'urban' category of monastic site, discussed in chapter 6.

The aim of this chapter is to assess the distribution of Buddhist sites beyond the Vidisha/Sanchi orbit, and to examine the degree to which these sites correspond to patterns at Sanchi in terms of location, architectural assemblage, internal organisation and wider landscape setting. The chapter is divided into two sections: Part I consists of a detailed site gazetteer and forms the basis for the discussion in Part II, which amongst other things, deals with chronology, site hierarchy and internal site organisation, the dynamics of the relic cult, and inter-site relationships within the 'Buddhist landscape'.

The 35 hilltop Buddhist sites documented during the SSP are listed in the gazetteer according to their position within the four main geographical sectors outlined in chapter 8 (Figure 11.1 colour). Whilst most of these sites were documented for the first time during the SSP, this list also includes the four previously published 'Bhilsa Tope' sites (Cunningham 1854) and Bighan (Lake 1910b), whose re-examination formed a central focus of this study. A list of Buddhist remains occurring within habitational settlements rather than their more usual hilltop monastic settings is also provided at the end of the gazetteer. This includes stupa and monastery remains within ancient Vidisha itself, with similar Buddhist remains identified at four smaller urban settlements in other parts of the SSP study area. A third category of Buddhist remains was also identified: those occurring in larger ritual settings whose predominant cultic affiliation can be defined as non-Buddhist or 'mixed'. Included in this category is Ahmadpur, a mixed ritual complex in Sector 4, Lohangi hill in the middle of Vidisha, and Udayagiri, better known for its Gupta-period Brahmanical cave temples, but also yielding evidence for some form of Buddhist presence during earlier periods. The last two sites can also be classified as 'urban', as both fall within the limits of the ancient city of Besnagar.

PART I: GAZETTEER

Hilltop Buddhist sites

Sector 1b: the western hills

Fourteen Buddhist hilltop Site Groups were documented in this area, including the previously documented 'Bhilsa Tope' site of Satdhara. The hills in this sector can be divided into three sub-groups: i) those in the immediate vicinity of Sanchi, including Nagauri to the south, and the long hill range to the west; ii) several smaller, isolated hills scattered across the otherwise agricultural terrain to the west as far as Satdhara on the eastern bank of the River Bes; and iii) the extended hill range to the west of the River Bes.

I) SOUTH AND WEST OF SANCHI

Nagauri (SG003a)

The early-historic quarry, settlement remains and *nāga* sculpture on Nagauri hill, situated c. 350 m south of Sanchi, were described in chapter 9. Prehistoric remains include extensive microlith scatters and a cluster of painted rock-shelters on the eastern edge of the hill. One of these shelters contains a later painting which may have Buddhist associations (Plate 48; Figure 11.3).[1] The shelter is two-tiered, the painting covering much of its upper wall. At either end of the panel is a parasol (or tree?), possibly a reference to the royal and/or divine status of the couple seated on a throne below; before them are two smaller individuals who seem to be in a position of supplication. To their right is a procession of horses and elephants, both with riders, and hunters holding spears. The unusual manner in which the subjects have been stencilled out of a background block of red paint represents a striking departure from the style and content of earlier paintings, both here and in other shelters throughout the study area (Plates 46–7); these usually consist of hunting scenes painted in red directly onto the rock. The stencilling treatment could be a kind of 'copy' of the reductive process of stone carving at Sanchi which may also provide dating clues for the painting: both in subject matter and style, there are similarities with the processional friezes on the Phase IIIa gateway carvings of Stupa 1. Another instructive parallel is the Besnagar *yakṣa* sculpture (Plate 140), discussed in chapter 12, whose turban is comparable with the hunters' 'piled-up' headdresses. However, even if the painting was informed by the wider sculptural repertoire at Sanchi and Vidisha, it could well have been executed at a much later date, and further may have had no formal connection with Buddhism.

Figure 11.3 Drawing of rock-painted frieze at Nagauri

The latter scenario is not unlikely given Nagauri's strong economic links with Sanchi including the fact that most of Sanchi's building material was quarried from here. Similarly, it is difficult to assess whether the shelter was used for monastic purposes, especially since it lacks additional evidence of adaptation as in the case of many of the shelters at Sanchi and other Buddhist sites.

Dargawan hills 1 and 2 (SG028 and SG029)

More unambiguously Buddhist remains are found on the hills to the west of Sanchi. There are two separate site groupings, one (Dargawan 1) on the smaller hillock to the north of the modern Sanchi-Gulgaon road, the other (Dargawan 2) spread over the larger hill range to its south.[2] The short valley between these hills bears the remains of a small dam, with another at Karondih to the south of the larger hill. As discussed in chapter 14, these would have formed small reservoirs for feeding into the main reservoir, itself held up by the ruined embankment between Sanchi and Nagauri hills.

The northern hilltop complex consists of over 100 heavily damaged structures including rectangular and apsidal buildings, and numerous cairn-like stupas with exposed relic chambers at their centre.[3] With diameters of just 1–3 m, the latter may be compared with some of the smaller stupas scattered throughout the main stupa complex on Sanchi hill, as well as the more recently revealed stupa cluster on its southern slopes (Plate 20). As discussed in chapter 9, these stupas are generally understood to have contained mortuary remains of ordinary monks and possibly even the laity and, like burial *ad sanctos* traditions in the Christian world, were positioned so as to benefit ritually from their proximity to more important relic deposits (Schopen 1987; 1994c). The large number of stupas on Dargawan hill suggests that we are dealing with a kind of dedicated burial ground; similar sites consisting solely of extensive clusters of small stupa 'burials' have been noted in the vicinity of the Buddhist site of Thotlakonda in Andhra Pradesh (Fogelin 2004; 2006). Dargawan's removed distance from Sanchi meant that its stupas, possibly containing lay burials, were positioned in deference to the hierarchical structure of the relic cult. At the same time, however, the site was sanctified by virtue of its visual link with the relic stupas on Sanchi hill, situated less than 1 km away on the opposite side of the valley.

The southern hilltop complex (Dargawan 2) is more dispersed, with Buddhist remains scattered all over the hill. The best preserved monuments, consisting of four stupas, are situated on the eastern edge of the hill, within direct visual range of Sanchi Stupas 1 and 2 (Figure 11.2 colour; Plate 60). The largest stupa has a diameter of 8 m, and is surrounded by three smaller stupas with diameters of 4.4, 4.8 and 5.6 m. All four survive to a height of about 1.5 m, with heavy damage at the top where local digging has exposed the central relic-chambers. Morphologically they are similar to the Phase II stupas at Sanchi (Marshall 1940, 41), with cores of stone blocks and rubble, and dressed masonry facing, portions of which are still *in situ*.

Three similar stupas, with diameters of 4.2, 4.4, and 8 m, are perched on the hill's southern edge, about 1.3 km from the eastern cluster; the Karondih dam mentioned earlier is situated in the short valley below. Various structural outlines, including two small apsidal structures,[4] were noted on the intervening hilltop, although precise systematic planning was hampered by dense vegetation cover and heavy site disturbance.

The only water source is a circular tank (diameter: 48 m) designed to collect monsoon rainfall, situated on the SW edge of the hill, overlooking Gulgaon village. It is of the same excavated type as similar tanks on Sanchi hill (Agarwal and Narain 1997, 170–1), and is lined on all sides with seven courses of dressed masonry slabs (Plate 97).

Kanchanpura (SG143)

There are also Buddhist remains on the summit of Kanchanpura hill, immediately to the north of Dargawan. These include a Phase II-type stupa (diameter: 5 m; surviving height: 1 m) and, 280 m further to the east, four heavily disturbed rectangular structures. Their similarity to those at Satdhara suggest that they were simple monasteries. The habitational settlement remains below the stupa, and above the modern village of Kanchanpura, are discussed in chapter 13.

Dhakna (SG032c)

In the opposite direction, around 2.5 km south of Dargawan, is a line of three small hillocks, the westernmost of which is occupied by the modern village of Dhakna.[5] A post-Mauryan bull capital, discussed later, is stored here, while ancient settlement and temple remains cover the lower ground to the south.[6] The summit of the easternmost hillock is occupied by five small stupa outlines (diameter: 3 m) and surrounded on all sides by a 0.8 m thick boundary wall. This follows the 'early' type of construction, i.e. with a rubble core and dressed masonry facing.

II) THE WESTERN VALLEY AREA

Satdhara (SG007)

Satdhara, situated about 8.5 km west of Sanchi, is the largest and best-preserved Buddhist site in this sector (Figure 11.2).[7] The principal monuments are situated on the summit of a low hill on the eastern bank of the River Bes (Figure 11.4), but also extend into the surrounding area, and opposite bank of the river. The total area covered by these remains is almost as large, if not larger, than Sanchi (Agrawal 1997, 407). The nearest habitational settlements, described in chapter 13, are Murlikheri-Naroda in the south and Sehor to the NE.[8]

Following Cunningham's (1854) early excavations of the principal stupas, the site has recently been taken up by the ASI for renewed excavation and conservation (Agrawal 1997); however, a detailed excavation report is still awaited. The central stupa (no. 1) (Plate 63), with a diameter of 34 m, and standing at a height of over 12 m, is of a smilar scale as Sanchi Stupa 1, and also follows a similar chronology and mode of construction: on account of the size of brick used in its core, the earliest construction phase has been dated to the Mauryan period (Agrawal 1997, 413). This is corroborated by fragments of a ribbed parasol and a small elephant capital discovered recently in the debris between the core and the outer stone facing (Plates 114–15).[9]

As at Sanchi, the outer facing was added in c. second century BC, along with a carved ground balustrade, individual railings from which are stored on site and also in the ASI storehouse (Willis 2000, fig. 74).[10] These later additions provide a Phase II *terminus post quem* for the elephant, while further indications of a Mauryan date are provided by its high polish, a typical feature of Mauryan sculpture. However, it is carved from local sandstone, and not the Chunar variety, as stated in recent accounts (Willis 2000, 80). Rough comparisons are provided by the elephant capital from Sanchi, Temple 40 (Plate 116), although the latter is unpolished and also double the size. Another parallel is the elephant-with-rider capital from Besnagar although it is over ten times the size of the Satdhara example (Plate 117).[11] Nevertheless both sculptures have a similarly high polish, and both have the same row of three vertical folds on their lower chests. A similar detail occurs on one of the elephant medallions on the Stupa 2 railings at Sanchi (Plate 118), which may imply a common date for all three works.[12]

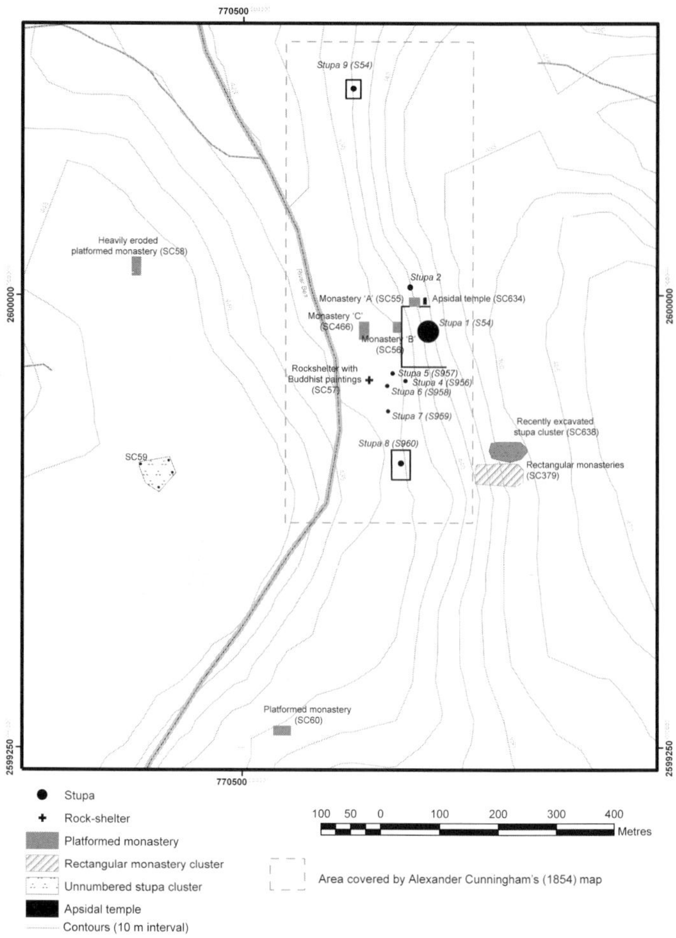

Figure 11.4 Site plan of Satdhara (with AC's mapping area indicated)

All of the other monuments at Satdhara date to Phase II or later, with the exception of a recently revealed apsidal temple (11.50 x 5.60 m) to the east of the Stupa 1 (Plate 95). Associated NBPW has suggested a Mauryan date (Agrawal 1997, 406; fig. 4), which is also in keeping with the chronology of apsidal temples at Sanchi and Vidisha.

Distributed at various points over the site are about 34 smaller stupas, all datable to Phase II. Of these, Stupas 2 and 8 were found to contain reliquaries (Cunningham 1854) (Table 6.1).[13] That from the former was uninscribed, while one of the reliquaries from Stupa 8 bore the inscribed names of Sariputta and Mahamoggalana, the two chief disciples of the Buddha (Willis 2000, 81);[14] the relics of these disciples were also retrieved from Sanchi, Stupa 3. By contrast, no reliquaries have been retrieved from Stupa 1, although a lidded stone box found within the rubble integument on the south side may have held a relic or consecratory deposit (Willis 2000, 80, n. 4, fig. 76). Further, as discussed in Part II in relation to the spatial dynamics of the relic cult, the relative positioning of Stupas 1 and 2 provides strong suggestions that, as at Sanchi, Stupa 1 may have contained the relics of the Buddha himself.

Many of the Stupa 1 railings, coping stones and paving slabs, all datable to Phase II, bear single-lined donative inscriptions, attesting to a system of collective patronage as found at Sanchi (Singh 1996). However, the rough and irregular carving style suggests a lower level of formality in the gift-recording procedure than at Sanchi (Agrawal 1997, 413–14).

Recent ASI clearance in the SE corner of the complex has revealed several Phase II stupas and narrow rectangular structures, both single- and double-roomed, and ranging in size from 9.60 x 4 m to 23.40 x 5.10 m (Plate 93; Agrawal 1997, 408, figs. 7–8). As discussed in chapter 10, these represent the most basic category of monastic dwellings in the study area. Their distance from the main stupas suggests that they were used by junior monks or pilgrims. Agrawal (*ibid.*) provides no dating suggestions, but their rubble-core, dressed-faced walls and their proximity to Phase II-type stupas indicate an early date; Agrawal's suggestion that the buildings originally had a thatched roofing may also imply an early date.[15]

By contrast, the senior monks probably resided in the principal monasteries clustered around Stupa 1. These have survived in the form of three solid ashlar platforms, one built against the northern wall, and the other two immediately outside the western wall of the main stupa enclosure (Figure 11.4; Plates 78–9). Ranging in size from 16.80 x 14.60 m to 30 x 16.80 m, they reach a height of over 5 m, and were probably surmounted by high, vertically orientated monasteries, possibly built of brick and timber.[16] All three have staircases cut into their body, which, as discussed later, appear to have been aimed at controlling access into the upper monastery.

Two more monastery platforms, not mentioned by Cunningham, were noted during the SSP (Figure 11.4). Both are situated at a removed distance from, but nevertheless within visual range of, the main stupa complex. The first (28.10 x 15.50 m; height: 2 m) stands on the opposite (western) bank of the River Bes in close proximity to a number of small stupa outlines. Like the other platforms, a staircase at the SW corner is cut into the main plinth. A second, much larger platform (35 x 18 m; height: 4 m) is built into the hillside around 1.7 km SE of Stupa 1.

Later additions to the site include five square projections on the outer edges of Stupa 1. These are datable to c. sixth or seventh centuries AD, but also incorporate coping stones and pillars from earlier structures (Willis 2000, 80). A painted panel in a rock shelter overlooking the river belongs to roughly the same period. The painting consists of a Buddha image, two stupas and an inscription of the Buddhist creed (Agrawal 1997, 410–11, figs. 9–10). Although the shelter reveals no additional signs of adaptation as found at Sanchi and other sites, such as platforms or 'beds', it no doubt formed an integral part of the wider site. The beauty of the view from here is hard to ignore, and it was no doubt an ideal place for meditation and contemplation.

Murlikheri (SG162)

Another monastery platform (25 x 19 m; height: 2 m) was noted on the northern slopes of the same hill about 2 km to the north of Satdhara: the extensive early-historic settlement of Murlikheri-Naroda occupies the valley below.[17] According to villagers, the main stupa at Satdhara is visible from here during the dry summer months. Given that no stupa remains were found in the immediate vicinity, it is possible that it was dependent in some way on Satdhara.

Naroda Pathari (SG162d)

More Buddhist remains, including a rectangular platform (10 x 6 m; height: 0.80 m), and four stupa bases (Plate 61; average dimensions: 3 x 3 m) were documented on a small sandstone outcropping c. 1 km NE of the modern village of Naroda. This type of stupa does not appear at Sanchi until the sixth or seventh centuries AD (Table 9.1), suggesting, therefore, a Phase V date. However, the nearby settlement remains at Mulikheri-Naroda evidently belong to a much earlier period.

Goldoria (SG022)

Around 500 m to the north of Naroda Pathari is a small hillock, known locally as Goldoria; this type of small, solitary hillock is a particularly favoured location for Buddhist sites. At its summit is a heavily damaged Phase II stupa (diameter: 5.10 m), surrounded on all sides by numerous single- and double-roomed rectangular structures.[18] The walls are constructed from a homogeneous mass of solid, undressed blocks, which, as discussed in chapter 10, are thought to date to a later period than the less robust rubble-core, dressed-facing variety. However, both wall types could easily have co-existed, and the choice as to which type was used may simply have reflected varying construction budgets. Similarly, the large quantity of terracotta tiles strewn throughout the site, need not imply a later date than the presumed thatched structures at Satdhara (Agrawal 1997).

Ferozpur (SC011c)

Ferozpur hill, situated immediately NE of Murlikheri hill, forms the northern point of a triangle with Satdhara and Goldoria. Ancient settlement remains occupy the southern slope behind the modern village where a group of fifth-century-AD serpent sculptures (Plates 166–7) are stored in a modern temple (Shaw and Sutcliffe 2003a, 86–9; Shaw 2004a, 45–6). To the west is a large dam, which, prior to being breached, would have created an extensive reservoir. As discussed in chapter 14, the *nāga*s would originally have stood at the edge of this water body.

At the summit of Ferozpur hill are a number of interconnected courtyard monasteries lined with rectangular rooms (Plate 91). These remains were first noted in Stage I, but mapped in 2004–5 (Plate 42).[19] The walls (average width: 0.60–0.85 m) are of the rubble-core, dressed-facing variety. Large quantities of terracotta tiles were found throughout the site. While precise dating awaits future excavation, the fifth-century-AD date for the *nāga* sculptures below (Williams 1976; Shaw 2004a) may be instructive; this date also fits with the generally accepted chronology for courtyard-type monasteries at Sanchi. However, the rather haphazard layout of the monastery here may suggest an earlier date, further supported by the abundance of early-historic potsherds amongst the settlement remains below. Further, the rectangular rooms are similar to the single-roomed buildings at Satdhara, and appear to represent an earlier, dormitory-style of monastery. Finally, similar plans are found at Mawasa, which can be dated quite confidently to Phase II. The only stupas found were of the small 1 m-diameter variety within the monastery compounds themselves. Although heavy vegetation cover means that the existence of additional remains cannot be ruled out, the apparent lack of larger stupas is an interesting point in itself. It is possible that Ferozpur performed a subsidiary monastic function to nearby sites such as Goldoria and Satdhara, to which it may well have been attached.

III) HILLS TO THE WEST OF THE RIVER BES

Sayargaon, Bamhora, Bagoda and Bala Barkhera
(SG042b, SG078, SG076, SG077)

Although the hills to the west of the River Bes, strictly speaking, lie outside the boundaries of the SSP, a number of Buddhist sites in this area are mentioned here in order to assess the wider applicability of the patterns in the survey area. Only one of these, Sayargaon, was examined during SSP; the others were documented during the Madhya Pradesh State Archaeology regional survey (Maheswari 1997), to which I refer here.

Sayargaon hill is the most prominent landmark in this area, its dramatic cliffs and painted rock-shelters on the eastern edge dominating the skyline for miles around. These create a kind of natural fortification, supplemented on the western edge by a 2 m-wide wall. Roughly at the centre of the hill are several rectangular structures which, according to local folklore, were built in 'ancient times' by *banjaris*, or travelling traders. Bad preservation and dense vegetation coverage made it difficult to ascertain their original function, but it may not be without significance that similar associations are attached to less ambiguously Buddhist remains on the three neighbouring hills (Maheswari 1997): on Bamhora hill, about 2 km to the NW, are the remains of a stupa (diameter: 5 m), faced with dressed masonry slabs but with a core reportedly containing typically 'Mauryan'-sized bricks (*ibid.*). Nearby is a rectangular platform (no dimensions given) and a number of painted rock-shelters (*ibid.*). Another stupa, '*vihāra*', and a cluster of painted shelters, are reported on Bagoda hill, 2 km to the north, with a third stupa on Bala Barkhera hill, 2 km further to the north still.

Sector 3: the southern hills

The area to the south of the Sanchi-Raisen road consists of extensive, densely vegetated hill ranges, interspersed by narrow, cultivated valleys. The key archaeological sites in this area are illustrated in Figure 11.5 (colour).

Sonari (SG004)

Sonari, situated approximately 8 km south of Sanchi, is the largest and best-preserved Buddhist site in Sector 3. A perennial stream flows down the western side of the hill, its source, which is marked by a modern *devī* shrine, providing the site's main water supply. This is connected to the stupas by a paved pathway. There are two large stupas (Plate 64), each set within a walled enclosure, with a cluster of six smaller stupas to the east (Figure 11.6). Since Cunningham's (1854) excavations, little work has been conducted here, apart from various bouts of ASI conservation (*ASIAR* 1978–9, 123; 1979–80, 127; 1981–2, 117; 1982–3, 186; 1986–7, 62). Cunningham (1854) retrieved reliquaries from Stupas 1 and 2 (Table 6.1); those from the latter are inscribed with the names of the Hemavata monks (Willis 2000, 84–8). As discussed in chapter 6, the Hemavata school was closely connected with the Phase II embellishments at Sanchi and Satdhara, and the establishment of new centres here at Sonari, as well as Andher and Morel khurd, where relics of the same monks have been found (*ibid.*). Further discussion of the relative configuration of the Hemavata relic stupas at these sites is given in Part II of this chapter.

The principal monastery is represented by the large ashlar platform (11 x 11 m; height: 4.6 m) built against the SW corner of the Stupa 1 enclosure. As at other sites it would have originally been surmounted by a superstructure, possibly several storeys high, and is approached by an internal stairway (width: 1.40 m) at its NE corner, cut into the body of the podium. Additional residential quarters may be represented by the cluster of heavily disturbed foundations to the NE.

Willis (2000, 83) suggests that Sonari would have been approached from Satdhara, to which Sonari was attached as a kind of subsidiary site. While this may indeed be true, one should not

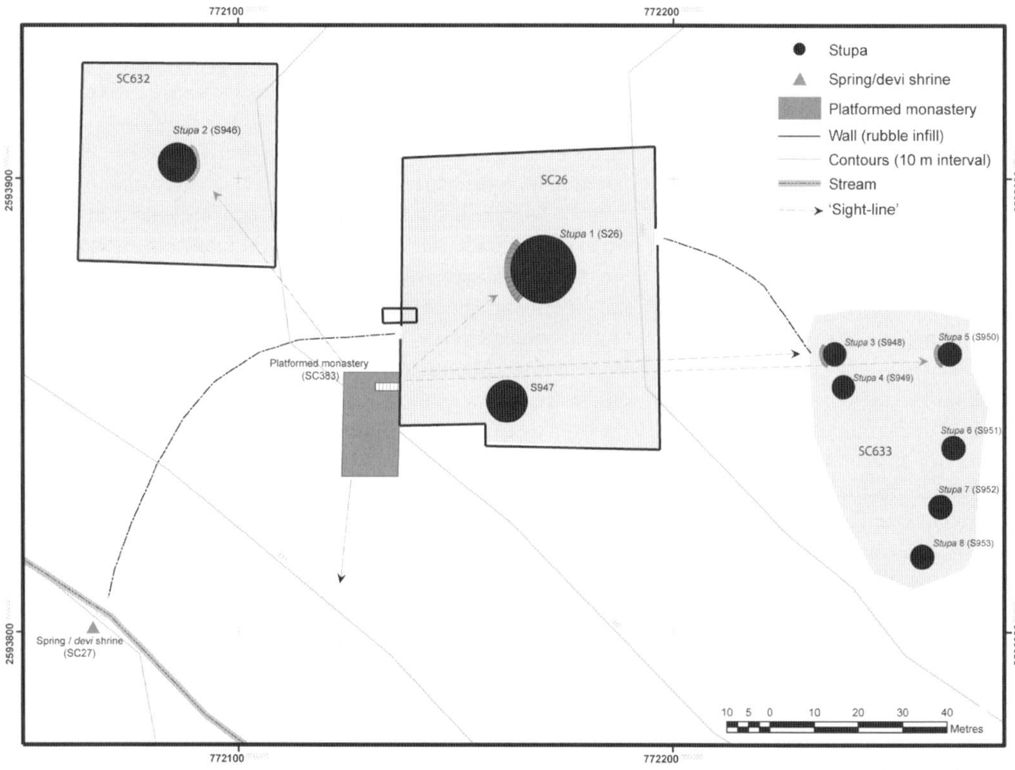

Figure 11.6 Site plan of Buddhist remains at Sonari (showing 'sight lines')

rule out other approaches, as discussed below. Further, since Sonari is separated from Satdhara by around 5 km, it is important to look at more localised communication routes, not only with other Buddhist sites, but with contemporary habitional settlements, which can provide important insights into Sonari's wider socio-economic function in the landscape: to the north, surrounded by a cluster of early settlements (Figure 11.5 colour), is the village of Sonari,[20] from where one approaches the site today. Sukhasen village in the east,[21] also surrounded by a number of early settlements, is linked to the Sonari stupas by an ancient pathway, whose paving stones are visible in places. Finally, several major settlements are located in the fertile valley 3 km to the south of Sonari hill. Of these, Besar talai is the largest and most important (Figure 11.5 colour),[22] and also includes remains of an urban stupa, discussed later. As discussed in chapter 13, the spatial and temporal link between Sonari and Besar talai fits with wider textually and anthropologically generated theories regarding the ritual and economic relationship between monks and local populations.

Sukhasen/Bari bir (SG150)
Just to the north of Sukhasen village, mentioned above, is a small, densely forested hillock, on the upper slopes of which are two small stupas (diameter: 1.70 m; surviving height: 0.70 m). At a lower level, there are around 25 stone platforms (average dimensions: 3 x 3 m), possibly stupa bases. Given their size and quantity, the site may be regarded as a single-purpose 'burial ground', as in the case of Dargawan 1, discussed earlier. Whilst the latter deferred to Sanchi for ritual legitimisation, this time, the main source of sanctification would have been Sonari, situated 1.5 km to the west.

Barahi Khas (SG059b)
The area to the SE of Sonari is dominated by a fertile valley dotted with several isolated hillocks and also containing a number of important settlements. The hill at Barahi Khas (around 5 km SE of Sonari) is occupied by a courtyard-type monastery (45 x 40 m), its outer walls (width: 1.05 m; surviving height: 0.65 m) being of the rubble-core, dressed-facing variety. The northern, eastern and southern faces are lined with narrow rectangular rooms (average dimensions: 9 x 4 m), while a rectangular platform (10 x 3.80 m; height: 0.50 m) abuts the western wall. A smaller platform (1.10 x 1.40 m; height: 0.30 m), possibly a stupa base, occupies the centre of the inner courtyard. While the accepted chronology for the courtyard monastery at Sanchi suggests a Phase V date, the rectangular rooms appear to be a hallmark of Phase II.

Mori/Karariya Kherai (SG135c)
There are more Buddhist remains at Mori, the first in a long line of hills which runs north–south from Pagneswar to Raisen on the eastern bank of the River Betwa. The lower western slopes are occupied by a square platform (10 x 10 m), possibly a stupa or temple base, with a heavily disturbed stupa outline close by (diameter: 4 m). There are several prehistoric painted shelters at the eastern edge of the hill, and ancient settlement remains at its southern foot.[23]

Raisen (SG137)
Raisen is situated outside the study area's southernmost boundary, but is included here so as to demonstrate the wider manifestation of the patterns in the study area. The hill is occupied by a large medieval fort (Day 1965, 315) which dominates the landscape for miles around. However, the steep drop on all sides of the hill, and the dramatic cliffs, create a naturally fortified aspect. We know from Andher and Kotra that such sites were favoured locations for Buddhist stupas and monasteries. Indeed, the earlier presence of the *saṅgha* at Raisen is attested by a well-preserved Phase II-type stupa (diameter: 3.50 m; surviving height: 1.50 m) on the SW part of the hill (Plate 66). More stupas and monastery structures are also reported on other parts of the hill, now covered in dense vegetation.[24] A ruined irrigation dam in the valley to the west is discussed in chapter 14, its spatial relationship to Raisen's Buddhist monuments fitting with wider patterns in the study area.

Sector 2b: the eastern hills
The hills in this sector, which contain eleven Buddhist Site Groups, can be divided into three main groupings (Figure 11.7 colour): i) those clustered around the first hill to the east of Sanchi, extending from from Sonthiya to Morel khurd, one of the 'Bhilsa Tope' sites (Cunningham 1854); ii) a second group of hills further to the east, which includes another of the 'Bhilsa Tope' sites, Andher; iii) several low, isolated hills, to the south of the Dabar *nāla*, with numerous Buddhist remains both on their summits and intervening lower ground. In this area it is often difficult to determine where one Buddhist site ends and another begins, thus providing justification for viewing it as a continuous 'Buddhist landscape'.

I) THE FIRST LINE OF HILLS
Murwara (SG118)
Several stupas were documented midway along the first line of hills behind the ancient settlements of Murwara and Bishankara (Figure 11.7 colour).[25] The two largest examples have diameters of 4 m, one following a brick construction, the other modelled on the Phase II type. Nearby are eight slightly smaller stupas (average diameter: 3 m), one of which is set on a square base (3.70 x 3.70 m). Following the stupa typology at Sanchi (Table 9.1), the latter may date to Phase IV or V.

Morel khurd (SG005)
Morel khurd, situated at the southern extent of the first line of hills, is the largest and best-preserved Buddhist site in Sector 2b. The Dabar *nāla*, a large perennial stream which supports several major early settlements,[2] flows by at the southern base of the hill. It is connected to the main site by an ancient paved pathway (Figure 11.8). Midway along is an underground spring, providing fresh drinking water to the site.[27] Additional water-storage facilities are provided by a now dried-up tank to the north of the main complex.[28] The site was first discovered by J. D. Cunningham (1847), with detailed descriptions provided subsequently by his brother, Alexander Cunningham (1854), who carried out the first excavations here. More recently, some excavation and conservation work has been conducted by the ASI (*IAR* 1984–5, 217). Systematic re-exploration during Stage I of the SSP revealed numerous features which are not mentioned in earlier reports and extend beyond the area presently under ASI conservation. These include many stupas, rock-shelters and miscellaneous structural remains mostly concentrated in the north and NE areas. Detailed site-planning, aided by Quickbird satellite imagery (Plate 43), was carried out in Stage II (Figure 11.8).

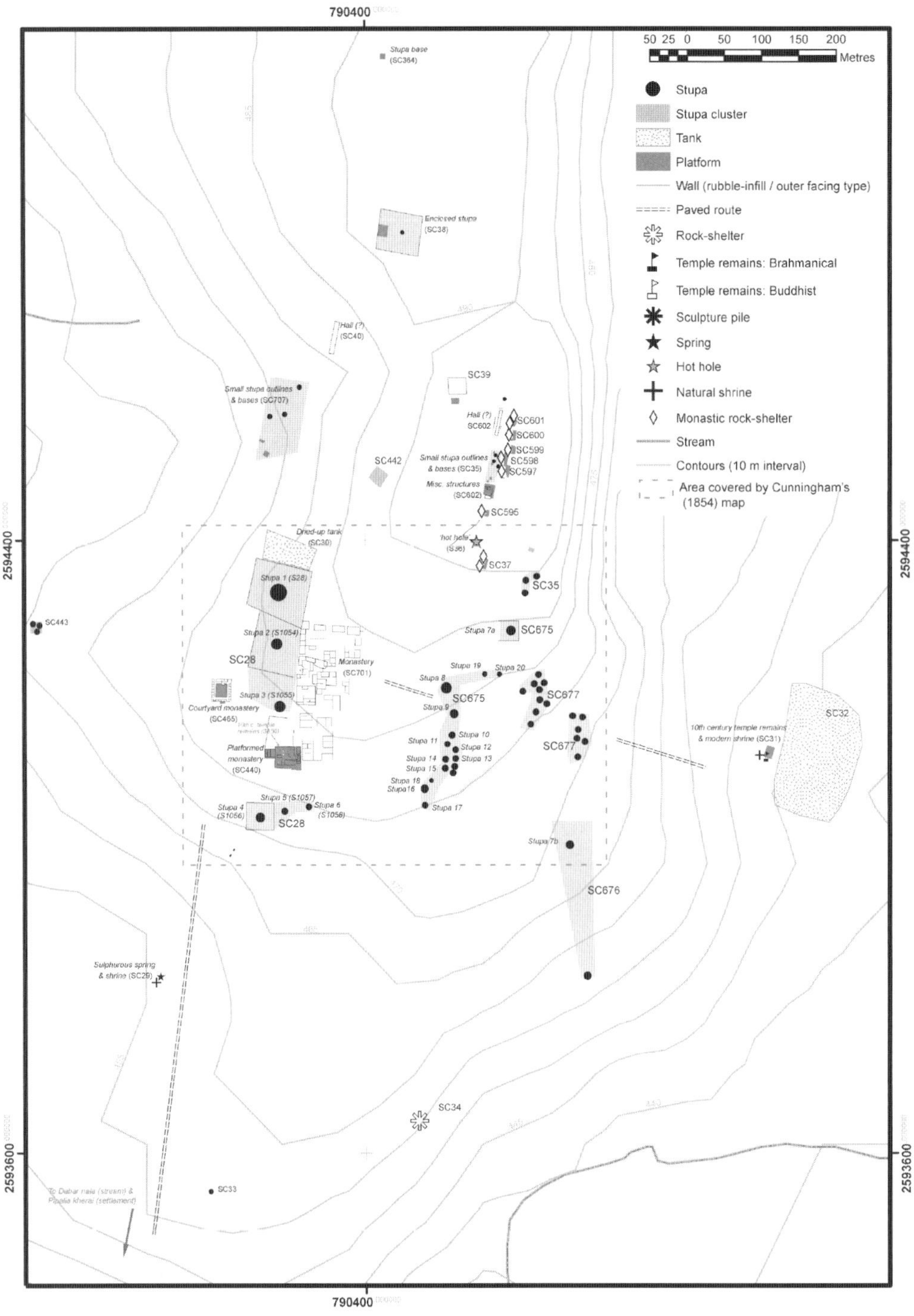

Figure 11.8 Site plan of the Buddhist remains at Morel khurd following renewed mapping in 2004/5 (with AC's mapping area indicated)

The best-preserved structures are spread over three levels: the four largest stupas, and the three principal monasteries, are on the upper plateau, with more than twenty smaller stupas spread over the two lower terraces. During Cunningham's (1854) excavations, inscribed reliquaries, although not connected with the Hemavata school, were retrieved from Stupas 2, 4 and 7 (Willis 2000, 89–94). More unusual deposits were found in some of the smaller stupas on the lower two terraces (nos. 9c, 10, 11, 17, 23), including large quantities of human bones (Table 6.1).[29] Schopen (1997, 8, 183) has suggested that these stupas were connected to a local 'cult of the monastic dead', as attested also at other well-known north Indian sites. Various fragments from stupa railings are scattered around the site and are described in chapter 9.

The upper plateau is dominated by an imposing ashlar platform (Plates 80–1). It measures 35 x 25 m and reaches a height of almost 9 m.[30] The principal remains on the summit include a pile of temple pilasters, a sculpture podium datable to c. tenth century AD (Plate 82), and a Buddha image (Plate 83), now stored in the Sanchi Museum.[31] These remains influenced Cunningham's original supposition that the platform was a temple-base. However, the temple was evidently a later addition, and with the exception of Phase VI and VII structures at Sanchi, represents the latest-known Buddhist monument in the area. The identification, during the SSP, of large quantities of brick fragments, as well as various outlines of rubble-infill, outer-faced walls on the summit (Figure 11.8), suggests that the platform was surmounted by an additional structure, possibly several storeys high. Its fortress-like appearance is accentuated by the remains of four square towers at each corner. As at Sanchi, Satdhara and Sonari, an internal stairway at its NE corner cuts into the podium. Traces of an external stairway on the east side of the platform were also identified. As discussed in Part II, these features attest to a preoccupation with monitoring access to the upper monastery, whose original appearance may not have been dissimilar to the kind of towering, multi-storeyed monasteries that survive today in the Himalayas (Shaw 2000).

A second monastery (29 x 26 m) to the west (Plate 89; Figure 11.8), has also been described in earlier publications as a 'platform' (Cunningham 1854, 328; Willis 2000, 89).[32] However, reaching a height of just 1.55 m, it appears to be of a somewhat different order to the aforementioned structure. Detailed site-mapping in 2004/5 revealed a courtyard plan, lined on all sides by small square cells. Given the accepted chronology for the courtyard monasteries at Sanchi, it may belong to Phase IV or V, although as discussed in chapter 10, the chronology of courtyard-style monasteries is still an unsettled matter.

A third area of monastery structures, included in Cunningham's site-plan (Plate 90), survives to the north of the main platformed monastery and consists of a cluster of irregularly shaped buildings containing one or more rectangular rooms.[33] Similar complexes occur at Devrajpur to the east and Kotra to the west and, as discussed later, may represent an intermediate stage in the development from single-roomed rectangular monasteries, as found, for example, at Satdhara, to the more regular courtyard monastery. However, on account of the homogeneous wall construction of the Morel khurd buildings, together with surface finds of late, coarse grey wares, it is possible that they belong to the site's latest phase of construction, as represented by the tenth-century-AD temple on the summit of the monastery platform. The foundations of a temple and water-tank (160 x 70 m) on the eastern side of the hill date to the same period (Figure 11.8). The question of whether this building phase represents the final stage in a continuous occupational sequence, or a brief period of 'reinvigoration' following a gap in the Buddhist occupation of the site (Willis 2000, 66), clearly deserves further investigation.[34]

Simpler residential facilities, belonging to earlier periods, were also documented in the form of a group of rock-shelters on the lower, NE ledge of the hill. Ten shelters were counted in total, many of which contain prehistoric paintings and microlithic tools. At least seven of these show signs of adaptation for residential use: as at Sanchi (Plate 49) and Ahmadpur in the SSP area, and Pangurariya in the Narmada valley (*IAR* 1975–6, 28–30) (Plate 52), the entrances have been built up into 2 m-high stone platforms, whilst some shelters are separated by stone walls (Plate 50). Some have stupas built directly on top of their overhang (Figure 11.8). Indeed, the narrow plateau above is strewn with small stupas (average diameter: 1–2 m) both with and without square bases.[35]

On the same plateau, there are a number of natural holes which emit hot, sulphurous vapours.[36] Various structural outlines in the immediate vicinity indicate that they were originally enclosed in buildings. These structures may have housed hot baths (*Jantaghara*), described in the Buddhist Canon as one of the ten structural components of a *Saṅgharama* (*Mahavagga* I, 30, 4; *Cullavagga* VI, 1, 2; Marshall 1940, 62). Alternatively they may have been steam rooms for therapeutic 'sweating' (*swedana*) practices of the kind described in ancient medical texts (*Caraka Samhita*, *Sutrasthana*, vol. 1, ch. 14, 268–85).[37] Some of the rock-shelters have large internal openings which may also have been connected to the same network of fault lines, thus possibly representing an early 'central-heating' system!

Systematic exploration revealed a much larger site than suggested by Cunningham's original sketch plan. Outside the formal site boundaries, too, a large dam was identified between Morel khurd hill and Binjoli kherai to the west; this is discussed in chapter 14.[38] On the actual hill, stupas were documented right up to its northern, western and southern-most edges (Figure 11.8). Three square-platformed stupas, set within walled enclosures, were identified in the densely vegetated northern area. Two of these have diameters of 4 m; the other measures 8.40 m.[39] Perched on the northern edge of the hill is a smaller stupa (diameter: 3 m), set on a two-tiered, square platform (6.40 x 6.40 m).[40] Following the stupa typology at Sanchi, all four of these stupas may be assigned to Phase IV or V.

The outlines of miscellaneous square and rectangular structures were also identified in the area between these stupas and the eastern plateau.[41] These may be interpreted variously as store-rooms, congregation halls or refectories. As discussed in chapter 2, one may assume that by the late centuries BC, monks were not compelled to beg for their daily meals, but probably ate together, drawing on stored food resources built up from localised exchange networks. Fogelin (2006, 163–4) has documented similar buildings at Thotlakonda in Andhra Pradesh, suggesting that they would have been largely the responsibility of non-monastic staff. Most monks would only have come into contact with such staff during mealtimes in the refectory, which was purposely kept at a removed distance from the residential and ritual areas of the monastic complex (*ibid.*). Such buildings are rarely commented upon at Sanchi or the 'Bhilsa Topes' sites, but evidently these sites comprised more than stupas, monasteries and temples.[42]

Another cluster of Phase II-type stupas (average diameter: 4.80 m) was noted on the westernmost 'finger' of the hill.[43] Another stupa, set on a circular drum (total diameter: 4 m), is positioned at the southern edge of the hill, several metres from the stone pathway which runs between the central complex and the Dabar *nāla*.[4] The distance between these stupas and the principal monuments may be an indication of their burial *ad sanctos* function.

Immediately below the southern stupa, and overlooking the Dabar *nāla*, are two rock-shelters, one of which contains three painted *śankhalipi* inscriptions (Plate 53),[45] following a similarly 'experimental' style as those found at Ahmadpur in Sector 4 (Plate 54).[46] The second shelter contains a historical painted frieze consisting of a cow, horse-with-rider and camel-with-rider. As at Nagauri, this may be a kind of 'copy' of the processional panels on Buddhist stupa gateways or railing pillars, although no such prototypes have survived at Morel khurd itself.

As at Sanchi, a number of Buddhist remains that may have originated from Morel khurd are now stored in neighbouring settlements and villages. This includes a fragment of a corner railing, now stored at Pipaliya kherai, a prominent settlement mound on the southern bank of the Dabar *nāla*, immediately opposite the aforementioned shelters (Figure 11.7 colour; Plates 5, 100).[47] It has two sockets for receiving the crossbar (*sucika*) (Plate 103) and is decorated on both sides with a closed bud meander and bead motif border, both of which are comparable with carvings on the northern gateway of Sanchi Stupa 1. It was probably taken from Morel khurd, although it bears no

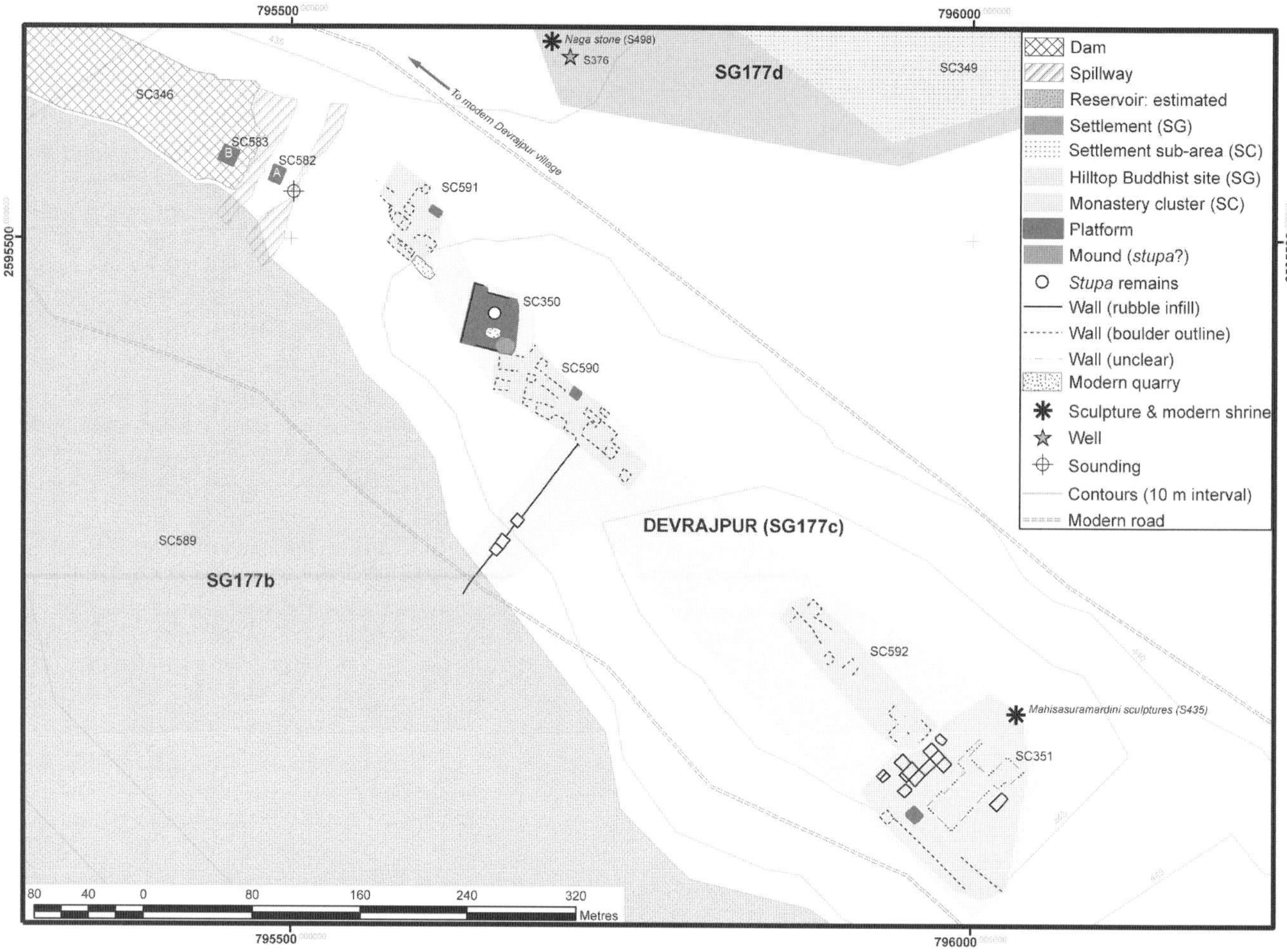

Figure 11.9 Site plan of Buddhist remains on Devrajpur hill

resemblance to any of the carved railings there. A group of Buddhist sculptures was also found at the ancient settlement of Binjoli kherai.[48] The latter is situated on a sandstone outcropping about 1 km to the NW of Morel khurd hill with which it is joined by the remains of an ancient dam discussed in chapter 14. The sculptures, all datable to c. fifth century AD, include a *yakṣa* seated on stool in *lalitāsana* (Plate 134); the lower half of a female figure standing in *sampada* (Plate 135), similar to the Temple 31 *nāginī* at Sanchi; and the lower half of a Bodhisattva-type figure wearing an opaque garment down to the ankles. A small *vedika*, carved with the image of a woman standing on a large fish or crocodile (Plate 104), is currently stored at Devalkhera, one of the major settlements on the bank of the Dabar *nāla*, around 2 km to the west.[49] The manner in which the cloth on the right side of the body falls into a pointed fold shows close similarities with the Besnagar Kubera *yakṣa*[50] discussed in chapter 12, while the heavy, piled up anklets are directly comparable with his *yakṣini* counterpart. However, the highly transparent quality of the cloth, which accentuates the area around the genitals, shows closer parallels with Kusana sculpture of the Mathura region. This piece, which may have come from Morel khurd itself, can thus be placed some time between the first century BC and second century AD. Iconographically, one recalls later images of the goddess Ganga, as typified for example by the doorway carvings found on Gupta temples. However, what may be taken as early prototypical forms of the same goddess are found at Buddhist sites from the late centuries BC. For example, direct comparisons may be drawn with a carved railing from Bharhut, showing Sudarsana *yakṣa* standing on top of a crocodile (Bachhoffer 1939, pl. 19b); and a bas-relief from Nadsur in the Deccan, depicting a couple standing on a large fish (Dehejia 1972, pl. 15).

II) SECOND LINE OF HILLS

Devrajpur (SG177c)

Devrajpur is the largest Buddhist site on the eastern line of hills and is spread out over a narrow escarpment to the north of Karhaud (Figure 11.7 colour). It was first documented in Stage I of the SSP, with systematic mapping conducted in Stage II (Shaw and Sutcliffe 2005; Shaw *et al.*, 2007). The Buddhist remains form part of a series of interrelated Site Groups which taken together constitute an 'early-historic complex'. These include a large reservoir to the west and south (Plate 223; Figure 14.10), and a settlement area to the north, which amongst other things includes temples belonging to the Brahmanical and Jain traditions.[51] The Buddhist site centres on a large stupa (diameter: 9 m), now reduced to several courses of eroded stone blocks (Plates 70–1) situated towards the western end of the escarpment (Figure 11.9). It is set on a 2 m-high platformed area which also includes another possible stupa, seriously damaged by modern quarrying activity. Scattered over the platform, and the area to the west, are outlines of single- and double-roomed rectangular structures, which represent the simplest form of monastic dwelling in the study area. Some of the walls consist of the rubble core, dressed-outer-masonry variety; others are formed from large free-standing boulders, the intervening spaces between which were presumably originally filled with mud or mortar (Plate 94). This simpler wall-construction is also found at Mawasa to the south, but is otherwise less common than the rubble-infill variety. Approximately 500 m to the east is a more complex monastery, consisting of a series of interconnected dwellings, some of which are loosely arranged around a central court. The individual rooms vary in shape and size, possibly indicating an early date.

Karhaud kherai (SG012b)

More Buddhist remains are situated at Karhaud kherai, a low-lying rocky outcrop about 2 km to the south of Devrajpur, between Karhaud and Morel khurd (Figure 11.7 colour). These include a heavily damaged stupa now reduced to a mound (diameter: 6.5 m; surviving height: 2 m) strewn with dressed and undressed stone masonry blocks. Around the stupa is a series of interconnected courtyards (average dimensions: 30 x 30 m), lined by narrow, rectangular rooms with walls (average width: 1 m; surviving height: 1 m) of the rubble-core, dressed-facing variety. This is also datable to Phase II.

All of these remains have been heavily damaged due to modern quarrying activity which has exposed sections up to 1 m deep. These contained numerous pottery fragments which were collected and studied during the SSP, a rare occurrence at Buddhist sites where surface collections are seldom available due to unploughed ground conditions. The assemblage, datable between Phases II and IV, was dominated by micaceous wares (type 13), burnished red wares (types 10a–b and 14a) and grey slipped wares (type 5a). While proving fortuitous for dating purposes, the rapid level of quarrying damage provided a forceful reminder of the urgency for systematic mapping at other, hitherto undisturbed sites.

Bawaliya hill (SG175)

More Buddhist remains were identified at Bawaliya, an isolated hill between Karhaud and Andher. The dramatic cliffs and rocky outcrops on its northern and eastern edges create a naturally fortified aspect,[52] while the western edge is protected by a massive fortification wall (width: 3.20 m; surviving height: 1.50 m). The entrance is situated midway along this wall, with the remains of a small room (10 x 10 m), possibly a guard-tower, to the south, and an additional five platforms (3.20 x 3.20 m), separated by c. 15 m intervals, further to the north. These create a distinctly military tone, reasons for which are discussed in Part II. Another wall to the south runs west–east across the hill. The resulting enclosure (c. 130 x 130 m) contains several heavily disturbed rectangular outlines, possibly simple monasteries, and five square platforms (c. 3.50 x 3.50 m), presumably stupa bases. A large stone-paved pathway runs north–south across the length of the compound. This site may have been the residential counterpart for nearby Andher which consists mainly of stupas.

Andher (SG013)

The stupas at Andher are perched on the edge of a solitary hill c. 1 km to the south of Bawaliya hill. As at Bawaliya, the hill has a naturally fortified appearance: it is defended on one side by a sheer cliff, and has a long gradual slope on the other (Plates 2, 142). The site has been more or less neglected since Cunningham's (1854) time, apart from some basic forest clearance carried out by the ASI in the 1920s (Willis 2000, 96). No water source has been located on the hill itself; the nearest being the small *bauri* next to the Phase III Bhagavata cult spot at its eastern base;[53] a number of ancient tanks were also identified at Hakimkheri c. 750 m to the south (Figure 11.7 colour).[54]

The central stupa (no. 1) is surrounded by a ground balustrade, most of which is still *in situ* (Plate 65). As discussed in chapter 9, the carved railings are closely related, both in style and content, to those of Sanchi, Stupa 2. Lying to the south is a corner post, decorated with a scene from the story of Buddha's conception (Willis 2000, fig. 117; Behrendt 2000). There are also several smaller stupas, all without balustrades (Figure 11.10). Reliquaries were found in Stupas 1–3, those from nos. 2–3 bearing inscriptions associated with the Hemavata school (Table 6.1; Willis 2000, 96–9; Cunningham 1854, 222–5). To the south of Stupa 1 is a heavily eroded platform (18.30 x 12 m) which was probably the base of a several-storeyed monastery. Supplementary residential quarters of a simpler nature were available at Bawaliya just to the north, which was probably attached to Andher.

Exploration during the SSP revealed additional remains not mentioned in Cunningham's report. These included a Phase II-type stupa (diameter: 3.20 m; standing height: 1.20 m) to the north of the main complex (Figure 11.10) and a square-platformed stupa (4 x 4 m), possibly dating to Phase IV or V, at the southern edge of the hill in an area now covered with dense, prickly scrub. It is situated at some distance from the main complex and is further cut off by a massive fortification wall (width: 2 m; surviving height: 1 m), which runs east–west across the northern edge of the enclosure and continues along the hill's western edge (Plate 98). However, despite this deliberate demarcation from the main complex, Stupa 1 is still in clear visual range. As discussed in Part II, this may reflect a level of deference to the hierarchical structure of the relic cult, the central complex being reserved for the stupas of the Hemavatas.

As at the main complex, this part of the site has a striking military appearance: the fortification wall has a large rectangular bastion at its SW corner and a circular tower positioned midway along its western length, while the southern and eastern edges of the hill are naturally defended by a line of cliffs and a sheer drop below. The objective behind these and similar defensive provisions at other Buddhist sites is taken up in Part II.

Bawaliya/Dharoyi hill (SG172)

Structural remains, with possible Buddhist associations, were also documented on the hill immediately to the east of Andher. These consisted of four faint circular outlines (average diameter: 4 m), positioned directly within visual range of Andher, Stupa 1. However, due to poor preservation their identification as stupas remains tentative. Close by, on the northern edge of the hill, are a large number of rock-shelters containing both prehistoric and early-historic paintings.

III) ISOLATED HILLS TO THE SOUTH

Mawasa (SG090)

The best-preserved Buddhist site in this area is Mawasa, which covers the lower slopes and summit of an isolated hill approximately 2.5 km south of Morel khurd (Figure 11.11) and overlooking the ancient settlement remains in and around the modern village of Nihalpur.[55] The site, also known as Atari or Kacheri (literally 'court') after the monumental, platformed

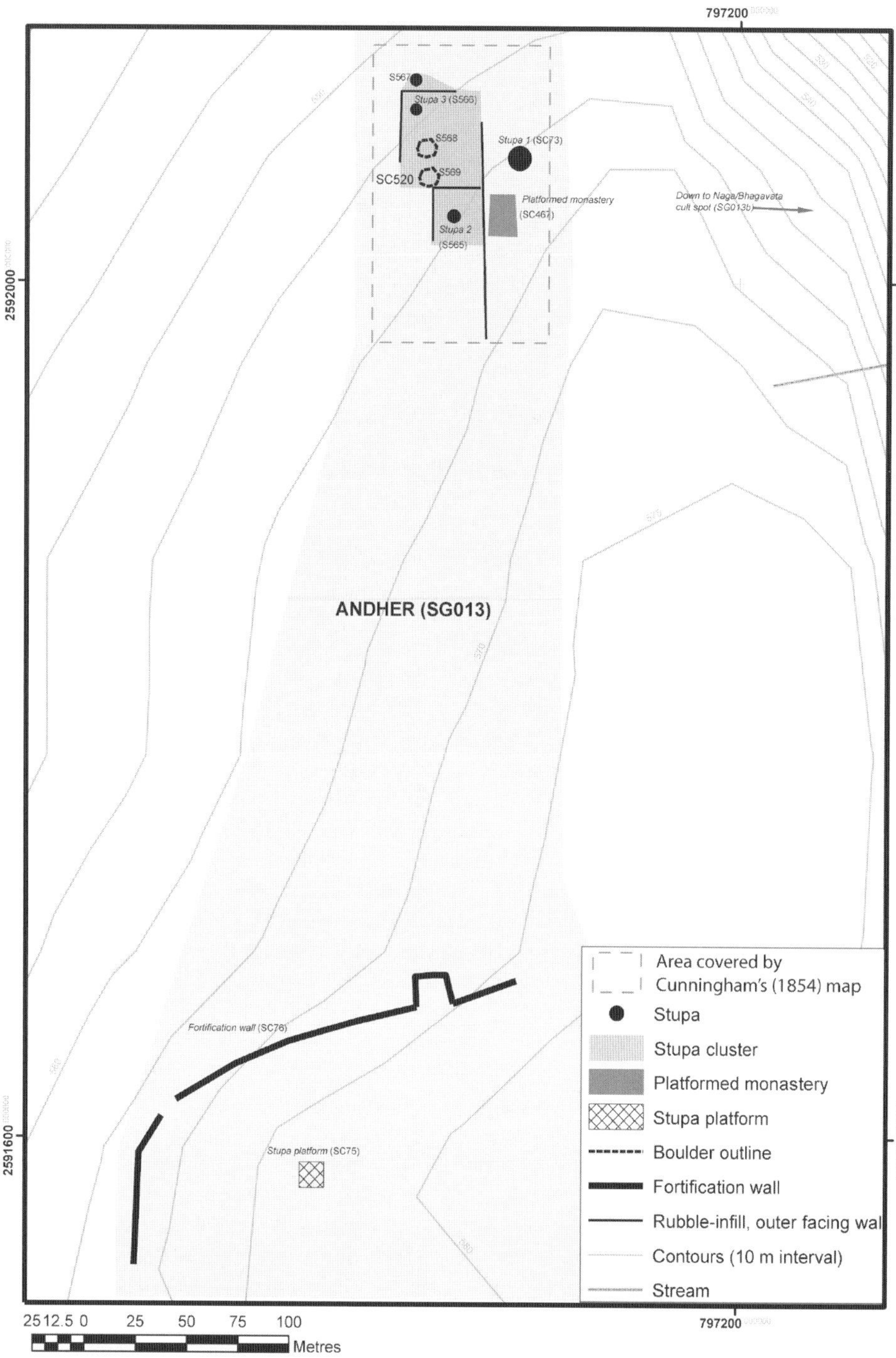

Figure 11.10 Site plan of Andher following renewed mapping (with AC's mapping area indicated)

entrance on the lower east side of the hill (Plate 84), was first documented in Stage I, with detailed mapping work carried out during Stage II. The site is organised over three tiers, the lower two consisting of monastery complexes set on high platforms, with a well-preserved stupa, surrounded by monastery structures, on the uppermost tier.

The structures on the lowest tier all occur on top of a 4 m-high platform (approximately 20 x 20 m) built into the eastern edge of the hill. The platform is approached by two sets of external stairways (width: 1.80 m), at its NE and SE corners. Both the platform and stairways are constructed from large dressed blocks up to 1 cubic metre in size. At the foot of the NE stairway is a small square platform (c. 4 x 4 m), possibly a stupa base. At either side of the platform, a 2 m-wide boundary wall, made up of a homogeneous core of unhewn boulders and dressed masonry facing, extends along the southern and northern edges of the hill. The platform itself is lined on its eastern, western and southern edges by a series of narrow rectangular rooms which may have been used for residential purposes.

At the centre of the platform are additional structures, surviving either as faint outlines, or actual standing walls, the most prominent being a single-roomed building intact up to its collapsed roof (Plates 84, 86; Figure 11.12). It measures 10 x 8 m at its base and survives to a height of 2.35 m, the outer walls consisting of six courses of massive stone masonry blocks of similar proportions to those used in the main platform and staircases. The entrance way, cut into the western wall, is 1.35 m high with a lower, 1 m-high, doorframe set further into the building by 1 m. The precise

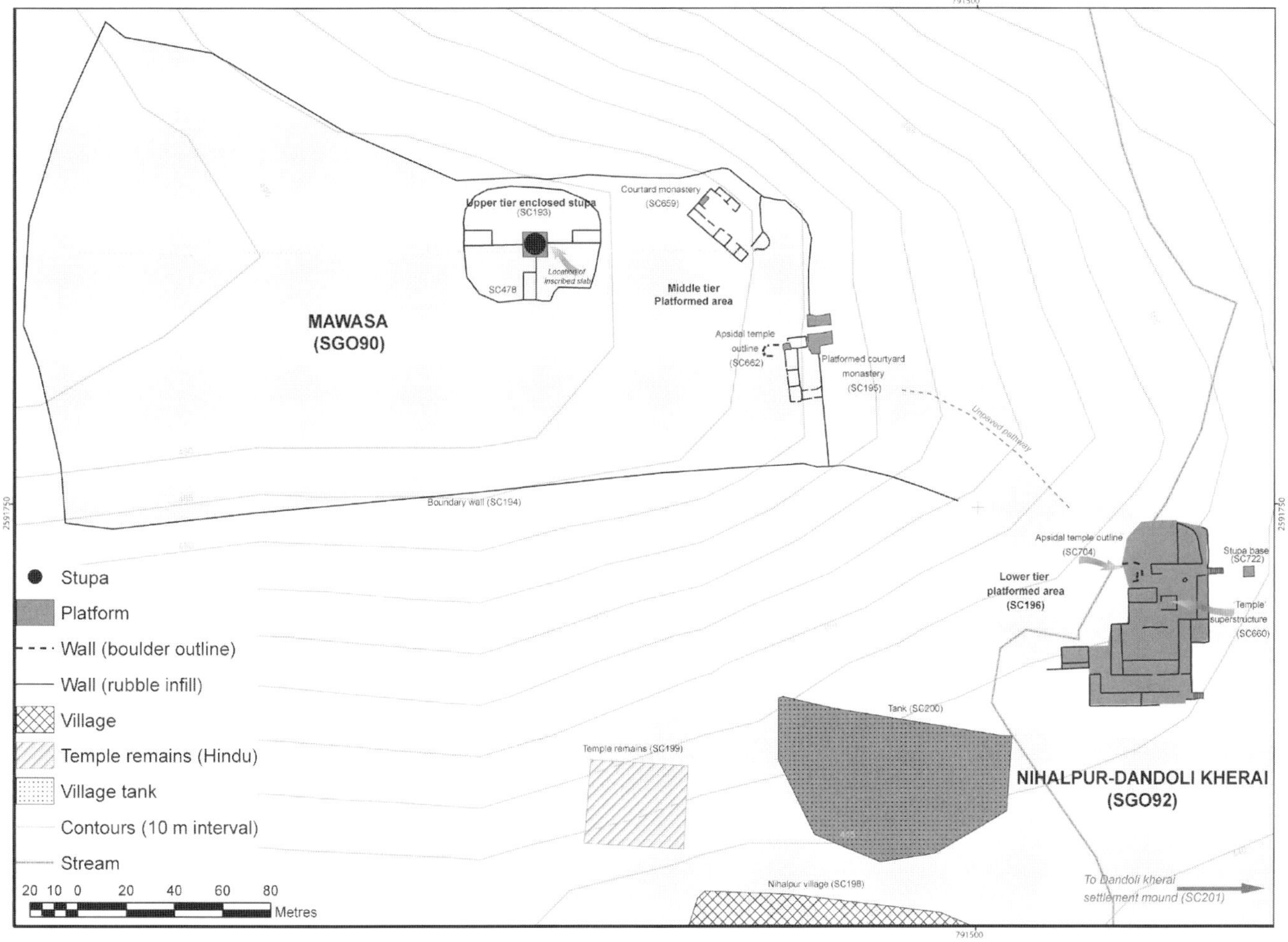

Figure 11.11 Site plan of Buddhist complex at Mawasa

function of this remarkably well-preserved building is unclear, but a guard room or shrine are strong possibilities.

The similarity between the stone blocks used in this structure and those in the platform and staircase provides strong evidence for a single building phase for both elements. Further, that the lower tier, as the entrance to the whole complex, was built around the same time as the two upper tiers, and thus formed part of the original design, is suggested by its overall formal and monumental appearance. As discussed later, a Phase II date is indicated by the method of construction of the stupa on the uppermost tier, and an associated donative inscription datable to the second or first century BC. If the structure in question is indeed a shrine, then it would represent the earliest-known standing example in India.

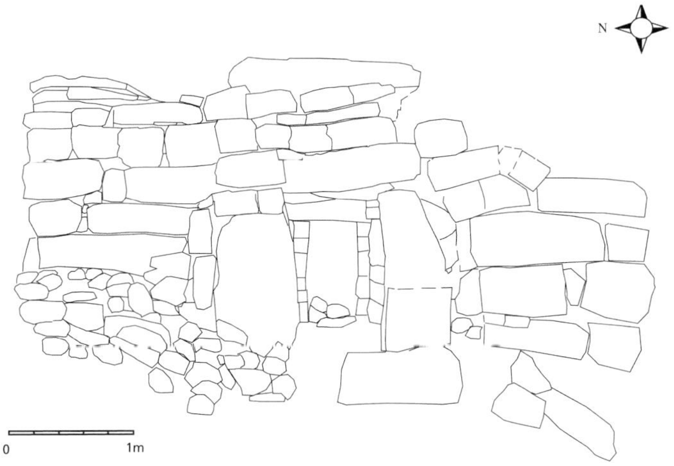

Figure 11.12 Plan of 'temple' at Mawasa

Immediately behind this structure to the NW is the outline of an apsidal structure, its entrance opening out to the east. The walls are not of the commonly used rubble-infill, outer-facing variety, but rather consist of large upright boulders set into the ground. Similar boulder-walled structures are used in some of the simple rectangular monastic structures at Devrajpur (Plate 94), and may originally have been filled in with mud or mortar. As discussed later, a similar apsidal structure occurs on the second tier. The apsidal-ended plan is suggestive of an early date, the closest parallels being provided by excavated Mauryan temple foundations at Sanchi, Satdhara and Vidisha, and Mauryan and post-Mauryan rock-cut *caityas* in Bihar and the Deccan.

The second tier is situated further up the eastern side of the hill, and linked to the lower terrace by a stone-paved pathway. It too consists of a massive platform, but this time approached via a narrow corridor cut through its main body (Plate 85). On either side of the platform is a 2 m-wide wall which skirts the eastern edge of the hill. Like the lower platform, its summit is covered with various structural remains. To the south of the entrance is a courtyard monastery (26 x 14 m) (Figure 11.11), comprising a central hall lined on the west, north and south by rectangular rooms as found on the lower tier. The walls, of the rubble-infill, outer-facing variety, vary between 0.6 and 1.0 m in width. The large rectangular rooms form a contrast to the single-occupancy cells found in the more regularly planned courtyard monasteries at Sanchi, and may have provided dormitory-style accommodation, possibly for junior monks and pilgrims. These structures, together with the interlinked courtyard monasteries at Devrajpur and Kotra, may thus represent an elaboration on the simple single- or double-roomed rectangular monasteries found at sites such as Devrajpur or Satdhara. Further, the platformed plinths on both the lower and middle tiers are sufficiently similar to the monastery platforms at the 'Bhilsa Tope' sites to suggest that both the platforms and the overlying monastery structures date to Phase II. As discussed in Part II, this evidence provides a crucial key for dating similar rectangular monasteries, whether standing as independent structures or within a larger courtyard setting, at other sites in the study area.

A second, less well-preserved monastery is situated approximately 80 m to the NW. This also follows a courtyard plan (30 x 17 m), with rectangular rooms lining the inner south, west and east wall, and a raised platform on the inner northern wall.

At the NW outer corner of the first monastery, the outline of an apsidal-ended structure, following the same boulder-walled construction as the aforementioned outline on the lower tier, was documented. It is oriented on a west–east axis, its entrance looking eastwards towards the monastery (Figure 11.11; Plate 96).

The upper tier, situated on the summit of the hill, is also reached by a stone pathway. It is protected on its northern, southern and eastern edges by another 2 m-wide boundary wall surviving to a height of 1 m. Roughly in the centre is a relatively well-preserved stupa (surviving height: 1.5 m; diameter: 7.5 m) set on a square platform (10 x 10 m; height: 1.40 m) (Plate 72). It is surrounded by a variety of structural remains, difficult to map due to dense vegetation cover. Notable features, however, include three radial walls which extend perpendicularly from the southern, western and eastern sides of the stupa platform to join the outer boundary wall mentioned above (Figure 11.11). Various rectangular rooms were also identified, including one (30 x 10 m) built against the southern radial wall. These may have performed a residential function as in the case of the rectangular rooms set within the courtyard monasteries on the lower tiers.

Many of the stupa's dressed-stone-facing slabs remain *in situ*, whilst others have collapsed, forming piles of adjoining debris. One slab, measuring 44 x 28 x 20 cm, was discovered in 2000, lying amidst fallen debris on the eastern side of the stupa (Plates 73–4). It bears an engraved inscription in Brahmi characters datable to between the second and first centuries BC. Palaeographically, it is comparable to the Phase II railing inscriptions at Sanchi, and the Heliodorus pillar inscription at Vidisha. Its current location suggests that it was originally positioned within the main body of outer facing. The inscription, a rubbing of which is reproduced in Figure 11.13, reads *makaḍeyena karapite*. This translates as '[This was] caused to be made by Makadeya', the proper name being combined with the third person instrumental singular suffix *-ena*.[56] Grammatically it is idiosyncratic, combining as it does the western 'r' with the eastern nominative singular ending, 'e'. This particular combination has been noted in a number of Asokan inscriptions, the usual explanation being that it represents the work of a scribe who, having received an exemplar containing the usual eastern 'l' and 'e', was not very consistent in his 'translation' to 'r' and 'o' (K.R. Norman, pers. comm.). If the block inscription is complete, i.e. if we can be sure that *karapite* is the complete word

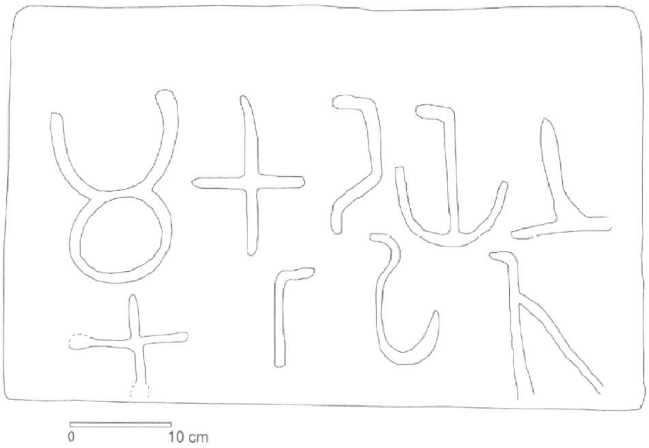

Figure 11.13 Rubbing of inscribed slab at Mawasa

and that 'e' is the end of it, we can probably rule out any 'incomplete translation' theory. We should simply have to accept therefore that the word was written this way for reasons known only to the scribe.

Interestingly, this particular wording is not found in any of Phase II donative inscriptions known from Sanchi or Satdhara. These usually end in the word *danam*, referring to the gift of individual components such as railing parts and paving slabs. By contrast, the Mawasa inscription probably refers to the construction of the *whole* stupa, and perhaps even the surrounding buildings, although we cannot say so for sure.[57] The buildings on the two lower tiers, which evidently form part of an integrated three-tiered site design datable to Phase II, may also have been funded by the same donor.

It is interesting to note that the stupas at Morel khurd to the north and Andher to the NE are in direct visual range from Mawasa. Despite the absence of donative inscriptions at these sites it has been assumed that they were funded by similar collective forms of patronage as attested at Sanchi and Satdhara. Furthermore, inscribed reliquaries show that all of the 'Bhilsa Tope' sites were under the control of the Hemavata school. The Mawasa inscription, therefore, provides crucial insights into the nature of patronage beyond the context of these sites. Whoever Makadeya was, his ability to fund an entire complex as opposed to single architectural components marks him out as an important figure. Further, the inscription's causative construction combined with the use of the nominative singular indicates Makadeya's stature as one who has the ability to get things done. The possibility that Makadeya was indeed a member of royalty is strengthened by early Brahmi inscriptions from Sri Lanka in which *karapite* occurs in a similar way. For example, in at least two inscriptions recording the donation of rock-shelter dwellings, the agents of the 'karapite' act are members of royalty (Paranavitana *IC*, I, Nos. 500, 813).[58]

The level of monumentality represented by the remains on the lower platformed terraces also raises questions about the identity of the relic held within the stupa at the site's summit. It is possible that, being in direct visual range of Morel khurd and Andher, it held some kind of burial *ad sanctos* function, with its sanctity being derived by reference to the Hemavata sites. However, it may also have been an important stupa in its own right, and operating in direct competition to the Hemavata tradition as

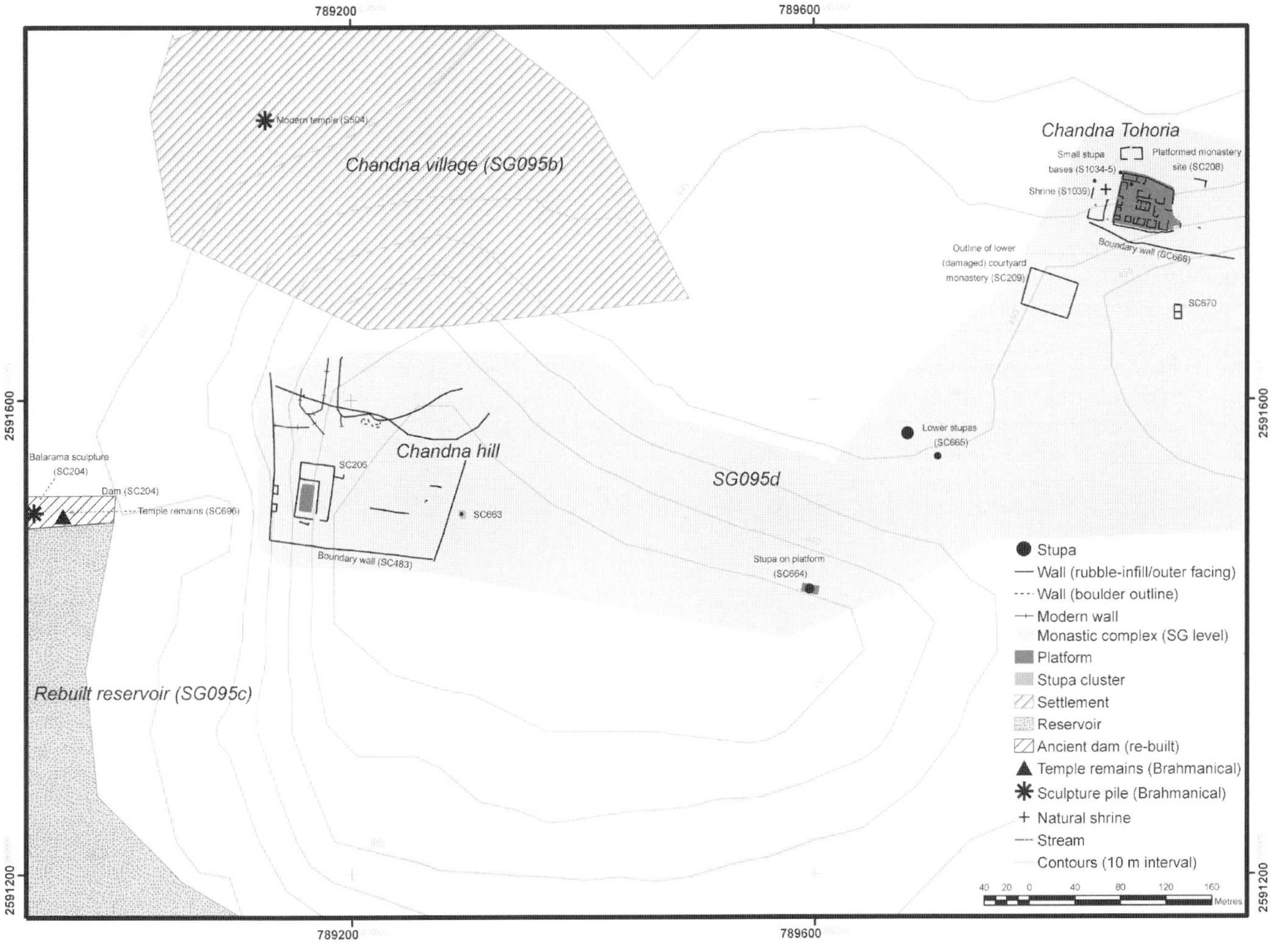

Figure 11.14 Site plan of Buddhist remains in and around Chandna and Chandna Tohoria

embodied in the network of associated relics in the Sanchi area. A similar story may well apply to neighbouring sites which have not yet yielded relics or indeed epigraphical evidence of the kind found at Mawasa.

Such an important and well-preserved site is obviously urgently in need of state protection, especially given its proximity to other ASI-protected sites. Due to the portability of the inscribed slab it is recommended that it be taken into safekeeping, while some of the structural remains are in need of careful conservation to prevent further damage. This applies especially to the remarkable free-standing structure on the lower tier. The fact that it is still standing is due in part to the support afforded by surrounding trees. However, the lintel could collapse at any moment, and conservation measures are urgently required.

Chandna hill and Chandna Tohoria (SG095d)

This extensive Buddhist Site Group is made up of a number of separate 'sites' which are spread over distinct topographical settings but are classified here as a single site entity due to their continuous distribution and the difficulty in determining where one 'site' ends and another begins.[59] There are two hilltop Buddhist complexes, the first, on Chandna hill, overlooking the modern village of Chandna, and the second, on Chandna Tohoria hill, situated immediately to the east. Additional Buddhist remains cover the intervening valley, while a third hillock (Chandna Tohoria-b), which according to villagers also bore structural remains prior to their destruction during recent quarrying activity, may also have formed part of this larger Buddhist Site Group. Taken together, these remains form part of a wider 'early-historic complex' comprising several other types of Site Groups including ancient settlement remains behind Chandna village, and a recently constructed reservoir to the south.[60]

The principal structure on Chandna hill is a walled enclosure (40.70 x 40.70 m) at the SW edge of the hill. An entrance way is cut into its northern wall, and at its centre is a 1 m-high platform (29.6 x 16.3 m) similar in appearance to monastery platforms found at other Buddhist sites. Several faint outlines of small stupas (diameter: 1 m) are scattered around the surrounding area. A larger stupa set on a 1 m-high square platform (8 x 8 m) is situated on a narrow outcropping at the easternmost edge of the hill. Both elements are constructed from very large blocks, reminiscent in scale and appearance to those used in the lower platformed terrace at Mawasa.

Like many other hilltop Buddhist sites, the main complex to the SW is protected by a fortification wall of the rubble-core, dressed-facing variety (width: 2 m). This skirts the southern and western edges of the hill and continues across its centre at the eastern side of the complex (Plate 99; Figure 11.14). Two small rectangular structures built into the southern wall may have functioned as guard towers.

A similar fortification wall (width: 1.6 m) protects the southern edge of Chandna Tahoria hill immediately to the east (Figure

11.14). The southern part of the hill is built up into a platformed terrace, and surmounted by a large courtyard (60 x 60 m) which bears faint traces of cells, their walls following the rubble-infill, outer-facing construction method. Unlike the courtyard monasteries at Sanchi, these are of an irregular shape and size and include both square (c. 4.5 x 4.5 m) and rectangular rooms, representing single and dormitory-type accommodation respectively. As at Mawasa, these may be an earlier prototype of the more regular monastery form found at Sanchi from the late Gupta period onwards. Scattered throughout the site are various small square stupa bases (c. 1.2 x 1.2 m) (Plate 62). At the centre of the courtyard is a raised platform surmounted by a three-roomed structure with walls surviving to a height of c. 1 m. As opposed to the rubble-infill, outer-facing type used in the courtyard monastery, these are constructed from homogeneous rubble. This may thus represent a later addition to the site, together with a rectangular structure at the northern foot of the monastery, which has similar walls.

The unploughed valley between the two hillocks also bears Buddhist remains, including a courtyard-style monastery (35 x 35 m) at the southern foot of Chandna Tohoria (Figure 11.14).[61] Its small, regularly sized cells (3 x 3 m) are similar to late-Gupta examples at Sanchi, suggesting therefore that it dates to a later period than its hilltop counterpart. Further to the west, immediately below the platformed stupa at the eastern edge of Chandna hill, are two heavily damaged stupas (diameters: 9 m and 4.5 m; surviving height: 0.3 m). The unusual setting of these remains may be explained by the fact that, due to shallow soil coverage in this area, the valley is unfit for cultivation.

The sheer extent of Buddhist remains on and between Chandna and Chandna Tohoria hills justifies viewing the area as a single extended Buddhist Site Group. Variations in monastery plan and wall typologies suggest a time range between Phases II to IV or V, with additional chronological insights provided by wider contextual information such as the Phase IIIa Balarama-*nāga* sculpture on the dam in the valley to the west of Chandna hill (Plates 141, 221) discussed in chapters 12 and 14.

Salera (SG170b)

Similarly dispersed Buddhist remains are found on Salera hill, about 2.5 km to the SW of Chandna (Figure 11.15):[62] from the hill's northernmost to southernmost ends, this Site Group covers a distance of 2 km. Originally documented in Stage I, but systematically mapped during Stage II, it forms part of a larger 'early-historic complex' comprising ancient settlement remains in and around the modern village of Salera, a now-dried up village tank, and important Brahmanical sculpture and temple remains datable between Phases IIIb and VII.[63] At the northern end of the hilltop is a well-preserved Phase II-type stupa (diameter: 5.15 m), known locally as Tegri.[64] It is set on a circular plinth

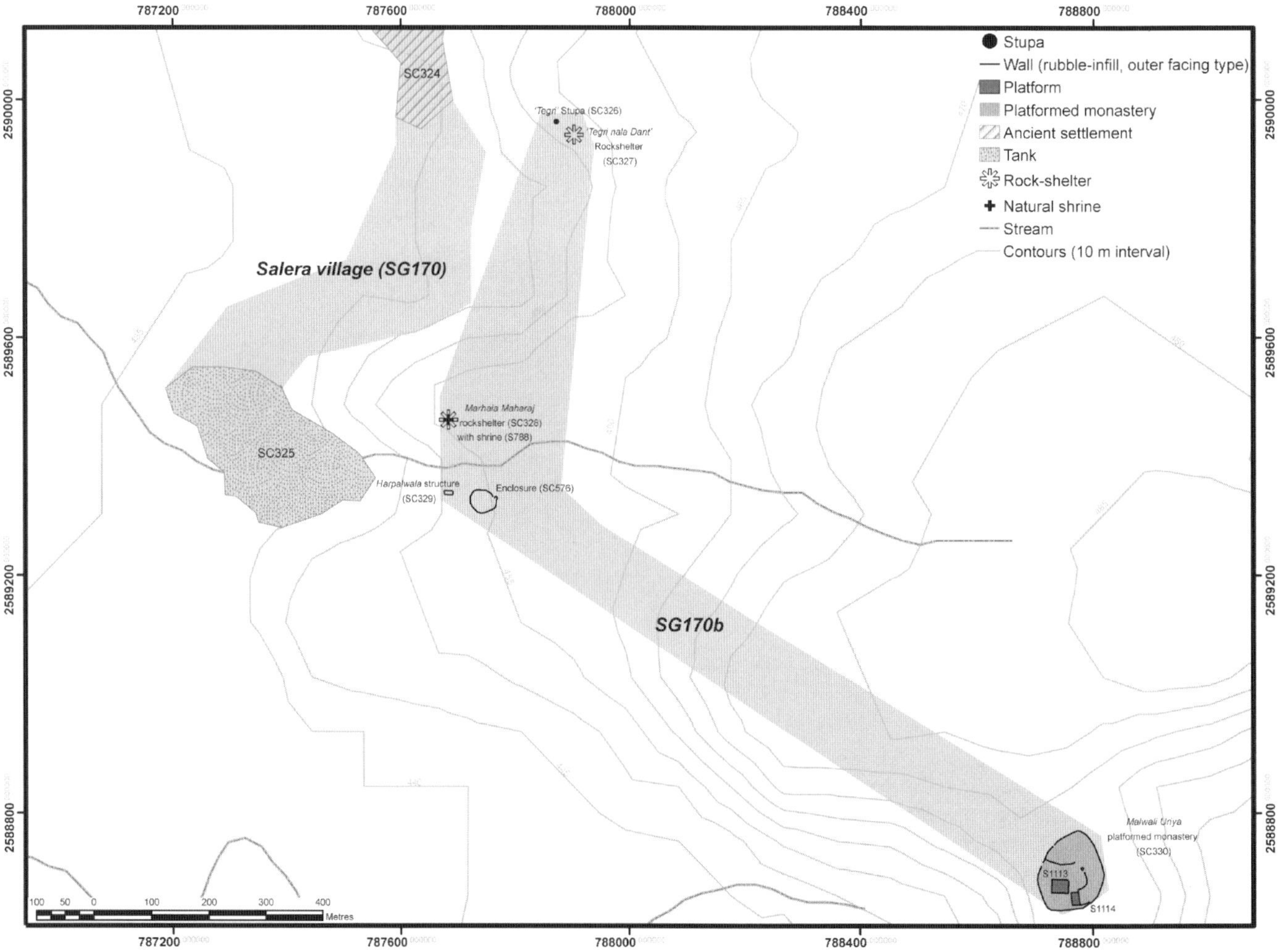

Figure 11.15 Site plan of Buddhist remains on Salera hill

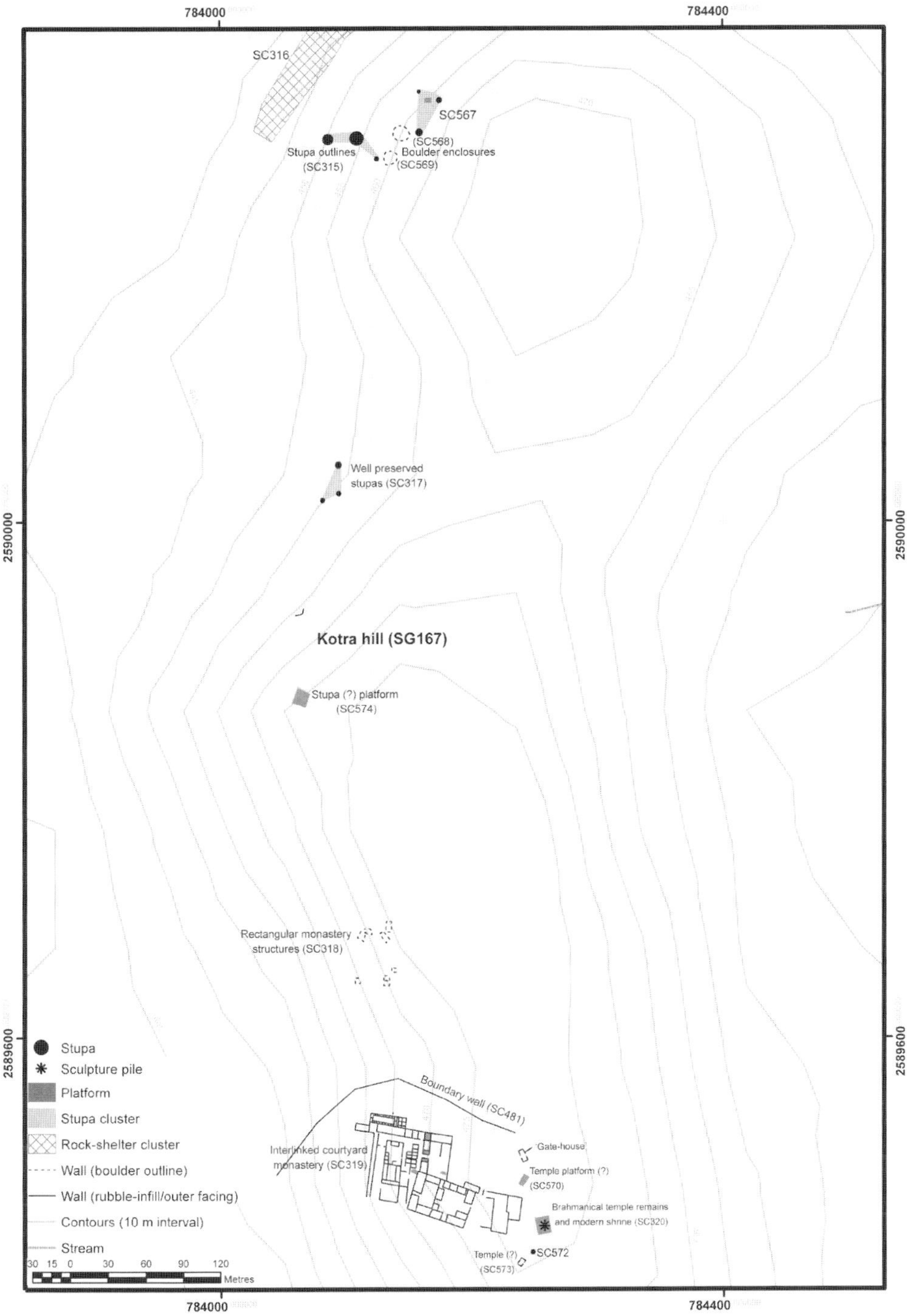

Figure 11.16 Site plan of Buddhist complex on Kotra hill

(width of *pradakṣinapatha*: 0.70 m) (Plate 75), creating a total height of 2 m. Around nine courses of dressed masonry facing remain *in situ*.

Nearby, in a rock-shelter known locally as *dant* ('teeth'), is a fresh-water spring which supplies a large perennial stream, the primary feeder for the now dried-up tank in the valley below. On the northern bank of this stream, about 600 m to the SW, is a site known locally as Harpalwala,[65] which consists of two additional structures of a more ambiguous nature: i) a 1 m-high platform (9.80 x 7.50 m), possibly a temple or stupa base; and ii) a large circular enclosure (diameter: 30 m) with walls (height: 0.75 m) of the rubble-infill, outer-facing variety and six courses of masonry surviving to a height of 0.8 m (Figure 11.15). A circular feature on one side of the entrance in the NE may have been a tower; however, the overall function of this enclosure remains unknown.

Approximately 1.25 km to the SE is a large, roughly circular (diameter: 100 m) platformed structure, known locally as Malwali Uriya (Plate 87).[66] It is surrounded on all sides by a 1 m-thick boundary wall (inner-rubble, outer-facing type), entered at its NW corner. The entire southern part of the enclosure is built up into a 3 m-high mound, further heightened by two more platforms, one (40 x 50 m; height: 3 m) near the western wall and another (15 x 15 m) to the south. The eastern area of the enclosure is partitioned off by an inner wall and contains a large amount of building debris including several circular outlines (diameter: 1 m). The overall function of this unusual platformed structure remains unknown, but it is possible that it bore a similar residential purpose to the better-preserved monastery platforms at Morel khurd or Mawasa.

Kotra (SG167)

Another large Buddhist Site Group covers most of Kotra hill about 3.5 km to the west of Salera (Plate 44; Figure 11.16).[67] Its wider 'early-historic complex' comprises an ancient settlement and a stone-lined tank at the northern foot of the hill.[68] The Buddhist remains are distributed over two main zones which largely follow topographical divisions: most of the monasteries are situated on the southern plateau, while the stupas are mainly restricted to the north and the intervening, lower saddle.

The northern plateau is protected by a 2 m-wide boundary wall on its western edge above a line of prehistoric painted rock-shelters. Several heavily damaged stupa outlines (average diameter: 3 m), miscellaneous platforms and a well-preserved stupa set on a square platform (8 x 8 m) were documented here. Further to the south, on the low saddle between the two plateaus, are three stupas (diameter: 3 m; surviving height: 1 m), with dressed masonry facing still intact in places.

The southern monastic zone is cordoned off from the north by a massive fortification wall (width: 1.6 m; surviving height: 1.5 m) which runs from the western to eastern edge of the escarpment and continues along the eastern edge of the hill. Midway along the eastern wall is an entrance-way with platforms on either side, presumably forming the bases of guard rooms. The enclosed area is occupied by a series of interconnected courtyard monasteries (Plate 44; Figure 11.16), each measuring an average of 15 x 30 m and lined on all sides by small regularly shaped square cells (3 x 3 m). Their similarity to courtyard monasteries at Sanchi is suggestive of a late date. Additional monastic structures were documented outside the enclosed area towards the saddle in the north. These consist of square and rectangular structures, surviving as boulder-wall outlines. Similar structures are found at Devrajpur and may be earlier in date to the courtyard monasteries to the south. However, it is also possible that both types of monasteries co-existed and simply provided accommodation to different ranks of monks.

Various other structural remains were documented around the southern monastic complex including a rectangular platform (8.5 x 4.5 m), possibly a temple base; and a small stupa outline (diameter: 2.5 m). Also in this area is a ruined tenth-century-AD Brahmanical temple, now incorporated into a modern Hanuman shrine. Together with additional Brahmanical remains within the ancient settlement on the lower slopes of the northern plateau, this late addition to the site forms part of a body of evidence, discussed in chapter 12, for the shifting balance between Buddhist and Brahmanical patronage networks in the latter part of the first millennium AD.

Sector 4: the northern hills

Sector 4, to the north of the River Bes, is dominated by flat, agricultural terrain, interspersed by just five small, but distinctive, hillocks (Figure 11.17 colour), three of which have Buddhist associations. However, whilst two of these, Torin and Bighan, can be defined as exclusively Buddhist sites, Ahmadpur in the far north has more varied ritual affiliations, of which Buddhism forms only a single component. It thus belongs to a somewhat different category, as do the mixed ritual sites of Udayagiri and Lohangi hill in the vicinity of Vidisha (Figure 11.1 colour). Beyond Ahmadpur, the land levels out until it joins the hilly region of Shamshabad around 50 km to the north. Although lying beyond the northern boundary of the study area, a Buddhist site in this area, Budha Pahar, is also included in the following discussion in order to demonstrate the wider manifestation of patterns outside the Sanchi-Vidisha area.

Bighan (SG035)

Bighan is the largest and best-preserved Buddhist Site Group in this sector. Its principal monuments are spread over two tiers of a low oblong-shaped hill, about 3 km NW of Udayagiri, on the northern bank of the River Bes (Figure 11.17 colour).[69] During the summer months, the river is fordable at Bighan village and Udayagiri,[70] but at other times of the year, the site is reached via the Vidisha-Ahmadpur road. Bighan village is positioned on the opposite bank (SG110). Nearby Site Groups which may have formed part of a single, interrelated 'early-historic complex' include the ruined dam at the northern foot of the Bighan hill and ancient settlement remains on Bagri-Jamwar hill to the NE.[71]

Captain Fell's report on Sanchi (reproduced in Prinsep 1834) contains the earliest known reference to the site: here he quotes Dr. Yeld's advice to visit the buildings at 'Jhinneah ka purar, 3 miles northwest of Oodyagiri' (*ibid.*, 489). Several years later, the brother of Alexander Cunningham, J.D. Cunningham (1847, 756), refers to a 'Jain hill, 3 miles northwest of Udayagiri'. Although the site is not mentioned by name, and no Jain monuments have subsequently been identified here,[72] it probably corresponds to the 'Bigan [*sic*] topes', the subject of H. Lake's (1910b, 145-6) short note which follows his better-known report on Besnagar (Lake 1910a). Despite the site's description by Lake, together with its proximity to Vidisha and its visual prominence from Sanchi (Lake 1910b, 145), it has not figured in subsequent literature,[73] and has consequently had little impact on the received understanding of the region's religious geography. It has also been excluded from any state-level conservation or protection measures.[74] Remarkably, however, in spite of increasing quarrying activity at the site, the principal structures appear to have undergone little deterioration since being described by Lake.

The hilltop complex is spread over two tiers with a variety of well-preserved stupas and other structures on the lower plateau to the south (Figures 11.17, 11.18), and a large, but heavily eroded stupa on the summit. Only the remains on the lower plateau figure in Lake's report, possibly due to their better-preserved condition.

The lower plateau is dominated by a large stupa (diameter: 17 m; surviving height: 2.60 m) built on top of a circular terrace (height: 2 m) (Plate 67). This creates a 1.8 m wide *pradakṣinapatha*, reached by a double set of steps (width: 1.65 m) on the east. The total original height, according to Lake's (1910b, 146) calculations, would have been around 13 m. Lake (*ibid.*) suggests a date of 'not ... later than Asoka's time'. However, with its homogeneous core and dressed facing, a Phase II date is more likely (Plate 68).

Approximately 130 m to the NE is a smaller, less well-preserved stupa (no. 2) (diameter: 8 m; surviving height: 1.8 m) on a roughly square platform (13 x 14 m)[75] It follows a similar Phase II construction method as the first. Lake sunk shafts into both stupas, only to discover that local 'spoilers' had already dug through as far as the base.

Approximately 150 m to the NE of Stupa 2 is a heavily damaged platform (22 x 25 m), reduced to less than 0.30 m in

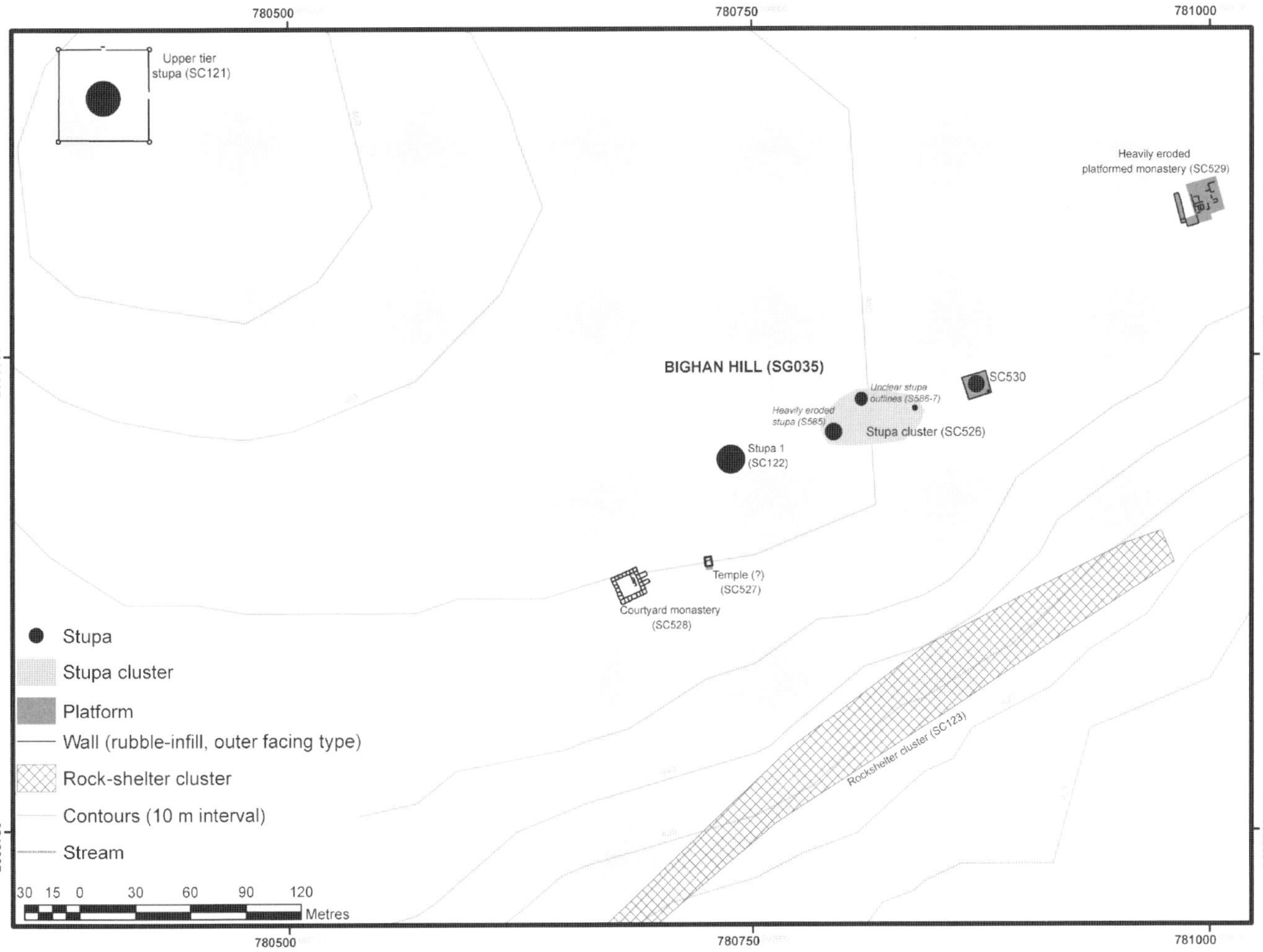

Figure 11.18 Map of Buddhist complex at Bighan

height. Lake (*ibid.*) described it as a 'monastery platform' on account of large quantities of brick strewn all over the site. Unfortunately the accompanying site-plan mentioned in Lake's report was omitted (presumably in error) from the final publication. However, further assessment of his interpretations was made possible by detailed mapping carried out during Stage II of the SSP. This identified some internal detailing including various walls of the rubble-infill, outer-facing variety (Figure 11.18). Taken together with the surface brick remains, these walls are suggestive of a brick and stone superstructure, presumably of a similar appearance to the 'platformed monasteries' at Morel khurd and related sites.

A second, better-preserved platform (24 x 24 m; height: 1.10 m) survives about 80 m SW of Stupa 1. Lake interpreted it as a temple base, but detailed mapping during the SSP revealed the outlines of a courtyard monastery structure lined with regularly sized square cells. While the stupas and platformed monastery evidently belong to Phase II, this type of courtyard monastery does not appear at Sanchi until Phase IV or V, and possibly represents a late addition to the site; earlier prototypes do seem to exist in the area, but these generally follow a more haphazard plan.

Additional structural outlines, not mentioned by Lake, were also noted during the present study. Most were too heavily disturbed to plan, with the exception of three heavily eroded stupa outlines (diameters: 2, 6 and 8 m) between Stupas 1 and 2 (Figure 11.18), and a small rectangular, 'shrine'-like structure (5.4 x 4.6 m) c. 90 m SW of Stupa 2 (Plate 67; Figure 11.18). It is divided into two rooms by a central wall and approached by an external staircase, the outlines of which are still visible on the south side.

Also absent from Lake's study is a line of rock-shelters on the southern edge of the hill. Some of these contain prehistoric and early-historic paintings,[76] the latter including a 'tree-in-railing' motif which is suggestive of some form of Buddhist association. Although additional signs of adaptation, as found at Morel khurd and Sanchi, were not identified, it is possible that some of these shelters acted as simple monastic dwellings, in addition to the more sophisticated monastery structures on the plateau above.

As mentioned earlier, an additional stupa, not included in Lake's report, was also documented on the summit of the hill (Figure 11.18). With a diameter of 17.60 m, it is even larger than Stupa 1 on the lower plateau, but was probably missed by Lake due to its heavily eroded condition.[77] It is set within a square enclosure (49.6 m x 49.6 m), with a circular tower (diameter: 1.60 m) surviving in outline form at each of its four corners. Similar towers, built into fortification walls, are found at other Buddhist sites in the study area. However, the Bighan structure is somewhat different, in that it comprises a compact structural unit. Similar plans have also been noted at other northern Indian Buddhist sites. For example, Sanchi, Building 43, is equipped with circular towers at each of its four corners, although unlike the Bighan

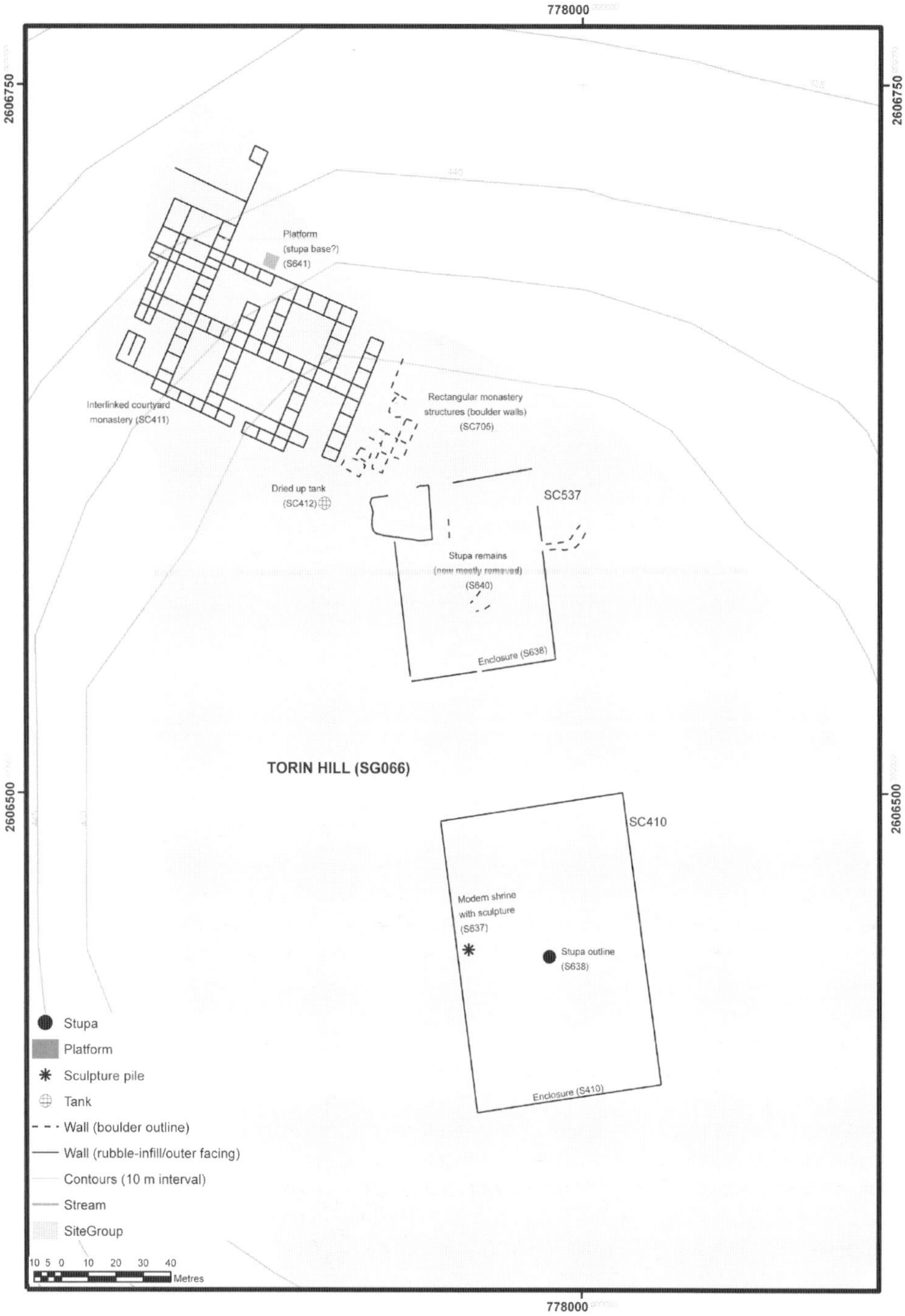

Figure 11.19 Map of Buddhist complex on Torin hill

example, it is set on a high platform and is probably at least 1000 years younger in date. While the Bighan stupa is too eroded to date with certainty, the rubble-core, dressed-facing construction of the enclosure walls, together with the post-Mauryan stupas on the lower plateau, are all suggestive of a Phase II date. For closer parallels, one may refer to the misnamed 'Bimbisara's jail' at Rajgir (Jackson 1914, 269; Hamid 1951, 30) or the Mahabodhi monastery at Bodh-Gaya (Cunningham 1892, 42–5).[78] The layout of all of these structures is almost identical to the typical Indian fort (Davison-Jenkins 1988, 46), possible reasons for which are explored in Part II.[79]

Torin (SG066)

Torin hill, another isolated hillock about 2 km to the north of Bighan hill also has Buddhist remains on its summit (Figure 11.17 colour). The hill is roughly oblong and divided into a southern and northern zone, the former containing two heavily damaged stupas (diameters: 10.5m; 8.15 m) arranged in a SE–NW alignment, and the latter, an interconnected courtyard monastery complex (Figure 11.19). The stupa in the SE survives to a height of 0.5 m, while the other has been reduced to a faint outline.[80] Both are set within square enclosures (103 x 69 m; 68 x 55 m) with entrances cut into their southern walls (rubble-core, outer-facing type).

The interconnected courtyard monasteries (Plate 92; Figure 11.19) are similar to those at Kotra (Plate 44) and extend to the northern edge of the hill. The walls, of the rubble-infill, outer-facing variety, are relatively well preserved, surviving to a height of about 0.8 m. A total of eight complete courtyards lined with regularly sized, square cells were identified, the latter suggesting

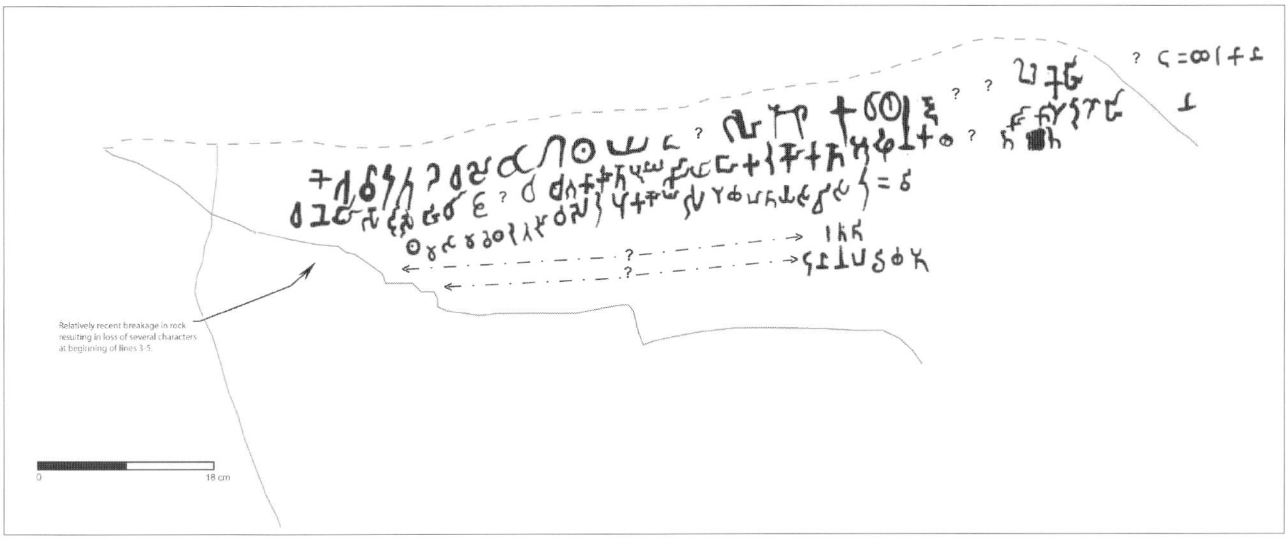

Figure 11.20 Hand copy of Brahmi inscription at Ahmadpur

a Phase IV/V date. To the east of the complex are a number of simpler, single-roomed structures, surviving as boulder-walled outlines. Some of these may have been store-rooms or refectories, or possibly dormitory-type accommodation for guests, or junior members of the monastic order.

Ahmadpur hill (SG037a)

As mentioned earlier, Ahmadpur, about 11.5 km NW of Udayagiri, is somewhat different to the hilltop Buddhist sites discussed so far, in that its Buddhist elements form part of a much larger, mixed Site Group category (Figure 11.17 colour).[81] This includes a Brahmanical temple complex on the summit of the hill (Plate 205) and an ancient settlement on its lower slopes.[82] The hill, situated on the northern bank of the Sahodra *nāla*, a perennial tributary of the River Betwa, itself forms part of a larger archaeological complex including a prominent settlement mound, partly occupied by the modern village of Ahmadpur on the opposite bank of the stream (Plate 6), and a number of important temples, both Jain and Brahmanical, in the immediate vicinity.[83]

Although these aspects of the site were documented for the first time during the SSP, Ahmadpur hill is well known for its prehistoric remains: its lower slopes are strewn with dense microlithic tool scatters (Pandey 1990), while 58 rock-shelters have been documented around the crest of the hill (Khare 1976b; *ASIAR*, 1976–7, 32–3). Approximately 28 of these contain paintings datable between the Chalcolithic and early-historic periods (*ibid.*). It is also renowned as one of the richest *śankhalipi* ('shell script') sites in India; 92 inscriptions have been documented within just seven of the rock-shelters (Sharma 1990, 90–4; Salomon 1986).[84] Some of these are unusual and highly experimental (Plate 55), especially those in caves 2, 4, 7 and 8.[85] For example, the standard *śankha* script is frequently accompanied by variants whose shell-shaped basal component is now replaced by rows of horned animals.

In addition to the aforementioned Brahmanical temple complex on the summit, discussed further in chapter 12, two major Buddhist sites were documented during the SSP. The first, situated midway up the southern side of the hill, is a well-preserved stupa surviving with two courses of intact dressed masonry facing to a height of 0.4 m (Plate 69). It is set on a square platform (10.4 x 10.4 m; height: 0.4 m) and enclosed by a 1 m-wide boundary wall. The chronology of square-platformed stupas at Sanchi suggests a Phase IV or V date (Marshall 1940, 47).

An earlier phase of Buddhist occupation, however, was identified at a second site on the western edge of the hill.[86] Here, the entrance-way of one of the rock-shelters (assigned no. 9 by the ASI) has been built up into a high stone platform. Similar platforms are found at some of the 'adapted' shelters at Sanchi and Morel khurd which as discussed elsewhere were probably used as simple monastic dwellings. Additional indications that the Ahmadpur shelter performed a similar monastic function are provided by some of the historical paintings inside the shelter, which include a 'tree-in-railing' motif (also found in Shelter no. 3)[87] and a *yakṣa*-type figure holding a spear, which finds its direct equivalent in the painted rock-shelter panel at Nagauri, discussed earlier.

However, the strongest evidence to this effect is provided by a five-lined, painted Brahmi inscription which covers a smooth rock-face (2.80 x 0.33 m) on the inner wall of the shelter (Plate 51). Raised at about 3 m above ground level, the entire inscription is executed in a dark red pigment, and overlies earlier black paintings, traces of which can still be seen. A hand-copy was made on-site, followed up by photographic examination. In total, 107 characters were identified, but allowing for the areas of illegibility, a total estimate of about 170 characters may be suggested: while most of the characters in lines 1–3 are fairly well preserved, those towards the right-hand side of these lines are more faded, and most of those in lines 4 and 5 are now illegible due to heavy erosion. Consequently, only some of the hand-copied characters in Figure 11.20 come out in the accompanying photograph (Plate 51). Further, approximately four characters from the beginning of line 3 have been completely removed by a breakage in the surface of the rock. The same breakage has also removed a considerable portion from the left-hand side of lines 4 and 5.

On the basis of palaeographic comparisons with the Phase II donative inscriptions at Sanchi, and the Heliodorus pillar inscription at Vidisha, the Ahmadpur inscription could be placed somewhere between the first century BC and first century AD, making it, therefore, one of the earliest-known painted epigraphs in north India (Harry Falk, pers. comm.). It is important to stress, however, that direct palaeographic comparisons between painted and engraved inscriptions may not yield entirely accurate results.[88] The Ahmadpur script is highly cursive, with considerable variety in size, spacing and palaeography. For example, the average character size in the first half of lines 1 and 2 is 6 x 3 cm. For the second half of the same two lines, as well as for most of lines 3–5, there is marked overcrowding, with the average character size reducing further to 3 x 1.8 cm. The last few characters in lines 1 and 2 spill over onto the unhewn rock-face to the right of the prepared surface, which indicates a lack of adequate foreplanning on the part of the 'scribe'. Further, two additional characters have been squeezed into the tight space between lines 2 and 3, as a kind of after-thought; one of these has even been scored out in error (Figure 11.20). Finally, there is some stylistic inconsistency between individual characters, particularly with regard to 's'. Each of these points stands in direct contrast to the well-planned, standardised format of the donative inscriptions at Sanchi.[89] As well as the fundamental differences in media, these contrasts may also reflect differences between the *type* of monasticism practised at the two sites. Whilst the 'monastic rock-shelters' at Sanchi and Morel khurd appear to perform a supplementary role to the structural monasteries within the central complexes, the shelter at Ahmadpur was probably a solitary 'forest' (*āvasā*) dwelling. It is no surprise therefore, that whilst the Sanchi inscriptions were carved by professional masons (Dehejia 1992), the rather haphazard inscription at Ahmadpur was probably carried out by a resident monk, presumably untrained in epigraphical conventions.

Unfortunately it has not been possible to identify, and even then with very little certainty, more than a very few words in the inscription.[90] This is due both to the cursive script, as well as an apparently highly localised dialect. In line 1, characters 7–9, the word *vase*, has been tentatively identified, followed by what may be the number 'ten' (= 'in the year 10'). The word *vase* occurs again in line 3, characters 10–11. This possible reference to a date is suggestive of some kind of donative record. Line 2 is slightly more edifying, with characters 1–11 possibly reading, *vanehi soḍas-ehi 10 6 ca* (= 'with sixteen 16 *vane-s* ['forests'?]'). The last phrase confirms that the language is Prakrit rather than Sanskrit,[91] whilst *vane* may possibly refer to the forest tradition of monasticism represented by the shelter here.

Until a fuller reading and translation is possible, it is difficult to assess the precise role that this peripheral Buddhist site played within the wider monastic territorial network, or how it related to larger monastic sites such as Bighan or Sanchi. Similarly, in the absence of a complete reading, comparisons with other Buddhist rock-shelter inscriptions in South Asia remain rather futile. Nevertheless, two preliminary points in this respect can be made at this stage. First, the term *lena* (literally 'cave-dwelling'), which features in most other known rock-shelter inscriptions in India and Sri Lanka, is conspicuously absent, although one cannot rule out its occurrence in one of the eroded or illegible parts of the inscription. The second notable feature is its length, which is considerably greater than other known examples from similar contexts. The early Sri Lankan rock-shelter inscriptions (over 1200 in total), for example, generally consist of no more than a few words, to announce the identity of the donor and the recipient of the shelter in question (Paranavitana 1970, vol. 1). In central India, the Bhimbetka rock-shelter inscription consists simply of two words, *Simhakasa lena*, indicating the name of the shelter's occupant (Gupta, 1967, 83).

Budha Pahar (SG098)

Ahmadpur is the northernmost hill in the study area, beyond which the land is predominantly flat and devoid of hills as far as Shamshabad district, approximately 50 km to the north (Figure 3.1). One of the first hills in this area, Budha Pahar, was selected randomly in order to test the consistency with which the topographical setting of Buddhist sites in the study area is replicated in other regions.

Like many of the Buddhist hilltop sites in the SSP study area, it is lined with prehistoric painted rock-shelters and strewn with microlithic tools. On its summit is a large Phase II-type stupa (diameter: 16 m; surviving height: 3 m) set within a square enclosure.[92] Nearby is the lower fragment of a Phase IIIb Buddha or Bodhisattva image, carved in local white sandstone (Plate 136) but following the Kusana style of the Mathura region.[93] Only the base and lower legs survive, revealing the figure to be seated in *padmāsana*, with the hands in *dhyānamudrā*.

'Urban' Buddhist sites

All of the Buddhist sites described above are bound within spatially distinct topographical units, that is, they are situated on hilltop locations at a removed distance from habitational settlements. The social and ritual significance of this trend is discussed later in Part II, but first let us examine the exception to this model, as represented by the limited number of Buddhist remains that occur within habitational contexts.

Vidisha (SG006)

The best known urban Buddhist monuments in the area occur within the ancient city of Vidisha itself, although precise provenances for individual remains are still lacking. The main evidence is provided by Phase II Buddhist railings found by Cunningham (1880, 38–9) and Lake (1910a) at various locations in and around Bes village (Figure 11.1 colour).[94] Whether or not these came from Cunningham's Mounds 'M' and 'N' (Figures 9.2, 11.21 colour), which he tentatively identified as stupas, has never been confirmed through follow-up investigations.[95] In addition to stupas, there were also monasteries, as attested by Phase II donative inscriptions from Sanchi which refer to a nunnery in Vidisha (Marshall 1940; Inscription nos. 137, 174, 220, 318, 344, 388).

Additional Buddhist remains were documented during the SSP within the 'modern' town of Vidisha. These include a dense clustering of individual architectural components, some of them half-submerged in the ground, inside a modern water-tower complex in the walled part of the town.[96] Clearly datable to c. second century BC is a long sculpted frieze with an interlinked lotus motif, presumably part of a stupa railing lintel (Plates 106–7). This evidence sheds doubt on the received understanding, discussed in chapter 9, that this area was only settled during the post-Gupta period following a period of urban decline at the older city site to the north. Notwithstanding the methodological weaknesses of the 'urban decline' model as far as its archaeological underpinnings are concerned, the traditional polarisation between the site's 'ancient' and 'modern' zones clearly needs to be backed up by excavations carried out within Vidisha town itself.

Further support for the suggestion that the two zones originally formed part of a larger extended urban centre is provided by additional Buddhist remains on Lohangi pir, a naturally fortified,

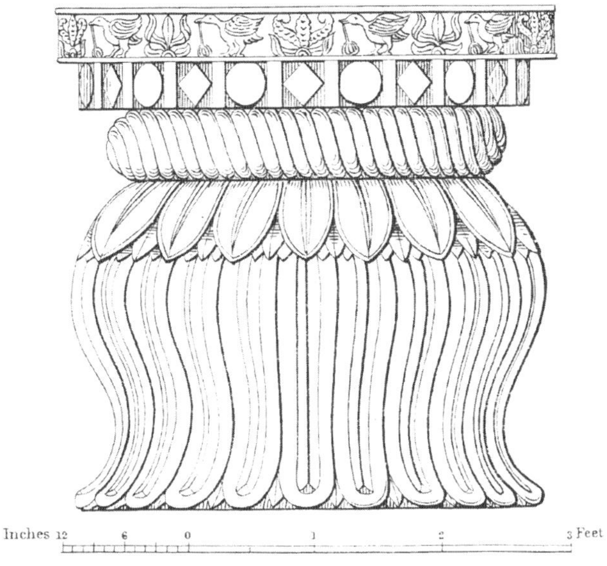

Figure 11.22 Lohangi hill: pillar capital (Cunningham 1880)

rocky outcropping which rises out of the 'modern' town of Vidisha (Figure 9.2).[97] It is a prominent landmark, clearly visible from many of the hilltop sites discussed above (Plate 3). Its summit is currently dominated by a mosque which partly incorporates a Phase VI temple, although much earlier remains have also survived. Embedded in the ground is a large lotus capital which would originally have surmounted a pillar of massive proportions (Plate 32; Figure 11.22). One might plausibly surmise that it would have dominated the skyline for miles around. That it may have held Buddhist associations was first suggested by Cunningham (1880, 34–5), who described it as a 'Buddhist capital'. Cunningham provides no further qualification for this suggestion apart from commenting on the fact that the annual festival here was held on the anniversary of the Buddha's death. However, a number of details noted during the SSP shed further light on the pillar's chronology and ritual affiliation. Although it is considerably larger than any of the post-Mauryan capitals discussed in chapter 9, the overlapping petals on the lotus, together with the cable-necking, bead-and-lozenge, pecking geese and honey-suckle decorations on the abacus, all find direct equivalents in the Heliodorus pillar, which, as discussed in chapter 9, provides one of the major keys for dating Phase II sculpture. Secondly, notably absent from Cunningham's report as well as the accompanying illustration (Figure 11.22) is any reference to the four pairs of animal feet which can still be seen on top of the lotus capital (Plate 32). Two of these are clearly those of an elephant, the other two of a lion, attesting therefore to an addorsed lion-elephant capital, similar in appearance to the carved representations of post-Mauryan capitals on some of the Phase II gateways at Sanchi, Stupa 2 (Plate 33). However, as discussed in chapter 12, although both the lion and elephant are popular motifs in Buddhist art, this particular combination is not unknown within early Bhagavata contexts.

Nevertheless, the likelihood that the Lohangi pillar was indeed a specifically Buddhist monument is strengthened by additional evidence for the site's continued link with Buddhism during the Gupta period. This takes the form of a previously unpublished sculpture, which is now stored in the Vidisha Museum but which, according to the museum accession book, originally stood on the summit of Lohangi hill (Plate 137).[98] The sculpture of a two-armed male figure, with long ringleted hair, strong muscular chest and stomach, torque necklace with central *srivatsa* motif, and transparent dhoti decorated with a delicately carved, widely spaced rosace pattern, all showing close parallels with Gupta sculptures from Sanchi and Udayagiri. In particular, the rope-like sash arranged over the thighs and supported by the left hand finds its direct equivalent in the Vajrapani Bodhisattva image from Sanchi (Plate 37).[99] The identification remains uncertain, but both the ringlets and the two- rather than four-armed aspect are suggestive of a Boddhisatva, rather than a Buddha, image.

Although Vidisha's religious reputation during the Gupta period is more closely associated with the Brahmanical tradition, as represented by major sculptures and temples both within the city and at nearby Udayagiri, further evidence for the continued presence of Buddhism in the city during this period is attested by another male image with strong Buddhist associations (Plate 172), this time from a site on the western bank of the River Betwa between the Heliorodus pillar and Amacchar village to the NE.[100] The sculpture, originally documented by Lake (1910a, 140–1, figs. 7, 9, 10), was found on a ghat, together with a group of free-standing *saptamātṛkā* figures, the latter datable to the early fifth century AD (Willis 1982, 51, pl. 48; Harle 1974, pls. 27–30; Agrawala 1971, figs. 19–24).[101] The treatment of the sash at the back of the male figure's neck (Lake 1910a, fig. 10) is sufficiently similar to that of the *saptamātṛkās* to warrant viewing all eight sculptures as belonging to a single group, both in denominational and chronological terms. Further indications of an early fifth-century-AD date are provided by the similar treatment of the figure's robust upper body to that of the Udayagiri Varaha (Plate 169). However, while the *saptamātṛkā*s are commonly interpreted along Brahmanical lines, the long locks of the male figure, the large circular halo behind the head, and the *vajra* held in the left hand, all led Lake to identify him as a Bodhisattva. The *class* of Bodhisattva was not specified, but the *vajra* suggests that we may be dealing with Vajrapani (Plate 37), as found for example at Sanchi (Marshall 1940, 391).[102] If this identification is correct, the puzzling question of why a Bodhisattva should be grouped together with *saptamātṛkā* sculptures will need to be addressed. It is possible, for example, that the group represents a Buddhist counterpart to the standardised Brahmanical grouping in which the goddesses are accompanied by an ithyphallic male figure. On the other hand, it is quite possible that the stylistic links between the Bodhisattva and the female sculptures are simply coincidental, and that the former was taken from another place with formerly Buddhist links.

Udayagiri (SG031)

The Brahmanical rock-cut temples and associated inscriptions on Udayagiri hill, approximately 1 km to the west of Vidisha's city rampart (Figure 11.21 colour), are central to discussions in chapter 12 regarding the consolidation of orthodox Hinduism, and its close alignment with royal authority, during the Gupta period. Despite the hill's present-day rural setting, it should be regarded as an 'urban' or 'suburban' site. The area between Udayagiri hill and the city ramparts is actually one continous settlement zone: three habitational mounds were documented during the SSP, at Udayagiri, Sonapura and Madhupuri, although early-historic pottery is found throughout.[103] Udayagiri would thus have fallen within Vidisha's wider suburban sprawl, an impression which fits

Kalidasa's descriptions (*Meghdūta* I, 25) of Nicaih hill and its Silavesma (caves), usually equated with Udayagiri, as a popular pleasure-spot for Vidisha's urban elite (Upadhyayan 1947; Mirashi 1960, 13; Bhattacharyya, 1977, 73).

Comparatively little is known, however, about the hill's pre-Gupta religious history. Given Udayagiri's suburban setting, and the ritual function of most of the other neighbouring hills, it would be surprising if it did not also have some kind of ritual significance, prior to being landscaped in the Brahmanical mould during the early fifth century AD. I am not suggesting here that we follow blindly the popular, but problematic, model that underneath every Hindu temple is a Buddhist stupa,[104] but it is important to examine whatever evidence there is for the site's pre-Gupta history. A notable phenonenon, for example, as one approaches the summit of the southern hill via the central passageway, is that the Gupta rock-cut shrines, alcoves and carved panels here, including the Sesa Narayana panel, are not executed on virgin rock but rather cut through pre-existing carvings. The latter consist of enormous *śankhalipi* inscriptions, each occupying areas of up to 2 x 6 m in size (Plate 58). Most are incomplete or damaged, large chunks having been broken off to make way for rock-cut chambers, or simply cut into by sculptural reliefs. The ostentatious manner in which the inscriptions were originally displayed is matched by the bold and public manner in which they are defaced, a fact which raises important questions about inter-religious relations during the Gupta period.

The *śankhalipi* script is generally placed somewhere in the Gupta period, with some scholars (e.g. Salomon 1980, 53) interpreting the inscriptions, found at a wide variety of sites in northern and central India, as pilgrims' records, possibly operating within a Saiva framework. However, agreement regarding their chronology and sectarian orientation has not yet been reached, and despite claims to the contrary (Mukherjee 1990), the script has not yet been convincingly deciphered. Central India is particularly renowned as a rich centre for *śankhalipi* inscriptions, although none of the known examples, whether painted or carved, come anywhere near the gigantic proportions of those at Udayagiri. As discussed earlier, particularly high concentrations of painted *śankhalipi* inscriptions occur in the Ahmadpur rock-shelters (Plate 54),[105] with similar examples at Morel khurd (Plate 53),[106] while beyond the study area, numerous painted examples have been recorded at Bhimbetka (Sharma 1990). At Sanchi, a carved *śankhalipi* inscription can be seen on the shaft of the Asokan pillar, currently stored on-site (Plate 57), with similar occurrences on Asokan pillars at Kausambi, Vaisali and Lauriya Araraj.

It may or may not be relevant that all of these sites are associated in some way with Buddhism, although it is possible, particularly in the case of the Asokan pillars, that the *śankhalipi* inscriptions represent a later overlay from a different and competing religious framework. The question of when and by whom they were executed, however, cannot be determined with certainty until the script has been convincingly deciphered. At Udayagiri, the Cave 6 inscription of Candragupta II dated to GE 82 (AD 400/1) provides a *terminus post quem* for the defaced *śankhalipi* inscriptions beneath the Gupta sculpture programme (Fleet *CII*, III, 21–5; Sircar 1969, 271–2).

An additional detail, noted during a site visit in January 2005, may provide further insights into their ritual affiliation.[107] Framed by one of the *śankhalipi* swirls to the right of the Sesa Narayana panel is a small carved element with a spherical roof (Plate 58). Overall it bears a close resemblance to a stupa motif carved on one of the railing pillars at Bodh Gaya (Plate 59). Some, especially those who view *śankhalipi* as a predominantly Saiva script, may prefer to interpret it as Saiva burial monument or a Saiva fire, as found, for example, on the eastern gateway panel of Sanchi, Stupa 1. However, even if it *is* a stupa, it may bear no temporal link to the surrounding inscriptions at all, but rather stem from an earlier, 'pre-*śankhalipi*' phase in the site's seemingly multi-religious trajectory.

Whichever way we interpret this detail, it is not the only piece of evidence at Udayagiri which suggests some form of Buddhist presence in earlier periods. For example, a cross-bar (*sucika*) from a railed balustrade was first noted by Cunningham (1880, 55) on the main village platform at Sonapura village, where it is still stored.[108] By comparing its dimensions (0.64 x 0.56 x 0.18 m) with those of the Bharhut stupa, Cunningham (*ibid.*) inferred the existence of a 'great Buddhist stupa' with a diameter of at least 20 m (*ibid.*). A second railing fragment, of a *vedika* (20 x 20 cm in section)[109] decorated with a lotus medallion of the same 'simple' type as that on the Phase II railings of Sanchi, Stupa 2, was also found at the same spot (*ibid.*) (Plate 105). Although these fragments could have been transported from elsewhere, possible provenances at Udayagiri itself include a site on the northern plateau where the faint outlines of two circular structures were identified during the SSP.[110] Given their heavily eroded condition, their identification as stupas remains highly speculative, and moreover, as Cunningham (*ibid.*, 55) himself realised, given the thoroughness of the Brahmanical re-ordering of the landscape during the Gupta period, the search for a stupa at Udayagiri may turn out to be futile: 'While Buddhism flourished, the stupa was safe; but when it became a persecuted faith, every stone would have found ready acceptance by the Brahmanical persecutors in the neighbouring city of Bhilsa [Vidisha]'. It may be relevant here to note that in the *Dīpavaṁsa*, the Vedisagiri monastery is described as being located in the city of Vessanagara (Dey 1927, 28), although most scholars prefer to equate it with Sanchi (Cunningham 1880, 37). Given its position within the suburbs of Vidisha, Udayagiri may turn out to be a much more likely contender.[111]

The foregoing descriptions show that from at least the second century BC, the *saṅgha* had a visible presence in the main capital city. The aim of the following section is to assess the distribution of Buddhist sites in Vidisha's wider hinterland that occur in urban, or other non-monastic, settings.

Marha kherai (SG141)

Marhai kherai is a small, isolated mound situated about 500 m south of Marha village in the fertile valley to the NW of Sanchi (Sector 1a),[112] approximately midway between Sanchi and Udayagiri (Figure 11.21 colour). As discussed in chapter 9, the shortest route to Sanchi from ancient Besnagar is via this valley, as opposed to the modern road which is about double the distance. The site is dominated by a heavily damaged stupa with a diameter of 10 m, and surviving only as a 0.5 m-high mound strewn with large quantities of stone debris. No associated settlement remains were identified in the immediate vicinity, meaning that it should be regarded more as a 'road-side', rather than 'urban' stupa , which would have been visible to anyone passing along this presumably busy route. Its location in the midst of ploughed, cultivated fields means that it is in a much more ruinous condition than many of its hilltop counterparts. However, that it belonged to the highest monumental order is indicated by a large stone panel (3.0 x

0.38 x 0.14 m) found semi-embedded in a field at a short distance to the west (Plates 108–9). Only the carved, upper face is visible, above which is a shallow overhanging element (height: 8 cm). The panel is broken on the far right, but its complete form may be inferred from the curved element on the left side. The overall shape and composition is similar to a coping stone from Besnagar which is carved on both sides.[113] However, unlike the Besnagar example, which curves round to follow the line of a circular stupa balustrade, the Marha panel is quite straight. A possible suggestion therefore is that it surmounted a square balustrade, or a simple gateway. However, it is quite different to the cross-bars on the Sanchi Stupa 1 *toraṇas*, which lack the overhanging element.

The carved face is decorated with a processional scene consisting of, from left to right, an elephant ridden by a couple; horse-and-rider; elephant-and-couple; buffalo-and-rider; elephant-and-couple; horse-and-rider; elephant-and-couple; and finally lion-and-rider.[114] A thick stalk, with sprouting, open lotus flowers, meanders above and below each animal, while a bead-and-lozenge border frames the entire panel. Each of these details has local parallels: first, the general composition and subject matter are similar to the relic processions depicted on the southern and western gateway panels of Sanchi Stupa 1. However, a number of stylistic features suggest a somewhat earlier date than these first-century-AD carvings. First, the lotus meander with its 'flatly' carved, sprouting flowers finds an almost direct equivalent on the inner face of the Besnagar coping (Cunningham 1880, pl. XIII).[115] Secondly, the bead-and-lozenge border is replicated almost exactly on the Heliodorus pillar abacus (Plate 27), as well as some of the Phase II carved railings at Sanchi, Stupa 2, and Andher (Plate 102). These comparisons suggest that the Marha Kherai stupa, or at least its railing, was constructed some time between the late second and early first centuries BC.

Besar talai colony (SG041)

Another 'non-hilltop' stupa, this time occurring within an urban context, was documented in the southern part of the study area (Sector 3). Besar talai is one of several major early-historic settlements situated in the narrow river valley about 3 km to the south of the stupas at Sonari (Figure 11.5 colour). The site centres on a prominent settlement mound, but pottery scatters continue for several km in the surrounding fields. The existence of a large stupa is attested by individual architectural and sculptural fragments stored at various locations throughout the site.[116] Although no stupa mound has been identified, one may assume that all of these fragments originated from a single find-spot, possibly around the NW corner of the village tank. Six plain cross-bars (*sucika*) are stored around the main village platform (Plate 110). Their dimensions (c. 1.15 x 0.54 x 0.20 m) may be compared with the railings at Bharhut, which, following a similar deduction as that followed by Cunningham for the railing at Udayagiri discussed earlier, suggests that the associated stupa had a diameter of at least 20 m.

An upright railing pillar (*vedika*) was also noted in the fields to the west of the main settlement mound. This has a long, narrow socket on one side (Plates 111–12) which would have received a 'solid' railing, of the type excavated at the Heliodorus pillar site in Vidisha (Bhandarkar 1913–14, 192–3, pl. LVIa).[117] Its obverse face is decorated with open and closed lotus buds, which are interspersed by a stalk meander (Plate 111); similar decorations are found at Sonari (Plate 101) and discussed in chapter 9. The reverse side is decorated with open lotus medallions, carved in high relief, and interspersed by open, upward-facing lotuses (Plate 112). Lying nearby is an incomplete *sucika* fragment (height: 33 cm; width: 10 cm) (Plate 113).[118] It is carved on its obverse side only with a geometric design consisting of open lotus flowers from which smaller buds sprout forth. The design is framed by a lotus stalk, tied in a knot at the right and set within an outer border of triangular motifs which run around the edge of the railing. The latter is also found on some of the Phase II stupa railings at Sanchi and Andher.

These local comparisons suggest a Phase II date for the Besar talai railings. However, an ASI report gives details of a polished Chunar sandstone fragment found here, inscribed with the words, *kudugaru karikha(ta)* (*IAR* 1978–9, 13) ('caused to be made by Kudugaru'). Whether or not this refers to the stupa itself is unknown, and we cannot be sure that the polished stone really *is* from Chunar and not of a local variety, as the so-called polished Chunar elephant capital at Satdhara turned out to be. Unfortunately, the single-line report provides no further details, but the legend's wording and grammatical construction are sufficiently similar to the Phase II Mawasa inscription described earlier, to suggest that it was issued around the same time and that, as at Mawasa, it referred to the construction of a stupa. Further, the causative construction suggests that the donor in question was a figure of considerable authority, possibly a king; the town's obvious political and economic importance is further illustrated by coins of the Eran type found here and discussed in chapter 13.

In addition to railings, several Phase II pillar fragments and associated capitals, possibly originating from the same stupa, were also documented at various locations throughout the site. The pillar remains consist of three separate lotus capital fragments stored on and around the central village platform (Plate 123).[119] Embellished with overhanging petals, they follow the typical post-Mauryan model as represented by the Heliodorus pillar and related material at Vidisha. It may safely be assumed that the pillar shafts, of which no remains have been found, were also of the Heliodorus type. Their crowning capitals in the form of three elephants and a humped bull are stored nearby and, as discussed later, form part of a larger group of animal capitals found at several other 'urban' Buddhist sites in the study area (Figure 9.4; Table 11.1).

The humped bull capital currently lies half-submerged in the ground on the eastern side of the mound (Plate 124).[120] Its head is missing, but a sash, decorated with a finely carved criss-cross pattern, is still visible around its neck, as are its ithyphallic features and heavily protruding backbones. Nearby is an elephant capital, also half-submerged in the ground. It too is ithyphallic, and stands on all fours (Plates 119–20).[121] Its underbelly and upper neck are carved with fleshy 'ripple' folds, while the back legs are decorated with incised swirling patterns. The resulting naturalism is accentuated further by the delicately modelled ridges and indentations on the hanging ear-flaps, and the prominent humps on either side of the head. The second elephant capital, lying on the northern bank of the ancient tank, is smaller and more rotund, with deeply incised eye-sockets and unusual fan-like detailing on the ear-flaps (Plate 121).[122] The third elephant capital, half-submerged in a ditch to the north of the mound, is slightly thinner and more elongated, with protruding backbones and hollow stomach (Plate 122).[123]

Broad comparisons can be made with the elephant capitals from Satdhara (Plate 114) and Sanchi (Plate 116), particularly the

Table 11.1 Animal capitals in the Sanchi-Vidisha area

Site SG no.	SC/ Installation no.	Present location	Animal type	lgt x ht (from stomach) x wd (at stomach) (m)	Stone type
Sanchi SG001	SC609/I-8	SAMRC	Elephant	0.70 (without rear part) x 0.51 x 0.36	Light buff sandstone
Sanchi Kanakhera SG002	SC17/I-253	On site	Bull	0.97 (without head) x 0.42 x 0.45	Light buff sandstone
Satdhara SG006	SC54/I-101	On site	Elephant	0.42 x 0.17 x 0.18	Light buff sandstone with high polish
Vidisha SG006	SC715/I-181	VM	Bull	1.0 x 0.38 x 0.42	Light buff sandstone
	SC715/I-182	VM	Bull	1.02 x 0.29 x 0.38	Light buff sandstone
	SC715/I-1137	Bhopal Museum	Bull	0.89 x 0.30 x 0.30	Light buff sandstone
	SC45/I-95	NMD	Elephant with rider	1.06 x 0.43 (with legs: 0.86) x 0.41	Polished grey sandstone
Besar talai SG041	SC142/I-134	On site	Bull (3)	115 x 0.32 x 0.40	Light buff sandstone with purple mottling
	SC142/I-135	On site	Bull (2)	0.96 (without head) x 0.32 x 0.27	Light buff sandstone
	SC380/I-142	On site	Elephant (1)	1.15 x 0.49 x 0.56	Light buff sandstone
	SC380/I-143	On site	Elephant (2)	? x 0.38 x 0.40	Light buff sandstone
	SC380/I-114	On site	Elephant (3)	1.10 x 0.33 x 0.32	Light buff sandstone
	SC380/I-145	On site	Bull (1)	0.92 (without head) x 0.27 x 0.34	Light buff sandstone
Dhakna village SG032	SC468/I-395	On site	Bull	0.97 (without head) x 0.34 x 0.38	Light buff sandstone
Tajpura shur SG064	SC404/I-296	On site	Bull	1.14 x 0.36 x 0.34	Light buff sandstone with purple mottling

latter whose head and ears are strikingly similar to those of elephant no. 2. As discussed earlier, these two examples are usually dated to the Mauryan period. Whilst we should not lose sight of the tendency for continuity between the two periods,[124] the clear post-Mauryan context of the Besar talai capitals may call for some revision of this framework.

The precise provenance of these pillar fragments and capitals, now stored at various locations, is unknown. However, there are strong suggestions that they all originated from a single architectural context. Although both the bull and elephant embody a wide range of religious and cultural references in ancient India, both animals are closely associated with Buddhism. The elephant refers to the story of the Buddha's conception, while the bull is one of the epithets of the Buddha, both as Sakya Pungava and 'Gautama' (or Gotama in Pali), literally 'the best bull' (Vajracharya 1999, 75). Elephants and bulls are also amongst the 'four noble animals' that feature prominently in Buddhist art, mythology and architecture.[125] These animals are also connected with directional symbolism and are often found at cardinal points of stupas, monasteries and temples.[126] All of these factors provide strong indications that the four pillar capitals at Besar talai were originally placed around the central stupa, possibly at each of its cardinal points.

Two more bull capitals are stored at a separate location about 600 m to the west of the main settlement mound.[127] The site consists of a small temple mound strewn with sculptures and architectural fragments datable to the ninth and tenth centuries AD. The bull capitals, however, belong to the same period as the others on the main settlement mound, and possibly attest to an earlier ritual structure here. The smaller capital is of the same order as the bull on the main mound. It too has a striated sash around the neck and, apart from a slightly fuller stomach, is also anatomically similar (Plate 125).[128] The head is missing, but one of the fleshy folds of dewlap is still visible. The tail loops up and over the right side of the body, to hang down on the left. The arrangement of the tail of the second, slightly larger capital is precisely the inverse: it loops up and over the left side of the body, to hang down on the right (Plate 126).[129] From this we may infer that the two animals originally crowned pillars arranged side-by-side, most probably at the entrance of an associated stupa or temple. The practice of placing pillars at the entrance of sacred buildings is a well-known phenomenon in ancient India (Khare 1976a, 177).

The second bull is by far the most elaborately carved of the Besar talai capitals. The buff sandstone contains an unusual purple variegation, which accentuates the soft, velvety texture of the animal's skin. The variegation also features in the decorative detailing: the swirling movement of the purple streaks is mirrored by the curved shape of the narrow length of rope, presumably part of a harness, which glides over the bridge of the nose. The robust sculptural volume of the body is combined with a heightened sensitivity to detail: the fine folds around the eyelids, the slightly flaring nostrils, the conical tassel at the end of the tail and the undulating, fleshy folds of the dewlap, all intensify the sense of tactility. Around the neck hangs a thick garland of lotuses, each decorated with overlapping petals and separated by a narrow 'cable' band. Both these details feature on post-Mauryan lotus capitals, of which the garland appears to be a direct derivative.

Six more bull capitals, all belonging to the same sculptural tradition, are known from the Sanchi-Vidisha area (Figure 9.4). All have the same prominent humps and fleshy dewlaps and, as shown in Table 11.1, follow broadly similar dimensions. First, two previously unpublished bull capitals from Besnagar are stored in the Vidisha Museum (Plates 128–9).[130] A third, also from Besnagar, is stored in the Bhopal Archaeology Museum (Plate 130).[131]

Other sites with animal capitals

Three more previously unpublished capitals were noted at separate settlement sites during the survey. The first lies on the SW corner of Kanakhera talai, a dried-up tank around 300 m east of Kanakhera (Plate 131),[132] the ancient settlement closest to Sanchi. The second lies half embedded in the middle of a field near Tajpur Shur (Plate 132),[133] a major early-historic settlement around 3 km east of Sanchi. Unlike the other two examples, its head is still intact, revealing delicate carving around the ears and eyes, and a rope-like sash around the neck. Finally, a third bull capital comes from the summit of Dhakna village hill, where it stands embedded in the ground at stomach level (Plate 133).[134] Close by are the remains of a square platform (c. 10 x 10 m), which may have been the base of either a stupa or temple. Indications as to the bull's original context are suggested by the frequency with which pillars are found at the entrance of such monuments. Furthermore, that the site was Buddhist in orientation is suggested by the evidence at Besar talai. Further consideration of the ritual function of this previously unstudied group of capitals, and their impact on our understanding of the nature of patronage at urban Buddhist sites, is discussed in the following section.

Summary

The material presented in this chapter provides a starting point for establishing a basic chronology of Buddhism in the local landscape; for establishing local stupa and monastery typologies; and for understanding aspects of internal site organisation. These various aspects of Buddhist monasticism are discussed in Part II of this chapter, drawing in particular on the issue of site-hierarchy; the development of institutionalised monasticism; patronage networks; inter-site relationships within the 'Buddhist landscape'; and the functional, ritual and symbolic significance of the topographical setting of monastic sites. This enables a consideration of the wider archaeological setting of monastic sites, including the relative configuration of non-Buddhist cult spots, settlements and agricultural systems, to be discussed further in chapters 13 and 14.

PART II: PATTERNS IN THE BUDDHIST LANDSCAPE

The history of local monasticism: a chronological framework

From the material described in the foregoing account, it is possible to delineate four major strands in the formation of Sanchi's 'Buddhist landscape' (Table 11.2; Figure 11.23 colour).

i) The first Buddhist monuments: Phase Id

The earliest period of monumental construction is represented by the Mauryan brick stupa, Asokan pillar and apsidal temples at Sanchi, and the brick stupa and apsidal temple at Satdhara (Figure 11.1 colour), but this is not to rule out the possibility of dispersed monastic communities during preceding periods: quite clearly, the 'monastic rock-shelters' found at Sanchi, Morel khurd and Ahmadpur require further investigation and, ideally, excavation in order to establish the chronology of their relationship to Buddhism. Further, as discussed in chapter 9, the fact that the schism edict, otherwise only known at sites in the Gangetic valley long since connected with Buddhism, is found at Sanchi does provide suggestions of some kind of pre-Mauryan Buddhist presence in the area.

ii) The second propagation: Phase II stupas and monasteries

The second propagation of Buddhism involved the elaboration of existing monuments at Sanchi and Satdhara and the establishment of numerous new monastic centres throughout the surrounding countryside. The main chronological indicators are Phase II stupas, found at a total of 27 sites (Table 11.2), and three major categories of monastic dwellings (Figure 11.23 colour; Appendix IIb): the first category survives in the form of prominent stone platforms, the best-preserved examples being at Sanchi and the four other 'Bhilsa Tope' sites, with close parallels at Mawasa, Salera, Murlikheri, Chandna Tohoria and Bighan. Brick fragments and stone walls on their summits suggest that they formed the bases of towering superstructures. Some of the wall outlines are clear enough to make inferences about their internal organisation. For example, the platform on the lowest tier of Mawasa hill is surmounted by a series of rectangular rooms, while the middle platform has a courtyard monastery also surrounded by rectangular rooms. Similar rectangular structures arranged around a courtyard, although without the underlying platformed element, were found nearby at Mawasa, Barahi Khas, Ferozpur, Karhaud kherai and Devrajpur (Appendix IIb).[135] These comprise the second major Phase II monastery category and sometimes follow a haphazard, interlinked plan. The rectangular rooms appear to have provided communal, dormitory-style accommodation, in contrast to the single-occupancy, square cells of the more regularly planned courtyard monasteries at Sanchi. The late appearance of the latter during Phase IV or V has to a large extent informed the accepted chronology of the courtyard monastery in central India. However, my principal argument is that prototypical variants, as represented by the platformed and non-platformed versions in the SSP study area, already existed during the late centuries BC. This should not really come as a surprise given that rock-cut versions of the courtyard monastery were already being produced in the Deccan around the same time, while the idea of building a courtyard monastery on top of a high platform finds its direct parallel in the second-century-BC rock-cut monastery at Pitalkhora. The rectangular rooms found in both the platformed and non-platformed versions in the SSP study area also occur at Satdhara and eight other smaller sites in the SSP study area (Appendix IIb). Comprising the third, and most basic, category of Phase II monastery, these consist of free-standing, single- or double-roomed buildings, without the addition of a central courtyard. Most have rubble-infill, outer-facing walls, although a few survive as boulder outlines which were presumably filled in with mortar. The fourth monastic, albeit only semi-structural, category consists of

Table 11.2 Buddhist sites: chronology and hierarchy

					Construction phases		Other indicators				Monastery type					
SG no.	**Name**	**Rank**	**Sector**	**Max. Stupa diam.**	**From**	**To**	**Rail-ings**	**Pillar**	**Relics**	**Don. inscrip**	**Mon-astery plat-form**	**Early CY**	**Regu-lar CY (IV)**	**Late CY (VI)**	**Rect.**	**Mon r-s**
SG001	Sanchi hill	1	1b	32	Id	VII	Y	Y	Y	Y	1	0	8	2	0	3
SG007	Satdhara	1	1b	30.8	Id	V	Y	Y	Y	Y	5	0	0	0	1	1
SG005	Morel khurd	2	2b	20	II	VI	Y	N	Y	N	1	0	1	1	0	9
SG031	Udayagiri	2	4	20	II	II	Y	Y	N	N	0	0	0	0	0	0
SG035	Bighan hill	2	4	17.6	II	IV	N	N	N	N	1	0	1	0	0	0
SG098	Budha pahar	2	4b	16	II	IIIb	N	N	N	N	0	0	0	0	0	0
SG004	Sonari hill	2	3	14.6	II	II	Y	N	Y	N	1	0	0	0	1	0
SG013	Andher	2	2b	12.6	II	V	Y	N	Y	N	1	0	0	0	0	0
SG066	Torin hill	2	4	10.5	II	IV	N	N	N	N	0	0	1	0	1	0
SG090	Mawasa	2	2b	7.5	II	IV	N	N	N	Y	2	3	0	0	0	0
SG095d	Chandna	3	2b	9	II	IV	N	N	N	N	0	0	2	0	0	0
SG177c	Devrajpur	3	2b	8.8	II	IV	N	N	N	N	0	1	0	0	1	0
SG167	Kotra	3	2b	4.5	II	IV	N	N	N	N	0	0	1	0	1	0
SG170b	Salera	3	2b	5.8	II	II	N	N	N	N	1	0	0	0	0	0
SG076	Bagoda	4	1b	?	II	II	N	N	N	N	0	0	0	0	1	0
SG077	Bala barkhera	4	1b	?	II	II	N	N	N	N	0	0	0	0	0	0
SG135c	Mori/Karariya kherai	4/'late'	3	9	IV	IV	N	N	N	N	0	0	0	0	0	0
SG029	Dargawan hill (2)	4	1b	8.1	II	II	N	N	N	N	0	0	0	0	1	1
SG012b	Karhaud kherai	4	2b	6.5	II	IV	N	N	N	N	0	1	0	0	0	0
SG022	Goldoria	4	1b	5.1	II	II	N	N	N	N	0	0	0	0	1	0
SG078	Bamhora	4	1b	5	II	II	N	N	N	N	0	0	0	0	1	1
SG143	Kanchanpura	4	1b	5	II	II	N	N	N	N	0	0	0	0	1	0
SG137	Raisen	4	3	3.5	II	II	N	N	N	N	?	?	?	?	?	?
SG028	Dargawan hill (1)	5	1b	3	II	II	N	N	N	N	0	0	0	0	0	0
SG032c	Dhakna	5	1b	3	II	II	N	Y	N	N	0	0	0	0	0	0
SG118	Murwara hill	5	2b	3	II	IV	N	N	N	N	0	0	0	0	0	0
SG162d	Naroda Pathari	5/'late'	1b	3	IV	IV	N	N	N	N	0	0	0	0	0	0
SG175	Bawaliya hill	5	2b	3	II	IV	N	N	N	N	0	0	0	0	1	0
SG150	Sukhasen	5	3	2	II	II	N	N	N	N	0	0	0	0	0	0
SG059b	Barahi khas	Monastery only	3	1	II	II	N	N	N	N	0	1	0	0	0	0
SG162	Murlikheri	Monastery only	1b	n/a	II	II	N	N	N	N	1	0	0	0	0	0
SG011c	Ferozpur	Monastery only	1b	1	II	II	N	N	N	N	0	1	0	0	0	0
SG006	Vidisha	Urban	1a	?	II	IV	Y	Y	N	Y	0	?	0	0	0	0
SG041	Besar talai	Urban	3	20	II	II	Y	Y	N	Y	0	0	0	0	0	0
SG141	Marha kherai	Urban	1a	10	II	II	Y	N	N	N	0	0	0	0	0	0
SG003a	Nagauri	Forest	1b	n/a	IIIA	IIIA	N	N	N	N	0	0	0	0	0	1
SG037a	Ahmadpur	Forest	4	9	II	IV	N	N	N	Y	0	0	0	0	0	1

Abbreviations: Don: Donative; CY: Courtyard; Rect: Rectangular; Mon r-s: Monastic rock-shelter

'monastic rock-shelters': prehistoric shelters showing signs of adaptation in the form of platformed terraces built up in front of their entrances, Buddhist paintings/inscriptions and often nearby stupas. At Sanchi, Morel khurd and Bighan, they perch on the outer edges of larger Buddhist architectural complexes, while at Ahmadpur, which may be viewed as a solitary 'forest dwelling', the only additional Buddhist evidence is a single stupa which may date to a much later period. Given that apparently unadapted rock-shelters occur at 14 Buddhist sites, it is not unlikely that some of these were also used by monks (Figure 11.1 colour).

iii) Phase IV to V stupas and courtyard monasteries

The Phase IV/V square-platformed stupas and regular courtyard monasteries at Sanchi provide the primary chronological markers for dating the third major phase of Buddhist construction, represented at 14 other sites in the SSP study area (Table 11.2; Figure 11.1 colour); of these, only Mori and Naroda Pathari show no evidence for Buddhist building activity in earlier periods, but given the high level of erosion at these sites, an earlier phase cannot be ruled out. These courtyard monasteries are lined with single-occupancy regular-sized square cells as at Sanchi, rather than the larger rectangular rooms of Phase II, and are found at

Morel khurd, Bighan and Chandna Tohoria,[136] while at Kotra and Torin they form part of large interconnected complexes.[137] As discussed in chapter 12, this renewed building activity coincided with a massive proliferation of Brahmanical temple construction. However, the latter does not appear to have undermined the *saṅgha*'s prominent place in the ritual landscape; nor is there evidence for any significant overlap in the spatial boundaries of Buddhist and Brahmanical sites which appear to occupy quite distinct topographical positions in the landscape, with the latter being largely confined to urban or village contexts.

iv) Phase VI monuments and the decline of Buddhism

The latest Buddhist monuments at Sanchi, including Temple 45 and Building 43, date to the ninth or tenth centuries AD. Monasteries 45 and 46, which follow the regular courtyard plan, also date to this period. At most other sites, however, bad preservation, the lack of surface ceramics and sketchy understanding of later structural forms mean that it is usually only possible to provide a loose *terminus* marker for the final phase of Buddhist occupation. At Satdhara, for example, the latest archaeological material dates to c. sixth or seventh century AD, while at Sonari, the *absence* of 'late' markers, such as the regular courtyard monastery, may indicate that abandonment had already taken place by this time.[138] However, quite how long Buddhist occupation continued after the construction of the latest archaeologically diagnostic feature is difficult to tell. The only clearly datable Phase VI Buddhist structure outside Sanchi is the tenth-century-AD temple at Morel khurd, built on top of the Phase II monastery platform, which was presumably already in ruins by this time. The interlinked monastery complex to the NW of the platform probably dates to the same period.[139] Whether these later structures represent the culmination of an unbroken history of Buddhist occupation at the site or, as suggested by Willis (2000, 66), a later 'reinvigoration' is difficult to determine in the absence of a complete ceramic sequence.

However, other forms of evidence throughout the SSP study area, *do* suggest that the demise of Buddhism had already set in by this time. As discussed in chapter 12, the enormous proliferation in Brahmanical temple construction during Phase IV reaches a climax between the ninth and tenth centuries AD.[140] The number of Brahmanical temples built within, or in close proximity to, Buddhist hilltop complexes during this period signals the *saṅgha*'s diminishing role in the ritual landscape (Table 11.3). At Kotra, Barahi khas and Karhaud, for example, the fact that tenth-century-AD Brahmanical temple remains are found within the actual monastic compound implies that these sites had already been abandoned by Buddhist monks (Figure 11.24; Table 11.3). At Udayagiri, where there is evidence, albeit tentative, for some form of early Buddhist presence, now obscured by Gupta-period, Brahmanical landscaping, this kind of re-orientation in ritual affiliation may have taken place much earlier. However, a more complex and heterogeneous religious dynamic is suggested by the archaeological patterns at other sites. As shown in Table 11.3, 12 sites, including Ferozpur and Ahmadpur, appear to have been part of a multi-denominational landscape from at least the Gupta period onwards, with Buddhist and Brahmanical centres co-existing in close proximity to each other, but nevertheless in distinct spatial spheres. Thus, at Ferozpur, the hilltop monastery co-exists with a major Brahmanical temple in the village at the foot of the hill. At Ahmadpur, the multi-phase Brahmanical temple on the hilltop co-exists during Phase IV with the Buddhist stupa on the lower slopes of the hill. A similar level of religious heterogeneity is attested at Vidisha, Besar talai and Marhai, where Buddhist remains are found outside the context of spatially discrete monastic centres. By Phase VI, some of these temples perch on the edges of hilltop Buddhist complexes. For example, at Sanchi, which was apparently still flourishing during the tenth century AD, there is a Saiva temple built into the side of the hill immediately *below* the main complex, and another at the northern foot of the hill. These patterns, also found at Morel khurd, which was still active as a Buddhist site during this period, attest to the contrasting ritual roles of Buddhism and Brahmanism, the former being predominantly a monastic tradition with less direct ritual involvement on the part of the laity, the latter being embedded in the everyday ritual lives of villagers.[141] However, at other sites such as Andher, Salera, Kanchanpura, Kotra, Barahi khas or Karhaud, where there is no such evidence for continued Buddhist occupation, the construction of Brahmanical temples in, or in close proximity to, monastic compounds implies that the balance of patronage had already began to tip towards Brahmanism, at the expense of Buddhist power.

Site hierarchy

In addition to chronology, it is also important to assess each site's relative position within the local Buddhist hierarchy. The primary starting point is stupa type and size (Table 11.4; Figure 11.23 colour), followed by criteria such as monastery type; presence or absence of stupa railings and enclosures; presence or absence of temples and halls; quantity and type of donative inscriptions; and identity of any associated relic or reliquary deposit (Table 11.2).

Stupa size

Beginning with the diameter of the largest stupa at each site, it is possible to build a five-tiered site hierarchy, with further adjustments made on the basis of the other variables outlined above (Table 11.4):

1) Sites with stupas with diameters of 30 m and above. Only Sanchi and Satdhara belong to this class. Notably, the central stupas here were established during Phase I, apparently under state patronage.
2) Sites with stupa diameters of between 16 and 21 m, i.e. of a similar scale to the main stupa at Bharhut (Cunningham 1879). Of the five sites belonging to this class, it is interesting to note that two are 'urban', rather than hilltop sites.
3) Sites with stupa diameters of between 8 and 15 m, that is of the same order as Sanchi, Stupas 2 and 3, which contain the relics of the Hemavata monks, and Mahamoggalana and Sariputta respectively. There are eight such sites in the study area, including Sonari, Morel khurd and Andher, all of which are associated with the Hemavata relics. The others include Dargawan 2, Mawasa, Torin hill and the two non-hilltop stupa sites, Vidisha[142] and Marha kherai.
4) Sites with stupa diameters of between 3 and 8 m, that is comparable to the lesser stupas at Satdhara, Sonari, Morel khurd and Andher. Eleven sites belong to this class.
5) Sites with stupas, with or without bases, that have diameters of less than 3 m. These conform to what are variously known as 'votive' or burial *ad sanctos* stupas

Table 11.3 Buddhist sites and Brahmanical temples (Phases IV–VII)

	Buddhist building phases				Brahmanical temple		
Site name	**Sector**	**From**	**To**	**SC/site no.**	**Phase from**	**Phase to**	**Location**
Hilltop Buddhist sites with no known evidence for nearby Brahmanical temples							
Sonari – SG003	3	II	II				
Satdhara – SG007	1b	II	V				
Goldoria – SG022	1b	II	II				
Dargawan (1) – SG028	Ib	II	II				
Dargawan (2) – SG029	1b	II	II				
Bighan – SG035	4	II	V				
Torin hill – SG066	4	II	V/V				
Bagoda – SG076	1b	II	II				
Bala barkhera – SG077	1b	II	II				
Bamhora – SG078	1b	II	II				
Mori/Karariya kherai – SG135c	3	IV	IV				
Sukhasen – SG150	3	II	II				
Bawaliya/Dharoyi baba hill – SG172	2b	II	II				
Hilltop sites with nearby Brahmanical temples (Phase IV onwards)							
Ferozpur – SG011	1b	?	IV	SC377	IV	VII	Village on lower slopes of Ferozpur hill
Dhakna hill – SG032c	1b	II	II	SC468, SC680	IV	VI	Dhakna village and Dhakna basti on lower slopes of hill
Ahmadpur – SG037a	4	II	IV	SC131, SC133	IV	VI	Summit of Ahmadpur hill, and in Ahmadpur village
Murwara hill – SG118b	2b	II	IV/V	SC449	IV	VII	Temple in Murwara village at base of hill
Murlikheri hill – SG162	1b	II	II	SC566	IV	VII	Temple in Naroda village
Raisen – SG137	3	II	II	SC456	IV	IV	Temple on site, on summit of Raisen hill
Devrajpur – SG177c	2b	II	IV/V	SC347, 582–586	V	VI	Temple remains on summit of dam below Devrajpur hill.
Mawasa – SG090	2b	II	IV/V	SV199	V	VI	In Nihalpur village at foot of Mawasa hill
Chandna hill – SG095d	2b	II	V	SC696	V	VI	Temple on dam at foot of Chandna hill
Mawasa – SG090	2b	II	V	090	V	VI	Nearby village
Bawaliya hill – SG175	2b	IV/V	IV/V	175	IV	VI	Nearby village
Naroda pathari – SG163	1b	IV/V	IV/V	SC566	IV	VII	Temple in Naroda village
Hilltop sites with nearby Brahmanical temples (Phase VI onwards)							
Sanchi – SG001	1b	Id	VII	SC12, SC19	VI	VI	Base of hill, and on eastern slopes, below temple 45, and at base of hill (also Phase II *nāga* on Nagauri hill)
Morel khurd – SG005	2b	II	VI	SC31	VI	VI	Lower eastern slopes of Morel khurd hill
Andher – SG013	2b	II	IV	SC78	VI	VI	Base of Andher hill (also Phase IIIa *nāga*)
Kanchanpura – SG143	1b	II	II	143	VI	VI	Nearby village
Salera – SG170b	2b	II	V	SC575	VI	VII	Temple remains in Salera village on lower slopes (also Phase IIIb *nāga*)
Hilltop Buddhist sites with Brahmanical temples on site							
Udayagiri – SG031/SC488 (?)	1a	II	II	SC108, 110, 693, 694, 220	IV	VI	Rock-cut and free-standing temples on Udayagiri hill and nearby villages
Karhaud kherai – SG012b	2b	?	?	SC344	VI	VI	Temple on site
Kotra hill – SG167	2b	II	V	SC320, SC313	VI	VI	Temple on site (on summit of Kotra hill) and settlement on lower slopes
Barahi khas – SG059b	3	IV/V	IV/V	SC691	VI	VI	Summit of Barahi khas hill
Urban (multi-denominational) sites							
Vidisha – SG006/SC49	1a	II	IV	SC44, 642–644, 654, 718	II	VII	Various temples on site (urban)
Besar talai – SG041/SC380	3	Id	II	SC142,	V	VI	Temple remains on site (urban)
Marha kherai – SG141	1a	II	II	SC558	VI	VI	Possible temple on site (urban)

Table 11.4 Buddhist site hierarchy based on stupa size

Stupas: class and diameter										**Square stupa platforms**			
1 30–32 m		**2 16–21 m**		**3 8–15 m**		**4 3–8 m**		**5 3 m and less**		**< 4 x 4 m**		**> 4 x 4 m**	
Sanchi Stupa 1	32	Bharhut	20.6	Sonari Stupa 2	14.6	Bighan Stupa 2	8	Satdhara others	3	Ahmadpur	10.4 x 10.4	Kotra	4 x 2
Satdhara Stupa 1	30.8	Udayagiri	20	Bighan Stupa 1	14	Mawasa	7.5	Murwara hill	3	Mori/Karaiya kherai	10 x 10	Morel Khurd north	3.6 x 3.6
		Morel khurd Stupa 1	20	Andher Stupa 1	12.6	Satdhara Stupa 2	7.3	Dhakna hill	3	Naroda Pathari	10 x 6	Murwara hill	3.7 x 3.7
		Besar Talai	20	Sanchi Stupa 3	12.2	Karhaud kherai	6.5	Dargawan 1	3	Sanchi	8.5 x 8.5	Bawaliya hill	3.5 x 3.5
		Bighan (summit)	17.6	Sanchi Stupa 2	12	Salera	5.8	Morel khurd tiers 3–4	2.5	Morel Khurd north	8.4 x 8.4	Naroda Pathari	3 x 3
		Buddha Pahar	16	Morel khurd Stupa 2	12	Andher Stupa 2	5.5	Morel khurd NE terrace	2	Kotra	8 x 8	Karhaud kherai	2.5 x 2.5
				Torin	10.5	Morel khurd tier 3	5.2	Sukhasen/ Bari bir	1.7	Chandna hill east	8 x 8	Sukhasen/ Bari bir	2 x 2
				Morel khurd tier 2	10	Goldoria	5.1	Sanchi	1	Morel khurd north	4 x 4	Morel khurd north	1.6 x 1.6
				Marha kherai	10	Kanchanpura	5	Chandna hill	1	Andher north	4 x 4	Chandna tohoria	1.2 x 1.2
				Chandna lower	9	Bamhora	5	Chandna tohoria	1	Kotra	5 x 3	Barahi khas	1.1 x 1.4
				Devrajpur	8.8	Morel khurd west	4.8	Kotra	1			Ferozpur	1 x 1
				Sonari Stupa 2	8.4	Morel khurd south	4.8						
				Dargawan 2	8.1	Dargawan 2	4.8						
						Andher Stupa 3	4.6						
						Chandna lower	4.5						
						Kotra	4.5						
						Sonari others	4						
						Mori/Karaiya a kherai	4						
						Bawaliya/ Dharoyi baba hill	4						
						Raisen	3.5						
						Kotra	3.5						

(Schopen 1987; 1994c), and usually occur in three main settings: a) at peripheral parts of major monastic sites such as Sanchi and Morel khurd; b) in large 'burial grounds' consisting predominantly of such stupas, as at Dargawan and Sukhasen;[143] and c) positioned within later courtyard monasteries or other monastic enclosures, as at Mawasa, Chandna Tohoria and many other sites. The former two contexts conform to the hierarchical dynamics of the relic cult, which require that the mortuary remains of ordinary monks and laity are placed at a removed distance from those of the Buddha and important saints (Schopen 1994c, 31–80). The latter example is well illustrated at Andher, where the Phase IV or V stupa, enclosed within a fortified enclosure to the south of the main Phase II complex, still maintains a clear visual link with Stupa 1.

Monastery type

There are also linkages between site hierarchy and monastery *type*. As shown in Table 11.4 with the exception of Salera, all ten sites at which platformed monasteries occur have stupas belonging to size classes 1 to 3. On the basis of stupa type alone, Salera belongs to class 4, but the presence of a platformed monastery led to a slight adjustment of this scheme: as shown in Table 11.2, Salera was placed in an overall Rank 3 position. With the exception of Satdhara, all of the single- or double-roomed rectangular monasteries belong to sites which on the basis of stupas alone conform to class 4. As shown in Table 11.2, Satdhara has an overall Rank 1 position, with five platformed monasteries. Significantly, the rectangular monasteries are located at a distance from the principal stupas and monasteries. This suggests that they were used by junior monks and/or pilgrims, while the platformed monasteries were reserved for the senior members of the *saṅgha*.

The relic deposit

The internal hierarchy of the 'Buddhist landscape' may also be related to the dynamics of the relic cult: much of the perceived ritual efficacy of the principal stupas (no. 1) at Sanchi and Satdhara derives from the nature of their relic deposit (Table 6.1). As yet, no relics have been retrieved from these stupas, but there are strong suggestions that they originally contained, and perhaps still do, the relics of the Buddha himself. This may be inferred from the fact that at both sites, the stupas containing the relics of Sariputta and Mahamoggalana are situated next to principal stupas (Figures 9.1, 11.4). This arrangement appears to conform to rules in the *Vinaya*, which stipulate that a monk's stupa should be positioned according to his rank in life and, more specifically, that the stupas of the Buddha's chief disciples, Sariputta and Mahamoggalana, should be appropriately situated beside that of the Buddha (*Mahaparinirvanasutra* 95.2.7; Roth 1980, 184–5; Willis 2000; Shaw 2000a, 30).

Also in keeping with the *Vinaya* rules is the fact that Sanchi Stupa 2 is set outside the main compound wall, seemingly because it contained the relics of the Hemavatas who post-dated the Buddha by several hundred years. Since Stupa 1 was built in Phase Id (by which time the *Vinaya* had been substantially codified), the Hemavatas' stupa, constructed a hundred years later, was possibly conforming to an earlier power structure. By contrast, Sonari, Andher and Morel khurd were built anew in Phase II, probably by the Hemavatas. Because the sites were 'new' the Hemavatas were able to manipulate the rules and position their own monument directly beside the main stupa at the site. This would seem to be a blatant statement of Hemavata eminence, corroborated by the fact that the most important stupas at these sites are set within enclosures. As shown in Table 11.2, stupa enclosures occur only at site Categories 1–3. Thus, while the identity of the relic deposits at the other sites is unknown, the presence of an enclosure is a strong indicator of their relative ritual importance. The correspondence between stupa size and ritual status is illustrated further by sites such as Morel khurd, where smaller stupas, most probably containing burials of ordinary monks and laity (Schopen 1996b), are positioned at a lower level, presumably in deference to the Hemavatas' ritual seniority.

There is also a link between site-hierarchy and sculptural grandeur. Notably, all of the sites connected with the Hemavatas have carved railings, conspicuously absent at most of the other hilltop sites. The size and relative sculptural opulence of these sites provide confirmation of the view that the Hemavata school played a key role in the 'second propagation' of Buddhism (Willis 2000) and were clearly at the top of the local hierarchical scale. As shown in Table 11.2, the only other sculpted railings are found at Vidisha, Besar talai and Marha kherai, all of which, being non-hilltop sites, clearly belong to a separate category.

The 'monastic landscape'

These criteria form the basis for defining five major ranks of Buddhist sites listed in Table 11.2. An additional four classes, 'monastery only', 'forest dwelling', 'late' and 'urban', are also defined: i) 'monastery only' refers to sites such as Ferozpur or Bawaliya hill where no associated stupas have been found; ii) 'forest dwelling' refers to sites such as Ahmadpur and, possibly, Nagauri, where there are no other residential facilities apart from 'monastic rock-shelters'; iii) 'late' refers to sites where there are no monastic remains prior to the sixth or seventh centuries AD, that is, consisting only of the square-platformed stupa and/or courtyard monastery type; iv) 'urban' refers to Buddhist remains such as stupas or pillar capitals found outside the boundaries of hilltop monastic boundaries. Their urban, or road-side setting in the case of Marha kherai, suggests that they were geared primarily towards lay ritual activity. Apart from Vidisha, no associated monastery remains have been found in such settings, suggesting that at some of the smaller sites, officiating monks may have resided at nearby hilltop monastic centres (e.g. Sonari for Besar talai, Sanchi for the others). However, the high rate of stone-removal at settlement sites means that the existence of associated monasteries cannot be ruled out.

In summary, therefore, there were two major centres during the Mauryan period, Sanchi and Satdhara. During the second propagation of Buddhism, Sanchi remains the most important site, followed closely by Satdhara. The three other geographical sectors also possessed at least one major site during this period: Bighan in the north, Sonari in the south and Morel khurd in the east, with Mawasa, one of the newly discovered sites in the eastern sector, representing a similarly important centre. Not all of these sites are of equal status, with Morel khurd being clearly larger than Sonari and Bighan. How these sites related to each other, and to the lesser sites in the intervening area, clearly deserves further consideration. There is also the question of how the different monastic territories (*sīma*) were delineated, or to what degree the monastic landscape was divided according to different schools: we have already established that Sanchi, Satdhara, Sonari and Andher were linked together under the Hemavata school and the leadership of Gotiputa. Willis (2000, 95) has suggested that Sonari was a kind of subsidiary to Satdhara, while Andher was dependent on Morel khurd. While there may be some truth in this, the documentation during the SSP of so many additional hilltop Buddhist sites in the area calls for an examination of more localised inter-site relationships. For example, although the nature of the relic deposits at these newly documented sites is presently unknown, one may assume that their closest allegiances were to the nearest major centre in the area. Thus, the stupa complexes on the northern and southern hillocks at Dargawan would have deferred to Sanchi, Ferozpur and Murlikheri to Satdhara, Torin to Bighan, Chandna and related sites to Mawasa, and so on. At the same time, Sanchi would have remained the pivotal site for the area as a whole. Finally, while these inter-site relationships, and internal hierarchies of the 'Buddhist landscape', are important for our understanding of local monastic history, equally important is the question of how these monastic sites related to other forms of social and religious hierarchies, as manifested for example in the configuration of non-Buddhist cult spots, settlements or land-use systems.

Buddhist patronage networks

On the basis of the donative inscriptions at Sanchi and Satdhara, it is generally assumed that in contrast to the state-patronised building campaigns during Phase I, the 'second propagation' of

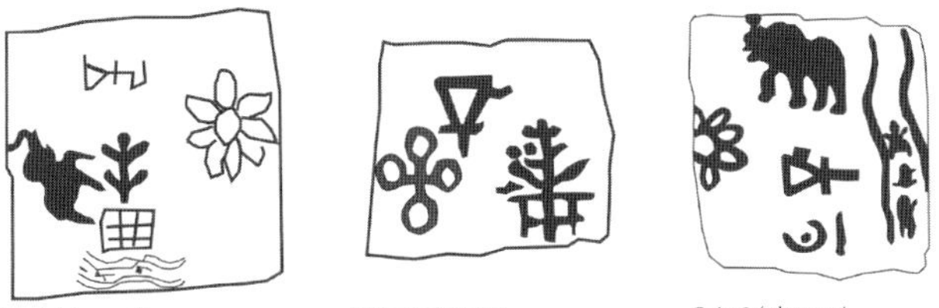

Coin 1 (obverse)
Dimensions: 2.3 x 2.3 x 0.2 cm
Weight: 10.3 grams

Coin 2 (obverse)
Dimensions: 1.8 x 1.8 x 0.15 cm
Weight: 4.6 grams

Coin 3 (obverse)
Dimensions: 2 x 2 x 0.1 cm
Weight: 5.8 grams

0 2 cm

Figure 11.25 Coins from Besar talai

Buddhism was funded chiefly by collective patronage. No donative inscriptions have been found at the three other Hemavata sites, Sonari, Morel khurd or Andher. However, the fact that all three sites are linked under a single school of Buddhism, as well as a single pan-Indian *sculptural* style, suggests that they were supported by similar means as Sanchi and Satdhara. Interestingly, however, the newly discovered Brahmi inscription at Mawasa demonstrates the existence of other non-collective forms of patronage during Phase II. The wording of the Mawasa inscription implies that the whole stupa, and perhaps the entire site, was funded by a single patron, who was possibly of royal status. This scale of patronage is more commonly associated with state sponsorship, as illustrated by the Phase I evidence at Sanchi. It is important to note, however, that whole structures, usually monasteries, are amongst the lay donations mentioned in texts such as the *Mūlasarvāstivāda-Vinaya* (Schopen 1994b). As discussed in chapter 2, these texts are rarely dated before the Kusana period, drawing largely on correlations with a limited set of archaeological evidence thought to indicate the emergence of institutionalised monasticism. Although the precise identity of Makadeya, the patron mentioned in the Mawasa inscription, remains unknown, this evidence is important for demonstrating that by at least the second century BC, the *saṅgha* had become sufficiently integrated in local society to attract single-person patronage of whole buildings.

Further evidence for non-collective, and possibly royal, forms of patronage occurs at a number of stupa sites situated within habitational settings. At Besar talai, for example, the fragmentary inscription which reads *kudugaru karikha(ta)* ('caused to be made by Kudugaru') (*IAR* 1978–9, 13) follows a similar causative structure to the Mawasa inscription. The assumption is that Kudugaru, like Makadeya, was a local king or oligarch and that the stupa whose railings are found at various points across the site is being referred to as the object of donation. As noted earlier, the quality of sculpture found at Besar talai finds its equivalent only at the most important hilltop sites in the area, which reinforces the idea that we are dealing with the highest order of patronage. Further evidence to this effect is provided by the post-Mauryan pillar and capital remains found at Besar talai and several other major settlements in the study area. This sets them apart from the hilltop complexes, where pillars only occur at the two most important centres, Sanchi and Satdhara. Furthermore, the fact that similar capitals are found at Vidisha shows not only that these urban sites were part of a unified socio-political system but that pillar construction was reserved only for the most important sites. This is partly explainable by the strong regal associations of pillars in ancient India, as typified by the imperial symbolism of the earlier Mauryan pillars and their capitals.[144] The most frequently depicted animal in this respect is the lion, which represents Sakyasimha, the lion among the Sakya clan, as well as the imperial force of the Mauryan empire. However, both the elephant and bull also embody a similar set of religio-political symbolic references.[145] It is possible therefore that the post-Mauryan elephant and bull capitals also embody a wider set of dynastic references. This supposition is strengthened by the fact that both bulls and elephants occur frequently on early coins from the Vidisha, Eran and Ujjain area (Bopearachchi and Pieper 1998, 94–8, 117–27).[146] In many cases, the animal is depicted as a pillar or standard capital, often in association with 'Buddhist' motifs such as the tree-in-railing. Coins of the elephant type were documented at Besar talai during the present survey (Figure 11.25; Plate 127).[147] There would appear therefore to be a significant link between 'state' forms of patronage and ritual sites where the presence of the laity was at its greatest. Secondly, it is no coincidence that these sites are also the ones with the most visually impressive displays of both sculpture and patronage, either in the form of inscriptions or 'regal' capitals. By contrast, although similar forms of patronage may have contributed towards the construction and upkeep of less 'public' monastic sites (visited by fewer lay visitors or pilgrims), it was not recorded in such an ostentatious manner.

The 'topography' of monastic sites

Apart from a limited number of urban Buddhist remains, the majority of Buddhist monuments in the SSP study area occur on hilltops. That these locations were actively sought out by the *saṅgha* is demonstrated most forcefully in areas where hills occur in limited numbers. For example, three out of five of the small hillocks immediately to the north of Vidisha are occupied by Buddhist remains. The predictability of this model was demonstrated at Budha Pahar, a small hill in Shamshabad district about 50 km north of Vidisha. This particular hillock was selected randomly as a likely spot for a stupa in order to test the wider applicability of the patterns in the SSP study area. These hilltop locations create a clear-cut, topographical delineation between monastic sites and wider aspects of the archaeological landscape, such as settlements, irrigation works and non-Buddhist cult spots. At the same time, the distance between these sites is usually insignificant. While the patterns discussed in this chapter offer crucial insights into the internal dynamics of the *saṅgha*, it is also important to assess patterns beyond the formal boundaries of hilltop monastic sites. These wider points will be taken up further in the following chapters.

Hilltops: practical and ritual associations

The purpose of this section is to explore the possible practical, ritual, symbolic and social reasons why these hilltop locations were so consistently sought out by the *saṅgha*. The most obvious advantage of hilltops is that they provide refuge from monsoon flooding. This is why so many settlements are situated on some form of raised ground. However, as shown in Figure 4.1, very few villages, either modern or ancient, are found on the summits of hills, but are much more likely to be situated on the lower slopes. This may be because hilltops are comparatively difficult to reach. They also have low agricultural value and deficient water supplies.

As discussed later, they may also have been considered too susceptible to siege. On the other hand, the forests which they support are a valuable natural resource for wild plants and animals. While these are used by agriculturalists, as well as hunter-gatherers, hilly areas have, since ancient times, been closely associated with non-producing, hunter-gatherer groups. This is attested by the large number of rock-shelters and microlith scatters found throughout the Vindhyan range. Studies in other parts of Madhya Pradesh have shown that similar types of sites are often favoured by other peripatetic or 'property-renouncing' groups, such as ascetics and sages (Jacobson 1975, 81). Notwithstanding the problems over its date and authorship, *Kautilya's Arthaśāstra* (2.2.5) also offers interesting insights into such sites, referring to the designation of non-agricultural land for the purposes of scholarly and ascetical activities. The level of correspondence between the kind of sites chosen by prehistoric hunter-gatherers and later ascetic groups is attested in the Sanchi area by the frequency with which painted rock-shelters and/or microlithic tools occur at Buddhist sites. As shown in Figure 11.1 (colour), these kinds of prehistoric remains were found at 14 hilltop sites showing evidence for later Buddhist activity. It is possible therefore that, as a 'non-producing' group, the incoming *saṅgha* had little other choice when it came to finding a place for itself in the landscape but to occupy areas which had little or no other economic value. A similar set of restricting factors may explain the tendency for Buddhist sites, particularly in the Deccan, to overlie older, 'protohistoric' burial grounds (Schopen 1996b). Being unsuitable for agricultural purposes, such locations obviously suited the *saṅgha*'s 'non-producing' status, but, due to their mortuary function, they would have had extremely polluting associations, according to the orthodox Brahmanical worldview. In both economic and spiritual terms, therefore, the Buddhists were relegated to the peripheral zones of the social landscape.

Hilltops also hold particular symbolic and mythological associations, described in ancient texts as the abode of *yakṣas* and other place-bound spirits (Misra 1981, 50; e.g. *Digha Nikāya*, 41). These shrines, often referred to as *caitya* (Misra 1981, 42; Coomaraswamy 1980, 17; *Aṅguttara Nikāya* II. 550), provided the focus of hilltop festivals (*gir-agga-samajjan*) of the kind known to have been held annually at Rajagaha (Hardy, 1903, 61–6). The same kind of hilltop festival is listed in Asoka's edicts nos. 1 and 9 as one of the events prohibited to monks and nuns (*Vinaya* II. 107, 150; III. 71; IV. 85, 267, 360; *Jātaka* III. 538). The suggestion that the configuration of the ritual landscape followed certain topographical conventions, supports other archaeological and ethnographic accounts relating to the predominance of pre-Buddhist ritual practices at major monastic sites (Cunningham 1892, 40; Byrne 1995; Kosambi 1962). The influence of these cults has also been traced in elements of Buddhist architecture.[148] Whether the *saṅgha* actively sought out places already regarded as sacred spots, is difficult to determine, especially since *yakṣa* or *nāga* worship rarely took on durable forms during the time in question. As discussed in chapter 12, stone images of these deities do not appear in the Sanchi area until the first century BC, that is, long after the arrival of Buddhism. Further, their sculptural representation may say more about the Buddhist worldview than 'local' religious practices. However, by simply occupying spaces in the landscape which in the minds of the local populace were associated with revered local deities, the *saṅgha* was already making a statement about its position in the local religious hierarchy. This may have been an early attempt to 'localise' itself in the area; it may also have embodied an element of proselytisation, that is, by asserting the Buddha's supremacy over local deities whose precise identity remains obscure.[149]

Hilltop stupas: 'seeing' the Buddha

Hilltops would have helped to further these proselytising aims by ensuring that stupas were seen throughout the surrounding landscape. At Sanchi, the main stupa can be seen for miles around, and at Andher, the principal stupa perches dramatically on the edge of a cliff, creating a striking silhoutte on the horizon. Those living in neighbouring villages would have been constantly aware of the monks' presence above. This is illustrated clearly at Andher, where the Phase IV/V stupa at the southern edge of the hill directly overlooks the village of Hakimkheri below. The other monastic sites all show a similar concern with maximising the stupas' visual presence. This line of influence also works the other way around: standing on the southernmost edge of Andher hill, not only does one get a bird's-eye view of the activity in the village below, but the sounds of the village are strikingly audible. The monks were apart from village life but were fully aware of its day-to-day activities; it is possible that not everyone would have welcomed the feeling of being scrutinised by monks overlooking them from the hill above! A similar level of surveillance comes across in the relative positioning of the main stupas, and the Phase IIIa Bhagavata cult spot below (Plate 142).

The element of intervisibility between stupa sites is also notable. From Sanchi, it is possible to see the stupas at Morel khurd; further in the distance are the stupas at Andher; and to the SW is a line of hills, immediately behind which are the monasteries of Sonari and Satdhara.[150] The main stupa at Sanchi is visible from as far away as Bighan in the north, and appears to have provided the main orientation for the smaller stupas and burials on Dargawan hills (1 and 2) to the west of Sanchi.

This level of intervisibility may have been an important way of maintaining linkages between key ritual sites. This arrangement was far from a passive network. Texts and inscriptions describe stupas not simply as repositories of the Buddhist relic, but containers of a 'living presence' which projected the power of the Buddha, the *dharma* and respected monks into and across the surrounding space (Schopen 1997). The highly visible setting of these stupas highlights the importance of 'seeing' (*dassana*) at Buddhist sacred sites. Both Trainor (1997, 174–7) and Schopen (1997, 117, n. 9) have noted the analogy between 'seeing' and worshipping at monastic sites, a feature which receives sanction in the Buddhist Canon. More specifically, the dynamics of the relic cult suggest that simply 'seeing' stupas is equivalent to beholding and worshipping the Buddha or saint whose relics the stupa contains. The objects of this 'seeing' are not merely sacred places, but 'relics of use' (*pāribhogika dhātu*); the places where the Buddha was born, gained enlightenment, taught and died were transformed into 'relics' because they had been 'used' by the Buddha. The parallel concept of *darśana*, found in varying degrees in other Indian faiths, ensures that through the auspicious sight of the venerated object, a devotee gains spiritual merit (Eck 1981). This adds a powerful new dimension to our understanding of the proselytising quality of stupa architecture, whose trajectory of influence could transcend its material boundaries by the very fact of its visual dominance. For the Buddhist monks, this mechanism was a means of quite literally 'presencing' the *dharma* in foreign ground. Furthermore, the visual prominence of Sanchi Stupa 1, which most probably contained the Buddha's relic, allowed the Buddha to be 'seen' by monks residing at distant monasteries. By the same logic, the efficacy of the *dharma* was being cast over the local population, whether or not they knew or wished it![151]

A similar concern with maximising the visual presence of stupas is also discernible in the internal layout of monastic sites. Studies by Schopen (1997) and Trainor (1997) have helped dispel the view, to some extent a product of Protestant-influenced historical analysis, that the veneration of relics was the exclusive concern of the lay followers of Buddhism. As part of a body of evidence on the 'cult of the monastic dead', Schopen (1997, 258; cf. Roth 1980, 186) has noted how the entrances to early monastic buildings tended to be orientated upon the principal stupa, albeit at some distance, while later quadrangular monasteries were built around a stupa in the central courtyard; in other cases, small stupas can be found distributed at various points within monastery compounds, as found, for example, in the courtyards of the eastern monasteries at Sanchi (Figure 9.1), as well as many of the outlying Buddhist sites in the study area. However, the spatial dynamics of early monastic complexes have not been fully understood, partly because the platforms described in this chapter have not hitherto been recognised as monasteries. Furthermore, with the recent exception of Satdhara (Agrawal 1997), none of the other Phase II monastery types, such as the simple rectangular buildings or the early courtyard monasteries lined with rectangular rooms, have been reported previously. In all cases, the monastery platforms are positioned in close proximity to, or in direct view of, the central stupa. Even without their superstructure, the platforms provide an all-encompassing panorama of the site as a whole. Going back to our discussion of 'seeing', this would have allowed the monks (or at least the senior monks who no doubt occupied these buildings) to keep the most important stupas within their line of vision, and therefore to contemplate the auspicious sight and presence of the Buddha and the *Arhats*. This helps to explain why Stupas 1 and 2 at Morel khurd are not in a straight line but are slightly staggered in order that both monuments could be seen from the monastery (Figure 11.8). This not only allowed the stupas to be admired but also provided an efficient means of surveillance. At Satdhara, 'Monastery platform B' not only offers a view of the main stupa but doubles as a 'lookout' for the river valley below (Figure 11.4). Similar arrangements are found at Sonari, where the staggering of the line of Stupas 1, 3 and 5 allows for all three to be kept in clear view from the platform (the lines of vision are shown by the arrows in Figure 11.6).[152] At Andher, too, the main stupa bears a visual link with the now heavily damaged platform to the SW (Figure 11.10). These provisions ensured that maximum spiritual merit was accrued through the act of 'seeing' (Shaw 2000a, 33).

The positioning of the monuments not only allowed the stupas to be admired but may also be explained as part of the need to protect the relics by regulating access to the stupas and maintaining close surveillance of them. On account of its ritual status as a human being, the stupa was not only open to the gaze of the devout, but also to more malevolent types of 'seeing'. The staggered gates at Sanchi Stupa 1 may have been aimed at diverting the gaze of the 'evil eye', traditionally thought to travel only in straight lines. The ritual and political efficacy of the relic also called for protection against theft (Trainor 1997, 117–35). As the reliefs on the Sanchi gateways show, relics were sources of contention from the earliest days of Buddhism. This was because relics lent themselves to use as instruments of political legitimacy, the spread of the *dharma* being easily appropriated by kings who sought to draw on analogies between themselves and the Buddha as *dharmarāja* and *cakravartin*. Although the use of relics as instruments of polity received its fullest elaboration in Sri Lanka, Strong (1983) has put forward convincing arguments that this mode of kingship was first developed by Asoka in the third century BC (see also Duncan 1990). As shown in Figures 11.8 and 11.6, the part of the stupa upon which the monasteries are most consistently orientated is the staircase leading to the upper terrace (Plate 64). This part was singled out not only because it offered the possibility of ascending to a higher spiritual plane,[153] but also because it took one as close as it was possible to get to the relic chamber, where one could circumambulate the sacred 'traces' of the Buddha (Falk 1977, 288).

The fortified hilltop: surveillance and defence

Stupas were also open to the threat of 'mundane' human action, which may help to explain why so many hilltop Buddhist sites are equipped with strategic mechanisms befitting their fortress-like location. Many of the hills are naturally defended by sheer cliffs and jagged rocks, which as shown at Andher, can set them apart from the surrounding landscape in a dramatic manner; Plate 142 depicts the Phase IIIa Bhagavata site as seen from the stupa site above. As shown in Figure 11.23 (colour), over half the sites include some form of fortified structure.

At Morel khurd, the Phase II platformed monastery has towers at each of its four corners. Even without towers, the height of this and other platforms creates a fortress-like aspect, which would have been an effective deterrent against attack, while the internal, covered staircases, enhanced at Satdhara by a bent entrance, would have enabled effective monitoring of movement in and out of the building.[154] Finally, the towering superstructures not only provide all-encompassing views of the stupas, for both ritual and defensive purposes, but would have doubled as 'look-outs' over the surrounding area. They are also highly 'visible': the Morel khurd platform, when seen from Andher or Sanchi, is even now the most conspicuous architectural feature at the site; in its complete form, it would have been double the present height and would have dominated the entire monastic complex. This would have increased the level of intervisibility between sites, which, in addition to enforcing the continuous presence of the *śāsana* across the landscape, may have allowed for forms of emergency signalling between sites.[155] Other elements of fortification include substantial boundary walls (Plate 98), often provided with towers and bastions, found at ten of the Buddhist sites in the area, including Sanchi and Andher. It is difficult to date these walls with certainty; the rubble-infill outer-facing construction at most sites is suggestive of an early date, but the wall on the eastern edge of Sanchi hill was probably built during the tenth or eleventh century AD. Building 43, one of Sanchi's latest structures, dates to around the same time. With its four corner towers it has a distinctly military appearance, closely mirrored by the fortified stupa enclosure at Bighan to the north of Vidisha. Similar military plans have been noted at medieval monasteries in eastern India.[156] The reason for building these later defences may well be related to the forces behind the eventual decline of Buddhism in the area: there is little evidence for ongoing occupation after the post-Gupta period at interior sites, and after the eleventh or twelfth century AD at Sanchi.

However the evidence discussed above suggests that these sites were subject to hostile threats during earlier periods also. The post-Mauryan king Pusyamitra seems to have been inimical to heterodoxy, especially Buddhism. Traditions which associate the horse sacrifice with the Sungas and identify them as Brahamanas lend support to their position as representatives of the vigorously orthodox (*smārta*). This has led to suggestions that the main stupa at Sanchi could have been intentionally damaged in the post-Mauryan era (Marshall 1940, 23–4; Verardi 1996, 230–1). While there is no direct proof that Sanchi was attacked by the Sungas, the circumstances are sufficiently compelling to see the injury to Sanchi as an assault on the *śāsana* and, quite literally, the 'body' of Buddhism.

However, it was not simply a question of heterodox versus orthodox views. As already noted, relic theft took place within Buddhist circles from the earliest times, and schisms appeared frequently, from as early as the Asokan period.[157] Finally, the fortification of the central Indian sites may have been less to do with inter-religious conflict, than with the fact that hilltops are in general more vulnerable to siege than other parts of the landscape. This is perhaps why habitational sites are usually built on the lower slopes, rather than the actual summit of hills.

The hilltop monastery: social and economic implications

Further suggestions that monastic sites were susceptible to attack or pillage, draw on theories regarding the wider social and economic function of monasteries. First, in addition to meditational retreats, many monasteries were centres of learning and scholarship (Ray 1994, 122) and would have contained valuable libraries in need of protection. Secondly, the larger sites attracted numerous pilgrims, whose donations would have resulted in the accumulation of considerable wealth. The large quantity of precious items found in Monastery 51 at Sanchi (Hamid 1940, 85–6), was possibly accumulated in this way.[158] Finally, many of the Deccan rock-cut monasteries occupied commanding positions on major trade-routes, suggesting that the *saṅgha* played an active role in facilitating inter-regional trade (Heitzman 1984; Ray 1986; Morrison 1995a). This view is corroborated by epigraphical and textual evidence which shows that the *saṅgha* supported the trading interests of travelling merchants by providing a safe haven for traders' caravans, offering secure lodging facilities, storing cash and lending out interest on permanent endowments (Schopen 1994b).[159] It also appears to have promoted the commercial value of traded goods, such as silk or the 'seven precious things', by incorporating them into the Buddhist framework as objects of ritual gift-giving (Liu 1988, 101). All of these factors would have increased the need for the kind of defence mechanisms seen in the Sanchi area.

The development of Buddhist monasticism

By highlighting the commercial interests of the *saṅgha*, these studies have been helpful for offering an alternative to the 'passive' model of Buddhism, which presents the 'ideal' monk as one engaged in a life of meditation, his subsistence based entirely on alms-begging. They have also shown that, despite their isolated locations, monastic centres were not cut off from the wider social and economic infrastructure. This we know from the Phase II donative inscriptions at Sanchi. Further evidence of the *saṅgha*'s ability to integrate itself in the economic infrastructure is provided by newly documented donative inscriptions at Besar talai and Mawasa discussed earlier.

As discussed in chapter 2, however, there is little understanding of how the *saṅgha* interacted with agricultural populations in the surrounding countryside, the prevalent view being that integrated systems of exchange did not begin until the fifth century AD with the appearance of 'ordered' courtyard monasteries and inscriptional evidence for permanent endowments of land and villages. As far as the earlier donative inscriptions relating to one-off gifts of stupa parts are concerned, these are not considered to have involved any ongoing financial obligation on the part of the donor. Furthermore, although the *saṅgha* may have reciprocated through the bestowal of merit (Schopen 1996a), this form of reciprocation is generally seen as superficial and ultimately 'passive'.

This framework may be challenged on a number of counts. First, Strenksi's (1986, 475) theory that the early donative inscriptions at Sanchi represented a kind of precursor to forms of 'generalised' exchange, as typified for example by 'monastic landlordism', calls for deeper recognition of the levels of social acceptance, not to mention administrative efficiency, involved in such fund-raising exercises.[160] One may assume, however, that for their daily needs, the monks would have relied for the most part on the local communities living in the immediate vicinity of the monastery. These villages may have had a similar status to the 'service villages' (*aramīkagāma*) described in early Buddhist texts such as the *Culavaṁsa* (v. 46.115) as providing labour to the monastery and meeting the nutritional needs of its inhabitants. Although during the post-Mauryan period some monks may have continued to practise mendicancy based on pre-existing alliances with individual families in specific villages, it is generally accepted that a more integrated, sustainable system of exchange between monastic and non-monastic sections of society would have been necessary as monasteries became larger and more institutionalised (Bailey and Mabbett 2003, 70–2). These issues are discussed further in chapter 14, drawing on the distribution of irrigation systems in the Sanchi area and their relationship to Buddhist sites and settlements.

The second major problem is that the early platformed and simple rectangular monasteries described in this chapter show that the fundamental criteria that underlay the development of exchange networks described in the texts already existed during the late centuries BC. As discussed in chapters 2 and 9, traditional theories regarding the chronology of monasteries and the development of institutionalised monasticism are mutually intertwined: the view that 'there are no monastery remains [at Sanchi] clearly datable before the Gupta period' (Trainor 1996, 32) refers solely to the chronology of the courtyard type of monastery which, according to Marshall (1940, 63-4), moved down to central India after appearing in the North-West during the Kusana period. This scheme is already challenged by the second-century-BC rock-cut monasteries of the Deccan, many of which follow a courtyard plan, while pre-Kusana monasteries (of the non-courtyard type) are known at many north Indian sites such as Taxila (Marshall 1951, i, 320), Rajgir, Kausambi and Sravasti.[161] However, as far as scholars of Buddhist history are concerned, it is not so much the existence or absence of monastery structures which matters, but rather whether their *architectural* complexity or 'order' is seen as matching the *administrative* order expected of a domesticated *saṅgha*. According to Marshall (*ibid.*), early monasteries at Taxila were merely makeshift structures with 'irregularly sized rooms' and devoid of outer boundary walls. Although there is little difference in the layout of many of the rock-cut courtyard-type monasteries of the Deccan and the later structural versions of the Kusana period, the former are usually regarded as lacking the 'internal organisation' accredited to a fully institutionalised *saṅgha* (Schopen 1994b). By contrast, the structural version is seen as the primary marker of a transition to socially embedded forms of monasticism.

A similar unilinear mode of reasoning, which places rock-cut architectural forms lower down the evolutionary scale than their structural equivalents, has also shaped academic perceptions of the type of 'monastic rock-shelters' described in this chapter. The fact that rock-shelters (*guha*) are described in the Pali *Vinaya* as one of the five types of temporary dwellings permitted to Buddhist monks during the rainy season, has meant that shelters of this type are generally seen as representing a 'pre-monumental' and therefore 'pre-domesticated' phase of Buddhism (Schopen 1994b, 548). More to the point, the large number of 'drip-ledge' shelters in Sri Lanka corroborate the traditional view that there were no *permanent* monasteries during the pre-Kusana period. This view can also be challenged from a number of angles. First, the distinction between forest (*āvāsa*) and village (*ārāma*) retreats had already become well defined during the Buddha's lifetime (Dutt 1962, 58). Despite the textual view of an overarching movement towards a 'village' tradition, the perpetuation of a two-tier system in later years is attested archaeologically by the fact that many of the Sri Lankan 'drip-ledge' shelters continued to be occupied long after part of the *saṅgha* had adopted permanent establishments (Schopen 1996a, 122). The dual existence of village-dwelling (*gamavasin*) and forest-dwelling (*arannavasin*) monks in Sri Lanka, and parts of Southeast Asia, is also well attested ethnographically (Tambiah 1984; R. Ray 1994).

In India, these issues remain largely unexplored, partly because there is no ongoing Buddhist tradition, but also because of the 'monumental' focus of archaeological research. The attention paid to 'Buddhist caves' rarely extends beyond the sphere of the elaborate rock-cut caves of the Deccan. Despite limited evidence to the contrary at Pangurariya (*IAR* 1975–6: 28–30; Sarkar 1983, 403–5; Sircar 1979, 94–103) and Bhimbetka (Gupta, 1967, 83), both in central India, it is generally believed that 'Indian monks normally did not occupy or "improve" natural caves' (Schopen 1994a, 151). Many questions remain regarding the 'monastic rock-shelters' in the Sanchi area, and their relation to the 'monumental' manifestation of Buddhism. However, it is likely that both the solitary forest dwellings and those clustered around the outer edges of larger monastic compounds continued to be occupied following the construction of structural monasteries. The question of whether this two-tier model was based on individual choice, or on internal hierarchies within the *saṅgha* (at Morel khurd for example, the shelters may have housed the junior monks, while the senior members resided in the platformed monasteries), can only be addressed effectively through focused collaborative research between textual scholars and archaeologists.

As pointed out by Strenski (1986), the study of the 'domestication' of the *saṅgha* has been hampered by a limited set of defining criteria based largely on the issue of the *saṅgha*'s transition from peripatetic mendicancy to sedentary monasticism. It has also been heavily influenced by the 'passive' model of Buddhism which regards the development of sustainable exchange networks between monastic and lay populations as evidence for the deterioration of true Buddhist values. Further misconceptions have arisen from the uncritical manner in which secondary archaeological material has been used by text-based scholars to 'prove' theories regarding Buddhist history. In Trainor's (1997, 61) words, archaeology 'offers a perspective on what people actually did, as opposed to what they were supposed to do according to an idealized textual tradition composed and preserved by a religious elite'.[162] This awakening, however laudable, is problematic (and ironic) in that it perpetuates the classic opposition of text as text and archaeology as 'fossil'. Generally absent is an awareness of developments within archaeological theory and method, such as those which acknowledge the similarity between archaeological sites and texts (e.g. Tilley 1991). Finally, the attempt to establish causal links between architectural and social meaning is (perhaps coincidentally) reminiscent of structuralist spatial analyses, whose essentialist reasoning came under heavy attack as part of the 'post-processual' critique (Hodder 1991, 35–55).

Returning to the Phase II monastery platforms and rectangular structures, a number of concluding points should be made. First, their identification as monasteries provides a crucial basis for establishing a revised chronological and typological framework of monastic architecture in the Sanchi area. Further, the symbolic and strategic positioning of the monastery platforms, together with aspects of their internal planning (especially at Mawasa), shows that they were far from haphazard, unplanned buildings. Finally, while insights into the social and ritual dynamics of the *saṅgha* may be inferred from the physical remains of monastic structures, it is important to look for other signs of 'domestication'. These may be manifested in the form of gifts recorded in the donative inscriptions, as well as other 'services' such as medicine and water-harvesting skills discussed in chapter 6. However, further insights are provided by situating this material within its broader archaeological setting.

Conclusion

The precise manner in which monks in the Sanchi area attended to their everyday needs remains uncertain. However, one of the major contentions of this study is that it is not possible to understand the social and economic background of the *saṅgha* without going beyond the formal boundaries of monastic sites. Thus, having discussed the dynamics of the local *saṅgha* on the basis of the topographical and archaeological patterns in the 'Buddhist landscape', we must now give consideration to other aspects of the archaeological landscape. Despite their topographically distinct hilltop setting, monastic sites cannot be separated from nearby non-Buddhist cult spots, settlements and land-use systems. As discussed in chapter 9, Sanchi itself should be regarded as an integral part of a larger archaeological complex comprising all of these elements. The aim of the following three chapters is to describe these other aspects of the landscape; how they relate to the configuration of Buddhist sites; and how they impact on our understanding of Buddhist history in the area.

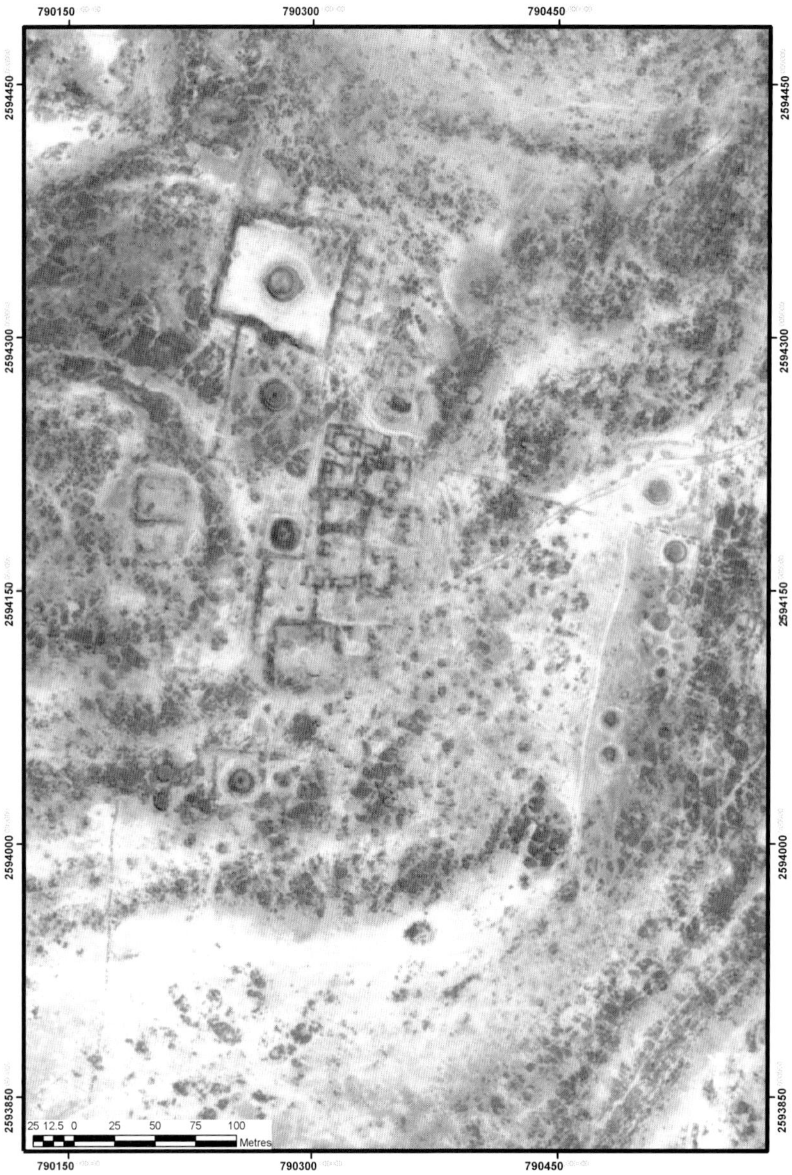

43 Morel khurd (Quickbird satellite imagery)

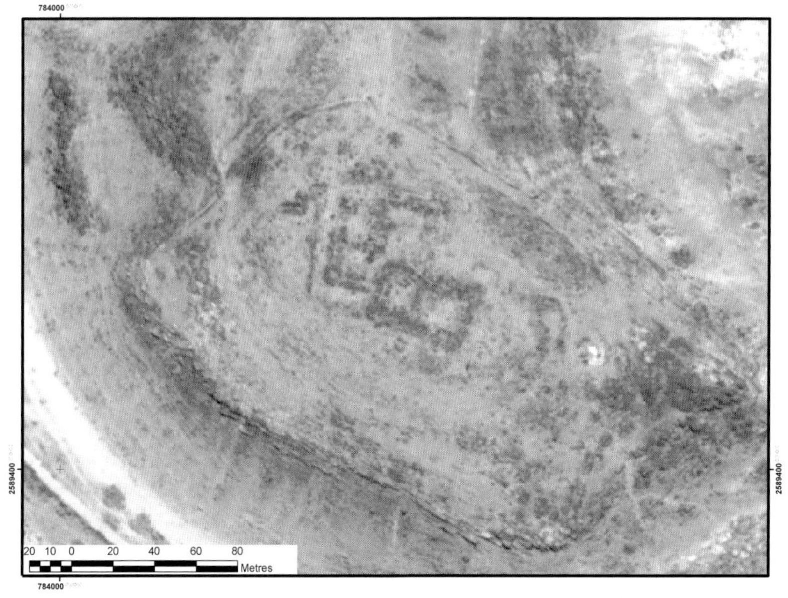

44 Kotra: hilltop monastery remains (Quickbird satellite imagery)

45 Sanchi: rock-shelters on eastern edge of hill

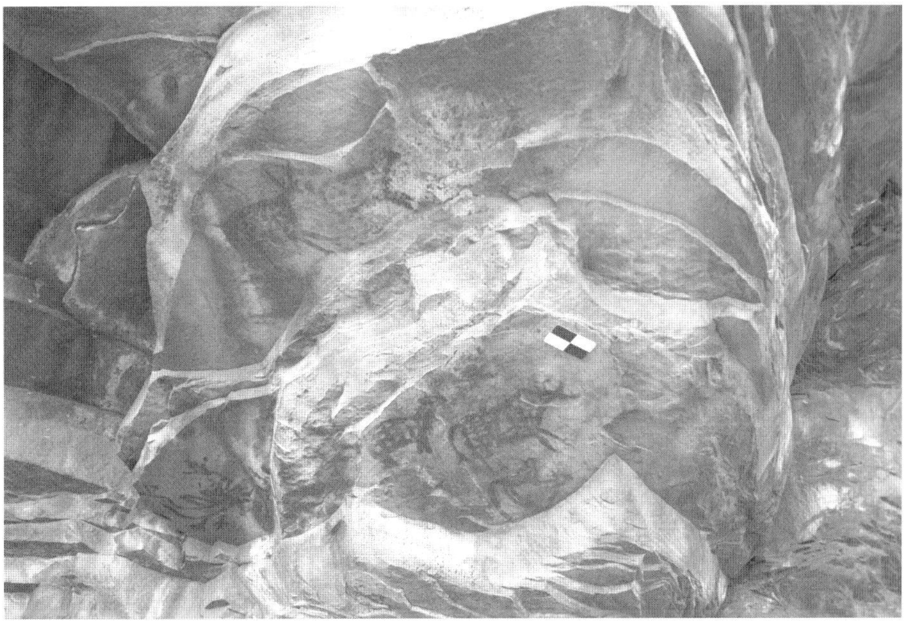

46 Ahmadpur: prehistoric paintings

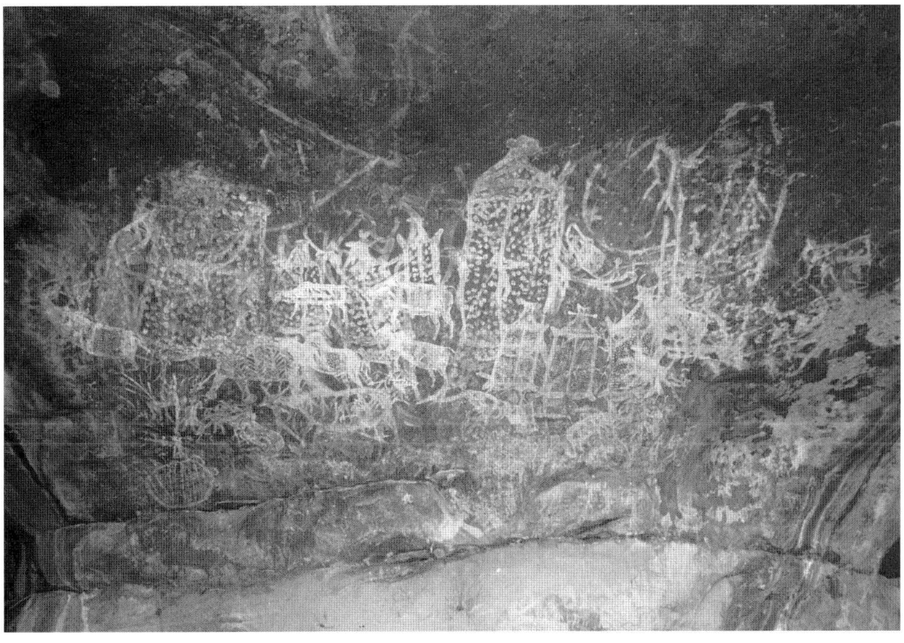

47 Kharwai: prehistoric paintings

48 Nagauri: historical painted frieze in rock-shelter

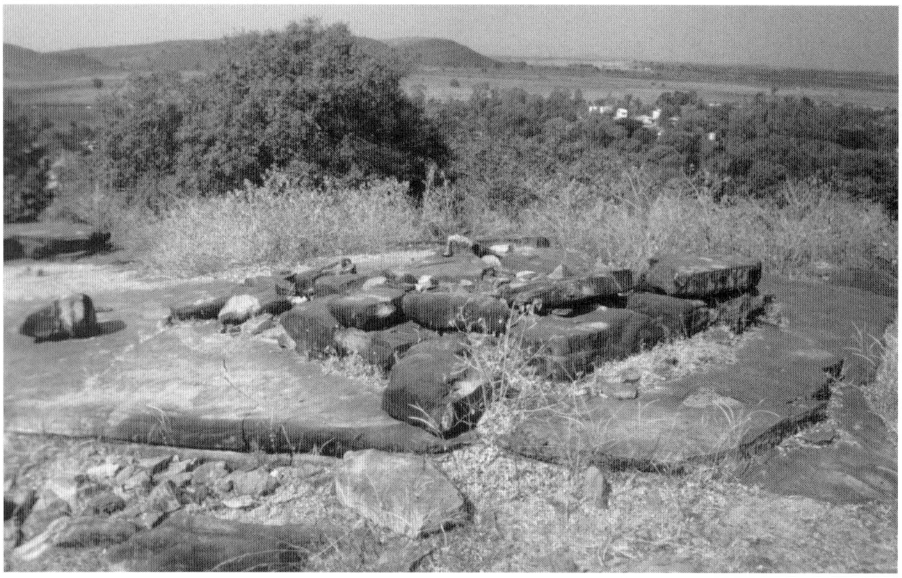

49 Sanchi: monastic rock-shelter with stupa on overhang

50 Morel khurd: monastic rock-shelters

51 Ahmadpur: rock-shelter 9 – Brahmi inscription

52 Pangurariya: monastic rock-shelter

53 Morel khurd: rock-shelter with *śankhalipi*

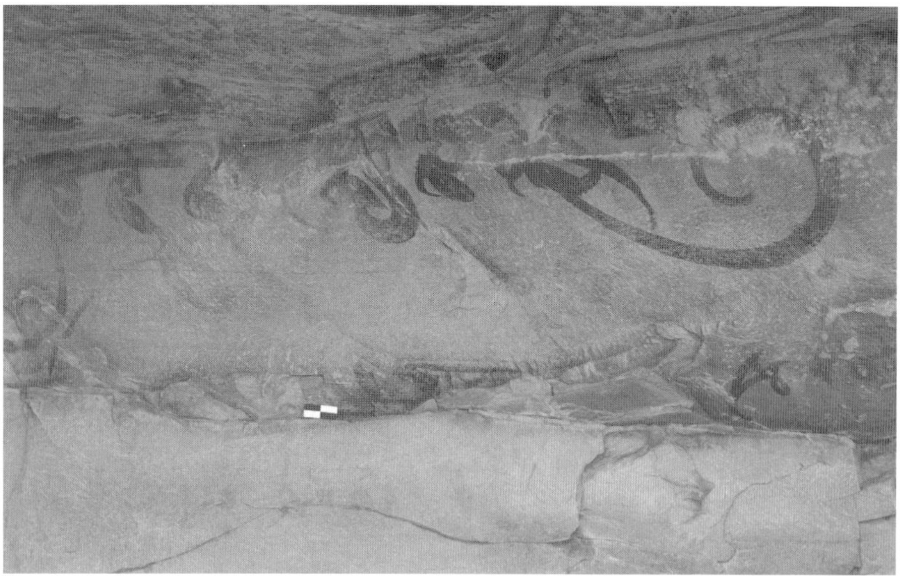

54 Ahmadpur: rock-shelter with *śankhalipi* (conventional)

55 Ahmadpur: rock-shelter with *śankhalipi* (experimental)

56 Udayagiri: *śankhalipi* inscriptions

57 Sanchi: *śankhalipi* on Asokan pillar shaft

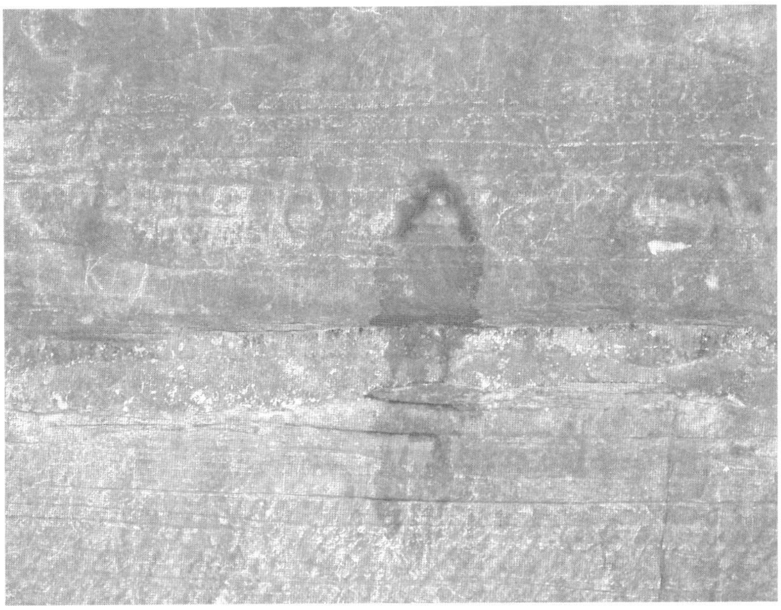

58 Udayagiri: stupa-like motif surrounded by *śankhalipi* swirls

59 Bodh-Gaya: stupa carving

60 Dargawan hill: stupas

61 Naroda Pathari: small stupa base

62 Chandna Tohoria: small stupa base

63 Satdhara: Stupa 1 (during excavations, showing inner brick core and outer facing)

64 Sonari: Stupa 1

65 Andher: Stupa 1

66 Raisen: stupa

67 Bighan: main stupa with shrine in foreground

68 Bighan: main stupa showing dressed masonry (from south)

69 Ahmadpur hill: stupa on lower slopes

70 Devrajpur: stupa remains (using kite aerial photography)

71 Devrajpur: stupa remains (using conventional photography)

72 Mawasa: stupa on summit

73 Mawasa: inscribed slab showing position on stupa

74 Mawasa: inscribed slab (detail)

76 Sanchi: platformed monastery (Building 8)

75 Salera: hilltop stupa

77 Pitalkhora: entrance to rock-cut monastery showing *nāga* drainage pipe on left

78 Satdhara: monastery platform 1 (from summit of Stupa 1)

79 Satdhara: monastery platform 2 (from summit of Stupa 1)

80 Morel khurd: monastery platform

81 Morel khurd: monastery platform, looking through entrance from summit

82 Morel khurd: temple remains on summit of monastery platform

83 Morel khurd: Buddha image from summit of monastery platform (c. tenth century AD) (SAM; SG005/I-633)

84 Mawasa: lower tier/entrance, showing 'temple' on summit

85 Mawasa: second-tier monastery, taken from below

86 Mawasa: 'temple' (SG090/SC660)

87 Salera: monastery platform

88 Sanchi: monastery 51

89 Morel khurd: courtyard monastery

90 Morel khurd: 'irregular' interlinked monastery

91 BELOW LEFT AND RIGHT
Ferozpur: interconnected courtyard monasteries

92 Torin hill: interlinked courtyard monastery

93 Satdhara: rectangular monastery in southern part of site

94 Devrajpur: boulder-walled structures

95 Satdhara: apsidal temple outline

96 Mawasa: apsidal temple (SG090/SC662)

97 Dargawan hill: tank (SG029/SC106)

98 Andher: fortification wall in northern part of site

99 Chandna hill: boundary wall

101 Sonari: lotus meander on stupa coping stone

102 Andher: bead-and-lozenge medallion

100 Pipalia kherai: linked with monastic remains by paved pathway

103 Pipalia kherai: carved railing
(c. second century BC) (SG005b/I-520)

104 Devalkhera: carved railing
(c. first to second century AD) (SG123/I-252)

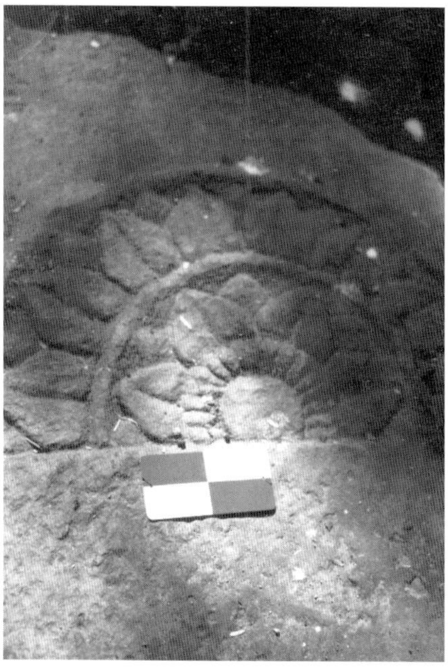

105 Udayagiri: carved railing with lotus medallion
(c. second to first century BC) (SG031/I-7)

106 Vidisha: water-tower complex – stupa railing
(c. second to first century BC) (SG006/I-953)

107 Vidisha: water-tower complex – stupa railing (side showing sockets for cross-bars)

108 Marha: carved panel (c. second to first century BC) (SG141/I-200)

109 Marha: carved panel (c. second to first century BC)

110 Besar talai: plain railing cross-bars stored around village platform (SG146/I-415)

111 Besar talai: railing with lotus meander (obverse) (c. second to first century BC) (SG146/I-410)

112 Besar talai: railing with lotus medallions (reverse)

113 Besar talai: carved railing cross-bar (SG146/I-411)

114 Satdhara: elephant capital from Stupa 1 (c. third century BC) (SG007/I-101)

115 Satdhara: elephant capital (underside)

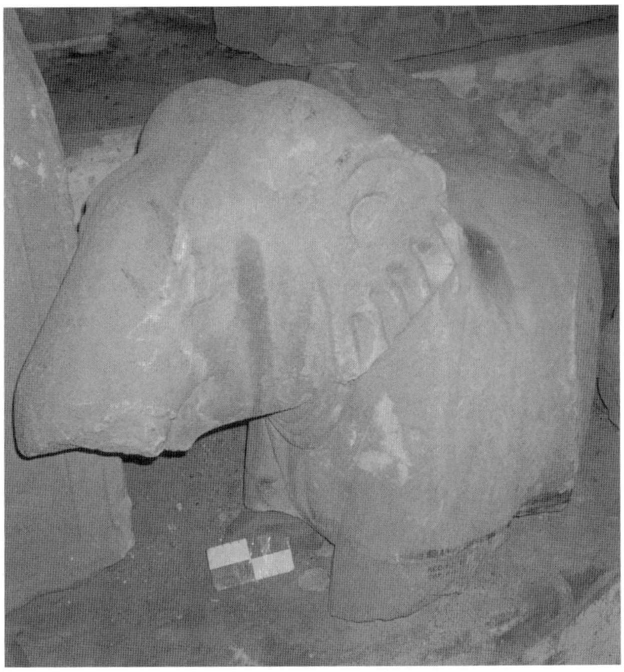

116 Sanchi: Temple 40 – elephant capital (c. third to second century BC) (SG001/I-8)

117 Vidisha: elephant-and-rider capital (c. second century BC) (SG006/I-95)

118 Sanchi: Stupa 2 – elephant medallion on railings

119 Besar talai: elephant capital 1 (c. second century BC) (SG041/I-142)

120 Besar talai: elephant capital 1 (underside)

121 Besar talai: elephant capital 2 (SG041/I-143)

122 Besar talai: elephant capital 3 (SG041/I-144)

123 Besar talai: lotus capital from post-Mauryan pillar (SG041/I-412)

124 Besar talai: bull capital 1 (SG041/I-145)

125 Besar talai: bull capital 2 (SG041/I-135)

126 Besar talai: bull capital 3 (SG041/I-134)

127 Besar talai: coins

128 Vidisha Museum: bull capital 1 (SG006/I-181)

129 Vidisha Museum: bull capital 2 (SG006/I-183)

130 Bhopal Archaeology Museum: bull capital (SG006/I-333)

131 Sanchi-Kanakhera: bull capital (c. second century BC) (SG002/I-253)

132 Tajpur Shur: bull capital (SG064/I-296)

133 Dhakna village: bull capital (SG032/I-395)

134 Binjoli kherai: *yakṣa* (c. fifth century AD) (SG005c/I-193)

135 Binjoli kherai: female figure (c. fifth century AD) (SG005c/I-202)

136 Budha Pahar: base of Buddha image (c. second to third century AD) (SG098/I-704)

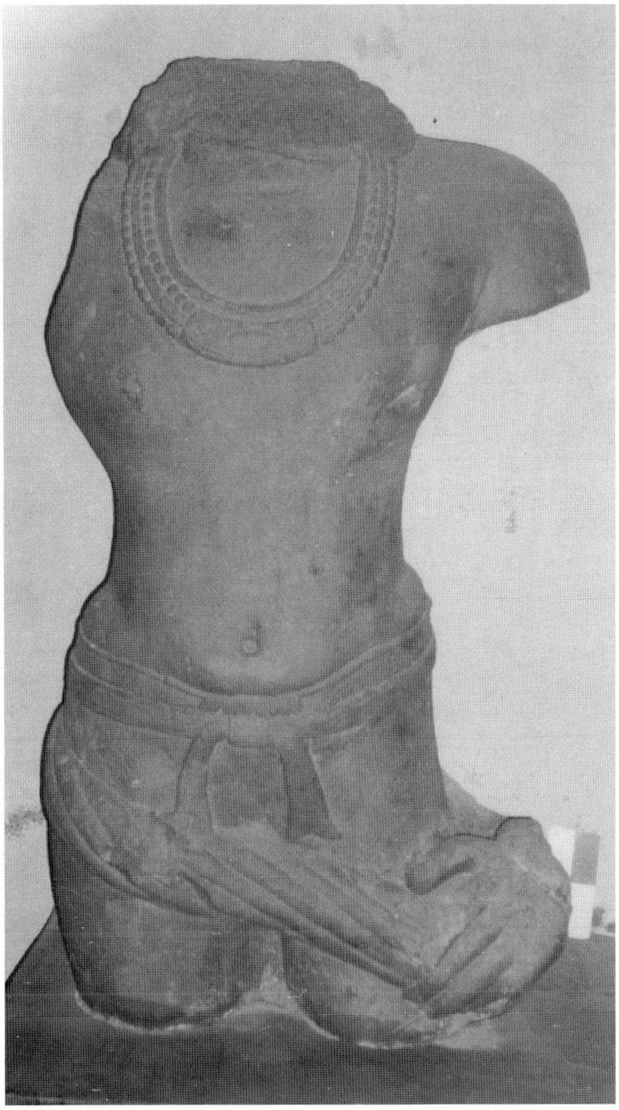

137 Lohangi hill: Bodhisattva (Vidisha Museum) (SG006/I-98)

CHAPTER 12

Non-Buddhist Ritual Sites

Introduction: non-Buddhist sculptural and architectural remains

Having discussed the spatial and temporal patterns in the Buddhist landscape, it is important to stress that this landscape was never exclusively Buddhist. The aim of this chapter is to examine other strands of Sanchi's multi-religious geography, based on the distribution of architectural and sculptural remains, whether previously published or documented for the first time during the SSP (Table 12.1). By thus separating Buddhist and non-Buddhist material into different chapters, there is a danger of overlooking the degree of fluidity that no doubt existed, both in time and space, between different denominational zones. However, this was the most convenient way of ordering the survey data. The primary focus will be on material datable between Phases Id (third to second century BC) and IV (fourth to sixth century AD); about 110 newly documented sculptures, documented at 62 find-spots, belong to this category. A number of previously unpublished sculptures stored in the Gwalior Gujari Mahal Museum (GGMM), the Sanchi Archaeological Museum (SAM) and the Vidisha Museum (VM) are also included in the discussion. For the later period between Phases V (seventh to eighth century AD) and VI (ninth to twelfth century AD), it is more difficult to provide precise quantifications, because finds usually consist of large piles of sculpture and temple fragments, often dislocated from their original architectural context. Approximately 1,190 sculpture and architectural fragments from this period are listed in Appendix IIa; however, it is more accurate to refer to the number of find-spots rather than individual sculptures. As shown in Figure 12.1, around 197 ritual find-spots of this period were documented, while Appendix IIc lists non-Buddhist cult spots and temples based on the primary context (where known) of associated material. Similarly, the overall spatial and temporal patterning of the ritual landscape, in both the earlier and later periods, reflects a site-by-site analysis rather than the total number of sculptures. As elsewhere in the study, these fragments are listed in the endnotes by their Site Group and Installation numbers.

The chapter is divided into two main sections. Part I is a site gazetteer arranged according to the seven major phases and their sub-phases defined in chapter 10. On the basis of this material, Part II deals with issues of style and ritual context, and examines the changing geographical and temporal patterns in the configuration of the multi-layered ritual landscape over the timeframe covered by this study.

Table 12.1 Newly documented sculptures

Ritual affiliation	Phase								
	Id	II	IIIA	IIIB	IV	V	VI	VII	Total
Buddhist		31	1	1	4		5		42
Bhagavata			3	2					5
Brahmanical				3	43	13	956	163	1197
Naga				6	5	1	3		15
Yaksa				2	6				8
Jain							14		14
Total	**0**	**31**	**4**	**14**	**58**	**14**	**978**	**163**	**1281**

PART I: GAZETTEER

Phase Id (third century BC)

Our understanding of religious history during the late centuries BC has been hampered by the 'monumental' focus of archaeological research, with excavations carried out at only a limited number of sites. It is likely that much ritual activity during this period would have involved non-durable materials such as wood and terracotta; the probability that we are dealing with an incomplete archaeological record therefore needs to be made quite explicit. Until more information about the cultic associations of 'non-monumental' sites such as shrines and rock-shelters is made available through excavation, we are limited to an assessment of a single aspect of the ritual landscape, that is the adoption of stone as a medium of representation. While imposing limitations on our understanding of religious history, this particular bias can also be used to our advantage, in so far as it provides insights into the history and development of stone sculpture workshops, as well as the patronage networks and administration systems that supported them.

As shown in Figure 12.1 (colour), the current framework of knowledge based on archaeological remains, suggests that the primary ritual centres during the third century BC formed a triangle between Sanchi, Satdhara and Vidisha. The first two are Buddhist in orientation, while the last, represented by the Heliodorus pillar site, was associated with the proto-Pancaratra system of the Bhagavata tradition, an early form of Vaisnavism.

As discussed in chapter 6, the pillar and the temple mentioned in the associated inscription are datable to the late second century BC following the chronology of Antialcidas, the Indo-Greek king named in the inscription. However, the wooden foundations of an earlier apsidal building underlying the temple remains probably date to c. third century BC (Khare 1967; *IAR* 1963–4, 17; 1964–5, 19–20).[1]

Phase IIa (late second to mid-first century BC)

The final quarter of the second century BC witnessed a proliferation of Buddhist building activity throughout the rural hinterland. Most of the Bhagavata material at the Heliodorus pillar site also dates to this period and is discussed in detail in chapter 6. The pillar was set up in honour of a Vasudeva temple, the stone remains of which overlie the earlier apsidal foundations mentioned above.

There are also Bhagavata remains at other sites in and around Vidisha: the problematic identity of a lotus bell capital on the summit of Lohangi hill in Vidisha was discussed in chapter 11.[2] It is much larger than the Heliodorus pillar capital, but it clearly belongs to the same post-Mauryan idiom. The remains of animal feet on top of the lotus, indicate that it was originally crowned by an addorsed elephant-and-lion capital (Plate 32), a combination often found within Buddhist contexts. However, composite lion-elephant capitals, found on coins datable to c. first century BC, as well as terracottas, have also been interpreted as symbols of Samkarsana and Vasudeva respectively (Joshi 1979, 23, fig. 1b; Allan 1936, 281, pl. XVI.5). The site's possible proto-Pancaratra associations during the late centuries BC cannot therefore be ruled out. The second major group of Bhagavata-related sculpture, discussed below, dates to a slightly later period, between the late first century BC and first century AD, and consists of a group of *nāga* sculptures which embody elements of Balarama iconography. As discussed in chapter 6, *nāga*s were often assimilated into Buddhist and Brahmanical frameworks meaning that a discussion of this material involves reference to a complex array of different and often entwined, religious histories.

Phases IIb–IIIa (first century BC to first century AD)

Nāga, yakṣa and Bhagavata sculptures

Much of the sculpture of this period relates to the *nāga* and *yakṣa* cults, ancient spirits connected with water, fertility and the natural elements. In contrast to the urban context of the Heliodorus pillar material, many of these sculptures are found in rural locations, and in particular, next to water bodies. Their importance in local cultic practice made them susceptible to assimilation into both Buddhist and Brahmanical frameworks, ruling out a strictly sectarian-based framework of discussion in the following sections. As discussed in chapter 6, the identification of ancient *nāga* cult spots is hampered by the non-durable nature of the earliest shrines. However, the antiquity of the cult is attested by descriptions in early Buddhist texts (Joshi 1979; Misra 1981), while its prevalence in the Sanchi area is attested by the number of donors in the Sanchi inscription whose names contain allusions to the *nāga* cult (Schopen 1996c).

Although allusions to *nāga*s can be found in the stupa railing carvings and inscriptions at Sanchi (Misra 1982), there is no evidence for free-standing sculptural representations of anthropomorphic deities of any kind prior to the first century BC. The earliest-known group, published in an earlier study by Joanne Williams (1976), consists of a *nāga-nāginī* couple from Gulgaon, a village about two km to the west of Sanchi, and another similar couple from Nagauri hill, immediately to the south of Sanchi. Slightly later in date is a group of four *yakṣa* and *yakṣini* sculptures from Vidisha (Chandra 1966), including the well-known Kubera *yakṣa* now stored in the Vidisha Archaeological Museum. The generally accepted date range for these sculptures, in the above order, is between the middle and the end of the first century BC. Williams's study also includes a later group of *nāga* sculptures, datable to the Gupta period (c. fifth century AD). This consists of i) two *nāga*s and a *nāginī* at Sanchi, and ii) a *nāga-nāginī* couple and a *nāga* pillar capital at Ferozpur, a village to the west of Sanchi whose hilltop monastic remains were discussed in chapter 11 (Table 12.2; Figure 12.2 colour).

The newly documented *nāga*s described below also fit into Williams's 'early' and 'late' phases, which, following the chronological framework used in this book, correspond to Phases IIb and IV. This new material also includes an additional, intermediary phase, datable to the second or third century AD (Phase IIIb). These are closely related to Kusana images of the Mathura region, in distinct contrast, therefore, to the lack of locally produced images of this period at Sanchi itself. However, as discussed in chapter 5, the lack of evidence for Kusana dynastic control of the area, makes it inappropriate to refer to these sculptures as 'Kusana'; a more appropriate designation would be Ksatrapa/Naga. There are also differences in geographical distribution: Williams's group is concentrated in and around Sanchi, extending into the hilly area immediately to the west. By contrast, most of the sculptures introduced in this chapter are situated on the flat agricultural plain to the east of Sanchi, with the two sculptures at Amacchar on the western bank of the River Betwa immediately to the north of Vidisha. Another difference is that when both groups of *nāga*s are viewed together, an element of cultic diversity becomes evident that was not immediately apparent on the basis of Williams's group alone. Not only can we identify 'independent' *nāga* cult spots, it is also possible to identify Brahmanical (particularly Vaisnava) and Buddhist serpent deities. Jain *nāga*s, most of them datable to the post-Gupta period, are also known in the area, and are dealt with later. The role of the *nāga* cult in relation to each of these religious traditions was discussed in chapter 6.

In total, six sets of *nāga* sculptures are known from Phase IIb; two of these, which happen to be the earliest, were dealt with in Joanna Williams's study; the remainder were documented for the first time during the SSP (Table 12.2; Figure 12.2 colour). Three of these appear to represent Samkarsana-Balarama in his serpent aspect; an additional sculpture of Samkarsana-Balarama in his non-serpent form also belongs to this period. I will now describe these in chronological order, beginning with the two already known sets of sculptures before introducing the 'new' ones. Such an approach is necessary for the purposes of context and for building up a comprehensive picture of the temporal and spatial patterns throughout the study area.

Gulgaon and Nagauri *nāga*s

The earliest-known serpent sculptures in the area come from Gulgaon, an ancient settlement (and modern village) around two km to the west of Sanchi (Figure 12.1 colour). Here a *nāga-nāginī*

Table 12.2 Selected early sculptures related to the *nāga*, *yakṣa* and Saiva traditions

Site name	Inst no.	SG no.	SC no.	Sculpture type	Context	Present position	Phase	Date	Height
Amacchar	I-392	SG169	SC323	*Nāga*	Brahmanical temple complex in village, on river bank	Under worship, embedded into mud platform	IV	Early 5th century AD	Seated 86 cm
	I-393	SG169	SC323	*Nāginī*	Ditto	Ditto	IV	Early 5th century AD	From waist downwards: 38 cm
Andher	I-109	SG013b	SC78	*Nāga*/Balarama	Temple site at foot of hilltop Buddhist site. Next to small bauri	Embedded into mud platform, under worship	IIIa	25 AD	227 cm
	I-110	SG013b	SC78	Samkarsana–Balarama	Ditto	Under worship on platform	IIIa	25 AD	From chest upwards: 43 cm
Andol	I-237	SG101	SC720	*Nāgakal*	Cult spot by river	Under worship	VI	10th century AD	135 cm
Bamnor	I-464	SG173	SC337	*Nāgakal*	Cult spot by village tank	Under worship	IV	5th century AD	50 cm
Chandna	I-1	SG095c	SC204	*Nāga*/Balarama	Independent shrine on summit of dam, with nearby village and hilltop Buddhist site	Under worship	IIIa	50 BC–25 AD	From thighs upwards: 52 cm
Devalkhera	I-250	SG123	SC684	*Nāga*/Visnu	Brahmanical temple complex in village, next to perennial stream	Embedded into mud platform, under worship	IV	405–415 AD	Broken into three parts. Upper three parts. Upper fragment: 39cm; lower fragment: 46 cm. Section in between is missing
Devrajpur	I-690	SG177d	SC349	*Nāgakal*	Next to ancient well, downstream of reservoir	Under worship	IV	5th century AD	100 cm
Ferozpur	I-336	SG011b	SC377	*Nāga*	Brahmanical temple complex in village at foot of hilltop Buddhist site. Edge of ancient reservoir	Embedded into mud platform in modern shrine, under worship	IV	Ditto	From knees upwards: 154 cm
	I-371	SG011b	SC377	*Nāginī*	Ditto	Ditto	IV	Early 5th century AD	From knees upwards: 115 cm
	I-372	SG011b	SC377	*Nāga–Nāginī* capital	Ditto	Ditto	IV	Ditto	155 cm
Gehunkheri	I-337	SG134	SC550	*Nāga*	Ditto	Ditto	IIIb	130 AD	From thighs downwards: 22 cm
	I-338	SG134	SC550	*Nāginī*	Temple remains in ancient settlement	Embedded in mud platform, under worship	IIIb	130 AD	From waist downwards: 30 cm
	I-339	SG134	SC550	Siva *liṅga*	Ditto	Ditto	IIIb	130 AD	95 cm
	I-340	SG134	SC550	*Yakṣa*	Ditto	Ditto	IIIb	130 AD	From neck to thighs: 44 cm
Gulgaon	I-105	SG010b	SC64	*Nāginī*	Ditto	Unknown	II	80–50 BC	147 cm
	I-104	SG010b	SC64	*Nāga*	Independent shrine on summit of ancient dam. Part of early-historic settlement	Sanchi Archaeological Museum	II	80–50 BC	190 cm
Mehgaon	I-156	SG056	SC389	*Nāga*/Balarama	From embankment of village tank	Embedded in mud platform in centre of village, under worship	IIIa	50 AD	82 cm

Morel kala	I-232	SG099	SC211	*Nāga*	Summit of ancient dam	Under worship propped up on dam	IIIb	125–130 AD	From waist to ankles: 94 cm
Murlikheri	I-362	SG162b	SC298	Siva *liṅga*	Cult spot on bank of perennial stream	Under worship	IIIb	130 AD	65 cm
Nagauri	I-627	SG003a	SC21	*Nāginī*	Ditto	Unknown	II	80–50 BC	130 cm
	I-626	SG003a	SC21	*Nāga*	Cult spot on lower slopes of hill, overlooking reservoir	*In situ*, under worship	II	80–50 BC	183 cm
Pagneswar	I-494	SG061	SC697	*Nāginī*	Multi-phase/multi-ritual temple complex in ancient settlement	Under worship	IIIb	130 AD	Snake canopy only: 4 cm
	I-290	SG061	SC697	*Yakṣa*/ Bodhisattva	Ditto	Ditto	IIIB	130 AD	80 cm
Pathari kativarat	I-187	SG084b	SC539	*Nāgakal*	From reservoir embankment	Under worship in rock-shelter shrine	VI	10th century AD	64 cm
Salera	I-458	SG170	SC575	*Nāga*	Temple complex at edge of ancient tank. Part of settlement below Buddhist hilltop site	Under worship	IIIb	2nd century AD	Base only: 50 cm
Sanchi	I-255	SG001	SC628	*Nāga*	Buddhist monastic complex. Possibly from one of temples to east of Stupa 1	Sanchi Archaeological Museum (Acc. 2859; formerly A103)	IV	5th century AD	172 cm
	I-256	SG001	SC628	*Nāga*	Ditto	Sanchi Archaeological Museum (Acc. 2858; formerly. A102)	IV	5th century AD	183 cm
	I-31	SG001	SC608	*Nāginī*	Ditto	Outside Temple 31	IV	AD 450	183 cm
Tijalpur	I-162	SG058	SC691	*Nāgakal*	From edge of village tank	Under worship with other sculptures in village	IV	5th century AD	80 cm
Vidisha	I-531	SG006	SC715	*Nāgakal*	Unknown	Vidisha Museum (Acc. 34)	IV	5th century AD	
	I-950	SG006	SC673	*Nāga*/ Balarama	Cult spot near bank of River Bes	Under worship in Forestry Commission park	IIIb	2nd century AD	67 cm
	I-536	SG006	SC714	Kubera *yakṣa*	From confluence of rivers Betwa and Bes	Vidisha Museum	II/IIIa	50 BC–25 AD	200 cm
	I-526	SG006	SC714	*Yakṣinī*	Ditto	Vidisha Museum	II/IIIa	50 BC–25 AD	150 cm
	I-169	SG006	SC715	*Yakṣa*	From road between Vidisha and Udayagiri	Vidisha Museum (Acc. 75)	IIIb	125–130 AD	From knees to neck: 98 cm

couple originally stood on the embankment of an ancient irrigation reservoir discussed in chapter 14 (Shaw and Sutcliffe 2001, 68–9).[3] During the 1980s, the *nāga* (Plate 138) was shifted to the SAM, following the theft of the *nāginī* partner. Another, almost identical *nāga* (Plate 139) stands on Nagauri hill immediately to the south of Sanchi, whose monuments it overlooks (Shaw 2000b, 35, fig. 14).[4] When it was first described by Marshall (1940, 244), it was still part of a couple, but, like its Gulgaon counterpart, the smaller *nāginī* has been stolen. Like the Gulgaon example, there is a close link with water: as it stands, it is only metres from the southern edge of what would have been a reservoir held up by the ancient embankment that runs between Sanchi and Nagauri hills (Figure 9.3; Shaw and Sutcliffe 2001, 55, 69).[5]

In keeping with early anthropomorphic serpent sculptures from other parts of India, both *nāga*s consist of larger-than-life standing deities, with the body of a coiled serpent rising up the back, and an outspread serpent canopy over the head (Joshi 1979). Both wear circular turbans piled up in a spiral on the head. Similar turbans are found at western Deccan cave sites such as Pitalkhora or Bhaja (Deshpande 1959; Bachhofer 1939, pl. 63).[6] Despite these pan-Indian comparisons, Williams (1976, 176–7) has argued that the Nagauri and Gulgaon *nāga*s belong to a 'localized' style, which gives the impression of a folk tradition not fully accustomed to working in stone. This view rests on the low relief of the sculptures as well as their stocky, rather stiff, frontal stance; the feet protrude straight out from the body, in contrast to the natural standing position of the Sanchi, Stupa 1 gateway figures. At the same time, there are also close points of convergence, such as the 'soft' modelling of the stomach and the prominent breasts which are not dissimilar to the first-century-AD Stupa 1 gateway figures. Other notable features such as the tightly clinging *dhoti*, the deep-set eyes and the pouting lips are uncommon before the early centuries AD. Such observations led Marshall (1940, pl. 125a) to assign the Nagauri *nāga* to around the first or second centuries AD. Yet, despite these 'late' stylistic features, dating is complicated by the overall awkwardness of the sculptures and the 'flat' modelling technique. It is therefore important to go beyond the isolated iconographic particularities to a holistic appraisal of the complete image. Williams (1976, 176–7), pursuing a similar logic, assigned both *nāga*s to a period midway between the carved railings on Stupas 2 and 1, by which time much of the rigidity and flat appearance has been remedied. Following this line of reasoning, together with the latest understanding regarding the relative chronology between Stupas 2 and 1,[7] a date of c. AD 50 for both the Nagauri and Gulgaon *nāga*s seems acceptable.

Vidisha *yakṣa*s

Closely connected in date is the well-known Kubera *yakṣa* (Plate 140) and three related sculptures from Vidisha. The Kubera *yakṣa* is stored along with its *yakṣini* counterpart in the VM.[8] Both were discovered in the 1960s at the convergence of the Rivers Bes and Betwa (Chandra 1966, figs. 4–6). The famous 'Besnagar *yakṣini*', now in the Calcutta Museum, was discovered much earlier by Cunningham (1880, 44; also Chandra 1966, fig. 1) on the bank of the River Betwa about one km NE of the Heliodorus pillar (S48; Figure 9.2). A *kalpadruma* capital (Cunningham 1880, 43–4, pl. XV), also kept in the Calcutta Museum, was found at the same site. Cunningham's suggestion that this was originally part of the Heliodorus complex is unconvincing given the distance between the two sites. Furthermore, taking into account the shared symbolic reference of the *kalpadruma* and the *yakṣini* to wealth and fertility, it is more likely that the two formed part of a single pillar capital (Dass and Willis 2002, 30–1). The upper portion of a second *yakṣini* from Besnagar is now stored in the Bhopal Archaeology Museum (Bakshi 1945). All four sculptures share the same erect and frontal posture, with the body weight distributed evenly between both legs. Although the overall stance is much more 'natural' than the Nagauri and Gulgaon *nāga*s, there is a similar incorporation of both early and late stylistic influences from central and western India. According to Chandra (1966, 163), the Kubera *yakṣa* retains the older Bharhut features, such as the multiple flower-and-bead bracelets, the fleur-de-lys armlets and the large spiral earrings. However, the solid sculptural volume and the broad chest and shoulders are more closely related to later developments in the Deccan. For example, the dhoti falls over the legs in two angular points, a characteristic also found at Pitalkhora (Deshpande 1959, 80–1, pl. 56a). Similar influences are seen in the fleshy modelling of the stomach, reminiscent of the Stupa 1 gateway figures at Sanchi. Chandra thus assigns the *yakṣa* to midway between Stupas 2 and 1. In general, this is the chronology followed here, although it is important to stress that the dating of the railings at Sanchi, Stupas 1 and 2, upon which this framework is based, is in itself an unsettled matter. Thus, a late first-century BC date or even later diverges somewhat from the earlier date-range posited by Chandra.[9]

Chandna Balarama

Four 'new' sculptures belonging to this early phase were documented during the SSP. All of these are serpent representations of Balarama, who, as discussed in chapter 6, is synonymous with Vasudeva's elder brother, Samkarsana. In contrast to his aniconic representation at the Heliodorus pillar site, he is now shown as an anthropomorphic deity, with a serpent canopy outspread over his head. The earliest examples in the study area come from an ancient irrigation embankment at Chandna, around 1.5 km to the south of the Buddhist stupas at Morel khurd (Figure 12.1 colour; Plate 141).[10] Broken from the thighs downwards (surviving height: 52 cm), it is markedly smaller than the other sculptures discussed so far. It consists of a standing anthropomorphic deity, with a five-headed serpent hood spread out over the head. The serpent rises up the back in a single column rather than the more usual horizontal coils. Local parallels, such as the lower portion of a second-century-AD *nāga* in the village of Salera (Plate 155),[11] indicate that it would have risen from a pile of coils beneath the standing figure. The body is small and squat, with a stocky chest and stomach, between which there is little differentiation. The right arm is missing, but the damaged, upper section of what appears to be a plough (*hala*) can be seen rising behind the left shoulder. This detail justifies identifying the *nāga* as Balarama.[12] A thick, plain sash is hung low over the hips and tied in a simple cross-knot at the centre. Both the sash and knot find close parallels in the Vidisha Kubera *yakṣa* (Plate 140), as do the long chunky necklace and bulky, piled-up turban. Although the Chandna image is considerably smaller than the Vidisha *yakṣa*, this broader set of stylistic parallels suggests a similar date of c. 25 BC.

Andher Balarama sculptures

Two more previously unrecorded sculptures, representing Balarama in both his serpent and non-serpent forms, were noted at the western base of Andher hill, immediately below the Buddhist stupas discussed in chapter 11 (Plate 142).[13] The larger of the two figures (height: 2.27 m), shown in serpent form, is set in a mud platform facing away from the stupas above (Plate 143).[14] The second, purely anthropomorphic, image lies in a broken state on the same platform (Plate 144).[15] Again, there is a link with water: the platform is positioned several metres to the south of a small stone tank (*bauri*).[16] The larger deity is four-armed, with a serpent that rises up the back in horizontal coils and terminates in a seven-headed canopy over the head. Unfortunately, much of the detail has been obscured by recent clay remodelling of the face and upper torso, while the entire image has been painted as Siva. The original stone of the serpent canopy is still visible, however, and one of its individual serpent heads was found nearby (Plate 145). A fragment of a heavily eroded circular headdress lies on the same platform (Plate 146). Its halo-like appearance and central medallion are comparable to the tall circular cockade seen in Kusana images of the Mathura region, not to the Deccan-inspired, spiral turbans of the Nagauri and Gulgaon *nāga*s described earlier.[17]

Both of the upper arms are upraised. The upper right hand holds what appears to be a pestle (*musala*). Extended horizontally over the head, it is carved with circular bands, each of which is decorated with vertical cross-spokes. The upper left hand supports the extended end of the pestle; the palm faces outwards to reveal an object of an indeterminate nature.[18] The lower right arm, of which the hand is missing, hangs down by the side of the body, while the lower left hand rests on the hip in a position similar to that of the Gulgaon *nāga*. The pestle (*musala*), referred to in the *Harivaṁśa* as one of the objects associated with Balarama, is seen in some of the earliest-known Balarama sculptures, such as the example from Jansuti, Mathura district (Plate 149) (Härtel 1987, pl. 7).[19] The latter, however, simply holds the *musala* against the shoulder. There are also similarities with another early Balarama sculpture from Tumain; in this case the long object that rests on the ground, supported by the right arm, is more like a club (*gadā*) or staff, than a *musala* (Joshi 1979, pl. 8a–c). Quite a different type of iconography emerges during the Kusana period: the right arm, now empty-handed, simply rises up and over the head in a similar manner to the Andher figure. Meanwhile, instead of a plough, the left hand holds a wine goblet against the chest. This type of Balarama occurs in large numbers in the Mathura region (Joshi 1979, pls. 20–2), the best-known example being the misnamed '*nāga*' from Chargaon, dated year 40 of the Kaniska era (Bachhofer 1939, pl. 97a). In all of the known examples from Mathura, however, the extended right hand remains empty, although in later four-armed versions, the *musala* sometimes reappears in one of the back hands (Härtel 1987, 582). It seems, therefore, that the Andher example combines elements that elsewhere belong to two quite distinct stages of Balarama iconography.[20]

The second image on the same platform (Plate 144) provides further indications that we are dealing with Balarama. It survives only from the waist upwards (surviving height: 43 cm) and, when complete, would have been less than half the size of the standing figure. Unlike the larger sculpture, it is entirely anthropomorphic, with no serpent attributes. However, close iconographic similarities between the two sculptures suggest that both belong to a single religious tradition: the position of the right hand, raised over the head, and the pestle-like object which it holds is almost identical to the larger image. The pestle is carved with the same circular bands, although the vertical cross-spokes found on the larger sculpture are absent. Unique to the smaller figure, however, are the remains of what looks like the upper portion of a ploughshare (*hala*) emerging from behind the left shoulder; as discussed in chapter 6, the *hala* is a distinguishing feature of the earliest Balarama-Samkarsana images in other parts of India. Other dating clues are provided by the bulbous, piled-up turban, secured by two bands and fastened in the centre by a large circular medallion. Similar, albeit not identical, turbans occur in many of the gateway panels of Sanchi Stupa 1, datable to c. AD 25 on the basis of the Satavahana inscription there. Further corroboration of an early first-century-AD date is provided by an interesting detail on the right side of the image (Plate 147). Hanging from the lower end of the club, at the proper left side of the image, is a long garland of *Aśoka* leaves, the large bulbous fruit of which can be seen on the top left corner of the sculpture. Although the *Aśoka* tree occurs on the Stupa 2 railings, it is not until the Stupa 1 gateway carvings that we encounter the realistic three-dimensionality of the Andher carving. An almost exact parallel can be made with the *Aśoka* fruit and leafy foliage shown in the background of the eastern gateway figure of Stupa 1 (Plate 148). This evidence for a first-century-AD Samkarsana in his non-serpent form calls for a rethinking of Härtel's view that there are no known images of Vira Samkarsana during the pre-Kusana period. It also raises important questions regarding the changing relationship between the *vīravāda* and the *nāga*-Balarama traditions, which at least during the earlier period, were assumed to have operated as independent cultic strands.[21]

Mehgaon Balarama

A fourth image with close iconographic links to the Balarama tradition was noted at Mehgaon, a major early-historic settlement to the east of Sanchi (Plate 150).[22] The image is now embedded at thigh level in the central village platform, but according to villagers it originally stood on the embankment of a dried-up tank to the north of the village.[23] The sculpture (total height: 82 cm) is two-armed and intact apart from a missing right hand. A thick serpent shaft rises up the deity's back, expanding into a five-headed canopy above the head. The individual serpent heads, each of which have protruding two-pronged tongues, are arranged in an almost horizontal line, as opposed to the circular, halo-like serpent canopies already described. A similarly shaped canopy occurs on the two-armed Balarama from Jansuti, Mathura (Plate 149). Stylistically, the closest local parallel is the standing figure on the Sanchi Stupa 3 gateway (Plate 151), datable to c. AD 50, that is slightly later than the Stupa 1 gateway figures (Willis 2000, 60–1, fig. 37). The tightly framed composition, the slight, upright stance of the body, the soft, fleshy modelling around the chest and stomach, and the treatment of the thick sash, wrapped around the waist and secured at the front with a barely visible knot, are all features directly comparable to the Sanchi figure. However, despite these similarities, the Mehgaon figure belongs to a more localized school: clumsy modelling has resulted in heavy distortion on the proper right shoulder; the flat, rounded face and the rope-like plait of hair, pulled over the top of the head and hanging in straight braids on either side, all create a reductive, 'folky' style. A disproportionately large, bulbous turban balances in an unnatural and precarious manner on the proper right side of the head. It is a far cry from the natural ease and symmetry of the Sanchi figure.

There are also iconographic idiosyncrasies and uncertainties: the left hand holds a long staff surmounted by what at first looks like a three-pronged fork (*triśūla*), with a missing third prong on the proper left side. It is not impossible that we are dealing with a Saiva image: although most of the early texts present Samkarsana as a Vaisnava deity, there are occasionally some interesting Saiva allusions.[24] Alternatively, there could be some allusion to Samkarsana's three-forked palm standard (Jaiswal 1967, 54). Further inspection, however, suggests that the missing prong may have extended further out and down to the left in the form of a ploughshare. The same can be said of the three-pronged object held in the left hand of a fifth newly documented Phase IIb *nāga*-Balarama image just to the west of the Heliodorus pillar site at Vidisha (Plate 152).[25] Its current *triśūla*-like appearance no doubt explains why the image is currently under worship as Siva, but a breakage on the proper left side evidently marks the spot where it originally continued into a ploughshare shape. Additional insights into the original appearance of these objects are provided by the Samkarsana-Balarama figure depicted on second-century-BC coins of Agathocles from Ai Khanoum, discussed in chapter 6. The object held in the deity's left hand could quite easily be mistaken for a *triśūla* if not for the down-turned element of the ploughshare, this time on its proper right-hand side.

Returning to the Mehgaon image, emerging from the proper right side of the pole, at the point where it meets the 'ploughshare', is a grooved, spherical object. A precise identification is difficult, but it is possible that we are dealing with a roughly carved lion head, a feature of Balarama iconography that sometimes occurs on top of ploughs or maces.[26] Further still to the right is what looks like a bulbous vase, with a narrow neck and flared rim, placed on its side directly on top of the deity's head. The vase, although more commonly held in the hand than balanced on the head, is a common attribute of *nāgas*. There may also be some indirect reference to another of Balarama's traditional attributes: a wine glass (Joshi 1979, 48–9).[27] Alternative interpretations, though, cannot be ruled out: it is possible that this object is merely an extension to what is already a rather unwieldy turban! This level of iconographic syncretism, and indeed confusion, acts as a powerful reminder that while textual iconographic formulas provide a basic framework for interpreting ritual images, the trajectory of iconographic development at the village level often unfolds in a less predictable, non-linear manner.

Phase IIIb sculptures (c. second to third century AD)

Five of the newly documented *nāga* sculptures belong to Phase IIIb.[28] Unfortunately, unlike earlier examples, their fragmentary nature means there are often no distinguishing features directly associated with Balarama, and it is thus difficult to fit them into a specific sectarian bracket. With the exception of the *nāga*-Balarama sculptures described in the foregoing account, non-Buddhist sculpture was, prior to the second century AD, restricted to the immediate vicinity of Sanchi and Vidisha. In addition to these serpent sculptures, several *yakṣas* and, for the first time, Saiva material, too, begin to appear throughout the study area, thus marking the unfolding of a heterogeneous Brahmanical landscape.

Morel kala *nāga*

The first example is an anthropomorphic *nāga* image from Morel kala, a settlement around 2.5 km SE of the well-known Buddhist complex at Morel khurd (Plate 153).[29] The lower half of the sculpture (total height from waist to ankles: 94 cm) lies propped up on an ancient irrigation embankment (Shaw and Sutcliffe 2001, 70, fig. 15). Both arms are missing, but serpent coils, rising in horizontal piles up the back, are still visible, as are the remains of a *kamaṇḍalu* in the left hand. A transparent dhoti terminates in a light hem just below the knees, with extra cloth falling in spiral, zigzag folds between the legs. A heavily striated sash skims the knees in a 'square-on' angle, rising to the left of the body, where it would have hung over the left arm. The remaining length of cloth flanks the left side of the body, terminating in a finely fluted border. A small loop, which presumably formed part of a knotted waist sash, is visible below the left hip. For a possible date, one may turn to early Kusana sculptures from the Gangetic valley area, which share the same sense of solid, yet refined, strength of bearing. The striated sash, its fluted border and the way in which it is arranged on the body are all comparable to the Sarnath Bodhisattva, datable to the first quarter of the second century AD (Williams 1982, pl. 6).[30] The spiral, zigzag pleating between the legs is also a feature of early Kusana images, such as the Ahicchatra Indra, datable to the early second century AD (Czuma *et al.*, 1985, pl. 57).

These pan-Indian parallels may also be tempered with local comparisons: an unpublished male sculpture from Vidisha, now stored in the VM, belongs to broadly the same style (Plate 154).[31] This deity's identity is unknown, but the sacred thread (*yajñopavita*) worn over the left shoulder provides evidence of its Brahmanical orientation. The face and arms are missing, but the surviving height (98 cm) suggests that the complete sculpture was approximately the same size as the Morel kala image. The figure has a robust physique, with a broad, expanded chest and fleshy modelling around the waist. A transparent dhoti with extra fabric gathered in folds between the legs is held in place by a striated hip belt, while another striated sash skims the knees in the same square-on angle as the Morel kala image; tucked into the belt at both hips, it forms a small loop on the left side, falling in folds on either side of the body. Strong muscular thighs are visible beneath the tightly clinging garment, which accentuates the area around the genitals. All of these are features shared by the Mathura sculptures discussed above, but both the stone and the slightly distorted treatment of the legs provide confirmation of the figure's local provenance.

Salera

Around 2.5 km to the west of Morel kala is the ancient settlement of Salera, whose extensive Buddhist remains on the adjoining hill were described in chapter 11. A *nāga* image is currently under worship amongst a multi-phase pile of sculpture in the modern village, next to a ruined tank (Plate 155).[32] Only the lowermost portion of the image survives: a single mass of serpent coils, upon which the deity's feet are still visible. Clues as to the original appearance of its upper portion are provided by the Chandna Balarama described earlier, as well as a Gupta-period *nāga* from Amacchar described later (Plate 173): in contrast to the Nagauri and Gulgaon examples, they stand on a pile of serpent coils which ascend the back in a single shaft. Similar images, such as the Brooklyn Museum *nāga* or the Cleveland Museum *nāginī*, are known from the Mathura region (Czuma *et al.*, 1985, 83–7, pl. 26). A c. second-century-AD date for the Salera *nāga* is supported by the treatment of the two heads (Plate 156) lying on a nearby platform, one of which may have originally belonged to the *nāga* in question.

Pagneswar

The locational context of the *nāgas* at Morel kala and Salera is in keeping with the traditional association between *nāgas* and water. However, a major shift takes place during this phase: rather than standing aloof, *nāgas* are now found within multi-denominational religious complexes, including *yakṣas*, *yakṣinis* and, for the first time, Saiva sculptures. An example of this new development, at least as far as its manifestation in stone is concerned,[33] occurs at Pagneswar, a large settlement situated at a major crossing on the River Betwa about 3.5 km south of Sanchi. Lying in the middle of the village, amidst a multi-phase pile of half-buried sculptural fragments, are three well-preserved sculptures, all of which are closely related to the Mathura school.

The first is an anthropomorphic *nāginī*, of which only the face and seven-headed serpent canopy survive (Plate 157).[34] The dimensions of the canopy (40 x 50 x 20 cm) give some indication of the size of the complete image. The face is full and rounded, with protruding eyes, a snub nose and thick lips set deeply in a grimacing smile. Thick, heavy ringlets are piled on top of the head. This particular hair arrangement is quite unusual, but the facial type is closely related to a wide range of Kusana images datable to the second century AD, such as the Bala Bodhisattva (Bachhofer

1939, pl. 79) or a *caturmukhaliṅga* from Mathura, now stored in the National Museum, Delhi.[35]

The second sculpture from Pagneswar is a large male figure (total surviving height: 80 cm), now semi-embedded in the ground in an upright position (Plate 158).[36] Both arms as well as the head are missing. The particular iconographical features which may have helped to determine whether we are dealing with a *yakṣa* or Bodhisattva are thus missing. The heavy sculptural volume conveys a sense of monumentality and powerful robustness, while the broad chest, deep-set navel and strong muscular stomach are all features shared by some of the Mathura sculptures described in the foregoing account. The figure wears a transparent dhoti which reaches down to the ankles, and through which solid athletic legs and an accentuated genital area are visible. The hemline is slightly heavier than the Morel kala *nāga* already described, hanging opaquely at the ankles. Extra folds of deeply incised fabric cascade down the right side of the body. The dhoti is supported by a belt, fastened in the centre by a large rectangular buckle and overlain by a thick, rope-like sash. A large knot, presumably belonging to the type of bulky scarf (*utterīya*) seen on many Kusana images from Mathura, is visible on the left hip. Another part of the same scarf falls in a 'U' shape over the knees. A massive pair of flat 'spade-like' feet emerge from under the garment. Their unusual downward angle gives the impression that the figure is standing on a steep slope. A close comparison in terms of apparel and general anatomical treatment is the Brooklyn Museum *nāga*, which exudes a similarly powerful physical presence, as well as sharing a number of similarities in the arrangement of sashes and belts. The latter image is usually dated to between the first and second centuries AD (Czuma 1985, pl. 25).

The third sculpture from Pagneswar is a Siva *liṅga* (Plate 181);[37] it is one of the earliest in the area, and provides further support of a second-century-AD date for the *nāginī*. Standing at a height of 70 cm, it belongs to the 'realistic' category as opposed to the stylised version that becomes common in later years. Rather than rising from a *yoni* base, a common attribute of later *liṅgas*, it emerges straight from the ground, terminating in a nut-shaped element representing the glans penis (*rudrabhāga*).[38] Similar *liṅgas* occur at widely dispersed locations throughout India from the second century BC to the early centuries AD (Sharma 1982, 47). The best-known example is the Gudimallam *liṅga*, dated variously between the second century BC and first century AD.[39] Apart from the two-armed Siva carved on one side of the shaft, its shape is similar to the Pagneswar *liṅga*. Other inter-regional parallels provide a broad framework for dating the Pagneswar *liṅga* to c. second century AD.[40]

Gehunkheri

Although it is possible that the Pagneswar *liṅga* dates to a slightly earlier period (cf. Dass and Willis 2002, 42, n. 88), a c. second-century-AD date is consistent with the chronology of sculptural and ceramic remains at two other sites in the area where similar *liṅgas* were noted: Murlikheri-Naroda (Plate 182),[41] a large settlement near Satdhara, and Gehunkheri (Plate 183),[42] to the east of Sanchi. Like Pagneswar, the latter forms part of a larger group of second-century-AD sculptures including a *yakṣa* and a *nāga-nāginī* couple. The *nāga* survives only from the waist down and the feet are missing, but the current dimensions suggest a total height of c. 60 cm, smaller than the *nāgas* described so far (Plate 159).[43] The *nāginī*, in an equally fragmentary condition, is of similar proportions (Plate 160).[44] Both stand in *samapāda*, with serpent coils rising up the back in horizontal piles. The *nāga* wears a transparent garment down to the ankles, falling in striated folds on either side. It flares out at the lower hem, in a manner similar to the *saṅghati* robe worn by Kusana Buddha and Bodhisattva images from Mathura.[45] The *nāginī* wears a transparent skirt secured by a jewelled belt fastened low on the waist. Above the waistline, the slightly protruding stomach is modelled in such a way as to accentuate the fleshy, rippled quality of the skin. The upper fragment of a deity consisting only of the head and shoulders (Plate 159), which may have belonged to the *nāginī* figure, is also embedded in the same platform. The rounded face, elongated earlobes, and piled-up hairstyle set in a high bun all find close equivalents in Mathura sculpture of the Kusana period. These comparisons are all supportive of a c. second-century-AD date.

Part of a *yakṣa* stands embedded at thigh level in the same platform (Plate 160).[46] Both its arms and head are missing. The figure has a broad, chunky chest and protruding stomach, between which there is little differentiation. The only piece of clothing is a wide sash, wrapped around the waist, and slung between the legs in the manner of a 'g-string'. Both in terms of anatomy and apparel, it is closely related to two *yakṣas* now stored in the Sanchi Museum reserve collection (Plate 40).[47] The latter differ from the Gehunkheri *yakṣa* in that they were not free-standing images, but rather stood with upraised arms, in the manner of the load-bearing *yakṣas* on the Stupa 1 gateways; a similar load-bearing *yakṣa* is now stored in the SAM.[48] By contrast, the angle of the arm-sockets of the Gehunkheri *yakṣa* show that the arms were not upraised, but rather that the image was intended to be free-standing. It may indeed be as early as the Sanchi *yakṣas*, datable to c. AD 25, but given the date of the accompanying sculptures already described, a Phase III date is more likely.

Phase IV (c. fourth to sixth century AD)

The gradual embracement of a stone-working tradition across an increasingly broad religious spectrum during the early centuries AD reaches a climax around the beginning of the fifth century AD. *Yakṣas*, *nāgas* and Siva *liṅgas* continue to be produced. However, the introduction of a wide variety of 'new' deities reflects the unfolding of a more heterogeneous Brahmanical landscape, at least as far as its manifestation in stone is concerned.

Vidisha and Udayagiri

One of the most significant changes is the appearance of large Brahmanical complexes, which, rather than representing a single sectarian strand, now reflect the growing movement towards pantheistic Brahmanism. The most important site in this respect is Udayagiri, whose sculptural programme reflects wider theological shifts, such as the first specific references to Visnu and his *avatāras*, as objects of worship.[49] Accordingly, Visnu now appears as an independent deity in Cave 6 (Plate 168),[50] while his *avatāras*, Varaha (Plate 169) and Ananta-Narayana, are depicted in excavations 5 and 13 respectively. The site's strong Saiva associations indicate an increasing movement towards a pluralistic form of Brahmanism which transcends sectarian divisions: Cave 4 is dedicated to Siva, in the form of an *ekamukhaliṅga*. Outside Cave 6 is what is usually considered to be one of the earliest depictions of Ganesa. Cave 6 includes two carvings of a twelve-armed *Mahiṣāsuramardinī*[51] and two *saptamātṛkā* panels. Although these goddesses are associated with Saivism, their connection with the main Vaisnava panels at Udayagiri also receives mythological sanction in the *Purāṇas* (Williams 1982, 42–3). However, some scholars believe that the development of the Brahmanical 'Great Goddess' tradition largely took the form of the wide-scale assimilation of local folk deities (Tiwari 1985), a factor which may explain their comparatively late 'monumentalisation'.

These developments are mirrored closely by the appearance of free-standing goddess sculptures in Vidisha. An enormous *Mahiṣāsuramardinī*, datable to the early fifth century AD, originally stood in the Bes village area (Cunningham 1880, 40),[52] while a group of seven seated *mātṛkā*s (mothers) stood on a platform on the bank of the River Betwa, around 1 km to the NE of the Heliodorus pillar site (Lake 1910a, 140).[53] What appear to be the remains of a Saiva temple in the Bes village area (SC643) were also noted during the SSP. The lower part of the temple can be assigned to the Gupta period on account of the size of the stone blocks (Plate 185), while a 'squat' Ganesa (Plate 186),[54] similar in form to the Udayagiri example and a number of Siva *liṅga*s, attest to the site's Saiva associations. The *liṅga*s (Plate 184)[55] are undecorated and rise straight up from the ground like the *liṅga* from Pipariya (Plate 187), which, as discussed later, also has Gupta temple remains. Vidisha's continued association with the proto-Pancaratra system is also attested by a sculpture, originally described as Visnu (Lake 1910a, 139; Harle 1974, fig. 18) but later identified as 'Balarama without snake and snakehood', i.e. Vira Samkarsana (Härtel 1987, 584, n. 34), on account of the *musala* in the right hand and lion-faced standard in the other.[56]

The wider Brahmanical landscape

To what degree do these developments as represented by the sculptural programmes at Udayagiri and Vidisha reflect trends throughout the area as a whole? The largest number of exclusively Vaisnava, or syncretic Vaisnava-Saiva, images were found in the area closest to the two main Brahmanical centres. One such find comes from Eran, a large settlement around 1 km north of Gulgaon. Here, a Visnu head was found among a large pile of sculptural and architectural remains (Plate 191)[57]. The associated torso is missing, but the high *kirīṭamukuṭa* crown, decorated with a quatrefoil pattern and central medallion depicting a lion with pearls issuing from its mouth, is directly comparable to the two Cave 6 Visnu images at Udayagiri (Plate 168), as well as the aforementioned Samkarsana image from Besnagar. Another head from the same site is identifiable as Harihara by the dreadlocks pulled into a top-knot on the right side of the head, the other side showing a *kirīṭamukuṭa* crown decorated with a rosace pattern (Plate 192).[58] The rounded face, with its shallow-set eyes and pouting lips, is typical of the Gupta period. That these images were originally housed in a temple is attested by the fragmentary remains of a number of pilasters and large stone blocks, both of which are typical of the Gupta period.

The remains of another large Harihara image were discovered at Amacchar, a large settlement on the bank of the River Betwa, 1.5 km to the east of the Heliodorus pillar site. Only two fragments survive: two hands, one of which holds a trident, the other a *śaṅkha* (Plate 193).[59] However, their size shows that the complete image was of considerable proportions. This, too, appears to have been associated with a large temple complex, as attested by the discovery of two lion-cornered abacuses measuring 65 x 55 x 32 cm (Plates 197–8).[60] At each corner is a lion, the hindquarters of which spread one-third of the way along the two adjoining faces. Closely related, albeit significantly smaller, are the lion-cornered abacuses in the outer porch of Sanchi Temple 17 (Plate 199; Williams 1982, pl. 32), and a very similar abacus from a large temple mound to the west of the Besnagar city rampart (Lake 1910a, 142–3, fig. 12).[61] In the place of trees, however, each of the four faces is carved alternately with female and male dwarfs, who hold a lotus and a sword. Their heads are disproportionately large compared to the rest of the body and covered with a long mass of tightly curled hair. Dwarfs with similar hairstyles are found on some of the temple carvings at Nachna (Williams 1982, pl. 155), while the way in which the transparent, deeply incised dhoti is pulled tightly between the legs, is in keeping with local sculptures datable to the first half of the fifth century AD.[62]

Other newly documented Vaisnava sculptures, although of a less unambiguously orthodox orientation, include part of a male figure now embedded in a mud platform just 500 m north of Udayagiri hill, in what is now part of a new landscaped garden complex (Plate 171).[63] Only the upper half survives, and much of the detail has been obscured by multiple layers of red paint. There is also some uncertainty as to how much of the image has been remodelled in mud. In its present condition, both of the figure's arms are bent at the elbows and held out in front of the body. The left hand holds a large *śaṅkha*, while held in the cupped palm of the left hand is a small bowl-shaped object decorated with several circular protrusions; this appears to be a form of lotus. Although both objects are common elements of Vaisnava iconography, their position in relation to the rest of the body appears to be the reverse of the standard pattern, as typified by the smaller of the Cave 6 Visnu images at the main Udayagiri site: there, the *śaṅkha* is held in the right hand (Williams 1982, pl. 35). The lotus does not appear at Udayagiri, but when it occurs elsewhere, it is usually held in the lower-right hand of four-armed images (Krishna 1980, 64).[64] By contrast, the heavy sculptural volume of its chest and shoulders is almost identical to the powerful robustness of the Varaha at Udayagiri (Plate 169). Furthermore, both figures wear an almost identical broad torque across the chest. Although torques are a regular feature of Gupta figures, there are no other examples in the area which so effectively bring out the quality of finely beaten gold. It is important to stress, however, that the anatomical parallels between the two images do not necessarily point to a shared religious identity.[65] Furthermore, neither the arm position, nor the long locks and bowl-cut fringe are features generally associated with Visnu. Is it possible that we are dealing with a syncretic *yakṣa*/Visnu image? This would hardly be surprising given the fact that *yakṣa*s seem to have provided one of the major prototypes for the development of figurative representations in both Brahmanical and Buddhist sculptural traditions (Misra 1981). Another 'syncretic' Visnu image, this time closely aligned with the *nāga* tradition, was found in the eastern sector (2b) at Devalkhera (Plate 174) and is discussed later on in relation to the increasing Visnuisation of *nāga* images during the Gupta period.

A number of 'new' Saiva cult spots datable to the Gupta period were also discovered during the survey. The first is situated at the village of Pipariya, directly opposite Udayagiri on the northern bank of the River Bes. Here, an undecorated *liṅga* is embedded in the ground (Plate 187).[66] The lack of decoration makes it difficult to date, but indications of a Gupta date are provided by the discovery, close by, of a fragment of an 'L'-shaped relief (Plate

201) which occurs at the lintel ends of Gupta doorways.[67] It is heavily eroded, but the surviving detail reveals the lower legs of a goddess, to the left of which a small figure stands on a crocodile's tail. To the right is another small figure wrestling with the crocodile's mouth. It is almost identical, although in inverse form, to one of the two doorway reliefs of Ganga, discovered by Cunningham at Besnagar (Plate 202; Cunningham 1880, 41; Williams 1982, pl. 45). Being half the size of the Besnagar example, however, there is no doubt that the two fragments belong to separate temples. Further indications of a Gupta date are provided by the fact that the *liṅga*s found next to the Gupta temple remains in Bes village, discussed earlier, are almost identical to the Pipariya example.

Another Saiva cult spot consists of an *ekamukhaliṅga*, still under worship on the bank of the River Bes, just outside the village of Neemkhera, about 6 km NW of Vidisha (Plate 188).[68] Standing at a height of 1.45 m, it is significantly larger than the Cave 4 *ekamukhaliṅga* at Udayagiri (Plate 190; Williams 1982, pl. 113), but the rounded Siva face, with its long dreadlocks and top knot, is directly comparable to the latter, suggesting therefore an early fifth-century-AD date. A similar *ekamukhaliṅga* still forms the central cult image in a cave-shrine at Karhaud, a hillside settlement around 1 km north of Andher (Plate 189).[69] Finally, a small anthropomorphic male figure, identifiable as Siva by its ithyphallic features, stands on the central village platform in Bawaliya village, immediately NE of Andher (Plate 194).[70] It is unfinished, as indicated by the rough chisel dressing and, as discussed later, seems to have come from the same workshop as a similarly unfinished *yakṣa* image, found *in situ* at the original quarry site about 500 m further to the north (Plate 195).[71]

As shown in Table 12.1, apart from the previously published *Mahiṣāsuramardinī* and *saptamātṛkā* examples at Udayagiri and Besnagar, very few Gupta-period Brahmanical goddesses were discovered during the survey. It is not until the post-Gupta period that they appear in significant numbers throughout the wider countryside, with two notable Gupta-period exceptions: i) at Mehgaon, already mentioned with reference to the Phase IIb Balarama image discussed earlier, where two seated *mātṛkā*s (Plate 208)[72] form part of a large multi-phase collection of sculptures on the main village platform and probably come from the large temple mound in the northern part of the village;[73] and ii) at Katarsi, a settlement in an 'interior' valley to the south of Sonari, where a *saptamātṛkā* panel is now embedded in a mud platform.[74]

As already mentioned, some of the Gupta sculptures described in the foregoing account appear to have been housed in temple complexes, the remains of which have been described at relevant points in this chapter. Significant Phase IV temples include those at Ratanpur Girdhari, Mehgaon, Ferozpur, Eran, Tajpura Shur, Raisen, Pipariya Bes, Amacchar, Dhakna, Dhakna basti and Devalkhera (Figure 12.1 colour; Appendix IIc).

Other temple sites were also found, which in the absence of associated sculpture, remain unclassified in terms of denominational affiliation. Near Sonapura on the bank of the River Betwa, just to the east of Udayagiri, the former existence of a large Gupta temple is indicated by a lion-cornered abacus (Plate 200),[75] almost identical in form to the Amacchar examples already described. The main difference is that its sides are decorated not with dwarfs but with large *kirīṭamukuṭa*s, whose tiny hands reach out to clutch the tails of two lions standing on either side. At nearby Madhupuri, a fragment of an 'L'-shaped relief which occurs at the lintel ends of Gupta doorways is stored on the main village platform (Plate 203).[76] It shows a leaf-clad branch, under which the doorway goddess would have stood. It is directly comparable to a second doorway fragment from Besnagar, datable to the early fifth century AD (Plate 204; Cunningham 1880; Williams 1982, pl. 46).

Around 7 km to the north of Udayagiri is Ahmadpur hill, whose extensive rock-shelters and Buddhist remains were described in chapter 11. On the summit of the hill, part of a Gupta temple survives in the form of an early fifth-century AD doorway (Plate 205), incorporated into a 10th-century-AD temple complex.[77] It is directly comparable to the doorway of Sanchi Temple 17 (Plate 199; Williams 1982, pl. 32), and Temple 1, Udayagiri. Finally, at Tajpur Shur, whose second-century-BC bull capital is discussed in chapter 11, the discovery of a pilaster (Plate 206)[78] closely related to the Gupta pilaster incorporated into Sanchi Temple 31 (Plate 207) attests to a temple constructed in the first quarter of the fifth century AD.

Nāgas and nāginīs

The changing ritual context of *nāga* sculptures during Phase III culminates during the Gupta period with the incorporation of *nāga* images into both Brahmanical and Buddhist ritual complexes. There are also changes in terms of style and iconography, the most notable of which is a pronounced 'Visnuisation' of *nāga* images. As I shall argue, these developments can be interpreted from three points of view. First, they are important for assessing current models of religious change regarding the relationship between Buddhism, orthodox Brahmanism and 'local' cults. Second, they reflect internal developments in Vaisnava theology discussed in chapter 6, namely the reorientation from the *vyūha* to *avatāra* systems. Finally, they may also be positioned within the political framework provided by epigraphical evidence discussed in chapter 5 for the changing dynamics between the Guptas and the local Naga Dynasty.

In order to provide the necessary context for evaluating the newly documented Phase IV *nāga*s, I shall first discuss a group of *nāga* sculptures from this period. This includes *nāga*s from Sanchi and Ferozpur in the western sector (Ib), both included in Williams's (1976) study, as well as the Brahmanical rock-cut complex at Udayagiri, where despite the absence of free-standing *nāga* sculptures, the serpent idiom is powerfully present in two of its carved Vaisnava panels.

Sanchi

The Phase IV *nāginī* (Plate 162) and two *nāga*s (Plate 161) at Sanchi were described in chapter 9. The former stands outside Temple 31, but may have originally been housed in its own shrine to the east of Stupa 1, along with one of the *nāga*s, now stored in the SAM. Their incorporation into the main monastic complex conforms to wider evidence from north India for *nāga* worship having become an integral component of Buddhist practice by the Gupta period. However, as discussed in chapters 6 and 9, despite the spatial dislocation between Buddhist and *nāga* cult spots during earlier periods, there is evidence that *nāga* worship was still central to the *saṅgha*'s wider concerns with agricultural productivity. Broadly speaking, the *nāga*s follow a similar iconographic programme to earlier examples, e.g. the outspread serpent canopies, the lotus flowers held in the right hand, and the *kamandalu* in the left. There is however, a marked 'Visnuisation' in terms of apparel and ornamentation: the dhoti, *vanamālā* and elaborate torque are all similar in style to those worn by the two Cave 6 Visnu images at Udayagiri (Plate 168). These parallels suggest a date somewhere in the first half of the fifth century AD, although Harle (1974, 42), noting a certain 'meanness and lack of vitality', assigns them slightly later than the Udayagiri sculptures. Also notable is the fact that in contrast to earlier periods the *nāgas* now wear crowns distinguished by 'three high circular lobes, the central of which bears a lion's head (*kirīṭamukuṭa*) from whose mouth festoons of pearls are draped' (Harle 1974, 42). The similarity to the crown worn by the Udayagiri Visnu figures is striking. Apart from the fact that the crowns of the latter follow a square rather than circular outline, the central *kirīṭamukuṭa* motif, which in shape can be seen as a continuation of the *maulimaṇi* turban of the Kusana period, is almost identical.[79] The *kirīṭamukuṭa* motif, which becomes increasingly popular in the Gupta period as a symbol of noble birth (Sircar 1966, *s.v.*), is just one of several factors that lie behind my twofold contention regarding the changing ritual and political status of the *nāga* cult during the Gupta period: i) *nāgas* begin to look more and more like Visnu; and ii) they begin to incorporate more allusions to royalty.

Ferozpur

The suggestion that some of the *nāgas* at Sanchi were actually housed in independent temples marks a shift in the configuration of the ritual landscape during the Gupta period. An increasing Visnuisation of *nāga* sculptures has also been noted. A third development that is intricately bound up with the second is an increasing 'royalisation' of *nāga* iconography. These processes are also evident at Ferozpur, an early settlement about 2.5 km to the west of Gulgaon, where a group of *nāga* sculptures are now housed in a makeshift temple at the western edge of the modern village. The group, consisting of a free-standing *nāga* and *nāginī* (Plate 166)[80] and a grooved lotus bell capital surmounted by two *nāga-nāginī* couples standing back-to-back (Plate 167),[81] was described in some detail by Williams (1976, pls. 1-9). However, no consideration was given to their wider archaeological context, a situation which has been remedied following the discovery, during the present study, of Buddhist monastic remains on the summit of Ferozpur hill, and a large irrigation embankment further to the west, discussed in chapters 11 and 14 respectively.

In terms of style, iconography and ornamentation, the Ferozpur sculptures belong to a unified idiom typified by the Gupta *nāgas* already discussed. For example, the *nāga*'s dhoti, *vanamālā*, torque and crown, with its three circular lobes and central *kirīṭamukuṭa*, are all closely related to the Sanchi *nāgas*. Also notable is the treatment of the *nāginī*'s anatomy and clothing which is almost identical to that of the Temple 31 *nāginī* (Plate 162). There are also stylistic and iconographic parallels with the *nāga* in the Udayagiri Varaha panel (discussed later). For example, the aquatic plants on the abacus of the bell capital are treated in almost an identical manner to those on the Varaha panel (Plate 170). This feature means that the standing *nāgas* are, like the kneeling *nāga* figure at Udayagiri, conceived as rising out of the primordial waters. It is also significant here that, as with the other *nāgas*, there are obvious iconographic parallels with the Visnu figures at Udayagiri (Plate 169). Despite these similarities, Williams (1976, 174) suggests that the Ferozpur sculptures are closer to the Sanchi *nāgas* in date (first half of the fifth century AD), largely on account of the 'planar organisation, static pose, and heaviness in the articulation of the legs.'

The significance of these chronological and iconographic observations is made clearer by the powerful regal associations of the Ferozpur sculptures which strengthen the view that the kneeling *nāga* at Udayagiri is a symbolic reference to the Naga dynasty and its relationship to the Guptas, as discussed in chapter 5. The first royal allusions at Ferozpur are the crowns worn by the free-standing *nāga* and the *nāgas* depicted on the pillar capital, which are similar to those worn by the kneeling figure at Udayagiri (Plate 169). The second imperial reference is the pillar capital, which, as noted by Williams (1976, 174), is closely related to the Budhagupta pillar at Eran. Many of the free-standing pillars in the Gupta period embodied much older imperial symbolism developed during the Mauryan period. Indeed, some, such as the small four-lioned pillar capital at Sanchi and the Iron Pillar at Delhi, are direct copies of Mauryan originals (Williams 1982, pl. 141). In light of the Guptas' archaizing tendencies, therefore, it is not too far-fetched to suggest that the back-to-back arrangement of the *nāga-nāginī* capital at Ferozpur may also have been a pun on the original Asokan pillar at Sanchi crowned by two pairs of addorsed lions. In William's (1976, 179) words, 'the elegant recasting of Mauryan-derived clichés to represent serpents rising from a pond and crowned by celestial hoods shows the sophistication of the *alaṃkaras*, or poetic conceits, favoured in Sanskrit poetry. The folk image had been taken over by the "great" or uniformitarian tradition.' A similar process has been noted in Orissa, where the 'ritual royalisation' of local deities appears to have been a key component in the rise of major royal-patronised pilgrimage centres during the mid-first millennium BC (Kulke 1993). Kulke (*ibid.*, 11) argues that this process 'became the best and most visible legitimation of royal power and wealth of the "divine kings" on the earth', although it is unclear whether the attribution of royal features to deities simply reflected royal patronage, or because 'the priests had ascribed these features of divine kingship to their gods in order to glorify them'.

Returning to Ferozpur, the *nāgas*' transposition into a sculptural idiom usually reserved for symbols of royalty or for 'orthodox' deities certainly suggests some reorientation in the ritual and political status of the *nāga* cult during the Gupta period. However, I would argue that the process may have been more complex than a simple case of 'cultic integration' or 'Sanskritisation', as suggested by Williams and Kulke. The *nāga* cult had long since been aligned with the 'great' tradition in the form of the Bhagavata cult; the fact that the *nāgas* during the Gupta period begin to look more and more like Visnu is merely the culmination of a long-standing ambivalence between Vaisnava and *nāga* traditions. Further, I would argue that the Ferozpur sculptures, with their strong imperial references, have a deeper political significance connected with the changing dynamics of the relations between the Naga and Gupta houses during the first half of the fifth century AD. The epigraphical evidence discussed in chapter 5 suggests that the conflict between the western and eastern halves of the Gupta empire may have led to a reassertion of the Nagas' power in the Vidisha area. I suggest, therefore, that the Ferozpur sculptures, by symbolically conflating the political power of the Nagas as kings with the divine power of *nāgas* as deities, can be seen as a direct competitive reference to the Gupta's symbolic identification with Visnu. Further support for viewing the *nāgas* as having both cultic and regal associations is provided by their location at the edge of a dried-up irrigation reservoir. On the one hand this reflects the traditional link between *nāgas* and water; it may also be a symbolic reference to the patronage of the Naga clan.[82]

Udayagiri

The serpent idiom also figures prominently at Udayagiri, whose sculpted panels and caves are direct products of the patronage of the Gupta court and its alignment with Vaisnavism. The most obvious illustration is the Sesa Narayana panel in Cave 13, in which Visnu is shown reclining on a bed of serpent coils in the interval between two periods of creation (Williams 1982, pl. 39). Although the iconographic roots of the Sesa Narayana idea, formally speaking, follow a trajectory distinct from that of the Balarama-*nāga* images discussed earlier, it would be surprising if the panel did not trigger more place-bound identifications in the minds of local visitors, given the long-entwined history of Bhagavata and *nāga* iconography in the region: the *nāga*, quite literally, is *supporting* Visnu. Elsewhere, for example, it has been suggested that the image of Visnu resting on the serpent Sesa 'indicates the subordination of the non Brahmanical divinity of the agricultural masses to the Brahmanical god Narayana Visnu' (Jaiswal 1967, 59). At the same time, however, the coils can also be seen as *part* of Visnu's body, just as in earlier free-standing images, the *nāga* coils were part of Balarama's body.

This possible appropriation, or even subordination, metaphor is even clearer in the second serpent reference at Udayagiri: the lower right-hand corner of the Varaha panel in Cave 5 shows a *nāga* kneeling in a position of supplication at Varaha's feet, belittled by the latter's gigantic proportions (Plate 169). With its anthropomorphic body and thirteen-headed serpent canopy, it is similar to the earlier free-standing *nāgas* in the area. Although the *nāga* wears a turban rather than a crown, the central, circular *kirīṭamukuṭa* torque is almost identical to that on the crowns of the Sanchi examples: although the lion element is damaged, the triangular fan of pearls below is clearly visible.

Central to the debates regarding the political dimensions of the panel is the question of the identity of the second kneeling figure behind the *nāga* just described.[83] Some scholars (e.g. Willis 2004) have viewed him as Candragupta II, whose depiction as a supreme devotee of Visnu (*paramabhāgavata*) kneeling before Varaha, his chosen deity, accords with the associated Cave 6 inscription, dated GE 82 (AD 400/1), which uses a similar terminology (Fleet *CII*, III, 21–5; Sircar 1965, 271–2). The second theory, which may not be mutually exclusive to the first, is that Varaha, shown rescuing the goddess Earth (Bhumi) from the primordial ocean, is an allegoric reference to Candragupta's restoration of political and moral order after years of Ksatrapa domination.[84] The supplicant *nāga* figure, from either standpoint, is viewed as a representative of the Naga dynasty, whose complex relationship of alliance, loyalty, rivalry and subordination to the Gupta empire is borne out in the textual and epigraphical sources discussed in chapter 5. Further, it has been argued that the site was intricately bound up with astronomical principles aimed at predicting major events in the agricultural year; the manipulation of water, in particular, seems to be a key element at the site (Willis 2004). Willis argues that the site was chosen by Candragupta II because its position on the Tropic of Cancer allowed for the effective tracking of the movement of the sun, which in turn provided the means for predicting the start and end of the monsoon. The Sesa Narayana panel signifies the beginning of the monsoon when Visnu is put to sleep, while the Varaha panel alludes to the ritual awakening of Visnu from his long sleep in order to mark the end of the monsoon. Following this narrative, Varaha rescues the earth goddess from the waters because he is restoring agrarian order after the end of the monsoons, and in the process stands on the head of the *nāga*, because he is the custodian of these monsoon waters. Given the Guptas' known involvement in agrarian expansion in the form of Brahmanical land grants, it is tempting to see an additional layer of meaning in the relationship between Varaha and the *nāga* in the Udayagiri panel. Both are shown emerging from the primordial waters, with the *nāga* being pushed back down with the force of Varaha's foot on his head: could it be that the Guptas are presenting themselves as the new masters of the land, thus usurping the position of the local Naga dynasty on the one hand and the Buddhists on the other, both of whom appear to have been closely connected with the irrigation works in the area? This association is most apparent during the Gupta period, but was probably already in place much earlier, as attested by the spatial and chronological link between *nāga* sculptures, monasteries and dams from the first century BC onwards (Shaw and Sutcliffe 2003a; 2005). Further evidence is provided by the Naga coins at Vidisha and the Naga appellations in the Sanchi inscriptions discussed in chapter 5. Both the Nagas' role as facilitators of agrarian expansion and their identification with a totemic deity are features more commonly associated with the Guptas (and their link with Visnu), who from the fourth century AD appear to have usurped their authority in the area.

Beyond the political allegory, the Udayagiri panel's most obvious message is of course religious: Visnu emerges from the primordial waters, which, being the traditional abode of *nāgas*, also give rise to the worshipping serpent king. Again, there seem to be several layers of meaning. First, we have the pun on the ambivalent relationship between Visnu and snakes: although Garuda is the traditional slayer of *nāgas*, Visnu paradoxically embodies the attributes of the latter, as illustrated by his Sesa manifestation in Cave 13. Second, there may also be some reference to a Sanskritisation or 'conversion' narrative, whereby a local spirit is being demoted to the position of a Vaisnava devotee. There is also a third layer, which only begins to emerge when we situate the panel within the wider body of *nāga* sculptures discussed in this chapter: from the first century BC onwards, most *nāgas* in the area are closely aligned with the Bhagavata tradition; the process of 'cultic absorption' or appropriation, therefore, goes back to the much earlier conflation between Balarama and *nāga* iconography. The major shift that occurs during the Gupta period is that Balarama becomes replaced by Visnu in keeping with the shift from the *vyūha* to *avatāra* systems of Vaisnavism. It is tempting to suggest, therefore, that the Udayagiri panel also contains some indirect reference to these internal theological developments, the kneeling *nāga* representing Balarama's submission to the power of Visnu in his boar incarnation. Finally, the full potency of the panel derives from a complex intertwining of both religious and political symbolic references. The *nāga* image is at the same time the deity *and* the dynastic symbol, just as Varaha is at the same time Visnu and the royal power of the Guptas.

Amacchar

The two-fold suggestion that Gupta *nāgas* increasingly adopt the attributes of Visnu on the one hand and royalty on the other is further supported by three newly documented Phase IV *nāga* sculptures. The first two, a *nāga* and *nāginī*, were noted at Amacchar, a large settlement on the bank of the River Betwa, 1.5

km to the east of the Heliodorus pillar site. The *nāga* (Plate 173),[85] the more complete of the two sculptures, stands semi-embedded in the ground amidst a large pile of Brahmanical sculptures ranging in date from around the fifth to the tenth century AD. This includes fragments from a large Harihara figure (Plate 193) and two lion-cornered abacuses from a Gupta temple (Plate 197) discussed earlier, which, taken together, attest to the increasing rarity of independent *nāga* cult spots during the Gupta period.[86] The *nāga* image also follows a slightly different stylistic formula to previously described examples. Rather than standing in the customary *samapāda* posture, the two-armed deity sits in *lalitāsana* on a pile of serpent coils which rise up the back in a single shaft, extending over the head in a five-headed canopy. Significantly, this position of 'royal ease' accords with other indicators of royal stature noted at Sanchi, Ferozpur and Udayagiri.[87]

Further idiosyncrasies include the fact that instead of the usual circular halo-like canopy, the individual serpent heads overlap each other and protrude at a pronounced horizontal angle to form a protective shelter over the deity's head. The figure's body is heavily eroded, but the lines of a transparent dhoti, and a sash tied in a simple knot at the centre of the waist, can still be made out. A sacred thread (*yajñopavita*) is visible over the left shoulder, strong evidence of the deity's Brahmanical identity. The right arm is bent at the elbow, with an unidentifiable object held against the chest. The fact that Balarama images are often shown in a similar pose, with a wine-glass held against the chest (Joshi 1979, 48–9), provides clues as to the image's possible Vaisnava associations. Multiple-beaded bangles, found on some of the earlier *yakṣa* figures, adorn the wrists. Dating is complicated by the absence of direct parallels, as well as the heavily eroded state of the sculpture. Yet one detail in particular suggests a Gupta date: the left hand holds a bunch of lotus flowers, the stalks of which bend with pronounced fluidity upwards and over the shoulders, leaving the flowers to adorn the left side of the body. One of the flowers is a closed bud, the other is fully expanded, its concave appearance accentuated by the deeply carved striations on its inner surface. This kind of lively three-dimensionality finds an almost direct parallel in the flowers held by the Ferozpur *nāga* (Plate 167). Comparisons can also be made with the aquatic plants on the Varaha panel at Udayagiri (Plate 170).

Additional support for a Gupta date is provided by the accompanying *nāginī* (Plate 163), which, with serpent coils piled horizontally up the back, follows a more conventional iconography.[88] Although only the lower half survives, enough detail remains to make direct comparisons with the *nāginī* outside Temple 31 at Sanchi (Plate 162): the position of the left hand, resting on the hip and gripping a fold of the transparent garment between the second and third fingers, is almost identical to the Sanchi figure. Another shared attribute is the manner in which the striated sash is looped over the right hip.

Devalkhera

The increasing dissolution of the distinction between Vaisnava and *nāga* iconographic programmes during the Gupta period reaches a climax in the final image in this group, a syncretic Visnu-*nāga* sculpture at Devalkhera, an early settlement near Morel khurd in the eastern sector (Plate 174).[89] The four-armed image is broken in two, but, apart from the missing upper right hand and a small section below the chest, the sculpture is almost complete. The upper left hand holds a *śankha*, with a personified *gadā* and *cakra* in the lower right and left hands respectively. The most obvious parallel is the larger of the two Cave 6 Visnu images at Udayagiri (Plate 169). Unfortunately, the outer detail of the face and headdress has been damaged but the square outline of the latter is so close to the crown worn by the Udayagiri Visnu that it can quite confidently be regarded as a proper *kirīṭamukuṭa* crown. A transparent dhoti that accentuates the outline of the knees and clings tightly to the area around the genitals is secured by a waist belt; a *vanamālā* is arranged over the knees. Quite clearly, we are dealing with a standing Visnu closely related to the Udayagiri Visnu figures, although the rather stocky legs may be suggestive of a slightly later date, more in line with the Sanchi *nāga*s. The most obvious difference, however, is that the Devalkhera image has a serpent rising up its back in horizontal coils, expanding into a seven-headed canopy above its head (Plates 174–5). This rare form of Visnu may be seen as a variation of the Ananta Narayana theme at Udayagiri, but given the local importance of the Balarama cult in earlier periods, a more plausible explanation is that it forms the culmination of a long history of syncretism between the Vaisnava and *nāga* traditions: just as the proto-Pancaratra tradition had spread into this part of the study area through the appropriation of *nāga* iconography, so does the first Visnu image appear in the guise of a *nāga*.

Nāgakals

While the anthropomorphic *nāga* sculptures are increasingly incorporated into Brahmanical or Buddhist complexes during the Gupta period, the only *nāga*s that appear to have retained their older status as independent folk-deities, are the theriomorphic *nāgakal*s, a number of which were found during the survey. These are stone slabs with an average height of 80 cm, carved on one side with either one or two serpents. Similar depictions of theriomorphic serpents already occur during the second century BC on the railing carvings of Sanchi Stupa 2. However, there is no evidence for free-standing *nāgakal*s in the Sanchi area prior to the Gupta period. One such example was found near Devrajpur kherai, around 2 km north of Andher (Plate 176).[90] Its proximity to a large irrigation complex discussed in detail in chapter 14 is in keeping with the traditional link between *nāga*s and water. The stone slab is carved with a single serpent which rises in four coils to join a single-headed cobra canopy. A similar Jain *nāgakal*, datable to c. fifth century AD, is stored in the VM (Plate 177).[91] An almost identical *nāgakal*, with the addition of a smaller cobra on either side, stands on the bank of the dried-up village tank at Bamnor, around 1.5 km east of Andher (Plate 178).[92] Another *nāgakal*, this time consisting of two rearing serpents with outspread cobra hoods, stands at the hillside settlement of Tijalpur, around 6 km south of Sanchi (Plate 179).[93] It, too, may be assigned to c. fifth century AD. Examples datable to the seventh or eighth century AD, and even as late as the tenth century AD were found at Parsora Haveli in Sector 2a (Plate 180) and Pathari kativarat in Sector 2b respectively. The comparatively late appearance of theriomorphic serpent stones, which one may assume were a continuation of much older wooden images, warrants further investigation. It may be that their aniconic appearance made them less susceptible to assimilation into orthodox ritual frameworks than their anthropomorphic counterparts.

Yakṣas and yakṣinis

There is also a notable change in the ritual setting of *yakṣa* sculptures during the fifth century AD. As discussed in chapter

9, three independent *yakṣa* images are incorporated into the monastic complex at Sanchi for the first time during this period (Plates 38–9).[94] All three figures are seated in *lalitāsana* on stools similar in form to those of the seated mothers at Besnagar (Williams 1982, pl. 48). A similar *yakṣa*, also seated on a stool in *lalitāsana*, was noted during the survey on a hillside just to the south of Bawaliya village, less than 1 km east of Andher (Plates 195–6)[95] Its existence only came to light in 2000 when it was unearthed by villagers during stone-cutting activities. It was evidently carved on site, as demonstrated by its unfinished state: the entire surface is covered with a preliminary dressing of rough chisel marks, the circular patterning of which is especially prominent on the face. An almost identical dressing is found on the Siva image (Plate 194) described earlier, which is stored on a platform in Bawaliya village itself, the suggestion being that both images were products of the same workshop. It is quite possible that the second-century-BC stupa railings at nearby Andher originated from the same quarry, and possibly even workshop, thus attesting to a remarkable level of continuity in the production of stone sculpture. Only the broad outline features have been applied, while the back remains completely uncarved. However, sufficient details, such as the protruding stomach and money-bag, enable one to identify the image as Kubera, the chief of the *yakṣas* (Misra 1981). Both the posture and anatomical detailing are strongly reminiscent of the three seated Sanchi *yakṣas* just described, while the outline of a *kirīṭamukuṭa* crown places it firmly within the Gupta period.

Yakṣini sculptures also continue during the Gupta period, but in noticeably smaller numbers than in earlier years. No *yakṣini* figures have been reported from Sanchi, and only two were documented during the SSP, both at Ratanpur Girdhari, a hillside settlement around 4.5 km south of Sanchi. The first, of which only the lower portion survives, has strong athletic legs adorned with chunky anklets, and a striated sash falling on the left side (Plate 164).[96] The general composition and modelling, as well as the square tenon on which it stands, are strikingly similar to the Temple 31 *nāginī* at Sanchi (Plate 162), thus supporting a c. fifth-century-AD date. The second *yakṣini* (Plate 165), of which only the lower torso remains, belongs to the same stylistic category.[97]

Phase V (c. seventh to late eighth century AD)

As discussed in chapter 6, the 'post-Gupta'/early Pratihara period corresponded to the third major phase of Buddhist propagation in the area. This appears to have been matched by an equal degree of Brahmanical expansion. Twelve Brahmanical ritual sites, consisting of 13 individual sculptural pieces, datable between c. seventh and eighth centuries AD, were documented during the SSP. As shown in Figure 12.1 (colour), eleven of these are directly linked to the goddess tradition, with a predominance of *Mahiṣāsuramardinī* and Durga figures (Plates 209–12), with the remainder consisting of a Visnu and Ardhaneswara image. The *Mahiṣāsuramardinī* images of this period are quite distinct from those found in Phases VI and VII. As shown by the examples at Pali, Dhakna and Devrajpur (Plates 209–10, 212), the goddess is usually four-armed and wears a flat cap-like headdress, while the buffalo head is still intact on the ground, rather than severed and held in the goddess's hand as in the case of later examples (Plate 213).[98] As discussed in the foregoing section, in contrast to the preceding period when goddess sculptures had been restricted to the Vidisha/Sanchi area, these are now found throughout the study area. However, the patterns in Figure 12.1 reveal an uneven distribution of Brahmanical sites, with the majority in the eastern sector (2a and 2b). There is a notable absence of Brahmanical sites in the northern sector (4).

Phase VI (c. ninth to tenth century AD)

As shown in Figure 12.1 (colour) and Table 12.3 there is a significant increase in temple construction during the late Pratihara - Paramara period (ninth to tenth century AD), with 103 individual temple sites identifiable in the study area. Approximately 1,010 'new' sculptures were recorded at a total of 199 find-spots; more precise quantification is precluded by the fact that many of the sites now consist of multi-phase temple sites, with large piles of sculptural and architectural fragments. The overwhelming majority of these sites are Brahmanical in orientation, but in contrast to earlier periods, it is now difficult to distinguish between different sectarian strands: only eight were specifically Saiva in orientation, and five belonged exclusively to the Devi tradition. The remainder represented a more generic, pantheistic form of Brahmanism (Plate 216). Brahmanical sites are distributed fairly evenly throughout the four major geographical sectors, although there is slightly more activity in the western (1a and 1b) and eastern (2a and 2b) sectors. A notable departure from earlier trends is the increase in the number of Hanuman sculptures: 25 such sculptures were documented during the SSP. In addition, two theriomorphic *nāgakal*s (Plates 176–9), as well as a semi-anthropomorphic *nāgakal* (Plate 180), all in Sectors 2a or 2b, were documented.

Six Jain temple sites were identified, at Vidisha (Sector 1a), Naroda-Murlikheri (Sector 1b), Morel kala and Devrajpur (Sector 2b), Besar talai (Sector 3) (Plate 214), and Ahmadpur (Sector 4) (Plate 215). This varied geographical distribution contrasts to the previous period, when Jain temples were restricted to the Vidisha/Udayagiri area only.

The proliferation of Brahmanical temple construction during this period presents a striking contrast to the near absence of building activity at hilltop monastic sites. Both of these points attest to the diminishing influence of the *saṅgha* and a major reorientation in the focus of religious patronage. Additional factors, discussed in chapter 11, suggest that many monastic sites had already been abandoned by this time. For example, as shown in Table 11.3 and Figure 11.25, ten of the Phase VI Brahmanical temples were built in, or in close proximity to, older monastic sites. Even those temples which remain in a village setting are built in such large numbers as to belittle the scale of the former 'Buddhist geography'. The unbalanced configuration of the ritual landscape is clearly illustrated in Figure 12.1. The only two monastic sites showing evidence for ongoing Buddhist occupation during this period are Sanchi and Morel khurd. However, the scale of Brahmanical temple construction in their immediate vicinity provides a clear indication that the *saṅgha* no longer occupied a central position in local patronage networks.

Phase VII (eleventh to twelfth century AD)

As shown in Table 12.1 (colour) and Figure 12.1, Brahmanical temples continued to be built during Phase VII, but in fewer numbers than the previous two centuries (Plate 218). Approximately 173 individual sculptural or architectural pieces (both previously known and newly documented) are distributed over 38 separate find-spots. These can be related to 33 actual temple sites. With few exceptions, such as the base of a female deity at Ratanpur Girdhari[99] which is closely related to Chandella examples (Plate 218), the sculpture of this period is generally of a lower quality than before, and with a reductive carving style (Plate 213). As discussed in chapter 9, the Jain temple complex which possibly stood on the Nagauri hill is included in this figure. No other Jain temples were documented in the surrounding area. With the exception of Sanchi, where there is limited evidence for building activity in c. eleventh century AD, most of the hilltop monastic sites appear to have been abandoned by this time.

PART II: PATTERNS IN THE MULTI-LAYERED RITUAL LANDSCAPE

Introduction

The material presented in Part I provides a starting-point for identifying the broad spatial and temporal trends in the ritual landscape between c. third century BC and twelfth century AD (Figure 12.1 colour; Table 12.3). Key questions include: why do some religious traditions use stone as a medium of representation earlier than others and why are certain areas 'monumentalised' earlier than others? As I shall argue, the appearance of stone sculptures has more to do with the changing focus of religious patronage than with the development of the religious landscape *per se*. These patterns also provide a basis for assessing theories of religious change and patronage, summarised in chapter 6, and for building a regional model for understanding the changing relationship between Buddhism, Brahmanism and 'local' cults.

Temporal and spatial trends in the Brahmanical landscape

Several key phases in the development of the ritual landscape may be delineated. First, the enormous proliferation in the quantity and geographical extent of Buddhist monuments in Phase IIa forms a striking contrast to the previous period when the known ritual geography is confined to Sanchi and Satdhara (Buddhist) and Vidisha (proto-Pancaratra/Bhagavata). During Phase IIa, the proto-Pancaratra system still remains confined to Vidisha, and it is not until Phase IIb that the first Balarama images begin to appear in the rural hinterland. As shown in Figure 12.1, the eastern sector (2a and 2b) is the main area of proto-Pancaratra expansion. As far as other non-Buddhist cults are concerned, it is not until Phase IIIb, that sculptures connected to the *nāga* and *yakṣa* cults, as well as to the Saiva tradition, appear in significant numbers in the rural hinterland. *Nāgas* and *yakṣas* are found in the Sanchi area during earlier periods, but not beyond the immediate vicinity of Sanchi and Vidisha. Now they are found throughout the study area, but with a particularly high concentration in the eastern sector.

The last point needs to be viewed against the local settlement patterns and agricultural trends discussed in chapters 13 and 14: the eastern sector has special social and economic value, largely because of the particular topographical combination of fertile black-cotton soil plains and small 'manageable' hills. Not only do the latter provide refuge from monsoon flooding, but their short valleys provide a suitable basis for downstream irrigation systems. This topographical combination may be contrasted to the predominantly flat land to the north, or the dense impenetrable hills of the south, lacking both suitable terrain for reservoir construction as well as extensive cultivable areas.

The gradual movement towards a multi-layered ritual landscape during the early centuries AD reaches a climax during Phase IV, when a number of major changes begin to take place. There is a significant increase in the number of sculptures related to the Brahmanical tradition. More importantly, there is enormous diversification in the *variety* of Brahmanical deities. These shifts

Table 12.3 Ritual sites: phases Id–VII (SC level)

Ritual sites		**Phase**								
Ritual group	**Ritual sub-group**	**Id**	**II**	**IIIa**	**IIIb**	**IV**	**V**	**VI**	**VII**	**Total**
	Buddhist	6	101	2	3	29	21	8	1	171
	Nāga		2		4	8	1	3		18
	Yakṣa/yakṣini		3	2	3	6				14
Bhagavata	Bhagavata (non-*Nāga*)	1	2	1		1				5
" "	Bhagavata (*Nāga*)		1	1	1					3
Total Bhagavata (combined)		1	3	2	1	1				8
Brahmanical	Devi					8	9	26	11	54
" "	*Nāga*-Vaisnava					1				1
" "	Saiva				3	8	1	46	4	62
" "	Vaisnava					3	1	24	1	29
" "	Brahmanical					23	1	96	28	148
Total Brahmanical (combined)					3	43	12	192	44	294
	Jain				1			9	1	11
	Total	7	109	6	15	87	34	212	46	516

reflect wider theological developments, such as the promotion of an overarching, pantheistic form of Brahmanism in the contemporary Puranic texts. As shown in Figure 12.1, however, the archaeological manifestation of orthodox Brahmanism during the Gupta period does not extend much beyond the immediate vicinity of Vidisha and Udayagiri. This is entirely in keeping with the area's strong links with the proto-Pancaratra tradition. Interestingly, the Brahmanical developments in the eastern sector also follow on directly from earlier trends: just as the proto-Pancaratra tradition had spread into this area through the appropriation of *nāga* iconography, so does the first Visnu image appear in the guise of a *nāga*. This brings me to my final point regarding the reorientation of the ritual landscape during the Gupta period. The increase in the total number of Brahmanical sculptures, not to mention the first free-standing Buddhist deities at Sanchi, coincides with a radical change in the ritual and social context of local folk deities. Apart from the theriomorphic *nāgakals*, which appear to retain their independent ritual identity, all of the *nāga* sculptures now appear as components of either Buddhist or Brahmanical complexes. Referred to variously as 'syncretism' or 'inclusivism' (Gonda 1970, 95), the dissolution of the independent character of local folk-cults reaches its climax in the later periods, when it becomes increasingly difficult to distinguish between the so-called 'high' and 'low' religious traditions. Secondly, although there is a notable proliferation of sites connected to the 'goddess' tradition during the 'post-Gupta' period (Phase V), from the ninth century AD onwards (Phase VI) the character of the ritual landscape has become overwhelmingly and overarchingly 'Brahmanical' in orientation. As shown in Figure 12.1 and Table 12.3, by this time it is usually not possible to distinguish between different sectarian strands within the Brahmanical tradition.

However, it should be reiterated that these patterns reflect the adoption of a stone-working tradition rather than the formation of a ritual landscape *per se*. It is important to stress that many aspects of non-Buddhist religious practice in ancient times would have revolved around 'non-monumental' shrines which would leave little in the way of archaeological traces. Insights into the nature of these shrines are provided by the nature of present-day religious practice in much of the rural countryside where shrines often consist of sculptural fragments reinstalled on village platforms (*cabutra*), or simple unhewn stones worshipped beneath trees (Plates 13–14). As discussed in chapter 8, the makeshift quality of these shrines represents a striking contrast to the grandiose scale of the original temples, which until the Muslim conquests of the thirteenth century AD, would have been part of a 'high' orthodox religious framework. The reuse of these sculptures therefore constitutes a transformation to an overtly 'folk' level of worship. Thus, although there is an element of continuity between the ritual geography of the past and present, we are dealing only with the reconstitution of the ruins of an orthodox religious tradition, which says little about more localised religious practices. Insights into these practices are provided by the 'non-monumental' cult spots documented during the survey (Figure 8.4). These help to remind us that much in the religious life of north India is based on a reverence for the inherent sacredness, or what Rudolph Otto (1923) called the *numen loci*, of particular places. These 'natural' shrines are located in rock-shelters, next to springs or on prominent hilltops. They are often found beneath large trees (Plate 13), which on account of their size are sometimes indicated on maps. They often consist of nothing more than a pile of unhewn stones placed on a platform (Plate 14). In other cases, they resemble small cairns (Plate 12). Many shrines are dedicated to place-bound deities known simply as *devī*, *bīr baba*, *bhūmia* or *djinn Maharāja*. Although these may be modern, their antecedents may be extremely ancient.[100] Above all, these patterns are important for highlighting the fact that the apparent paucity of archaeological evidence relating to religion beyond the Buddhist and orthodox Brahmanical framework may reflect partly the 'non-monumental' focus of local cultic practice.

Inter-religious dynamics

Buddhism and Brahmanical traditions

These spatial and temporal patterns also provide insights into the socio-political dynamics of ritual 'monumentalisation', especially the changing focus of religious patronage. It is possible that some of the variation in the distributional trends outlined in the foregoing account may stem from the divergent nature of the religious groups concerned. For example, as opposed to the largely devotional nature of the proto-Pancaratra system, the *saṅgha*, being a monastic community, actively sought out places away from urban centres. We also need to consider the degree to which the *saṅgha*'s comparatively early and prolific spread into rural areas was related to its preferential access to patronage and, furthermore, to a different *kind* of patronage to the proto-Pancaratra tradition. While both traditions were closely connected to state patronage during the Mauryan period, by the post-Mauryan period Buddhism is set apart by the prevalence of a collective patronage system.

The comparatively late extension of the proto-Pancaratra system into the rural hinterland in Phase IIIb may have been an attempt to redress this balance. The stylistic similarities between the earliest Balarama sculptures and developments at neighbouring Buddhist sites show that the same local artisans were now working for an increasingly varied set of patrons. Secondly, the physical orientation of these early Brahmanical sculptures belies an element of competitive reference to the Buddhist domination of the ritual landscape. The element of proselytisation in the positioning of stupas was considered in chapter 11, particularly with regard to their symbolic function as mechanisms for projecting the physical 'presence' of the Buddha and his *dharma* across the landscape. In the light of these discussions, the positioning of the Andher Balarama sculpture directly below the stupas on the hill above may have been an attempt to forestall this line of influence. Furthermore, the way in which it is orientated *away* from the stupas, may be a conscious symbol of resistance to the Buddhist stake over the ritual landscape (Plate 142).

A number of observations should also be made regarding the relationship between Buddhist and Brahmanical strands of the ritual landscape in later years. As shown in Figures 11.1, 11.25 and 12.1, the third major programme of Buddhist building construction in Phase V (sixth to seventh century AD) coincides with an acceleration in Brahmanical temple construction. The two traditions therefore seem to flourish at roughly equal rates in the post-Gupta period. From around the eighth century AD, however, the accelerated rate of construction at Brahmanical sites forms a striking contrast with the near absence of building activity at most Buddhist sites (Figures 11.25, 12.1). Despite this shift in the balance of the ritual landscape, the patterns shown in Figure 11.25 demonstrate that monastic and Brahmanical ritual sites continued to occupy quite distinct topographical spaces in the landscape: with the exception of the 'urban' Buddhist remains discussed in chapter 11, the majority of Buddhist sites occupy solitary hilltops, while most Brahmanical sites are situated in villages or towns. This difference reflects the fact that both performed quite different functions: while most Buddhist sites were primarily monastic, the majority of Brahmanical sites were geared towards public worship. As discussed in chapter 11, this pattern changes between the ninth and tenth centuries AD, when many Brahmanical temples are built in increasingly close proximity to monastic sites. In some cases, they are built directly within the compounds of older monastic sites, which one may assume had already been abandoned by this time (Figure 11.25); possible reasons for this abandonment are discussed in chapter 15.

Buddhism and 'local' cults

The *nāgas*' relationship to both Vaisnavism and Buddhism was touched upon in chapter 6, and is taken up again in the following two sections. Attention is also paid to another aspect of the *nāgas*' archaeological setting, that is the ancient reservoirs on whose banks they are often situated. Taken together, these patterns provide a basis for building an integrated model of religious change which considers both the ritual and economic dimensions of the changing dynamics between these religious traditions and their position within the wider cultural landscape.

As discussed in chapter 6, scholarship on religious change with regard to early Indian Buddhism has tended to focus on the ritual dimensions of religious experience, drawing heavily on textual accounts of the subordination and ultimate conversion of local deities through the power of the Buddha's teachings. Because *nāgas* preside over specific places, their assimilation into Buddhism is viewed as a crucial element of the *saṅgha*'s 'localisation' in new areas (Cohen 1998, 377–8). The assumption behind this kind of approach is that there was a pan-Indian *nāga* cult which was assimilated by Buddhism. It is important to assess the degree to which the patterns at Sanchi fit with these models.

The first point to stress is that in central India, there is no material evidence for *nāgas* or *yākṣas* prior to the mid-first century BC. The earliest free-standing *nāgas* at Nagauri and Gulgaon post-date the establishment of Buddhism by around two hundred years, while in the outlying areas they do not appear before the first century BC. It is important to consider explanations for these patterns. Whilst there is every possibility that these 'local' deities were worshipped in non-durable forms, there are serious challenges to the validity of the traditional polarisation between 'Buddhist' and 'non-Buddhist' deities, which presupposes that *nāgas* were suppressed or appropriated by Buddhism. As stressed in chapter 6, a distinction needs to be made between the practice and representation of the *nāga* cult, while there are reasons to suppose that the *saṅgha* was actively involved in the development of standardised iconographic models for representing deities that already existed in many divergent regional forms.

As discussed in chapter 6 and Part I of this chapter, all of the pre-Gupta *nāgas* in the Sanchi area were situated at a distance from Buddhist sites as typified by the spatial dislocation between the Nagauri *nāga* and the stupas on Sanchi hill. This forms a contrast to later patterns during the Gupta period, when *nāga* shrines appear within the monastic complex on Sanchi hill itself. This is the first time, therefore, that any direct parallel can be drawn with examples of 'cultic assimilation' as observed by Cohen (1998) at Ajanta. However, the motives behind this kind of assimilation appear to be quite different: given that Buddhism had already been established in the area for around seven hundred years, it is doubtful that we are dealing with a mechanism for 'localising' the *saṅgha*, which is what Cohen puts forward as an explanation for the positioning of the Cave 16 *nāga* at Ajanta. Rather, I have argued that the installation of these shrines was a culmination of a much older history of interaction between monks and *nāgas*. Despite the Nagauri *nāga*'s removed distance from Sanchi, its position is less at odds with later patterns than it at first appears: once the Buddhist monuments on Sanchi hill are viewed as components of an interconnected early-historic complex including the reservoir and settlement at Nagauri, the *nāga* ceases to be 'external' to the monastic site.

Elsewhere (Shaw 2000b) I have suggested that the *nāga* was placed here to guard the Buddhist relic at Sanchi from afar. At the same time, it overlooks the reservoir because of its association with water and fertility. Fa Hsien's accounts from eastern India show that by the Gupta period, *nāga* shrines were placed within monastic settings precisely because of the *nāgas*' ability to ensure adequate rainfall and, in turn, agricultural success; the positioning of *nāga* shrines on dams is entirely in keeping with such a model, particularly since, as suggested elsewhere (Shaw and Sutcliffe 2003a; 2005), the *saṅgha* appears to have played a role in the management of local irrigation. *Nāga* worship was thus part of Buddhist practice, not because the *saṅgha* sought to convert local populations, but rather because its effects were in harmony with the *saṅgha*'s wider economic interest in water-harvesting and agrarian production. This hypothesis, based on the relative configuration of dams, settlements and monasteries in the Sanchi area, as well as similar patterns in western India and Sri Lanka, forms part of an active model of religious change which suggests that monks moved into new areas with a set of 'practical' incentives for locals to give their economic support to the monastery (Shaw and Sutcliffe 2003a; 2005).[101]

This view is supported further by observations regarding the ostentatious display of water-harvesting facilities at rock-cut monasteries in western India (Shaw and Sutcliffe 2003a, 92–5). The development of sophisticated water-harvesting systems was a means of alleviating suffering (*dukkha*) as well as an instrument for generating patronage networks. Additional evidence, discussed in chapter 6, for the *saṅgha*'s monopolisation of the rain-making business supports the impression of a religious institution deeply embedded in the rural infrastructure. That the *nāgas* which provided the ritual channel for the *saṅgha*'s rain-making activities were placed next to the reservoirs – the ultimate symbol of the effects of timely rainfall on the one hand and of skilful water-storage techniques on the other – would have helped further to build up trust between the *saṅgha* and local farming communities.

Brahmanism and 'local' cults

Another important point regarding the appearance of *nāga* images at Sanchi during the Gupta period is that, when we examine the complete sculptural record across the study area as a whole, we realise that for at least the previous 350 years, local *nāga* deities had already been undergoing a process of cultic integration: when they first move into the rural, hinterland areas, they do so within a Brahmanised mould, that is as Balarama. While this point could be taken as evidence against their posited link with Buddhism, it should be reiterated that as a deity of fertility and agriculture, Balarama is simply a *nāga* with the addition of a plough and pestle. It is possible that the question of his sectarian affiliation was of little concern to local inhabitants who may have seen him as a *nāga* standing, as expected, at the edge of a water body. The assumption is, therefore, that Buddhist monks were less concerned with the *nāgas*' shifting sectarian affiliations than with their inherent power, that is their ability to ensure climatic stability. However, while we cannot assume a direct sectarian link between Balarama in his *nāga* form and the proto-Pancaratra material at Vidisha, it is significant to note that Balarama's position on ancient dams accords with evidence for similar linkages between the Pañcavīra tradition and water bodies in other parts of Madhya Pradesh.[102] By the first century AD, the link between *nāga*-Balarama and *vīra*-Samkarsana manifests itself in the sculptural record as demonstrated by the co-existence of Balarama in both his serpent and non-serpent form at Andher. It is not until the Gupta period, though, that the Vaisnava orientation of these images becomes explicit, with many shown either as Visnu himself or with attributes closely associated with Visnu. Interestingly, this is also when *nāga* shrines become incorporated into the monastic compound at Sanchi for the first time. In this light, the *nāgas* at Sanchi are less a concession to 'local' folk cults than to the Brahmanical tradition. Indeed, it is from the Gupta period onwards that we start to witness the increasing prominence of Brahmanical deities at Buddhist sites. These points raise interesting questions regarding the changing focus of religious patronage between c. second century BC and fifth century AD. They are also suggestive of a growing level of competition between Buddhism and Brahmanism as far as the involvement of these religious institutions in agrarian production was concerned. This view is supported by evidence for the growth of Brahmanical land-grants during the Gupta period, as well as recent scholarship on the Gupta kings' support of agricultural, calendrical rituals connected with orthodox Vaisnavism at nearby Udayagiri (Willis 2002).

Conclusion

This chapter has attempted to delineate the main temporal and spatial trends in the non-Buddhist ritual landscape through the documentation of sculpture and temple remains. While detailed descriptions and illustrations have been given for individual sculptures belonging to Phases II to IV, the sheer quantity of material belonging to later periods has precluded more than generalised overviews, with only selected sculptures being accompanied by illustrations. To remedy this situation, the complete database will be provided in web format in due course.

138 Gulgaon: *nāga* (c. first century AD) (SAM; SG010b/I-104)

139 Nagauri: *nāga in situ* (c. first century AD) (SG003a/I-626)

140 Vidisha: Kubera *yakṣa* (c. first century BC) (SG006/I-536)

141 Chandna: *nāga*-Balarama sculpture (c. first century BC) (SG095c/I-1)

142 Andher hill: looking down to first-century-AD Bhagavata site below

143 Andher: *nāga*-Balarama (c. first century AD) (SG013b/I-109)

144 Andher: Balarama in non-serpent form (c. first century AD) (SG013b/I-110)

145 Andher: individual head from a *nāga*'s serpent canopy

146 Andher: headdress

147 Andher: Detail of 'Asoka' tree garland on side of Balarama image

148 Sanchi: Stupa 1 – gateway guardian holding 'Asoka' tree chowrie (c. first century AD)

149 Two-armed Balarama from Jansuti, Mathura district (c. second to first century BC) (State Museum, Lucknow)

150 Mehgaon: *nāga* image (c. first century AD) (SG056/I-156)

151 Sanchi: Stupa 3 gateway image (c. first century AD)

152 Vidisha Forestry Commission site: *nāga*-Balarama (c. second century AD) (SG006/I-997)

153 Morel kala: *nāga* (c. second century AD) (SG099/I-232)

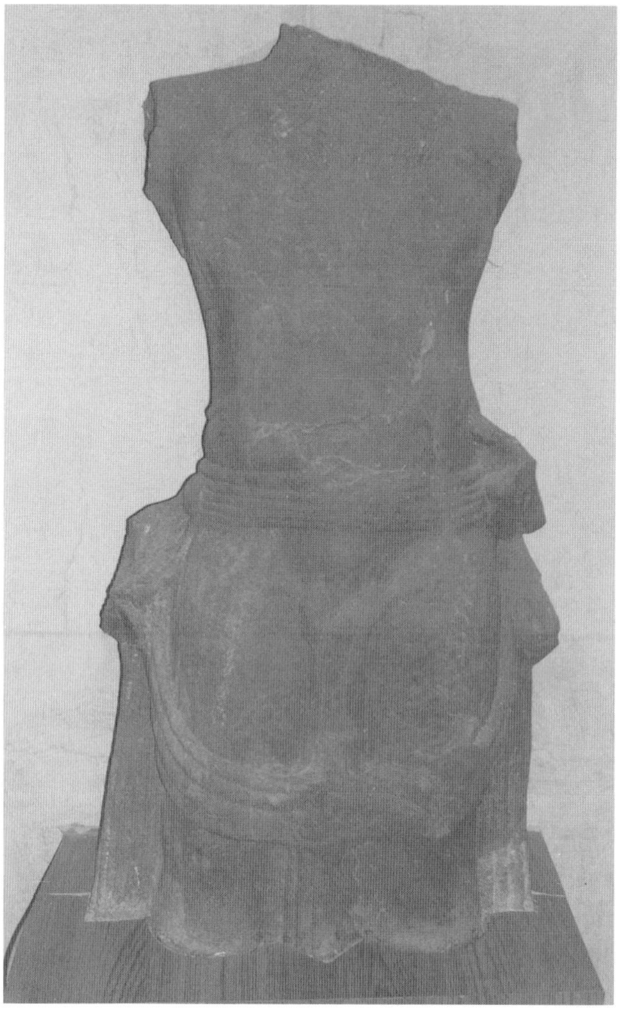

154 Vidisha Museum: *yakṣa* (c. second century AD) (SG006/I-169)

155 Salera: base of *nāga* image (c. second century AD) (SG170/I-458)

156 Salera: heads, one of which possibly belongs to a *nāga* (SG170/I-459)

157 Pagneswar: *nāginī* (c. second century AD) (SG061/I-494)

158 Pagneswar: *yakṣa*/Bodhisattva (c. second century AD) (SG061/I-290)

159 Gehunkheri: lower half of *nāga* image (right), and separate upper portion (left), possibly belonging to *nāginī* (SG134/I-337)

160 Gehunkheri: *nāginī* (left) and *yakṣa* (right) (SG134/I-338; I-340)

161 Sanchi: *nāga* sculpture from one of temples to the east of Stupa 1 (c. fifth century AD) (SG001/I-256)

162 Sanchi: *nāginī* outside Temple 31 (c. fifth century AD) (SG006/I-31)

163 Amacchar: lower half of *nāginī* (c. fifth century AD) (SG169/I-393)

164 Ratanpur Girdhari: female deity 1 (c. fifth century AD) (SG038/I-545)

165 Ratanpur Girdhari: female deity 2 (c. fifth century AD) (SG038/I-546)

166 Ferozpur: *nāga* and *nāginī* (c. fifth century AD) (SG011b/I-366; I-371)

167 Ferozpur: *nāga-nāginī* couple on pillar capital, and detail of flowers held in *nāga's* right hand (c. fifth century AD) (SG011b/I-372)

169 Udayagiri: cave 5 Varaha panel

168 Udayagiri: cave 6 Visnu (RHS of door)

170 Udayagiri: detail of cave 5 Varaha panel

171 Udayagiri: *yakṣa*/Visnu image (c. fifth century AD) (SG031/I-638)

172 Vidisha: 'Bodhisattva' (?) from *saptamātṛkā* site (Lake 1910a) (SG001/I-565)

173 Amacchar: *nāga* (c. fifth century AD) (SG169/I-392)

174 ABOVE Devalkhera: Visnu in *nāga* form (in two parts) (c. fifth century AD) (SG123/I-250)

175 RIGHT Devalkhera: Visnu in *nāga* form (back)

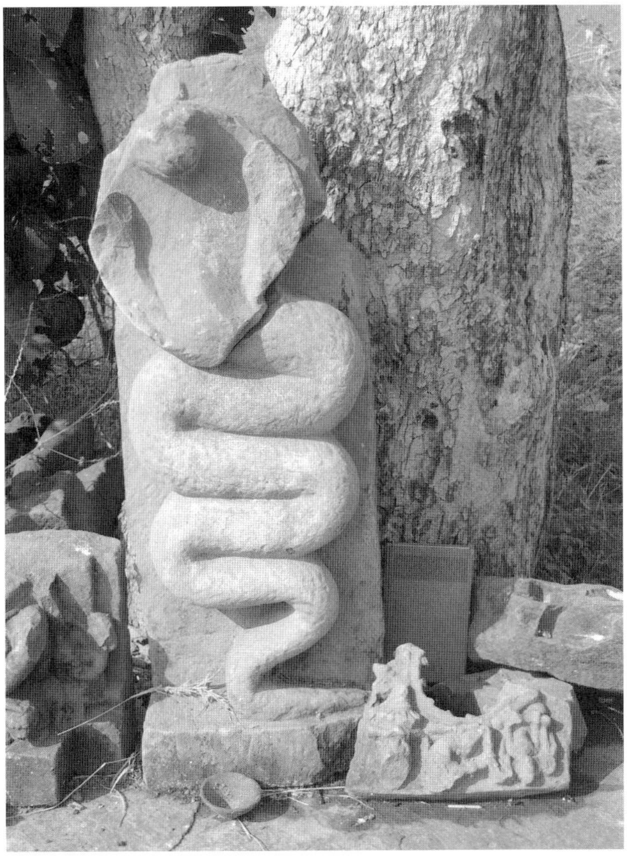

176 Devrajpur kherai: *nāgakal* (c. fifth century AD) (SG177d/I-690)

177 Vidisha Museum: Jain *nāgakal* (c. fifth century AD) (SG006/I-531)

178 Bamnor: *nāgakal* (c. fifth century AD) (SG173/I-464)

179 Tijalpur: *nāgakal* (c. fifth century AD) (SG058/I-162)

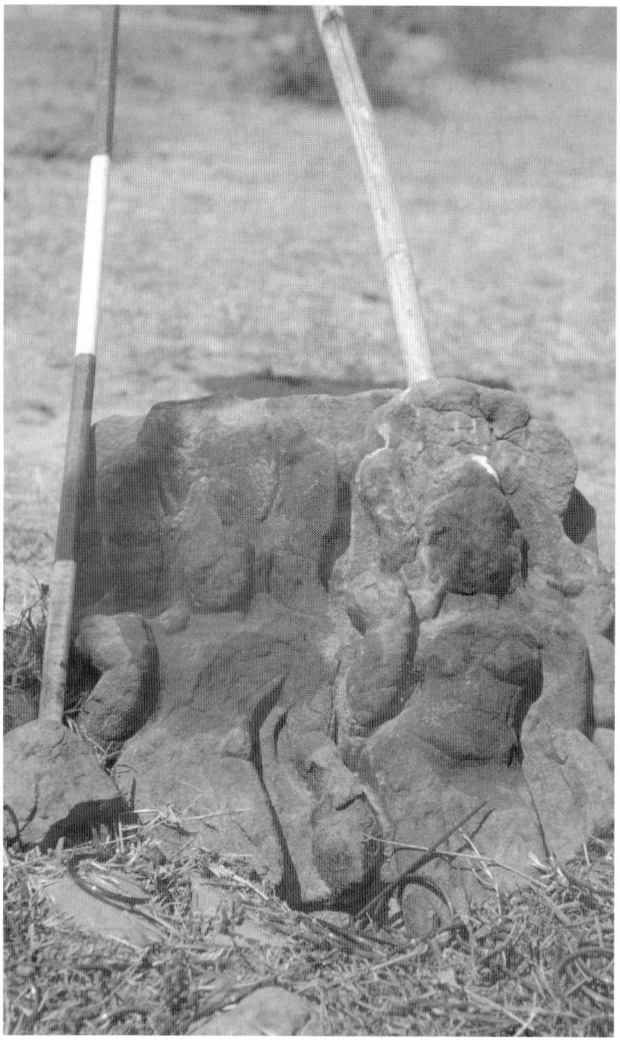

180 Parsora: *nāga-nāginī* couple (c. seventh to eighth century AD) (SG133/I-657)

181 Pagneswar: Siva *liṅga* (c. second century AD) (SG061/I-495)

182 ABOVE Murlikheri-Naroda: Siva *liṅga* (c. second century AD) (SG162b-I-366)

183 RIGHT Gehunkheri: Siva *liṅga* (c. second century AD) (SG134/I-339)

184 Vidisha: Siva *liṅga* outside Saiva temple (c. fifth century AD) (SG006/I-943)

185 ABOVE Vidisha: Saiva temple (c. fifth century AD)

186 Vidisha: Ganesa image (c. fifth century AD) (SG006/I-945)

187 Pipariya: undecorated Siva *liṅga* (c. fifth century AD) (SG146/I-661)

188 Neemkhera: *ekamukhaliṅga in situ* (c. fifth century AD) (SG164/I-389)

190 Udayagiri: *ekamukhaliṅga* (c. fifth century AD)

189 Karhaud: *ekamukhaliṅga in situ* in rock-shelter shrine (c. fifth century AD) (SG012/I-376)

191 Eran: Visnu head (c. fifth century AD) (SG010/I-279)

192 Eran: Harihara head (c. fifth century AD) (SG010/I-281)

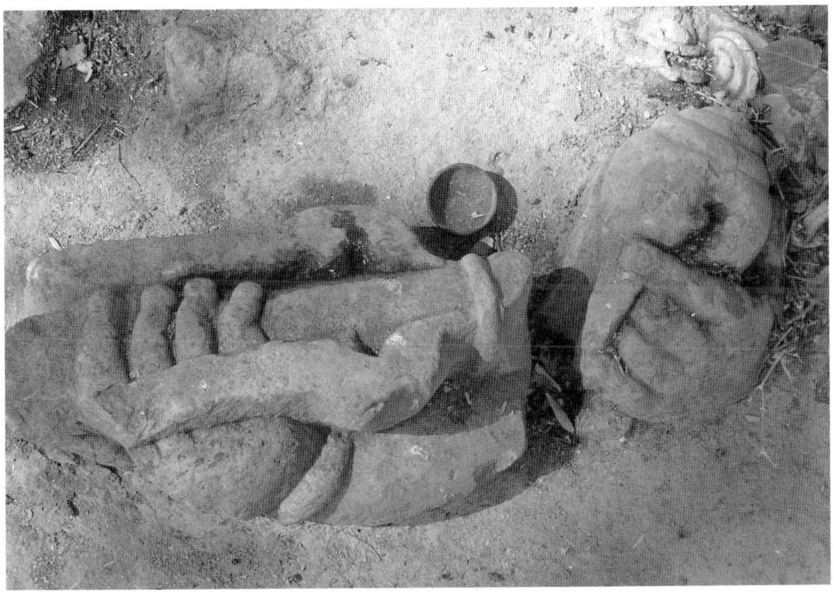

193 Amacchar: Harihara fragment (SG169/I-435)

194 Bawaliya: unfinished Siva image (c. fifth century AD) (SG171/I-153)

195 Bawaliya quarry: unfinished Kubera *yakṣa* (c. fifth century AD) (SG172b/I-687)

196 Bawaliya quarry: unfinished Kubera *yakṣa* – back

197 Amacchar: abacus with lions and dwarfs (1) (c. fifth century AD) (SG169/I-453)

198 Amacchar: abacus with lions and dwarfs (2)

199 Sanchi: Temple 17 lion abacus (c. fifth century AD)

200 Sonapura: abacus with lions at corners (c. fifth century AD) (SG031b/I-247)

201 Pipariya: 'L'-shaped fragment from temple doorway (c. fifth century AD) (SG146/I-666)

202 Vidisha: 'L'-shaped doorway fragment discovered by Cunningham (Williams 1982, pl. 45)

203 Madhupuri: fragment of 'L'-shaped relief (c. fifth century AD) (and c. tenth-century-AD Jain head) SG031b/I-587; I-593)

204 Vidisha: 'L'-shaped fragment discovered by Cunningham (Williams 1982, pl. 46)

205 Ahmadpur: temple doorway (c. fifth century AD) (SG037a/SC131)

206 Tajpur Shur: temple pilaster (c. fifth century AD) (SG064/I-574)

207 Sanchi: Temple 31 – pilasters incorporated from an earlier Gupta (c. fifth century AD) structure

208 Mehgaon: seated *mātṛkā* (c. fifth century AD) (SG134/I-559)

209 Pali: Durga *Mahiṣāsuramardinī* (c. seventh to eighth century AD) (SG100/I-233)

210 Dhakna basti: Durga *Mahiṣāsuramardinī* (c. seventh to eighth century AD) (SG032b/I-130)

211 Devrajpur: Durga *Mahiṣāsuramardinī* (c. seventh to eighth century AD) (SG177c/I-693)

212 Devrajpur: Durga *Camundai* and other sculptural fragments (c. eighth century AD) (SG177b/I-430)

213 Late Durga *Mahiṣāsuramardinī* (c. tenth century AD)

214 Devrajpur: Jain sculptures and temple remains (c. tenth century AD) (SG177/I-428; I-1075)

215 Ahmadpur: Jain sculpture from large temple (c. tenth century AD) (SG037/I-542)

216 Amkhera 2: Visnu and Uma Maheswar (c. tenth century AD) (SG177/I 439; I 438)

217 Sanchi: Kal Bhairav site: c. tenth-century-AD sculptures (SG001/SC12)

218 Ratanpur girdhari: female deity (c. eleventh century AD) (SG038/I-184)

CHAPTER 13

Habitational Settlement Sites

Introduction

A total of 134 settlements were documented at the Site Group level during the survey. When viewed at a Site Cluster level, this figure increases to 161 to account for Site Groups that contain more than one settlement area (Table 13.1; Figure 13.1). Of these Site Clusters, 82 survive as mounds formed from denuded mud structures (Plates 5, 9) and 44 as clusters of sandstone buildings on the lower slopes of hills (Plate 8; Table 13.1; Figure 13.1). Also included in the overall figure are 30 modern villages where, in addition to sculptures or temple fragments, no settlement mounds or evidence for residential buildings were recorded, but may nevertheless overlie earlier remains. There is also a fourth category that I refer to as 'memory site'. These sites are commemorated locally as ancient or 'ancestral' settlements, but in all five cases, no supporting archaeological evidence was identified.[1] As suggested in chapter 8, this belief appears to stem from assumptions regarding the so-called 'archaeological' character of material found in the immediate vicinity of these sites.

As before, this chapter is divided into two parts, with a site gazetteer in Part I and a thematic discussion on spatial and temporal patterns across the habitational landscape in Part II. The site gazetteer is ordered according to settlements' positioning within the major geographical sectors, and smaller sub-sectors therein. Sites are listed by name, with the provision of SG and SC numbers to enable easy cross-referencing with the tables, ordered on SG number, in Appendix I, which also provides additional details on each Site Group's non-habitational elements. Basic details on settlement type, size and topographical setting are given, as well as sculptural and ceramic phasing (with sample numbers), the latter of which relates to more detailed tables in Appendices IIa and III. Settlement distribution over the study area is illustrated in Figure 13.1; while smaller-scale inter-site patterns are illustrated in the sector-by-sector maps in chapter 11.

Site size

Each settlement is graded according to size, following the six-tier structure outlined in Table 13.2 and illustrated in polygon-outline form in Figure 13.2. However, it should be stressed that this framework refers only to the overall situation, rather than to a particular phase in each site's history. Attempts to build a phase-by-phase hierarchical framework on the basis of size alone were avoided, largely because of the inherent shortcomings of this approach as shown by earlier studies. For example, both Erdosy's (1988, 20) and Lal's (1984, 206–9) central hypotheses concerning shifts in population trends at the onset of the early-historic period were based on inferences about site hierarchies calculated according to the relative coverage of pottery scatters at different phases of each site. The major weakness of both studies was that the susceptibility of surface pottery analysis to distortions caused by site-formation and post-depositional processes was not made sufficiently explicit. For example, both lateral displacement and the differential survival rates of different types and periods of artefacts are major factors to be considered when making such inferences (Hodder and Malone 1984). More recent 'village-to-village' surveys in India have avoided the issue of size-based hierarchy altogether, because the question as to whether the size of a single site can be distinguished from one period to another from surface analysis alone has come under serious doubt (Lahiri *et al.*, 1996).

PART I: GAZETTEER

Sector 1a: central agricultural plains

Agricultural plain between Sanchi and Udayagiri
Neemkhera (SG164)
Mound (height: 3 m) c. 8 km WNW of Vidisha on east bank of River Bes (Size level: 6). Partially occupied by modern village. Temple and sculpture remains under worship on village platform

Table 13.1 Settlements documented during the survey

Hillside *basti*	Mound	Modern village with sculptural remains	'Memory site'	Total no. of settlements
44	82	30	5	161

Table 13.2 Settlement size hierarchy

Rank	Area
1	More than 100 ha
2	More than 45 ha
3	More than 30 ha
4	More than 14 ha
5	More than 7 ha
6	Less than 7 ha

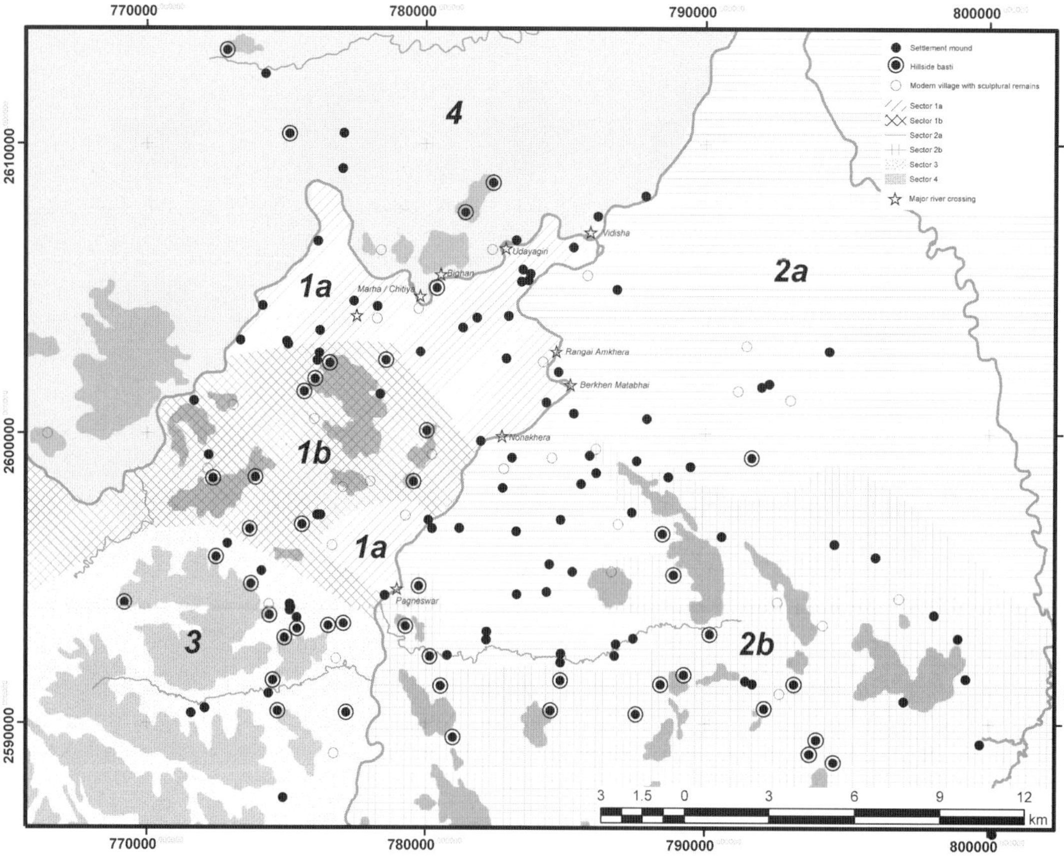

Figure 13.1 Map showing settlement distribution arranged according to type and sector (SC level): Phases Ib–VII

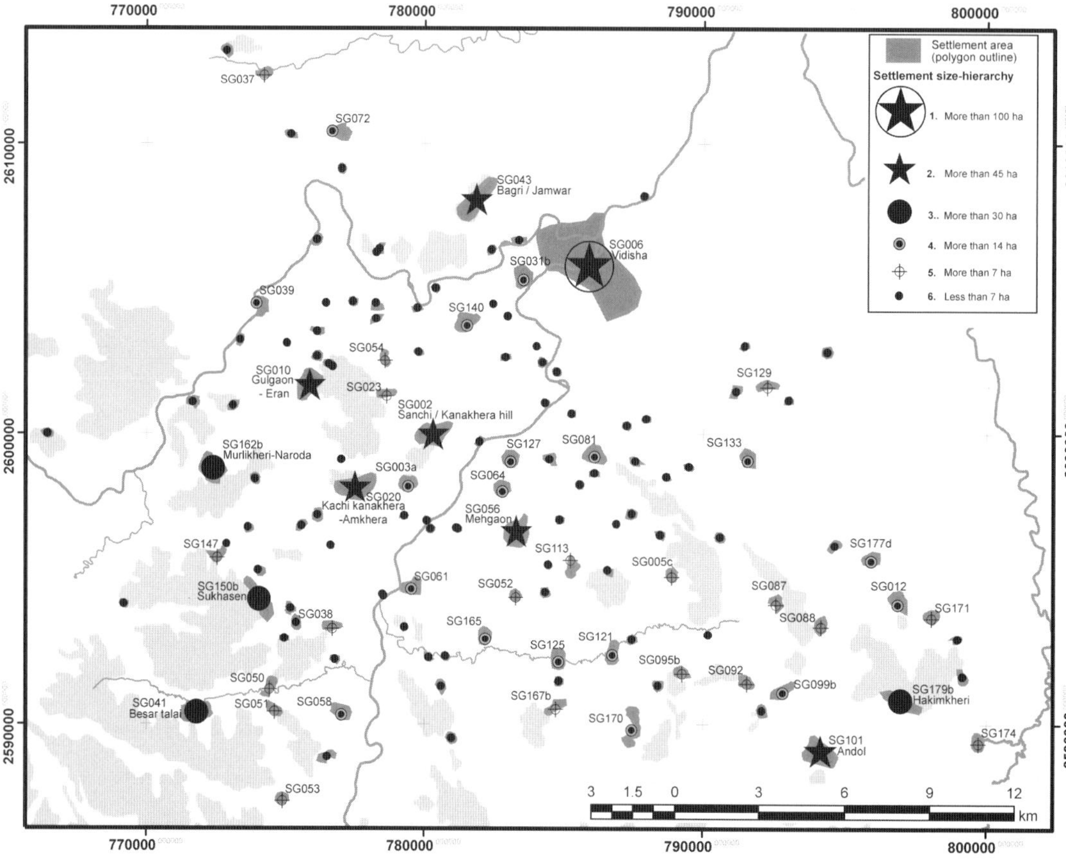

Figure 13.2 Map showing settlements as polygon outlines with corresponding six-tier site hierarchy (SG level)

(Phase VI), with additional *in situ* sculpture at Saiva cult spot to the SW (S308): Phase IV. Pottery phasing: Id-VII (BSM48).

Fatehpur Marmata (SG039)
Mound (height: 3 m; partially ploughed), c. 6 km NE of Satdhara on east bank of River Bes (Size level: 4). Partially occupied by modern village. Large quantities of pottery, and several courses of boundary wall visible in the mound section. Sculptures (probably from Pathar) under worship on village platform: Phase VI. Pottery phasing: Id-IV (SM61a, b). Pottery and sculpture reported in *IAR* 1978–9, 14.

Berkheri (SG055)
Mound (ploughed; height: 2 m) c. 3.5 km NW of Sanchi on west bank of large perennial stream, which runs W-E to join River Bes (Size level: 6). Partially occupied by modern two-house dwelling. Heavily disturbed outlines of two stone structures at the western edge of mound. Sculptures under worship in stone enclosure at eastern edge, beside modern *Bir baba* temple: Phase VI. Natural shrine. Pottery phasing: Id-VI (SM79).

Barkheri/Amapura (SG149): 'memory site'
Modern village, c. 4 km WNW of Udayagiri, on the northern bank of a perennial stream which runs W–E to join the River Bes. An area dominated by a large palm-tree, immediately north of the village, is commemorated as an ancient settlement and sacred site. However, no archaeological remains were found, apart from a few dispersed potsherd scatters. These may have been spread as manure. Natural shrine.

Dhongari (SG105): 'memory site'
Site between Udayagiri and Sonapura Chak commemorated as an ancient settlement. However, no archaeological remains to that effect were found on site. It appears that the site's reputation as an ancient settlement stems largely from the 'big stones' found in the surrounding fields. Natural shrine.

Utari guhar (SG106)
Mound (ploughed; height: 3 m), immediately south of Dhongari, c. 250 m west of River Betwa (Size level: 6). Enclosed on the north and east by perennial streams. Pottery phasing: Ic-IIIb. (BSM18).

Karhaiya (SG109)
Mound between Udayagiri and Sanchi, occupied by modern village (Size level: 6). Sculptures under worship outside modern temple: Phase VII.

Bighan village (SG110)
Modern village on southern bank of River Bes (Size level: 6). Ancient ford leads over to Buddhist site on Bighan hill (SG035). Ancient temple site (SC446) at southern end of village, with associated sculptures under worship: Phases VI-VII.

Marwai (SG140)
Large settlement, partly occupied by modern village, c. 2 km NW of Udayagiri (Size level: 4). Octagonal stepwell in centre of village (Phase VI). Small mound (unploughed; height: 1 m) immediately NE of the village, with surface brick scatters extending into adjoining hills for c. 30 m. Remains of tank (SC263), with 225 m-long embankment (height: 3 m) faced in places. Temple mound (SC259) and associated sculptures in centre of village, with additional sculptures under worship next to tank: Phase VI. Pottery phasing: Id-VII (BSM39a, b).

Marha kherai (SG141)
Mound (ploughed; height: 1–2m) midway between Udayagiri and Sanchi (Size level: 6). Stupa remains (Phase II) on summit of mound and adjoining field. Sculptures (probably from Marwai) under worship beneath *chola* tree c. 75m to the east: Phase VI.

Chitiya (SG142)
Modern village c. 3 km NNW of Udayagiri on the southern bank of the River Bes (Size level: 6). Ancient ford joins site to Marha. Sculptures (probably from Marwai) under worship in modern village: Phase VI.

Dhaniakheri (SG144)
Barren settlement mound (unploughed; height: 3 m) immediately south of modern Dhaniakheri village, 5 km NW of Sanchi (Size level: 6). Southern bank of perennial stream. Remains of tank (SC269), with 260 m-long embankment running E–W. Stone facing visible on northern face at west end of embankment. Ancient temple mound (SC459), now occupied by modern temple, to the north, with associated sculpture under worship: Phase VI. Pottery phasing: Id-IIIb (BSM37).

Sukha/Umakhera (SG145)
Mound (ploughed; height 2 m) dominated by large *Barghat* tree, and marked by 418 m spot-height on Survey of India map (Size level: 6). Situated immediately NW of modern Sukha village, c. 4 km west of Udayagiri, on north bank of perennial *nāla*, which flows W–E to meet the River Bes. Pottery phasing: Id-VII (BSM38).

Nonakhera (SG018)
Mound (height: 2 m), c. 1.5 km NE of Sanchi on the western bank of River Betwa (Size level: 6). Occupied by modern village. Sculpture under worship on village platform: Phases II-VI, with Phase II sculpture from Sanchi.

Parariya (SG154)
Mound (ploughed: height: 1.75 m) immediately north of modern Parariya village, on western bank of River Betwa (Size level: 6). Sculpture under worship outside modern Hanuman temple: Phase V. Natural shrine. Pottery phasing: Id-VII (BSM42).

Udayagiri/Madhupuri/Sonapura (SG031b)
Extensive settlement area consisting of four separate mounds between modern villages of Udayagiri, Madhupuri and Sonapura (Size level: 4). Pottery scatters extend up to Besnagar ramparts implying that this area was part of Vidisha's suburban sprawl. Pottery phasing: Ic-VII (BSM15, 16, 17).

i) Udayagiri (SC112)
Mound (ploughed, height: 4 m) at southern base of Udayagiri hill, on eastern bank of village tank (SC113). Pottery scatters extend into fields in south, merging with settlement remains at Sonapura basti, and eventually with the main mounds of Besnagar proper.

ii) Sonapura basti (SC221)
Mound (heavily ploughed; height 1 m) in the fields to the east of Udayagiri, spread over either side of the track to Madhupuri.

Ancient temple on northern bank of River Betwa (SC220), Phases IV-VI, with additional sculptures under worship on central village platform: Phases II-VI.

iii) Madhupuri (SC222)
Mound (unploughed; height: 4 m) occupied by modern village. Medieval *bauri* to NW of village. Sculpture stored on village platform: Phases IV-VI. Natural shrine.

iv) Madhupuri kherai (SC223)
Mound (ploughed: height: 2 m) immediately east of Madhupuri, on the north side of Besnagar–Madhupuri road.

Vidisha area

Vidisha (SG006)
Large city site (Size level: 1) extending from the ancient mounds and rampart at Besnagar in the north to the 'modern' town of Vidisha in the south.

i) Besnagar (SC45)
Ancient city mounds, situated within fork of Rivers Bes and Betwa. Temples, stupas and sculpture fragments at various locations: Phases II-VII. The best known is the Heliodorus pillar site to the NE of the main city mounds (SC44): Phases Id-IV. Pottery phasing: Ib-V (BSM6). References: Bhandarkar 1914; 1915; Khare 1969; *IAR* 1963–4, 17; 1964–5, 19–20.

ii) Vidisha (SC52)
Modern town with ancient sculptures stored at various locations: Phases II-VII. Ancient temple remains and sculptures on Lohangi hill (SC53): Phases II-VI.

iii) Bes tila (SC321)
Mound (ploughed; height: 2.60 m) between Heliodorus pillar site and Amacchar (SG169). Remains of dried-up village tank (SC322) immediately east of mound, consisting of ploughed-over mound running E–W (length: 80 m; height: 2 m). Sculptures under worship beneath *palah* tree on summit of mound: Phase V.

Rangai Amkhera (SG017)
Mound (ploughed; height: 3 m) opposite modern Rangai village, on eastern bank of River Betwa, south of Vidisha (Size level: 6). Occupied by single farmhouse. Excavations carried out in the 1970s revealed a three-phase sequence consisting of two pre-pottery, microlithic levels, overlain by a chalcolithic level. The earliest chalcolithic occupation was dated to c.1900–1800 BC on the basis of the similarity of the ware to Kayatha II, continuing to beginning of first millennium BC (contemporary with PGW). Ancient temple, with sculpture, outside modern Rangai village (SG017b): Phase VI. Pottery phasing: Ib-c (SM22). Other finds: microliths. References: Khare 1980, 55–7; IAR 1976–77, 33–4.

Bari (SG155): 'memory site'
So-called ancient settlement situated c. 1 km to the east of Rangai village. The villagers of Rangai regard it as their ancestral village and have hence marked it out as a sacred site. However, no archaeological remains were found, despite villagers' claims that many potsherds and hewn stone slabs are found in the surrounding fields. Natural shrine.

Amacchar (SG169)
Large settlement mound (height: 4 m) immediately north of Vidisha, on west bank of River Betwa (Size level: 6). Partially occupied by modern village, but with several ploughed fields at northern edge of mound. The *ghat* and platform with the seven seated mothers (SG006/SC653), described by Lake (1910a), is situated around 1 km further to the south along the river. Ancient temple remains and associated sculpture under worship at the western edge of the village (SC463) and on the main village platform overlooking the river: Phases IV-VI. Pottery phasing: Id-VII (BSM47b).

South of Sanchi

Piparia village (SG014)
Mound (height: 1 m), c. 2 km SE of Sanchi, on western bank of River Betwa (Size level: 6). Occupied by modern village. Sculpture under worship on village platform: Phase VI. Other finds: iron slag, stone tools.

Chapna (SG030)
Modern village, c. 3.5 km south of Sanchi (Size level: 6). According to local tradition, the inhabitants moved here from the ancient settlement at Dhakna. Other finds: 'lower palaeolithic tools' reported in *IAR* 1978–9, 13.

Berkheri ghat kherai (SG156)
Small mound (ploughed; height: 2.75 m), c. 3.5 km SSW of Sanchi, on the western bank of the River Betwa, just above crossing to Pagneswar (Size level: 6). Occupied by single farmhouse. Sculptures (probably from Pagneswar) under worship beneath *imli* tree at western edge of mound: Phase VI. Pottery phasing: Id-VII (BSM43).

Sector 1b: hilly region around Sanchi and western sector

Sanchi-Kanakhera (SG002)
Lower, northern plateau of Sanchi hill (Size level: 2). Cunningham (1854, 117) noted remains of 'large town' on the lower saddle of the hill between the two modern villages of Kanakhera and Sanchi. Kanakhera well-inscription attests to ongoing occupation in the fourth century AD (Marshall 1940, 392). Large rectangular tank at the eastern base of the hill (SC15), and another further to the north (SC16). A third tank (70 x 90 x 20 cm) in the middle of Sanchi village split into two by a large embankment, faced on both sides by dressed stone slabs (SC18). Temple remains (SC19) and sculpture piles (S363, S877): Phases II-VII. Other finds: painted rock-shelters, microliths.

Nagauri (SG003a)
Low hill c. 350 m south of Sanchi (Size level: 4). Modern village on lower slopes of hill, with ancient quarry remains on summit. Finished and unfinished sculpture stored at various locations: Phases II-VI. Pottery phasing: Id-VII (SM11, 19a, 18, 20). Other finds: rock-shelters with prehistoric and historical paintings, 'monastic rock-shelter', microliths.

Kachi kanakhera/Amkhera (SG020)
Large settlement area comprising the modern villages of Kachi kanakhera and Amkhera (SC444) spread over the hill, c. 1 km west of Nagauri hill (Size level: 2).

i) Kachi kanakhera (SC86)
Modern village situated on eastern side of hill. Assumed to overlie ancient settlement, given sculptural remains and its important location at the western end of the embankment

which runs from Nagauri hill. Mainly unploughed, apart from small field midway up hill. Sculptures under worship on village platform: Phases VI-VII. Natural shrine.

ii) Amkhera (SC87)
Modern village on eastern side of hill. According to villagers, large amounts of red and black pottery are found when digging house foundations. Large village tank (SC444), and two ancient wells (S88, S542) on eastern side of the Sanchi–Raisen road. Sculptures under worship on village platform, Phases VI-VII. Other finds: stone tools.

Bilori 1 (SG009)
Modern village on small hillock, c. 2 km south of Sanchi (Size level: 6). Sculptures (some from Sanchi) under worship outside modern temple: Phases IIIa-VI.

Hills to west of Sanchi
Dargawan (SG023)
Low mound (unploughed; height: 0.5m), on lower eastern side of Dargawan hill, c. 2 km NW of Sanchi (Size level: 5). Partially occupied by single farmhouse. Covered with outlines of around 25 stone structures. Much of the stone has been removed. Walled village tank (SC439) to east of settlement. Early date suggested by proximity to dam at western base of Dargawan hill (SG028b). Sculpture under worship on platform in middle of mound: Phase VII. Natural shrine. Pottery phasing: Id-IIIa (SM40a). Brief reference to sculpture in *IAR* 1978–9:14.

Karondih (SG029c): 'memory site'
Narrow valley to south of long hill immediately opposite Sanchi. Enormous *banyan* tree with modern *djinn* shrine in the middle of agricultural fields, immediately NW of the ancient dam (SG029b). The suffix *dih* (= mound) in the name Karondih is used locally to refer to ancient settlement mounds. No such remains have been found in the immediate vicinity, apart from the nearby settlement remains at Gulgaon. It is possible that the tree, which could be as much as 1,000 years old, has been linked to a settlement for which there is no archaeological evidence. Buddhist remains on hill above (SG029). Natural shrine.

Gulgaon-Eran (SG010)
Large settlement complex on lower slopes of large hill-range, c. 3 km NW of Sanchi (Size level: 2). Consists of two main habitational areas extending south to north between the modern villages of Gulgaon and Eran, and connected by an ancient route (SC94).

i) Gulgaon kherai (SC63)
Remains of around 70 ancient stone structures on western bank of irrigation embankment (SG010b) at northern end of modern village. A large boundary wall, with a rubble-core and dressed facing, runs across the site from east to west (surviving length: 49.6 m; width: 1 m). Sculpture, mostly from dam area, is stored at modern shrine and in the Sanchi Archaeological Museum: Phases II-VI. Pottery phasing: Id-VII (sample: SM29).

ii) Eran 1 (SC91)
Large modern village at lower eastern base of hill. Further up hill are remains of around 20 ancient structures. Sculpture stored outside two temple ruins (SC93, SC378), and at various points in village: Phases IV-VI. Brief reference to sculpture in *IAR* 1978–9, 14.

Eran 2 (SG010c)
Ancient settlement immediately north of Gulgaon-Eran (Size level: 6). The main mound (ploughed, height: 1m) is on the southern bank of unwalled tank (SC96), with a smaller mound on the northern side. Natural shrine. Pottery phasing: IV-VII (SM48).

Kanchanpura (SG143b)
Hillside settlement, consisting of about 30 structural outlines, on lower, northern slopes of hill, c. 3.5 km NW of Sanchi (Size level: 6). Overlooks modern village below, with Buddhist remains on hill above (SG143).

Baheriya (SG024)
Large settlement mound (unploughed; height: 1.5 m), now eroded into two separate mounds (Plate 9), c. 2 km NW of Eran (Size level: 6). Several outlines of stone structures on the top of both mounds. Pottery phasing: Id-VII (SM44a, b).

Ucher (SG054)
Modern village situated on eastern lower slopes of hill and extending into ploughed fields below, c. 3 km NNW of Sanchi (Size level: 5). Possible temple remains situated at edge of dried-up village tank (SC171), to the north of modern village. Associated sculptures under worship on four separate platforms in the village (S618-S621): Phase VI. Pottery phasing: Id-VII (SM78).

Dhakna basti (SG032b)
Low barren mound (unploughed; height: 1 m) at the NE base of hill (easternmost in a line of three hillocks on the Sanchi–Raisen road), c. 2.25 km SW of Sanchi (Size level: 6). Remains of about 20 structural outlines. Pottery scatters extend for c. 200 m into ploughed fields on eastern side of road, where there is an ancient well (S115). Sculpture under worship on platform in middle of mound: Phases IV-V. Pottery phasing: Ic-IIIb (SM51; SM53).

Dhakna village (SG032)
Modern village situated on southern slopes of hill (westernmost in line of three hillocks on the Sanchi–Raisen road), south of Sanchi (Size level: 6). Overlooks ancient embankment (SG032d) to the south. Sculpture under worship on central village platform, and at ancient temple site (SC468), Phase II-VI.

Rajatalai (SG067)
Hillside settlement on lower, SE slope of large hill, c. 2.5 km SW of Gulgaon (Size level: 6). Approximately 30 heavily damaged structural outlines. Large dried-up tank (SC415), with no sign of stone facing, at base of hill. Sculptures under worship on platform to NE of tank: Phase VII. An early *yakṣa* sculpture, mentioned by B.N. Misra (1982, 295), apparently stands somewhere in this vicinity, visible from the train which passes by around 600m to the south (*ibid*., pers. comm.). Having explored the entire valley between Salamatpur and Sanchi, there was no sign (or local knowledge) of this. Pottery phasing: IV-VII (SM80).

Further west, up to Satdhara
Ferozpur (SG011b)
Modern village situated on lower SE slopes of hill, c. 5 km west of Sanchi (Size level: 6). Buddhist site on summit of same hill (SG011c), and ancient reservoir remains to the SW (SG011). Sculpture stored around ancient temple remains (SC377), Phase IV-VII. Pottery phasing: Id/II-VII (SM32a; SM32b; SM33).

Naroda-Murlikheri (SG162b)
Large settlement situated in narrow valley c. 1 km south of Buddhist hilltop site at Satdhara (Size level: 3). Comprises modern villages of Murlikheri in the west and Naroda in the east.

i) Murlikheri basti (SC298)
Mound (ploughed; height: 1 m) on eastern edge of modern village, next to perennial stream. Buddhist monastery situated on upper slopes of adjoining hill (SG162). Sculptures under worship on platform at western edge of modern village, and at cult spot (S299) to the east on the bank of a perennial stream: Phases IIIb-VII. Pottery phasing: Id-IIIb (BSM44).
ii) Naroda
Hillside settlement on lower slopes of hill to south of modern Naroda village. Approximately 20 structural outlines. Ancient dried-up tank (SC303) (c. 150 x 150 m) at easternmost edge of settlement. Faced embankments (height: 2 m) on west and north side, the southern side being held up by the large hill, and the eastern side by a rocky outcrop which bears Buddhist remains (SG162d). Jain temple site (SC304) and associated sculptures under worship by tank, and Brahmanical temple (SC566) and sculpture remains on and around modern village platform: Phases IV-VI.

Sehor (SG021)
Mound (ploughed; height: 1m) at northern base of Satdhara hill, on eastern bank of River Bes (Size level: 6). Partially occupied by single house. Sculpture under worship outside modern shrine: Phases II (from Satdhara)-VII. Pottery phasing: Ic-VII (SM34a, b). Other finds: stone tools.

Chirauli (SG033)
Mound (height: 2 m), c. 3 km NE of Satdhara (Size level: 6), on east bank of River Bes. Partially occupied by modern village, with ploughed fields on northern edge of mound. Sculptures under worship on village platform: Phase VI.

Anori (SG065)
Modern village situated on slightly raised ground at the junction of two perennial streams, c. 4.5 km NW of Sanchi (Size level: 6). Ancient *bauri* (SG065b) with well-built stone masonry facing, situated at some distance to the SW.

Sayargaon (SG042)
Modern village situated on lower eastern slopes of hill, c. 3 km west of Satdhara, on the northern bank of the River Bes (Size level: 6). Sculptures (possibly from Pachmarhi) under worship in rock-shelter above (SG042b): Phase VI.

Sector 2a: agricultural plains to the east of the River Betwa

Mehgaon (SG056)
Large mound (height: 2 m), c. 3 km east of Sanchi (Size level: 2). Partially occupied by modern village, with several ploughed fields on the eastern side of village. Remains of large, dried-up village tank (SC390) to the NW, enclosed on the west and south side by large, stone-faced embankments (surviving height: 1.90 m). Ancient temple mound (SC368) in centre of village, with associated sculptures under worship on main village platform (S625). Some of these sculptures also came from the ancient tank; others supposedly from Kherai khera (SG052), with which Mehgaon is considered to have ancestral links: Phases IIIa-VI. Pottery phasing: Id/II-IIIb (BSM21). Brief reference to sculpture in *IAR* 1978–9, 14.

Kherai khera (SG052)
Mound (heavily ploughed; height: 0.70 m), c. 1.5 km south of Mehgaon (Size level: 5). Considered to be the 'ancestral village' of Mehgaon (SG056). Many of the sculptures stored in Mehgaon are thought to come from here. Sculptures under worship beneath *imli* tree at southern edge of mound: Phase VII. Pottery phasing: Id/II-VII (SM75). Natural shrine.

Dhobakheri (SG062)
Mound (height: 1 m) east of Sanchi (Size level: 2). Occupied by modern village. Sculptures under worship on main village platform: Phases V-VII.

Dhaniakheri (SG063)
Mound (height: c. 0.70 m) east of Sanchi (Size level: 6). Occupied by modern village. Sculptures under worship on platform at southern entrance to village (possibly from temple site at Tajpura Shur): Phase VI.

Tajpura Shur (SG064)
Mound (unploughed; height: 2.5 m), c. 2.25 km east of Sanchi (Size level: 4). Partially occupied by modern village, but extending for about 1 km to the east and SE. Ancient, dried-up tank (SC405), around 200 m SE of main settlement mound. No evidence of stone facing. Ancient temple site and associated sculptures (SC406) on eastern bank of tank, with additional sculptures on village platform (S513) and at isolated site in middle of field (S407): Phases II-VI. Pottery phasing: Id-VII (BSM30).

Jhirniya (SG180)
Modern village c. 750 m SW of Murwara and c. 3 km east of Mehgaon (Size level: 6). Sculptures (possibly from Alamkhera) under worship on village platform: Phase VII.

Suakhera (SG181)
Mound (height: 4.50 m), c. 3 km south of Vidisha (Size level: 6). Partially occupied by modern village. Natural shrine.

Daulatpur (SG112)
Low mound (unploughed; height: 1 m) between Mehgaon and Alamkhera (Size level: 6). Considered to have ancestral links with Mehgaon, to which the land belongs. Dried-up *bauri* (S232) in middle of site. Natural shrine.

Alamkhera (SG113)
Large mound (ploughed; height: 2 m), c. 5.5 km east of Sanchi (Size level: 5). Surmounted by small temple mound and sculptures (SC234), with a second temple site (SC235) c. 750 m to the north: Phases IV-VII. Natural shrine. Pottery phasing: Id-VII (BSM22).

Bhauliya kherai (SG114)
Mound (ploughed; height: 2 m) immediately south of Alamkhera, on the west bank of perennial stream (Size level: 6). Temple mound (SC448), c. 185 m to the east, with associated sculptures under worship: Phase VII. Pottery phasing: Id-II (BSM26).

Bhaijakhera (SG115)
Mound (height: 2 m) between Meghaon and Jhirniya (Size level: 6). Occupied by single house. Sculptures (possibly from Alamkhera) under worship by *imli* tree on eastern edge of settlement: Phase VII.

Sankheri (SG120)
Modern village situated on slightly raised ground, c. 3 km NW of Morel khurd (Size level: 6). Ancient well (S426) lined with brick-sized stone facing, situated in ploughed fields c. 250 m to west of village.

Chopra (SG126)
Small modern village situated on slightly raised ground amidst low-grade agricultural land, c. 2 km west of Sonthiya (Size level: 6). According to locals, pottery is found when digging house foundations. Ancient well (S433), with sculptures (probably from Tajpur Shur), situated in the fields, c. 300 m east of village: Phase VI.

Chirohli kherai (SG127)
Mound (ploughed; height: 1.50 m), immediately north of modern Chirohli village, c. 2.5 km east of Sanchi (Size level: 4). Sculptures stored on platform under *imli* and *bargat* trees, at northern edge of mound. More sculpture stored at modern temple in Chirohli village: Phases V-VI. Pottery phasing: Id-IIIb (BSM31).

Pagneswar (SG061)
Modern village covering most of hillock, c. 4 km south of Sanchi, above major crossing over the River Betwa (Size level: 4). Three ancient temple sites (SC400, SC507, SC697), with associated sculptures under worship, and additional sculptures lying half-submerged in centre of village: Phases IIIb-VII.

Dabar nāla (southern, eastern plains)
Girbhar (SG165)
Large settlement area comprising mounds on both sides of the Dabar *nāla*, c. 5 km south of Sanchi (Size level: 4). The northern mound (SC309) (height: 1 m) is occupied by modern village; the southern mound (SC310) (height: 4 m) is partially occupied by a temporary settlement. Phase IV temple foundations (SC165) on its summit with associated sculptures under worship: Phase VI. Pottery phasing: Ic-IV (BSM45)

Mungawali kherai (SG166)
Low rocky outcropping in the agricultural plain south of Dabar *nāla*, c. 4 km NW of Morel khurd. Tributary of Dabar *nāla* runs through site (Size level: 6). Heavily disturbed structural outlines, on slightly raised, unploughed ground to the west of modern Mungawali village. Temple remains and sculptures under worship on village platform: Phase VI.

Mahuakhera/Himatgarh (SG121)
Two large mounds (height: 3-4 m) occupied by modern villages on either side of the Dabar *nāla*, c. 3 km west of Morel khurd (Size level: 4). Evidently originally one large settlement. At Mahuakhera on the south bank of the stream, pottery is visible all the way down to the top of the *nāla* bank, with pottery scatters continuing for c. 1 km in the fields to the south. Temple mound, with associated sculptures by *imli* tree to the south of Mahuakhera, with additional sculptures under worship on platform in Himatgarh: Phases VI-VII. Pottery phasing: Ic-VII (BSM28).

Devalkhera (SG123)
Mound (height: 4 m), c. 2.5 km west of Morel khurd, on north bank of Dabar *nāla* (Size level: 6). Partially occupied by modern village. Pottery visible in section formed by *nāla*, to depth of 3 m. Temple and sculptural remains stored under *imli* tree on main village platform: Phases IV-VI (with additional Phase II fragments, probably from Morel khurd). Pottery phasing: Id/II-IIIb (BSM29).

Parwariya/Arwariya (SG125)
Two mounds (height: 3 m) on either side of the Dabar *nāla*, c. 5 km west of Morel khurd (Size level: 4). Occupied by modern villages, and evidently originally one large settlement. Sculpture (possibly from Mungawali) lying half-submerged in ground in middle of Arwariya village on southern bank: Phase VI.

Agricultural plains SE of Vidisha (to NW of hills)
Chiroriya village (SG128)
Modern village, c. 4 km SE of Vidisha (Size level: 6). Ancient temple remains, and associated sculptures under worship: Phase VI.

Chiroriya kherai (SG129)
Mound (height: 2.5 m) to the east of modern Chiroriya village, c. 4 km SE of Vidisha (Size level: 5). Now ploughed down into two separate mounds, the second, lower one situated c. 150 m further east. Various structural outlines on barren ground towards summit of mound. Small temple mound c. 150 m east to the east, with associated sculptures under worship: Phase VI. Pottery phasing: Id-VII (BSM32).

Bhauriya (SG130)
Modern village, c. 1.5 km east of Chiroriya (Size level: 6). Small temple mound at the southern edge of the village, with associated sculptures under worship: Phase VI.

Karaiya khera (SG131)
Modern village, c. 4.5 km SE of Vidisha (Size level: 6). Sculptures (possibly from Chiroriya kherai) under worship on village platform: Phase VI.

Madankheri/Dharukheri (SG132b)
Mound (ploughed; height: 2 m), c. 500 m west of modern Madankheri village and c. 7 km SE of Vidisha (Size level: 6). Temple remains (SG132) situated beneath large *imli* tree, between here and Karaiya kherai, with associated sculptures under worship: Phase VII. Pottery phasing: Id-VII (BSM33).

Parsora haveli (SG133)
Modern village situated on lower slopes of solitary hillock, c. 5 km SE of Vidisha (Size level: 4). Ancient well in field to south of village. Modern Hanuman temple on summit of hill, overlying ancient temple site (SC251). Associated sculptures under worship on platform SE of village: Phases V-VI. Natural shrine.

Gehunkheri/Bhairav (SG134)
Mound (ploughed; height: 1.5 m), c. 500 m north of Gehunkheri village and c. 3 km south of Vidisha (Size level: 6). Occupied by single farmhouse. Temple remains with associated sculptures under worship: Phases IIIb-VI. Pottery phasing: IIIa-b (BSM35).

Dhuladev (SG138)
Naturally raised (ploughed) ground (440 m contour shown on map) between Sonthiya and Gehunkheri, c. 3.5 km south of Vidisha. Dominated by large *bargat* tree (indicated on toposheet). The locals insist that this is an ancient settlement, probably because of the raised ground and tree. However, neither pottery nor structural remains were found on site. Natural shrine.

Low-grade agricultural land to the east of hills
Pathari kapasia (SG083)
Mound (partially ploughed; height: 4 m) c. 800 m NW of Pathari village, east of the long line of hills between Sonthiya and Morel khurd (Size level: 6). Pottery phasing: Id-VII (BSM3).

Pathari kativarat (SG084)
Mound (height: 2 m) formed from accumulated stone structures, at base of second in line of hills between Sonthiya and Morel khurd (Size level: 6). Immediately below small dam (SG084c). Several heavily disturbed structural remains on the summit. Small ploughed area at the lower edges of mound. Small temple mound situated immediately below the hill. The sculptural remains from here are now stored in nearby rock-shelter (SG084b): Phase VI. Pottery phasing: Id-VII (BSM4).

Pathari/Gehunkheri (SG084d)
Mound formed from stone structures, at base of hill, less than 1 km west of Pathari Kativarat (Size level: 6). Pottery scatters extend for c. 225 m into ploughed fields to north. Sculpture under worship on two separate platforms: Phase VI.
Pottery phasing: Id-VII (BSM34).

Dhanora kherai (SG085)
Mound (height: 7 m), covered with heavily disturbed structural outlines, c. 500 m SW of modern Dhanora village, amidst low-grade agricultural land east of Morel khurd (Size level: 6). Positioned on the bank of a small stream which flows from NE to SW. Small ploughed section at NE edge of mound. Pottery phasing: Id-IIIb (BSM5).

Sector 2b: hills in the east

First line of hills
Umariya kherai (SG139)
Mound (ploughed; height: 3 m) SW of modern Umariya village, and c.1 km south of Sonthiya (Size level: 6). Situated on the western bank of the Kariya *nāla*, a perennial stream which runs south–north from Morel khurd to join the Betwa immediately east of Sanchi. Pottery phasing: Id-II (sample: BSM36).

Sonthiya-Shiampur basti (SG081)
Mound (unploughed; height: 1 m), formed from accumulated stone structures, on stony waste-land c. 300 m south of modern Sonthiya village (Size level: 4). Structural outlines visible on the summit. Dried-up village tank (SC181) with faced embankments, situated between mound and modern Sonthiya village. Pottery phasing: Id-II (BSM1).

Sonthiya kherai 2 (SG082)
Mound (ploughed; height: 3 m), c. 700 m south of Sonthiya-Shiampur basti (Size level: 6). Positioned on eastern bank of Kariya *nāla*, a large perennial stream which acts as the demarcation for the boundary between districts Vidisha (NE) and Raisen (SW). Pottery phasing: Ic-VII (BSM2).

Murwara village (SG118b)
Mound (height: 2 m) at base of large hill, south of Morel khurd (Size level: 6). Partially occupied by modern village. Section formed by modern road at SE edge of village, where mound has been ploughed down to height of c. 1 m, reveals pottery all the way down to the base. Phase IV stepwell (S424) at eastern edge of village. High temple mound (SC449) to the west of the settlement, with associated sculptures under worship: Phase VII. Natural shrine. Pottery phasing: Id-VII (BSM23; BSM24).

Bishankhera (SG117)
Hillside settlement on low outcropping at western base of hill on opposite side of Pathari Kativarat (Size level: 6). Numerous structural outlines visible on summit. Site surrounded by boundary wall. Natural shrine. Pottery phasing: II-VII (BSM25).

Binjoli kherai (SG005c)
Hillside settlement on low rocky outcropping c. 1.5 km NW of Morel khurd (Size level: 5). Remains of large interconnected building complex consisting of approximately 17 structures. Line of three high monoliths (height: c. 6 m) in the centre of the settlement. Terminal date of c. second century BC suggested by irrigation embankment linking the outcropping with Morel khurd. Sculptures stored in middle of settlement (possibly taken from Morel khurd): Phases IV-VI.

Pipalia kherai (SG005b)
Barren mound (unploughed; height: 4 m) on the southern bank of Dabar *nāla*, c. 500 m south of Morel khurd (Size level: 6). Pottery scatters extend into surrounding ploughed fields. Sculptures under worship on main platform (one of which is possibly from Morel khurd): Phases II-V. Pottery phasing: Id/II-VII (BSM10).

Second line of hills
Morel khurd village (SG087)
Modern village situated on the lower western slopes of rocky scrubland c. 1.5 km east of Morel khurd (Size level: 5). Sculpture (probably from temple at Morel khurd: SG005/SC031) under worship in modern temple: Phase VII.

Kanpohra village (SG088)
Modern village situated on side of hill behind Morel khurd village (Size level: 5). Surrounded by extensive quarry (SG088b) which is thought to have been the source for the Phase II railings at the Heliodorus pillar site in Vidisha (Bhandarkar 1913–14, 192). Sculpture from temple mound (SC191) under worship in stone enclosure at stone quarry: Phase VII.

Morel kala (SG099b)
Hillside settlement on northern slopes of hill, overlooking modern Morel kala village, c. 2.5 km SE of Morel khurd (Size level: 4). Numerous structural outlines, surrounded by large boundary wall (80 x 150 m). Ancient dam in valley below (SG099). Jain and Brahmanical temple sites (SC371; SC687) with associated sculptures in worship, and another sculpture stored on the dam itself: Phases IIIb-VI.

Pali (SG100)
Modern village situated on NW slopes of hill (Size level: 6), c. 500 m SW of Morel kala, to which it is joined by ancient dam (SG099). Sculpture under worship in modern temple at eastern base of hill and rock-shelter shrine (SC213): Phases V-VI.

Third line of hills (Andher and further east)
Bawaliya (SG171)
Large mound (height: 3 m), c. 1 km NW of Andher (Size level: 5). Partially occupied by modern village, with ploughed fields at western edges. Dried-up ancient tank (SC332) (90 x 90 m) with three unfaced embankments (height: 2 m), situated between village and hill to west. Phase IV stepwell (S333) at SW corner of tank. Sculptures under worship here, and on central village platform (Phases IV-VI). Additional sculpture at quarry site (SG172b) to the north (Phase IV), and below Andher hill (SG013b) (Phase IIIb-VI). Pottery phasing: II-VII (BSM50).

Bamnor (SG173)
Mound (height: 3 m), situated at eastern base of hill which forms centre of line of three hills, c. 1.75 east of Andher (Size level: 6). Partially occupied by modern village, with ploughed fields at eastern edges. Overlooks ancient tank (SC338), with embankments (standing height: 1 m), constructed from unhewn boulders. Sculptures under worship beneath *pipal* tree at northern edge of village, in modern temple to west of village, and at additional cult spot in fields to east: Phases IV-VI. Pottery phasing: Id-II (BSM52).

Karhaud (SG012)
Modern village situated on SE slope of hill, c. 1.5 km north of Andher (Size level: 4). Circular village tank (SC71), with loose stone facing, at southern foot of hill. Two ancient temple complexes (SC72, SC519) and rock-shelter shrine (SC69) with sculpture under worship: Phases IV-VI.

Devrajpur (SG177)
Large modern village, c. 3 km NW of Andher (Size level: 6). Occupied by modern village. Ancient dam to the south (SG177b). Jain temple remains and associated sculpture at western edge of village (Phase VI), with additional Brahmanical temples on the summit of the dam itself (Phases V-VI).

Devrajpur kherai (SG177d)
Mound (ploughed; height: 1.5 m) to the east of modern Devrajpur village (Size level: 4). Situated at base of hill, with Buddhist remains on its summit (SG177c), and to SE of ancient dam (SG177b). Dried-up *bauri* (S376) on SW edge of mound, next to sculptures under worship beneath *kakra* tree: Phases IV-VI. Pottery phasing: Id-IIIb (BSM55).

Semra kherai (SG178)
Mound (recently ploughed; height: 1 m) at northern base of hill (northernmost in line of three hills), immediately east of Andher (Size level: 6). Overlooks dried-up, circular tank (diameter: 105 m) (SC353). Stone facing of embankments (height: 1m) still visible in places. Sculptures under worship beneath *neem* tree next to tank: Phase VI.

Hakimkheri (SG179b)
Mound (height: 3 m), at southern base of hill (southernmost in a line of three hills) immediately east of Andher (Size level: 3). Partially occupied by modern village. Three dried-up tanks in SE (SC356), west (SC368) and centre (SC593) of village. Temple remains and associated sculptures under worship beneath *mahua* tree, next to first tank. More temple ruins to north of village (SC360): Phases VI-VII.

Hills to the south
Nihalpur/Dandoli kherai (SG092)
Large settlement area (Size level: 5) below Buddhist remains on Mawasa hill(SG090). Includes mound (height: 1 m), occupied by Nihalpur village (SC198), and a second barren mound (Dandoli kherai: SC201) to the east. The latter is encircled on all sides by a perennial stream, which has created a deep section (5–6 m) on north side of mound. Walls of stone structures are visible at a depth of 3.5 m, overlying pottery deposits. Pottery continues up to 2 m above water level, where natural black-cotton soil is reached. Medieval, stone-lined *bauri* (S202) in fields 100 m to north of Dandoli kherai. Temple mound (SC199) to the south of Nihalpur, next to dried-up village tank. Associated sculptures under worship outside modern temple in village: Phases V-VI. Pottery phasing: Id-VII (BSM12, BSM13).

Chandna/Gorpur kherai (SG095a)
Hillside settlement on NE slope of hillock, c. 2.5 km south of Morel khurd, and immediately SW of Chandna village (Size level: 6). Remains of about 20 heavily disturbed stone structures. Ancient reservoir below (SG095c). Ancient temple remains (SC696), and sculptures under worship on ancient dam: Phases II-VI.

Chandna hill (SG095b)
Hillside settlement on upper slopes of hillock, c. 500 m NE of Chandna/Gorpur kherai and overlooking modern Chandna village below (Size level: 5). Various structural outlines. Buddhist remains on summit of hill (SG095d). Sculptures (possibly from temple site on Chandna dam) (SG095c/SC696) under worship in modern shrine at centre of villages: Phase V-VI.

Salera (SG170)
Modern village on lower western slopes of hill, c. 4 km SW of Morel khurd (Size level: 4). Buddhist remains on summit of hill (SG170b). Ancient dried-up tank (SC325), with three ploughed down embankments, at the western base of the two hills. Ancient temple remains and associated sculpture stored on two village platforms outside modern Hanuman temple on western slopes of northern hill (SC575) and in modern Siva temple on lower slopes of southern hill: Phases IIIb-VII.

Kotra hill north (SG167b)
Hillside settlement on lower eastern slopes of hill, c. 3.5 km west of Salera and north of modern Kotra village (Size level: 4). Numerous structural outlines. Buddhist remains on summit (SG167). Dried-up tank (SC314) (110 x 340 m), with three stone-faced embankments, immediately below settlement. Ancient temple remains in middle of settlement (SC313), with associated sculptures under worship on platform beneath *pipal* tree at temple site. Additional Brahmanical sculptures under worship at modern temple amidst Buddhist complex on southern hilltop (SG167/SC320): Phase VI.

Gyasabad/Dhanasari (SG174)
Mound (height: 3 m), c. 3 km SE of Andher, on the southern bank of a perennial stream which runs NE to SW (Size level: 5). Partially occupied by modern village of Gyasabad. The modern village of Dhanasari on the opposite bank appears to be beyond the boundaries of the ancient settlement. Temple remains and associated sculptures (SC578) under worship on two platforms at centre of Gyasabad and on platform in Dhanasari: Phase VI. Pottery phasing: Id-IV (BSM53).

Sachet (SG102)
Mound (height: 7 m), c. 6 km SE of Andher (Size level: 4). Occupied by modern village. Ancient temple site (SC473) in middle of village, with associated sculptures under worship on village platform: Phases V-VI. Pottery phasing: Ib-VII (BSM14). Malwa Ware (Phase Ib) pottery reported in *IAR* 1984–5, 47–8.

Andol (SG101)
Large settlement area, c. 3 km SW of Andher (Size level: 2). Incorporates modern Andol village, and two additional settlements consisting of structural outlines on raised ground to the south (SC218) and SW (SC216). Ancient, dried-up tank (SC217) below latter site, with remains of stone facing still visible. Ancient temple site (SC372), and associated sculpture, in fields to east of modern Andol village, with additional sculptures under worship on platform in middle of SC216: Phase VI.

Southern line of hills to east of Betwa
Mori khauri (SG152)
Mound (height: 2 m) at eastern foot of long line of hills between Pagneswar and Raisen (Size level: 6). Occupied by modern village, and dominated by large *barghat* tree. Temple remains and sculpture under worship beneath *khinni* tree on western edge of mound: Phase VI.

Katsari kherai (SG158)
Hillside settlement on lower NE slopes of hill between Pagneswar and Raisen (Size level: 6). Approximately 50 heavily disturbed structure outlines. Late medieval well at south side of Nyal Karka hill.

Barla hill (SG159)
Modern village on lower slopes of hill (third in a line of hillocks) between Pagneswar and Raisen (Size level: 6). Ancient temple site and associated sculptures. Additional sculptures in one of a series of rock-shelters on eastern edge of hill above: Phase V-VI. Other finds: prehistoric rock-paintings and ancient dam (SG159b).

Ghatla kherai (SG160)
Hillside settlement on slightly raised ground at southern base of hill (fourth in a line of hills) between Pagneswar and Raisen (Size level: 6). Approximately 100 heavily disturbed structural outlines. Phase IV stepwell (160/2b) in fields to the east. Sculptures under worship on platform at centre of settlement, and on a second platform just below rock-shelters to the north: Phases V-VI. Other finds: rock-shelters with prehistoric paintings (SC295).

Sector 3: hilly region to the south

Hills to south and east of Sonari
Khamkhera (SG057).
Modern village situated at northern base of solitary hillock, c. 7 km south of Sanchi (Size level: 6). Sculptures under worship outside modern temple, possibly taken from ancient temple in Tijalpur (SG058): Phase VII.

Tijalpur (SG058)
Modern village on solitary hillock, c. 7.5 km south of Sanchi (Size level: 4). Large village tank (SC445) at western base of hill. Temple remains on western side of hill, with associated sculptures under worship: Phases IV-VI.

Barahi khas (SG059)
Modern village situated at western base of solitary hillock, c. 9 km south of Sanchi (Size level: 6). Buddhist remains on summit of hill (SG059b). Ancient tank (SC396) and sculptures under worship, probably from temple next to hilltop Buddhist site: Phase VI.

Salamatpur hill (SG068)
Modern village situated on western slope of solitary hillock, c. 5 km SW of Sanchi (Size level: 6). Structural outlines continue as far as modern Salamatpur village. Natural shrine. Pottery phasing: Ic-VII (SM81a-b).

Sonari village (SG147)
Modern village situated at northern base of hill, c. 1.5 km north of Sonari and c. 5.5 km SW of Sanchi (Size level: 5). Ancient well and temple site (SC461) now occupied by modern Hanuman temple to the NE of modern village. Associated sculpture under worship here: Phase VI.

Sonari basti (SG148)
Mound (ploughed; height: 4 m) NE of modern Sonari village (Size level: 6). Occupied by single farmhouse. Sculpture (probably from Sonari temple) under worship beneath *imli* tree at eastern edge of mound: Phase VII. Pottery phasing: Id-VI (BSM40).

Sukhasen (SG150b)
Hillside settlement on NE slopes of Sonari hill, c. 5 km SW of Sanchi. Heavily disturbed structural outlines and ancient *bauri*, immediately south of modern Sukhasen village (SC278), with over 100 additional outlines (SC275) on lower, eastern slopes of hill, immediately NW of Sukhasen village. Sculptures under worship at modern temple site in middle of former site and on platform in middle of modern village: Phase VI. Natural shrine.

Suakheri basti (SG151)
Mound (partially ploughed; height: 3 m), immediately east of Sonari hill (Size level: 6). Partially occupied by two-house settlement. Sculpture under worship beneath *babul* tree at southern edge of mound: Phase VI. Pottery phasing: Id/II-VII (BSM41).

Ratanpur girdhari (SG038)
Hillside settlement on NE slope of hill, immediately above modern Ratanpur village, c. 5 km south of Sanchi (Size level: 5). About 25 structural outlines. Temple remains to the west of settlement (SC136) and in middle of modern village (SC690), with

sculptures under worship: Phases IV-VI. Natural shrine. Reference to sculpture in *IAR* 1978-9, 15-16.

Kharetiya 1 (SG044)
Mound (ploughed; height: 3.50 m), c. 1.5 km east of Sonari hill, on west bank of stream which flows from west to join River Betwa in east (Size level: 6). The heavily ploughed mounds to the NW and south appear to have been part of the main mound. Pottery scatters extend for some distance into the surrounding agricultural plains. Several stone structural remains on the top. Small temple mound (SC381) to south of settlement, with sculptures under worship on platform to the north: Phase VI. Natural shrine. Pottery phasing: Id-VII (SM70a). Other finds: iron slag.

Burakhera/Kharetiya 2 (SG046)
Hillside settlement on summit and northern slopes of small hillock, c. 2 km SE of Sonari hill (Size level: 6). Consists of about 50 stone structures. Small settlement mound (heavily ploughed; height: 1 m) at the northern base of the hill. Pottery phasing: Ic-VII (SM71a, b).

Baleiya (SG048b)
Settlement of around 10 rectangular stone structures (average dimensions: 16.30 x 5.20 m), situated on western slopes of hill, around 400 m SW of Kharetiya 2 (Size level: 6). Natural shrine.

Southern valleys
Bhartipur (SG040)
Modern village on lower slopes of hillock west of Sonari (Size level: 6). Sculpture (probably from Besar talai) under worship on village platform: Phase VI.

Besar talai colony (SG041)
Mound (height: 4 m) situated in long, narrow valley 2.5 km south of Buddhist remains at Sonari (Size level: 3). Partially occupied by modern village, with several ploughed fields. Situated on the east bank of the perennial *nāla* which joins the River Betwa in the east. Pottery scatters continue for nearly 1 km into the surrounding fields. The approximate western boundary is marked by a large solitary farmhouse. Circular village tank (SC147) immediately south of the main settlement mound. Scattered remains of large stupa (Phase II) under worship at various locations, with additional sculptural remains at two ancient temple sites (SC142, SC144) and a rock-shelter shrine on the hill above (SC145): Phases II-VI.

Collection of coins (Plate 127; Figure 11.25) in possession of local farmer, including three die-struck, square copper coins. Coin 1 dimensions: 2.3 x 2.3 x 0.2 cm; weight: 10.3 grams; symbols: tree-in-railing, elephant, flower, triangular standard. Coin 2 dimensions: 1.8 x 1.8 x 0.15 cm; weight: 4.6 grams; symbols: tree-in-railing, Ujjain symbol, triangular standard. Coin 3 dimensions: 2.0 x 2.0 x 0.1 cm; weight: 5.8 grams; symbols: flower, triangular standard, elephant, river with fishes. Almost identical symbol combinations are found on published examples from Eran, Vidisha and Ujjain. These are datable to c. third to second century BC but, unlike the Besar talai examples, are inscribed with the names of the issuing city (Bopearachchi and Pieper 1998, 94–8; 117–27).

Pottery phasing: Ic-VII (SM65). Other finds: iron slag. Brief mention of sculptures and fragment of 'Mauryan' donative inscription in *IAR* 1978–9, 13.

Amkhera bhauji colony (SG050)
Large settlement area on SW slopes of Kharitol hill (Size level: 5), including about 50 ruined stone structures immediately behind modern Amkhera bhauji colony (SC160), and a settlement mound (ploughed; height: 3 m) on the southern bank of stream to the west (SC163). Remains of several stone structures at summit of mound. Pottery scatters continue for c. 250 m into fields in west, where there is an ancient well (S162). Like Besar talai colony, this village was established in the 1970s as part of a government forest-clearance project.

Two ancient temple sites in nearby vicinity (SC161, SC367), with associated sculpture under worship on platform in Amkhera bhauji colony (S510), in modern temple on mound (S508), and a second modern temple situated at the southern edge of the mound (S509), en route to Katsari: Phase VI. Pottery phasing: Ic-VII (SM72, SM74a, b). Other finds: iron slag.

Katsari (SG051)
Hillside settlement on northern slopes of hillock, c. 1 km south of Amkhera Bhauji, on the southern bank of a perennial *nala* (Size level: 5). Approximately 20 structural outlines above modern Katsari village, and dried-up village tank (SC165) to the west. Sculptures under worship on platform to the south: Phase IV. Natural shrine.

Amoni ka khera (SG053)
Mound (ploughed; height: 3 m), surrounded by several converging streams, in narrow valley, c. 4 km south of Sonari (Size level: 5). Pottery phasing: Id-VII (SM76).

Sector 4: hills and plains to the north of the River Bes

Pipariya (Bes) (SG146)
Mound (height: 2 m) immediately north (c. 0.75 km) of Udayagiri, on the northern bank of the River Bes (Size level: 6). Partially occupied by modern village. Ancient temple site (SC460) now occupied by modern Durga temple, to the east of the village. Associated sculpture under worship here and in middle of village: Phases IV-VI.

Neemkheria (SG008)
Modern village situated on the southern slopes of Bighan hill, c. 2 km NW of Udayagiri (Size level: 6). Buddhist remains on summit (SG035). Sculptures under worship on main platform: Phase VII.

Jamwar/Bagri (SG043)
Large settlement area covering low hill, c. 2 km north of Udayagiri (Size level: 2). Incorporates modern villages of Jamwar (SC153) and Bagri (SC151). Ancient temple site (SC532) in Jamwar, with sculptural fragments stored at various locations in two villages: Phases V-VI.

Ahmadpur village (SG037)
Mound (height: 4 m) on the southern bank of the Sahodra *nāla*, opposite Ahmadpur hill (Size level: 5). Partially occupied by modern village, with unploughed fields on southern, lower parts of mound. Ancient well on northern bank of *nāla* (S134). Sculpture stored on village platform and two temple mounds (S133, 135), Phase VI. Pottery phasing: Ib-IIIb (sample: BSM7).

Ahmadpur hill kherai (SG037b)
Hillside settlement midway up SW slope of Ahmadpur hill (Size level: 6). Heavily damaged structural outlines. Rock-shelters with prehistoric and historical paintings, Buddhist and Brahmanical remains on summit and lower slopes of hill (SG037a): Phases IV-VI. Pottery phasing: Id-IIIb (BSM11).

Torin (SG066b)
Modern village on lower, SE slopes of solitary hillock, c. 4 km NNW of Udayagiri, on the east bank of the River Bes (Size level: 6). Buddhist remains on summit of hill (SG066). Sculptures under worship in modern shrine on hilltop: Phase VI.

Bilori 2 (SG071)
Modern village situated on lower, southern slopes of solitary hillock, c. 2.25 km south of Ahmadpur hill (Size level: 6). Ritual complex on summit of hill (SG071b). Quarrying activity has revealed section at southern edge of hill, showing walls built directly on the bedrock, at a depth of c. 1.5 m. Pottery visible all the way down. Ancient temple and sculpture remains incorporated into modern Hanuman temple just above the modern village: Phases VI-VII. Pottery phasing: Id-VII (SM83a-b).

Khamtala (SG072)
Mound (height: 2.5 m), c. 1.5 km north of River Bes (Size level: 4). Partially occupied by modern village. Ancient village tank (SC421) with faced embankments, still holding water. Temple and sculpture remains in worship on platform at eastern edge of tank: Phases IV-VI. Two medieval pillars, one at southern base of mound, another in middle of tank. Pottery phasing: Id-VII (SM89).

Bankheri (SG073)
Mound (heavily ploughed; height: 1 m) surrounded by several streams, c. 5.5 km NW of Udayagiri (Size level: 6). Sculptures (possibly from Khamtala) under worship on platform at centre of mound: Phase VII.

PART II: SETTLEMENT DISTRIBUTION PATTERNS

Site hierarchy

Basic details regarding site size were provided in Part I, following the six-tier structure outlined in Table 13.2 and further illustrated in polygon-outline form in Figure 13.2. Unsurprisingly, Vidisha, which covers an area of c. 630 ha, is the largest settlement in the area (Level 1), with an additional six sites in Level 2; 23 in Levels 3–4, 19 in Level 5, and the remaining 84 belonging to the smallest category (Level 6). As discussed earlier, it is not possible to build up a phase-by-phase site hierarchy on the basis of size alone. However, by drawing on additional archaeological criteria discussed during this study, it is still possible to construct a broad local settlement hierarchy for the early-historic period.

One major marker of rank, for example, is the group of post-Mauryan pillars and capitals discussed in chapter 11. Important examples were found at the capital city, as well as the principal Buddhist sites of Sanchi and Satdhara. However, the other four settlements at which they occur (Besar talai, Dhakna, Sanchi-Kanakhera and Tajpur Shur) obviously ranked high in the local hierarchical structure, at least as far as political and economic ties to the capital city was concerned (Table 13.3). Further indications of Besar talai's political status are provided by coins, which, albeit uninscribed, bear symbols almost identical to the Eran and Ujjain series; and a major urban stupa surrounded by post-Mauryan pillars. The stupa's possible connection with royal patronage is suggested by the wording of a fragmentary inscription which reads *kudugaru karikha(ta)* (*IAR* 1978–9, 13) ('caused to be made by Kudugaru'). As discussed in chapter 11, the variant term *karapite* which occurs in the similarly constructed Mawasa stupa inscription is also used in several Sri Lankan inscriptions whose subject matter is the donation of rock-shelter dwellings by members of royalty. Quite clearly, the personages mentioned in the Besar talai and Mawasa inscriptions had significant economic and political clout, but precisely how they fitted within the wider local or inter-regional political scene remains unknown.

Additional indicators of economic status within the regional settlement hierarchy are provided by the distribution of irrigation dams, which, as described in chapter 14, are associated with high construction and maintenance costs, probably covered by local landlords or oligarchs. Accordingly, the sites which may be regarded as occupying high ranks in the local hierarchical structure, following criteria other than size alone, are listed in Table 13.3.

Site distribution

Topographical zones
Settlement distribution over the principal geographical sectors is illustrated in Figure 13.1. The geographical trends are similar to those noted for Brahmanical temple sites described in chapter 12: the highest settlement density occurs in Sectors 1a–b and 2a–b, with the lowest to the north of the River Bes (Sector 4). The areas with the highest density of settlement mounds are the central agricultural plain (Sector 1a) and the agricultural terrain to the east of the River Betwa (Sector 2a). These patterns possibly reflect variations between the total size of each sector, with Sectors 1a and 2a being the largest in the study area. However, they may equally reflect 'real' trends related to the topographic particularities of each sector discussed in chapter 7: the low quantity (five) of hillside settlements in Sector 4 clearly reflects the limited number of hills in this area, while settlement of the surrounding agricultural plains is hampered by the high risk of monsoon flooding in this area. By contrast, although the eastern bank of the River Betwa is also flood-prone, the large expanse of black-cotton soil plain further east is better drained and consequently more suitable for settlement; a total of 27 mounds were documented in Sector 2a, including Mehgaon which is one of the largest in the study area (Level 2), and nine others belonging to Level 4. Further, the ratio of mounds to hillside settlements (approximately 2:1) throughout the overall eastern sector (2a–b) reflects the particular balance between agricultural and hilly terrain in this area: many important hillside settlements such as Sonthiya, Pathari kativarat or Pathari-Gehunkheri[2] are located on the lower slopes of the three major lines of hills running north to south, around the Buddhist hilltop sites of Morel khurd and Andher. Another, more dispersed group of solitary hillocks continues in a west–east line to the south of the Dabar *nāla*, with major settlements, such as Salera, Chandna and Kotra,[3] situated on their lower slopes and Buddhist complexes on their summits.

Similar observations can be made about the settlement patterns in the hilly areas of the western (1b) and southern (3) sectors. The

Table 13.3 Site hierarchy: sites in Ranks 1–3, and corresponding criteria (Phases Id–IV)

SG No.	Name	Sector	Pottery range	Sculpture phase	Area hierarchy	Additional criteria
SG006	Vidisha	1a	1b to 5	1d to 7	1	Temples, stupas, pillars
SG010	Gulgaon-Eran	1b	1d to 7	2 to 7	2	Dam, early sculpture
SG002	Sanchi/Kanakhera hill	1b	n/a	2 to 7	2	Temple, well inscription
SG056	Mehgaon	2a	1d to 3b	4 to 6	2	Sculpture, large village tank
SG101	Andol	2b	n/a	6 to 6	2	Sculpture, size
SG162b	Murlikheri-Naroda	1b	1d to 3b	3b to 7	3	Dam, major temple, associated Buddhist sites
SG179b	Hakimkheri	2b	n/a	6 to 7	3	Temple
SG041	Besar talai	3	1c to 7	2 to 6	3	Dam, Post-Mauryan pillar, urban stupa
SG140	Marwai	1a	1d to 7	6 to 6	4	Temple
SG031b	Udayagiri/Madhupuri/Sonapura	1a	1b to 7	3c to 6	4	Major temples
SG039	Fatehpur marmata	1a	1d to 4	n/a	4	Strategic location
SG003a	Nagauri	1b	1d to 7	2 to 7	4	Dam, quarry, proximity to Sanchi
SG003a	Nagauri	1b	1d to 7	2 to 7	4	Dam, early sculpture
SG064	Tajpura shur	2a	1d to 7	2 to 6	4	Post-Mauryan pillar
SG125	Parwariya/Arwariya	2a	n/a	n/a	4	Strategic location
SG102	Sachet	2a	1b to 7	6 to 6	4	Major temple
SG121	Mahuakhera-Himatgarh	2a	1c to 7	6 to 7	4	Large temple. Strategic position
SG165	Girbhar	2a	1c to 4	4 to 6	4	Large temple. Strategic position
SG133	Parsora haveli	2a	n/a	5 to 6	4	Major temple
SG099b	Morel kala	2b	n/a	3b to 6	4	Major dam, sculpture
SG177d	Devrajpur	2b	1d to 4	2 to 6	4	Dam, adjoining Buddhist site
SG012	Karhaud	2b	n/a	4 to 6	4	Major temples
SG170	Salera	2b	n/a	2 to 7	4	Major village tank, sculpture, adjoining Buddhist site
SG061	Pagneswar	3	n/a	3b to 7	4	Major crossing, and sculpture/temples
SG058	Tijalpur	3	n/a	4 to 7	4	Temple
SG072	Khamtala	4	1d to 7	4 to 7	4	Temple
SG095b	Chandna/Gorpur kherai	2b	n/a	2 to 6	5	Major dam and adjoining Buddhist sites

relatively high number of hillside settlements is in keeping with the predominance of hilly terrain in both sectors. In Sector 1b, the majority are situated in the immediate vicinity of Sanchi, for example Sanchi-Kanakhera and Nagauri,[4] or amongst the cluster of small hills immediately to the west, for example Gulgaon-Eran, Ferozpur and Murlikheri-Naroda.[5] Many of the hills in Sector 3 are comparatively large and inaccessible, which may explain the high concentration of hillside settlements around the group of smaller hillocks to the south of Sonari, such as Baleiya, Ratanpur Girdhari or Katsari.[6] Again, the distribution of mounds is highest in Sectors 1a and 2a due to the predominance of flat agricultural land. By contrast, agricultural land is more limited in Sector 3 due to the predominance of extensive hill ranges: most of the nine settlement mounds documented during the SSP are restricted to two narrow valleys to the south of Sonari. The first valley includes Besar talai and Kharetiya 1, with Amoni ka khera in the second, further south.[7]

Other criteria such as accessibility and proximity to the capital city may also have determined site distribution. It is notable, for example, that the majority of sites belonging to Size Level 2, as well those containing additional indicators of 'importance' (Table 13.3) occur either in the hilly sector around Sanchi (1b) or in the agricultural plains to the east of the River Betwa (2a). Although there are potentially issues of accessibility for the latter due to limited crossing places over the River Betwa,[8] this seems not to have been a major deterrent against settlement of this area during the early-historic period. By contrast, the River Bes is comparatively easy to cross, with fords at Vidisha, Bighan and Udayagiri, although the area to the north (Sector 4) has a particularly low concentration of settlement mounds.[9]

Rivers and nālas

While the distribution of hillside settlements and mounds is influenced largely by the availability of suitable terrain, another major factor, especially with regard to mound distribution, is the orientation of rivers and perennial streams. As shown in Figure 13.1, several major settlements, such as Fatehpur Marmata and Neemkhera in Sector 1a, are located along the River Bes, with a marked preference for its southern bank.[10] A number of settlements also occur on both banks of the River Betwa, the largest being Nonakhera, Parariya and Pagneswar.[11] However, a more stable setting is provided by the banks of small perennial streams, which offer year-round water supplies without the risk of inundation. Thus in Sector 1a, the triangle enclosed by the southern bank of the River Bes and a major perennial *nāla* which flows W–E provides the setting for a large cluster of settlements, notably Berkheri.[12] As already mentioned, the highest settlement density in Sector 4 occurs in the narrow valley immediately to the south of Sonari, an area dominated by a large perennial stream flowing W–E. Besar talai, one of the most important settlements in the study area as a whole, forms one of a series of major sites situated on this stream. Amoni ka khera, in the even narrower valley further south, is also situated on the banks of a large *nāla* which rises from a perennial spring about 1 km to the west.[13] Despite its remote location, a small shrine, maintained by a resident priest, has grown up around the spring. This important

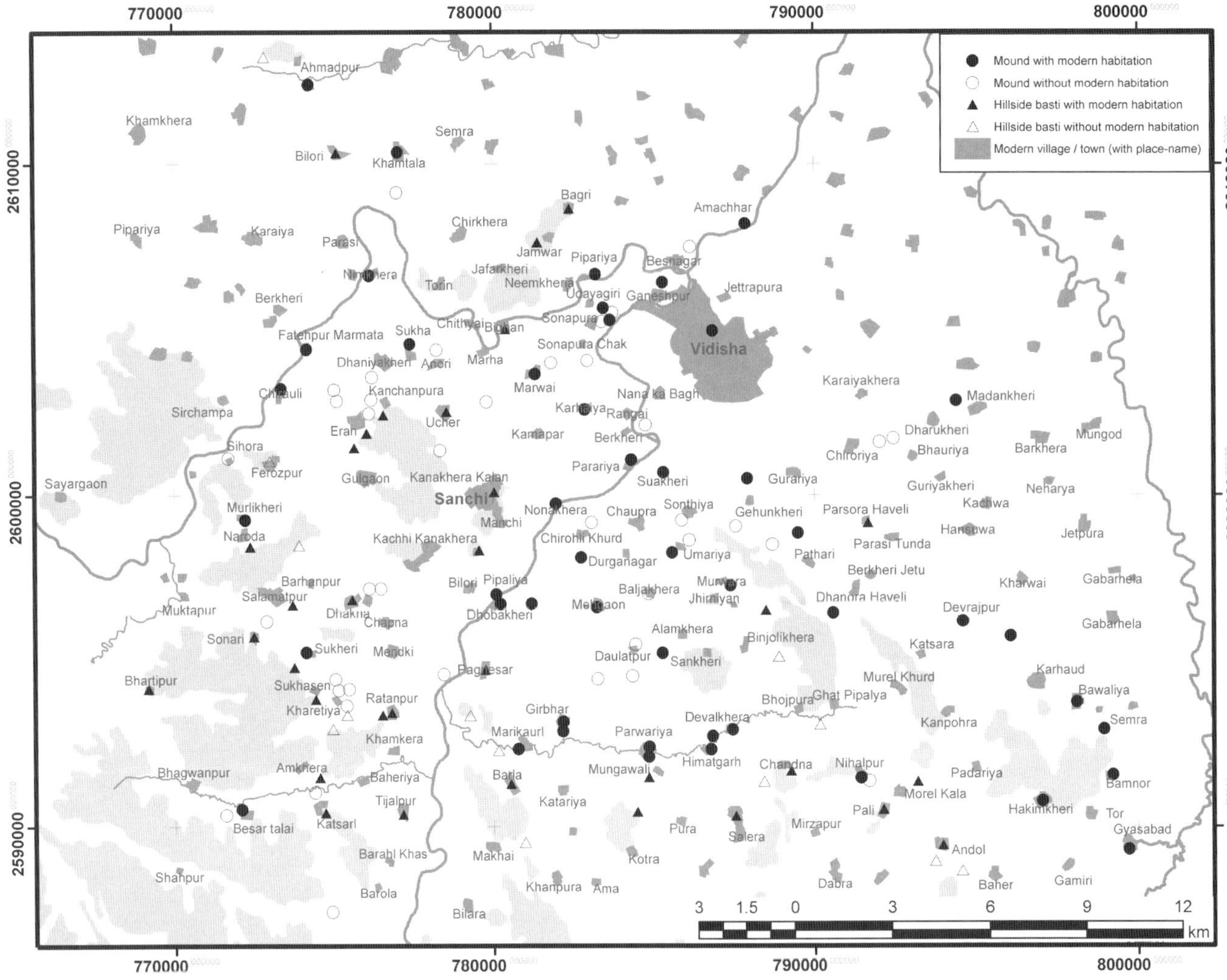

Figure 13.3 Map showing settlement continuity (SC level): relationship between modern and ancient habitations

cult spot, known locally as Rajanal, is almost always busy with large groups of hunters, herders and foragers, for whom the promise of all-year water supplies in an otherwise arid area has a major impact on their daily livelihood. This example illustrates the close link between practical realities such as the need for water, the configuration of local settlements, and popular perceptions of the divine. Finally, in Sector 2a, another perennial stream called the Dabar *nāla* forms the focus for a large number of major mounds, notably Devalkhera, Mahuakhera-Himatgarh and Pipalia kherai,[14] close to the stupas at Morel khurd.

Both the perennial and non-perennial streams could also be dammed for irrigation purposes. As discussed in chapter 14, the abundance of short valleys, combined with the black-cotton soil downstream, afforded ideal conditions for the construction of irrigation embankments to store runoff from the surrounding hills. The fact that the area's balance of hills and agricultural plains does not extend northwards of Vidisha may be taken as a major factor in the high density of settlements in the SSP study area. However, whilst recognising the relationship between topography and settlement distribution, this is not to suggest a wholly 'environmentally determinist' argument. Before we consider other factors behind local settlement patterns, it is necessary to discuss the issue of chronology and, in particular, whether any major shifts in settlement location can be identified over the period covered by this study.

Chronology

Dating the settlements

A basic chronological framework was constructed using a combination of sculptural, architectural and ceramic typologies; the range of criteria for dating the various settlement phases is summarised in Table 10.1. The various weaknesses of internal pottery typologies established from surface collections alone, particularly those related to the complexities of site formation processes, were discussed in chapter 7. These problems are exacerbated by the fact that the stratified sequence from Vidisha was never published beyond summary form. It should be stressed therefore that the chronology presented here only reflects the presence or absence of a certain sculptural or architectural phase, or diagnostic ceramic ware. A large number of individual sherds summarised in Appendix IIIa are still lacking verified stratified parallels, meaning that the resolution of the present chronological framework is subject to re-evaluation at a later stage.[15]

Another bias which needs to be made explicit stems from the disparity between the dating capacity of ceramic and sculptural evidence. The most obvious point is that the dates suggested by ceramic samples are often significantly earlier than those based on sculptural evidence. As discussed in chapter 12, this is directly related to the fact that the appearance of stone sculpture is a relatively late occurrence in India. This bias is reinforced by the

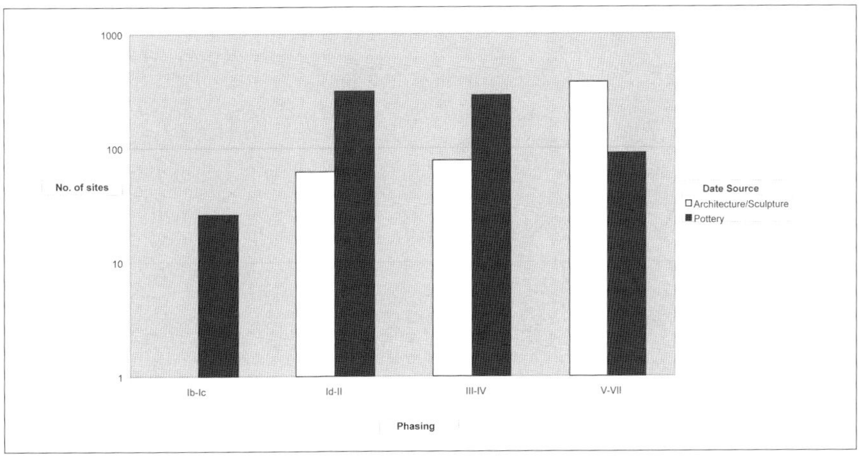

Figure 13.4 Graph showing settlement phasing Ib–VII and corresponding dating evidence (SG level)

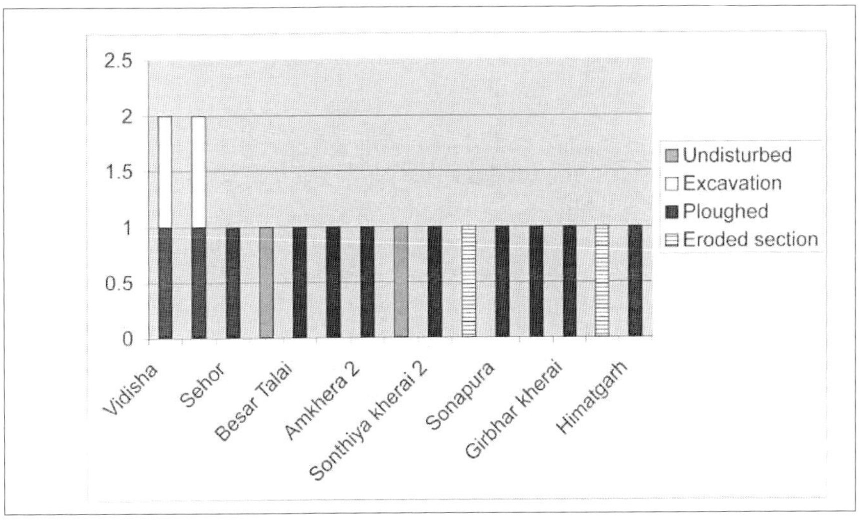

Figure 13.5 Graph showing relationship between sites yielding ceramics datable prior to Phase II and surface ground conditions

fact that, as shown in Figure 13.3, approximately two-thirds of the settlements documented during the SSP (both mounds and hillside settlements) are currently occupied by modern villages (Plate 6). Since the availability (and representativeness) of ceramic samples is determined by the presence of ploughed surfaces or exposed sections, the ongoing occupation of settlements has a direct impact on dating resolution. Even more problematic when it comes to dating are the hillside settlements, which are often completely devoid of ploughed surfaces or sections.

The mutual interrelationship between the earliest date obtained for each site, the type of available dating evidence, and ground conditions is illustrated in Figures 13.4 and 13.5. Given that there are no stone sculptures at any of the settlements prior to the second century BC (Phase II), an identification of an earlier date is dependent entirely on ceramic evidence. It should therefore come as no surprise that, of the 15 settlements yielding pottery datable between Phases Ib and Id, all, with the exception of two, had ploughed surfaces, exposed sections or had been excavated in the past (Figure 13.5). Further, prior to Phase Id, ceramics constitute the only available dating evidence, while between Phases Id and IIIa, ceramics still far outweigh sculpture as a dating tool. It is only in Phase IIIb and later that sculpture becomes the dominant dating tool (Figure 13.4). Quite obviously, therefore, the possible existence of buried ceramic evidence dating to earlier periods at these sites cannot be ruled out.

Despite these shortcomings, the available evidence is adequate for the purposes of providing a broad chronological framework within which to examine the archaeological setting of early Buddhist sites in the SSP study area. In some cases, it was possible to adjust the chronology suggested by sculptural and ceramic evidence on the basis of immediate archaeological context. For example, despite the absence of pottery at Binjoli kherai,[16] a large settlement NW of Morel khurd, the earliest available dating evidence was a group of sculptures datable to c. fifth century AD (Phase IV). However, a Phase II or earlier date is suggested by the proximity of a large irrigation embankment, which, as described in chapter 14, runs between here and Morel khurd.[17] A similar line of reasoning informed the dating of Barla in the south and Dargawan to the west of Sanchi.[18]

Temporal and spatial patterns in the rural hinterland

Quite clearly, further archaeological research is required to attain a more secure chronological framework in which to situate the settlement patterns in the study area. Three main steps for future research in this direction can be envisaged: i) carrying out more detailed petrographic analysis and C14 dating of existing surface-ceramic collections; ii) supplementing the existing characterisation analysis with a systematic, comparative study of stratified sequences from excavated sites in central India; and iii) carrying out renewed excavations at Vidisha, coupled with test pits at selected settlements in the surrounding area.

However, on the basis of the available evidence, a number of preliminary observations can be made regarding the temporal and spatial distribution of settlements in the study area. First, it should be noted that, apart from Vidisha and Rangai Amkhera, no Kayatha-type pottery (Phase Ib) was collected during the study.[19] However, Chalcolithic 'painted black on orange' (i.e. 'Malwa Ware') is reported from Sachet in Sector 3 (*IAR* 1984–5, 47–8) (Figure 13.1).[20] The earliest group of newly documented settlements belong to Phase Ic, that is between c.1000 and 600 BC. Twenty-nine settlements were dated to this phase, largely on the basis of Black and Red Ware (fabric type 1), Black Slipped Wares (fabric types 2, 4, 5), and Coarse Grey Ware (fabric types 6 and 6b). A number of vessel types in Red Slipped Wares were also dated to this period. As shown in Figure 13.1, the settlement area immediately in front of Udayagiri hill is included in this group.[21] However, given its proximity to the city mounds at Besnagar (the rampart is just over 1 km to the east) and the continuous spread of pottery scatters between the two sites, one may consider it as part of the city's suburban sprawl. Interestingly, settlements of this phase are evenly spread throughout the study area and are often situated next to smaller streams. As illustrated at Besar talai and Amoni ka kherai, even the most 'interior valleys' appear to have been settled by this time.[22] Sites such as Fatehpur Marmata and Amacchar, which are located directly on the Rivers Bes and Betwa, only appeared to yield pottery of Phase Ib and later.[23] Another major point to note is that, as illustrated by the pottery and sculpture phasing in Table 13.4, all of the Phase Ic sites show evidence for continued occupation into later periods. This suggests therefore that the sequence at Rangai Amkhera, which shows evidence for abandonment after c. 1000 BC, is an exception to wider regional trends. The latter appear not to fit with the Gangetic-valley settlement patterns discussed in chapters 2 and 9, which were characterised by a shift from major river banks to interior locations between the Chalcolithic and Iron Age.

The next phase (Id) was dated to between c. 600–200 BC, which was tentatively identified at 24 of the newly documented settlements (Figure 13.1). Although the major diagnostic ware of this period is NBPW, only a single sherd was collected during the SSP. However, a number of the Black Slipped Wares and Red Slipped Wares are directly relatable to associated wares from excavated NBPW horizons. Having said this, given the degree of continuity between Phases Ic and Id in many of the Black Slipped Wares, an earlier date for many of these sites cannot be ruled out. As shown in Figure 13.1, four of the Phase Id settlements, Parariya, Berkheri ghat kherai, Fatehpur Marmata and Amacchar, are situated next to the Rivers Betwa or Bes.[24] Further, there is a fairly even distribution of Phase Id sites throughout Sectors 1–3, which may be contrasted to their near absence in Sector 4.

The next settlement phase (II) is datable to between the second and first centuries BC. Seventeen sites, whose earliest archaeological material dated to this period, were documented during the SSP. The diagnostic ceramic types of this period consist largely of Red Slipped Wares, with the most common vessel types being jars such as nos. 148a–b, 175a–d, 141a–b, and 163. Sculptural evidence also becomes available for the first time. As shown in Figure 13.6, the two main areas of settlement during this period are Sectors 1a and 2a, with a particularly high concentration in the latter area to the east of the Betwa. Many of these sites are situated in direct proximity to Buddhist sites. The spatial and temporal relationship between the two types of sites will be discussed later; however, the main point to note is that there is no significant change in the topographical or geographical location of settlements between Phases Ic and II. With regard to the remaining settlements, five were positioned in the first-to-third century-AD time bracket (Phase III). In addition to sculpture, the main diagnostic ceramic types for this period are micaceous wares (type 13) and highly polished red wares (type 14a). Eight settlements were dated to Phase IV (c. fourth to sixth centuries AD); with a further 44 assignable to between the seventh and twelfth centuries AD (Phases V–VII). However, as already discussed, many of these sites may well be earlier. The distribution of settlements datable between c. fifth and twelfth century AD is illustrated in Figure 13.1.

Brief mention should also be made of the relationship between ancient and modern-day settlement patterns. As shown in Figure 13.3, most settlements are situated in close proximity to modern villages, while 105 sites recorded at the Site Cluster level are actually overlain by modern villages. Others are situated at the edge of modern villages, indicating a shift in location some time in the past. As discussed in chapter 9, a similar phenomenon occurs at Vidisha, which appears to have shifted (or simply shrunk?) from the original city site in the fork of the River Betwa and Bes to its present location some time after the Gupta period. In some cases, however, there *is* evidence for complete abandonment, as represented by ancient settlements which show no signs of having been shifted to a new location in the immediate vicinity. Approximately 51 sites to which this situation applies were

Table 13.4 Phase Ic sites (c. 1000–600 BC): occupational sequences

SG no.	Name	Sector	Area hierarchy	Pottery phasing	Sculpture phasing
SG006	Vidisha	1a	1	Ic to IIIb	II to VII
SG021	Sehor	1b	6	Ic to VII	n/a
SG031b	Udayagiri/Madhupuri/Sonapura	1a	4	Ic to VII	IIIb to VI
SG032b	Dhakna basti	1b	6	Ic to IIIb	IV to VI
SG041	Besar talai	3	3	Ic to VII	II to VI
SG046	Burakhera/Kharetiya 2	3	6	Ic to VII	n/a
SG050	Amkhera bhauji	3	5	Ic to VII	IV to VI
SG068	Salamatpur hill	3	6	Ic to VII	n/a
SG082	Sonthiya kherai 2	2a	6	Ic to VII	n/a
SG106	Utari guhar	1a	6	Ic to IIIb	n/a
SG121	Mahuakhera-Himatgarh	2a	4	Ic to VII	VI to VII
SG165	Girbhar	2a	4	Ic to IV	IV to VI

recorded during the SSP; their geographical distribution is illustrated in Figure 13.3. This number would be somewhat higher, if we include Besar talai and neighbouring settlements in the narrow valley to the south of Sonari. As mentioned briefly in chapter 11, most of the modern villages in this area are recently established government 'colonies', set up during the 1970s as part of an extensive forest-clearance programme: it appears that, following the abandonment of major settlements such as Besar talai, the whole valley had been allowed to revert to natural forest. These patterns would appear to tally with historical records, already mentioned in chapter 4, of a series of serious droughts, and consequent depopulation, from the fourteenth century AD onwards. These events may, in part, explain the considerable disparity between ancient and modern-day settlement patterns demonstrated in this study.

Settlements and Buddhist sites

The temporal and spatial distribution of settlements provides a starting point for evaluating the wider social and economic setting of the hilltop Buddhist sites discussed in previous chapters. In particular, the relative configuration of monasteries and settlements provides an empirical basis for assessing theories regarding the link between Buddhist propagation and wider economic, political and social transformations during the early-historic period. For example, it has been suggested that, despite its 'property-renouncing' status, the *saṅgha*, through its pioneering spirit, encouraged the movement of populations into new areas (Ray 1994, 5). Quite clearly, in order to assess such hypotheses, the loose chronological framework presented here would require corroboration through excavation and rigorous statistical ceramic analysis. However, at this stage, a number of preliminary propositions may be offered. First, the majority of Buddhist sites described in chapter 11 show evidence for occupation during much earlier periods: the large number of painted rock-shelters and microlithic scatters at these sites attest to peripatetic, possibly hunter-gatherer, occupation from at least the Chalcolithic period (Figure 11.1). Secondly, the chronology of early village settlements discussed above suggests that much of the low-lying area surrounding these hills had been occupied by sedentary communities from at least 1000 BC, if not earlier.

To state the obvious, despite the solitary setting of the hilltop Buddhist monasteries, the incoming *saṅgha* did not choose completely unsettled areas. However, a number of these sites appear to be more or less contemporary with settlements in their immediate vicinity. As shown in Figure 13.6, for example, neither Pipalia kherai, nor Binjoli kherai, situated within less than 1 km of Morel khurd, have yielded archaeological evidence datable to before c. third or second century BC.[25] The same applies to Nagauri, less than 500 m south of Sanchi, although Dhakna basti contains some Phase Ic pottery.[26] However, given the uncertainties over the dating of surface ceramics from these settlements, any inferences regarding their chronological relationship to Buddhist sites remain speculative.

Nevertheless, one point of certainty is that whether or not they predate the establishment of Buddhism, a number of significant changes take place within these settlements during Phase II. First, as discussed in chapter 11, the earliest stone sculptures to appear in the study area outside the context of the capital city and the hilltop Buddhist sites are the Phase II pillar and capital remains, as found at Besar talai, Tajpur shur, Kanakhera and Dhakna. The 'imperial' nature of these pillars and their similarity to examples from Vidisha itself suggest that these places operated as political and economic 'nodes' in a larger interlinked network. Secondly, the strong Buddhist associations of the animal capitals at these sites provide clear indications of the focus of religious patronage during this period. The third point is that, prior to the last quarter of the first century BC, there is no clear evidence for non-Buddhist sculpture in these 'interior' areas. When examples do appear, the influence of artistic developments at neighbouring monastic sites is obvious. Both these last two points support the view that the growing patronage base of Buddhism between c. third and second century BC was closely related to the increasingly urban character of settlements. The previous sentence was worded in such a way as to emphasise the element of patronage rather than Buddhism *per se*: this is so as to avoid suggestions of a causal link between the establishment of Buddhism and these wider changes in the archaeological landscape. As argued by H.P Ray (1994, 122) in her study of the relationship between Buddhist propagation and the expansion of trading networks in the Deccan area, it is important to view both processes as part of a much larger set of economic and ideological changes involving the spread of urbanisation and monarchical systems from their base in the Gangetic valley. Buddhism did not 'cause' the proliferation of trade, but rather both processes were linked to the emergence of an 'interactive support system' between monastic and lay sections of society that 'constantly evolved and adapted itself between 300 BC and AD 300' (*ibid.*).

Examples of similar forms of 'interactive support systems' include textual and epigraphical descriptions of the ritualised exchange of gifts and religious merit (*pūnya*) between the *saṅgha* and the laity. As discussed in chapter 2, these descriptions lie at the heart of theories, hitherto untested archaeologically, regarding the development of institutionalised monasticism. It is interesting to speculate as to whether the spatial relationship between monastic sites and local settlements accords in any way with these theories. The first point to note is that, as shown in Figure 13.6, each of the Phase II hilltop Buddhist sites is situated within 1 to 2 km of the nearest habitational settlement. For example, Morel khurd should be viewed in relation to Binjoli kherai and Pipalia kherai; Andher to Hakimkheri; Mawasa to Naroda; Sonari to Besar talai; and Satdhara to Naroda and Sehor. This spatial relationship would appear to conform to the *Patimokka* rules in the *Vinaya* which stipulate that monasteries should be situated close, but not too close, to towns (*Vinaya* III, 155). As argued by Gombrich (1988, 95, 156) in his study of the present-day relationship between monasteries and settlements in Sri Lanka, both in spatial and social terms the position of the monastery is dialectical and 'ambivalent', because although it is 'outside' society, it is also dependent upon society for financial support. The paradox, but also the key to the success of this arrangement, is that, in the eyes of the Sri Lankan Buddhist laity, the extremity of a monk's detachment from society is considered an indication of his religious standing; and by extension, the perceived power of his renunciation is likely to determine the level of patronage that he receives from society. In return, the donor is granted *pūnya* in quantities corresponding to the value of his donation (Gombrich, 1988, 156). The fact that the *saṅgha* in the Sanchi area would not have been able to survive in their secluded hilltop locations without some level of integration within the local social and economic infrastructure has already been stressed at various

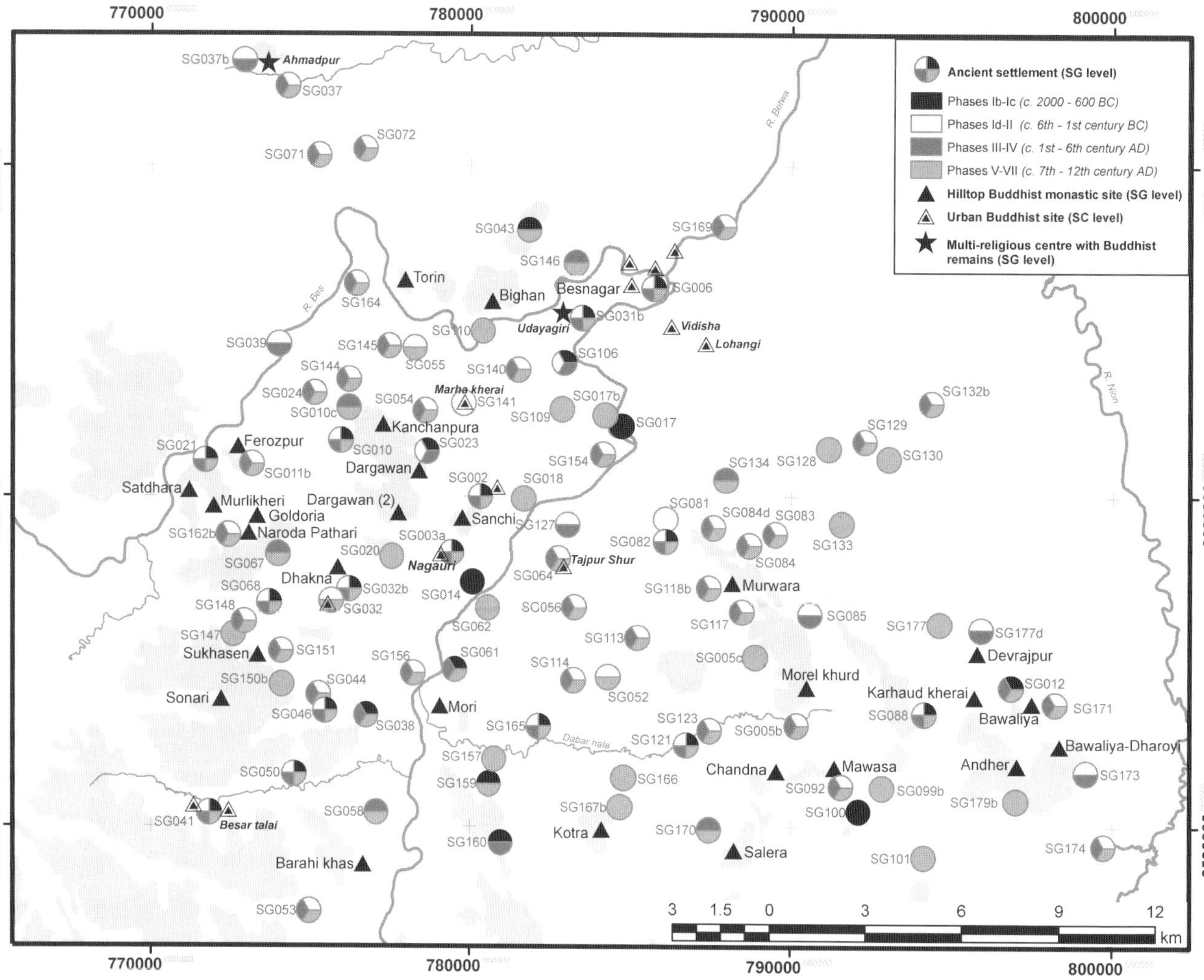

Figure 13.6 Settlements Phases Id–VII (SG) and Buddhist sites (hilltop monastic, urban and mixed ritual contexts)

points throughout this study. Whilst the *saṅgha*'s livelihood may have rested heavily on inter-monastery allegiances, the need to view monasteries side by side with local settlements and evidence for patronage networks is illustrated by Sonari's spatial relationship with Besar talai in the valley to the south. As discussed in chapter 11, the close art-historical parallels between Besar talai's large urban stupa and those at Sonari provide ample evidence that both sites were part of an inter-linked socio-religious infrastructure. Further insights into the possible nature of this relationship are provided by the group of ancient irrigation embankments discussed in the next chapter.

Although based on the relationship of a single Buddhist site to its immediate archaeological setting, Fogelin's (2006) recent survey in and around Thotlakonda in Andhra Pradesh offers useful parallels to the inter-site patterns discussed here. On the basis of close similarities between ceramics at Thotlakonda and nearby settlements, Fogelin (*ibid.*, 152–3) suggests that there was a high level of localised exchange between monks and local populations. This is in contrast to earlier theories (e.g. Ray 1994) which have stressed the importance of long distance trade as a determining factor in the positioning of Buddhist monasteries. Further, the abundance of storage jars at Thotlakonda supports the view that food was stored and prepared on site, rather than acquired through begging rounds (Fogelin 2006, 165). This food was probably cooked by non-monastic staff who, as discussed in chapter 2, are mentioned in early Buddhist texts and inscriptions.

Conclusion

The settlement patterns discussed in this chapter are central to my aim of providing a social context to the 'ritual' aspects of the landscape described in previous chapters. Such an integrated approach is particularly important in light of the fact that the majority of non-Buddhist sculpture described in chapter 12 occurs within habitational settings. While providing insights into the configuration of the ritual landscape, at least with regard to the development of a stone-working tradition, this material indicates little about habitational history. The ceramic evidence discussed in this chapter has therefore been crucial for the identification of longer-term temporal rhythms in the landscape. Finally, by stepping beyond the physical boundaries of the Buddhist monastic sites that form the focus of this study, and looking back from neighbouring settlements, we have gained a new perspective of the *saṅgha*'s position in wider society.

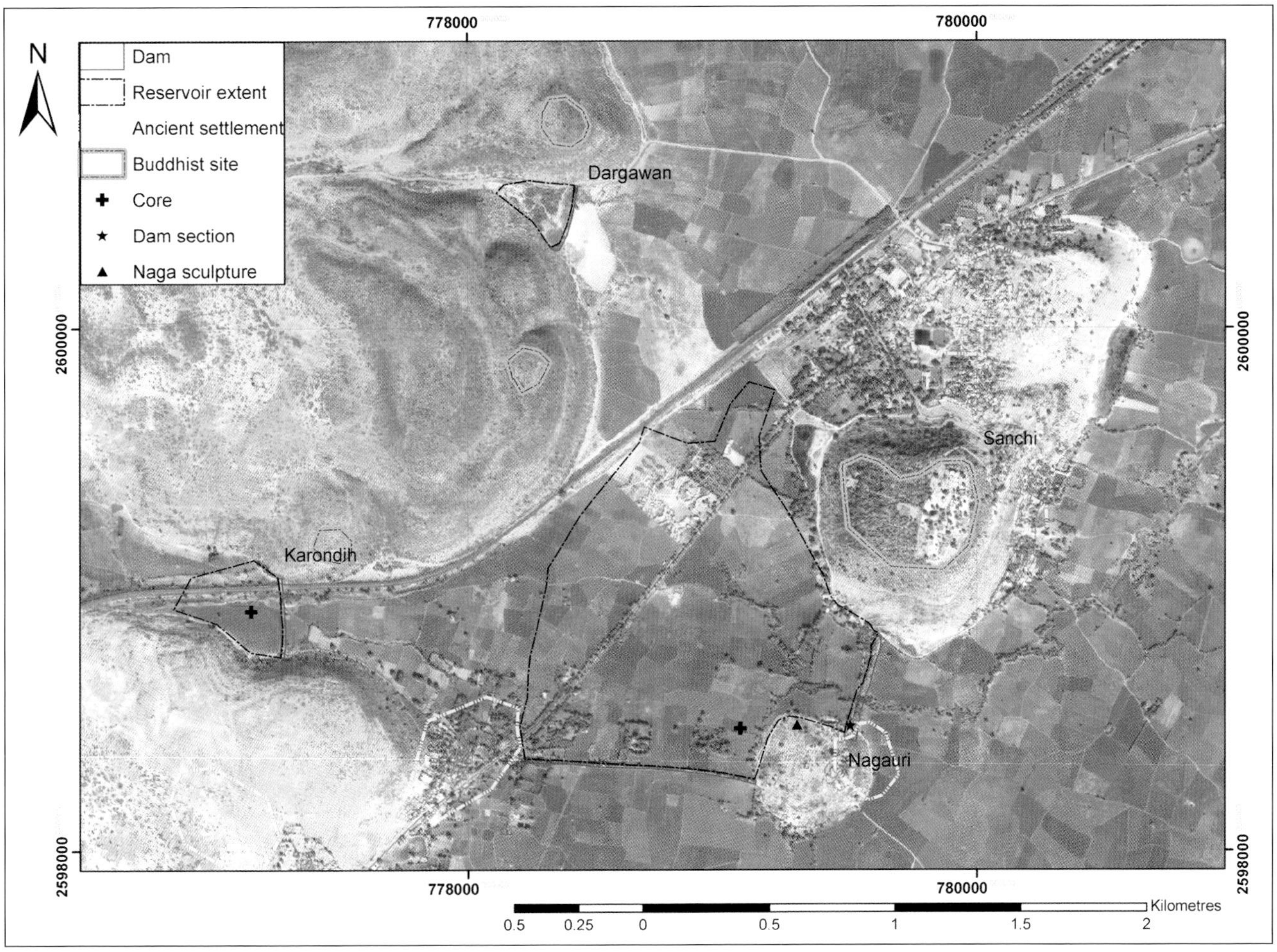

Plate 15 Sanchi hill and surroundings: Quickbird satellite imagery

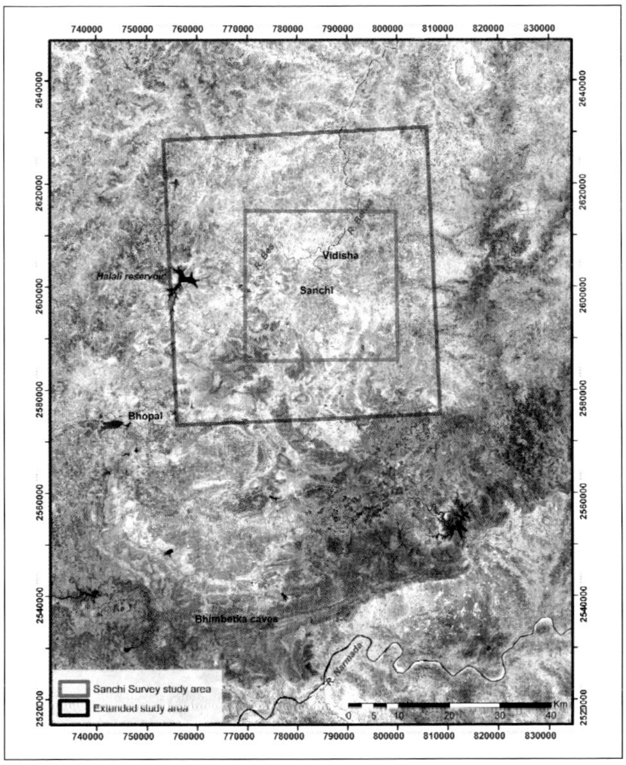

Figure 3.1 Physical map of Bhopal/Vidisha area, showing smaller study area

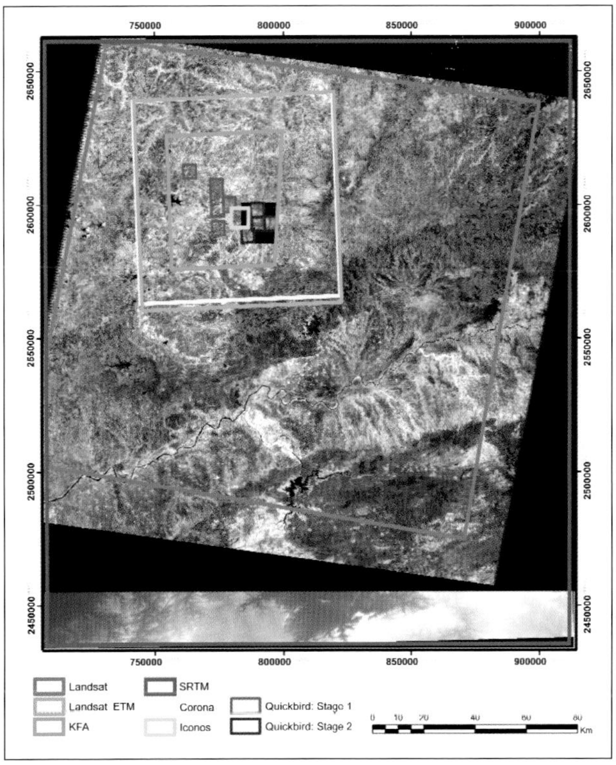

Figure 8.1 Map showing satellite imagery purchased in 2003–5 (Stage I)

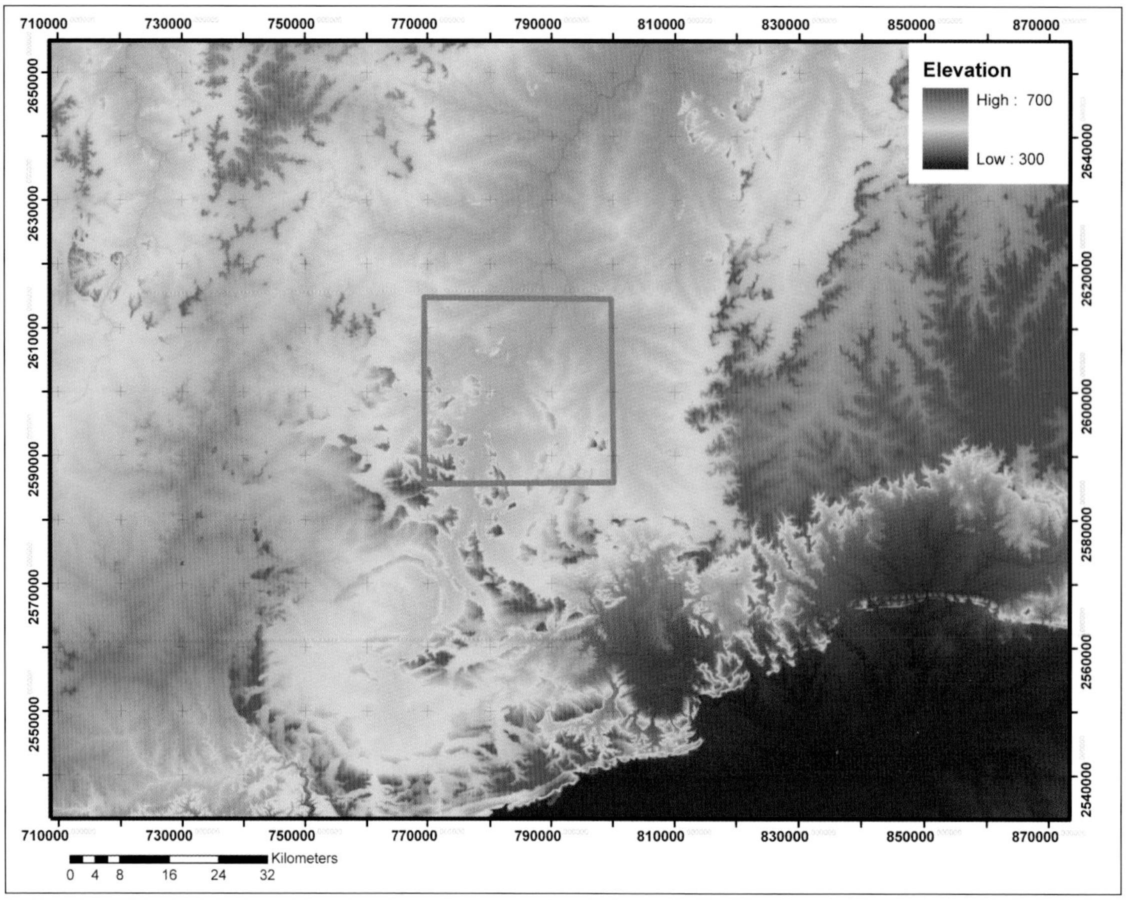

Figure 4.2 Relief map of study area, and wider geographical setting

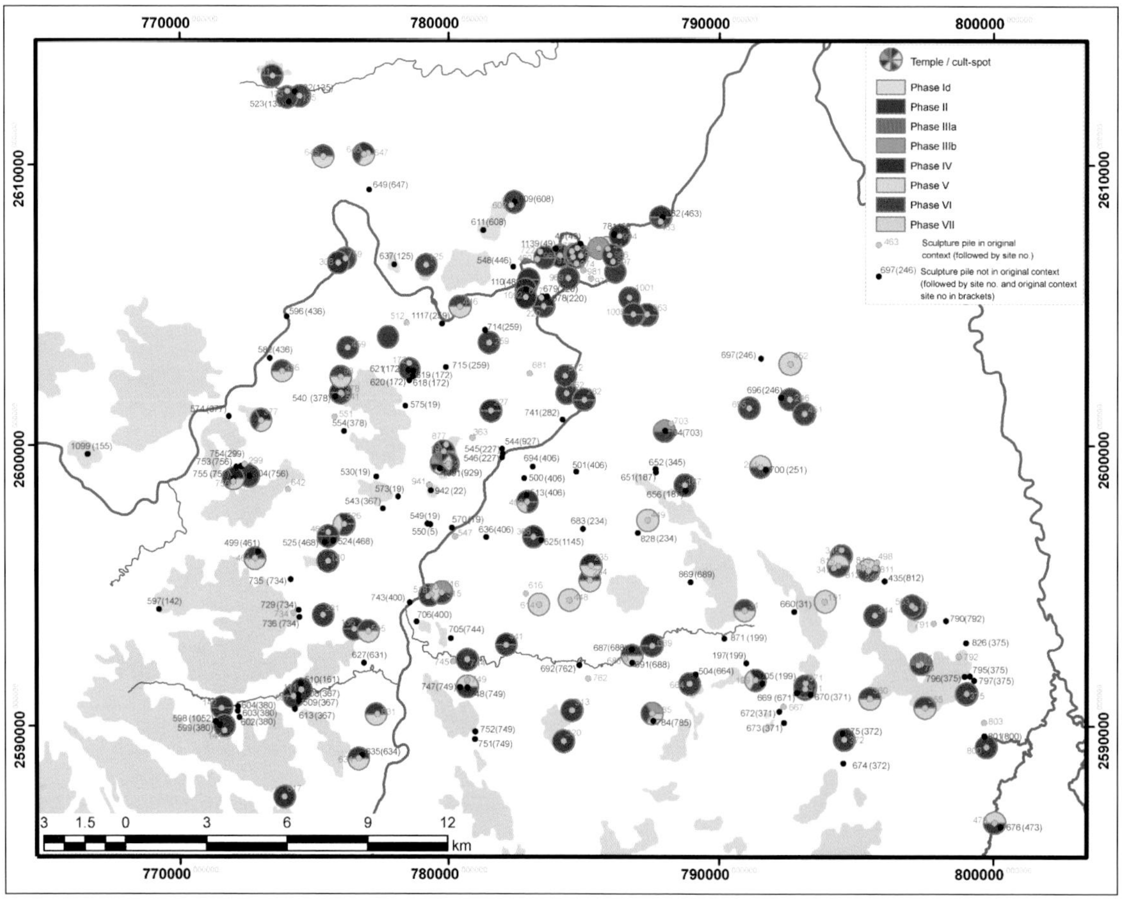

Figure 8.4 Map showing distribution of cult spots and temples, with sculpture piles (in original context and out of original context)

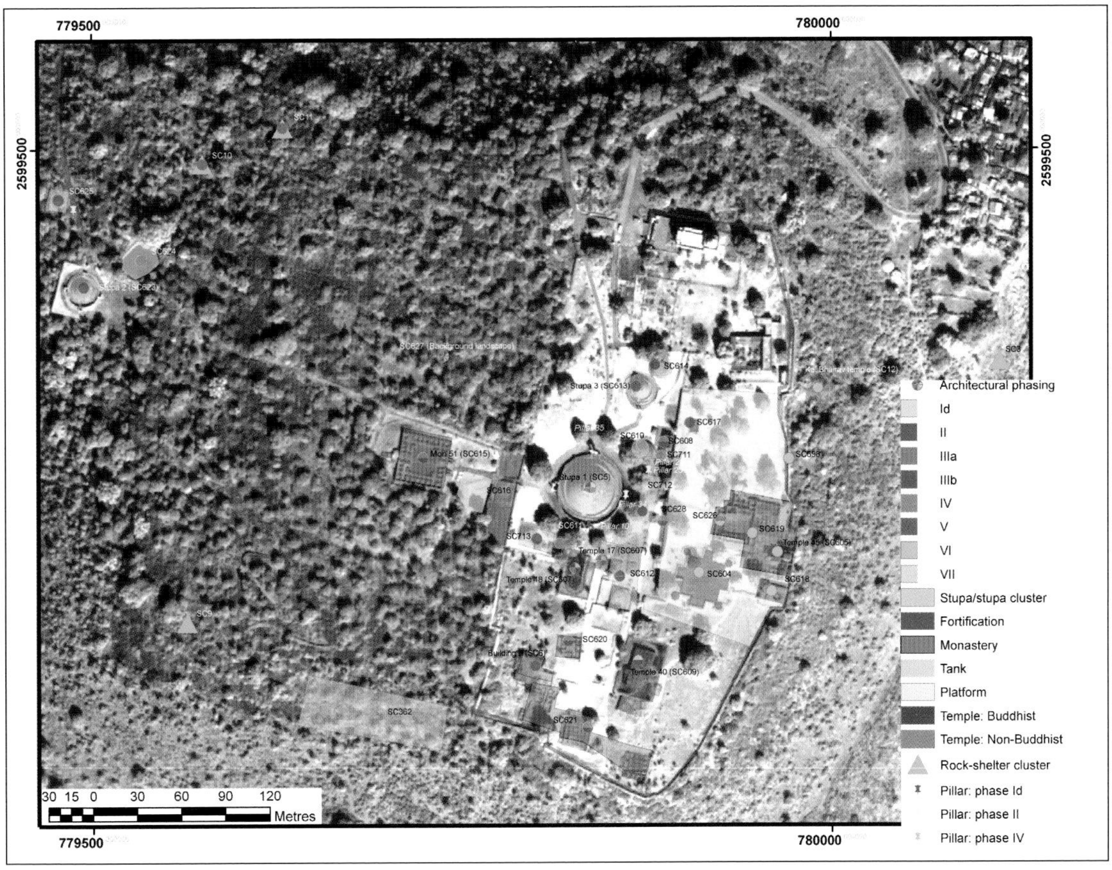

Figure 9.1 Map of Sanchi showing main architectural building phases (with Quickbird imagery background)

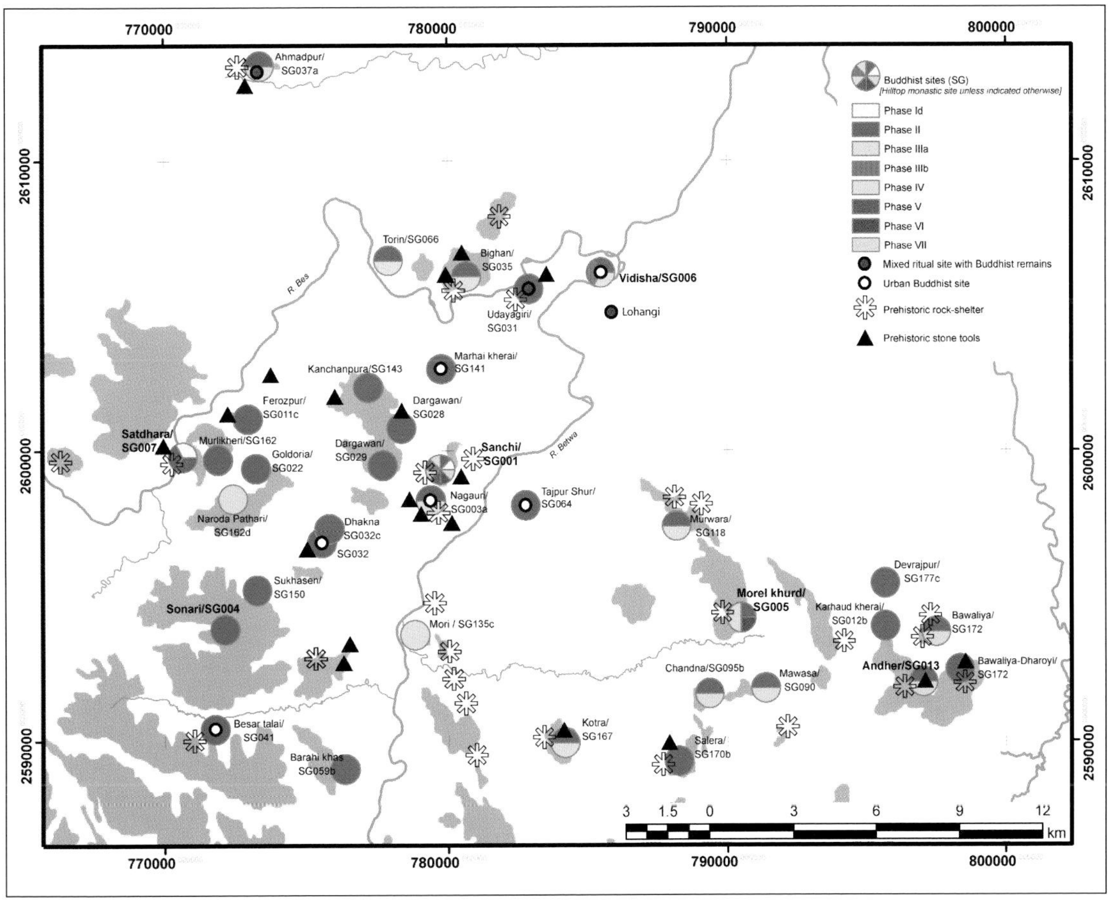

Figure 11.1 Map of Buddhist sites in the Sanchi area according to earliest building phase (SG level), and prehistoric sites (rock-shelters and stone tools)

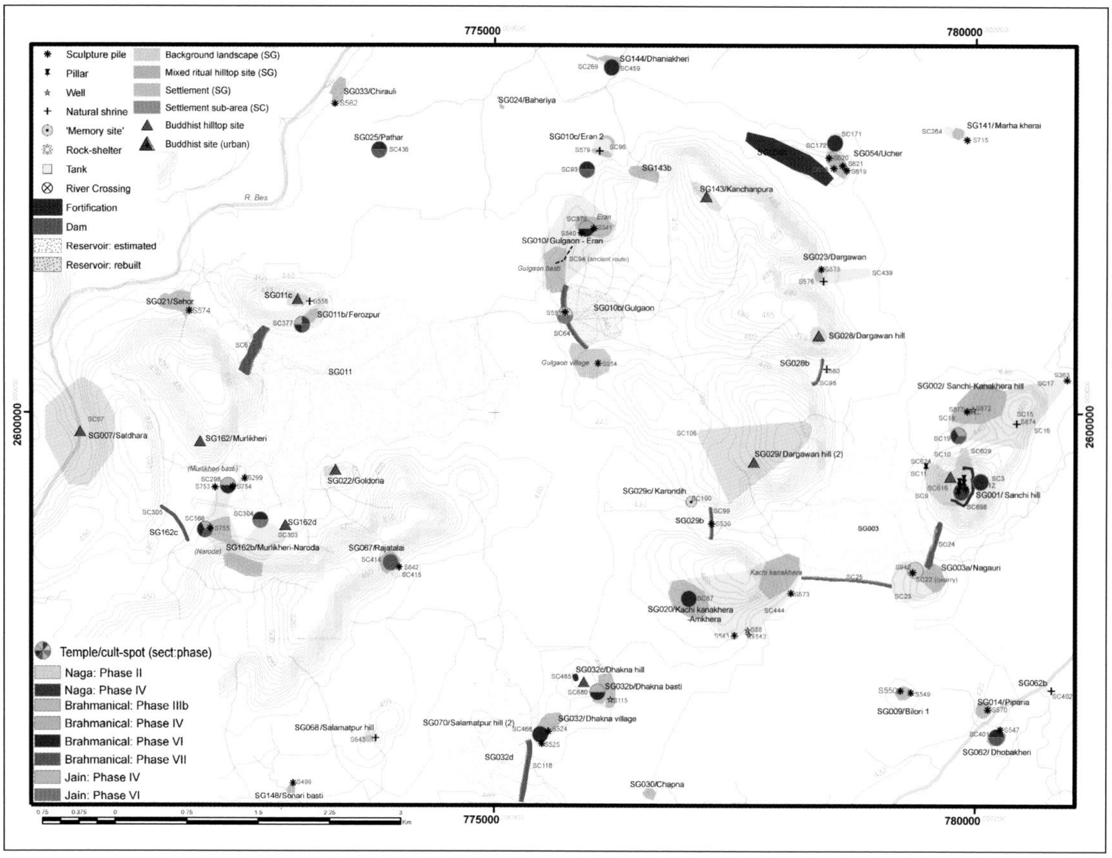

Figure 11.2 Map of archaeological sites in the western sector

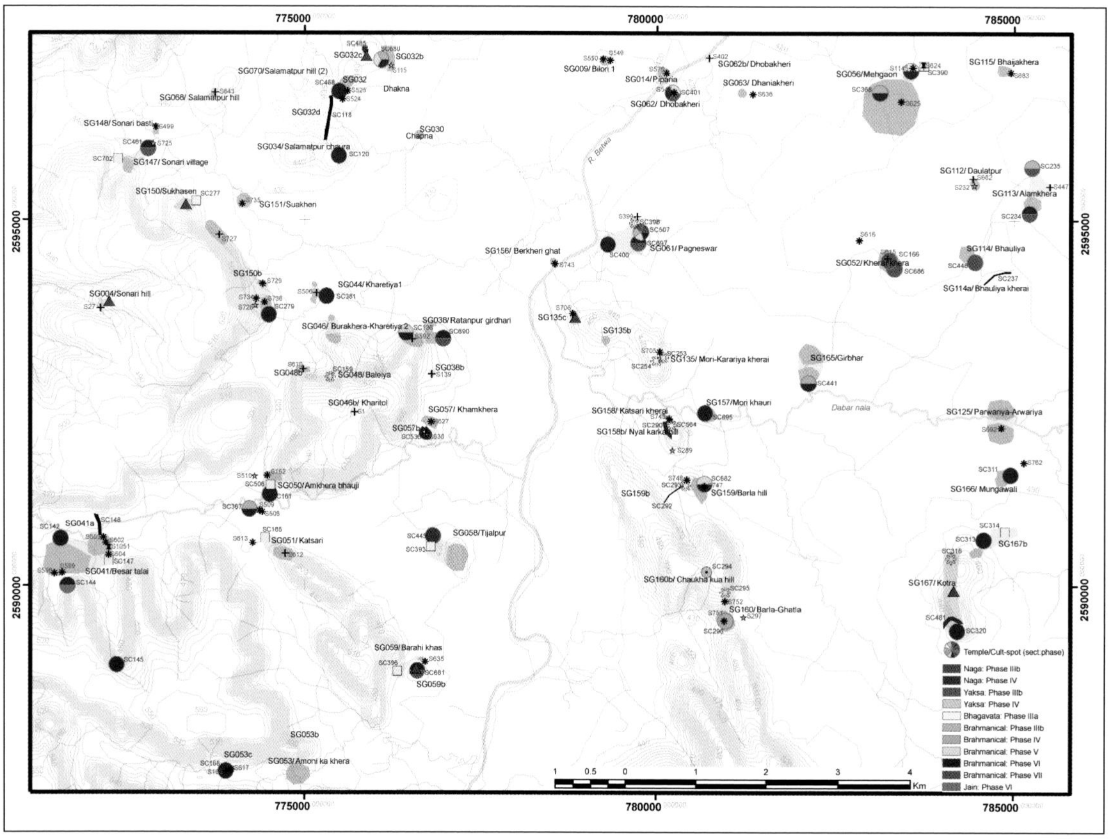

Figure 11.5 Map of archaeological sites in the southern sector (for complete map key, see Figure 11.2)

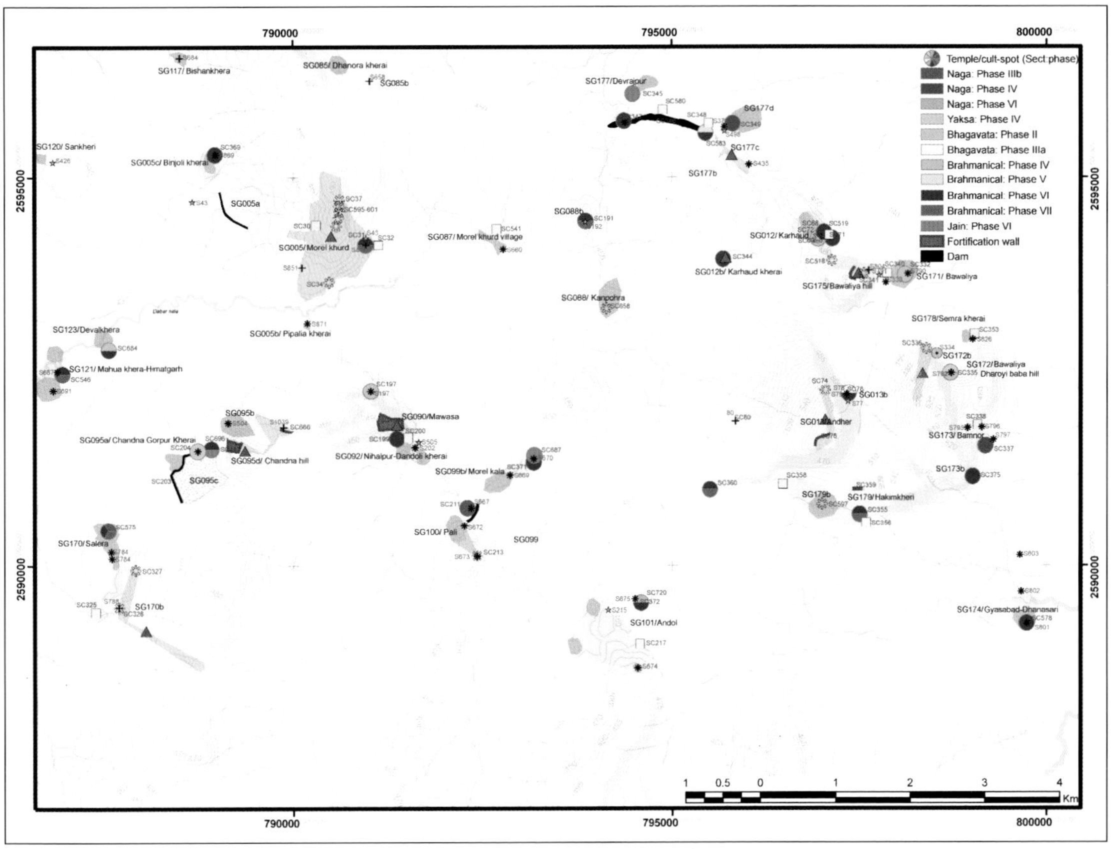

Figure 11.7 Map of archaeological sites in the eastern hilly sector (for complete map key, see Figure 11.2)

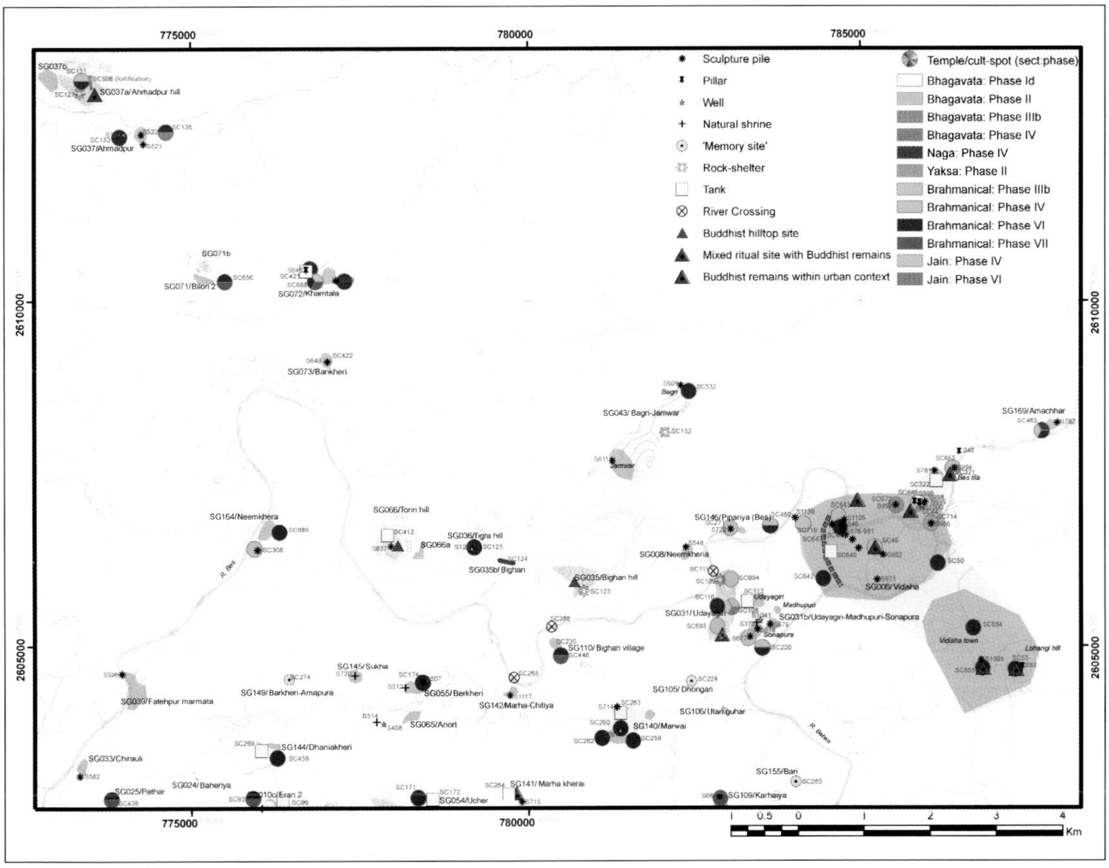

Figure 11.17 Map of archaeological sites in the northern sector (for complete map key, see Figure 11.2)

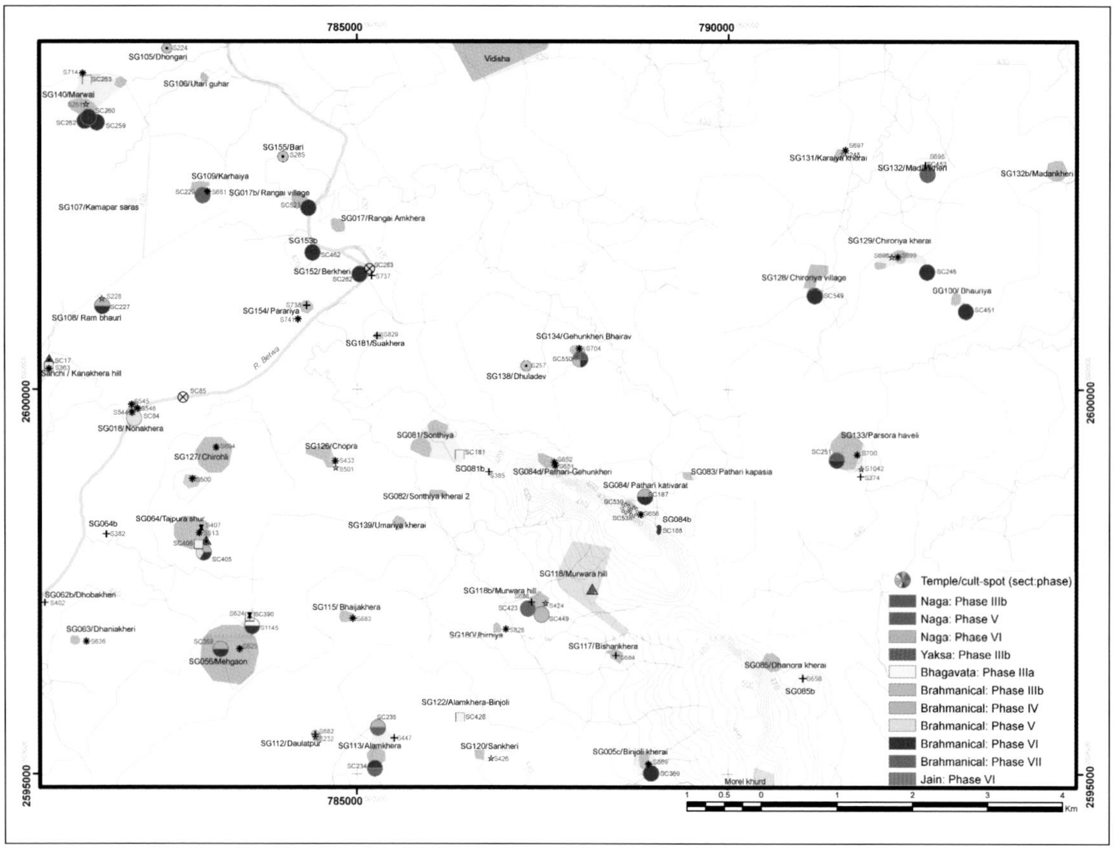

Figure 11.21 Archaeological sites in Sectors 1a and 2a, between Sanchi and Vidisha, and to east of River Betwa (for complete map key, see Figure 11.2)

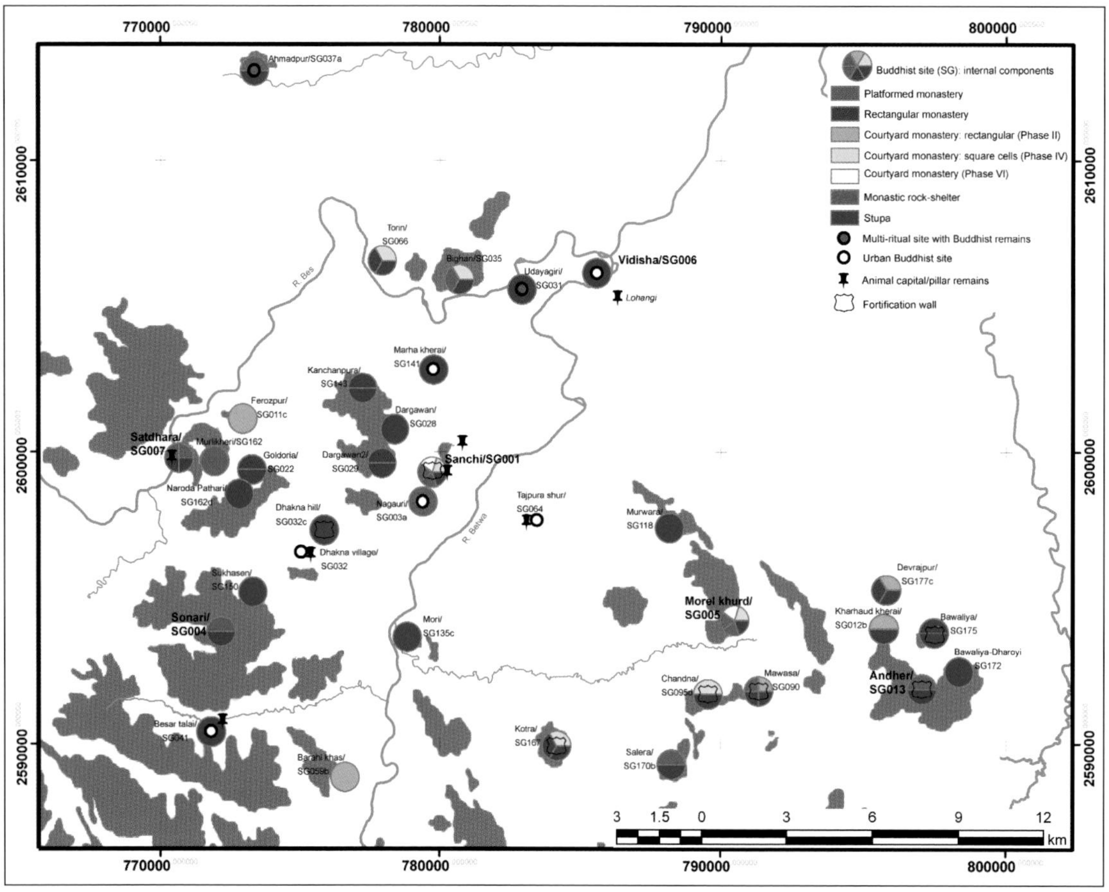

Figure 11.23 Map showing components of Buddhist sites: monastery types, stupas, elements of fortification

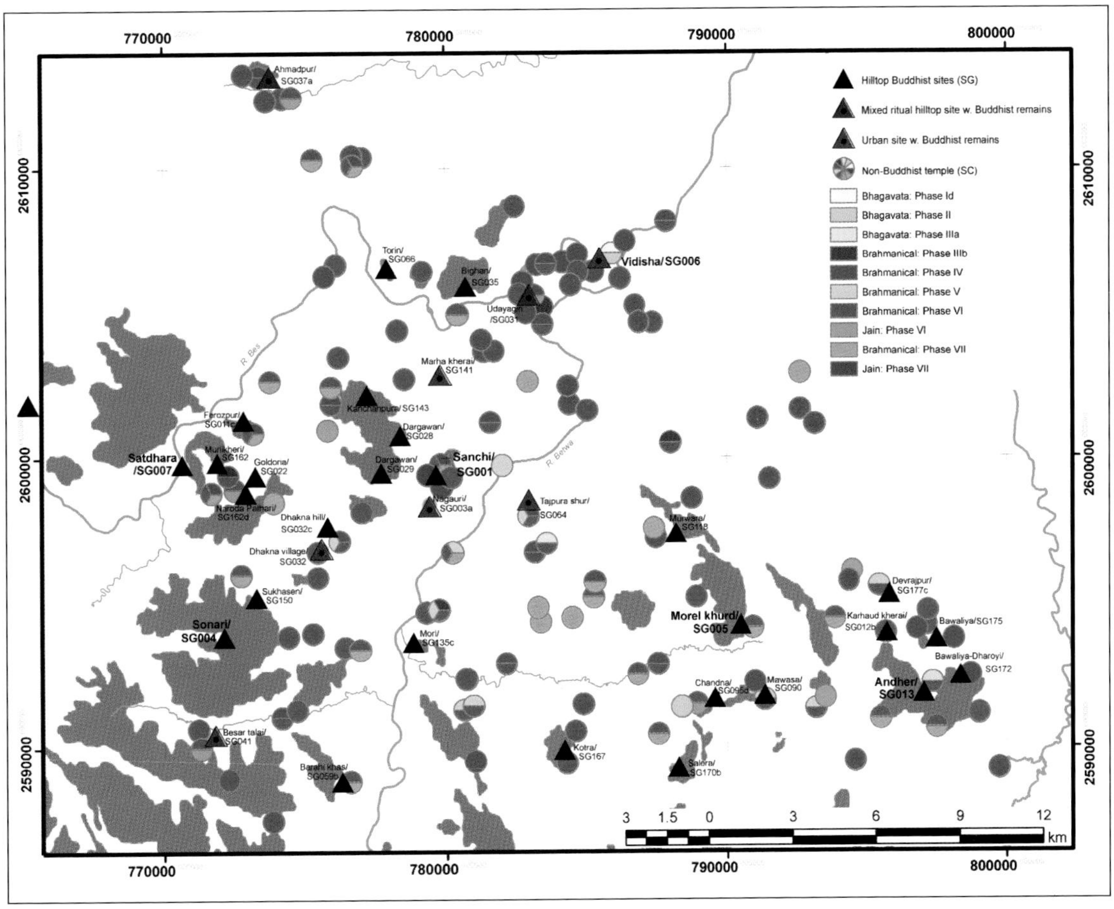

Figure 11.24 Map showing Buddhist sites and Brahmanical temples and cult spots (Phases Id–VII)

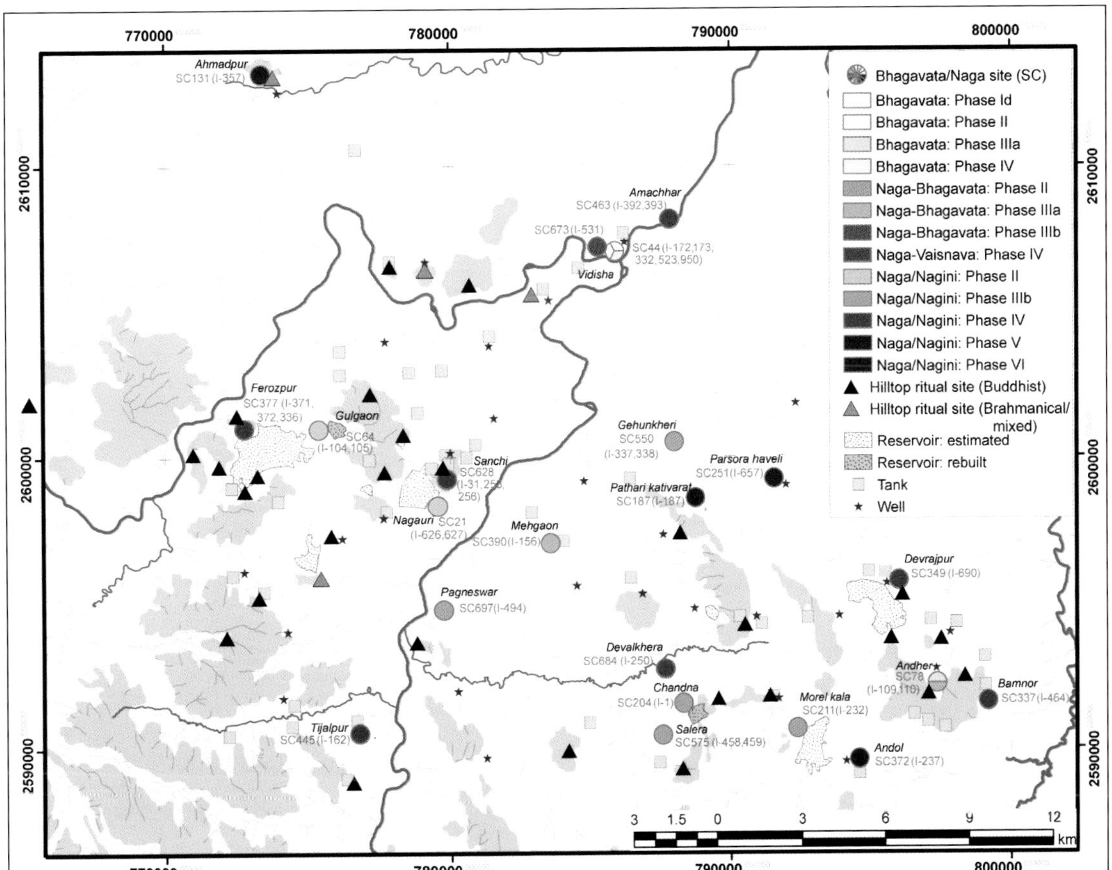

Figure 12.2 Distribution of Naga/Bhagavata cult spots (SC) in relation to reservoirs, tanks, wells and rivers/streams (individual sculpture details given in brackets)

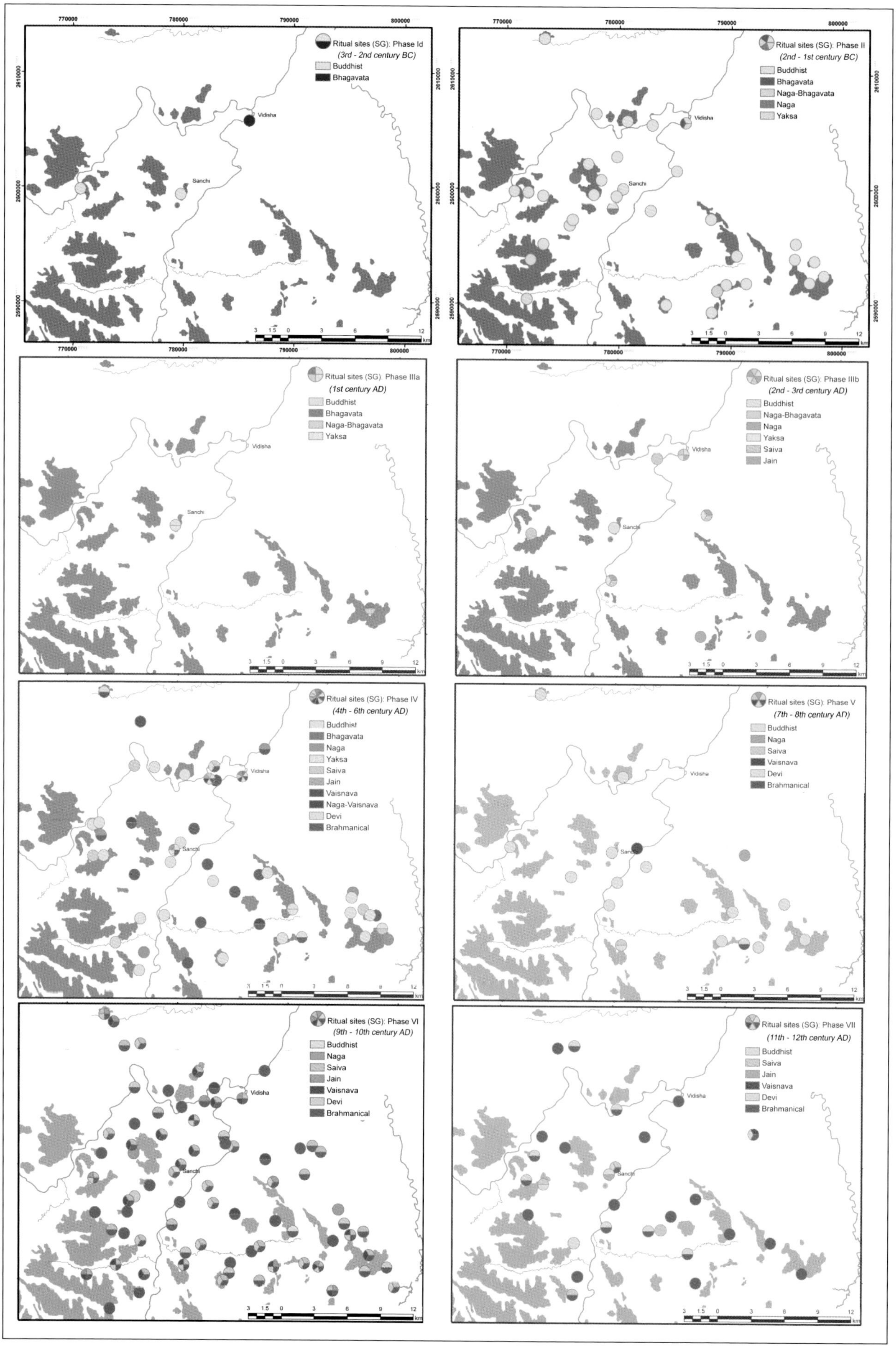

Figure 12.1 The development of the ritual landscape: building Phases Id–VII (SG level)

CHAPTER 14

Irrigation Systems

Introduction

Several of the dams discussed in this chapter have already been mentioned in the course of relating key ritual and habitational sites to their archaeological landscape. These were built to dam streams for irrigation purposes and are distinguishable from 'excavated' village tanks, usually fed by rainwater and local runoff. Further suggestions of their irrigation function are provided by their design efficiency in terms of storage capacity and inflow, and by evidence for spillways and other mechanisms for controlling water levels during the monsoon.[1] The earliest scholarly reference to these dams was by Alexander Cunningham (1854, 365), who commented on a number of ruined embankments in the short valleys between Sanchi and Satdhara (Sector 1b). No precise locations or descriptions were given, but the following observation, although not substantiated by any historical or theological evidence, has a special relevance to the present study: '[The embankments] show that the Buddhist monks were as famous for practical agricultural, as for philosophical learning' (*ibid.*). Almost a century later, Marshall (1940, 13; 1918, pl. XV), in the course of his excavations at Sanchi, made passing reference to the remains of a dam in the 350 m-long valley between Sanchi hill and Nagauri to the south (Figures 1.2 and 9.3; Plate 219). A second dam runs for just over 1 km between Nagauri and Kacchi Kanakhera hill to the west. Again, no detailed descriptions were given, although Marshall suggested that they were designed for downstream irrigation and that they were probably built in c. second century BC, in keeping with the second and most prolific building phase at Sanchi. However, in contrast to Cunningham, Marshall refused to see any connection with Sanchi's Buddhist history, following the canonical prohibition against monks' involvement in agriculture. The documentation of an additional fifteen dams in the SSP study area, together with other aspects of their archaeological context (Figure 1.2; Table 14.1), provided an opportunity to assess Marshall's understanding of the Sanchi dam, both in terms of its chronology and its relationship to Buddhist monasticism.[2]

The dam-based component of the SSP has undergone several phases of research:[3] Stage I focused on dam distribution and form, with estimates of reservoir areas and volumes based on the analysis of surface remains, combined with local present-day hydrological and climate data (Shaw and Sutcliffe 2001; 2003a;

Table 14.1 Dams in the Sanchi area (dimensions in metres unless stated otherwise)

			Dams			Reservoir						Catchment			
Site name	**SC no.**	**Sector**	**Lgt**	**Ht**	**Rev. ht (Stage II)**	**Gradient**	**Lgt**	**Area (m^2)**	**Rev. area (Stage II)**	**Vol. ($m^3 x 10^6$)**	**Rev. vol. (Stage II)**	**Area (m^2)**	**Runoff vol. ($m^3 x 10^6$)**	**Spillway**	**Sluice**
Sanchi-Karondih	99	1b	500	2.3		0.003	770	0.4		0.44		1.95	0.975	N	N
Chandna	204	2b	450	6		–	–	0.25		0.75		1.29	0.645	Y	Y
Dhakna	118	1b	630	4.5		0.007	630	0.4		0.9		4.11	2.055	N	N
Gulgaon	64	1b	600	1.5		0.006	250	0.15		0.11		4.3	2.148	N	N
Sanchi-Dargawan	98	1b	300	2.1		0.008	250	0.08		0.079		0.38	0.19	N	N
Bighan	124	4	250	2.2		0.002	1100	0.28		0.3		1.5	0.75	N	N
Sanchi-Nagauri 1	24	1b	350	2.8	3.5	0.002	1261	1.3	3	1.85	3.6	7.63	3.815	Y	Y
Ferozpur	67	1b	500	4	9	0.003	1300	1	2.3	2	4.7	17	8.5	N	N
Raisen	455	3													
Bhauliya kherai	237	2a	500	1		0.002	5000	0.25		0.13		2.06	1.03	N	N
Morel khurd	42	2b	1100	3.6		–	–	0.6		1.08		2	1	N	N
Devrajpur	346	2b	1100	4	4.5	0.003	1380	1.5	1.86	3.04	3.8	13.49	6.745	Y	Y
Besar talai	148	3	1000	3		0.002	1290	1.29		1.94		8.53	4.265	N	N
Naroda	305	1b	500	2.2		0.005	440	0.22		0.24		1.19	0.592	N	N
Barla hill	292	2b	500	2		0.007	285	0.14		0.14		0.74	0.37	N	N
Morel kala	211	2b	350	6		0.002	2500	0.88		2.63		12.83	6.415	Y	Y
Pathari kativarat	188	2b	80	1.5		0.003	500	0.04		0.03		0.37	0.185	N	N

2003b). During Stage II these estimates were refined following the availability of high-resolution contour maps generated by 'total station' mapping and SRTM data (Shaw and Sutcliffe 2005; Shaw *et al.*, 2007; Beck and Shaw, forthcoming). In Stage I, *terminus ante quem* dates of between c. first century BC and fifth century AD were provided by *nāga* sculptures located on or near some of the dams, with additional chronological indicators provided by morphological and contextual data. During Stage II, a programme of Optically Stimulated Luminescence (OSL) analysis aimed at providing actual construction dates for selected dams. The most successful OSL samples, from the Sanchi dam, suggested a construction date some time between the third and second centuries BC; this fits closely with Marshall's original supposition. Another major objective was to identify the kinds of land use and crops with which the dams were associated: estimates of the reservoirs' storage capacity led to the suggestion that they were designed for rice irrigation as a response to the increased population levels indicated by the distribution of habitational and Buddhist sites in the SSP study area. During Stage II, this hypothesis was tested through the study of ancient pollen sequences from selected reservoir beds (Shaw *et al.*, 2007). Finally, analysis of the relative configuration of dams, ritual sites and settlements led to the working hypothesis that they were part of a cultural package that accompanied the westward spread of Buddhism, urbanisation and the development of centralised state polities during the late centuries BC; and further, that they were central to the development of sustainable exchange networks between Buddhist monks and the local laity, just as similar irrigation systems in Sri Lanka formed the basis of monastic landlordism from c. second century BC onwards (Shaw and Sutcliffe 2003a; 2005).

The chapter is divided into three main sections: Part I deals with general issues of dam morphology and local hydrology, and explains the methods used for reconstructing original reservoir areas, volumes and land use. Part II consists of a site gazetteer arranged by geographical sector. Individual dam descriptions are given, with details on morphology, chronology and land use, as well as ritual and habitational aspects of the wider archaeological landscape. In Part III, these details provide the basis for further discussion of land use and, in particular, the hypothesis that the dams were associated with wet-rice cultivation and that they played a role in the development of reciprocal exchange networks between monks and local agricultural populations.

PART I: PRELIMINARIES

Distribution

All of the sixteen dams documented during the SSP are built across short valleys. The associated reservoirs were filled up through the damming of streams and by collecting runoff from the higher ground upstream (Figure 1.2; Table 14.1). Their distribution is largely determined by the availability of suitable terrain. The study area occupies a transitional area between two major topographical zones (flat agricultural land to the north and dense hilly zones to the south), which may partly explain the high density of reservoirs in a relatively small area. However, due to micro-regional variations in topography, there are also variations in dam distribution across the study area. Sector 1b to the west of Sanchi, with its even balance of hills and short valleys, is particularly suitable for dam construction. Here the hills provide runoff for water supply, while the black-cotton soils in the agricultural plains are suitable for irrigated cultivation. Dam building is more restricted in the central and eastern agricultural plains (Sectors 1a and 2a), and to the north of Vidisha (Sector 4), where open plains are interspersed only occasionally by small, distinctive hillocks. Further, while the gradually sloping terrain in Sector 1b is well suited to the construction of inundation tanks for upstream irrigation, as illustrated by the Sanchi, Ferozpur and Dhakna dams,[4] the deeper valleys in Sector 2b to the east are better suited to downstream irrigation, as illustrated by the Devrajpur and Morel kala dams (Figure 1.2).[5]

Form and structure

All of the dams are in a ruinous state with multiple breaches, although the Chandna and Gulgaon dams are now partly overlain by modern constructions. With the exception of the Murlikheri-Naroda and Bhauliya kherai dams, which have been ploughed over, they usually survive as fairly prominent earthworks (Plate 220).[6]

All the dams have homogeneous earthen cores, with dressed sandstone facing slabs (average dimensions: 1.5 x 0.4 x 0.6 m), mainly on the upstream side, but occasionally downstream too. In some places these are laid horizontally (Plate 222), but in others

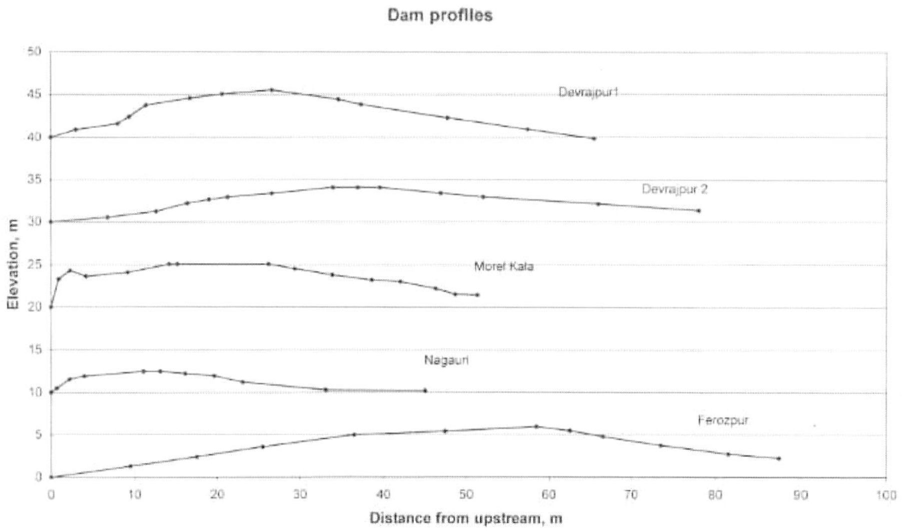

Figure 14.1 Dam profiles

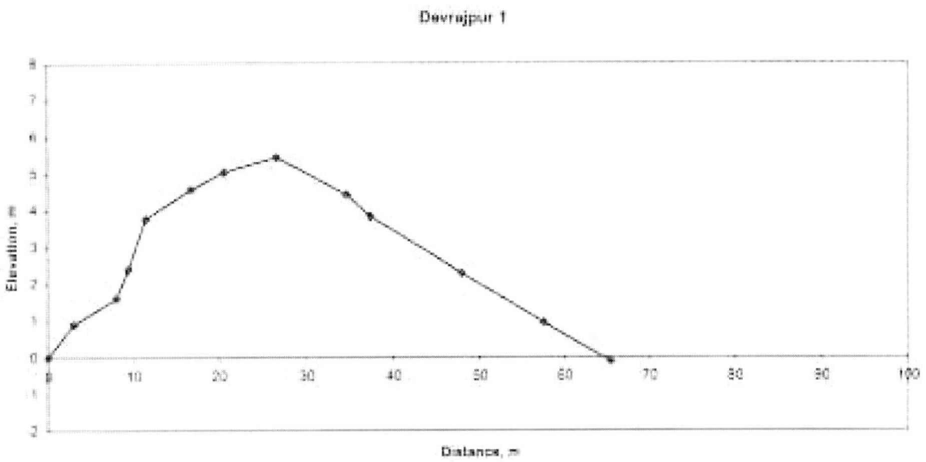

Figure 14.2 Devrajpur: dam profile (with distorted vertical axis)

they are interlocked, with lateral blocks laid parallel to the face, and head-on slabs slotted in perpendicular to the main line of the dam; this arrangement occurs mainly at points where water velocities would have been highest. During Stage II, examination of selected dam profiles (Shaw and Sutcliffe 2005) revealed an additional lining of small fragments behind the masonry, evidently a mechanism for filtration and drainage.

Dam heights range from 1 to over 6 m (Table 14.1), lengths from 80 to 1400 m, and total base widths from 10 to nearly 90 m. On the larger dams, the upstream face is usually much steeper than the downstream face which is relatively flat with a typical gradient of about 1:10 (Figures 14.1, 14.2). There is the possibility that the profile of the lower dams was designed to limit damage in case of overtopping (Shaw and Sutcliffe 2003, 75–6).

Reconstructing reservoir areas and volumes

Assuming that the distribution of dams in Figure 1.2 represents the total number of dams across the study area, it is possible to evaluate their total impact on irrigation and land-use practices, as discussed in Part III. First I will explain the methods used to calculate the original reservoir areas, volumes, catchments and inflows, upon which these discussions are based. Primary measurements were made through a combination of field investigation and map work, with additional information on hydrology, hydrogeology and climate provided by water balance studies carried out in the Betwa basin between 1976 and 1980 (Sutcliffe *et al.*, 1981; Sutcliffe and Green 1986; Hodnett and Bell 1986). Each of these methodologies is described below.

Field measurements and map work

During Stage I dam heights (h) were estimated by taking tape-measured heights at arbitrary points along each dam, with an allowance of 20 cm added to allow for erosion for well-preserved sites, and higher allowances for others. Dam lengths (l) were also measured in the field; for less well-preserved dams, the original length was estimated from topographic maps on the assumption that dams generally extend from the base of one hill to another. The gradient of the reservoir floor α was estimated using 20 m-interval contours provided by Survey of India 1:50,000 maps. These measurements (h, l, α) provided the basis for reconstructing the original reservoir dimensions, with further improvements made in Stage II following the availability of 1 m-interval contours generated from 'total station' mapping and SRTM data (Shaw and Sutcliffe 2005; Beck and Shaw, forthcoming). The dimensions of the dams are listed in Table 14.1, which also includes the estimated reservoir areas and volumes.[7]

A relatively simple model was used for estimating reservoir shape. In most cases, a rectangular outline was assumed, with the embankment length (l) providing the width of the reservoir. The length of the reservoir, in the direction of the land slope, was estimated from the dam height (h) and the gradient (α) as h/α. The surface area (A) of the reservoir is estimated from the product of length and width as lh/α. The average depth of the rectangular reservoir, when full to the top of the embankment, is half the height of the dam, or h/2. The storage volume (V) of the reservoir is hA/2, or $lh^2/2\alpha$. These estimates are used consistently over the study area, and therefore comparisons of reservoir volumes with inflow are valid.

In a few cases, these assumptions were adjusted to correspond to details revealed in maps. For example, because the recently restored reservoirs at Chandna and Ferozpur are now under water (Figure 1.2), it is difficult to estimate their gradients; the surface areas of these reservoirs were thus estimated from maps. At Ferozpur (Figure 14.9), several tributaries converged at the dam site and the estimated area took this into account, after the length of the reservoir had been estimated from the gradient.

During Stage II, the areas between 1 m-interval contours were measured from scaled maps using transparent graph paper and converted to areas in km^2. The cumulative reservoir areas up to successive contour levels were calculated and listed in Table 14.2; these areas are plotted against elevation in Figure 14.3 for Sanchi, Devrajpur and Ferozpur. It will be noted that these relations are essentially linear, except in the immediate vicinity of the dams, indicating a plain sloping gently towards the dam; in the case of the Sanchi dam the slope is approximately 2 m per 1 km, as assumed in the previous estimates.

The incremental and total volumes corresponding to each contour elevation were calculated from the measured area between successive contour levels and the mean elevation of this area. The total volumes are also listed in Table 14.2 and plotted against elevation in Figure 14.4. Because the relations between area and elevation are essentially linear, those between volume and elevation are parabolic. The total areas and volumes were calculated using estimates of the highest continuous level of

Table 14.2 **Reservoir areas and volumes at various elevations: Sanchi, Ferozpur, Devrajpur**

Sanchi			Ferozpur			Devrajpur		
Elevation (m)	**Area (km^2)**	**Volume (m^3x10^6)**	**Elevation (m)**	**Area (km^2)**	**Volume (m^3x10^6)**	**Elevation (m)**	**Area (km^2)**	**Volume (m^3x10^6)**
421	0	0	427	0	0	433	0	0
422	0.22	0.05	428	0	0	434	0.02	0.01
423	1.03	0.68	429	0.01	0.01	435	0.03	0.03
424	2.35	2.37	430	0.04	0.03	436	0.36	0.23
425	3.76	5.43	431	0.19	0.15	437	0.71	0.76
			432	0.53	0.51	438	1.11	1.67
			433	1.09	1.31	439	1.61	3.03
			434	1.73	2.72	440	2.11	4.89
			435	2.31	4.74			
			436	2.99	8.18			

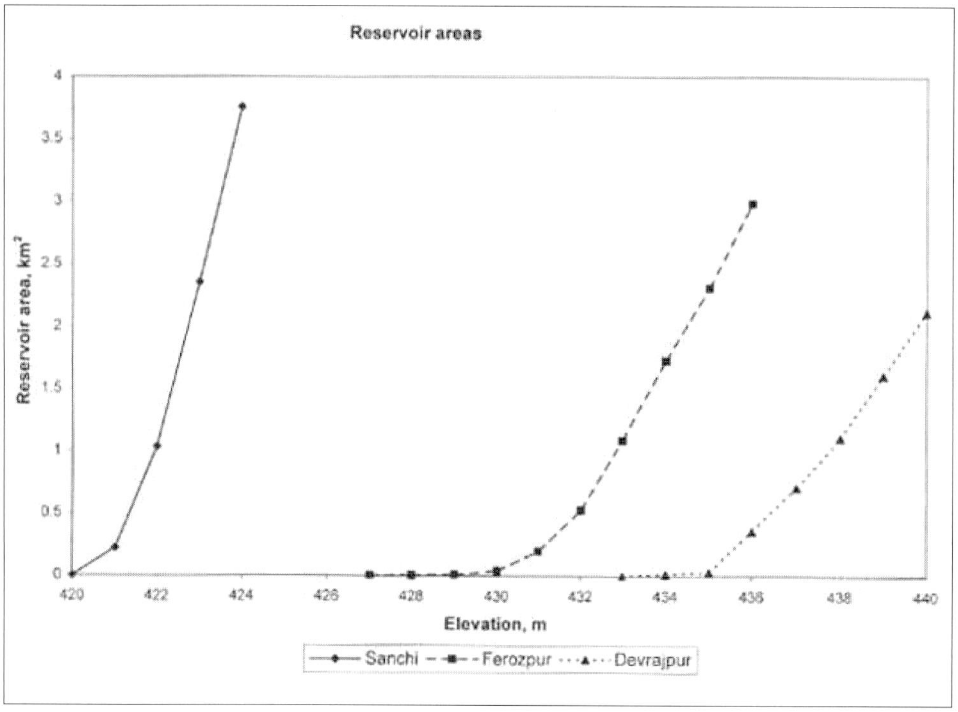

Figure 14.3 Reservoir areas related to elevation: Sanchi, Ferozpur, Devrajpur

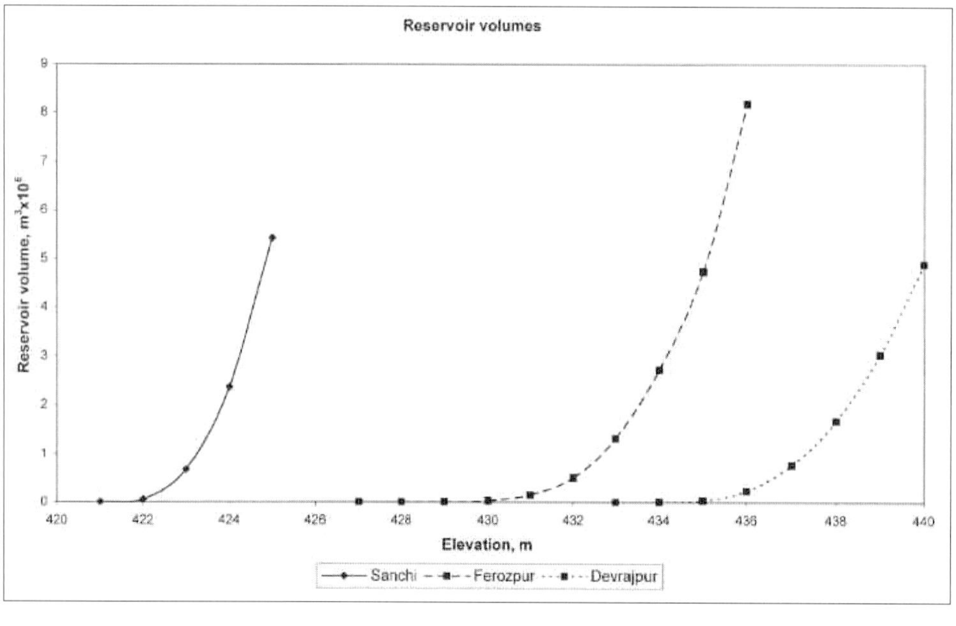

Figure 14.4 Reservoir volumes related to elevation: Sanchi, Ferozpur, Devrajpur

each dam. However, this level may not be precise and the volumes in particular are very sensitive to any level uncertainty.

Reservoir inflow

In order to assess reservoir function and land use, it is necessary to compare the topography and the evidence of historical reservoir dimensions with the present climate and hydrology. The average annual inflow was estimated drawing on the results of the Betwa basin water balance studies mentioned earlier.

The dams are all situated within a radius of about 15 km of Vidisha, where the 50-year annual average rainfall is 1334 mm, with 1230 mm during the monsoon, i.e. June–September (Sutcliffe *et al.*, 1981, 354). These figures correspond to an average annual runoff depth of about 500 mm (Figure 14.6), which, when combined with the measured basin areas, provide estimates of the annual inflow to each reservoir; these estimates of mean annual runoff are included in Table 14.1. These figures are based on the present rainfall regime and basin conditions, and would be conservative if the rainfall over the last 2000 years had been higher than current levels. However, bearing in mind the impact which relatively recent changes to basin vegetation might have had on runoff depths, coupled with suggestions of localised climatic change, discussed in chapter 4, it should be stressed that the most important factor here is the correspondence between the two sets of volumes; the evidence shows that reservoir capacities are strongly related to average inflow, and consistent under- or over-estimation of either would not affect this result. Furthermore, the estimated runoff volumes are in general greater than the estimated reservoir volumes, so the reservoirs are the limiting factor rather than the runoff.

It is interesting to note that the reservoir volumes are in fact closely related to the estimated runoff volumes. The two are compared in Figure 14.5, which shows that the average runoff is sufficient to fill the reservoirs in most cases. In fact the equation linking runoff volumes Q to reservoir capacity V, both in m^3x10^6, may be expressed as Q = 1.598 V + 0.397; this relation is highly significant, with a correlation coefficient (R^2) of 0.859. This implies that the runoff is sufficient to fill the reservoirs easily in an average year under present conditions. If it is assumed that the typical reservoir is 1.60 times the mean annual runoff, and that the distribution of annual runoff is normal with the basin-wide standard deviation of 45% of the average, the statistical properties of the normal distribution imply that the average reservoir would be filled in 9 out of 10 years.

It is perhaps more important to note that the reservoir sizes are reasonably well related to the drainage basin and the expected runoff, which implies that the reservoir dimensions were well adapted to their positions and the runoff available at the site. During Stage II the examination of dam sections at Sanchi and Devrajpur revealed homogeneous cores built in a single phase, and with no evidence of serial construction. This suggests that they were not built through trial and error, but rather were constructed to an appropriate size with an empirical understanding of the principles of water balance. The dimensions of the Devrajpur spillway, discussed later, suggest that the principles of flood control were also understood.

Transpiration

The potential transpiration, or the water loss from a moist crop surface, and also open water evaporation were estimated from the climate variables: temperature, humidity, sunshine and wind speed (Sutcliffe *et al.*, 1981; Sutcliffe and Green 1986; Hodnett and Bell 1986). The monthly values for Bhopal, which may be taken as typical of the Betwa basin, are also included in Table

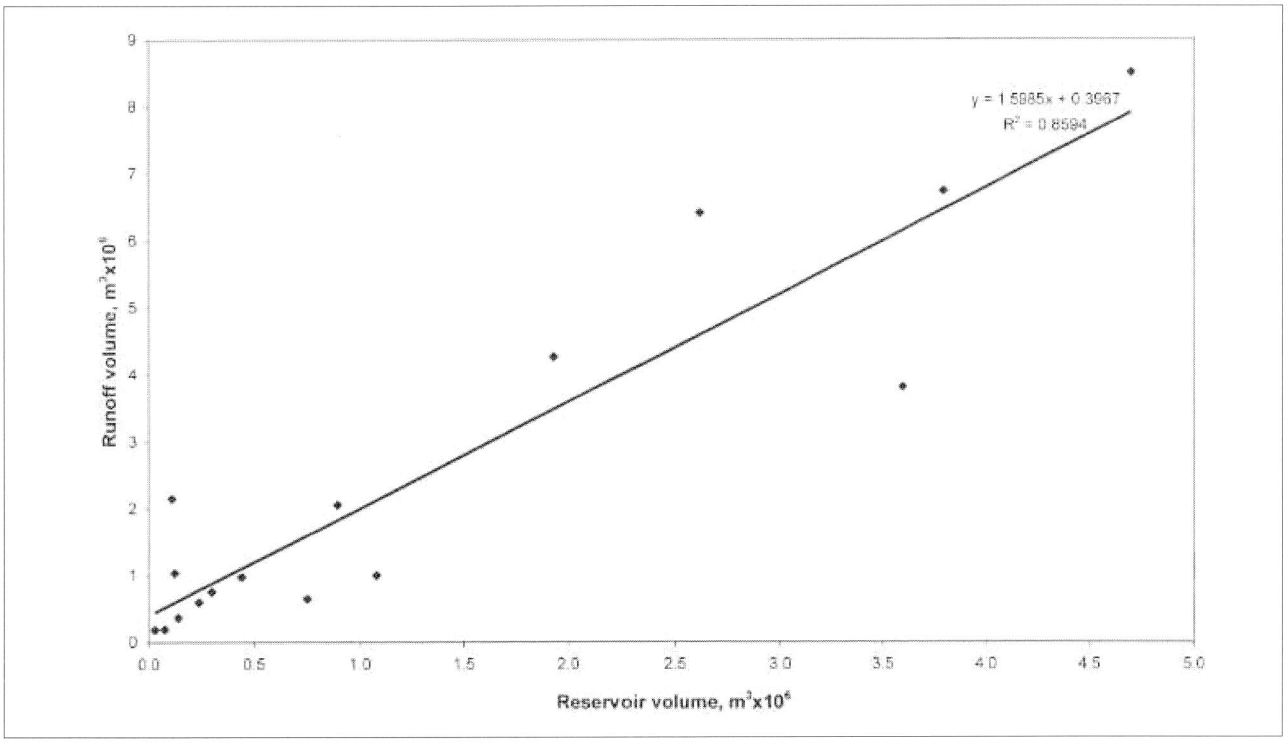

Figure 14.5 Reservoir volume and runoff

Figure 14.6 Monsoon rainfall and runoff: Betwa basin, 1926–79 (after Sutcliffe and Green 1981, fig. 15)

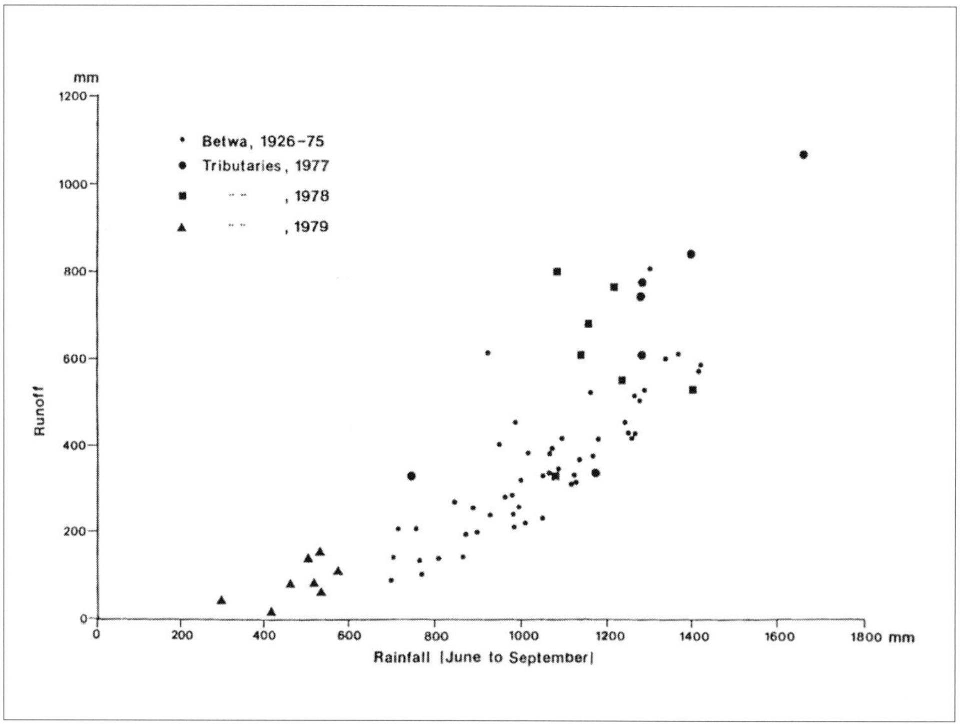

4.1 and Figure 4.3, and total 1640 mm over the year. This water loss is relatively low in winter, rises to a peak in May as the temperature increases, and is depressed in July–September as the humidity rises during the monsoon. Because of the annual balance between rainfall and open water evaporation (Table 4.1), the reservoirs would fill on average towards the end of the monsoon, and the net evaporation from October to June is 1400 mm. Thus the reservoir would retain water throughout the dry season in the absence of abstraction or leakage, provided that the dam height was greater than about 1.4 m. This is the case with nearly all the dams, so that water would be available throughout the year.

Seasonal cycle of climate

The typical seasonal climate cycle is illustrated in Figure 4.3 by the balance between average monthly rainfall and potential transpiration. From January to June there is a period of water deficit, when rainfall is much lower than potential transpiration, and vegetation is unable to transpire without water supply from irrigation. As a result, deciduous forest species such as teak shed their leaves during this time. From July to September the rainfall exceeds transpiration, and a period of soil moisture recharge or replenishment is followed by a period of water surplus when almost all the runoff occurs. From October the rainfall again falls below the potential transpiration rate, and the transpiration from crops or other green vegetation is only maintained for a while by using the soil moisture store, which was recharged at the beginning of the monsoon. The soil moisture store is limited by soil capacity and rooting depth, and is equivalent to a depth of about 200 mm, as estimated by water balance studies and by soil moisture measurements (Sutcliffe *et al.*, 1981).

Runoff

The runoff from the Betwa basin is the residual after the rainfall has contributed to transpiration or evaporation, and also to soil moisture recharge. It was measured over a period of 50 years, from 1926 to 1975, at Dhukwan at the lower end of the basin of 20600 km^2 with an average runoff of 351 mm (Sutcliffe *et al.*, 1981.). This runoff is also concentrated between June and September, though there is some residual baseflow from groundwater reserves after the monsoon. The rainfall on which the runoff depends varies widely from year to year, and the standard deviation over the 50-year period was 211 mm, or 18.5% of the average rainfall of 1138 mm. Because the runoff is a residual of the hydrological cycle, the standard deviation of the annual runoff is high at 157 mm, or 44.7% of the average. Thus the annual variation of the runoff is relatively higher than that of basin rainfall. In fact the relation between basin rainfall and runoff, derived from the whole Betwa basin record, supplemented by records from various tributaries in 1977–9 (Figure 14.6), provides a means of estimating runoff from monsoon rainfall. This provides an indication of the possible effect on runoff of historical changes of climate and in particular rainfall.

An indication of the runoff regime of the smaller streams in the Vidisha area is given by a detailed study of the Nion at Kuakheri (Sutcliffe and Green, 1986). During 1978, average monsoon rainfall first recharged the soil moisture store, then gave rise to groundwater recharge and runoff of 555 mm over the basin of 921 km^2. In 1979, when monsoon rainfall was exceptionally low at 40% of average, the sequence was similar but runoff was only 80 mm. The runoff pattern was sporadic in both years and confined to two spates in 1979. The benefits of reservoir storage are thus clear.

Comparative framework

Before discussing additional aspects of the design of the Sanchi dams and their implications for land use and chronology, it is necessary to discuss the comparative framework for interpreting this material. In India, the closest parallel is provided by the well-known Sudarsana lake (*tataka*) at Junagadh, discussed in chapter 2. A second-century-AD inscription by the Ksatrapa ruler Rudradaman is carved onto the Girnar rock, which also bears the earlier Asokan edicts, at the head of the reservoir (Shaw and Sutcliffe 2003). The inscription refers to the king's repair to the dam, and to its earlier construction and subsequent improvement by Candragupta Maurya and Asoka respectively (Kielhorn 1905–6). Later repairs are also mentioned in Skandagupta's inscription carved on the same rock (Bhandarkar *CII*, III, 296–304; Fleet *CII*, III, 56–65).[8] Following several unsuccessful attempts to locate the dam, the first reliable archaeological identification was by Mehta (1968) who gives its length as 1 km, height as 17 m, and reservoir area as 1 km^2 (*ibid.*, 24). Following the same method used for the SSP study area, its total volume can be estimated at around 8.500 m^{3}x 10^6 (Shaw and Sutcliffe 2003a). This is somewhat larger than the Sanchi reservoirs, but other structural parallels, to be discussed below, place them in a similar category. Furthermore, the fact that many of these structural features find reference in the Rudradaman inscription makes the Sudarsana dam invaluable for understanding the Sanchi dams.

By far the richest body of scholarship on ancient irrigation in South Asia relates to the complex network of reservoirs and canals in Sri Lanka's Dry Zone. The development from village tanks to much larger reservoirs, often fed by a supply canal and supplying water for distant irrigation, appears to have taken place around the third century BC (Gunawardana 1978b, 73). This included the development of sluice technology to control outflow into the supply canal network, and also the development of spillways to protect the larger dams. Based on the dimensions given in Table 14.1, it is possible to compare the area and volume of Sri Lankan and central Indian reservoirs. If this comparison is based on reservoir size alone, the Sanchi reservoirs may be placed somewhere between the average 'village tank' and the larger Sri Lankan reservoirs such as the Basawakkulam and Tissawewa in Anuradhapura (Shaw and Sutcliffe 2003a). It is, however, noted that the overall dam heights are much larger than the mean depths of the reservoirs, indicated by comparison of reservoir volumes and surface areas; this may indicate sluice control at lower reservoir levels. This comparison is important for assessing the irrigation function and associated land use in the SSP study area. However, the comparison may be misleading as the irrigation contexts of the Sri Lankan Dry Zone and central India are so different. The two-fold evolutionary scheme which developed in Sri Lanka may not be relevant to central India because of the very different conditions. In Sri Lanka the irrigation system was based on an advanced network of canal-fed reservoirs, which in several cases supplemented the yield of local catchments by exploiting rivers draining from neighbouring wet zones, and which supplied water through feeder canals to areas suitable for irrigation. The range of rainfall in Sri Lanka is much greater than in central India, and the timing of the two rainfall seasons is less predictable than the single monsoon in central India. The soil moisture storage capacity of Sanchi's black-cotton soils, in close proximity to sites suitable for the construction of medium-sized reservoirs, means that there is no need to draw on additional supplies from perennial rivers or to supply irrigation water though long canals.

Despite these differences, however, the early Sri Lankan reservoirs provide important markers for evaluating various structural features of the Sanchi dams. Furthermore, the foregoing observations are important for reassessing the received understanding of irrigation in ancient India. Comparisons with Sri Lankan irrigation systems helped to shape the view that reservoirs played a marginal role in ancient Indian irrigation and that they did not progress beyond the level of the 'village tank' (Parker 1909, 349). This assumption appears to be unfounded, due largely to the geomorphological differences between the two areas already described. Furthermore, comparisons based largely on size alone without regard to hydrological factors have overlooked the fact that reservoirs like those in the Sanchi area represent the peak of a local irrigation tradition. There was no need or advantage for them to be made bigger or more complex, as they already served their function quite adequately and made the best use of the runoff available.

Flood control and water distribution

Spillways

Only three of the dams in the SSP study area revealed evidence of spillways, or 'waste-weirs', as they are sometimes referred to in South Asian literature. Examples noted at Devrajpur, Morel kala and possibly Sanchi consist of a cutting through the bedrock between one end of the dam and the adjoining hillside (Plate 223). Similar spillways are found at some of the early Sri Lankan reservoirs (Parker 1909, 358), with close equivalents in Gujarat, at Junagadh (Mehta 1968, 24), as well as a group of smaller dams in the Devnimori area (Mehta 1963, 359). A rocky weir situated to the east of the north abutment of the Junagadh dam, and examined by the present author in 2002 (Shaw and Sutcliffe 2003, 90), appears to correspond to the term '*parivāha*' used in Rudradaman's inscription (Kielhorn 1905–6; Mehta *ibid.*). The weir consists of a 'natural' (i.e. unexcavated) ravine (c. 10 x 10 m in plan) between the embankment and the adjacent hillside and contains the remains of a 'temporary' dam as found at many of the Sri Lankan reservoirs (Shaw and Sutcliffe 2003a).

Apart from the three aforementioned examples, no other rock-cut spillways were located in the SSP study area. However, evidence from smaller dams in Sri Lanka suggests that rocky outcrops adjacent to embankments could have provided natural spillways without excavation. It is also possible that spillways have been destroyed by modern roads, dam reconstruction, and the building of modern spillways as at Chandna and Gulgaon; it is significant to note that the design and location of the simple modern spillway at the northern end of the Gulgaon dam (Shaw and Sutcliffe 2003a, fig. 6), positioned about 1.5 m below the dam crest, is not dissimilar to the ancient spillways at Devrajpur and Morel kala.

In addition, the lower embankments could have relied on a reasonably level top and shallow downstream gradients, so that any overtopping would be distributed over a wide section of the downstream face, limiting the depth and thus the effect of spill. However, there is evidence for multiple breaching at some smaller dam sites, in particular at Dargawan and Karondih, to the west of Sanchi. For higher and potentially more vulnerable dams, spillways were excavated to minimise the risk of damage.

Control structures

Additional mechanisms for flood control were also noted in the study area, individual examples of which are described in Part II. The dams are usually pierced by a stream channel at their deepest point or, in other words, at the natural drainage point for the dam catchment. Clear examples of this pattern were noted at the four highest dams, Sanchi, Devrajpur, Morel kala and Ferozpur (Figure 1.2). At Sanchi and Morel kala, the main feeder pierces the main dam at its southern limit, and at Devrajpur at its western limit. In all cases, except for those sites where recent reconstruction has occurred (e.g. Chandna and Gulgaon), there is clear evidence for dam-failure at some time in the past. The location of this failure, at the deepest point of the dam where it is pierced by the main feeder stream, suggests that flood damage was the principal cause.

Masonry remains, attesting to some kind of monumentalised control structure, have been found in the feeder streams of the four highest dam sites mentioned above, and will be described in detail in Part II. Their location at the dam's most vulnerable point is in keeping with patterns from other parts of South Asia: as discussed later, the repair and upkeep of dams are often commemorated in a monumental manner due to the merit (both ritual and social) associated with such acts (Morrison 1993; Venkayya 1906).

Sluices

No evidence for sluices or outlets for downstream irrigation has been located at any of the dams, although future excavation may shed light on the subject. The complex distribution systems of the kind found in Sri Lanka to supply irrigation water over large distances would not have been necessary in the study area, and several of the dams, for example Sanchi and Gulgaon, appear to have been designed for upstream, rather than downstream irrigation. It is possible that the smaller dams used simple pipes that have not survived in the archaeological record. A similar arrangement is implied by the term *praṇālī* in the aforementioned Rudradaman inscription at Junagadh. As argued elsewhere (Shaw and Sutcliffe 2003, 91), this term is more likely to have referred to a simple sluice than a canal as suggested by Mehta (1968, 26). The literal meaning of *praṇālī* is 'pipe' (Monier Williams, 1899, 660), thus implying a small channel for distributing water to the downstream fields. A variant of this term, *niddhamana-panālī* ('drainage pipe'), occurs in the *Samantapāsādikā* (vol. II, 344) a fifth-century-AD Sri Lankan commentary on the Buddhist Canon, to describe a system for removing water from a reservoir using simple bailing devices, or 'water wheels' such as those described in the *Culavaṁsa* (v. 79: 31-8). In this text, the term is contrasted with *nibbāhana-udaka* ('spout for removing water'), which refers to an actual sluice for releasing water from a tank into a network of canals (Gunawardana 1978b, 70).

Similar devices may have been used on the larger of the Sanchi dams, and may even in later years have developed along the lines of the Sri Lankan *bisokotuva* sluice (Gunawardana 1978b; Bohingamuwa 2005) and its close equivalents in South India. At Vijayanagara, for example, water was discharged through pipes laid at bed level, and regulated by the vertical movement of a stone board attached to a rod (Davison 1997). Some of the smaller dams in the SSP area may have been deliberately breached in order to allow for water-release during the monsoon, and filled up again during the dry season (Willcocks 1930). Another suggestion, to be discussed later, is that cultivation could have taken place at the edges of the reservoir as the water level subsided. Finally, there is evidence that some of the lower-gradient reservoirs were used directly for the upstream irrigation of rice paddy.

Chronology

Dams are difficult to date due to the nature of their construction, with building material often sourced from multiple locations, and frequent repairs. Assigning an original context to associated archaeological material is rarely straightforward. The dating of Sri Lankan and South Indian dams has traditionally relied on inscriptions and constructional (particularly sluice) typologies (Venkayya 1906; Parker 1909; Brohier 1934 [reprint 1979]; Davison-Jenkins 1997), although in recent years, some advances in the dating of canals have been made in Sri Lanka (Myrdal-Runebjer 1994; Risberg *et al.*, 2002) and southern Cambodia (Bishop *et al.*, 2004, 321[9]) through the use of C14 and OSL techniques respectively.

During Stage I, the main chronological markers were *nāga* sculptures situated on or near some of the embankments (Shaw 2004a; Shaw and Sutcliffe 2001, 68–71; 2003a, 84–5). Although *nāgas* became closely aligned with Buddhist and Brahmanical traditions, their reputed control over the natural elements, and particularly rainfall, was often maintained through their close spatial link to sources of water; of the 18 groups of serpent sculptures (total individual pieces: 24) whose original provenance is known, seven are associated with irrigation reservoirs, five with village tanks, one with a well and four with rivers or streams (Figure 12.2; Table 12.2). A body of archaeological, textual and epigraphical evidence testifying to similar linkages in other parts of north India (Puri 1963, 50; Härtel 1993) and Sri Lanka (Parker 1909, 657; Gunarwardana 1979, 215) means that even when *nāga* sculptures have been relocated in modern shrines, it is often possible to trace them back to their original position. On the basis of these linkages, *terminus ante quem* dates varying between c. first century BC and fifth century AD were provided for the dams. Other chronological pointers were provided by morphological factors such as stone-facing type, and by the dates of associated settlements and Buddhist sites.

As discussed in chapter 12, the earliest *nāgas* are those from Gulgaon and Nagauri, both datable on art-historical grounds to about 50 BC. The former, now stored in the Sanchi Archaeological Museum, originally stood on the Gulgaon dam (Plate 138), while the Nagauri *nāga* which is still in its original location stands just metres from the edge of the former Sanchi reservoir (Plate 139). The similarity between the size and shape of the stone blocks used in the facing of both dams further suggests a similar date (Table 14.1). To state the obvious, the *nāga* sculptures must have been installed some time after the completion of the dams and thus provide reliable *terminus ante quem* dates in the mid-first century BC. A similar link between *nāga* images and dams was found at Chandna and Morel kala, providing terminal dates of, respectively, the early first century AD and c. second to third century AD.

As far as the dams' actual construction dates are concerned, our working hypothesis accords closely with Marshall's (1940, 13) suggestion that the Sanchi dam was roughly contemporary to either Phase I or II at Sanchi. In Stage II this hypothesis was tested through a programme of OSL dating (Shaw and Sutcliffe 2005; Shaw *et al.*, 2007). The project was underlain by the assumption that the OSL clock was reset to zero when the sediments were last exposed to light during the original excavation of the dams; because sediments need to be disturbed prior to being deposited in a dam, we should be able to date the last disturbance by measuring the amount of accumulated trapped charge, or time elapsed, since the sediment's last exposure to light. Sediment samples were collected from the two largest dams, Sanchi and Devrajpur, having scraped back existing road-cuttings to reveal clean sections. Sediment samples for supplementary OSL dating were also collected from cores hand-drilled in the dried-up reservoir beds at Sanchi and Devrajpur, as well as Karondih. The results confirmed the suitability of local sediments for geological dating methods, as well as our working hypothesis that the dams were constructed during the late centuries BC: the two most successful OSL samples were from the Sanchi dam, which produced dates of c. 450 BC (+- 240 years) and c. 210 AD (+- 190 years).

Pollen analysis

Coring carried out within the Sanchi, Devrajpur and Karondih reservoir beds was also aimed at establishing Holocene pollen sequences for testing our working hypothesis, discussed further in Part II, that the dams were built principally for wet-rice cultivation, as opposed to wheat, the main staple today. Nine sediment core samples were studied using the standard technique of acetolysis (Erdtman 1943), which yielded an average pollen sum of 105 to 175 (Shaw *et al.*, 2007).[10] Although these sequences cannot lead to the identification of specific agricultural crops, they are useful for providing a broad palaeovegetative and climatic setting for the dams (Shaw *et al.*, 2007, figs. 9–11, table 2, pl. 11).

At all three coring locations, samples were selected for pollen analysis from three different levels within the sediment core: i) the middle of the reservoir silts; ii) the base of the silts; and iii) the underlying buried sediment. The resulting sequences were all roughly similar, with most variation reflecting differences in reservoir area and volume at the three sites. The results show that all three reservoirs were surrounded by open grassland vegetation during the course of sediment accumulation. Grasses (Poaceae) were the dominant species, followed by Asteraceae (Tubuliflorae and Liguliflorae) and sporadic distribution of other herbaceous plants such as Ranunculaceae, Malvaceae (*Hibiscus*), *Chrozophora* and *Justicia*. Marshy taxa, such as sedges (Cyperaceae), *Polygonum*, *Polygala*, *Solanum* and *Hygrophila*, also appeared in high numbers, particularly at Devrajpur, the largest reservoir in the area. Also well represented were the pollens of aquatic plants such as *Lemna*, *Potamogeton* and *Typha* (elephant grass); freshwater algae such as *Zygnema*, *Spirogyra* and *Botryococcus*; and monolete and trilete ferns. These pollens all attest to extensive areas of waterlogged, marshy terrain. The predominance of moisture-loving trees such as *Madhuca indica* (mahua), *Holoptelea* (chilbil) and others further supports the picture of a warm, swampy environment. The occurrence of cerealia pollens, along with commonly associated ruderal plants such as Chenopodiaceae/Amaranthaceae (spinach/amaranth), Caryophyllaceae, Brassicaceae (mustard) and *Cannabis sativa* (hemp), confirms that much of the surrounding terrain was under cultivation. As discussed in chapter 4, the identification of specific cereal crops is not possible through pollen analysis alone and will require supplementary phytolith sampling in the future at nearby habitational sites. Further, the pollen sequences remain undated due to the unsatisfactory nature of the OSL samples from the reservoir cores, a problem which will be remedied through future C14 dating programmes. However, despite these weaknesses, the predominance of spores from wet, marshland plant species accords closely with the kind of water-logged environment expected of a rice-growing regime (Shaw and Sutcliffe 2005).

PART II: GAZETTEER

Western hilly sector (1b)

A total of seven dams were documented in Sector 1b (Table 14.1); some of these probably correspond to the ruins seen by Cunningham (1854, 365), mentioned earlier, in the short valleys between Sanchi and Satdhara.

Sanchi

The dam between Sanchi hill and Nagauri, described earlier, stands at a height of 2.8 m (or 424.5 m above sea level) and would have formed a reservoir covering an area of about 3 km^2 with a storage capacity of about 3.6 m^3 x 10^6, fed by streams draining from the hills to the west (Figures 9.3, 14.7). Earlier uncertainties over the function of the second dam between Nagauri and Kacchi Kanakhera in the west (Shaw and Sutcliffe 2003a), due to the higher ground levels to the south, were clarified by contour planning during Stage II (Shaw and Sutcliffe 2005). The dam's position outside the basin's natural drainage channel suggests that it acted as a retaining wall rather than a storage dam.

Other developments during Stage II included the examination of a road-cutting at the southern limit of the main dam, which was cleaned back to form a vertical section down to the present road surface. This revealed additional aspects of dam construction and allowed for the collection of sediment and ceramic samples for OSL dating, described below. The dam section revealed an earthen core, with stone facing and an inner lining of stone packing on the upstream side (Figure 14.8; Plates 224–5). As shown in Figure 14.8, the earthen core consists of several layers. These reflect the process by which the dam was built up by piling layers of earth one upon the other.

Water control

Although no sluice gate was found, comparisons with patterns at Devrajpur, Morel kala and Ferozpur suggest that the central control structure was probably located over the main feeder stream which has breached the dam approximately midway along its length (Figure 14.7). A number of dressed masonry slabs noted in the stream about 15 m downstream of the breach support this suggestion. A possible spillway was also identified in the form of a low depression between the northern end of the dam and the lower outcroppings of Sanchi hill. As discussed earlier, similar spillways, either cut out of the bedrock or utilizing the lower ground between the dam and the adjoining escarpment, occur at Devrajpur and Morel kala, with close parallels in Gujarat and Sri Lanka (Shaw and Sutcliffe 2001, 67; 2003a, 76–7). Immediately downstream of the probable spillway at the edge of a cultivated field, a small depression may correspond to a ploughed-out overspill tank, as found, for example, downstream of the Devrajpur spillway described later.

Dating considerations

As discussed earlier, the first-century-BC *nāga* sculpture at the foot of Nagauri hill provides a *terminus ante quem* for the main Sanchi dam, by virtue of the fact that its current position corresponds with the edge of the ancient water-body (Figure 9.3). The aim of the Stage II OSL sampling programme was to test working hypotheses about the dam's actual construction date (Shaw *et al.*, 2007).

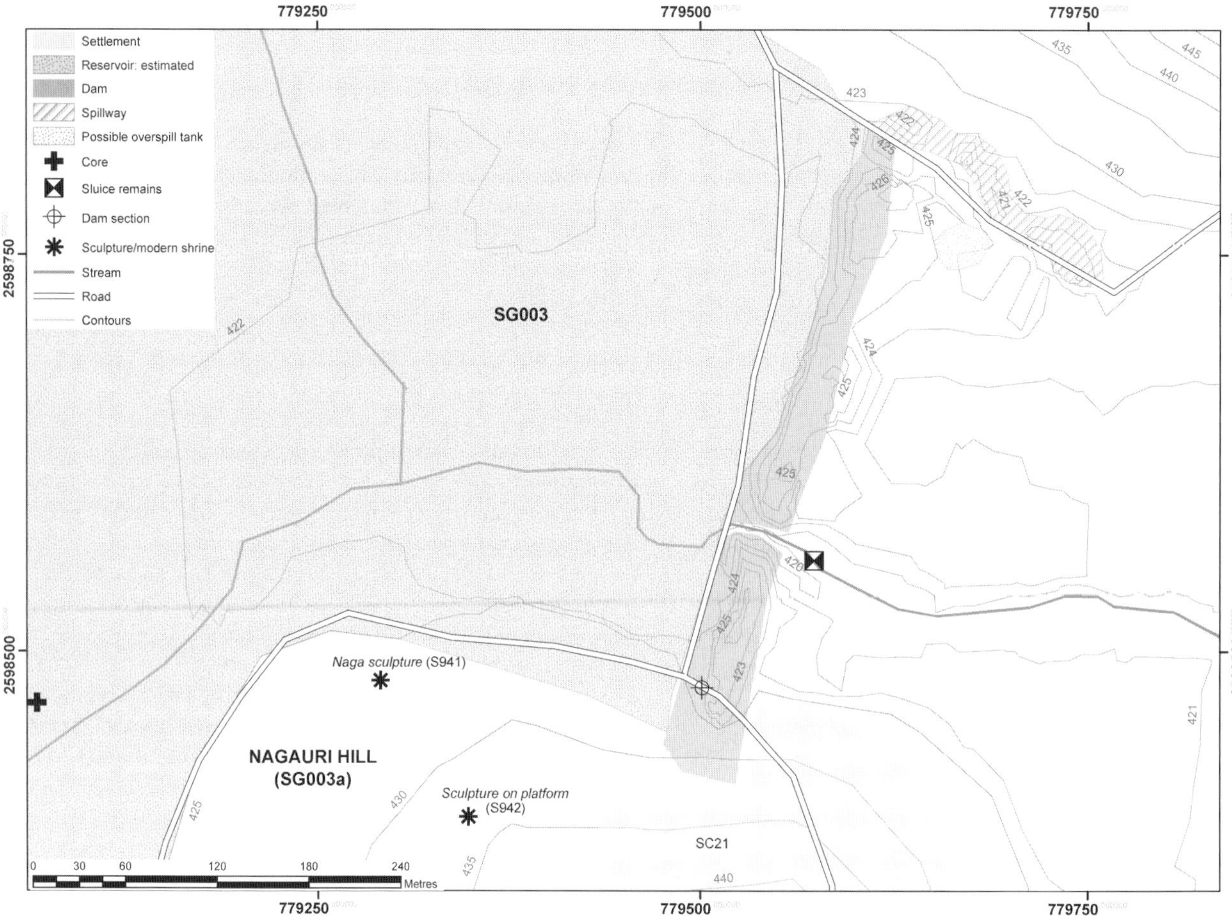
779250
779500
779750
Settlement
Reservoir: estimated
Dam
Spillway
Possible overspill tank
Core
Sluice remains
Dam section
Sculpture/modern shrine
Stream
Road
Contours
2598750
2598500
SG003
Naga sculpture (S941)
NAGAURI HILL
(SG003a)
Sculpture on platform
(S942)
SC21
0 30 60 120 180 240
Metres

Figure 14.7 Detailed map of the Sanchi dam

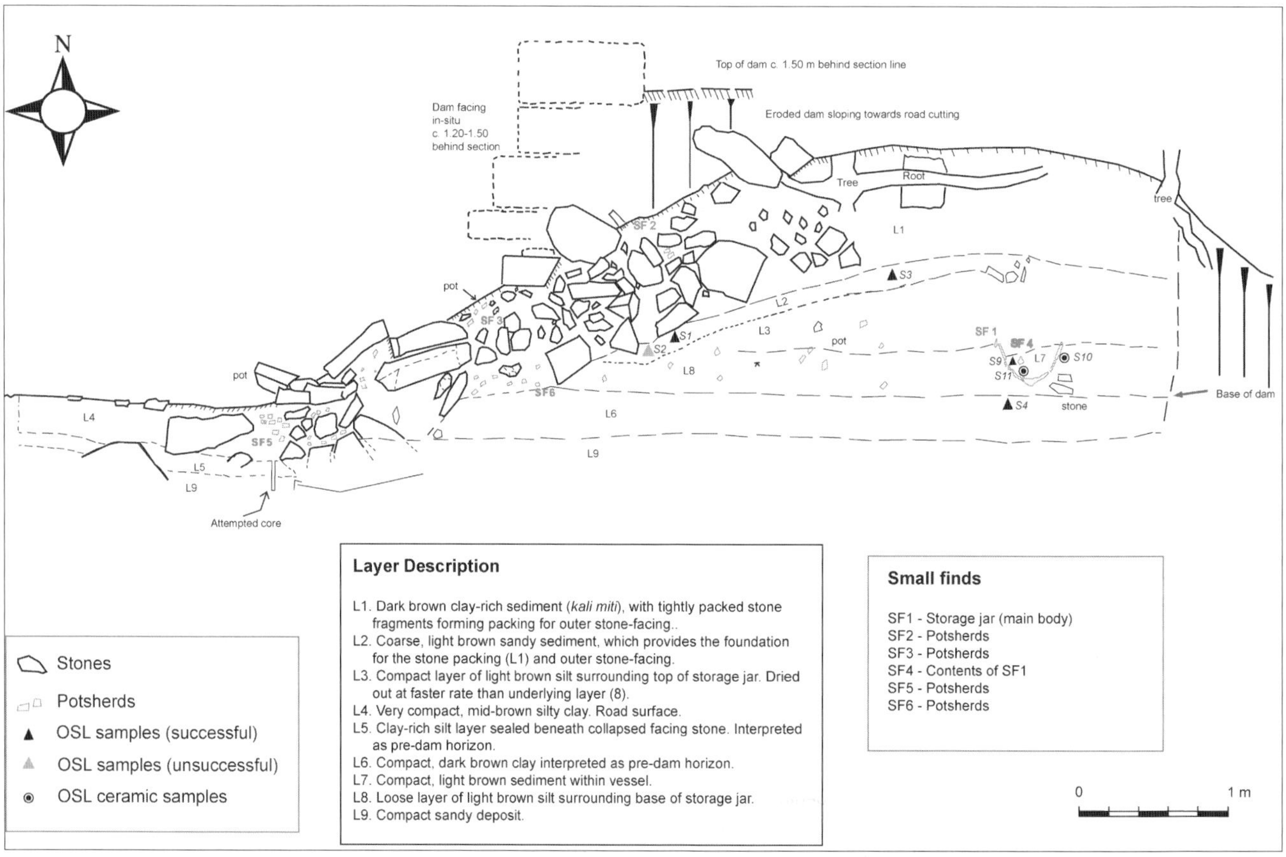
N
Top of dam c. 1.50 m behind section line
Dam facing
in-situ
c. 1.20-1.50
behind section
Eroded dam sloping towards road cutting
Tree
Root
tree
L1
L2
L3
L4
L5
L6
L7
L8
L9
SF 1
SF 2
SF 3
SF 4
SF5
SF6
S1
S2
S3
S4
S9
S10
S11
pot
stone
Base of dam
Attempted core
Stones
Potsherds
OSL samples (successful)
OSL samples (unsuccessful)
OSL ceramic samples
Layer Description
L1. Dark brown clay-rich sediment (*kali miti*), with tightly packed stone fragments forming packing for outer stone-facing..
L2. Coarse, light brown sandy sediment, which provides the foundation for the stone packing (L1) and outer stone-facing.
L3. Compact layer of light brown silt surrounding top of storage jar. Dried out at faster rate than underlying layer (8).
L4. Very compact, mid-brown silty clay. Road surface.
L5. Clay-rich silt layer sealed beneath collapsed facing stone. Interpreted as pre-dam horizon.
L6. Compact, dark brown clay interpreted as pre-dam horizon.
L7. Compact, light brown sediment within vessel.
L8. Loose layer of light brown silt surrounding base of storage jar.
L9. Compact sandy deposit.
Small finds
SF1 - Storage jar (main body)
SF2 - Potsherds
SF3 - Potsherds
SF4 - Contents of SF1
SF5 - Potsherds
SF6 - Potsherds
0
1 m

Figure 14.8 Sanchi dam section (scaled drawing)

Three OSL dates were obtained from samples collected from separate contexts within and below the dam (Table 14.3; Figure 14.8; Plate 224); two dates from fragments of a storage jar at the base of the dam (Figure 14.8; Plate 225; Shaw *et al.*, 2007, pl. 8); and a further two from a sediment sample and a separate pottery sherd collected from the deposit (L7) inside the jar (Shaw *et al.*, 2007).

The first OSL sample (S1) was collected from the sandy layer (L2) immediately beneath the lowest level of stone packing, the assumption being that the OSL clock was reset to zero before the sediment was sealed by the stone slabs above. This yielded a date of c. 450 BC (+- 240 years), which accords closely with our working hypothesis that its construction took place around the same time as Phase I or II at Sanchi. The second sample (S3), from the same layer further towards the centre of the dam, gave an unexpectedly early date of c. 1780 BC (+- 460 years). This is probably due to the fact that the OSL in the sediment failed to be reset to zero prior to its deposition in the dam and therefore retained the time signature of the presumably Chalcolithic spoil heap from where it was excavated. The third sample (S4) from the buried pre-dam layer (L4) beneath the aforementioned storage jar provided an even earlier date of c. 3680 BC (+- 630 years), probably representing Holocene alluvial deposits washed in from river action over the years prior to the construction of the dam.

Two more OSL dates, of c. 2930 BC (+- 770 years) and c. 1740 BC (+- 750 years) were obtained from separate fragments of the conical-based storage jar (S10a-b). This disparity of over 1000 years is possibly the result of irregularly released luminescence throughout the vessel, due to ill-firing.[11] Additional distortions were possibly introduced by the clay's high feldspar content, a known factor in reducing the efficacy of silica-based analysis.[12] However, it is interesting to note that the date-range for S10b is similar to S3, which, as discussed above, probably came from a Chalcolithic spoil heap. Further, these dates are in keeping with chronology of similarly shaped vessels from Chalcolithic sites in central and north India (Rakesh Tewari, pers. comm.).

Finally, OSL dates were obtained from a sherd of a separate vessel (S8), and sediment sample (L9), both collected from the deposit (L7) inside the storage jar. These produced highly divergent dates of c. 1360 BC (+- 270 years) and c. AD 210 (+- 190 years) respectively. Such widely divergent dates might reasonably be explained thus: the storage jar was dug out, along with its contents, from Chalcolithic levels at a nearby mound, some time in the late centuries BC. While the single potsherd (S8) inside retained its original time signature, that is roughly contemporary to S10b and S3, the actual sediment (S9) was exposed to light during the transportation and deposition of the jar, and thus had its OSL clock reset to zero. Taking into account the error-margin of S9 (+- 190 years), together with the date range for S1 from L2 (450 BC+- 240 years), the most reliable OSL sample from the main body of the dam, one may propose a third to second century BC date for the dam's actual construction.

This accords closely with the suggested chronology of over 500 potsherds recovered from the dam core as well as the inner lining (L1) (Shaw *et al.*, 2007, pl. 6) (Plate 226).[13] Insights into their original provenance and function within the dam are provided by house-building practices in local villages where ancient potsherds often turn up in the walls of modern houses (S.B Ota, pers. comm.). This is because the mortar used to bind stone courses sometimes contains pottery-rich earth, which is collected from ancient settlements due to its especially sticky consistency. It is likely that the ceramics in the Sanchi dam were also introduced as part of a mortar composed of sediment dug out from a nearby settlement mound or spoil heap.

The sherds are mostly thinly slipped red wares, with several black wares also. The absence of distinctive slips or decoration, together with the paucity of detailed ceramic descriptions and illustrations in relevant excavation reports, precludes comparisons with material from stratified contexts. However, broad comparisons can be made with red wares from late centuries-BC levels at Vidisha, as well as Nandour, Ninnore and Dangawada (Figure 3.2; Sharma and Misra 2003).[14] There are also similarities with some of the red wares (particularly type 14) collected from surface contexts during the SSP (Appendix III), suggesting a date range, therefore, of sometime between c. third and second centuries BC.

Table 14.3 OSL sediment and ceramic samples from dam sections and reservoir cores

Site	Sample no.	Context	Layer/depth	Notes	Material	OSL	Dates	Reliability
Sanchi	S1	Section	L2	Below stone facing	Sediment	OSL (tube)	c. 450 BC (±240 years)	High
Sanchi	S3	Section	L2	Below stone facing	Sediment	OSL (tube)	c. 1780 BC (±460 years)	Low
Sanchi	S4	Section	L6	Pre-dam horizon	Sediment	OSL (tube)	c. 3680 BC (±630 years)	High
Sanchi	S8	Section	L7	Contents of storage jar	Potsherd	OSL (ceramic)	c. 1360 BC (±270 years)	High
Sanchi	S9	Section	L7	Contents of storage jar	Sediment	OSL (bag)	c. 210 AD (±190 years).	High
Sanchi	S10a	Section	L8	Storage jar fragment	Potsherd	OSL (ceramic)	c. 2930 BC (±770 years)	High
Sanchi	10b	Section	L8	Storage jar fragment	Potsherd	OSL (ceramic)	c. 1740 BC (±750 years)	High
Sanchi	S19	Core 4	0.73–0.82 m	Reservoir deposit	Sediment	OSL (bag)	c. 590 AD (±220 years)	Low
Sanchi	S21	Core 4	0.90–1.00 m	Pre-dam horizon	Sediment	OSL (bag)	c. 790 AD (±120 years)	Low
Karondih	K3	Core 1	1.29–1.38 m	Reservoir deposit	Sediment	OSL (bag)	c. 7210 BC (±740 years)	Low
Karondih	K4	Core 1	1.38–1.47 m	Pre-dam horizon	Sediment	OSL (bag)	c. 13,600 BC (±1322)	High
Devrajpur	D20	Section	N/A	Below stone packing	Sediment	OSL (tube)	c. 4160 BC (±580 years)	Low
Devrajpur	D21	Section	N/A	1 m below stone packing in southern sounding	Sediment	OSL (tube)	c. 1275 BC (±457 years)	Low
Devrajpur	D26	Section	N/A	Behind packing stone	Sediment	OSL (tube)	c. 2797 BC (±489 years)	Low
Devrajpur	D5	Core 1	2.25–2.36 m	Reservoir deposit	Sediment	OSL (bag)	c. 1764 BC (±640 years)	Low
Devrajpur	D8	Core 1	2.96–3.04 m	Pre-dam horizon	Sediment	OSL (bag)	c. 2726 BC (±882 years)	High

Four cores were drilled at two separate locations (Figure 9.3) with the aim of establishing reservoir depth, and collecting samples for supplementary OSL dating and pollen analysis: three cores within the main reservoir bed, approximately 180 m north of the east–west retaining dam, and a fourth core approximately 100 m upstream of the smaller dam at Karondih to the west, described later. All four cores produced a similar sequence reaching a total depth of 1.40–1.45 m at Sanchi, and 1.70 m at Karondih. Two OSL samples were collected from each of the coring locations at Sanchi, and an additional two at Karondih. All yielded unreliable dates for different reasons. At Sanchi, S19 from within the reservoir sediment and S21 from the buried subsoil produced dates of c. 590 AD (+- 220 years) and c. 790 AD (+- 120 years) respectively. Given the date-range of the OSL samples from the dam itself, these are unfeasibly young, and may be regarded as erroneous, probably due to light contamination incurred during sampling or some other disturbance in historic times. By contrast, at Karondih, samples from similar contexts (K3 and K4) produced excessively early dates of c. 7210 BC (+- 740 years) and c. 13,610 BC (+- 1320 years) respectively. These probably reflect the depositional age of pre-existing Holocene alluvial deposits.

Dargawan and Karondih

Immediately upstream, and to the west of the Sanchi reservoir, are two smaller dams, Dargawan and Karondih (Figure 9.3).[15] The former, in the narrow valley to the north, is situated between the Buddhist 'burial ground' on Dargawan hill to the north and the extensive stupa site on Dargawan 2 hill to the south.[16] The total dam length is 300 m, with an estimated reservoir area and volume of approximately 0.08 km^2 and 0.079 $m^3 \times 10^6$ respectively (Shaw and Sutcliffe 2001, 58). About 3 km to the south is the Karondih dam which runs for 500 m across the narrowest point of the short valley that drains into the main Sanchi reservoir. The estimated area and volume are 0.4 km^2 and 0.44 $m^3 \times 10^6$ respectively (*ibid.*). The northernmost end of the dam is traversed by the main Bhopal–Vidisha railway line.[17] Although the embanked line, built between 1886 and 1889,[18] may have had an impact on the course and size of the main feeder stream, these changes will not have affected the overall reservoir volume: runoff ratios.[19]

Land use

These three dams formed an integrated, 'cascading', irrigation complex, with the smaller reservoirs at Dargawan and Karondih evidently designed to maintain water levels in the main Sanchi reservoir as part of an upstream irrigation system (Shaw and Sutcliffe 2005). Whether the smaller dams were part of the original design cannot be confirmed in the absence of adequate OSL dates from these sites. However, patterns in the wider archaeological landscape discussed below do suggest that they were contemporary to the main Sanchi dam. Crops (probably rice) would have been cultivated in the main reservoir itself with additional water being supplied from the upstream tanks as the reservoir level fell. As discussed later, a similar form of upstream irrigation is attested at two nearby dam sites, Ferozpur and Dhakna. This hypothesis is further supported by the graph in Figure 14.3 which illustrates the reservoir areas at different elevations and thus reinforces the contour maps in giving information about the reservoir topographies. At Sanchi, the potential for upstream irrigation, especially for rice, is demonstrated by the curve linking area and elevation which highlights the extensive plain above the dam, a factor which is also illustrated by the outline of the reservoir in the contour map (Figure 9.3).

These observations help to explain the function of the second embankment of the main reservoir which runs east–west from Nagauri hill. As noted previously (Shaw and Sutcliffe 2003a, 80), the crest of this dam appears to be a continuation of the ground level to the south, which itself is higher in elevation (by approx. 1.5 to 2.0 m) than the level to the north. Although its stone facing is similar to the main dam, its position away from the basin's natural drainage point implies that it functioned as a retaining wall rather than a storage dam. A similar difference in levels was noted at Dhakna to the SW (*ibid.*) which seems also to have been designed to provide upstream flooding, so that crops could be cultivated on the residual soil moisture.

Wider archaeological landscape

The three dams that comprise the Sanchi reservoir system also form part of a larger archaeological complex, the internal patterns of which are replicated at other dam sites in the study area. As discussed in chapter 11, in addition to the Buddhist monuments on Sanchi hill, Phase II stupas are also found on the hills to the north and south of the Dargawan dam, and immediately above the Karondih dam.[20] Many of the modern villages in the area, such as Kanakhera and Nagauri to the north and south of Sanchi respectively, overlie ancient settlements. Two more settlements, consisting of ruined stone structures, occur on the eastern and northern slopes of the hill to the north of the Dargawan dam, while the surrounding agricultural plains are dotted with early-historic settlement mounds. As discussed in Part III, a similar relationship between dams, settlements and Buddhist sites across the study area provides an empirical basis for positing a direct link between changes in agriculture and the histories of Buddhism and urban culture.

Ferozpur

The Ferozpur dam (Plate 220) is situated about 11 km west of Sanchi and also forms part of a larger archaeological complex, including an ancient settlement at the foot of the hill, which abuts the northern end of the dam, and a large Buddhist monastery complex on its summit (Plate 42; Figure 14.9) (Shaw and Sutcliffe 2001; 2003a; 2005).[21] The dam stands at a height of 6 m (or 436 m above sea level).[22] However, in order to prevent overtopping of a dam of this height, it is likely that the water level would have been controlled at around 435 m, which provides an estimated reservoir area and volume of 2.3 km^2 and 4.7 $m^3 \times 10^6$ respectively (Shaw and Sutcliffe 2005). The high river action caused by the convergence of a number of streams at the dam site has led to considerable soil erosion which probably explains why preliminary coring carried in the reservoir bed during Stage II yielded little in the way of reservoir sediment (Shaw *et al.*, 2007).

As shown by the relation between area and elevation (Figure 14.3), the extremely limited cultivable land downstream of the dam as far as the River Bes contrasts with the extensive area upstream. It seems likely therefore that, as at Sanchi, the upstream area, i.e. the reservoir bed itself, would have been cultivated directly, with supplementary irrigation provided by the Gulgaon tank further to the west. The case for this is even clearer than at Sanchi, lending further weight to our argument that the main irrigated crop in the area was rice.

A *terminus ante quem* date of c. fifth century AD is provided by a group of *nāga* sculptures stored in a modern temple in

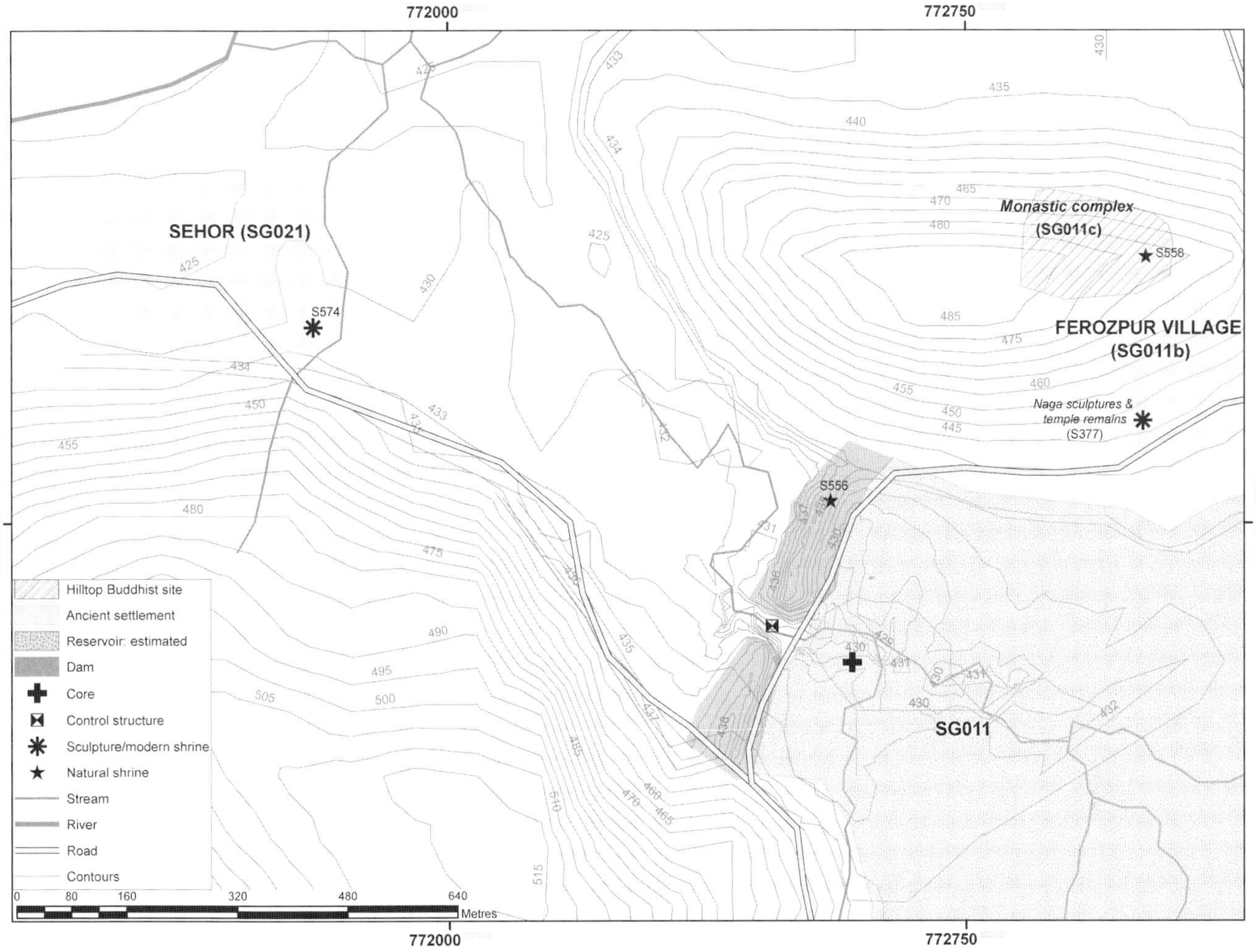

Figure 14.9 Map of Ferozpur dam and surrounding archaeological landscape

Ferozpur village, a location which corresponds to the eastern bank of the original reservoir. As discussed in chapter 11, however, the monastery structures on Ferozpur hill may be much older, possibly Phase II, and the dam is likely to be contemporary with the Gulgaon and Sanchi dams to the east.

Dhakna

Passing reference has already been made to the Dhakna dam, to the south of Sanchi, in relation to the anomaly of its reservoir bed being set at a lower level than the fields downstream. As at Sanchi, this suggests that crops were cultivated directly within the reservoir bed itself as part of an upstream irrigation regime. The Dhakna dam also accords with the internal dynamics of the 'early-historic complex' as typified at Sanchi and Ferozpur, with a hilltop Buddhist site and several habitational settlements in its immediately vicinity.[23]

Gulgaon

The Gulgaon dam to the east of Ferozpur underwent reconstruction in the 1970s; however, the original dam, together with several *in situ* facing slabs, is still visible behind the modern concrete embankment. As discussed above, the Gulgaon reservoir appears to have formed part of a cascading irrigation system, with water being distributed downstream to the larger reservoir at Ferozpur, in order to maintain levels necessary for an upstream irrigation regime. A *nāga* sculpture which originally stood, along with its *nāginī* counterpart, on the dam's summit, provides a *terminus ante quem* of c. 50 BC, as in the case of the Nagauri *nāga* at the Sanchi dam. Other points of comparison between the two sites, which provide suggestions of a single construction date in the third or second century BC, include the similar dimensions of the facing stones (Table 14.1).

As in the previous examples, the Gulgaon dam also forms part of a larger early-historic complex, with several Buddhist hilltop remains in the immediate vicinity, notably Dargawan 2 to the east, and Ferozpur and Goldoria to the west.[24] The modern village of Gulgaon partially overlies an ancient settlement which extends as far as modern Eran in the north, and also includes an ancient paved road.[25]

Murlikheri-Naroda

The Naroda dam is situated in a narrow valley behind Satdhara hill, about 2 km SE of the Buddhist monuments there. The earthen embankment has been more or less ploughed out, although when first documented in Stage I, several slabs of stone facing were scattered over the site.[26] The dam forms part of a larger archaeological complex including a Buddhist monastery platform on Murlikheri hill to the north and, to the east, a large settlement area incorporating the modern villages of Murlikheri and Naroda, and extending as far as the stupas at Naroda Pathari further to the NE.[27]

Eastern hilly sector (2b)

Four dams, Devrajpur, Morel kala, Chandna and Morel khurd, were documented in the deep valleys formed by the escarpments to the east of the flat agricultural terrain on the eastern bank of the River Betwa. All four dams appear to have been designed for downstream irrigation in contrast to the upstream irrigation regimes practised on the low-gradient reservoirs in Sector 1b.

All of the dams form part of larger 'early historic complexes' including contemporary settlements and hilltop Buddhist sites: the agricultural plain between Sanchi and Andher is scattered with early-historic mounds, some of which are overlain by present-day villages. Many of the hills further to the east have ancient settlements on their lower slopes, about half of which are associated with modern villages (Figure 13.3). Although from Phase IV onwards there is an increase in the number of Brahmanical and Jain temples, during the preceding period the ritual landscape is dominated by Buddhist sites. Practically every hilltop in this sector is occupied by stupas or monasteries (Figure 11.7), which in some areas, especially around Chandna and Mawasa, form part of a continuous interlinked Buddhist complex.

Devrajpur

The Devrajpur dam, situated about 14 km SE of Sanchi, is the largest and best-preserved dam in the study area with an effective length of 1 km, although this is increased to approximately 2 km by the long sandstone ridge to the east with which the dam is aligned (Plate 223).[28] This acts as a 'natural embankment' and performs a similar function as the east–west retaining wall at Sanchi. However, since it runs parallel to the main feeder stream, it does not alter earlier reservoir calculations. At the other end of the dam, elevated terrain encloses lower ground to the west: beyond the western abutment of the dam, there is a drop of 3–4 m to a narrow valley with a large stream flowing to the north about 200 m beyond the dam (Figure 14.10). As this stream is continuous with the channel which approaches the dam diagonally near the spillway at its eastern end, and then turns back to bypass its western end, it is possible that this is the result of erosion and river capture following the construction of the dam: it may be relevant, for example, that a channel continues NE of the dam from the spillway towards the River Nion. The contour map in Figure 14.10, derived from a combination of 'total station' mapping and SRTM data, suggests a dam height of about 4.5 m (440.5 m above sea level). However, the existence of a spillway, described below, suggests that the reservoir water level was held below the crest to avoid overtopping. On the basis of an estimated water level of 1 m below the crest, one may calculate a reservoir area of 1.86 km^2 and a volume of 3.8 $m^3 \times 10^6$ (Shaw and Sutcliffe 2005).[29]

During Stage II, an exposed section formed by a modern road-cutting, approximately midway along the dam, was scraped back to obtain an intact profile. As at Sanchi, this revealed an earthen core, faced on the upstream side with large stone blocks,

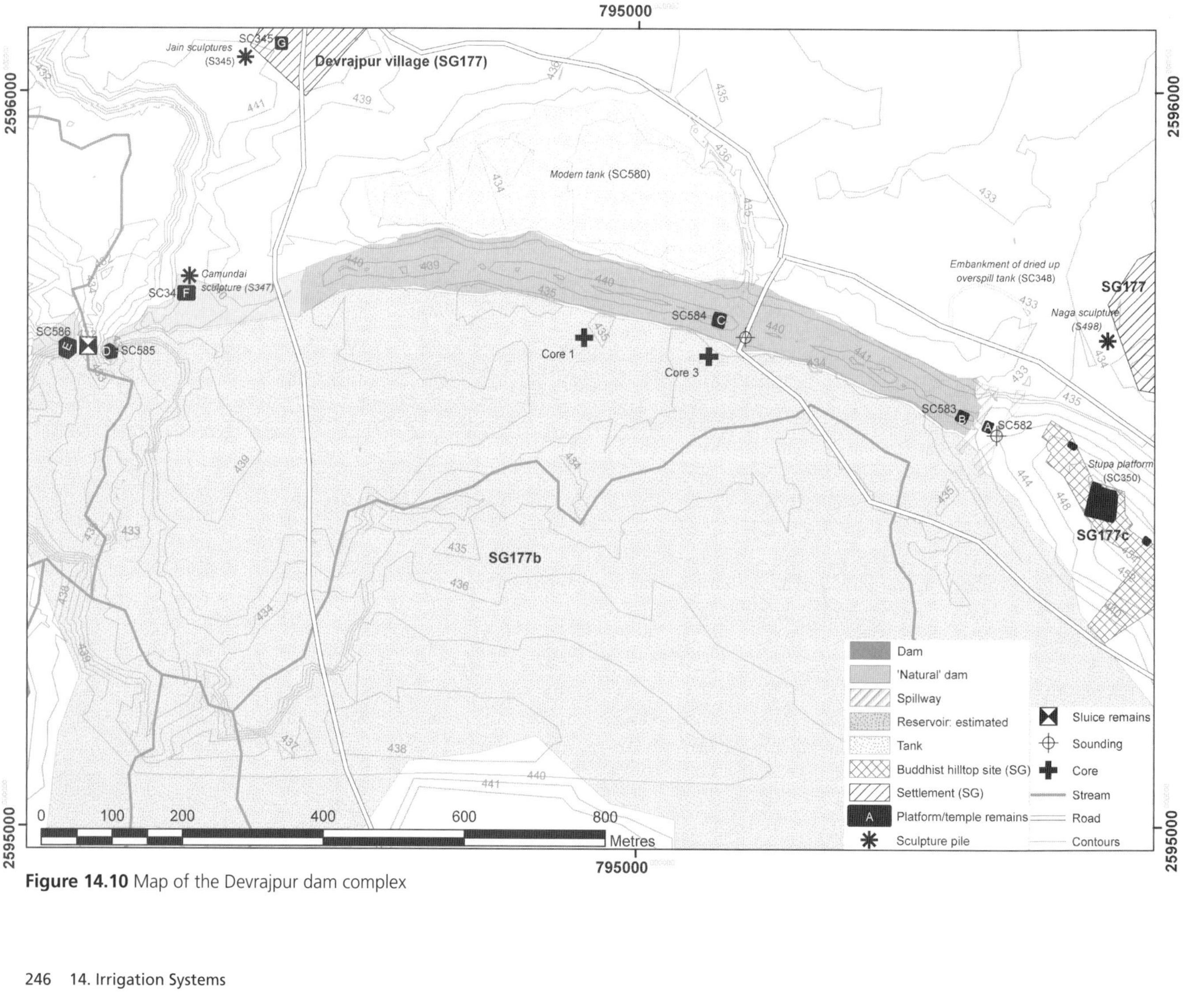

Figure 14.10 Map of the Devrajpur dam complex

interspersed by smaller packing stones. However, unlike the Sanchi dam which contains different sediment layers, the Devrajpur core consists entirely of homogeneous black-cotton soil with no discernible stratigraphy (Plate 227; Figure 14.11). While the Sanchi dam section contained high levels of sand due to its proximity to the adjoining hill, the Devrajpur road-cutting was situated midway along the dam where it is difficult to distinguish between the black-cotton soil in the embankment and the black-cotton soil beneath the lowest course of stone facing; the same homogeneous deposit continued to the base of the two 1 m-deep soundings sunk at either end of the section. This factor had a negative impact on the effectiveness of the OSL dating programme discussed later.

Water control

A spillway cut out of the raised bedrock at the right (eastern) abutment of the dam was mentioned earlier (Plate 223). Where the embankment reaches the outcrop, a channel about 10 m wide and 1.3 m deep has been excavated in the rock, with curved masonry restraining walls at the entrance. The spillway passes through the section of the dam and then bends to the west, meandering back in an easterly direction for around 50 m, where it joins a small overspill tank (110 x 110 m). An approximate estimate of a 50-year return period flood, based on 50-year daily rainfall of 240 mm over a basin of 13.5 km^2 and a runoff coefficient of 70%, would correspond with a flow of 26 m^3 and a water depth of about 1.5 m. Thus the spillway would be adequate for a 50-year flood without overtopping of the embankment. An additional spillway cut into the rock at a higher level on the hill (width: 5.0 m) was noted in Stage II (Shaw and Sutcliffe 2005). A small sounding (1.40 x 0.50 m) sunk through its centre revealed 0.60 m of sediment accumulation, which implies an original height differential of about 2 m between the lower and upper spillways.

Remains of a monumentalised control structure over the main feeder stream to the west were also mentioned earlier. These include a number of light buff sandstone blocks, both plain and decorated, datable to Phases V and VI. The earlier fragments (Plates 230, 231) are comparable to mouldings from Pratihara temples in other parts of central India (Shaw and Sutcliffe 2003a, 78, figs. 7, 8),[30] thus attesting to the possible existence of a Pratihara-period temple somewhere on the dam. This would conform to the widespread tradition in India of building temples next to streams and tanks. However, it is more likely that they belonged to a control structure that incorporated shrine-like elements, a suggestion strengthened by the fact that their location at the most vulnerable part of the dam is in keeping with patterns from other parts of South Asia: as discussed later, the repair and upkeep of dams are often commemorated in a monumental manner due to the merit (both ritual and social) of such acts (Morrison 1993; Venkayya 1906).

Land use and hydrology

The contour map (Figure 14.10) and the derived curves linking elevation and area, which are linear above a certain level (Figure 14.3), illustrate the extensive reservoir area. The low-lying ground to the west of the dam reinforces the possibility that erosion has occurred in this area. Although the reservoir area itself could have been used for cultivation, the height of the dam and the evidence for spillways and control structures suggest alternatively that it was part of a downstream irrigation regime.

Archaeological setting

The dam forms part of a larger interrelated archaeological complex including a settlement mound to the NE of the spillway and a series of hillside settlements further to the east (Figure 11.7). There are also temple and sculpture remains at various locations along the crest of the Devrajpur dam. The earliest example is a theriomorphic serpent stone (*nāgakal*) propped up next to a tree NE of the eastern spillway, and datable to the Gupta period or slightly later (Plate 176). In keeping with the link between *nāga*s and water bodies throughout the study area, one may assume that it originally stood overlooking the reservoir, thus providing a *terminus ante quem* date for the dam (Shaw and Sutcliffe 2001, 70).

A platform stands between the lower and upper spillways ('A'

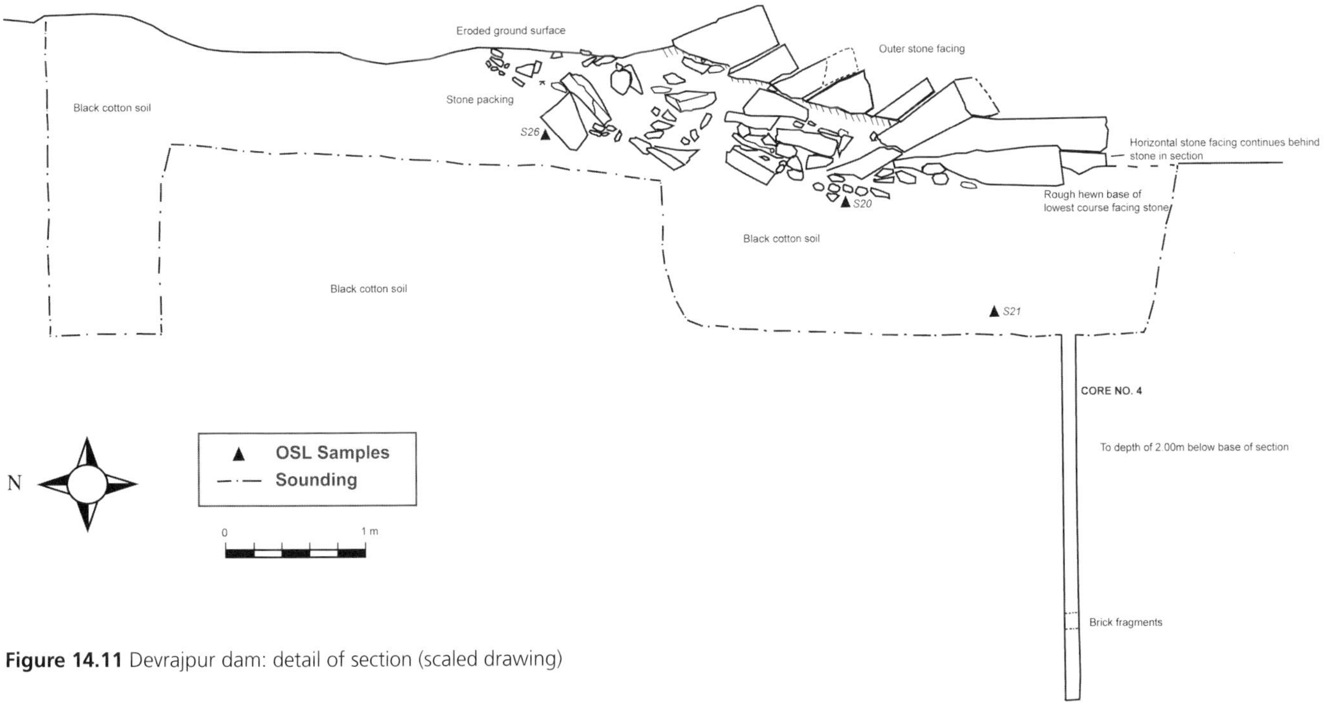

Figure 14.11 Devrajpur dam: detail of section (scaled drawing)

in Figure 14.10), with another immediately to the west of the lower spillway ('B'). These were evidently building foundations, with which a large quantity of broken stone and brick fragments found in the small sounding in the upper spillway, discussed earlier, could have been associated. A third platform ('C') is situated to the west of the road-cut section, with another ('D') on the high ground to the east of the presumed control structure in the lower basin; a fifth mound ('E') is visible on the west bank of the stream. Foundations of a sixth structure ('F') survive in the form of a low platform midway between mound 'D' and the western end of the dam. At least some of these were evidently temples, as suggested by associated sculptural and architectural fragments found at various locations. Architectural fragments belonging to Phases V and VI found within the feeder stream were mentioned earlier. Although some of these evidently belonged to the monumentalised control structure built over the stream, others may have come from temples represented by mounds 'D', 'E' or 'F'. The same applies to a pile of sculptures stored at 'F'. This comprises tiny purple sandstone fragments datable to Phase VI, and a buff sandstone *Camundai* image (Plate 212), belonging to Phase V.[31] Remains of a third, Jain, temple, were also found about 300 m to the north. These include several large, purple sandstone *tirthankara* images and architectural fragments datable to Phase VI (Plate 214).[32]

These sculpture and temple remains show that by the mid-first millennium BC, the Devrajpur dam was closely connected with Brahmanical and Jain institutions. However, a number of Phase II stupas and monastery remains on the long escarpment at the eastern end of the dam (Figure 11.10) accord with the close link between dams and Buddhist sites throughout the study area (Shaw and Sutcliffe 2005). Based on similar inter-site relationships across the SSP study area, it seems not unreasonable to suggest a Phase II date for the construction of the Devrajpur dam; a Phase II date is supported further by similarities in stone-facing at Devrajpur, Sanchi and Gulgaon (Table 14.1).

As at Sanchi, the OSL dating project initiated in Stage II aimed at testing this hypothesis. To this end, samples were collected from three locations within the road-cutting section described earlier (Figure 14.8; Table 14.3): i) directly under the base of the stone packing (D20); ii) 1 m below the stone packing, at the base of the southern sounding (D21); and iii) directly behind a medium-sized inner packing stone laid on top of the earthen core (D26). However, all produced unfeasibly early dates: D20 = c. 4160 BC (+- 580 years); D21 = c. 1270 BC (+- 460 years); and D26 = c. 2800 BC (+- 490 years). A likely explanation is that the OSL signal from these samples was not fully reset during the excavation of the sediment used to construct the dam. It might be relevant that the black-cotton soil was probably dug out nearby, and thus had less chance of being exposed to light. However, the general date-range is in keeping with that expected of pre-dam alluvial deposits from the Holocene, washed in from river action over the years prior to the construction of the dam. The same applies to two unfeasibly early OSL dates obtained from a core (no. 1 in Figure 14.10) sunk in the main reservoir bed (Shaw *et al.*, 2007).

Morel khurd

Approximately 5 km to the west of Devrajpur are the well-known Buddhist monuments on Morel khurd hill. Amongst the newly documented elements of the site's immediate archaeological setting is the large dam which runs from the western foot of the hill to a small outcropping further to the west. The latter bears ancient settlement remains and some Phase IV Buddhist sculptures. The dam is heavily damaged, and ploughed out in parts, although several stone facing slabs can still be seen. Based on wider study area patterns, the dam is roughly contemporary with the Phase II Buddhist monuments at Morel khurd.

Morel kala

The Morel kala dam, to the south of Morel khurd, is built across a 350-m long valley between the modern villages of Morel kala and Pali. The former overlies the remains of an extensive ancient settlement which includes several Phase VI Brahmanical and Jain temples. Standing at a height of over 6 m, the dam is one of the most imposing in the study area, with well-preserved stone facing on the upstream side and additional facing, in places, on the downstream side (Plate 222; Shaw and Sutcliffe 2001, fig. 6). Previous estimates of area and volume have been given as 0.9 km^2 and 2.63 $m^3 \times 10^6$ respectively (*ibid.*, table 1), while a *terminus ante quem* date of c. second century AD is provided by a *nāga* image propped up on the dam's summit (Plate 153).

As at Devrajpur, the remains of a control mechanism have been noted over a major breach caused by the feeder stream. This includes a wall-like structure consisting of over 22 courses of masonry on either side of the channel (Plate 228). Several fragments from a Phase V temple incorporated into the structure's upper four courses (Plate 229) are probably the results of repair. Not only does this support the suggestion that we are dealing with a control structure built at the point of the dam most vulnerable to flood damage, it also indicates continued use and repair in the period following the Muslim conquests when the temple in question was presumably destroyed. This is not to preclude the possibility, however, that the temple was destroyed by flood action some time during the pre-Sultanate period. Whichever the case, the question of whether the dam was in use continuously from its original construction or whether this represented a later revival cannot be determined without excavation or geoarchaeological investigation.

There is also evidence for a rock-cut spillway, similar to the Devrajpur example, which occupies a gap of 13.5 m between the northern abutment of the dam and the adjoining hillside (Shaw and Sutcliffe 2003a, fig. 5). As indicated by quarrying marks visible in places, it appears to have been deliberately lowered to its present level, about 1.5–1.8 m below the crest of the dam (Shaw and Sutcliffe 2003, 78–9). With a catchment area of about 12.8 km^2, this would pass the flood of a similar return period or frequency as at Devrajpur without overtopping (Shaw and Sutcliffe 2003a).

Chandna

The Chandna dam is situated about 4 km west of Morel kala and, like Gulgaon, has undergone recent renovation (Plate 221). However, the large facing blocks of the older dam can be seen underneath the smaller blocks used in the modern construction. A *terminus ante quem* date of c. 50 BC is provided by a *nāga*-Balarama sculpture on the dam's summit, and described in chapter 12. However, a somewhat earlier construction date is suggested by the similarity of the original stone facing to that at Sanchi, as well as the proximity of Phase II Buddhist sites: most of the surrounding hills bear Buddhist remains, and the entire area between here and Mawasa to the east can justifiably be regarded as a continuous interlinked Buddhist complex.[33] Ancient settlement remains are also found on the sandstone outcropping at the NE corner of reservoir, and behind Chandna village to the SE.[34]

Southern sector (3)

A possible explanation for the unusually low occurrence of dams in this sector is the predominance of large, impenetrable hill ranges with limited areas of intervening land for cultivation. The single exception here is the narrow valley several km to the south of the Buddhist monuments at Sonari. A major perennial stream runs through this fertile valley which contains a significant number of major settlement mounds, including Besar talai which has yielded early-historic pottery and coins, as well as evidence for a major Phase II stupa surrounded by free-standing pillars. The dam, which probably dates to around the same period, runs from the northern end of the mound to the adjoining hillside. It is heavily damaged with most of its stone facing and earthen core having been reused in houses in the modern village of Besar talai.

Further to the south, and outside the formal boundaries of the study area, is Raisen dam, situated at the western base of the imposing hill famous for its medieval fort. However, its earlier Buddhist associations are attested by various stupa and monastery remains in and around the fortified area.

Northern sector (4)

There is also a paucity of dams in this sector, this time due to the obverse topographical combination to that in the south: an expanse of predominately flat terrain with a limited number of hillocks and, thus, sufficiently short valleys. The single exception is the short valley between the hills of Bighan and Tigra to the west. As described in chapter 11, the former is occupied by a major Phase II Buddhist complex, which, following wider patterns discussed so far, provides a rough indicator of the dam's construction date.

Summary
Despite the morphological similarities between the dams discussed above, it is clear that each reservoir was custom-designed to suit its particular environment. The gradually sloping terrain in the western sector (1b) was well suited to the construction of inundation tanks for upstream irrigation, as illustrated by the Sanchi, Ferozpur and Dhakna dams, while in the eastern sector (2b), dams built across deeper valleys, as at Devrajpur and Morel kala, provided the basis for downstream irrigation. The total impact that these dams had on irrigation and land-use practices across the study area, as well as their relationship to neighbouring Buddhist and settlements sites, is discussed further in Part III. I will also present additional evidence in support of two central hypotheses: i) that the dams were built principally for the irrigation of rice, as a response to increased levels of social complexity represented by local settlement patterns and the distribution of Buddhist sites; and ii) that they played a central role in the development of exchange networks between monastic and non-monastic sections of society.

PART III: PATTERNS IN THE AGRARIAN LANDSCAPE

Land use

A notable feature of the Sanchi reservoirs is that their storage capacity is at variance with the irrigation needs of present-day farmers (Shaw and Sutcliffe 2001; 2003a; 2005). Since historical times, local agriculture has been based primarily on rain-fed wheat cultivation. The near absence of irrigation is usually attributed to the high moisture storage capacity of the local black-cotton soils, which are recharged by the annual monsoon rains and provide sufficient water to carry the wheat crop from planting to maturity. In recent years some supplementary irrigation has been applied to increase yields, but this has relied on cheap on-field pumping of shallow ground water. However, there is another, less frequently discussed factor: compared to other parts of India, eastern Madhya Pradesh is relatively under-populated, mainly due to a series of catastrophic famines since the fourteenth century; the notorious drought of 1899–1900 reputedly accounted for many of the abandoned settlements in the area (*Imp. Gaz*, vol. ix, pp. 374–5). As noted by Watt (1889, vol. 6, 151), the low intensity of local agriculture may have more to do with demography than soil type: it is likely that any significant rise in population would bring about increased production demands and hence the need for irrigation. This raises obvious questions regarding land-use practices prior to the demographic changes outlined above.

The first point is that the distribution of ancient settlements across the study area attests to a much higher population density in the past, while the abundance of sculpture and the remains of elaborate temples present a striking contrast to the overwhelmingly rural nature of the present-day landscape. Both of these factors reflect the wider processes of urbanisation and political centralisation that began with the expansion of the Mauryan empire in c. third century BC. Secondly, most of the surrounding hilltops are covered with extensive Buddhist remains. Today, they lie empty, with settlements restricted to the lower slopes or intervening valleys. Both of these processes, that is urbanisation and Buddhist propagation, would have exerted significant pressure on local food supplies, calling for the kind of intensive agriculture represented by the Sanchi dams; a useful avenue for future research would be to estimate how many monks resided at each monastic centre, in order to measure the impact that Buddhist propagation had on local population densities. Quite clearly, it would have been in the interests of the monks, as non-producing sections of society, to be embedded in an agriculturally efficient environment, as their livelihood depended on the availability of local patronage. The link between rising population levels and wet-rice agriculture is a familiar one and, for example, forms the central focus of Geertz's (1963) seminal work on 'agricultural involution' in Southeast Asia. According to Geertz, the complex water management and distribution systems upon which wet-rice cultivation is dependent, calls for a high degree of specialised organisation and labour force. Wet-rice regimes thus predicate a particular set of economic circumstances which are quite different to those which underlie swidden shifting agriculture. Of particular importance is the 'marked tendency (and ability) [for wet-rice cultivation] to respond to a rising population through intensification; that is, through absorbing increased numbers of cultivators on a unit of cultivated land'. While densely populated areas supported by swidden agriculture tend to undergo rapid deterioration as new land is brought into cultivation to cope with rising population levels, the opposite phenomenon occurs in a wet-rice regime which results in the 'support of an ever-increasing number of people within an undamaged habitat' (*ibid.*, 31).

Decline/disuse

By extension, this line of enquiry might also shed light on whether there was any causal link between the decline of Buddhism and the eventual disuse of local irrigation schemes: although the relatively recent depopulation is an important factor, the earlier disappearance of monks, possibly around the tenth century AD, would have had a significant impact on the local economy. As noted earlier, it seems likely that flood damage rather than sedimentation was the physical cause of disuse, sedimentation not being a known problem in the Sanchi area. Additional explanations for decline include factors such as the collapse of associated administrative systems. Interesting parallels are provided by the south Indian dams and associated Cola and Pallava inscriptions, whose principal aim was to record terms and conditions for de-siltation (Davison-Jenkins 1997, p. 93). In many cases, it was the drying up of these sources of patronage that led to the eventual abandonment of the reservoirs (Venkayya 1906). In the Sanchi area, changes in the local economy following the decline of Buddhism might have led to a similar breakdown; without the monasteries there would have been less pressure on agricultural production, and changes in patronage networks might have caused the reservoirs to cease to operate as irrigation works. This is not to suggest that some of them did not continue to be used for other purposes such as domestic water supplies. This is implied by fragments of a seventh- or eighth-century-AD Brahmanical temple, presumably destroyed during Muslim incursions in the twelfth and thirteenth centuries AD, incorporated into the control structure at Morel kala. Other possible explanations for their reuse in later years come from the massive Bhojpur lake to the south of Bhopal, which was destroyed in 1434 by Hoshang Shah (Dey 1965, 55; appendix c, 419–21),[35] and the series of recorded famines from the fourteenth century AD. However, their final abandonment probably resulted from the radical depopulation following the most serious of these famines between 1899 and 1900; future archaeometric research is likely to clarify some of these questions.

Rice cultivation in central India?

Our working hypothesis therefore is that the Sanchi reservoirs were built in c. third to second century BC in order to increase agricultural output and support the increased population levels indicated by local settlement patterns. Their main function was irrigation, but they evidently doubled as domestic water-supplies, animal watering-holes or fish sources (Shaw and Sutcliffe 2003a). A major question, however, is whether they were built to irrigate pre-existing wheat crops or whether they were part of a new land-use system, such as wet-rice cultivation. Both are possible suggestions: it is generally accepted that in most parts of India artificial irrigation can increase agricultural output by as much as 30% (Brown 1912, 8; Davison-Jenkins 1997, 92). However, while today it is relatively simple to provide supplementary irrigation of say 50 mm by pumping recharged ground water where it is required without the need for canal transfer, it would require a complex and extensive canal system to distribute this water from a reservoir over a large area, which would be very much larger than the concentrated area of rice cultivation on which a depth of about 800 mm might be required. The high costs involved in constructing and maintaining the dams would have made more sense if they were used for rice cultivation, largely because of the dramatically increased depth and intensity of irrigation. Other factors include the superior yields and nutritional value of rice relative to irrigated wheat.[36] As discussed later, a rice-based economy is also in keeping with Buddhist views of food, medicine and the body, and justifies a focus on the cultural and economic factors behind food change in the late centuries BC. Finally, to construct dams and canals to improve wheat yields would seem illogical compared with bringing new land into cultivation, especially when the availability of cultivable land was not a limiting factor in the area.

Water requirements for wet-rice cultivation

An account of possible cultivation of irrigated rice in the SSP study area must take account of the seasonal pattern of cultivation and the climate and physical environment of the area. The climate is highly seasonal, with over 90% of the total rainfall (average 1300 mm) occurring between June and September. This highly seasonal rain cycle was a crucial factor behind the development of irrigation technologies in ancient India. Not only do water-storage facilities act as a crucial insurance policy in periods of drought, they also play an important role in controlling monsoon floods (Agarwal and Narain 1997, 90–2). Interestingly, we know from nineteenth-century famine records that those parts of Bihar and Madhya Pradesh where traditional reservoir systems were still in use (e.g. Gaya, Bijapur and Sambalpur districts) were immune to the series of severe droughts in the latter part of the century (*ibid.*, 182–3).

Measurement has shown (Sutcliffe 2004, 45–9, 108–16) that rainfall surplus first recharges soil-moisture storage and then contributes to groundwater and runoff. After the monsoon, this soil-moisture storage is sufficient to maintain wheat until harvest with some contribution from winter rainfall. This information can also be used to estimate water requirements for wet-rice cultivation, assuming the climate was similar to the present (Shaw and Sutcliffe 2001, 62–4). We may carry out a 'feasibility analysis' of rice cultivation, based on the methodology of Clark *et al.* (1982); therein it is observed that 'of all the world's irrigated land 90% is used for growing rice' and that the seed is first grown in a nursery and then grown in standing water until maturity. As ancient rice varieties would have needed longer growing periods and thus higher water requirements (Greenland 1997; pers. comm.), estimates have been derived rather conservatively based on present climate and soil conditions.

The growing season is limited by the need to flood the cultivated area at the beginning of the season, which thus depends on the timely start of the monsoon and the onset of soil moisture recharge, groundwater recharge and runoff. A growing period of 150 days from germination to harvesting is assumed. The water requirements include the need to create initial flooding and to maintain flooding, including evaporation and downward percolation. During the growing season, water will be required to maintain crop transpiration, open-water evaporation and also continued percolation. The crop factors (a multiplier, linking crop water use to evaporation) derived from field experiments (Clark *et al.* 1982) include evaporation from the water surface but not percolation; account should also be taken of reliable rainfall during the irrigation season.

Thanks to earlier hydrological investigations in the Betwa river basin near Sanchi (Sutcliffe and Green 1986), the necessary climate and physical evidence for assessing these requirements is available. Assuming the start date for ground preparation at 15 June, the average start of the monsoon, the season would last until the end of November. The saturation needs may be taken as the measured soil moisture deficit (250 mm), plus the groundwater recharge (50 mm) and the required water depth of 100 mm. To maintain this depth through July, open water evaporation (164 mm) must be added to early percolation (1–2 mm/day) to give a total of 595 mm.

From August to November, the crop water requirement can be estimated from the crop factors listed by Clark *et al.* (*ibid.*), which rise from 1.20 to a peak of 1.40 and fall to 1.12 before maturity and harvesting. We have multiplied open-water evaporation rates (Shaw & Sutcliffe 2001, 62) by these crop factors to give a total crop water requirement of 680 mm. The reliable effective rainfall, taken as the 1 in 10 monthly values for the Betwa basin, totals 504 mm for the period July to November.

Thus the water required to recharge the soil and groundwater profile and provide 100 mm of flooding would be 595 mm, including percolation and evaporation in July. The crop water requirement from August to November would be 680 mm, offset by rainfall of 500 mm. The net water requirement may be rounded to 800 mm. The total reservoir storage of 19.5 $m^3 \times 10^6$ (Shaw and Sutcliffe 2005) would be sufficient to irrigate 24 km^2. This illustrates the intensive nature of rice irrigation, requiring significant water storage to supply a relatively small but highly productive area, and thus feed an increased population. It is unlikely that the water requirement would be greatly affected if the rice crop were grown upstream of the dam.

It is interesting here to speculate on the total yield which might have been obtained on such an area of irrigated rice. Compared to modern yields of 2000–2500 kg/ha, the estimated yield for early rice varieties is around 1000–1500 kg/ha (Greenland, pers. comm.; Greenland 1997). On this basis, the average annual crop in the SSP study area would be of the order of 2400–3600 t/year. These figures may be compared with the average yield obtainable from crops of unirrigated wheat. In 1878, the average yield of wheat for all districts in the Central Provinces was said to range from 90 to 135 kg/ha (Watt 1889–93, iv, 153). This comparison is obviously a gross simplification, but is enough to illustrate the impact which the introduction of irrigated rice would have had on the local economy.

At first glance, some may suggest that the Sanchi dams were part of a double-cropping system with rice grown in the summer and wheat in the winter: the medieval irrigation systems in the western Deccan appear to have been built precisely for this purpose (Morrison 1995a, 212), as were the traditional *ahar* dams of southern Bihar, many of them still in use today (Agarwal and Narain 1997, 86–98).[37] Despite being designed for downstream irrigation of rice during the summer, the reservoir bed itself was used for *rabi* crops (wheat, barley and sometimes rice) during the winter (*ibid.*). However, this practice is largely a means of counteracting the low-moisture retaining capacity of the soils in south Bihar which unlike the clay-rich soils of central India are unable to support a winter crop without irrigation. Further, the rice-growing cycle described above would have not left adequate time for a second, winter crop. Rather, it is more likely that the Sanchi reservoirs were part of a complementary cropping system: by providing intensive irrigation for rice cultivation, they could have supplemented rain-fed cultivation of both *kharif* and *rabi* crops in surrounding areas.

Urbanisation, Buddhist propagation and agricultural/dietary change

Although the results of preliminary pollen analysis were in keeping with the kind of water-logged environment expected of a wet-rice cultivation regime, the foregoing suggestions require further verification through phytolith analysis, which has the potential of identifying specific cereal crops. This is especially important since there is no recorded tradition of commercial rice production in central India. As discussed in chapter 4, with few exceptions, archaeobotanical research on the history of rice agriculture has hitherto been restricted to eastern India which appears to have been the epicentre of domestic rice cultivation from at least the second millennium BC (Fuller 2002). Limited samples from the Deccan and south India suggest that the introduction of rice to these areas was part of a wider set of processes during the early-historic period including urbanisation and the spread of Buddhism from the Gangetic valley area.

Not only would the introduction of rice, with its superior yields and nutritional value, have been an appropriate measure in the face of rising population levels associated with growing urbanisation, it could also have been an inevitable outcome of a general spread of cultural influences from eastern India, where wet-rice cultivation had long since formed the backbone of the agrarian economy. A growing demand for rice would seem quite natural as these influences became more deeply embedded in the Sanchi area. At first, rice could have been introduced as a traded commodity, only later becoming a locally produced crop. Useful analogies here include the spread, between the eighth and tenth centuries AD, of new crops such as rice, sugar-cane, citrus fruits and cotton, together with advanced irrigation technologies such as the water-wheel, from Asia into the Middle East and the Mediterranean (Sherratt 1999; Watson 1983). Some of these crops were known during much earlier periods as attested by Greek sources;[38] small amounts of sugar and rice, for example, were imported from India as medicines, but were not cultivated locally until the introduction of Islam when they became staple crops rather than elite goods (Watson 1983, 15–16; 99–100). While the demand for these new crops came largely as a response to rising population levels associated with widespread urbanisation from the eighth century AD onwards,[39] it is interesting to note that in many cases they were promoted not only for their superior calorific value, but also for reasons of prestige or simply improved taste. For example, most were irrigated summer crops, which, like some of the Indian *kharif* crops, were supplementary, and secondary, to the winter (*rabi*) staples (Sherratt 1999, 30–1).

Analyses of early Brahmanical and Buddhist texts show that rice was not only central to the Gangetic valley diet; it also had a wide range of ritual, medicinal and economic uses (Ghosh and Chakrabarti 1980). Rice was considered an auspicious item in Brahmanical ritual; it was also an important object of donation within the Buddhist context. More indirect references to paddy fields and rice cultivation in Buddhist texts, either as the backdrop to particular narratives or as a metaphor for Buddhist practices, suggest that in eastern India the earliest Buddhist *saṅgha*, along with the earliest city dwellers, grew up within a predominantly rice-growing culture.[40] The major question, however, is what happened when large communities, either monastic or otherwise, moved into non rice-growing areas? Given the far-ranging importance of rice, from everyday meals to funerary ceremonies, it is not unlikely that some would have wanted to cultivate it in these new areas. For ordinary people the desire for familiarity may have been the main reason; for monks there may have been others. Future avenues of research combining ethnographic research and detailed textual analysis include the question of whether wheat or rice was considered more suited to monastic aims or to perceptions of the 'ideal body'. While a distinction between minor ritual use and large-scale production needs to be made, the argument here is that sustained use of rice within a monastic context would require rice cultivation becoming embedded in the local agrarian infrastructure. Secondly, textual evidence, such as references in the *Dhammapada* (xxvi. 21) to rice being donated to the *saṅgha* by all sections of society, suggests that rice played an integral role in the earliest exchange systems between monks and lay populations. It would not be surprising if these systems were reproduced in new areas with rice figuring prominently in the *saṅgha*'s propagation strategies. What is being suggested here is that, although intensive rice cultivation would have been an effective way of coping with the growing number of non-producing populations in the area, changes to the central Indian diet were also the direct result of the spread of new religious and cultural trends from eastern India that brought with them changing attitudes towards food and the body.[41]

Buddhism and water: 'practical' models of religious change

Within the theological model of Buddhist scholarship, the response to these issues is not difficult to predict: because monks are supposed to eat whatever is put in their begging bowl, they would have little power in influencing their daily diet. Such a view is based on a 'passive' model of Buddhism (e.g. Conze 1951), which sees the *saṅgha*'s participation in social relations as a distortion of its original position as a body of renouncers, concerned solely with individual enlightenment. Accordingly, Marshall's (1940, 13) reluctance to deduce any connection between the Sanchi dam and the history of local Buddhism was based on a passage in the *Anguttara Nikaya* (V, 17) which prohibits monks from owning or managing agricultural land. As discussed in chapter 2, evidence for Sri Lankan 'monastic landlordism' has been important for building a more 'active' model of Buddhist propagation: many of the ancient dams there bear inscriptions linking them to nearby monasteries, whose involvement in agrarian modes of production as instruments of lay patronage played a major role in the emergence of socially integrated monasticism from the second century BC onwards (Gunawardana 1971). In particular, the development of the sophisticated *bisokoṭuva* sluice was central to the development of 'monastic landlordism', which depended heavily on the controlled allocation of irrigation facilities to selected sections of society (Gunawardana 1978b, 69).

In addition to offering an alternative model to the 'Oriental despot' theory (Wittfogel 1957), the Sri Lankan material has been important for challenging received models of early Buddhist monks as passive mendicants and social parasites. As discussed in chapter 6, it accords closely with 'practical' models of religious change, the indication being that monks moved into new areas with a set of motives for local communities to extend their economic support to the monastery. The view that water management was central to Buddhist propagation is supported further by observations regarding the ostentatious display of water-harvesting facilities at the Deccan rock-cut monasteries of western India (Shaw and Sutcliffe 2003a, 92–5). It appears that the monastery's monopoly over the business of water harvesting and management was not only central to the generation of lay patronage, but that it accorded directly with Buddhist theology and its preoccupation with the alleviation of suffering (*dukkha*): in a region of the world where 90% of the annual rainfall occurs in two to three months, it provided a very practical solution to drought and flood, some of the key causes of everyday suffering.[42]

As yet, no inscriptions have been found in association with the Sanchi dams that might shed light on the kind of local patronage networks and modes of administration that underlay their construction, upkeep and management. The first point to note, however, is that the dams' 'monumentality' closely rivals that of even the largest Buddhist structures in the area, serving as a reminder that the latter were not the only large-scale construction projects during the late centuries BC. Insights into the levels of manpower involved in their construction may be provided at a future stage by comparing their volume with that of major stupas and monasteries. A preliminary comparison between the Sanchi dam and Stupa 1 on the hill above shows that the volume of the dam is approximately nine times that of the latter. This rather crude comparison needs to be tempered with consideration of the high costs represented by the elaborate railing and gateway carvings on Sanchi, Stupa 1. However, it gives an indication of the significant size of investment represented by local dam-building programmes. Quite clearly, the high investment involved in the construction of the dams would only have made sense if an efficient system for ensuring profitability was already in place, including a developed administrative framework for overseeing the use and supply of irrigation.

Secondly, the internal dynamics of the 'early historic complex' at Sanchi are consistently repeated throughout the study area: as shown in Figure 1.2, ten of the dams bear a direct spatial reference to monastic sites. This relative configuration of monasteries, reservoirs and settlements is so similar to those in Sri Lanka that there are grounds for suggesting that they were underlain by similar religio-economic systems.

Patronage

While the earliest phase (Id) of construction at Sanchi was closely related to the patronage of the Mauryan empire, we know from the numerous donative inscriptions at Sanchi and nearby sites that most of the Phase II monuments were funded by the pooled resources of individual patrons from widely dispersed locations across central India. One may assume, however, that for their daily needs, the monks would have relied heavily on the local communities living in their immediate vicinity. Further, we may assume that these same communities were closely involved with the running of the dams and the irrigation facilities that they provided. These villages may have had a similar status to the 'service villages' (*aramīkagāma*), described in early Buddhist texts such as the *Culavaṁsa* (v. 46.115) as providing labour to the monastery and meeting the nutritional needs of its inhabitants.

Although during the post-Mauryan period some monks may have continued to beg for a living, drawing on pre-established alliances with individual families in specific villages, it is generally accepted that a more integrated, sustainable system of exchange between monastic and non-monastic sections of society would have been necessary as monasteries became larger and more institutionalised (Bailey and Mabbett 2003, 70–2). Further, a system based on a high degree of agricultural surplus, as opposed to a simple subsistence economy, would have been necessary to support the large monasteries that developed during the post-Mauryan period (*ibid.*, 71).

While it is too early to posit a direct causal link between the establishment of Buddhism and the construction of dams in the Sanchi area, one may still suggest a more general link, that Buddhism spread from eastern India as part of a wider package, including urbanisation and new forms of political administration, that brought with it the need for more intensive agriculture. As both monasteries and urban centres grew in size and number, irrigated agriculture would have been an important means of catering for increased food demands.[43]

While the water-resource structures in the Sanchi area seem to be spatially and economically related to largely contemporary Buddhist monasteries, their later history was evidently linked to other religious traditions, as suggested by the growing number of Brahmanical and Jain temples, and the corresponding decrease in Buddhist building projects, from Phase IV onwards. This pattern fits with wider changes in the relationship between religion and agriculture across northern India: from the Gupta period onwards we begin to find epigraphical evidence for Brahmanical land grants and the rise of temple-owned land and water-resource structures. It is no coincidence, therefore, that the most significant Brahmanical temple mounds on the Devrajpur dam are situated next to spillways and sluices, at the sources of water control and manipulation, and where, in other parts of South Asia, the associated donative inscription is usually located (Shaw and Sutcliffe 2003a, 78–80).

Putting aside the precise nature of the link between Buddhism and dam construction, another important question is 'who were the principal patrons who paid for their construction?' As discussed in chapter 5, there are strong grounds for arguing that the *nāga* sculptures located on, or near to, many of the dams had a deeper political significance, as symbols of the local oligarchy of the same name. The argument that these sculptures, which particularly during the Gupta period underwent a process of 'royalisation', doubled as representations of the local Naga dynasty supports the view, also suggested by numismatic and epigraphic evidence, that the Nagas were powerful local oligarchs closely connected with the patronage of Buddhist and agricultural building projects in the area. Both their role as facilitators of agrarian expansion and their identification with a totemic deity are features more commonly associated with the Guptas (and their link with Visnu), who from the fourth century AD appear to have usurped the Nagas' authority in the area (Shaw 2004; Shaw and Sutcliffe 2003a): as discussed in chapter 12, the royal cave-temples at Udayagiri seem to have been closely bound up with rituals aimed specifically at predicting the start and finish of the monsoon, and thus maximising the efficacy of local agriculture (Willis 2004).

Conclusion

The archaeological and hydrological analyses presented in this chapter demonstrate that the Sanchi dams were indeed designed for irrigation purposes and that their size is in harmony with local catchments and runoff volumes, while some of the larger reservoirs show a familiarity with the problems of flood control. This suggests that they were built by engineers who were already accustomed to reservoir irrigation. The insights regarding associated land-use patterns introduce fresh evidence into debates regarding the history of rice in central India, and its possible relationship to wider social and religious processes taking place during the late centuries BC. More importantly, an analysis of the relative position of dams, contemporary settlements, Buddhist sites and cult spots provides a starting point for considering alternative models to the canonical 'ideal' of the 'antisocial' Buddhist monk, disconnected from social relations and, in particular, agrarian modes of production.

It is germane to consider possible centres of influence behind this irrigation technology, and the time frame over which it developed in the Sanchi area. As discussed earlier, the impetus for rice cultivation probably came from eastern India. However, it does not automatically follow that the irrigation technology also came from the same area. Although some analogies have already been suggested with the *ahar* reservoir system in southern Bihar (Agrawal and Narain 1997, 86–98), major differences in soil types and climate between eastern and central India call for quite different irrigation solutions. Other possible areas of influence have been explored elsewhere (Shaw and Sutcliffe 2003a). For example, given the historical link between the Buddhist traditions of Sanchi and Sri Lanka, a level of technological exchange between the two areas cannot be ruled out (*ibid.*, 95–100). There are also close similarities between the Sanchi dams and the Junagadh dam, which itself may have been influenced by dam-building traditions in Baluchistan (Shaw and Sutcliffe 2003a, 89–92; Possehl 1975). However, we should not assume a ready-made model for dam-based irrigation technology: the close relationship between runoff and reservoir volume in the Sanchi area suggests a high level of understanding of water-balance which must have been based on a considerable period of observation and understanding of local conditions. That the construction of the dams occurred in the late centuries BC around the same time as the widespread establishment of Buddhist and urban centres in the area is confirmed by OSL dates from the Sanchi dam. The need for more intensive forms of agriculture probably unfolded over time as monasteries became more institutionalised and embedded in local society, and local populations grew in size.[44] This could have been tackled by building on pre-existing, indigenous irrigation traditions, and applying them to new crops with the help of advanced irrigation technologies known from other parts of South Asia. These early dams could have been of a makeshift, temporary nature and were then greatly developed, and made more permanent, during the early historic period.[45] Useful analogies may be sought in traditional land-use practices in other parts of Madhya Pradesh, such as the *haveli* system which utilised temporary embankments for impounding monsoon runoff and improving the moisture content of the soil over the dry season (Agarwal and Narain 1997, 166–75; Shaw and Sutcliffe 2003a, 80–1). This suggests a gradual evolution of the archaeological landscape as represented by the intra-site patterns of the 'early-historic complexes' recorded during the SSP. However, in order to 'prove' these propositions, it would first be necessary to build an improved chronological and palaeo-environmental framework for the Sanchi area. This would involve a focused programme of excavation at selected settlements and Buddhist sites as a basis for refining regional architectural and ceramic typologies, and for establishing secure geological and radiocarbon dating, as well as archaeobotanical, sequences.

219 Sanchi-Nagauri dam viewed from southern end of Sanchi hill

220 Ferozpur dam viewed from summit of Ferozpur hill

221 Chandna dam (reconstructed) taken from top of Chandna hill

222 Dam facing (Morel kala)

223 Devrajpur dam from eastern escarpment, with spillway in foreground (the line of trees marks the location of the road cutting)

224 Sanchi dam section taken from east showing details

225 Sanchi dam section taken from west showing location of samples and stone facing

226 Red ware potsherds from stone packing layer

227 Devrajpur dam section

228 Morel kala: monumentalised control structure

229 Morel kala: temple fragments (c. seventh century AD) reused in feeder stream structure

230 Devrajpur dam: torus moulding amongst structural remains in main feeder stream (c. seventh century AD)

231 Devrajpur dam: eave moulding (c. seventh century AD)

CHAPTER 15

Conclusion: Towards an Integrated Model of Religious Change

Buddhist landscapes in central India

The task of providing an archaeological and cultural setting for Sanchi's Buddhist monuments has been achieved in two ways in this study: i) by filling in the gaps in the 'Buddhist landscape' through the documentation of 'new' Buddhist sites beyond the context of Sanchi and the four other 'Bhilsa Tope' sites; and ii) through a systematic documentation of other aspects of the archaeological landscape beyond the formal boundaries of monastic sites, including rock-shelters, habitational settlements, water-resource structures and non-Buddhist ritual locations.

The sheer number of newly documented Buddhist sites has shown that Buddhist propagation in this area during the late centuries BC was substantially more prolific than previously assumed. The identification of early monasteries which appear to predate the regular courtyard monastery, assumed not to have appeared at Sanchi before the Gupta period, has been useful for challenging received assumptions about the history and chronology of monasticism. Further, observations of the strategic positioning and, in some cases, fortified aspect of Buddhist sites have raised interesting questions regarding the symbolic, ritual and practical incentives behind the positioning of early stupas and monasteries in the landscape. Fresh insights into local patronage networks have been provided by the discovery of a donative inscription at Mawasa, while new evidence relating to the reuse of prehistoric rock-shelters has raised questions regarding the early history of Buddhist occupation in central India. While attesting to the co-existence of forest and village monastic communities from the late centuries BC onwards, the possibility that these 'monastic rock-shelters' represent a pre-Mauryan and 'pre-monumental' phase of local Buddhism cannot be ruled out. It is expected that future investigation of this type of shelter both in the Sanchi area and further afield, such as Pangurariya, will enable assessment of whether the widespread construction of stupas and monasteries during the late centuries BC represented a 'new' cultural movement or a 'monumentalisation' of an earlier forest tradition. This is an important distinction, as the existence of small, dispersed communities of monks would have meant that a level of local integration had already been in place before the large-scale propagation programmes had begun. This would have played a crucial role in easing relations between the incoming *saṅgha* and local populations and, above all, in generating the patronage networks upon which the Buddhist building programmes were dependent.

The second approach followed in this study has been the examination of the ritual, social and economic background of Buddhist propagation beyond the monastery walls. On the one hand, this rich and varied archaeological dataset has shown that the establishment of Buddhism was not an isolated process, but rather formed part of a wider set of cultural and economic developments between the late centuries BC and early centuries AD. On the other hand, the internal dynamics of the 'early-historic complex', typified by the relative configuration of Buddhist sites, settlements, dams and non-Buddhist cult spots at Sanchi and replicated with some regularity throughout the study area, provide an empirical basis for assessing models regarding the nature of social and economic interactions between the *saṅgha* and local lay populations beyond the framework of inscriptions and monastery chronologies. Further, these inter-site patterns have raised interesting questions regarding the applicability of current models of religious change for understanding the *saṅgha*'s relationship to local cults. Each of these issues is considered further in the following three sections.

Finally, a rich body of new sculptural and architectural material has shed important light on aspects of the non-Buddhist religious landscape. By examining the spatial and temporal distribution of this material throughout the study area, it has been possible to investigate the key phases in the development of a multi-tiered religious landscape and the changing dynamics of religious patronage between c. third century BC and twelfth century AD. While Buddhism is the dominant force during the first half of this time-frame, by the second half, the Brahmanical identity of the landscape has become overwhelmingly apparent. The proliferation of Brahmanical temple construction from Phase IV onwards is mirrored by the gradual decline in Buddhism, with its eventual disappearance probably occurring sometime after the twelfth century AD.

Urbanisation and agrarian change

The disproportionate attention which sites such as Sanchi and the four other 'Bhilsa Tope' sites have hitherto received in comparison to the surrounding archaeological landscape largely reflects the enduring 'monumentality', itself a result of the vagaries of archaeological preservation, of many Buddhist structures. However, the present-day rural setting of these sites represents a striking contrast to the 'suburban' quality of the surrounding landscape as suggested by settlement patterns discussed in chapter 13. In ancient times, much of the intervening valleys and lower slopes of the hills on whose summits these Buddhist sites are positioned, would have been occupied by large villages and towns; the full extent of these built-up zones is illustrated in the polygon-based maps (e.g. Figures 11.8, 13.2, etc.). The rise of urbanisation at Vidisha is usually viewed alongside the westward spread of the Mauryan empire during the third century BC. Given the uncertainties over the archaeological sequence at Vidisha, we should not rule out the possibility that this process had already began somewhat earlier. However, it is not until the Mauryan and post-Mauryan periods that the influence of 'pan-Indian' developments becomes evident in the form of visual representation, as found for example at Sanchi and Vidisha. The intertwined processes of urbanisation and the spread of pan-Indian art are also evident in Vidisha's rural hinterland, as illustrated by the appearance of Phase II urban stupas and pillars at 'interior' settlements such as Besar talai. The main point to note, however, is that the latter, if not both, of these processes were evidently closely related to the movement of large monastic communities into these areas. As discussed in chapters 11–12, the only evidence for stone sculpture outside the context of Vidisha and Sanchi occurs within hilltop monastic settings or else at urban stupas or shrines with a strong link to Buddhism. Without suggesting direct causal linkages between Buddhist propagation and social change, the former process does appear to have acted as one of the major vehicles for the spread of a larger set of cultural influences from the Gangetic valley area. That this role was not exclusive to Buddhism is attested by the c. third- to second-century-BC Bhagavata cult centre at Vidisha and the later proliferation of related sculpture throughout the surrounding countryside. The apparent absence of Vaisnava and Saiva sculpture outside the capital city until the mid-first century BC does support theories regarding the pioneering nature of early Buddhist propagation.

Further insights into the wider social and economic setting of monastic sites have been provided by the irrigation embankments discussed in chapter 14. The high investment involved in their construction would only have made sense if an efficient system for ensuring profitability was already in place. This raises obvious questions regarding the factors which led to such increased food-production demands. At this stage, two possible explanations have been considered. First, the acceleration of urban growth which began with the spread of the Mauryan empire in the third century BC would have led to increased food consumption levels. Secondly, the establishment of large numbers of monastic complexes throughout the hinterland would have added significant pressure on local resources, calling for intensive wet-rice agriculture with which the reservoirs appear to have been connected. Parallels can be drawn here with processes of 'agricultural involution' in Southeast Asia, where wet-rice regimes were a to increasing population levels that could not be supported through existing shifting swidden agriculture alone (Geertz 1963).

The *saṅgha* and local society: exchange networks

The above observations highlight the importance of viewing monastic sites, settlements and dams in the Sanchi area as related components in an interdependent socio-economic system. While the increased agricultural efficiency brought about by the local irrigation systems would have played an important role in catering for the *saṅgha*'s needs, one of the underlying questions throughout this book has been 'what were the terms of exchange between the *saṅgha* and the local food-producing sections of society?' In other words, did monks beg for a living or were they involved in more formal, socially integrated and, hence, stable forms of exchange? Possible answers to this question have been situated within wider discussions regarding the 'domestication' of the *saṅgha*. As discussed in chapters 2 and 6, it is generally accepted that the movement away from mendicancy coincided with the *saṅgha*'s transition from peripatetic to sedentary forms of monasticism (Dutt 1962). This is because, while the dietary needs of small mobile groups of forest-dwelling monks could have been met by local populations with little difficulty, those of large permanent monastic communities would have called for more sustainable forms of patronage. It is highly unlikely that even the most altruistic patrons could have carried on supporting a settled *saṅgha* unless they were receiving some form of tangible benefit in return. With regard to the Sanchi area, the received view is that 'domestication' did not take place until at least the early centuries AD. Although this view stems, in part, from a 'theological' model of Buddhism which views the departure from mendicancy as a deterioration of 'true' Buddhist values, it also reflects the narrow framework of reference through which archaeological material has been used by text-based scholars of Buddhist history. This chronology is challenged by newly documented evidence for the existence of permanent monastic structures during earlier periods and by the sheer quantity of Buddhist complexes, coupled with their size and architectural sophistication, which provide strong evidence that institutional forms of monasticism were already in place by c. second century BC.

Suggestions as to how the *saṅgha* might have negotiated reciprocal terms of exchange with local agricultural communities in the Sanchi area have been posited by comparisons with examples of Sri Lankan 'monastic landlordism'. Inscriptions from the second century BC onwards attest to the monastic ownership of land and water-resource structures, donated to the *saṅgha* not only by local chieftains but also by private individuals (Gunawardana 1971, 24; Paranavitana 1970, vol. I, lxii; lxxxiv). In fact, the social composition of the donors is roughly comparable to that of the earlier, third-century-BC inscriptions, generally associated with the donation of drip-ledged rock-shelters (Paranavitana 1970, vol. I). The major difference between the earlier and later inscriptions is the shift in the principal object of donation from rock-shelters to water-resource structures and agricultural land. This shift is usually regarded as one of the primary factors behind the 'domestication' of the *saṅgha* in Sri Lanka and the corresponding shift from 'passive' mendicancy to 'active' forms of socially embedded monasticism, as well as from forest to village forms of monasticism.

In India, by contrast, the study of monastic landlordism is in its infancy. This is because the subject has hitherto been approached from a predominantly epigraphical framework which finds no evidence for monastery-owned land prior to the first century AD. Furthermore, the full institutionalisation of religious-based landownership is not generally thought to have occurred until the appearance of Brahmanical land-grants during the Gupta period (Kosambi 1955, 229; Kulke 1993). This system is typified by the Pallava and Cola tank inscriptions of south India (Stargardt 1990, 133–40), culminating in the temple-owned tanks of the medieval period. At Vijayanagara, for example, kings, queens and local elite would donate land or cash grants to local temple councils, which would then reinvest the original donation in the form of hydraulic construction projects (Morrison 1993,

145). The consequent increase in yields presented obvious benefits for local agriculturalists, while a percentage of the profits would be returned to the temple in the form of a 'donation'. This would then be 'transformed' into *prasād*, some of which would be repaid to the original donor, with the remainder sold to pilgrims. The ingenuity of this system lay in the pooling of small donations or investments, which enabled the construction of large-scale irrigation systems whose high investment levels would otherwise have required 'centralized initiative of control' (Morrison 1993, 146).

The above examples are useful for assessing how local patrons, monks and farmers might have worked together in the Sanchi area. The grounds for viewing monastic sites and dams as part of a unified economic system are particularly compelling at sites such as Morel khurd, Sanchi, Ferozpur and Devrajpur, where not only is there a major dam directly below the Buddhist complex, but where the latter clearly outweighs neighbouring settlements in terms of size and 'monumentality'. At this point, however, there is no way of 'proving' that monastic landlordism was prevalent in the area. Furthermore, the suggestion that religious institutions played a major role in the control and management of water resources is not restricted to the context of Buddhism, as attested for example by the first-century-BC Balarama sculpture on the Chandna dam and later Brahmanical and Jain temples on the Devrajpur dam. However, the main point is that the temporal and spatial relationships between monasteries, dams and settlements provide an empirical basis for viewing the establishment of Buddhism, the spread of urbanisation and the intensification of agrarian production as parts of a complex socio-economic system which functioned through an interdependent exchange network between local rulers, landowners, labourers and monks.

Non-monastic staff

Whilst suggesting that the saṅgha was engaged in localised exchange networks rather than relying on long-distance trade or individual monks' begging rounds, this is not to say that monks themselves were involved directly in the building, upkeep or running of irrigation works, or indeed in agricultural production. These activities were prohibited to monks according to canonical rules, which is why earlier scholars such as Marshall dismissed the possibility that monks at Sanchi had any direct connection with the dam at the foot of the hill. However, it should by now be clear that the *saṅgha* was adept at getting around such rules so that on an institutional level it could participate in the wider commercial world without its individual monastic members breaking their vows. Such activities, along with other jobs inherent to any large institution, such as cooking, cleaning and financial administration, would have been carried out by non-monastic staff. As discussed in chapter 2, these work forces are referred to by a range of titles in Buddhist texts and inscriptions, and were often the object of lay gifts to the *saṅgha*. They were responsible for work that monks were not permitted to carry out themselves, thus allowing monks to pursue a life of asceticism and learning, whilst ensuring the prosperity and efficacy of the larger Buddhist institution within the community at large. Striking this balance between enabling monks to follow their renunciate path whilst attending to institutional duties is at the very heart of the monastic phenomenon. Here there are obvious parallels to other religious traditions. We may refer, for example, to the thirteenth-century Duiske Abbey in Ireland, which 'for about 330 years ... continued to exist through good times and bad, turbulent and peaceful. It was the hub of the local community, upon which it had an enormous influence – introducing new farming methods and good management of natural resources, as well as tending the poor and the sick' (Graiguenamanagh: *A Visitor's Guide*, n.d.).[1]

An end to suffering: practical models of religious change

The suggestion that the *saṅgha* was from an early period involved in reciprocal forms of exchange with local agricultural populations also contributes to discussions of 'religious change'. As discussed in chapter 6, the understanding of religious change in respect to early Buddhism is still open to debate. Current models have tended to focus solely on the 'ritual' dimensions of religious experience rather than considering social or economic forms of interaction between monastic and lay sections of society. For example, theories regarding the *saṅgha*'s assimilation of local deities have drawn heavily on textual accounts describing the Buddha's subordination and ultimate 'conversion' of powerful *nāgas* and *yakṣas*. Others have viewed the presence of 'non-Buddhist' sculpture at major monastic sites as evidence of the *saṅgha*'s participation in 'localisation' strategies (Cohen 1998; Bloss 1973). However, neither of these models is borne out by the archaeological patterns discussed in this book: as shown by the sculptural material considered in chapter 8, there is little to suggest that prior to the Gupta period local cultic elements were being assimilated into monastic settings.

The approach described in this book has, by breaking down the arbitrary distinction between 'ritual' and 'non-ritual' dimensions of the landscape and viewing Buddhist and non-Buddhist ritual centres side by side with settlement patterns and agrarian systems, provided an empirical basis for assessing the applicability of alternative, more socially integrated models of religious change. Of particular relevance in this respect are a number of studies, based largely on ethnographic and historical sources, of the 'functional' or 'practical' aspects of religious change in Islamic or Christian contexts. For example, Eaton (1993) has shown how local populations in east Bengal were attracted to Islam not for exclusively religious reasons, but because of the superior agricultural resources to which it provided access. Eaton refers to the process not as one of 'conversion' but rather as 'creative adaptation', a term coined earlier by Smail (1961, 91) in the context of colonial Indonesia. Since the essence of this process is 'the acceptance of change by the acculturating group', the question of 'forced cultural change' is inappropriate.

Eaton's study offers useful suggestions for understanding the dynamics of religious change in the Sanchi area, with regard to both the *saṅgha*'s attitude towards local cults and its position within the economic infrastructure. Thus, while the incoming *saṅgha* seems not to have actively assimilated local cultic elements either as a means of 'conversion' or 'localisation', the concept of 'creative adaptation' offers a possible explanation for why the production of *nāga* and *yakṣa* sculptures only appear in stone media after the establishment of Buddhism and, further, seem to mirror developments already seen within monastic contexts. Similarly, in Sri Lanka, the introduction of Buddhism was less to do with the conversion of local populations than with providing an effective vehicle for generating patronage networks. Not only was this essential for the survival of the *saṅgha*, but by acting as agents for economic development and the alleviation of everyday suffering (*dukkha*), it enabled the propagation of Buddhist ideology to the most interior areas. Additional 'services' that I have only mentioned in passing in this book, as they are dealt with in detail by other scholars, included medicine and mortuary rituals (Zysk 1991; Schopen 1994c; 1996b). It appears therefore that Buddhism moved into new areas with resources that were intended to complement, rather than replace, the existing religious framework; hence the two-tiered religious structure of most 'Buddhist' countries where many of the laity's ritual requirements are taken care of by the 'native' religious tradition rather than Buddhism.

Ironically, just as the selective and 'practical' role that monks played in the lives of local non-monastic populations was a major factor in the success of Buddhist propagation programmes, it may also have contributed to the eventual downfall of Indian Buddhism. While Buddhism flourished in neighbouring Asian regions, in India its patronage base was already on the decline from the Gupta period onwards, and by the Muslim conquests of the twelfth and thirteenth centuries AD, only a few marginal Buddhist outposts were surviving in eastern India (Verardi 1996). Although the coming of Islam was the final straw, Buddhism's decline had already set in much earlier, due to a combination of internal monastic disputes and external Brahmanical oppression (Verardi 2003). Jainism also suffered a similar fate but, unlike Buddhism, managed to survive into the present day by emulating Brahmanical practices and, perhaps even more importantly, by providing a strong and inclusive ritual identity to the laity. According to some scholars (Jaini 1980; Verardi 1996), it was precisely because of Buddhism's failure to do the same for its own laity that some of its more practical functions were appropriated by competing religious traditions, especially Saiva and Vaisnava institutions, and it was reduced to a handful of communities with few tangible services to give back to society. By the time of the late Muslim incursions of the twelfth century, monks played a marginal economic role in wider society, and with the majority of local ritual activity set within a Brahmanical framework, the last remnants of Buddhist monasticism soon vanished from the landscape altogether.

Notes

Chapter 1

1 Notable exceptions to this trend include Hans Bakker's pioneering work on the religious and political history of Ayodhya (1986) and Ramtek (1997), which applies a 'synthetic method of investigation' to philological, art-historical and archaeological sources within their geographical setting. Other recent examples of integrated approaches to sites in the landscape, to be discussed further in chapter 7, include Dass and Willis's work at Udayagiri (Dass and Willis 2002; Willis 2004) and Dilip Chakrabarti's (2004) extensive explorations in the Gangetic valley.
2 Since the SSP began, a number of other studies on the wider archaeological setting of major Buddhist sites including Bharhut (Hawkes, in press), Amaravati (Shimada, in press), and Fogelin (2004; 2006) have also been initiated.
3 A summary of field investigations, excavations, and conservation work at Sanchi is given in Mitra 1996.
4 Similar stupa*s* have been found throughout the study area during the SSP, closely paralleled by recent discoveries in Andhra Pradesh (Fogelin 2004; 2006).
5 I am grateful to the Madhya Pradesh Directorate of Archaeology, Archives, and Museums (Bhopal) for granting me access to these reports in 1999–2000.
6 Details available on http://www.britac.ac.uk/institutes/SSAS/projects/sanchi.htm.
7 This is less of a problem in India itself, where students of ancient Indian history, like those following a Classical training in Europe, are exposed to a more balanced combination of textual, language and archaeological training from their earliest schooldays. However, this level of interdisciplinarity is undermined by the narrow geographical focus, with limited theoretical or methodological insights from regions outside India.

Chapter 2

1 Other important textual sources include the *Sūtra* literature, especially the *Gṛhya* and *Dharmasūtras*, and the Grammar of Panini, particularly the *Aṣṭādhyāyī*, generally dated to fifth/fourth century BC. The *Purāṇas*, especially the *Viṣṇu Purāṇa*, are also important for understanding genealogies; however, since these are based on oral histories, there are significant problems when it comes to establishing fixed chronologies, as discussed later with reference to the problematically dated *Arthaśāstra*.
2 The observations of the Greek historian Megasthenes (fl. 300 BC), an ambassador sent by the first Seleucus to the court of Candragupta Maurya at Pataliputra (McCrindle 1979), were later reproduced in Strabo's *Geography* (c. 64 BC–AD 21).
3 For a recent discussion of this problem in relation to central India, see Kennet 2004.
4 The *jati* (occupational caste) hierarchy was not defined until several centuries later (Mabbett and Bailey 2003).
5 Sequences based on dynastic rule lie at the heart of both the 'Historiographic'/ 'Colonial' model and 'Feudal' models. For further discussion, see Kulke 1995a; Thapar 1984; and Sinopoli 2003.
6 For other recent case-studies, see Kulke, ed., 1995.
7 See Miller 2006 for a discussion of the role of irrigation in the rise of cities during the Bronze Age Harappan.
8 See Scarborough 2003, ch. 3, for broader discussion.
9 Similar revisions have also been made in Mesopotamia and Egypt on the basis of village-based water-management systems (Adams 1974).
10 Another Sudarsana dam mentioned in a Vakataka inscription from Ramtek, Maharashtra (Bakker 1997, appendix I, v. 5), has recently been taken up for investigation (Bakker, Cork, Sutcliffe, Shaw and Bosma, forthcoming). See also: http://www.britac.ac.uk/institutes/SSAS/projects/sanchi.htm.
11 A similar Brahmanical patronage system is attested at the Ramtek Sudarsana lake mentioned in n. 10.
12 For a more recent discussion of the latter and their possible connection with the 'Gabarbands' of Baluchistan, see Possehl 1975.
13 It has also been suggested that merchant groups and trade networks themselves 'compensated for the disappearance of the democratic tribal political structures that were being absorbed by the large political entities then emerging in Northwest India' (Benavides 2005, 85; Heitzman 1984, 131).
14 As discussed later, although Weberian capitalist strands that are compatible with Buddhism have been identified in these modern contexts, others have argued for a distinctly 'Buddhist economics' which differs from either capitalist or communist ideas (Schumacher 1973; Harvey 2000, 215–19; Green 1992).
15 Evidence for the role of trade in Buddhist monasticism is discussed in chapter 11.

Chapter 3

1 I am grateful to Emma Read, whom I accompanied to Kharwai and Satkunda during the course of her PhD research (Cambridge University) on painted rock-shelter sites in Raisen district.
2 For recently excavated Chalcolithic sites in Madhya Pradesh, see Sharma and Misra 2003.
3 As discussed in chapter 8, the establishment of reliable, regionally specific ceramic sequences is an urgent requirement in South Asian archaeology. At present, the basic framework for establishing local typologies is usually provided by well-known 'type' sites in the Gangetic valley such as Kausambi and Ahicchatra. The reliability of this approach is obviously undermined by the lack of attention to local variations, but just as problematic is the fact that most of the Gangetic valley 'type' sites were excavated prior to the development of sophisticated sampling, dating or petrographic analysis techniques.
4 This site is listed as SG017 in the SSP database.

Chapter 4

1 Ancient pollen sequences suggest that the appearance of *sāl* forests in central India was a relatively late occurrence, datable to c. 1200 years BP (Chauhan 1995).
2 The most reliable dates are from Damadama (Fuller 2002; 2003) and more recently Lahuradewa (Fuller, in press); earlier dates in the fifth and fourth millennium BC have been suggested for Koldihawa and Chopani Mando respectively (Sharma *et al.*, 1980), although these are no longer considered reliable.
3 Grateful thanks to Emma Harvey for carrying out this preliminary work and for giving advice over future phytolith-based research in the Sanchi area.
4 The channels at Udayagiri were partly fed by a tank on top of the hill. Although the rainfall should have been adequate for filling this tank (Sutcliffe, pers. comm.), there is evidence that it was refilled using a manually operated pulley system connected to the Bes river below (Willis 2004); Dass 2006.

Chapter 5

1 A similar point is made in Willis (1997) with regard to later periods of central Indian history.
2 A recent revision of Satavahana chronology is given in Cribb 2000.

3 Numismatists are now in general agreement that the king in question is Satakarni I, who ruled in the Malwa area from c. AD 25, and not Satakarni II or the later Gautamiputra Satakarni (Cribb 2000).
4 For a discussion of the impact of 'imprecise' archaeological techniques and poor ceramic sequences on Sharma's urban decay theory, with specific reference to the Vakataka realm, see Kennet 2004.
5 Scholars are divided, however, in their opinion as to whether in the *Purāṇas* the word *nava* refers to the 'nine' Naga rulers (Trivedi 1957) or to the three 'new' houses at Mathura, Kantipurya and Pawaya as opposed to the older, aforementioned lineage at Vidisha (Bhandarkar *CII*, III, 20–21).
6 Hitherto these have been interpreted within a religious framework, being seen as evidence for the strong influence of local cultic practice in the area (Schopen 1996c; Misra 1981). Such an approach illustrates the general dislocation between the study of religious and political history in South Asia. There are also suggestions that the Nandin kings who succeeded the so-called Sungas had Naga affiliations (Bhandarkar *CII*, III, 10).
7 Grateful thanks to Shailendra Bhandare for directing me to this inscription, which is also renowned for containing the earliest reference to Maharashtra as a geographical entity. I am also grateful to Michael Willis for alerting me to the Parivrajaka and Ucchakalpa plates (Fleet *CII*, III), which refer to Naga oligarchs working as subordinates to local kings.
8 E.g. in the *Bhāgavata Purāṇa*, Garuda, the symbol of birth and light, slays the serpent Kaliya, the epitome of darkness and poison. However, 'Viṣṇu combines both of these symbols within himself for he sleeps on the serpent of eternity (Ananta or Śeṣa – the good *alter ego* of the evil Kāliya) and then awakens to ride on the Garuda bird' (O'Flaherty 1975, 221).

Chapter 6

1 Also known as Besnagar, after the village Bes, which occupies a key position amidst the ancient city mounds. For the inscription, see Sircar 1965, 88; Salomon 1998, 265–6. For the associated Vasudeva temple, see Khare 1967. For the history and archaeology of the Pancaratra system, see Härtel 1987; Srinivasan 1979; Bakker 1997.
2 For an art-historical and iconographic study of the Udayagiri caves, see Williams 1982, 40–52. For new insights into the architectural programme, see Dass 2001; Dass and Willis 2002; Willis 2005.
3 However, see Shaw 2004a, and Dass and Willis 2002, where this issue is taken up.
4 The precedent for this regulation was set when king Bimbasara donated a bamboo grove at Rajagaha to the *saṅgha* (Gombrich 1997, 96, 156; *Vinaya Piṭaka* I, 39).
5 Only three of the inscriptions have direct royal associations.
6 As discussed in chapter 5, Kurara probably refers to the city-state of the same name mentioned on coins, and may correspond with the modern village of Kurawar to the north of Vidisha.
7 For a revised chronology of the Hemavata school, see Willis 2000.
8 By contrast, the full development of a pan-Hindu geography based on inter-regional pilgrimage centres appears not to have been fully consolidated until the 16th century (Bakker 1986; 1992).
9 The best-known example, in which the site is now referred to as Kakanadabota, is dated in the Gupta year 93 (AD 412–13) and records a grant of land by Amarakarddava, a military officer in Candragupta II's army (Marshall 1940, 388–9; inscrip. 833; Fleet *CII*, III, 29–34; Bhandarkar *CII*, III, 247–51; Sircar 1965, 280–2. Another which dates to the Gupta year 131 (AD 450–1), records the donation of a lamp 'in the place of the four Buddhas' (Marshall 1940, 389–90; inscrip. 834; Fleet *CII*, III, 29–34).
10 See chapter 5 for discussion on the dating of the pillar and inscription. The foundations of an earlier apsidal building underlying the associated temple remains are dated to c. third century BC (Khare 1967; *IAR* 1963–4, 17; 1964–5, 19–20).
11 Härtel (1987, 580) attributes the coining of these terms to J.N. Banerjea. See also Srinivasan 1979 for distinctions between *vīravāda*, *vyūhavāda* and *avatāravāda*. For a more recent discussion, see Bakker 2004.
12 Vasudeva's association with the Vrsni race is mentioned in the *Mahābhārata* (Poona Edition, 6.32.37).
13 See Fussman (1989, 3–7, pl. 4; 15–16, pl. 18) for examples at Chilas on the River Indus; and Neumayer (1992–3) for a group of paintings at Tikula (Gwalior district, Madhya Pradesh).
14 E.g. the second-century-BC Nanaghat cave inscription (Pune district, Maharashtra) invokes Samkarsana and Vasudeva in a list of other gods (Chanda 1920; Sircar 1965, vol. 1, 192). Another example is the roughly contemporary Ghosundi inscription (Chitogarh, Rajasthan) which refers to the erection of a stone railing for the purpose of worship (*pūjā-śilā-prākāra*) of the Blessed Ones, Samkarsana and Vasudeva (Sircar 1965, vol. 1, 90; Jayaswal 1921–2; Bhandarkar 1920; for the remains of an elliptical shrine at nearly Nagari, see Chanda 1920, 163). Vasudeva and Baladeva (Samkarsana) are also mentioned in a list of heterodox sects in the early Buddhist text, the *Mahānidessa* (I, 89).
15 The Mora well inscription from Mathura, inscribed during the time of Sodasa (early first century AD), describes the installation of cult idols of the five heroes (*Pañcavīra*) of the Vrsni race in a stone temple (Sircar 1965, vol. 1, 122; Lüders 1937–8, 194–200). These deities are also listed by name in the *Vāyumahāpurāṇa*, cited in Härtel, 1987, 575, n. 6.
16 Härtel (1987, 581) argues that although the system reaches full maturity in the Pancaratra texts of the ninth century AD, earlier sanctions are provided by the *Nārāyanīya* section of the *Śanti-Parvan* of the *Mahābhārata* (XII, 326, 31–41), which describes the cosmic Narayana as the god of fourfold form. Here, Narayana announces himself to be the god of creation, Vasudeva, from whom his other forms emanate one after the other: from Vasudeva emanates Samkarsana; from Samkarsana emanates Pradyumna; and so on. However, given that this text is generally believed to have been compiled in the Gupta period, such sanctions need to be viewed with caution.
17 These developments correspond with the appearance, during the late Kusana period, of sculptural representations of the *caturvyūha* concept. A well-known example, now in the Mathura Museum (Acc. no. 13. 392–95), depicts Samkarsana emerging from Vasudeva's shoulder (Härtel, 1987, 584, pl. IX). A four-sided image from Bhita datable to c. first century BC, now in the Lucknow State Museum, has also been interpreted as an earlier representation of the *caturvyūha* principle (Srinivasan 1979), but as urged by Bakker (1999, 341–2), this argument is unconvincing.
18 However, there are early images from Mitaoli, now stored in the ASI Museum, Gwalior Fort.
19 As illustrated, for example, by a Gupta image from Vidisha, which was originally described as Visnu (Lake 1910a, 139; Harle 1974, fig. 18) but, on account of the *musala* in the right hand and lion-faced standard in the other, has been convincingly re-identified as 'Balarāma without snake and snakehood', i.e. Vira Samkarsana (Härtel 1987, 584, n. 34).
20 The temple is described as the 'excellent temple' (*prāsādottama*) of the Bhagavata, the latter being thought to correspond to Vasudeva-Krsna, the principle deity of the Bhagavata tradition.
21 Cf. Cunningham (1880, 42, pl. xiv), who suggested that the Heliodorus pillar was crowned by one of the fan capitals lying nearby.
22 The capital illustrated in Plate 30 remains on site; the other two are stored in the GGMM.
23 Two fan-palm capitals from Pawaya are stored in the GGMM, while another from Kausambi is stored in the Allahabad University Museum (Acc no. AM2; Sharma 1982, 32). Another example from Mathura is stored in the State Museum, Lucknow (acc. no. J584; Joshi 1979, pl. 5). Samkarsana's association with the fan-palm capital is also supported by later sculptural evidence, such as the well known Kusana-period *caturvyūha* image from Mathura in which he is shown emanating from Vasudeva's shoulder in his serpent manifestation (see n. 17). An additional feature that has hitherto attracted little interest is a small fan-palm capital upon which Samkarsana appears to be standing. This final observation provides a useful key for relating the serpent and non-serpent forms of Samkarsana-Balarama.
24 E.g. in *Mahābhārata* 9.22.2 (also 9.36.20e and 9.53.10b) Balarama is given the epithet *tāladhvaja:* 'he who has the fan-palm standard'. Thanks to Alexis Sanderson for this reference.
25 In the *Viṣṇudharmottarapurāṇam* (ed. Kṛṣṇadāsa, 3.85.28), for example, it is stated, 'O King, fine standards on poles with their appropriate banners should be fashioned at the left side of [each of] the deities' (*vāmapārśvagāḥ kāryā devānām pravarā dhvajāḥ/svapatākāyutā rājan yaṣṭisthās*). Translation by Alexis Sanderson, to whom I am indebted for help with this material. However, whilst acknowledging the continuity of older idioms in later texts, there are obvious problems with using a post-Gupta Kashmiri text for interpreting second-century-BC sculpture in central India.
26 This was found about 1 km to the east, en route to Amacchar, along with a typical post-Mauryan abacus, discussed in chapter 9. For the capital, see Härtel 1987, 56–7, who also discusses the vehicles of Samba and Aniruddha, the remaining two *Pañcavīras*. See also Banerjea 1985, 387–8; Chanda 1920: 162. A crocodile capital from Kausambi, now stored in the Allahabad Museum, has been dated to the same period and used to infer the existence of an associated temple of Pradyumna (Chandra 1970, 56–7).
27 Others, such as Banerjea (1985, 387–8, n. 1), interpret these standards as symbols of the four *vyūhas*, rather than the five *vīras*.
28 See n. 23.
29 For the Parkham *yakṣa*, see Vogel 1930; and the Noh *yakṣas*, Agrawala 1933.
30 State Museum, Lucknow (acc. no. G215; Härtel 1987, 582, pl. 7).
31 Hari Singh Gaur Museum, Sagar (Joshi 1979, pl. 8a–c).
32 Other than the tradition of Balarama's habitual drunkenness (Joshi 1979, 48–9), it is difficult to locate the textual sanction for this association. One possible source is the rule given in Varahamihira's *Bṛhatsaṃhitā* that images of Baladeva should be white, have their eyes rolling with

intoxication and should carry a plough and 'one pot' (*kuṇḍakam*) (57.36: *baladevo halapāṇir madavibhramalocanaś ca kartavyaḥ/bibhrat kuṇḍakam ekam śaṅkhendumṛṇālagauratanuḥ*). I am grateful to Alexis Sanderson for this reference.

33 See n. 19.

34 Grateful thanks to Lance Cousins who helped me think more clearly about these matters.

35 For example, Visnu appears as an independent deity in Cave 6; there are two examples, the larger of which (Plate 168), stands to the right of the door with his two personified weapons: *cakrapuruṣa* and *gadādevī*. The smaller Visnu to the left of the doorway holds a *cakra* and *gadā* in their unpersonified forms (Williams 1982, pl. 35). Two of his *avatāras*, Varaha (Plate 169) and Narasimha, are depicted in excavations 5 and 12 respectively. Bakker (1986) gives a detailed discussion of the relationship between the textual and archaeological manifestations of these developments.

36 In this respect, comparisons can be made with the growth of Christian sites in Europe (Harbison 1994; Stopford 1994), which often developed around pre-existent cult spots in order to facilitate the greatest number of conversions.

37 See also Cohen (1998), who draws largely on references in the *Jātaka* stories and the *Mūlasarvāstivāda Vinaya*.

38 Close parallels in the Brahmanical tradition include the story of Garuda's defeat of the snakes guarding the elixir (*MBh* I:5: 29) and Krsna's destruction of the *nāga* Kaliya (*Viṣṇu Purāṇa*).

39 E.g. Dāvs 4: 28–37.

40 As discussed in chapter 9, it may also explain the removed distance between Sanchi and the *nāga* on Nagauri hill.

41 Composed sometime between the middle of the second and end of the fourth century AD, this 'proto-tantric' text contained rituals and invocations that were to become part of the state-sponsored apparatus of state-protection in the Far East (A. Sanderson, *pers comm.*; Sanderson 2004).

42 It may not be coincidental that some depictions of the Mucalinda story, with the *nāga* coiled up and over the Buddha's body, are similar to standardised representations of *nāgarājas* which embody the same combination of human and serpent attributes. It is possible that, in addition to the usual 'conversion' narrative, this story also embodies an element of localisation whereby the Buddha is appropriating the powers and very identity of the *nāga* itself. That the Buddha is no longer distinguishable from the *nāga* is what comes across from the second part of the story where the maidservant Sujata brings an offering to the Buddha, whilst he sits meditating under the tree, and is startled to see what she believes to be a *nāgarāja* sitting in his place.

43 Other evidence of the *saṅgha*'s direct participation in commercial activities comes from Tibet, Southeast Asia and China where monasteries were operating as banks, money-lenders, bridge-builders, and as agents for bringing new land into cultivation (Gernet 1956, 13, 117).

44 As discussed in chapter 15, the 'practical' model also helps to explain the prevalence of a two-tiered religious system in most 'Buddhist' countries (Willis, forthcoming a, ch. 2). Because Buddhism never infiltrated the everyday ritual lives of India's villagers, its more practical functions were easily usurped by competing religious traditions (Jaini 1980).

Chapter 7

1 It is an interesting irony that 'phenomenological archaeology' was invented by the 'phenomenologically challenged', i.e. those with rather few phenomena to study (Andrew Sherratt, pers. comm., 2004).

2 Maclean (1996) notes a similar problem in many parts of Africa.

Chapter 8

1 OSL refers to the levels of luminescence (light) emitted on exposure to light as the result of released energy accumulated in crystalline materials through the action of ionizing radiation from natural radioactivity. When a sediment is exposed to sunlight prior to deposition, the OSL acquired over geological time is removed; the luminescence clock is thus set to zero. The OSL then accumulates in response to the ionizing radiation received during the burial period of the sediment. The level of OSL observed in ancient samples is thus dependent on the absorbed radiation dose, and hence it can be related to the time elapsed since last illumination/heating once the dose received per year (during burial) has been calculated (http://www.rlaha.ox.ac.uk/lumin/lumindx.html).

2 Funded by the British Academy and the Society for South Asian Studies, this part of the project has been carried out in collaboration with Anthony Beck.

3 Whilst modern ploughs can reach depths of up to 1 m, the ox-drawn plough rarely exceeds 15 cm.

4 This situation, however, is rapidly changing, with the recent proliferation of stone-quarries and tree plantations, not to mention the illicit sculpture trade.

5 Map nos: 55E10, 55E11, 55E14, 55E15.

6 Total-station-based contour mapping was carried out using the services of Nikhil Land Survey and Civil Consultancy, Bhopal. Grateful thanks to S.R. Patidar for help and assistance.

7 See Appendix IIb for a list of cult spots and temples based on the primary context of associated installations.

8 For example, between the modern bridges at Rangai (SG017) and Pagneswar (SG061), places where the river can be crossed during the dry season have only been identified at Berkheri (SG152/SC283) and Nonakhera (SG018/SC85).

9 This applies as much to 'Buddhist' remains as to wider aspects of the landscape such as the dam below Sanchi hill, for example, which, notably, has not yet come under ASI protection. Such examples serve as a reminder of the mutually entwined relationship between archaeological theory and heritage legislation: landscape archaeology is not simply a whim of European theoreticians but rather, through bringing previously sidelined site-categories into the scholarly arena, holds the potential of saving them from imminent destruction.

10 See Agrawal 1997 for illustration of the Buddhist rock-shelter painting at Satdhara.

11 A analogous situation has been observed in Syria (Beck *et al.*, in press; Donoghue *et al.*, 2000).

12 E.g. at Pipariya village (SG146/I-663), where an image of Visnu is currently under worship as the village goddess, Durga.

13 See n. 5.

14 As discussed in chapter 12, the diminishing influence of Buddhism is archaeologically discernible in the Sanchi area from c. seventh century AD, with its final disappearance attested in c. twelfth century AD. For the scholarly 'rediscovery' of Buddhism in India in the early nineteenth century, see Allen 2002.

15 E.g. SG017b/SC285, SG029c/SC100, SG105/SC224, SG138/SC257, SG149/SC274, SG160b/SC294, SG172b/SC334.

Chapter 9

1 This corresponds to 'Period II' in the earlier five-phase sequence published in *IAR* 1975–6.

2 SG141.

3 SG002.

4 SG002/SC15; SG001/SC3.

5 SG002/SC14.

6 The lighter coloured stone used in the Phase III gateways of Stupa 1 was quarried from Udayagiri hill.

7 SG003a/SC23/S487.

8 SG003a/SC21.

9 SG003.

10 The apsidal plan is a hallmark of the earliest shrines in India such as the Bhagavata temples at Vidisha and Nagari, Rajasthan (Chapter 6), as well as the rock-cut *caitya* temples in Bihar and the Deccan (Sarkar 1965; 1966).

11 Most of the pillar shaft, though, is stored in an open-sided shelter slightly further to the east.

12 For the distribution of other Asokan capitals, see Ghosh 1967; Gupta 1980; Ray 1952. For their symbolism, see Vajracharya 1999; Verardi 2000.

13 This was suggested by a Brahmi inscription, dated palaeographically to c. second century BC and carved on one of the pillars overlying the original apsidal foundations. However, another fragmentary inscription bearing the name, 'Vimdu-sa-ra du-tara', led to the new suggestion that Sanchi's Buddhist significance dated to the time of Asoka's father, Bindusara (Raghava Varier and Narayanana 1976). The validity of this argument has not yet been confirmed.

14 SG001/I-8; SAMRC, acc. 2726.

15 For the elephant's three-fold Buddhist, folk and political symbolic function, see Verardi 2000; Vajracharya 1999.

16 There is evidence that the original stupa had been subjected to 'wanton' and deliberate damage. Marshall (1940, 23) attributed this act to Pusyamitra, who is supposed to have been inimical to Buddhism. However, the cause of this apparent destruction remains unknown.

17 This was confirmed by the discovery of a section of the original pavement at a depth of 14 feet (5.30 m) below the NW bastion of Building 43, a tenth-century-AD building situated on top of the high retaining wall to the east of Stupa 1.

18 Charred remains found between Phases I and II of the temple, led Marshall (1940, 64–5) to suggest that like Stupa 1, the original apsidal shrine had been deliberately destroyed.

19 A Chunar sandstone reliquary bowl (Marshall 1940, 53; Mus. Cat. A10) and a bone relic (Maisey 1892, 74; Cunningham 1854, 112) were found in the apse. However both appear to have been deposits of a later stupa built on the spot during the medieval period. The original shrine was not dated to Phase I, because the earliest floor rests on a layer of rubble filling rather

than bedrock. Secondly, as argued by Marshall (1940, 56), had the shrine been built at the same time as the earliest brick stupa, it would have followed the alignment of the Asokan pillar which represents a true north–south alignment. Instead, it follows the alignment of the second phase of Stupa 1, which was shifted slightly to the north-east in anticipation of the gateways which were added during the third phase.

20 The present facing and plinth were added in the seventh or eighth centuries AD (Willis 2000, 69–75).

21 For a summary of the arguments regarding the 'Buddhist' nature of the Stupa 2 carvings, see Taddei 1996.

22 SG037a.

23 The two floors were separated by 3 feet (c. 90 cm) of debris.

24 Similar material, although in less complete form, is found at other sites in the Gangetic valley such as Mathura and Pratapgarh. There are also close parallels with Bharhut period sculpture from sites further south such as Bhaja and Amaravati (Willis 2000, 58).

25 Cf. Behrendt (2000) who, in his study of a sculpted panel from Andher, assigns comparative material at Bharhut to c. 80 BC.

26 The custom of 'copying' Mauryan capitals was particularly prevalent during the Gupta period, as typified for example by the small four-lioned capital, which originally crowned Pillar no. 26 to the east of Stupa 1, and is now stored in the Sanchi Museum (Marshall, 1940, 49-50; Williams 1982, 96-7, pl. 141).

27 SG001/I-14.

28 SG001/I-36; SAMRC, acc. 2850.

29 SG001/I-32; SAMRC, acc. 18.

30 SG001/I-15.

31 SG001/I-72; SAMRC, acc. 2772.

32 SG006/I-560; GGMM.

33 SG006/I-524; GGMM, acc. 10a. This supposition is further supported by the fact that the honey-suckle motif on the abacus is interspersed by crocodiles rather than the pecking geese, as in the case of the Heliodorus pillar.

34 SG006/I-171.

35 For comparisons with an addorsed lion-elephant capital (SG006/I-99) on Lohangi hill in Vidisha, see chapter 11.

36 The lion represents Sakyasimha, the lion among the Sakya clan, as well as the imperialism of the Mauryan empire, while the elephant refers to the story of the Buddha's conception.

37 However, as discussed in chapter 11, additional railings with more complex designs are now stored at nearby settlements, including Pipalia kherai (SG005b) and Devalkhera (SG123).

38 A tenth-century-AD Buddha image from the temple is now stored in the Sanchi Museum (SG005/I-633).

39 Marshall (1940, 63) refers to instructions in the *Vinaya* that buildings should be built on high platforms (*caya*) to protect them from floods.

40 SG001/SC11; SG001/SC10.

41 Acceptance of this date rests largely on the argument that the three separate inscriptions referring to a donor named Nagapiya (two of which were found on gateway pillars, and another on the Stupa 2 balustrade) refer to two different generations of the same family. Those who suggest that they refer to one and the same person argue that the two monuments may only be separated by 30–40 years (arguments summarised in Taddei 1996). Given the difference in wording of the inscriptions, and the stylistic gap between the two monuments, this particular argument does not present any serious challenge to the accepted AD 25 date for the gateways of Stupa 1.

42 SG 010b/I-106. Unfortunately, when the author first visited Gulgaon in 1998, the whereabouts of this image was no longer known.

43 For example, a Gupta pilaster datable to c. AD 405–15 (Williams 1982, pl. 40) was reincorporated into the tenth-century-AD superstructure of Temple 31 (Plate 207). A number of similar pilasters, possibly from the same temple, are also stored in the SAMRC (SN 001/1, 8, 26, 38). One of these may correspond to the Gupta pilaster found beneath the tenth-century-AD monastery complex around Temple 45 (Marshall 1940, 77).

44 The Mathura sandstone images from Stupas 12 and 14 were described earlier. Stupa 29 also contained a reliquary made of two earthenware cups, one inverted above the other. Inside it were a small piece of bone and a broken vase of 'Maurya or Sunga date [*sic*] which no doubt had once held some holy relic' (Marshall 1940, I, 48; III, pl 105d).

45 See chapter 6 for the changing nature of patronage and local exchange networks during this period, and chapter 6, n. 9, for the inscription of Candragupta II, dated AD 412–13.

46 SG001/I-227; SAM, acc. 2720. The dedication of a Vajrapani pillar is recorded in an inscription (Marshall 1940, inscrip. 835) carved on another Gupta pillar (no. 26) to the east of Sanchi.

47 SAM, acc. 2857, 2848, only the latter of which is illustrated here (Plate 36). For the iconography of Padmapani, see De Mallman 1948, 219–20.

48 Given that the two Padmapani images are the largest free-standing images at Sanchi, one can be quite certain that Cunningham was referring to them in his account.

49 The distinctive, geometric motif on the pillars is known as the 'unfinished medallion'. This becomes common in central India in the sixth to seventh century AD, but in the Deccan, earlier examples go back to the second to third century AD (Williams 1982, 140).

50 Cf. Marshall (1940, 52-3), who dated it to the tenth century AD. Most of the gateway is *in situ* apart from a section now stored in the SAMRC, acc. 2863.

51 The obvious question of what was behind such destruction has not been addressed.

52 Building 21 may be Gupta on the basis of the torus moulding at its base.

53 Suggestions for prototypical forms of the courtyard monastery during earlier periods are given in chapter 10, drawing on new data from the SSP, as well as existing evidence for rock-cut monastery sites in the Deccan.

54 Similar boundary walls are found at many of the newly documented Buddhist sites in the study area. Their possible date and function are considered in chapter 11.

55 The Avalokitesvara image is now in the Victoria and Albert Museum (Irwin 1972). The Maitreya is stored in the SAMRC, acc. 2728/61.538.

56 Misidentified by Marshall (1940, 74) as Majuravidhyaraja. Carvings of Manjusri also appear on some of the votive stupas scattered around the site, thereby refuting Marshall's (*ibid.*, 254) argument that Manjusri was entirely absent at Sanchi.

57 For other dated ninth-century-AD remains, including the Bhimgaja temple in Badoh Pathari, see Willis 1997, 121; *ibid.*, 2000, 76.

58 For the Gyaraspur inscription, see chapter 5.

59 SG035/SC121.

60 SG001/SC3.

61 SG008/SC84.

62 SG009/SC62.

63 SG001/I-255, I-256; SAM, acc. 2859 and 2858. The latter, the larger of the two, is illustrated here (see also Williams 1976, 174, fig. 6; n. 5). For the former, see Marshall 1940, pl. 125b; Harle 1974, 42, fig. 40.

64 SG001/I-31.

65 India Office Library, photograph nos. 1413; 1875; 1877. No. 1413 was reproduced in Irwin 1972, figs. 4–5.

66 Marked 'F' on Fell's map. However, given the number of inaccuracies in Fell's report, this may not be entirely reliable.

67 They may have stood in one of the no-longer extant Gupta temples (19, 20 or 22) to the east of Stupa 1, the existence of which is attested by the number of Gupta pilasters found beneath tenth-century-AD structures.

68 SG001/ I-12, I-13, the former illustrated here (Plate 38)

69 SG001/I-24, I-34, I-39; SAMRC, acc., 2741, 2654, 2773, the last illustrated here (Plate 39).

70 SG001/SC12.

71 SG002/SC19.

72 Unfortunately, the accompanying sketch-map (prepared by Captain Murray) mentioned in Prinsep's report, and indicating the location of this temple, was omitted from the final publication owing to its bad quality. It is possible that it is still held in the Asiatic Society's archives (Calcutta).

Chapter 10

1 Listed as Period IIIb in the final sequence from Vidisha (Table 9.2).

2 Periods IIb and IIIa in Table 9.2.

3 Similar stupas have more recently been noted in large numbers around the Buddhist site of Thotlakonda in Andhra Pradesh (Fogelin 2004; 2006).

4 E.g. Mawasa, Salera, Murlikheri, Chandna Tohoria and Bighan.

5 Individual sherd descriptions are provided in the SSP database, shortly to be launched in a web-based format.

6 http://www.rlaha.ox.ac.uk/lumin/lumindx.html.

7 Grateful thanks to Norman Hammond for this reference.

Chapter 11

1 SG003a/SC23/S487.

2 Dargawan follows the name of the ancient settlement at the foot of the northern hillock (SG023).

3 Precise quantification and planning was hampered by dense vegetation coverage and a high rate of stone removal from the site.

4 SG029/SC104.

5 SG032.

6 SG023b.

7 Not 15 km, as given by Willis (2000, 80).

8 SG162b and SG021.

9 SG007/I-101. The capital is currently stored in the site storehouse.

10 Two more railing crossbars, originally from Satdhara, are stored outside a modern farmhouse on the ancient settlement mound of Sehor (SG021), just over 1 km to the NE.

11 SG006/I-95.

12 Cf. Chandra (1966, 163) who places the Besnagar elephant in the mid-first century BC, along with the Besnagar Kubera *yakṣa*, discussed in chapter 12.
13 Listed in the original publication as nos. 2 and 7 (Cunningham 1854, 323).
14 Details of the present whereabouts of this reliquary are provided in Willis 2000, 81.
15 This may be compared to the rectangular structures at Goldoria and Ferozpur, where large quantities of terracotta tiles were found.
16 Agrawal (1997, 406) also identifies them as two-storeyed monasteries, although no qualification for this interpretation is given aside from observations of pillars and beams on top of the western platform.
17 SG162b.
18 Dense vegetation cover precluded the possibility of a clear photograph or detailed mapping.
19 The Buddhist remains here were mentioned briefly in earlier publications (Agrawal 1997; Shaw and Sutcliffe 2001, 70; Shaw 2004a, 45), although with no intra-site detail. The offset of approximately 20 m between the site-plan and the Quickbird satellite imagery in Plate 42 is a result of the inherent error margin of hand-held GPS technology, with further errors related to the projection system of the satellite imagery (Shaw 2005; Beck and Shaw, forthcoming).
20 SG147.
21 SG150b.
22 SG041.
23 SG135b.
24 ASI Site Warden, pers. comm.
25 SG118b; SG117.
26 SG005b; SG121; SG123; SG125; SG165.
27 SG005/SC29. Apparently the spring, known locally as 'Ganga-Yamuna', was only rediscovered by villagers in recent years.
28 SG005/SC30.
29 SG005/SC675.
30 SG005/SC440.
31 SG005/I-633.
32 SG005/SC465.
33 SG005/SC701.
34 Possible reasons for the decline of Buddhism from the post-Gupta period onwards are discussed in chapter 12.
35 SG005/SC35; SC365.
36 SG005/SC36.
37 Grateful thanks to Sebastian Pole for this reference. For the medical function of Buddhist monasteries, see Zysk 1991, who also discusses the possible Buddhist underpinnings of the Ayurvedic medical tradition.
38 SG005a.
39 SG005/SC38; SC442; SC49.
40 SG005/SC364.
41 SG005/SC40; SC602.
42 Cf. Ota and Khamari 2006, who suggest that the southern cluster of courtyard structures at Sanchi was used by lay employees.
43 SG005/SC443.
44 SG005/SC33.
45 SG005/SC34.
46 SG037a/SC127.
47 SG005b.
48 SG005c.
49 SG123.
50 SG006/I-536.
51 SG177b; SG177d.
52 A large rock-shelter perched on the edge of the cliffs is a local cult spot known as Durgasthan (SC340).
53 SG013b.
54 SG179b.
55 SG092.
56 Grateful thanks to Thera Somaratna, Harry Falk, K.R. Norman, Michael Willis and Jonathan Walters for help in studying this inscription.
57 As discussed later, a similarly worded inscription has been recorded at Besar talai (*IAR* 1978–9, 13), a major settlement in Sector 3, which also contains an 'urban' stupa.
58 Grateful thanks to Jonathan Walters for this important insight.
59 These remains were recorded summarily in Stage I, with detailed mapping carried out in Stage II.
60 SG095b; SG095c.
61 The monastery was originally recorded in 2000, but when revisited in 2005, most of its walls had been dismantled for reuse in modern constructions. The imprint of the original outline can still be discerned on the ground, although this too will disappear in time.
62 Originally documented in 2000, these remains were mapped in detail in 2004.
63 SG 170.
64 SG170b/SC326.
65 SG170b/SC329.
66 SG170b/SC330.
67 First noted in Stage I, with detailed mapping carried out in Stage II.
68 SG167b.
69 The site was first documented in Stage I of the SSP, with detailed mapping carried out in Stage II.
70 SG110/SC388; SG031/SC111.
71 SG035b; SG043.
72 Either the Jain identification was based on ignorance or on Jain sculpture which has subsequently been removed from the site.
73 One exception is a passing reference in the unpublished report of Madhya Pradesh State Archaeology Department's village-to-village survey (Maheswari 1997). Here, the site is referred to not as Bighan but as Jafalkheri, the name of a village to the north.
74 One possible explanation for this neglect is that Bighan falls within Vidisha District, formerly part of the Princely State of Gwalior. By contrast, Sanchi and the other 'Bhilsa Tope' sites fall within Raisen, formerly part of the Bhopal State whose Begum rulers were the principal funders behind Marshall's excavations at Sanchi.
75 Described by Lake (1910b, 146) as 'oblong'.
76 These are listed in summary form elsewhere (*IAR* 1976–7, 77; Shukla 1990) under the name Neemkheria, the village immediately below Bighan hill.
77 Between 1998 and 2000, visibility levels were reduced further due to a recent Eucalyptus planting programme.
78 Kaniska's stupa in the North-West also bears a superficial resemblance to the Bighan structure. However, the four corner projections are not towers, but rather bases for stupas or pillars. Rather than following a fort-plan, it belongs to a similar tradition to the later Pancaratra temples (Dobbins, 1971, 18).
79 There are also examples of fortified Brahmanical temples during later periods (Davison-Jenkins *ibid.*, 47).
80 The site was first documented in Stage I, but by the time it was revisited in 2005, all that survived of the second stupa was a pile of boulders.
81 Grateful thanks to Sarpanch, Jagalahars Yadav for many kindnesses during various visits to the site.
82 SG037b.
83 SG037.
84 Although there have been claims to the contrary (Mukherjee 1990), the shell script has not yet been convincingly deciphered. There are also uncertainties over its chronology, as well as its sectarian affiliations. Both of these issues are discussed later with regard to carved, and more conventional, versions of the script found at Udayagiri and Sanchi.
85 SG037a/SC127.
86 SG037a/SC127/S128.
87 SG037a/SC127/S836.
88 A modern analogy might be, for example, the comparison between commercially printed documents and handwritten letters.
89 These factors further complicated the recording process, already difficult due to poor preservation: it was often difficult to determine whether certain paint-strokes should be read as idiosyncratic vowel endings, or whether they were the result of clumsiness or fallen paint during the rendering of the inscription.
90 Grateful thanks to Harry Falk and K.R. Norman for comments regarding the palaeography and content of the inscription.
91 Were it in Sanskrit, it would read, *ṣoḍaśebhi* (Harry Falk, pers. comm., with additional help from Jonathan Walters)
92 Only the core of unhewn blocks and chippings survive, most of the dressed facing evidently having been removed.
93 Cf. Sanchi, where most of the Kusana images are Mathura imports.
94 SG006/SC45; SC719; SC49; Most of these are now stored in the Gujari Mahal Museum, Gwalior.
95 SG006/SC49; SC646.
96 SG006/SC655.
97 SG006/SC53.
98 SG006/SC53/I-98. VM, acc. 1673.
99 SG001/I-227; SAM, acc. 2720.
100 SG006/SC653/I-565.
101 The *saptamātṛkā* figures, described in chapter 12, are stored in the GGMM and National Museum, Delhi; however, the whereabouts of the Bodhisattva image, unmentioned since Lake's report, are no longer known.
102 SG001/I-227. SAM, acc. 2720.
103 SG031b.
104 For a recent critique of this view, see Dass and Willis 2002; Bakker 2004.
105 Other rich *śankhalipi* sites in central India are discussed by Sharma 1990, including the UNESCO World Heritage site of Bhimbetka to the south of Bhopal, where 33 *śankhalipi* inscriptions have been found in 10 out of the 130 known rock-shelters.

106 SG005/SC34.
107 I am grateful to Alexandre G. Mitchell, a specialist in Greek archaeology, for alerting me to this detail.
108 SG031b/SC221/I-592.
109 Now stored at a new location at the western base of Udayagiri hill: SG031/SC110/I-7.
110 SG031/SC488.
111 For Lohangi rock as another contender, see Bhattacaryya 1977, 73.
112 SG141.
113 Further comparisons are provided by a carved coping stone from Bharhut, now stored in the National Museum, Delhi (accession no. 68.168).
114 A lion-with-rider also occurs on the west gate of Sanchi, Stupa 1. Thanks to Justin Meiland for this insight.
115 Now stored in the GGMM, acc. 7, 8. For further discussion of the Besnagar railings, see Willis 2000, 58.
116 As explained in chapter 13, prior to a government tree-clearance programme in the 1970s, the entire valley was covered with dense forest. This may explain the relatively well preserved condition of this important body of early sculpture.
117 SG041/I-410.
118 SG041/I-411.
119 SG041/I-59, I-412, I-413.
120 SG041/I-145.
121 SG041/I-142.
122 SG041/I-143.
123 SG041/I-144.
124 The custom of 'copying' Mauryan capitals was particularly prevalent during the Gupta period, as typified for example by the small four-lioned capital, which originally crowned Pillar no. 26 to the east of Stupa 1 and is now stored in the Sanchi Museum (Marshall, 1940, 49–50; Williams 1982, 96–7, pl. 141).
125 The other two are the lion and horse. According to Buddhist mythology, the four noble animals reside at the four quarters of Lake Anottata in the Himalayas (Paranavitana 1936, 24). The elephant is the most frequently depicted animal at Sanchi and Bharhut. It also occurs on Asokan pillars but, like the bull, in much less numbers than the lion. Only one example, from Sankisa, has survived. However, a carved railing at Bharhut suggests that the pillar at Bodh Gaya was also crowned by an elephant capital (Irwin 1983, fig. 10). Another elephant is carved on a rock-face at Dhauli. Similarly, only one Mauryan bull capital, at Rampurva (*ASIAR* 1907–8, 181–88; Irwin, 1987, pl. I), survives, but that there were others is attested by Chinese pilgrims' reports of a bull capital outside the Jetavana monastery (*ASIAR* 1907–8, 187). There are also theories that the Allahabad pillar was originally crowned by a bull, rather than a lion (Irwin 1979; 1983). Another bull capital from Malhai (labelled incorrectly as a horse) in the Allahabad University Museum is datable to c. second century BC. Apart from these examples, however, there is a paucity of published examples of animal capitals (cf. Jha 2004).
126 For the directional symbolism of animals at monastic sites in Sri Lanka, see Paranavitana 1936, 24. The same group is also found on the Sarnath abacus (Agrawala 1965). See Jha 2004, 99–101 for further discussion.
127 SG041/SC142.
128 SG041/I-135.
129 SG041/I-134.
130 SG006/I-181, I-183; VM, acc. 273, 269.
131 SG006/ I-333.
132 SG002/I-253.
133 SG064/I-296.
134 SG032/I-395.
135 SG090/SC659/SC478; SG059b/SC394; SG011c/SC65; SG012b/SC482; SG177c/SC351.
136 SG005/SC465; SG035/SC538; SG095d/SC208;SC209
137 SG167/SC319; SG066/SC411.
138 Cf. Willis 2000, 81.
139 SG005/SC701.
140 Theories regarding the decline of Buddhism in India are discussed in chapter 15 (see also Jaini 1980; Verardi 1996; 2003).
141 As discussed in chapter 15, this very factor may have played a major role in the eventual downfall of Buddhism in India.
142 Calculations regarding stupa diameter at these sites were made on the basis of the railing dimensions (Cunningham 1880).
143 SG028; SGSG150.
144 For the distribution of Mauryan capitals, see Gupta 1980; Ghosh 1967; for symbolism of capitals, see Irwin 1976; Vajracharya 1999, 75; Verardi 2000.
145 The elephant, for example, refers to the Buddha's appropriation of the powers of Indra, the traditional rain god and archetypal king (Verardi 2000, 70).
146 In some cases, the bull and elephant occur on the same coin (e.g. Pieper 1998, 121, no. 36).
147 SG041/SC146. Grateful thanks to Natru Ram Chaudhary for granting access to these coins.
148 The fact that early *yakṣa* shrines were referred to as *caitya* offers a gloss on the possible antecedents of the stupa (Law 1931; Misra 1981, 91–3; Irwin 1987; Van Kooij 1995). There are also suggestions that the carved *toraṇa* panels at Sanchi are based on the *charaṇa chitras*, the pictorial scrolls whose public display was, according to texts such as the *Saṃyutta Nikāya*, or *Arthaśāstra*, an integral component of the banned hilltop festivals (Ray 1945, 69). For the link between stupas and megalithic burials, see Stargardt 1990: 346; Schopen 1996b; and Bakker, forthcoming.
149 That this theme continued in later years is suggested by the theory that the Mahayana deity, Avalokitesvara, was commonly placed on hilltop locations as a 'relic or revival of the old worship of the hill gods' (Getty 1914, 55). Images of Avalokitesvara appear at Sanchi in significant numbers from the fifth century AD.
150 Similar observations were made by Cunningham (1854, 342), who periodically commented on what could be seen from principal spots in the landscape.
151 As discussed in chapter 6, this local Buddhist geography with its individual stupas also formed part of a much larger Buddhist World Map conceived of an ever-expanding Buddha corpse (Walters 2002).
152 Over a century and a half ago, Cunningham (1854, 315) noticed that the angle between Stupas 1 and 2 at Sonari was remarkably similar to that at Sanchi. He even suggested that 'there must have been some peculiar significance in this particular angle' but failed to pursue this line of investigation any further. Other explanations for this arrangement, related to the internal hierarchies of the *saṅgha*, are discussed above.
153 Adrian Snodgrass (1985, 282–5) discusses this connection with reference to the stairways of south-east Asian terrace stupas, paying particular attention to their serpent-balustrades, as symbols of the 'rainbow bridge' which links heaven and earth, but whose role as guardians of the Buddhist relic should not be forgotten.
154 The guardian figures (*dvārapāla*) that frequently flank the doors of later temples also reinforce the idea that entrances needed to be protected and regulated. They appear in about the fifth century AD, but *yakṣa* figures on earlier Buddhist monuments were, it seems, already serving the same purpose.
155 It is interesting to note that the terracotta lamps found by Garrick during excavations of the massive platformed structure known as Nandangarh at Lauriya Nandangarh were, according to local legend, used to signal across to similar structures in the area (*ASIR*, XVI, 106). Although the force of this argument is lessened by the fact that the structure in question was subsequently identified as a stupa (*ASIAR* 1935–6, 55; Ghosh 1950, 59–61; 1990, 255), the importance of intervisibility between sites is still made clear.
156 For example, Antiachak Vikramaśīla appears to have been fortified in c. eleventh century AD (*ASIAR* 1972–3, 4, fig. 1). Its plan is almost identical, albeit on a much larger scale, to many of the hilltop sites in the Sanchi area: 'The outer wall of the monastery shows a circular projection like a tower in the corner with similar circular projections alternately with rectangular projections at regular intervals' (Prasad 1987, 86). Verardi (1996, 244) also suggested that the monastery at Uddandapura may have been attacked by Muslims because of its resemblance to a fortress (see also Sinha *et al.*, 1983, 37).
157 It has been suggested that the fortification of Antiachak Vikramasila in c. eleventh century AD arose not from the threat of Muslim invasion, but rather from internal conflicts between tantric and non-tantric elements of the *saṅgha* (Chaudhary 1978, 227).
158 Hamid's (1940) argument that this material proved the structure to be queen Devi's monastery is a reflection of the 'theological' model of Buddhist scholarship which views commercial pursuits as the sign of a degenerate *saṅgha*.
159 It is interesting to note that in later years, many of these facilities were taken over by the fortified Śaiva *maths* (Misra 1999, 71).
160 For example, Strenski (1986, 475) points out that the merit-bestowing rituals are often held several days after the initial donation to disguise the *saṅgha*'s involvement, prohibited in the Canonical rules, in 'restricted' forms of exchange with the laity. By the same token, monastic landlordism, by allowing the benefits to 'trickle down to society as a whole', helped to perpetuate the orthodox image of the *saṅgha*'s refusal to enter into direct social relations.
161 For the elliptical monastery at Rajgir, see Ghosh 1951; IAR 1954–5: 16–17; Sarkar 1965; 1966; for Ghositarama at Kausambi, see *IAR* 1953–4, 9; 1954–5, 16; 1955–6, 20; for Śravasti, see Vogel 1911, 108–9.
162 Trainor makes this statement with reference to Schopen 1987, 193–4.

Chapter 12

1 Apsidal and elliptical plans are associated with the earliest free-standing

and rock-cut temples in India, with known examples from other Bhagavata sites such as Nagari in Rajasthan (Chanda 1920, 163), as well as Ajivika and Buddhist contexts; the latter include Temples 18 and 40 at Sanchi. Quite clearly, therefore, temple plans at the time transcended sectarian affiliation.
2 SG006/I-99.
3 SG010b/I-104, I-105.
4 SG003a/I-626.
5 The significance of the *nāga* as a means of providing a *terminus ante quem* date for the dam is discussed in chapter 14.
6 The small cockade visible in the centre has also led to comparisons with the circular crest ornament with the central tassel standard (referred to as the *maulimaṇi* type of turban) found in Kusana sculpture from Mathura (Czuma and Morris 1985, pl. 20). However, as discussed later on, the full development of the *maulimaṇi* in the Sanchi area does not become apparent until the first or second centuries AD.
7 As discussed in chapter 9, similarities between the carvings on the Heliodorus pillar and Stupa 2 suggest a date range of c. 115–80 BC for the latter.
8 SG006/I-536, I-526.
9 This follows the assumption that the Stupa 1 gateways date to c. AD 25, as opposed to the 'middle of the first century BC,' as maintained by Chandra (1966, 160).
10 SG095c/I-1. For an earlier illustration of the sculpture, including a rear view, see Shaw and Sutcliffe 2001, 69, figs. 13–14.
11 SG169/I-392.
12 See chapter 6 for iconography of Balarama.
13 SG013b/SC78.
14 SG013b/I-109.
15 SG013b/I-110. The sculptures were first noted by the author in 1998. Unfortunately by 2004, the smaller image was no longer to be found.
16 Significantly, this appears to be the nearest source of water for the monastic site on the hill above, which may have played some role in the level of religious competition discernible in the relative positioning of the stupa and Balarama images.
17 A close parallel is provided by the turban worn by the Brooklyn Museum *nāga* datable to the first or second century AD (Czuma *et al.*, 1985, pl. 25).
18 This is not clear, but closely resembles a miniature female figure.
19 See chapter 6, n. 35, for references.
20 The only other context I am aware of in which this particular arm posture occurs *together* with a *musala* is in a carved panel from Amavarati, now in the Musée Guimet, Paris (acc. no. MG 17066), depicting the attack of Mara. One of Mara's troop of demons is shown holding a pestle-like object in the right hand and extended over the head; the other end of the pestle is supported by the left hand (Okada 2000, 50, fig. 50).
21 See discussion in chapter 6.
22 SG056/I-156.
23 SG056/SC390.
24 In the proto-Pancaratra *Saṁhitā*s, for example, Samkarsana is sometimes linked with Rudra Siva (Jaiswal 1967, 54).
25 SG006/SC673/I-997. First noted during field investigations in January 2004, this image is currently under worship in the grounds of the Forestry Department on the northern bank of the River Bes. Its cultic relationship to the Heliodorus pillar site, less than 1 km to the east, deserves further investigation.
26 The textual sanction is provided in the *Harivaṁśa* (*Viṣṇuparvan*, 121, 100, 705). Early sculptural examples include a first-century-AD Balarama from Mathura (Mathura Museum, acc. no. C19; Joshi 1979, pl. 18) and another in the Bharat Kala Museum, Varanasi (acc. no. 279; Joshi 1971, 245). This identification continues in later non-serpent forms of Balarama, as illustrated by a Gupta image from Vidisha discussed later (Lake 1910a, 139; Harle 1974, fig. 18; Härtel 1987, 584, n. 34).
27 Possible textual sanctions for this association are explored in chapter 6, n. 32.
28 As discussed in chapter 9, the identification of sculptures belonging to this stage is of some significance for local religious and political history in that it presents a striking contrast to the absence of locally produced Phase IIIb sculpture at Sanchi itself.
29 SG099/I-232.
30 The Sarnath Bodhisattva is usually placed several years earlier than the Bala Bodhisattva, the latter being dated year 3 of Kaniska's era. Given the revised thinking on the dating of the Kaniska era (year 1 = AD 126), the Bala Bodhisattva is assignable to c. AD 129 as opposed to the usually accepted date of AD 81 (Bachhofer 1939, pl. 79).
31 SG006/I-169; VM, acc. 75. The exact provenance is unknown, but according to the accession book, it was found 'on the road between Besnagar and Udayagiri.'
32 SG170/I-458.
33 It should be stressed that this movement towards durable media of representation probably indicates major shifts in religious patronage rather than religious practice *per se*.
34 SG061/I-494.
35 NMD, acc. 65.172. A similar *caturmukhaliṅga* from Kausambi is kept in the Allahabad Museum (Chandra 1970, pl. 88).
36 SG061/I-290.
37 SG061/I-495.
38 However, there is no textual evidence that the notion of the *rudrabhāga* and the portions assigned to Brahma (*brahmabhāgaḥ*) and Visnu (*viṣṇubhāgaḥ*) existed during this period; these terms are unlikely to be earlier than the sixth-century-AD *Bṛhatsaṃhitā* (57.53–54) (Alexis Sanderson, pers. comm.).
39 For a second-century-BC date, see Sharma 1982, 61. Others, such as Sivaramamurti (1964, 46-7) assign it to the first century AD.
40 E.g. a similar, undecorated *liṅga* is depicted on a carved frieze from Mathura datable to c. second century BC to first century AD. 'Realistic' *liṅga*s are also depicted on early coins (Sharma 1982, 60, pl. 36). An early free-standing example is the early Kusana *ekamukhaliṅga* from Aghapur which differs from the Pagneswar *liṅga* only in respect of the central Siva face (Agrawala 1967, pl. 2).
41 SG162b/I-366.
42 SG134/I-339.
43 SG134/I-337.
44 SG134/ I-338.
45 See, for example, the second-century-AD standing Buddha in the Mathura Museum (Czuma and Morris 1985, 30, fig. 6).
46 SG134/ I-340.
47 SG001/I-24; I-34; SAMRC, acc. 2654, 2741, the former illustrated here (Plate 40).
48 SAMRC, acc. 2654.
49 For the distinction between the iconographic representation of Visnu and Vasudeva, see Härtel 1987. For art-historical and iconographic analysis of the Udayagiri caves, see Williams 1982, 40–52. For new insights into the architectural programme at the site, see Dass 2001.
50 The larger of the two Visnu images to the right of the doorway is illustrated here (Plate 168). For the smaller image on the left, see Williams 1982, pl. 35.
51 For discussion of the iconography of the *Mahiṣāsuramardinī* images, see Harle 1970; 1971–2. For chronology, see Yokochi 2004.
52 SG006/S979/I-525. Marked 'G' on Cunningham's (1880, pl. xii) map. Stored in the Gujari Mahal Museum, Gwalior. The image's identity was unknown to Cunningham at the time of its discovery when it was known only by its local name, 'Telin'.
53 SG006/ SC653. Six of the *mātṛkā*s (/I-85-89) are stored in the GGMM. The seventh (I-91) is stored in the NMD, acc. 51.101. An eighth, previously unrecorded *mātṛkā*, evidently from another location in Besnagar, is kept in the VMRC (SG006/I-540). This figure depicts Camunda, apparently absent from the larger group, throttling the child lying across her lap.
54 SG006/I-945.
55 SG006/I-943.
56 The sculpture is currently stored in the AMG.
57 SG010/I-279.
58 SG010/I-281.
59 SG169/I-435.
60 SG169/I-453.
61 SG006/ SC718. Referred to by Cunningham (1880, 45, pl. xii) as Mound R, and Lake (1910a, 142–3) as Mound 12.
62 A close comparison is the garment worn by the doorway goddess discovered at Besnagar by Cunningham (Williams 1982, pl. 45), and the Vajrapani and Padmapani Bodhisattvas at Sanchi (Marshall 1940, 254, pls. 125a, c; 108b).
63 SG031/I-638.
64 E.g. a four-armed Visnu image from Unchdih, Allahabad district (Chandra 1970a, pl. 223).
65 Indeed, the Bodhisattva figure (SG006/I-565;Plate 172) which was found by Lake (1910a, 140–1) alongside the seated mothers at Besnagar had an almost identical body-type. This figure is discussed in more detail in chapter 11.
66 SG146/I-661.
67 SG146/I-666.
68 SG164/I-389.
69 SG012/I-376.
70 SG171/I-153.
71 SG172b/I-687.
72 SG056/I-556, I-559.
73 SG056/SC368.
74 SG051/I-443.

75 SG031b/SC220/I-247.
76 SG031b/SC222/I-597.
77 SG037a/SC131.
78 SG064/I-574.
79 An almost identical *kirīṭamukuṭa* torque is worn by the Gupta Samkarsana figure from Vidisha referred to in ch. 6, n. 17 (Harle, 1974, fig. 18).
80 SG011b/I-366, I-371.
81 SG011b/I-372.
82 Similarly, Bakker (2004b) has suggested that the Vakataka-period *nāga* image found in a 'burial shaft' at Mansar was part of a memorial to Prabhavati Gupta, the Vakataka queen descended from mixed Naga-Gupta stock.
83 Harle (1974, 11) also notes that a similar figure is shown kneeling at the base of the Sesa Narayana in cave 13.
84 The rescue of Bhumi has also been linked to the story, retold in a Sanskrit drama, of Candragupta's rescue of Dhruvadevi, the wife of his elder brother, Ramagupta (Asher 1983). The latter's shameful surrender of his wife to the Sakas is presented as one of the primary factors behind Candragupta's final campaign against the Sakas. Although some have doubted the historicity of Ramagupta, the local presence of a king of that name in the latter half of the fourth century AD is attested by the discovery of coins and three inscribed Jain images at Vidisha bearing the name Ramagupta (Williams 1982, 25). Further discussion of these debates and their position with nationalistic Indian historiography is given in Willis 2004.
85 SG169/I-392.
86 See Shaw 2004a for more illustrations.
87 Another parallel is the well-known *Nāgarāja* outside cave 16 at Ajanta (Harle 1974, fig. 84), whose royal status is suggested by the *lalitāsana* pose and elaborate crown, which follows the same three-lobed circular form as examples from Sanchi and Ferozpur. Interpretations of this figure are usually confined to a purely religious framework. E.g. Cohen (1998), following on from the associated inscription, views it as a local spirit 'assimilated' into the complex as part of the *saṅgha*'s localisation strategies. Consequently, the possibility for wider dynastic references has not been explored. I would argue that given the political and genealogical links between the Vakataka and Naga houses discussed in chapter 6, some reference to a Naga ruler would not have been out of place at Ajanta.
88 SG169/I-393.
89 SG123/I-250.
90 SG177d/I-690.
91 SG006/I-531; VM, acc. 34. Its Jain affiliations are attested by two small *tirthankaras* visible on either side of the *nāga* slab.
92 SG173/I-464.
93 SG058/I-162.
94 Two of these (SG001/I-12, I-13) are positioned on the raised terrace to the east of Stupa 1. The third (SG001/I-39) is stored in the SAMRC, acc. 2773.
95 SG172b/I-687.
96 SG038/I-545.
97 SG938/I-546.
98 See Yokochi 2004 for chronology of *Mahiṣāsuramardinī* images in central India.
99 SG038/I-184. See *Image of Man: Khajuraho Archaeology Museum, 1821*, no. 83, for a close comparison.
100 For the link between modern aniconic goddess shrines and an 'upper palaeolithic' shrine at Bagor I, Madhya Pradesh, see Kenoyer *et al.*, 1983.
101 See chapter 6 for parallels with 'functional' models of religious change developed in relation to the spread of Islam and Christianity (Eaton 1993; Peel 1968).
102 Of particular note is a painted Brahmi inscription from a rock-shelter in Shivpuri district, not far from the rock-painted depiction of Samkarsana and Vasudeva at Tikula (Gwalior district) mentioned in chapter 6, n. 13. This refers to a person called Sivarakhi who, as a devotee of Krsna, caused a rock-shelter (?) and a tank to be constructed (Neumayer 1992–3).

Chapter 13
1 SG155/SC285, SG029c/SC100, SG105/SC224, SG138/SC257, SG149/SC274.
2 SG081; SG084; SG084d.
3 SG170; SG095a-b; SG167b.
4 SG002; SG003a.
5 SG010; SG011b; SG162b.
6 SG048b; SG038; SG158.
7 SG041; SG044; SG053.
8 For example, even today, the only permanent bridging points are at Rangai just to the south of Vidisha (SG017), and Pagneswar (SG061), in Sector 3, with dry-season fords occurring between these points only at Berkheri (SG152/SC283) and Nonakhera (SG018/SC85).
9 SG006/SC50; SG110/SC388; SG031/SC111.
10 SG039; SG164.
11 SG018; SG154; SG061.
12 SG055.
13 SG053; SG053c.
14 SG123; SG121; SG005b.
15 Details of individual sherds can be consulted on the web-based database to be made available shortly.
16 SG005c.
17 SG005a.
18 SG159; SG023.
19 SG006; SG017.
20 SG102.
21 SG031b.
22 SG041; SG053.
23 SG039; SG169.
24 SG154; SG156; SG039; SG169.
25 SG005b; SG005c.
26 SG003a; SG032b.

Chapter 14
1 This is not to overlook the probability that the reservoirs served additional functions such as 'watering-holes' for water-buffalo and other farm animals.
2 Another dam was also noticed at Raisen (SG137b), but since this falls outside the southern boundary of the survey, it is not included in calculations for the region as a whole.
3 This included interdisciplinary research with John Sutcliffe, a hydrologist who had undertaken water balance studies in the Betwa river region between 1976 and 1980.
4 SG003; SG011; SG032d.
5 SG177b; SG099.
6 SG162c; SG114a. Only the former was too damaged to be measured.
7 The figures given for Devrajpur, Ferozpur and Sanchi reflect revised estimates in Stage II.
8 Interestingly, another Sudarśana reservoir is mentioned in a Vakataka inscription from Ramtek, Maharashtra (Bakker 1997, appendix I, v. 5). The associated dam was investigated during a field-visit in December 2006 (Bakker, Cork, Sutcliffe, Shaw and Bosma, forthcoming). See also: http://www.britac.ac.uk/institutes/SSAS/projects/sanchi.htm.
9 Grateful thanks to Norman Hammond for this reference.
10 Grateful thanks to M.S. Chauhan for carrying out this analysis.
11 A minimum heat of 350º C is required for the OSL clock to be reset to zero.
12 For this reason, re-analysis was carried out which involved soaking the samples in acid over three weeks. The new results are awaited.
13 SF 2, 3, 5, and 6.
14 Grateful thanks to O.P Misra for help in studying this material.
15 Dargawan follows the name of the modern village at the foot of the long hill slightly further to the north. The Karondih dam is listed as Swami Par in a previous publication (Shaw and Sutcliffe 2001, 58).
16 SG028; SG029.
17 Crossing no. 267.c/1-E; 878 EP. 31, Delhi–Bombay line (first crossing SW of Sanchi).
18 Thanks to H. Gunston (citing I.J. Kerr, *Building the Railways of the Raj, 1850–1900.* Delhi: Oxford University Press, 1995) for this information.
19 Further clarification of this issue might be obtainable from high-resolution satellite imagery (Beck and Shaw, forthcoming).
20 SG028; SG029.
21 SG011b; SG011c.
22 This is higher than original estimates (2001) following the availability of high-resolution satellite imagery.
23 SG032c; SG032; SG032b.
24 SG029; SG011c; SG022.
25 SG010.
26 Almost all traces of the dam, including the stone facing slabs, had been removed by the time it was revisited in 2003–4. The height in Table 14.1 relates to the height from the bottom of the eroded stream.
27 SG162; SG162b; SG162d.
28 However, the removal of stone facing blocks for commercial purposes has increased at an alarming rate in recent years and, if allowed to continue, will result in a similar situation as at Ferozpur where hardly a single facing block remains.
29 As at Sanchi, these are higher than earlier estimates following the availability of closely spaced contours generated from 'total station' mapping and SRTM data.
30 The main indicator to this effect is the upturned profile on the torus moulding (Shaw and Sutcliffe 2003a, fig. 7), a feature which in later years is usually replaced by a simple semi-circle. Another seventh-century-AD

indicator is the semi-circular curve above the torus; by the eighth century AD this usually becomes square. A close comparison occurs on the seventh-century-AD Siva temple at Mahua (Willis 1997, 37, fig. 3, nos. 2–3; pl. 1). The simple knobs on the eave moulding (Shaw and Sutcliffe 2003a, fig. 8) are frequently found on *śikhara*s in Pratihara temple architecture.

31 SG177b/SC347.

32 SG177/SC345.

33 SG095d.

34 SG095a; SG095b.

35 The Bhojpur lake covered about 650 km^2 according to one estimate (Kincaid 1888, 352). Local tradition attests to it having led to the aridification of the Betwa river in the Vidisha region and the need for well and tank storage during the hot season. With the destruction of the lake, the flow returned to the Betwa, rendering the use of tanks at Vidisha unnecessary. The area draining to the Bhojpur lake would have been about 1400 km^2, compared with a total area of 2500 km^2 above Vidisha, so the lake would have had a significant effect on flows at the city. It is important to stress that the tanks being referred to are of the excavated variety as opposed to the dammed reservoirs described here; it is unlikely that the latter would have been affected by these events because they were built well before the Bhojpur lake, traditionally attributed to king Bhoja (c. AD 1000–55). However, the chronology of the Bhojpur lake is far from settled and, given its enormous impact on the local environment, cannot be entirely ruled out as an influencing factor.

36 For a detailed discussion of the impact of irrigated rice cultivation in ancient South East Asia, and south India, see Stargardt 1990, especially chapter III, and 1998, 169–76.

37 Until the nineteenth century, the *ahar* reservoirs, together with the *pyne* canals with which they were sometimes connected, were responsible for irrigating nearly 75% of the total irrigated area in south Bihar (Agarwal and Narain 1997, 86–98).

38 E.g. rice and other plants are mentioned in Theophratus' (370–c. 285 BC) *Enquiry into Plants* (I. 319, bk IV 4), following Alexander the Great's expeditions to the Persian Gulf and India (Watson 1983, 15–16, n. 13; Bretzl 1903, 201–3). The same crops appear slightly later in Greek medical texts such as Dioscorides' (fl. first century AD) *Materia Medica* (I, 173, bk II, 95) or Celsus' (fl. first century) *De Medicina* (I. 197, 201, 331, 411, 490).

39 The refined eating habits of the emerging wealthy urban class are seen as major influences in the introduction and diffusion of new crops (Watson 1983, 101, 132), just as later on, in the fourteenth century, the spread of new crops into temperate Europe beyond the Alps, was largely a result of the sophisticated spice-based cuisine that was emerging in the courts of Christian Europe (Sherratt 1999).

40 In Southeast Asia, the link between Buddhism and rice is demonstrated powerfully in a series of myths based loosely on the *Aggañña Sutta* of the *a* (v. 27), mentioned in chapter 2. As discussed by Benavides (2005, 80), the main gist of these myths is that 'after appearing as the results of meritorious acts, rice grows as long as Buddhism spreads'.

41 This is not to imply that all of the monks in the Sanchi area came from eastern India; many would have been recruited from local families.

42 For the link between the introduction of new irrigation technology and the spread of Buddhism in eighth-century Tibet, see Dalton 2004.

43 For a similar link between population growth, political change and the introduction of new rice species into southern China from Champa in central Vietnam during the eleventh century AD, see Glover and Higham 1996, 414.

44 One suggestion, for example, that needs to be tested by future excavation, is that small communities of Buddhist monks were already resident in the area (possibly in the 'monastic rock-shelters' documented at some hilltop Buddhist sites), before Asoka's patronage fuelled the construction of the first free-standing monuments at Sanchi.

45 Tentative evidence to this effect was revealed while coring at Devrajpur. A core sunk at the lowest point of the reservoir immediately upstream of the modern tank to the north of the dam (no. 1 in Figure 14.14) consisted of over 3 m of shell-rich reservoir silts. It is possible that this surprisingly deep sequence is testament to a pre-existent palaeotank that was incorporated into the reservoir design.

Chapter 15

1 I am grateful to John Sutcliffe for this reference.

APPENDIX I

Site groups (SG), site complexes (SC) and sites (S)

SG001 Sanchi hill (ritual). Sector: 1b

Published Buddhist monastic site.
SC3 Rock-shelter cluster (780115, 2599361) *Manchi*
Line of rock-shelters on eastern side of Sanchi hill, one of which has been adapted into modern shrine. Phasing: Paintings (1b): Stone tools (1b)
S3 (5) – Rock-shelter cluster
S938 – Rock-shelter/shrine (in worship)
SC5 Stupa (779836, 2599278) *Stupa 1*
Phasing: Architecture (1d to 2): Inscriptions (published) (2 to 4): Sculpture (1d to 4)
S5 – Stupa
S 916 'Pillar 10', S917 'Pillar 26', S918 'Pillar 35', S925 'Pillar 25', S926 'Pillar 34'
SC6 Monastery (779798, 2599160) *Building 8*
Phasing: Architecture (2)
S6 – Platformed monastery
SC7 Stupa (779899, 2598916)
Badly damaged stupa on lower west ledge of Sanchi hill. Phasing: Architecture (2)
S7 – Stupa
SC8 Ancient route
Remains of old route leading up western side of Sanchi hill.
S8 – Ancient route
SC9 Rock-shelter (779564, 2599189)
Three rock-shelters on western side of Sanchi hill.
S9 (3) – Rock-shelter
SC10 Rock-shelter cluster (779575, 2599491)
Group of rock-shelters, with cluster of small stupas (diameter: c. 50 m) in front. Phasing: Rock-shelter (2)
S10, S935 – Monastic rock-shelter
S934 – Stupa complex
SC11 Rock-shelter (779629, 2599514)
Rock-shelter, with square stupa platform (c. 2.5 x 2.5 m) built on top. Phasing: Rock-shelter (2)
S11 (3) – Monastic rock-shelter
S936 – Stupa
SC12 Temple: Brahmanical (779990, 2599343) *Kal Bhairav*
Rock-shelter shrine with Kal Bhairav image set into rock-face. Immediately below Temple 45. Remains of 10th century Saiva temple complex. Phasing: Sculpture (6)
S12 (2 W) – Temple remains: Brahmanical
S937 – Rock-shelter/modern shrine (in worship)
SC362 Stupa (779689, 2599130)
Group of small 'burial ad sanctos' stupas .
S362 (15) – Stupa
SC604 Temple: Buddhist (779910, 2599221) *Temple 43*
Phasing: Architecture (6): Inscriptions (published) (6)
S878 – Temple remains: Buddhist
SC605 Temple: Buddhist (779963, 2599235) *Temple 45*
Phasing: Architecture (6): Sculpture (6)
S879 – Temple remains: Buddhist
SC607 Temple: Buddhist (779843, 2599229) *Temple 18*
Phasing: Architecture (2 to 5): Sculpture (4)
S881 – Temple remains: Buddhist
SC608 Temple: Buddhist (779886, 2599307) *Temple 31*
Phasing: Architecture (5): Sculpture (4)
S1091 – Sculpture pile
S882 – Temple remains: Buddhist
SC609 Temple: Buddhist (779868, 2599164) *Temple 40*
Phasing: Architecture (1d to 2): Sculpture (1d/2)
S883 – Temple remains: Buddhist
SC610 Stupa (779871, 2599306) *Stupa 5*
Phasing: Architecture (4)
S884 – Stupa
SC611 Temple: Buddhist (779815, 2599241) *Temple 9*
Phasing: Architecture (4)
S885 – Temple remains: Buddhist
SC612 Stupa (779856, 2599219) *Southern* stupa *cluster*
Cluster of 7th century AD stupas on square platforms to east of Temple 18. Phasing: Architecture (5): Sculpture (3b)
S886 'Stupa 11', S887 'Stupa 12', S888 'Stupa 13', S889 'Stupa 16', S890 'Stupa 14', S891 'Stupa 6'
SC613 Stupa (779867, 2599344) *Stupa 3*
Phasing: Architecture (2): Reliquary (2)
S903 – Stupa
SC614 Stupa (779880, 2599358) *Stupa 4*
Phasing: Architecture (5)
S904 – Stupa
SC615 Monastery (779723, 2599297) *Monastery 51*
Courtyard monastery to west of Stupa 1. Phasing: Architecture (4/5)
S905 – Courtyard monastery
SC616 Tank (779757, 2599275) *Monastery 51 tank*
S906 – Tank
SC617 Temple: Buddhist (779904, 2599320) *Temple 32*
Phasing: Architecture (5)
S907 – Temple remains: Buddhist
SC619 Monastery (779946, 2599247) *Eastern Mon Complex*
Courtyard monastery complex on summit of eastern platform. Phasing: Architecture (6)
S909 'Monastery 47', S910 'Monastery 45', S911 'Monastery 46'
SC620 Monastery (779821, 2599177) *Monastery 36*
Phasing: Architecture (4/5)
S912 – Courtyard monastery
SC621 Monastery (779833, 2599120) *Southern Mon complex*
Cluster of courtyard monasteries, including nos. 37 and 38. Phasing: Architecture (4/5)
S913 'Monastery 37', S914 'Monastery 38', S915 – Courtyard monastery
SC623 Stupa (779494, 2599410) *Stupa 2*
Phasing: Architecture (2): Reliquary (2): Sculpture (2)
S920 – Stupa
SC624 Tank (779533, 2599428) *Stupa 2 tank*
Excavated tank by Stupa 2. Phasing: Sculpture (4)
S921 – Tank
SC625 Stupa (779477, 2599468)
Small stupa platform NW of Stupa 2. Phasing: Architecture (2): Sculpture (2)
S922 – Stupa
S923 – Pillar
SC626 Platform (779924, 2599255) *Eastern Terrace*
High platformed area to the east of Stupa 1. Phasing: Architecture (6): Sculpture (4)
S924 – Platform
SC627 Background landscape (779737, 2599364) *Unprovenanced sculptures*
Sculptures from Sanchi where exact context is unknown. Phasing: Sculpture (1d to 7)

S919 – Begging bowl
S927 – Background landscape
SC628 Temple: Buddhist (779885, 2599256) *Lower eastern temple cluster*
Various structural remains to east of Stupa 1, now overlain by 10th century AD platform. Phasing: Architecture (5): Sculpture (4)
S1136 'Route 21' – Ancient route
S928 'Temple 22', S929 'Temple 20', S930 'Temple 19'
SC629 Tank (779896, 2599627)
Small tank at northern foot of Sanchi hill.
S931 – Tank
SC630 Tank
Large tank at western foot of Sanchi hill.
S932 – Tank
SC698 Fortification wall (779865, 2599267) *Sanchi east*
Runs around eastern summit of Sanchi hill. Phasing: Fortification (6)
S1101 – Fortification wall

SG002 Sanchi/Kanakhera hill (settlement). Sector: 1b

Lower, northern part of Sanchi hill.
SC13 Settlement (780030, 2600101)
Modern village on NW slopes of Kanakhera hill, partially ovelying ancient settlement.
S366 – Hillside basti
S872 – Well
S877 – Sculpture pile (in worship)
SC14 Ancient route (780317, 2599674) *Rani Jhansi ki Ghori*
Stretch of rock, (lgth: 8.60 m) with petroglyphs in shape of horse hooves, hence the name, meaning 'The Rani of Jhansi's horse-prints'. Part of 'Chikni ghat' ('Shiny rocks'), an ancient route which leads to the monastic site from Puraina talab below.
S14 – Ancient route
SC15 Rock-shelter cluster (780385, 2599943) *Vasantol, Churelatol, Manitol*
Three rock-shelters on eastern side of Kanakhera hill. Vasantol contains prehistoric painting of rock-shelter with person squatting infront of a fire. Manitol contains painting of horned/winged animal with a bird on its back. The paintings in Chirelatol are modern. Phasing: Paintings (1b)
S15 'Vasantol', 875 'Manitol', 876 'Churelatol'
S874 – Natural shrine. Durga shrine on summit of Churelatol.
SC16 Tank (780552, 2599833) *Puraina talab*
Large rectangular tank (400 x 150 m) at the eastern base of Kanakhera hill. Lined with stone facing on all sides apart from western side which is held up by base of hill.
S16 – Tank
SC17 Tank (780863, 2600298) *Kanakhera talai*
Phasing: Sculpture (2)
S17 – Tank
S363 – Sculpture pile (in worship)
SC18 Tank (779836, 2599959) *Dahori/Madagan*
Village tank, split into two by a large embankment, faced on both sides by dressed stone slabs (70 x 90 x 20 cm). The embankment has a form of spillway (now blocked up) in the middle to allow for water flow between both sides. The two halves of the tank are known locally as Dahori and Madagan respectively. A third, smaller tank is situated just to the east. This too is split into two by a stone-faced embankment. According to Marshall, the tank is probably contemporary with the two Sati stones situated within the village to the south. One of these bears an inscription dated AD 1294–5.
S18 – Tank
S873 – Mosque
SC19 Temple: Brahmanical (779818, 2599779)
Between Sanchi Museum and Government Rest House. Phasing: Sculpture (4 to 7)
S19 – Temple remains: Brahmanical

SG003 Sanchi-Nagauri (reservoir). Sector: 1b

Reservoir remains at southern foot of Sanchi hill.
SC24 Dam (779563, 2599033)
Phasing: Pottery (1d to 7): Sediment sample (1d/2)
S24 (2) – Dam
SC25 Dam (778676, 2598302)
Phasing: Sediment sample (1d/2)
S25 – Dam
SC631 Reconstructed reservoir (777309, 2590411)
Phasing: Sediment sample (1d/2)
S944 – Reconstructed reservoir

SG003a Nagauri (settlement). Sector: 1b

Low hill c. 350 m south of Sanchi.
Ancient hillside settlement overlain by modern village.
SC21 Settlement (779568, 2598341)
Phasing: Pottery (1d to 7): Sculpture (2): Stone tools (1a to 1b)
S21 – Hillside basti
S941, S942 – Sculpture pile (both in worship)
SC22 Quarry (779280, 2598314)
Ancient quarry and stone-cutting centre, from where much of the stone for the monuments at Sanchi was taken. Western side of hill covered with mining marks, with some unfinished sculpture. Phasing: Sculpture (2 to 4)
S22 – Quarry
SC23 Rock-shelter cluster (779391, 2598182)
Line of rock-shelters on the eastern and southern side of hill, around five of which contain prehistoric paintings in dark red and orange. Phasing: Paintings (1b to 3a): Stone tools (1a to 1b)
S23 (4) – Rock-shelter cluster (in worship)
S487 'Churlela ka dant' – Monastic rock-shelter

SG004 Sonari hill (ritual). Sector: 3

Large hill (525m), running N-S, situated c. 7km south-west of Sanchi.
Published Buddhist monastic site.
SC26 Stupa (772167, 2593875) *Stupa 1*
Two stupas set within square enclosure. Phasing: Reliquary (2)
S26, S947 – Stupa
SC27 Background landscape (772067, 2593801)
Perennial spring situated c. 500 m SE of monastic complex. This forms the source of a major *nāla* which flows down the hill in a westerly direction. Reached by a pathway, whose stone slabs are still visible in places.
S27 – Natural shrine
SC383 Monastery (772131, 2593847)
Platformed monastery (11 x 11 m; ht: 3.6–4.6 m) abutting southern wall of stupa enclosure. Flight of steps (wd: 1.4 m) cut into body of platform in NE corner. Phasing: Architecture (2)
S383 – Platformed monastery
SC632 Stupa (772086, 2593905) *Stupa 2*
Phasing: Architecture (2): Reliquary (2)
S946 – Stupa
SC633 Stupa (772252, 2593839)
Stupa cluster at eastern end of site.
S948 'Stupa 3', S949 'Stupa 4', S950 'Stupa 5', S951 'Stupa 6', S952 'Stupa 7', S953 'Stupa 8'

SG005 Morel khurd (ritual). Sector: 2b

Long, low hill running N-S, overlooking Dabar *nāla*.
Published Buddhist monastic site.
SC28 Stupa (790308, 2594301) *Upper tier*
Main stupa complex on upper tier. Phasing: Pottery (3a to 3b)
S28 'Stupa 1', S1054 'Stupa 2', S1055 'Stupa 3', S1056 'Stupa 4', S1057 'Stupa 5', S1058 'Stupa 6'
SC29 Background landscape (790117, 2593831) *Ganga-Yamuna*
Perennial, sulphurous spring to the south of main complex.
S29 – Spring
S851 – Natural shrine : Shine developed around spring.
SC30 Tank (790297, 2594388)
Dried up tank to the north of main stupa complex.
S30 – Tank
SC31 Temple remains: Unknown/mixed cult (790946, 2594125)
Linked to upper terrace by stone pathway. Phasing: Architecture (6): Sculpture (6 to 7)
S31 – Temple: Unknown/mixed cult (in worship)
S852 – Natural shrine: Devi shrine (unhewn, painted stone installed on platform).
SC32 Tank (791012, 2594123)
Dried up tank (160 x 70 m) east of SC31. Earthen embankments (ht: 3 m) on western and eastern sides. Sloping stone facing intact on western side.
S32 – Tank
SC33 Stupa (790189, 2593551) *Morel khurd south*
Stupa at southernmost point of hill, en-route to Pipalia kherai. Diameter, including pradaksina patha: 4 m. Phasing: Architecture (2)
S33 – Stupa
SC34 Rock-shelter cluster (790474, 2593642)
Two rock-shelters on SE slope of hill, on northern bank of Dabar *nāla*. Three

śankhalipi inscriptions in easternmost shelter. Heavily eroded paintings of cow, horse with riders, and camel with rider in westernmost shelter. Phasing: Paintings (2)

S34, S853 – Rock-shelter

SC35 Stupa (790626, 2594496) *Morel khurd east*
Several small stupas on narrow plateau below upper terrace. Average diameter: 2 m. Also, square stupa platform (1.50 x 1.50 m). Phasing: Architecture (2)

S35 (4), S863 (3), S1106 (2), S1107 (3), S1110, S1111 – Stupa

SC36 Hot hole (790551, 2594399)
Several holes and crevices on the eastern plateau, from which hot sulphorous vapours emanate. The same system appears to extend into the rock-shelters below.

S36 – Hot hole (in worship)

SC37 Rock-shelter cluster (790563, 2594369)
Line of ten rock-shelters below eastern terrace. Some bear faint remains of rock-paintings, heavily damaged by stone-cutting activity and water erosion. Many have holes extending far into hillside. Possibly connected to 'hot-air' system above. Nos. 1, 2, 6, 7, 8, 9 and 10 have been built up in the front with large stone platforms, standing at a height of up to 2 m. Shelter 8 has stupa built directly above it. Phasing: Rock-shelter (1b to 2)

S37 'Cave 1' (10), S854 'Cave 2' – Monastic rock-shelter

SC38 Enclosure (790463, 2594787)
Large walled enclosure (1) with the remains of a square platform (13 x 14 m) on the western wall. Situated NE of the main stupa complex.

S38 (3) – Enclosure

SC39 Stupa (790527, 2594603) *Morel khurd north*
Square stupa platform (8.40 x 8.40 m) set within square enclosure. Phasing: Architecture (4)

S39 (4) – Stupa

SC40 Building Religious (790358, 2594667)
Long narrow building (67 x 4.2 m) north of stupa 1. Possibly dining room/assembly hall.

S40 – Building Religious

SC364 Stupa (790425, 2595033) *Morel khurd north*
Two-tiered stupa base at northern edge of hill. Inner platform: 3.60 x 3.60 m; outer platform: 6.40 x 6.40 m. Phasing: Architecture (4/5)

S364 – Stupa

SC365 Stupa *Morel khurd East*
Stupa platform (1.60 x 1.60 m), directly above rock-shelter no. 8. Phasing: Architecture (2)

S365 – Stupa

SC440 Monastery (790288, 2594118) *Siddh ka makan, or Madhu deo ka mandar (i.e. Krsna's temple)*
Solid ashlar platform at the southern edge of the upper terrace of the hill (35 x 25 m), with smaller platform projecting on southern side. Height varies from 5.20 m on the north and east side, to 8.50 m on the south and west. The walls slope considerably and have square towers at each corner. A flight of steps cuts into the body of the platform in the NE corner. Remains of walls of superstructure revealed during mapping in 2004–5. Evidence for second stairway (width: 1.30 m) on east side of platform. Remains of a 10th century temple at the western edge of the platform. Phasing: Architecture (2): Sculpture (6)

S440 'Platformed monastery

S850 – Temple remains: Buddhist

SC442 Stupa (790418, 2594483) *Morel khurd north*
Square stupa platform (4.0 x 4.0 m) set within square enclosure. Phasing: Architecture (4/5)

S442 – Stupa

SC443 Stupa (789955, 2594287) *Morel khurd west*
Group of small stupas on western 'finger' of hill. Diam: 4.80 m.

S443 (3) – Stupa

SC465 Monastery (790205, 2594204)
Low platform (29 x 25.8 m; ht.1.55 m) at western side of upper terrace. Small projecting platform on southern side. Faint outlines of a series of square cells along inner wall. Phasing: Architecture (4/5)

S465 – Courtyard monastery

SC595 Rock-shelter (790566, 2594435)
Single rockshelter with platform built up infront.

S855 'Cave 3' – Monastic rock-shelter

SC596 Rock-shelter (790588, 2594489)
Phasing: Rock-shelter (2)

S856 'Cave 4' – Monastic rock-shelter

SC597 Rock-shelter (796996, 2594505)

S857 'Cave 5' – Monastic rock-shelter

SC598 Rock-shelter (790600, 2594514)
Phasing: Rock-shelter (2)

S858 'Cave 6' – Monastic rock-shelter

SC599 Rock-shelter (790602, 2594536)
Phasing: Rock-shelter (2)

S859 'Cave 7' – Monastic rock-shelter

SC600 Rock-shelter (790601, 2594547)
Single rockshelter.

S860 'Cave 8' – Rock-shelter

SC601 Rock-shelter (790604, 2594553)
Two rockshelters with platform built up in front.

S861 'Cave 9', S862 'Cave 10' – Monastic rock-shelter

SC602 Building Religious (790583, 2594583)
Miscellaneous buildings on the eastern terrace.

S864, S1108, S1109 – Building Religious

SC675 Stupa (790596, 2594285) *Morel khurd tier 2*
Mid tier stupa complex. Phasing: Architecture (2)

S1059 'Stupa 7a', S1061 'Stupa 8', S1062 'Stupa 9c', S1063 'Stupa 10', S1064 'Stupa 11', S1065 'Stupa 12', S1066 'Stupa 13', S1067 'Stupa 14', S1068 'Stupa 15', S1069 'Stupa 16', S1070 'Stupa 17', S1071 'Stupa 18', S1072 'Stupa 19', S1073 'Stupa 20'

SC676 Stupa (790682, 2593930) *Morel khurd lower tier*
Stupa cluster on lowermost tier. Phasing: Architecture (2)

S1060 'Stupa 7b', S1075 – Stupa

SC677 Stupa (790691, 2594192) *Morel khurd tier 3*
Two separate clusters of stupas on third tier. Phasing: Architecture (2)

S1076, S1077, S1078, S1079, S1080, S1081, S1082, S1083, S1084, S1085, S1086, S1087, S1088, S1089 – Stupa

SC701 Monastery (790350, 2594206)
Interconnected, haphazard, courtyard monastery originally mapped by Cunningham. Phasing: Architecture (6)

S1103 – Interconnected courtyard monastery

SC721 Background landscape
Sculptures from Morel khurd, but with no precise location.

S1098 – Unprovenanced sculptures

SG005a Morel khurd (reservoir). Sector: 2b

SC42 Dam (789205, 2594579)
Massive embankment running SW-NE from the western base of Morel khurd hill, to Binjoli hill. Faced on north side with upslanting slabs as at Nagauri. Would have held in body of water flowing from hill in the north. Phasing: Dam (2)

S42 – Dam

SC700 Reconstructed reservoir (789277, 2594623)

S1102 – Reconstructed reservoir

SG005b Pipalia kherai (settlement). Sector: 2b

Agricultural plain directly to the south of Morel khurd hill.
Large barren, settlement mound situated on the southern bank of Dabar *nāla*. Situated around 500 m south of the main stupa complex. The two sites are connected by a stone paved pathway which leads from the spring to the south of the main complex, and continues over the plateau, all the way to the *nāla* at the foot of the hill.

SC41 Settlement (790177, 2593086)
Phasing: Pottery (1d to 7)

S41 – Hillside basti

S871 – Sculpture pile (in worship)

SG005c Binjoli kherai (settlement). Sector: 2b

Low rocky outcrop c. 1.5 km NW of Morel khurd.
Settlement situated on slightly raised ground formed by lower slopes of one of the western projections of Morel khurd hill. Situated around 1.5 km NW of the main stupa complex. Remains of heavily disturbed structures throughout settlement. Most prominent feature are three high monoliths (height: c. 6 m) which form a line in the centre of the settlement.

SC369 Settlement (788894, 2595181)
Phasing: Architecture (6): Water architecture (6)

S369 – Hillside basti

S43 – Well

S869 – Sculpture pile

S870 – Building cluster

SG006 Vidisha (settlement). Sector: 1a

Agricultural plain.
Large city site extending from the ancient mounds and rampart in the north, to the 'modern' town of Vidisha in the south.

SC44 Temple: Brahmanical (785875, 2607057) *Khambaba/ Heliodorus pillar*
Heliodorus pillar site. Phasing: Architecture (1d/2): Sculpture (2 to 4)
S1000 – Well
S44 'Heliodorus pillar' – Temple remains: Brahmanical (in worship)
S995, S998 – Pillar
S999 – Sculpture pile (in worship)

SC45 Settlement (785220, 2606425) *Besnagar*
Phasing: Pottery (1c to 3b): Pottery (published) (1b to 5): Sculpture (2 to 4)
S45 – Settlement mound
S46 'Site L', S971 'Site F', S976 'Site T', S977 'Site J', S978 'Site H', S979 'Site G', S980 'Site K', S981, S982 'Site Y' – Sculpture pile (in worship)

SC49 Stupa (784947, 2607112) *Mound M*
Large mound to north of River Bes. May correspond to Lake's 'site 10'. Excavated by Cunningham who found the corner pillar of a Buddhist pillar, decorated with lotus medallions. Cunningham concluded that may have been the site of a stupa, temple, or monastery. Phasing: Sculpture (2)
S49 – Stupa

SC50 Background landscape (786168, 2606192) *Charan tirth*
Modern temple containing various 10th century fragments. Supposed to contain Visnupad, but this could not be found. Phasing: Architecture (6)
S50 – Modern temple (in worship)

SC52 Settlement (786816, 2604908) *Modern Vidisha*
See Ch. 13.
S52 – Settlement mound

SC53 Temple: Brahmanical/Buddhist (?) (787339, 2604660) *Lohangi*
Fortified rock in the centre of Vidisha town. Phasing: Sculpture (2 to 6)
S53 – Pillar (Buddhist?) *(in worship)*
S962 – Mosque
S963 – Temple remains: Brahmanical (in worship)

SC321 Settlement (786168, 2607490) *Bes tila*
S321 – Settlement mound
S781 – Sculpture pile (in worship)

SC322 Tank (786147, 2607387) *Bes tila*
Remains of dried up village tank just to the south of settlement mound. Embankment survives as ploughed over mound running E-W (length: 80 m; height: 2 m).
S322 – Tank

SC640 Tank (784549, 2606363) *Besnagar*
Small tank immediately to east of city rampart.
S967 – Tank

SC641 Temple: Unknown/mixed cult (784379, 2606154) *Mound S/Dungari*
Mound S (AC). Mound 1 (Lake)
S968 – Temple: Unknown/mixed cult

SC642 Temple: Unknown (784428, 2605968) *Mound Rs*
Low mound to south of Vidisha-Udayagiri road, at SW corner of city rampart. Phasing: Sculpture (6)
S969 – Temple remains: Unknown (in worship)

SC643 Temple: Brahmanical (784661, 2606796) *Site X*
Gupta temple remains on bank of River Bes Phasing: Architecture (4): Sculpture (4)
S972 – Temple remains: Brahmanical (in worship)

SC644 Temple: Brahmanical (784688, 2606712) *Site W*
Remains of Visnu temple with sculptures under worship on platform. Phasing: Sculpture (6)
S974 – Temple remains: Brahmanical

SC645 Building Religious (785364, 2606654) *Mound P/Kaliya*
High mound east of the village Bes, to the south of the River Bes. Cunningham was unable to excavate due to the presence of a house, but he concluded that 'this was certainly the site of a large building'.
S983 – Building Religious (in worship)

SC646 Stupa (785750, 2606954) *Mound N*
High mound just to the sw of the Heliodorus pillar site, and just beyond crossing over River Bes. Identified as a stupa mound by Cunningham, but no excavations carried out due to modern building on top. Some of the stupa railings now stored in the Gujari Mahal museum, Gwalior, may come from here.
S987 Stupa

SC647 Fortification wall (784543, 2606424) *Besnagar*
Phasing: Fortification (1d/2): Pottery (published) (1d)
S988 – Fortification wall

SC653 Background landscape (786344, 2607481) *Site 11 (Lake)*
Ghat with saptamatrikas and bodhisattava. Phasing: Sculpture (4)
S994 – Sculpture pile

SC654 Temple: Brahmanical (786699, 2605259) *Bijalmandal*
Site under protection of ASI. Phasing: Architecture (6): Islamic architecture (to): Sculpture (6)
S1001 – Temple remains: Brahmanical (in worship)
S1002 – Mosque

SC655 Background landscape (786841, 2604677) *Modern Vidisha*
Extensive architectural remains set within modern water-tower compound in the middle of the walled town of Vidisha. Phasing: Sculpture (2 to 6)
S1005 – Sculpture pile

SC673 Background landscape (785538, 2607034) *Forestry Commission*
Forestry Department on the northern bank of the River Bes to the west of the Heliodorus pillar. Phasing: Sculpture (3b)
S997 – Sculpture pile (in worship)

SC703 Background landscape (784751, 2606819) *Site X*
Lingas in the river to east of Gupta temple (972).
S1105 – Sculpture pile

SC718 Temple: Brahmanical (784126, 2606760) *Mound R/12*
Low mound outside city ramparts to the west of Bes village. Labelled Mound R by Cunningham, and appears to correspond to Mound 12, revisited by Lake. Here Lake noticed a large Gupta-period abacus, with eight lions back to back, very similar to that noted at Amacchar during the Sanchi survey. Mound occupied by a modern temple with a modern Ganesh sculpture. Phasing: Sculpture (4)
S965 – Brahmanical

SG007 Satdhara (ritual). Sector: 1b

Long hill (513 m) on eastern bank of River Bes.
Published Buddhist monastic site.

SC54 Stupa (770806, 2600343) *Stupa 1*
Stupa set within walled enclosure. Phasing: Architecture (1d to 2): Inscriptions (published) (2): Sculpture (1d/2 to 2)
S54 – Stupa

SC55 Monastery (770790, 2599990) *Monastery A*
Platformed monastery (16.8 x 14.6 m; ht: 5.5 m) abutting northern boundary wall around Stupa 1. Two internal staircases, one at the NW corner, the other at the NE. Phasing: Architecture (2)
S55 – Platformed monastery

SC56 Monastery (770761, 2599948) *Monastery B*
Platformed monastery (24.4 x 18.3 m) abutting western wall of stupa 1 enclosure. Highly ruinous state. Phasing: Architecture (2)
S56 – Platformed monastery

SC57 Rock-shelter (770712, 2599858)
Rock-shelter with painting of stupa, datable to Gupta period (Agrawal 1997). Phasing: Paintings (4): Rock-shelter (1b): Stone tools (1b)
S57 – Monastic rock-shelter

SC58 Monastery (770318, 2600049)
Platformed monastery (28.1 x 15.5 m) on western bank of River Bes. Internal stairway on SW corner. Phasing: Architecture (2)
S58 – Platformed monastery

SC59 Stupa (770354, 2599703)
Several small stupa outlines c. 20 m west of SC58. Phasing: Architecture (2)
S59 (5) – Stupa

SC60 Monastery (770568, 2599279)
Large platform c. 1 km south of main stupa complex, built into side of hill. Phasing: Architecture (2)
S60 – Platformed monastery

SC379 Monastery (770935, 2599702)
Group of rectangular monasteries (average: c. 9.6 x 4 m; 23.4 x 5.1 m; average wall wd: 60 cm) in recently cleared area in southern part of site. Phasing: Architecture (2)
S379 (6) – Rectangular monastery

SC466 Monastery (770705, 2599942) *Siddh ka makan/Monastery C*
Platformed monastery (30 x 16.8 m; Ht: 4.9 m) on edge of cliff overlooking River Bes. Staggered, internal stairway on eastern side. Phasing: Architecture (2)
S466 – Platformed monastery

SC634 Temple: Buddhist (770807, 2599991)
Outline of apsidal temple revealed during 1997 excavations. Immediately to the north of Stupa 1. Phasing: Architecture (1d)
S954 – Temple remains: Buddhist

SC635 Stupa *Stupa 2*
Phasing: Architecture (2): Reliquary (2)
S955 – Stupa

SC636 Stupa (770752, 2599834) *Southern cluster*
Cluster of small stupas to the south of Stupa 1. Phasing: Architecture (2)
S956 'Stupa 4', S957 'Stupa 5', S958 'Stupa 6', S959 'Stupa 7'

SC637 Stupa (770767, 2599720) *Stupa 8*
Phasing: Architecture (2): Reliquary (2)
S960 – Stupa
SC638 Stupa (770950, 2599740)
Group of newly revealed stupas immediately north of SC379. Phasing: Architecture (2)
S961 (6) – Stupa complex

SG008 Neemkheria (settlement). Sector: 4

Long hill (480 m) running W-E, c. 2 km NW of Udayagiri.
Modern village situated on the southern slopes of Bighan hill, just below the Buddhist monastic site. Absence of pottery makes it difficult to establish chronology, but ancient habitation attested by sculptural remains.
SC61 Settlement (782381, 2606343)
S548 – Sculpture pile (in worship)
S61 – Modern settlement

SG009 Bilori 1 (settlement). Sector: 1a

Prominent, low hill (440 m) in the flat plain south of Sanchi.
Hillside settlement overlain by modern village.
SC62 Settlement (779261, 2597181)
S549, S550 – Sculpture pile (both in worship)
S62 – Modern settlement

SG010 Gulgaon-Eran (settlement). Sector: 1b

Based around large hill-range, c. 3 km NW of Sanchi.
Large settlement complex consisting of three main habitational areas extending from Gulgaon kherai, behind the ancient dam, Eran and Eran 2.
SC63 Settlement (775633, 2601444) *Gulgaon kherai*
Phasing: Pottery (1d to 7): Stone tools (1a)
S63 – Hillside basti
SC91 Settlement (776053, 2601877) *Eran*
Phasing: Stone tools (1b)
S540 'Khotama', S541 'Dhuladev' – Sculpture pile (both in worship)
S91 – Hillside basti
SC92 Mosque (775970, 2601745) *Eran*
Remains of mosque on summit of hill.
S92 – Mosque (in worship)
SC93 Temple: Brahmanical (775966, 2602455) *Eran*
10th century temple remains set on high platform NW of modern Eran village.
Phasing: Architecture (6): Sculpture (6 to 7)
S93 – Temple remains: Brahmanical (in worship)
SC94 Ancient route (775769, 2601606) *Gulgaon-Eran*
Remains of ancient road between Eran and Gulgaon kherai.
S94 – Ancient route
SC378 Temple: Brahmanical (775963, 2601864) *Eran*
Phasing: Sculpture (4 to 6)
S378 – Temple remains: Brahmanical (in worship)
SC515 Settlement (776000, 2600532) *Gulgaon village*
Modern village possibly underlain by ancient site.
S553 – Modern settlement
S554 – Sculpture pile (in worship)

SG010b Gulgaon (reservoir). Sector: 1b

SC64 Dam (775840, 2600969)
Ancient dam, reconstructed in the 1970s. Phasing: Dam (1d/2): Sculpture (2 to 6)
S551 – Sculpture pile (in worship)
S64 – Dam
SC516 Reconstructed reservoir (776052, 2600986)
Phasing: Dam (1d/2)
S555 – Reconstructed reservoir

SG010c Eran 2 (settlement). Sector: 1b

SC95 Settlement (776176, 2602751)
Phasing: Pottery (4 to 7)
S579 – Natural shrine: modern shrine under Banyan tree.
S95 – Settlement mound

SC96 Tank (776150, 2602705)
Unwalled village tank just to north of settlement mound.
S96 – Tank

SG011 Ferozpur (reservoir). Sector: 1b

Prominent hill (500 m), c. 5 km west of Sanchi.
SC67 Dam (772491, 2600627)
Faced on both sides. Core made up of occupational debris. Phasing: Dam (1d/2 to 4): Pottery (1d to 7)
S1046 – Sluice
S556 – Platform (in worship)
S67 – Dam
SC517 Reconstructed reservoir (773751, 2600058)
Phasing: Dam (2)
S557 – Reconstructed reservoir

SG011b Ferozpur (settlement). Sector: 1b

Ancient settlement situated on lower SE slopes of hill, below monastic site. Overlain by modern village.
SC66 Settlement (773092, 2600986)
Phasing: Pottery (1d to 7)
S66 – Modern settlement
SC377 Temple: Brahmanical (773012, 2600894)
Phasing: Sculpture (4 to 7)
S377 – Temple remains: Brahmanical (in worship)

SG011c Ferozpur (ritual). Sector: 1b

SC65 Monastery (772970, 2601141)
Interconnected courtyard monasteries lined with rectangular rooms. Rubble-infill, stone faced walls. Average wd: 60–85 cm. Phasing: Architecture (2): Stone tools (1b)
S1007, S1008 – Stupa
S558 – Natural shrine: tree shrine at far west of monastery complex, on edge of hill.
S65 (6) – Interconnected courtyard monastery (rectangular)

SG012 Karhaud (settlement). Sector: 2b

Long, low hill (460 m), c. 1.5 km north of Andher.
Settlement situated on SE slope of hill. Overlain by modern village.
SC68 Settlement (796828, 2594345)
S562 – Modern temple (in worship)
S68 – Modern settlement
SC69 Rock-shelter (796946, 2594209) *Mahadev gufa*
Large rock-shelter overlooking village tank. Phasing: Sculpture (4)
S69 – Rock-shelter (in worship)
SC71 Tank (797095, 2594255) *Djinn Maharaj*
Circular village tank, with loose stone facing. Still holds water.
S71 – Tank (in worship)
SC72 Temple: Brahmanical (797137, 2594211) *Durgasthan*
Remains of 10th century temple built into modern shrine. Phasing: Architecture (6): Sculpture (6)
S72 – Temple remains: Brahmanical (in worship)
SC518 Rock-shelter (797129, 2593920) *Godariawali gufa*
Empty cave to the east of rock-shelter shrine.
S70 – Rock-shelter (in worship)
SC519 Temple: Brahmanical (797023, 2594291)
Two small Paramara shrines to the west of village tank. Phasing: Architecture (6): Sculpture (6)
S563 (2) – Temple remains: Brahmanical (in worship)

SG012b Karhaud kherai (ritual). Sector: 2b

Low hill north of Andher, west of Karhaud, and east of Pohra.
SC344 Temple: Brahmanical (795690, 2593940) *Mata Mandir*
Western edge of hill. Phasing: Sculpture (6)
S344 – Temple remains: Brahmanical (in worship)
SC482 Monastery (795749, 2593981)

Series of interconnected courtyard-type structures (c. 30 x 30 m), lined with rectangular cells. Phasing: Architecture (2)

S482 – Interconnected courtyard monastery (rectangular)

SC579 Quarry (795749, 2593968)
Modern excavations/quarry (show up in satellite imagery). Pottery found throughout.

S805 (3) – Quarry

SC672 Stupa (795748, 2593980)
Stupa mound in centre of monastery complex. Diameter: 6.5 m; surviving height: c. 2 m. Small square platform (c. 2.5 x 2.5 m) immediately to the west. Phasing: Architecture (2): Pottery (1d to 7)

S343 (4), S1045 – Stupa

SG013 Andher (ritual). Sector: 2b

Prominent hill (596 m) c. 10 km east of Sanchi.
Published Buddhist monastic complex.

SC73 Stupa (797094, 2592060) *Stupa 1*
Contains uninscribed reliquary Phasing: Architecture (2): Inscriptions (published) (2): Sculpture (2): Stone tools (1b)

S73 – Stupa

SC74 Rock-shelter cluster (797039, 2592247)
Series of rock-shelters formed by cliffs on eastern side of the hill. Phasing: Rock-shelter (1b)

S74 (6) – Rock-shelter cluster

SC75 Stupa (796993, 2591584)
Square stupa platform situated within the fortified enclosure in the southern-most part of the hill. Stupa has been dug down to its relic chamber. Phasing: Architecture (4/5)

S75 – Stupa

SC76 Fortification wall (796998, 2591609)
Massive fortification wall enclosing stupa (75), running along southern and eastern edge of hill. Undressed boulders. Ht: 1 m; wd: 2 m). Outlines of rectangular bastion at SW corner. Circular bastion midway along the western wall.

S76 – Fortification wall

SC80 Background landscape (795858, 2591847)
Three stone platforms with triangular Devi stones and flags, on the lower western slope of Andher hill.

S80 (3) – Natural shrine

Three stone platforms with triangular Devi stones and flags, on the lower western slope of Andher hill.

SC467 Monastery (797085, 2592033)
Monastery platform (18.3 x 12 m; surviving ht: 1–2 m) abutting southern wall of stupa 1 enclosure. Phasing: Architecture (2)

S467 – Platformed monastery

SC476 Stupa (796997, 2592232)
Stupa on lower tier to north of main complex. Diam: 3.20 m. Surviving ht: 1.20 m.

S476 (2) – Stupa

SC520 Stupa (797052, 2592064)
Cluster of smaller stupas to west of stupa 1 Phasing: Architecture (2)

S565 'Stupa 2', S566 'Stupa 3', S567, S568, S569 – Stupa

SG013b Andher (background landscape). Sector: 2b

Ancient cult spot at the eastern foot of Andher hill.

SC78 Temple: Brahmanical (797357, 2592212)
Temple and sculptural remains. Phasing: Scatter (3a): Sculpture (3a to 6)

S77 , S78 – Sculpture pile (both in worship)

S79 – Well

SG014 Piparia (settlement). Sector: 1a

Agricultural plain 2 km SE of Sanchi, on western bank of River Betwa.
Low settlement mound, overlain by modern village.

SC81 Settlement (780085, 2597009)

S570 – Sculpture pile (in worship)

S81 – Settlement mound

SC82 Background landscape (780128, 2597529)
Rocky outcrop with microlithic scatters in midst of fields. Phasing: Stone tools (1b)

S82 – Locale

SG017 Rangai Amkhera (settlement). Sector: 1a

Agricultural plain midway between Sanchi and Vidisha, on eastern bank of River Betwa.
Roughly circular settlement mound, c.200 m to east of Betwa river. Occupied partially by single house. Excavations carried out in the 1970s, revealed a 3 phase chalcolithic layer over two pre-pottery microlithic levels. The earliest chalcolithic occupation was dated to c.1900–1800 BC on the basis of the similarity of the ware to Kayatha II, continuining up to beginning of 1st millenium BC (contemporary with PGW).

SC83 Settlement (784745, 2602142)
Phasing: Pottery (1b): Pottery (published) (1b to 1c)

S83 – Settlement mound

SG017b Rangai village (settlement). Sector: 1a

Agricultural plain midway between Sanchi and Vidisha, on eastern bank of River Betwa.
Modern village with ancient temple remains.

SC521 Settlement (784229, 2602456)

S571 – Modern settlement

SC523 Temple: Brahmanical (784317, 2602482)
Phasing: Architecture (6): Sculpture (6)

S572 – Temple remains: Brahmanical

SG018 Nonakhera (settlement). Sector: 1a

Agricultural plain 1.5 km NE of Sanchi on western bank of River Betwa.
Small settlement mound on the western bank of River Betwa, overlain by modern village.

SC84 Settlement (781964, 2599743)
Phasing: Sculpture (5)

S 544 , S545 , S546 – Sculpture pile (all in worship)

S84 – Settlement mound

SC85 Ford (782661, 2599889)
Ancient ford, c. 250 m north of village.

S85 – Ford

SG020 Kachi kanakhera-Amkhera (settlement). Sector: 1b

Small hill (480 m) 1.5 km SW of Sanchi.

SC86 Settlement (777987, 2598355) *Kachi kanakhera*

S573 – Sculpture pile (in worship)

S86 – Modern settlement

SC87 Settlement (777041, 2598128) *Amkhera*
Modern village on eastern side of hill. According to villagers, large amounts of red, and black pottery are found when digging house foundations. Phasing: Sculpture (6): Stone tools (1a)

S543 – Sculpture pile (in worship)

S87 – Modern settlement

S88, 542 – Well

SC444 Tank (777776, 2598005) *Amkhera*
Large village tank on eastern side of the Sanchi-Raisen road opposite Amkhera village.

S444 – Tank

SG021 Sehor (settlement). Sector: 1b

Agricultural plain at northern base of Satdhara hill, on eastern bank of River Bes.
Low settlement mound separated by *nāla* which flows S-N from Satdhara hill, and joins River Bes. Partially occupied by single house and small temple.

SC89 Settlement (771666, 2601093)
Phasing: Pottery (1c to 7): Stone tools (1a)

S574 – Sculpture pile (in worship)

S89 – Settlement mound

SG022 Goldoria (ritual). Sector: 1b

Small hillock (480m) east of Ferozpur.

SC90 Monastery (773268, 2599407)
Phasing: Architecture (2): Pottery (1d to 2)

S90 (20) – Rectangular monastery

SC477 Stupa (773258, 2599405)
Stupa outline at centre of site. Diam: 5.10 m. Phasing: Architecture (2)
S477 – Stupa

SG023 Dargawan (settlement). Sector: 1b

Northern hillock (520 m), in line of hills opposite Sanchi, c. 1 km to the NW.
Low mound on lower eastern side of Dargawan hill, occupied partially by single house. Covered with outlines of around 25 stone structures. Much of the stone has been removed.
SC437 Settlement (778384, 2601393)
Phasing: Pottery (1d to 3a): Stone tools (1b)
S437 – Settlement mound
S575 – Sculpture pile (in worship)
S576 – Natural shrine: p*latform beneath banyan tree with unhewn stones*
SC439 Tank (778860, 2601414)
Walled village tank to east of settlement. Only fills up during the monsoon.
S439 – Tank (in worship)

SG024 Baheriya (settlement). Sector: 1a

Agricultural plain 2 km NW of Eran.
Large settlement mound, now eroded into two separate mounds. Several outlines of stone structures remain on the top of both mounds.
SC438 Settlement (775076, 2603181) *CH(B)*
S438 – Settlement mound

SG025 Pathar (background landscape). Sector: 1b

Natural raised outcrop (20 m) c. 300 m SE of Chirauli village.
SC436 Temple: Brahmanical (773795, 2602653)
Remains of 10th century temple on top of natural raised outcrop. Phasing: Sculpture (6 to 7): Stone tools (1b)
S436 – Temple remains: Brahmanical (in worship)

SG028 Dargawan hill (ritual). Sector: 1b

Northern hillock (520 m), in line of hills opposite Sanchi, c. 1 km to the NW.
SC97 Stupa (778383, 2600788)
Outlines of many (over 100) stone structures all over the top of the hill, and continuing on the lower tiers of the eastern slopes. Most of the outlines are circular, and appear to be of small stupas (average diameter: 3 m). Several of the others are of rectangular form with apsidal-shaped ends.
Phasing: Architecture (2)
S97 (100) – Stupa complex

SG028b Dargawan hill (reservoir). Sector: 1b

Northern hillock (520 m), in line of hills opposite Sanchi, c. 1 km to the NW.
SC98 Dam (778376, 2600420)
Slightly concave embankment running N-S from the southern base of Dargawan hill, to Dargawan 2. Faced with stone masonry on the east side, several course of which are still visible towards the southern end of the embankment. Possibly faced on the west side as well, as attested by the large number of fallen stone blocks on this side. Would have enclosed small body of water to the west of the embankment. Phasing: Dam (1d/2)
S580 (2) – Natural shrine: *platforms on dam under worship*
S98 – Dam
SC525 Reconstructed reservoir (778264, 2600436)
Phasing: Dam (1d/2)
S581 – Reconstructed reservoir

SG029 Dargawan hill (2) (ritual). Sector: 1b

Southern hillock (520m) in line of hills opposite Sanchi, c. 1 km to the west.
Various Buddhist remains distributed over the hill.
SC101 Stupa (778265, 2599857) *Eastern complex*
Stupa complex on eastern edge of hill, consisting of one large stupa (diameter: 8.10 m; surviving height: 1.5 m); and three smaller st¨pas (diameters: 4.40 m; 4.80 m; 5.70 m). Dressed masonry edges still visible at the base, but all of them show evidence of having been dug by villagers, and what look like relic-chambers lie exposed in the centres. Phasing: Architecture (2)
S101 'Stupa 1', S531 'Stupa 2', S532 'Stupa 3', S533 'Stupa 4'
SC102 Stupa (777460, 2599176) *Southern complex*
Cluster of small stupas to the south of stupa 1. Phasing: Architecture (2)
S102, S103, S538 – Stupa
SC104 Temple (?): Buddhist (777374, 2599332)
Very disturbed outline of an apsidal structure (incomplete length: 9 m; width: 6.30 m), situated to the north of 4a.. Contains two stupa outlines (diameter: 1.10 m and 1.90 m). Another heavily damaged apsidal structure (c.8.40 x 6 m) c. 20 m further north. Phasing: Architecture (2)
S104 – Temple remains: Buddhist (x 2)
S105 (2), S539 – Stupa
SC106 Tank (777173, 2599801)
Circular tank, c. 1.10 km SW of 029/3a. Diam: 48 m. Embankment (ht: 1 m), with seven surviving courses of dressed facing.
S106 – Tank
SC480 Rectangular monastery (778252, 2599896)
Badly damaged rectangular structures next to stupas (3a). Phasing: Architecture (2)
S480 (3) – Rectangular monastery
SC513 Stupa (778210, 2599785)
Small votive stupas Phasing: Architecture (2)
S535, S537 – Stupa

SG029b Dargawan hill (2) (reservoir). Sector: 1b

Southern hillock (520m) in line of hills opposite Sanchi, c. 1 km to the west.
SC99 Dam (777272, 2598893) *Karondih*
Slightly concave embankment running N-S, immediately below stupas on Dargawan 2 hill. Stone facing on west side only, several blocks of which survive towards the northern end. Stone masonry joined with lime mortar. Cut through at northern side by railway at point occupied by crossing no. 267.c/1 E; 878 EP. 31 (from Bombay). Phasing: Dam (1d/2)
S530 – Sculpture pile (in worship)
S99 – Dam
SC512 Reconstructed reservoir (777056, 2598927) *Karondih*
Phasing: Dam (1d/2)
S529 – Reconstructed reservoir

SG029c Karondih (settlement). Sector: 1b

Narrow valley to south of long hill immediately opposite Sanchi.
Enormous Banyan tree in the middle of agricultural fields, NW of the ancient embankment. It is interesting to note that the suffix dih (= mound) in the name Karondih, is used locally to refer to ancient settlement mounds. No such remains have been found in the immediate vicinity, apart from the nearby settlement remains at Gulgaon. It is possible that the tree at Karondih, which could be as much as 1000 years old, has been linked to a settlement for which there is no archaeological evidence.
SC100 Memory site (777010, 2599111)
S100 – Natural shrine: modern Devi shrine beneath Banyan tree.

SG030 Chapna (settlement). Sector: 1a

Agricultural plain 3.5 km south of Sanchi.
Modern village, whose inhabitants, according to local tradition, moved here from the ancient settlement at Dhakna.
SC107 Settlement (776638, 2596155)
S107 – Modern settlement

SG031 Udayagiri (ritual). Sector: 4

Long hill running N-S, c. 1.5 km west of Vidisha city ramparts.
Published rock-cut temple complex.
SC108 Rock-cut ritual complex (783018, 2605933)
Phasing: Architecture (4): Sculpture (4 to 6)
S108 'Cave 4', S1095 'Caves 5–6', S1096 'Cave 13', S1097 Jain cave
SC109 Rock-shelter cluster (782883, 2605949)
Rock-shelters with prehistoric rock paintings situated on western and northern cliff-fronts. Phasing: Stone tools (1b)
S109 (5) – Rock-shelter cluster

SC110 Temple: Brahmanical (782843, 2605571)
Cult spot with early Buddhist and later, Vaisnava, remains. Phasing: Sculpture (4 to 6)
S110 – Temple remains: Brahmanical (in worship)
SC111 Ford (782779, 2606077)
Ancient ford, with large stone slabs, immediately to the west of Udaigiri hill.
S111 – Ford
SC488 Stupa (782797, 2605215)
Circular outline on summit of northernmost hill. Various railings (SC110/ I-7; SC221/I-592) attest to existence of large stupa, of comparable size to Bharhut stupa. Phasing: Sculpture (2)
S488 – Stupa
SC693 Temple: Brahmanical (782843, 2605280) *Temple 1*
Phasing: Architecture (4)
S1092 – Temple remains: Brahmanical
SC694 Temple: Brahmanical (782954, 2605913)
Gupta temple on northern hill. Phasing: Architecture (4): Sculpture (2 to 4)
S1094 – Temple: Buddhist

SG031b Udayagiri/Madhupuri/ Sonapura (settlement). Sector: 1a

Long hill running N-S, c. 1.5 km west of Vidisha city ramparts.
Series of interconnected settlement mounds to east of Udayagiri hill.
SC112 Settlement (783459, 2605659) *Udayagiri*
Phasing: Pottery (1d to 7)
S112 – Settlement mound
SC113 Tank (783301, 2605639) *Udayagiri*
Village tank to west of settlement.
S113 – Tank
SC220 Temple: Brahmanical (783518, 2604970) *Sonapura Maujimara*
High temple mound on northern bank of River Betwa. Height of mound: 7 m above river bank. Phasing: Architecture (6): Sculpture (4 to 6)
S220 – Temple remains: Brahmanical (in worship)
SC221 Settlement (783418, 2605217) *Sonapura basti*
Phasing: Pottery (1c to 7): Sculpture (3b)
S221 – Settlement mound
S677 , S678 – Sculpture pile (in worship)
SC222 Settlement (783680, 2605301) *Madhupuri*
See chapter 13.
S222 – Settlement mound
S679 – Sculpture pile (in worship)
SC223 Settlement (783741, 2605514) *Madhupuri kherai*
Phasing: Pottery (1d to 2)
S223 – Settlement mound

SG032 Dhakna village (settlement). Sector: 1b

Small hillock (460 m), which forms the easternmost hillock of a line of three, c. 2.25 km SW of Sanchi. The modern village of Dhakna occupies the western most hillock. Modern village situated on southern slopes of hill. Early sculptural remains demonstrate that overlies ancient settlement.
SC117 Settlement (775590, 2596842)
S117 – Hillside basti
S524 , S525 – Sculpture pile (both in worship)
SC468 Temple remains: Unknown/mixed cult (775489, 2596755)
Base of temple at southern edge of village (summit of hill). Phasing: Architecture (2): Sculpture (2 to 6)
S1053 – Pillar
S468 – Temple remains: Unknown/mixed cult (in worship)

SG032b Dhakna basti (settlement). Sector: 1b

Small hillock (460 m), which forms the easternmost hillock of a line of three, c. 2.25 km SW of Sanchi. The modern village of Dhakna occupies the western most hillock.
Low barren mound at NE base of Dhakna hill. Formed from eroded stone, rather than mud structures. Extends in a westerly direction from edge of Sanchi-Raisen road, as far as the western base of the hill; and for c. 200 m across the ploughed fields to the east of the road. On the unploughed part of the mound, the remains of around 40 stone structures can still be seen.
SC114 Settlement (776224, 2597214)
Phasing: Pottery (1c to 3b)
S114 – Settlement mound
S115 – Well

SC680 Temple: Brahmanical (776086, 2597182)
Phasing: Sculpture (4 to 6)
S526 – Temple remains: Brahmanical (in worship)

SG032c Dhakna (ritual). Sector: 1b

SC116 Stupa *Dhakna hill*
Damaged stupa outlines. Average diam: 3 m. Phasing: Architecture (2)
S116 (8) – Stupa
SC485 Fortification wall (775855, 2597326) *Dhakna hill*
Rubble-infill, dressed facing type. Wall wd: 80 cm.
S485 – Fortification wall

SG032d Dhakna (reservoir). Sector: 1b

SC118 Dam (775335, 2596390) *Dhakna village*
Remains of ancient embankment runs from Dhakna village hill and joins hill in SE, on other side of modern Sanchi-Salamatpur road. Cut through by stream running from west. Faced on west side with stone masonry, very similar to Nagauri embankment. At highest point, the upper levels of stone masonry jut out at extreme angle, levelling out towards the base Curved, out-turning to east. Highest standing height: 4.50 m. Phasing: Dam (1d/2)
S118 – Dam
SC511 Reconstructed reservoir (774993, 2596750)
Phasing: Dam (1d/2)
S528 – Reconstructed reservoir

SG033 Chirauli (settlement). Sector: 1a

Agricultural plain, c. 3 km NE of Satdhara, on eastern bank of River Bes. Settlement mound on east bank of River Bes, partially occupied by modern village.
SC119 Settlement (773363, 2603242)
S119 (3) – Settlement mound
S582 – Sculpture pile(in worship)

SG034 Salamatpur chaura (ritual). Sector: 1b

Small hill (460m), c. 4.5km south-west of Sanchi, and 1 km SE of Salamatpur.
SC120 Temple: Brahmanical (775484, 2595874)
Temple remains on summit of hill, incorporated into modern shrine and sadhu's residence. Phasing: Sculpture (6)
S120 – Temple remains: Brahmanical (in worship)

SG035 Bighan hill (ritual). Sector: 4

Prominent hill (480 m, now largely deforested) to the north of Bighan village, and around 2km NW of Udayagiri.
Buddhist remains spread over hill.
SC121 Stupa (780400, 2606139) *Upper tier*
Stupa outline (diam: 17.6 m) in middle of walled enclosure(49.6 x 49.6 m). Outlines of round towers at each corner (diam: 1.6 m). Walls of rubble-infill, dressed facing type. Phasing: Architecture (2): Stone tools (1b)
S121 – Stupa
S584 – Fortification wall
SC122 Stupa (780738, 2605947) *Stupa 1*
Phasing: Architecture (2)
S122 – Stupa
SC123 Rock-shelter cluster (780825, 2605796) *Lower tier*
Around 25 rock-shelters on the southern side of Bighan hill. Many contain heavily eroded rock-paintings ranging from chalcolithic to early-historic period (e.g. tree-in-railing motif). Corresponds to 'Neemkheria' shelters described elsewhere (*IAR* 1976–7, 77; Shukla 1990). Phasing: Paintings (1b to 2)
S123 (25) – Rock-shelter cluster
SC526 Stupa (780808, 2605968) *Lower tier*
Cluster of three stupas to the east of Stupa 1. Phasing: Architecture (2)
S585 'Stupa 2', S586, S587 – Stupa
SC527 Temple: Buddhist (780727, 2605892) *Lower tier*
Small rectangular, 'shrine'-like structure (5.4 x 4.6 m) c. 90 m SW of *Stupa* 2.
Phasing: Architecture (2)
S588 – Temple remains: Buddhist

SC528 Monastery (780684, 2605880) *Lower tier*
Courtyard monastery set on low platform at western extent of site. Phasing: Architecture (4/5)
S589 – Courtyard monastery
SC529 Monastery (780994, 2606082) *Lower tier*
Low monastery platform in NE of site, with evidence of some internal walls revealed during mapping in 2004–5. Phasing: Architecture (2)
S590 – Platformed monastery
SC530 Stupa (780873, 2605985) *Lower tier*
Phasing: Architecture (2)
S591 – Stupa

SG035b Bighan (reservoir). Sector: 4

SC124 Dam (779668, 2606224)
Embankment running S-N across the short valley between Bighan and Tigra hill. Faced with stone blocks on the west side. Would have held in water to the east of the embankment. Phasing: Dam (2)
S124 – Dam

SG036 Tigra hill (ritual). Sector: 4

Small prominent hill (460m) c. 1 km NW of Bighan hill.
SC125 Temple: Brahmanical (779180, 2606430)
Modern Hanuman temple complex situated on summit of hill. Earlier 10th century temple attested by various incorporated fragments. Directly comparable to Bijal mandal at Vidisha (SG006). Phasing: Sculpture (6)
S125 – Temple remains: Brahmanical (in worship)
S126 – Well

SG037 Ahmadpur (settlement). Sector: 4

High settlement mound partially occupied by modern village, on the southern bank of the Sahodra *nāla*, opposite Ahmadpur hill. Much of height is due to river silltation, but the upper part is formed from settlement debris.
SC132 Settlement (774252, 2612429) *Ahmadpur village*
Phasing: Pottery (1d to 3b): Sculpture (6)
S132 – Settlement mound
S522, S523 – Sculpture pile (in worship)
SC133 Temple: Brahmanical (773994, 2612417) *Ahmadpur village*
Temple mound on north bank of river to the west of the village mound. Phasing: Architecture (6): Sculpture (6)
S133 – Temple remains: Brahmanical (in worship)
S134 – Well
SC135 Temple: Jain (774456, 2612455) *Ahmadpur village*
East of the main settlement. According to villagers, the Jain sculptures now stored in the village, originally came from this site. Phasing: Architecture (6): Sculpture (6)
S135 – Temple remains: Jain

SG037a Ahmadpur hill (ritual). Sector: 4

Prominent hill (522 m) on north bank of Sahodra *nāla*, a tributary of River Betwa. Ahmadpur village is situated on the opposite bank. This is the northernmost hill in a series of prominent hills which punctuate the otherwise flat landscape. Various prehistoric and historic remains scattered over lower slopes and summit of hill.
SC127 Rock-shelter cluster (773362, 2613133)
Over 58 rock-shelters situated on the southern and western slopes of the hill. 28 contain paintings ranging from chalcolithic to historical periods. Phasing: Inscriptions (published) (2): Paintings (1b to 2): Rock-shelter (2): Sankalipi (3b): Sculpture (6): Stone tools (1a to 1b)
S127 (58 W) – Rock-shelter cluster (numbered by ASI)
S128 'Shelter no. 9b' – Monastic rock-shelter
S834 'Cave 1', S835 'Cave 2', S836 'Cave 3' (in worship), S837 'Cave 4', S838 'Cave 7',S 839 'Cave 8', S840 'Cave 13/14' (in worship), S841 'Cave 15', S842 'Cave 16', S843 'Cave 17, S844 'Cave 18', S845 'Cave 19'
SC129 Stupa (773435, 2612859)
Platform (10.4 x 10.4 m; surviving ht: 0.45 m) enclosed by boundary wall, which traverses southern edge of the hill. Phasing: Architecture (4/5)
S129 – Stupa (in worship)
SC131 Temple: Brahmanical (773436, 2613174)
10th century temple complex, built around older Gupta temple remains, the doorway of which has been incorporated into later structure. Phasing: Architecture (4 to 6): Sculpture (4 to 6)
S131 – Temple remains: Brahmanical (in worship)
SC508 Fortification wall (773510, 2613181)
Remains of massive fortification wall to east of temple site.
S521 – Fortification wall

SG037b Ahmadpur hill kherai (settlement). Sector: 4

Settlement situated midway up SW slope of the hill. Consists of badly damaged structural remains.
SC130 Settlement (772869, 2613207) *Ahmadpur hill*
Phasing: Pottery (1d to 3b)
S130 – Hillside basti

SG038 Ratanpur girdhari (settlement). Sector: 3

Large hill (558 m) c. 5 km south of Sanchi. Settlement on lower, NE slope of hill, consisting of c. 25 stone structures. Ground conditions prevented pottery collection, but terminal date provided by early sculpture. Modern village is situated immediately below.
SC136 Temple: Brahmanical (776450, 2593459)
West of settlement. Phasing: Sculpture (4 to 6)
S136 – Temple remains: Brahmanical (in worship)
SC137 Settlement (776832, 2593461)
S137 (2) – Modern settlement
S593 , S594 – Sculpture pile (both in worship)
SC138 Settlement (776551, 2593368)
Phasing: Stone tools (1b)
S138 – Hillside basti
S592 'Thakur baba ka sthan' – Natural shrine: modern shrine in middle of ancient settlement, below Imli tree (platform with uncarved stones and white flags).
SC690 Temple: Brahmanical (776981, 2593381)
Phasing: Sculpture (6 to 7)
S595 – Temple remains: Brahmanical (in worship)

SG038b Ratanpur Girdhari (background landscape). Sector: 3

SC139 Background landscape (776821, 2592899) *Matabhai ka sthan*
Modern cult spot situated on the summit of small hillock. Phasing: Stone tools (1b)
S139 – Natural shrine: three platforms with uncarved stones.

SG039 Fatehpur marmata (settlement). Sector: 1a

Agricultural plain, c. 6 km NE of Satdhara, on eastern bank of River Bes. High mound situated on east bank of River Bes. Partially covered with modern village. Large quantities of pottery, and several courses of boundary wall visible in the natural section on the river side of the mound.
SC140 Settlement (774146, 2604362)
Phasing: Pottery (1d to 4)
S140 – Settlement mound
S596 – Sculpture pile (in worship)

SG040 Bhartipur (settlement). Sector: 3

Small, prominent hill in valley to west of Sonari. Modern village on lower slopes of hill, possibly overlying ancient settlement.
SC141 Settlement (769184, 2594150)
S141 – Hillside basti
S597 – Sculpture pile (in worship)

SG041 Besar talai (settlement). Sector: 3

Long, deep valley which lies south of Sonari hill. From here, it is about a 2.5 km walk over the hill to the stupas at Sonari. The valley is dominated by a large perennial stream which flows through a series of important early historic settlements, joining River Betwa in the east.
The modern village here is one of a series of modern 'colonies' in the valley, which were established in the 1970s, as part of an extensive jungle-clearance

programme. The fact that the entire valley was deeply entrenched with jungle coverage partly explains the well-preserved condition of the early sculptures found here.

SC142 Temple remains: mixed cult (771537, 2590641) *Bhagvanpur colony*
Remains of 2nd century BC, possibly Buddhist, temple in form of two animal capitals. Also remains of later 10th century Brahmanical temple. Phasing: Sculpture (2 to 6)

S1052 – Temple remains: Buddhist
S142 – Temple remains: Brahmanical (in worship)

SC143 Settlement (771624, 2590361) *Bhagvanpur colony*
Large settlement mound (height: 4 m), partially covered by modern village, which nevertheless includes a number of ploughed fields. Situated on the east bank of the perennial *nāla*. Pottery scatters continue for nearly 1 km into the agricultural plains in the east, and all along the edge of the hill-range in the south.

S143 – Settlement mound
S598 , S599 – Sculpture pile (both in worship)

SC144 Temple: Brahmanical/Jain (771634, 2589998)
Remains of square temple on lower slopes of hill, just behind farm-house. Phasing: Architecture (6): Sculpture (6)

S144 – Temple remains: Brahmanical/Jain(in worship)

SC145 Rock-shelter (772323, 2588918)
Rock-shelter c. 1 km from main mound. Situated at edge of perennial *nāla*, which rises c. 300 m further up the hill. Contains perennial spring. Phasing: Sculpture (6)

S145 – Rock-shelter (in worship)

SC146 Settlement (772089, 2590544)
Phasing: Coins (2): Pottery (1c to 7).

S146 – Settlement mound
S602 , S603 , S604 – Sculpture pile (all in worship)

SC147 Tank (772213, 2590338)
Circular village tank just to the south of the main settlement mound.

S147 – Tank

SC380 Stupa (772132, 2590518)
Remains scattered at various points through site. Phasing: Sculpture (2)

S1051 (4) – Pillar
S380 – Stupa

SG041a Besar talai (reservoir). Sector: 3

SC148 Dam (772058, 2590831)
Large embankment running N-S from edge of Sonari hill, and running to the west of the main settlement mound. Built in a curve, bending outwards to the east. It would have formed a body of water to the west. All the stone facing appears to have been removed. Phasing: Dam (1d/2)

S148 – Dam

SG042 Sayargaon (settlement). Sector: 1b

Prominent hill (548 m), on the northern bank of the River Bes, c. 3 km west of Satdhara. Densely forested. Hill dominates much of the surrounding area, due to the dramatic rocky outcroppings on its eastern edge.
Modern village situated on lower eastern slopes of hill. Sculpture from here stored in rock-shelter (1a). Attests to underlying ancient settlement.

SC4 Settlement (766458, 2600004)

S4 – Modern settlement

SG042b Sayargaon (ritual). Sector: 1b

SC149 Rock-shelter (766580, 2599686)
Large rock-shelter containing heavily eroded rock-paintings in dark red: animals with x-ray stomachs and elongated stick-like figures. Phasing: Paintings (1b)

S1099 – Sculpture pile (in worship)
S149 – Rock-shelter

SC150 Building cluster (766265, 2599739) *Banjari ka sthan*
Several square outlines.

S150 (4) – Building Religious

SC486 Fortification wall (766143, 2599648)
Fortification wall on western edge of hill.

S486 – Fortification wall

SG043 Bagri/Jamwar (settlement). Sector: 4

Low hill consisting largely of sheet rock (442 m), c. 2 km north of Udayagiri.
Large settlement area incorporating modern villages of Jamwar and Bagri.

SC151 Settlement (782410, 2608680) *Bagri*

S151 – Hillside basti

SC152 Rock-shelter (782056, 2608088) *Bagri*
Series of rock-shelters on SE edge of hill, many of which have been destroyed by recent stone-quarrying activity.

S152 (6), S606 (in worship) – Rock-shelter

SC153 Settlement (781404, 2607627) *Jamwar*

S153 – Hillside basti
S611 – Sculpture pile (in worship)

SC532 Temple: Brahmanical (782413, 2608685) *Jamwar*
Large number of sculptural and architectural fragments, evidently belonging to a large temple of early 10th century AD, are scattered over various locations throughout the village. The majority of these are piled up on the main platform in the centre of the village. Phasing: Sculpture (6)

S608 – Temple remains: Brahmanical (in worship)
S609 – Sculpture pile (in worship)

SG044 Kharetiya 1 (settlement). Sector: 3

Agricultural plain c. 1.5 km from stupa complex at Sonari.
Large mound, on west bank of *nāla* which flows W-E, towards River Betwa. The heavily ploughed mounds to the NW and south appear to have been part of the main mound. Pottery scatters extend for some distance into the surrounding agricultural plains. Several stone structural remains on the top, but difficult to reach because of poisonous plant (*kranch*).

SC154 Settlement (775175, 2594117)
Phasing: Pottery (1d to 7)

S154 – Settlement mound
S506 – Natural shrine: unhewn stone installed on platform beneath Imli tree. Worshipped as Pathar baba . According to local folk-lore, the village was abandoned when stones began to fall from the sky as punishment from the gods after a Muslim had killed a cow in the village.

SC381 Temple: Brahmanical (775309, 2593953)
Small temple mound to south of settlement. Phasing: Architecture (6): Sculpture (6)

S381 – Temple remains: Brahmanical (in worship)

SG045 Pachmarhi (ritual). Sector: 1b

Western cliffs of a large hill range directly overlooking the River Bes, on whose eastern bank the caves are situated. Satdhara is situated 7 km further to the east.

SC155 Rock-cut ritual complex (762260, 2601793)
Series of three semi-structural cave temples, incorporating a mixture of 10th century AD and modern architectural elements. Complex is reached directly from the bank of the River Bes by a series of much damaged stone steps which ascend a high terrace built in stepped layers. Phasing: Architecture (6): Sculpture (6)

S155 (3 W) – Rock-cut ritual complex

SG046 Burakhera/Kharetiya 2 (settlement). Sector: 3

Small prominent, spherical shaped hill (480 m).
Ancient settlement on its summit and northern slopes. Consists of c. 50 stone structures. Despite lack of pottery, likely dates provided by the pottery from Kharetiya 2, a small settlement mound at the northern base of the hill, which appears to be a direct extension of the hillside settlement.

SC156 Settlement (775403, 2593375) *Burakhera.*

S156 – Hillside basti

SC157 Settlement (775376, 2593658) *Kharetiya (2)*
Phasing: Pottery (1c to 7)

S157 – Settlement mound

SG046b Kharitol (background landscape). Sector: 3

One of the highest hills (558m) in the area, acting as a prominent landmark thoughout the area, due to the 'stupa' like, spherical shaped hump on the summit. The entire hill is covered with dense jungle.
Known locally as Kharitol, but apart from a modern platform, situated on the spherical hump on the top of the hill, there are no other 'monumental' remains. According to villagers, this was built by the forestry departement in order to

cover up a 2 m deep hole, which had, in earlier years, been worshipped (Munshilal Chowkse of Ratanpur Girdhari, *pers. comm*). Further exploration of the hill was precluded by the extremely dense, prickly jungle, and the abundance of the poisonous bush, *'kranch'*.
SC699 Background landscape (775691, 2592366)
S1 – Natural shrine

SG048 Baleiya (background landscape). Sector: 3

Small spherical shaped hill (540 m), directly opposite (SE) of Sonari hill.
SC159 Rock-shelter (775363, 2592850) *Shankar gufa*
Rock-shelter situated on eastern side of hill, at the top of monsoon stream, just to the south of Baleiya. Unable to reach the site, because of the density of thorny jungle, and abundance of poisonous bushes (*'kranch'*), Binoculars revealed a very large rock-shelter with a stone platform built up outside. According to villagers, the shelter contains rock-paintings and sculptures.
S159 – Rock-shelter (in worship)

SG048b Baleiya (settlement). Sector: 3

Settlement situated on western slopes of hill, c. 400 m SW of Kharetiya 2. Settlement extends for around 150 m along side of hill.
SC158 Settlement (774972, 2592965)
S158 – Hillside basti
S610 – Natural shrine: unhewn stone set on small platform beneath Banyan tree at centre of settlement.

SG050 Amkhera bhauji (settlement). Sector: 3

Large hill, surmounted by Kharitol (558 m) west of Sonari. The large perennial stream which passes through Bhagvanpur colony,passes to the south.
Large settlement extending from hillside remains on SW slopes of hill, just behind the Amkhera bhauji colony, to large mound situated on the southern bank of *nāla* to the west. The hillside site consists of around 50 ruined stone structures, which extend as far as the base of the hill. Remains of several stone structures at summit of mound, but difficult to make out due to surface disturbance, and thick jungle coverage. Pottery scatters in the field to the west suggest that the original settlement extended for c.250 m up to the ancient well.
SC160 Settlement (774544, 2591495) *Amkhera bhauji colony*
Phasing: Pottery (1d to 7)
S160 – Hillside basti
S162 – Well
S510 – Sculpture pile (in worship)
SC161 Temple: Brahmanical (774503, 2591286) *Amkhera bhauji colony*
Temple remains situated in the fields c. 250 m to the south of the main settlement site. Phasing: Sculpture (6)
S161 – Temple remains: Brahmanical (in worship)
SC163 Settlement (774378, 2591035) *Amkhera 2*
Phasing: Pottery (1c to 6)
S163 – Settlement mound
S508 , S509 – Sculpture pile (both in worship)
SC367 Temple: Brahmanical (774210, 2591048) *Shankar ji ka sthan*
Temple remains to north of mound, on other side of *nāla*. Phasing: Architecture (6): Sculpture (4 to 6)
S367 – Temple remains: Brahmanical (in worship)
SC506 Tank (774512, 2591376)
S511 – Tank

SG051 Katsari (settlement). Sector: 3

Small hill c. 1 km south of Amkhera Bhauji colony, on the southern bank of the perennial *nāla* which flows W-E from Bhagvanpur colony to the River Betwa. Settlement situated on northern slopes of hill, just above modern village. Consists of c. 20 stone structures.
SC164 Settlement (774704, 2590439) *Katsari kherai*
S164 – Hillside basti
S612 – Natural shrine: modern cult-spot in centre of settlement, consisting of 'wishing' tree, decorated with numerous cloth bundles.
S613 – Sculpture pile (in worship)
SC165 Tank (774438, 2590655)
Dried up village tank situated to the west of the modern village.
S165 – Tank

SG052 Kherai khera (settlement). Sector: 2a

Agricultural plain east of Sanchi, c. 1.5 km south of Mehgaon.
SC166 Settlement (783263, 2594446)
Low, heavily eroded mound. Phasing: Pottery (1d to 7): Sculpture (7)
S166 – Settlement mound
S615 – Natural shrine: Djinn Maharaj platform beneath Pipal tree, in centre of mound, with modern terracotta horses.
S616 – Sculpture pile (in worship)
SC686 Temple: Brahmanical (783333, 2594334)
Phasing: Sculpture (7)
S614 – Temple remains: Brahmanical (in worship)

SG053 Amoni ka khera (settlement). Sector: 3

Agricultural land situated in narrow valley, set amidst densely forested hills c. 4 km south of Sonari. Forms the next valley below Bhagvanpur colony.
SC167 Settlement (774911, 2587433)
Large mound, situated in the midst of several converging nålas, the largest one of which is perennial. Phasing: Pottery (1d to 7)
S167 – Settlement mound

SG053c Amoni ka khera (background landscape). Sector: 3

SC168 Background landscape (773875, 2587471) *Rajanal*
Popular cult-spot situated at the source of perennial *nāla*, c. 1.10 km NW of Amoni ka khera. The modern shrine here is occupied by a resident priest. Despite the remote location, the promise of all-year round water attracts farmers and goatherders for many miles around. At the time of our visit, there were over 30 people congregated here. Phasing: Sculpture (6)
S168 – Natural shrine
S617 – Sculpture pile (in worship)

SG054 Ucher (settlement). Sector: 1b

Small, isolated hill (450 m), 3 km NNW of Sanchi.
Modern village situated on eastern lower slopes of hill, and extending into ploughed fields below. That the site overlies ancient settlement is attested by pottery and sculptural remains.
SC170 Settlement (778575, 2602513)
Phasing: Pottery (1d to 7)
S170 – Hillside basti
S618 , S619 , S620 , S621 – Sculpture pile (all in worship)
SC171 Tank (778568, 2602779)
Dried up village tank situated to north of modern village.
S171 – Tank
SC172 Temple: Unknown/mixed cult (778543, 2602727)
Outlines of various stone structures at edge of tank. Phasing: Sculpture (6)
S172 (2) – Temple: Unknown/mixed cult

SG054b Ucher (ritual). Sector: 1b

Small, isolated hill (450 m), 3 km NNW of Sanchi.
SC173 Terraced fortification (778077, 2602567)
The southern side of the hill is built up into a high stepped terrace, following the contours, and forming a kind of encasement around the hill. Seems to have acted as a kind of fortification, whereas the NE side of the hill is 'naturally' protected by sheer cliffs.
Phasing: Pottery (1c to 3b)
S173 – Terraced fortification (in worship)
SC534 Building cluster (778227, 2602553)
Various structural outlines on summit of hill, but too heavily disturbed for planning.
S622 – Building cluster

SG055 Berkheri (settlement). Sector: 1a

Agricultural plain c. 3.5 km NNW of Sanchi.
SC174 Settlement (778298, 2604409)
Large oblong shaped mound situated on west bank of large perennial *nāla*, which flows W-E towards River Bes. Partially occupied by modern two-house dwelling. Heavily disturbed outlines of two stone structures at the western

edge of mound. Phasing: Pottery (published) (1d to 6): Sculpture (6)

S174 – Settlement mound

S507 – Natural shrine: modern shrine, known as Mahmbai ka sthan or Gosai baba, built into roots of large Pipal tree. Situated at western edge of mound.

S512 – Sculpture pile (in worship)

SG056 Mehgaon (settlement). Sector: 2a

Agricultural plain east of Sanchi. Situated c. 3 km SE of Sanchi.
Large modern village situated on slight mound, which becomes more prominent on the east side of the village. Given the number of early sculptures, one may assume that this was an important settlement in ancient times. Even today, it is the largest village in the area.

SC368 Temple: Brahmanical (783127, 2596739)
Temple mound standing at height of 2 m in middle of village. Phasing: Architecture (6): Sculpture (4 to 6)

S368 – Temple remains: Brahmanical

SC389 Settlement (783280, 2596547)
Phasing: Pottery (1d to 3b)

S389 – Settlement mound

S625 – Sculpture pile (in worship)

SC390 Tank (783553, 2597043)
Remains of large, dried up village tank NE of the village. Enclosed on the west and south side by large embankments (surviving height: 1.90 m). Most of the facing has been removed, but a remaining portion, consisting of four courses of dressed stone masonry (surviving height: 0.80 m) has survived on the western inner face. Phasing: Sculpture (6)

S390 – Tank

S624 – Pillar

SG057 Khamkhera (settlement). Sector: 3

Small solitary hill (460 m), immediately east of Kharitol hill. Overlooks the northern bank of the perennial stream which flows W-E from Besar Talai colony to the River Betwa. Modern village situated at northern base of hill. Most probably overlies ancient settlement as attested by sculptural fragments.

SC392 Settlement (776788, 2592228)

S392 – Modern settlement

S627 – Sculpture pile

SG057b Khamkhera (ritual). Sector: 3

SC391 Terraced fortification (776736, 2592079) *Kot Toriya*
Summit of hill encased by stepped terrace, similar to Ucher hill. Rises from within few metres of large boundary wall (solid, homogeneous core) running approx. midway around hill. Large quantities of brick fragments strewn all over the site.

S391 – Terraced fortification

S630 – Natural shrine: Djinn Maharaj shrine (terracotta horses set on platform) on summit of hill.

SC535 Building cluster (776701, 2592114)
A number of heavily disturbed structural outlines are situated in the area between the boundary wall and the terracing.

S629 (6) – Building cluster

SC536 Fortification wall (776734, 2592079)

S628 – Fortification wall

SG058 Tijalpur (settlement). Sector: 3

Small, solitary hill (450 m). One of series of prominent hills in otherwise flat, agricultural plain. Situated c. 7.5 km south of Sanchi.
Most of hill occupied by modern village, which given sculptural remains, clearly overlies ancient settlement.

SC393 Settlement (777181, 2590390)

S393 – Hillside basti

SC445 Tank (776813, 2590537)
Large village tank at western base of hill. Phasing: Sculpture (4)

S445 – Tank

SC691 Temple: Brahmanical
Phasing: Sculpture (6 to 7)

S631 – Temple remains: Brahmanical

SG059 Barahi khas (settlement). Sector: 3

Small isolated hill (440 m), set amidst agricultural plain c. 2 km SE of Katsari. River Betwa flows around 1 km to the east. Modern village situated at western base of hill.

SC395 Settlement (776705, 2588980)

S395 – Modern settlement

S635 – Sculpture pile (in worship)

SC396 Tank (776330, 2588835)
Ancient village tank situated at western base of hill.

S396 – Tank

SG059b Barahi khas (ritual). Sector: 3

SC394 Monastery (776588, 2588874)
Square enclosure (45 x 40 m) lined on north, east, and south walls with narrow rectangular rooms (c. 9 x 4 m). Walls of outer-facing, rubble-infill variety. Surviving ht: 0.65 m; wd: 1.05 m. Low platform (1.10 x 1.40 m) in centre of courtyard. High, rectangular platform (10 x 3.80 m) abuts inner western wall. Phasing: Architecture (2)

S394 – Courtyard monastery (rectangular)

S632 , S633 – Stupa bases (both in worship)

SC681 Temple: Brahmanical (776621, 2588839)
Phasing: Sculpture (6 to 7)

S634 – Temple remains: Brahmanical (in worship)

SG061 Pagneswar (settlement). Sector: 2b

Small hillock (440 m), situated c. 300 m SE of a major crossing over the River Betwa.
Entire hill occupied by modern village. Evidently overlies ancient settlement as attested by sculptural remains.

SC397 Settlement (779760, 2594733)

S397 – Hillside basti

S517 – Sculpture pile (in worship)

SC398 Rock-shelter (779693, 2594955)
Number of heavily eroded rock-shelters on eastern side of hill.

S398 (3) – Rock-shelter

S399 (2) – Natural shrine: two prominent shaped rocky outcrops at northern base of hill. Daubed with red paint, indicating their 'sacred' status.

SC400 Temple: Brahmanical (779306, 2594662)
Incorporated into two modern temples on east bank of River Betwa. Situated next to bridge. The only crossing over River Betwa south of Rangai. Phasing: Sculpture (6)

S 400 , S518 – Temple remains: Brahmanical (both in worship)

SC507 Temple: Brahmanical (779743, 2594740)
Converted mosque Phasing: Islamic architecture (to): Sculpture (6 to 7)

S515 – Temple remains: Brahmanical (in worship)

SC697 Temple: Brahmanical (779751, 2594763)
Phasing: Sculpture (3b to 6)

S516 – Temple remains: Brahmanical

SG062 Dhobakheri (settlement). Sector: 2a

Agricultural plain east of the River Betwa, directly opposite Pipalia. Although only 2 km SE of Sanchi, belongs to a distinct geographical sector because of the lack of adequate crossing places on this part of the Betwa. At present in order to reach Dhobakheri, it is necessary to go via Pagneswar, which results in a round-trip of c. 8 km. Given the importance of the eastern area in ancient times, it is possible that the two areas were linked by ferry-boats.

SC401 Settlement (780220, 2596735)
Low mound on the east bank of the River Betwa, occupied by modern village. Phasing: Sculpture (5 to 7)

S401 – Settlement mound

S547 – Sculpture pile (in worship)

SG062b Dhobakheri (background landscape). Sector: 2a

SC402 Background landscape (780741, 2597217)
Modern cult spot situated c. 800 m NE of Dhobakheri, on the eastern bank of River Betwa, and eastern bank of perennial *nāla* which flows from the south (therefore a '*sangham*'). The site is also shared by villagers from Dhaniakheri,

situated 300 m further south. Phasing: Sculpture (9)

S402 – Natural shrine: small enclosure, dominated by a large Banyan tree. A modern Hanuman image stands on the central platform.

SG063 Dhaniakheri (settlement). Sector: 2a

Agricultural land east of the River Betwa, directly opposite Pipalia.
SC403 Settlement (781207, 2596742)
Low mound situated around 300 m south of the River Betwa. Occupied by modern village.

S403 – Settlement mound
S636 – Sculpture pile

SG064 Tajpura shur (settlement). Sector: 2a

Agricultural land on the eastern side of the River Betwa, c. 2.25 km east of Sanchi.
SC404 Settlement (782774, 2598131)
Low settlement mound, occupied by modern village. Original settlement was much larger than it is today, extending to the east and SE of the main mound, in the vicinity of the ancient village tank. Here, a raised bit of scrub land is known locally as 'kherai'. Phasing: Pottery (1d to 7)

S404 – Settlement mound
S407, S513 – Sculpture pile

SC405 Tank (782864, 2597981)
Ancient, dried-up village tank, around 200 m SE of main settlement mound. No evidence of stone facing.

S405 – Tank

SC406 Temple: Brahmanical (782900, 2597998)
Temple remains on eastern bank of ancient village tank. Phasing: Sculpture (2 to 6)

S406 – Temple remains: Brahmanical (in worship)

SG064b Tajpura shur (background landscape). Sector: 2a

SC382 Background landscape (781628, 2598117) *Birvan Baba*
Modern cult spot between main settlement mound and River Betwa to the east.

S382 – Natural shrine: painted stones installed under a Chola (Palash) tree;worshipped as Birvan Baba.

SG065 Anori (settlement). Sector: 1a

Agricultural plain, c. 4.5 km NW of Sanchi, on the southern bank of perennial *nāla* which flows W-E towards the River Bes.
SC409 Settlement (778260, 2603963)
Modern village situated on slightly raised ground at the junction of two perennial streams. No archaeological remains discernable but presence of ancient settlement suggested by bauri in fields to SW.

S409 – Modern settlement

SG065b Anori (background landscape). Sector: 1a

SC408 Background landscape (777728, 2603866)
Ancient, square bauri, lined with well-built stone masonry facing, situated in fields SW of modern village.
Phasing: Water architecture (6)

S408 – Well
S514 – Natural shrine: Djinn Maharaj shrine next to bauri, under Banyan tree (terracotta horses set on platform).

SG066 Torin hill (ritual). Sector: 4

Solitary, oval-shaped hill (452 m), running NW to SE. Situated around 4 km NNW of Udayagiri, on the east bank of the River Bes.
SC410 Stupa (777989, 2606445)
Entire hilltop covered with heavily disturbed remains of various monastic structures. The most discernible features include: square, walled enclosure (71.5 x 71.5 m) with stupa in centre (diameter: 10.5 m; surviving height: 0.5 m). Entrance in south. Walls of outer-facing, rubble-infill variety (average width: 97 cm). Second walled compound (64.1 x 64.1 m) to NW. Entrance on southern wall, and stupa remains in centre (diameter: 8.15 m). Walls of outer-facing, rubble-infill variety (average width: 1.16 m). Phasing: Architecture (2)

S410 – Enclosure
S637 – Sculpture pile (in worship)
S638 – Stupa

SC411 Monastery (777878, 2606679)
Series of interconnected courtyard monasteries with regular-sized, square cells. Phasing: Architecture (4)

S411 (30) – Interconnected courtyard monastery
S641 – Stupa

SC412 Tank (777905, 2606602)
Small, dried up tank NW of the northern-most stupa enclosure. No signs of stone facing.

S412 – Tank

SC537 Stupa (777957, 2606578)
Phasing: Architecture (2)

S639 – Enclosure
S640 – Stupa

SC705 Monastery (777929, 2606635)
Cluster of single and double roomed structures with boulder walls, to east of courtard monastery complex. Phasing: Architecture (2)

S1116 – Rectangular monastery

SG066a Torin (settlement). Sector: 4

Modern village situated on lower, SE slopes of hill.
SC413 Settlement (778374, 2606383)

S413 – Modern settlement

SG067 Rajatalai (settlement). Sector: 1b

Large hill (520 m), c. 2.5 km SW of Gulgaon. Goldoria hill is situated directly to the NW (1 km) on opposite side of the hill.
SC414 Settlement (773923, 2598486)
Settlement situated on lower, SE slope of hill. Consists of around 30 heavily disturbed, stone structures. Difficult to quantify due to dense jungle coverage. Phasing: Pottery (4 to 7): Sculpture (7)

S414 – Hillside basti
S642 – Sculpture pile (in worship)

SC415 Tank (773978, 2598376)
Large, dried up tank situated at base of hill. No sign of stone facing.

S415 – Tank

SG068 Salamatpur hill (settlement). Sector: 1b

Small, isolated hill (460 m), c. 5 km SW of Sanchi.
SC416 Settlement (773695, 2596709)
Modern village situated on western slope of hill, extending as far as modern Salamatpur, situated on the low-lying ground. Evidently overlies ancient settlement, as attested by discovery of several heavily disturbed structural outlines on the summit of the hill. Phasing: Pottery (1c to 7)

S416 – Hillside basti
S643 (3) – Natural shrine: several Devi shrines (unhewn, painted stones set on platforms).

SG070 Salamatpur hill (2) (locale). Sector: 1b

Small, isolated hill (height: 440m), situated midway between Salamatpur and Dhakna hill.
SC417 Locale (774835, 2596907)
Prehistoric 'locale' as attested by numerous microlithic flakes and cores. Any evidence for any structural remains was precluded by stone-quarrying damage. Phasing: Stone tools (1b)

S417 – Locale

SG071 Bilori 2 (settlement). Sector: 4

Small, isolated hill (471 m), c. 2.25 km south of Ahmadpur hill. Situated in otherwise flat, agricultural plain north of the River Bes.
SC419 Settlement (775193, 2610329)
Modern village situated on lower, southern slopes of hill. Most probably occupies site of ancient settlement, as attested by sculptural remains. Phasing: Pottery (1d to 7)

S419 – Hillside basti
SC656 Temple: Brahmanical (775318, 2610305)
Phasing: Sculpture (6 to 7)
S645 – Temple remains: Brahmanical (in worship)

SG071b Bilori 2 (ritual). Sector: 4

Small, isolated hill (471 m), c. 2.25 km south of Ahmadpur hill. Situated in otherwise flat, agricultural plain north of the River Bes.
SC418 Building cluster (775115, 2610456)
Large number of heavily disturbed structural outlines, covering most of the summit of the hill. The majority are rectangular or square in shape. In the centre, is a stone platform. At the southern edge of the hill, stone quarrying has resulted in large section. The remains of stone walls are visible at a depth of c. 1.5 m, built directly on top of the natural bedrock.
S418 – Building cluster
S644 – Platform

SG072 Khamtala (settlement). Sector: 4

Agricultural plain, c. 1.5 km north of River Bes.
SC420 Settlement (777055, 2610376)
Settlement mound. Partially occupied with modern village. Phasing: Pottery (1d to 7): Sculpture (6)
S1021 – Pillar (in worship)
S420 – Settlement mound
S646 – Sculpture pile
SC421 Tank (776721, 2610431)
Ancient village tank (with water), to west of village. Embankments faced with stone. Phasing: Sculpture (6)
S421 – Tank (in worship)
S648 – Pillar (in worship)
SC685 Temple: Brahmanical (776823, 2610385)
Phasing: Sculpture (4 to 7)
S647 – Temple remains: Brahmanical (in worship)

SG073 Bankheri (settlement). Sector: 4

Agricultural plain, c. 0.5 km north of River Bes, and 5.5 km NW of Udayagiri.
SC422 Settlement (777022, 2609146)
Low mound, situated c, 1 km south of modern Bankheri (the latter is now more or less conflated with Khamkhera). Regarded in local memory as the old settlement of Khamtala. Encircled by several *nālas*.
S422 – Settlement mound
S649 – Sculpture pile (in worship)

SG076 Bagoda (ritual). Sector: 1b

Large hill (552 m), c. 2 km north of Bamhora
SC175 Rock-shelter (763728, 2603226)
Painted rock-shelter (Maheswari 1997). Phasing: Paintings (1b)
S175 – Rock-shelter
SC176 Stupa (763688, 2603150)
Outline of stupa and rectangular monastery (Maheswari 1997) Phasing: Architecture (2)
S176 – Stupa

SG077 Bala barkhera (ritual). Sector: 1b

Small hill (480 m), c. 2 km north of Bagoda.
SC177 Stupa (762126, 2603510)
Stupa outline (Maheswari 1997). Phasing: Architecture (2)
S177 (3) – Stupa

SG078 Bamhora (ritual). Sector: 1b

Small, isolated hill (480 m), c. 1.5 km NW of Sayargaon.
SC178 Rock-shelter (765220, 2601899)
Two painted rock-shelters (Maheswari 1997). Phasing: Paintings (1b)
S178 (2) – Rock-shelter
SC179 Stupa (765198, 2601880) *Banjari ka cabutra*
Outline of stupa (diameter: 5 m), and platform, 'Typically Mauryan sized bricks' (Maheswari 1997). Phasing: Architecture (2)
S179 – Stupa

SG081 Sonthiya (settlement). Sector: 2b

Small hill (480 m) east of River Betwa, which forms the northernmost part of a series of hills, beginning with Morel khurd in the south.
SC180 Settlement (785873, 2599238) *Sonthiya-Shiampur basti*
Low mound, formed from eroded stone, rather than mud structural remains. Situated on stoney waste-land around 300 m south of modern Sonthiya village. Several heavily disturbed structural outlines still visible, but most of the stones have been removed (apparently by stone-merchants from Vidisha). Situated on southern bank of *nāla*, which has a perennial pool. Phasing: Pottery (1d to 2)
S180 – Settlement mound
SC181 Tank (786390, 2599149) *Sonthiya-Shiampur basti*
Dried up village tank between Shiampur and modern Sonthiya village. Stone faced embankment on the western side, with seven courses of masonry still standing.
S181 'Sonthiya/Shiampur basti' – Tank
SC384 Settlement (786096, 2599485) *Sonthiya village*
S384 – Modern settlement

SG081b Sonthiya (background landscape). Sector: 2b

SC385 Background landscape (786751, 2598977) *Sonthiya village*
Modern cult spot on summit of hill, consisting of platform with unhewn stones.
S385 – Natural shrine

SG082 Sonthiya kherai 2 (settlement). Sector: 2a

Agricultural plain 1 km SW of Sonthiya village.
SC182 Settlement (786101, 2598649) *Sonthiya kherai*
Oblong settlement mound, running W-E. Situated in agricultural plain, c. 700 m south of Shiampur basti. Positioned on eastern bank of Kariya *nāla*, a large perennial stream which flows S-N towards River Betwa. It also acts as the demarcation for the boundary between districts Vidisha (NE) and Raisen (SW). Phasing: Pottery (1c to 7)
S182 – Settlement mound

SG083 Pathari kapasia (settlement). Sector: 2a

Agricultural plain to east of the long line of hills, which begins at Morel khurd in the south.
SC183 Settlement (789459, 2598876)
High settlement mound c. 800 m NW of Pathari. Phasing: Pottery (1d to 7)
S183 – Settlement mound
S650 – Modern temple (in worship)

SG084 Pathari kativarat (settlement). Sector: 2b

Scattered around hill (490 m), second in line of hills, which ends in the SE with Morel khurd.
SC184 Settlement (788701, 2598505) *Kativarat*
Low mound formed from eroded stone, rather than mud structural remains. Several heavily disturbed structural remains on the summit of the mound. Phasing: Pottery (1d to 7)
S184 – Settlement mound
SC187 Temple: Brahmanical (788735, 2598592) *Kativarat*
Sculptural remains stored in one of rock-shelters above (657) Phasing: Architecture (6): Sculpture (6)
S187 – Temple remains: Brahmanical

SG084b Pathari kativarat (background landscape). Sector: 2b

Hill (490 m), second in line of hills, which ends in the SE with Morel khurd.
SC185 Rock-shelter *Kativarat*
Series of rock-shelters formed by the tilting uplift action of the rocky outcrops at the NE edge of the hill. Some of these contain heavily eroded paintings, mainly in red. The best preserved painting is situated in the southern-most shelter, consisting of a spiral pattern, a goose, and a series of horned animals. Large

scatters of microlithic tools outside the shelters. Phasing: Paintings (1b)

S186 (5 W) – Rock-shelter cluster

SC538 Rock-shelter (788632, 2598449) *Kativarat*

S185 – Rock-shelter (in worship)

SC539 Rock-shelter (788740, 2598405) *Kativarat*

Rock-shelter containing sculpture from temple mound below (187)

S656 – Sculpture pile (in worship)

S657 – Rock-shelter

SG084c Pathari kativarat (reservoir). Sector: 2b

SC188 Dam (789076, 2598174) *Kativarat*

Between the line of rock-shelters formed by the uptilting rocks, and the hill immediately above, is a flat rocky plateau. The remains of an earthern embankment runs N-S, which originally would have stored water in the area over the rocky plateau. Few blocks of stone facing survive on the inner (western) side. Phasing: Dam (2)

S188 – Dam

SC657 Reconstructed reservoir (789059, 2598175)

Phasing: Dam (2)

S1023 – Reconstructed reservoir

SG084d Pathari/Gehunkheri (settlement). Sector: 2a

Remains of settlement on raised, rocky ground which abutts northern base of hill, and extends over the ploughed area c. 225 m to the NE.

SC475 Settlement (787592, 2599071) *Gehunkheri*

Phasing: Pottery (1d to 7)

S475 – Settlement mound

S651 , S652 – Sculpture pile (both in worship)

SG085 Dhanora kherai (settlement). Sector: 2b

Low-grade agricultural land east of Morel khurd hill.

SC189 Settlement (790591, 2596449)

High settlement mound, c. 500 m SW of modern Dhanora village. Positioned on the bank of a small *nāla* which flows NE to SW. Covered with heavily disturbed structural outlines. Most of the surface stone has been removed (apparently by stone-merchants from Vidisha). Phasing: Pottery (1d to 3b)

S189 – Settlement mound

SG085b Dhanora kherai (background landscape). Sector: 2b

SC540 Background landscape (791006, 2596241)

Muslim cult spot on small hill to south-east of Dhanora kherai settlement mound.

S658 – Natural shrine

SG087 Morel khurd village (settlement). Sector: 2b

Low-lying rocky scrub (460 m) c. 1.5 km east of Morel khurd stupa site. Surrounded by poor, sandy agricultural land.

SC190 Settlement (792611, 2594161)

Modern village situated on the lower western slopes of rocky scrubland, with ancient tank.

S190 – Modern settlement

S660 – Sculpture pile (in worship)

SC541 Tank (792669, 2594335)

Dried up tank with stone embankments.

S661 – Tank

SG088 Kanpohra (settlement). Sector: 2b

Low rocky hill beyind Morel khurd village.

SC191 Temple: Brahmanical (793845, 2594436) *Agrola*

Small temple mound next to quarry. Sculpture from here stored in stone enclosure at stone quarry. Phasing: Architecture (7): Pottery (1d to 7): Sculpture (7): Water architecture (6)

S191 – Temple remains: Brahmanical (in worship)

S192 – Well

SC387 Settlement (794170, 2593444)

Modern village situated on side of hill.

S387 – Modern settlement

SC658 Rock-shelter (794121, 2593309) *Gufa Mandir*

Modern temple (Gufa mandir) built around natural cave.

S1024 – Rock-shelter/shrine (in worship)

SG088b Kanpohra (Quarry). Sector: 2b

Huge sandstone quarry (still in use), which Bhandarkar (1913–14, 192) suggested was one of the major sources for the stone railings at the Heliodorus pillar site.

SC386 Quarry (793791, 2594566) *Agrola*

S386 – Quarry

SG090 Mawasa (ritual). Sector: 2b

Prominent, isolated hill (491 m), c. 1 km south of Morel khurd hill. Surrounded on all sides by agricultural plain. Known locally as Mawasa, but the nearest village is Nihalpur, situated at the SE base of the hill.

Buddhist complex built on three levels.

SC193 Stupa (791316, 2591858) *Upper tier*

Large stupa (diameter: 7.5 m; surviving ht: 1.20 m), set on square platform (10 x 10 m; ht: 1.40 m; stone facing: c. 45 x 30 x 150 cm. One of stone facing slabs on eastern side (44 x 28 x 20 cm) bears inscription in Brahmi: *makaḍeyena karapite*). Surrounded by walled enclosure (74 x74 m), lined with rectangular rooms (30 x 10 m). Phasing: Architecture (2): Inscription (unpublished) (2)

S193 – Stupa

SC194 Fortification wall (791271, 2591845) *Upper tier*

Massive boundary wall runs around hill on NE, SW and east sides. Wd: 2 m; Surviving ht: 1 m. Homogeneous core of large unhewn boulders, dressed stone masonry facing.

S194 – Fortification wall

SC195 Monastery (791427, 2591808) *Middle tier*

Middle-tier monastic complex. Linked with upper and lower tiers by stone-paved pathway. Boundary wall on eastern edge. Two solid platforms, one on either side of the main entrance. Surmounted by single-roomed structure. Courtyard type monastery c. 20 m to the north. Phasing: Architecture (2)

S195 – Courtyard monastery (on platform)

SC196 Monastery (791567, 2591708) *Atari/Kacheri ('court'). Lower tier*

Lower-tier monastic complex set on solid platform (20 x 20 ml ht: 4 m) constructed from large stone blocks (1.0 x 0.50 m). Approached from east by external stairway (wd: 1.80 m) at the northern and southern corners. Lined with rectangular rooms. Boundary wall runs along eastern edge of hill (wd: 2 m). Connected to middle tier by paved pathway. Phasing: Architecture (2)

S196 – Platformed monastery (with rectangular rooms)

SC197 Background landscape (791011, 2592243)

Remains of temple at northern base of hill. Phasing: Sculpture (4)

S197 – Sculpture pile

SC478 Monastery (791315, 2591858) *Upper tier*

Rectangular rooms formed by radials projecting from central stupa Phasing: Architecture (2)

S478 (3) – Rectangular/courtyard monastery

SC659 Monastery (791395, 2591866) *Middle tier*

Around 80 m to the North-West of the second tier's entrance is a second monastery (30 x 17 m), in a much worse state of repair than the first. This also follows a courtyard plan (30 x 17 m) surrounded by rectangular rooms on the south, west and east sides, and with a raised platform at the northern end. Phasing: Architecture (2 to 4)

S1025 – Courtyard monastery (rectangular)

SC660 Temple: Buddhist (791581, 2591713) *Lower tier*

Well-preserved single-roomed structure (10 x 8 m at the base, surviving up to about 6 courses, to a height of 2.35 m at the base of the collapsed roof). Constructed from massive stone masonry blocks of similar proportions to those used in the main platform and staircases. The building is entered from the west by a 1.35 m-high doorway, with a lower, 1m-high, door frame set behind the outer doorway by 1 m. Phasing: Architecture (2)

S1026 – Temple remains: Buddhist

SC662 Temple: Buddhist (791414, 2591815) *Middle tier*

Boulder outline of apsidal temple (?) on middle tier to west of monastery. Phasing: Architecture (2)

S1028 – Temple remains: Buddhist

SC704 Temple: Buddhist (791565, 2591724) *Lower tier*

Boulder outline of apsidal temple on lower tier to NW of free-standing temple (SC660). Phasing: Architecture (2)

S1112 – Temple: Buddhist

SC722 Stupa (791615, 2591726) *Lower tier*
Small square stupa platform on lower ground to east of lower monastic platform.
S1027 – Stupa

SG092 Nihalpur/Dandoli kherai (settlement). Sector: 2b

Agricultural plain immediately south of Mawasa hill.
Large settlement area extending from low settlement mound, occupied by Nihalpur village, to second barren mound (Dandoli kherai) to the east. The latter is encircled on all sides by perennial *nāla*, which has created a deep section (5–6 m), on north side of mound. Walls of stone structures are visible at a depth of 3.5 m, overlying pottery deposits. Pottery continues up to 2 m above water level, when natural black cotton soil is reached.
SC198 Settlement (791445, 2591477) *Nihalpur*
Phasing: Pottery (1d to 7)
S198 – Settlement mound
S505 – Sculpture pile (in worship)
SC199 Temple: Brahmanical (791357, 2591630) *Nihalpur*
Situated south of settlement within Mango and Neem plantation (45 x 50 m; ht: 1 m). Phasing: Architecture (6): Sculpture (5 to 6)
S199 – Temple remains: Brahmanical
SC200 Tank (791466, 2591640)
Dried up village tank 100 m east of temple mound.
S200 – Tank
SC201 Settlement (791706, 2591391) *Dandoli kherai*
Phasing: Pottery (1d to 2)
S201 – Settlement mound
S202 – Well

SG095a Chandna Gorpur Kherai (settlement). Sector: 2b

Small hill (440 m) c. 1 km SW of modern Chandna village.
SC203 Settlement (788416, 2591335)
Settlement situated on NE slope of hill. Consists of c. 20 heavily disturbed stone structures. Overlooking ancient tank to the east.
S203 – Hillside basti

SG095b Chandna hill (settlement). Sector: 2b

Small hill (460 m), c. 2 km south of Morel khurd hill.
SC205 Settlement (789258, 2591821)
Ancient settlement situated on northern slopes of hill. Most of the site is now occupied by modern village, but few structural remains are still visible, around 150 metres to the SW of the village.
S205 – Hillside basti
S504 – Sculpture pile (in worship)

SG095c Chandna hill (reservoir). Sector: 2b

Small hill (460 m), c. 2 km south of Morel khurd hill.
SC204 Dam (788676, 2591167)
Ancient embankment running with slight curve, from NE to SW, between Chandna hill, and Chandna Gorpur kherai (SG095a). A second embankment runs west to join Salera hill. Sloped facing on inner side. Blocks are of small brick-size variety, as opposed to the large rectangular slabs at Nagauri. Recently rebuilt, and now holds water. Phasing: Dam (2): Sculpture (2)
S1100 – Sculpture pile
S204 – Dam
SC542 Reconstructed reservoir (788737, 2591148)
Phasing: Dam (2)
S665 – Reconstructed reservoir
SC696 Temple: Brahmanical (788911, 2591498)
Remains of temple on dam. Phasing: Sculpture (6)
S664 – Temple remains: Brahmanical (in worship)

SG095d Chandna hill (ritual). Sector: 2b

Extensive, interlinked Buddhist complex covering Chandna and Chandna Tohoria hills and some of the intervening low-lying land.
SC206 Building Religious (789168, 2591523) *Chandna*
Walled enclosure with entrance in north. (40.70 x 40.70 m; wall wd: 1 m). Large platform (29.60 x 16.30 m) in the SW corner. Small room (5.20 x 5.20 m) in the NE corner. Several circular outlines (diam: 1 m).
S206 – Platform
SC483 Fortification wall (789224, 2591541) *Chandna*
Boundary wall runs around SW and northern edges of hill, the eastern wall cutting the hill roughly in half (150 x 150 m). Walls (Wd: 1.55 m) of outer-facing, rubble-infill variety.
S483 – Fortification wall
SC663 Stupa (789295, 2591504) *Chandna*
Small stupa outline to east of outer boundary wall.
S1029 – Stupa
SC666 Fortification wall (789904, 2591735) *Chandna tohoria*
Summit of hill surrounded on all sides by boundary wall (60 x 60 m; width of wall: 1.60 m). Rubble infill, outer facing type.
S1033 – Fortification wall
SC208 Monastery (789879, 2591769) *Chandna tohoria*
Phasing: Architecture (2, 4)
S1034, S1035, S1036 – Stupa
S1039 – Natural shrine: small platform with stone painted in red at western extent of courtyard monastery.
S208 – Courtyard monastery
SC209 Monastery (789801, 2591692) *Chandna tohoria (lower)*
Outline of enclosure (35 x 35 m), lined with small cells (c. 3 x 3 m). Entrance in northern wall. Phasing: Architecture (4/5)
S209 – Courtyard monastery
SC665 Stupa (789697, 2591561) *Chandna tohoria*
Phasing: Architecture (2)
S1031, S1032 – Stupa
SC668 Building Religious (789887, 2591762) *Chandna tohoria*
Small building built on top of 0.5 m-high platform at centre of monastery complex, with three rooms. This may be later than the rest, due to homogeneous rubble appearance of walls (11 x 8 m).
S1037 – Building Religious
SC669 Building Religious *Chandna tohoria*
Rectangular roomed structure in the north (wall thickness: 80 cm) May be later. Rubble infill.
S1038 – Building Religious
SC670 Building Religious (789918, 2591675) *Chandna tohoria*
Outline of small (6 x 12 m) double-roomed structure at southern base of hill, to the east of the no-longer extant courtyard monastery.
S1040 – Building Religious
SC664 Stupa (789597, 2591442) *Chandna*
Heavily damaged stupa on square platform (c. 8 x 8 m; ht: 0.8 m), on the eastern finger which overlooks Chandna Tohoria. Very large blocks, rather like the scale of architecture at Mawasa. Phasing: Architecture (2)
S1030 – Stupa
SC207 Locale (789519, 2591929) *Chandna tohoria (b)*
According to locals, hill was once covered with structural remains, no longer visible due to stone quarrying activity.
S207 – Locale

SG098 Budha pahar (ritual). Sector: 4b

Prominent hill (480 m) in Shamshabad District.
SC471 Stupa (780221, 2629930)
Phasing: Architecture (2): Sculpture (3b)
S471 – Stupa
SC472 Rock-shelter (780260, 2629809)
Phasing: Paintings (1b)
S472 (5) – Rock-shelter

SG099 Morel kala (reservoir). Sector: 2b

Scrub land interspersed by number of small hillocks (440 m), c. 1 km SE of Mawasa.
SC211 Dam (792344, 2590678)
Large embankment which runs N-S from Morel Kala to Pali. Lined on both sides with well preserved facing, and upward slanting slabs. Phasing: Dam (2): Sculpture (3b)
S1120 – Spillway
S211 – Dam
S667 – Sculpture pile (in worship)
SC543 Reconstructed reservoir (792892, 2590037)
Phasing: Dam (2)
S666 – Reconstructed reservoir

SG099b Morel kala (settlement). Sector: 2b

Scrub land interspersed by number of small hillocks (440 m), c. 1 km SE of Mawasa.
Settlement situated on northern slopes of hill north of modern village. Consists of numerous structural outlines. Hill surrounded on all sides by large boundary wall (80 x 150 m). Various sculptural piles scattered through settlement, belonging to two (Jain and Śaiva) temples.
SC210 Settlement (793159, 2591369)
S210 – Hillside basti
SC371 Temple: Brahmanical (793158, 2591329)
Centre of settlement. Phasing: Sculpture (5 to 6)
S371 – Temple remains: Brahmanical (in worship)
S670 – Sculpture pile (in worship)
SC544 Settlement (792685, 2591073)
S668 – Modern settlement
S669 – Sculpture pile (in worship)
SC687 Temple: Jain (793165, 2591422)
Phasing: Sculpture (6)
S671 – Temple remains: Jain

SG100 Pali (settlement). Sector: 2b

Small hill/rocky scrub, 500 m SW of Morel kala.
Modern village situated on NW slopes of hill. Most probably underlain by ancient settlement as attested by sculptural remains, and ancient dam (SG099).
SC212 Settlement (792202, 2590377)
S212 – Hillside basti
S672 – Sculpture pile (in worship)
SC213 Rock-shelter (792405, 2590122) *Gufa mandir*
Rock-shelter adapted into shrine.
S213 – Rock-shelter
S673 – Sculpture pile (in worship)

SG101 Andol (settlement). Sector: 2b

Small hill (460 m), c. 200 m SW of modern village.
Large settlement including modern Andol village, two additional settlement areas to the south and SW.
SC214 Settlement (793943, 2589463) *Andol village*
Phasing: Water architecture (6)
S214 – Hillside basti
S215 – Well
SC216 Settlement (794536, 2588673) *Andol kherai (1)*
S216 – Hillside basti
S674 – Sculpture pile (in worship)
SC217 Tank (794572, 2588989) *Andol kherai (1)*
Ancient, dried up tank at northern base of hill, just below ancient settlement. Remains of stone facing still visible.
S217 – Tank
SC218 Settlement (793701, 2588965) *Andol kherai (2)*
S218 – Hillside basti
SC372 Temple: Brahmanical (794585, 2589519)
Fields to east of modern Andol village. Phasing: Sculpture (6)
S372 – Temple remains: Brahmanical (in worship)

SG102 Sachet (settlement). Sector: 2a

Agricultural plain c. 6 km SE of Andher.
SC219 Settlement (800156, 2586243)
High settlement mound occupied by modern village. Phasing: Pottery (1b to 7): Pottery (published) (1b)
S219 – Settlement mound
S676 – Sculpture pile (in worship)
SC473 Temple: Brahmanical (800038, 2586555)
Base of temple at western foot of mound, with four courses of masonry. Phasing: Architecture (6): Sculpture (5 to 6)
S473 – Temple remains: Brahmanical (in worship)

SG105 Dhongari (settlement). Sector: 1a

Agricultural plain between Udayagiri and Sanchi.
'Site' situated between Udayagiri (SG031) and Sonapura Chak (SG031b). The site's local reputation as an ancient settlement is not supported archaeologically, and probably stems from the 'big stones' found in surrounding fields.
SC224 Memory site (782446, 2604479)
S224 – Natural shrine

SG106 Utari guhar (settlement). Sector: 1a

Agricultural plain between Udayagiri and Sanchi.
SC225 Settlement (782953, 2604063)
Settlement mound, just to the south of Dhongari, c. 0.25 to the west of River Betwa. Enclosed on the north and east by perennial *nālas*. Phasing: Pottery (1c to 3b)
S225 – Settlement mound

SG107 Kamapar saras (background landscape). Sector: 1b

Small rocky outcrop (from surrounding plain: 2 m), surrounded by agricultural plain between Sanchi and Udayagiri.
SC226 Background landscape (781945, 2602388)
Prehistoric 'locale' between Karhaiya and Kamapur, just to the west of the Sanchi-Bhopal railway. Extensive microlithic scatters.
S226 – Locale

SG108 Ram bhauri (background landscape). Sector: 1a

Agricultural plain between Udayagiri and Sanchi.
SC227 Temple: Brahmanical (781539, 2601224)
Ancient temple site c. 1.5 km NE of Sanchi, on the west side of the Vidisha-Sanchi road. Occupied by modern temple. Phasing: Sculpture (4 to 6): Water architecture (6)
S227 – Temple remains: Brahmanical (in worship)
S228 – Well

SG109 Karhaiya (settlement). Sector: 1a

Agricultural plain between Udayagiri and Sanchi.
SC229 Settlement (782890, 2602647)
Low settlement mound, occupied by modern village. Phasing: Sculpture (7)
S229 – Settlement mound
S681 – Sculpture pile (in worship)

SG110 Bighan village (settlement). Sector: 1a

Agricultural plain between Udayagiri and Sanchi.
SC230 Settlement (780392, 2605026)
Modern village situated on southern bank of River Bes.
S230 – Hillside basti
SC388 Ford (780342, 2605275)
Ancient ford, used for crossing river during summer months. One of the most direct routes to Bighan stupa site on opposite side of river.
S388 – Ford
SC446 Temple: Brahmanical (780418, 2604954)
Temple mound at southern edge of village. Phasing: Sculpture (6 to 7)
S446 – Temple remains: Brahmanical (in worship)

SG112 Daulatpur (settlement). Sector: 2a

Agricultural plain to east of Sanchi. Situated between Mehgaon and Alamkhera.
SC231 Settlement (784450, 2595494)
Low settlement mound with low-density pottery scatters. Ancestral connections with Mehgaon, to which the land belongs.
S231 – Settlement mound
S232 – Well
S682 – Natural shrine: Devi shrine (unhewn stone set on platform).

SG113 Alamkhera (settlement). Sector: 2a

Agricultural plain to east of Betwa, c. 5.5 km east of Sanchi.
SC233 Settlement (785261, 2595219)
Phasing: Pottery (1d to 7)

S233 – Settlement mound

SC234 Temple: Brahmanical (785211, 2595190)
Small temple mound on the summit of settlement mound. Phasing: Sculpture (6 to 7)

S234 – Temple remains: Brahmanical

SC235 Temple: Brahmanical (785252, 2595716)
Small temple mound c. 750 m to north of settlement mound. Large stone foundation blocks. A late medieval *sati* stone now stands on the site. Phasing: Architecture (4): Sculpture (7)

S235 – Temple remains: Brahmanical

SC706 Background landscape (785515, 2595462)
Modern cult spot to the east, midway between settlement mound and modern Alamkhera village.

S447 – Natural shrine: platform under large banyan tree.

SG114 Bhauliya (settlement). Sector: 2a

Agricultural land on east side of River Betwa.

SC236 Settlement (784334, 2594544)
Settlement mound situated to the south of Alamkhera, on the west bank of perennial *nāla*. Phasing: Pottery (1d to 2)

S236 – Settlement mound

SC448 Temple: Brahmanical (784456, 2594484)
Temple mound, c. 185 m east of settlement mound, situated on small piece of scrub-land. Existing trench behind main platform (3 x 0.50 m; depth, c. 0.80 m) reveals the following sequence:
level 1 – black cotton soil; level 2 – light pebbly soil (5 cm); level 3 – ashy layer (4 cm); level 4 – pottery and brick (20 cm). Phasing: Sculpture (7)

S448 – Temple remains: Brahmanical (in worship)

SG114a Bhauliya kherai (reservoir). Sector: 2a

SC237 Dam (784769, 2594210)
Heavily damaged embankment which would have dammed *nāla* running from north. Phasing: Dam (2)

S237 – Dam

SG115 Bhaijakhera (settlement). Sector: 2a

Agricultural plain to east of River Betwa, between Meghaon and Jhirniya.

SC238 Settlement (784863, 2597047)
Settlement mound occupied by single house.

S238 – Settlement mound

S683 – Sculpture pile (in worship)

SG117 Bishankhera (settlement). Sector: 2a

Agricultural land to east of River Betwa. Site situated on rocky ground (depth of soil over bedrock: c. 30cm), which skirts the western base of large hill (490 m), the other side of which is occupied by Pathari Kativarat.

SC239 Settlement (788478, 2596526)
Settlement situated on slightly raised ground at base of hill, SE of modern village. Large number of stone structural remains, with an average of one course of masonry still standing. Surrounded by boundary wall. Phasing: Pottery (2 to 7)

S239 – Hillside basti

S684 – Natural shrine: Devi shrine (large number of unhewn stones set on platform).

SG118 Murwara hill (ritual). Sector: 2b

Large hill (490 m), immediately south of Morel khurd hill. The other side of the hill is occupied by Pathari Kativarat.

SC240 Stupa (788585, 2596860)
Brick stupa immediately behind Bishankara (SG117).

S240 – Stupa

SC241 Stupa (788348, 2597916)
Stone stupa to the north of SC240. Phasing: Architecture (2)

S241 – Stupa

SC242 Stupa complex (787908, 2597942)
Around eight stone stupa outlines, to the north of SC242. Average diam: 3 m. Phasing: Architecture (4)

S242 (7) – Stupa complex

S685 – Stupa

SG118b Murwara hill (settlement). Sector: 2b

Large hill (490 m), immediately south of Morel khurd hill. The other side of the hill is occupied by Pathari Kativarat.

SC423 Settlement (787448, 2597247)
Settlement mound, partially occupied by modern village. Pottery found throughout existing section formed by modern road at SE edge of village, where mound has been ploughed down to height of c. 1 m. Phasing: Pottery (1d to 7): Water architecture (4)

S423 – Settlement mound

S424 – Well

S686 – Natural shrine: Djinn Maharaj shrine built into roots of large Banyan tree at centre of village.

SC449 Temple: Brahmanical (787373, 2597335)
High temple mound immediately west of settlement mound. Phasing: Sculpture (7)

S449 – Temple remains: Brahmanical (in worship)

SG120 Sankheri (settlement). Sector: 2b

Slightly raised ground amidst the agricultural plain east of the River Betwa, c. 3 km NW of Morel khurd.

SC425 Settlement (786651, 2595246)
Modern village situated on slightly raised ground. Ancient well lined with brick-sized stone facing, situated in ploughed fields c. 250 m to west of village.

S425 – Modern settlement

S426 – Well

SG121 Mahuakhera-Himatgarh (settlement). Sector: 2a

One of a series of ancient settlements on the bank of the Dabar *nāla*, a perennial stream which flows E-W, to the south of Morel khurd.
Two modern villages on either side of the Dabar *nāla*, evidently originally one large settlement.

SC427 Settlement (786833, 2592741) *Mahuakhera*

S427 – Settlement mound

SC430 Settlement (786748, 2612812) *Himatgarh*
Phasing: Pottery (1c to 7)

S430 – Settlement mound

S691 – Sculpture pile (in worship)

SC546 Temple: Brahmanical (786798, 2592522) *Mahuakhera*
Small temple mound (c.1m high) immediately east of *imli* tree with tiny 10th century fragments buried under *nāla* siltation. Phasing: Sculpture (6 to 7)

S687 – Sculpture pile (in worship)

S688 – Temple remains: Brahmanical

SG122 Alamkhera/Binjoli (background landscape). Sector: 2a

Agricultural land to east of River Betwa.

SC428 Tank (786398, 2595729)
Dried up circular tank, situated between Alamkhera and Binjoli kherai. Few remaining slabs of stone facing on east and south sides.

S428 – Tank

SG123 Devalkhera (settlement). Sector: 2a

One of a series of ancient settlements on the bank of the Dabar *nāla*, a perennial stream which flows E-W, to the south of Morel khurd.

SC429 Settlement (787478, 2592931)
High settlement mound, occupied by modern village. Situated on north bank of Dabar *nāla*, c. 2.5 km west of Morel khurd. Pottery visible in section formed by *nāla*, to depth of 3 m.Phasing: Pottery (1d to 3b)

S429 – Settlement mound

SC684 Temple: Brahmanical (787532, 2592871)
Phasing: Sculpture (4 to 6)

S689 – Temple remains: Brahmanical (in worship)

SG125 Parwariya/Arwariya (settlement). Sector: 2a

One of a series of ancient settlements on the bank of the Dabar *nāla*, a perennial stream which flows E-W, to the south of Morel khurd.
Two villages on either side of the Dabar *nāla*, evidently originally one large settlement.
SC431 Settlement (784820, 2592421) *Parwariya*
S431 – Settlement mound
SC450 Settlement (784816, 2592093) *Arwariya*
S450 – Settlement mound
S692 – Sculpture pile (in worship)

SG126 Chopra (settlement). Sector: 2a

Low-grade agricultural land c. 2 km west of Sonthiya.
SC432 Settlement (784511, 2599133)
Small modern village situated on more or less flat ground. According to locals, pottery is found when digging house foundations.
S432 – Modern settlement
S433 – Well (in worship)
S501 – Sculpture pile

SG127 Chirohli (settlement). Sector: 2a

Agricultural plain 2.5 km east of Sanchi
SC243 Settlement (783070, 2599150) *Chirohli kherai*
Low settlement mound, immediately north of modern Chirohli village. Phasing: Pottery (1d to 3b)
S243 (3) – Settlement mound
S694 – Sculpture pile
SC548 Settlement (782777, 2598800)
S500 – Sculpture pile (in worship)
S693 – Modern settlement

SG128 Chiroriya village (settlement). Sector: 2a

Agricultural plain, 4 km SE of Vidisha
Modern village with ancient temple remains.
SC244 Settlement (791164, 2601473)
S244 – Modern settlement
SC549 Temple: Brahmanical (791115, 2601338)
Phasing: Sculpture (6)
S695 – Temple remains: Brahmanical (in worship)

SG129 Chiroriya kherai (settlement). Sector: 2a

Agricultural plain, 4 km SE of Vidisha
Large settlement mound, now ploughed down into two separate mounds, the second, lower one situated c. 150 m further east. Situated amidst fields to east of modern Chiroriya village. Various stone structural fragments on barren ground towards summit of mound.
SC245 Settlement (792279, 2601728)
Phasing: Pottery (1d to 7)
S245 – Settlement mound
S696 – Sculpture pile (in worship)
S699 – Well
SC246 Temple: Brahmanical (792606, 2601649)
Small temple mound c. 150 m east of settlement mound. Phasing: Sculpture (6)
S246 – Temple remains: Brahmanical (in worship)

SG130 Bhauriya (settlement). Sector: 2a

Agricultural plain to SE of Vidisha, c. 1.5 km east of Chiroriya.
SC247 Settlement (793024, 2601175)
S247 – Modern settlement
SC451 Temple: Brahmanical (793123, 2601140)
Southern edge of village. Phasing: Sculpture (6)
S451 – Temple remains: Brahmanical (in worship)

SG131 Karaiya kherai (settlement). Sector: 2a

Agricultural plain, c. 4.5 km SE of Vidisha.
Modern village with sculpture stored on village platform.
SC248 Settlement (791470, 2603047)
S248 – Modern settlement
S697 – Sculpture pile

SG132 Madankheri (background landscape). Sector: 2a

Agricultural plain, c. 7 km SE of Vidisha.
SC452 Temple: Brahmanical (792609, 2602925)
Temple remains situated beneath large *imli* tree, between Karaiya kherai and Madankheri mound.
Phasing: Sculpture (7)
S452 – Temple remains: Brahmanical (in worship)
S698 – Natural shrine: imli tree with platform of unhewn stones.

SG132b Madankheri (settlement). Sector: 2a

Agricultural plain, c. 7 km SE of Vidisha.
SC249 Settlement (794366, 2602849)
Settlement mound c. 500 m west of modern Madankheri village. Phasing: Pottery (1d to 7)
S249 – Settlement mound

SG133 Parsora haveli (settlement). Sector: 2a

Small, prominent, isolated hill (480 m), surrounded by flat, agricultural land between Vidisha and Morel khurd, c. 5 km SE of Vidisha.
SC250 Settlement (791579, 2599216)
Modern village situated on lower slopes of hill. Evidently overlies ancient settlement, as attested by sculpture, and large quantities of pottery found by villagers when digging house foundations.
S250 – Hillside basti
S700 – Sculpture pile (in worship)
SC251 Temple: Brahmanical (791534, 2599248)
Modern Hanuman temple on summit of hill overlying an ancient stone platform. The surrounding area contains high quantities of brick fragments. Phasing: Sculpture (5 to 6)
S251 – Temple remains: Brahmanical (in worship)

SG134 Gehunkheri Bhairav (settlement). Sector: 2a

Agricultural land, c. 3 km south of Vidisha.
SC252 Settlement (787974, 2600518)
Low mound c. 500 m north of Gehunkheri village, occupied by a single house. Phasing: Pottery (3a to 3b)
S252 – Settlement mound
SC550 Temple: Brahmanical (787981, 2600513)
Sculptures, under worship, embedded in mud platform. Phasing: Sculpture (3b to 6)
S703 – Temple remains: Brahmanical
S704 – Sculpture pile (in worship)

SG135 Mori/Karariya kherai (background landscape). Sector: 2b

Large hill (480 m), first in long line of hills running roughly N-S from Pagneswar (c. 4 km south of Sanchi) to Raisen.
SC253 Rock-shelter (780088, 2593119)
Large rock-shelter on west side of Sanchi-Raisen road. Contains heavily eroded paintings in dark red (animals, and human hand-prints). Phasing: Paintings (1b)
S253 – Rock-shelter
S705 – Sculpture pile (in worship)
SC254 Rock-shelter (779998, 2593072)
Rock-shelter c. 30 m south of SC253. Contains prehistoric paintings of spotted animals. Phasing: Paintings (1b)
S254 – Rock-shelter

SG135b Mori/Karariya kherai (settlement). Sector: 2b

Remains of settlement at southern base of hill, consisting of large number of square and rectangular stone remains. Possibly the supporting settlement for the Buddhist site on the west of the hill (SG135c).

SC256 Settlement (779278, 2593354)
S256 (8) – Hillside basti

SG135c Mori/Karariya kherai (ritual). Sector: 2b

SC255 Stupa (778825, 2593688)
Stone platform (c. 10 x 10 m) and a stupa outline (diamater: 4 m). Phasing: Architecture (4)
S706 – Sculpture pile (in worship)
S707, S708 – Stupa
SC671 Building cluster (778856, 2593693)
Low mound on lower western slopes of hill, formed from ruined stone structures. Large number of faint structural outlines.
S255 (8) – Building cluster

SG137 Raisen (ritual). Sector: 3

Large prominent hill (540 m), c. 16 km SE of Sanchi.
SC453 Medieval fort/palace (783813, 2582431)
S453 – Palace
SC454 Stupa (783122, 2582179)
Well-preserved stupa (diam: 3.50 m; surviving ht: 1.50 m. Phasing: Architecture (2)
S454 – Stupa
SC456 Temple: Brahmanical (783584, 2582190)
Centre of fort area. Phasing: Sculpture (4)
S456 – Temple remains: Brahmanical
SC551 Fortification wall (783616, 2582078)
S709 – Fortification wall

SG137b Raisen (reservoir). Sector: 3

SC455 Dam (783090, 2583003)
Large dam running from western base of hills to large hill in west. Would have held up water on the southern side (*nālas* flowing from south and west). Phasing: Dam (1d/2)
S455 – Dam

SG138 Dhuladev (settlement). Sector: 2a

Agricultural land to south of Vidisha (c. 3.5 km). Between Sonthiya and Gehunkheri.
Naturally raised ground (440 m contour shown on Survey of India map), dominated by large *barghat* tree. Both of these features probably form the basis of the site's local repuation as an ancient settlement. However, no pottery or structural remains were found here to support this suggestion.
SC257 Memory site (787267, 2600287)
S257 – Natural shrine: memory site

SG139 Umariya kherai (settlement). Sector: 2a

Agricultural land to east of Sanchi, on the western bank of the Kariya *nāla*, a perennial stream which flows S-N from Morel khurd, meeting Betwa immediately east of Sanchi.
SC258 Settlement (785574, 2598260)
Settlement mound SW of the modern village of Umariya, and c. 1 km south of Sonthiya.
S258 – Settlement mound

SG140 Marwai (settlement). Sector: 1a

Agricultural land between Udayagiri and Sanchi (c. 2 km NW of Udayagiri). Large ancient settlement site, now partly occupied by modern village. A second smaller mound is situated just to the NE of the modern village.
SC259 Temple: Brahmanical (781468, 2603664)
Temple remains set on low mound in centre of village. Phasing: Sculpture (6)
S259 – Temple remains: Brahmanical
SC260 Math (781359, 2603734)
Remains of 10th century AD Saiva *math* in centre of village. Phasing: Architecture (6)
S260 – Math

SC262 Settlement (781310, 2603684)
Phasing: Water architecture (6)
S261 – Well
S262 – Settlement mound
SC263 Tank (781373, 2604024)
Remains of village tank in fields just to NW of SC474. Consists of embankment (height: 3 m; length: 225 m) orientated W-E. Several stone slabs visible at western end. Would have enclosed water body to south.
S263 – Tank
S714 – Sculpture pile (in worship)
SC474 Settlement (781824, 2603998)
Phasing: Pottery (1d to 7)
S474 – Settlement mound
S713 – Modern temple (in worship)

SG141 Marha kherai (settlement). Sector: 1a

Agricultural plain midway between Sanchi and Udayagiri.
Ploughed mound, standing at height of 1–2m in the midst of wheat fields. Dimensions: c. 70 x 70m. Stupa remains on summit.
SC264 Tank (779698, 2602856)
Low depression in field, c. 150 west of mound, which according to villagers, marks the site of an ancient tank.
S264 – Tank
SC458 Stupa (779806, 2602867)
Heavily disturbed stupa mound in middle of field. Diam: 10 m; surviving ht: 0.50 m. Phasing: Sculpture (2)
S458 – Stupa
SC558 Settlement (779808, 2602826)
Ploughed mound, standing at height of 1–2m in the midst of wheat fields. Dimensions: c. 70 x 70m.
S1140 – Settlement mound
S715 – Sculpture pile (in worship)

SG142 Marha/Chitiya (settlement). Sector: 1a

Agricultural plain c. 3 km WNN of Udayagiri on the southern bank of the River Bes.
SC265 Ford (779777, 2604540)
S265 – Ford
SC560 Settlement (779726, 2604341) *Marha*
Modern settlement with ancient sculpture pile.
S1117 – Sculpture pile
S718 – Modern settlement

SG143 Kanchanpura (ritual). Sector: 1b

Large hill (500 m), c. 3.5 km NW of Sanchi, on the lower western slopes of which Eran is situated.
SC267 Stupa (777104, 2602336)
Stupa remains. Diam: 5 m; surviving ht: 1m. Phasing: Architecture (2)
S267 – Stupa
SC479 Monastery (777295, 2602099)
Several heavily damaged rectangular structures c. 280 m east of stupa. Phasing: Architecture (2)
S479 (8) – Rectangular monastery

SG143b Kanchanpura (settlement). Sector: 1b

Large hill (500 m), c. 3.5 km NW of Sanchi, on the lower western slopes of which, Eran is situated.
SC266 Settlement (776563, 2602412)
Ancient settlement on lower, northern slopes of hill, just above modern village. Consists of around 30 heavily damaged structural remains.
S266 – Hillside basti

SG144 Dhaniakheri (settlement). Sector: 1a

Agricultural plain 5 km NW of Sanchi, on southern bank of perennial *nāla*.
SC268 Settlement (776138, 2603561)
Barren settlement mound immediately south of modern Dhaniakheri village. Phasing: Pottery (1d to 3b)

S268 – Settlement mound

SC269 Tank (776132, 2603529)
Remains of village tank immediately north of temple site, surviving as embankment (length: 260 m) orientated E-W. Stone facing visible on northern face, at west end of embankment.
S269 – Tank

SC459 Temple: Brahmanical (776223, 2603488)
Temple remains on low mound, occupied by modern temple, immediately north of settlement mound. Phasing: Sculpture (6)
S459 – Temple remains: Brahmanical (in worship)

SG145 Sukha (settlement). Sector: 1a

Agricultural land, c. 4 km west of Udayagiri. Situated on north bank of perennial *nāla*, which flows W-E towards River Bes.

SC270 Settlement (777423, 2604562) *Umakhera*
Settlement mound dominated by large *barghat* tree. NW of modern Sukha village (marked by 418 m spot-height on Survey of India map). Phasing: Pottery (1d to 7)
S270 – Settlement mound
S720 – Natural shrine: small Devi shrine set into roots of Barghat tree.

SG146 Pipariya (Bes) (settlement). Sector: 4

Agricultural land immediately north (c. 0.75 km) of Udayagiri, on the northern bank of the River Bes.

SC271 Settlement (783217, 2606669)
Low settlement mound partially occupied by modern village. Phasing: Sculpture (4)
S271 – Settlement mound
S722 – Sculpture pile

SC460 Temple: Brahmanical (783553, 2606694)
Ancient temple site occupied by modern Durga temple, immediately east of the modern village. Phasing: Architecture (4 to 6): Sculpture (4 to 6)
S460 – Temple remains: Brahmanical (in worship)

SG147 Sonari village (settlement). Sector: 3

Large hill (525 m), c. 5.5 km SW of Sanchi.

SC272 Settlement (772488, 2595738)
Modern village situated at its northern base, c. 1.5 km north of hilltop stupa site (SG007). Evidently overlies ancient settlement, as attested by sculptural remains.
S272 – Hillside basti

SC461 Temple: Brahmanical (772774, 2595969)
Ancient temple site occupied by modern Hanuman temple NE of modern village. Phasing: Sculpture (6 to 7)
S461 – Temple remains: Brahmanical (in worship)
S725 – Well

SC702 Tank (772343, 2595827)
S1104 – Tank

SG148 Sonari basti (settlement). Sector: 3

Agricultural plain NE of modern Sonari village.

SC273 Settlement (772878, 2596207)
Oblong settlement mound, 0ccupied by single farmhouse. Phasing: Pottery (1d to 7)
S273 – Settlement mound
S499 – Sculpture pile (in worship)

SG149 Barkheri/Amapura (settlement). Sector: 1a

Agricultural plain, c. 4 km WNN of Udayagiri, on the northern bank of a perennial stream which flows W-E towards the River Bes.

SC274 Memory site (776454, 2604519)
An area dominated by a large palm tree, just to the north of the modern village, is commemorated as an ancient settlement, and therefore revered as an a sacred site. However, no archaeological remains were found, apart from a few scattered sherds.
S274 – Natural shrine: palm tree

SG150 Sukhasen (ritual). Sector: 3

Lower slopes of Sonari hill, c. 5 km SW of Sanchi.

SC276 Stupa (773318, 2595205) *Sukhasen bari bir*
Faint outlines of c. 25 heavily disturbed square platforms. Two small stupa outlines behind. Diam: 1.70 m; surviving ht: 0.70 m. Phasing: Architecture (2)
S276 (25) – Stupa

SC277 Tank (773450, 2595255) *Sukhasen bari bir*
Small, unlined tank (15 x 15 m) east of SC276.
S277 – Tank

SC562 Stupa
Remains of circular structure, further up hill from SC276. Too heavily damaged for proper planning.
S730, S731, S732 – Stupa

SG150b Sukhasen (settlement). Sector: 3

Large, extensive hill (525 m),the top of which is occupied by Sonari stupas (SG007). Situated c. 5 km SW of Sanchi.
Series of settlements including modern Sukhasen village and two more habitational areas to the south and SW.

SC275 Settlement (773740, 2594822) *Sukhasen hill basti*
S275 – Hillside basti
S727 – Natural shrine: Devi shrine beneath imli tree (large stone cairn with white flag).

SC278 Settlement (774441, 2593833) *Sukhasen village basti*
Phasing: Sculpture (6)
S278 – Hillside basti
S728 – Well
S734 (in worship), S736 – Sculpture pile

SC280 Settlement (774392, 2594124) *Sukhasen village*
S280 – Modern settlement
S729 – Sculpture pile (in worship)

SG151 Suakheri (settlement). Sector: 3

Agricultural plain just east of Sonari hill.

SC281 Settlement (774132, 2595256)
Settlement mound partially occupied by two-housed Adivasi settlement. Phasing: Pottery (1d to 7)
S281 – Settlement mound
S735 – Sculpture pile (in worship)

SG152 Berkheri (background landscape). Sector: 1a

Agricultural plain midway between Sanchi and Vidisha, on western bank of River Betwa.

SC282 Temple: Brahmanical (785001, 2601626) *Mathabhai ka sthan*
Temple mound c. 1 km NE of modern Berkheri village, on the western bank of the River Betwa, opposite island in middle of village. Marks ancient crossing place across the river. Phasing: Architecture (2): Sculpture (6)
S282 – Temple remains: Brahmanical (in worship)

SC283 Ford (785172, 2601561) *Isa baba ka sthan*
Ancient ford which crosses river via island in middle of river.
S283 – Ford (in worship)
S737 – Natural shrine: on the eastern side of the river, slightly further south are some prominently shaped rocks which are painted red to indicate their sacred status. Known locally as Isababa. Apparently an image, worshipped as Bhairav baba, is lying in the middle of the river, but only appears during low water levels in the summer months.

SG153b Berkheri (background landscape). Sector: 1a

SC462 Temple: Brahmanical (784362, 2601854)
Beneath *pipal* tree to south of Berkheri village. Phasing: Sculpture (6)
S462 – Temple remains: Brahmanical (in worship)

SG154 Parariya (settlement). Sector: 1a

Agricultural plain midway between Sanchi and Vidisha.

SC284 Settlement (784325, 2601069)
Low settlement mound north of modern Parariya village, on western bank of

River Betwa. Phasing: Pottery (1d to 7)

S284 – Settlement mound

S738 – Natural shrine: Djinn baba shrine, and Devi platform with unhewn painted stones in centre of mound.

S741 – Sculpture pile (in worship)

SG155 Bari (settlement). Sector: 1a

Agricultural land c. 1 km E of Rangai.
Area marked out as a sacred site due to its reputation as an ancient settlement with ancestral links to modern Rangai village. However, no archaeological remains could be found, despite villagers' claims that many potsherds and hewn stone slabs are found in the surrounding fields.

SC285 Memory site (784016, 2603030)

S285 – Natural shrine

SG156 Berkheri ghat (settlement). Sector: 1a

Agricultural plain to SSW of Sanchi (c. 3.5 km), on the western bank of the River Betwa, above crossing to Pagneswar.

SC286 Settlement (778535, 2594427)
Small settlement mound occupied by modern farmhouse. Phasing: Pottery (1d to 7)

S286 – Settlement mound

S743 – Sculpture pile (in worship)

SG157 Mori khauri (settlement). Sector: 2a

Agricultural land at eastern foot of long line of hills between Pagneswar and Raisen.

SC287 Settlement (780767, 2592345)
Small settlement mound occupied by modern village, and dominated by large *barghat* tree.

SC695 Temple: Brahmanical (780685, 2592362)
Phasing: Sculpture (6)

S744 – Temple remains: Brahmanical (in worship)

SG158 Katsari kherai (settlement). Sector: 3

Large hill (520 m) between Pagneswar and Raisen.

SC288 Settlement (780153, 2592298)
Ancient settlement on NE lower slopes of hill. Consists of around 50 heavily disturbed stone structures.

S288 – Hillside basti

S289 – Well

S745 – Sculpture pile (in worship)

SG158b Nyal karka hill (Hilltop site). Sector: 2b

Fortified hill, with jagged cliffs (and rock-shelters) east side, and a large wall (width: 1.70 m) on the west side. This has square bastions at both corners.
No structural remains found.

SC290 Fortification wall (780152, 2592145)

S290 – Fortification wall

SC564 Rock-shelter (780207, 2592191)
Line of rock-shelters on eastern edge of hill.

S746 – Rock-shelter

SG159 Barla hill (settlement). Sector: 2b

Third in a line of small prominent hills (460 m) between Pagneswar and Raisen, the first two being Mora and Nyal karka, and the fourth, further to the south, Chaukha kua.

SC291 Settlement (780603, 2591304)
Large settlement on lower slopes of hill, partially occupied by modern village. No structural remains, but embankment and sculpture attests to existence of ancient settlement. May also have been connected with Katarsi kherai (SG158). Phasing: Sculpture (5 to 6)

S291 – Hillside basti

S747 – Sculpture pile (in worship)

SC293 Rock-shelter cluster (780412, 2591370)
Line of rock-shelters on eastern edge of hill, above modern village. One contains prehistoric paintings (horned animals with x-ray stomach). Phasing: Paintings (1b)

S293 (5) – Rock-shelter

S748 – Sculpture pile (in worship)

SC682 Temple: Brahmanical (780682, 2591393)
Phasing: Sculpture (5 to 6)

S749 – Temple remains: Brahmanical (in worship)

SG159b Barla hill (reservoir). Sector: 2b

SC292 Dam (780243, 2591257)
Large embankment running from Barla hill to hill in west. Heavily damaged with six surviving courses of stone masonry facing on southern side. Jagged, upward slanting facing, of Nagauri type. Fed by small *nāla* flowing S-N. Width: 2m.
Phasing: Dam (2)

S292 – Dam

SG160 Barla/Ghatla (settlement). Sector: 3

Fourth in line of series of hills between Pagneswar and Raisen, the first three in the north being Mori, Nyal karka, and Barla.

SC295 Rock-shelter cluster (780980, 2589909) *Chaukha kua*
Line of rock-shelters on southern edge of hill. Many contain well-preserved, prehistoric paintings (mainly hunting scenes). Phasing: Paintings (1b)

S295 (5) – Rock-shelter cluster

SC296 Settlement (780984, 2589527) *Ghatla kherai*
Ancient settlement on slightly raised ground at southern base of hill. Consists of heavily disturbed outlines of around 100 stone structures. Phasing: Water architecture (4)

S296 – Hillside basti

S297 – Well

S751 , S752 – Sculpture pile (both in worship)

SG160b Chaukha kua hill (Background landscape). Sector: 2b

Recognised as 'ancient site' by villagers, but consists of no more than a depression in the ground at the summit of the hill, and an outline of a circular platform (c. 10 m diameter), constructed from unhewn stones.

SC294 Memory site (780716, 2590187) *Chaukha kua*

S294 (2) – Natural shrine

SG162 Murlikheri (ritual). Sector: 1b

Small hill (513 m) which adjoins Satdhara hill to the NE.

SC300 Monastery (771932, 2599702)
Large square platform (25 x 19 m; ht: 2 m) constructed from massive boulders. Situated midway up hill to north of Murlikheri village. Phasing: Architecture (2)

S300 – Platformed monastery

SG162b Murlikheri-Naroda (settlement). Sector: 1b

Small hill (513 m) which adjoins Satdhara hill to the NE.
Large settlement extending from Murlikheri in the west to Naroda kherai in the east.

SC298 Settlement (772212, 2599264) *Murlikheri basti*
Phasing: Pottery (1d to 3b): Sculpture (3b to 6)

S298 – Settlement mound

S299 (in worship), S753, S754 (in worship) – Sculpture piles

SC301 Settlement (772151, 2598784) *Naroda*

S301 – Modern settlement

SC302 Settlement (772371, 2598467) *Naroda kherai*

S302 – Hillside basti

SC303 Tank (772682, 2598769) *Naroda*
Ancient dried up tank (c. 150 x 150,) at eastern edge of settlement, abutting the northern base of the main hill, and the western base of Naroda Pathari hill (SG12d). Embankments (surviving ht: 2 m) with inner stone facing on western and northern sides, the southern side being held up by the large hill, and the eastern side by the rocky outcrop extending in a northerly direction from the hill.

S303 – Tank

SC304 Temple: Jain (772553, 2598916) *Naroda*
Temple remains on western bank of village tank. Phasing: Sculpture (6)

S304 – Temple remains: Jain (in worship)
SC566 Temple: Brahmanical (771972, 2598818) *Naroda*
Temple remains distributed between platform and modern buffalo yard. Phasing: Architecture (6): Sculpture (4 to 7)
S755 – Sculpture pile (in worship)
S756 – Temple remains: Brahmanical

SG162c Murlikheri-Naroda (reservoir). Sector: 1b

SC305 Dam (771653, 2598881)
Large embankment heavily ploughed to less than 1 m in height, running from just north of modern Naroda village, to Murlikheri hill in the north. Would have held in body of water to the west. Most of the stone facing has been removed, although several stone slabs have been piled up in the middle of the field. Phasing: Dam (1d/2)
S305 – Dam

SG162d Naroda Pathari (ritual). Sector: 1b

Long hill (500 m), immediately opposite Satdhara hill, c. 1 km to the south.
SC306 Stupa (772815, 2598868)
Four small stupa platforms (c. 3 x 3 m), and a rectangular platform (10 x 6 m). Phasing: Architecture (4)
S306 (4) – Stupa complex
S758 – Stupa

SG164 Neemkhera (settlement). Sector: 1a

Agricultural plain, c. 8 km WNW of Vidisha, situated on the eastern bank of River Bes.
SC307 Settlement (776125, 2606690)
High settlement mound partially occupied by modern village, on eastern bank of River Bes. Phasing: Pottery (1d to 7)
S307 – Settlement mound
SC308 Background landscape (775875, 2606508)
In situ Siva *liṅga* on eastern bank of River Bes, SW of village. Phasing: Sculpture (4)
S308 – Sculpture pile (in worship)
SC689 Temple: Brahmanical (776144, 2606664)
Phasing: Sculpture (6)
S759 – Temple remains: Brahmanical (in worship)

SG165 Girbhar (settlement). Sector: 2a

Agricultural plain c. 5 km south of Sanchi. Two high mounds on either side of the Dabar *nāla*.
SC309 Settlement (782177, 2593176) *Girbhar village*
Phasing: Pottery (1c to 4)
S309 – Settlement mound
SC310 Settlement (782147, 2592893) *Girbhar kherai*
S310 – Settlement mound
SC441 Temple: Brahmanical (782103, 2592898) *Girbhar kherai*
Temple platform on summit of mound (c. 20 x 20 m). Faced with large dressed stone blocks similar to those used in Gupta temples. Phasing: Architecture (4 to 6): Sculpture (6)
S441 – Temple remains: Brahmanical (in worship)

SG166 Mungawali (settlement). Sector: 2b

Low rocky outcropping in the midst of agricultural land south of Dabar *nāla* (c. 4 km NW of Morel khurd). Tributary of Dabar *nāla* flows through site.
SC311 Settlement (784838, 2591488)
Ancient settlement on slightly raised ground to the west of modern Mungawali village. Consists of heavily disturbed outlines of stone structures. Most of the stone has been removed by stone merchants from Vidisha. Phasing: Sculpture (6)
S311 – Hillside basti
S762 – Sculpture pile (in worship)

SG167 Kotra (ritual). Sector: 2b

Long hill running N-S. Consists of two main parts, separated by lower saddle.
SC315 Stupa (784106, 2590292). *Kotra north.*
Cluster of heavily disturbed stupa outlines at western edge of hill. All dug down to their relic chambers. Phasing: Architecture (2)
S315, S765, S766 – Stupa
SC316 Rock-shelter cluster (784125, 2590378). *Kotra north.*
Group of c. 15 rock-shelters on western edge of hill, immediately below stupa complex. Many contain heavily eroded prehistoric paintings. Most are executed in red, with much superimposition. Subject matter includes horned animals, dancing figures, and hunting scenes. Phasing: Rock-shelter (1b): Stone tools (1b)
S316 (15) – Rock-shelter
SC317 Stupa (784089, 2590032). *Kotra north.*
Three well-preserved stupas (surviving ht: 1 m; diam: 3 m. stone facing: 40 x 20 x 15 cm) on saddle between northern and southern summits. Phasing: Architecture (2)
S317, S774, S775 – Stupa
SC318 Monastery (784124, 2589667). *Kotra south*
Heavily disturbed outlines of around six rectangular structures. Phasing: Architecture (2)
S318 (6) – Rectangular monastery
SC319 Monastery (784178, 2589496). *Kotra south*
Number of interconnected courtyard-type monasteries (c. 15 x 30 m), lined with small cells (c. 5 x 5 m). Phasing: Architecture (4)
S319 (5) – Interconnected courtyard monastery
SC320 Temple: Brahmanical (784255, 2589456). *Kotra south*
Temple remains on eastern edge of hill, occupied by modern Hanuman temple. Phasing: Architecture (6): Sculpture (6)
S320 – Temple remains: Brahmanical (in worship)
SC481 Fortification wall (784146, 2589532). *Kotra south*
Runs around southern and western edges of hill (c. 150 x 150; wd: 1.50 m; surviving ht: 1.50 m) Outlines of circular towers at each corner. High platform to south of NE corner (6 x 6 m; ht: 2.5 m).
S481 – Fortification wall
SC567 Stupa (784167, 2590318). *Kotra north*
Cluster of heavily disturbed stupa outlines and rectangular platform. The former are all dug down as far as the relic chamber. The western edge of the hill is protected by a large boundary wall, too heavily damaged to be measured. Phasing: Architecture (4)
S767, S768, S769, S770 – Stupas
SC568 Enclosure (784145, 2590301). *Kotra north*
One of two enclosures (12 x 12 m) bounded by large boulders (diam: 0.8 m).
S771 – Enclosure
SC569 Enclosure (784137, 2590282). *Kotra north*
One of two enclosures (12 x 12 m) bounded by large boulders (diam: 0.8 m).
S773 – Enclosure
SC570 Platform (784240, 2589491). *Kotra south*
Rectangular platform to east of main monastery platform, possibly the base of a temple.
S777 – Platform
SC572 Stupa (784248, 2589435). *Kotra south*
Small circular stupa base to the east of main monastery complex. Phasing: Architecture (2)
S778 – Stupa
SC573 Building Religious (784238, 2589428). *Kotra south*
Rubble infill wall outline of rectangular structure oriented NW-SE. Entrance in the SE.
S779 – Building Religious
SC574 Stupa (784065, 2589865). *Kotra south*
Large stupa platform at northern end of southern hill. Phasing: Architecture (4)
S780 – Stupa

SG167b Kotra (settlement). Sector: 2b

Eastern base of Kotra hill north.
SC312 Settlement (784480, 2590460)
Large number of heavily disturbed structural outlines surrounding temple complex.
S312 – Hillside basti
SC313 Temple: Brahmanical (784562, 2590551)
Eastern side of Kotra hill. Consists of large temple base with boundary wall (wd: 1 m). Phasing: Architecture (6): Sculpture (6)
S313 – Temple remains: Brahmanical (in worship)
SC314 Tank (784876, 2590745)
Dried up village tank (110 x 340 m) at eastern base of Kotra hill north, just below temple site. Held in by stone faced embankments on north, south and east sides. Western side is held in by eastern edge of hill.
S314 – Tank

SG169 Amacchar (settlement). Sector: 4

Agricultural land immediately north of Vidisha on western bank of River Betwa. The ghat and platform with the seven seated mothers, described by Lake (1910a), are situated around 1 km further to the south along the river.

SC323 Settlement (787891, 2608202)
Large settlement mound (total height from river: 10m, habitational debris depth: 4m), partially occupied by modern village. Phasing: Pottery (1d to 7)
S323 – Settlement mound
S782 – Sculpture pile (in worship)

SC463 Temple: Brahmanical (787837, 2608156)
Western edge of village. Phasing: Sculpture (4 to 6)
S463 – Temple remains: Brahmanical (in worship)

SG170 Salera (settlement). Sector: 2b

Two hills running N-S in a horse-shoe shape, c. 4 km SW of Morel khurd.

SC324 Settlement (787518, 2590254)
Modern village straddles lower western slopes of northern hill, and continues on lower western slopes and the basin formed by the northern and southern hill. Given other archaeological evidence in and around the site, it is likely to overlie an ancient settlement.
S324 – Hillside basti
S784 – Sculpture pile (in worship)

SC325 Tank (787371, 2589399)
Ancient dried up tank at the western base of the two hills. Would have been fed by the perennial stream which flows E-W. Held up by three embankments, now almost completely ploughed down, whilst the eastern side is held up by the base of the hill.
S325 – Tank

SC575 Temple: Brahmanical (787538, 2590453)
Modern Hanuman temple in upper village, on western slopes of northern hill. Large collection of sculpture stored on two separate platforms outside. Phasing: Sculpture (3b to 7)
S785 – Temple: Brahmanical (in worship)

SG170b Salera (ritual). Sector: 2b

SC326 Stupa (787873, 2589964) *Tegri*
Well-preserved stupa immediately behind village. Set on circular plinth (total diam: 5.85 m; surviving ht: 2 m; facing: c. 55 x 25 x15 cm). Phasing: Architecture (2)
S326 – Stupa

SC327 Rock-shelter (787903, 2589940) *Tegri Nāla Dant*
Large rock-shelter immediately south of SC326. Contains spring, which feeds *nāla* that flows into village-tank (170/1b) below. Phasing: Stone tools (1b)
S327 'Dant' – Rock-shelter (in worship)

SC328 Rock-shelter (787684, 2589461) *Marhaia Maharaj*
Large rock-shelter perched on edge of western 'finger' of southern hill, overlooking settlement and the surrounding basin.
S328 – Rock-shelter
S788 – Natural shrine (unhewn stones)

SC329 Stupa (787685, 2589340) *Harpalwala*
Rectangular platform (9.80 x 7.50 m; surviving ht: 1 m) south of SC328.
S329 – Stupa

SC330 Monastery (788761, 2588705) *Malwali Uriya*
Massive platform (150 x 75 m; surviving ht: 3 m) south of SC576. Entrance in NW corner. Surmounted by central platform (38 x 45 m; surviving ht: 3 m). Smaller platform against SW edge (15 x 15 m). Large number of unclear structural outlines, including small stupa bases (diam: 1 m). Walled enclosure (75 x 37 m), divided into several rooms at northern edge of platform. Phasing: Architecture (2)
S1113, S1114 – Building Religious
S1115 – Stupa
S330 – Platformed monastery

SC576 Enclosure (787745, 2589325)
Large circular, walled compound (diam: 30 m; surviving wall ht: 75 cm) 30 m east of SC329.
S789 – Enclosure

SG171 Bawaliya (settlement). Sector: 2b

Low grade agricultural land surrounded on west, south and east by hills, c. 1 km NW of Andher.

SC331 Settlement (798113, 2593741)
Large settlement mound, partially occupied by modern village. Phasing: Pottery (2 to 7): Water architecture (4)
S331 – Settlement mound
S333 – Well
S790 'Shankar Bhagwan ka sthan', S791 – Sculpture pile (both in worship)

SC332 Tank (797874, 2593763)
Dried up ancient tank (90 x 90 m) between village and hill to west. Unfaced embankments (ht: 2 m) on north, south and east side (west side held up by base of hill).
S332 – Tank

SG172 Bawaliya/Dharoyi baba hill (ritual). Sector: 2b

Large hill (544 m), third in line of hills directly opposite (east) of Andher, and c. 500 m south of Bawaliya village.

SC336 Rock-shelter (798396, 2592789) *Dharoyi baba hill*
Long line of rock-shelters to NW of SC577. The largest shelter contains numerous early-historic paintings in red, mostly of elephants. Superimposed over heavily eroded prehistoric hunting scenes. Phasing: Paintings (1b to 2)
S336 (6), S793 (2) – Rock-shelters

SC577 Stupa (798279, 2592192)
Number of heavily disturbed circular outlines (average diam, c. 4m). Phasing: Architecture (2)
S794 – Stupas

SG172b Bawaliya (quarry). Sector: 2b

SC334 Memory site (798536, 2592728) *Dharoyi baba hill*
Situated on lower NE slope of hill. Phasing: Stone tools (1b)
S334 – Natural shrine: small pile of stones which apparantly marks ancient site.

SC335 Quarry (798718, 2592482) *Dharoyi baba hill*
Unfinished sculpture attesting to ancient mine and sculpture production site on lower slopes of small hill immediately to SE of SC334. Phasing: Sculpture (4)
S335 – Quarry
S792 – Sculpture pile

SG173 Bamnor (settlement). Sector: 2b

Large hill (540 m) which forms centre of line of three hills directly opposite Andher, c. 1.75 km to the west.

SC337 Settlement (799186, 2591537)
Settlement mound, situated at eastern base of hills, partially occupied by modern village. Phasing: Pottery (1d to 2): Sculpture (4)
S337 – Settlement mound
S795, S796, S797 – Sculpture piles (all in worship)

SC338 Tank (799076, 2591807)
Ancient tank between village and hill to west, with embankments (surviving ht: 1 m), constructed from unhewn boulders.
S338 – Tank

SG173b Bamnor (background landscape). Sector: 2b

SC375 Temple: Brahmanical (799025, 2591157)
Remains of two stone structures on lower eastern slopes of hill to the south of Bamnor (en-route to Tor). Consists of rectangular building (9 x 13 m), with walls of outer facing, rubble infill construction; and a platform (9 x 7 m), standing on a mound (ht: c. 750 m).
S375 (2) – Temple remains: Brahmanical

SG174 Gyasabad/Dhanasari (settlement). Sector: 2b

Agricultural land SE of the range of hills around Andher (c. 3 km distance). Large settlement mound (ht. above *nāla*: 4 m; Occupation debris depth: 3m), on the southern bank of a perennial stream which flows NE to SW. Partially occupied by modern village of Gyasabad. On the northern bank of the *nāla* is the modern village of Dhanasari, which appears to be beyond the boundaries of the ancient settlement.

SC339 Settlement (799705, 2589308)
Phasing: Pottery (1d to 4)

S339 – Settlement mound
S802 (in worship), S803 – Sculpture pile
SC578 Temple: Brahmanical (799740, 2589253)
Phasing: Sculpture (6)
S800 'Shiv Bhagvan ka sthan' – Temple remains: Brahmanical (in worship)
S801 'Shiv Bhagvan ka sthan' – Sculpture pile (in worship)

SG175 Bawaliya hill (ritual). Sector: 2b

Prominent, isolated hill (520 m), c. 500 m west of Bawaliya, and immediately opposite (north) of Andher hill.
SC340 Rock-shelter (797564, 2593754) *Durgasthan*
Large rocky outcrop on the NE corner of hill, whose dramatic, craggy shape dominates the horizon throughout the area.
S340 (5) – Rock-shelter
S804 – Natural shrine
SC341 Fortification wall (797414, 2593757)
Runs along western and southern edges of hill forming enclosure (c. 130 x 130 m; surviving ht: 1.50 m; wd: 3.20 m). Entrance midway along western wall. Small room (10 x 10 m) to north of entrance, followed by five square platforms (c. 3.20 x 3.20 m) each separated by c. 15 m.
S341 – Fortification wall
SC342 Stupa (797415, 2593735)
Several square platforms (c. 3.50 x 3.50 m). Pathway with large stone slabs (c. 2.0 x 1.60 x 0.12 m) runs across site. Phasing: Architecture (2 to 4)
S342 (8) – Stupas
SC726 Monastery (797415, 2593735)
Large number of heavily damaged structural outlines. Phasing: Architecture (2)
S1146 – Rectangular monasteries

SG177 Devrajpur (settlement). Sector: 2b

Long, thin hill which projects in a SE-NW direction from Karhaud hill into otherwise agricultural land. Situated c. 3 km NW of Andher.
SC345 Temple: Jain (794476, 2596073)
Western edge of village. Many large stone blocks lying around on site. Phasing: Architecture (6): Sculpture (6)
S345 – Temple remains: Jain (in worship)
SC464 Settlement (794689, 2596211)
Large modern village at NW corner of irrigation embankment. Most probably overlies ancient settlement.
S464 – Settlement mound

SG177b Devrajpur (reservoir). Sector: 2b

SC346 Dam (794811, 2595673)
Massive dam which runs from west side of hill up to the large perennial *nāla* in the west (see Ch. 13). Phasing: Dam (1d/2): Sculpture (5 to 6)
S346 – Dam
S809 – Sluice
S816, S817 – Spillways
SC347 Temple: Brahmanical (794360, 2595724)
Temple base situated at western end of dam. Phasing: Sculpture (6)
S347 – Temple remains: Brahmanical (in worship)
SC348 Tank (795491, 2595691)
Small tank (110 x 100 m) on east (downstream) side of dam, west of Devrajpur kherai, and abutting the hill to the south of the dam. Probably acted as overspill tank. Three of the sides are supported by stone faced embankments, while the west side is held up by the base of the hill itself. Phasing: Dam (1d/2)
S348 – Tank
SC580 Tank (794878, 2595867)
Modern tank downstream of dam.
S808 – Tank
SC582 Temple remains: Unknown (795489, 2595546)
Temple platform/foundations between the lower and upper spillways. Large quantity of broken stone and brick fragments found in the small sounding in the upper spillway probably came from here.
S811 – Temple remains: Unknown/mixed cult
SC583 Temple remains: Unknown (795453, 2595559)
Temple platform/foundations to the west of lower spillway. Large quantity of broken stone and brick fragments found in the small sounding in the upper spillway probably came from here. Phasing: Sculpture (5 to 6)
S812 – Temple remains: Unknown/mixed cult
SC584 Temple remains: Unknown (795113, 2595689)
Temple platform situated to the west of the road-cutting through the dam.
S813 – Temple remains: Unknown/mixed cult
SC585 Temple: Brahmanical (794253, 2595645)
Temple platform on the high ground to the east of the control structure in the lower basin.
S814 – Temple remains: Buddhist
SC586 Temple: Brahmanical (794194, 2595649)
Mound on the west bank of the stream overlooking control structure. May have belonged to temple or part of monumentalised control structure.
S815 – Temple remains: Brahmanical
SC589 Reconstructed reservoir (795167, 2594784)
Reconstructed reservoir Phasing: Dam (1d/2)
S818 – Reconstructed reservoir

SG177c Devrajpur (ritual). Sector: 2b

Extensive Buddhist remains on hill to the east of Dam.
SC350 Stupa (795658, 2595447)
Heavily damaged stupa outline (diam: 7.80 m), on square platform (8.80 x 8.80 m; surviving ht: 1 m; stone facing: c. 40 x 20 x 10 cm). Enclosed by boundary wall (44.40 x 44.40 m). Further to the east is a similar kind of enclosure, and a heavily damaged stone platform further east still. Both have been heavily damaged by modern stone quarrying. Phasing: Architecture (2)
S350 (2), S820 – Stupas
S823 – Platform
SC351 Monastery (795981, 2595104)
Large number of interconnected courtyard monastery structures, with haphazardly sized rectangular rooms. Phasing: Architecture (2)
S351 (3) – Interconnected courtyard monastery (rectangular)
S435 'Devi sthan' – Sculpture pile (in worship)
SC590 Monastery (795706, 2595374)
Cluster of single and double-roomed monastery buildings with boulder walls. Situated to east of platform and stupas. Phasing: Architecture (2)
S819 (15) – Rectangular monasteries
S824 – Platform
SC591 Monastery (795588, 2595517)
Cluster of single and double-roomed monastery buildings with boulder walls, west of stupa (SC350). Phasing: Architecture (2)
S821 (6) – Rectangular monasteries
S822 – Platform
SC592 Monastery (795918, 2595192)
Cluster of single roomed structures with boulder walls on eastern part of hill. Phasing: Architecture (2)
S825 (6) – Rectangular monasteries

SG177d Devrajpur (settlement). Sector: 2b

SC349 Settlement (796005, 2595738) *Devrajpur kherai*
Settlement mound situated at the western base of Devrajpur hill. Phasing: Pottery (1d to 3b): Sculpture (4)
S349 – Settlement mound
S376 – Well
S498 – Sculpture pile (in worship)

SG178 Semra kherai (settlement). Sector: 2b

Large hill (544 m), northernmost in line of three hills directly opposite (east) of Andher hill.
SC352 Settlement (798922, 2592947)
Low settlement mound at northern base of hill.
S352 – Settlement mound
S826 – Sculpture pile (in worship)
SC353 Tank (799040, 2592984)
Dried up, circular tank (diam: 105 m; surviving ht: 1 m) at northern base of hill. Most of stone facing blocks have been removed.
S353 – Tank

SG179 Hakimkheri (background landscape). Sector: 2b

Large hill (540 m); the southernmost in a line of three hills immediately opposite (east) of Andher hill.

SC359 Fortification wall (797479, 2590981)
Remains of large wall (outer-facing, rubble infill variety) running W-E up northern edge of hill. Inner face lined with rectangular cells.
S359 – Fortification wall

SG179b Hakimkheri (settlement). Sector: 2b

Large hill (540 m); the southernmost in a line of three hills immediately opposite (east) of Andher hill.
SC354 Settlement (797017, 2590766)
Large settlement mound, at southern base of hill, partially occupied by modern village.
S354 – Settlement mound
SC355 Temple: Brahmanical (797504, 2590659) *Kharamata ka sthan*
Temple remains on NW bank of dried up tank (SC356). Sculptures stored beneath *Mahua* tree. Phasing: Sculpture (6 to 7)
S355 – Temple remains: Brahmanical (in worship)
SC356 Tank (797594, 2590550)
Dried up remains of circular tank (diam: 110 m), with embankments on all sides (surviving ht: 1 m), immediately SE of modern village.
S356 – Tank
SC358 Tank (796477, 2591045)
Dried up circular tank (diam: 150 m) west of village, on lower ground between Andher and Hakimkheri hill. Faced on inner side with stone slabs, but most of these have been removed.
S358 – Tank
SC360 Temple: Brahmanical (795510, 2590976)
Temple platform (8 x 8 m) situated on SW lower slopes of Andher hilll, midway between Hakimkheri and Padariya. Phasing: Architecture (6): Sculpture (7)
S360 – Temple remains: Brahmanical
SC593 Tank
Heavily disturbed remains of embankment with stone facing in centre of modern village. Difficult to plan because much of the original tank has been built over by modern structures.
S357 – Tank

SG180 Jhirniya (settlement). Sector: 2a

Agricultural plain to east of River Betwa, c. 3 km east of Mehgaon.
SC361 Settlement (786891, 2596904)
Modern village c. 750 m SW of Murwara.
S361 – Modern settlement
S828 – Sculpture pile (in worship)

SG181 Suakhera (settlement). Sector: 2a

Agricultural plain c. 3 km south of Vidisha.
SC434 Settlement (785286, 2600700)
High settlement mound, partially occupied by modern village.
S434 – Settlement mound
S829 – Natural shrine (unhewn stones beneath large Barghat tree)

APPENDIX IIa

Sculpture and architectural fragments

Abbreviations: *B.S. – buff sandstone; L.B.S. – light buff sandstone; P.S. – purple sandstone; W.S. – white sandstone; P.C.S. – polished Chunar sandstone; R.M.M.S. – red mottled Mathura sandstone.*
Qty – Quantity; Ht – Height; Circumf – Circumference; Diam – Diameter; Lgt – Length; Wd – Width; Acc. – Museum accession number.

NB: Unless otherwise indicated, sculptures are in their primary context.

SG001 Sanchi hill (ritual)

SC3 Manchi (Rock-shelter cluster)
S938 – Rock-shelter (in worship)
I-6: Votive stupa. 5th century AD (Phase 4). Material: B.S. Primary context: SG001/S927
Votive stupa with image of Manjusri in niche.

SC5 Stupa 1
S5 – Stupa 1
I-937: Buddha. Qty: 4. AD 450 (Phase 4). Published (Fleet *CII*, III, 29 34; Marshall 1940, 389 90; inscrip. 834)
Four Buddha images, each at cardinal points of stupa inside gateway. Associated railing inscription, dated to the Gupta year 131 (AD 450–1), records the donation of a lamp 'in the place of the four Buddhas'.

S916 – Pillar 10 (south of Stupa 1)
I-20: Pillar remains (Ht: 1280 cm; Circumf: 240 cm). 3rd century BC (Phase 1d). Material: P.C.S. Published (Marshall 1940). Remains of Asokan pillar outside south entrance of Stupa 1.
I-302: Animal capital from Asokan pillar. 3rd century BC (Phase 1d). Material: P.C.S. Museum: SAM (Acc. 2868). Published (Marshall 1940).

S917 – Pillar 26 (east of Stupa 1)
I-16: Pillar remains. 5th century AD (Phase 4). Published (Marshall 1940, inscrip. 835). Bears an inscription recording the dedication of a Vajrapani pillar (no. 35) to north of Stupa 1. Originally crowned by four-lioned capital (now in SAM). Copy of Mauryan examples.

S918 – Pillar 35 (north of Stupa 1)
I-17: Pillar remains (Ht: 176 cm; Circumf: 293 cm). 5th century AD (Phase 4). Published (Marshall 1940). Lotus capital surmounted by cable-necking and railed element.
I-227: Vajrapani Bodhisattva from summit of pillar (Ht: 136 cm). Broken from below knees. 5th century AD (Phase 4). Material: G.S. Museum: SAM (Acc. 2720/A99). Published (Marshall 1940, 391).

S925 – Pillar 25 (east of Stupa 1)
I-15: Pillar remains (Lgt: 50 Wd: 46 Ht: 460 Circumf: 172 cm). 115–80 BC (Phase 2). Published (Marshall 1940, 49).
Divided into two sections: lower octagonal section, and upper sixteen-sided section. Lotus capital with overlapping petals. Surmounted by cable necking and beed and lozenge moulding; and cuboid 'railed' element'.
I-72: Animal capital, possibly from Pillar 25. 115–80 BC (Phase 2). Material: L.B.S. Museum: SAMRC (Acc. 2772).
Winged lion capital with elongated body, and inscription on side. Deeply incised curls on mane.

S926 – Pillar 34 (eastern gateway of Stupa 1)
I-29: Lion capital. Head missing. 115–80 BC (Phase 2). Material: L.B.S. Museum: SAMRC (Acc. 2721). Published (Marshall 1940, pl. 108c; Cunningham 1954, pl. 7).
Stands on haunches on circular abacus, decorated with honey suckle and pecking geese motif. Rotund and compact body, in contrast to the elongated form of the lion capital from the pillar next to Stupa 2. The treatment of the mane however is almost identical to the latter: thick curls, deeply incised. Ithyphallic.

SC12 Kal Bhairav (Temple: Brahmanical)
S12 – Temple remains (in worship)
I-80: Miscellaneous (Temple architecture). Qty: 8. 10th century AD (Phase 6). Material: P.S. Includes pilaster with overflowing *kumbha*, and *kirīṭamukuṭa* design, carved in high relief. Also pilasters with 'flat' overflowing pot.
I-81: Nandi. 10th century AD (Phase 6). Material: P.S.
I-82: Miscellaneous (Sculpture). Qty: 5. 10th century AD (Phase 6). Material: P.S.

S937 – Rock-shelter/modern shrine
I-79: Kal Bhairav. Covered with *sindhur*. 10th century AD (Phase 6). Primary context: S12

SC604 Building 43 (Buddhist)
S878 – Building 43
I-1026: Temple remains. 9th century AD (Phase 6). Published (Marshall 1940, 394; *ASIAR*, 1912–13 (I): 21).

SC605 Temple 45 (Buddhist)
S879 – Temple 45
I-9: Maitreya Bodhisattva. 9th century AD (Phase 6). Material: G.S. Museum: SAMRC (Acc. 2728/61538). Published (Marshall 1940). Forms the pair to Irwin's (1972) Avalokitesvara, now in the Victoria and Albert Museum, London.

SC608 Temple 31 (Buddhist)
S882 – Temple 31
I-22: Pilaster 405–415AD (Phase 4). Museum. SAMRC (Acc. 2665/75). Similar to in-situ pilaster in Temple 31 (Williams 1986, pl. 40).
I-38: Pilaster. 405–415AD (Phase 4). Material: L.B.S. Museum: SAMRC (Acc. 2630/137). Similar to in-situ pilaster in Temple 31 (Williams 1986, pl. 40).
I-61: Pilaster. 405–415AD (Phase 4). Material: P.S. Museum: SAMRC (Acc. 2662/138).
I-223: Pilaster. 405–415AD (Phase 4). Material: L.B.S. Museum: SAMRC (Acc. 2703/136).

S1091 – Sculpture
I-31: *Nāginī* (Wd: 27 cm; Ht: 163 cm; Depth: 15 cm). AD 450 (Phase 4). Material: L.B.S. Published (Marshall 1940, 59; Shaw 2004a). Primary context: S929 (possibly from one of temples to east of Stupa 1). Five-headed serpent canopy. Left hand rests on hip, clutching fold of garment. Right hand holds lotus, raised to shoulder. Heavy anklets.

SC609 Temple 40 (Temple: Buddhist)
S883 – Temple 40
I-8: Elephant capital (Lgt: 70 Wd: 32 Ht: 59 cm). Trunk and half of back missing. 3rd–2nd century BC (Phase 1d/2). Material: L.B.S. Museum: SAMRC (Acc. 2726/ A11). Published (Marshall 1940, 68; pl. 104i). Back part of capital broken off. Excavated from debris between Phase I and II.

SC612 Southern stupa cluster
S887 – Stupa 12
I-988: Bodhisattva. 2nd–3rd century AD (Phase 3b). Material: RMMS. Broken pedestal with part of the left foot of a standing image, wearing sandals. Retrieved from the relic chamber of Stupa 12.To the right of the pedestal is a dwarf pilaster with foliate cap. In the sunk panel, the partly mutilated figure of the Bodhisattva Maitreya, seated cross-legged and holding a small flask in his left hand. To his left, two female votaries clad in saris, each holding a lotus stalk in the right and and the hem of the sari in the left. Kusana Brahmi inscription on the borders above and below the panel (no. 830) recording the image's dedication by the daughter of Vishakula.

S890 – Stupa 14
I-985: Bodhisattva (Ht: 2 ft. 7.5 inches) 3rd century AD (Phase 3b). Material: RMMS.
Image of Buddha seated cross legged in *dhyāna mūdra*. Retrieved from the relic chamber of Stupa 14 where it had evidently been enshrined after removal from a previous location. The head, broken off when originally found, has been refixed. The figure wears a *saṅghati* which covers both shoulders, and emerges on the throne beneath his legs. Cakra symbol on the palms, and cakra and triratna on the soles of the feet. Mortice hole at the back of the head hole for the attachment of a nimbus.

SC625 Stupa 2
S923 – Pillar remains
I-14: Pillar remains. 115–80 BC (Phase 2). Published (Marshall 1940, 82).
Fragment (Lgt: 180cm) of the sixteen-sided pillar which originally stood to the southwest of Stupa 2.
I-32: Lion capital (Lgt: 107 Ht: 43 cm). 115–80 BC (Phase 2). Material: L.B.S. Museum: SAMRC (Acc. 2861/A31). From summit of pillar to southwest of Stupa 2. Elongated body. Tail hangs between legs. Ithyphallic. Deeply incised curls on mane.
I-36: Pillar remains (Ht: 85 Diam: 51 Circumf: 112 cm). 115–80 BC (Phase 2). Material: L.B.S. Museum: SAMRC (Acc. 2850). Inverted lotus capital from pillar to southwest of Stupa 2. Overlapping petals, cable necking, and octagonal tenon.

SC626 Eastern Terrace (Platform)
S924 – Sculpture pile
I-12: *Yakṣa* (Wd: 39; Ht: 93; Depth: 24 cm). 5th century AD (Phase 4). Material: L.B.S.
Yakṣa with outspread legs, seated on stool. Flat, broad chest, with protruding stomach. Sash worn around the waist, tied at front in simple knot. Chunky torque necklace around neck.
I-13: *Yakṣa* (Wd: 35; Ht: 81; Depth: 23 cm). Broken from chest upwards. Damaged stomach. 5th century AD (Phase 4). Material: L.B.S.*Yakṣa* seated in *lalitāsana* (right leg on ground on stool). Flat, broad chest and protruding stomach. Remains of upright object resting on left leg. May have formed pair to *yakṣa* in SAMRC (I-39).

SC627 Unprovenanced sculptures (Background landscape)
S927 – Miscellaneous sculpture
I-24: *Yakṣa* (Ht: 61 cm). c. 25 AD (Phase 3a). Material: B.S. Museum: SAMRC (Acc. 2654/B21). Published.
Missing head, and lower legs. Damaged stomach. Standing *yakṣa*. Thick chest and bulky stomach. Heavy folds of skin at the waist, similar to I-34 to which it was possibly a pair. Both arms missing, but angle of left shoulder indicates that it was originally extended upwards to support part of architectural structure. Striated sash around waist, tied at front in simple cross-knot. Two-stringed necklace, with three chunky beads, two in the shape of a *nandipada*.
I-34: *Yakṣa* (Ht: 58 cm). Broken off at thighs and shoulders. Left shoulder in separate piece. C. 25 AD (Phase 3a). Material: L.B.S. Museum: SAMRC (Acc. 2741/30). Published.
Standing *yakṣa* with protruding belly. Fleshy folds of skin shown around back and waist. Angle of left shoulder similar to no. I-24. Part of waist band drawn between legs (cf. *yakṣa* at Udayagiri). Double-stringed necklace, with three chunky beads.
I-39: *Yakṣa* (Wd: 79 cm; Ht: 79 cm; Depth: 28 cm). Head and arms missing, and part of right leg below knee broken off. 5th century AD (Phase 4). Material: L.B.S. Museum: SAMRC (Acc. 2773/N38). Published.
Yakṣa seated in *lalitāsana* (left leg on ground) on stool. Obverse seated position to *yakṣa* on eastern terrace (I-13), to which it may have formed a pair. Broad chest, and protruding stomach, heavy folds of skin at side of waist. Chunky necklace.
I-68: Buddha (Wd: 49 cm; Ht: 36 cm). Head missing. 4th century AD (Phase 3b). Material: R.M.M.S. Museum: SAM (Acc. 2701). Published.
Buddha seated in *Padmāsana* on lotus throne. Kusana-type cloth.
I-74: Buddha (Wd: 49 cm; Ht: 106 cm). Both arms damaged. 4th century AD (Phase 3b). Material: R.M.M.S. Museum: SAM (Acc. 2782/2). Published.
Standing Buddha in *sampada*. Wears transparent *saṅghati*, with lightly incised pattern. Very little distinction between fabric and surface of the body, accentuating lean, muscular quality of the legs. Extra cloth falls in spiral, zig-zag folds on proper left side of body.
I-78: Buddha (Wd: 25 cm; Ht: 38 cm). Right arm damaged, head missing. 4th century AD (Phase 3b). Material: R.M.M.S. Museum: SAM (Acc. 2790). Published.
I-221: Pillar remains. 115–80 BC (Phase 2). Museum: SAMRC (Acc. 2627/131). Published.
Top of octagonal pillar with attached inverted lotus capital with overlapping petals, cable necking, and plain circular abacus and tenon.
I-262: Tirthankara. 11th–12th century AD (Phase 7). Material: W.S. Museum: SAM. Published.
I-263: Door attendant. 11th century AD (Phase 7). Material: L.B.S. Museum: SAM. Published.
I-264: Door attendant. 11th century AD (Phase 7). Material: L.B.S. Museum: SAM (Acc. cf 29). Published.
I-268: Buddha. 3rd century AD (Phase 3b). (Wd: 1 foot, 4 inches). Material: R.M.M.S. Museum: SAM (Acc. 2785). Published (Marshall *et al.*, 1940, 386, inscrip. 829.).
Pedestal surmounted by the feet of a standing Buddha and to his right the lower part of an attendant figure. On the front face of the pedestal is a dentil cornice above and a Persepolitan pilaster to either side; and framed between them a group of 12 figures. In the centre, a Bodhisattva seated in *dhyana mudra*; to the right of him, six male worshippers, and to his left, five females. The male figures war long tunics of the Kusana pattern held in by a belt at the hips. The women wear saris and bodices. Some of the worshippers bear lotuses or other offerings; others hold their hands in prayer. Bears an inscription dated to the year 22 (c. AD 222–247) and mentions a king called Vaskusana, thought to be a member of the Kusana dynasty.
I-303: Padmapani Bodhisattva (Ht: 196 cm). 5th century AD (Phase 4). Material: G.S. Museum: SAM (Acc. 2848). Published (Cunningham 1854, 200, pl. IV).
Appears to correspond to one of the 'two colossal figures' described by Cunningham as leading 'past no. 3 stupa to the road leading to Sanchi village'. Marked on Cunningham's map, just to the west of Stupa 3, immediately to the south of the entrance to the main Stupa 1 enclosure.
I-304: Padmapani Bodhisattva (Ht: 192 cm). 5th century AD (Phase 4). Material: G.S. Museum: SAM (Acc. 2857/A101). Published
See note above re. I-303.
I-987: Bodhisattva. Material: L.B.S. Museum: SAM (Marshall 1940, vol. 1, 202; 253, inscrip. 828; vol. III, pl. 124b; Hamid 1920, no. A82)
Seated cross legged in *dhyana mudra*. Pedestal bears an inscription in Brahmi characters of the Kusana period dated to the year 28, which records a gift during the reign of King Vasiska. Following recent revisions of the Kusana era (Willis 1999/2000, 269–70), this can now be viewed as year 128 (c. AD 228–253). From inscription it appears that the image represents Siddhartha seated beneath the *jambu* tree on the occasion of his first meditation.

SC628 Lower eastern temple cluster
S929 – Sculpture
I-255: *Nāga* (Wd: 30 cm; Ht: 172 cm; Depth: 14 cm). 5th century AD (Phase 4). Material: L.B.S. Museum: SAM (Acc. 2859/A103). Published (Maisey 1892, 76; Marshall 1940; Williams 1976, 174, n. 5; Shaw 2004a). Possibly from one of the temples now partly obscured by the eastern terrace.
I-256: *Nāga* (Wd: 32 cm; Ht: 183 cm; Depth: 15 cm). 5th century AD (Phase 4). Material: L.B.S. Museum: SAM (Acc. 2858/A102). Published (as above). Possibly from one of the temples now partly obscured by the eastern terrace.

SG002 Sanchi/Kanakhera hill (settlement)

SC13 (Settlement)
S877 – In situ memorial (in worship)
I-936: Sati. Qty: 2.

SC17 Kanakhera talai (Tank)
S363 – Pillar remains (lower ground to the east of Kanakhera hill)
I-253: Bull capital (Lgt: 97 cm; Wd: 45cm; Ht: 42 cm). Legs and head missing. 115–80 BC (Phase 2). Material: B.S.
Bull capital with small hump, and flat, bony back. Accentuated bony structure. Tail hangs down behind body.

SC19 (Temple: Brahmanical)
S19 – Miscellaneous sculpture
I-19: Laksmi. 10th century AD (Phase 6). Museum: SAMRC. Published.
I-23: Siva. 10th century AD (Phase 6). Museum: SAMRC (Acc. 61.583). Published.

I-30: Uma Maheswar. Lower half only. 10th century AD (Phase 6). Museum: SAMRC (Acc. 2649/61.618). Published.
I-43: *Saptamātṛkā*. Heavily damaged. 5th century AD (Phase 4). Material: L.B.S. Museum: SAMRC (Acc. 2597). Published.
I-44: Agni. 10th century AD (Phase 6). Material: P.S. Museum: SAM (Acc. 2674). Published.
I-46: Siva (Wd: 60 cm; Ht: 47 cm). 11th–12th century AD (Phase 7). Material: B.S. Museum: SAM (Acc. 2727). Published.
I-49: Siva (Wd: 67 cm; Ht: 34 cm). 10th century AD (Phase 6). Material: P.S. Museum: SAM (Acc. 2871). Published.
I-60: Gajalaksmi. 10th century AD (Phase 6). Material: B.S. Museum: SAM (Acc. 2870). Published.
I-62: Kartikkeya (Wd: 36 cm; Ht: 84 cm). 9th century AD (Phase 6). Material: B.S. Museum: SAM (Acc. 2805/42). Published.
I-63: Nairriti. Top half broken off. 11th–12th century AD (Phase 7). Museum: SAM (Acc. 2623). Published.
I-65: Chund (Wd: 62 cm; Ht: 112 cm). Entire outer part of face and breasts have been cut off. 11th–12th century AD (Phase 7). Material: W.S. Museum: SAM (Acc. 2638). Published.
I-66: Varuna (Ht: 84 cm; Depth 43 cm). 10th century AD (Phase 6). Material: B.S. Museum: SAM (Acc. 2804). Published.
I-198: Varaha. 10th century AD (Phase 6). Museum: SAMRC (Acc. 2878). Published.
I-220: Uma Maheswar. Material: L.B.S. Museum: SAMRC (Acc. 2659/A25). Published.
I-254: Miscellaneous (Sculpture). Qty: 10. 10th century AD (Phase 6). Material: P.S.

SG003a *Nagauri* (settlement)

SC21 (Settlement)
S941 – In situ sculpture (in worship)
I-626: *Nāga* (Wd: 34 Ht: 183 Depth 17 cm). c. 80–50 BC (Phase 2). Material: B.S. Published (Marshall 1940; Williams 1976; Shaw 2004a).
Intact, anthropomoprhic *nāga* with seven-headed snake canopy. Horizontal serpent coils on back. Opaque garment. Spiral turban. Right hand in *abhayamudra*, holding lotus. Left hand holds water flask (*kamandalu*).
I-627: *Nāginā* (Ht: 130 cm). c. 80–50 BC (Phase 2). Material: B.S. Published (as above). Female counterpart of I-626. Current whereabouts unknown.

S942 – Sculpture pile (in worship)
I-628: Pillar remains (Ht: 38 cm; Diam: 18 cm; Circumf: 56 cm). 115–80 BC (Phase 2). Material: B.S. Primary context: SG003a/S22.
Small, crudely carved lotus capital, with six overlapping petals, cable-necking and small tenon.
I-629: Miscellaneous (Sculpture). Qty: 8. 10th century AD (Phase 6). Material: P.S. Primary context: SG003a/S19
I-630: *Sucika*. C. 115–80 BC (Phase 2). Material: B.S. Primary context: SG003a/S19
Small railing crossbar decorated with simple lotus medallion. Unfinished.
I-632: Votive stupa. Upper portion only, unfinished. 5th century AD (Phase 4). Material: P.S. Primary context: SG003a/S19 (quarry).

SC22 (Quarry)
S22 – In situ sculpture (unfinished)
I-631: Animal capital. 115–80 BC (Phase 2). Material: B.S.
Ithyphallic horse capital. Crudely carved. Unfinished. Tenon at base visible.

SG005 Morel khurd (ritual)

SC31 (Temple remains: unknown)
S31 – Temple remains (in worship)
I-634: Sculpture base. 10th century AD (Phase 6). Material: P.S.

SC440 Siddh ka makan, or Madhu deo ka mandar/ Krsna's temple) (Monastery/Temple remains: Buddhist).
S850 – Temple remains
I-83: Pilaster. Qty: 4. 10th century AD (Phase 6). Material: P.S. From temple built on summit of earlier (Phase II) platformed monastery.
I-633: Buddha. 10th century AD (Phase 6). Material: P.S. Museum: SAM
Seated in *padmāsana* on lotus throne, elaborately carved side-attendants and *vyālas*.

SG005b Pipalia kherai (settlement)

SC41 (Settlement)
S871 – Sculpture pile (in worship)
I-519: Durga. Embedded in mud platform from waist downwards. 7th–8th century AD (Phase 5). Material: B.S. Primary context: SG092/S199 (?). Four-armed, with sword in upper right hand. Round face and flat cap-like headdress.
I-520: *Vedika* (Lgt: 23 Wd: 16 cm). Broken in half length-wise. 115–80 BC (Phase 2). Material: B.S. Primary context: SG005/S1098. Fragment of carved corner railing of stupa balustrade. Obverse side: two sockets for receiving *Sucika*. Reverse side: lotus bud meander design and beaded border.

SG005c Binjoli kherai (settlement)

SC369 (Settlement)
S869 – Sculpture pile
I-192: Durga *Mahiṣāsuramardinī*. 10th century AD (Phase 6). Material: P.S. Primary context: SG123/S689 (?).
'Early' type: head still intact on ground. However style is reductive and 'folky'.
I-193: *Yakṣa* (Wd: 40 cm; Ht: 33 cm; Depth: 38 cm). 5th century AD (Phase 4). Material: L.B.S. Primary context: SG005/S1098.
Fragment of male figure seated on stool in *lalitāsana*. Broad chest, protruding stomach. Traces of chunky necklace strung low over chest. Sacred thread over left shoulder.
I-202: *Yakṣini* (Wd: 40 cm; Ht: 60 cm; Depth: 18 cm). Broken from waist downwards. Feet missing. 5th century AD (Phase 4). Material: L.B.S. Primary context: SG005/S1098.
Lower half of *yakṣini* standing in *sampada*. Transparent skirt, reaching to below knees. Bulky folds of cloth at either side of hips. Heavy scarf skims knees at square-on angle. Cf. *Nāginī* at Sanchi (SG001/S1091/I-31).
I-203: Bodhisattva (Wd: 20 cm; Ht: 24 cm; Depth: 8 cm). Broken from waist downwards. 5th century AD (Phase 4). Material: L.B.S. Primary context: SG005/S1098.
Lower fragment of small, roughly hewn stone slab showing standing male figure set in niche. Legs held tightly together. Opaque garment reaching ankles. Thin sash around waist.
I-204: Hanuman. 10th century AD (Phase 6). Material: P.S. Primary context: SG123/S689.

S870 – Building cluster
I-191: Monolith. Qty: 3 (Ht: 500 cm). 10th century AD (Phase 6). Material: B.S. Three roughly hewn monoliths set in line across centre of settlement (separated by c. 10m).

SG006 Vidisha (settlement)

SC44 Khambaba/ Heliodorus pillar (Temple: Brahmanical)
S995 – Pillar remains
I-170: Pillar remains. 115–80 BC (Phase 2). Material: L.B.S. Published (Sircar 1965, 88; Salomon 1998, 265–266; Irwin 1976; Khare 1967; Shaw 2004a).
Pillar bearing inscription of Heliodorus. Divided into three sections: octagonal, sixteen-sided, and tapering sperical section. Surmounted by post-Mauryan inverted lotus capital, overlapping petals, cable necking; bead and lozenge moulding; abacus with pecking geese and honey-suckle motif.
I-561: Garuda capital (Lgt: 57 cm; Wd: 53 cm; Depth: 27 cm). 115–80 BC (Phase 2). Material: L.B.S. Museum: GGMM. (Acc. 52). Published (Dass 2002–3). Railing abacus surmounted by large claws of bird pinning down snake. Most probably formed crowing capital of Heliodorus pillar.

S998 – Pillar remains
I-332: Fan palm capital (Ht: 78 cm). c. 115–80 BC (Phase 2). Material: L.B.S. Museum: GGMM. (Acc. 452). Published (Cunningham 1880). Small fan-palm capital with four upraised palms.
I-522: Pillar remains. 115–80 BC (Phase 2). Material: L.B.S. Museum: GGMM. (Acc. 1). Published (Lake 1910, 144).
Fragment of octagonal pillar with inscription. Reads 'Bhāgavata, son of Gatami, caused a Garuda standard to be made in connection with the best temple of Bhāgavat (Vāsudeva) when Mahārāja Bhāgavata had been crowned 12 years'.
I-523: Fan palm capital (Wd: 20 cm; Ht: 220 cm). Upper portion broken. 115–80 BC (Phase 2). Material: B.S. Published (Cunningham 1880, 41). Fan-palm capital, leaves and bunches of fruit on all sides.
I-524: Crocodile capital (Lgt: 150 cm; Wd: 9 Ht: 51 Depth: 9 cm). 115–80 BC (Phase 2). Material: B.S. Museum: GGMM. (Acc. 10a). Published (Cunningham 1880, pl. XIV; Härtel, 1987, 579–8; Bhandarkar 1914–15, 190, fig. D).

Chunky crocodile (*makara*) capital, with hole on base.
I-560: Pillar remains (Ht: 600 cm). 115–80 BC (Phase 2). Material: L.B.S. Museum: GGMM. Published (Cunningham 1880).
Inverted lotus capital with overlapping petals; cable necking; beed and lozenge moulding; abacus with *makara* and honey-suckle motif. Surmounted by cuboid 'railing' motif and sixteen-sided faceted circular element. Possibly crowned by *makara* capital found at same location (I-524).

S999 – Pillar remains/Sculpture pile (in worship)
I-173: Fan palm capital (Lgt: 110 cm; Circumf: 90 cm). 115–80 BC (Phase 2). Material: L.B.S. Primary context: SG006/S998. Long fan-palm capital, four palm leaves, bunches of berries on either side.
I-331: Railing coping. 115–80 BC (Phase 2). Material: L.B.S. Plain balustrade from top of curved railing.

SC45 Besnagar (Settlement)
S46 – Sculpture pile (Site L)
I-96, I-97, I-311, I-312, I-325, I-326: Sucikas. 115–80 BC (Phase 2). Museum: GGMM (Acc. 8c). Published (Cunningham 1880). Primary context: SG006/S49.
I-334: Gateway railing. 115–80 BC (Phase 2). Material: B.S. Museum: GGMM. (Acc. 8a). Published (Cunningham 1880). Primary context: SG006/S49.
Upright railing from gateway, carved with devotees before tree, with two holes for railings.

S971 – Pillar remains (Site F)
I-95: Animal capital (Wd: 141 Ht: 133 Depth 65 cm). 115–80 BC (Phase 2). Material: L.B.S. NMD. Published (Cunningham 1880, 40). Large ithyphallic elephant with rider, only the lower half of which remains. Striated sash visible on left side of body. Elephant set on large stone slab. Striated sash around neck. Three vertical creases on upper chest (cf. Satdhara elephant capital (SG007), and elephant medallions on Stupa 2, Sanchi).

S979 – Sculpture pile (Site G)
I-525: Durga *Mahiṣāsuramardinī* (Ht: 210 cm). Known locally as 'telin'. 5th century AD (Phase 4). Material: B.S. Museum: GGMM. Published (Cunningham 1880, 40)

SC50 Charan tirth (Background landscape)
S50 – Modern temple (in worship)
I-1042: Temple remains. 10th century AD (Phase 6).

SC53 Lohangi (Temple: Brahmanical/Buddhist (?)
S53 – Pillar remains (in worship)
I-98: Bodhisattva (Wd: 32 cm; Ht: 80 cm; Depth 23 cm). Only torso from shoulders to just above knees survives. Head and arms (apart from left hand) missing. 4th century AD (Phase 3b). Material: L.B.S. Museum: VM. (Acc. 1673). Standing male figure. Torque necklace with *srivatsa*. Ringlets visible down back. Transparent *dhotī* with finely carved, widely spaced rosace pattern. Narrow string around waist tied in spiral knot at front. Bulky *utterīya* held in place by left hand.
I-99: Pillar remains (Ht: 77cm; Depth: 81 cm). 115–80 BC (Phase 2). Material: L.B.S. Published (Cunningham (1880, 34–5; Shaw 2004a).Inverted lotus capital with overlapping petals; cable necking; beed and lozenge moulding; abacus with pecking geese and honey-suckle motif. Remains of two pairs of feet (elephant and lion) on top. Buddhist/Bhagavata (?).

S963 – Temple remains (in worship)
I-1222: Miscellaneous (Temple architecture). 10th century AD (Phases 6).

SC321 Bes tila (Settlement)
S781 – Sculpture pile (in worship)
I-680: Miscellaneous (Sculpture). Only two sides visible. Other two sides remain submberged in ground. 9th century AD (Phase 6). Material: P.S. Primary context: SG169/S463.
Fragment of four sided stone block, only two sides of which are visible. One face carved with Visnu image, the other with Laksmi.

SC642 Mound Rs (Temple: Brahmanical)
S969 – Sculpture pile (in worship)
I-702: Miscellaneous (Sculpture). Qty: 5. 10th century AD (Phase 6). Material: P.S. Published (Cunningham 1880).

SC643 Site X (Temple: Brahmanical)
S972 – Sculpture pile (in worship)
I-943: *Liṅga (in situ)*. Qty: 2. 5th century AD (Phase 4).
Two undecorated *liṅga*s which rise straight up from the ground.
I-945: Ganesa. 5th century AD (Phase 4).
Small 'squat' Ganesa similar in form to the Udayagiri rock-cut example.

SC644 Site W (Temple: Brahmanical)
S974 – Sculpture pile (in worship)
I-947: Sesa Narayana. 10th century AD (Phase 6).
I-948: Miscellaneous (Sculpture). Qty: 10. 10th century AD (Phase 6).

SC653 Site 11 (Background landscape)
S994 – Sculpture pile
I-564: *Saptamātṛkā*. 5th century AD (Phase 4). Material: L.B.S. Museum: GGMM.Published (Lake 1910a, 140)
I-565: Bodhisattva (Ht: 106 cm). 5th century AD (Phase 4). Material: L.B.S. Published.
Yakṣa/Bodhisattva (?), with round face and solid bulky shoulders. Arm band, and large torque necklace. Garland around forehead. Holds *vajra* in left hand. Circular nimbus behind head.

SC654 Bijalmandal (Temple: Brahmanical/Mosque)
S1001 – Temple remains (worship)
I-952: Miscellaneous (Sculpture). 10th–13th century AD (Phases 6–7). Published.

SC655 Modern Vidisha/Water tower (Background landscape)
S1005 – Sculpture pile (in worship)
I-953: Railing coping. 2nd–1st century BC (Phase 2).
Stupa railing decorated with interlinked lotus flowers on one face, and with three sockets for receiving cross bars visible on sides. Evidently from a large stupa structure.
I-954: Miscellaneous (Temple architecture). 10th century AD (Phase 6).

SC673 Forestry Commission (Background landscape)
S997 – Sculpture pile (in worship)
I-950: *Nāga*/Balarama (Wd: 35 cm; Ht: 67 cm). 2nd century AD (Phase 3b). Published (Shaw 2004a).
Anthropomorphic *nāga* image, surviving from the waist upwards, with five-headed serpent canopy. Holds three-pronged object in left hand. Its current *triśula*-like appearance (painted over with a flower) evidently explains why the image is currently under worship as Siva, but a breakage on the proper left side possibly marks the spot where it originally continued into a ploughshare shape.

SC703 Site X (Background landscape)
S1105 – In situ sculpture (in River Betwa)
I-1161: *Liṅga*. Qty: 2. 5th century AD (Phase 4).

SC714 Triveni (Background landscape)
S986 – Sculpture/cult spot
I-526: *Yakṣini* (Ht: 150 cm). Broken in two at waist 50 BC–25 AD (Phase 2/IIIa). Material: B.S. Museum: VM. Published (Chandra 1966). Found half buried in river Betwa.
I-536: *Yakṣa* (Ht: c. 200 cm). 50 BC–25 AD (Phase 2/IIIa). Material: L.B.S. Museum: VM.Published (Chandra 1966). Besnagar Kubera *yakṣa* found alongside I-526.

SC715 Unprovenanced sculptures (Background landscape)
S1137 – Miscellaneous sculpture
I-169: *Yakṣa* (Wd: 34 cm; Ht: 98 cm; Depth: 28 cm). Embedded in stand just below knees. Head and arms missing. Erosion over stomach. 125–130 AD (Phase 3b). Material: L.B.S. Museum: VM. (Acc. 75). Published (Shaw 2004a).
Standing *yakṣa*, broad chest. Sacred thread over left shoulder. Tranparent *dhotī* fabric gathered between legs. Striated belt tied in flat knot on right side. Flat striated *vanamālā* above knees.
I-171: Pillar remains (Ht: 300 cm). 115–80 BC (Phase 2). Material: L.B.S. Museum: VM (garden). (Acc. 103 (pillar); 341 (capital)). Published (Hartel 1987, pl. VIb).
Pillar shaft divided into three sections. Lower and upper section octagonal, with sixteen sided section in between. Spherical object separates pillar from capital. Surmounted by railing element, bead and lozenge moulding, cable necking and uninverted lotus capital. Since this is in reverse order to other capitals, it has been described as 'upside down' (Härtel 1987). However this appears not to be the case, as at the top of the lotus, as it presently stands, are the remains of what appear to be elephant feet interspersed by rearing cobras.
I-181: Bull capital (Lgt: 100 cm; Wd: 42 cm; Ht: 38 cm). Missing head and hump. Broken from upper legs downwards. Damage along spine as a result of someone's attempt to split the capital in two. 115–80 BC (Phase 2). Material: L.B.S. Museum: VM. (Acc. 273).
Humped bull capital. According to records, found 'near Udayagiri',
I-182: Bull capital (Lgt: 102 cm; Wd: 38 cm; Ht: 29 cm). Part of face missing; embedded in stand at upper legs. 115–80 BC (Phase 2). Material: L.B.S. Museum: VM. (Acc. 269).
Humped bull capital. Five pronounced creases at top of chest. Fleshy, heavy dewlap. Delicate carving around eyes.

I-333: Bull capital (Lgt: 89 cm; Wd: 30 cm; Ht: 46 Depth 12 cm). 115–80 BC (Phase 2). Material: L.B.S. Museum: BAM.
Humped bull capital. Ithyphallic; tail hanging straight down behind body. Heavy, fleshy dewlap. Short legs with disproportionately large feet. Set on large stone slab, with hole in centre, presumably for receiving tenon on pillar.
I-531: *Nāgakal*. 5th century AD (Phase 4). Material: L.B.S. Museum: VM. (Acc. 34). Published (Shaw 2004a).
Theriomorphic *Nāgakal*, with depictions of *tirthankaras* on either side of serpent canopy.
I-540: *Saptamātṛkā*. 5th century AD (Phase 4). Material: L.B.S. Museum: VMR (Acc: A1465)
Seated mother/Durga *Camundai* throttling child. Possibly formed part of group from Site 11 (SC653).
I-563: *Vedika*. 115–80 BC (Phase 2). Material: B.S. Museum: GGMM. (Acc. 8a). Published (Cunningham 1880).
Upright carved post. Two holes for *Sucika*. Devotees around tree.

SC716 Site A-B (Background landscape)
S48 – Pillar remains
I-530: Pillar remains. C. 50 BC–25 AD (Phase 2). Material: B.S. Published (Cunningham 1880)
Railed capital surmounted by 'wishing tree' in the round (*kalpadruma*).
I-1221: *Yakṣini*. 2nd–1st century BC (Phase 2). Calcutta Museum. Published (Cunningham 1880; Chandra 1966).
The 'Besnagar *yakṣini*'.

SC718 Mound R/12 (Temple: Brahmanical (?))
S965 – Temple remains
I-1224: *Abacus*. 5th century AD (Phase 4). Published (Lake 1910a, 142–3, fig. 12).
Large abacus with eight lions back to back, two lions on each of the four sides of the abacus, interspersed with trees. Very similar to those found at Amacchar (SG169).

SG007 Satdhara (ritual)

SC54 Stupa 1
S54 – Pillar/architectural remains
I-101: Elephant capital (Wd: 13 cm). Upper part of body broken. 3rd–2nd century BC (Phase 1d/2). Material: L.B.S.
Small rotund elephant capital with prominent humps on either side of head. Remains of striated sash around neck. Three vertical creases on upper chest (cf. elephant-with-rider from Besnagar (SG006/I-95), and one of the elephant medallions from Stupa 2, Sanchi).

SG008 Neemkheria (settlement)

SC61 (Settlement)
S548 – Sculpture pile (in worship)
I-50: Miscellaneous (Sculpture). Qty: 5. 11th–12th century AD (Phase 7). Material: P.S. Primary context: SG110/S446.
I-102: Durga *Mahiṣāsuramardinī* ('late' type). 11th century AD (Phase 7). Material: P.S. Primary context: SG110/S446.
I-103: *Saptamātṛkā*. 11th century AD (Phase 7) Material: P.S. Primary context: SG110/S446.

SG009 Bilori 1 (settlement)

SC62 (Settlement)
S549 – Sculpture pile (in worship)
*I-51:**Śalabanjika* (Wd: 15 cm; Ht: 20 cm; Depth: 10 cm). Lower half only. 25 AD (Phase 3a). Material: L.B.S. Primary context: SG001/S5.
Lower half of naked *Śalabanjika*. Double beaded belt around waist. Long braids of hair hang down over back. Miniature version of *Śalabanjika* from the bracket of Stupa 1 gateway. Probably from Sanchi.
I-52: Miscellaneous (Sculpture). Qty: 5. 10th century AD (Phase 6). Material: P.S. Primary context: SG002/S19.

S550 – Sculpture pile (in worship)
I-53: Siva (Wd: 14 cm; Ht: 28 cm). 10th century AD (Phase 6). Material: P.S. Primary context: SG002/S19.

SG010 Gulgaon-Eran (settlement)

SC91 Eran (Settlement)
S540 – Sculpture pile (in worship)
I-276: Pilaster. Qty: 2. 10th century AD (Phase 6). Material: P.S. Primary context: SG010/S378.
Fragment of pilaster with diamond motif.
I-277: Miscellaneous (Temple architecture). 10th century AD (Phase 6). Material: P.S. Primary context: SG010/S378.

S541 – Sculpture pile (in worship)
I-282: Hero stone. Material: P.S.

SC93 Eran (Temple: Brahmanical)
S93 – Temple remains (in worship)
I-285: Pilaster (Wd: 40 cm; Ht: 123 cm). 11th century AD (Phase 7). Material: L.B.S.
Temple pilaster with decorative floral border. Front face shows four-armed bearded figure, wearing rudrax *mala*. High crown. Upper right hand: spear; lower right hand: *varadamudra*.
I-286: Pilaster. Qty: 3 (Wd: 30 cm; Ht: 128 cm). 11th century AD (Phase 7). Material: L.B.S.
Pilaster with diamond pattern, and flat floral carving. Cf. Sas Bahu temple entrance door at Gwalior, dated VS 1150 (c. AD 1093–4) (Willis 1996, pl. 10).
I-287: Nandi. Fragmentary. 10th century AD (Phase 6). Material: L.B.S.

SC378 Eran (Temple: Brahmanical)
S378 – Temple remains (in worship)
I-278: Sesa Narayana. 10th century AD (Phase 6). Material: P.S.
I-279: Visnu. Head only; heavy damage to face. C. 400–415 AD (Phase 4). Material: W.S.
Wears high *kirīṭamukuṭa* crown, decorated with quatrefoil pattern. Circular medallion in centre with lion head, and string of pearls emerging from mouth.
I-280: Uma Maheswar. 10th century AD (Phase 6). Material: G.S.
I-281: Harihara (Wd: 14 cm; Ht: 18 cm; Depth: 14 cm). Head only. C. 430–460AD (Phase 4). Material: W.S.
Right side: Siva's dreadlocks; left side: Visnu's *kirīṭamukuṭa* crown decorated with rosace pattern.
I-283: Visnu. 10th century AD (Phase 6). Material: P.S.
Large Visnu image with side images, and *vyala*.
I-284: Miscellaneous (Sculpture). Qty: 20. 10th century AD (Phase 6). Material: P.S.

SC515 Gulgaon village (Settlement)
S554 – Sculpture pile (in worship)
I-736: Miscellaneous (Sculpture). 10th century AD (Phase 6). Primary context: SG010/S378.

SG010b Gulgaon (reservoir)

SC64 (Dam)
S551 – Sculpture pile (in worship)
I-104: *Nāga* (Wd: 76 cm; Ht: 190 cm; Depth: 11 cm). 80–50 BC (Phase 2). Material: B.S. Museum: SAM Published (ASIAR 1972–3 (pl. XLIV); Misra 1982; 1990; Williams 1976; Shaw 2004a)
Intact anthropomorphic *Nāgarāja* with thirteen-hooded snake canopy. Horizontal serpent coils. Lotus held in right hand. Spiral arm band; thick bracelets; Short torque, with three oval stones, and long, six-stringed necklace; chunky earrings, with beaded tassles. Spiral turban; opaque garment.
I-105: *Nāginī* (Ht: 147 cm). 80–50 BC (Phase 2). Material: B.S. Published (as above).
Female counterpart of I-104. Current whereabouts unknown.
I-106: Buddha. Torso only. 2nd–3rd century AD (Phase 3b). Material: R.M.M.S. Published (ASIAR 1972–3 (pl. XLIV). Primary context: SG001/S927.
Appears to have disappeared since earlier description in IAR 1972–3).
I-107: Miscellaneous (Sculpture). Qty: 5. 10th century AD (Phase 6). Material: P.S. Primary context: SG010/S378.
I-108: Tirthankara. 10th century AD (Phase 6). Material: B.S. Primary context: (?)
Standing Parsvanatha image, with seven headed snake canopy, and seven horizontally piled up coils behind body. Two female side deities, and *apsāra*. Below the main figure, to the left, is a male seated in *lalitāsana* holding a staff in his the hand and a pot in the right. Lion and two *apsāras* above main deity's head.

SG011b Ferozpur (settlement)

SC377 (Temple: Brahmanical)
S377 – Temple/pillar remains (in worship)
I-336: *Nāga* (Wd: 33 cm; Ht: 154 cm; Depth: 20 cm). Well-preserved. Painted. early 5th century AD (Phase 4). Material: B.S. Published (Williams 1976; Shaw 2004a).
Anthropormorphic *Nāgarāja* with seven-hooded canopy. Right hand holds bunch of half-closed lotus flowers. Left hand holds water jar (*kamandalu*). *kirīṭamukuṭa* crown with central lion head.
I-371: *Nāginī* (Wd: 30 cm; Ht: 115 cm; Depth: 14 cm). Painted. early 5th century AD (Phase 4). Material: B.S. Published (as above).
Nāginī with five-headed serpent canopy. Horizontal serpent coils behind back. Left hand resting on hip. Right hand upraised to shoulder, and holding lotus. Heavy anklets.
I-372: *Nāga* capital (Ht: 155 cm; Circumf: 165 cm). Bell capital half-submerged in ground. Painted. early 5th century AD (Phase 4). Material: B.S. Published (as above).
Lotiform bell capital, surmounted by cable moulding. Abacus decorated with aquatic plants and birds. Surmounted by two *nāgas* and two *Nāginīs* standing back to back. Both *nāgas* and *Nāginīs* hold bunch of lotus flowers in right hand.
I-373: *Makara* waterspout. 5th century AD (Phase 4). Material: P.S.
I-374: Miscellaneous (Temple architecture). Qty: 5. 11th century AD (Phase 7). Material: P.S.
Temple remains including pilaster with spiral cork-screw design, overflowing pot and diamond motif. Overflowing pot carved in reductive, 'flat' style. Cf. Gwalior Sas Bahu temple entrance door, dated VS 1150 (c. AD 1093–94) (Willis 1996, pl. 10).
I-375: Miscellaneous (Sculpture). Qty: 10. 10th century AD (Phase 6). Material: P.S.

SG012 Karhaud (settlement)

SC69 Mahadev gufa (Rock-shelter)
S69 – Rock-shelter/in situ sculpture (in worship)
I-376: *Liṅga*. Covered with *sindhur*. 5th–6th century AD (Phase 4). Material: B.S.
Ekamukhaliṅga with wide face. Rather crudely carved.

SC72 Durgasthan (Temple: Brahmanical)
S72 – Temple remains (in worship)
I-379: Durga *Mahiṣāsuramardinī*. 10th century AD (Phase 6). Material: P.S.
I-380: Uma Maheswar. 10th century AD (Phase 6). Material: P.S.
I-381: Hero stone. 10th century AD (Phase 6). Material: P.S.

SG012b Karhaud kherai (ritual)

SC344 Mata Mandir (Temple: Brahmanical)
S344 – Temple remains (in worship)
I-423: Hanuman. Covered with *sindhur*. 10th century AD (Phase 6). Material: P.S.
I-424: *Liṅga*. Covered with *sindhur*. 10th century AD (Phase 6). Material: P.S.
I-425: Durga *Mahiṣāsuramardinī* ('early' type). Covered with *sindhur*. 10th century AD (Phase 6). Material: P.S.
I-426: Hero stone (Ht: 300 cm). Material: P.S.
I-427: Visnu. Covered with *sindhur*. 10th century AD (Phase 6). Material: P.S.
I-478: Miscellaneous (Sculpture). Qty: 5. Covered with *sindhur*. 10th century AD (Phase 6). Material: P.S.

SG013 Andher (ritual)

SC73 Stupa 1
S73 – Architectural remains
I-383: *Vedika* (Wd: 40 cm; Ht: 186 cm; Depth: 15 cm). 115–80 BC (Phase 2). Material: B.S. Published (Bechert 2000). Railing bearing carving of Maya's dream.

SG013b Andher (background landscape)

SC78 (Temple: Brahmanical)
S77 – Sculpture/cult-spot (in worship)
I-109: *Nāga*/Balarama (Wd: 46 cm; Ht: 227 cm). Repainted as Siva. Headdress lying on ground separately. C. AD 25 (Phase 3a). Material: B.S.
Standing *Nāga*/Balarama with seven headed cobra canopy. Possibly four-armed. Upraised upper arms. Left hand holds club horizontally over head. Part of headdress on same platform.
I-110: Samkarsana/Balarama (Wd: 14 cm; Ht: 43 cm). Broken from chest upwards c. AD 25 (Phase 3a). Material: B.S.
Upper half of small male figure. Rounded face. Bulky turban. Right hand holds club horizontally over head. Remains of plough-share emerging from behind left shoulder. Details of Asoka tree fruit visible just below the left side of the plough. Leafy foliage cascading down in a looped garland. Cf. chowrie held by *yakṣa* on Stupa 1, eastern gateway.

S78 – Sculpture pile (in worship)
I-111: Uma Maheswar. Fragmentary. 10th century AD (Phase 6). Material: P.S.
I-112: Laksmi Narayana. Fragmentary. 10th century AD (Phase 6). Material: P.S.
I-113: Miscellaneous (Sculpture). Qty: 5. 10th century AD (Phase 6). Material: P.S.

SG014 Piparia (settlement)

SC81 (Settlement)
S570 – Sculpture pile (in worship)
I-114: Ganesa. Covered with *sindhur* and set upside down within mud. 10th century AD (Phase 6). Material: P.S. Primary context: SG002/S19.

SG017b Rangai village (settlement).

SC523 (Temple: Brahmanical)
S572 – Sculpture pile
I-115: Durga *Mahiṣāsuramardinī*. 10th century AD (Phase 6). Material: P.S.
I-117: Miscellaneous (Sculpture). Qty: 10. 10th century AD (Phase 6). Material: P.S.

SG018 Nonakhera (settlement)

SC84 (Settlement)
S544 – Sculpture pile (in worship)
I-732: Visnu. Primary context: SG108/S227.

S545 – Sculpture pile (in worship)
I-118: Votive stupa. 5th century AD (Phase 4). Material: B.S. Primary context: SG001/S927.
Votive stupa with niche containing Manjusri
I-119: *Vedika* (Wd: 5 cm; Ht: 12 cm). Fragmentary form, with heavy water erosion. c. 115–80 BC (Phase 2). Material: L.B.S. Primary context: SG001/S927.
Fragment of *vedika*, with sockets for *sucika*. Obverse side bears carving of naked goddess.
I-120: Visnu (Wd: 11 cm; Ht: 20 cm; Depth: 2.5 cm). 7th century AD (Phase 5). Material: L.B.S. Primary context: (?). Small plaque carved with four armed Visnu. Long staff in upper right hand. *Śaṅkha* in lower left hand.

S546 – Sculpture pile (in worship)
I-121: *Liṅga*. 10th century AD (Phase 6). Material: P.S. Primary context: SG108/S227.
I-122: Nandi. 10th century AD (Phase 6). Material: P.S. Primary context: SG108/S227.
I-123: *Makara* (not pipe). 5th–6th century AD (Phase 4). Material: B.S. Primary context: SG108/S227.

SG020 Kachi kanakhera-Amkhera (settlement)

SC86 Kachi kanakhera (Settlement)
S573 – Sculpture pile (in worship)
I-124: Hanuman. Head only. 10th century AD (Phase 6). Material: P.S. Primary context: SG002/S19.
I-125: Miscellaneous (Sculpture). Qty: 8. Badly eroded fragments. 11th–12th century AD (Phase 7). Material: P.S. Primary context: SG002/S19.

SC87 Amkhera (Settlement)
S543 – Sculpture pile (in worship)
I-126: Miscellaneous (Sculpture). Qty: 8. 10th century AD (Phase 6). Material: B.S. Primary context: SG050/S367
I-127: Hanuman. Head only. 10th century AD (Phase 6). Material: P.S. Primary context: SG050/S367
I-128: Hero stone. 10th century AD (Phase 6). Material: B.S.

SG021 Sehor (settlement)

SC89 (Settlement)
S574 – Sculpture pile (in worship)
I-129: *Mahiṣāsuramardinī* ('late' type) Heavily eroded. Very reductive carving style. 11th century AD (Phase 7). Material: P.S. Primary context: SG011b/S377.
I-635: *Sucika.* 115–80 BC (Phase 2). Material: B.S. Primary context: SG007/S54. Carved with lotus medallion.
I-636: *Sucika.* 115–80 BC (Phase 2). Material: B.S. Primary context: SG007/S54. Carved with lotus medallion.

SG023 Dargawan (settlement)

SC437 (Settlement)
S575 – Sculpture pile (in worship)
I-269: Durga *Mahiṣāsuramardinī.* 11th century AD (Phase 7). Material: P.S. Primary context: SG002/S19.

SG025 Pathar (background landscape)

SC436 (Temple: Brahmanical)
S436 – Temple remains (in worship)
I-270: Miscellaneous (Temple architecture). Qty: 3. 10th century AD (Phase 6). Material: P.S.
I-271: Miscellaneous (Sculpture) (Wd: 10 cm; Ht: 15 cm). Lower half of female figure. 9th century AD (Phase 6). Material: L.B.S.
I-272: Durga *Mahiṣāsuramardinī.* 10th century AD (Phase 6). Material: P.S.
I-273: *Liṅga.* 10th century AD (Phase 6). Material: P.S.
I-274: Sati (*in situ*) 1619 AD (Phase 8). Material: P.S.
I-275: Samadhi (*in situ*). Qty: 2. Material: P.S.

SG029b Dargawan hill (2) (reservoir)

SC99 Karondih (Dam)
S530 – Sculpture pile (in worship)
I-288: Siva (Wd: 14 cm; Ht: 20 cm). Heavily eroded. 10th century AD (Phase 6). Material: P.S. Primary context: SG002/S19.
I-289: Ganesa (Wd: 14 cm; Ht: 13 cm). Heavily eroded. 10th century AD (Phase 6). Material: P.S. Primary context: SG002/S19.

SG031 Udayagiri (ritual)

SC108 (Rock-cut temple complex)
S108 – Rock-cut cave no. 4 (Brahmanical)
I-1172: *Ekamukhaliṅga.* 5th century AD (Phase 4). Published (Williams 1982).

S1095 – Rock-cut cave nos. 5 and 6 (Brahmanical)
I-1173: Varaha. 5th century AD (Phase 4). Published (Williams 1982; Shaw 2004a).
I-1176: Visnu. 5th century AD (Phase 4). Published (Williams 1982, pl. 35)
I-1177: Visnu. 5th century AD (Phase 4). Published (Williams 1982; Shaw 2004, fig. 25)
I-1178: Durga *Mahiṣāsuramardinī.* Qty: 2. 5th century AD (Phase 4). Published (Williams 1982; Harle 1970; 1971–2).
I-1179: *Saptamātṛkā.* Qty: 2. 5th century AD (Phase 4). Published (Williams 1982)
I-1180: Ganesa. 5th century AD (Phase 4). Published (Williams 1982).

S1096 – Rock-cut cave no. 13 (Brahmanical)
I-1174: Sesa Narayana. 5th century AD (Phase 4). Published (Williams 1982; Willis 2004).

S1097 – Rock-cut cave (Jain)
I-1175: Tirthankara. 5th–6th century AD (Phase 4). Published (Williams 1982).

SC110 (Temple: Brahmanical)
S110 – Temple remains (in worship)
I-7: *Vedika* (Lgt: 20 cm; Wd: 20 cm). Incomplete. 115–80 BC (Phase 2). Material: B.S. Published (Cunningham 1880, 55). Primary context: SG031/S488. Bears carving of with half lotus medallion, similar in style to Heliodorus pillar medallions. At side is remains of socket for receiving *sucika.*
I-638: *Yakṣa* (Wd: 40 cm; Ht: 76 cm). 400–415 AD (Phase 4). Material: obscured by *sindhur.*
Upper half of massive standing male figure, possibly composite *Yakṣa*/Visnu image. Separate portion of buttocks lying separately.
I-982: Miscellaneous (Temple architecture). 9th century AD (Phase 6).

SC694 (Temple: Unknown)
S1094 – Temple/pillar remains on summit of hill
I-650: Lion capital. 115–80 BC (Phase 2). Museum: GGMM. (Acc. 54). Published (Dass and Willis 2002).
I-651: Pilaster. 5th century AD (Phase 4). Museum: GGMM. (Acc. 18). Published (Dass and Willis 2002).

SG031b Udayagiri/Madhupuri/ Sonapura (settlement)

SC220 Sonapura Maujimara (Temple: Brahmanical)
S220 – Temple remains (in worship)
I-246: Miscellaneous (Sculpture). Qty: 10. 10th century AD (Phase 6). Material: P.S.
I-247: Lion abacus (Wd: 45 cm; Ht: 45 cm; Depth: 42 cm). 5th century AD (Phase 4). Material: W.S.
Pilaster abacus with four lions at each corner. *Kirīṭamukuṭa* between each lion, arms reaching out to hold lions' tails.
I-586: Surya (Lgt: 25 cm; Wd: 26 cm). 10th century AD (Phase 6). Material: P.S. Fragment with carving of seven rearing horses of Surya.
I-587: Miscellaneous (Temple architecture). 9th century AD (Phase 6). Material: W.S.

SC221 Sonapura basti (Settlement)
S677 – Sculpture pile (in worship)
I-5: Siva. Head only. 2nd century AD (Phase 3b). Material: B.S.
I-588: Miscellaneous (Sculpture). Qty: 5. 10th century AD (Phase 6). Material: P.S. Primary context: SG031b/S220
I-589: Laksmi. 10th century AD (Phase 6). Material: P.S. Primary context: SG031b/S220
I-590: Laksmi Narayana. 10th century AD (Phase 6). Material: P.S. Primary context: SG031b/S220
I-591: Nandi. 10th century AD (Phase 6). Material: P.S. Primary context: SG031b/S220
I-592: *Sucika* (uncarved).(Lgt: 64 cm; Wd: 56 cm; Depth: 18 cm). 115–80 BC (Phase 2). Material: G.S. Primary context: SG031/S488.
I-593: Tirthankara. Head only. 10th century AD (Phase 6). Material: B.S. Primary context: SG031/S1097.
Head of Jain Tirthankara, with tightly curled hair.

S678 – Sculpture pile
I-594: Pilaster. 5th century AD (Phase 4). Material: B.S. Primary context: SG031b/S220.
Octagonal pilaster with overflowing pot/foliage capital.

SC222 Madhupuri (Settlement)
S679 – Sculpture pile (in worship)
I-595: Miscellaneous (Sculpture). Qty: 10. 10th century AD (Phase 6). Material: P.S. Primary context: SG031b/S220.
I-596: Tirthankara. 10th century AD (Phase 6). Material: B.S. Primary context: SG031/S1097.
Head of Jain tirthankara , with tightly curled hair.
I-597: Miscellaneous (Temple architecture). 405–415AD (Phase 4). Material: B.S. Primary context: SG031/S1094.
Fragment from L shaped relief from lintel of Gupta temple doorway. Shows leaf and foliage-clad branch, under which Goddess would have stood.

SG032 Dhakna village (settlement)

SC117 Dhakna village (Settlement)
S524 – Sculpture pile (n worship)
I-360: Miscellaneous (Sculpture). Qty: 3. 9th century AD (Phase 6). Material: B.S. Primary context: SG032/S468.
I-397: Visnu. Qty: 3. 10th century AD (Phase 6). Material: P.S. Primary context: SG032/S468.
I-398: Uma Maheswar. 10th century AD (Phase 6). Material: P.S. Primary context: SG032/S468.

S525 – Sculpture pile (in worship)
I-399: Deva. Head only. Detail obscured by heavy *sindhur.* 9th century AD (Phase 6). Material: B.S. Primary context: SG032/S468.
Male head with high headdress, consisting of square-shaped, jewelled crown, and protruding element on top.

SC468 Dhakna village (Temple remains: Unknown/mixed cult)
S1053 – Pillar remains (in worship)
I-395: Bull capital (Lgt: 97 cm; Wd: 38 cm; Ht: 34 cm). Half submerged in ground, and painted white. Head missing. 115–80 BC (Phase 2). Material: L.B.S. Pronounced hump. Flat back. Tail hangs straight down the back.

SC680 Dhakna basti (Temple: Brahmanical)
S526 – Temple remains (in worship)
I-130: Durga *Mahiṣāsuramardinī* (Wd: 37 cm; Ht: 52 cm). 8th century AD (Phase 5). Material: W.S.
'Early' type: four armed with Bufalo head still intact on ground. Robust lion attacking from right side. Wears flat cap-like headdress. Rotund modelling.
I-131: Durga. Head missing. 9th century AD (Phase 6). Material: W.S.
I-132: Pilaster. 5th–6th century AD (Phase 4). Material: R.S.
Obverse carved with lotus medallion.
I-394: Pilaster. 5th–6th century AD (Phase 4). Material: B.S.
Small pilaster with overflowing pot.

SG033 Chirauli (settlement)

SC119 (Settlement)
S582 – Sculpture pile (in worship)
I-400: Brahma. 10th century AD (Phase 6). Material: P.S. Primary context: SG025/S436.
I-401: Miscellaneous (Sculpture). Qty: 5. 10th century AD (Phase 6). Material: P.S. Primary context: SG025/S436.

SG034 Salamatpur chaura (ritual)

SC120 (Temple: Brahmanical)
S120 – Temple remains (in worship)
I-402: Miscellaneous (Temple architecture). Qty: 5. 10th century AD (Phase 6). Material: P.S.

SG036 Tigra hill (ritual)

SC125 (Temple: Brahmanical)
S125 – Temple remains (in worship)
I-403: Miscellaneous (Temple architecture). Qty: 2. 10th century AD (Phase 6). Material: P.S.
Fragment of temple base with diamond/flower motif.
I-404: Miscellaneous (Sculpture). Qty: 3. 10th century AD (Phase 6). Material: P.S.

SG037 Ahmadpur (settlement)

SC132 Ahmadpur village (Settlement)
S522 – Sculpture pile
I-542: Tirthankara. 10th century AD (Phase 6). Material: P.S. Primary context: SG037/S135.
Possibly Adinatha, with tight curls, and long locks at back of head. Similar in general appearance to Morel Khurd Buddha (SG005).
I-543: Hero stone. 10th century AD (Phase 6). Material: P.S.

S523 – Sculpture pile (in worship)
I-544: Laksmi Narayana. 10th century AD (Phase 6). Material: P.S. Primary context: SG037/S133.

SC133 Ahmadpur village (Temple: Brahmanical)
S133 – Sculpture pile (in worship)
I-541: Sesa Narayana. 10th century AD (Phase 6). Material: P.S.

SG037a Ahmadpur hill (ritual)

SC127 Ahmadpur hill (Rock-shelter cluster)
S836 – Rock-shelter/sculpture pile (in worship)
I-405: Uma Maheswar. Lower half only. 10th century AD (Phase 6). Material: P.S.

SC131 Ahmadpur hill (Temple: Brahmanical)
S131 – Temple remains (in worship)
I-175: Natarāja. Heavily eroded. Head missing. 9th century AD (Phase 6). Material: L.B.S.
Eight-armed, with two side images, carved on plaque. Transparent garment. Sinuous, elongated limbs.
I-357: *Nāgakal*. 10th century AD (Phase 6). Material: B.S.
Single serpent head from canopy of anthropomorphic *nāga*.
I-358: Durga *Mahiṣāsuramardinī* ('late' type). Upper half only. 10th century AD (Phase 6). Material: P.S.
I-359: Durga *Mahiṣāsuramardinī*. Lower half only. 10th century AD (Phase 6). Material: P.S.
'Late' type: severed head of bufalo lies on ground, with chunky lion biting from behind.
I-361: Devi. Qty: 5. 10th century AD (Phase 6). Material: P.S.
I-407: Miscellaneous (Sculpture). Small fragment from just below knees to above ankles. 5th century AD (Phase 4). Material: L.B.S.
Lower legs of male figure. Transparent *dhotī*, thick sash set at square-on angle below the knees. Sineous legs.
I-912: Inscribed slab. Lying outside temple (Lgt: 53 cm; Wd: 28 cm). Bears a *śankhalipi* inscription.

SG038 Ratanpur girdhari (settlement)

SC136 (Temple: Brahmanical)
S136 – Temple remains (in worship)
I-545: *Yakṣini* (Wd: 30 cm; Ht: 40 cm; Depth: 24 cm). Lower half only. 5th century AD (Phase 4). Material: L.B.S.
Lower legs of a large *yakṣini* image, set on tenon. Transparent skirt reaching ankles. Striated folds of cloth hanging down on proper left side. Heavy anklets. Cf. *Nāginī* outside temple 31, Sanchi (SG001).
I-546: *Yakṣini* (Wd: 22 cm; Ht: 36 cm; Depth: 15 cm). 5th century AD (Phase 4). Material: L.B.S.
Lower half of standing *yakṣini*. Fleshy stomach, prominent muscles around navel. Transparent skirt reaching ankles. Secured by tight hip belt (*katibandha*) tied by a buckle on the right hip. Striated scarf looped over left hip. Cf. *Nāginī* outside temple 31, Sanchi (SG001).
I-547: Durga *Mahiṣāsuramardinī* (Wd: 26 cm; Ht: 39 cm). Lower half only. 10th century AD (Phase 6). Material: P.S.
Follows unusual pattern whereby the head of the buffalo is being held upwards by the goddess, rather than being killed.
I-548: Durga. Feet of Durga standing on two lions. 10th century AD (Phase 6). Material: P.S.
I-566: Devi. Qty: 5. 10th century AD (Phase 6). Material: P.S.

SC137 (Settlement)
S593 – Sculpture pile (in worship)
I-567: Uma Maheswar. 10th century AD (Phase 6). Material: P.S. Primary context: SG038/S595.
I-568: Ganesa. 10th century AD (Phase 6). Material: P.S. Primary context: SG038/S595.

S594 – Sculpture pile (in worship)
I-184: Devi (Wd: 72 cm; Ht: 62 cm; Depth: 34 cm). 11th century AD (Phase 7). Material: L.B.S. Primary context: SG038/S595.
Lower half of large female deity. Right foot stands on the ground, while the left foot raised to stamp on forehead of small kneeling figure of indeterminate gender. Deity wears a decorated crown, with a round 'bun'; chunky anklets. Left arm wrapped around upper body of kneeling figure, with sword held in hand. Camundai and another female attendant on the left. Cf. 11th century AD Chandella image of 'flying female warriors' from Ratanpur (no. 83, in *Image of Man: Khajuraho Archaeology Museum*, 1821)
I-569: Hanuman (Wd: 25 cm; Ht: 33 cm). Broken into three parts. 10th century AD (Phase 6). Material: P.S. Primary context: SG038/S595.

SC690 (Temple: Brahmanical)
S595 – Temple remains (in worship)
I-185: Miscellaneous (Sculpture). Qty: 10. Fragmentary. 10th century AD (Phase 6). Material: P.S.

SG039 Fatehpur marmata (settlement)

SC140 (Settlement)
S596 – Sculpture pile (in worship)
I-570: Durga *Mahiṣāsuramardinī* ('early' type) (Wd: 25 cm; Ht: 27 cm). Lower half only. 10th century AD (Phase 6). Material: P.S. Primary context: SG025/S436.
I-571: Devi. Qty: 6. Fragmentary. 10th century AD (Phase 6). Material: P.S. Primary context: SG025/S436.

SG040 Bhartipur (settlement)

SC141 (Settlement)
S597 – Sculpture pile (in worship)
I-572: Uma Maheswar. Heavily eroded. 10th century AD (Phase 6). Material: P.S. Primary context: SG041/S142.

SG041 Besar talai (settlement)

SC142 Bhagvanpur colony (Temple remains: Brahmanical/Buddhist)
S142 – Temple remains (in worship)
I-133: Miscellaneous (Temple architecture). Qty: 5. 10th century AD (Phase 6). Material: B.S.
I-136: Uma Maheswar. 9th century AD (Phase 6). Material: P.S.
I-549: Visnu. 9th century AD (Phase 6). Material: P.S.
I-550: Sesa Narayana. 9th century AD (Phase 6). Material: W.S.
I-573: Nandi. Broken into two parts. 10th century AD (Phase 6). Material: G.S.

S1052 – Pillar remains
I-134: Bull capital (Lgt: 115 cm; Wd: 40 cm; Ht: 32 cm). Submerged in the ground at stomach level. 115–80 BC (Phase 2). Material: L.B.S.
Pronounced hump and flat back. Rope over bridge of the nose. Heavy dewlap. Thick garland around neck, decorated with lotuses, reminiscent in form to post-Mauryan lotus capitals. Tail looped over left side of body, hanging down on right. Terminates in conical tassel.
I-135: Bull capital (Lgt: 96 cm; Wd: 27 cm; Ht: 32 cm). Submerged in the ground at stomach level. Head and neck missing. 115–80 BC (Phase 2). Material: L.B.S.
Pronounced hump and flat back. Thick, striated sash around neck. Heavy dewlap. Ithyphallic. Tail looped over right side of body, hanging down on left.

SC143 Bhagvanpur colony (Settlement)
S598 – Sculpture pile (in worship)
I-408: *Makara* waterspout (Lgt: 28 cm; Wd: 18 cm). Neck only. Broken at mouth. 115–80 BC (Phase 2). Material: B.S. Primary context: SG041/S1052
Fragment of makara spout with garland around neck.
I-409: Miscellaneous (Sculpture) (Wd: 19 cm; Ht: 58 cm; Depth: 18 cm). 10th century AD (Phase 6). Material: B.S. Primary context =SG041/ S144.
Carved plaque with couple. Crude 'folky' style.
I-411: *Sucika*. 115–80 BC (Phase 2). Material: L.B.S. Primary context: SG041/S380.
Fragment with border of triangular beads. Lotus rosace in centre with smaller buds emerging from below. Enclosed by stalk, tied in knot at right side of rosace.

S599 – Sculpture pile (in worship)
I-410: *Vedika*. 115–80 BC (Phase 2). Material: L.B.S. Primary context: SG041/S380.
Carved railing pillar with indentation on one side for receiving solid cross bar. Obverse: lotus meander enclosing lotus rosaces. Reverse: high relief lotus rosaces.

SC144 Besar talai (Temple: Brahmanical/Jain)
S144 – Temple remains (in worship)
I-54: Miscellaneous (Temple architecture). Qty: 8. 10th century AD (Phase 6). Material: P.S.
I-137: Ambika (Wd: 40 cm; Ht: 60 cm). Two arms missing. 9th century AD (Phase 6). Material: P.S.
Four-armed Ambika (Jain goddess), seated on stool, in *lalitāsana*, with lion below. Side attendants, set within pilasters. Holds child on lap. Lotuses held in two surviving hands.
I-138: Ganesa. 10th century AD (Phase 6). Material: P.S.
I-139: Devi. 9th century AD (Phase 6). Material: P.S.
Standing, four-armed female deity, with side attendants, set within square pilasters. Lotus held in both right hands. Surviving left hand holds club.
I-140: *Liṅga*. 10th century AD (Phase 6). Material: P.S.
Standard yoni shaped stone carved with five individual *panchmukhaliṅgas*.
I-141: Nandi. Material: P.S.

SC145 Besar talai (Rock-shelter)
S145 – Rock-shelter/sculpture pile (in worship)
I-55: Uma Maheswar (Wd: 51 cm; Ht: 72 cm). 10th century AD (Phase 6). Material: P.S. Primary context: SG041/S144.
I-56: Nandi (Lgt: 75 cm; Wd: 45 cm). 10th century AD (Phase 6). Material: P.S. Primary context: SG041/S144.
I-57: Miscellaneous (Temple architecture). Qty: 5. 10th century AD (Phase 6). Material: P.S.
I-58: *Liṅga*. Qty: 3. 10th century AD (Phase 6). Material: P.S. Primary context: SG041/S144.

SC146 Besar talai (Settlement)
S602 – Sculpture pile (in worship)
I-412: Pillar remains. Qty: 2. 115–80 BC (Phase 2). Material: L.B.S. Primary context: SG041/S380.
Fragment of inverted lotus capital, with overlapping petals.

S603 – Sculpture pile (in worship)
I-413: Pillar remains. 115–80 BC (Phase 2). Material: L.B.S. Primary context: SG041/S380.
Fragment of inverted lotus capital, with overlapping petals.
I-414: *Sucika (uncarved)*. 115–80 BC (Phase 2). Material: L.B.S. Primary context: SG041/S380.

S604 – Pillar remains/Sculpture pile (in worship)
I-59: Pillar remains. Qty: 2. 115–80 BC (Phase 2). Material: L.B.S. Primary context: SG041/S380.
Fragment of inverted lotus capital, with overlapping petals.
I-415: *Vedika*. Qty: 3 (Lgt: 115 cm; Wd: 54 cm). 115–80 BC (Phase 2). Material: L.B.S. Primary context: SG041/S380.

SC380 (Stupa site)
S1051 – Pillar remains
I-142: Elephant capital (Lgt: 115 cm; Wd: 56 cm; Ht: 49 cm). Trunk and entire left portion of body missing. 115–80 BC (Phase 2). Material: L.B.S.
Elongated body. 'Ripple' folds on underbelly and upper neck. Swirly pattern on back legs. Prominent humps on either side of head. Ithyphallic.
I-143: Elephant capital (Wd: 40 cm; Ht: 38 cm). Legs and trunk missing. 115–80 BC (Phase 2). Material: L.B.S.
Small rotund elephant capital with prominent humps on either side of head. Ear-flaps spread out like a fan. Accentuated eye-sockets, with deep carving around lids.
I-144: Elephant capital (Lgt: 110 cm; Ht: 33 cm). Embedded in the ground at stomach level. Lower face also obscured by ground. 115–80 BC (Phase 2). Material: L.B.S.
Prominent bones on the lower back; hollow stomach.
I-145: Bull capital (Lgt: 92 cm; Ht: 27 cm). Head missing. Embedded in the ground at stomach level. 115–80 BC (Phase 2). Material: L.B.S.
Humped, with flat back, with prominent back bones. Wears sash around neck decorated with fine criss-cross pattern. Tail loops up and over right side of body.

SG042b Sayargaon (ritual)

SC149 (Rock-shelter)
S1099 – Rock-shelter/Sculpture pile (in worship)
I-416: Kal Bhairav. Broken into five parts, which have been pieced together. 9th century AD (Phase 6). Material: B.S. Primary context: SG045/S155 (?).
Four armed, standing in *tribangha*. Elongated body, sinuous limbs.

SG043 Bagri/Jamwar (settlement)

SC153 Jamwar (Settlement)
S611 – Sculpture pile (in worship)
I-419: Uma Maheswar. 10th century AD (Phase 6). Material: P.S. Primary context: SG043/S608.

SC532 Jamwar (Temple: Brahmanical)
S608 – Temple remains (in worship)
I-417: Miscellaneous (Sculpture). Qty: 20. 10th century AD (Phase 6). Material: P.S.
I-418: Hanuman (Ht: 49 cm). Broken from waist downwards; head missing. 10th century AD (Phase 6). Material: P.S.
I-454: Sesa Narayana. 10th century AD (Phase 6). Material: P.S.
I-456: *Makara* waterspout. 10th century AD (Phase 6). Material: P.S.

S609 – Sculpture pile (in worship)
I-455: Miscellaneous (Temple architecture). Qty: 5. 9th century AD (Phase 6). Material: P.S. Primary context: SG043/S608. Temple remains including pilasters with undecorated, overflowing *kumbhas*. Elaborately carved doorway. Cf. Maladevi temple, Gyaraspur.

SG044 Kharetiyal (settlement)

SC381 (Temple: Brahmanical)
S381 – Temple remains (in worship)
I-420: Miscellaneous (Sculpture). 10th century AD (Phase 6). Material: L.B.S. Fragment of *vastukand* from large *Devi* image.
I-421: Hero stone. Qty: 3. 10th century AD (Phase 6). Material: P.S.

SG050 Amkhera bhauji (settlement)

SC160 Amkhera bhauji colony (Settlement)
S510 – Sculpture pile (in worship)
I-431: Visnu. 10th century AD (Phase 6). Material: G.S. Primary context: SG050/S161.
I-432: Uma Maheswar. 10th century AD (Phase 6). Material: G.S. Primary context: SG050/S161.

SC161 Amkhera bhauji colony (Temple: Brahmanical)
S161 – Temple remains (in worship)
I-433: Uma Maheswar. 10th century AD (Phase 6). Material: P.S.
I-434: Miscellaneous (Temple architecture). 10th century AD (Phase 6). Material: P.S.

SC163 Amkhera 2 (Settlement)
S508 – Sculpture pile (in worship)
I-437: Durga *Mahiṣāsuramardinī*. Main image in shrine, covered with *sindhur* and dressed in clothes. 10th century AD (Phase 6). Primary context: SG050/S367.
I-438: Uma Maheswar. 10th century AD (Phase 6). Material: G.S. Primary context: SG050/S367.

S509 – Sculpture pile (in worship)
I-439: Visnu. 10th century AD (Phase 6). Material: G.S. Primary context: SG050/S367.
I-440: Miscellaneous (Sculpture). Qty: 8. 10th century AD (Phase 6). Material: P.S. Primary context: SG050/S367.

SC367 Shankar ji ka sthan (Temple: Brahmanical)
S367 – Temple remains (in worship)
I-441: Nandi. 10th century AD (Phase 6). Material: P.S.
I-442: *Liṅga*. 10th century AD (Phase 6). Material: P.S.

SG051 Katsari (settlement)

SC164 Katsari kherai (Settlement)
S613 – Sculpture pile (in worship)
I-443: *Saptamātṛkā*. Heavily damaged. Semi-submerged in mud platform. 5th century AD (Phase 4). Primary context: SG050/S367.
Saptamātṛkā panel, with Virabadra and Ganesa at either side of mothers. Rounded faces.

SG052 Kherai khera (settlement)

SC166 (Settlement)
S616 – In situ memorial (in worship)
I-447: Sati. Qty: 2. 11th–12th century AD (Phase 7). Material: obscured by *sindhur*.

SC686 (Temple: Brahmanical)
S614 – Temple remains (in worship)
I-444: Hanuman. 11th century AD (Phase 7). Material: P.S.
I-445: Hanuman. 11th century AD (Phase 7). Material: P.S.
I-446: Durga. 11th century AD (Phase 7). Material: P.S.

SG053c Amoni ka khera (background landscape)

SC168 Rajanal (Background landscape)
S617 – Sculpture pile (in worship)
I-448: Miscellaneous (Sculpture). Covered with *sindhur*. 10th century AD (Phase 6). Material: P.S. Primary context: (?).
Composite image made up of tiny, broken 10th century AD sculptural fragments.

SG054 Ucher (settlement)

SC170 (Settlement)
S618 – Sculpture pile (in worship)
I-154: Miscellaneous (Sculpture). 10th century AD (Phase 6). Material: P.S. Primary context: SG054/S172.
I-479: Visnu. 10th century AD (Phase 6). Material: P.S. Primary context: SG054/S172.
I-480: Miscellaneous (Sculpture). 10th century AD (Phase 6). Material: P.S. Primary context: SG054/S172.

S619 – Sculpture pile (in worship)
I-155: Miscellaneous (Sculpture). Qty: 3. 10th century AD (Phase 6). Material: P.S. Primary context: SG054/S172.

S620 – Sculpture pile (in worship)
I-449: Uma Maheswar. Lower half only. 10th century AD (Phase 6). Material: P.S. Primary context: SG054/S172.
I-450: Miscellaneous (Sculpture). Qty: 2. 10th century AD (Phase 6). Material: P.S. Primary context: SG054/S172.

S621 – Sculpture pile (in worship)
I-551: Miscellaneous (Sculpture). Qty: 3. 10th century AD (Phase 6). Material: P.S. Primary context: SG054/S172.
I-552: Nandi. 10th century AD (Phase 6). Material: P.S. Primary context: SG054/S172.

SG055 Berkheri (settlement)

SC174 (Settlement)
S512 – Sculpture pile (in worship)
I-553: Miscellaneous (Sculpture). Qty: 5. Heavily damaged fragments. 10th century AD (Phase 6). Material: P.S. Primary context: (?).
I-554: Uma Maheswar. Heavily damaged. 10th century AD (Phase 6). Material: P.S. Primary context: (?).

SG056 Mehgaon (settlement)

SC368 (Temple: Brahmanical)
S368 – Temple remains
I-510: Miscellaneous (Temple architecture). Qty: 5. 10th century AD (Phase 6). Material: P.S.

SC389 (Settlement)
S625 – Sculpture pile (in worship)
I-156: *Nāga*/Balarama (Wd: 50 cm; Ht: 82 cm; Depth: 8 cm). 50 AD (Phase 3a). Material: L.B.S. Primary context: SG056/S623.
Anthropomorphic figure with five-headed hood set horizontally over head. Two-pronged tongue protrudes from each of the *nāga* mouths. 'Folky' carving style. Rope-like plaits. Lopsided, bulbous turban. Pot, turned on its side, on top of head. Long pole supported by left arm, surmouted by 'trident' and lion's head. One of the former's prongs is broken and evidently extended to form a ploughshare.
I-176: Ganesa (seated on stool). 10th century AD (Phase 6). Material: P.S. Primary context: SG056/S368.
I-177: Durga *Mahiṣāsuramardinī*. Lower half only. 10th century AD (Phase 6). Material: P.S. Primary context: SG056/S368.
'Later' type: head of the buffalo lies severed on the ground.
I-178: Miscellaneous (Sculpture). Qty: 10. 10th century AD (Phase 6). Material: P.S. Primary context: SG056/S368.
I-555: Miscellaneous (Sculpture). Qty: 10. 10th century AD (Phase 6). Material: B.S. Primary context: SG056/S368.
I-556: *Saptamātṛkā*. Lower half only. 5th century AD (Phase 4). Material: B.S. Primary context: SG056/S368.
I-557: Durga. Upper half only. 10th century AD (Phase 6). Material: P.S. Primary context: SG056/S368.
I-558: Devi. 10th century AD (Phase 6). Material: P.S. Primary context: SG056/S368.
Four armed goddess, possibly Varahi, seated in *lalitāsana*. Set within two rounded pilasters. Boar-hooved feet. Tortoise below. Lower left hand holds water pot; upper left hand holds *cakra*.
I-559: *Saptamātṛkā*. Lower half only. 5th century AD (Phase 4). Material: B.S. Primary context: SG056/S368.
Seated mother, holding child on lap. Latter holds *daṅda*-type object.

SC390 (Tank)
S624 – In situ pillar
I-157: Pillar remains (Ht: 380 cm; Circumf: 100 cm). 10th century AD (Phase 6). Material: P.S.
Pillar in three sections: octagonal/16 sided /spherical, surmounted by tenon and remains of railed capital.

SG057 Khamkhera (settlement)

SC392 (Settlement)
S627 – Sculpture pile
I-158: Miscellaneous (Sculpture). Qty: 5. 11th century AD (Phase 7). Primary context: SG058/S631.

SG058 Tijalpur (settlement)

SC691 (Temple: Brahmanical)
S631 – Temple remains (in worship)
I-159: Visnu. 10th century AD (Phase 6). Material: P.S.
I-160: Uma Maheswar. 10th century AD (Phase 6). Material: P.S.
I-161: Miscellaneous (Sculpture). Qty: 5. 10th century AD (Phase 6). Material: P.S.
I-162: *Nāgakal* (Wd: 50 cm; Ht: 80 cm; Depth: 18 cm). 5th century AD (Phase 4). Material: L.B.S. Primary context: SG058/S445.
Theriomorphic *Nāgakal*, two rearing serpents with outspread cobra hoods.

SG059 Barahi khas (settlement)

SC395 (Settlement)
S635 – Sculpture pile (in worship)
I-2: Hero stone. 10th century AD (Phase 6). Material: B.S. Primary context: SG059b/S634.
I-3: Ganesa. 10th century AD (Phase 6). Material: P.S. Primary context: SG059b/S634.

SG059b Barahi khas (ritual)

SC681 (Temple: Brahmanical)
S634 – Temple remains (in worship)
I-163: Nandi. 11th century AD (Phase 7). Material: P.S.
I-164: *Liṅga*. 11th century AD (Phase 7). Material: P.S.
I-165: Miscellaneous (Sculpture). Qty: 4. 11th century AD (Phase 7). Material: P.S.

SG061 Pagneswar (settlement)

SC397 (Settlement)
S517 – Sculpture pile (in worship)
I-639: Durga *Camundai*. 10th century AD (Phase 6). Material: P.S. Primary context: SG061/S515.
I-640: Uma Maheswar. Qty: 3. 10th century AD (Phase 6). Material: P.S. Primary context: SG061/S515.
I-641: Nataraja. 10th century AD (Phase 6). Material: P.S. Primary context: SG061/S515.
I-642: Miscellaneous (Sculpture). Qty: 5. 10th century AD (Phase 6). Material: P.S. Primary context: SG061/S515.
I-643: Miscellaneous (Sculpture). Qty: 5. 11th century AD (Phase 7). Material: P.S. Primary context: SG061/S515.
I-644: Durga *Mahiṣāsuramardinī* ('late' type). 11th century AD (Phase 7). Material: P.S. Primary context: SG061/S515.

SC400 (Temple: Brahmanical)
S400 – Temple remains (in worship)
I-499: Miscellaneous (Sculpture). Qty: 5. 10th century AD (Phase 6). Material: P.S.

S518 – Sculpture pile (in worship)
I-725: Miscellaneous (Sculpture). Qty: 20. Material: P.S.

SC507 (Temple: Brahmanical)
S515 – Temple remains (in worship)
I-645: Miscellaneous (Temple architecture). Qty: 20. 10th century AD (Phase 6). Material: P.S.
Various temple elements re-incorporated into late medieval mosque.

SC697 (Temple: Brahmanical)
S516 – Temple remains
I-290: *Yakṣa* /Bodhisattva (?). (Wd: 59 cm; Ht: 80 cm; Depth: 37 cm). Head and arms missing; lying horizontally, half-submerged in ground. 130 AD (Phase 3b). Material: L.B.S.
Standing male figure, broad chest, deep-set navel, fleshy stomach. Transparent *dhotī*, reaching to ankles. Prominent genitalia. Massive spade-like feet. Striated folds of cloth fall on right side of body. Waist belt with large rectangular buckle. Thick rope-like sash falls over knees in 'U' shape.
I-291: Varaha. Lower fragment only. 9th century AD (Phase 6). Material: B.S. Carved in the round, showing snake, and kneeling female figure.
I-292: Varaha (?) (Lgt: 110 cm; Ht: 50 cm). Part of head only. 10th century AD (Phase 6). Material: P.S.
Large animal resembling an elephant. However, front part of head is missing, therefore not possible to confirm. Body carved with 1000 gods, more commonly associated with Varaha images.
I-293: Ganga (Lgt: 25 cm; Wd: 13 cm; Depth: 15 cm). Base and feet only. 8th century AD (Phase 5). Material: B.S.
Feet of goddess, with delicately carved crocodile and two side images on lower base.
I-494: *Nāginī* (Wd: 50 cm; Ht: 40 cm; Depth: 20 cm). Head and snake canopy only. 130 AD (Phase 3b). Material: L.B.S.
Nāginī with seven-headed serpent canopy. Rounded face, thick lips, grimacing smile. Heavy ringlets piled up on top of head.
I-495: *Liṅga*. 130 AD (Phase 3b). Material: B.S.
I-496: Hanuman. 10th century AD (Phase 6). Material: P.S.
I-497: Makara waterspout. 10th century AD (Phase 6). Material: P.S.
I-498: Miscellaneous (Sculpture). 10th century AD (Phase 6). Material: P.S.

SG062 Dhobakheri (settlement)

SC401 (Settlement)
S547 – Sculpture pile (Site in worship)
I-500: Durga *Mahiṣāsuramardinī*. Covered with *sindhur*. 7th–8th century AD (Phase 5). Material: G.S. Primary context: (?)
'Early' type: Buffalo's head still intact, being held by Goddess.
I-501: Ganesa. 10th century AD (Phase 6). Material: G.S. Primary context: (?)
Plaque with 'squat' Ganesa seated in *lalitāsana*.
I-502: Miscellaneous (Sculpture). Fragment only. 11th–12th century AD (Phase 7). Material: P.S. Primary context: (?). Fragment of Vaisnava image.
I-503: Hanuman. 11th–12th century AD (Phase 7). Material: P.S. Primary context: (?).

SG063 Dhaniakheri (settlement)

SC403 (Settlement)
S636 – Sculpture pile
I-504: Durga *Camundai*. 10th century AD (Phase 6). Material: P.S. Primary context: SG064/S406.
I-505: Devi. Qty: 5. Heavily damaged. 10th century AD (Phase 6). Material: P.S. Primary context: SG064/S406.

SG064 Tajpura shur (settlement)

SC404 (Settlement)
S407 – Sculpture pile
I-296: Bull capital (Lgt: 114 cm; Wd: 30 cm; Ht: 36 cm). 115–80 BC (Phase 2). Material: L.B.S. Primary context: SG064/S406.
Pronounced hump,and protruding back bones. Tail hangs straight to the ground. Decorated floral garland around neck. Ears extend forward. Eye sockets carved with two circular bands.

S513 – Sculpture pile
I-506: Miscellaneous (Sculpture). Qty: 10. 10th century AD (Phase 6). Material: B.S. Primary context: SG064/S406.
I-517: Durga *Camundai*. 10th century AD (Phase 6). Material: B.S. Primary context: SG064/S406.
I-518: Durga *Mahiṣāsuramardinī*. 10th century AD (Phase 6). Material: B.S. Primary context: SG064/S406.
'Early' type: buffalo's head, still intact on ground; hind legs being held by Goddess.

SC406 (Temple: Brahmanical)
S406 – Temple remains (in worship)
I-294: Uma Maheswar. 10th century AD (Phase 6). Material: P.S.
I-295: Devi. Lower fragment only. 10th century AD (Phase 6). Material: P.S. Feet of female figure with side attendants.
I-574: Pilaster. 405–415AD (Phase 4). Material: L.B.S.
Similar to pilaster in temple 31, Sanchi, datable to c. AD 405–15 AD (Williams 1986, pl. 40).

SG066 Torin hill (ritual)

SC410 Stupa site
S637 – Sculpture pile (in worship)
I-297: Miscellaneous (Sculpture). Qty: 4. 10th century AD (Phase 6). Material: P.S. Primary context: SG036/S125.

SG067 Rajatalai (settlement)

SC414 (Settlement)
S642 – Sculpture pile (in worship)
I-298: Durga *Mahiṣāsuramardinī* 11th century AD (Phase 7). Material: P.S. Primary context: (?).
'Early' type: buffalo's head still intact on ground; hind legs held by Goddess. Lion biting buffalo neck from behind. However, stylistically, very reductive and 'folky'. Primary context: (?).
I-299: Nandi. 11th century AD (Phase 7). Material: P.S. Primary context: (?).
I-300: *Liṅga*. 11th century AD (Phase 7). Material: P.S. Primary context: (?).

SG071 Bilori 2 (settlement)

SC656 Temple: Brahmanical
S645 – Temple remains (in worship)
I-313: Pilaster. Qty: 4. 10th century AD (Phase 6). Material: P.S. Incorporated into modern temple.
I-314: Nandi. 10th century AD (Phase 6). Material: P.S.
I-315: Miscellaneous (Sculpture). Qty: 10. 11th century AD (Phase 7). Material: P.S.

SG072 Khamtala (settlement)

SC420 (Settlement)
S646 – In situ memorial
I-316: Samadhi. Qty: 2. Material: B.S.

S1021 – Pillar remains (in worship)
I-577: Pillar remains. 10th century AD (Phase 6). Material: P.S.
Pillar with square base, followed by octagonal/four-sided/octagonal/cylindrical sections. Square tenon to receive capital. Recarved as Sati pillar.

SC421 (Tank)
S648 – In situ pillar remains (in worship)
I-578: Pillar remains. 10th century AD (Phase 6). Material: P.S.
Fragment of pillar set in middle of tank. Consists of octagonal and four-sided section, surmounted by plain, spherical capital.

SC685 Temple: Brahmanical
S647 – Temple remains (in worship)
I-317: Ganesa. Heavily eroded and defaced. 5th–6th century AD (Phase 4). Material: L.B.S.
I-318: Durga *Mahiṣāsuramardinī* ('late' type). Lower half only. 10th century AD (Phase 6). Material: P.S.
I-575: Uma Maheswar. Lower half only. 10th century AD (Phase 6). Material: P.S.
I-576: Miscellaneous (Sculpture). Qty: 5. 10th century AD (Phase 6). Material: P.S.

SG073 Bankheri (settlement)

SC422 (Settlement)
S649 – Sculpture pile (in worship)
I-481: Miscellaneous (Sculpture). Qty: 5. 11th–12th century AD (Phase 7). Material: P.S. Primary context: SG072/S647.
I-579: Durga *Mahiṣāsuramardinī*. 11th–12th century AD (Phase 7). Material: P.S. Primary context: SG072/S647.
I-580: Ganesa. 11th–12th century AD (Phase 7). Material: P.S. Primary context: SG072/S647.

SG084b Pathari kativarat (background landscape)

SC539 Kativarat (Rock-shelter)
S656 – Rock-shelter/Sculpture pile (in worship)
I-186: Durga *Mahiṣāsuramardinī*. 10th century AD (Phase 6). Material: P.S. Primary context: SG084/S187.
I-187: *Nāgakal* (Wd: 25 cm; Ht: 64 cm; Depth: 12 cm). 10th century AD (Phase 6). Material: P.S. Primary context: SG084/S187.
Theriomorphic *Nāgakal*: stone slab decorated with two entwined serpents. Coils arranged in knotted design, outspread cobra canopies.
I-188: Miscellaneous (Sculpture). Qty: 10. 10th century AD (Phase 6). Material: P.S. Primary context: SG084/S187.
I-482: *Saptamātṛkā*. 10th century AD (Phase 6). Material: P.S. Primary context: SG084/S187.

SG084d Pathari/Gehunkheri (settlement)

SC475 (Settlement)
S651 – Sculpture pile (in worship)
I-701: Hanuman. 10th century AD (Phase 6). Material: P.S. Primary context: SG084/S187.

S652 – Sculpture pile (in worship)
I-700: Tirthankara. 10th century AD (Phase 6). Material: P.S. Primary context: SG177/S345 (?).

SG087 Morel khurd village (settlement)

SC190 (Settlement)
S660 – Sculpture pile (in worship)
I-189: Miscellaneous (Sculpture). Qty: 8. 11th century AD (Phase 7). Material: P.S. Primary context: SG005/S31 (?).

SG088 Kanpohra (settlement)

SC191 Agrola (Temple: Brahmanical)
S191 – Temple remains (in worship)
I-146: Miscellaneous (Sculpture). Qty: 5. Heavily eroded. 11th–12th century AD (Phase 7). Material: P.S.

SG090 Mawasa (ritual)

SC197 Background landscape
S197 – Sculpture pile
I-147: Pilaster. 5th–6th century AD (Phase 4). Material: B.S. Primary context: SG092/S199 (?).

SG092 Nihalpur/Dandoli kherai (settlement)

SC198 Nihalpur (Settlement)
S505 – Sculpture pile (in worship)
I-148: Ardhaneśwara. 8th century AD (Phase 5). Material: B.S. Primary context: SG092/S199.
Rounded face; flat, cap-like headdress.
I-149: *Saptamātṛkā*. 10th century AD (Phase 6). Material: B.S. Primary context: SG092/S199.
I-150: Durga. Feet and base only. 10th century AD (Phase 6). Material: P.S. Primary context: SG092/S199.
Carved in the round, with massive sculptural volume. Lions carved on lower base.
I-151: Kal Bhairav. 10th century AD (Phase 6). Material: P.S. Primary context: SG092/S199. 'Folky' style.
I-152: Miscellaneous (Sculpture). Qty: 10. 10th century AD (Phase 6). Material: P.S. Primary context: SG092/S199.
I-190: Hero stone. Qty: 6. 10th century AD (Phase 6). Material: P.S. Primary context: SG092/S199.

SG095b Chandna hill (settlement)

SC205 (Settlement)
S504 – Sculpture pile (in worship)
I-485: Hero stone. 10th century AD (Phase 6). Material: P.S. Primary context: SG095b/S664.
I-486: Pilaster. 9th century AD (Phase 6). Material: G.S. Primary context: SG095b/S664.
Decorated with inverted lotuses, and Hanuman image.
I-487: Hanuman. 10th century AD (Phase 6). Material: G.S. Primary context: SG095b/S664.
I-488: Durga *Mahiṣāsuramardinī* ('late' type). 10th century AD (Phase 6). Material: G.S. Primary context: SG095b/S664.
I-489: Makara waterspout. 10th century AD (Phase 6). Material: G.S. Primary context: SG095b/S664.
I-490: Laksmi Narayana. 10th century AD (Phase 6). Material: G.S. Primary context: SG095b/S664.
I-491: Tirthankara (Wd: 20 cm; Ht: 30 cm; Depth: 8 cm). 10th century AD (Phase 6). Material: G.S. Primary context: SG095b/S664.
Small Tirthankara image seated in *padmāsana*. Possibly side image of larger deity.
I-492: Miscellaneous (Sculpture). Qty: 10. 10th century AD (Phase 6). Material: G.S. Primary context: SG095b/S664.

SG095c Chandna hill (reservoir)

SC204 Dam
S1100 – Sculpture pile (in worship)
I-1: *Nāga*/Balarama. 50 BC–25 AD (Phase 2). Material: L.B.S. Published (Shaw 2004a; Shaw and Sutcliffe 2003a).
Standing anthropomorphic *nāga* with five headed serpent hood spreading out over his head. No coils can be seen, but rather the shaft of the snake rises in a single column behind the back. Probably originally stood directly on top of a pile of coils, similar to the arrangement at Salera (SG170). Small squat body, with stocky chest and stomach, with little differentiation between the two. Wears thick sash, set low over hips, tied in a simple cross-knot at the front. The treatment of the sash and knot is very similar to the Besnagar Kubera *Yakṣa*, as is the remains of a long plain necklace, and a piled-up turban. Face has been heavily damaged, but the long curly locks are still visible hanging over shoulders. Just behind the remaining left shoulder, is the upper remaining section of a long vertical object, probably a plough; this justifies the Balarama interpretation.

SC696 Temple: Brahmanical
S664 – Temple remains
I-4: Miscellaneous (Temple architecture) around base of dam. Qty: 5. 10th century AD (Phase 6). Material: P.S. Temple mouldings and sculpture bases.

SG098 Budha Pahar (ritual)

SC469 Ravangav (Background landscape)
S469 – In situ sculpture (in worship)
I-703: *Yakṣa*. 2nd century BC (Phase 2).

SC471 Stupa site
S471 – Sculpture pile
I-704: Buddha. Base and lower legs only (in *padmāsana*). 2nd century AD (Phase 3b). Material: L.B.S.

SG099 Morel kala (reservoir)

SC211 Dam
S667 – Sculpture pile (in worship)
I-232: *Nāga* (Wd: 33 cm; Ht: 94 cm). Broken from waist downwards; feet missing. 125–130 AD (Phase 3b). Material: L.B.S.
Lower half of anthropomophic *Nāgarāja*. Horizontal serpent coils. Transparent cloth. Zig-zag folds between legs. Striated sash skims knees at square-on angle.

SG099b Morel kala (settlement)

SC371 (Temple: Brahmanical)
S371 – Temple remains (in worship)
I-582: Siva. 10th century AD (Phase 6). Material: P.S.

S670 – Sculpture pile (in worship)
I-493: Miscellaneous (Sculpture). Qty: 5. 10th century AD (Phase 6). Material: P.S. Primary context: SG099b/S371.
I-581: *Mahiṣāsuramardinī*. 10th century AD (Phase 6). Material: P.S. Primary context: SG099b/S371.

SC544 Settlement
S669 – Sculpture pile (in worship)
I-511: Ambika. 10th century AD (Phase 6). Material: P.S. Primary context: SG099b/S671.
I-512: Uma Maheswar. 10th century AD (Phase 6). Material: P.S. Primary context: SG099b/S371.
I-787: Visnu. 10th century AD (Phase 6). Primary context: SG099b/S371.

SC687 (Temple: Jain)
S671 – Temple remains
I-583: Tirthankara. Qty: 2 (Wd: 53 cm; Ht: 68 cm). Head missing. 10th century AD (Phase 6). Material: B.S.
Seated in *Padmāsana*, with hands resting on knees in *dhyānamūdra*. Well formed chest, and stomach muscles. Lower plinth carved with two lions.
I-584: Tirthankara. 10th century AD (Phase 6). Material: P.S.
Standing image, possibly Adinatha, with long tresses of hair. Side panels carved in similar style as Buddha from Morel Khurd (SG005)
I-585: Tirthankara. Heavily eroded. 10th century AD (Phase 6). Material: P.S.
Seated in *padmāsana*, with hands resting on knees in *dhyānamūdra*.

SG100 Pali (settlement)

SC212 (Settlement)
S672 – Sculpture pile (in worship)
I-233: Durga *Mahiṣāsuramardinī*. Covered with *sindhur*. 7th–8th century AD (Phase 5). Material: B.S. Primary context: SG099b/S371.
Four-armed/'early' type: buffalo head still intact on ground, tail held by goddess. Rounded face, flat 'cap' like headdress.
I-234: Visnu. Covered with *sindhur*. 10th century AD (Phase 6). Material: P.S. Primary context: SG099b/S371.
I-235: Hero stone. Covered with *sindhur*. 9th century AD (Phase 6). Material: B.S. Primary context: SG099b/S371.

SC213 Gufa mandir (Rock-shelter)
S673 – Rock-shelter/Sculpture pile (in worship)
I-236: Miscellaneous (Sculpture). Qty: 5. Heavily eroded. 10th century AD (Phase 6). Material: P.S. Primary context: SG099b/S371.

SG101 Andol (settlement)

SC216 Andol kherai (1) (Settlement)
S674 – Sculpture pile (in worship)
I-241: Miscellaneous (Sculpture). Qty: 5. 10th century AD (Phase 6). Material: P.S. Primary context: SG101/S372.

SC372 Andol (Temple: Brahmanical)
S372 – Temple remains (in worship)
I-238: Parvati (four-armed). 10th century AD (Phase 6). Material: P.S.
I-239: Visnu (four-armed). 10th century AD (Phase 6). Material: P.S.
I-240: Miscellaneous (Sculpture). 9th century AD (Phase 6). Material: W.S.

SC720 (Background landscape)
S675 – Sculpture pile (in worship)
I-237: *Nāgakal* (Wd: 60 cm; Ht: 135 cm; Depth: 12 cm). 10th century AD (Phase 6). Material: P.S. Primary context: SG101/S372.
Small *Nāgakal* with very simple snake carving. Three headed cobra hood.

SG102 Sachet (settlement)

SC219 (Settlement)
S676 – Sculpture pile (in worship)
I-242: Durga. Covered with *sindhur*. 7th century AD (Phase 5). Material: L.B.S. Primary context: SG102/S473.
I-244: Miscellaneous (Sculpture). Qty: 8. 10th century AD (Phase 6). Material: P.S. Primary context: SG102/S473.

SC473 (Temple: Brahmanical)
S473 – Temple remains (in worship)

I-243: Miscellaneous (Sculpture). Qty: 10. Covered with *sindhur*. 10th century AD (Phase 6). Material: P.S.

SG108 Ram bhauri (background landscape)

SC227 (Temple: Brahmanical)
S227 – Temple remains (in worship)
I-598: Varaha. 10th century AD (Phase 6). Material: P.S. Body carved all over with '1000 gods'.

SG109 Karhaiya (settlement)

SC229 (Settlement)
S681 – Sculpture pile (in worship)
I-599: Miscellaneous (Sculpture). Qty: 10. 11th–12th century AD (Phase 7). Material: P.S. Primary context: (?),

SG110 Bighan village (settlement)

SC446 (Temple: Brahmanical)
S446 – Temple remains (in worship)
I-600: Miscellaneous (Temple architecture). 10th century AD (Phase 6). Material: P.S.
I-601: Durga *Mahiṣāsuramardinī* ('late' type), very reductive style. 11th–12th century AD (Phase 7). Material: P.S.
I-602: Miscellaneous (Sculpture). Qty: 10. 10th century AD (Phase 6). Material: P.S.

SG113 Alamkhera (settlement)

SC234 (Temple: Brahmanical)
S234 – Temple remains
I-603: Miscellaneous (Sculpture). Qty: 5. Heavily eroded; semi-submerged in jungle foliage. 10th century AD (Phase 6). Material: P.S.
I-604: Visnu. Semi-submerged in ground. 10th century AD (Phase 6). Material: P.S.

SC235 (Temple: Brahmanical)
S235 – In situ memorial (in worship)
I-606: Sati. Late Medieval (Phase 8). Material: P.S.

SG114 Bhauliya (settlement)

SC448 Temple: Brahmanical
S448 – Temple remains (in worship)
I-607: Uma Maheswar. 11th century AD (Phase 7). Material: P.S.

SG115 Bhaijakhera (settlement)

SC238 (Settlement)
S683 – Sculpture pile (in worship)
I-608: Miscellaneous (Sculpture). Qty: 8. Late Medieval (Phase 8). Material: P.S. Primary context: SG113/S234.

SG118b Murwara hill (settlement)

SC449 (Temple: Brahmanical)
S449 – Temple remains (in worship)
I-609: Hero stone. Late Medieval (Phase 8). Material: P.S.
I-610: Miscellaneous (Sculpture). Qty: 8. Late Medieval (Phase 8). Material: P.S.

SG121 Mahuakhera-Himatgarh (settlement)

SC430 Himatgarh (Settlement)
S691 – Sculpture pile (in worship)
I-195: Miscellaneous (Sculpture). Qty: 8. Heavily damaged. Late Medieval (Phase 8). Material: P.S. Primary context: SG121/S688.

SC546 Mahuakhera (Temple: Brahmanical)
S687 – Sculpture pile (in worship)
I-613: Miscellaneous (Sculpture). Qty: 8. 11th–12th century AD (Phase 7). Material: P.S. Primary context: SG121/S688.
I-614: Durga *Mahiṣāsuramardinī* ('late' type). 11th–12th century AD (Phase 7). Material: P.S. Primary context: SG121/S688.

S688 – Temple remains
I-615: Miscellaneous (Sculpture). 10th century AD (Phase 6). Material: P.S.

SG123 Devalkhera (settlement)

SC684 (Temple: Brahmanical)
S689 – Temple remains (in worship)
I-248: Durga *Mahiṣāsuramardinī* ('late' type). 10th century AD (Phase 6). Material: P.S.
I-249: Uma Maheswar. 10th century AD (Phase 6). Material: P.S.
I-250: *Nāga*/Visnu (Ht: 46 cm). Broken into three parts, of which only the upper and lower part remain. Upper part is broken at chest; lower half is broken just above waist. Section in between is missing. 405–415AD (Phase 4). Material: B.S. Four-armed Visnu as *nāgarāja*. Seven headed snake canopy, horizontal serpent coils. Lower right hand: personified *gadā*; lower left hand: personified *cakra*; upper left hand: *Śaṅkha*; upper right hand: missing. Wears *kirīṭamukuṭa* crown. Distended ear-lobes with chunky earrings; heavy torque necklace. Transparent cloth.
I-251: Miscellaneous (Temple architecture). 405–415AD (Phase 4). Material: B.S. Part of lintel from temple doorway, showing dwarf holding tail of crocodile.
I-252: *Vedika* (Lgt: 13 cm; Wd: 11 cm; Ht: 22 cm). 1st century BC (Phase 2). Material: W.S. Primary context: S1098.
Lower fragment of carved *vedika* with one socket and a half visible on the side for receiving *sucika*. Carved on obverse side with female figure standing on crocodile. Transparent garment reaching lower calves. 'Naked' appearance of genitalia. Folds of cloth fall in criss-cross pattern down left side, held back by left hand. Folds on right side fall in sharp point. Heavy anklets.
I-616: Miscellaneous (Sculpture). Qty: 10. 10th century AD (Phase 6). Material: P.S.

SG125 Parwariya/Arwariya (settlement)

SC450 Arwariya (Settlement)
S692 – Sculpture pile (in worship)
I-194: Hanuman. Qty: 2 (Ht: 92 cm). 10th century AD (Phase 6). Material: L.B.S. Primary context: SG166/S762.

SG126 Chopra (settlement)

SC432 (Settlement)
S501 – Sculpture pile (in worship)
I-507: Nandi. 10th century AD (Phase 6). Material: P.S. Primary context: SG064/S406(?).

SG127 Chirohli (settlement)

SC243 Chirohli kherai (Settlement)
S694 – Sculpture pile (in worship)
I-319: Devi. Heavily damaged. 10th century AD (Phase 6). Material: P.S. Primary context: SG064/S406(?).

SC548 (Settlement)
S500 – Sculpture pile (in worship)
I-320: Durga *Mahiṣāsuramardinī*. Heavily damaged; covered with *sindhur*. 8th century AD (Phase 5). Material: B.S. Primary context: SG064/S406(?). 'Early' type: buffalo's head still intact, lying on ground. Robust lion biting into buffalo's behind.

SG128 Chiroriya village (settlement)

SC549 (Temple: Brahmanical)
S695 – Temple remains (in worship)
I-321: Miscellaneous (Sculpture). Qty: 20. 10th century AD (Phase 6). Material: P.S.
I-1104: Miscellaneous (Temple architecture). 10th century AD (Phase 6).

SG129 Chiroriya kherai (settlement)

SC245 (Settlement)
S696 – Sculpture pile (in worship)
I-803: Hanuman. Primary context: SG129/S246.

SC246 (Temple: Brahmanical)
S246 – Temple remains (in worship)
I-322: Sculpture base. 10th century AD (Phase 6). Material: P.S.
I-323: Hanuman. 10th century AD (Phase 6). Material: P.S.
I-324: Sati. Qty: 2. 10th century AD (Phase 6). Material: P.S.
I-611: Uma Maheswar. 10th century AD (Phase 6). Material: P.S.
I-612: Miscellaneous (Sculpture). Qty: 10. 10th century AD (Phase 6). Material: P.S.
I-646: Hero stone. Qty: 2. 10th century AD (Phase 6). Material: P.S.

SG130 Bhauriya (settlement)

SC451 (Temple: Brahmanical)
S451 – Temple remains (in worship)
I-647: Miscellaneous (Sculpture). Qty: 8. 10th century AD (Phase 6). Material: P.S.
I-977: Uma Maheswar. 10th century AD (Phase 6).

SG131 Karaiya kherai (settlement)

SC248 (Settlement)
S697 – Sculpture pile (in worship)
I-648: Miscellaneous (Sculpture). Qty: 5. 10th century AD (Phase 6). Material: P.S. Primary context: SG129/S246.
I-649: Uma Maheswar. 10th century AD (Phase 6). Material: P.S. Primary context: SG129/S246.

SG132 Madankheri (background landscape)

SC452 (Temple: Brahmanical)
S452 – Temple remains (in worship)
I-652: Miscellaneous (Sculpture). 11th–12th century AD (Phase 7). Material: P.S.
I-653: Visnu. 11th–12th century AD (Phase 7). Material: P.S.
I-654: Durga *Mahiṣāsuramardinī* ('late' type). 11th–12th century AD (Phase 7). Material: P.S.
I-655: Hanuman. 11th–12th century AD (Phase 7). Material: P.S.

SG133 Parsora haveli (settlement)

SC250 (Settlement)
S700 – Sculpture pile (in worship)
I-656: Hanuman. 10th century AD (Phase 6). Material: P.S. Primary context: SG133/S251.
I-657: Anthropomorphic *nāgarāja nāginī* couple (Wd: 41 cm; Ht: 47 cm). Broken just above knees. 7th–8th century AD (Phase 5). Material: B.S. Primary context: SG133/S251.
Plaque carved with anthropomorphic *nāga* and *nāginī* couple. Rounded faces. *Tribhanga* pose. Five-headed snake canopy. Both hold lotuses in right hand. Horizontal serpent coils.
I-658: *Liṅga* (Lgt: 24 cm; Wd: 24 cm). 10th century AD (Phase 6). Material: B.S. Primary context: SG133/S251.
Small, flat *chaumukhaliṅga*: bears small *liṅga* at each corner of upper surface, divided by central cross element.

SG134 Gehunkheri Bhairav (settlement)

SC550 (Temple: Brahmanical)
S703 – Temple remains (in worship)
I-337: *Nāga* (Wd: 20 cm; Ht: 20 cm; DepthL 8 cm). Broken from thighs downwards. Covered with *sindhur* and white powder paint. 130 AD (Phase 3b). Material: B.S.
Lower portion of standing male image. Horizontal serpent coils. *Sampada*. Transparent garment. Stands on base.
I-338: *Nāginī* (Wd: 15 cm; Ht: 30 cm; Depth: 8 cm). Broken from waist downwards. Feet missing. Covered with *sindhur* and white powder paint. 130 AD (Phase 3b). Material: B.S.
Lower half of *nāginī*. Horizontal serpent coils. Transparent skirt. Striated folds fall on either side of body. Jewelled belt at waist. Fleshy stomach, deep-set navel.
I-339: *Liṅga* (Ht: 95 cm). Covered with *sindhur* and white powder paint. 130 AD (Phase 3b). Material: B.S.
I-340: *Yakṣa*. Surviving from neck to thighs (44cm). Arms and head missing. Covered with *sindhur* and white powder paint. 130 AD (Phase 3b). Material: B.S. Standing *yakṣa*, chunky, wide chest, pot belly. Sash drawn between legs. Similar to standing *yakṣa*s from Sanchi (e.g., SG001/I-24) but free-standing rather than load-supporting.

S704 – Sculpture pile (in worship)
I-341: Miscellaneous (Sculpture). Qty: 5. 10th century AD (Phase 6). Material: P.S. Primary context: SG134/S703.
I-342: Laksmi Narayana. 10th century AD (Phase 6). Material: P.S. Primary context: SG134/S703.

SG135 Mori/Karariya kherai (background landscape)

SC253 (Rock-shelter)
S705 – Rock-shelter/Sculpture pile (in worship)
I-343: Hanuman. 10th century AD (Phase 6). Material: P.S. Primary context: SG157/S744.

SG135c Mori/Karariya kherai (ritual)

SC255 (Stupa site)
S706 – Sculpture pile (in worship)
I-808: Uma Maheswar. 10th century AD (Phase 6). Primary context: SG06a/S400 (?).
I-809: Sati (*in situ*).

SG137 Raisen (ritual)

SC456 (Temple: Brahmanical)
S456 – Temple remains
I-508: Miscellaneous (Sculpture). Qty: 10. 5th–6th century AD (Phase 4). Material: P.S.

SG140 Marwai (settlement)

SC259 (Temple: Brahmanical)
S259 – Temple remains (in worship)
I-344: Miscellaneous (Sculpture). Qty: 15. Covered with *sindhur*. 10th century AD (Phase 6). Material: P.S.
I-345: Ganesa (four-armed). Covered with *sindhur*. 10th century AD (Phase 6). Material: P.S.
I-346: Varaha. Fore-part of body badly damaged. Covered with *sindhur*. 10th century AD (Phase 6). Material: P.S.
Body carved with '1000 gods.
I-347: Hanuman. Upper half only. Covered with *sindhur*. 10th century AD (Phase 6). Material: P.S.

SC260 (Śaiva math)
S260 – Śaiva math remains
I-811: Architectural remains. 10th century AD (Phase 6).

SC263 (Tank)
S714 – Sculpture pile (in worship)
I-348: *Saptamātṛkā* panel. 10th century AD (Phase 6). Material: P.S. Primary context: SG140/S259

SG141 Marha kherai (settlement)

SC458 (Stupa site)
S458 – Architectural remains
I-200: *Toṛana* crossbar/berm (Lgt: 300 cm; Wd: 38 cm; Ht: 8 Depth: 14 cm). Semi submerged in ground. 115–80 BC (Phase 2). Material: L.B.S.
Long panel (cross-bar, or berm of stupa gateway). Front face carved with procession (from left to right): lion with rider elephant with couple; horse with single rider; elephant with couple; buffalo; elephant with couple; horse with single rider; elephant with couple. Interspersed by sprouting lotus meander. Bead and lozenge border on upper and lower edges.

SC558 (Settlement)
S715 – Sculpture pile (in worship)
I-514: Hanuman. Heavily eroded. 10th century AD (Phase 6). Material: L.B.S. Primary context: SG140/S259.
I-515: Miscellaneous (Sculpture). Heavily eroded. 10th century AD (Phase 6). Material: L.B.S. Primary context: SG140/S259.
Fragment of fish, but given state of erosion, not certain. May represent one of incarnations of Visnu.

SG142 Marha/Chitiya (settlement)

SC560 Marha (Settlement)
S1117 – Sculpture pile
I-516: Laksmi. Broken from waist upwards. 10th century AD (Phase 6). Material: P.S. Primary context: SG140/S259.
Female figure seated *lalitāsana* on lotus. Side attendants hold lotus stalks. Jewelled belt around waist.

SG144 Dhaniakheri (settlement)

SC459 (Temple: Brahmanical)
S459 – Temple remains (in worship)
I-659: Miscellaneous (Temple architecture). Qty: 5. 10th century AD (Phase 6). Material: P.S.
I-660: Sati (*in situ*). Qty: 2. Material: P.S.

SG146 Pipariya (Bes) (settlement)

SC271 (Settlement)
S722 – In situ sculpture
I-661: *Liṅga*. 5th century AD (Phase 4). Material: P.S. Plain *liṅga*, emerging directly from the ground.

SC460 (Temple: Brahmanical)
S460 – Temple remains (in worship)
I-662: Doorway pilasters. Qty: 2. 10th century AD (Phase 6). Material: P.S.
I-663: Visnu (four-armed). Lower arms missing. 10th century AD (Phase 6). Material: P.S. (under worship as Durga)
I-664: Miscellaneous (Sculpture). Qty: 10. 10th century AD (Phase 6). Material: P.S.
I-665: *Saptamātṛkā*. Broken from waist upwards. 5th century AD (Phase 4). Material: B.S. Lower half of Camundai seated on stool.
I-666: Temple remains (Wd: 34cm; Ht: 30 cm). Heavily eroded. Lower half only. 405–415AD (Phase 4). Material: W.S.
Fragment of L-shaped relief from lintel end of Gupta temple doorway. Carved with Ganga standing on elephant, inverse of relief from Besnagar (Williams, 1986, pl. 45).

SG147 Sonari village (settlement)

SC461 (Temple: Brahmanical)
S461 – Temple remains (in worship)
I-667: Miscellaneous (Sculpture). Qty: 10. Heavily damaged. 10th century AD (Phase 6). Material: P.S.

SG148 Sonari basti (settlement)

SC273 (Settlement)
S499 – Sculpture pile (in worship)
I-668: Miscellaneous (Sculpture). 11th–12th century AD (Phase 7). Material: G.S. Primary context: SG147/S461.

SG150b Sukhasen (settlement)

SC278 Sukhasen village basti (Settlement)
S734 – Sculpture pile (in worship)
I-669: Hanuman. 9th century AD (Phase 6). Material: L.B.S.

S736 – Sculpture pile (in worship)
I-513: Hanuman. 10th century AD (Phase 6). Material: P.S. Primary context: SG150b/S734.

SC280 Sukhasen village (Settlement)
S729 – Sculpture pile (in worship)
I-670: Kal Bhairav (four-armed). 10th century AD (Phase 6). Material: L.B.S. Primary context: SG150b/S734. 'Folky' style.

SG151 Suakheri (settlement)

SC281 (Settlement)
S735 – Sculpture pile (in worship)
I-671: Miscellaneous (Sculpture). Qty: 5. Heavily damaged. Covered with *sindhur*. 10th century AD (Phase 6). Material: P.S. Primary context: SG150b/S734.
Various sculptural fragments including Visnu, Uma-Maheswar and Laksmi.

SG152 Berkheri (background landscape)

SC282 Matabhai ka sthan (Temple: Brahmanical)
S282 – Temple remains (in worship)
I-617: Brahma (six-armed). Covered with *sindhur*. 9th century AD (Phase 6). Material: L.B.S. Seated in *padmāsana*.
I-618: Uma Maheswar. Qty: 2. Covered with *sindhur*. 9th century AD (Phase 6). Material: L.B.S.
I-619: *Sahsamātṛkā* panel (six mothers). Covered with *sindhur*. 9th century AD (Phase 6). Material: L.B.S.
I-620: Devi. 9th century AD (Phase 6). Material: L.B.S.
Side deities from Devi image, with sinuous curvaceous bodies.
I-672: Miscellaneous (Sculpture). Qty: 7. Covered with *sindhur*. 9th century AD (Phase 6). Material: L.B.S.

SG153b Berkheri (background landscape)

SC462 (Temple: Brahmanical)
S462 – Temple remains (in worship)
I-509: Miscellaneous (Sculpture). Qty: 6. 9th century AD (Phase 6). Material: P.S.

SG154 Parariya (settlement)

SC284 (Settlement)
S741 – Sculpture pile (in worship)
I-621: Miscellaneous (Sculpture). Qty: 10. Heavily eroded. Covered with *sindhur*. 9th century AD (Phase 6). Material: P.S. Primary context: SG152/S282.
I-622: Devi. Much of detail obscured due to *sindhur* and white paint. 9th century AD (Phase 6). Material: B.S. Primary context: SG152/S282.
Lower half of *yakṣini* standing in *tribhanga*. Transparent skirt. Long sinuous legs. Heavy, beaded belt at waist.

SG156 Berkheri ghat (settlement)

SC286 (Settlement)
S743 – Sculpture pile (in worship)
I-623: Miscellaneous (Sculpture). Heavily damaged. 10th century AD (Phase 6). Material: P.S. Primary context: SG061/S400.

SG157 Mori khauri (settlement)

SC695 (Temple: Brahmanical)
S744 – Temple remains (in worship)
I-624: Miscellaneous (Sculpture). Qty: 10. 10th century AD (Phase 6). Material: P.S.
I-625: Hanuman. Qty: 2. 10th century AD (Phase 6). Material: P.S.
I-840: Miscellaneous (Sculpture). 9th century AD (Phase 6). Material: L.B.S.
I-841: Durga *Mahiṣāsuramardinī*. 10th century AD (Phase 6).

SG158 Katsari kherai (settlement)

SC288 (Settlement)
S745 – In situ memorial (in worship)
I-842: Sati.

SG159 Barla hill (settlement)

SC291 (Settlement)
S747 – Sculpture pile (in worship)
I-673: Hanuman. 10th century AD (Phase 6). Material: B.S. Primary context: SG159/S749.

SC293 Rock-shelter cluster)
S748 – Rock-shelter/Sculpture pile (in worship)
I-201: Durga *Mahiṣāsuramardinī*. 8th century AD (Phase 5). Material: B.S. Primary context: SG159/S749.
'Early' type: head of buffalo still intact on ground, hind leg held by goddess. Robust lion biting from behind.
I-349: *Liṅga* (Lgt: 10 cm; Wd: 10 cm; Depth: 5 cm). 10th century AD (Phase 6). Material: B.S. Primary context: SG159/S749.
Flat *panchmukhaliṅga*: consists of four spheroid *liṅgas* at each corner, separated by central cross element. Surmounted by fifth spheroid *liṅga* in the centre.
I-350: Visnupad. Qty: 2. 10th century AD (Phase 6). Material: B.S. Primary context: SG159/S749.
I-676: Miscellaneous (Sculpture). 10th century AD (Phase 6). Material: B.S. Primary context: SG159/S749.
I-677: Kal Bhairav (four-armed/ithyphallic). 9th century AD (Phase 6). Material: L.B.S. Primary context: SG159/S749.

SC682 (Temple: Brahmanical)
S749 – Temple remains (in worship)
I-674: Miscellaneous (Sculpture). Qty: 5. Heavily damaged. 10th century AD (Phase 6). Material: P.S.
I-675: Durga *Mahiṣāsuramardinī* ('late' type). 10th century AD (Phase 6). Material: P.S.

SG160 Barla/Ghatla (settlement)

SC296 Ghatla kherai (Settlement)
S751 – Sculpture pile (in worship)
I-351: Miscellaneous (Sculpture). Qty: 5. Heavily damaged. 10th century AD (Phase 6). Material: P.S. Primary context: SG159/S749.
I-352: *Makara* waterspout. 10th century AD (Phase 6). Material: P.S. Primary context: SG159/S749.
I-353: Sati (*in situ*). Material: P.S. Primary context: SG159/S749.

S752 – Sculpture pile (in worship)
I-354: Surya (Wd: 50 cm; Ht: 50 cm). 9th century AD (Phase 6). Material: L.B.S. Primary context: SG159/S749.
Stone slab with carved Surya image.

SG162b Murlikheri-Naroda (settlement)

SC298 Murlikheri basti (Settlement)
S299 – In situ memorial/cult spot (in worship)
I-363: Sati. 10th century AD (Phase 6). Material: P.S.

S753 – Sculpture pile (in worship)
I-355: Miscellaneous (Sculpture). Qty: 5. Heavily damaged. 11th–12th century AD (Phase 7). Material: P.S. Primary context: SG162b/S756.
I-356: Durga *Mahiṣāsuramardinī* ('late' type). 11th–12th century AD (Phase 7). Material: P.S. Primary context: SG162b/S756.

S754 – Sculpture pile (in worship)
I-362: *Liṅga*. Split in half down middle, with one side missing. 2nd century AD (Phase 3b). Material: B.S. Primary context: SG162b/S299. Undecorated.

SC304 Naroda (Temple: Jain)
S304 – Temple remains (in worship)
I-384: Miscellaneous (Sculpture). Qty: 3. 10th century AD (Phase 6). Material: P.S. Primary context: SG162b/S756.
I-385: Uma Maheswar. 10th century AD (Phase 6). Material: P.S. Primary context: SG162b/S756.
I-386: Tirthankara (Jain). Lower half only. Broken from chest downwards. 10th century AD (Phase 6). Material: B.S.
Small slab of stone with standingTirthankara in niche.

SC566 Naroda (Temple remains: Brahmanical)
S755 – Sculpture pile (in worship)
I-364: Miscellaneous (Sculpture). Qty: 8. 10th century AD (Phase 6). Material: P.S. Primary context: SG162b/S756.
I-365: Miscellaneous (Sculpture). Qty: 10. 10th century AD (Phase 6). Material: P.S. Primary context: SG162b/S756.
I-366: Siva. Head only. 5th century AD (Phase 4). Material: B.S. Primary context: SG162b/S756.
Siva head with dreadlocks and top knot. Set on plaque. Rounded face, and fringe.
I-367: Durga *Mahiṣāsuramardinī*. 10th century AD (Phase 6). Material: P.S. Primary context: SG162b/S756.
Follows unusual model belonging neither to the 'early' nor 'late' type: goddess holds buffalo's head up in the left. Cf Durga *Mahiṣāsuramardinī* from Mathura (c. 3rd–4th century AD), now in Los Angeles County Museum: of Art (Czuma 1985, pl. 61).
I-368: Uma Maheswar. 10th century AD (Phase 6). Material: P.S. Primary context: SG162b/S756.

S756 – Temple remains
I-369: Hero stone. 10th century AD (Phase 6). Material: P.S.
I-370: Temple remains. 10th century AD (Phase 6). Material: P.S.
Part of temple doorway with three tiers of side-deities and *vyālas*.

SG164 Neemkhera (settlement)

SC308 (Background landscape)
S308 – In situ sculpture (in worship)
I-389: *Liṅga* (Ht: 145 cm; Circumf: 130 cm). Most of face cut off. Semi submerged in ground. Covered with *sindhur*. 5th century AD (Phase 4). Material: B.S.
Large *ekamukhaliṅga*, with rounded face, long dreadlocks and top-knot. Distended earlobes. Torque necklace.

SC689 (Temple: Brahmanical)
S759 – Temple remains (in worship)
I-387: Miscellaneous (Sculpture). Qty: 10. 10th century AD (Phase 6). Material: P.S.
I-388: Durga *Mahiṣāsuramardinī* (with personified buffalo). 10th century AD (Phase 6). Material: P.S.

SG165 Girbhar (settlement)

SC441 Girbhar kherai (Temple: Brahmanical)
S441 – Temple remains (in worship)
I-205: Miscellaneous (Sculpture). Qty: 5. 10th century AD (Phase 6). Material: P.S.
I-206: Temple remains. 10th century AD (Phase 6). Material: P.S.
Fragment of sikhara.
I-207: Sati (*in situ*). Material: P.S.
I-390: Durga *Mahiṣāsuramardinī* ('late' type). 10th century AD (Phase 6). Material: P.S.
I-391: *Liṅga* (Lgt: 20 Wd: 20 Depth 8 cm). 10th century AD (Phase 6). Material: P.S.
Flat *panchmukha liṅga*: spherical *liṅgas* at each of four corners, separated by cross element. Surmounted by central *liṅga* with carved face.

SG166 Mungawali (settlement)

SC311 (Settlement)
S762 – Sculpture pile (in worship)
I-208: Miscellaneous (Sculpture). Qty: 5. 10th century AD (Phase 6). Material: P.S.
I-209: Hanuman. Heavily damaged. 10th century AD (Phase 6). Material: P.S.
I-210: Pilaster. 10th century AD (Phase 6). Material: P.S. Temple pilaster with niche containing small Visnu carved in 'folky' style.
I-211: Miscellaneous (Temple architecture). 10th century AD (Phase 6). Material: P.S. *Jala* from top of *gavakṣa*.

SG167 Kotra (ritual)

SC320 (Temple: Brahmanical)
S320 – Temple remains (in worship)
I-483: Miscellaneous (Sculpture). Qty: 5. Heavily damaged. 10th century AD (Phase 6). Material: P.S.
I-484: Hanuman. Heavily damaged. 10th century AD (Phase 6). Material: P.S.

I-678: *Liṅga*. Heavily damaged. 10th century AD (Phase 6). Material: P.S.
I-679: Durga. Heavily damaged. 10th century AD (Phase 6). Material: P.S.

SG167b Kotra (settlement)

SC313 (Temple: Brahmanical)
S313 – Temple remains (in worship)
I-212: Miscellaneous (Sculpture). Qty: 10. 10th century AD (Phase 6). Material: P.S.
I-213: Durga *Mahiṣāsuramardinī*. 10th century AD (Phase 6). Material: P.S.

SG169 Amacchar (settlement)

SC323 (Settlement)
S782 – Sculpture pile
I-392: *Nāga* (Wd: 50 cm; Ht: 86 cm). Face and chest heavily eroded. Right hand missing. early 5th century AD (Phase 4). Material: L.B.S. Primary context: SG169/S463.
Anthropomorphic *Nāgarāja* seated in *lalitāsana*. Left hand holds bunch of lotus flowers, slung over left shoulder. Right hand bent at elbow, holding indiscernible object, possibly a wine-cup, against chest. 'Beaded' bangles on wrist. Sacred thread (*yajñopavita*) worn over left shoulder. Serpent ascends back in single shaft, rising from mass of coils below body.
I-393: *Nāginī* (Wd: 17 cm; Ht: 38 cm; Depth: 16 cm). Broken from waist upwards. Feet missing. Both arms missing apart from left hand resting on hip. early 5th century AD (Phase 4). Material: L.B.S. Primary context: SG169/S463.
Lower half of *nāginī*. Horizontal serpent coils. Transparent garment reaching to below knees. Striated folds fall on left side of body. Three-stringed beaded belt. Surviving left hand rests on left hip, clutching fold of garment between 2nd and 3rd fingers. Striated sash looped over right hip. Cf. *nāginī* outside Temple 31, Sanchi.
I-435: Harihara. Qty: 2 (Wd: 8 cm; Ht: 30 cm). early 5th century AD (Phase 4). Material: B.S. Primary context: SG169/S463.
Two separate hands of large Harihara image. One holds a *triśula*, the other a conch.
I-436: Hanuman. 10th century AD (Phase 6). Material: P.S. Primary context: SG169/S463.
I-451: Miscellaneous (Sculpture). Qty: 7. 10th century AD (Phase 6). Material: P.S. Primary context: SG169/S463.
I-452: Sati. Qty: 3. Material: P.S. Primary context: SG169/S463.

SC463 (Temple: Brahmanical)
S463 – Temple remains (in worship)
I-453: Lion abacus. Qty: 2 (Lgt: 65 cm; Wd: 55 cm; Diam: 8 cm; Depth 32 cm). early 5th century AD (Phase 4). Material: B.S.
Two square abacuses with lion head at each corner. 'Dwarf' figure (females and males) stand between each lion. Each carries lotus in left hand, a sword in the other. Large heads with full-bodied curly hair. Deeply incised *dhotīs*, pulled tightly between legs.
I-457: Pillar remains (Lgt: 37 cm; Ht: 155 cm; Diam: 30 cm). Lower section only. 5th century AD (Phase 4). Material: B.S.
Lower fragment of unusual pillar with square base and cylindrical shaft. At the lower end of of the cylindrical section, are two humps on either side of the pillar. Reminiscent, in a very reduced form, of the fan palm capitals from the Heliodorus pillar site (SG006).

SG170 Salera (settlement)

SC324 (Settlement)
S784 – Sculpture pile (in worship)
I-682: *Liṅga*. Qty: 3. 10th century AD (Phase 6). Material: P.S. Primary context: SG170/S785.
I-683: Makara waterspout. 10th century AD (Phase 6). Material: P.S. Primary context: SG170/S785.

SC575 (Temple: Brahmanical)
S785 – Temple remains (in worship)
I-458: *Nāga* (Wd: 50 cm; Ht: 50 cm; Depth: 38 cm). Only coiled base with feet survives. 2nd century AD (Phase 3b). Material: B.S.
Mass of serpent coils surmounted by feet of *nāgarāja.*
I-459: *Nāga*. Head only. Face heavily eroded. 2nd century AD (Phase 3b). Material: G.S.
Possibly belongs to *nāgarāja* (I-458). Distended ear-lobes and heavy chunky ear-rings.

I-460: Miscellaneous (Sculpture). Qty: 10. 10th century AD (Phase 6). Material: P.S.
I-461: Hanuman. 10th century AD (Phase 6). Material: G.S.
I-462: Hanuman. 11th century AD (Phase 7). Material: P.S.
I-681: *Liṅga*. Qty: 2 (Lgt: 12 Wd: 10 Depth 12 cm). 10th century AD (Phase 6). Material: B.S.
Two small *panchmukha liṅgas*: spherical *liṅgas* at each of the four corners, separated by cross element. Surmounted by fifth *liṅga* in centre.

SG171 Bawaliya (settlement)

SC331 (Settlement)
S790 – Sculpture pile (in worship)
I-153: Siva. Unfinished. 5th century AD (Phase 4). Material: B.S. Primary context: SG172b/S792.
Two-armed, standing male figure. Ithyphallic. Sash wrapped over shoulder and reaching to beneath knees. Unfinished,with circular chisel marks over body and face. Same workshop as Kubera *yakṣa* (SG172b/I-687).
I-684: Miscellaneous (Sculpture). Qty: 5. Heavily eroded. 10th century AD (Phase 6). Material: P.S. Primary context: SG012/S563.

S791 – In situ memorial (in worship)
I-685: Sati. Material: P.S.

SG172b Bawaliya (quarry)

SC335 Dharoyi baba hill (Quarry)
S792 – Unfinished sculpture (in worship)
I-687: *Yakṣa* (Wd: 88 cm; Ht: 133 cm; Depth: 37 cm). early 5th century AD (Phase 4). Material: B.S.
Unfinished sculpture of Kubera *yakṣa* seated on stool in *lalitāsana*. Fleshy breasts and protruding stomach. Main details 'sketched' in: large, heavy torque; distended ears with chunky earrings. Right hand rests on knee holding round object. Left hand: broken. Chunky arm-band. Same workshop as SG171/I-153.

SG173 Bamnor (settlement)

SC337 (Settlement)
S795 – Sculpture pile (in worship)
I-463: Hero stone (Wd: 35 cm; Ht: 75 cm; Depth: 35 cm). Heads of wrestlers missing. 9th century AD (Phase 6). Material: L.B.S. Primary context: SG173b/S375.
I-464: *Nāgakal* (Wd: 35cm; Ht: 50 cm; Depth: 15 cm). 5th century AD (Phase 4). Material: L.B.S.
Lower half of unentwined theriomorphic *nāgakal*, with tenon below. Smaller cobras on either side.
I-688: Hero stone. 10th century AD (Phase 6). Material: P.S. Primary context: SG173b/S375.

S796 – Sculpture pile (in worship)
I-465: Ganesa (seated in *lalitāsana*). Covered with *sindhur*. 10th century AD (Phase 6). Material: P.S. Primary context: SG173b/S375.

S797 – Sculpture pile (in worship)
I-466: Durga *Mahiṣāsuramardinī* ('late' type). 10th century AD (Phase 6). Material: P.S. Primary context: SG173b/S375.
I-467: Miscellaneous (Sculpture). Qty: 4. 10th century AD (Phase 6). Material: P.S. Primary context: SG173b/S375.

SG174 Gyasabad/Dhanasari (settlement)

SC339 Gyasabad (Settlement)
S802 – Sculpture pile (in worship)
I-475: Uma Maheswar. 10th century AD (Phase 6). Material: G.S. Primary context: SG174/S800.
I-476: Miscellaneous (Sculpture). Qty: 5. 10th century AD (Phase 6). Material: G.S. Primary context: SG174/S800.
I-477: Durga *Mahiṣāsuramardinī* ('late' type). 10th century AD (Phase 6). Material: G.S. Primary context: SG174/S800.

S803 – In situ memorial
I-469: Hero stone. Material: P.S.

SC578 (Temple: Brahmanical)
S800 – Temple remains (in worship)
I-468: Miscellaneous (Sculpture). Qty: 10. 10th century AD (Phase 6). Material: G.S.
I-470: Durga *Mahiṣāsuramardinī* ('late' type). 10th century AD (Phase 6). Material: G.S.
I-471: Nandi. 10th century AD (Phase 6). Material: G.S.
I-472: Siva. 10th century AD (Phase 6). Material: G.S.

S801 – Sculpture pile (in worship)
I-473: Miscellaneous (Sculpture). Qty: 50. 10th century AD (Phase 6). Material: G.S. Primary context: SG174/S800.
I-474: Siva. 10th century AD (Phase 6). Material: G.S. Primary context: SG174/S800.

SG177 Devrajpur (settlement)

SC345 (Temple: Jain)
S345 – Temple remains (in worship)
I-428: Tirthankara. Qty: 3. 10th century AD (Phase 6). Material: G.S. Standing Tirthankaras, with round faces and *srivatsas* on chest.
I-1075: Temple remains (Jain). 10th century AD (Phase 6).

SG177b Devrajpur (reservoir)

SC346 (Dam)
S809 – Sluice remains
I-889: Sluice remains. Qty: 4. 7th century AD (Phase 5). Material: L.B.S.
I-989: Sluice remains. 9th century AD (Phase 6).

SC347 (Temple: Brahmanical)
S347 – Temple remains (in worship)
I-429: Miscellaneous (Temple architecture). 10th century AD (Phase 6). Material: P.S.
I-430: Durga Camundai. Heavily eroded below waist. 9th century AD (Phase 6). Material: L.B.S.
Eight-armed; sinuous, curvaceous body.
I-689: Devi. Qty: 5. 9th century AD (Phase 6). Material: L.B.S.
Various fragments of Devi sculptures.

SG177c Devrajpur hill (ritual)

SC351 Devrajpur hill east (Buddhist monastery)
S435 – Sculpture pile (in worship)
I-693: Durga *Mahiṣāsuramardinī* ('early' type). 7th–8th century AD (Phase 5). Material: G.S. Primary context: SG177b/S812. Four-armed, with rounded face.
I-694: Durga *Mahiṣāsuramardinī* ('early' type). Lower half only. 8th century AD (Phase 5). Material: P.S. Primary context: SG177b/S812.
I-695: Hanuman. 10th century AD (Phase 6). Material: G.S. Primary context: SG177b/S812.

SG177d Devrajpur (settlement)

SC349 Devrajpur kherai (Settlement)
S498 – Sculpture pile (in worship)
I-690: *Nāgakal* (Wd: 30 cm; Ht: 100 cm; Depth: 25 cm). Next to ancient well. Broken into two parts; cracked at joint between serpent body and canopy. 5th century AD (Phase 4). Material: L.B.S.
Consists of unentwined serpent with single-headed canopy. Cf. *nāgakal* in VM (SG006/I-531)
I-691: Uma Maheswar. 8th century AD (Phase 5). Material: L.B.S. Primary context: SG177/S347.
I-692: Miscellaneous (Sculpture). Qty: 3. 10th century AD (Phase 6). Material: P.S. Primary context: SG177/S347.

SG178 Semra kherai (settlement)

SC352 (Settlement)
S826 – Sculpture pile (in worship)
I-686: Miscellaneous (Sculpture). Qty: 5. Heavily eroded. 10th century AD (Phase 6). Material: P.S. Primary context: SG173b/S375.

SG179b Hakimkheri (settlement)

SC355 Kharamata ka sthan (Temple: Brahmanical)
S355 – Temple remains (in worship)
I-696: Miscellaneous (Sculpture). Qty: 8. Heavily damaged. 11th–12th century AD (Phase 7). Material: P.S.
I-906: Durga *Mahiṣāsuramardinī*. 10th century AD (Phase 6). Material: P.S.

SC360 (Temple: Brahmanical)
S360 – Temple remains
I-698: Miscellaneous (Sculpture). Qty: 5. 11th–12th century AD (Phase 7). Material: P.S.

SG180 Jhirniya (settlement)

SC361 (Settlement)
S828 – Sculpture pile (in worship)
I-699: Miscellaneous (Sculpture). Qty: 5. Heavily damaged. 11th century AD (Phase 7). Material: P.S. Primary context: SG113/S234.

SG182 Saleiya (background landscape)

SC490 (Background landscape)
S830 – In situ memorial (in worship)
I-910: Samadhi. Late Medieval (Phase 8).

APPENDIX IIb
Monastery architecture: dates and classifications

Free-standing rectangular monasteries: Phase II

Rubble-infill/outer-facing type walls

SG no.	*SC no.*	*Site name*
SG007	SC379	Satdhara
SG022	SC90	Goldoria
SG029	SC480	Dargawan 2
SG076	SC708	Bagoda
SG143	SC479	Kanchanpura
SG175	SC726	Bawaliya hill

Boulder walls

SG no.	*SC no.*	*Site name*
SG177c	SC590; SC591; SC592	Devrajpur
SG066	SC705	Torin
SG167	SC318	Kotra

Monastery platforms: Phase II

SG no.	*SC no.*	*Site name*
SG001	SC6	Sanchi building 8
SG004	SC383	Sonari
SG005	SC440	Morel khurd monastery 1
SG007	SC55, 56, 446	Satdhara monastery a, b, c
SG007	SC60	Satdhara south
SG007	SC50	Satdhara west
SG013	SC467	Andher
SG035	SC529	Bighan
SG162	SC300	Murlikheri
SG170b	SC330	Salera

Courtyard monasteries with rectangular rooms: Phase II

On platform

SG no.	*SC no.*	*Site name*
SG090	SC195	Mawasa middle tier: courtyard mon with rectangular rooms
SG090	SC196	Mawasa lower tier: Line of rectangular rooms

Without platform

SG no.	*SC no.*	*Site name*
SG059b	SC394	Barahi khas
SG011c	SC65	Ferozpur (interconnected)
SG090	SC659	Mawasa: middle tier
SG090	SC478	Mawasa: upper tier
SG012b	SC482	Karhaud kherai
SG177c	SC351	Devrajpur (interconnected)

Courtyard monasteries: Phases IV/V and VI

Phase IV/V (regular-sized square cells)

SG no.	*SC no.*	*Site name*
SG001	SC620, 621,	Sanchi: monasteries 36, 37, 38.
SG005	SC465	Morel khurd: monastery 2
SG035	SC538	Bighan
SG095d	SC209	Chandna Tohoria lower
SG095d	SC208	Chandna Tohoria upper
SG066	SC411	Torin (interconnected)
SG167	SC319	Kotra (interconnected)

Phase VI courtyard monastery

SG no.	*SC no.*	*Site name*
SG005	SC701	Morel khurd (interconnected/haphazard)
SG001	SC619	Sanchi: monasteries 45, 46, 47 (regular, interconnected)

APPENDIX IIc

Phase-by-phase list of non-Buddhist cult spots and temples

PHASE	SG Name	SG No	SC No	SG context	SC type	Ritual
Id	Vidisha	SG006	SC44	Settlement	Temple	Bhagavata
II	Vidisha	SG006	SC44	Settlement	Temple	Bhagavata
	"	"	SC714	Settlement	Free-standing	*Yakṣa*
	"	"	SC715	Settlement	Free-standing	Bhagavata
	"	"	SC717	Settlement	Free-standing	*Yakṣa*
	Nagauri	SG003a	SC21	Settlement/quarry	Free-standing	*Nāga*
	Gulgaon	SG010b	SC64	Ancient dam	Free-standing	*Nāga*
	Chandna	SG095c	SC204	Ancient dam	Free-standing	*Nāga* -Bhagavata
IIIa	Sanchi	SG001	SC297	Hilltop ritual	Free-standing	*Yakṣa*
	Andher	SG013b	SC78	Background landscape	Free-standing	Bhagavata/*Nāga* -Bhagavata
IIIb	Mehgaon	SG056	SC390	Ancient dam	Free-standing	*Nāga* -Bhagavata
	Pagneswar	SG061	SC697	Settlement	Temple	*Nāga*/Saiva
	Gehunkheri Bhairav	SG134	SC550	Settlement	Temple	*Nāga*/Saiva/*Yakṣa*
	Murlikheri-Naroda	SG162b	SC298	Settlement	Free-standing	Saiva
	Salera	SG170	SC575	Settlement	Temple	*Nāga*
IV	Sanchi	SG001	SC626	Hilltop ritual	Free-standing	*Yakṣa*
	"	"	SC628	Hilltop ritual	Temple	*Nāga*
	"	"	SC627	Hilltop ritual	Free-standing	*Yakṣa*
	Morel khurd	SG005	SC721	Hilltop ritual	Free-standing	*Yakṣa*
	Vidisha	SG006	SC44	Settlement	Temple	Bhagavata
	"	"	SC643	Settlement	Temple	Saiva
	"	"	SC653	Settlement	Free-standing	Devi
	"	"	SC703	Settlement	Free-standing	Saiva
	"	"	SC718	Settlement	Temple	Brahmanical
	Gulgaon-Eran	SG010	SC378	Settlement	Temple	Brahmanical
	Ferozpur	SG011b	SC377	Settlement	Temple	Brahmanical/*Nāga*
	Karhaud	SG012	SC69	Settlement	Rock-shelter shrine	Saiva
	Udayagiri	SG031	SC108	Hilltop ritual	Temple	Brahmanical
	"	"	SC108	Hilltop ritual	Temple	Jain
	"	"	SC693	Hilltop ritual	Temple	Brahmanical
	"	"	SC694	Hilltop ritual	Temple	Brahmanical
	Udayagiri/Madhupuri/ Sonapura	SG031b	SC220	Settlement	Temple	Brahmanical
	Dhakna basti	SG032b	SC680	Settlement	Temple	Brahmanical
	Ahmadpur hill	SG037a	SC131	Hilltop ritual	Temple	Brahmanical
	Ratanpur girdhari	SG038	SC136	Settlement	Temple	*Yakṣa*
	Amkhera bhauji	SG050	SC367	Settlement	Temple	Devi
	Mehgaon	SG056	SC368	Settlement	Temple	Devi
	Tijalpur	SG058	SC445	Settlement/tank	Free-standing	*Nāga*
	Tajpura shur	SG064	SC406	Settlement	Temple	Brahmanical
	Khamtala	SG072	SC685	Settlement	Temple	Brahmanical
	Nihalpur/Dandoli kherai	SG092	SC199	Settlement	Temple	Brahmanical
	Ram bhauri	SG108	SC227	Background landscape	Temple	Brahmanical
	Alamkhera	SG113	SC235	Settlement	Temple	Brahmanical
	Devalkhera	SG123	SC684	Settlement	Temple	Brahmanical/*Nāga*-Vaisnava
	Raisen	SG137	SC456	Hilltop ritual	Temple	Brahmanical
	Pipariya (Bes)	SG146	SC247	Settlement	Free-standing	Saiva
	"	SG146	SC460	Settlement	Temple	Brahmanical/Devi
	Murlikheri-Naroda	SG162b	SC566	Settlement	Temple	Saiva
	Neemkhera	SG164	SC308	Background landscape	Free-standing	Saiva
	Girbhar	SG165	SC441	Settlement	Temple	Brahmanical
	Amacchar	SG169	SC463	Settlement	Temple	Brahmanical/*Nāga*

	Bawaliya	SG172b	SC335	Quarry/ stone-cutting centre	In situ/ unfinished	Saiva/*Yakṣa*
	Bamnor	SG173	SC337	Settlement/tank	Free-standing	*Nāga*
	Devrajpur	SG177d	SC349	Settlement/tank	Free-standing	*Nāga*
V	Dhakna basti	SG032b	SC680	Settlement	Temple	Devi
	Pagneswar	SG061	SC697	Settlement	Temple	Devi
	Tajpura shur	SG064	SC406	Settlement	Temple	Devi
	Nihalpur/Dandoli kherai	SG092	SC199	Settlement	Temple	Brahmanical/Devi
	Morel kala	SG099b	SC371	Settlement	Temple	Devi
	Sachet	SG102	SC473	Settlement	Temple	Devi
	Parsora haveli	SG133	SC251	Settlement	Temple	*Nāga*
	Barla hill	SG159	SC682	Settlement	Temple	Devi
	Devrajpur	SG177b	SC347	Ancient dam	Temple	Saiva
	"	SG177b	SC583	Ancient dam	Temple	Devi
VI	Sanchi	SG001	SC12	Hilltop ritual	Temple	Saiva
	Sanchi/Kanakhera	SG002	SC19	Settlement	Temple	Brahmanical
	Morel khurd	SG005	SC31	Hilltop ritual	Temple	Brahmanical
	Vidisha	SG006	SC53	Settlement	Temple	Brahmanical
	"	"	SC642	Settlement	Temple	Brahmanical
	"	"	SC644	Settlement	Temple	Vaisnava
	"	"	SC654	Settlement	Temple	Brahmanical
	Gulgaon-Eran	SG010	SC378	Settlement	Temple	Brahmanical
	"	"	SC93	Settlement	Temple	Brahmanical
	Ferozpur	SG011b	SC377	Settlement	Temple	Brahmanical
	Karhaud	SG012	SC519	Settlement	Temple	Brahmanical
	"	"	SC72	Settlement	Temple	Brahmanical
	Karhaud kherai	SG012b	SC344	Hilltop ritual	Temple	Brahmanical
	Andher	SG013b	SC78	Background landscape	Temple	Brahmanical
	Rangai village	SG017b	SC523	Settlement	Temple	Brahmanical
	Pathar	SG025	SC436	Background landscape	Temple	Brahmanical
	Udayagiri	SG031	SC108	Hilltop ritual	Temple	Jain
	Udayagiri	SG031	SC110	Hilltop ritual	Temple	Brahmanical
	Udayagiri/Madhupuri/Sonapura	SG031b	SC220	Settlement	Temple	Brahmanical
	Dhakna village	SG032	SC468	Settlement	Temple	Brahmanical
	Dhakna basti	SG032b	SC680	Settlement	Temple	Devi
	Salamatpur chaura	SG034	SC120	Hilltop ritual	Temple	Brahmanical
	Tigra hill	SG036	SC125	Hilltop ritual	Temple	Brahmanical
	Ahmadpur	SG037	SC133	Settlement	Temple	Brahmanical
	"	SG037	SC135	Settlement	Temple	Brahmanical
	"	"	"	Settlement	Temple	Jain
	Ahmadpur hill	SG037a	SC131	Hilltop ritual	Temple	Brahmanical
	Ratanpur girdhari	SG038	SC136	Settlement	Temple	Brahmanical/Saiva/Devi
	Besar talai	SG041	SC142	Settlement	Temple	Brahmanical
	"	"	"	Settlement	Temple	Brahmanical
	"	"	"	Settlement	Temple	Jain
	Bagri/Jamwar	SG043	SC532	Settlement	Temple	Brahmanical
	Kharetiya 1	SG044	SC381	Settlement	Temple	Brahmanical
	Pachmarhi	SG045	SC155	Hilltop ritual	Temple	Brahmanical
	Amkhera bhauji	SG050	SC161	Settlement	Temple	Brahmanical
	"	SG050	SC367	Settlement	Temple	Brahmanical
	Ucher	SG054	SC172	Settlement	Temple	Brahmanical
	Mehgaon	SG056	SC368	Settlement	Temple	Brahmanical
	Tijalpur	SG058	SC691	Settlement	Temple	Brahmanical
	Barahi khas	SG059b	SC681	Hilltop ritual	Temple	Brahmanical
	Pagneswar	SG061	SC400	Settlement	Temple	Brahmanical
	"	"	SC507	Settlement	Temple	Brahmanical/Saiva
	"	"	SC697	Settlement	Temple	Brahmanical
	Tajpura shur	SG064	SC406	Settlement	Temple	Brahmanical
	Bilori 2	SG071	SC656	Settlement	Temple	Brahmanical
	Khamtala	SG072	SC685	Settlement	Temple	Brahmanical
	Pathari kativarat	SG084	SC187	Settlement	Temple	Brahmanical/*Nāga*
	Kanpohra	SG088	SC191	Settlement	Temple	Brahmanical
	Nihalpur/Dandoli kherai	SG092	SC199	Settlement	Temple	Brahmanical
	Chandna hill	SG095c	SC696	Ancient dam	Temple	Brahmanical
	"	"	"	Ancient dam	Temple	Jain
	Morel kala	SG099b	SC371	Settlement	Temple	Brahmanical
	"	SG099b	SC687	Settlement	Temple	Jain
	Andol	SG101	SC372	Settlement	Temple	Brahmanical/*Nāga*
	"	"	"	Settlement	Temple	Vaisnava
	Sachet	SG102	SC473	Settlement	Temple	Brahmanical
	Ram bhauri	SG108	SC227	Background landscape	Temple	Brahmanical
	Bighan village	SG110	SC446	Settlement	Temple	Brahmanical
	Alamkhera	SG113	SC234	Settlement	Temple	Brahmanical
	Mahuakhera-Himatgarh	SG121	SC546	Settlement	Temple	Brahmanical
	Devalkhera	SG123	SC684	Settlement	Temple	Brahmanical
	Chiroriya village	SG128	SC549	Settlement	Temple	Brahmanical

	Chiroriya kherai	SG129	SC246	Settlement	Temple	Brahmanical
	Bhauriya	SG130	SC451	Settlement	Temple	Brahmanical
	Parsora haveli	SG133	SC251	Settlement	Temple	Brahmanical
	Gehunkheri Bhairav	SG134	SC550	Settlement	Temple	Brahmanical
	Marwai	SG140	SC259	Settlement	Temple	Brahmanical
	"	"	SC260	Settlement	Temple	Saiva
	Dhaniakheri	SG144	SC459	Settlement	Temple	Brahmanical
	Pipariya (Bes)	SG146	SC460	Settlement	Temple	Brahmanical
	Sonari village	SG147	SC461	Settlement	Temple	Brahmanical
	Berkheri	SG152	SC282	Background landscape	Temple	Brahmanical
	"	SG153b	SC462	Background landscape	Temple	Brahmanical
	Mori khauri	SG157	SC695	Settlement	Temple	Brahmanical
	"	SG157	SC695	Settlement	Temple	Devi
	Barla hill	SG159	SC682	Settlement	Temple	Brahmanical
	Murlikheri-Naroda	SG162b	SC304	Settlement	Temple	Jain
	"	SG162b	SC566	Settlement	Temple	Brahmanical
	Neemkhera	SG164	SC689	Settlement	Temple	Brahmanical
	Girbhar	SG165	SC441	Settlement	Temple	Brahmanical
	Kotra	SG167	SC320	Hilltop ritual	Temple	Brahmanical
	"	SG167b	SC313	Settlement	Temple	Brahmanical
	Amacchar	SG169	SC463	Settlement	Temple	Brahmanical
	Salera	SG170	SC575	Settlement	Temple	Brahmanical
	Bamnor	SG173b	SC375	Background landscape	Temple	Brahmanical
	Gyasabad/Dhanasari	SG174	SC578	Settlement	Temple	Brahmanical
	Devrajpur village	SG177	SC345	Settlement	Temple	Jain
	Devrajpur dam	SG177b	SC347	Ancient dam	Temple	Brahmanical
	"	"	SC583	Ancient dam	Temple	Brahmanical
	Hakimkheri	SG179b	SC355	Settlement	Temple	Devi
	"	"	SC360	Settlement	Temple	Brahmanical
VII	Sanchi/Kanakhera	SG002	SC19	Settlement	Temple	Brahmanical
	Morel khurd	SG005	SC31	Hilltop ritual	Temple	Brahmanical
	Gulgaon-Eran	SG010	SC93	Settlement	Temple	Brahmanical
	Ferozpur	SG011b	SC377	Settlement	Temple	Brahmanical
	Pathar	SG025	SC436	Background landscape	Temple	Brahmanical
	Ratanpur girdhari	SG038	SC690	Settlement	Temple	Devi
	Kherai khera	SG052	SC686	Settlement	Temple	Brahmanical
	Tijalpur	SG058	SC691	Settlement	Temple	Brahmanical
	Barahi khas	SG059b	SC681	Hilltop ritual	Temple	Brahmanical
	Pagneswar	SG061	SC507	Settlement	Temple	Brahmanical
	Bilori 2	SG071	SC656	Settlement	Temple	Brahmanical
	Khamtala	SG072	SC685	Settlement	Temple	Brahmanical
	Kanpohra	SG088	SC191	Settlement	Temple	Brahmanical
	Bighan village	SG110	SC446	Settlement	Temple	Brahmanical
	Alamkhera	SG113	SC234	Settlement	Temple	Brahmanical
	"	"	SC235	Settlement	Temple	Brahmanical
	Bhauliya	SG114	SC448	Settlement	Temple	Saiva
	Murwara hill	SG118b	SC449	Settlement	Temple	Brahmanical
	Mahuakhera-Himatgarh	SG121	SC546	Settlement	Temple	Brahmanical
	Madankheri	SG132	SC452	Background landscape	Temple	Brahmanical
	Sonari village	SG147	SC461	Settlement	Temple	Brahmanical
	Murlikheri-Naroda	SG162b	SC566	Settlement	Temple	Brahmanical
	Salera	SG170	SC575	Settlement	Temple	Brahmanical
	Hakimkheri	SG179b	SC355	Settlement	Temple	Brahmanical
	"	"	SC360	Settlement	Temple	Brahmanical

APPENDIX IIIa

Pottery: Sample numbers and corresponding site details

BSM1
SG081/ SC180/ S180
Sonthiya-Shiampur basti
Settlement mound
Red Ware: 1; Black Ware: 2

BSM2
SG082/ SC182/ S182
Sonthiya kherai 2
Settlement mound
Red Ware: 29; Black Ware: 7;
Red and Black Ware: 1

BSM3
SG083/ SC183/ S183
Pathari kapasia
Settlement mound
Red Ware: 12

BSM4
SG084/ SC184/ S184
Pathari kativarat
Settlement mound
Red Ware: 6; Black Ware: 3

BSM5
SG085/ SC189/ S189
Dhanora kherai
Settlement mound
Red Ware: 4; Black Ware: 3

BSM6
SG006/ SC45/ S45
Besnagar
Settlement mound
Red Ware: 4; Black Ware: 2

BSM7
SG037/ SC132/ S132
Ahmadpur village
Settlement mound
Red Ware: 8; Black Ware: 4

BSM8
SG088/ SC191/ S191
Kanpohra/Agrola
Temple remains
Red Ware: 10; Black Ware: 1

BSM9
SG005/ SC28/ S28
Morel khurd
Monastery site
Red Ware: 6; Black Ware: 4

BSM10
005b/ SC41/ S41
Pipalia kherai
Hillside basti
Red Ware: 12; Black Ware: 4

BSM11
SG037b/ SC130/ S130
Ahmadpur hill
Hillside basti
Red Ware: 7; Black Ware: 4

BSM12
SG092/ SC198/ S198
Nihalpur
Settlement mound
Red Ware: 1; Black Ware: 2

BSM13
SG092/ SC201/ S201
Dandoli kherai
Settlement mound
Red Ware: 11

BSM14
SG102/ SC219/ S219
Sachet
Settlement mound
Red Ware: 11; Black Ware: 10

BSM15
SG031b/ SC221/ S221
Sonapura basti
Settlement mound
Red Ware: 19; Black Ware: 4

BSM16
SG031b/ SC112/ S112
Udayagiri
Settlement mound
Red Ware: 27; Black Ware: 5

BSM17
SG031b/ SC223/ S223
Madhupuri kherai
Settlement mound
Red Ware: 6

BSM18
SG106/ SC225/ S225
Utari guhar
Settlement mound
Red Ware: 11; Red and Black Ware: 2

BSM19
SG003/ SC24/ S24
Nagauri
Dam
Red Ware: 7

BSM21
SG056/ SC389/ S389
Mehgaon
Settlement mound
Red Ware: 4; Black Ware: 3

BSM22
SG113/ SC233/ S233
Alamkhera
Settlement mound
Red Ware: 16; Black Ware: 7

BSM23
SG118b/ SC423/ S423
Murwara village
Settlement mound
Red Ware: 16; Black Ware: 8

BSM24
SG118b/ SC423/ S423
Murwara village
Settlement mound
Red Ware: 7

BSM25
SG117/ SC239/ S239
Bishankhera
Hillside basti
Red Ware: 1; Black Ware: 3

BSM26
SG114/ SC236/ S236
Bhauliya kherai
Settlement mound
Red Ware: 9; Black Ware: 1

BSM27
SG121/ SC430/ S430
Himatgarh
Settlement mound
Red Ware: 6; Black Ware: 1; Red and Black Ware: 2

BSM28
SG121/ SC430/ S430
Himatgarh
Settlement mound
Red Ware: 4; Black Ware: 3

BSM29
SG123/ SC429/ S429
Devalkhera
Settlement mound
Red Ware: 7; Black Ware: 4

BSM30
SG064/ SC404/ S404
Tajpura Shur
Settlement mound
Red Ware: 5; Black Ware: 3

BSM31
SG127/ SC243/ S243
Chirohli kherai
Settlement mound
Red Ware: 18; Black Ware: 8

BSM32
SG129/ SC245/ S245
Chiroriya kherai
Settlement mound
Red Ware: 11; Black Ware: 7

BSM33
SG132b/ SC249/ S249
Madankheri/Dharukheri
Settlement mound
Red Ware: 12; Black Ware: 15

BSM34
SG084d/ SC475/ S475
Pathari/Gehunkheri
Settlement mound
Red Ware: 18

BSM35
SG134/ SC252/ S252
Gehunkheri Bhairav
Settlement mound
Red Ware: 2; Black Ware: 3

BSM36
SG139/ SC258/ S258
Umariya kherai
Settlement mound
Red Ware: 2; Black Ware: 5

BSM37
SG144/ SC268/ S268
Dhaniakheri/Pathari
Settlement mound
Red Ware: 2; Black Ware: 7

BSM38
SG145/ SC270/ S270
Umakhera
Settlement mound
Red Ware: 10; Black Ware: 1

BSM39a
SG140/ SC474/ S474
Marwai
Settlement mound
Red Ware: 15; Black Ware: 4

BSM39b
SG140/ SC474/ S474
Marwai
Settlement mound
Red Ware: 12; Black Ware: 2

BSM40
SG148/ SC273/ S273
Sonari basti
Settlement mound
Red Ware: 13; Black Ware: 2

BSM41
SG151/ SC281/ S281
Suakheri basti
Settlement mound
Red Ware: 8; Black Ware: 10

BSM42
SG154/ SC284/ S284
Parariya
Settlement mound
Red Ware: 11; Black Ware: 15

BSM43
SG156/ SC286/ S286
Berkheri ghat kherai
Settlement mound
Red Ware: 5; Black Ware: 6

BSM44
SG162b/ SC298/ S298
Murlikheri basti
Settlement mound
Red Ware: 8; Black Ware: 5

BSM45
SG165/ SC309/ S309
Girbhar kherai
Settlement mound
Red Ware: 16; Black Ware: 15; Red and Black Ware: 2

BSM47b
SG169/ SC323/ S323
Amachhar
Settlement mound
Red Ware: 14; Black Ware: 10

BSM48
SG164/ SC307/ S307
Neemkhera
Settlement mound
Red Ware: 13; Black Ware: 5

BSM50
SG171/ SC331/ S331
Bawaliya village
Settlement mound
Red Ware: 10; Black Ware: 2

BSM52
SG173/ SC337/ S337
Bamnor
Settlement mound
Red Ware: 3; Black Ware: 5

BSM53
SG174/ SC339/ S339
Gyasabad
Settlement mound
Red Ware: 7

BSM54a
SG012b/ SC672/ S343
Karhaud kherai
Monastery site
Red Ware: 16; Black Ware: 7

BSM54b
SG012b/ SC672/ S343
Karhaud kherai
Monastery site
Red Ware: 11; Black Ware: 4

BSM55
SG177d/ SC349/ S349
Devrajpur kherai
Settlement mound
Red Ware: 13; Black Ware: 3

SM11/19a
SG003a/ SC21/ S21
Nagauri
Hillside basti
Red Ware: 8; Black Ware: 6

SM14
SG003/ SC24/ S24
Nagauri
Dam
Red Ware: 5

SM21
SG014/ SC81/ S81
Piparia village
Settlement mound
Red Ware: 2

SM26
SG020/ SC86/ S86
Kachi kanakhera
Modern settlement
Red Ware: 3; Black Ware: 2

SM28c
SG020/ SC87/ S87
Amkhera
Modern settlement
Red Ware: 2

SM29
SG010/ SC63/ S63
Gulgaon kherai
Hillside basti
Red Ware: 1; Black Ware: 9

SM32a
SG011b/ SC66/ S66
Ferozpur
Modern settlement
Red Ware: 7; Black Ware: 2

SM32b
SG011b/ SC66/ S66
Ferozpur
Modern settlement
Black Ware: 6

SM34a
SG021/ SC89/ S89
Sehor
Settlement mound
Red Ware: 9

SM34b
SG021/ SC89/ S89
Sehor
Settlement mound
Black Ware: 4

SM35a
SG011/ SC67/ S67
Ferozpur
Dam
Red Ware: 2; Black Ware: 4

SM35b
SG011/ SC67/ S67
Ferozpur
Dam
Red Ware: 6; Black Ware: 10

SM37
SG022/ SC90/ S90
Goldoria
Monastery site
Red Ware: 3; Black Ware: 3

SM40a
SG023/ SC437/ S437
Dargawan
Settlement mound
Red Ware: 2; Black Ware: 3

SM44a
SG024/ SC438/ S438
Baheriya
Settlement mound
Red Ware: 11; Black Ware: 5;
Red and Black Ware: 1

SM44b
SG024/ SC438/ S438
Baheria
Settlement mound
Black Ware: 8

SM48
SG010c/ SC95/ S95
Eran 2
Settlement mound
Red Ware: 4; Black Ware: 1

SM49
SG010/ SC94/ S94
Eran
Ancient route
Black Ware: 5

SM51
SG032b/ SC114/ S114
Dhakna basti
Settlement mound
Red Ware: 1; Black Ware: 4

SM53
SG032b/ SC114/ S114
Dhakna basti
Settlement mound
Red Ware: 2; Black Ware: 2

SM57
SG035/ SC122/ S122
Bighan hill
Stupa/monastery
Red Ware: 2
site

SM61a
SG039/ SC140/ S140
Fatehpur Marmata
Settlement mound
Red Ware: 13; Black Ware: 5

SM61b
SG039/ SC140/ S140
Fatehpur Marmata
Settlement mound
Red Ware: 7; Black Ware: 3

SM62
SG039/ SC140/ S140
Fatehpur Marmata
Settlement mound
Red Ware: 1

SM63
SG039/ SC140/ S140
Fatehpur Marmata
Settlement mound
Red Ware: 1

SM65
SG041/ SC146/ S146
Besar Talai
Settlement mound
Red Ware: 2

SM66c
SG041/ SC146/ S146
Besar Talai
Settlement mound
Red Ware: 9; Black Ware: 4

SM70a
SG044/ SC154/ S154
Kharetiya (1)
Settlement mound
Red Ware: 11; Black Ware: 7

SM71a
SG046/ SC157/ S157
Kharetiya (2)
Settlement mound
Red Ware: 3; Black Ware: 3

SM71b
SG046/ SC157/ S157
Kharetiya (2)
Settlement mound
Red Ware: 2; Black Ware: 4

SM72
SG050/ SC160/ S160
Amkhera bhauji
Hillside basti
Red Ware: 4

SM74a
SG050/ SC163/ S163
Amkhera 2
Settlement mound
Red Ware: 10; Black Ware: 3

SM74b
SG050/ SC163/ S163
Amkhera 2
Settlement mound
Red Ware: 6; Black Ware: 1

SM75
SG052/ SC166/ S166
Kherai khera
Settlement mound
Red Ware: 13; Black Ware: 9

SM76
SG053/ SC167/ S167
Amoni ka khera
Settlement mound
Red Ware: 12; Black Ware: 5

SM77a
SG054b/ SC173/ S173
Ucher
Terraced
Red Ware: 1; Black Ware: 1; Red and Black Ware: 1
fortification

SM77b
SG054b/ SC173/ S173
Ucher
Terraced
Red Ware: 1; Black Ware: 1
fortification

SM78
SG054/ SC170/ S170
Ucher
Hillside basti
Red Ware: 3

SM79
SG055/ SC174/ S174
Berkheri
Settlement mound
Red Ware: 4; Black Ware: 7

SM80
SG067/ SC414/ S414
Rajatalai
Hillside basti
Red Ware: 3

SM81b
SG068/ SC416/ S416
Salamatpur hill
Hillside basti
Black Ware: 5

SM83a
SG071/ SC419/ S419
Bilori 2
Hillside basti
Red Ware: 6; Black Ware: 4

SM83b
SG071/ SC419/ S419
Bilori 2
Hillside basti
Red Ware: 4; Black Ware: 1

SM89
SG072/ SC420/ S420
Khamtala
Settlement mound
Red Ware: 7; Black Ware: 4

APPENDIX IIIb
Pottery: Fabric types

1 Black and Red ware
Medium thickness fabric. Well levigated.
10th century BC–3rd century BC (Phase 1c–1d)
Most common in excavated contexts in c. 1000 BC, but also continues into early-historic period, in association with NBPW (Ansari and Dhavalikar 1975, 96).

Feel: Very hard with smooth texture and smooth feel.
Slip: Medium slip. Outer: weak red (10r 5/4); inner: black (7.5yr n2/n3). High polish/burnish.
Void: Identified vegetal voids: frequency of <5, size range of 0.5–2mm.
Colour: Core = 2.5Y N/2 (black).
Inclusions: Opaque grey/cream rounded (hs) clay pellets (good sorting, size range 0.5–1.0 with a frequency of 5).

2 Thick Black Slipped Ware
Medium thickness fabric.
10th century BC–3rd century BC (Phase 1c–1d)
Similar wares occur in excavated contexts in association with Black and Red ware (BRW), datable to c. 1000–600 BC (Sinha 1971, 10–11; Narain and Roy 1976, 68–9). Also continues in NBPW levels, as represented for example by the sequence at Sravasti (Aboshi and Sonada 1997, 30; figs.19; 67–8; 72–3). Very few intact rims in SSP assemblage;mainly fragments of grooved necks of jars and bowls.

Feel: Very hard with smooth texture and smooth feel
Slip: Thick slip. Black (7.5yr n2). High polish/burnish, sometimes crackled.
Void: Identified vegetal voids: frequency of 20, size range of 0.5–2mm
Colour: Core = 2.5Y N/2 (black).
Inclusions: Opaque grey/cream rounded (hs) clay pellets (good sorting, size range 0.5–1.0 with a frequency of 5).Opaque grey subrounded (hs) grog (good sorting, size range 0.5–2.0 with a frequency of 20).

3 Northern Black Polished Ware (NBPW)
Thin thickness fabric. Very well levigated.
5th century BC–2nd century BC (Phase 1d–2)
Generally accepted date range in eastern India: c. 600–200 BC (Ghosh 1990, 255–6). Slightly later in central India. No intact rims in SSP assemblage.

Feel: Very hard with smooth texture and smooth feel
Slip: Thin slip. Black (2.5yr n2.5). High polish.
Void:
Colour: Core = 10YR 6/2 (light brownish grey).
Inclusions: None

4 Thin Black Slipped Ware
Medium thickness fabric.
10th century BC–3rd century BC (Phase 1c–1d)
Similar wares found in excavated contexts datable to c. 1000–200 BC, i.e. in association with BRW and NBPW (Sinha 1971, 10–11; Narain and Roy 1976, 68–9).

Feel: Very hard with irregular texture and smooth feel
Slip: Thin slip. Black/very dark grey (2.5yr n2.5/7.5yr n3). High polish/burnish.
Void: Identified vegetal voids: frequency of 20, size range of 0.5–2mm
Colour: Core = 2.5Y N/2 (black).
Inclusions: Opaque brown/brey angular (ls) straw (good sorting, size range 0.5–3.0 with a frequency of 20).Opaque black/brown subangular (hs) opaque stone (good sorting, size range 2.0–3.0 with a frequency of 10).Opaque grey subrounded (hs) grog (good sorting, size range 0.5–2.0 with a frequency of 20).

4b Black Polished Ware
Thin thickness fabric. Very well levigated.
10th century BC–3rd century BC (Phase 1c–1d)
Similar wares found in excavated contexts datable to c. 1000–200 BC, i.e. in association with BRW and NBPW (Sinha 1971, 10–11; Narain and Roy 1976, 68–9).

Feel: Very hard with smooth texture and smooth feel
Slip: 7.5yr n.2. slip. Brown. High polish.

5a Grey Slipped Ware
Medium thickness fabric. Well levigated. Similar to red ware, type 10a.
5th century BC–2nd century BC (Phase 1d–2)
Similar date range as Type 4.

Feel: Hard/very hard with irregular texture and smooth feel
Slip: Thin/medium slip. Dark grey (7.5y n4); or reddish brown (5yr 5/3). High polish /burnish.
Void: Identified vegetal voids: frequency of 20, size range of 0.5–2mm
Colour: Core = 2.5Y N/2 (black).
Inclusions: Opaque grey angular (ls) vegetal/straw (good sorting, size range 0.5–1.0 with a frequency of 20).Opaque grey/cream rounded (hs) clay pellets (good sorting, size range 0.5–1.0 with a frequency of 5).Opaque grey subrounded (hs) grog (good sorting, size range 0.5–2.0 with a frequency of 20).

5b Buff Slipped Ware
Thin thickness fabric. Well levigated. Thinner, lighter coloured version of 5a.
5th century BC–2nd century BC (Phase 1d–2)
Similar date range as Type 4.

Feel: Hard/very hard with irregular texture and smooth feel
Slip: Thin/medium slip. Reddish grey (5yr 5/2); or weak red (10r 4/3). Polish.
Void: Identified vegetal voids: frequency of 10, size range of 0.5–3mm
Colour: Core = 2.5YR N/0.25 (black); Surface = 10YR 5/2 (greyish brown).
Inclusions: Opaque grey angular (ls) vegetal/straw (good sorting, size range 0.5–3.0 with a frequency of 5).Opaque grey/cream rounded (hs) clay pellets (good sorting, size range 0.5–1.0 with a frequency of 5).Opaque black/brown subangular (hs) opaque stone (good sorting, size range 2.0–3.0 with a frequency of 10).

5c Heavy Buff Slipped Ware
Thick thickness fabric. Heavier version of 5a.
5th century BC–2nd century BC (Phase 1d–2)
Similar date range as Type 4.

Feel: Hard with fine texture and smooth feel
Slip: Thick slip. Pinkish brown (5yr 5/4); or pinkish grey (7.5yr 6/4). Polish/burnish.
Void: Identified vegetal voids: frequency of 20, size range of 0.5–2mm
Colour: Core = 2.5Y N/4 (dark grey); Margin = 2.5YR 15/2 (greyish brown); Surface = 2.5Y 15/2 (greyish brown).
Inclusions: Opaque grey angular (ls) straw (good sorting, size range 0.5–2.0 with a frequency of 20).Opaque white/grey rounded (ls) calcitic (good sorting, size range 0.5–1.0 with a frequency of 10).Opaque white/cream subrounded (hs) quartzite (good sorting, size range 0.5–2.0 with a frequency of 5).

6 Coarse Grey Ware
Medium thickness fabric.
10th century BC–1st century BC (Phase 1c–2)
Similar wares from excavated contexts occur between pre-NBPW levels and c. 1st century BC (Ansari and Dhavalikar 1975, 98).

Feel: Hard/very hard with irregular texture and smooth feel
Slip: Generally unslipped slip. Occasionally light grey (2.5y n7); or pink (7.5yr 7/4).
Void: Identified vegetal voids: frequency of 10, size range of 0.5–3mm
Colour: Core = 2.5YR N/0.25 (black); Surface = 10YR 5/2 (greyish brown).
Inclusions: Opaque grey angular (ls) vegetal/straw (good sorting, size range 0.5–3.0 with a frequency of 5).Opaque grey/cream rounded (hs) clay pellets (good sorting, size range 0.5–1.0 with a frequency of 5).

6b Coarse Grey Ware
Medium thickness fabric. Slightly rougher version of 6a.
10th century BC–1st century BC (Phase 1c–2)
Similar wares from excavated contexts occur between pre-NBPW levels and c. 1st century BC (Ansari and Dhavalikar 1975, 98).

Feel: Hard/very hard with irregular texture and rough feel
Slip: Generally unslipped slip. Occasionally grey (7.5yr n7); or brown (7.5yr 5/4).
Void: Identified vegetal voids: frequency of <5, size range of 0.5–2mm
Colour: Core = 7.5R N/2.5 (black); Surface = 10YR 6/2 (light brownish grey).
Inclusions: Opaque grey angular (ls) vegetal/straw (good sorting, size range 0.5–3.0 with a frequency of 5).Opaque grey/cream rounded (hs) clay pellets (good sorting, size range 0.5–1.0 with a frequency of 5).

7 Unslipped, Incised Grey Ware
Thin thickness fabric.
(Phasing unknown)

Feel: Hard/very hard with irregular texture and smooth feel
Slip: Generally unslipped slip. Dark brown (7.5yr 3/2); or very dark grey (7.5yr n3). Smooth with incised decoration.
Void: identified vegetal voids: frequency of 20, size range of 0.5–2mm
Colour: Core = 2.5Y N/2 (black).
Inclusions: Opaque grey angular (ls) straw (good sorting, size range 0.5–2.0 with a frequency of 20).Opaque white/grey rounded (ls) calcitic (good sorting, size range 0.5–1.0 with a frequency of 10).

8 Crude Grey Ware
Thin-Medium thickness fabric. Fast wheel.
11th–12th century AD–Late Medieval (Phase 7 and later)

Feel: Hard with irregular texture and rough and brittle feel
Slip: Generally unslipped slip.
Void: Identified vegetal voids: frequency of 10, size range of 0.5–2mm
Colour: Core = 2.5Y N/3 (very dark grey); Margin = 2.5YR 4/2 (dark greyish brown); Surface = 10YR 6/4 (light yellowish brown).
Inclusions: Opaque grey angular (ls) straw (good sorting, size range 0.5–2.0 with a frequency of 10).Opaque brown subrounded (hs) iron/opaque stone (good sorting, size range 0.5–1.0 with a frequency of 20).

9 Crude Black and Red Ware
Medium thickness fabric. Poorly levigated.
2nd century BC–2nd century AD (Phase 2–3b)
Similar wares are common in excavated contexts between c. 2nd century BC and 2nd century AD (Ansari and Dhavalikar 1975, 96; Mehta and Chowdhary 1966, 84).

Feel: Soft with irregular texture and rough feel
Slip: Unslipped slip.

10a Red Slipped Ware/Red Burnished Ware
Medium thickness fabric. 'Hard baked', metallic ring.
5th century BC–1st century BC (Phase 1d–2)
Similar wares occuring in association with NBPW are described at Kausambi (Sharma 1969, 150). Paste usually has inclusions of sand, straw, and husk, with frequent voids. Usually has ochrous slip. May also be related to 'highly glazed pottery' which occurs at Tripuri from c. 400–100 BC (Dikshit 1955, 44). Described as hard baked, with orange red slip, metallic ring, and high gloss, probably caused by salt being added to kiln. Usually burnished. 'Red burnished ware' also occurs during the same period at Tumain (Bajpai and Pandey 1985).

Feel: Very hard with fine texture and smooth feel
Slip: Medium slip. Light red (2.5yr 6/6); or red (10r 4/6); or weak red (10r 5/4). Smooth, sometimes light polish.
Void: Identified vegetal voids: frequency of 5, size range of 0.5–4mm
Colour: Core = 2.5YR N/3 (very dark grey); Margin = 10YR 5/3 (brown); Surface = 2.5YR 5/8 (red).
Inclusions: Opaque grey/cream rounded (hs) clay pellets (poor sorting, size range 0.5–2.0 with a frequency of 5).Opaque white/cream rounded (ls) calcitic (good sorting, size range 0.5–2.0 with a frequency of 10).Opaque white/grey subangular (ls) vegetal/straw (good sorting, size range 0.5–4.0 with a frequency of 20).Opaque orange/brown subrounded (hs) grog (good sorting, size range 0.5–1.0 with a frequency of 5).

10b Red Slipped Ware/Red Burnished Ware
Medium thickness fabric. Slightly less hard version of 10a.
5th century BC–1st century BC (Phase 1d–2)
See Type 10a.

Feel: Hard with fine texture and smooth feel
Slip: Thin/medium slip. Red (10r 4/6); or weak red (10r 5/4). Smooth, sometimes light polish.
Void: Identified vegetal voids: frequency of 5, size range of 0.5–4mm
Colour: Core = 2.5YR N/3 (very dark grey); Margin = 10YR 5/3 (brown); Surface = 2.5YR 5/8 (red).
Inclusions: Opaque grey/cream rounded (hs) clay pellets (poor sorting, size range 0.5–2.0 with a frequency of 5).Opaque white/cream rounded (ls) calcitic (good sorting, size range 0.5–2.0 with a frequency of 10).Opaque white/grey subangular (ls) vegetal/straw (good sorting, size range 0.5–4.0 with a frequency of 20).Opaque orange/brown subrounded (hs) grog (good sorting, size range 0.5–1.0 with a frequency of 5).

10c Red Slipped Ware (crude)
Medium-Thick thickness fabric. Fast wheel.
5th century BC–1st century BC (Phase 1d–2)

Feel: Very hard with irregular/brittle texture and smooth feel
Slip: Unslipped or trace only slip. Light red (10r 6/6); or red (10r 4/6).
Void: Identified vegetal voids: frequency of 5, size range of 0.5–4mm
Colour: Core = 2.5YR N/3 (very dark grey); Margin = 10YR 5/3 (brown); Surface = 2.5YR 5/8 (red).
Inclusions: Opaque grey/cream rounded (hs) clay pellets (poor sorting, size range 0.5–2.0 with a frequency of 5).Opaque white/cream rounded (ls) calcitic (good sorting, size range 0.5–2.0 with a frequency of 10).Opaque white/grey subangular (ls) vegetal/straw (good sorting, size range 0.5–4.0 with a frequency of 20).Opaque orange/brown subrounded (hs) grog (good sorting, size range 0.5–1.0 with a frequency of 5).

11 Heavyweight Red Ware
Medium thickness fabric. Dense, heavy fabric, ill-fired.
(Phasing unknown)

Feel: hard with irregular texture and rough feel
Slip: Trace only slip. Red (10r 5/6).
Void: identified vegetal voids: frequency of 10, size range of 0.5–2mm
Colour: Core = 7.5YR N/2.5 (black); Margin = 10R 4/3 (weak red); Surface = 2.5YR 6/8 (light red).
Inclusions: Opaque white/grey angular (ls) vegetal/straw (good sorting, size range 0.5–3.0 with a frequency of 5).Opaque red/brown subangular (hs) clay pellets (good sorting, size range 0.5–2.0 with a frequency of <5).Opaque red/brown subrounded (hs) iron stone (good sorting, size range 0.5–3.0 with a frequency of 5).

12 Thin Lightweight Red Ware
Thin thickness fabric. Biscuit-like texture.
(Phasing unknown)

Feel: hard with fine texture and smooth and rough feel
Slip: Thin slip. Red (10r 5/6).
Void: identified vegetal voids: frequency of 5, size range of 0.5–1mm
Colour: Core = 2.5YR 5/2 (greyish brown); Margin = 5YR 4/6 (yellowish red); Surface = 5YR 4/6 (yellowish red).
Inclusions: Opaque white/grey angular (ls) vegetal/straw (good sorting, size range 0.5–3.0 with a frequency of 10).Clear clear/white rounded (hs) quartzite (good sorting, size range 0.5–1 with a frequency of <5).Opaque red/brown subrounded (hs) iron stone (good sorting, size range 0.5–3.0 with a frequency of 5).Opaque white/cream well rounded (hs) calcitic (?) (good sorting, size range 0.5–2 with a frequency of 5–10).

13 Micaceous Ware
Thin-Medium thickness fabric. Well levigated.
1st century AD–3rd century AD (Phase 3a–3b)
Micaceous wares, in a similar repertoire of shapes, occur at numerous sites in central and north India between c. 1st–2nd century AD, e.g., Pauni (Deo and Joshi 1972, 65), Tumain (Bajpai and Pandey 1984, 31), and Devnimori where it is described as a 'costlier and less used ware' (Mehta and Chowdhary 1966, 77). Mica is an effective flux (Allchin 1960, 27).

Feel: Hard with smooth texture and smooth feel
Slip: Thin/trace only slip. Reddish yellow (5yr 7/6); or pink (5yr 7/4); or pale red (10r 6/4). Micaceous.
Void: Unidentified vegetal voids: frequency of <5, size range of 0.5–1.1mm
Colour: Core = 10YR 6/2 (light brownish grey); Margin = 2.5YR 6/6 (light red).
Inclusions: Opaque white/grey rounded (hs) calcitic? (good sorting, size range 0.5–2.0 with a frequency of 5).Clear clear/silver subrounded (hs) mica (very good sorting, size range 0.5–1.0 with a frequency of 20).

14a Burnished Red Ware
Thin-Medium thickness fabric. Poorly levigated. Metallic sound.
1st century AD–3rd century AD (Phase 3a–3b)
Some similarities to Red Polished Ware (RPW), common in 1st-to-2nd century AD levels at sites such as Amreli (Rao 1966) and Baroda (Subbarao 1953, 57–62) in Gujarat, and Maheswar (ibid, 62) and Vidisha (IAR 1964–5, 19) in Madhya Pradesh. Most commonly associated vessel types are sprinklers; and globular pots, as represented in the SSP assemblage by Vessel Type 99b (Appendix IIIb). However, examples from the SSP assemblage are much less well levigated and cannot be described as true RPW.

Feel: Very hard with fine texture and smooth feel
Slip: Medium slip. Reddish brown (2.5yr 5/4); dark red (10r 3/6); or red (10r 4/8). High polish/burnish.
Void: Identified vegetal voids: frequency of 5, size range of 0.5–3mm
Colour: Core = 2.5YR N/3 (very dark grey); Margin = 7.5YR 7/6 (reddish yellow); Surface = 2.5YR N/3 (very dark grey).

Inclusions: Opaque white/grey angular (ls) vegetal/straw (good sorting, size range 0.5–3.0 with a frequency of 5).Opaque red/brown subangular (hs) clay pellets (good sorting, size range 0.5–2.0 with a frequency of <5).

14b Black Painted Red Ware
Thin thickness fabric. Well levigated.
5th century AD–7th century AD (Phase 4–5)
A similar ware is found at Sonkh from c. 5th century AD, where it occurs most commonly in the form of spouted jars (Hartel 1993, 361; fig. 92).

Feel: Very hard with fine texture and smooth feel
Slip: Medium slip. Dark red (10r 3/6); or red (10r 5/8) with yellow or black stripe. High polish/burnish.
Void: Identified vegetal voids: frequency of 5, size range of 0.5–3mm
Colour: Core = 2.5YR N/3 (very dark grey); Margin = 7.5YR 7/6 (reddish yellow); Surface = 2.5YR N/3 (very dark grey).
Inclusions: Opaque white/grey angular (ls) vegetal/straw (good sorting, size range 0.5–3.0 with a frequency of 5).Opaque red/brown subangular (hs) clay pellets (good sorting, size range 0.5–2.0 with a frequency of <5).

15a Micaceous Slipped Ware
Medium thickness fabric. Very well levigated. Occurs mainly in the form of spouts.
1st century AD–3rd century AD (Phase 3a–3b)

Feel: Hard with smooth texture and smooth feel
Slip: Thin slip. Red (10r 5/8). Very fine micaceous slip.
Void: Irregular voids: frequency of <5, size range of -mm
Colour: Core = 2.5Y 5/2 (greyish brown); Margin = 2.5YR 5/2 (greyish brown); Surface = 2.5YR 5/2 (greyish brown).
Inclusions: Clear clear rounded (hs) mica (good sorting, size range <0.5 with a frequency of 10).

15b Micaceous Polished Ware
Medium thickness fabric. Well levigated. Slightly less smooth version of 15a.
1st century AD–3rd century AD (Phase 3a–3b)

Feel: Hard with fine texture and smooth feel
Slip: Thin slip. Dark grey (5yr 4/1); or light grey (5yr 7/1); or weak red (10r 4/4). Micaceous polish.
Void: Identified vegetal voids: frequency of 5, size range of 0.5–4mm
Colour: Core = 2.5YR N/3 (very dark grey); Margin = 10YR 5/3 (brown); Surface = 2.5YR 5/8 (red).
Inclusions: Opaque grey angular (ls) vegetal/straw (very good sorting, size range 0.5–2.0 with a frequency of 5).Opaque white/grey rounded (hs) calcitic (good sorting, size range 0.5–1.0 with a frequency of 5).Opaque black/brown subangular (hs) opaque stone (good sorting, size range 2.0–3.0 with a frequency of 10).

16 Rough, Hand-made Red Ware
Medium thickness fabric. Occurs most frequently in the form of cups.
(Phasing unknown)

Feel: Soft with hackly texture and rough feel
Slip: Unslipped slip. Reddish brown (5yr 4/4).
Void: irregular voids: frequency of 10, size range of 0.5–4mm
Colour: Core = 10YR 4/1 (dark grey); Margin = 2.5YR 6/8 (light red); Surface = 2.5YR 6/8 (light red).
Inclusions: Opaque grey angular (ls) vegetal/straw (fair sorting, size range 0.5–3.0 with a frequency of 10).Opaque brown rounded (ls) opaque stone (good sorting, size range 0.5–2.0 with a frequency of 5).Opaque white well rounded (hs) calcitic (good sorting, size range 0.5–3.0 with a frequency of 20).

17 Rough, Unslipped Red Ware
Thin-Medium thickness fabric.
(Phasing unknown)

Feel: hard with irregular texture and harsh feel
Slip: Unslipped or eroded slip slip. Unslipped, occasionally red (10yr 4/8).
Void: identified vegetal voids: frequency of 20, size range of 0.5–2mm
Colour: Core = 5R 6/2 (pale red); Margin = 5YR 7/8 (reddish yellow); Surface = 5YR 7/8 (reddish yellow).
Inclusions: Opaque grey angular (ls) straw (good sorting, size range 0.5–2.0 with a frequency of 10).Opaque white rounded (hs) calcitic (good sorting, size range 0.5–1.0 with a frequency of 20).Opaque red/brown subrounded (hs) iron stone (fair sorting, size range 0.5–3.0 with a frequency of 10).

18 Heavy Stone Ware
Medium-Thick thickness fabric. Heavy, dense fabric.
(Phasing unknown)

Feel: hard with irregular texture and smooth feel
Slip: Thin/traces only slip. Unslipped, occasionally dark red (10r 3/6); or red (10r 5/8).
Void: identified vegetal voids: frequency of 5, size range of 0.5–2mm
Colour: Core = 2.5YR N/2 (black); Margin = 2.5YR 5/8 (red); Surface = 2.5YR 5/8 (red).
Inclusions: Opaque white/grey angular (ls) vegetal/straw (good sorting, size range 0.5–3.0 with a frequency of 20).Clear white/clear angular (hs) quartzite (good sorting, size range 0.5–2.0 with a frequency of <5).Opaque black rounded (hs) iron stone/silver (good sorting, size range 3.0 with a frequency of 5).Opaque orange/pink subangular (hs) grog (good sorting, size range 0.5–2.0 with a frequency of 10).Opaque white/cream well rounded (hs) calcitic (fair sorting, size range 0.5–3.0 with a frequency of 10).

19 Medieval Unslipped Ware (red or black)
Medium thickness fabric. Well levigated. Fast wheel.
11th–12th century AD–Late Medieval (Phase 7 and later)

Feel: Hard with fine/brittle texture and smooth feel
Slip: Unslipped slip. Red (10r 5/6); or weak red (10r 5/4).
Void: Identified vegetal voids: frequency of 5, size range of 0.5–3mm
Colour: Core = 10R 6/6 (light red); Margin = 5YR 6/6 (reddish yellow).
Inclusions: Opaque grey angular (ls) vegetal (good sorting, size range 0.5–3.0 with a frequency of 20).Opaque orange rounded (hs) grog (good sorting, size range 0.5–1.0 with a frequency of <5).Opaque white/grey subangular (hs) straw (good sorting, size range <0.5 with a frequency of 5).Opaque white/cream subangular (ls) calcitic (good sorting, size range 0.5–1.0 with a frequency of 20).

20 Heavily Pitted, Unslipped Red-Ware
Medium-Thick fabric. Well levigated. Biscuit-like texture.
(Phasing unknown)

Feel: hard with laminated texture and rough feel
Slip: Unslipped slip. Unslipped.
Void: identified vegetal voids: frequency of 30, size range of 0.5–3mm
Colour: Core = 5YR 6/6 (reddish yellow); Margin = 5YR 6/6 (reddish yellow); Surface = 5YR 6/6 (reddish yellow).
Inclusions: Opaque grey subangular (ls) vegetal/straw (good sorting, size range 0.5–3.0 with a frequency of 20).

29 Unclassified
Miscellaneous fabric.
(Phasing unknown)
Unclassified wares

30 Kayatha Ware
Thin fabric.
2000 BC–1800 BC (Phase 1b)
Wheel-made with a dark brown slip and linear paintings in deep red. Occurs at Kayatha in the Chambal valley in c. 2000–1800 BC (Wakankar 1967), and related sites in central India.

31 Malwa Ware
Thin fabric.
1500 BC–1200 BC (Phase 1b)
Buff/orange slipped ware with black or dark brown designs. Occurs at Maheshwar-Navdatoli (Sankalia et al., 1971) Eran (IAR 1960–1) and many other central Indian sites.

APPENDIX IIIc

Pottery: Vessel types with common fabric-type occurrences (and associated sample numbers)

Abbreviations:
B&P 1984 = Bajpai, K.D., and S.K. Pandey. 1984. *Excavation at Tumain*
MGD 1955 = Dikshit, M.G. 1955. *Tripuri – 1952: being the account of the excavations at Tripuri, Madhya Pradesh*
HH 1993 = Härtel, H. 1993. *Excavations at Sonkh: 2500 Years of a Town in Mathura District.*
M&C 1966 = Mehta, R.N., and S.N Chowdhary. 1966. *Excavations at Devnimori*
GRS 1969 = Sharma, G.R. 1969. 'Excavations at Kausambi, 1957–59'
Lal 1954 = Lal, B.B. 1954. 'Excavation at Hastināpura and other explorations, 1950–2'

1 Carinated dish
10th century BC to 3rd–2nd century BC (Phase 1c–1d/2)
Dish. Lenticular base with slightly carinated edge, incurved or straight wall, direct rim.

COMPARATIVES:
Occurs in BRW at Sonkh, c. 1000 BC (HH 1993, fig. I.19).

FABRIC OCCURRENCES:
1 (Black and red ware): x1: BSM27-i
10a (Red slipped ware/Red burnished ware): x4: BSM18-vi; BSM8-I; BSM18-xii; BSM16-vii
12 (Thin lightweight red ware): x2: BSM23-iv; BSM18-viii

2 Carinated bowl
10th century BC to 6th century BC (Phase 1c)
Bowl, lenticular base with carinated edge. Conical, inleaning wall, direct rim.

COMPARATIVES:
Bowls of this shape occur in PGW and black burnished wares at Sonkh, c. 1000 BC (HH 1993, figs. I.1; I.10).

FABRIC OCCURRENCES:
1 (Black and red ware): x2: BSM27-ii; BSM18-i

3a Shallow dish
10th century BC to 3rd century AD (Phase 1c–3b)
Bowl/dish with inturned, featureless rim, and carinated upper body.

COMPARATIVES:
Similar, but not identical, shapes occur at Kausambi in c. 1000 BC (GRS 1969, fig. 12 A), mainly PGW. Similar bowls occur in black slipped ware and red slipped ware in c. 7th–3rd century BC (*ibid.*, fig. 12.XV).

FABRIC OCCURRENCES:
10b (Red slipped ware/Red burnished ware): x3: BSM14-iv; SM66c-h; BSM43-i 12 (Thin lightweight red ware): x1: SM75-i 13 (Micaceous Ware): x1: BSM15-xxi

3b Bowl/dish
6th century BC to 5th century AD (Phase 1c–4)
Variation of 3a, but with slightly out-turned, rounded rim, and more pronounced carination at neck, possibly to receive lid.

COMPARATIVES:
Occurs at Kausambi, c. 7th–4th century BC (GRS 1969, fig. 12.XX). Black slipped ware; also in unslipped grey ware at Tumain, c. 1st–5th century AD (B&P 1984, fig. 15.199).

FABRIC OCCURRENCES:
10a (Red slipped ware/Red burnished ware): x5: BSM33-viii; BSM33-vi; BSM38-vii; BSM31-xiii; BSM32-viii

3c Shallow dish
1st century AD to 4th century AD (Phase 3a–3b)
Variation of 3a, with ledge on outer side for receiving lid. Rim is pointed with inner ledge, rather than rounded like 3a.

FABRIC OCCURRENCES:
13 (Micaceous Ware): x3: BSM16-xxiii; SM74a-g; BSM54b-iv

4 Bowl/dish
(Phasing unknown)
Lower portion of bowl/dish with carinated base, and rounded bottom. Incised pattern just above carination.

FABRIC OCCURRENCES:
2 (Thick black slipped ware): x1: SM34a-c 5a (Grey slipped ware): x1: SM34a-f 5b (Buff slipped ware): x1: SM34a-f 7 (Unslipped, incised grey ware): x1: SM34a-d

5 Lidded bowl
1st century AD to 4th century AD (Phase 3a–3b)
Small shallow bowl with outflaring rim, and prominent carinated shoulder forming ridge for receiving lid.

FABRIC OCCURRENCES:
13 (Micaceous Ware): x1: SM61a-j

6a Shallow dish
1st century AD to 4th century AD (Phase 3a–3b)
Broad mouthed, shallow dish with bevelled rim, ledge at shoulder.

COMPARATIVES:
Occurs in micaceous wares at Devnimori, c. 4th century AD (M&C 1966, fig. 32.66).

FABRIC OCCURRENCES:
13 (Micaceous Ware): x2: BSM10-xvi; BSM55-iii

6b Shallow dish
(Phasing unknown)
Variation of 6a: with bevelled rim, internally thickened to form triangular shape. Pronounced carination at shoulder.

FABRIC OCCURRENCES:
6 (Coarse grey ware): x2: BSM30-I; BSM37-i
29 (Unclassified): x1: BSM45-vii

8 Shallow dish
(Phasing unknown)
Shallow, wide mouthed dish with incurved rim, and slight collar on outer side.

FABRIC OCCURRENCES:
5a (Grey slipped ware): x1: SM34b-iv

9 Shallow carinated dish
(Phasing unknown)
Shallow, wide mouthed dish with slight incurve on inner, and straight on outer. Carination at shoulder.

FABRIC OCCURRENCES:
4 (Thin black slipped ware): x1: BSM7-ii 6 (Coarse grey ware): x2: BSM39a-i; BSM54a-i 11 (Heavyweight red ware): x1: SM75-l

10 Carinated dish
10th century BC to 6th century BC (Phase 1c)
Small, shallow dish with featureless rim, straight slanting inner wall, prominent carination at shoulder. Base slants in heavily below.

FABRIC OCCURRENCES:
1 (Black and red ware): x1: BSM45-i 4 (Thin black slipped ware): x1: BSM15-i

11 Small lidded dish
10th century BC to 3rd–2nd century BC (Phase 1c–1d/2)
Small, shallow dish, with featureless rim, straight slanted inner wall, and prominent ridge on outer side for receiving lid.

FABRIC OCCURRENCES:
5a (Grey slipped ware): x1: BSM54a-ii

12 Shallow dish
3rd–2nd century BC (Phase 1d/2)
Shallow dish with heavily out-flaring rim, decorated with zig-zag incised pattern.

FABRIC OCCURRENCES:
1 (Black and red ware): x1: BSM41-i
5a (Grey slipped ware): x1: BSM31-iii

13 Shallow dish
1st century AD to 4th century AD (Phase 3a–3b)
Shallow dish, with featureless rim, flat bottom, and straight out-curved inner wall, decorated with horizontal, incised lines. Externally thickened at base.

FABRIC OCCURRENCES:
13 (Micaceous Ware): x1: BSM9-vii

15 Bowl
10th century BC to 4th century AD (Phase 1c–3b)
Fragment of deep, hemispherical bowl with flat topped, straight rim.

COMPARATIVES:
Occurs in coarse red ware at Sonkh, c. 1000 BC (HH 1993, fig. I. 31). Similar shapes occur in micaceous wares at Tripuri, c. 2nd century AD (MGD 1955, fig. 23.123); and Devnimori, c. 4th century AD.

FABRIC OCCURRENCES:
10a (Red slipped ware/Red burnished ware): x3: BSM55-x; BSM48-xv; BSM34-v 13 (Micaceous Ware): x1: BSM34-vi 17 (Rough, unslipped red ware): x2: BSM48-ii; BSM2-xxvii 29 (Unclassified): x1: BSM50-viii

16 Bowl
5th century BC to 3rd–2nd century BC (Phase 1d–1d/2)
Deep bowl with slightly rounded rim, outcurving at shoulder.

COMPARATIVES:
Occurs in red burnished ware at Tumain, c. 5th – 4th century BC (B&P 1984, fig. 1.63).

FABRIC OCCURRENCES:
5a (Grey slipped ware): x2: BSM12-iii; BSM31-ii 8 (Late medieval grey ware): x1: SM29-a 12 (Thin lightweight red ware): x1: SM77a-a 17 (Rough, unslipped red ware): x4: BSM27-v; SM76-e; BSM23-iii; BSM10-xi 29 (Unclassified): x1: BSM39a-ix

17a Bowl
7th–8th century AD to 9th–10th century AD (Phase 5–6)
Hemispherical, rimless bowl, tapering at sides.

FABRIC OCCURRENCES:
29 (Unclassified): x2: BSM14-iii; BSM54b-viii

18 Large, deep bowl
(Phasing unknown)
Wide mouthed bowl, with slightly incurved rim.

FABRIC OCCURRENCES:
17 (Rough, unslipped red ware): x1: SM35b-vi

19 Bowl
1st century AD to 4th century AD (Phase 3a–3b)
Large shallow bowl with heavily sloping walls, slightly rounded, featureless rim.

FABRIC OCCURRENCES:
13 (Micaceous Ware): x2: BSM55-vii; BSM39a-iv

20 Miniature bowl
1st century AD to 2nd century AD (Phase 3a–3b)
Miniature shallow funnel bowl. Flat bottom, beaded rim.

COMPARATIVES:
Occurs in unslipped red ware at Sonkh, c. 1st century AD (HH 1993, fig.IV.47).

FABRIC OCCURRENCES:
6 (Coarse grey ware): x1: SM44b-vii 14b (Black painted red ware): x1: SM74a-d 29 (Unclassified): x2: BSM45-iii; BSM2-viii

21a Bowl/cover
5th century AD to 11th–12th century AD (Phase 4–7)
Small bowl with heavily slanting, straight walls, and concave rim. Perhaps used as cover.

COMPARATIVES:
Occurs in red slipped ware at Tumain, c. 5th–12th century AD (B&P 1984, fig. 21.215).

FABRIC OCCURRENCES:
14a (Burnished red ware): x1: SM89-f

21b Small bowl/cover
5th–6th century AD (Phase 4)
Variation of 21a.

FABRIC OCCURRENCES:
14a (Burnished red ware): x1: BSM45-xi29 (Unclassified): x2: BSM34-vii; BSM30-i

21c Bowl
1st century AD to 5th–6th century AD (Phase 3a–4)
Larger version of 21a, with horizontal incised lines below inner rim. Probably flat bottoms.

FABRIC OCCURRENCES:
4 (Thin black slipped ware): x1: SM34a-b 6 (Coarse grey ware): x2: BSM2-iv; SM66c-b 10c (Red slipped ware (crude)): x1: SM75-k 14a (Burnished red ware): x1: SM34a-f 18 (Heavy stone ware): x1: SM34a-g

21d Bowl
5th–6th century AD (Phase 4)
Variation of 21a, with knife edge, outflaring rim. Cut rim base.

FABRIC OCCURRENCES:
5a (Grey slipped ware): x6: BSM54a-vii; BSM38-vii; BSM54a-vi; BSM45-xii; BSM31-x; BSM54a-iv 6 (Coarse grey ware): x1: BSM22-viii 18 (Heavy stone ware): x1: SM66c-f 29 (Unclassified): x2: BSM23-xiii; BSM26-iii

22 Bowl
(Phasing unknown)
Bowl with concave rim, and curved inner wall.

FABRIC OCCURRENCES:
5a (Grey slipped ware): x2: SM37-a; BSM42-xi 10b (Red slipped ware/Red burnished ware): BSM15-xv x1: 15b (Micaceous polished ware): x1: BSM3-xi 19 (Medieval unslipped ware (red or black)): x1: SM34a-e 29 (Unclassified): x2: BSM29-iv; BSM5-iii

23 Bowl/cup
(Phasing unknown)
Lower fragment of bowl/cup, with flat bottom, cut off with string. Possibly base of 21c.

FABRIC OCCURRENCES:
16 (Rough, hand-made red ware): x9: BSM13-I; BSM13-vii; BSM13-v; BSM13-ix; SM70a-h; BSM13-viii; BSM13-ii; BSM13-iv; BSM53-vii; BSM16-iv; BSM16-v; BSM1-i; BSM13-iii 17 (Rough, unslipped red ware): x6: SM14-c; SM14-d; BSM17-vi; BSM2-xix; BSM19-ii; BSM17-iii

24a Bowl
2nd–1st century BC (Phase 2)
Bowl with funnel shaped, thick in-beaded rim.

COMPARATIVES:
Occurs in unslipped red ware at Sonkh, c. 2nd century BC (HH 1993, fig.II.48).

FABRIC OCCURRENCES:
4 (Thin black slipped ware): x1: BSM7-iv 10a (Red slipped ware/Red burnished ware): x1: BSM43-iii 19 (Medieval unslipped ware (red or black)): x1: SM71a-c 29 (Unclassified): x2: BSM50-ix; SM44a-k

24b Bowl
6th century BC to 3rd–2nd century BC (Phase 1c–1d/2)
Bowl with inturned rim, convex on interior side, possibly lid.

COMPARATIVES:
Roughly similar shape occurs in red slipped ware at Tumain in c. 6th century BC (B&P 1984, fig. 3.60).

FABRIC OCCURRENCES:
5a (Grey slipped ware): x1: BSM33-iii 6 (Coarse grey ware): x3: BSM21-i; BSM41-viii; SM81b-iv 8 (Late medieval grey ware): x1: 10b (Red slipped ware/Red burnished ware): x2: BSM54a-xiv; SM71a-b

26 Bowl
3rd–2nd century BC (Phase 1d/2)
Bowl with out-turned rim, slight carination in centre, and roundish base.

COMPARATIVES:
Occurs in unslipped grey ware at Tumain in c. 3rd century BC (B&P 1984, fig. 7.122).

FABRIC OCCURRENCES:
10a (Red slipped ware/Red burnished ware): x3: BSM33-v; BSM34-ix; BSM89-e 10b (Red slipped ware/Red burnished ware): x1: BSM7-vii 13 (Micaceous Ware): x1: BSM54a-viii 17 (Rough, unslipped red ware): x2: BSM16-xxx; BSM22-xv 29 (Unclassified): x7: BSM38-x; BSM24-v; BSM23-vii; BSM45-viii; BSM26-ix; BSM54b-vii; BSM50-ii

27 Basin
6th century BC to 3rd–2nd century BC (Phase 1c–1d/2)
Basin with incurved, externally collared rim. Sometimes externally grooved.

COMPARATIVES:
Occurs at Kausambi in c. 6th–3rd century BC (GRS 1969, fig. 19.20) and Hastinapura (Lal 1954, fig. 16.XXIIa), c. 3rd century BC. Both red slipped ware; also in unslipped grey ware at Tumain, c. 3rd century BC (B&P 1984, fig. 7.52b).

FABRIC OCCURRENCES:
6 (Coarse grey ware): x5: SM35b-iii; BSM11-i; BSM4-ii; SM29-c; BSM44-i 9 (Crude black and red ware): x1: SM61b-iv 10a (Red slipped ware/Red burnished ware): x2: SM89-g; BSM5-ii 10b (Red slipped ware/Red burnished ware): x9: BSM44-iii; BSM31-iv; SM74a-a; BSM48-I; BSM44-ii; BSM32-ii; BSM18-iii; BSM7-ii; BSM18-ii 15b (Micaceous polished ware): x1: SM61a-b

28 Basin
(Phasing unknown)
Deep basin with incurved, externally thickened rim, inner groove.

FABRIC OCCURRENCES:
5a (Grey slipped ware): x2: BSM44-ii; SM51-ii 5c (Heavy buff slipped ware): x2: SM32b-ii; SM32b-v 10b (Red slipped ware/Red burnished ware): x2: SM72-d; BSM38-v 29 (Unclassified): x1: SM81b-iii

29 Basin
(Phasing unknown)
Basin with prominent out-turned rim.

FABRIC OCCURRENCES:
6 (Coarse grey ware): x8: BSM33-ix; BSM43-iii; BSM11-iii; BSM4-iii; BSM33-xi; SM79-f; BSM47b-v; BSM33-x

30a Bowl
5th–6th century AD (Phase 4)
Bowl with out-turned collared rim, triangular section.

COMPARATIVES:
Occurs in red slipped ware at Tumain, c. 5th century AD (B&P 1984, fig. 21.216).

FABRIC OCCURRENCES:
2 (Thick black slipped ware): x1: SM51-iv 6 (Coarse grey ware): x4: SM81a-c; SM35b-ix; BSM33-xii; BSM32-iv 10b (Red slipped ware/Red burnished ware): x2: BSM33-iii; SM32a-e

30b Carinated bowl
(Phasing unknown)
Variation of 30a, incurved, with slight carination at shoulder.

FABRIC OCCURRENCES:
6 (Coarse grey ware): x2: SM44a-c; SM29-b

32 Bowl
2nd–1st century BC to 3rd century AD (Phase 2–3b)
Bowl with prominent out-turned rim, ridge inside, straight slanted sides.

FABRIC OCCURRENCES:
6 (Coarse grey ware): x1: BSM33-viii 10b (Red slipped ware/Red burnished ware): x2: SM61a-e; SM76-h 14a (Burnished red ware): x1: BSM40-i 19 (Medieval unslipped ware (red or black)): x1: SM83a-b

33 Basin
2nd–1st century BC (Phase 2)
Basin/pan with outflaring, out-turned rim, forms ridge at top, sometimes grooved inside.

COMPARATIVES:
Occurs in red slipped ware at Tumain, c. 2nd century BC (B&P 1984, fig. 14.161).

FABRIC OCCURRENCES:
6 (Coarse grey ware): x2: SM89-d; SM61a-b 10a (Red slipped ware/Red burnished ware): x2: BSM22-xvii; BSM48-viii

34 Bowl
5th–6th century AD (Phase 4)
Deep bowl, with straight, insloping sides, internally thickened, featureless rim.

COMPARATIVES:
Occurs in coarse ware with red wash at Tumain, c. 5th century AD (B&P 1984, fig. 18. 213).

FABRIC OCCURRENCES:
20 (Heavily pitted, unslipped red-ware): x1: SM76-f

35 Bowl
(Phasing unknown)
Bowl with straight, incurved rim, quadrangular section.

FABRIC OCCURRENCES:
5a (Grey slipped ware): x1: BSM1-ii 10b (Red slipped ware/Red burnished ware): x2: BSM40-iii; BSM15-viii 29 (Unclassified): x2: BSM38-iv; BSM26-iv

37a Bowl
5th century BC to 5th century AD (Phase 1d–4)
Bowl with horizontally splayed out, internally thickened rim, triangular section. Rim has internal groove.

COMPARATIVES:
Occurs at Kausambi in c. 5th–3rd century BC (GRS 1969, fig. 18.5); also in red slipped ware at Tumain, c. 5th century AD (B&P 1984, fig. 18.212).

FABRIC OCCURRENCES:
10a (Red slipped ware/Red burnished ware): x2: BSM40-ix; BSM39b-ii 14b (Black painted red ware): x1: BSM40-vi

37b Bowl
3rd century BC to 9th–10th century AD (Phase 1d–6)
Bowl, convex base with flat centre, flaring in-beaded rim.

COMPARATIVES:
Occurs at Tripuri, c. 3rd/2nd century BC (MGD 1955, fig. 22.117a); also Sonkh, c. 10th century AD (HH 1993, fig. VII.31). Both in red slipped ware.

FABRIC OCCURRENCES:
14a (Burnished red ware): x1: BSM16-xx

38a Small bowl
7th–8th century AD to 9th–10th century AD (Phase 5–6)
Small bowl with flaring rim.

FABRIC OCCURRENCES:
5a (Grey slipped ware): x1: BSM40-i 6 (Coarse grey ware): x2: SM74a-a; BSM5-iii 14a (Burnished red ware): x1: SM74b-i

38b Small bowl
(Phasing unknown)
Variation of 38a.

FABRIC OCCURRENCES:
6 (Coarse grey ware): x1: BSM31-xii 17 (Rough, unslipped red ware): x1: SM76-k

39 Bowl
(Phasing unknown)
Bowl with flaring, slightly internally thickened rim.

FABRIC OCCURRENCES:
5a (Grey slipped ware): x1: BSM48-ii

40 Bowl
2nd–1st century BC (Phase 2)
Heavy bowl, shallow funnel shaped, beaded rim.

COMPARATIVES:
Occurs in coarse, red-slipped ware at Sonkh, c. 2nd century BC (HH 1993, fig. II.77).

FABRIC OCCURRENCES:
5a (Grey slipped ware): x3: SM75-d; BSM45-xi; BSM52-iii

41a Bowl
(Phasing unknown)
Small, spherical bowl with downturned collared rim.

FABRIC OCCURRENCES:
8 (Late medieval grey ware): x1: SM81a-f

41b Small bowl
(Phasing unknown)
Variation of 41a.

FABRIC OCCURRENCES:
8 (Late medieval grey ware): x1: SM71a-b 19 (Medieval unslipped ware (red or black)): x2: BSM16-xxi; SM26-a

43 Bowl
(Phasing unknown)
Shallow bowl, narrow, out-turned rim.

FABRIC OCCURRENCES:
19 (Medieval unslipped ware (red or black)): x2: SM48-d; BSM39b-xi

44 Miniature jar
(Phasing unknown)
Miniature jar.

FABRIC OCCURRENCES:
4b (Black polished ware): x1: SM83a-d

45 Shallow dish
10th century BC to 6th century BC (Phase 1c)
Shallow bowl/dish with flaring sides. Slightly out-curved, banded rim.

COMPARATIVES:
Occurs in unslipped grey ware at Sonkh, c. 8th century BC (HH 1993, fig. II.34).

FABRIC OCCURRENCES:
4 (Thin black slipped ware): x1: SM66c-c

46a Bowl
1st century AD to 4th century AD (Phase 3a–3b)
Small hemispherical bowl, with groove on top of rim, for receiving lid.

FABRIC OCCURRENCES:
10b (Red slipped ware/Red burnished ware): x7: BSM34-xv; BSM38-iii; BSM30-ii; BSM16-viii; BSM45-v; BSM54a-xii; BSM54a-x 13 (Micaceous Ware): x1: BSM54a-xi

46b Basin
4th century BC to 9th–10th century AD (Phase 1d–6)
Small bowl with thickened rim, and groove on top for lid.

COMPARATIVES:
Occurs in c. 4th–2nd century BC at Kausambi (GRS 1969, fig. 19.24) and Tripuri (MGD 1955, fig. 17.63-68). Unslipped red wares.

FABRIC OCCURRENCES:
6 (Coarse grey ware): x3: BSM52-iv; BSM55-i; SM29-d 10a (Red slipped ware/Red burnished ware): x2: BSM54a-vii; BSM34-iii

47 Lidded basin/cooking vessel
3rd–2nd century BC to 3rd century AD (Phase 1d/2–3b)
Small basin/cooking vessel, recurved neck, flaring rim, prominent grooves at top for receiving lid.

COMPARATIVES:
Occurs in unslipped grey ware at Tumain, c. 3rd century BC (B&P 1984, fig. 5.43); also in unslipped red ware at Sonkh, c. 2nd–3rd century AD (HH 1993, fig. V.55).

FABRIC OCCURRENCES:
10b (Red slipped ware/Red burnished ware): x1: SM83a-e

48 Lidded basin
(Phasing unknown)
Small basin with heavily slanting walls, flaring rim, prominent ridge at top for receiving lid.

FABRIC OCCURRENCES:
10a (Red slipped ware/Red burnished ware): x2: SM80-b; SM35b-iv

49 Small lidded bowl
(Phasing unknown)
Small hemispherical bowl, with slightly collared rim, two grooves on top, possibly for receiving lid.

FABRIC OCCURRENCES:
5a (Grey slipped ware): x1: BSM32-vi 6 (Coarse grey ware): x2: BSM14-iii; BSM54b-ii 10a (Red slipped ware/Red burnished ware): x1: BSM55-xii

50 Lidded basin
1st century AD to 4th century AD (Phase 3a–3b)
Heavy basin with externally thickened, flat topped, ridged rim, possibly for receiving lid.

FABRIC OCCURRENCES:
10a (Red slipped ware/Red burnished ware): x1: BSM55-viii 13 (Micaceous Ware): x1: BSM55-iv 15b (Micaceous polished ware): x1: BSM39b-i

51 Basin
7th–8th century AD to 9th–10th century AD (Phase 5–6)
Basin, with broad spread rim, in-slanting sides.

FABRIC OCCURRENCES:
5a (Grey slipped ware): x1: BSM52-i 5c (Heavy buff slipped ware): x2: SM51-I; SM75-e 7 (Unslipped, incised grey ware): x1: SM76-d 14a (Burnished red ware): x1: BSM38-i

52 Basin
(Phasing unknown)
Basin, with broad spread rim, slightly ribbed on top, inward-slanting sides.

FABRIC OCCURRENCES:
18 (Heavy stone ware): x1: SM44a-f

53a Small lidded bowl
(Phasing unknown)
Small shallow, spherical bottomed bowl, broad spread rim, slightly ridged, possibly for receiving lid.
FABRIC OCCURRENCES:
5c (Heavy buff slipped ware): x1: SM32b-vi

53b Small basin
(Phasing unknown)
Small basin, broad spread, collared neck, slightly ridged.
FABRIC OCCURRENCES:
5a (Grey slipped ware): x2: BSM7-iii; BSM23-ix

54 Lidded bowl
(Phasing unknown)
Small, light bowl with externally thickened rim, slightly ridged for receiving lid.
FABRIC OCCURRENCES:
5a (Grey slipped ware): x1: BSM45-viii

55 Basin
(Phasing unknown)
Wide mouthed basin, insloping sides, outflaring collared rim, with incised decoration on inner rim.
FABRIC OCCURRENCES:
5a (Grey slipped ware): x1: SM75-f

56 Lidded basin
1st century AD to 4th century AD (Phase 3a–3b)
Wide mouthed, basin, externally thickened collared rim, with ridge for receiving lid. Decorated on outer rim with row of small incised dots.
FABRIC OCCURRENCES:
6 (Coarse grey ware): x1: BSM45-xiv
7 (Unslipped, incised grey ware): x1: BSM47b-ii;

57 Basin
(Phasing unknown)
Wide mouthed basin, with outsplayed ribbed rim.
FABRIC OCCURRENCES:
5a (Grey slipped ware): x1: SM32a-b

58 Basin
(Phasing unknown)
Deep bowl/basin, externally thickened collared rim. Sometimes has ridge on outer body.
FABRIC OCCURRENCES:
5a (Grey slipped ware): x2: BSM47b-ix; BSM33-vi 6 (Coarse grey ware): x2: SM26-a; BSM11-ii 10a (Red slipped ware/Red burnished ware): x1: SM75-j 10c (Red slipped ware (crude)): x3: BSM23-v; BSM3-vii; BSM23-ix 29 (Unclassified): x1: BSM4-v

59 Lidded basin
1st century AD to 4th century AD (Phase 3a–3b)
Deep bowl/basin, with slight ridge at top to receive lid.
FABRIC OCCURRENCES:
13 (Micaceous Ware): x2: BSM3-viii; BSM39a-xi
29 (Unclassified): x1: SM83b-iii

60 Bowl
1st century BC to 6th century AD (Phase 2–4)
Large bowl, incurved wall, beaded rim, lenticular base.
COMPARATIVES:
Occurs in red slipped ware at Sonkh, c.1st century BC–1st century AD (HH 1993, fig. III.43), continuing at Tumain in c. 6th century AD (B&P 1984, fig. 53.57).
FABRIC OCCURRENCES:
17 (Rough, unslipped red ware): x7: BSM3-xii; BSM41-iv; BSM23-x; BSM19-vii; SM76-g; BSM10-vi; BSM25-i

61 Small bowl
(Phasing unknown)
Small bowl with flat topped, externally thickened rim, incised horizontal lines on body.
FABRIC OCCURRENCES:
17 (Rough, unslipped red ware): x4: BSM23-xv; BSM15-xviii; BSM24-viii; BSM24-vii

62 Small bowl
(Phasing unknown)
Small bowl with flat topped, externally thickened rim.
FABRIC OCCURRENCES:
17 (Rough, unslipped red ware): x1: BSM31-xv

63 Small carinated bowl
(Phasing unknown)
Small bowl with featureless rim, slight carination at base.
FABRIC OCCURRENCES:
17 (Rough, unslipped red ware): x1: SM34a-d

64 Basin
5th century BC to 2nd century BC (Phase 1d–2)
Deep basin with slightly out-turned, thickened externally grooved rim, tapering sides.
COMPARATIVES:
Occurs at Kausambi, c. 5th–2nd century BC (GRS 1969, fig. 19.23). Red ware, slipped on both sides.
FABRIC OCCURRENCES:
10a (Red slipped ware/Red burnished ware): x1: SM35b-vii

65 Large bowl
2nd–1st century BC (Phase 2)
Large bowl with thick flaring side, and flat base. Rounded, grooved rim, with ridge just below.
COMPARATIVES:
Occurs in red ware with thick slip on both sides, at Tumain, c. 2nd century BC (B&P 1984, fig. 11.167).
FABRIC OCCURRENCES:
4 (Thin black slipped ware): x1: BSM30-ii 5a (Grey slipped ware): x1: BSM30-iii 6 (Coarse grey ware): x1: BSM25-i 10a (Red slipped ware/Red burnished ware): x1: BSM15-iii

66 Basin
(Phasing unknown)
Large basin with incurved rim.
FABRIC OCCURRENCES:
29 (Unclassified): x1: BSM12-ii

67a Heavy basin/jar
(Phasing unknown)
Basin or storage jar with externally thickened, rounded collared rim.
FABRIC OCCURRENCES:
18 (Heavy stone ware): x2: BSM48-iv; BSM18-i

67b Heavy jar
(Phasing unknown)
Large heavy storage jar with externally thickened, rounded collared rim.
FABRIC OCCURRENCES:
10a (Red slipped ware/Red burnished ware): x1: SM61b-vi

68 Large, heavy basin
2nd century BC to 1st century BC (Phase 2)
Large, heavy basin with straight edges, out-turned, rounded rim, finger tip decoration on outer side. Thick section.
COMPARATIVES:
Occurs in red ware with thick slip on both sides, at Tumain, c. 2nd century BC (B&P 1984, fig. 11.168).
FABRIC OCCURRENCES:
10a (Red slipped ware/Red burnished ware): x1: BSM16-i

69 Deep bowl
3rd–2nd century BC (Phase 1d/2)
Heavy, deep bowl with bulbous, out-flaring rim, flat at top.
COMPARATIVES:
Similar shaped rim occurs on jar with red wash, at Tumain, c. 3rd century BC (B&P 1984, fig. 7.109).
FABRIC OCCURRENCES:
10a (Red slipped ware/Red burnished ware): x1: BSM29-i

70 Deep basin
(Phasing unknown)
Heavy, deep basin, with incurved rim, and applique wheel-like design on exterior surface.
FABRIC OCCURRENCES:
17 (Rough, unslipped red ware): x1: BSM17-i

71a Bowl
2nd century AD to 3rd century AD (Phase 3b–3b)
Heavy bowl, shallow funnel shaped, grooved club-rim, flat bottom.
COMPARATIVES:
Occurs in unslipped red ware at Sonkh, c. 2nd–3rd century AD (HH 1993, fig. V.58).
FABRIC OCCURRENCES:
18 (Heavy stone ware): x1: BSM12-i

71b Large bowl
(Phasing unknown)
Deep, large bowl with outsplayed, ribbed collared rim.
FABRIC OCCURRENCES:
6 (Coarse grey ware): x1: BSM22-xiv

72 Basin
1st century AD to 4th century AD (Phase 3a–3b)
Deep, large basin, with outsplayed collared rim, sometimes with incised decoarations, such as horizontal lines and triangular pattern.
FABRIC OCCURRENCES:
4 (Thin black slipped ware): x1: BSM33-i 6 (Coarse grey ware): x1: BSM23-xi 7 (Unslipped, incised grey ware): x2: SM76-c; SM75-g

73 Cooking vessel
(Phasing unknown)
Cooking pot with out splayed collared rim, decorated on top rim with horizontal, incised lines, and comb pattern.
FABRIC OCCURRENCES:
10a (Red slipped ware/Red burnished ware): x1: SM75-m

74 Jar/cooking vessel
(Phasing unknown)
Small jar/cooking vessel with outcurved collared neck. Hand joined at shoulder.
FABRIC OCCURRENCES:
14a (Burnished red ware): x1: SM34a-a 29 (Unclassified): x2: BSM36-iii; BSM32-xi

75 Cooking vessel
(Phasing unknown)
Cooking pot with outcurved round collared neck.
FABRIC OCCURRENCES:
4 (Thin black slipped ware): x3: SM34b-i; SM34b-iii; BSM26-i 10a (Red slipped ware/Red burnished ware): x1: BSM18-xi

76a Cooking vessel
10th century BC to 3rd–2nd century BC (Phase 1c–1d/2)
Cooking pot with straight neck, splayed out rim, and globular body. Shortly raised edge on the rim.

FABRIC OCCURRENCES:
4 (Thin black slipped ware): x4: SM71a-a; BSM45-iv; SM71b-ii; BSM6-ii 5a (Grey slipped ware): x1: SM34a-a 5b (Buff slipped ware): x1: SM11/19a-d

76b Cooking vessel
(Phasing unknown)
Variation of 76a.

FABRIC OCCURRENCES:
2 (Thick black slipped ware): x2: SM81b-ii; BSM6-i 6 (Coarse grey ware): x1: SM35b-viii 6b (Coarse grey ware): x3: BSM41-v; BSM23-viii; BSM23-iv 10a (Red slipped ware/Red burnished ware): x1:

76c Cooking vessel
(Phasing unknown)
Variation of 76a, with prominent ridges on inner and outer rim.

FABRIC OCCURRENCES:
6 (Coarse grey ware): x1: BSM14-v

79 Cooking vessel
1st century AD to 4th century AD (Phase 3a–3b)
Small cooking vessel, globular body, short neck. Outcurved, collared rim.

COMPARATIVES:
Occurs at Kausambi, c. 1st–4th century AD (GRS 1969, fig. 29. 88). Red or "chocolate" slipped ware.

FABRIC OCCURRENCES:
5a (Grey slipped ware): x2: BSM14-I; SM83a-a 6 (Coarse grey ware): x1: BSM14-v 14a (Burnished red ware): x4: BSM15-vii; BSM15-xx; BSM40-xii; BSM6-viii 15b (Micaceous polished ware): x1: BSM35-iii 29 (Unclassified): x2: SM83b-I; BSM15-xvi

80a Cooking vessel
6th century AD to 7th–8th century AD (Phase 4–5)
Cooking vessel with short neck and out-turned mouth. Down-oblique rim.

COMPARATIVES:
Occurs at Sravasti, c. 6th century AD (16 D1). Red ware.

FABRIC OCCURRENCES:
6 (Coarse grey ware): x2: SM83b-i 18 (Heavy stone ware): x1: SM76-d

80b Cooking vessel
(Phasing unknown)
Variation of 80a with grooves on inner neck.

FABRIC OCCURRENCES:
17 (Rough, unslipped red ware): x1: SM44a-a

90 Cooking vessel
2nd–1st century BC (Phase 2)
Cooking vessel with splayed out rim, and fine indentations on inner rim.

COMPARATIVES:
Occurs at Sravasti, (23A), in red slipped ware; also in brown slipped ware at Tripuri (MGD 1955, fig. 28.144). Both c. 2nd century BC.

FABRIC OCCURRENCES:
4 (Thin black slipped ware): x1: BSM15-iii 5a (Grey slipped ware): x2: SM75-a; SM75-b 6 (Coarse grey ware): x1: SM35a-c 6b (Coarse grey ware): x1: SM34b-ii

91a Cooking vessel
2nd century AD to 4th century AD (Phase 3b–3b)
Cooking vessel with shortly splayed out rim and globular body, probably with round base. Featureless rim.

COMPARATIVES:
Occurs in red ware at Sravasti, c. 2nd–3rd century AD (23A); also in crude black and red ware at Devnimori, c. 4th century AD (M&C 1966, fig. 36.105).

FABRIC OCCURRENCES:
6 (Coarse grey ware): x1: BSM39a-iv 9 (Crude black and red ware): x1: SM61a-d 14a (Burnished red ware): x1: BSM31-iii

91b Cooking vessel
2nd century AD to 4th century AD (Phase 3b)
Heavier version of 91a.

FABRIC OCCURRENCES:
6 (Coarse grey ware): x1: SM70a-d

92 Cooking vessel
1st century AD to 4th century AD (Phase 3a–3b)
Cooking vessel with shortly splayed out rim and globular body, probably with round base. Featureless rim.

COMPARATIVES:
Occurs in micaceous ware at Tripuri, c. 4th century AD (MGD 1955, fig. 64.122).

FABRIC OCCURRENCES:
6 (Coarse grey ware): x2: BSM50-i; SM70a-a 10a (Red slipped ware/Red burnished ware): x5: BSM53-ii; BSM53-vi; SM74a-j; BSM40-xi; BSM34-xi 14a (Burnished red ware): x3: BSM2-xv; BSM2-iii' BSM15-xiii 29 (Unclassified): x2: BSM44-vii; BSM14-xi

93 Cooking vessel
(Phasing unknown)
Cooking vessel with shortly splayed out rim and globular body, probably with round base. Featureless rim.

FABRIC OCCURRENCES:
13 (Micaceous Ware): x1: BSM2-xx 15b (Micaceous polished ware): x1: BSM48-vi 29 (Unclassified): x2: BSM45-xiii; BSM27-ii

94 Cooking vessel
1st century AD to 4th century AD (Phase 3a–3b)
Cooking pot with externally thickened rim, flat top, incised with thin ridges. Incised pattern on outer rim.

FABRIC OCCURRENCES:
13 (Micaceous Ware): x1: SM61a-i

95 Carinated cooking vessel
1st century AD to 4th century AD (Phase 3a–3b)
Cooking pot with out-flaring rim, heavily carinated.

COMPARATIVES:
Occurs in micaceous wares at Tumain, c. 1st century AD (B&P 1984, fig. 15.98); and Tripuri, c. 3rd–4th century AD (MGD 1955, figs. 23.119; 23.121; 23.122).

FABRIC OCCURRENCES:
5a (Grey slipped ware): x3: BSM45-v; BSM45-iii; BSM45-ii 13 (Micaceous Ware): x28: BSM54b-vi; BSM55-v; BSM3-iv; BSM16-xii; BSM22-xii; BSM16-xix; BSM34-i; BSM39b-v; BSM10-x; BSM22-vii; BSM55-vi; BSM31-xii; BSM16-xviii; BSM16-xxvii; BSM34-xix; SM74a-i; BSM48-xviii; BSM3-ii; BSM34-xiii; BSM16-xxv; BSM22-xxiii; BSM54b-v; BSM2-iv; BSM40-xvi; BSM16-x; BSM39a vii; BSM16-xi, SM44a-b 17 (Rough, unslipped red ware): x1: BSM10-vii 29 (Unclassified): x2: BSM22-vi; BSM39b-ix

96a Cooking vessel
(Phasing unknown)
Cooking pot, internally thickened rim.

FABRIC OCCURRENCES:
5a (Grey slipped ware): x1: BSM45-vi 11 (Heavyweight red ware): x2: BSM15-v; SM14-b

96b Cooking vessel
(Phasing unknown)
Variation of 96a, with groove on inner neck.

FABRIC OCCURRENCES:
5a (Grey slipped ware): x1: SM75-c 6 (Coarse grey ware): x3: BSM36-iii; BSM23-v; BSM31-ix

96c Cooking vessel
(Phasing unknown)
Variation of 96a, with triangular section.

FABRIC OCCURRENCES:
5a (Grey slipped ware): x1: BSM33-xv 6 (Coarse grey ware): x1: BSM48-iv 6b (Coarse grey ware): x1: SM37-b 10b (Red slipped ware/Red burnished ware): x1: SM61a-f 18 (Heavy stone ware): x1: SM76-l 29 (Unclassified): x1: BSM9-v

98 Carinated cooking vessel
1st century AD to 4th century AD (Phase 3a–3b)
Small cooking pot, with short neck, globular body, carination on upper part. Shallow groove on shoulder, flared slanted rim.

COMPARATIVES:
Occurs at Devnimori, usually in micaceous wares, c. 4th century AD (M&C 1966, fig. 32.61). Given the high occurrence of micaceous wares at other sites, an earlier date cannot be ruled out.

FABRIC OCCURRENCES:
11 (Heavyweight red ware): x1: SM11/19a-c

99 Cooking vessel
1st century AD to 4th century AD (Phase 3a–3b)
Cooking pot with internally thickened rim, triangular section.

FABRIC OCCURRENCES:
13 (Micaceous Ware): x1: BSM2-xxxi 29 (Unclassified): x1: BSM4-i

99b Globular pot
1st century AD to 4th century AD (Phase 3a–3b)
Upper part of globular pot with small, slightly outcurved, rim.

COMPARATIVES:
Occurs in red polished ware at Devnimori, c. 4th century AD (M&C 1966, fig. 32.68).

FABRIC OCCURRENCES:
14a (Burnished red ware): x1: SM74b-i

100a Jar
1st century AD to 5th–6th century AD (Phase 3a–4)
Small jar with outflaring rim, flat at top, roughly triangular section.

COMPARATIVES:
Occurs in coarse, red slipped ware at Tumain, c. 1st–5th century AD (B&P 1984, fig. 16.256).

FABRIC OCCURRENCES:
6 (Coarse grey ware): x4: BSM33-xiv; SM81a-b; BSM5-ii; SM40a-a 10b (Red slipped ware/Red burnished ware): x3: BSM48-xiv; BSM48-vii; BSM24-ii 10c (Red slipped ware (crude)): x1: SM78-b 14a (Burnished red ware): x3: BSM11-vi; BSM11-vii; BSM11-ii

100b Jar
7th–8th century AD to 11th–12th century AD (Phase 5–7)
Variation of 100a with groove on inner neck.

FABRIC OCCURRENCES:
19 (Medieval unslipped ware (red or black)): x1: SM83a-f

101 Jar
10th century BC to 3rd–2nd century BC (Phase 1c–1d/2)
Small jar with externally thickened collared rim.

FABRIC OCCURRENCES:
6 (Coarse grey ware): x6: SM89-c; SM44a-a; BSM2-v; SM29-g; SM29-f; SM40a-b 10b (Red slipped ware/Red burnished ware): x2: SM37-c; SM44a-c

102 Large jar or cooking pot
7th–8th century AD to 11th–12th century AD (Phase 5–7)
Large jar or cooking pot, with out-turned rim of square section.

FABRIC OCCURRENCES:
19 (Medieval unslipped ware (red or black)): x3: SM72-a; BSM8-v; BSM14-ii

103 Jar
10th century BC to 3rd–2nd century BC (Phase 1c–1d/2)
Jar with out-turned rim, triangular section. Incised ridge on outer shoulder, hand-joined at shoulder.

FABRIC OCCURRENCES:
5a (Grey slipped ware): x1: SM35a-a

104 Jar
1st century AD to 5th–6th century AD (Phase 3a–4)
Broad mouthed, globular vessel with out-flaring rim, horizonal ridges on outer rim.

COMPARATIVES:
Occurs in Black and red ware at Tumain, c. 1st to 5th century AD (B&P 1984, fig. 16.253).

FABRIC OCCURRENCES:
14a (Burnished red ware): x2: BSM16-xiv; BSM2-vii 15b (Micaceous polished ware): x2: BSM35-I; BSM48-xvi

105a Lidded jar
2nd century BC to 5th–6th century AD (Phase 2–4)
High necked globular vessel with downward facing, outflaring rim, grooved ridge at top for receiving lid.

COMPARATIVES:
Occurs in ill-fired, unslipped red ware at Tumain, c. 2nd century BC (B&P 1984, fig. 12.165; 13.176); and in black-slipped wares during 5th century AD (17.274).

FABRIC OCCURRENCES:
10b (Red slipped ware/Red burnished ware): x8: BSM31-x; BSM31-vii; BSM42-vi; BSM31-vi; BSM54a-xvi;
BSM54a-xv; BSM13-xi; 10b-BSM14-v 15b (Micaceous polished ware): x1: BSM47b-ix 17 (Rough, unslipped red ware): x2: BSM30-v; BSM10-iv 29 (Unclassified): x5: BSM9-ii; BSM47b-ii; BSM31-xvi; SM72-c; SM83b-iv

105b Lidded vase
5th–6th century AD to 11th–12th century AD (Phase 4–7)
Same as 105a, apart from fact that both parts of upper ridge slant upwards, rather than downwards. Also, inner neck has inner groove, rather than being straight.

COMPARATIVES:
Occurs in red slipped ware at Tumain, c. 5th–12th century AD (B&P 1984, fig. 19.244).

FABRIC OCCURRENCES:
10b (Red slipped ware/Red burnished ware): x5: BSM2-xiii; BSM30-iii; 10b-BSM34-viii; SM74a-b; BSM16-xiii

106 Lidded jar
2nd century BC to 9th century AD (Phase 2–6)
Low necked vessel with outflaring rim, ridge at top for receiving lid.

COMPARATIVES:
Occurs in ill-fired, unslipped red ware at Tumain, c. 2nd century BC (B&P 1984, fig. 12.163); also red slipped ware at Ahichchhatra, in c. AD 850–1100 (6.64).

FABRIC OCCURRENCES:
10b (Red slipped ware/Red burnished ware): x4: BSM39b-iv; BSM55-xi; BSM39b-iii; SM75-d 14a (Burnished red ware): x1: BSM11-iv 17 (Rough, unslipped red ware): x1: BSM34-xxi

107 Large, short necked, lidded jar
10th century BC to 3rd–2nd century BC (Phase 1c–1d/2)
Large jar with short neck, prominent ridge on top of rim for receiving lid.

FABRIC OCCURRENCES:
5a (Grey slipped ware): x1: BSM33-v

108 Small lidded jar
(Phasing unknown)
Small jar with incurved, collared rim, prominent ridge on inner rim for receiving lid.

FABRIC OCCURRENCES:
17 (Rough, unslipped red ware): x1: BSM50-vii

109 High necked, lidded jar
(Phasing unknown)
High necked jar, with out-turned rim, ridge for receiving lid.

FABRIC OCCURRENCES:
17 (Rough, unslipped red ware): x1: BSM19-iii

110 Spouted jar
(Phasing unknown)
Spouted jar.

FABRIC OCCURRENCES:
14a (Burnished red ware): x2: BSM21-ii; BSM15-ii 15a (Micaceous slipped ware): x4: BSM54b-xii; BSM34-xviii; BSM34-xvii; SM61a-m

111 Vase
1st century AD to 1st century AD (Phase 3a)
Vase with out-turned pointed nail-head rim, and flaring neck.

COMPARATIVES:
Occurs in red slipped ware at Hastinapura, c. 1st century AD (Lal 1954, fig. 21. XXXVI).

FABRIC OCCURRENCES:
5a (Grey slipped ware): x1: BSM32-v 6 (Coarse grey ware): x1: SM44a-b 10a (Red slipped ware/Red burnished ware): x5: BSM2-vi; BSM28-i; BSM32-x; BSM39a-xii; BSM2-xxiii 14a (Burnished red ware): x1: BSM45-vi 17 (Rough, unslipped red ware): x4: BSM34-iv; BSM10-xiii; SM44a-i; SM44a-j 19 (Medieval unslipped ware (red or black)): x1: SM32b-iii

112 Small basin
10th century BC to 3rd–2nd century BC (Phase 1c–1d/2)
Basin with collared rim, and prominent ridge on inner neck.

FABRIC OCCURRENCES:
5a (Grey slipped ware): x1: BSM32-i

113 Jar
(Phasing unknown)
Jar with collared rim, and incised ridges on inner neck.

FABRIC OCCURRENCES:
10a (Red slipped ware/Red burnished ware): x1: SM81a-a

114 Jar
6th century BC to 3rd century AD (Phase 1c–3b)
Large jar, with concave, recurved neck, externally rib-collared rim. Notches above, grooved shoulder.

COMPARATIVES:
Occurs at Kausambi, c. 5th century BC (GRS 1969, fig. 22.8); also Hastinapura, c. 1st century AD (Lal 1954, fig. 21. XXXVII); and Sonkh, c. 2nd–3rd century AD (HH 1993, fig. V. 22). All in red slipped ware.

FABRIC OCCURRENCES:
10a (Red slipped ware/Red burnished ware): x9: SM74b-iv; SM74b-vi; BSM43-v; BSM32-v; BSM8-ix; BSM42-ix; BSM42-viii; BSM42-xi; SM70a-f 10c (Red slipped ware (crude)): x2: BSM24-iii; BSM42-iii

115 Jar
4th century BC to 3rd century AD (Phase 1d–3b)
Jar with vertical rim, externally thickened and grooved.

COMPARATIVES:
Occurs in red slipped ware at Kausambi, c. 4th century BC (GRS 1969, fig. 22.83); also in unslipped red wares at Sonkh, c. 2nd–3rd century AD (HH 1993, fig. V.17).

FABRIC OCCURRENCES:
10b (Red slipped ware/Red burnished ware): x2: BSM41-iii; SM70a-c

116 Jar
(Phasing unknown)
Large jar, with concave, recurved neck, externally rib-collared rim.

FABRIC OCCURRENCES:
10a (Red slipped ware/Red burnished ware): x3: BSM42-vii; BSM7-iv; SM11/19a-b

118 Jar
3rd–2nd century BC (Phase 1d/2)
Jar with out-turned externally collared rim.

COMPARATIVES:
Occurs in unslipped red ware at Hastinapura, c. 3rd century BC (Lal 1954, fig. 18.XXXVII).

FABRIC OCCURRENCES:
5a (Grey slipped ware): x1: BSM47b-i 10a (Red slipped ware/Red burnished ware): x1: BSM8-iii

119a Vase
6th century BC to 4th century BC (Phase 1c–1d)
Vase with vertical round nail-head rim, and long corrugated neck.

COMPARATIVES:
Occurs at Kausambi, c. 6th–4th century BC (GRS 1969, fig. 21.65). Internal and external red slip.

FABRIC OCCURRENCES:
6 (Coarse grey ware): x1: SM11/19a-b 10a (Red slipped ware/Red burnished ware): x2: BSM21-iii; BSM14-vi

119b Vase
2nd century BC to 5th century AD (Phase 2–4)
High necked vessel with outflaring rim, tapering towards outer side. Incised ring on inner side of mouth.

COMPARATIVES:
Occurs at Tripuri, c. 2nd century BC (MGD 1955, fig. 19.97), in burnished red ware. Continues in black slipped wares at Tumain, c. 5th century AD (B&P 1984, fig. 21.248).

FABRIC OCCURRENCES:
6 (Coarse grey ware): x2: SM81a-e; SM81a-d 19 (Medieval unslipped ware (red or black)): x2: SM83b-ii; SM83a-d

120a Vase
3rd–2nd century BC (Phase 1d/2)
Vase, globular, out-curved featureless rim, ridged above neck.

COMPARATIVES:
Occurs at Hastinapura, c. 3rd century BC (Lal 1954, fig. 18.XXXId). Unslipped red ware.

FABRIC OCCURRENCES:
10c (Red slipped ware (crude)): x2: BSM27-vi; BSM55-i

120b High necked vase
10th century BC to 3rd–2nd century BC (Phase 1c–1d/2)
Variation of 120a, with slightly flaring neck.

FABRIC OCCURRENCES:
5a (Grey slipped ware): x1: BSM39a-iii 10b (Red slipped ware/Red burnished ware): x4: BSM54a-iv; BSM8-ii; BSM54a-iii; BSM47b-v 29 (Unclassified): x1: BSM54a-xiii

120c Jar
6th century BC to 3rd–2nd century BC (Phase 1c–1d/2)
Jar, globular or pyriform. Carinated neck. Vertically sharpened, slightly out-curved rim. Variation of 120a.

COMPARATIVES:
Occurs at Kausambi, c. 500–250 BC (GRS 1969, fig. 21.66), in red ware, externally and internally slipped; also in smooth, black slipped wares in c. 3rd century BC levels at Sonkh (HH 1993, fig. II.56); and Hastinapura (Lal 1954, fig. 18. XXXIe).

FABRIC OCCURRENCES:
18 (Heavy stone ware): x2: SM44a-d; SM76-b

120d Vase
6th century BC to 3rd century BC (Phase 1c–1d)
Vase, high neck, with vertical, externally double beaded rim.

COMPARATIVES:
Occurs at Kausambi (GRS 1969, fig. 21.61), c. 6th–3rd century BC. Red ware with wash. Voids from husk.

FABRIC OCCURRENCES:
15b (Micaceous polished ware): x1: SM11/19a-c 17 (Rough, unslipped red ware): x1: BSM24-iv

121 Pipe
(Phasing unknown)
Pipe.

FABRIC OCCURRENCES:
13 (Micaceous Ware): x1: BSM38-x 14a (Burnished red ware): x1: BSM16-xvii 15a (Micaceous slipped ware): x2: SM44a-e; BSM23-vii 17 (Rough, unslipped red ware): x2: BSM47b-viii; BSM16-xxix

123a Jar
3rd–2nd century BC to 2nd–1st century BC (Phase 1d/2–2)
Short-necked, globular vessel with out-turned rim, flat at top, and incised deep broad line inside neck.

FABRIC OCCURRENCES:
10a (Red slipped ware/Red burnished ware): x10: BSM39b-xii; SM11/19a-g; BSM7-ix; BSM31-ii; BSM31-v; BSM4-iii; BSM15-xvii; BSM14-ix; BSM11-iii; SM61b-v 10c (Red slipped ware (crude)): x1: SM76-a

124 Jar
3rd–2nd century BC to 2nd–1st century BC (Phase 1d/2–2)
High bottle-necked vessel, with incurved rim, prominent groove on inner rim. Protruding ridge on outer neck.

FABRIC OCCURRENCES:
10b (Red slipped ware/Red burnished ware): x1: SM34a-c

125 Jar
10th century BC to 3rd–2nd century BC (Phase 1c–1d/2)
Open mouthed vessel, with collared neck, and groove on inner side.

FABRIC OCCURRENCES:
2 (Thick black slipped ware): x1: SM74b-i

126 Pyriform jar
5th century BC to 2nd–1st century BC (Phase 1d–2)
Pyriform jar, slender neck, bevelled rim (beak rim), i.e., out-curved, externally thickened.

COMPARATIVES:
Occurs at Kausambi, c. 5th–3rd century BC (GRS 1969, fig. 22.80), in red ware, internally and externally slipped; also in red-slipped wares at Tumain, (B&P 1984, fig. 12.164); and unslipped red wares at Sonkh (HH 1993, fig. III.11), both in c. 2nd–1st century BC levels.

FABRIC OCCURRENCES:
4 (Thin black slipped ware): x2: BSM33-ii; BSM54b-iii 6 (Coarse grey ware): x1: BSM42-ix 10a (Red slipped ware/Red burnished ware): x2: BSM2-xxiv; BSM47b-iii 17 (Rough, unslipped red ware): x5: SM44a-h; SM80-a; SM66c-b; BSM38-ii; BSM54a-vi

127 Jar
2nd–1st century BC (Phase 2)
Globular jar, thin walled, funnel neck, bevelled collar rim.

COMPARATIVES:
Occurs in unslipped red wares at Tumain (B&P 1984, fig. 12.239) and Sonkh (HH 1993, fig. III.5), both in c. 2nd–1st century BC levels.

FABRIC OCCURRENCES:
17 (Rough, unslipped red ware): x2: SM35a-a; BSM39b-viii 18 (Heavy stone ware): x1: SM44a-g

128 Jar
1st century AD to 4th century AD (Phase 3a–3b)
Jar with sharp-edged, collared rim.

FABRIC OCCURRENCES:
5a (Grey slipped ware): x1: BSM42-vii 6 (Coarse grey ware): x3: BSM42-xiii; BSM41-vi; BSM43-ii 10c (Red slipped ware (crude)): x1: BSM40-xiii

129 Jar
5th century AD to 11th–12th century AD (Phase 4–7)
Jar with collared, upturned rim, flat at top.

FABRIC OCCURRENCES:
10c (Red slipped ware (crude)): x4: BSM32-ix; BSM8-vi; BSM47b-vii; BSM39b-vi

130 Jar
2nd century BC to 9th–10th century AD (Phase 2–6)
High necked vessel. Rim squarely turned towards outer side.

COMPARATIVES:
Occurs in unslipped red ware at Tumain, c. 2nd century BC (B&P 1984, fig. 12.182).

FABRIC OCCURRENCES:
10a (Red slipped ware/Red burnished ware): x4: SM37-b; BSM47b-iv; SM75-g; BSM8-iv 17 (Rough, unslipped red ware): x1: BSM50-vi

131 Jar
(Phasing unknown)
Jar with out-turned, collared rim, triangular section.

FABRIC OCCURRENCES:
6b (Coarse grey ware): x1: BSM52-v 10a (Red slipped ware/Red burnished ware): x5: BSM53-v; BSM47b-xiii; BSM18-vii; BSM11-v; BSM37-i 10c (Red slipped ware (crude)): x1: SM35b-iii 29 (Unclassified): x2: BSM54a-ix; BSM55-ii

132a Jar
10th century BC to 3rd–2nd century BC (Phase 1c–1d/2)
Jar/pouring vessel, with high-neck, slightly outflaring rounded rim.

COMPARATIVES:
Occurs in red slipped ware at Tumain, c. 8th century BC levels (B&P 1984, fig. 2.32b).

FABRIC OCCURRENCES:
5a (Grey slipped ware): x1: BSM41-ix 6 (Coarse grey ware): x2: BSM10-iv; BSM42-iii 10b (Red slipped ware/Red burnished ware): x5: BSM11-I; BSM2-I; BSM10-xv; BSM33-ii; BSM38-ix

132b Jar
10th century BC to 3rd–2nd century BC (Phase 1c–1d/2)
Variation of 132a with more outflaring on rim.

FABRIC OCCURRENCES:
5b (Buff slipped ware): x1: SM74a-c 6 (Coarse grey ware): x1: SM11/19a-f 10b (Red slipped ware/Red burnished ware): x5: BSM2-xiv; BSM15-xii; BSM14-viii; BSM17-iv; BSM27-iv 12 (Thin lightweight red ware): x1: SM74a-e 29 (Unclassified): x1: BSM3-vi

132c Jar/pouring vessel
10th century BC to 3rd–2nd century BC (Phase 1c–1d/2)
Variation of 132a with thickened external rim.

FABRIC OCCURRENCES:
10b (Red slipped ware/Red burnished ware): x3: BSM22-xx; BSM27-iii; BSM33-ix

133 Vase
3rd–2nd century BC to 1st century AD (Phase 1d/2–3a)
Vase with out-curved, internally thickened rim, concave neck.

COMPARATIVES:
Occurs at Hastinapura, c. 3rd century BC (Lal 1954, fig. 18.XXXIV), and c. 4th century BC–1st century AD in Kausambi (GRS 1969, fig. 22.85). All red slipped wares.

FABRIC OCCURRENCES:
5a (Grey slipped ware): x1: BSM47b-vii 10a (Red slipped ware/Red burnished ware): x3: BSM31-xviii; BSM37-ii; BSM30-iv

137 Jar
(Phasing unknown)
Globular or pyriform jar/pouring vessel, short, recurved neck. Upturned, banded rim. Probably convex base.

FABRIC OCCURRENCES:
10b (Red slipped ware/Red burnished ware): x1: SM70a-e

138 Small jar/pouring vessel
(Phasing unknown)
Small globular or pear-shaped jar, with short, recurved neck. Upturned, grooved, banded rim.

FABRIC OCCURRENCES:
10b (Red slipped ware/Red burnished ware): x1: BSM4-i

139 Small jar/pouring vessel
10th century BC to 6th century BC (Phase 1c)
Small jar/pouring vessel with lenticular trunk, funnel shaped collar rim.

COMPARATIVES:
Occurs in black-slipped grey ware at Sonkh, c. 1000 BC (HH 1993, fig. I.54).

FABRIC OCCURRENCES:
10b (Red slipped ware/Red burnished ware): x1: BSM19-i

140 Jar
3rd–2nd century BC to 2nd–1st century BC (Phase 1d/2–2)
Globular or pear-shaped jar, with short, recurved neck. Incurved, featureless banded rim. Convex base.

COMPARATIVES:
Very common type at Sonkh (HH 1993, fig. II.54), Kausambi (GRS 1969, fig. 21.44), and Hastinapura (Lal 1954, fig. 18. XXXI) during c. 3rd–2nd centuries BC. Mainly red slipped wares; also occurs in unslipped grey ware at Tumain, c. 2nd century BC (B&P 1984, fig. 8.142).

FABRIC OCCURRENCES:
10b (Red slipped ware/Red burnished ware): x3: BSM18-ix; BSM18-xiii; BSM2-v

141a Jar/pouring vessel
2nd–1st century BC (Phase 2)
High necked vessel with out-flaring rim, ridge at top, and tapering towards the outer side to form triangular section.

COMPARATIVES:
Occurs in unslipped red ware at Tumain, c. 2nd century BC (B&P 1984, fig. 12.177).

FABRIC OCCURRENCES:
10a (Red slipped ware/Red burnished ware): x8: BSM16-ix; BSM54a-ii; BSM54a-I; BSM26-vii; BSM23-xvi; BSM48-v; BSM45-xvi; BSM54b-i

141b Jar
2nd–1st century BC to 4th century AD (Phase 2–3b)
Variation of 141a with prominent groove(s) on inner side of rim. Sometimes with narrow protruding ridge on outer neck below rim.

FABRIC OCCURRENCES:
10a (Red slipped ware/Red burnished ware): x5: SM61a-g; BSM2-xi; BSM26-vi; BSM2-x; BSM28-ii; 10b (Red slipped ware/Red burnished ware): x1: BSM2-ix 29 (Unclassified): x2: BSM54a-v; BSM8-xi

141c Jar
2nd–1st century BC (Phase 2)
Variation of 141a with curved rim.

FABRIC OCCURRENCES:
10a (Red slipped ware/Red burnished ware): x2: SM75-f; BSM40-ii

141d Jar
2nd–1st century BC (Phase 2)
Variation of 141a with groove on inner rim, and prominent incurve below rim.

FABRIC OCCURRENCES:
10a (Red slipped ware/Red burnished ware): x1: SM75-b

147 Jar/pouring vessel
5th century AD to 11th–12th century AD (Phase 4–7)
High necked vessel with out-turned rim, depressed decoration on inner mouth, and groove on outer rim.

COMPARATIVES:
Occurs in black slipped ware at Tumain, c. 5th–12th century AD (B&P 1984, fig. 19.248).

FABRIC OCCURRENCES:
16 (Rough, hand-made red ware): x2: BSM39a-xiv; BSM4-iv

148a Jar
2nd century BC to 5th–6th century AD (Phase 2–4)
Vessel with out-curved, clubbed rim and concave neck.

COMPARATIVES:
Very common ware at Kausambi from c. 2nd century BC to 3rd century AD (GRS 1969, fig. 22.86). Red ware, internally and externally slipped.

FABRIC OCCURRENCES:
10a (Red slipped ware/Red burnished ware): x3: BSM45-iv; SM14-a; BSM31-ix

148b Jar
2nd–1st century BC (Phase 2)
High necked vessel, rim portion outflaring, forming ridge on top, and tapering outwards.

COMPARATIVES:
Occurs in ill-fired, unslipped red ware at Tumain, c. 2nd century BC (B&P 1984, fig. 12.160).

FABRIC OCCURRENCES:
10a (Red slipped ware/Red burnished ware): x3: SM74a-f; SM11/19a-a; SM61a-d

148c Jar
2nd–1st century BC (Phase 2)
High necked, broad mouthed vessel. Outflaring rim, ridge at top. Grooved rim below rim on exterior.

COMPARATIVES:
Occurs in red slipped ware at Tumain, c. 2nd century BC (B&P 1984, fig. 13.166).

FABRIC OCCURRENCES:
10a (Red slipped ware/Red burnished ware): x3: BSM32-iii; BSM52-ii; BSM48-iii 17 (Rough, unslipped red ware): x1: SM70a-a

148d Jar/pouring vessel
2nd century AD to 4th century AD (Phase 3b)
Vessel with out-turned, thickened rim. Grooved concave neck, and grooved shoulder.

COMPARATIVES:
Occurs in red slipped ware at Kausambi, c. 2nd century AD (GRS 1969, fig. 30.103).

FABRIC OCCURRENCES:
16 (Rough, hand-made red ware): x1: BSM3-ix

148e Jar
1st century AD to 4th century AD (Phase 3a–3b)
Variation of 148a with ridge on outer neck, and triangular, downfacing collar.

FABRIC OCCURRENCES:
13 (Micaceous Ware): x1: BSM10-viii 29 (Unclassified): x1: BSM9-viii

148f Jar/pouring vessel
3rd–2nd century BC(Phase 1d/2)
Vessel with under-cut rim.

COMPARATIVES:
Occurs in grey ware with black wash, at Tumain, c. 3rd century BC (B&P 1984, fig. 7.109).

FABRIC OCCURRENCES:
5b (Buff slipped ware): x1: BSM27-i 17 (Rough, unslipped red ware): x1: BSM43-vi

155 Vase
2nd–1st century BC(Phase 2)
High-necked vase with out-turned rim. Groove on inner mouth.

COMPARATIVES:
Similar rim occurs on a thick red slipped ware vase at Tumain, c. 2nd century BC (B&P 1984, fig. 14.149).

FABRIC OCCURRENCES:
6 (Coarse grey ware): x1: BSM54b-i10b (Red slipped ware/Red burnished ware): x5: SM76-c; BSM47b-x; BSM4-vi; BSM29-iii; BSM33-xi

158 Vase/pouring vessel
3rd–2nd century BC (Phase 1d/2)
Vessel with our-flaring rim, tapering towards inner side.

COMPARATIVES:
Occurs in thin fabric with red slip at Tumain, c. 3rd century BC (B&P 1984, fig. 6.90a).

FABRIC OCCURRENCES:
6 (Coarse grey ware): x1: BSM41-ii

160 Jar
(Phasing unknown)
Vessel with externally thickened rim, triangular section, groove on inner mouth.

FABRIC OCCURRENCES:
6 (Coarse grey ware): x1: SM89-b 17 (Rough, unslipped red ware): x2: BSM15-x; SM71a-a

161 Vase/pouring vessel
(Phasing unknown)
Vessel with out-turned rim, square section, groove inside mouth.

FABRIC OCCURRENCES:
17 (Rough, unslipped red ware): x2: SM61b-ii; BSM22-xxi

162 Vase/pouring vessel
(Phasing unknown)
Vessel with outturned collared rim, square section.

FABRIC OCCURRENCES:
10a (Red slipped ware/Red burnished ware): x1: BSM45-ii 14a (Burnished red ware): x2: BSM48-I; SM61b-i

163 Jar
6th century BC to 4th century AD (Phase 1c–3b)
Small vessel, perhaps for holding water, splayed out, featureless rim, and constricted neck.

COMPARATIVES:
Occurs at Kausambi, c. 7th–4th century BC; also at Devnimori, c. 4th century AD (M&C 1966, fig. 29.37). Both in red slipped ware (unburnished).

FABRIC OCCURRENCES:
10a (Red slipped ware/Red burnished ware): x4: BSM3-v; SM75-c; BSM3-iii; SM89-d 10b (Red slipped ware/Red burnished ware): x1: SM76-i 10c (Red slipped ware (crude)): x2: SM66c-d; SM75-e 14a (Burnished red ware): x1: BSM33-x 17 (Rough, unslipped red ware): x1: SM48-b 18 (Heavy stone ware): x2: BSM23-vi; SM34a-b

165 Jar
10th century BC to 5th–6th century AD (Phase 1c–4)
Broad mouthed, short necked vase with slanting collar, flat at the top. Sometimes ridged on outer rim.

COMPARATIVES:
Similar shapes occur at Hastinapura, c. 1000 BC (Lal 1954, fig. 11.XIII), in red ware, internally and externally slipped; also in unslipped red wares at Tumain, c. 5th century AD (B&P 1984, fig. 17.271). Micaceous wares, however, common in phase IIIa-b.

FABRIC OCCURRENCES:
5a (Grey slipped ware): x2: BSM1-I; BSM33-xvi 6 (Coarse grey ware): x2: BSM10-v; BSM31-xi 10a (Red slipped ware/Red burnished ware): x1: BSM45-xii 13 (Micaceous Ware): x3: BSM16-iii; BSM35-ii; BSM39a-x

167 Jar
(Phasing unknown)
Globular jar with ribbed collared rim.

FABRIC OCCURRENCES:
19 (Medieval unslipped ware (red or black)): x1: SM48-a

168 Jar
(Phasing unknown)
Jar, globular body, outcurved, collared rim, with prominent groove on inner neck. Wheel-made neck, and joined with rest of body by hand (finger/looting marks are visible at the joint). The vessel is then beaten out with a paddle and anvil, in order to produce the necessary degree of thinness for a water pot.
FABRIC OCCURRENCES:
6 (Coarse grey ware): x1: SM32a-a

169 Jar
(Phasing unknown)
Jar with carinated collar rim and globular body.
FABRIC OCCURRENCES:
10c (Red slipped ware (crude)): x1: SM44a-e

170 Jar
(Phasing unknown)
Jar, globular, with flat top, ribbed collared rim.
FABRIC OCCURRENCES:
6 (Coarse grey ware): x1: BSM14-vi

171 Jar
1st century AD to 4th century AD (Phase 3a–3b)
Jar, globular, with ribbed, over-turned rim. Hand made on turntable,and joined with lower wheel thrown part (looting marks still visible).
FABRIC OCCURRENCES:
6 (Coarse grey ware): x1: SM61a-a

172 Jar
(Phasing unknown)
Jar, globular, with slightly out-curved, ribbed rim.
FABRIC OCCURRENCES:
10a (Red slipped ware/Red burnished ware): x2: SM81a-c; SM80-c

173 Jar
1st century AD to 4th century AD (Phase 3a–3b)
Jar, with ribbed rim.
FABRIC OCCURRENCES:
5a (Grey slipped ware): x1: BSM47b-iii 6 (Coarse grey ware): x1: BSM44-iii

174 Jar
(Phasing unknown)
Jar with incurved, ribbed, collared rim.
FABRIC OCCURRENCES:
5b (Buff slipped ware): x2: SM79-a; SM79-a

175a Jar
(Phasing unknown)
Jar, globular, with externally thickened rim, triangular section.
FABRIC OCCURRENCES:
5b (Buff slipped ware): x2: BSM47b-x; SM35b-ii 6 (Coarse grey ware): x1: BSM36-ii 10a (Red slipped ware/Red burnished ware): x10: SM74a-h; BSM50-iii; BSM44-vi; BSM47b-I; BSM47b-vi; BSM44-iv; BSM50-i; BSM52-i; BSM40-xiv; BSM21-i

175b Jar
(Phasing unknown)
Variation of 175a.
FABRIC OCCURRENCES:
5a (Grey slipped ware): x2: BSM29-iv; BSM5-i 6 (Coarse grey ware): x2: BSM50-ii; BSM31-iv 10a (Red slipped ware/Red burnished ware): x5: BSM9-iv; SM53-I; SM51-I; BSM41-ii; BSM52-iii 13 (Micaceous Ware): x1: BSM37-v 19 (Medieval unslipped ware (red or black)): x1: SM65-a

175c Jar
(Phasing unknown)
Variation of 175a, with groove on inner neck.
FABRIC OCCURRENCES:
10a (Red slipped ware/Red burnished ware): x2: SM70a-b; SM79-b 20 (Heavily pitted, unslipped red-ware): x1: SM57-a

175d Jar
1st century AD to 4th century AD (Phase 3a–3b)
Variation of 174a with ribbing on outer rim.
FABRIC OCCURRENCES:
10a (Red slipped ware/Red burnished ware): x3: BSM39b-I; BSM21-iv; BSM7-i

179 Jar
2nd century AD to 4th century AD (Phase 3b)
Vase with out-turned, externally grooved rim, and short ledge on inner rim.
COMPARATIVES:
Occurs in "chocolate" red slipped ware at Kausambi, c. 2nd century AD (GRS 1969, fig. 30.99).
FABRIC OCCURRENCES:
14a (Burnished red ware): x2: BSM47b-xi; SM70a-g

180 Jar
(Phasing unknown)
Jar with externally thickened, externally grooved rim, rounded section, sometimes with prominent ridge on inner mouth.
FABRIC OCCURRENCES:
6 (Coarse grey ware): x1: SM79-b; 10a (Red slipped ware/Red burnished ware): x3: BSM29-v; SM81a-b; BSM32-vi

181 Jar
(Phasing unknown)
Vessel with externally thickened, externally grooved rim, square section.
FABRIC OCCURRENCES:
6 (Coarse grey ware): x1: SM89-a

182 Lid
(Phasing unknown)
Lid with upper knob, square section.
FABRIC OCCURRENCES:
10a (Red slipped ware/Red burnished ware): x2: SM61b-vii; SM79-c

183 Jar
1st century AD to 4th century AD (Phase 3a–3b)
Large, heavy jar with upturned rim, ridged on inner side.
FABRIC OCCURRENCES:
13 (Micaceous Ware): x1: BSM28-iv

185 Jar
1st century AD to 2nd century AD (Phase 3a–3b)
Globular jar, with wide-mouthed, cylindrical neck. Middle ridge and ridge below. Beaked rim. Joined with body using paddle and anvil.
COMPARATIVES:
Occurs in unslipped ochre/red ware (chaff tempered) at Sonkh, c. 1st century AD (HH 1993, fig. IV.4).
FABRIC OCCURRENCES:
5a (Grey slipped ware): x1: BSM42-viii 6 (Coarse grey ware): x2: SM29-e; BSM38-i 10a (Red slipped ware/Red burnished ware): x3: SM32a-c; SM37-a; BSM2-ii 10b (Red slipped ware/Red burnished ware): x1: SM83a-a 17 (Rough, unslipped red ware): x1: SM35a-b

186 Jar
3rd–2nd century BC (Phase 1d/2)
High necked vessel with flaring, out-turned rim. Perhaps globular. Band around the neck.
COMPARATIVES:
Occurs in well-fired, red burnished ware at Tumain, c. 3rd century BC (B&P 1984, fig. 5.106).
FABRIC OCCURRENCES:
5a (Grey slipped ware): x1: BSM45-i 6 (Coarse grey ware): x1: BSM42-vi 10b (Red slipped ware/Red burnished ware): x2: BSM23-xvii; BSM23-xii

187 Jar
6th century BC to 4th century AD (Phase 1c–3b)
Vase/jar, with vertical, round nail-head rim, and long corrugated neck.
COMPARATIVES:
Occurs at Kausambi, c. 6th–3rd century BC (GRS 1969, fig. 21.65), in red ware, internally and externally slipped. Similar vessels, with more out-flaring rim, occur at Ahichchhatra, c. 2nd–4th century AD (3.40).
FABRIC OCCURRENCES:
6 (Coarse grey ware): x1: SM29-a 10a (Red slipped ware/Red burnished ware): x1: BSM39a-i

189a Jar/cooking vessel
2nd century AD to 6th century AD (Phase 3b–4)
Fragment of globular jar/cooking vessel with short neck. Outcurved, round-collared rim.
COMPARATIVES:
Occurs in ill-fired red wares at Sonkh, c. 2nd–3rd century AD (HH 1993, fig. V.26); also at Hastinapura in c. 6th century AD (Lal 1954, fig. 11. XXII), in red ware slipped on both sides.
FABRIC OCCURRENCES:
5a (Grey slipped ware): x1: SM76-b 6 (Coarse grey ware): x6: BSM55-ii; SM35a-b; BSM55-iii; BSM45-x; BSM39a-ii; BSM45-xvi 15b (Micaceous polished ware): x1: BSM35-ii

189b Jar/cooking vessel
5th–6th century AD (Phase 4)
Large jar/cooking vessel, presumably globular. Short, vertical neck, out-leaning banded collar-rim.
COMPARATIVES:
Occurs in slurry daubed red ware at Sonkh, c. 5th century AD (HH 1993, fig. VI. 6).
FABRIC OCCURRENCES:
19 (Medieval unslipped ware (red or black)): x1: SM83a-c

190 Large jar/cooking vessel
5th–6th century AD (Phase 4)
Large jar/cooking pot, globular, angular, out-curved neck, with externally and internally grooved band-rim.
COMPARATIVES:
Occurs in red slipped ware with painted black stripes, at Sonkh, c. 5th century AD (HH 1993, fig. VI.11).
FABRIC OCCURRENCES:
6b (Coarse grey ware): x1: SM76-a

191 Small vase/pouring vessel
1st century AD to 5th century AD (Phase 3a–4)
Small vessel with out-flaring rim, and restricted neck. Prominent ridge at top for receiving lid.
COMPARATIVES:
Occurs in unslipped grey/black ware at Tumain, c. 1st–5th century AD (B&P 1984, fig. 15.202).
FABRIC OCCURRENCES:
15b (Micaceous polished ware): x1: BSM15-ix 17

(Rough, unslipped red ware): x2: BSM15-xxii; BSM14-vii

192 Small vase/pouring vessel
(Phasing unknown)
Small vessel with out-turned rim, constricted neck.

FABRIC OCCURRENCES:
10a (Red slipped ware/Red burnished ware): x1: BSM23-xi

195a Jar
2nd–1st century BC (Phase 2)
Small jar, steep shoulder, concave neck, banded collar rim, flattened globular body.

COMPARATIVES:
Occurs in unslipped red ware at Sonkh, c. 2nd century BC (HH 1993, fig. II.93).

FABRIC OCCURRENCES:
17 (Rough, unslipped red ware): x2: BSM2-xxi; BSM2-xxvi

195b Jar
5th–6th century AD (Phase 4)
Variation of 195a. With channelled and bevelled collar rim.

COMPARATIVES:
Occurs in red slipped ware painted with horizontal black stripes, at Sonkh, c. 5th century AD (HH 1993, fig. VI.20).

FABRIC OCCURRENCES:
10c (Red slipped ware (crude)): x4: BSM14-x; SM75-a; BSM33-i;BSM41-i

195c Jar
5th–6th century AD (Phase 4)
Variation of 195b, with flat top, and more triangular section.

FABRIC OCCURRENCES:
15a (Micaceous slipped ware): x1: BSM44-i 29 (Unclassified): x2: BSM39a-v; BSM29-ii

199 Jar
(Phasing unknown)
Wide mouthed vessel with out-turned, ribbed rim.

FABRIC OCCURRENCES:
10b (Red slipped ware/Red burnished ware): x2: SM40a-a; SM66c-a

200a Jar
1st century AD to 5th century AD (Phase 3a–4)
High necked jar/vase with gently outflaring rim, with grooves on outer face of rim. Examples at Tumain and Sravasti are spouted.

COMPARATIVES:
Occurs in unslipped grey ware at Tumain, c. 1st–5th century AD (B&P 1984, fig. 16.242), and red ware at Sravasti (18. B1).

FABRIC OCCURRENCES:
10a (Red slipped ware/Red burnished ware): x2: SM89-b; BSM41-v

200b Spouted vase
1st century AD to 2nd century AD (Phase 3a–3b)
Variation of 200a, gently out-turned neck, splayed-out rim, grooves on outer face of rim.

COMPARATIVES:
Occurs at Sravasti in spouted variety, c. 1st–2nd century AD (18. B10). Red ware.

FABRIC OCCURRENCES:
10b (Red slipped ware/Red burnished ware): x2: SM72-b; SM78-c 10c (Red slipped ware (crude)): x2: BSM38-vi; SM89-a 14a (Burnished red ware): x3: SM75-h; BSM33-iv; BSM32-iv 14b (Black painted red ware): x1: SM32a-b

202 Small jar
(Phasing unknown)
Small jar, with ribbed rim.

FABRIC OCCURRENCES:
10b (Red slipped ware/Red burnished ware): x1: BSM42-x

203 Jar
2nd century AD to 5th century AD (Phase 3b–4)
Jar, globular, carinated shoulder with upturned edge. High, upcurved neck, grooved band-rim.

COMPARATIVES:
Occurs in slurry daubed red ware at Sonkh, c. 2nd–3rd century AD (HH 1993, fig. V.29); and in coarse black and red ware at Tumain, c. 1st–5th century AD (B&P 1984, fig. 16.253).

FABRIC OCCURRENCES:
14a (Burnished red ware): x2: BSM43-ii; BSM43-iv

204 Jar
(Phasing unknown)
Jar with out-turned, ribbed rim.

FABRIC OCCURRENCES:
10a (Red slipped ware/Red burnished ware): x2: SM89-c; BSM27-i

205 Large pouring vessel
5th–6th century AD (Phase 4)
Vessel with funnel wall, thick concave banded rim.

COMPARATIVES:
Occurrs in unslipped red ware at Sonkh, c. 5th century AD (HH 1993, fig. VI.58).

FABRIC OCCURRENCES:
5c (Heavy buff slipped ware): x1: SM51-iii 10b (Red slipped ware/Red burnished ware): x2: BSM39a-iii; BSM45-i

206 Large pouring vessel
(Phasing unknown)
Heavy wide mouthed vessel with ribbed rim.

FABRIC OCCURRENCES:
10b (Red slipped ware/Red burnished ware): x1: BSM31-i

207 Jar
(Phasing unknown)
Short-necked jar with over-turned collared rim, square section.

FABRIC OCCURRENCES:
8 (Late medieval grey ware): x1: SM83a-c 10a (Red slipped ware/Red burnished ware): x5: SM61a-c; SM61a-a; SM32a-a; SM78-a; SM32a-f

208 Jar
(Phasing unknown)
Large jar, short necked, with straight, collared rim, grooved on inner mouth.

FABRIC OCCURRENCES:
18 (Heavy stone ware): x1: SM66c-c

210 Jar
(Phasing unknown)
Short-necked jar, with out-turned collared rim, slight ridge under outer rim, groove on inner mouth.

FABRIC OCCURRENCES:
6 (Coarse grey ware): x7: SM70a-f; SM70a-e; SM61a-c; SM79-d; SM79-c; SM70a-b; SM79-e

99999 Body sherd
(Phasing unknown)
Undiagnostic body sherd

COMPARATIVES:
Varies

FABRIC OCCURRENCES:
1 (Black and red ware): x1: SM77a-a

2 (Thick black slipped ware): x9: BSM28-ii; BSM28-iii; BSM2-ii; BSM15-iv; SM71a-c; BSM2-i; SM66c-d; SM53-ii; SM74a-b; SM53-ii

3 (Northern Black Polished Ware): x2: SM32b-iv; BSM2-vi

4 (Thin black slipped ware): x8: SM71b-i; BSM14-iv; BSM16-v; BSM33-iv; SM61a-e; BSM16-ii; SM61b-ii; SM61b-iii

5a (Grey slipped ware): x22: BSM33-xiiil BSM40-ii; BSM48-iii; BSM38-iv; BSM38-vi; BSM41-iv; BSM54b-iv; SM75-h; BSM28-i; SM75-i; SM35b-i; BSM41-iii; SM44a-d; BSM7-i; BSM37-vi; SM66c-a; BSM54a-v; BSM54a-iii; BSM42-xv; BSM45-xv; SM48-a; BSM22-iv;

5b (Buff slipped ware): x5: BSM9-v; SM35b-v; BSM10-vi; BSM53-iii; BSM9-ii

5c (Heavy buff slipped ware): x3: SM26-c; SM70a-c; BSM38-iii

6 (Coarse grey ware): x54 (not listed)6b (Coarse grey ware): x3: BSM41-x; SM37-c

7 (Unslipped, incised grey ware): x3: (not listed)

10a (Red slipped ware/Red burnished ware): x11: SM11/19a-d; SM48-c; SM32a-g; SM81a-e; BSM34-xii; BSM2-xii; SM79-d; SM32a-d; SM81a-f; SM81b-I; BSM32-vii; -99999-10b-BSM24-i

10b (Red slipped ware/Red burnished ware): x7: BSM4-ii; SM70a-d; BSM8-vii; SM11/19a-e; SM66c-I; SM61a-k

10c (Red slipped ware (crude)): x3: SM66c-g; SM35b-ii; SM81a-a

13 (Micaceous Ware): x6: BSM28-iii; BSM14-ix; BSM16-vi; BSM14-ii; BSM23-i; BSM45-x; -99999-

14a-BSM22-v 14a (Burnished red ware): x18: BSM22-xiii; BSM2-xxix; BSM40-iv; BSM2-xxii; BSM22-xxiv; BSM5-iv; SM61a-L; SM61b-iv; BSM23-viii; SM74b-vii; BSM16-xxvi; BSM47b-xv; BSM7-v; BSM39a-vi; BSM54b-xi; BSM29-vi; BSM31-xiv; -99999-14b-SM61b-iii

14b (Black painted red ware): x3: BSM53-iv; BSM41-viii

15b (Micaceous polished ware): x3: BSM42-xii; BSM35-i;SM11/19a-f; SM34a-i

17 (Rough, unslipped red ware): x2: BSM10-xiv; SM34a-i

18 (Heavy stone ware): x2: SM66c-e; SM76-j

19 (Medieval unslipped ware (red or black)): x1: SM65-b

29 (Unclassified): x130 (not listed)

30 (Kayatha ware): x2: SM22; BSM1431 (Malwa ware): x2: SM22; BSM14

APPENDIX IIId

Pottery: Vessel-type illustrations

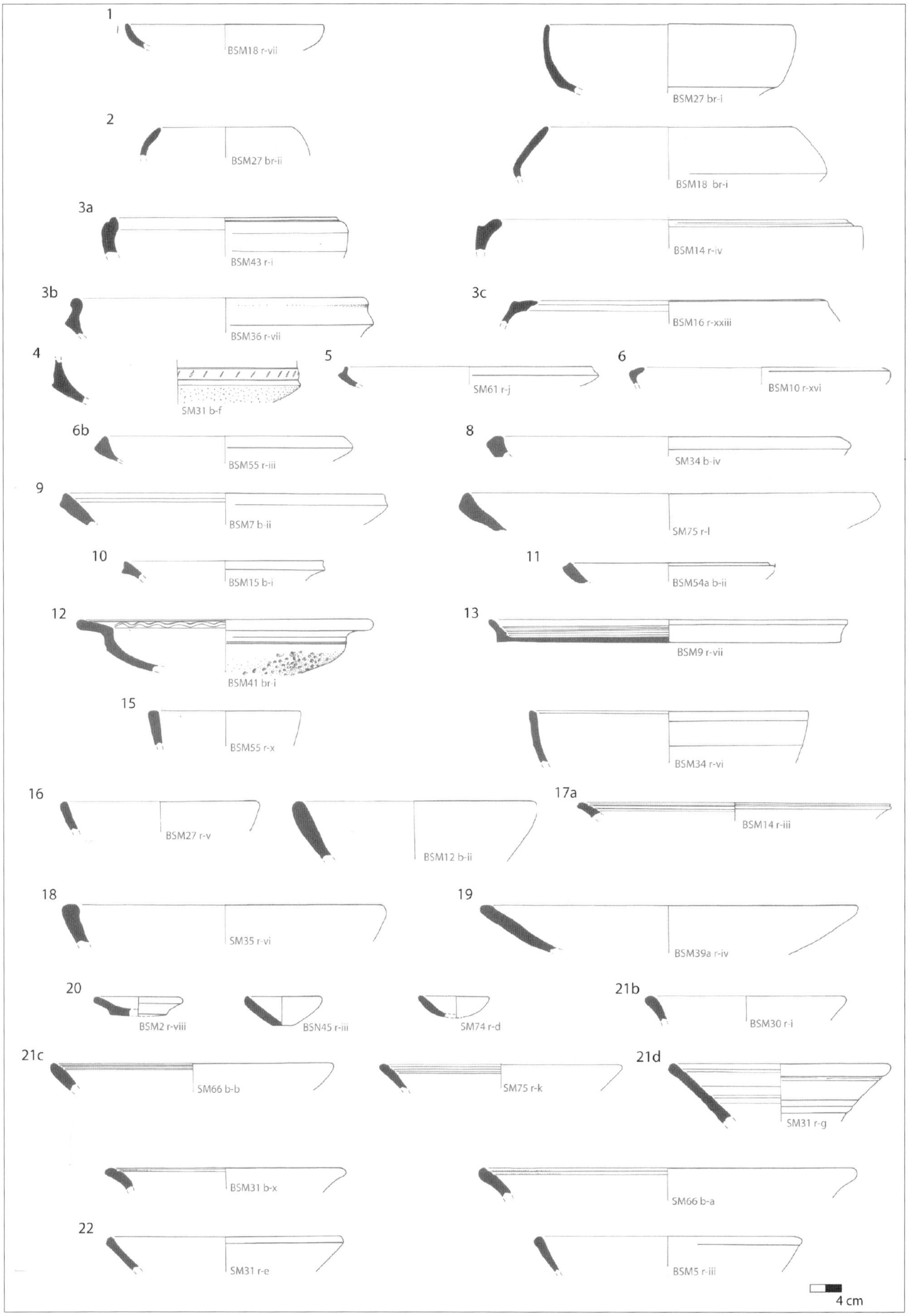
1
BSM18 r-vii
BSM27 br-i
2
BSM27 br-ii
BSM18 br-i
3a
BSM43 r-i
BSM14 r-iv
3b
BSM36 r-vii
3c
BSM16 r-xxiii
4
SM31 b-f
5
SM61 r-j
6
BSM10 r-xvi
6b
BSM55 r-iii
8
SM34 b-iv
9
BSM7 b-ii
SM75 r-l
10
BSM15 b-i
11
BSM54a b-ii
12
BSM41 br-i
13
BSM9 r-vii
15
BSM55 r-x
BSM34 r-vi
16
BSM27 r-v
BSM12 b-ii
17a
BSM14 r-iii
18
SM35 r-vi
19
BSM39a r-iv
20
BSM2 r-viii
BSN45 r-iii
SM74 r-d
21b
BSM30 r-i
21c
SM66 b-b
SM75 r-k
21d
SM31 r-g
BSM31 b-x
SM66 b-a
22
SM31 r-e
BSM5 r-iii
4 cm

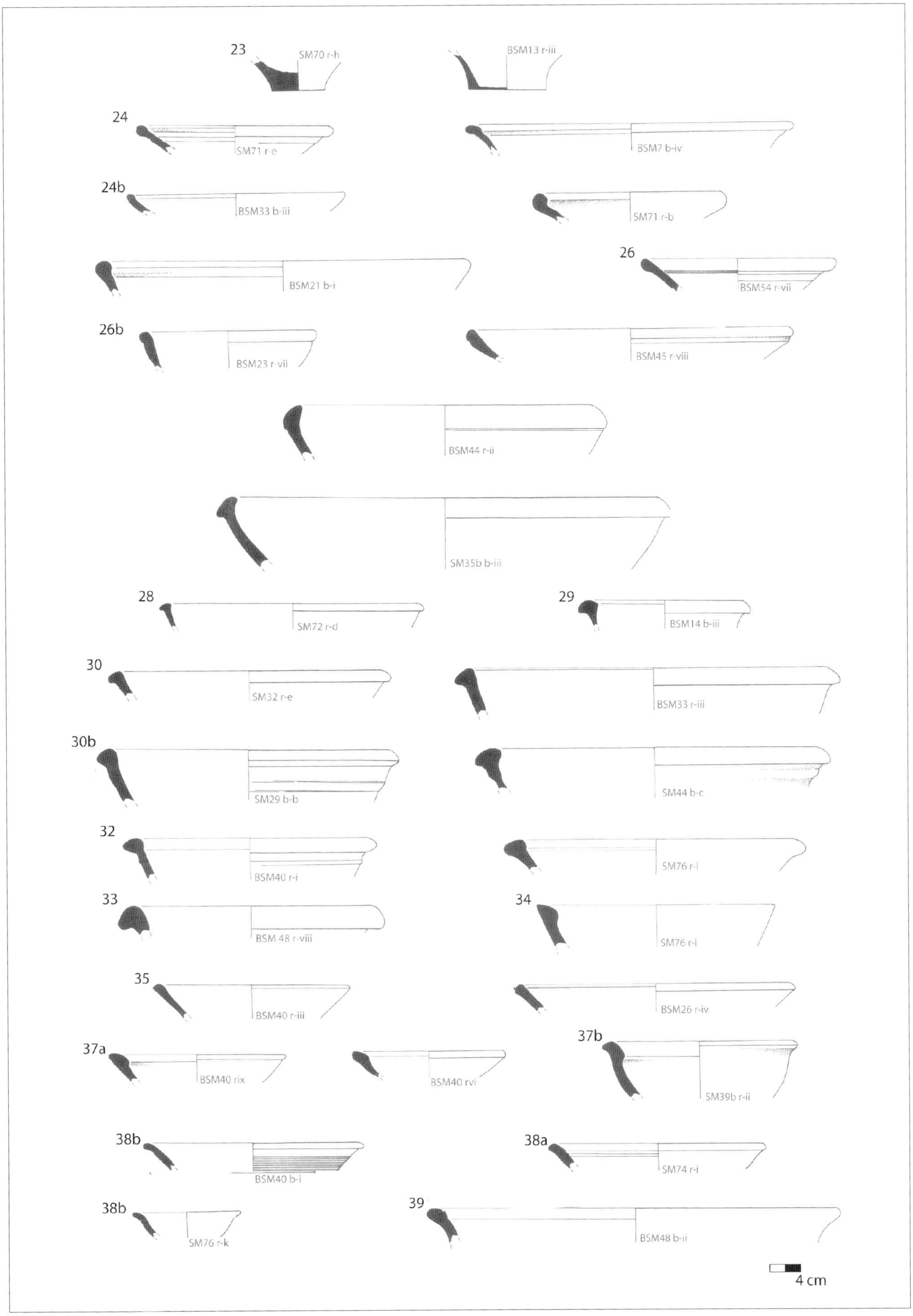
23
SM70 r-h
BSM13 r-iii
24
SM71 r-e
BSM7 b-iv
24b
BSM33 b-iii
SM71 r-b
BSM21 b-i
26
BSM54 r-vii
26b
BSM23 r-vii
BSM45 r-viii
BSM44 r-ii
SM35b b-iii
28
SM72 r-d
29
BSM14 b-iii
30
SM32 r-e
BSM33 r-iii
30b
SM29 b-b
SM44 b-c
32
BSM40 r-i
SM76 r-l
33
BSM 48 r-viii
34
SM76 r-i
35
BSM40 r-iii
BSM26 r-iv
37a
BSM40 rix
BSM40 rvi
37b
SM39b r-ii
38b
BSM40 b-i
38a
SM74 r-i
38b
SM76 r-k
39
BSM48 b-ii
4 cm

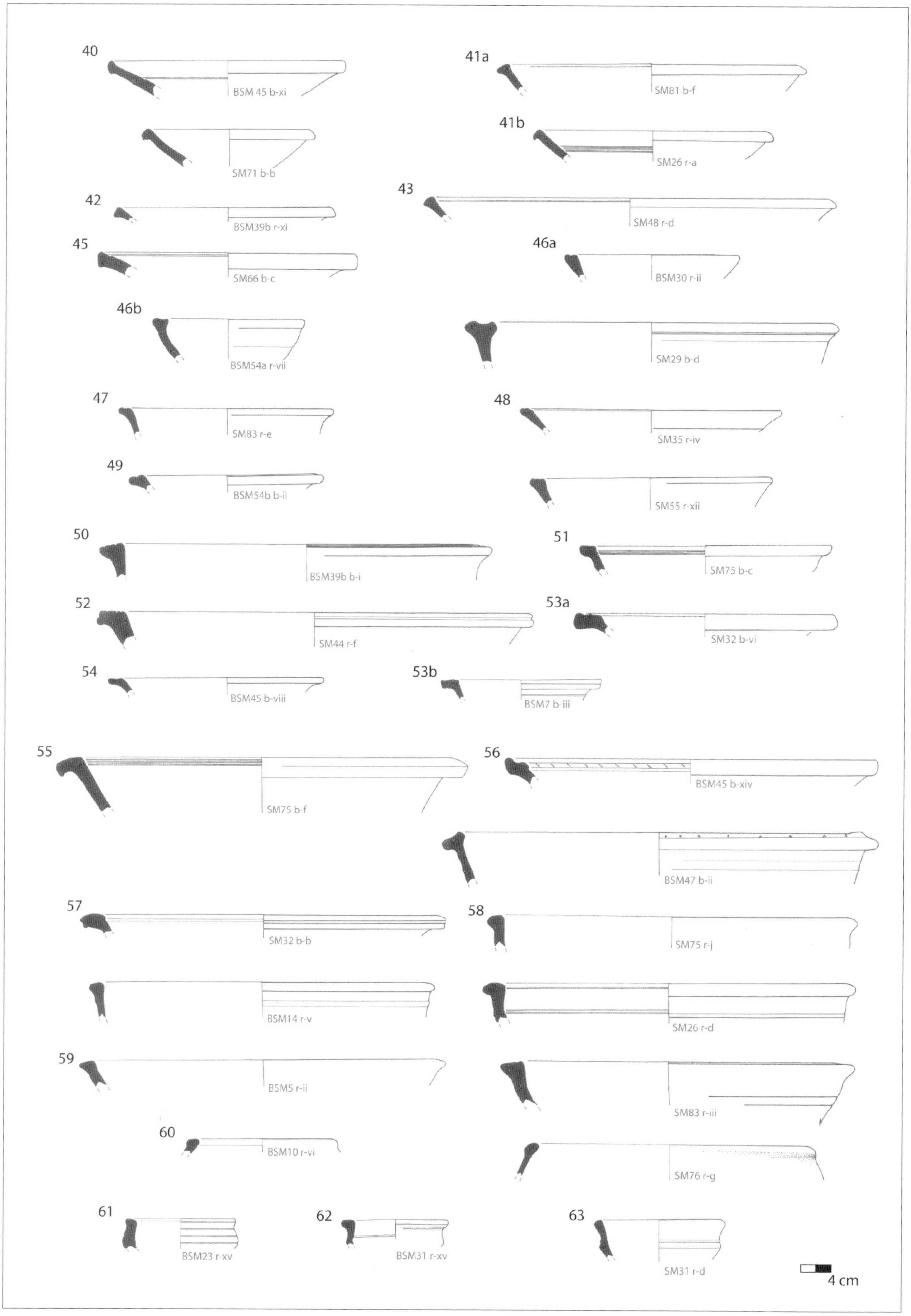
40
BSM 45 b-xi
41a
SM81 b-f
SM71 b-b
41b
SM26 r-a
42
BSM39b r-xi
43
SM48 r-d
45
SM66 b-c
46a
BSM30 r-ii
46b
BSM54a r-vii
SM29 b-d
47
SM83 r-e
48
SM35 r-iv
49
BSM54b b-ii
SM55 r-xii
50
BSM39b b-i
51
SM75 b-c
52
SM44 r-f
53a
SM32 b-vi
54
BSM45 b-viii
53b
BSM7 b-iii
55
SM75 b-f
56
BSM45 b-xiv
BSM47 b-ii
57
SM32 b-b
58
SM75 r-j
BSM14 r-v
SM26 r-d
59
BSM5 r-ii
SM83 r-iii
60
BSM10 r-vi
SM76 r-g
61
BSM23 r-xv
62
BSM31 r-xv
63
SM31 r-d
4 cm

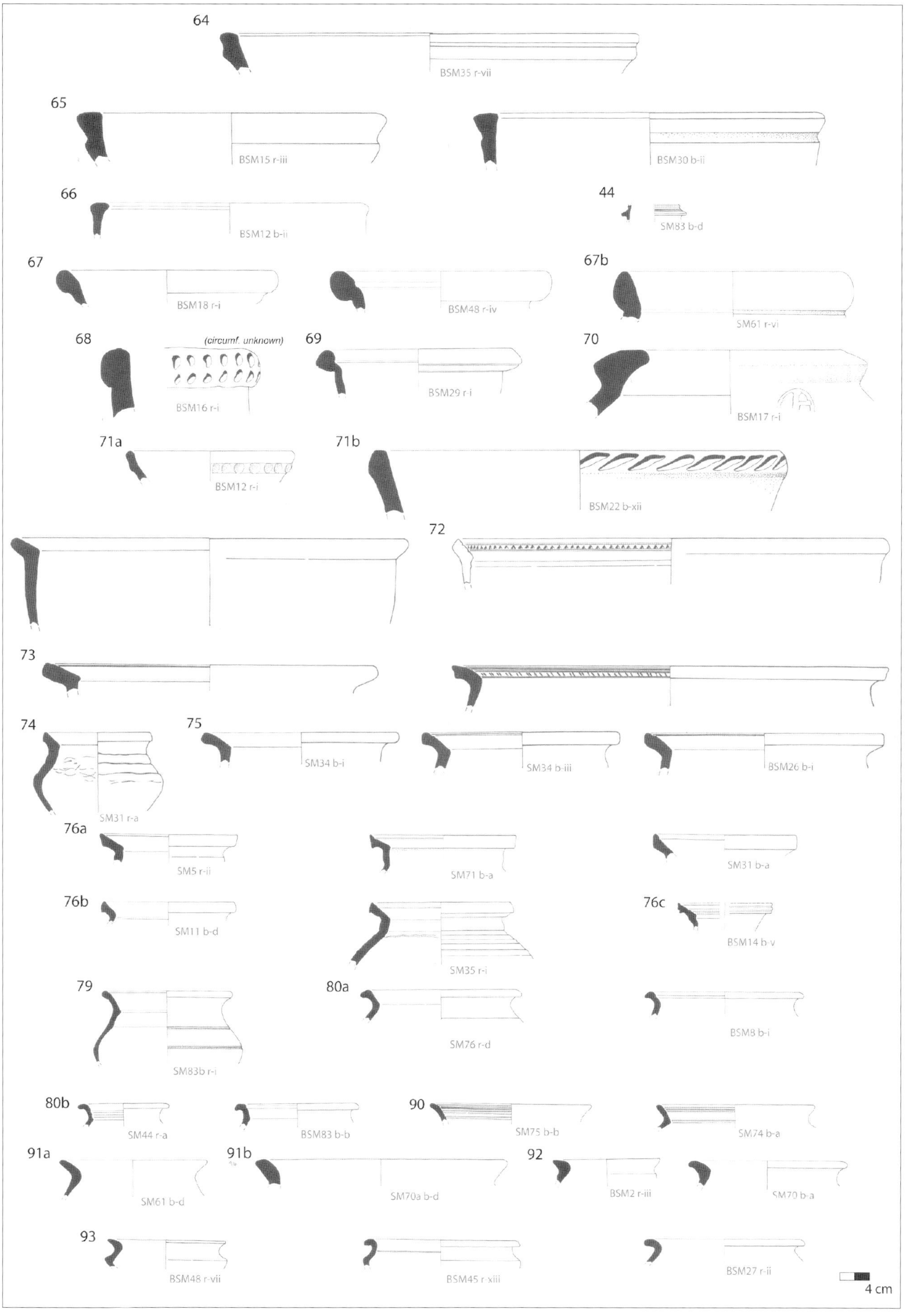
64
BSM35 r-vii
65
BSM15 r-iii
BSM30 b-ii
66
BSM12 b-ii
44
SM83 b-d
67
BSM18 r-i
BSM48 r-iv
67b
SM61 r-vi
68
(circumf. unknown)
BSM16 r-i
69
BSM29 r-i
70
BSM17 r-i
71a
BSM12 r-i
71b
BSM22 b-xii
72
73
74
SM31 r-a
75
SM34 b-i
SM34 b-iii
BSM26 b-i
76a
SM5 r-ii
SM71 b-a
SM31 b-a
76b
SM11 b-d
SM35 r-i
76c
BSM14 b-v
79
SM83b r-i
80a
SM76 r-d
BSM8 b-i
80b
SM44 r-a
BSM83 b-b
90
SM75 b-b
SM74 b-a
91a
SM61 b-d
91b
SM70a b-d
92
BSM2 r-iii
SM70 b-a
93
BSM48 r-vii
BSM45 r-xiii
BSM27 r-ii
4 cm

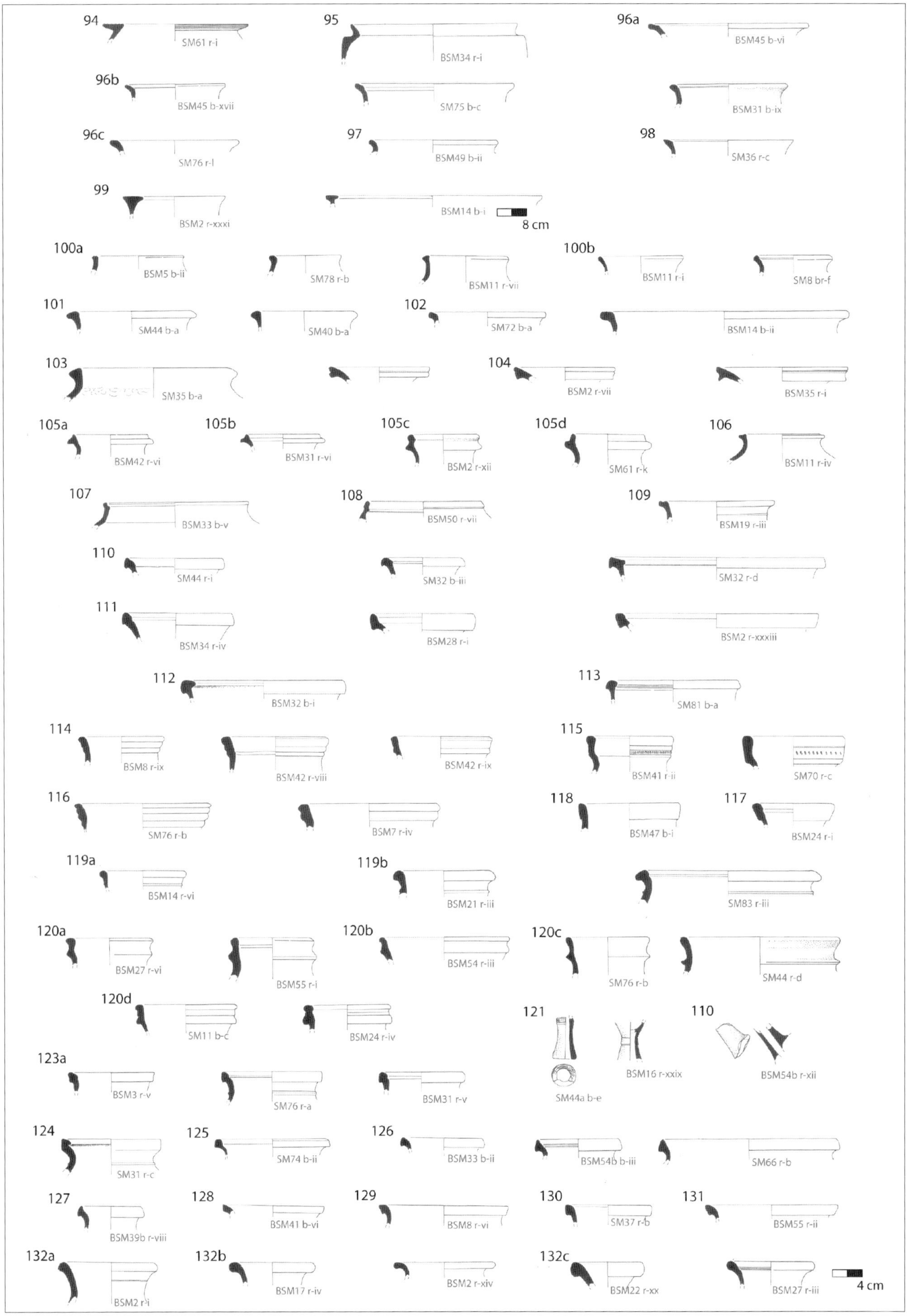

94
SM61 r-i
95
BSM34 r-i
96a
BSM45 b-vi
96b
BSM45 b-xvii
SM75 b-c
BSM31 b-ix
96c
SM76 r-l
97
BSM49 b-ii
98
SM36 r-c
99
BSM2 r-xxxi
BSM14 b-i
8 cm
100a
BSM5 b-ii
SM78 r-b
BSM11 r-vii
100b
BSM11 r-i
SM8 br-f
101
SM44 b-a
SM40 b-a
102
SM72 b-a
BSM14 b-ii
103
SM35 b-a
104
BSM2 r-vii
BSM35 r-i
105a
BSM42 r-vi
105b
BSM31 r-vi
105c
BSM2 r-xii
105d
SM61 r-k
106
BSM11 r-iv
107
BSM33 b-v
108
BSM50 r-vii
109
BSM19 r-iii
110
SM44 r-i
SM32 b-iii
SM32 r-d
111
BSM34 r-iv
BSM28 r-i
BSM2 r-xxxiii
112
BSM32 b-i
113
SM81 b-a
114
BSM8 r-ix
BSM42 r-viii
BSM42 r-ix
115
BSM41 r-ii
SM70 r-c
116
SM76 r-b
BSM7 r-iv
118
BSM47 b-i
117
BSM24 r-i
119a
BSM14 r-vi
119b
BSM21 r-iii
SM83 r-iii
120a
BSM27 r-vi
BSM55 r-i
120b
BSM54 r-iii
120c
SM76 r-b
SM44 r-d
120d
SM11 b-c
BSM24 r-iv
121
SM44a b-e
BSM16 r-xxix
110
BSM54b r-xii
123a
BSM3 r-v
SM76 r-a
BSM31 r-v
124
SM31 r-c
125
SM74 b-ii
126
BSM33 b-ii
BSM54b b-iii
SM66 r-b
127
BSM39b r-viii
128
BSM41 b-vi
129
BSM8 r-vi
130
SM37 r-b
131
BSM55 r-ii
132a
BSM2 r-i
132b
BSM17 r-iv
BSM2 r-xiv
132c
BSM22 r-xx
BSM27 r-iii
4 cm

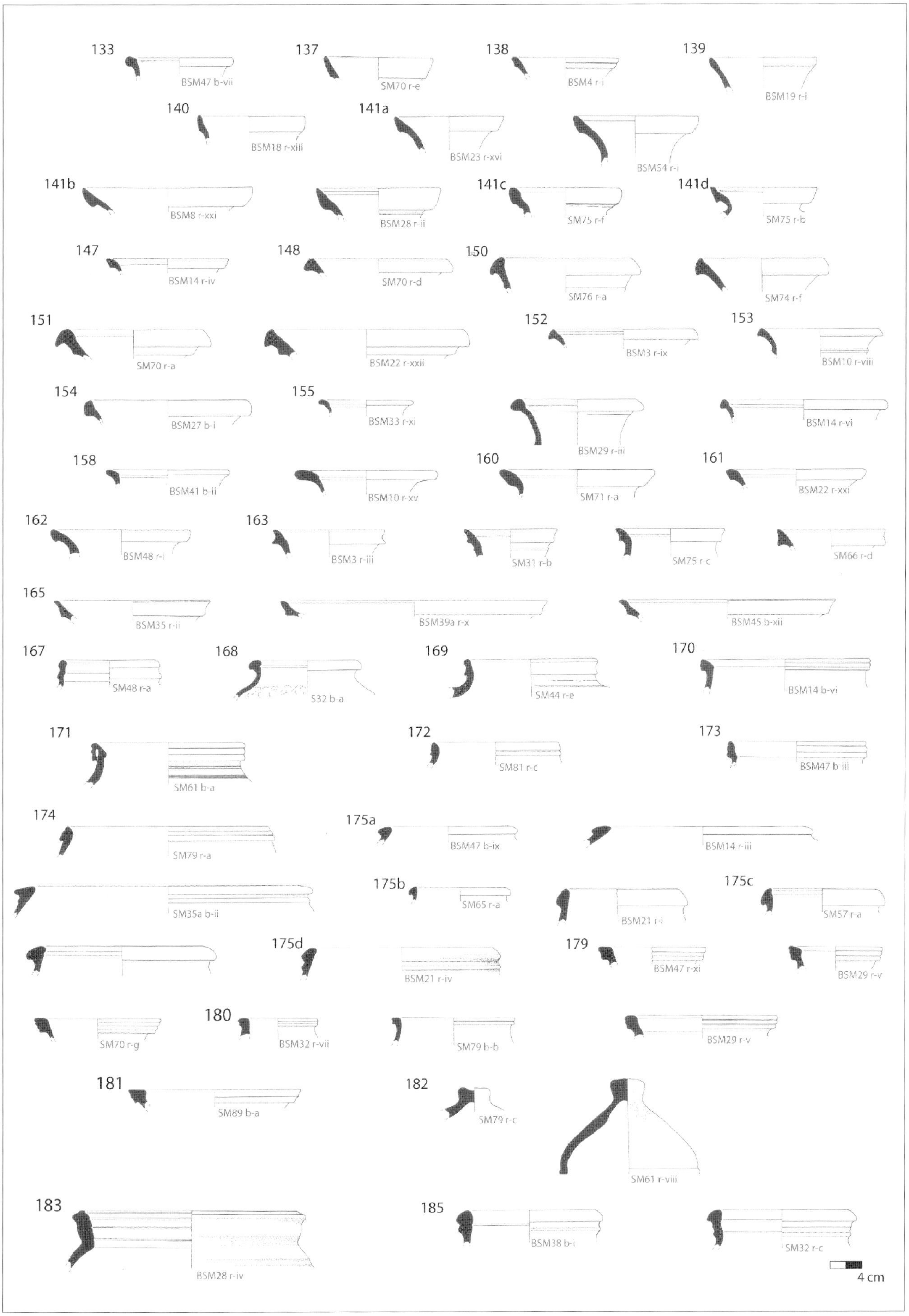

133
BSM47 b-vii
137
SM70 r-e
138
BSM4 r-i
139
BSM19 r-i
140
BSM18 r-xiii
141a
BSM23 r-xvi
BSM54 r-i
141b
BSM8 r-xxi
BSM28 r-ii
141c
SM75 r-f
141d
SM75 r-b
147
BSM14 r-iv
148
SM70 r-d
150
SM76 r-a
SM74 r-f
151
SM70 r-a
BSM22 r-xxii
152
BSM3 r-ix
153
BSM10 r-viii
154
BSM27 b-i
155
BSM33 r-xi
BSM29 r-iii
BSM14 r-vi
158
BSM41 b-ii
BSM10 r-xv
160
SM71 r-a
161
BSM22 r-xxi
162
BSM48 r-i
163
BSM3 r-iii
SM31 r-b
SM75 r-c
SM66 r-d
165
BSM35 r-ii
BSM39a r-x
BSM45 b-xii
167
SM48 r-a
168
S32 b-a
169
SM44 r-e
170
BSM14 b-vi
171
SM61 b-a
172
SM81 r-c
173
BSM47 b-iii
174
SM79 r-a
175a
BSM47 b-ix
BSM14 r-iii
SM35a b-ii
175b
SM65 r-a
BSM21 r-i
175c
SM57 r-a
175d
BSM21 r-iv
179
BSM47 r-xi
BSM29 r-v
SM70 r-g
180
BSM32 r-vii
SM79 b-b
BSM29 r-v
181
SM89 b-a
182
SM79 r-c
SM61 r-viii
183
BSM28 r-iv
185
BSM38 b-i
SM32 r-c
4 cm

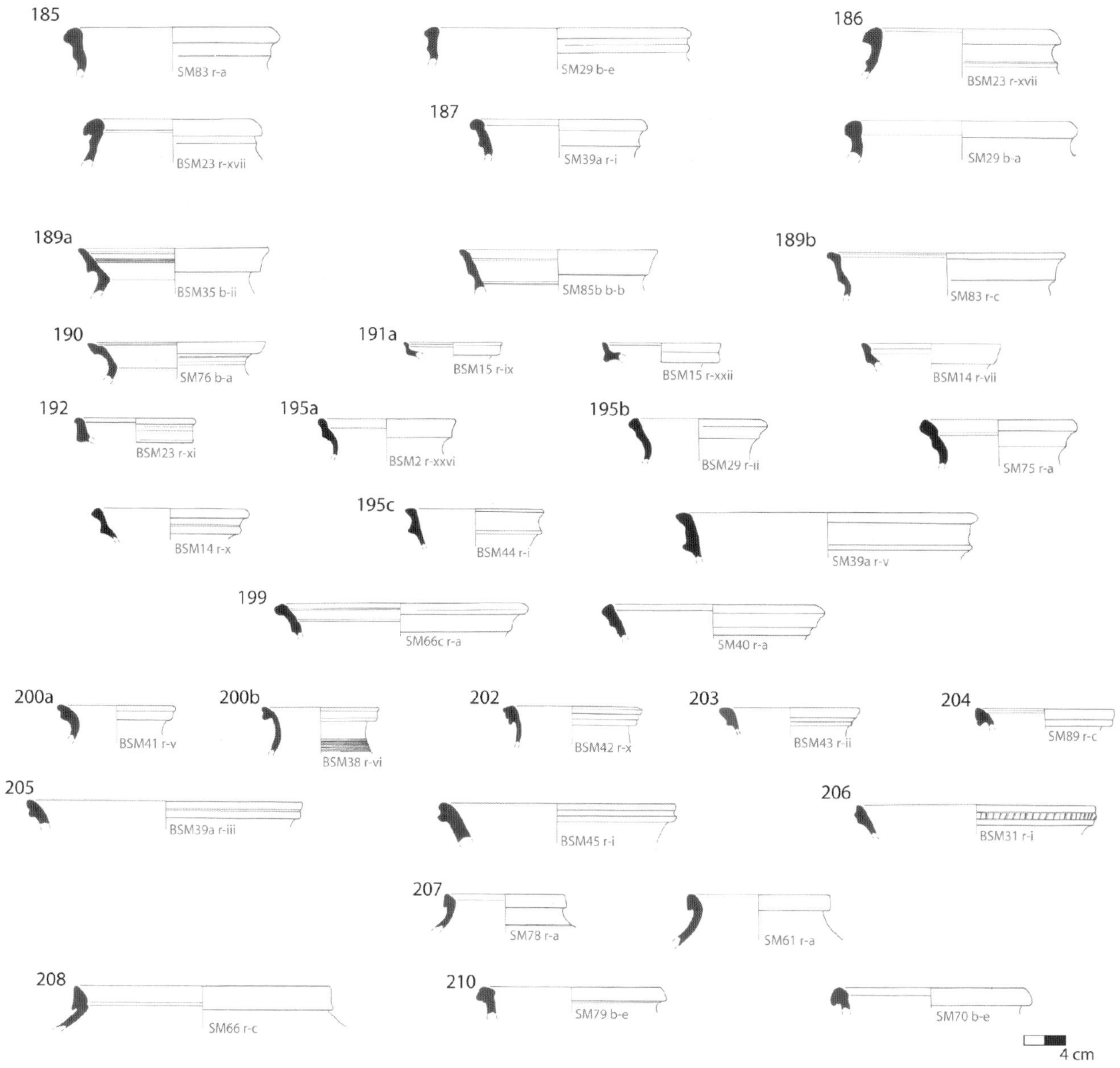
185
SM83 r-a
SM29 b-e
186
BSM23 r-xvii
BSM23 r-xvii
187
SM39a r-i
SM29 b-a
189a
BSM35 b-ii
SM85b b-b
189b
SM83 r-c
190
SM76 b-a
191a
BSM15 r-ix
BSM15 r-xxii
BSM14 r-vii
192
BSM23 r-xi
195a
BSM2 r-xxvi
195b
BSM29 r-ii
SM75 r-a
BSM14 r-x
195c
BSM44 r-i
SM39a r-v
199
SM66c r-a
SM40 r-a
200a
BSM41 r-v
200b
BSM38 r-vi
202
BSM42 r-x
203
BSM43 r-ii
204
SM89 r-c
205
BSM39a r-iii
BSM45 r-i
206
BSM31 r-i
207
SM78 r-a
SM61 r-a
208
SM66 r-c
210
SM79 b-e
SM70 b-e
4 cm

Bibliography

Primary sources

The Ain I Akbari by Abul Fazl Allami. Translated by H. Blochmann. Calcutta: Asiatic Society of Bengal (1873).
Anguttaranikaya. Edited by R. Morris. London: Pali Text Society (1955).
Charaka Samhita. Translated by Dr. R.K. Sharma and Vaidhya Bhagwan Dash. Chowkambika series (1995).
The Cūḷavaṃsa. Edited by W. Geiger, London: Pali Text Society, Oxford University Press (1925-1927; 1980).
De materia medica libri quinque by Dioscorides, Pedanios (fl. 1st century). Edited by M. Wellmann, 3 vols. Berlin (1906-14).
De Medicina by Celsus, Aulus Cornelius (fl. 1st century). Edited and Translated by W.G. Spencer. 3 vols. London (1948-53).
Dhammapada: The Word of the Doctrine, Translated, with an introduction and notes by K.R.Norman. Oxford: Pali Text Society. (1997).
Dīgha Nikāya. See Walshe 1987 below.
The Dīpavaṃsa: an ancient Buddhist historical record. Edited and translated by Hermann Oldenberg. London; Edinburgh: Williams and Norgate (1879). Reprint, London: Pali Text Society.
Enquiry into plants by Theophrastus (370 BC – c. 285 BC). Edited and translated by Sir A. Holt. 2 vols. London; New York (1916).
The Geography of Strabo. Edited and translated by H. L. Jones. vol. 7. London: Heinemann, (1930).
Harsha Carita of Banabhatta. Edited and translated by E.B Cowell, and F.W. Thomas, Delhi: Motilal Banarsidass (1961, reprint).
Kama Sutra of Vatsyayana. Translated by Sir Richard Burton, and F.F. Arbuthnot. Edited by W.G. Archer. London: Unwin (1981).
Kautilya's Arthasastra. Translated by R. Shamasastri, with introductory note by J. F. Fleet (2nd edition). Mysore: Wesleyan Mission Press (1923).
The Mahāvaṃsa, or the great chronicle of Ceylon. Translated by Wilhelm Geiger. London. Oxford: Oxford University Press (1912). Reprint, London: Pali Text Society (1980).
Samantapāsādikā. Edited by J. Takakusu and M. Nagai. London: Pali Text Society (1927).
Śrīviṣṇudharmottarapurāṇam. Edited by K. Kṛṣṇadāsa, 1912. Bombay: Venkatesvara Steam Press. Reprint, Delhi: Nag Publishers (1984).
Tāranātha's History of Buddhism in India. Translated by L. Chimpa and A. Chattopadhyaya. Edited by D. Chattopadhyaya. Delhi: Motilal Banarsidass (1970).
Viṣṇudharmottara Purāṇa. Edited by P. Shah. Vadodara: Oriental Institute, Maharaja Sayajirao University of Baroda (1958).

Secondary sources

Aboshi, Y., and K. Sonoda 1997. *Excavations at Jetavana.* Kansai: Kansai University.
Adams, Mc. R. 1974. 'Historic patterns of Mesopotamian irrigation agriculture', in T.E. Downing and McGuire Gibson (*eds.*), *Irrigation's Impact on Society.* Tucson: University of Arizona Press, 1-6.
——. 1981. *Heartlands of Cities: surveys of ancient settlement and land use on the central floodplain of the Euphrates.* Chicago: Chicago University Press.
Adams, W.Y. 1986. *Ceramic industries of Medieval Nubia.* Memoirs of the UNESCO Archaeological Survey of Sudanese Nubia, 1. Lexington: University Press of Kentucky.
Agarwal, A., and S. Narain. 1997. *Dying Wisdom: rise, fall and potential of India's traditional water harvesting systems.* New Delhi: Centre of Science and Environment.
Agrawal, R.C. 1997. 'Stupas and Monasteries: a recent discovery from Satdhara', India. *South Asian Archaeology 1995*: 403-15.
Agrawala, V.S. 1933. 'Pre Kushāna sculpture of Mathura', *Journal of the U.P. Historical Society*, 6: 87-9.
Agrawala, R.C. 1967. 'Unpublished sculptures and terracottas in the National Museum, New Delhi, and some allied problems', *East and West* 17 (3-4): 276-286.
——. 1971. 'Mātṛkā reliefs in early Indian art', East and West 21: 79-89.
Alcock, S., and J. Cherry, 1996. 'Survey at any price?', *Antiquity* 70: 207-11.
Alcock, S., and R. Osborne. 1996. *Placing the Gods: sanctuaries and sacred space in ancient Greece.* Oxford: Clarendon Press.
Ali, D. 1998. 'Technologies of the self: courtly artifice and monastic discipline in early India', *Journal of the Economic and Social History of the Orient* 41(2): 159-184.
Allan, J. 1936. *A Catalogue of the Indian Coins in the British Museum.* London: Trustees of the British Museum.
Allchin, F.R. 1954. *The Development of Early Culture in the Raichur district of Hyderabad.* Unpublished PhD Dissertation. University of London.
——. 1960. *Pikhlihal excavations.* Hyderabad: Government of Andhra Pradesh.
Allchin, F.R. (*ed.*), 1995. The Archaeology of Early Historic South Asia: the emergence of cities and states. Cambridge: Cambridge University Press.
Allchin, F.R., and K.R. Norman. 1985. 'Guide to the Aśokan inscriptions', *South Asian Studies* 1: 43-50.
Allen, C. 2002. *The Buddha and the Sahibs: the men who discovered India's lost religion.* London: John Murray.
Ammerman, A. 1981. 'Surveys and Archaeological Research', *Annual Review of Anthropology*, 10: 68-88.
Ansari, Z.D., and M.K. Dhavalikar 1975. *Excavations at Kayatha.* Pune: Deccan College.
Asad, T. 1983. 'Anthropological conceptions of religion: reflections on Geertz', *Man* (n. s.), 18: 237-59.
Asher, F.M. 1983. 'Historical and political allegory in Gupta art', in B.L. Smith (*ed.*), *Essays on Gupta Culture.* Delhi: Motilal Banarsidass.
Bachelard, G. 1964. *The Poetics of Space.* New York: Orion.
Bachhofer, L. 1939. *Early Indian Sculpture.* London: Pegasus Press.
Badam, G.L. and V. Sathe. 1995. 'Palaeontological research in India: retrospect and prospect', in V. Kale (*ed.*), *Quarternary Environments and Geoarchaeology of India.* Bangalore: Geological Society of India: 473-95.
Bailey, G., and I Mabbett. 2003. *The Sociology of Early Buddhism.* Cambridge: Cambridge University Press.
Bajpai, K.D., and S.K. Pandey. 1984. *Excavation at Tumain.* Bhopal: Directorate of Archaeology and Museums, Madhya Pradesh.
Bakker, H. 1986. *Ayodhya.* Groningen: Egbert Forsten.
——. 1992. *The Sacred Centre as the Focus of Political Interest: proceedings of the symposium held on the occasion of the 375th anniversary of the University of Groningen, 5-8 March 1989.* Groningen: Egbert Forsten.
——. 1997. *The Vākāṭakas: an essay in Hindu iconology.* Groningen: Egbert Forsten.
——. 1999. Review of 'Many Heads, Arms and Eyes: origin, meaning and form of multiplicity in Indian art', by D. M. Srinivasan, E.J. Brill, Leiden / New York, 1997. *Artibus Asiae* 58 (3/4): 339 – 343.
——. 2002. 'Religion and politics in the eastern Vakāṭaka kingdom', *South Asian Studies* 18: 1-24.
——. 2004. 'Mansar', in H. Bakker (*ed.*), *The Vākāṭaka Heritage: Indian Culture at the Crossroads.* Gonda Indological Studies XIII. Groningen: Egbert Forsten, 71-85.
——. 2006. 'A Theatre of Broken Dreams: Vidiśā in the Days of Gupta Hegemony', in M. Brandtner and S.K. Panda (*eds.*), Interrogating History: Essays for Hermann Kulke. New Delhi: Manohar.

——. Forthcoming. 'Monuments to the Dead in Ancient North India'.
Bakker, H., E. Cork, J.V. Sutcliffe, J. Shaw, and N. Bosma. Forthcoming. 'Preliminary results of fieldwork at Ramtek and Mansar, December 2006'.
Bakshi, K.G. 1945. 'A new pre-Mauryan statue discovered at Bhilsa', *Proceedings of the Indian History Congress*, 8: 20-22.
Ball, T., J.D. Brotherson, and J.S. Gardner. 1993. 'A typologic and morphometric study of variation in phytoliths from einkorn wheat (*Triticum monococcum*)', *Canadian Journal of Botany* 71: 1182-1192.
Banerjea, J.N. 1942. 'The holy Pañcavīras of the Vṛṣṇis', *Journal of the Indian Society of Oriental Art*, 10: 65-8.
——. 1985. *The Development of Hindu Iconography*. New Delhi: Munshiram Manoharlal.
Barker, G. 1995. *A Mediterranean Valley: landscape archaeology and Annales history in the Biferno valley*. London: Leicester University Press.
Barrett, J. 1990. 'The monumentality of death: the character of early Bronze Age mortuary mounds in southern Britain', *World Archaeology* 22: 179-89.
Bechert, H. 1982. 'The importance of Asoka's so-called schism edict', in L.A. Hercus (*ed.*), *Indological and Buddhist studies: volume in honour of Professor J. W. de Jong on his sixtieth birthday*. Canberra: Australian National University, Faculty of Asian Studies: 61-68.
Bechert, H. (*ed.*), 1991. *The Dating of the Historical Buddha*. Göttingen : Vandenhoeck & Ruprecht
Beck, A., G. Philip, M. Abdulkarim, and D. Donoghue. In press (2007). 'An Archaeological Evaluation of Corona and Ikonos High Resolution Satellite Imagery: settlement and landscape development in the Homs Region, Syria', *Antiquity*.
Beck, A., and Shaw, J. Forthcoming. 'The application of satellite imagery to the Sanchi Survey Project, central India'. For submission to *Antiquity*.
Bednarik, R.G. 1993, 'Palaeolithic art in India'. *Man and Environment* 18: 33-40.
Behrendt, K. 2000. 'An unnoticed relief from the Bhilsa Topes and its relationship to the sculpture of Sanchi', *South Asian Studies* 16: 1-11.
Benavides, G. 2005. 'Economy', in D.S. Lopez Jr (*ed.*), *Critical Terms for the Study of Buddhism*. Chicago; London: The University of Chicago Press, 77-102.
Bendall, C. 1880. 'The Meghasūtra (Partial edition and translation)', *Journal of the Royal Asiatic Society*: 236-311.
Bender, B. (*ed.*), 1993. *Landscape: Politics and Perspectives*. Oxford: Berg.
Bender, B., S. Hamilton, and C. Tilley. 1997. 'Leskernick: stone worlds; alternative narratives; nested landscapes', *Proceedings of the Prehistoric Society*, 63: 147-78.
Bernard, P. 1974. 'Trésor de monnaies indiennes et indo-grecques d'ai khanoum, Part II', *Revue Numismatique* 16: 7–41.
Bhandarkar, D.R. 1920. *Archaeological Remains and Excavations at Nagari.* Memoirs of the Archaeological Survey of India, IV.
Bhandarkar, J. 1914. 'Excavations at Besnagar', *Annual Report of Archaeological Survey of India 1913-14:* 186-226.
Bhandarkar, J. 1915. 'Excavations at Besnagar', *Annual Report of Archaeological Survey of India 1914-15*: 66-89.
Bhandarkar, R.G. 1913 (reprint, 1965). *Vaisnavism, Saivism and Other Minor Systems.* Varanasi: Indological Book House.
Bhattacharya, P.K. 1977. *Historical Geography of Madhya Pradesh from Early Records*. Delhi: Motilal Banarsidass.
Bintliff, J. (*ed.*), 1991. *Archaeology and the Annales School*. Leicester: Leicester University Press.
Bishop, P., D.C.W. Sanderson, *et al.* 2004. 'OSL and radiocarbon dating of a pre-Angkorian canal in Mekong delta, southern Cambodia', *Journal of Archaeological Science* 31: 319-336.
Bloss, L.W. 1973. 'The Buddha and the naga: a study in Buddhist folk religiosity', *History of Religions* 13 (1): 37-53.
Bohingamuwa, W. 2005. 'The ancient Panda Wewa: archaeological investigation, geographical and historical background', *Ancient Ceylon* 18, 82-124.
Boivin, N., R. Korisettar, P.C. Venkatasubbaiah *et al.* 2002. 'Exploring Neolithic and Megalithic south India: the Bellary District archaeological project', *Antiquity* 76 (294): 937-8.
Bopearachchi, O. 1989. 'Monnaies indo-grecques surfrappées' *Revue Numismatique* 31: 49-79.
Bopearachchi, O., and W. Pieper. 1998. *Ancient Indian Coins*. Brepols: Turhout, Indicopleustoi, vol. 11.
Bourdieu, P. 1977. *Outline of a Theory of Practice*. Cambridge: Cambridge University Press.
Bradley, R. 1991. *Altering the Earth: the origins of monuments in Britain and continental Europe*. Edinburgh: Society of Antiquaries of Scotland.
——. 1999. *The Archaeology of Natural Places*. London: Routledge.
Braudel, F. 1972. The Mediterranean and the Mediterranean World in the Age of Philip II. London: Fontana.
Brekke, T. 1997. 'The early *saṅgha* and the laity', *Journal of the International Association of Buddhist Studies* 20(2): 7-32.
Bretzl, H. 1903. *Botanische Forschungen des Alezanderzuges*. Leipzig: B.G. Teubner.
Brohier, R.L. 1934 (repr. 1979). *Ancient Irrigation Works in Ceylon*. vols. I-III. Colombo: The Ministry of Mahaweli Development, Sri Lanka.
Brown, R. H. 1912. *Irrigation: its principles and practice as a branch of engineering*. London: Archibald Constable & Co.
Burgess, J. 1902. 'The great stupa at Sanchi-Kanakheda', *Journal of the Royal Asiatic Society of Great Britain and Ireland*: 29-45.
Byrne, D. 1995. 'Buddhist stupa and Thai social practice', *World Archaeology*, 27 (2): 266-81.
Carmichael, D., J. Hubert, B. Reeves, and A. Schanches (*eds.*), 1994. *Sacred Sites, Sacred Places.* London: Routledge.
Chakrabarti, D.K. 1985. 'Iron and urbanisation: an examination of the Indian context', *Purattatva*, 15: 68-74.
——. 1995a. *The Archaeology of Ancient Indian Cities*. Delhi: Oxford University Press.
——. 1995b. 'Buddhist sites across South Asia as influenced by political and economic forces', *World Archaeology* 27: 185-202.
——. 1997. *Colonial Indology: Sociopolitics of the Ancient Indian Past.* Delhi: Munshiram Manoharlal.
——. 2001. *Archaeological Geography of the Ganga Plain: the lower and the middle Ganga.* New Delhi: Permanent Black.
Chakrabarti, D. K., R. Tewari and R. N. Singh 2003. 'From the Ganga plain to the eastern and western Deccan: a field-study of the ancient routes', *South Asian Studies* 19: 57-71.
Chakravarty, K.K., R.G. Bednarik *et al.* 1997. *Indian Rock Art and its Global Context.* Delhi; Bhopal: Motilal Banarsidass Publishers; Indira Gandhi Rashtriya Manav Sangrahalaya.
Chakravarty, K.K., V.S. Wakankar, and M.D. Khare. 1989. *Dangawada Excavations*. Bhopal: Archaeology and Museums, Madhya Pradesh.
Chakravarty, R. 1998. 'The creation and expansion of settlements and management of hydraulic resources in ancient India', in R.H. Grove, V. Damodaran, and S. Sangwan (*eds.*), *Nature and the Orient: the environmental history of south and southeast Asia*. Delhi: Oxford University Press, 87-106.
Chanda, Ramapradad. 1920. 'Archaeology and the Vaishnava tradition', *Memoirs of the Archaeological Survey of India*, no. 5.
——. 1921. 'Four ancient yaksha statues', *Journal of the Department of Letters, Calcutta University* 4: 3-6.
Chandra, G. C. 1938. 'Excavations at Rajgir', *Annual Report of the Archaeological Survey of India* 1935–36. Delhi, 52–4.
Chandra, P. 1966. 'Yaksha and yakshi images from Vidisa', *Ars Orientalis* VII: 157-63.
——. 1970a. *Stone sculpture in the Allahabad Museum.* Pune: American Institute of Indian Studies.
——. 1970b. A Vāmana temple at Maṛhiā and some reflections on Gupta architecture', *Artibus Asiae* XXXII: 125-145.
Chattopadhyaya, B.D. 1984. *A Survey of the Historical Geography of Ancient India*. Calcutta: Manisha Granthalaya.
——. 1994. *The Making of Early Medieval India*. Delhi: Oxford University Press.
Chattopadhyaya, S. 1970. *Evolution of Hindu Sects up to the time of Samkaracarya.* New Delhi: Munshiram Manoharlal.
Chauhan, M. S. 1995. 'Origin and history of tropical deciduous Sal (Shorea Robusta Gaernt.) forests in Madhya Pradesh, India', *Palaeobotanist* 43: 89-101.
——. 2000. 'Pollen evidence of late-Quaternary vegetation and climate change in Northeastern Madhya Pradesh', *Palaeobotanist* 49: 491-500.
——. 2002. 'Holocene vegetation and climatic changes in southeastern Madhya Pradesh, India', *Current Science* 83 (12): 1444-5.
Cherry, J.F. 1982. 'A preliminary definition of site distribution on Melos', in C. Renfrew and M. Wagstaff (*eds.*), *An Island Polity.* Cambridge: Cambridge University Press, 10-23.
——. 1983. 'Frogs around the pond: Current archaeological survey projects in the Mediterranean area', in D.R. Keller and D.W. Rupp (*eds.*), *Archaeological Survey in the Mediterranean Area.* Oxford: BAR International Series 155: 375-416.
——. 1994. 'Regional survey in the Aegean: the 'New Wave' (and after),' in P.N. Kardulias (*ed.*), *Beyond the Site: regional studies in the Aegean area.* Lanham Md: University Press of America, 91-112.
Cherry, J.F., J.L. Davis, and E. Mantzourani. 1991. *Landscape Archaeology as Long-Term History: Northern Keos in the Cycladic Islands.* UCLA Institute of Archaeology.
Chorley, R.J., and P. Haggett.1967. *Models in Geography.* London: Methuen.
Clark, J.D., and G.R. Sharma. 1983. 'Palaeoenvironments and Prehistory in the Middle Son Valley, Madhya Pradesh, North-Central India'. Allahabad: Abinash Prakashan.
Clark, J.G.D. and M.A.J. Williams. 1990. 'Resource strategies and cultural

change in the Son valley, northern Madhya Pradesh, Central India', *Man and Environment* 15: 13-28.
Clark, W.M., M.E. Bramley, and R.F. Thorp 1982, 'Water requirements for flooded rice cultivation', *Proceedings of the Institution of Civil Engineers, Part 2,* 73: 769-788.
Clarke, D.L. 1972. *Models in Archaeology.* London: Methuen.
Chowdhury, K.A. 1977. *Ancient Agriculture and Forestry in North India.* Bombay: Asia Publishing House.
Coccari, D. M. 1989. 'Protection and identity: Banaras' Bir babas', in S. B. Freitag (*ed.*), *Culture and Power in Banaras: Community, power and environment 1800-1980.* Berkeley; London: University of California Press. 130-46.
Cohen, R.S. 1998. 'Naga, yaksini, Buddha: local deities and local Buddhism at Ajanta', *History of Religions*, 37(4): 360-40.
Cohn, B. S., and Marriott, M. 1958. 'Networks and centres in the integration of Indian civilisation', *Journal of Sociology of Religion* 1: 1-9.
Coleman, S., and Elsner, J. 1994. 'The pilgrims progress: art, architecture and ritual movement at Sinai', *World Archaeology* 26 (1): 73-89.
Coningham, R.A.E. 1995. 'Monks, caves and kings: a reassessment of the nature of early Buddhism in Sri Lanka', *World Archaeology* 27: 222-42.
——.1998. 'Buddhism "rematerialized" and the archaeology of the Gautama Buddha', *Cambridge Archaeological Journal,* 8(1): 121-26.
——.2001. 'The archaeology of Buddhism', in T. Insoll (*ed.*), *Archaeology and World Religion.* London: Routledge, 60-95.
Conze, E. 1975. *Buddhism: its essence and development.* New York: Harper Torch books.
Coomaraswamy, A.K. 1980 (reprint). *Yakṣas.* Delhi: Munshiram Manoharlal.
Cribb, J. 2000. 'Early Indian history', in M. Willis, *Buddhist Reliquaries from Ancient India.* London: British Museum Press, 39-55.
Cunningham, A. 1854. *Bhilsa Topes.* London: Smith, Elder & Co.
——. 1879. *The Stupa of Bharhut.* London: W.H. Allen and Co.
——. 1880. *Archaeological Survey of India: Report of tours in Bundelkhand and Malwa in 1874–75 and 1876-77.* Vol. X. Calcutta: Office of the Superintendent of Government Printing.
——. 1892. *Mahabodhi, or the great Buddhist temple under the Bodhi tree at Buddha-Gaya.* London: W.H. Allen and Co.
——. 1924. *The Ancient Geography of India.* Calcutta: Chuckervertty and Chatterjee.
Cunningham, J.D. 1847. 'Notes on the Antiquities within the Bhopal Agency', *Journal of the Asiatic Society of Bengal*, 16 (2): 739-63.
Czuma, S.J. 1985. *Kushan Sculpture: images from early India.* he Cleveland Museum of Art.
Dalton, J. 2004. 'The Early Development of the Padmasambhava Legend in Tibet: a study of IOL Tib J 644 and Pelliot tibétain 307', Journal of the American Oriental Society 124 (4): 759-72.
Dass, M. 2001. *Udayagiri: a sacred hill, its art, architecture and landscape.* Unpublished PhD Dissertation. De Montford University, Leicester.
——. 2002–3. 'Heliodorus Pillar from Besnagar: its capital and worship', *Journal of the Asiatic Society of Mumbai* 77-78: 32-41.
——. 2006. 'Water Systems at Udayagiri: a search for its meaning ', in K.K. Chakravarty, G. L. Badam and Vijay Paranjpye (*eds.*), *Traditional Water Management Systems of India.* New Delhi: Aryan Books International, 34-45.
Dass, M., and M.D. Willis. 2002. 'The lion capital from Udayagiri and the antiquity of sun worship in central India', *South Asian Studies* 18: 25-46.
Davis, R.H. 1999. *The Lives of Indian Images.* Princeton: Princeton University Press.
Davison-Jenkins, D.J. 1997. *The Irrigation and Water Supply Systems of Vijayanagara.* Vijayanagara research project monograph series, vol. 5. New Delhi: Manohar.
Day, U.N. 1965. *Medieval Malwa: A political and cultural history 1401-1563.* Delhi: Munshiram Manoharlal.
Dehejia, V. 1972. *Early Buddhist Rock Temples: a chronological study.* London: Thames and Hudson.
——. 1992. 'Collective and popular bases of early Buddhist patronage: sacred monuments, 100 BC-AD 250', in B.Stoler-Miller (*ed.*), *The Powers of Art: patronage in Indian culture.* Delhi: Oxford University Press, 35-46.
Deo, S.G., and J.P. Joshi, 1972. *Pauni Excavation 1969-1970.* Nagpur: Nagpur University.
De Mallman, M.T. 1948. *Introduction a l'etude d'Avalokitesvara.* Paris: Musée Guimet.
De Polignac, F. 1984. *La Naissance de la cité Grecque* (translated in 1995 as *Cults, territory and the origins of the Greek city-state.* Chicago: Chicago University Press).
Deshpande, M.N. 1959. 'The rock-cut caves of Pitalkhora', *Ancient India* 15: 66-93.
De Terra, H. and T. T. Paterson 1939, *Studies on the Ice Age in India and Associated Human Cultures.* Washington, D.C: Carnegie Institution of Washington.
Dhavalikar, M.K. 1985. 'Cultural ecology of chalcolithic Maharashtra', in S.B. Deo, and K. Paddayya (*eds.*), *Recent Advances in Indian Archaeology.* Poona: Deccan College, 65-73.
——. 1995. 'Climate and early historic cultures: Satavahana cultural ecology', in S. Wadia, R. Korisettar, and V.S. Kale (*eds.*), *Quaternary Environments and Geoarchaeology of India: essays in honour of Professor S.N. Rajaguru.* Bangalore: Memoirs of the Geological Society of India 32, 353-59.
Dikshit, M.G. 1955. *Tripuri - 1952: being the account of the excavations at Tripuri, Madhya Pradesh.* Government of Madhya Pradesh.
Dobbins, K. W. 1971. *The Stupa and Vihara of Kanishka I.* Calcutta: The Asiatic Society.
Doelle, W. 1977. 'A multiple survey strategy for cultural resource management studies', in M.B. Schiffer and G.J. Gunnerman (*eds.*), A Guide for Cultural Resource Management Studies. New York: Academic Press, 201-9.
Donoghue, D.N.M., N. Galiatsatos, G. Philip, and A.R. Beck. 2000. 'Satellite imagery for archaeological applications: a case study from the Orontes Valley, Syria', in R.H. Bewley and W. Raczkowski (*eds.*), *Aerial Archaeology: developing future practice.* Leszno: IOS Press, 211-223.
Duncan, J.S. 1990. *The City as Text: the politics of landscape interpretation in the Kandyan kingdom.* Cambridge: Cambridge University Press.
Dunnell, R.C., and W.S. Dancey. 1983. 'The siteless survey: a regional scale data collection strategy', in M.B. Schiffer (*ed.*), *Advances in Archaelogical Theory and Method*, 6. New York: Academic Press, 267-87.
Dutt, S. 1962. *Buddhist Monks and Monasteries of India: their history and their contribution to Indian culture.* London: G. Allen and Unwin.
Eade, J., and Sallnow, S. 1991. 'Introduction', in J. Eade, and S. Sallnow (*eds.*), *Contesting the Sacred: the anthropology of Christian pilgrimage.* London: Routledge.
Eaton, R.M. 1993. *The Rise of Islam and the Bengal Frontier, 1204-1760.* Berkeley: University of California Press.
Eck, D. 1981. *Darśan: seeing the divine image in India.* Chambersberg: Anima Books.
Eighmy, J.L, and J.B. Howard. 1991. 'Direct dating of prehistoric canal sediments using archaeo-magnetism', *American Antiquity* 56(1): 88-102.
Eksambekar, S.P., S R. Sainkar, and M.D. Kajale, 1999. 'Phytolith study using scanning electron microscope (SEM): some initial considerations', *Bulletin of the Deccan College Post-Graduate Research Institute* 58: 85-92.
Entwistle, A.W. 1987. *Braj Centre of Krishna Pilgrimage.* Groningen: Egbert Forsten.
Epigraphica Zeylanica. Archaeological Department. Ceylon
Erdosy, G. 1988. *Urbanisation in Early Historic India.* Oxford: BAR International Series 430.
——. 1998. 'Deforestation in Pre- and Protohistoric South Asia', in R.H. Grove, V. Damodaran, and S. Sangwan (*eds.*), *Nature and the Orient: the environmental history of South and Southeast Asia.* Delhi: Oxford University Press, 51-70.
Eschmann, A., H. Kulke, and G.C. Tripathi (*eds.*), 1986. *The Cult of Jagannath and the Regional Tradition of Orissa.* Delhi: Manohar.
Falk, H. 2006. *Aśokan Sites and Artefacts: A Source-Book with Bibliography.* Mainz: Monographien zur indischen Archäologie, Kunst und Philologie, Band 18.
Falk, N.A. 1977. 'To gaze on the sacred traces', *History of Religions* 16: 281-93.
Fell, J. 1834 (reprint). 'Description of an ancient and remarkable monument, near Bhilsa', *Journal of the Asiatic Society* III: 490-94.
Flannery, K. V. (*ed.*), 1976. *The Early Mesoamerican Village.* New York: Academic Press.
Fogelin, L, 2004, 'Sacred Architecture, Sacred Landscape: Early Buddhism in Northern Coastal Andhra Pradesh', in H.P. Ray and C.M. Sinopol (*eds.*), *Archaeology as History in Early South Asia.* New Delhi: Aryan Books International, 376-91.
——. 2006. *Archaeology of Early Buddhism.* New York: Altamira Press.
Foley, R. 1981. 'Off-site Archaeology: an alternative approach for the short-sited', in I. Hodder (*ed.*), *Pattern of the Past.* Cambridge: Cambridge University Press, 157-83.
Fossey, J.M. 1983. 'The topography of Ancient Boiotia: the extensive survey', in D.R. Keller, and D.W. Rupp (*eds.*), *Archaeological Survey in the Mediterranean Area.* Oxford: BAR International Series 155, 233-5.
Fotiades, M. 1983. 'Surveying with limited resources', in D.R. Keller, and D.W. Rupp (*eds.*), *Archaeological Survey in the Mediterranean Area.* Oxford: BAR International Series 155, 207-10.
Frauwallner, E. 1956. *The Earliest Vinaya and the Beginnings of Buddhist Literature.* Rome: Is. M. E. O.
Fritz, J. 1978. 'Palaeopsychology today: ideational systems and human adaptation in prehistory', in C. Redman (*ed.*), *Social Archaeology: beyond subsistence and dating.* London: Academic Press, 37-60.
Fu, Chen Zhao. 2001. 'Rock Art of Southern Asia', in D.S. Whitley (*ed.*), *Handbook of Rock Art Research.* Walnut Creek: Altamira Press, 760-785.
Fujiwara, H, M.R. Mughal, A. Sasaki, and T. Matano. 1992. 'Rice and *ragi* at

Harappa: preliminary results by plant opals analysis', *Pakistan Archaeology* 27: 129-142.
Fuller, D.Q. 2002. 'Fifty years of archaeobotanical studies in India: laying a solid foundation',in, S. Settar, and R. Korisettar (*eds.*), *Indian Archaeology in Retrospect, vol III: Archaeology and Interactive Disciplines.* Publications of the Indian Council for Historical Research. New Delhi: Manohar, 247–363.
——. 2003. 'Indus and Non-Indus Agricultural Traditions: local developments and crop adoptions on the Indian Peninsula', in S.A. Weber and W.R. Belcher (*eds.*), *Indus Ethnobiology: New Perspectives from the Field.* New York; Oxford: Lexington Books, 343-95.
——. In press. 'The Ganges on the World Neolithic Map: the significance of recent research on agricultural origins in northern India' *Pragdhara (Journal of the Uttar Pradesh State Department of Archaeology)*
Fuller, D., and N. Boivin. 2002a. 'Beyond description and diffusion: a history of processual theory in the archaeology of south Asia', in S. Settar and R. Korisettar (*eds.*), *Indian Archaeology in Retrospect. Vol. IV: History, theory and method.* New Delhi: Manohar: 159-90.
——. 2002b. 'Looking for post-processual theory in south Asian archaeology', in S. Settar and R. Korisettar (*eds.*), *Indian Archaeology in Retrospect. Vol. IV: History, theory and method.* New Delhi: Manohar: 191-215.
Fussman, G. 1987–8. 'Central and provincial administration in ancient India: the problem of the Mauryan empire', *The Indian Historical Review* 14: 41-72.
——. 1989. 'Les inscriptions Kharoṣṭhi de la plaine de Chilas', in K. Jettmar, D. Konig, and V. Thewalt (*eds.*), *Antiquities of Northern Pakistan: Reports and Studies*. Vol. 1, *Rock Inscriptions in the Indus Valley*. Mainz: Verlag Philipp von Zabern, 1–39.
——. 2003. *Naissance et déclin d'une qasba: Chanderi du Xe au XVIIIe siècle.* Paris: Collège de France: Diffusion de Boccard.
Gai, G.S. 1969. 'Three inscriptions of Rāmagupa', *Journal of the Bhandarkar Research Institute* XVIII: 245-51.
Gallant, T.W. 1983. 'The Ionian islands palaeo-economy project', in D.R. Keller, and D.W. Rupp (*eds.*), *Archaeological Survey in the Mediterranean Area.* Oxford: BAR International Series 155, 223-6.
Gaur, R.C. 1983. Excavations at Atranjikhera: early civilization of the upper Ganga Basin. Delhi: Motilal Banarsidass.
Geertz, C. 1963. *Agricultural Involution: the process of ecological change in Indonesia.* Berkeley: Association of Asian Studies, University of California Press.
——. 1980. *Negara: The Theatres State in Nineteenth-Century Bali.* Princeton: Princeton University Press.
Gernet, J. 1956 (1995). *Buddhism in Chinese Society: An economic history from the fifth to the tenth centuries.* New York: Columbia University Press.
Getty, A. 1914. *The Gods of Northern Buddhism: their history, iconography and progressive evolution through the northern Buddhist countries.* Oxford: Clarendon Press.
Ghosh. A. 1950. *Archaeology in India*. Delhi.
——. 1951. 'Rājgir 1950', *Ancient India* , 7: 66-78.
——. 1967. 'The pillars of Asoka: their purpose', *East and West* 17: 273-275.
——. 1973. *The City in Early Historical India.* Simla: Indian Institute of Advanced Studies.
——. 1990. *An Encyclopaedia of Indian Archaeology*. Leiden: E.J. Brill.
Ghosh, A., and A.C. Panigrahi. 1946. 'The pottery of Achichchhatra, district Bareilly, UP', *Ancient India* I: 37-59.
Giddens, A. 1979. *Central Problems in Social Theory: action, structure and contradiction in social analysis.* London: Macmillan.
Glover, I.C. and C.F.W. Higham, 1996. 'New evidence for rice cultivation in South, Southeast and East Asia', in G.R. Harris (*ed.*), *The Origins and Spread of Agriculture and Pastoralism in Eurasia*, London: UCL Press, 413-41.
Gombrich, R. 1988. *Theravada Buddhism: a social history from ancient Benares to modern Colombo.* London: Routledge and Kegan Paul.
Gonda, J. 1970. *Viṣṇuism and Śivaism: a comparison.* London: Athlone Press.
Goody, J. 1975. 'Religion, social change, and the sociology of conversion', in, J. Goody (*ed.*), *Changing Social Structure in Ghana.* London: International African Institute: 91-106.
Goyal, S.R. 1984. *A Religious History of Ancient India.* Meerut: Kusumanjali Prakashan.
Green, R.M. 1992. 'Buddhist economic ethics: a theoretical approach', in R.F. Sizemore and D.K. Swearer (*eds.*), *Ethics, Wealth and Salvation: a study in Buddhist social ethics*. Columbia: University of South Carolina Press, 215-234.
Greenland. D. 1997. *The Sustainability of Rice Farming.* Wallingford: CABI.
Gregory, D. 1978. 'The discourse of the past: phenomenology, structuralism and historical geography', *Journal of Historical Geography* 4: 161-73.
——. 1995. 'Imaginative geographies', *Progress in Human Geography* 19: 447-85.
Grinsell, L.V. 1972. 'The individual fieldworker', in P.J. Fowler (*ed.*), *Field Survey in British Archaeology*. London: Council for British Archaeology, 10-12.
Grove, A.T. 1993. 'Africa's climate in the Holocene', in T. Shaw, P. Sinclair, B. Andah, and A. Okpoko (*eds.*), *The Archaeology of Africa: food, metals and towns*. London: Routledge, 32-42.
Gunawardana, R.A.L.H. 1971. 'Irrigation and hydraulic society in early medieval Ceylon', *Past and Present* 53: 3-27.
——. 1978a. 'Social function and political power: a case study of state formation in irrigation society', *Indian Historical Review* IV (2): 259-73.
——. 1978b. Hydraulic engineering in ancient Sri Lanka: the cistern sluices. In, Indrapala, Prematilleke and van Lohuizen-de Leeuw (*eds.*), *Studies in South Asian Culture*, VII: 61-74. Senerat Paranavitana Commemoration Volume. Leiden: E.J. Brill.
——. 1979. *Robe and Plough: monasticism and economic interest in early Medieval Sri Lanka.* Tucson: University of Arizona Press for the Association for Asian Studies.
Gupta, J. 1967. *Prāga Aitihasika Bhartiya Chitrikala*. New Delhi.
Gupta, S. 1992. 'Empirical time and the Vyūhāntara gods of the Pāñcarātra', in A.W. Van den Hoek, D.H.A. Kolff, and M.S. Oort (*eds.*), *Ritual, State and History in South Asia: essays in honour of J. C. Heesterman* . Leiden: E.J. Brill, 163-78.
Gupta, S.P. 1974. 'Two urbanisations in India: a study of their social structure', *Puratattva* 7: 53-60.
——. 1980. *The Roots of Indian Art.* Delhi: B.R. Publishing Corporation.
Hamid, M. 1940, Excavation at Sanchi. *Annual Report Archaeological Survey of India*, 1936-37, 85-7.
——. 1951. *Rājgir*. Archaeological Survey of India.
Hamid, M. M., R.C. Kale, and R.P. Chanda. 1922. *Catalogue of the Museum of Archaeology at Sanchi, Bhopal State*. Calcutta: Superintendent Government Printing.
Harbison, R. 1994. 'Early Irish pilgrim archaeology in the Dingle Peninsula', *World Archaeology*, 26 (1): 90-103.
Hardy, E. 1903. 'Ueber den upsprung des samajja', in Album Kern: opstellen geschreven ter eere Van H.K. Kern hem aangeboden. Leiden: E. J. Brill, 61-6.
Harle, J. C. 1974. *Gupta Sculpture: Indian Sculpture of the Fourth to the Sixth Centuries A.D.* Oxford: Clarendon Press.
Härtel, H. 1987. 'Archaeological evidence on the early Vāsudeva Worship', in G. Gnoli, and L. Lanciotti (*eds.*), *Orientalia Iosephi Tucci Memoriae Dicata.* Roma: Serie Orientale Roma, LVI, 2: 579-87.
——. 1993. *Excavations at Sonkh*: *2500 Years of a Town in Mathura District.* Berlin: Dietrich Reimer Verlag.
Harvey, E. L., D. Q. Fuller, and J. N. Pal *et al.* 2005. 'Early Agriculture of the Neolithic Vindhyas (North-Central India)', in U. Franke-Vogt and H.J. Weisshar (*eds.*), South Asian Archaeology*: Proceedings of the European Association for South Asian Archaeology Conference, Bonn, Germany, 7th – 11th July 2003.* Aachen: Linden Soft, 329-334.
Harvey, P. 2000. *An Introduction to Buddhist Ethics.* Cambridge: Cambridge University Press.
Hawkes, J. In press. 'The sacred and secular contexts of the Buddhist stupa site of Bharhut', in J. Hawkes and A. Shimada (*eds.*), *Buddhist Stupas in South Asia: Recent Archaeological, Art-Historical, and Historical Perspectives*. New Delhi: Oxford University Press.
Heitzman, J. 1984. 'Early Buddhism, trade and empire', in K.A. R Kennedy, and G.L. Possehl (*eds.*), *Studies in the Archaeology and Palaeoanthropology of South Asia.* New Delhi: Oxford and IBH Publishing Company, 121-37.
——. 1995. 'State formation in South India, 850 – 1280', in H. Kulke (*ed.*), *The State in India 1000 – 1700.* Delhi: Oxford University Press, 162-95.
Hodder, I. 1984. 'Burials, houses, women and men in the European Neolithic', in D. Miller, and C. Tilley (*eds.*), *Ideology, Power and Prehistory*. Cambridge: Cambridge University Press, 51-68.
——. 1987. 'Converging traditions: the search for symbolic meanings in archaeology and geography', in J.M. Wagstaff (*ed.*), *Landscape and Culture: geographical and archaeological perspectives*. Oxford: Basil Blackwell, 134-45.
——. 1991. *Reading the Past.* Cambridge: Cambridge University Press.
——. 2000. 'Developing a Reflexive Method in Archaeology', in I. Hodder (*ed.*), *Towards Reflexive Method in Archaeology: the example at Çatalhöyük.* Cambridge: The McDonald Institute for Archaeological Research: 1-16.
Hodder, I. (*ed.*), 1982. *Symbolic and Structural Archaeology*. Cambridge: Cambridge University Press.
Hodder, I., and C. Malone. 1984. 'Intensive survey of prehistoric sites in the Stilo region, Calabria', *Proceedings of the Prehistoric Society* 50: 121-50.
Hodder, I., and C. Orton. 1976. *Spatial Analysis in Archaeology*. Cambridge: Cambridge University Press.
Hodnett, M.G., and J.P. Bell, 1981. *Soil Physical Processes of Groundwater Recharge through the Black cotton soils of the Deccan traps*. Indo-British Betwa Groundwater Project. Summary Technical Report. Vol. III. Wallingford: Institute of Geological Studies.

——. 1986. 'Soil moisture investigations of groundwater recharge through black cotton soils in Madhya Pradesh, India', *Hydrological Sciences Journal* 31 (3): 361-381.
Hooja, R. 1988. *The Ahar Culture and Beyond: settlements and frontiers of 'Mesolithic' and early agricultural sites in south-eastern Rajasthan, c. 3rd-2nd Millennia B.C.* Oxford: BAR.
Hoskins, W.G. 1955 (reprint 1985). *The Making of the English Landscape*. London: Penguin Books.
Houyan, L., W. Naiqin and L. Baozhu, 1997. 'Recognition of rice phytoliths', in A. Pinilla, J. Juan-Tresserras and M. J. Machado (*eds.*), *The First European Meeting on Phytolith Research: the state of the art of phytoliths in soils and plants*. Madrid: Centro de Ciencias Medioambiantales, Consejo Superior de Investigaciones Cientificas, 159-174.
Huke. R.E., and E.H. Huke. 1988. *Human Geography of Rice in South Asia*. IRRI: Manila.
Hultzsch, E. 1925 (1991 reprint). *CII, I: Inscriptions of Aśoka*. Delhi: Archaeological Survey of India.
Ingold, T. 1993. 'The temporality of landscape', *World Archaeology* 25 (2): 152-74.
Ingram, K.T., and T.P. Tuong. 1995. 'Environmental characterization requirement for strategic research in rice grown under adverse conditions of drought, flooding or salinity', In K.T. Ingram (*ed.*), *Rainfed Lowland Rice*. IRRI: Manila.
Irwin, J. 1972. 'The Sanchi Torso', *Victoria and Albert Museum Year Book* 3: 7-28.
——. 1976. 'The Heliodorus pillar at Besnagar', *Puratattva* 8: 166-76.
——. 1987. 'Buddhism and the Cosmic Pillar', in G. Gnoli, and L. Lanciotti (*eds.*), *Orientalia Iosephi Tucci Memoriae Dicata*. Roma: Serie Orientale Roma, LVI (2), 635-660.
Jackson, V.H. 1914. 'Notes on old Rajgir', *Archaeological Survey of India Annual Report 1913-14:* 90.
Jacobson, J. 1975. 'Static sites and peripatetic peoples in the archaeology of population mobility in eastern Malwa'. in S. Leshnik, and G.D. Sontheimer (*eds.*), *Pastoralists and Nomads in South Asia*. Wiesbaden: O. Harrassowitz: 68-91.
——. 1980. 'Investigations of Late Stone Age Cultural Adaptations in the Central Vindhyas', *Man and Environment* 4: 65-82.
——. 1985. 'Acheulian surface sites in central India', in V. N. Misra and P. Bellwood (*eds.*), *Recent Advances in Indo-Pacific Prehistory*. Delhi: Oxford and IBH Publishers Co, 49-57.
Jaini, P.S. 1980. 'The disappearance of Buddhism and the survival of Jainism: a study in contrast', in A.K. Narain (*ed.*), *Studies in the History of Buddhism*. Delhi: B.R. Publishing Corp.
Jaiswal, S. 1967. *The Origin and Development of Vaiṣṇavism (from 200 B.C. to A.D. 500)*. Delhi: Munshiram Manoharlal.
Jameson, M.H., C.N. Runnels, and T.H. Van Andel. 1994. *A Greek Countryside: the southern Argolid from prehistory to the present day*. Stanford: Stanford University Press.
Jayaswal, K.P. 1921-1922. 'The Ghosundi Stone Inscription', *Epigraphica Indica* XVI: 25-27.
Jha, A., and D. Rajgor. 1994. *Studies in the Coinage of the Western Ksatrapas*. Nasik: Institute of Research in Numismatic Studies.
Jha, B. 2004. *Bull in Early Indian Art (up to sixth century AD)*. New Delhi: D.K. Printworld.
Jha, M. (*ed.*), 1985. *Dimensions of Pilgrimage: an anthropological appraisal*. New Delhi: Inter-India Publications.
——. (*ed.*), 1995. *Pilgrimage: concepts, themes, issues and methodology*. New Delhi: Inter-India Publications.
Johansen, P. G. 2003. 'Recasting the foundations: new approaches to regional understandings of South Asian archaeology and the problem of Culture history', *Asian Perspectives* 42(2): 193-206.
Johnson, W. 1908 (reprint 1971). *Folk Memory or The Continuity of British Archaeology*. Oxford: Clarendon Press.
Joshi, N.P. 1979. *Iconography of Balarama* . New Delhi: Shakti Malik.
Joshi, V. 1961. 'Stone age industries in the Damoh area, Madhya Pradesh', *Ancient India* 17: 5-37.
Kajale, M. D. and S. P. Eksambekar. 2001. 'Phytolith approach for investigating ancient occupations at Balathal, Rajasthan, India. Part 1: Evidence of crops exploited by initial farmers', in J. D. Meunier and F. Colin (*eds.*), *Phytoliths: applications in earth sciences and human history*. Abingdon: A A Balkema, 199-204.
Keller, D.R., and D.W. Rupp (*eds.*), 1983. *Archaeological Survey in the Mediterranean Area*. Oxford: BAR International Series 155.
Kennet, D. 2004. 'The transition from early historic to early medieval in the Vākāṭaka realm', in H. Bakker (*ed.*), *The Vākāṭaka Heritage: Indian Culture at the Crossroads*. Groningen: Egbert Forsten, 11-18.
Kenoyer, M. 1997. 'Early city-states in South Asia: comparing the Harappan phase and early historic period', in D.L. Nichols, and T.H. Charlton (*eds.*), *The Archaeology of city-states: cross-cultural approaches*. Washington and London: Smithsonian Institution Press, 51-70.
Kenoyer, J.M., J.D. Clark, J.N Pal, and G.R. Sharma. 1983. 'An upper palaeolithic shrine in India?' *Antiquity* 57: 88-94.
Khare, M.D. 1967. 'Discovery of a Vishnu temple near the Heliodorus pillar, Besnagar, Dist. Vidisha (M.P.)', *Lalit Kala* 13: 21-7.
——. 1976a. 'Comments on John Irwin's, "The Heliodorus pillar at Besnagar"', *Puratattva* 8: 176-8.
——. 1976b. 'Rock shelters of Ahmadpur hill, Vidisha district', *Madhya Pradesh Itihas Parishad*. 10: 18-20.
——. 1981. 'Neolithic-chalcolithic remains at Rangai (Vidisha)', *Puratattva* 12: 55-7.
Kielhorn, F. 1905-6. 'Junagadh rock inscription of Rudradāman: the year 72', *Epigraphica Indica* VIII, 36-49.
Kincaid, W. 1888. 'Rambles among ruins in central India', *The Indian Antiquary* XVII: 348-52.
Knapp, A.B. (*ed.*), 1992. *Archaeology, Annales and Ethnohistory*. Cambridge: Cambridge University Press.
Kosambi, D.D. 1955. 'The Basis of Ancient Indian History (I)', *Journal of the American Oriental Society* 75 (1), 35-45.
——. 1962. 'At the Crossroads: a study of Mother Goddess cult sites', in D.D. Kosambi (*ed.*), *Myth and Reality: Studies in the formation of Indian culture*. Bombay: Popular Prakashan, 82-109.
——. 1963. 'The beginning of the Iron Age in India', *Journal of Economic and Social History of the Orient* 6 (3): 309-318.
Krishna, N. 1980. *The Art and Iconography of Vishnu-Narayana*. Bombay: D.B. Taraporevala Sons and Co. Private Ltd.
Kulke, H. 1993. 'Royal temple policy', in H. Kulke (*ed.*), *Kings and Cults: state formation and legitimation in India and South-east Asia*. New Delhi: Manohar, 1-16.
——. 1995a. 'Introduction: the study of state in pre-modern India', in H. Kulke (*ed.*), *The State in Premodern India, 1000-1700*. Delhi: Oxford University Press, 1-47.
——. 1995b. 'The early and the imperial kingdom: a processural model of integrative state formation in early medieval India', in H. Kulke (*ed.*), 1995. *The State in Premodern India, 1000-1700*. Delhi: Oxford University Press, 233-62.
Kulke, H. (*ed.*), 1993. *Kings and Cults: state formation and legitimation in India and Southeast Asia*. Delhi: Manohar.
——. (*ed.*), 1995. *The State in Premodern India, 1000-1700*. Delhi: Oxford University Press.
Lahiri, N. 1992. *The Archaeology of Indian Trade Routes*. Delhi: Oxford University Press.
——. 1996. 'Archaeological landscapes and textual images: a study of the sacred geography of late medieval Ballabgarh', *World Archaeology* 28(2): 244-264.
Lahiri, N., and U. Singh. 1999. 'In the shadow of New Delhi: understanding he landscape through village eyes', in P.J. Ucko, and R. Layton (*eds.*), *The Archaeology and Anthropology of Landscape: shaping your landscape*. London: Routledge, 175-88.
Lahiri, N., U. Singh, and T. Uberoi. 1996. 'Preliminary field report on the archaeology of Faridabad-the Ballabgarh Tehsil', *Man and Environment* 11(1): 32-57.
Lake, H.H. 1910a. 'Besnagar', *Journal of the Bombay Branch of the Royal Asiatic Society* XXIII: 135-145.
——. 1910b. 'Bigan Topes'. *Journal of the Bombay Branch of the Royal Asiatic Society* XXIII: 45-6.
Lal, B.B. 1954. 'Excavations at Hastināpura and other explorations, 1950-2', *Ancient India* 10-11: 5-151.
Lal, M. 1984. *Settlement History and the Rise of Civilisation in the Ganga-Yamuna Doab (from 1500 BC-AD 300)*. Delhi: B.R. Publishing Corporation.
——. 1986. 'Iron tools, forest clearance and urbanization in the Gangetic plains', *Man and Environment* X: 83-90.
Lane, P. 1986. 'Past practices in the ritual present: examples from the Welsh Bronze Age', *Archaeological Review from Cambridge* 5 (2): 181-92.
Lansing, J. 1991. *Priests and Programmers: Technologies of Power in the Engineered Landscape of Bali*. Princeton, NJ: Princeton University Press.
Law, B.C. 1931. 'Cetiya in Buddhist literature', in Von W. Wust (*ed.*), *Studia Indo-Iranica Ehrengabe fur Wilhelm Geiger*. Leipzig: O. Harrassowitz, 42-8.
Layton, R. 1999. 'The Alawa totemic landscape: ecology, religion and politics', in P.J. Ucko and R. Layton (*eds.*), *The Archaeology and Anthropology of Landscape: shaping your landscape*. London: Routledge, 219-238.
Leach, E.R. 1959. 'Hydraulic society in Ceylon', *Past and Present* 15: 2-26.
Liu, X. 1988. *Ancient India and Ancient China: trade and religious exchanges AD 1-600*. New Delhi: Oxford University Press.
Lowenthal, D. 1961. 'Geography, experience and imagination: towards a geographical epistemology', *Annals of the Association of American Geographers* 51: 241-60.

Lowenthal, D., and M. Bowden (*eds.*), 1976. *Geographies of the Mind*. New York: Oxford University Press.

Ludden. D. 1979. 'Patronage and Irrigation in Tamil Nadu: A Long-term View', *Indian Economic & Social History Review* 16: 347-365.

Lüders, H. 1937-38. 'Seven Brahmi Inscriptions from Mathura and its Vicinity', *Epigraphica Indica* 24: 194-212.

Maclean, M.R. 1996. *The Social Impact of the Beginnings of Iron Technology in the Western Lake Victoria Basin: a district case study*. Unpublished PhD dissertation. University of Cambridge.

McCrindle, J.W. 1901 (1979). trans. Ancient India as Described in Classical Literature. New Delhi: Oriental Books Reprint 1979.

Madella, M. 2003. 'Investigating agriculture and environment in South Asia: present and future contributions from opal phytoliths', in S. Weber and W.R. Belcher (*eds.*), *Indus Ethnobiology: new perspectives from the field*. Lanham: Lexington Books, 199-249.

Maheswari, M.K. 1997. *Vidisha District Village-to-Village Survey, 1996-7*. Bhopal State Archaeology Department. Unpublished report.

Maisey, F.C. 1892. *Sanchi and its Remains: a full description of the ancient buildings, sculptures and inscriptions*. London: Kegan Paul, Trench, Trubner and Co.

Majumdar, R.C. 1953. *The History and Culture of the Indian People: the age of imperial unity*. Bombay: Bharatiya Vidhya Bhavan.

Majumdar, R.C., and A.D. Pusalker. 1954. *The Classical Age*. Bombay: Bharatiya Vidya Bhavan.

Malcolm, J. 1832. *A Memoir of Central India including Malwa and Adjoining Provinces; with the history, and copious illustrations of the past and present condition of that country*. London: Parbury & Allen.

Marinatos, N. and R. Hagg (*eds.*), 1993. *Greek Sanctuaries: new approaches*. London: Routledge.

Marshall, J. 1918. *A Guide to Sanchi*. Calcutta: Superintendent Government Printing.

——. 1951. *Taxila: an illustrated account of the archaeological excavations carried out at Taxila under the orders of the Government of India between the years 1913 and 1934*. London: Cambridge University Press.

Marshall, J., A. Foucher, and N.G. Majumdar. 1940. *The Monuments of Sanchi*. London: Probsthain (reprinted 1983, Delhi: Swati Publications).

Mathpal, Y. 1984. 'Prehistoric rock paintings of Bhimbetka, Central India'. New Delhi: Abhinav Publications.

Mehta, R.N. 1963. 'Ancient bunds in Sabarkantha district, Gujarat'. *Journal of Oriental Institute* (MS University, Baroda) 10 (4): 359-365.

——. 1968. 'Sudarsana lake', *Journal of Oriental Institute* (MS University, Baroda) 18: 18-28.

Mehta, R.N., and S.N, Chowdhary. 1966. *Excavations at Devnimori*. Baroda: University of Baroda.

Meinig, D.W. 1979. 'Reading the landscape: an appreciation of W.G. Hoskins and J.B. Jackson', in D.W. Meinig (*ed.*), *The Interpretation of Ordinary Landscapes*. Oxford: Oxford University Press.

Mejdahl, V. 1986. 'Thermoluminiscence dating of sediments', *Radiation Protection Dosimetry* 17: 219-227.

Miller, H.M.L. 2006. 'Water Supply, Labor Organization and Land Ownership in Indus Floodplain Agricultural Systems', in: C. Stanish and J. Marcus *(eds.), Agriculture and Irrigation in Archaeology*, Cotsen: Institute of Archaeology Press.

Mirashi, M.W. 1960. *Studies in Indology*. Vol. 1. Nagpur: Vidarbha Samshodhana Mandal.

Mirashi, V.V. 1955a. ''Kānākherā Stone Inscription of Śrīdharavarman: (Kalachuri) Year 102', *CII, IV: Inscriptions of the Kalachuri-Chedi Era, Part I*. Ootacamund: Government Epigraphist for India, 13-16.

——. 1955b. 'Eran stone pillar inscription of Śrīdharavarman', *CII, IV*, 605-611.

Misra, B.N. 1982. 'Sculptural representations of Naga Muchalinda', in R.K. Sharma (*ed.*), *Indian Archaeology: new perspectives. Proceedings of the 11th annual congress of the Indian Archaeological Society* 1980. Delhi: Agam Kala Prakashan, 291-301.

Misra, P. K. 2001. 'Excavations at the Buddhist site of Deor-Kothar (Barhat), District Rewa, Madhya Pradesh, India, 1999-2001', *Circle of Inner Asian Art Newsletter* 13: 3-13.

Misra, R.N. 1981. *Yaksa Cult and Iconography*. New Delhi: Munshiram Manoharlal.

——. 1994. 'Perceptions of India's past: tradition and the artist', in C.B. Asher, and T.R. Metcalf (*eds.*), *Perceptions of South Asia's Visual Past*. New Delhi: Oxford and IBH Publishing, 101-21.

——. 1999. 'Religion in a disorganised milieu: Saiva Siddhanta's institutionalization in the Gopadri region', in J.T. O'Connell, and T. Joseph (*eds.*), *Organisational and Institutional aspects of Indian Religious Movements*. Simla: IIAS, 59-78.

Misra, V. D., J. N. Pal and M. C. Gupta 2000-1, 'Excavations at Amilkoni, Rewa, Madhya Pradesh, and exploration around Amilkoni', *Pragdhara* 12: 145-52.

Misra, V.N., and Y. Mathpal. 1979. 'Rock art of Bhimbetka Region, Central India', *Man and Environment* 3: 27-33.

Mitra, D. 1971. *Buddhist Monuments*. Calcutta: Sahitya Samsad.

——. 1996. 'Discovery and restoration of the monuments' in V. Dehejia (*ed.*), *Unseen Presence: the Buddha and Sanchi*. Mumbai: Marg Publications, 1-17.

Monier Williams, J. 1899 (revised edition). *A Sanskrit-English Dictionary*. Oxford: Clarendon.

Moody, J.A. 1989. *The Environmental and Cultural Prehistory of the Khania Region*. Unpublished Phd Dissertation. University of Minnesota.

Morrison, K. 1993. 'Supplying the city: the role of reservoirs in Indian urban landscape', *Asian Perspectives* 32(2): 133-149.

——. 1995a. 'Trade, urbanism, and agricultural expansion: Buddhist monastic institutions and the state in early historic western Deccan'. *World Archaeology* 27 (2): 203-21.

——. 1995b. *Fields of Victory: Vijayanagara and the course of intensification*. Berkeley: University of California, Archaeological Research Facility.

Mughal, M.R. 1980. 'New Archaeological evidence from Bahawalpur', *Man and Environment* 4: 93-98.

——. 1992. 'The consequences of river changes for the Harappan settlements in Cholistan'. *Eastern Anthropologist* (Special Number on Indus Civilisation) 45 (1-2): 105-116.

Mughal, M.R., F. Iqbal, M.A. Khan, and M. Hassan. 1996. 'Archaeological Sites and Monuments in Punjab, Preliminary Results of Explorations 1992-6', *Pakistan Archaeology* 29: 1-474.

Munshi, S. 1979. 'Tribal absorption and Sanskritisation in Hindu society', *Contributions to Indian Sociology*, NS. 13 (2): 293-317.

Murti, M.L.K. 1989. 'Pre-Iron Age Agricultural Settlements in South India: an ecological perspective', *Man and Environment* 14: 65-81.

Myrdal-Runebjer, E. 1994. 'Vavala vava-Sigiri Mahavava irrigation system: preliminary results from an archaeological case study', in A. Parpola and P. Koskikallio (*eds.*), *South Asian Archaeology 1993*. Helsinki: Suomalainen Tiedeakatemia, 551-62.

Nagarch, B.L. 1990. 'Bijalmandal or Vijayamandira, Vidisha: a study', in K.K. Chakravarty (*ed.*), *Vidisha Through the Ages*. Delhi: Agam Kala Prakashan, 23-42.

Narain, A.K. 1973. 'The Two Hindu Divinities on the Coins of Agathocles from Ai Khanum', *Journal of the Numismatic Society of India* 35: 73-7.

Narain A.K. and T.N. Roy 1976. *Excavations at Rajghat (1957-1958; 1960-1965). Part 1: the cuttings, stratification and structures*. Varanasi: Banaras Hindu University.

Neumayer, E. 1978. *Lines on Stone: the prehistoric rock art of India*. New Delhi: Manohar.

——. 1992–3. 'On the Identification of Bhakti Deities in Rock Pictures', *Puratattva* 23: 53-60.

O'Flaherty, W. 1975. *Hindu Myths: A Sourcebook Translated from the Sanskrit*. London: Penguin Books.

Okada, A. 2000. *Sculptures indiennes du Musée Guimet*. Paris: Réunion des Musées Nationaux.

Ortner, S.B. 1978. *Sherpas Through their Rituals*. Cambridge: Cambridge University Press.

Ota, S.B., and D.K. Khamari. 2006. 'Sanchi during post Gupta period: some random thoughts', in B.R. Mani, and S.C. Saran (*eds.*), *Purābhāratī, Vol. II, Studies in Early Historic Archaeology and Buddhism (Commemoration Volume in Respect of Prof. B.P. Sinha)*. Delhi: Sharada Publishing House, 329-333.

Otto, R. 1925. *The Idea of the Holy*. London: Oxford University Press.

Padayya, K. 1995. 'Theoretical Perspectives in Indian Archaeology: a historical review', in P.J. Ucko (*ed.*), *Theory in Archaeology: A World Perspective*. London: Routledge, 110-149.

Pal, P. (*ed.*), 2002. *Indian Terracotta Sculpture: the Early Period*. Mumbai: Marg Publications.

Pandey, R.P. 1987. *Prehistoric Archaeology of Madhya Pradesh*. Delhi: Sundeep Prakashan.

——. 1990. 'Geomorphic setting of landscape around Ahmadpur rock-shelters', in K.K. Chakravarty (*ed.*), *Vidisha Through the Ages*. Delhi: Agam Kala Prakashan, 1-10.

Paranavitana, S. 1936. *Excavations in the citadel of Anuradhapura*. Memoirs of the Archaeological Survey of Ceylon, III. Colombo.

——. 1970. *Inscriptions of Ceylon*. 2 vols. Colombo: Department of Archaeology, Ceylon.

Parker, H. 1909 (1981). *Ancient Ceylon*. New Delhi. Asian Educational Services.

Peacock, D.P.S. 1977. 'Ceramics in Roman and Medieval archaeology', in D.P.S. Peacock (*ed.*), *Pottery and Early Commerce: characterisation and trade in Roman and later ceramics*. London: Academic Press, 21-33.

Peatfield, A. 1983. 'The topography of Minoan peak sanctuaries', *Annual of British School at Athens* 78: 273-280.

Peel, J.D.Y. 1968. 'Syncretism and religious change', *Comparative Studies in Society and History* 10: 121-41.

Plog, S., F. Plog, and W. Wait. 1978. 'Decision making in modern surveys', in M.B. Schiffer (*ed.*), *Advances in Archaeological Method and Theory*, vol. I. New York: Academic Press, 383-421.
Possehl, G.L. 1975. 'The chronology of Gabarbands and palas in Western South Asia', *Expedition* 17 (23), 33-37.
——. 1980. *Indus Civilisation in Saurashtra*. Delhi: B.R. Publishing Corporation.
Prasad, H.K. 1960. 'The Nāga cult in Bihar', *Journal of the Bengal Royal Asiatic Society* LXVI:129-34.
Prinsep, J. 1834. 'Second note on the Bhilsa inscription', *Journal of the Asiatic Society of Bengal* III: 488-93.
——. 1837.' Note on the facsmiles of inscriptions from Sanchi near Bhilsa, taken for the Society by Captain Smith, engineer; and on the drawings of the Buddhist monuments presented by Captain W. Murray, at the meeting of the 7th June', *Journal of the Asiatic Society of Bengal* VI (1): 451-63.
Puri, B.N. 1968. 'Irrigation and agricultural economy in ancient India', *Annals of the Bhandarkar Oriental Research Institute* 48-9: 383-90.
Raghava Varier, M.R., and M.G.S. Narayanan. 1976. 'Bindusara, Sanchi and Asoka', *Journal of Indian History* 54: 53-71.
Ramaswami, N.S. 1975. *Amaravati: the art and history of the stupa and the temple*. Hyderabad: Govt. of Andhra Pradesh.
Rao, M. 1994. *Sanchi Sculptures: an aesthetic and cultural study*. New Delhi: Akay Book Corporation.
Rao, S. R. 1966. *Excavations at Amreli: a Kshatrapa-Gupta town*. Baroda: Museum and Picture Gallery.
Ray, H.P. 1986. *Monastery and Guild: commerce under the Satavahanas*. Delhi: Oxford University Press.
——. 1994. *The Winds of Change: Buddhism and the maritime links of early South Asia*. Delhi: Oxford India.
Ray, N.R. 1945. *Maurya and Sunga art*. Calcutta: University of Calcutta Press.
——. 1952. 'Mauryan art', in N. Sastri (*ed.*), *Age of the Nandas and Mauryas*. Varanasi: Motilal Banarsidass.
Ray, R. 1994. *Buddhist Saints in India: a study in Buddhist values and orientations*. New York: Oxford University Press.
Relph, E. 1976. *Place and Placelessness*. London: Pion.
——. 1985. 'Geographical experience and being in the world: the phenomenological origins of geography', in D. Seamon, and R. Mugeraver (*eds.*), *Dwelling, Place and Environment: towards a phenomenology of person and world*. Dordrecht: Martinus Nijhoff, 15-32.
Renfrew, C., and M. Wagstaff (*eds.*), 1982. *An Island Polity*. Cambridge: Cambridge University Press.
Richards, C. 1993. 'Monumental choreography: architectural and spatial representation in late Neolithic Orkney, in C. Tilley (*ed.*), *Interpretative Archaeology*. Oxford: Berg: Steiner, 143-78.
Risberg, J., E. Myrdal-Runebjer, *et al.* 2002. 'Sediment and soil characteristics and an evaluation of their applicability to the irrigation history in Sigiriya, Sri Lanka', *Journal of Nordic Archaeological Science* 13: 27-42.
Rosen, A. M. 1986. *Cities of Clay: the geoarchaeology of tells*. Chicago: University of Chicago Press.
——. 1992. 'Preliminary identification of silica skeletons from Near Eastern archaeological sites: an anatomical approach', in G. Rapp Jr. and S. C. Mulholland (*eds.*), *Phytolith Systematics: emerging issues*. New York: Plenum, 129-147.
Roth, G. 1980. 'Symbolism of the Buddhist Stupa', in A.L. Dallapiccola (*ed.*), *The Stupa: its religious, historical and architectural significance*. Wiesbaden: Steiner, 183-217.
Salomon, R. 1986. 'New Śankalipi (shell character) inscriptions', *Studien zur Indologie und Iranistik*. Reinbek: 109-58.
——. 1996. 'British Museum stone inscription of the Tripurī Kalacuri Prince Valleka'. *Indo-Iranian Journal* 39: 133-61.
——. 1998. *Indian Epigraphy: a guide to the study of inscriptions in Sanskrit, Prakrit and other Indo-Aryan languages*. Oxford: Oxford University Press.
Sanderson, A. 2004. 'Notes on the *Mahāmeghasûtra*'. Unpublished paper, dated 16/04/04.
Sankalia, H.D. 1974. *The Prehistory and Protohistory of India and Pakistan*. Pune: Deccan College Postgraduate and Research Institute.
Sankalia, H.D., S.B. Deo, and Z.D. Ansari. 1971. *Chalcolithic Navdatoli: excavations at Navdatoli, 1957-9*. Pune: Deccan College Research Institute.
Sarcar, H. 1983. 'A post-Asokan inscription from Pangoraria in the Vindhyan range', in B.N. Mukherjee *et al.* (*eds.*), *Studies in Indology*. Shri D.C. Sircar Festschrift. Delhi: Sundeep.
Sarkar, H. 1965. 'Elliptical structures in ancient India', *Journal Asiatic Society, Bengal* 7: 83-7.
——. 1966. *Studies in Early Buddhist Architecture of India*. Delhi: Munshiram Manoharlal.
Saxena, A., V. Prasad, I. B. Singh, M. S. Chauhan, and R. Hasan. 2006. 'On the Holocene record of phytoliths of wild and cultivated rice from Ganga Plain: evidence for rice-based agriculture', *Current Science* 90: 11, 1547-52.
Scarborough, V.L. 2003. *The Flow of Power: ancient water systems and landscapes*. New Mexico: School of American Research.
Schiffer M.J., A.P. Sullivan, and T.C. Klinger. 1978. 'The design of archaeological surveys', *World Archaeology* 10. 1-28.
Schmithausen, L. 1997. *Maitri and Magic: Aspects of the Buddhist Attitude Toward the Dangerous in Nature*. Wien: Verlag der Österreichischen Akademie der Wissenschften.
Schopen, G. 1987. 'Burial "ad sanctos" and the physical presence of the Buddha in early Indian Buddhism: a study in the archaeology of religions', *Religion* 17: 193-225 (reprinted in Schopen 1997: 114-147).
——. 1993. 'Stūpa and Tīrtha: Tibetan mortuary practices and an unrecognised form of burial *ad sanctos* at Buddhist sites in India', in T. Skorupski (*ed.*), *Papers in Honour of D.S. Ruegg*. Buddhist Forum, II. London: School of Oriental and African Studies, 273-93.
——. 1994a. 'The monastic ownership of servants or slaves: local and legal factors in the redactional history of two Vinayas', *Journal of the International Association of Buddhist Studies* 17(2): 145-73.
——. 1994b. 'Doing business for the lord: lending on interest and written loan contracts in the Mūlasarvāstivāda-Vinaya', *Journal of the American Oriental Society* 114(4): 527-54.
——. 1994c. 'Ritual rights and bones of contention: more on monastic funerals and relics in the Mūlasarvāstivāda-Vinaya', *Journal of Indian Philosophy* 22: 31-80.
——. 1996a. 'The lay ownership of monasteries and the role of the monk in Mūlasarvāstivādin monasticism', *Journal of International Association of Buddhist Studies* 19: 81-126.
——. 1996b. 'Immigrant monks and the proto-historical dead: the Buddhist occupation of early burial sites in India', in F. Wilheln (*ed.*), *Festschrift Dieter Schlingloff.* Reinbek: Verlag fur Orientalistische Fachpublikationen, 215-238 (Reprinted in Schopen 2004, *Buddhist Monks and Business Matters: Still More Papers on Buddhist Monasticism in India*. Studies in the Buddhist Traditions. Honolulu: University of Hawaii Press, 360-81).
——. 1996c. 'What's in a name: the religious function of early donative inscriptions', in V. Dehejia (*ed.*), *Unseen Presence: the Buddha and Sanchi*. Mumbai: Marg Publications, 58-73.
——. 1997. *Bones, Stones, and Buddhist Monks: collected papers on the archaeology, epigraphy, and texts of monastic Buddhism in India*. Honolulu: University of Hawaii Press.
Schumacher, E.F. 1973. *Small is Beautiful: a study of economics as if people mattered*. London: Vintage.
Scully, V. 1961. *The Earth, the Temple and the Gods : sacred architecture*. New Haven: Yale University Press.
Shaffer, J.G., 1984. 'The Indo-Aryan Invasions: Cultural myth and Archaeological Reality', in J.R. Lukas (*ed.*), *The People of South Asia*. New York: Plenum Press, 77-88.
Sharma, G.R. 1969. 'Excavations at Kausambi, 1957-59', *Memoirs of the Archaeological Survey of India*, no. 74.
——. 1980. *From History to Prehistory: contributions of the department to the archaeology of the Ganga valley and the Vindhyas*. Allahabad: University of Allahabad.
Sharma, G. R. and J. D. Clark 1983. *Palaeoenvironments and Prehistory in the Middle Son Valley, Madhya Pradesh, north-central India*. Allahabad: Abinash Prakashan.
Sharma, G. R., V. D. Misra, D. Mandal, *et al.* 1980, *Beginnings of Agriculture (Epi-Palaeolithic to Neolithic: excavations at Chopani-Mando, Mahadaha and Mahagara)*. Allahabad: Abinash Prakshan.
Sharma, I.K. 1982. The Development of Early Śaiva Art and Architecture (with special reference to Āndhradeśa). Delhi: Sundeep Prakashan.
Sharma, R.L. (ed). 1990. *Studies in Shell Script*. Delhi: Agamkala Prakashan.
Sharma, R.S. 1983a. Material Culture and Social Formations in Ancient India. New Delhi: Macmillan.
——. 1983b. Perspectives in Social and Economic History of Early India. New Delhi: Munshiram Manoharlal.
——. 1987. *Urban Decay in India*. New Delhi: Munshiram Manoharlal.
Shaw, J. 2000a. 'The sacred landscape', in M. Willis, *Buddhist Reliquaries from Ancient India*. London: British Museum Press, 27-38.
——. 2000b. 'Ayodhya's sacred landscape: ritual memory, politics and archaeological "fact"', *Antiquity* (Special edition: *Archaeology and Identity in South Asia*, edited by R.A.E. Coningham and N. Lewer) 74 (285): 693-700.
——. 2002. *The Sacred Geography of Sanchi Hill: the archaeological setting of Buddhist monasteries in central India*. PhD dissertation. University of Cambridge.
——. 2004a. 'Nāga sculptures in Sanchi's archaeological landscape: Buddhism, Vaiṣṇavism, and local agricultural cults in Central India, first century BCE to fifth century CE,' *Artibus Asiae* LXIV(1): 5-59.
——. 2004b. 'Early historic landscapes in central India: recent archaeological investigations in districts Raisen and Vidisha, Madhya Pradesh, 2003-4,'

Journal of Interdisciplinary Studies in History and Archaeology (University of Allahabad) 1 (1): 143-150.

——. 2005. 'The archaeological setting of Buddhist monasteries in central India: a summary of a multi-phase survey in the Sanchi area, 1998-2000,' in C. Jarrige and V. Lefèvre (*eds.*), *South Asian Archaeology: proceedings of the 16th international conference of the European Association of South Asian Archaeologists*. Paris: Éditions Recherche sur les Civilisations, ADPF, 2, 665-676.

Shaw J., and J.V. Sutcliffe, 2001. 'Ancient irrigation works in the Sanchi area: an archaeological and hydrological investigation,' *South Asian Studies* 17: 55 - 75.

——. 2003a. 'Water management, patronage networks and religious change: new evidence from the Sanchi dam complex and counterparts in Gujarat and Sri Lanka,' *South Asian Studies* 19: 73-104.

——. 2003b. 'Ancient dams, settlement archaeology and Buddhist propagation in central India: the hydrological background,' *Hydrological Sciences Journal* 48 (2): 277 - 291.

——. 2005. 'Ancient dams and Buddhist landscapes in the Sanchi area: new evidence on irrigation, land use and monasticism in central India,' *South Asian Studies* 21: 1-24.

Shaw, J., J.V. Sutcliffe, L. Lloyd-Smith, J-L. Schwenninger, and M.S. Chauhan, with contributions by O.P. Misra and E. Harvey. 2007. 'Ancient Irrigation and Buddhist history in Central India: Optically Stimulated Luminescence and pollen sequences from the Sanchi dams', *Asian Perspectives* 46(1): 166-201.

Sherratt, A. 1996. '"Settlement patterns" or "landscape studies"? Reconciling reason and romance', *Archaeological Dialogues* 3(2): 140-59.

——. 1999, 'Cash-crops before cash: organic consumables and trade', in C. Gosden, and J.G. Hatler (*eds.*), *The Prehistory of Food: Appetites for Change*, London: Routledge, 13-34.

Shimada, A. In press. 'Amaravati and Dhanyakataka: social soles of Buddhist monasteries in ancient Indian cities', in J. Hawkes and A. Shimada (*eds.*), *Buddhist Stūpas in South Asia: Recent Archaeological, Art-Historical, and Historical Perspectives*. New Delhi: Oxford University Press

Shinde, V. 1988. 'Land use pattern during chalcolithic period in the Tapi basin', *Puratattva* 18: 54-60.

——. 1989. 'New light on the origin, settlement system and decline of the Jorwe culture of the Deccan, India', *South Asian Studies* 5: 59-72.

Shukla, S.K. 1990. 'Neemkheria: 4000 sāl purāne shailcitra', in K.K. Chakravarty (*ed.*), *Vidisha Through the Ages*. Delhi: Agam Prakashan, 191-95.

Singh, A.K. 1990. 'Donors of Korara', in K. K. Chakravarti (*ed.*), *Vidisha Through the Ages*. Delhi: Agam Prakashan, 74-6.

Singh, G. 1971. 'The Indus valley culture seen in the context of post-glacial climatic and ecological studies in northwest India'. *Archaeology and Physical Anthropology in Oceania* 6(2): 177-89.

Singh, G., R.D. Joshi, and A.B. Singh. 1972. 'Stratigraphic and radiocarbon evidence for the age and development of three salt lake deposits in Rajasthan, India', *Quaternary Research* 2 (4): 496-505.

Singh, R.L. (*ed.*), 1971. *India: a regional geography*. Varanasi: National Geographic Society of India.

Singh, Rana P.B. (*ed.*), 1994. *The Spirit and Power of Place: human environment and scarality (sic.): essays dedicated to Yi-Fu Tuan*. National Geographical Journal of India, 40 (1-4).

Singh, U. 1996. 'Sanchi: the history of the patronage of an ancient Buddhist establishment', *Indian Economic and Social History Review* 33(1): 1-35.

Sinha, B.P. 1971. 'Some problems of ancient Indian potteries', in B.P. Sinha (*ed.*), *Potteries in Ancient India*. Patna: The Department of Ancient Indian History and Archaeology, 9-14.

Sinha, B.P., S.H. Askari, and Q. Ahmad (*eds.*), 1983-87. *Comprehensive History of Bihar*. Patna: Kashi Prasad Jayaswal Research Institute.

Sinopoli, C. 1997. 'Nucleated settlements in the Vijayanagara metropolitan region', in R. Allchin and B. Allchin (*eds.*), *South Asian Archaeology 1995*. New Delhi: Oxford & IBH Pub., 475-87.

——. 2003. *The Political Economy of Craft Production: Crafting Empire in South India, c. 1350-1650*. Cambridge: Cambridge University Press.

Sinopoli, C.M., and K. Morrison, 1992. 'Archaeological survey at Vijayanagara', *Research and Exploration* 8 (2): 237-39.

Sircar, D.C. 1965. *Select Inscriptions Bearing on Indian History and Civilisation, from the 6th century BC to the 6th century AD*. 2nd edition. Calcutta: University of Calcutta.

——. 1966. *Indian Epigraphical Glossary*. Delhi: Motilal Banarsidass.

——. 1969. *Ancient Malwa and the Vikramaditya tradition*. Delhi: Munshiram Manoharlal.

——. 1970. 'Vidiśa Jain image inscriptions of the time of Rāmagupta', *Journal of Ancient Indian History III:* 145-51.

——. 1979. 'Western version of minor rock edict I at Panguraria', *Asokan Studies*. Calcutta: 94-103.

Śivaramamurti, C. 1964. *Indian Sculpture*. New Delhi: Indian Council of Cultural Relations.

Smail, J.R.W., 1961. 'On the possibility of an autonomous history of modern Southeast Asia, *Journal of Southeast Asian History* 2 (2): 72-102.

Smith, C. 1999. 'Ancestors, place and people: social landscapes in Aboriginal Australia', in P.J. Ucko and R. Layton (*eds.*), *The Archaeology and Anthropology of Landscape: shaping your landscape*. London: Routledge, 189-203.

Smith, L.M.V. 1996. 'Report on the pottery collection', in M.D.S. Mallinson, L.M.V. Smith, S. Ikram, C. Le Quesne and P. Sheehan-Road, *Archaeology in the Middle Nile*. Vol. I. The SARS Survey from Bagrawiya-Meroe to Atbara 1993. Sudan Archaeological Research Society Publication 1. London: Sudan Archaeological Research Society, 165-69.

Smith, M.L. 2001. *The Archaeology of an Early Historic Town in Central India*. Oxford: British Archaeological Reports.

——. 2002. 'Systematic survey at the Early Historic urban site of Sisupalgarh, Orissa', in G. Sengupta and S. Panja (*eds.*), *Archaeology of Eastern India: New Perspectives*. Calcutta: Centre for Archaeological Studies and Training, East India, 109-125.

Snodgrass, A. 1985. *Symbolism of the Stupa*. Ithaca: Cornell University.

Snodgrass, A.M. 1986. 'Interaction by design: the Greek city state', in C. Renfrew and J.F. Cherry (*eds.*), *Peer Polity Interaction and Socio-political Change*. Cambridge: Cambridge University Press.

Sonakia, A. 1986, 'Skull cap of an early man from the Narmada valley alluvium (Pleistocene) of central India', *American Anthropologist* 87: 612-6.

Srinivas, M. N. 1967. 'The cohesive role of Sanskritization', in P. Mason (*ed.*), *India and Ceylon: unity and diversity*. London: Oxford University Press, 67-82.

Srinivasan, D. 1979. 'Early Vaiṣṇava Imagery: Caturvyūha and variant forms', *Archives of Asian Art* XXXII: 39-54.

Stargardt. J. 1983. *Satingpra I, the environmental and economic archaeology of South Thailand*. Oxford: British Archaeological Reports and Institute for Southeast Asian Studies, Singapore.

——. 1990. *The Ancient Pyu of Burma*. Vol. 1: *Early Pyu cities in a man-made landscape*. Cambridge: Publications on Ancient Civilization in South East Asia. Cambridge University Press.

——. 1998. 'Earth, rice, and water: "reading the landscape" as a record of the history of Satingpra, south Thailand', in R.H. Grove, V. Damodaran, and S. Sangwan (*eds.*), *Nature and the Orient: the environmental history of South and Southeast Asia*. Delhi: Oxford University Press, 127-42.

Stillwell, R. 1954. 'The Siting of Classical Greek temples' *Journal of Society of Architectural Historians* 13(5): 3-8.

Stopford, J. 1994. 'Some approaches to the archaeology of Christian pilgrimage'. *World Archaeology* 26 (1): 57-77.

Strenski, I, 1983. 'On generalised exchange and the domestication of the Sangha'. *Man* 18: 463-77.

Strong, J.S. 1983. *The Legend of King Aśoka: a study and translation of the Aśokāvadāna*. Princeton: Princeton University Press.

Subbarao. 1953. Baroda Through the Ages, being the report of an excavation conducted in the Baroda area 1951-2. Baroda: Faculty of Arts, MS. University of Baroda.

Sugandhi, N.2003. 'Context, content , and composition: questions of intended meaning and the Aśokan edicts', *Asian Perspectives* 42 (2): 224-246.

Sutcliffe, J.V. 2004. *Hydrology: A Question of Balance*. Wallingford: International Association of Hydrological Sciences Press.

Sutcliffe, J.V., and C.S. Green. 1981. *The Surface Hydrology of the Betwa Basin, India*. Indo-British Betwa groundwater project. Betwa report 7. Summary Technical report. Vol 2. London: Institute of Geological Sciences.

Sutcliffe, J.V., and C.S. Green. 1986. 'Water balance investigation of recharge in Madhya Pradesh, India', *Hydrological Sciences Journal* 31(3):383- 394.

Sutcliffe, J.V., R.P. Agrawal, and J.M. Tucker. 1981. 'The water balance of the Betwa basin, India', *Hydrological Sciences Bulletin* 26(2): 149-158.

Taddei, M. 1996. 'The first beginnings: sculptures on stupa 2', in V. Dehejia (*ed.*), *Unseen Presence: the Buddha and Sanchi*. Mumbai: Marg Publications. 74-91.

Tambiah, S.J. 1970. *Buddhism and the Spirit Cults of Northeast Thailand*. Cambridge: Cambridge University Press.

——. 1976. *World Conqueror and World Renouncer: a study of Buddhism in Thailand against a historical background*. Cambridge: Cambridge University Press.

——. 1984. The Buddhist Saints of the Forest and the Cult of Amulets. Cambridge: Cambridge University Press.

Tewari, R. 2003. 'The Origins of Ironworking in India: New Evidence from the Central Ganga Plain and the Eastern Vindhyas', *Antiquity* 77: 536-544.

Thapar, R. 1984. *From Lineage to State: social formations in the mid-first millennium B.C. in the Ganga Valley*. Bombay: Oxford University Press.

——. 1998 (reprint). *Asoka and the Decline of the Mauryas*. Delhi: Oxford University Press.

——. 1999. 'Some appropriations of the Theory of Aryan Race Relating to the Beginnings of Indian History'. in D. Ali (*ed.*), *Invoking the Past: the Uses of History in South Asia*. Delhi: Oxford University Press, 15-35.
Thero, P.T. (undated). *Sanchi*. Mahabodhi Society of Ceylon.
Thomas, J. 1991. *Rethinking the Neolithic*. Cambridge: Cambridge University Press.
Tilley, C. 1991. *Material Culture as Text: the art of ambiguity*. London: Routledge.
——. 1994. *A Phenomenology of Landscape: Places, paths and monuments*. Oxford: Berg.
——. 1996a. 'The power of rocks: topography and monument construction on Bodmin Moor', *World Archaeology* 28 (2): 161-175.
——. 1996b. *Material Culture as Text: the art of ambiguity*. London: Routledge.
Tiwari, J.N. 1985. *Goddess Cults in Ancient India: with special reference to the first seven centuries A.D.* Delhi: Sundeep Prakashan.
Trainor, K. 1996. 'Constructing a Buddhist ritual site: stupa and monastery architecture', in V. Dehejia (*ed.*), *Unseen Presence: the Buddha and Sanchi*. Mumbai: Marg Publications, 18-35.
——. 1997. *Relics, Ritual, and Representation in Buddhism: rematerializing the Sri Lankan Theravada tradition*. Cambridge: Cambridge University Press.
Trautmann, T. 1971. *Kautilya and the Arthasastra: a statistical investigation of the authorship and evolution of the text*. Leiden: Brill.
Trivedi, H.V. 1957. *Catalogue of the Coins of the Naga Kings of Padmavati*. Gwalior: Department of Archaeology and Museums, Government of Madhya Pradesh.
——. 1991. *CII, VII* (1978-1991): *Inscriptions of the Paramāras, Chandellas, Kachchhapaghātas and two minor dynasties*. New Delhi.
Tuan, Yi Fu. 1974. *Topophilia: a study of environmental perceptions, attitudes and values*. New York: Columbia University Press.
——. 1977. *Space and Place: the perspectives of experience*. Minneapolis: University of Minnesota Press.
Turner, V. 1973. 'The centre out there: pilgrim's goal', *History of Religions* 12 (30): 191-230.
Upadhyayan, B.S. 1947. *India in Kalidāsa*. Allahabad: Kitabistan.
Upreti, G.B. 1997. *The Early Buddhist World Outlook in Historical Perspective*. Delhi: Manohar
Vajracharya, G.V. 1999. 'Symbolism of Asokan pillars: a reappraisal in the light of textual and visual evidence', *Marg* 51 (2): 53-76.
Van de Veer, P. 1988. *Gods on Earth: the management of religious experience and identity in a north Indian pilgrimage centre*. London: The Athlone Press.
Van Kooij, K. R. 1995. 'Remarks on festivals and altars in early Buddhist art', in K.R. Van Kooij, and H. Van der Veer (*eds.*), *Function and Meaning in Buddhist Art*. Groningen: Egbert Forsten, 33-44.
Vats, M.S. 1952. *The Deogaṛh temple of the Gupta period*. Memoirs of the Archaeological Survey of India, no. 71.
Venkayya, V. 1906. 'Irrigation in South India in ancient times', *Archaeological Survey of India Annual Review 1903-4*: 202-211.
Verardi, G. 1996. 'Religion, rituals and the heaviness of Indian history', *Annali* (Istituti universitario Orientale) 56: 215-253.
——. 2000. 'The Buddha-elephant'. *Silk Road Art and Archaeology* 6: 69-74.
——. 2003. 'Images of Destruction: an enquiry into Hindu icons in their relation to Buddhism', in G Verardi and S Vita (*eds.*), *Buddhist Asia I: Papers from the first conference of Buddhist Studies held in Naples in May 2001*. Kyoto: Italian School of East Asian Studies, 1-36.
Vogel, J. Ph. 1909. 'Naga worship in ancient Mathura', *Archaeological Survey of India Annual Report 1908-9*: 159-63.
——. 1911. *Excavations at Saheth-Maheth*. Archaeological Survey of India Annual Report 1907-8.
——. 1926. *Indian serpent-lore: the nagas in Hindu legend and art*. London: Arthur Probstain.
Wakankar, V.S. 1967. *Kayatha Excavation Number*. Ujjain: The Journal of Vikram University.
Wakankar, V.S. and R.R.R. Brooks, 1976. Stone Age Painting in India. Bombay: D.B. Taraporevala.
Walshe, M, trans. 1987 (1995). *The Long Discourses of the Buddha: A translation of the 'Dīgha Nikāya'*. Translated from the Pāli. Boston: Wisdom Publications.
Walters, J.S. 1997. 'Stūpa, story, and empire: constructions of the Buddha biography in early post-Aśokan India', in J. Schober (*ed.*), Sacred Biography in the Buddhist Traditions of South and Southeast Asia. Honolulu: University of Hawai'i Press, 160-194.
——. 2002. 'Mapping Sāñchi in a whole Buddhist world', in P.D. Premasiri-Peradeniya (*ed.*), *Buddhist Studies in Honour of Professor Lily de Silva*. Peradeniya: University of Peradeniya, Dept. of Pali and Buddhist Studies, 1-14,
Watson, A. 1983. *Agricultural Innovation in the early Islamic World: The Diffusion of Crops and Farming Techniques, 700-1100*. Cambridge: Cambridge University Press.
Watt, G. 1889–93. *A Dictionary of the Economic Products of India*. 6 vols. Calcutta and London: W.H. Allen and Co.
Weber, M. 1920 (reprint:1958). *The Religion of India: sociology of Hinduism and Buddhism*. Translated by H. Gerth and D. Martindale. Glencoe: Free Press.
Weber, M. 1963. *The Sociology of Religion*. Boston: Beacon Press
Williams, J.G. 1976. 'New naga images from the Sanchi area', *Oriental Art* 22: 174-79.
——. 1982. *The Art of Gupta India: maturity and crisis*. Princeton: Princeton University Press.
Willcocks, W, Sir. 1930. *Ancient Systems of Irrigation in Bengal*. Calcutta: University of Calcutta.
Willis, M. 1996a. 'Architecture in central India under the Kacchapaghāta rulers', *South Asian Studies* 12: 13-32.
——. 1996b. *Inscriptions of Gopakṣetra: materials for the history of central India*. London: British Museum Press.
——. 1997. *Temples of Gopakṣetra: a regional tradition of architecture and sculpture in central India*. London: British Museum Press.
——. 1999/2000. 'The Sānchī Bodhisattva dated Kuṣāṇa year 28', in E. Errington and O. Bopearachchi (*eds.*), Papers in Honour of Francine Tissot. *Silk Road Archaeology* 6: 269-73.
——. 2004. 'The Archaeology and Politics of Time', in H. Bakker (*ed.*), *The Vākāṭaka Heritage: Indian culture at the crossroads*. Groningen: Egbert Forsten, 33-58.
——. Forthcoming a. *The Archaeology of Ritual: Udayagiri and the Establishment of the Gods in Gupta India.*
——. Forthcoming b. 'Relics of the Buddha: body, essence, text', in J. Hawkes and A. Shimada (*eds.*), *Buddhist Stupas in South Asia: Recent Archaeological, Art-Historical, and Historical Perspectives*. New Delhi: Oxford University Press.
Willis, M., with contributions from J. Cribb and J. Shaw. 2000. *Buddhist Reliquaries from Ancient India*. London: British Museum Press.
Wittfogel, K.A. 1957 (reprint: 1973). Oriental Despotism: a comparative study of total power. New Haven and London: Yale University Press.
Yokochi, Y. 2004. 'The Mahiṣāsuramardinī icon, with special reference to the images made in the Vākāṭaka realm', in H. Bakker (*ed.*), *The Vākāṭaka Heritage: Indian culture at the crossroads*. Groningen: Egbert Forsten, 167-78.
Zysk, K. G. 1991. *Asceticism and Healing in Ancient India: medicine in the Buddhist monastery*. New York; Oxford: Oxford University Press.

Index

Chapter and note numbers refer to the notes on pp. 263–71

Morel khurd (Bhojpur) 18, 21, 115–8, 136
Brahmanical temples 137, 138; Buddha image 116; Buddhist landscape 122–3, 140; burial deposits 116; carved railings 88–90, 104–5, 117, 221, 222; courtyard monasteries 117, 136–7; dam 117, 233, 246, 248, 261; hot hole 117; monastery platform 90–1, 94, 105–6, 116–7, 142–4; monastic patronage 140–1; Phase VI temple 91, 137; relics 51–3, 116, 140, 142–4; rock-shelters 117, 135, 136, 145; sculptures 118; settlements 221, 222, 231; site hierarchy 140; stupas 104–5, 115–18, 139
Mortar 106, 119, 121, 135, 243
Multi-denominational ritual sites 110, 126, 129, 137, 138, 182–3
Munsell soil charts 106, 107
Musala (pestle), in sculpture 54, 56, 180–1, 184, ch. 6, n. 19, ch. 12, n. 20
Muslim-Hindu relations 55
Muslim incursions 75, 191, 248, 250, 262, ch. 11, n. 156, n. 157

Nachna, temples at 184
Nāga cult (see also 'Local' and pan-Indian religion; Rain-making rituals; Religious change; Visnu and *nāga* cult)
and Bhagavata system 54–5, 56, 177, 180–2, 186, 187, 191, 192–3; and Buddhism 7, 24, 55, 56–7, 58–9, 86, 94, 142, 185–6, 192–3, 261–2, ch. 6, n. 40, n. 42; and kingship 57; and Vaisnavism 49, 56, 185–8, 191; and water 24, 54, 55, 57, 108, 186–7, 188, 192–3, 240; as protectors of the Buddhist relic 57, 192, ch. 11, n. 153, 192; history of 55, 58–9, 177
Naga dynasty (see also Localised polities) 47, 48–9, 83, 177, 185, 186–7, 253, ch. 5, n. 5, n. 6, n. 7, ch. 12, n. 82, n. 87
coinage 48, 84, 187
Nāga Mucalinda 57, ch. 6, n. 42
Nāga pillar capitals 186–7
Nāga sculptures (see also Ajanta, *nāga*; Balarama-*nāga* images; Visnuisation of *nāga* images)
and dams 55, 57, 86, 94, 108, 113, 124, 179, 180, 181–2, 186–7, 192–3, 234, 240, 241, 244–5, 247, 248, 253; and Saivism 181, 182; as representations of the Naga dynasty 48, 186–7, 253, ch. 12, n. 82, n. 87; chronology of 55, 57, 177, 179–80, 190, 192, 261–2; Jain 177, 188, ch. 12, n. 91; royalisation of 48, 56, 186–8, 253, ch. 12, n. 82, n. 87; Sanchi 94–5, 185–6; SSP area 50, 86, 94, 110, 113, 177–184; 185–8, 190, 192
Nāga shrines within Buddhist compounds
Ajanta 57–9, 192; northern India 57, 94; Sanchi 86, 94, 185–6, 192–3
Nāga temples
Rajgir 58; Sonkh 58
Nāgakals (serpent stones) 188, 189, 191, 247
and reservoirs/dams 188
Nagari (Rajasthan) ch. 6, n. 14, ch. 9, n. 10, ch. 12, n. 1
Nagauri hill (see also Sanchi-Nagauri reservoir complex)
Jain temple 95, 190; microliths 86; *nāga* sculpture 86, 94, 138, 177–80, 192, 240, 214, ch. 6, n. 40; painted panel 110–11, 117, 129, 136, 140; quarry 42, 94; rock-shelters 22, 36, 86; settlement 70, 86, 94, 218, 227, 231, 244
Nanaghat Cave inscription, Maharashtra ch. 6, n. 14
'Natural' sites and shrines 56, 61–2, 64, 66, 69, 70, 75–7, 191, 217–25, 231
New archaeology (see Processual archaeology)
Nion river 238
'Non-site' data (see also (see 'Natural' sites and shrines) 60, 62, 64, 75–7
Northern Black Polished Ware (NBPW) 22, 28, 30, 106, 107
in SSP area 39, 46, 52, 83, 84, 104, 107, 112, 230
Northwest crop package 38, 43–4
Numen loci (see Otto, Rudolph)

Optically Stimulated Luminescence (OSL) dating 67, 71, 108–9, 234, 240–1, 243–4, 247, 248, 253, ch. 8, n. 1
Orientalism 23, 28–9, 30–1, 252
Orissa
ancient states 28, 29; kingship and royal cults 55, 56, 65, 186; irrigation 31
Orthodoxy v. orthopraxy 23
Otto, Rudolph 60–1, 191

Padmapani sculpture 84, 92, ch. 9, n. 47, n. 48, n. 62
Padmasambhava (see also Tibet) 59
Painted Grey Ware (PGW)
and Aryan theory 29; and Iron 29–30, 39; in central India 39, 83–5, 104, 218
Painted inscriptions
Brahmi 129–30, ch. 12, n. 102; *śankhalipi* 117, 132, ch. 11, n. 105
Painted rock-shelters
historic 86, 110–11, 113, 117, 127, 129; prehistoric 36–7, 40, 56, 62, 88, 105, 110, 114, 126, 127, 129, 130, 142, 231, ch. 3, n. 1; at Sanchi 86, 218
Palaeolithic
'shrine' ch. 12, n. 100; stone tools 36–7, 42, 218;
Pallava inscriptions 31, 250, 260
Pan-Indian art 24, 47, 53, 140–1, 179–80, 182, 260,
Pañcavīra 54, 56, 193, ch. 6, n. 15, n. 26
Pangurariya
Asokan edict 37, 40, 46, 87; monastic rock-shelters 37, 40, 74, 87, 117, 145; prehistoric rock-shelters 36; stupas 40; water channels 45
Paramaras 48, 104, 105, 189
Parivāha (see also Spillways) 239
Parivahana (see also Staff, non-monastic) 93
Passive v. active models of Buddhism (see Buddhism)
Patronage, Brahmanical 53, 54–5, 56, 126, 137, 186–7, 189, 190–2, 193, 259, ch. 2, n. 11
Patronage, Buddhist (see also Exchange networks)
collective 47, 49, 50–1, 112–3, 122, 140–1, 231–2, 252–3; royal/individual 18, 47, 49, 50, 122–3, 140–1, 226, 259;
Patimokka rules 50, 231
Pedology, in SSP area (see Soils)
Permanent endowments 35, 144–5
Pestle (see *Musala*)
Phenomenological approach
in archaeology 62–3, 75, ch. 7, n. 1; in geography 60–2
Phytolith analysis 38, 44
in SSP 241, 251, ch. 4, n. 3
Pilgrimage
Buddhist 27, 56; Brahmanical (see also Ayodhya) 55–6, 61, 62, 186, ch. 6, n. 8; Christian 61, ch. 6, n. 36
Pillars
Gupta 84, 92, 186–7, ch. 9, n. 46, ch. 11, n. 124; Mauryan 89, 105, 132, 135, 186, ch. 9, n. 12, ch. 11, n. 125; post-Mauryan 49, 54, 88–90, 141, 226, 227
Pitalkhora
nāga image 57; platformed monastery 91, 135; rock-cut architecture and sculpture 18, 179, 180
Ploughing methods, in SSP area 68, 69, 106
Ploughshare, in sculpture (see *Hala*)
Pollen analysis 44–5, ch. 4, n. 1
in SSP 44, 67, 234, 241, 244, 251
Polygon-based maps (see Maps)
Population shifts (see also Depopulation) 18, 31–3, 43, 66, 215, 231, 234, 249–53, 260, ch. 14, n. 43
Post-Mauryan polities (see also Pillars; State; Stupa railings) 23, 29, 46–7, 48–9, 53
Post-processual archaeology 60, 145
Pottery (see Ceramics)
Prabhavati Gupta (see also Vakatakas) 48–9, ch. 12, n. 82
Pradyumna 54, ch. 6, n. 16, n. 26
Pratiharas 48, 93, 104, 105, 189, 247, ch. 14, n. 30
Processual archaeology 29
Propagation of Buddhism
and Mauryan empire 23, 27, 49, 50; in SSP area 24; 'second' 18, 21, 49, 51–3, 87–91, 135–6, 140–1; social and economic background of (see also Religious change) 7, 18, 24, 27, 31, 33–4, 58, 77, 231–2, 249, 251–2, 259–62
Proselytisation 142, 191
Proto-Pancaratra system (see also Bhagavata cult) 40, 46, 50, 53–5, 56, 176–7, 184, 188, 190–3
Pūnya (merit) 8, 27, 33, 34, 58, 142–3, 144, 231–2, 240, 247, ch. 11, n. 160, ch. 14, n. 40
Purāṇas 55, 184, ch. 2, n. 1 , ch. 5, n. 5
Bhāgavata Purāṇa ch. 5, n. 8; *Vāyumahā Purāṇa* ch. 6, n. 15; *Viṣṇu Purāṇa* 48, ch. 2, n. 1, ch. 7, n. 38
Pusyamitra (see also Sungas) 46–7; attitude towards Buddhism 47, 143–4; ch. 9, n. 16

Quarries/quarrying, in SSP area
ancient 86, 94, 110, 185, 186, 218, 222, 223, 227; modern 42, 69, 73, 118, 119, 123, 126, 226

Rabi crops 43, 251
Railways 39, 45, 83, 244, ch. 14, n. 18
Rain-fed agriculture 43, 249, 251
Rainfall 43, 44–5, 55, 57–9, 233, 237–8, 249–52
Rainmaking rituals (see also *Nāgas*, and water) 57–9, 94, 192, 240, ch. 11, n.145
Rain retreats (see *Vessana*)
Raisen district 41
forests 45, rock-shelters 22, 36, 40, ch. 3, n. 1; tool-production sites 37
Raisen Fort 115
Buddhist remains 115, 136, 138, 139; Brahmanical temple 138, 185; dam 115, 233, 249
Rajgir
ancient city 18, 27, 28, 53, 58; Bimbisara's jail 128; Buddhist monasteries 144–5, ch. 11, n. 161; Hariti story 58; *nāga* temple 58
Ramagupta, king 47, ch. 12, n. 84
Ramtek (see also Mansar) ch. 1, n. 1,
dam ch. 2, n. 10, n. 11, ch. 14, n. 8
Rangai, Vidisha (see also Chalcolithic/early-historic transition) 22, 30, 38, 39, 83–5, 104, 218, 229–30
Reconnaissance (see Survey design)
Rectangular monasteries
arranged around courtyard 106, 113, 115, 119, 120, 121–2, 124, 135; free-standing 74, 106, 111, 112, 113, 114, 117, 118–19, 121, 126, 139–40, 143, 144–5; Red Polished Ware 106, 108